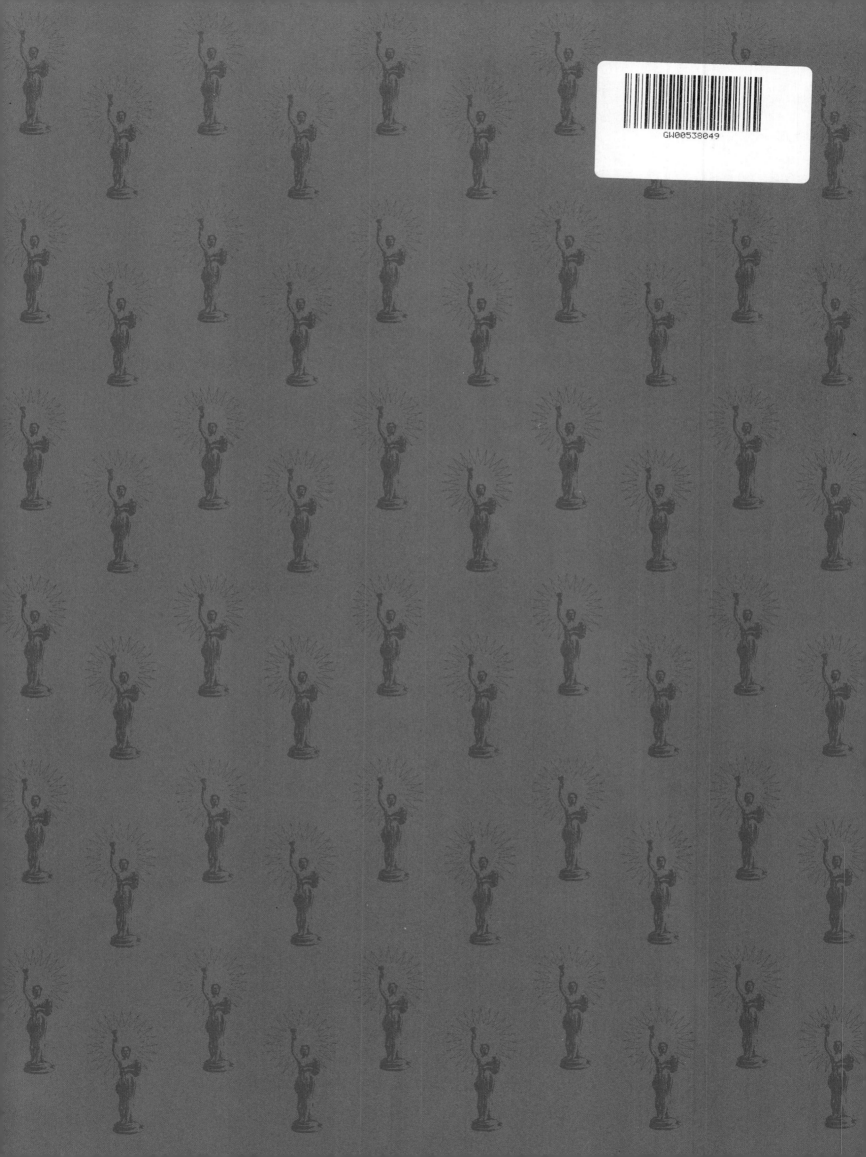

THE
COLUMBIA
STORY

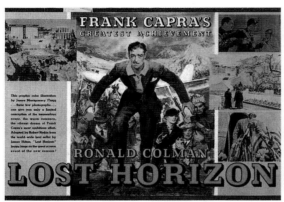

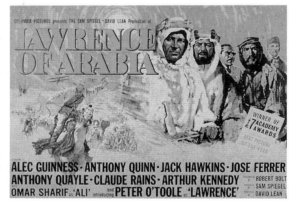

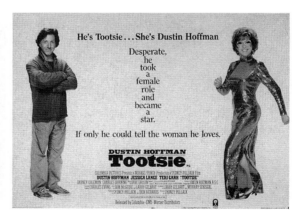

THE
COLUMBIA
STORY

Clive Hirschhorn

hamlyn

Once again for Pearl and Colin

Produced under licence from Columbia Pictures, a division of
Columbia Pictures Industries, Inc.

This edition published in Great Britain in 1999 by Hamlyn,
an imprint of Octopus Publishing Group Limited,
2-4 Heron Quays, London E14 4JP

Publishing Director Laura Bamford
Creative Director Keith Martin
Commissioning Editor Julian Brown
In-house Editor Tarda Davison-Aitkins
Editors Anne Lloyd and Robyn Karney
Designers Geoff Borin and Mike Moule
Picture Researcher Zoe Holtermann
Production Controller Lisa Moore

ISBN 0 600 59836 5

A catalogue record for this book is available from the British Library

Produced by Toppan
Printed in China

CONTENTS

PREFACE

As usual with this ongoing series of Hollywood studio histories, a preface is necessary to explain the thinking behind some of the decisions taken in the organisation of the book.

From the outset, I had to decide what, precisely, constitutes a Columbia picture. For example, was any film that carried the Columbia logo an automatic candidate for 'main entry' status in the body of the book, even when the film did not originate with the studio itself but was bought in from an independent company? From the mid-1950s onwards, and in common with the other major Hollywood studios, Columbia began to distribute movies that were not their own 'in house' creations; *Lawrence Of Arabia* (1962) and *Oliver!* (1968) are examples of these. Major films of this type should be regarded as an integral part of Columbia's history because of the studio's creative or financial (or both) involvement in them and for this reason they are fully described and illustrated in the main body of the book. I have, however, relegated to the appendices 'pick-ups' that were only released by Columbia in the USA and not in the UK; foreign-language films; movies made specifically for the British market by Columbia British; British films such as *The Great Manhunt* (1950), *The Clouded Yellow* (1951) and *Storm Over The Nile* (1956) which were made by British companies and released in the USA only; and, finally, films that do not easily fit into any definable category.

On the other hand, all the films made by Warwick in Britain, were given financial backing from Columbia and therefore appear in the book as main entries.

Inevitably some grey areas remain. *The Last Emperor* (1988), for example, which received no financial or creative input from Columbia, has been included on the strength of the studio's worldwide distribution deal with Yanko Films/Tao Film, *The Last Emperor*'s production company.

During the last 20 years, the whole question of what constitutes a studio's involvement with a production has become such a vexed one that, at times, making a decision had to be purely subjective. Should you, therefore, be struck by any inconsistencies, I beg your indulgence.

The silent movies made by the studio between 1923 and 1929 were, on the whole, of such minor interest that, over the years, the majority of them have been lost through neglect. Stills for many of these films also proved impossible to locate, and it was therefore decided to treat these early productions uncritically, and in an abbreviated form. The notable exceptions are, of course, the few made by Frank Capra in 1928 and 1929 which are included as main entries. It was also necessary, for reasons of space, to relegate the hundreds of B Westerns and series made by the studio between 1930 and 1958 to abbreviated appendix entries.

From 1970 onwards, as most films were photographed in colour, I have only specified those shot in black and white.

Acknowledgements
First and foremost I should like to thank Su Lesser of Columbia's legal department in Culver City, California, for her support, her unfailing willingness to assist in locating rare material and for being such a helpful chum in general. Working with her on this project was truly a pleasure. Dennis Doph did invaluable work in ferreting out and collating the many stills used in the book; his speed and efficiency were awesome. Also at Columbia, both in the USA and the UK, my thanks to Glenda Mojica, Bonnie Yohay, Becky Ford, Margarita Medina, Karen Spiegel, Bob Nafius, Colin Greene, Maggie Nelson, Grover Crisp, Lisa Davidson, Rob Word, Barbara Lakin, Michael Schlesinger, Donna Brainard, Arnie Shupack, Tony Roth, Patrick Schaefer, Hollace Davids, Damien Everly, Helen Lavarre, Alan Press, Sherry Sherman, Beverley Starr, Kythe Bramah, Susan Tyre, Pat Williamson and Dennis Wilson.

I am immeasurably indebted, too, to Ann Lloyd for the many hours of 'hard labour' she put into deciphering my original manuscript; for her enthusiasm, her expertise and her patience. She was vital to this project and she has my deep-felt gratitude. Thanks must also go to Dick Vosburgh and Jack Lodge for bringing their knowledge and expertise to bear on the book's material, to my 'in-house' editors Tessa Rose and Isabel Greenham and to Tony Holdsworth of Octopus Books. I should also like to thank Marc Wanamaker, Tom Vallance, Ken Sephton, Julian Fox, William C. Wilson, Joseph L. Lee Goss, Peter Schooley, Peter Strickland, Eric Spilker, Howard Mandelbaum and Photofest, Mary Corliss of the Museum of Modern Art, Joel Finler, Richard Chatten, Ian Cook and Garth Twa who, in their various ways, were most helpful to me. Finally, I am indebted to the following publications: *The New York Times*, *Variety*, *The Monthly Film Bulletin*, David Quinlan's *British Sound Films* (Batsford), Denis Gifford's *British Film Catalogue* (David and Charles), Joel Finler's *The Hollywood Story* (Octopus), Bob Thomas' *King Cohn* (Barrie and Rockliffe), Frank Capra's *The Name Above The Title* (W. H. Allen), and The *Motion Picture Guide* (Cinebooks).

To my long-time editor Robyn Karney, I owe a debt of gratitude for her expert copy editing beyond the call of duty.

Clive Hirschhorn

INTRODUCTION

The year 1924 was a busy one in Hollywood's history. Over 400 feature films were produced in the USA, including such fine movies as *The Thief of Bagdad* (United Artists) with Douglas Fairbanks, *Beau Brummel* (Warner Bros.) with John Barrymore, *The Iron Horse* (Fox) with George O'Brien and Madge Bellamy, and Buster Keaton's *The Navigator*.

It was the year Louis B. Mayer joined theatre-owner Marcus Loew (head of the Metro Company), merged with the Goldwyn Company, and formed Metro-Goldwyn-Mayer.

The world's obsession with Hollywood and the dreams it peddled reached fever pitch. As newspapers and fan magazines outdid each other with attention-grabbing headlines and stories that made public the private lives of superstars such as Fairbanks and Pickford, Gloria Swanson, Charlie Chaplin, Harold Lloyd, John Gilbert, Valentino and Clara Bow, a new company, light years away from the glitz and glamour of the Hollywood dream machine, modestly came into being.

The date was 10 January 1924.
The company was Columbia Pictures.
This is its story.

It begins in the New York of the 1880s. Joseph Cohn, a Jewish tailor who had emigrated from Germany, met a Polish-born woman called Bella, married her, and produced four sons and a daughter. Max was the oldest, Nathaniel and Anna the two youngest, and in the middle came Jacob (Jack) and Harry, who were born in 1889 and 1891 respectively. The family lived in a cramped, four-roomed apartment on East 88th Street. In common with most immigrant families trying to make their way in the New World, they had come to realise that America was not exactly waiting for them with open arms, and that to succeed required perseverance and resourcefulness. The opportunities were there all right, it was simply a matter of going after them.

With no responsibilities other than to find sufficient money to pay for their upkeep at home, it was, of course, far easier for second-generation sons of immigrants to risk putting a toe in the piranha-filled waters of commercial enterprise. Jack and Harry Cohn, both single men, had far less to lose than their father, who was not about to risk his meagre but regular income on fly-by-night, get-rich-quick schemes. A martinet of the old school, he was far more concerned with his sons' education than with their social status; ironically the only one of Joseph's boys to reach high-school – Max – would ultimately be the least materially successful of the four Cohn brothers.

The first of the Cohns to enter the fast-growing world of show-business was Jack. At the age of 19, in 1908, he quit his job at the Hampton Advertising Agency for one with Carl Laemmle's Film Service Company. When Laemmle began producing films and formed his IMP (Independent Motion Picture) Company, Jack went to work in the laboratory there. Tough, street-wise, ambitious and well versed in the ways of hustling, young Jack eventually graduated from the laboratory to other departments of the IMP organisation and in 1913 founded Universal Weekly, a newsreel which he both edited and produced for Laemmle. Jack was just as economy-

Below: The 35-acre ranch outside Burbank that, from 1935, became home to Buck Jones, Charles Starrett, Gene Autry – and the rest of the Columbia's B-Western unit.

minded as his avuncular boss (called 'Uncle Carl' by his employees), and soon he was also handling the job of seeing that IMP's one- and two-reel shorts came in on time and on budget.

After supervising IMP's output for a period of almost five years, Jack Cohn worked on his first feature, *Traffic In Souls*, a drama about the white-slave trade in New York. Directed by George Loane Tucker and costing $57,000, this was the first feature released by Laemmle, whose company was now called Universal. It was Jack's task to edit the film down from ten reels (150 minutes) to a more manageable six (90 minutes). This he did. The film opened on 24 November 1913 in New York, realised a profit of $450,000 and proved to the burgeoning motion-picture industry just how successful full-length features could be. *Traffic In Souls* was a major stepping-stone for Laemmle, who, encouraged by the film's success, decided to invest in his own studio on the West Coast. In 1915 he went over to Hollywood to open Universal City, which lay just off Lankershim Boulevard.

Jack, meantime, had persuaded Laemmle to hire Joe Brandt, an attorney friend of his with whom he had worked in the Hampton Advertising Agency. This was a most judicious appointment for all concerned, for Brandt so impressed Laemmle that he was soon made general manager of Universal, based in New York.

Harry Cohn was also making steady progress. In 1904, soon after his Bar Mitzvah, and against his father's wishes, he left school and found temporary employment as a choir boy in a play called *The Fatal Wedding*. This was followed by a lengthy stint as a shipping-clerk for the music-publishing firm of Francis, Day and Hunter. Then, in 1912, he joined forces with pianist Harry Ruby, and together they offered themselves to the Claremont Nickelodeon for $28 a week. Harry, who was the 'singing half' of the duo, 'managed' the act, pocketing $11 a week and giving the remaining $17 to his hard-working partner, who not only accompanied Harry during

Jack Cohn

Harry Cohn

Because of his brother's connections with Carl Laemmle at Universal, Harry naturally took his idea to Jack who, in turn, convinced his boss that it was worth pursuing. Harry's instinct proved correct. The series of shorts was a success and, in 1918, Harry Cohn (then aged 27) was invited to become Uncle Carl's secretary at Universal City in Hollywood. He could not refuse such an offer and packed his bags for California, leaving behind brother Jack and Joe Brandt in New York.

As Harry began his tenure with Universal, so Jack, after 12 years as a Laemmle employee, started to feel restless. He branched out on his own with a series of shorts (called Screen Snapshots) which gave audiences a chance to glimpse their favourite movie stars away from the set. The series was popular enough to tempt Joe Brandt away from his safe and lucrative job at the studio and to join Jack as a full-time partner. After a while, both men felt a third partner was necessary and Jack suggested Harry. It was an inspired choice.

Harry had always wanted to be self-employed and jumped at the opportunity. He bade adieu to Laemmle and returned to New York where, in 1919, he, Jack and Joe Brandt formed the triumvirate that would soon guide the fortunes of a new motion picture company known as CBC (Cohn-Brandt-Cohn) Film Sales.

CBC got off to a near-disastrous start and almost went bankrupt when the director they hired for a series of shorts, based on H. A. McGill's Hall Room Boys cartoon strip, and starring vaudevillians Flannigan and Edwards, pocketed most of the budget and despatched from Hollywood three awful shorts . After this experience the partners decided that Harry should return to the West Coast and supervise production of the two-reelers himself.

Harry was happy to put 3,000 miles between himself and his brother (throughout their lives the two men were fierce rivals) and returned to Hollywood as a fledgling producer itching to succeed in an industry that, by 1920, was attracting audiences of 35 million people a week, each willing to pay five cents a time to be drawn into a flickering, magical world of romance, excitement, thrills and drama. There was a fortune to be made in this sun-drenched land of dreams, and Harry was determined to make it, not as an employee, but as an employer.

He knew he would have to begin modestly, and no place was more modest in the Hollywood of the 1920s than the small area just off Sunset Boulevard – near Gower Street and Beachwood Drive – known as Poverty Row. Without as yet a studio of his own, the only way for Harry Cohn to become a producer was in the tried-and-tested Poverty Row tradition of borrowing money from a sympathetic banking house. Next, he would have to find a story that could be shot mainly out of doors, thereby eliminating the need to hire studio space for longer than was absolutely necessary. Finally, he would have to find an actor who was either on his way up or on his way down (and so did not cost too much), who did not mind being associated with Poverty Row, and who could play several roles in the same short (so he also needed to be good at disguises).

Short-ends of film (unexposed discards from reels of stock, usually about 50 feet or so in length) were easily and inexpensively purchased from the major studios such as Paramount and Universal. Cameras and other technical equipment could be hired from several sources for not too much money. The ideal producer could also direct, and his crew should comprise no more than a lighting cameraman and an assistant capable of being a Jack-of-all trades.

Such were the harsh dictates of Poverty Row at the beginning of the 1920s. The challenge appealed to Harry Cohn who, hardened by the realities of an under-privileged life in New York, was, at the age

the tinted-slide sing-a-longs five times a day, but also played the piano during the continuous movie shows from one in the afternoon to eleven at night. Under Cohn's influence, the duo attempted to improve their lot by taking cabaret engagements. As a team, however, they lacked style – and, more important, talent – and the act dissolved. Years later Ruby, together with lyricist Bert Kalmar, became a successful song-writer both on Broadway and in Hollywood; but although he and Harry Cohn remained friendly, Ruby worked only once more for Columbia.

Harry's next job found him collecting trolley fares. There was no future in that, so he decided to take advantage of the rising popularity of Tin Pan Alley and became a song plugger for the publishing firm of Waterson, Berlin and Snyder. A short stint in the army, from which he was released on the death of his 49-year-old father, was followed by Harry's decision to go into business on his own account. Music publishers would pay to have their new popular songs 'plugged' by singing pianists (or duos like Harry and Ruby) during the slide-show intervals at movie houses. Harry had the idea of extending the effectiveness of this song-plugging by substituting actual movies for static slides.

Gambling everything on this notion, he took a one-room office in the Strand Building on Broadway, and made his first movie-song plug for a mere $25. He sold the finished product (which was little more than a group of soldiers marching in step) for ten times that amount. These plugs proved so popular with exhibitors that Harry wondered whether it might not be a good idea to produce a series of song shorts which (though silent, of course) would feature established stars miming the words of the songs in appropriate situations (a forerunner, in fact, of contemporary pop videos).

of 29, ready to meet it head on. Even before he had a kingdom to command, Cohn was an abrasive, extremely crude operator. He had witnessed the power wielded by men such as Carl Laemmle and Adolph Zukor (at Paramount), and was determined to equal their impact on the industry.

Harry's first move on returning to Hollywood was to hire another director for the Hall Room Boys two-reelers. His choice was an ex-Sennett employee called Alfred Santell. Under Cohn's supervision at the Balshofer Studios on Hollywood Boulevard and the Independent Studios on Sunset and Gower, the films were economically yet efficiently made (a Cohn trademark).

Jack Cohn and Joe Brandt in New York were delighted with the results. They had no difficulty selling them, and each sale provided the financial wherewithal for the next production. After a few months, Cohn had not only absorbed all the finer points of survival on Poverty Row, but had added a few rules of his own to the manual – such as painting both sides of the scenic backdrops in order to maximise their value to the production. Another time-saving trick of his was to have an actress make-up one side of her face if her scenes required her to be shot from only one angle.

One other lesson Harry Cohn quickly learned in the first six months as production executive for CBC was that the big money was not to be found in one- and two-reel shorts. Power, prestige and Hollywood-style perks lay in the production of feature films (between four and six reels – 60–90 minutes), as Carl Laemmle had discovered way back in 1913. Both Jack and Joe in New York knew this to be the case but, being the 'money men', they were less willing to take risks with the company's funds (a situation that prevailed under Jack long after Brandt's departure). Harry, however, finally persuaded them to enter the arena with the big boys and, after raising $20,000, CBC released its very first feature on 20 August 1922. The film was called *More To Be Pitied Than Scorned*, and was a six-reeler which Harry produced and Edward Le Saint directed. Made at the Paulis Studios on Sunset and Gower, it was a melodrama in which a jealous husband brings untold misery to both himself and his wife when he mistakenly assumes she has been unfaithful. It starred J. Frank Glendon and Rosemary Theby.

After refusing an offer of $65,000 from Marcus Loew of Metro, CBC sold the film in the 'States-rights market' whereby individual distributors in individual States were able to buy the film outright and keep all the profits for themselves. CBC not only made a handsome $130,000 on the deal, but were contracted by the distributors for a further five features.

Between August 1922 and December 1923, CBC produced ten full-length features in all, six of them directed by Le Saint. Though none hit the jackpot, either commercially or artistically, none lost money. All the same, while CBC was more than holding its own among the maverick, here-today-gone-tomorrow outfits that populated Poverty Row, it was still no threat to the Warners, Zukors and Laemmles of the industry; the initials CBC were translated in the trade as Corned Beef and Cabbage, a sobriquet which stuck in the craw of Harry Cohn, a proud man who hated being ridiculed in any way. At Harry's behest the name of the company was officially changed, and on 10 January 1924 Columbia Pictures Corporation was born with new offices at 729 Seventh Avenue, New York, and leased premises at 6070 Sunset Boulevard, Hollywood.

The new company's President was Joe Brandt; Jack Cohn was Vice-President in charge of sales, and both men continued to operate out of New York. Harry Cohn was Vice-President in charge of production, and was Hollywood based. By 1924, the rivalry between Jack and Harry had established a pattern that would persist until Jack's death in 1956. The two men argued incessantly, wilfully disagreed with each other's decisions, and, in matters of artistic policy, were diametrically opposed on principle. In the end, though, both relied on the other's expertise, without ever admitting it. One-upmanship was the name of the game. Harry's deep need to prove to his brother that his artistic judgements were sound kept him constantly on his toes, while Jack's need to prove to the business community that the company was expanding, both artistically and commercially, ultimately resulted in Harry (usually) having his own

Joe Brandt

way. Harry, poorly educated though he was, nonetheless had a remarkable instinct for talent. The man in the middle was, of course, Joe Brandt, who more than earned his salary by acting as mediator between the two powerful sibling rivals; no easy task considering the foulness of Harry's language and the strength of his temper. Even in his more tranquil moments Harry subjected his stars and associates to constant verbal abuse; when aroused, he was a formidable adversary who went for the jugular. Cohn's second-in-command was Sam Briskin, who had joined CBC as a lowly-paid auditor during the company's early days. Briskin's opinion was often sought by Harry Cohn, who relied equally on his subordinate's tact in negotiating problem contracts.

In 1925 Harry Cohn decided that the only way Columbia could compete with the majors was by having a studio of its own. Renting space on Poverty Row was not the answer to a would-be mogul's prayer for power so, for a mortgage payment of $150,000, he bought two stages and an adjoining office at 6070 Sunset Boulevard, near the south-east corner of Sunset and Gower. This was the first of many acquisitions that, over the years, would comprise the burgeoning Columbia lot.

In 1926, a boom year in Hollywood, Columbia went public and changed its marketing system from selling outright franchises in the States-rights market to the more profitable 'exchange' system which operated on a percentage-of-profits basis. That same year, another important decision was taken that would shape the nature of the studio's product until Harry Cohn's death in 1958. This tiny company decided, unlike Paramount, Warner Bros. and MGM, not to invest its limited resources in theatres but to spend that money on making movies.

While this arrangement removed the financial burden of having to invest in real estate, or having to maintain the upkeep of such investments, it also meant that the product being churned out by Columbia had to maintain a consistently high quality otherwise exhibitors would refuse to book it. The wisdom of this decision was first illustrated in 1929 when, during the Depression, the drop in cinema attendance almost forced both Paramount and RKO into receivership; and again, in 1948, when the Consent Decree prohibited studios from both making and exhibiting their own product. In neither instance was Columbia forced to sell any real estate investments at a loss.

In 1927 the studio made its first bid for the big time with a feature called *The Blood Ship*, starring Hobart Bosworth – who had been a major star in the teens, but now, a decade later, at the age of 60, was a Hollywood also-ran. Bosworth owned the story and was so keen to re-establish himself in the eyes of the movie colony's hierarchy that he offered to play the central role for nothing. Cohn accepted his offer. The film was directed by George B. Seitz and shot mainly on location on a rented, three-masted schooner. It was the most costly production to date in Columbia's short history – and also its most prestigious. *The Blood Ship* opened at the Roxy Theatre, New York, in mid- July 1927, and was described by the critic of the *New York Times* as a 'vigorous, unalloyed melodrama'. For the first time, Harry Cohn's Columbia – with its torch-lady logo – was beginning to make a dent in an industry hitherto impervious to the company's existence.

Then a miracle happened. Harry Cohn agreed to pay Frank Capra, a director of slapstick comedies, $1,000 to direct a film for him. It was, in fact, a two-way miracle that would change the fortunes of both Columbia and Capra.

One of seven children of a Sicilian peasant, Frank Capra arrived in America with his family at the age of six. He sold newspapers to finance his years at grammar school, adding additional chores to his schedule – such as janitoring, and guitar-playing at a local bistro – when he graduated to high school. He completed his formal education at the California Institute of Technology, after which he tackled a variety of jobs across the country before returning to the West Coast where he developed an interest in movies. With 'chutzpah' substituting for experience, he directed his first short film, *Fultah Fisher's Boarding House*, a one-reeler about the San Francisco waterfront. Soon afterwards he became a gag-writer

9

for Hal Roach's Our Gang series, then moved to the Mack Sennett studio where he helped nurture the talent of comedian Harry Langdon through three successful full-length features, all of which he co-wrote and directed (although he received credit only for the last two). Langdon's egotistical temperament and his resentment of the part Capra had played in his success resulted in Capra's dismissal. The fledgling director then directed a failure called *For The Love of Mike* (1927) before being approached by Columbia.

Capra's first assignment for Harry Cohn was a domestic comedy called *That Certain Thing* (1928), with Ralph Graves and Viola Dana. Cohn was delighted with the result, instantly recognising Capra's special quality, and gave him a $1,500 bonus plus a contract for three further films at $2,500 a picture.

The next handful of features Capra made were typical low-budget B movies. Then came *Submarine* (1928), starring the lot's two most bankable male stars, Ralph Graves and Jack Holt. Originally assigned to director Irvin Willat, whose work on it failed to meet with Harry Cohn's approval, *Submarine* had been in production on location in San Pedro for several weeks when Capra was ordered to rescue it. After facing the initial hostility of the crew as well as his two leading men, Capra quickly set to work and turned a potential disaster into the studio's biggest-grossing film to date. *Submarine* was the first Columbia release to incorporate sound-effects, and it was soon followed by the company's first all-talkie, *The Donovan Affair* (1929), also directed by Capra.

The success of *Submarine* led to two further Holt-Graves-Capra collaborations, *Flight* in 1929 and *Dirigible* two years later; both were critical and financial hits. Capra then directed Jean Harlow in *Platinum Blonde* (1931), a breezy comedy that in lesser hands would almost certainly have been a pot-boiler. *American Madness* (1932) followed, and was his first truly 'Capraesque' comedy-drama, about the effects of bank failure on the 'little people' of a community during the Depression. Capra not only brought out the best in the stars with whom he worked but discovered in them qualities untapped by other directors. His biggest triumph in this respect was finding the key to Barbara Stanwyck's screen persona, and unlocking the talent she had kept discreetly hidden for her first three (non-Capra) films. Vulnerability coupled with strength was Stanwyck's professional trademark, and it was first seen in Capra's *Ladies Of Leisure* (1930) – though it would be less apparent in *The Bitter Tea of General Yen*, an exotic Oriental romance directed by

Sam Briskin

Capra in 1933. Although *Bitter Tea* was one of Capra's few box-office failures, the entire enterprise was a clear demonstration of the money-oriented Cohn's complete faith in, and respect for, his brilliant young director. No one else on the lot would have been given the green light on so patently uncommercial a project.

With his next film, *Lady For A Day* (1933), Capra raised Cohn and Columbia several degrees in prestige. A charming comedy about a fruit-pedlar (May Robson) who enlists the help of a gambler so that she can pretend to be a duchess and thereby not shame her daughter in front of the girl's fiancé, it was nominated for Best Picture. Capra was Oscar-nominated for Best Director, May Robson for Best Actress and Robert Riskin for Best Screenplay.

The following year Capra went one better with *It Happened One Night* (1934), for which the studio borrowed Claudette Colbert from Paramount and Clark Gable from MGM. Despite the two stars' misgivings over both the property and their Poverty Row surroundings, *It Happened One Night* was an overwhelming success. Gable and Colbert played off each other beautifully, Capra's direction was awash with warmth, humour and observation, and, at the Academy Awards Ceremony for 1934, the film won for Columbia its first Oscar for Best Picture – as well as Oscars for Best Actor, Best Actress, Best Director and Best Screenplay (adaptation).

For the rest of the decade, Capra's career at Columbia thrived. *Mr Deeds Goes To Town* (1936) and *You Can't Take It With You* (1938) were both scripted by Robert Riskin, Capra's favourite writer, and both linked comedy with social comment to superb effect. The Sicilian immigrant's son won two more Oscars for himself and one more for the studio (*You Can't Take It With You*). Capra's major project for 1937 was a screen adaptation of James Hilton's novel *Lost Horizon*, a fantasy set in a Tibetan paradise. His prestigious association with Columbia ended in 1939 after the controversial *Mr Smith Goes To Washington*.

Frank Capra and Harry Cohn did not always see eye to eye during their 12-year association. Indeed, they quarrelled regularly and, on several occasions, bitterly. However, there can be no doubt whatsoever that their stormy collaboration produced a fine body of work.

In the end, Harry Cohn was all too aware that, without Capra, the history of Columbia Pictures would have been very different. Equally, he knew that Capra would have found his niche in Hollywood just as easily without Harry Cohn, for such talent cannot be kept hidden. The bottom line was that he needed Capra more

Every Picture Will Have A Box Office Cast

Above: The impressive frontage of the Columbia lot on Poverty Row, as seen from the vantage point of North Gower Street, shortly after its purchase in 1925. **Right:** The broad sunny streets of the studio's inner lot which house the vital behind-the-scenes departments — electrical, maintenance, scenery and titles.

than Capra needed him – a fact that his pride found difficult to accept. For the next couple of decades, he set out to prove that, as far as Harry Cohn and Columbia were concerned, there was life after Capra.

The 1930s was a rich and varied time in Hollywood. MGM traded in glossy, star-studded musicals, comedies, and dramas that glorified women, motherhood, and America. Warner Bros. took more risks and brought a rough, tough, edge to their musicals, gangster films, and 'message' dramas. Universal produced some fine weepies and horror films before concentrating, in the latter half of the decade, on B pictures, Westerns, and song-filled Deanna Durbin comedies. There was a sophisticated European sheen and glamour to much of Paramount's 1930s output; while 20th Century-Fox had its sugar-coated heart in America's recent past and for the rest of the decade was the folksiest, least sophisticated of the majors. RKO, due to its turbulent management, was the most eclectic of Hollywood's studios, and, apart from the nine Astaire-Rogers musicals it produced between 1933 and 1939, its mercurial, chameleon-like personality resulted in several classics but no distinctive 'house' style.

Columbia also produced its share of classics throughout the 1930s but, unlike RKO, it did have a personality of its own. Extravagance was not one of its traits, and production values were rarely a substitute for a workable script. There was a sophistication about the studio's best product, especially its comedies, that contrasted sharply with the vulgar behaviour of Harry Cohn himself (whom Capra once referred to as 'His Crudeness'), and the unglamorous surroundings of the studio.

'Making the most with the least' might have been the studio's motto; and although the company's fortunes flourished throughout the decade, Harry Cohn, who became President of Columbia Pictures in 1932 when he bought out Joe Brandt, did not leave Poverty Row. Instead, he absorbed it bit by bit until he owned most of the area between Sunset Boulevard and Fountain Avenue, and Gower Street and Beachwood Drive. In addition, in 1935 he bought a 35-acre ranch near Burbank on which the studio's large output of Buck Jones and Charles Starrett Westerns was filmed.

By 1937 Columbia was producing a feature a week, sometimes more. Early in the decade Harry Cohn realised that to run a profitable studio all he needed were two or three successful A movies a year. In order to pay for the prestige pictures Columbia became the prime producer of 'programmers' (fillers) which could be relied on to generate a steady flow of income. (It is worth noting that from it's birth until the time of Harry Cohn's death, Columbia – unlike all the other major studios – never went into the red.) These programmers included a large quota of B Westerns and titles in Columbia's many popular series (i.e. Blondie, Boston Blackie, Jungle Jim etc.) – plus cheap and cheerful B movies of all kinds. In addition, the studio also specialised in one-reeler and two-reeler comedy shorts (featuring the likes of The Three Stooges, Charlie Chase), and had its own list of popular serials (The Shadow, Batman, Superman etc).

In 1937 Columbia's two big A features were Capra's *Lost Horizon* and Leo McCarey's *The Awful Truth*. The rest of the year's 'corned beef and cabbage' product comprised 13 Westerns and 38 other programmers, plus shorts and serials. Nevertheless, the attribute that every one of this motley collection displayed was solid craftsmanship. Cohn's proud boast was that all Columbia's films had a quality 'look' about them. If they didn't, they wouldn't be booked by exhibitors. And if they weren't booked, Columbia, as it owned no theatres of its own, would soon be out of business.

Director Howard Hawks, though never under contract to the studio, was nevertheless one of the directors responsible for some of Columbia's finest A features. In 1931 he made one of the best of the studio's early movies – *The Criminal Code*, which won the studio its first Oscar nomination (for Best Screenplay). In addition he made *Twentieth Century* (1934), a marvellous screwball comedy with John Barrymore and Carole Lombard, *Only Angels Have Wings* (1939), with Jean Arthur, Cary Grant and rising starlet Rita Hayworth, and the glorious black farce *His Girl Friday* (1940) with Cary Grant and Rosalind Russell.

During the 1930s, Cohn had refused to keep a roster of high-salaried stars on his books. He had learned from Jack Warner's experiences at Warner Bros., that contract stars were expensive trouble-makers who were rarely happy with the roles they were assigned. When he needed a big name, he borrowed one from outside. Apart from Barbara Stanwyck, who left the studio in 1933, and opera diva Grace Moore, who made five films at Columbia, starting in 1934 with the successful *One Night Of Love*, Cohn's only other bankable star was Jean Arthur. Unfortunately, she and her uncouth boss fought incessantly and, after making *The Impatient Years* in 1944, she persuaded him to release her from her contract. At Columbia, Irene Dunne discovered she could play comedy (indeed the studio gave many previously 'straight' stars their chance in this genre) and proved it in *Theodora Goes Wild* (1936), and in the Oscar-winning *The Awful Truth* (1937) alongside Cary Grant – Columbia's biggest male star, whom the studio shared under a non-exclusive arrangement with RKO. Katharine Hepburn, too, made one film, the delightful *Holiday* (1938), for director George Cukor at Columbia – but never returned during Cohn's lifetime.

As the 1930s drew to a close, Cohn realised more and more that an alternative to borrowing stars at inflated salaries (*vis à vis* Claudette Colbert in *It Happened One Night*) would be to develop some of his own. Rosalind Russell was not exactly a newcomer. She had been under contract to MGM for a couple of years, playing poised, intelligent heroines, but, when loaned out to Columbia, had made quite an impact in *Craig's Wife* (1936). Cohn was convinced that, with the right director and property, she could become a major talent. After her success at MGM in *The Women* (1939), it took just one more film at Columbia, Howard Hawks's *His Girl Friday* (1940) to prove Cohn right – and he signed her up.

Above: Director Frank Capra (left) with Claudette Colbert and Clark Gable, stars of his *It happened One Night* (1934). Well might they look merry, for the film earned Oscars for all of them. **Right:** Director Howard Hawks (left) with stars Carole Lombard and Lionel Barrymore on the set of *Twentieth Century*, another excellent Columbia comedy of 1934.

If Cohn wished to become a star-maker, he was given the opportunity in 1936 when a young dancer called Margarita Cansino came to the studio via a short and unmemorable stint at 20th Century-Fox. After three undistinguished B's for Columbia, she changed her name to Rita Hayworth and, for the rest of the decade, continued to appear in whatever junk she was handed, without much personal success. It was not until Howard Hawks cast her as Cary Grant's ex-lover in *Only Angels Have Wings* (1939) that Cohn became aware of the beauty he had under contract.

Even then, it took a loan-out to Warner Bros., for Raoul Walsh's *The Strawberry Blonde* (1941), and another to 20th Century-Fox for Rouben Mamoulian's big-budget, Technicolor romance *Blood and Sand* (opposite Tyrone Power) for Harry Cohn to realise just how major was the asset he had on his books. Hayworth's career at Columbia finally moved into top gear in the 1940s when, after starring in two black-and-white musicals with Fred Astaire – *You'll Never Get Rich* (1941) and *You Were Never Lovelier* (1942) – and being loaned out again to 20th Century-Fox for the Technicolor musical *My Gal Sal* (1942), she was given star-billing over Gene Kelly (on loan from MGM) in Columbia's first Technicolor musical, *Cover Girl* (1944). The film was a smash hit and Harry Cohn became the proud owner of a screen goddess whose beauty and allure made her one of the greatest sex symbols in Hollywood's history and a favourite pin-up of GIs everywhere.

Also on his books were two promising young male newcomers Glenn Ford, who previously co-starred with Hayworth in *Gilda* (1946) and William Holden would become major assets at Columbia in the 1940s, bringing both profit and prestige to their irascible boss.

If the 1930s saw Columbia struggling to throw off its Poverty Row associations, the war-torn 1940s, with its rapacious need for escapist entertainment, was the decade in which Harry Cohn became the powerful equal of Messrs. Warner, Mayer, Zanuck and Zukor. Old habits, however, die hard, and success did not change Cohn's attitude towards thrift and economy. He could certainly run the studio profitably enough by continuing with the policy he had adopted in the 1930s. At the same time, he knew that if he wanted to compete with the majors he would have to be prepared to gamble the company's money on many more A films than he had produced in the past. And having tasted prestige and gained an entrée into the film community – neither of which had come easily – Cohn had no desire to relinquish these glittering prizes by returning to the austerity tactics of the previous decade.

Instead of producing just a couple of big-budget films a year, Cohn decided to treble his quality output and pay less attention to his programmers. Sam Briskin was in charge of production of the general B features and the various series, with Jules White and Hugh McCollum handling the studio's numerous shorts. The rising number of high-quality films – plus the studio's first moves into colour features – brought about an influx of top-grade creative personnel: among them, cameramen (Rudolph Maté, Burnett Guffey and Charles Lawton Jr came to join head-of-department Joseph Walker), production designers (Rudolph Sternad, Cary Odell and Van Nest Polglase were brought in by supervising art director Stephen Goosson), costume designers (Jean Louis and for a short

time Travis Banton), and musicians (Marlin Skiles, Mischa Bakaleinikoff and George Duning came to work with Music Director Morris Stoloff).

Though Columbia's films had always made steady money, the studio did not really know the meaning of the word 'blockbuster' until the mid-1940s when *The Jolson Story*, with Larry Parks as Al Jolson, became the studio's biggest earner to date (and the sixth biggest for the decade in the whole of Hollywood). Other big earners were the Chopin biopic *A Song To Remember* (1945) with Cornel Wilde, and *Gilda* (1946), one of the great *films noires* of the 1940s – and, arguably, Rita Hayworth's most famous film. The most profitable decade in the studio's history so far ended with Hayworth flying off to Europe to marry Prince Aly Khan, with the release of the Oscar-winning *All The King's Men* (the studio's first Best Picture Oscar winner for 11 years), and with another financial bonanza in *Jolson Sings Again*, which grossed $5 million at the box-office. By the end of the 1940s, the only link between Columbia Pictures and Poverty Row was geographical.

No decade in Hollywood's chequered history was more turbulent than the 1950s. After the boom years of the 1940s, the 1950s began inauspiciously with weekly cinema attendance in America dropping drastically. The demon television was blamed. The upheaval in the film industry caused by the advent of television had repercussions that are still being felt today. Heavy tax laws, restrictive conditions imposed by the unions, and an overall increase in the cost of film production in Hollywood helped change the smiling face of the movie industry into a frown.

On the plus side Columbia was one of the first of the major studios to venture into TV (a case of feeding the hand that bites it) with its money-making Screen Gems subsidiary, headed by Jack Cohn's son Ralph, and as a result found itself better off financially than did some of its competitors. Also, the studio had found two bright and promising new stars in Judy Holliday and Jack Lemmon, and had put them to profitable use, both together and individually, in pictures such as *Born Yesterday* (1950) *The Marrying Kind* (1952), *It Should Happen To You* and *Phffft* (both 1954), and *The Solid Gold Cadillac* (1956). However, the studio was making fewer films than ever before – except, perhaps, during the silent era – and despite the success of *From Here To Eternity* (1953) and *The Caine Mutiny* (1954), dozens of employees were made redundant. The studio system, on which men like Harry Cohn thrived, was slowly beginning to sink under the weight of change as powerful independent producers, such as Sam Spiegel (whose *On The Waterfront* won Columbia yet another Best Picture Oscar in 1954) and Stanley Kramer, began to make their presence felt.

Harry Cohn, whose wrangles with the front-office were becoming more frequent and embittered, realised he was no longer the force he had been. Illness further undermined his position as President, and it came as a blow to the company's morale when, in 1954, he was operated on for cancer. The mood of uncertainty was reflected in the studio's product for the next couple of years and was heavily reinforced by Jack Cohn's death, at the age of 67, in 1956. The one bright spot in this sad process of decay was Sam Spiegel's triumph with *The Bridge On The River Kwai*, which won yet another Best Picture Oscar for the studio, in 1957. The triumph was

Below: Harry Cohn (left) discussing *When You're In Love* (1936) with Columbia star Grace Moore. Robert Riskin (right), the studio'd Oscar-winning screenwriter, also directed this film.

Below: On the set of She Wouldn't Say Yes (1945) with its star Rosalind Russell (left), director Alexander Hall (second left) and writer-producer Virgina Van Upp (second right).

Above: Rita Hayworth rose to stardom in the Forties, when she blossomed into on of the cinema's legendary *femmes fatales*.

short lived. The following year, at the age of 66, Harry Cohn died of a heart attack. His memorial was held on Stages 12 and 14 on the Columbia lot, and 200 people attended – which prompted several comments, now part of Hollywood lore, such as, 'Give the public what they want and they'll show up!' It was the end of an era – and, for the very first time in its history, the studio went into the red.

With both Jack and Harry dead, there was no way that the personality and working methods of Columbia could remain unchanged, even though Harry's long-time associate Sam Briskin was brought in as Head of Production. Other Cohn associates – such as Abe Schneider and Leo Jaffe, who had been connected with the studio since the 1930s – were also given positions of importance. Schneider became the company's President and Chief Executive, with Jaffe its Vice-President and Treasurer.

Two British productions, *The Guns Of Navarone* (1961) and Sam Spiegel's *Lawrence Of Arabia* (1962), kept Columbia's coffers healthy in the early part of the 1960s, though the profit margins were nothing like they had been in the mid-1940s. Only when the company opened its own production office in England in 1965 and released a series of British-made hits – such as *A Man For All Seasons* (1966), *To Sir With Love* (1967), *Georgy Girl* (1967) and *Oliver!* (1968) – did the situation appreciably improve. The only home-grown hit of the period was *Funny Girl* (1968), starring Barbra Streisand, directed by William Wyler and produced by Ray Stark.

Between 1970 and 1972 Columbia Pictures – which, in 1968, changed its corporate structure and became Columbia Pictures Industries, Inc. – moved out of its 14-acre lot at Gower, Sunset and Beachwood Drive, leaving behind a ghost town in which storage and office space were leased. Columbia Pictures Industries and Warner Communications then concluded a real-estate merger and became joint owners of the Burbank Studios. All Columbia personnel were moved to the new Burbank complex, and by late 1972 the last vestiges of the studio's Poverty Row associations had been removed, once and for all.

With the disappearance of the outmoded Motion Pictures Production Code at the end of the 1960s, a new permissiveness invaded the cinema, allied to the fast-growing youth market and

manifesting itself in profitable, 'new look' movies such as *Easy Rider* and *Bob And Carol and Ted And Alice* (both 1969). Despite these and other successes, notably *Five Easy Pieces*, *Getting Straight* and *The Owl And The Pussycat* (all 1970), the profits made by the company between 1966 and 1970 were soon dissipated by a string of failures, including *MacKenna's Gold* (1969), the appalling musical remake of *Lost Horizon* (1973) and such British-made duds as *Cromwell* (1970). The combined losses of these artistic, as well as commercial, disasters ended the company's operations in Britain. Indeed, had it not been for producer Ray Stark and his leading lady Barbra Streisand – who brought a Midas touch to *The Way We Were* (1973), *For Pete's Sake* (1974) and *Funny Girl* sequel, *Funny Lady* (1975) – the company would almost certainly have gone under.

Clearly something had to be done – and it was. In 1973, the investment banking company of Allen & Company Inc. was brought in as financial adviser to Columbia, and the firm and its president, Herbert A. Allen, became the largest shareholders. Thereafter, Allen, working with the new management team of Alan Hirschfield, David Begelman and Peter Guber, restored to it the wealth and prestige it had once enjoyed. Buoyed by the terrific successes of *Shampoo* (1975), *Murder By Death* (1976), *Taxi Driver* (1976), Steven Spielberg's *Close Encounters Of The Third Kind* (1977) and *The Deep* (1977), Columbia was soon flying high again. In 1979 Kramer vs. Kramer won for the studio its first Best Picture Oscar in 11 years. Even after a major embezzlement scandal led to the much publicised departure of Begelman, followed not long after by the departure of Hirschfield's departure, the company continued to prosper.

Dan Melnick, who was made Vice-President in charge of Worldwide Production in 1977 (having been second-in-command to Begelman), became President and Chief Executive Officer of Columbia Pictures in January 1978.

In June that year, Frank Price, who had begun his career as a reader for Columbia Pictures in the mid-1950s, and later spent two decades as head of Universal Studios' television division, was appointed President of Columbia Pictures Productions. It was an inspired appointment: Price immediately realised that a major change in the studio's outlook was necessary.

During the 1970s, the motion picture industry was still groping for a strategic management style to replace the dictatorial but undeniably successful approach of the long-gone movie moguls of the 1930s and 1940s. Columbia, which had prospered under what was arguably the tightest rein of all, was no exception to these uncertainties. Indecision concerning management style was matched by the challenges arising from fundamental changes in the way motion pictures were now being produced, marketed and distributed. The rise of the super-agent heralded the age of the 'package deal' in which a project, complete with star, director and writer was presented as a single unit – take it or leave it. Also, the venerable and well-tested theatrical distribution strategy of opening a film in a major downtown venue before slowly saturating the suburbs was suddenly irrelevant. The boom in suburban population meant that plentiful audiences were no longer confined to downtown areas. International distribution – hitherto just a tiny trickle of the overall

Below: Al Jolson (right) giving Harry Cohn the go-ahead to make *The Jolson Story* (1946) – Columbia's most successful film of the Forties.

revenue system – soon became a gushing torrent; while television, which continued its two-decade rise in popularity, was itself springing lucrative new tributaries such as the fledgling cable industry and the home video business.

In short, a tidal wave of change had engulfed the industry and Columbia, which had plummeted perhaps to its lowest point during the early 1970s, was able, under Frank Price, to regain its footing towards the end of the decade. From that point on, it became one of the most skilled of all the studios, both in its methods of responding to these new challenges and its profitable exploitation of them. And it was Price who managed to lay to rest the ghost of Harry Cohn's iron-handed personal rule by introducing a less flamboyant but solidly professional manager class, of which he was a perfect example.

During the late 1970s and early 1980s, Price gathered around him a brilliant supporting cast of executives, many of who shared his television background. Together they succeeded in establishing a new approach to running a major studio. Under Price, Columbia pioneered blanket releasing of its films in all markets while, with regard to the high-powered mega-agents and their all-inclusive package deals, Price not only adapted to this new development, but was able to turn it to advantage.

His first major move as President of Columbia Pictures was to appoint Victor A. Kaufman as vice-chairman. They were a formidable pair: keen to exploit the burgeoning home video market, they arranged a joint venture between the studio and the RCA Corporation to establish RCA/Columbia International Home Video, as well as RCA/Columbia Home Video for the domestic market.

Significantly for a man who had moved his sights from the small screen to the big, Price's interest in television and home entertainment – which had made him such a key player at Universal – continued with the same degree of commitment at Columbia, whose TV division had, by 1981, acquired Time-Life's library of 70 made-for-TV movies, all of which would be distributed by Columbia. By 1982 the studio was in such good shape under Price's leadership that it attracted the interest of the Coca-Cola Company who were willing to pay $750 million to own it. In addition to Columbia's recent hits such as *Kramer vs. Kramer* (1979), *The Electric Horseman* (1980), *The Blue Lagoon* (1980) *Seems Like Old Times* (1980), and the phenomenally successful *Tootsie* (1982), the purchase price also included an impressive film library and other valuable assets.

As far as Price was concerned, Coca-Cola's acquisition of the studio was good news – especially to shareholders whose stock was being purchased at double its market value. His own personal stock was equally high with the studio's new owners who, in a piece that appeared in the *Wall Street Journal*, remarked on the 'businesslike demeanour of Mr Price and other top officials.'

The honeymoon, however, was short-lived and a divorce quickly followed after Columbia Pictures, HBO and CBS pooled their considerable resources to form TriStar Pictures, a new studio that would profit from both network and pay-television by giving HBO exclusive pay-TV rights to a larger number of films.

For Price, the creation of TriStar and what it initially stood for (quantity rather than quality) was unacceptable. Mass production was

fine for the soft-drink business, but not for motion pictures. To exacerbate matters, Price equally disapproved of TriStar's poaching of key Columbia personnel for positions in the new company, among them Victor Kaufman, who became TriStar's first chairman and CEO.

Price exited Columbia in 1983. Over the next three years the studio was run first by Fay Vincent, then Guy McElwaine and, in 1986, by David Puttnam, a talented British film-maker whose high-profile appointment was as dramatically brief as it was heavily controversial. Having co-produced *Midnight Express* for Columbia in 1978 and produced the Academy Award-winning *Chariots of Fire* (20th Century-Fox 1981), Puttnam was a hot property whose credits, when stacked against such films as *Violets Are Blue*, *A Fine Mess*, *Armed and Dangerous* and *Jo-Jo Dancer*, *Your Life Is Calling*, all made or released by Columbia in 1986, were impressive, to say the least.

Puttnam's credo was quality rather than quantity. In order to achieve his aims and break away from the kind of profligacy and excess associated with the new Hollywood, he felt it would be necessary to restructure and streamline the company. He did so by reducing the number of independent producers on the lot – a highly unpopular move – by being selective in his choice of films to be made, and by making certain that reasonable budgets were maintained. Believing that his cost-cutting manifesto would endear him both to the industry in general and the Coca-Cola Company in particular, Puttnam's candour and finger wagging had the reverse effect. By his vociferous disapproval of such disasters as *Ishtar* (1987) he very soon began making powerful enemies.

Taking issue with accepted Hollywood practices was never an industry vote-getter – especially not for a Brit – and what the self-destructive Puttnam hoped would be deemed common sense by his peers, was seen as patronising. The lesson he quickly learned was that it was simply not possible to alienate the industry's pivotal movers and shakers and hope to survive. As a result, his brief tenure at Columbia ended on 1 December 1987, the same time that Coca-Cola announced that it was severing its entertainment sector from its soft-drink sector by merging the former with TriStar.

In effect, this meant that, after the sale, The Coca-Cola Company, which owned 100% of the entertainment sector and 36.9% of TriStar, would now own 80% of TriStar, 31% of which would be distributed to the stockholders as a dividend. A new company was born: Columbia Pictures Entertainment (CPE), 49% of which would be owned by The Coca-Cola Company, 31% by their shareholders, and 20% by TriStar shareholders. Victor Kaufman was its new President.

Puttnam departed from the studio in December 1987 with a $3 million payout. His job went to Dawn Steel, formerly Paramount's head of production. She was the first woman ever to hold the post at Columbia. But another wind of change – one that would eventually reach gale force – was about to blow through the studio, making it impossible for Steel to succeed, despite the fact that Columbia's merger with TriStar in 1989 made her potentially one of the most powerful studio heads in Hollywood.

By 1989 the Coca-Cola Company had stripped Columbia of a great deal of cash. The company had had to sell receivables, so that the money that would have accrued in future years was factored out

Below: Alec Guinness and Sessue Hayakawa in a fleeting moment of harmony as they survey *The Bridge On The River Kwai* (1957), one of Sam Spiegal's British productions.

Below: Dustin Hoffman and little Justin Henry in *Kramer vs. Kramer* (1979), which won Columbia's first Best Picture Oscar in over a decade.

of the studio and passed on to Coca-Cola – a move that subsequently hurt Columbia financially. Meanwhile, there was continued pressure from Columbia's shareholders, who didn't think it made any sense for a soft-drink company to own a movie studio, and this, plus the realisation on Columbia's behalf that it and Coke made uneasy bedfellows, led to a parting of the ways.

Though it took a while, Coca-Cola's executives came to realise that a film studio was not a conventional company whose profits could be predicated on the sheer number of products sold in any given year. The imponderable, maverick nature of film-making and the volatile creative personalities in charge, were light years away from anything experienced by Coke's rather conservative executives in Atlanta. It was as basic as that. Having initially believed that the motion picture business was about market-share, Coca-Cola's hierarchy was forced to confront and admit the misconceptions in its thinking. The variables of the soft-drink business were vastly different from that of motion pictures. There was a precise and predictable relationship in the dynamics of the beverage business that could not be applied to movies.

Not long into Coca-Cola's tenure at Columbia, Victor Kaufman had begun streamlining the company. It was common knowledge in the industry that Coke wanted out, and Kaufman's aim was to make Columbia look mean and lean. Thus, by producing the minimum number of films and television shows, and dramatically cutting back on overheads, the studio was in good shape when Mike Ovitz, acting less as an agent than as an adviser, brought in a potential buyer – the Japanese electronics giant Sony.

Believing that running a movie studio would be synergistic with their own business, on 25 September 1989, Sony offered the Coca-Cola Company a hefty $3.4 billion dollars for the studio and its assets. These included Columbia's library of over 3000 films, 25,000 episodes from 270 television shows, a theatre chain (Loew's Theatre Management comprising 850 screens), RCA/Columbia Home video, TriStar, and Triumph, a distributing arm of Columbia that had begun releasing product under its own banner.

Over the 10 years since Sony's acquisition of Columbia-TriStar, three distinct periods emerged. The first and most colourful involved the formidable team of Jon Peters and Peter Guber who, at the behest of Walter Yetnikoff, President of Sony's CBS Records, descended on the lot and regenerated it in a matter of months.

Since both Guber and Peters had always wanted to run a Hollywood studio, it did not take much persuading on Sony's behalf to bring them on board. There was, however, one initial snag: at the time, both men had still five years to run of an exclusive contract with Warner Bros. At some considerable cost to Sony, the situation was eventually resolved.

On 8 January 1990, it was officially announced that Dawn Steel would be leaving Columbia and, in the time-honoured tradition of such sudden exits, 'going into independent production'. Steel died tragically of a brain tumour in 1997.

Though Guber and Peters had more than proven themselves as high-flying producers, Peters had had no experience as a studio production head, and under his and Guber's guidance and direction, the company's costs went into orbit. Excess was a word that would

Below: Tommy Lee Jones (right) and Will Smith in *Men In Black* (1997).

come to define their tenure at Columbia – for example, the flamboyant Peters redecorated the studio as an art deco showpiece conceived by the designer of *Batman*.

Profligacy, however, was not confined to the cosmetic. The amounts the duo was prepared to pay for stars and scripts became seriously unrealistic. The result was a couple of disastrous years in terms of cash flow and profitability that inevitably led to Jon Peters being fired.

In 1992, Frank Price's position was filled by Mark Canton, a former colleague of Guber's at Warner Bros., but Canton and Guber did not prove a winning combination in terms of box-office returns. In October 1994, following the failure of *The Last Action Hero* (1993), which starred Arnold Schwarzenegger and cost the studio a massive $126 million, Peter Guber resigned. The studio then enjoyed something of a settled and stable period, characterised by the more reflective and businesslike approach of lawyer and chief executive Alan Levine, who succeeded Guber.

Though Columbia-TriStar's huge successes included *Sleepless In Seattle* (1993), *Philadelphia* (1993) and *Legends of the Fall* (1994), the disastrous summer of 1996, with such flops as *Multiplicity*, *The Fan* and *The Cable Guy* – allied to the poor box-office returns of *The Last Action Hero* and *I'll Do Anything* (1994) resulted in Canton's inevitable dismissal in September of 1996.

The third, and by far most successful, period of the Sony era began in the latter half of 1996 with key events in Tokyo and Culver City. In Tokyo, Sony CEO Norio Ohga chose Nobuyuki Idei as Sony's new president. Idei envisioned a unique entertainment electronics hybrid aimed squarely at the emerging opportunities of the Digital Age, and, in that new conception of Sony, the entertainment assets – especially Sony Pictures – rose to new levels of strategic importance.

Idei's vision for Sony overall was matched by a new conception of how Sony Pictures should be managed, which included installing a completely new senior management team, with emphasis on the word 'team'.

Leading that team was John Calley as the studio's new president. A former Warner Bros. executive and a past president of United Artists, Calley was an industry veteran, widely admired for his taste, intelligence and strong relationships with actors and film makers. His management style was just what the turbulent, troubled studio needed, and a new sense of calm and collegiality descended on the Sony lot almost from the day he arrived.

While Calley assumed responsibility for running the studio, he was joined by a fresh senior management team determined to make equal progress in strategic administrative and operational areas. The new team included Sony executive Yuki Nozoe, who assumed the post of Executive Vice-President. Instead of resisting 'interference' from Tokyo, as had previous regimes under the Sony banner, Calley installed Nozoe in the office next to his and welcomed the link to the studio's owners. As a result, Tokyo became much better educated in the vagaries of Hollywood economics and culture and did not interfere with the new management in the day-to-day running of the studio or the development of its products.

Co-President Jeff Sagansky and Executive Vice-President Bob Wynne filled two other senior positions in the new management team. Though Sagansky departed early in 1988, Wynne rose to become President and COO later that year. Idei's expectations of the new team were lofty: 'This team represents a new vision and new direction of the studio.'

Sony's president did not have long to wait for his faith to be rewarded. In 1997 Columbia-TriStar enjoyed the greatest box-office successes in its history, with such films as *Jerry Maguire*, *Men In Black*, *Air Force One* (released in the UK by Buena Vista), *My Best Friend's Wedding*, and *As Good As It Gets* generating an all-time industry record for a single year.

What Coca-Cola had tried, and failed, to do – i.e. bring an effective blend of creativity and financial acumen into the business of running a film production company, and to reshape an old-time Hollywood studio into a modern going concern – Sony has finally succeeded in doing. Long-range planning in how Columbia helps the parent company to grow, and vice-versa, is now Tokyo's prime concern. Equally significant is Sony Pictures' commitment to bring its business into the digital age, specifically in areas of interaction with the consumer.

For Calley, Nozoe and Wynne this innovation is the most important of all – akin to the invention of sound. And, it must be said, a most exciting way to launch not only the millennium, but also the studio's next 75 years.

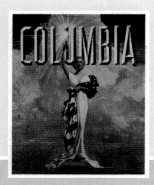

THE EARLY YEARS

Columbia's silent movies, with the exception of a handful directed by Frank Capra, were undistinguished. But with the arrival of Capra, as well as cameraman Joe Walker and sound-wizard John Livadary, the studio was, at least, well-equipped to enter the sound era. Confident of his behind-the-camera team, Harry Cohn invested $150,000 in the Ralph Graves-Jack Holt starrer *Submarine* (1928) – a silent film with sound effects and a music score. The happy box-office returns more than justified the gamble and paved the way for *The Donovan Affair* (1929), the studio's first talkie. If Columbia hadn't quite entered 'the big time', it was speedily approaching it in the fast lane.

1928

▷ After languishing as a gag-man and director of two reelers for Mack Sennett, then putting the great silent comedian Harry Langdon on the map with two excellent movies, *The Strong Man* (1926) and *Long Pants* (1927) – both for First National – director Frank Capra joined Columbia and was put to work on a 'quickie' called **That Certain Thing**. Made for less than $20,000, it admirably demonstrated that, with initiative and talent, the simplest story had potential – and they did not come any simpler than Elmer Harris's tale of a wealthy restaurant-chain magnate (Burr McIntosh) who disinherits his only son (Ralph Graves, centre left) when the lad decides to marry a cigar-stand drudge (Viola Dana, centre right) rather than take over the family business. Undaunted, the son and his new wife hit on an idea to market box lunches, and soon they are so successful that

old man McIntosh's restaurant chain is feeling the pinch. In the end, father and son settle their differences, merge businesses, and everyone lives happily ever after. The small cast, which included Aggie Herring as Miss

Dana's mother, worked wonders under Capra's guidance. Considering how little the film cost, it couldn't help but show a pleasing profit. For Capra it was a modest start to a spectacular career. (Silent – 7 reels)

OTHER RELEASES

Apart from a handful of Capra movies made in 1928 and 1929 (see above), Columbia's silents were unremarkable. By 1930 all their releases were talkies, bar one rogue silent which is also included here.

1922

More To Be Pitied Than Scorned
Domestic drama. An actor (J. Frank Glendon) mistakenly believes his wife (Alice Lake) has been unfaithful. Also cast: Rosemary Theby. Dir: Edward J. Le Saint.

Only A Shop Girl
Drama. Danny Mulvey (William Scott), just released from prison, is wrongly accused of murder. The real culprit is his sister (Estelle Taylor), who makes a deathbed confession. With Wallace Beery, Josephine Adair, Mae Busch. Dir: Edward J. Le Saint.

1923

The Marriage Market
Comedy. The story of a wealthy young flapper (Pauline Garon) and the amorous adventures she has after being expelled from a fashionable boarding school. Also cast: Jack Mulhall. Dir: Edward J. Le Saint.

Temptation
Domestic melodrama. A stockbroker (Phillips Smalley) successfully sets out to prove that most women are corrupted by wealth. With Eva Novak, Bryant Washburn. Dir: Edward J. Le Saint.

The Barefoot Boy
Rural drama. Mistreated by his stepfather and wrongly accused of setting fire to the schoolhouse, 12-year-old Dick (Frankie Lee) runs away, vowing vengeance. Years later he (now John Bowers) returns determined to close the mill he has inherited. However, his childhood sweetheart (Marjorie Daw) persuades him to change his mind. Dir: David Kirkland.

Forgive And Forget
Society drama. A woman (Estelle Taylor) is blackmailed by her lover's room-mate (Philo McCullogh). Her husband (Wyndham Standing) is then accused of the lover's murder. The resolution reveals the culprit to be the room-mate – who confesses before falling to his death. With Vernon Steele. Dir: Howard M. Mitchell.

Innocence
Melodrama. When Broadway star Fay (Anna Q. Nilsson) turns down Paul (Earle Foxe), her dancing partner, and instead marries a wealthy socialite (Freeman Wood), she finds herself rejected by her husband's snobbish family. Her problems really begin, though, when Paul re-enters her life at a party given for the newlyweds. With Marion Harlan, Wilfred Lucas. Dir: Edward J. Le Saint.

Mary Of The Movies
Melodrama. To earn some extra money for her brother's operation, Mary (Marion Mack) goes to Hollywood in an attempt to break into movies, but all she manages to do is become a waitress in a studio restaurant. Finally, because of her resemblance to a star who has taken ill, she lands the lead in a picture. With Harry Cornelli, Florence Lee. Dir: John McDermott.

Yesterday's Wife
Romantic drama. Megan (Irene Rich) and Gilbert (Lewis Dayton) are about to be married when a petty quarrel puts an end to their plans. Gilbert marries Viola (Eileen Percy) instead. He and Megan are reconciled, however, after Viola's death in a boating accident. Dir: Edward J. Le Saint.

Her Accidental Husband
Drama. After attempting to succeed in his father-in-law's fishing business, Gordon (Forrest Stanley) persuades his wife Rena (Miriam Cooper) to return to his home and wealthy family. There she learns to become a lady. Dir: Dallas M. Fitzgerald.

1924

A Fight For Honor
Melodrama in which a station foreman (Wilfred Lucas) discovers a plot to blow up a railway bridge. With William Fairbanks and Eva Novak. Dir: Henry MacRae.

The Fatal Mistake
Melodrama. After being fired from his job on the *Star*, cub reporter Jack Darwin (William Fairbanks), with the help of an undercover police woman (Eva Novak), prevents the theft of the valuable Rigo jewels, gets his job back – and marries the police woman. Dir: Scott Dunlap.

The Foolish Virgin
Melodrama. Jim (Robert Frazer), a reformed thief and successful inventor, meets quiet and refined Mary (Elaine Hammerstein) at a jazz party. They fall in love and all goes well until she learns about his past. It's only after he rescues her from a forest fire that she forgives him and confirms her love. Dir: George W. Hill.

◁ While **The Matinee Idol** (Johnny Walker, right) is in upstate New York waiting for his motor-car to be repaired, he mischievously decides to audition as an extra in the local Bolivar Players production of a Civil War melodrama. The show turns out to be so sublimely (and unintentionally) hilarious that Johnnie's producer, who just happens to be in the audience, invites the entire company, headed by Bessie Love (left) and her actor-director father (Lionel Belmore), to New York to appear in his forthcoming revue. Unaware that they are being exploited, the Bolivarians arrive on Broadway where, predictably, their over-the-top efforts are greeted with mirth. Deeply hurt, Bessie returns home, followed by Johnnie, who has fallen in love with her. Director Frank Capra, whose second feature for the studio this was, revealed a really strong sense of comedy in his handling of the show within the show. Though a small-budget movie, *The Matinee Idol* was generous with its laughs, and the original mood of the piece proved popular with audiences. Based on a story by Robert Lord and Ernest S. Pagano and scripted by Peter Milne and Elmer Harris, it gave Capra his first chance to mix comedy with romance, and, in its modest way, was the perfect showcase for the talented Miss Love. Also cast: Ernest Hilliard, Sidney D'Albrook and David Mir. Remade as *The Music Goes Round* in 1936. (6 reels)

Pal O' Mine
Drama. An opera singer (Irene Rich) returns to the stage when her husband (Josef Swickard) loses his job – and then gives him work secretly paid for by herself. When a temperamental artist (Pauline Garon) reveals the secret, the husband becomes disillusioned. Ultimately, though, his faith in his wife is restored. With Willard Louis. Dir: Edward J. Le Saint.

One Glorious Night
Domestic melodrama. Although she is in love with a poor draughtsman (Al Roscoe), Mary (Elaine Hammerstein) decides to marry a wealthy, mother-dominated lawyer (Freeman Wood). The marriage is a disaster, and Mary leaves. Her newborn baby is, unbeknown to Mary, adopted by the draughtsman who, five years later, sees Mary in a driving snowstorm on Christmas Eve and reunites her with her child. With Phyllis Haver, Lillian Elliott, Clarissa Selwynne. Dir: Scott Dunlap.

The Midnight Express
Melodrama. Disowned by his railroad-president father (George Nichols) for leading a dissolute life, Jack (William Haines) takes a job in the railroad yards and prevents a collision between the Midnight Express and a runaway freight train – thus redeeming himself in the eyes of both his sweetheart (Elaine Hammerstein) and his father. Dir: George W. Hill.

Traffic In Hearts
Melodrama. The story of the tribulations encountered by an architect (Robert Frazer) when a tyrannical politician (Charles Wellesley) – the father of his sweetheart – prevents him from erecting model tenements for the poor. With Mildred Harris. Dir: Scott Dunlap.

Tainted Money
Melodrama. A long-standing feud between two lumber magnates is brought to an end with the help of the antagonists' son (William Fairbanks) and daughter (Eva Novak) respectively. With Bruce Gordon. Dir: Henry MacRae.

The Price She Paid
Society drama. In order to save her extravagant mother (Eugenie Besserer) from bankruptcy, a young society girl (Alma Rubens) is forced to accept the proposal of a wealthy man (William Welsh) she loathes. Dir: Henry MacRae.

The Battling Fool
Melodrama. A minister's son (William Fairbanks) is taken in hand by an ex-prize fighter (Pat Harmon) and turned into a world champion. The finale finds him frustrating an embezzlement attempt and rescuing his sweetheart (Eva Novak) from a burning building. Dir: W.S. Van Dyke.

The Beautiful Sinner
Gangster melodrama. A wealthy young criminologist (William Fairbanks) and a secret serviceman (Carl Stockdale) set out to apprehend a gang of waterfront thieves. With Eva Novak. Dir: W.S. Van Dyke.

Discontented Husbands
Domestic melodrama. A tale that chronicles the problems encountered by an inventor (James Kirkwood) when his new can-opener turns him into a wealthy man. With Cleo Madison. Dir: Edward J. Le Saint.

Women First
Melodrama. Ex-jockey Billy (William Fairbanks) and stable-owner Jennie (Eva Novak) thwart a bribery attempt and win the big race. Dir: Reeves Eason.

After Business Hours
Society melodrama. By giving his wife (Elaine Hammerstein) everything that money can buy, but no money to spend herself, a wealthy man (Lou Tellegen) is soon made to see the error of his ways when she incurs gambling debts that she's unable to pay. Dir: Mal St Clair.

The Danger Signal
Melodrama. Twin boys (Gaston Glass and Robert Gordon), separated as youngsters, grow up to love the same girl (Dorothy Revier). With Jane Novak, Robert Edeson. Dir: Erle C. Kenton.

The Fate Of A Flirt
Romantic comedy. A young English lord (Forrest Stanley) takes a chauffeur's job in order to be near the girl (Dorothy Revier) he loves, and resorts to blackmail as a means of persuading his sweetheart's reluctant relatives (Tom Ricketts and Clarissa Selwynne) to agree to their marriage. Dir: Frank Strayer.

The Fearless Lover
Melodrama. A young patrolman (William Fairbanks) arrests the brother (Arthur Rankin) of his girlfriend (Eva Novak) then, learning that the boy was forced into a life of crime by a notorious crook (Tom Kennedy), sets out to bring the crook to justice. Dir: Henry MacRae.

A Fight To The Finish
Melodrama. A millionaire (Tom Ricketts), in despair at the antics of his playboy son (William Fairbanks), pretends he has lost his fortune. It is now, he says, the son's turn to support the father. With Phyllis Haver. Dir: Reeves Reason.

△ **The Way Of The Strong** was demonstrated by Mitchell Lewis (illustrated) playing a bootlegger called Handsome Williams. When Handsome, who is really rather ugly, realizes that Nora, his blind violinist sweetheart (Alice Day, being carried) is in love with a piano player called Dan (Theodore von Eltz), he sacrifices his own love for her (and, in the end, his life as well) so that she may find true happiness with his rival. This unashamed melodrama was scripted by Peter Milne from a story by William Conselman and directed by Frank Capra who would soon graduate to better things. Also cast: Margaret Livingston and William Norton Bailey. (65 mins)

▽ **The Power Of The Press** was one of the year's better B's, thanks, largely, to director Frank Capra who circumnavigated the clichés inherent in the Frederick A. Thompson-Sonya Levien scenario (story by Thompson) and surfaced with a taut, fast-paced crime thriller. Set in the world of newspapers, it starred an energetic Douglas Fairbanks Jr (centre) as a cub reporter who lands a Page One story when the daughter (Jobyna Ralston, centre left) of a man running for mayor (Edwards Davis) is implicated in the murder of a district attorney. Ralston, of course, is innocent of the charge and together she and Fairbanks bring the real culprit - Davis's corrupt political opponent – to justice. Also cast: Mildred Harris, Philo McCullough and Wheeler Oakman (seated, centre). (Silent – 7 reels)

Fighting The Flames
Melodrama. The only son (William Haines) of a judge (David Torrence) is disowned by his father for obstructing firemen during a hotel blaze. But he later redeems himself by rescuing a young woman (Dorothy Devore) and a street urchin (Frankie Darro) from a burning building, and capturing the urchin's wicked father – an escaped convict. Dir: Reeves Eason.

Fighting Youth
Action melodrama. Tired of the many fights and scrapes Dick (William Fairbanks), her fiancé, gets himself involved in, Jean (Pauline Garon) threatens to break off their engagement if he ever uses his fists again. He does, and Jean makes good her threat – but she relents when she learns that Dick is about to take on, in a charity bout, the man (Frank Hagney) who brutally knocked her brother to the ground. Dir: Reeves Eason.

A Fool And His Money
Melodrama. A hack writer (William Haines) inherits a fortune from a distant relative and buys a castle in Laupheim. On pursuing what appears to be the ghost of a beautiful woman (Madge Bellamy), he learns that the so-called ghost is the estranged wife of the castle's previous owner, a cruel count (Stuart Holmes). A romance blossoms, despite the efforts of the count to convict the writer for obstructing justice. Dir: Erle C. Kenton.

The Handsome Brute
Police melodrama. After losing his job on the force, Larry O'Day (William Fairbanks) reveals an internationally known detective (Lee Shumway) to be a cheap crook. He is reinstated and marries his sweetheart (Virginia Lee Corbin). Dir: Robert Eddy.

The Great Sensation
Romantic melodrama. Jack (William Fairbanks), the son of a wealthy family, pretends to be a chauffeur and goes to work for Peggy (Pauline Garon), a beautiful flapper. Not only does he save her from drowning, but recovers her mother's (Adelaide Hallock) jewels from a society crook (Lloyd Whitlock). Dir: Jay Marchant.

Justice Of The Far North
Melodrama. The trials and tribulations of Umluk (Arthur Jasmine), an eskimo chief, in the icy northwest. With Marcia Manon. Dir: Norman Dawn.

The Lure Of The Wild
Melodrama. Believing that his wife (Jane Novak) has committed adultery, Jim (Alan Roscoe) takes his small daughter (Billie Jean) to the Canadian wilderness. He is murdered, and his daughter is subsequently cared for by Shep, the family dog. Dir: Frank Strayer.

The New Champion
Action melodrama. When 'Knockout' Riley (Frank Hagney) injures his hand in a car accident, a blacksmith's assistant called Bob (William Fairbanks) enters a championship bout in his place – and wins. With Edith Roberts. Dir: Reeves Eason.

Speed Mad
Action melodrama. After being abducted on the eve of a race he hopes will win him $5,000, a young racing daredevil (William Fairbanks) escapes his captors and arrives at the track just in time to drive his speedster to victory. With the prize money he saves the father (Charles K. French) of his sweetheart (Edith Roberts) from losing the family home. Dir: Jay Marchant.

The Price Of Success
Melodrama. When, after five years of marriage, Ellen (Alice Lake) discovers that her husband George (Lee Shumway) is having an affair with another woman (Alma Bennett), she begins a flirtation with the wealthy son (Gaston Glass) of a millowner. George repents and the couple live happily ever after. Dir: Tony Gaudio.

Sealed Lips
Melodrama. Complications ensue when a young suitor (Cullen Landis) misunderstands the affections of his sweetheart (Dorothy Revier) for a man who turns out to be her father (Scott Turner). Dir: Tony Gaudio.

S.O.S. Perils Of The Sea
Action melodrama. A mother (Elaine Hammerstein) and daughter (Jean O'Rourke) sail for America, unaware that they've been left a fortune which, if not claimed within ten years, will go to charity. With Robert Ellis. Dir: James P. Hogan.

Steppin' Out
Comedy. Complications proliferate when an employer (Robert Agnew) allows his secretary (Dorothy Revier) to pose as his wife. With Ford Sterling, Ethel Wales. Dir: Frank Strayer.

The Unwritten Law
Melodrama. Employer John Randall (Forrest Stanley) tricks his private secretary, Helen (Elaine Hammerstein), into marrying him by falsely telling her that the man she really loves has been killed in a saloon brawl in Mexico. The repercussions end in Randall's murder and in Helen being arrested for the crime. The real culprit is Randall's housekeeper. With William V. Mong. Dir: Edward J. Le Saint.

△ Frank Capra's fifth film for the studio was **Say It With Sables**, a heavy-duty melodrama which starred Francis X. Bushman (right), Helene Chadwick, Margaret Livingston (left), and Arthur Rankin. Bushman played a wealthy widower who ends his affair with gold-digger Livingston in order to marry the more suitable Chadwick. Shortly afterwards, his son (Rankin) returns from college with a fiancée on his arm. The girl turns out to be none other than the opportunistic Miss Livingston. From this point onwards Dorothy Howell's scenario (from a story by Capra and Peter Milne) turned really nasty, ending with Livingston's death which may or may not have been accidental. Also cast: June Nash, Alphonz Ethier and Edna Mae Cooper. (Silent)

▷ For **Submarine**, which was the first Columbia film to use sound effects and a music score, producer Harry Cohn took his hand away from his heart and budgeted $150,000 for this stirring tale of men who plumb the depths in S-44 submarines. He also teamed, for the first time, Jack Holt with Ralph Graves (upper left). After firing Irving Willat from the directorship and settling on him a 'supervisor' credit, Cohn gave the job to up-and-coming Frank Capra. Very much a director with his own ideas, Capra caused of a stir on the set by insisting that no one wear make-up. Other directorial 'innovations' followed, and the end result was a taut, convincingly directed drama which found Holt, as an intrepid deep-sea diver, rescuing Clarence Burton and his crew when Burton's submarine lodges itself 400 feet underwater. Capra's grim depiction of men slowly dying for want of oxygen was powerfully realistic. He even managed to make something of the story's obligatory romantic elements, which found both Holt and his buddy Graves in love with attractive Dorothy Revier. Equally effective were the underwater photography was extremely effective, the sound effects and the thrilling sequence in which a destroyer crashes into the S-44. *Submarine* opened at the prestigious Embassy Theatre in New York, only the second Columbia film deemed worthy of a Broadway première. (103 mins)

When Husbands Flirt
Domestic comedy. Complications ensue after newlywed Henry (Forrest Stanley) lends his car to his partner (Tom Ricketts), and when Henry's wife (Dorothy Revier) finds some incriminating evidence. Dir: William Wellman.

Who Cares
Society drama. The 'companionate marriage' of Martin (William Haines) and Joan (Dorothy Devore) is threatened by the arrival of 'social freelancer' Gilbert Palgrave (Lloyd Whitlock) who becomes Joan's constant companion. Martin, however, rescues Joan from a fate worse than death and, in the end, the couple are reconciled. Dir: David Kirkland.

1926

Ladies Of Leisure
Melodrama. A confirmed bachelor (T. Roy Barnes) marries in order to protect a woman's (Elaine Hammerstein) reputation. With Robert Ellis. Dir: Thomas Buckingham.

When The Wife's Away
Domestic comedy. Mistaken identity and female impersonation loom large when indigent Billy (Georg K. Arthur) and Ethel (Dorothy Revier) rent a fashionable apartment for a few days in order to impress their uncle Hiram (Tom Ricketts). Dir: Frank Strayer.

The Truthful Sex
Domestic drama. After being happily married for several years, Sally (Mae Busch) and Robert (Huntley Gordon) drift apart and form other emotional attachments. In the end, though, they resume their life together. Dir: Richard Thomas.

The Belle Of Broadway
Romantic melodrama. A one-time star of the Paris theatre (Edith Yorke), now fallen on hard times, allows a young American revue artist (Betty Compson) to take her place and pose as her former self to become the darling of Paris all over again. With Herbert Rawlinson, Armad Kaliz. Dir: Harry O. Hoyt.

Obey The Law
Society melodrama. When his old pal's daughter is about to marry a wealthy man, an underworld confederate steals a valuable pendant which he gives the bride's father who, in turn, presents it as a gift to his daughter. When the law arrives to investigate, the confederate confesses all. With Bert Lytell, Edna Murphy, Hedda Hopper, Larry Kent, Eugenia Gilbert. Dir: Alfred Raboch.

The Thrill Hunter
Comedy. An author (William Haines) is mistaken for the King of Grecovia, kidnapped, and forced to marry Princess Zola (Alma Bennett). He escapes, the Grecovians dynamite themselves out of existence, and the author marries the daughter (Kathryn McGuire) of his publisher (E. J. Ratcliffe). With Frankie Darrow. Dir: Eugene De Rue.

The False Alarm
Melodrama. After failing to rescue his father (Ralph Lewis) from a burning building because of his fear of fire, fireman Joe Casey (John Harron) is branded a coward. He redeems himself by saving a colleague from a blazing steel mill. After that, he and his brother (George O'Hara) fight over the same girl (Dorothy Revier). Joe wins. With Mary Carr, Priscilla Bonner. Dir: Frank O'Connor.

Sweet Rosie O'Grady
Romantic comedy. Orphan Rosie (Shirley Mason), now grown to womanhood under the care of a genial pawnbroker (E. Alyn Warren) and an Irish cop (William Conklin), rescues a wealthy young man (Cullen Landis) from local ruffians – and marries him. Dir: Frank Strayer.

An Enemy Of Men
Melodrama. After her younger sister (Barbara Luddy) is deserted by her husband and dies in childbirth, Norma (Dorothy Revier) vows to make all men suffer. Which she does, until she meets a fine young man called Doctor Phil (Cullen Landis). Dir: Frank Strayer.

1927

Pleasure Before Business
Comedy. When an industrious cigar manufacturer (Max Davidson) falls into bad health, his daughter (Virginia Brown Faire) uses up her dowry to keep him in the style to which he has become accustomed. The money is retrieved after a horserace. With Pat O'Malley. Dir: Frank Strayer.

The Clown
Circus melodrama. The life of a circus owner William V. Mong is ruined after he finds his wife (Barbara Tennant) in the arms of a lion tamer (John Miljan). In the ensuing struggle, the wife is accidentally killed, and the husband jailed for life. Years later he escapes from prison dressed as a clown and turns a lion on the tamer. He, himself, is then killed in an elephant stampede. Dorothy Revier played his daughter and Johnny Walker the man the daughter loves. Dir: William James Craft.

△ Frank Capra came to the rescue (but only just) of **So This Is Love**, a lightweight comedy which starred William Collier Jr (left) as a dress designer in love with shop-girl Shirley Mason (right). The problem is that boxer Johnnie Walker loves her too. Undaunted by the obvious fact that, physically speaking, he is definitely no match for the bull-like Walker, Collier takes a few lessons in the ring himself and (aided by Miss Mason, who deliberately overfeeds Walker before the climactic fight between the two rivals) flattens his rival and, by pummelling him in the stomach, wins the girl. Rex Taylor and Elmer Harris scripted the concoction from a story by Norman Stringer. Also cast: Ernie Adams, Carl Gerard, William H. Strauss and Jean Laverty. (Silent – 6 reels)

The Bachelor's Baby
Comedy. To avoid being arrested for speeding, a couple (Helene Chadwick and Harry Myers) invent a 'sick baby'. When the officer (Pat Harmon) demands to see the child, a midget (Midget Gustav) is dragooned into impersonating it. Dir: Frank Strayer.

The Better Way
Romantic comedy. Unattractive Betty Boyd (Dorothy Revier), a broker's stenographer, overhearing a tip from a business associate, invests in the stock market. She makes a fortune, and, after spending time with beauty experts, blossoms from ugly duckling to swan. She's wooed by her boss, but won by Billie (Ralph Ince), the office book-keeper. Dir: Ralph Ince.

Birds Of Prey
Underworld melodrama. A well-known metropolitan banker – and former prison in-mate (William H. Tooker) – plots a bank robbery with a gang of thieves. All the bad guys perish in an earthquake. With Hugh Allen, Priscilla Dean, Ben Hendricks Jr. Dir: William James Craft.

The Price Of Honor
Melodrama. An innocent man (William V. Mong), sentenced to life imprisonment through circumstantial evidence, is paroled after 15 years because he is not expected to live. With Dorothy Revier, Malcolm McGregor. Dir: E. H. Griffith.

Paying The Price
Melodrama. A heavy loser at a gambling club confronts its owner with evidence of cheating and finds himself accused, on circumstantial evidence, of the owner's murder. With John Miljan, Mary Carr, George Fawcett. Dir: David Selman.

By Whose Hand?
Melodrama. A nightclub entertainer called Peg (Eugenia Gilbert) is suspected of being a jewel thief when some gems are stolen during a party on a Long Island estate. The real culprit turns out to be 'Society Charlie' (William Scott), a well-known confidence man. Also cast: Ricardo Cortez as Agent X-9. Dir: Walter Lang.

For Ladies Only
Romantic comedy. When a business manager (John Bowers) fires all the women on his staff believing them to be interested only in perfume and hosiery, he is outsmarted by his wily secretary (Jacqueline Logan) who tells a potential female buyer that he discriminates against women. In the end, all his female employees are reinstated. Dir: Scott Pembroke, Henry Lehrman.

Isle Of Forgotten Women
Melodrama. A fugitive from justice (Conway Tearle) arrives at Paradise Island having confessed to crimes committed by his father. His fiancée (Alice Calhoun), however, retains her faith in him and is prepared to wait until his name is cleared – which, in the end, it is. With Dorothy Sebastian as a young native girl called Marua. Dir: George B. Seitz.

Stage Kisses
Melodrama. A rich boy (Kenneth Harlan) falls in love with an actress (Helene Chadwick) and marries her against his mother's (Frances Raymond) wishes. When, later, the husband finds another man (John Patrick) in her boudoir, he goes to pieces, believing that his marriage, like stage kisses, is phony. The actress then sets out to show her husband that she has been the victim of a set-up. Dir: Albert Kelly.

The College Hero
Romantic comedy. A rivalry exists between a college freshman (Bobby Agnew) and his room-mate (Rex Lease). It all comes right in the end, though, with the popular freshman scoring a spectacular touchdown, despite being injured, and winning the game for his college. With Pauline Garon. Dir: Walter Lang.

Remember
Romantic drama. Though Ruth (Dorothy Phillips) secretly loves mechanic Jimmy (Earle Metcalfe), he loves Ruth's sister Connie (Lola Todd). When he goes off to war, Connie accepts his signet ring, but she's immediately unfaithful. When Jimmy returns from the war blinded, Ruth assumes Connie's place. When his sight is restored, Jimmy finally realizes that it is Ruth he has loved all along. With Lola Todd. Dir: David Selman.

The Romantic Age
Drama. Stephen (Eugene O'Brien) loves vivacious Sally (Alberta Vaughn) and proposes to her. Sally, however, seems to prefer his brother Tom (Bert Woodruff). But after Stephen manages to save her securities in an office fire, she realizes it is he who has been her hero all along. Dir: Robert Florey.

Sally In Our Alley
Romantic comedy. Sally (Shirley Mason), a girl of the tenements, is adopted by three foster fathers (Alec B. Francis, William H. Strauss, and Paul Panzer). But the group is broken up when the girl's wealthy aunt (Kathlyn Williams) invites her into her luxurious home in order to give her all the advantages of money and social position. With Richard Arlen as a plumber in love with Sally. Dir: Walter Lang.

1929

◁ Jean Hersholt (right) played Pa Goldfish, a pushcart peddler, in **The Younger Generation** – a lachrymose family drama, directed by Frank Capra, which charted the rise of the Goldfish family from New York's Lower East Side to Park Avenue. Responsible for the family's betterment is Morris Goldfish (Ricardo Cortez, left), Pa's ambitious, go-getting son whose constant attempts to improve his family's image (in order to impress his 'intended's' wealthy family) and deny his roots are the cause of much unhappiness. Jack Cohn's production – a part-talkie (but also issued as a silent) – was a pretty undistinguished effort all round. The stilted dialogue was by Howard J. Green (from the play *It Is To Laugh* by Fannie Hurst). Also cast: Lina Basquette (second right) as Birdie Goldfish – Cortez's flapper sister, Rosa Rosanova (second left) and Rex Lease. (75 mins)

◁ **The Broadway Hoofer** was a charming backstage comedy – with songs – in which a Broadway star (Marie Saxon, right) inadvertently finds herself auditioning for a chorus job in the Gay Girlies Burlesque touring show while taking a much-needed vacation in the country. The writer, director and star of the upcoming entertainment is the personable Jack Egan (left) who, unaware that Ms Saxon is a New York celebrity, is so impressed with her dancing that he not ony gives her a job but makes her a feature player in the company. Saxon's maid (Louise Fazenda) blows the gaff on her employer's prank. Egan has become romantically attached to Ms Saxon and does not take kindly to the deception, so he fires her. A short time passes. Saxon is back on Broadway and Egan is about to make his East Coast appearance in a night club. On his opening night he spots Saxon in the audience, forgets a routine, and is rescued by her when she hops onto the stage and assists him in one of the burlesque dances they had previously rehearsed together. Egan forgives her, and the couple live happily ever after. Harry Cohn produced from an original story by Gladys Lehman (who also supplied the dialogue), George Archainbaud directed and Jack Cunningham staged the numbers. Also cast: Ernest Hilliard, Gertrude Short, Eileen Percy, Charlotte Merriam, Fred MacKaye and Billy Franey. (63 mins)

The Blood Ship
Sea melodrama. A captain (Walter James); dreaded for his cruelty, is confronted by a man (Hobart Bosworth) whom, years ago, he had framed for murder, and whose wife and daughter he had kidnapped. With Jacqueline Logan as Bosworth's daughter. Dir: George B. Seitz.

Stolen Pleasures
Domestic drama. Two married couples (Helen Chadwick and Gayne Whitman; Dorothy Revier and Ray Ripley) each separate as a result of arguments. After certain misunderstandings and false accusations, peace is finally restored. Dir: Philip E. Rosen.

The Opening Night
Drama. When a theatrical producer (E. Alyn Warren), believed drowned, turns up as a lonely, broken anmnesiac three months later, he arrives just in time to see his wife (Claire Windsor) marrying her leading man (John Bowers). Rather than mar her happiness, he takes a job washing cars. Dir: Edward H. Griffith.

Poor Girls
Drama. When a young girl (Dorothy Revier) discovers that her mother (Ruth Stonehouse) is the owner of a notorious nightclub, she leaves home. A climactic reconciliation re-unites mother and daughter, the latter also being saved from a loveless marriage. With Edmund Burns. Dir: William James Craft.

The Wreck
Melodrama. A woman (Shirley Mason) unwittingly goes through a bogus marriage ceremony with a thief (Malcolm McGregor) and is held as an accomplice to his crimes by the police. Dir: William J. Craft.

The Kid Sister
Romantic drama. A young girl (Ann Christy) forsakes the quiet life of her village home and joins her chorus-girl sister (Marguerite De La Motte) in New York. She's soon disillusioned with the city, and returns home to her waiting beau. With Malcolm McGregor. Dir: Ralph Graves.

The Swell-Head
Melodrama. Lefty Malone (Ralph Graves) eschews business to become a prize-fighter, has his head turned by success, falls for the wrong girl (Mildred Harris), then realizes the error of his ways. With Johnnie Walker, Mary Carr. Dir: Ralph Graves.

The Tigress
Melodrama. In Spain a band of gypsies poach the deer in a neighbouring estate. The chief gypsy (Howard Truesdell) is murdered in cold blood, and the owner (Jack Holt) of the estate is blamed. The chief's daughter (Dorothy Revier), a crack knife-thrower, sets out to avenge her father. Dir: George B. Seitz.

Wandering Girls
Melodrama. A small-town, jazz-mad girl (Dorothy Revier) becomes involved with a pair of entertainers-cum-society-thieves (Armand Kaliz and Mildred Harris) and finds herself accused of possessing stolen jewels. With Robert Agnew, Eugenie Besserer. Dir: Ralph Ince.

The Warning
Melodrama. The captain (Jack Holt) of an opium-smuggling tramp steamer turns out to be the chief of the British Intelligence Service in China, in which capacity he saves secret service agent Mary Blake (Dorothy Revier) from death at the hands of an opium gang. Dir: George B. Seitz.

Rich Men's Sons
Drama. The idle son (Ralph Graves) of a railroad magnate meets the daughter (Shirley Mason) of an ironworks owner in a cafe, where he is accused of stealing her vanity case. She takes over the iron works when her father falls ill and puts Ralph to work. He wins his father's signature to a contract, and her hand. Dir: Ralph Graves.

1928

After The Storm
Melodrama. Believing his wife (Maude George) to have been unfaithful, a ship's captain (Hobart Bosworth) takes his young son (Charles Delavey) and leaves her. Twenty years later she stows away on his ship – and all is forgiven. The film ends with the captain sacrificing his life in a storm to save his son and daughter-in-law (Eugenia Gilbert). Dir: George B. Seitz.

Beware Of Blondes
Melodrama. A clerk (Matt Moore) in a jewellery store prevents a robbery and, as a reward, is given a vacation in Honolulu, provided that he transports a valuable emerald to the Islands. On the boat he meets a blonde called Mary (Dorothy Revier) whom he mistakes for a thief called Blonde Mary (Hazel Howell). Complications then arise. With Roy D'Arcy. Dir: George B. Seitz.

Court-Martial
Historical drama. James Camden (Jack Holt), a Union officer, is ordered by President Lincoln (Frank Austin) to break up a Confederate guerrilla band led by Belle Starr (Betty Compson). Cadman joins the band by posing as a gunman and soon falls in love with Belle. Dir: George B. Seitz.

△ If two men can fall for the same woman, why can't two women fall for the same man? They can, and in **Broadway Scandals** they did. The women in question were Carmel Myers and Sally O'Neill (right), and the man they both wanted was hoofer Jack Egan (left). As the film's title indicated, The Great White Way provided the setting for this routine backstage musical which found Broadway superstar Miss Myers coming between Egan and his singing sweetheart, O'Neill – but only temporarily. It was written by Norman Huston and Harold J. Green (who provided the dialogue) and Gladys Lehman (who provided the scenario), and directed by George Archainbaud – who overdid the chorus numbers and thereby ground the plot to a halt. Also cast: J. Barney Sherry, Johnny Hyams, Charles Wilson, Doris Dawson and, as a radio announcer, Charles Lane. (73 mins)

◁ Ralph Ince (left) starred in **Wall Street** as a steelworker-made-good. His co-star was Aileen Pringle (right), a lady with vengeance on her mind. Seems that Ince was once responsible for ruining her husband. When, finally, she succeeds in doing to Ince what he did to her spouse, love intrudes and they all live happily ever after. Norman Houston wrote it from a story by Paul Gangelin and Jack Kirkland, Roy William Neill directed both sound and silent versions of this programmer at a cracking pace and the photography was by Ted Tetzlaff. Also cast: Sam de Grasse, Philip Strange, Ernest Hilliard and James Finlayson. (68 mins)

◁ A feeble melodrama, **Acquitted** starred Margaret Livingston (illustrated) as a gangster's moll serving an eight-year prison sentence for a crime she did not commit. The villain of the piece is Sam Hardy. A gangster with a sentimental streak in his nature (and who also happens to have a weakness for Irving Berlin's popular song 'What'll I Do'), Hardy, in the course of Keene Thompson and James Seymour's silly screenplay, Hardy loses the affections of his moll to Lloyd Hughes, a doctor she has met in prison who just so happens to be serving a sentence for a crime committed by Hardy. Harry Cohn produced, Frank Strayer directed, and the cast included Charles Wilson, George Rigas and Otto Hoffman. (63 mins)

The Apache
Melodrama. After sending a woman's lover and partner to jail, a police offical then tries to seduce her. With Margaret Livingston, Warner Richmond, Don Alvarado, Philo McCullough. Dir: Philip Rosen.

Virgin Lips
Melodrama. American oil and mining concerns in Central America hire Barry Blake (John Boles) to protect their interests against bandit leader Carta (Richard Alexander). After being in a plane crash in the jungle, Blake meets Norma (Olive Borden) and falls in love. With Arline Pretty. Dir: Elmer Clifton.

The Desert Bride
Melodrama. A French Army intelligence officer (Allan Forrest) is captured by Arab nationalists while on an espionage mission. His sweetheart (Betty Compson) is also taken prisoner. Both are tortured by Kassim Ben Ali (Otto Matiesen), leader of the Arab nationalists, but they refuse to divulge any information. They're finally rescued by French troops who storm the fortress and kill Kassim. Dir: Walter Lang.

Driftwood
Melodrama. Jim Curtis (Don Alvarado), an alcoholic beachcomber, and Daisy Smith (Marceline Day), a proud woman of easy virtue, meet on an island, fall in love, and, together, search for a new start to life and a better tomorrow. Dir: Christy Cabanne.

Fashion Madness
Romantic drama. A shrewish young debutante (Claire Windsor) drags her dying lover (Reed Howes) ten miles to the nearest settlement in the Canadian wilds, saves his life, and is transformed. With Laska Winters. Dir: Louis J. Gasnier.

Broadway Daddies
Drama. A nightclub dancer (Jacqueline Logan) spurns her wealthy suitors in favour of poor but ambitious Richard Kennedy (Rex Lease). Richard, however, turns out to be the son of a wealthy businessman (Alec B. Francis) and is pretending to be poor to test his sweetie's love. A newspaper article lets the cat out of the bag. Dir: Fred Windemere.

Golf Widows
Comedy. Two golf widows (Kathleen Key and Sally Rand) decide to get even with their husbands (Will Stanton and Vernon Dent) by going to the Tijuana horseraces with a wealthy broker (John Patrick) and an insurance salesman (Harrison Ford). Complications follow in rapid succession. Also cast: Vera Reynolds as Ford's fiancée. Dir: Erle C. Kenton.

Lady Raffles
Comedy melodrama. Taken by surprise during a robbery, Lady Raffles (Estelle Taylor) seeks cover at the back of an adjoining mansion and is mistaken by the butler for a temporary maid hired to help serve at a party celebrating the homecoming of wealthy Warren Blake (Ronald Drew). Among the party guests are a pair of jewel thieves (Lilyan Tashman and Ernest Hilliard) who recognize Lady Raffles and assume she's there to steal a priceless necklace. In the end, Lady Raffles is revealed to be an agent of Scotland Yard. Dir: Roy William Neill.

The Siren
Melodrama. A society girl (Dorothy Revier) is charged with the murder of a gambler (Norman Trevor), but his partner proves her innocence. With Tom Moore. Dir: Byron Haskin.

Modern Mothers
Drama. A famous actress (Helene Chadwick) visits her daughter (Barbara Kent) whom she left with relatives as an infant. The visit has only been permitted because the mother has agreed to conceal her true identity. While she is there, the actress attracts the attention of her daughter's playwright boyfriend (Douglas Fairbanks Jr), one of whose plays she sells to a Broadway producer. A romance between the mother and the playwright blossoms, but when she realizes the hurt she is causing her daughter, the mother sacrifices her love by rejecting the writer – who returns to the daughter and marries her. Dir: Philip Rosen.

The Sporting Age
Melodrama. After being temporarily blinded in a train accident James (Holmes Herbert), whose wife (Belle Bennett) has been having an affair with his young secretary Phillip (Carroll Nye), regains his sight. He keeps this fact from his wife, who continues her affair. Finally, he invites his niece (Josephine Borio) to his home in the hope that she will fall for Phillip and vice versa. His ploy works, James reveals that he can see again, and husband and wife are reconciled. Dir: Erle C. Kenton.

Restless Youth
Society melodrama. After the father (Norman Trevor) of her sweetheart (Ralph Forbes) persuades her to give up his son and avoid ruining his career, Dixie (Marceline Day), who was once expelled from college for staying out after hours, is placed on trial for murdering a lecherous clerk. She is successfully defended by her erstwhile sweetheart, and, in the end, the couple are reconciled. With Robert Ellis. Dir: Christy Cabanne.

△ A backstage drama, with songs (though also issued in a silent version), **The Song Of Love** charted the vicissitudes of a show-biz family called The Gibsons. A slimmed-down Belle Baker made her film debut as the singer of the act. Ralph Graves (left) played her liquor-imbibing vaudevillian husband and young David Durand was their young son and applause-getter. The plot (by Howard J. Green, Dorothy Howell and Henry McCarthy) is activated when Ma Gibson realizes that she is depriving her youngster of a proper childhood and breaks up the act. Eunice Quedens, later Eve Arden (centre), played a flirtatious blonde and Arthur Housman (right), a Scottish acrobat. The producer was Edward Small and the director Erle C. Kenton. (76 mins)

△ (right) In her first film for the studio Barbara Stanwyck (left) was somewhat miscast, as the heroine of **Mexicali Rose** (GB: **The Girl From Mexico**). With more than a passing nod in the direction of Mae West, she played a hip-swinging man-eater who dallies with the affections of 'Happy' Manning (Sam Hardy, right), the carefree owner of a profitable gambling saloon somewhere along the Mexican border. Unable to appreciate a good thing when she sees it, Rose, who by any other name would smell . . . takes up with someone else, and is run out of town by Hardy. In revenge, she wilfully marries Hardy's younger brother (William Janney), after which she starts giving the eye to anything in pants – including the local idiot called Loco the halfwit (Arthur Rankin, centre). The

original scenario, by Norman Houston, called for Stanwyck's death at the hands of the loony Loco. Producer Harry Cohn opted instead for her come-uppance by suicide, which made no dramatic sense at all given Rose's anything-but-blushing behaviour. Stanwyck's own opinion of the movie – 'an abortion' – may be over-stating the case, but it was certainly no career-enhancer. Fortunately for Stanwyck, enough of her charisma penetrated the mediocre material to allow the trade paper *Variety* to remark, 'the girl shouldn't have any trouble in pictures'. The best notices, however, were reserved for Hardy. Erle C. Kenton directed both sound and silent versions, and his cast also featured Louis Natheaux, Harry Vejar, Louis King and Julia Beharano. (60 mins)

Ransom
Melodrama. A chemist (Edmund Burns) who is working for the government discovers the formula for a deadly gas, and the leader of the Chinese underworld (William V. Mong) sets out to rob him of it. With Lois Wilson. Dir: George B. Seitz.

Runaway Girls
Melodrama. A young girl (Shirley Mason), after leaving home and finding a job as a manicurist, soon becomes a modiste's model thanks to a lecherous man-about-town (Edward Earle) who has designs on her. Complications ensue when the girl's sweetheart (Arthur Rankin) is accused of shooting the cad. Dir: Mark Sandrich.

The Scarlet Lady
Melodrama. Denounced by the man (Don Alvarado) that she loves, a beautiful Russian revolutionary (Lya De Putti) returns to her people and becomes a terrorist. Dir: Alan Crosland.

The Sideshow
Circus melodrama. When the midget boss (Little Billy) of a travelling circus refuses to be bought out by a rival circus, all kinds of accidents begin to happen. Love interest is supplied by Ralph Graves and Marie Prevost. Dir: Erle C. Kenton.

Name The Woman
Drama. On trial for murder, a man (Gaston Glass) is acquitted when a masked lady (Anita Stewart) – the wife of a prosecuting attorney – who was with him on the night of the crime, risks her reputation and her husband's (Huntly Gordon) position by testifying on the accused's behalf. The accused is freed and the attorney, realizing that his wife's misconduct is a reflection of his own neglect, resigns. Dir: Erle C. Kenton.

Sinner's Parade
Melodrama. In order to support her sister and her sister's child, Mary (Dorothy Revier) leads a double life: by day she works as a schoolteacher, at night she dances in a cabaret show. The man in her life is club-owner Al Morton (Victor Varconi). With John Patrick, Marjorie Bonner. Dir: John G. Adolfi.

Stool Pigeon
Underworld melodrama. Jimmy (Charles Delaney), the apple of his mother's eye, joins a criminal gang in order to provide his ma with some of life's creature comforts. Trouble ensues when he falls for Goldie (Olive Borden), the gun moll of the gang's leader (Louis Natheaux). With Lucy Beaumont. Dir: Renaud Hoffman.

The Street Of Illusion
Drama. An egotistical but impecunious actor (Ian Keith), after being given a small part in a Broadway play, manages to secure for Sylvia, an aspiring young actress (Virginia Valli), the lead part in the play. When Sylvia, however, falls in love with the play's leading man (Kenneth Thomson), the actor, overcome with jealousy, substitutes real bullets for blanks in the play's prop pistol. Dir: Erle C. Kenton.

Object – Alimony
Drama. When Jimmy (Hugh Allan) discovers Renaud (Douglas Gilmore) in the embrace of his wife Ruth (Lois Wilson), he suspects the worst and walks out on her. His wife, however, is innocent – Renaud having forced himself on her – and it takes a best-selling novel and a play about the incident, written by a man (Roscoe Karns) whom Ruth meets in a boarding house, before Jimmy realizes how silly he's been. Dir: Scott R. Dunlap.

Nothing To Wear
Comedy. When husband Phil (Thoedore von Eltz) won't give her a fur coat, Jackie (Jacqueline Logan) tries to persuade former sweetheart Tommy (Bryant Washburn) to buy it. Phil buys the coat, but leads Jackie to think it came from Tommy. She gives it to Tommy to hide it from Phil, but Tommy's girl spots it and thinks it's for her. . . . Dir: Erle C. Kenton.

The Wife's Relations
Comedy. Complications beget complications when an aspiring young inventor (Gaston Glass) accepts a position as caretaker of a large estate and invites his impoverished friends to visit him when his employer is away. With Shirley Mason, Ben Turpin. Dir: Maurice Marshall.

A Woman's Way
Melodrama. A Parisian dancer (Margaret Livingston), joins the company of the Opéra, and falls in love with a wealthy American (Warner Baxter). When Jean (Armand Kaliz), a criminal she once shielded, escapes from prison, she assists the police in his capture and frees herself of the only blight on her otherwise happy life. Dir: Edmund Mortimer.

The Bachelor Girl
(Talking sequences)
Drama. A beautiful and efficient secretary (Jacqueline Logan) does her best to take in hand a shiftless stock clerk (William Collier Jr) with whom she is in love. Despite her tireless efforts he continues on the downward path. They separate, only to meet a couple of years later, at which point he promises to make himself worthy of her. Dir: Richard Thorpe.

△ Frank Capra's first all-talking effort was **The Donovan Affair**, a comedy-thriller based on Owen Davis's stage whodunnit of the same name. It was an enjoyable trifle which kept audiences guessing from the moment the lights are turned off at a dinner party and one of the guests is murdered. Enter Jack Holt (front right) as Inspector Killian, together with his inept side-kick (Fred Kelsey, front left). Holt has the suspects re-enact the incident, and, as he turns the lights off, there's a scream and another guest drops dead. Undaunted, he tries a third time – and, with a bit of help from some of the remaining guests, the culprit is duly apprehended. It was good, clean hokum which allowed Capra to indulge his flair for comedy. Also cast: Dorothy Revier and William Collier Jr (as the love interest), John Roche (as victim Donovan), Agnes Ayres, Wheeler Oakman, Ethel Wales and Hank Mann. Howard Green and Dorothy Howell wrote the script. Also issued in a silent version. (83 mins)

△ (right) Dedicated to the US Marines, **Flight** re-teamed Jack Holt (right) and Ralph Graves (left) as fliers in Curtis fighter-bombers – both vying for the love of pretty Lila Lee. Plot-wise *Flight*, based on a story by Graves, was old hat even in 1929, but when it took to the air over Nicaragua (the movie's setting) – it really soared. This was not surprising given that its director was Frank Capra. Without recourse to process shots or trick photography, Capra made brilliant use of the nine planes and flight crew loaned to him by the Marine Corps, expertly choreo-graphing the formation sequences, including one spectacular crash. The most daring scene, however, was one which received a mixed re-sponse from critics at the time and concerned the cremation, in one of the fighter bombers, of dead pilot Harold Goodwin by Graves who sets a match to the sheet in which the body has been wrapped. Effective, too, was the lighthearted opening sequence which finds Graves on a football field running with the ball towards his own goal – an incident based on a real-life occurrence at the Rose Bowl earlier that year. The screenplay was by Howard J. Green (dialogue by Capra). Also cast: Alan Roscoe, Jimmy De La Cruze and stuntmen Bill Williams and Jerry Jerome. Sound and silent versions. (116 mins)

The Quitter
Melodrama. A disgraced surgeon (Ben Lyon) regains his self respect after operating on a café owner (Fred Kohler) and saving the man's life. He is rewarded with the love of a café entertainer called Patricia (Dorothy Revier). Dir: Joseph Henabery.

The College Coquette
(Made as both a sound and a silent film)
Melodrama. When college flirt Betty (Ruth Taylor) realizes that her room-mate Doris (Jobyna Ralston) is about to be hurt in love by Tom (William Collier Jr), a sophisticated playboy, she makes a 'protective' play for Tom herself, hoping to show Doris how worthless he is. But the ploy misfires when Doris falls down an elevator shaft. With John Holland, Adda Gleason. Dir: George Archainbaud.

The Faker
Melodrama. The worthless disinherited son (Gaston Glass) of a wealthy man (Charles Hill Mailes) engages a phony spiritualist (Warner Oland) to arrange a fake séance in the hope that an invented message from his late mother will help change his father's mind. Dir: Phil Rosen.

Trial Marriage
(Made both with a music score and sound effects and as a silent film)
Drama. A woman (Sally Eilers) enters into a trial marriage and defies the wishes of her husband (Jason Robards Sr) by dancing at a charity ball in a revealing costume. Not knowing she is pregnant, her spouse dissolves the contract. There's a happy ending though, when, a year later, after marrying and divorcing other people, the couple marry for real. With Norman Kerry. Dir: Erle C. Kenton.

The Eternal Woman
Melodrama. The proud daughter (Olive Borden) of an innkeeper in the hills of Buenos Aires returns home to discover that her sister (Nina Quartaro) has been wronged and her father (Josef Swickard) murdered. She swears vengeance on the person responsible. With Ralph Graves, Ruth Clifford. Dir: John P. McCarthy.

Father And Son
(Talking sequences)
Drama. On his birthday, a young boy (Mickey McBan) receives a recording machine from his father (Jack Holt). Shortly afterwards, the father is tricked into marriage with an adventuress (Dorothy Revier) who soon alienates father and son. A quarrel between the woman and a former lover (Wheeler Oakman) ends in her death – for which her husband is blamed. A recording made by the son of the incident ultimately clears the father's name. With Helene Chadwick. Dir: Erle C. Kenton.

The Flying Marine
Drama. (Made as both a sound and a silent film) Mitch (Jason Robards Sr), a commercial flyer, takes his young brother Steve (Ben Lyon) under his wing. Sally (Shirley Mason), with whom Mitch is in love, promises to marry Steve. She soon discovers, however, that Steve is irresponsible and that it's Mitch she really wants. Dir: Albert Rogell.

The Fall Of Eve
(Made as both a sound and a silent film)
Farce. All sorts of problems arise when a businessman (Jed Prouty) introduces his secretary (Patsy Ruth Miller) as his wife. With Arthur Rankin (as Ms Miller's sweetheart), Ford Sterling, Gertrude Astor. Dir: Frank Strayer.

Light Fingers
(Made as both a sound and a silent film)
Crime melodrama. In which a jewel thief (Ian Keith), through the love of a good woman (Dorothy Revier), decides to go straight. Dir: Joseph Henabery.

Behind Closed Doors
Mystery melodrama. A foreign embassy in Washington is agog over the activities of a group of royalists attempting to raise funds to aid a revolution and restore the deposed emperor in a new republic. Within the embassy a mysterious individual known as 'The Eagle' (Fanny Midgley) is at work. With Virginia Valli, Gaston Glass. Dir: Roy William Neill.

1930

Hurricane
(Made as both a sound and a silent film)
Melodrama. Captain Black (Allan Roscoe) and his band of pirates are shipwrecked on a South Sea island where they hold in custody several shanghaied sailors, among them Dan (Johnny Mack Brown), a youth of good breeding. When Black observes the vessel of the feared Hurricane Martin (Hobart Bosworth) approaching, he plots to get his men aboard the vessel, incite a mutiny, and seize the cargo. With Leila Hyams. Dir: Ralph Ince.

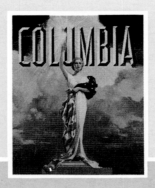

1930-1939

Because extravagance was an undreamed-of luxury at Columbia, the Depression didn't cause drastic cut-backs. Indeed, as the decade unfurled, the studio managed to produce a fair number of 'A grade' films and several of these Thirties movies have achieved classic status. Harry Cohn's commitment, however, was to quantity rather than quality. For every critical success made by Frank Capra or Leo McCarey or George Cukor, there were literally dozens of 'programmers' – though all were solidly crafted. By keeping a vigilant eye on budgets, Cohn ensured that Columbia was the only major studio to remain in the black through the turbulent, financially precarious Thirties.

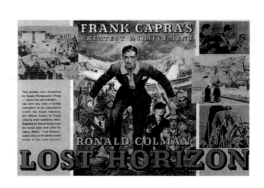

▽ **Around The Corner** was the corny story of an Irish policeman called O'Grady (Charlie Murray, right) and a Jewish pawnbroker called Kaplan (George Sidney, left) who come across a foundling and raise her as their own. Eighteen years later, the child – now a beautiful young woman called Rosie (Joan Peers) – finds herself loved by prizefighter Terry Callahan (Charles Delaney) as well as by socialite Tommy Sinclair (Larry Kent) and has to choose between them. When Tommy wins a boxing match against Terry (and a prize of $25,000), she chooses Tommy. It was written by Jo Swerling whose screenplay set out to capture the audiences that made *Abie's Irish Rose* such a success on Broadway, and directed by Bert Glennon. The cast also included Jess Devorska, Fred Sullivan and Harry Strang. (68 mins)

▷ **Brothers** (GB: Blood Brothers) was about identical twin brothers separated in infancy, one of whom is brought up as a lawyer in privileged circumstances while the less fortunate becomes a pianist in a speak-easy. The former, despite his advantages, is a drunk and a libertine; the latter is a man of impeccable character. When the wastrel commits murder, it is the good guy who is blamed. Finally, however, the rich man's conscience gets the better of him and, in the last reel, he confesses all, conveniently dies, and leaves his girl, as well as his fortune, to his wronged sibling. Audiences were left with brains numbed by the familiarity and downright implausibility of it all. Still, it gave its star, Bert Lytell (left), a chance to indulge in a spot of character acting. To portray the rich brother he donned a pair of tortoise-shell specs and a moustache, while the indigent sibling was identified by an Irish brogue; in neither case was he convincing. The best character work came from Maurice Black and Frank McCormack. Dorothy Sebastian (right) provided the obligatory female interest, with other roles under Walter Lang's indifferent direction going to William Morris, Richard Tucker, Claire McDowell and Howard Hickman. The film was based on a stage play of the same name by Herbert Ashton Jr, and scripted by Sidney Lazarus, John Thomas Neville and Charles R. Gordon. (63 mins)

▽ The second screen version of Brandon Thomas's 1892 farce **Charley's Aunt** (a silent version in 1925 starred Sydney Chaplin) was another moneymaker for the studio, utilizing, as it did, two modest sets and a cast of 10. There was no stinting in the talent department, however, and Charlie Ruggles (second left), as Lord Babberley, an Oxford student who agrees to chaperone two of his chums in the guise of their aunt Doña D'Alvadorez, from Brazil, hilariously chewed up what little scenery there was. Given his high-octane performance, it was a wonder that co-stars Hugh Williams, Halliwell Hobbes (left), Flora Le Breton and Doris Lloyd (second right) (as the real aunt) managed to make any impression at all. Romantic interest was supplied by June Collyer (right) as Amy, and Flora Sheffield as Kitty. Al Christie's direction kept the familiar material (scripted by F. M. Willis) brisk and bracing. A British version, with Arthur Askey, appeared in 1940; Jack Benny did a version for 20th Century-Fox in 1941; a musical version, called Where's Charley? (based on a Broadway musical), was presented by Warner Bros. in 1951, and a German version of the original play surfaced five years later. (88 mins)

△ Based on a couple of characters who frequently appeared on the covers of *Liberty Magazine*, **For The Love O' Lil** was about the marital tribulations of a bashful young lawyer whose wife has ideas way beyond her station. Jack Mulhall (left) played the husband and Sally Starr (centre) was his flapper wife, with other roles under James Tinling's direction going to Elliott Nugent (right), Margaret Livingston, Charles Sellon, Julia Swayne Gordon and Billy Bevan. The screenplay was by Dorothy Howell, with Bella Cohen and Robert Bruckner supplying the dialogue. (67 mins)

▽ A modest programmer, **Guilty?** told the tale of an ex-jailbird who decides to commit suicide so that his daughter may feel free to marry the son of a judge without fear of shame. Seen through the eyes of 10 people all familiar with the suicide victim – a senator accused of bribery on circumstantial evidence – the film starred John St Polis as the senator, Virginia Valli (right) as his daughter, John Holland (left) as her fiancé, and Erville Alderson as the judge. Also in the cast: Richard Carlyle, Clarence Muse, Eddie Layton and Robert T. Haines. George B. Seitz directed, and it was written by Dorothy Howell from her own story. (67 mins)

◁ Dorothy Sebastian (right) and Neil Hamilton (centre) played a secretary and boss respectively in **Ladies Must Play**, a comedy by Paul Hervey Fox. Though Dorothy loves Neil, he is unaware of her affections, goes broke and enters an arrangement with her whereby he'll find a wealthy husband for her to marry in return for a commission. The film ends with Dorothy taking Neil's last four bucks and giving him 40 cents change as *his* commission for getting *her* a husband – himself. Raymond Cannon directed, and the cast included Natalie Moorhead (left, miscast as a society *femme fatale*), Shirley Palmer and Pauline Neff. (64 mins)

▽ In a pairing not dissimilar to Victor McLaglen and Edmund Lowe in *What Price Glory?* (Fox, 1926), Jack Holt (right) and Ralph Graves (centre) lent their middleweight box-office names to **Hell's Island**, in which they played two Americans in the French Foreign Legion, both of whom are in love with the same girl (Dorothy Sebastian, left). In a military skirmish, Holt is shot and believes Graves culpable. Actually, it was a desert brigand who did the shooting, but the truth only emerges after Graves is tried for insubordination and sent to Hell's Island for ten years. On learning the facts, Graves sacrifices his life in a shooting incident, leaving the way clear for his rival and Miss Sebastian to live happily ever after. A somewhat unoriginal narrative, it was written by Jo Swerling from a story by Thomas Buckingham, directed by Edward Sloman (who drew crowd-pleasing performances from his leading men), and also featured Richard Cramer, Harry Allen, Lionel Belmore, Otto Lang and Carl Stockdale. (77 mins)

△ **Ladies Of Leisure** was the first film Barbara Stanwyck made for director Frank Capra. In it Stanwyck (right) played Kay Arnold, a single-minded gold-digger who sets out to ensnare socialite and would-be artist Jerry Strange (Ralph Graves, left). While she is posing for a portrait he is painting of her called 'Hope', Jerry manages to uncover the *real* Kay behind her brittle, wise-cracking exterior and the couple fall in love. But it's shock! horror! time in the Strange family. In order to prevent her son from marrying someone from the wrong side of the tracks, Mrs Strange (Nance O'Neill), borrowing a ploy from *Camille*, and one that would later be used in Robert Sherwood's *Waterloo Bridge*, implores Kay not to jeopardize Jerry's chances of success by allowing him to marry beneath him. Mr Strange (George Fawcett) makes a similar plea, after which a defeated Kay heads for Cuba on a cruise ship. She decides to jump overboard but is rescued and reunited with Jerry, who asks her to marry him. She accepts and, unlike Dumas and Sherwood's doomed heroines, the couple live happily ever after. Though Graves was far too wooden to elicit much sympathy or understanding as the weak-willed artist, Stanwyck, with her magical combination of toughness and vulnerability, scored a bull's-eye. She was seen at her very best in the film's two lengthy love scenes – and also in the scene in which Nance O'Neill begs Stanwyck to end her romance with Jerry. Director Capra wisely toned down much of the melodrama inherent in the original play (*Ladies Of The Evening* by Milton Herbert Gropper, which was produced on stage by David Belasco), and drew standout supporting performances from Marie Prevost as an overweight 'party girl', and from Lowell Sherman as an inebriated roué. It was scripted by Jo Swerling. Re-made in 1937 as *Women Of Glamor*. (102 mins)

▽ When May Fisher's sugar daddy is run over by a motor car and killed, the legacy she was hoping to inherit goes to the man's nephew, a San Francisco waterfront missionary. Undaunted, the grasping Miss F wheedles her way into the nephew's affections and marries him, only to discover that he intends to spend the family fortune on a rest home for itinerant hoboes and down-and-outs. Initially miffed, May comes to realize she is in love with her do-gooding missionary man and voluntarily settles into his unselfish lifestyle. Such was the women's-magazine content of **Madonna Of The Streets**, a sombre melodrama that starred Evelyn Brent (left) as the woman on the make, and Robert Ames as the man who converts her. With minimal lighting and only about three sets, director John S. Robertson (working from a script by Jo Swerling, which in turn was based on W. B. Maxwell's *The Ragged Messenger*) simply wasn't talented enough to lift this melodrama from its routine, programmer status. Also cast: Ivan Linow, Josephine Dunn (right), J. Edward Davis, Zack Williams and Richard Tucker. (72 mins)

△ In **Melody Man**, a drama with a fair amount of music and one song ('Broken Dreams' by Ballard McDonald, Arthur Johnston, Dave Dreyer, and sung by Buster Collier), John St Polis (centre), starred as a Viennese composer who, after murdering both his wife and her royal lover, flees to America with his young daughter. Eighteen years pass during which time he has become (under an assumed name) a musician in a Broadway restaurant, while his daughter (Alice Day, second right) earns her living arranging music for a jazz combo. Miss Day and her new-found band-leader beau (Buster Collier – aka William Collier Jr – right) re-arrange one of St Polis's Viennese compositions – and leads to the arrest of the elderly composer by the Austrian authorities. Based on a Rodgers and Hart musical of the same name, and boasting an opening 12-minute Technicolor sequence, the film still made little impact. It was directed by Roy William Neill, scripted by Howard J. Green, and, in supporting roles, featured Johnny Walker, Mildred Harris, Albert Conti and Anton Vaverka. (68 mins)

△ Living beyond one's means was the subject of **Personality**, a passable programmer that starred Johnny Arthur (right) and Sally Starr (left) as a young couple trying to extend their $40-per-week salary to three times its worth. A cautionary tale, it was written and directed by Victor Heerman, and, in supporting roles, featured stage actors Lee Kohlmar, Vivian Oakland and John T. Murray. Modest, but likeable. (67 mins)

△ The studio didn't waste much time or money on **Murder On The Roof**, confining most of the action in F. Hugh Herbert's screenplay (story by Edward Dougherty) to two sets – a café and a penthouse. The plot had a has-been criminal lawyer (William V. Mong) being wrongly accused of murder and followed the efforts of the accused's daughter, a nightclub singer (Dorothy Revier, right), to prove his innocence. Raymond Hatton co-starred as a newspaper reporter posing as a drunk, with other roles under George B. Seitz's direction going to David Newell (left), Paul Porcasi (centre front), Virginia Brown Faire, Margaret Livingston and Louis Natheaux. (55 mins)

△ Set mainly in England, and also in China, **Prince Of Diamonds** was a far-fetched adventure melodrama (with more than a soupçon of romance) in which a diamond merchant and an indigent English aristocrat vie for the affections of pretty Aileen Pringle (centre). Ian Keith (left) and Claude King (foreground) were the two men in Miss Pringle's life, with other roles in Paul Hervey Fox's screenplay (story by Gene Markey) going to Tyrrell Davis, Tom Ricketts, and Fritzi Ridgeway (right). Karl Brown and A. H. Van Buren directed. (67 mins)

◁ An enjoyable, lightweight comedy-thriller, **A Royal Romance** was the story of an impecunious young writer who, after inheriting a fortune from an uncle, moves into an allegedly haunted castle with his faithful black servant Rusty. In a secret chamber, the writer discovers the castle's former mistress; she is hiding there to escape detection as the kidnapper of her child, whom the court has awarded to her divorced husband. William (Buster) Collier Jr (front right) played the writer, Clarence Muse his servant and Pauline Starke (front left) the lady in the chamber. Her husband (the count) was Ullrich Haupt, and the cast also included Ann Brody, Eugenie Besserer and Walter P. Lewis. Erle C. Kenton directed and it was written by Norman Houston. (66 mins)

△ A romantic melodrama of no distinction whatsoever, **Sisters** chronicled the complicated affair between a sophisticated Manhattan model and a country hick-turned-city-census-taker. Sally O'Neill (right) was the model, Russell Gleason her beau. Also featured were Molly O'Day as O'Neill's sister, Jason Robards Sr (left) as O'Day's loving but jobless husband, and Morgan Wallace as a Chicago crook. It was written by Jo Swerling from a story by Ralph Graves, directed by James Flood, and also featured John Lee (centre) and Carl Stockdale. (66 mins)

▽ A musical-comedy hit in the Broadway season of 1928, **Rain Or Shine** reached the screen without its musical numbers but with the stage performance of comedian Joe Cook (left) more or less intact. A comedy set in a circus milieu, the film was little more than a fun-filled excuse to allow Cook – engagingly assisted by Dave Chasen (who would soon abandon acting for a more successful career as a Hollywood restaurateur) and Tom Howard – to indulge in several slapstick routines. The screenplay was by Jo Swerling and Dorothy Howell who had taken it from a stage show by James Gleason. The crux of the plot had Cook saving the circus of co-star Joan Peers (right) from closure by giving a one-man show when the rest of the performers go on strike. Harry Cohn, normally a very frugal studio boss, allowed director Frank Capra and the studio's special-effects team to stage an elaborate storm and a fire which saw (in one take) the big top reduced to ashes. Strong supporting performances from Louise Fazenda, William Collier Jr and Alan Roscoe contributed to the film's success at the box-office. (87 mins)

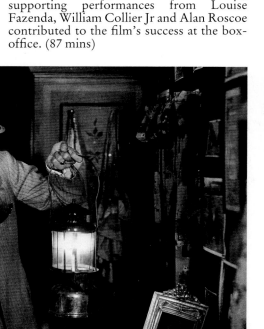

△ A thoroughly routine mystery yarn, **Soldiers And Women**, set in a Marine Corps post in Haiti, told of two women, both of whom are having an affair with a captain, and are implicated in the murder of the husband of one of them. Aileen Pringle (right) and Helen Johnson were the women in question, Grant Withers (left) was the captain of their dreams, and Walter McGrail the hapless husband. Emmett Corrigan, as a blundering general, stole the acting honours, and the cast, under Edward Sloman's serviceable direction, included Blanche Frederici, Wade Boteler, Ray Largay, William Colvin and Sam Nelson. The screenplay was written by Dorothy Howell from the 1928 play *The Soul Kiss* by Paul Hervey Fox and George Tilton – and betrayed its stage origins. (69 mins)

▽ A so-so crime melodrama by Dorothy Howell, Casey Robinson and Jo Swerling (title supplied for $500 by Mark Linder who, in 1928, wrote a stage play of the same name), **The Squealer** was the story of two bootleg gangsters – Jack Holt (right) and Robert Ellis – both of whom reach a sorry end. Ellis is shot by Holt who in turn takes his own life by walking into a spray of machine-gun bullets as soon as he realizes that his wife (Dorothy Revier) is innocent of framing him. It was a convenient solution for all concerned and allowed Revier to pursue her affair with Matt Moore (left), a far more suitable father-substitute for their young son (Davey Lee) than Holt could ever be. There weren't many laughs on offer, though the unique ZaSu Pitts, as a maid, did her best with what few there were. Director Harry Joe Brown's cast was rounded out by Arthur Houseman, Matthew Betz, Louis Natheaux, Eddie Kane and Elmer Ballard, all of whom brought a certain amount of underworld sleaze to characters called Red Majors, Ratface Edwards, Whisper, Mitter Davis and Pimply Face. (67 mins)

▽ A remake of the 1921 First National silent version, **Tol'able David**, based on the story by David Hergesheimer and scripted by Benjamin Glazer, was set in the hills of Virginia and told the story of how young David Kinemon finally became a man by driving the mail truck and rescuing its mail sacks from the villainous Hatburn family. In the role originally created by Richard Barthelmess, young Richard Cromwell (left) made a pleasing debut; and although his dialogue was kept to a minimum, he brought Hergesheimer's intrepid hero convincingly to life. Vigorous support was offered by Noah Beery as the evil Luke Hatburn, Edmund Breese as Hunter Kinemon, and James Bradbury Jr as the local custodian of the mail. The ladies were represented by Joan Peers (right) as Esther Hatburn, the girl David loves, and by Barbara Bedford and Helan Ware. **Tol'able David** was directed by John Blystone with one eye squarely on Henry King's original silent version. Though no masterpiece, it was an effective revenge drama which evoked all the hillbilly atmosphere that the simple tale demanded. (78 mins)

△ A romantic melodrama spawned from the criminal underworld, **Temptation** starred Lawrence Gray (left) as the victim of bad company who takes the rap for a crime he did not commit. After jumping parole he is wooed back into a life of crime by his former crooked associates. However, he flees to New York where he falls in love with Lois Wilson, a cashier in a cheap restaurant. But she is out to marry money – changing her mind just in time to prevent Gray from robbing a bank. Realizing she loves him, she insists he serve out the remaining year of his sentence so that they can start again from scratch. A melodrama demonstrating that behind every man there is always a woman, it was written by Leonard Praskins, directed by E. Mason Hopper, and also featured Eileen Percy (right), Billy Bevan, Bodil Rosing and Gertrude Bennett. (66 mins)

▷ A rough-and-not-so-ready comedy, **Sweethearts On Parade** was a vehicle for pretty Alice White who, in the course of the story provided for her by Al Cohn and James A. Starr (dialogue by Colin Clements), accepts a proposal of marriage from pugnacious marine Lloyd Hughes (centre right) – then promptly accepts another from millionaire Kenneth Thompson (centre right), who, it turns out, is already married and who once was the recipient of a punch in the nose from Hughes. The films ends with White and Hughes happily reconciled. Marie Prevost, Ray Cooke, Wilbur Mack, Ernest Wood and Max Asher were also in the cast. The film was produced by Al Christie and directed by Marshall Neilan. (67 mins)

◁ A retread of the British-made *White Cargo* (1930), **Vengeance** featured the Congo as an exotic locale for a steamy tale of love and hate in which hero Jack Holt (centre – without, for once, recourse to flying fists) manages to win the affections of leading lady Dorothy Revier after her dastardly English husband (Phillip Strange, left) offends everyone in sight and stops a poisoned dart. F. Hugh Herbert wrote it, Archie Mayo called the shots and the cast included George Pearce, Hayden Stevenson and Irma Harrison. The inclusion of newsreel footage of the African bush didn't help. (65 mins)

▽ Based on a play by Martin Flavin, **The Criminal Code** was a prison drama which benefited immeasurably from Walter Huston's strong central performance. Huston played a district attorney who, after successfully prosecuting a young man (Phillips Holmes, left) for murder, knowing that a good defence lawyer could have secured an acquittal, becomes the warden of the very prison to which Holmes has been sent. In an attempt to befriend Holmes, Huston makes him his chauffeur, in which capacity the convict meets Huston's pretty daughter (Constance Cummings making a rather tentative screen debut). Inevitably, the couple fall in love. The plot thickens when a stool pigeon called Runch (Clark Marshall) is murdered by ruthless killer Boris Karloff, and Holmes (who has seen the killing) obeys the criminal code by refusing to reveal the culprit's identity. As a result, Holmes is sent to solitary, where he languishes until Karloff confesses. As scripted by Fred Niblo Jr and Seton I. Miller, the screen version imposed a happy ending, with Holmes in line for a pardon. On stage, Holmes ruined his chances of parole by murdering the sadistic Captain Gleason, played by De Witt Jennings in the film. Tautly directed by Howard Hawks in characteristically macho fashion, and with Karloff repeating his chillingly effective stage portrayal as convict Galloway, *The Criminal Code* was one of the studio's better efforts for 1931 – and a critical as well as commercial success. Mary Doran (right), John Sheehan, Otto Hoffman, Arthur Hoyt and Paul Porcasi were featured too. The story was remade by the studio as *Penitentiary* in 1938, and again in 1950 as *Convicted*. A segment of *The Criminal Code* featuring Karloff was also used in Peter Bogdanovich's first film *Targets* (Paramount, 1967). (96 mins)

▽ Some unimpressive photography by the usually reliable Ted Tetzlaff all but kiboshed the efforts of **A Dangerous Affair**, starring Jack Holt (left) and Ralph Graves (right). A mystery melodrama with a fair quota of laughs (courtesy of scenarist Howard J. Green), it featured Holt as a police lieutenant and Graves as a local reporter who find themselves investigating the murder of a lawyer after a will-reading. As friendly rivals (what else?) Messrs Holt and Graves once again played themselves, with other roles under the directorial guidance of Edward Sedgwick going to Sally Blane, Susan Fleming, Blanche Frederici, Edward Brophy, De Witt Jennings, Tyler Brooks, William V. Mong and Fredric Santley. (75 mins)

△ Harry Cohn once again teamed Jack Holt (right) and Ralph Graves (centre), this time for **Dirigible**, and allowed director Frank Capra to spend more money on it than had been spent on any Columbia feature so far. Following in the adventurous footsteps of such airborne dramas as *The Lost Zeppelin* (Tiffany, 1930), *Wings* (Paramount, 1927), *Hell's Angels* (United Artists, 1930) and the studio's own *Flight* (1929), no expense was spared in bringing Lieutenant Commander Frank W. Wead's story about a rescue trip to the South Pole excitingly to life. The plot had an Admiral Byrd-like Graves flying over the Pole in a plane and agreeing to land so that one of the explorers on board could plant a US flag in its icy wastes. The landing goes wrong and the plane crashes, throwing its passengers clear of the burning wreckage – whence they must crawl home through the snow. Just as the situation is looking hopeless, Holt arrives in his dirigible and whisks the remaining survivors to safety – and a ticker-tape welcome on Broadway. Jo Swerling and Dorothy Howell's screenplay certainly deserved no ticker-tape welcome in itself but, given the Capra treatment, it was serviceable enough and furnished audiences

△ The deceiver in **The Deceiver** was a Shakespearean actor-cum-womanizer who pays for his philandering by being murdered. The question is, whodunnit? Set for most of its running time in a Broadway theatre housing a production of *Othello*, the film featured Ian Keith (right) as the lecherous victim, and starred Lloyd Hughes and Dorothy Sebastian (left) as the love interest – with Natalie Moorhead, Richard Tucker, George Byron, Greta Granstedt, Murray Kinnell and De Witt Jennings in support. Louis King was the director. Although the sound recording and the photography were perhaps below par, Jo Swerling's screenplay, adapted from the story 'It Might Have Happened' by Bella Muni (Mrs Paul Muni) and Abem Finkel, kept audiences guessing. (66 mins)

with several big set pieces, one of the most spectacular being an early sequence showing the destruction of a dirigible in mid-air. The rivalry between 'lighter-than-air' and 'heavier-than-air' crafts, as championed, respectively, by Holt and Graves, was, in a sense, the film's theme, and it was left to audiences to decide which was the more effective. Through the co-operation of the Navy, Capra was able to make use of the giant dirigible *Los Angeles* for many of the sequences. After an abortive attempt to shoot on location at Lakehurst, New Jersey (where the production was halted by warring Union officials), filming resumed in the San Gabriel Valley in temperatures of 95°F. To simulate arctic conditions, cornflakes were used as snow, and little cages of white ice fixed into the actors' mouths to create the illusion of vaporized breath. Capra's resourcefulness and inventiveness paid off handsomely. The film was premiered at the prestigious Grauman's Chinese Theater in Hollywood, and turned a tidy profit for the studio. Also cast: Fay Wray (left, as Graves' long-suffering wife), Hobart Bosworth, Roscoe Karns, Harold Goodwin, Clarence Muse and Emmet Corrigan. (100 mins)

▷ **Fifty Fathoms Deep** was a shallow adventure vehicle for Jack Holt (illustrated) in which the best was saved for the last: an heroic rescue attempt by juvenile lead Richard Cromwell on a scuttled yacht, 50 fathoms down. For the rest it was a routine tale involving a flinty diver (Holt), his young underwater student (Cromwell), and the girl (Loretta Sayers, illustrated) Cromwell marries. The plot by Dorothy Howell (script by Roy Chanslor) had Sayers turning her young husband against Holt, then abandoning him for a yachtsman – for which she pays the ultimate price: her life. Roy William Neill directed, and his cast included Mary Doran and Wallace MacDonald. (65 mins)

△ The breaking of a levee was the highspot of **The Flood** – a dispiriting drama that starred an inadequate Eleanor Boardman (left) as a woman torn between the man she loves and the one she eventually marries. Nothing in it worked – not even the climactic dam-burst. Monte Blue (right) made a colourless hero, and the rest of the cast – including Frank Sheridan, William V. Mong, Violet Barlowe, Eddie Tamblyn and Arthur Hoyt – didn't fare much better. It was written by John Thomas Neville from his own story and directed by James Tinling. (65 mins)

▷ **The Good Bad Girl** was a high-octane melodrama about the gangster's moll who dumps her racketeering boyfriend for a respectable rich man, then, after giving birth to a child, finds her questionable background a decided liability. Indeed, so embarrassed is her husband by his wife's shady erstwhile associations that he sues for divorce. It is only when her former gangster lover is gunned down by a detective that all is forgiven and a happy ending vouchsafed. Heading the cast were Mae Clarke (second right) as the moll, James Hall (second left) as her wealthy husband and Robert Ellis as her ex. Also in it were: Marie Prevost, Nance O'Neil (right), Edmund Breese (left), James Donlan, Paul Porcasi, Paul Fix and Wheeler Oakman. Jo Swerling wrote it from a story by Winifred Van Duzer, and Roy William Neill was the director. (67 mins)

◁ 'A throbbing story of young love', proclaimed the ads for **The Guilty Generation** – a spirited re-working of the *Romeo And Juliet* story. This time the feud is between rival beer barons Mike Palmero (Leo Carillo, left) and Tony Ricca (Boris Karloff). Palmero decides to move his activities to Florida, and at a party there his daughter (Constance Cummings, second right) meets and falls in love with John Smith (Robert Young, right), a handsome young architect. But he turns out to be Ricca's son, who has disavowed his father and changed his name – and so the star-crossed tragedy unfolds. The excellent cast was augmented by Emma Dunn (second left) as Palmero's mother, as well as Ruth Warden, Murray Kinnell and Elliott Rothe. It was scripted by Jack Cunningham, from a play by Joe Milward and J. Kirby Hawks, and directed by Rowland V. Lee. (82 mins)

◁ The first film produced by Harry Cohn's brother Jack, **The Last Parade** starred Jack Holt (left) and Tom Moore (right) in a Victor McLaglen-Edmund Lowe-type relationship – this time as war buddies. On returning from the front, Moore is given a job as a police sergeant; Holt finds his old post on the *Herald* no longer vacant and takes up with a bootlegger. The girl they both love is Constance Cummings (centre), a nurse who looked after them in a field hospital. Moore gets the girl and Holt the electric chair – for murdering his boss. The ironic twist in the story, provided by Casey Robinson and scripted by Dorothy Howell, is that it is Moore who arrests Holt for the crime. All three principals acquitted themselves favourably under Erle C. Kenton's direction, and the cast also included Gaylord Pendleton, Robert Ellis, Earle D. Bunn, Edmund Breese and Clarence Muse. (82 mins)

▽ A freight train careering off its tracks and an all-out fist-fight were the two highlights in **Lightning Flyer**, an action drama which starred James Hall (right) as the ne'er-do-well son of a railroad owner who redeems himself by working for his father (under a different name) and apprehending the villain of the piece. Scripted by Barry Barringer, this rather simple-minded yarn was directed with no distinction at all by journeyman William Nigh, featured Dorothy Sebastian (second right) as the female lead, plus (among others) Walter Merrill, Robert Homans and Albert J. Smith. (62 mins)

◁ A yawnsome drama with an office back-drop, **Lover Come Back** eschewed the eternal-triangle theme in favour of the eternal quartet – eternal, in this case, being the time the plot seemed to take to work itself out. A miscast Betty Bronson (in arms – who once played Peter Pan) played Vivian March, temptress, and the story-line (by Helen Topping Miller, tritely scripted by Robert Shannon and Dorothy Howell) found her luring personable Jack Mulhall (third right) away from stenographer Constance Cummings, the girl he really loves. Cummings, on the rebound, has an affair with her boss, Jameson Thomas (left). Not content with her successful conquest of Mulhall, Bronson decides to have a romantic liaison with Thomas as well. Mulhall discovers her infidelity, gets a divorce, and returns to Cummings whom, of course, he should never have abandoned in the first place. A cast that also included Fredric Santley, John Mack, Katherine Givney and Loretta Sayers (right) made no impact at all, and Erle C. Kenton's direction was powerless against the phony dialogue and the *el cheapo* programmer atmosphere into which the whole misguided undertaking was plunged. (68 mins)

▽ **The Lion And The Lamb** was a comedy thriller set in London. It uneasily cast Walter Byron (centre) as an earl called Dave who, through circumstances beyond his control, finds himself a gang member of London's underworld, out to kidnap a wealthy young woman. Byron's escape from his predicament and the revenge he plans on the gang formed the content of Matt Taylor's screenplay (story by E. Phillips Oppenheim). Montagu Love (right) played the heavy, Carmel Myers a femme fatale, and Raymond Hatton (left) the hero's lowbrow chum. It was directed by George B. Sertz. (75 mins)

△ **Maker Of Men** was the one in which a young footballer gets to prove his worth by running the length of the field to score the winning touchdown. Richard Cromwell (left), somewhat miscast, played the gridiron hero, though top billing went to Jack Holt (second left) as his football-coach father. Father and son do not see eye to eye for the bulk of Howard J. Green's screenplay (story by Green and director Edward Sedgwick), and the irony is that Cromwell, who is not playing for his father's team, scores the winning touchdown for the opposition. Joan Marsh was cast as the (perfunctory) female interest, with other roles going to Robert Alden, John Wayne, Walter Catlett, Natalie Moorhead, Joe Sawyer (second right) Richard Tucker and Edith Wales. (71 mins)

◁ Laura La Plante (left) turned clothes-horse to play a dumb, rattle-brained wife in **Meet The Wife**, a potential farce that, under A. Leslie Pearce's ham-fisted direction, gave the impression it was taking place in slow motion. The plot revealed the problems that beset Miss La Plante when husband number one (Lew Cody, second left) returns from the supposed dead to discover his wife ensconced with hubbie number two (Harry Myers). A sub-plot of sorts, involving La Plante's younger sister (Joan Marsh, second right) and her romance with two men – a newspaper reporter (William Janney, right) and an English fop (Claud Allister going way over the top) – didn't help. It was a dull piece of writing by F. McGrew Willis and Walter DeLeon from the play of the same name by Lynn Starling. (69 mins)

▽ The sight of leading lady Laura La Plante (left) wearing a sable coat in the middle of the Arizona desert was the best thing on offer in **Arizona** (aka **Men Are Like That**; GB: **The Virtuous Wife**). A re-make of a 1918 Douglas Fairbanks silent, and an adaptation by Robert Riskin and Dorothy Howell of Augustus Thomas's play *Arizona*, it also featured a young John Wayne (centre) based on an Army outpost in Arizona, who discovers that his erstwhile girlfriend (La Plante) is married to his best pal (Forrest Stanley, right), a commanding officer. June Clyde, Nina Quartero, Susan Flemming, Loretta Sayers and Hugh Cummings filled out the cast. The director was George B. Seitz. (70 mins)

▽ Lois Moran (second left) starred in **Men In Her Life**, as a 'woman with a past' who, after being lured to a rendezvous in the French countryside by an unscrupulous count (Victor Varconi), is blackmailed by him on the eve of her wedding to a senator's son (Donald Dillaway). Enter Charles Bickford (right) as a bootlegger who, after eliminating the troublesome count, finds himself on trial for murder. Moran testifies on his behalf – and the film ends with the two stars finding romance with each other. Luis Alberni, Adrienne D'Ambricourt, Barbara Weeks and Wilson Benge were in it too; it was written by Robert Riskin and Dorothy Howell (from the novel by Warner Fabian) and directed by William Beaudine. One of the studio's better Bs. (70 mins)

▷ **Pagan Lady** was yet another variation on the theme of a 'good' boy falling into the clutches of a 'bad' woman who then rejects him in marriage because 'she doesn't belong'. It starred a miscast Evelyn Brent (left) as the lady, a wimpish Conrad Nagel (right) as an evangelist's nephew, and Charles Bickford as a racketeer whose rough and ready lifestyle is far more appropriate to Miss Brent's than is the goody-goody Mr Nagel. A storm sequence, well directed by John Francis Dillon, who was clearly more at home with props than with people, was the film's single redeeming feature. Benjamin Glazer wrote it from a play by William DuBois, and the cast included Roland Young, William Farnum (as the evangelist), Lucille Gleason, Leslie Fenton, Gwen Lee and producer-to-be Wallace MacDonald. (70 mins)

△ **The Miracle Woman** again teamed director Frank Capra with Barbara Stanwyck. It was an expensive feature and one of Capra's few financial failures. Inspired by John Meehan and Robert Riskin's Broadway play *Bless You Sister*, which in turn was inspired by the real-life evangelistic antics of Aimee Semple MacPherson, it traversed *Elmer Gantry* territory in its exposé of phony religious exploitation. The villain of the piece is Sam Hardy, an opportunistic con-man and promoter who, after hearing Stanwyck (left), a pastor's daughter, preach to her late father's recalcitrant flock, persuades her to take up evangelism. She does, and in no time at all has amassed an enormous following. Realizing he is on to something big, Hardy hires 'cripples' whom Stanwyck miraculously heals. Commercially speaking, the duo are on an ascent that gathers momentum with each new prayer meeting. Then one day a blind pilot (David Manners, right), who was just about to hurl himself from a window when he heard Stanwyck preaching on a radio, enters her life. One of Stanwyck's crowd-pleasing gimmicks is to preach to her congregation from inside a lion's cage and Manners, in order to show his faith, volunteers to step into the cage with her. Faith soon turns to love – expressed by the shy Mr Manners through a ventriloquist's dummy. A series of plot contrivances follow as con-man Hardy unsuccessfully attempts to separate Stanwyck from Manners. The drama ended – not with Manners miraculously recovering his sight, but with Stanwyck about to confess to the world that she is a phony, and Hardy burning down the tabernacle in which she preaches. Unfairly dismissed by Capra as 'claptrap and corn' (he felt he had 'chickened out' by passing the burden of the villainy from Stanwyck to Hardy), the film was not without quality. Capra's sensitive handling of the Stanwyck-Manners relationship stayed well clear of sentimentality and his filming of the climactic fire was every bit as thrilling as the big-top blaze in his *Rain Or Shine* (1930). Joseph Walker's photography contributed a strong sense of mood and atmosphere to the many night shots, and the screenplay by Dorothy Howell and Jo Swerling went about as far as was permissible at the time in exposing a money-making racket as prevalent today as it was then. Stanwyck's performance was terrific and went some considerable distance in establishing her as an actress of quality – after the disappointing *Ten Cents A Dance* earlier in the year (see next page) – Beryl Mercer over-sweetened the role of Manners's housekeeper, but Russell Hopton was just right in the small part of a press-agent. The film was banned in the UK. (91 mins)

△ A 'quickie' about an irresponsible pilot who, after causing the death of his sweetheart's brother, redeems himself by apprehending a group of **Sky Raiders**, it starred Lloyd Hughes (left) and Marceline Day (centre), with Wheeler Oakman (right), Walter Miller, Kit Guard and Ashley Buck in support. Harvey Gates wrote it, and Christy Cabanne directed. (59 mins)

▷ Though called **Platinum Blonde**, the central character in this lively newspaper yarn, inspired by the hit play *The Front Page*, was Stew Smith, a likeable reporter whose integrity in handling a breach-of-promise (and blackmail) story involving the wealthy Schuyler family results in his abandoning his newsroom cronies for marriage to Miss Schuyler – the shapely blonde of the title. Turning from fact to fiction, Stew, with the help of a pretty girl reporter called Gallagher, decides to write a play. What happens, though, is that he realizes just how much he misses his less rarefied existence as a reporter, and how much he likes Gallagher. He also tires of being referred to as 'Cinderella Man' by his former colleagues and, after an argument with his wife, walks out on the Schuyler millions and into the welcoming arms of Gallagher – as you knew he was destined to do from reel one. In a triumph of style over content, what was basically programmer material was, in the capable hands of director Frank Capra, given a spit and polish that helped underplay the basic familiarity of the material. For once there was a ring of truth to the newsroom; and the contrast between the haves and the have-nots, as represented by the upper-crust Schuylers and the lowly reporters, was humorously handled in the screenplay fashioned by Jo Swerling, Dorothy Howell and Robert Riskin from a story by Harry E. Chandler and Douglas W. Churchill. Best of all, though, was the cast. Robert Williams (right, whose promising career was tragically truncated shortly after the film was completed) played reporter Smith and had the perfect light-comedy touch the role demanded. The titular heroine (pun intended) was blonde bombshell Jean Harlow (left – who was also not long for this world) while Loretta Young was under-used, though effective, as Gallagher. Edmund Breese played managing-editor Conroy; and there was good work from Walter Catlett, Louise Closser Hale, Reginald Owen, Claude Allister and, as Smythe, the butler, Halliwell Hobbes. (82 mins)

△ A 'thriller' about the murder of a subway passenger, **Subway Express** was set almost entirely in a single subway carriage. Earl Snell's adaptation from the play by Eva Kay Flint and Martha Madison was repetitive to the point of torture as each of the suspects underwent the same drawn-out process of questioning. Top-billed Jack Holt (centre) played the inspector called in to investigate the crime – and had his work cut out for him. The cast under director Fred Newmeyer included Aileen Pringle (left), Alan Roscoe, Jason Robards Sr (right), Sidney Bracy, Selmer Jackson, Fred Kelsey, Julianne Leighton and Mason Williams. (67 mins)

▽ An under-nourished pot-boiler, directed by Thornton Freeland and written by Samuel Spewack from his novel *Murder In The Gilded Cage*, **Secret Witness** was the story of a no-good cad (William Collier Jr, left) whose refusal to divorce his wife results in the suicide of his mistress, and of the vengeance exacted by the dead woman's brother. Una Merkel (right) received top billing, with other roles going to ZaSu Pitts, Purnell Pratt and Clyde Cooke. (66 mins)

▽ Noah Beery played a Bligh-like captain in **Shanghaied Love**, a salty cliché-encrusted tale of ships and the men who sail in them. As the skipper of the *Golden Bough*, Beery maltreats his men shamefully. Nor does he treat the opposite sex any better, as evidenced by his handling of a woman he has 'stolen', together with her baby daughter, from seaman Willard Robertson. When the woman dies as a result of his cruelty, he brings up her daughter (Sally Blane, right) as his own. Richard Cromwell (left) and Blane provided the romantic interest. The cast, under George B. Seitz's direction, included Sidney Bracey, Edwin J. Brady, Erville Alderson and, for comic relief, Fred Toomes and Dick Alexander. The screenplay was written by Roy Chanslor and Jack Cunningham from a story by Norman Springer. (75 mins)

△ After making *Illicit* for Warner Bros., Barbara Stanwyck (centre) returned to Columbia for **Ten Cents A Dance** in which she played Barbara O'Neill, a dance hostess (or taxi dancer) in a ten-cents emporium called Palais de Dance. ('What's a guy gotta do to dance with you gals?' enquires a customer. 'All ya need is a ticket and some courage,' comes the characteristic Stanwyck reply.) For such a smart cookie, though, Stanwyck's taste in men leaves a lot to be desired – as she discovers for herself when she marries a young clerk (Monroe Owsley, left), a failure, a louse, and a thief who steals money to pay the heavy debts he has incurred. Borrowing $5,000 from a wealthy admirer (Ricardo Cortez), Stanwyck repays her husband's debts only to be accused by the ingrate of having compromised herself in the process. Realizing just what a non-starter she's got herself hitched to, she leaves him, and although not in love with the generous Mr Cortez agrees to become his wife. Inspired by the popular Rodgers and Hart song, *Ten Cents A Dance* was an unabashed melodrama from first reel to last, and whatever efforts scenarists Jo Swerling and Dorothy Howell made to inject some spice into the characters and situations, they were sabotaged by director Lionel Barrymore, who, so the story goes, was taking so much medication to counteract the painful effects of his arthritis that more often than not he fell asleep on the set, leaving the cast (which also included Sally Blane, Blanche Frederici and Victor Potel) to fend for themselves. Nor was the film helped by the uncomfortably close resemblance between Monroe Owsley's ungrateful husband and the character he played in Paramount's *Honor Among Lovers* the same year. (75 mins)

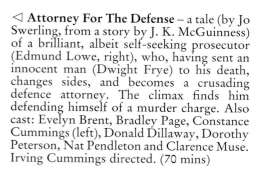

1932

▽ Attorney For The Defense – a tale (by Jo Swerling, from a story by J. K. McGuinness) of a brilliant, albeit self-seeking prosecutor (Edmund Lowe, right), who, having sent an innocent man (Dwight Frye) to his death, changes sides, and becomes a crusading defence attorney. The climax finds him defending himself of a murder charge. Also cast: Evelyn Brent, Bradley Page, Constance Cummings (left), Donald Dillaway, Dorothy Peterson, Nat Pendleton and Clarence Muse. Irving Cummings directed. (70 mins)

▽ Made shortly after President Franklin Delano Roosevelt's New Deal, and espousing all the theories The Deal implied, Frank Capra's **American Madness** marked the trail-blazing director's fruitful association with writer Robert Riskin and was his most blatantly Capraesque picture to date. The story, devised by Capra and scripted by Riskin, was a slap in the face to outdated Hooverism and a plea to bank managers to lend money on the collateral of their clients' good characters ('hoarding money in vaults makes as much sense as pouring oil back into oil wells . . .'). It had bank president Walter Huston (centre) putting this theory (against opposition from his board of directors) into practice. Panic ensues when cashier Gavin Gordon (right), to pay off a gambling debt, robs the bank of $50,000. The public's belief that the amount stolen was 10 times that figure results in a run on the bank. To prevent a catastrophe, Huston sinks his own resources into the bank. He is aided in his endeavours by ex-convict Pat O'Brien (left), one of the bank's cashiers. Together with employee Constance Cummings (second left), they set out to persuade the many small-time clients who have benefited in the past from Huston's generous loan-schemes to make immediate deposits in the bank. (Capra

would use the same narrative ploy in RKO's *It's A Wonderful Life*, 1946.) They succeed, and so moved are Huston's directors by the faith of these small investors that they agree to make up the balance of the losses themselves. The theme of wealth versus ideals and Big Money against the little people greatly appealed to Capra, who was proud of the fact that *American Madness* was one of the first movies that openly addressed itself to the Depression and the panic it engendered. Filmed almost entirely within the confines of The First National Bank, Capra 'kicked up the pace' of his narrative technique by eliminating long walks and prolonged entrances and exits, by increasing the speed of scenes one-third above normal and by overlapping speeches. This resulted in an energy and immediacy remarkable even by Capra's previous standards and was nowhere better demonstrated than in the sequence detailing the pyramiding panic as investors withdraw their savings while news of robbery spreads around the town. In addition to Walter Huston, who was quite superb as the idealistic banker, there was fine work from a handpicked cast that included Kay Johnson, Robert Ellis, Jeanne Sorel, Edwin Maxwell, Walter Walker, Berton Churchill, Arthur Hoyt and Edward Martindale. (80 mins)

△ **The Big Timer** was a prize-fight melodrama, written by Robert Riskin and Dorothy Howell (story by Riskin), that starred Ben Lyon (left) as a hamburger-stand operator who aspires to be a boxer. The girl who makes it happen for him is Constance Cummings, a female fight promotor who inherits her father's stable, and whom he marries. What happens to Lyon when he begins to make it and is seduced by socialite Thelma Todd (right) was the heart of Riskin's story. Tommy Dugan, Robert E. O'Connor, Charley Grapewin, Russell Hopton and Jack Miller completed the cast, and it was directed by Edward Buzzell. (60 mins)

◁ Set aboard an express train travelling from Los Angeles to San Francisco, **By Whose Hand?** was a fast-paced whodunnit involving the murder of a jewellery magnate (Kenneth Thomson, front) in his Pullman berth. Isadore Bernstein and Stephen Roe's screenplay, from a story by Harry Adler, made the most of the running time, while director Ben Stoloff not only managed to draw suspense from every plot point, but credible performances from Ben Lyon (second left, top cast), Barbara Weeks (centre back), William V. Mong (left), Ethel Kenyon (second right), Tom Dugan, Dwight Frye and, as the killer, Nat Pendleton. (63 mins)

△ Mae Clarke (right), who a year earlier in *The Public Enemy* (Warner Bros.) achieved some sort of screen immortality when James Cagney screwed a grapefruit into her face, was the female lead in **Final Edition**, a lively crime caper which, like *The Front Page* (United Artists, 1931) was set in the world of newspapers. It was no mere co-incidence that Pat O'Brien (left) had starring roles in both; for – relying on the axiom that if at first you succeed, try again – the studio clearly hoped to cash in on the success of the earlier film. Clarke had had a featured role in *The Front Page* as well, thus ensuring, if nothing else, that the chemistry between the leading players would keep the workaday plot crackling. She played the newspaper's sob sister who, after being fired for incompetence by O'Brien, proves herself by uncovering the murderer of a police commissioner – and the motive. Roy Chanslor's story, scripted by Dorothy Howell, found employment for Mary Doran, Bradley Page, Morgan Wallace and James Donlan. The director was Howard Higgin. (66 mins)

△ The man **Behind The Mask** was Edward Van Sloan (left), a lunatic doctor who disgraces the Hippocratic oath by murdering his victims, then filling their coffins with drugs. For Van Sloan is part of a drug syndicate which Jack Holt (centre), with a bit of help from the United States Secret Service, helps to uncover. Dangerous work – and dangerous for audiences, too, as they might easily have died laughing at the sheer ineptitude of the screenplay Jo Swerling based on his story *In The Secret Service*. Just as *Final Edition* used Pat O'Brien and Mae Clarke in the hope of replicating the success of *The Front Page*, so *Behind The Mask* recruited Van Sloan and, as a member of the Secret Service, Boris Karloff (right) – both fresh from their work in *Frankenstein* (Universal, 1931), clearly hoping to cash in on the popular horror vogue. But even director John Francis Dillon's use of atmospheric graveyard scenes, storm-tossed nights, and Frankenstein-like laboratories, could not save his film from the *shlock* horror it was. Constance Cummings, Claude King, Bertha Mann and Willard Robertson filled out the cast. (68 mins)

▽ When Barbara Stanwyck (right) demanded $50,000 to appear in **Forbidden** (after Helen Hayes had turned it down), Harry Cohn refused. Stanwyck, in turn, refused to make the film and a court case ensued. Cohn won – and capitulated. Stanwyck got more money and the world got another soap opera. Frank Capra directed and, liberally borrowing certain plot points from Fannie Hurst's novel *Back Street*, provided the story-line as well. Jo Swerling scripted it, and it went like this. . . . A country librarian (Stanwyck) becomes the mistress of a successful lawyer (Adolphe Menjou) who, though he loves her, cannot marry her because of the guilt he feels for having crippled his understanding wife in a car crash. With Stanwyck managing to remain in the background, yet always at his side, he enters politics and is hounded by newspaper man Ralph Bellamy (left) who also happens to be in love with Stanwyck. To complicate matters further, Stanwyck has Menjou's child (whom Menjou adopts). To help Menjou's political career, Stanwyck agrees to marry Bellamy, whom she does not love. Things go from bad to worse and, when her new husband threatens to ruin Menjou by exposing his past, she murders him and goes to prison. A three-handkerchief weepie, it was redeemed by Stanwyck's touchingly effective central performance and by Joseph Walker's striking photography. Directorially the film fell far short of Capra's best efforts to date, though a love scene between Stanwyck and Menjou, played out in masks, was both moving and effective. Dorothy Peterson played Menjou's ailing wife, with other roles going to Thomas Jefferson, Charlotte V. Henry and Halliwell Hobbes. (87 mins)

▽ Western star Buck Jones changed his saddle for the driver's seat in **High Speed**, an action-filled melodrama in which he played a policeman who not only proves his prowess on the speedway, but brings a gang of crooks to justice. He also gets the girl (Loretta Sayers). Wallace MacDonald, Mickey McGuire (soon to become Rooney), Ed Le Saint, William Walling and Ward Bond were also featured in the screenplay Adele Buffington wrote from a story by Harold Shumate, and it was directed by D. Ross Lederman. (60 mins)

▽ Strictly for fans of unsophisticated fan magazines, **Hollywood Speaks** was yet another behind-the-scenes peek at the machinations of Tinseltown. All about a young hopeful called Gertie Smith (Genevieve Tobin, right) whose suicide attempt outside Grauman's Chinese Theater is thwarted by a newspaper gossip columnist (Pat O'Brien), it homed in on the romance that develops between the two, and the unsuccessful attempts of the newspaperman to turn his protégée into a star by changing her name to Greta Swan, showing her the ropes, and introducing her to all the right people. When a scandal with a racketeer all but ruins her chances, O'Brien marries her instead. Lucien Prival (centre) hammed it up as a Von Stroheim-type director, and the cast was completed by Rita Le Roy (left), Leni Stengel, Ralf Harolde and Anderson Lawlor. The star-struck nonsense was written by Norman Krasna who would soon make a name for himself both on Broadway and in the movies. Jo Swerling received a dialogue credit too. Eddie Buzzell directed. (71 mins)

◁ A colour sequence did little to liberate **Last Man** from the trough of indifference into which it so easily slid. When a derelict vessel is found bobbing off the coast of Port Said, with a dead crew and one lone, loony man aboard, detective Charles Bickford (right) is called in to investigate. Keene Thompson's story (dialogue by Francis Faragoh and Sam Nelson) was directed by Howard Higgin. The cast included Constance Cummings (left), Alec B. Francis, Alan Roscoe, Robert Ellis, Jimmy Wang and Bill Williams. (65 mins)

▷ First published in an anthology of *The World's Best Short Stories*, Ursula Parrott's **Love Affair** clearly lost something in the translation from page to screen, and might euphemistically be described as 'tame romantic fare'. It starred ex-Ziegfeld girl Dorothy Mackaill (right) as a rich lass who falls in love with aviator Humphrey Bogart (left). The course of true romance, they soon discover, is anything but high flying. For a start, he's poor and she's rich – which for some reason proves an obstacle. Then she loses all her money and is unable to finance the new high-powered motor he has invented, bringing more problems. To complicate matters even further, a triangle situation develops when her financial adviser (Hale Hamilton) proposes to her. All is unravelled in the end, though, courtesy of scenarists Jo Swerling and Dorothy Howell. The other roles, under Thornton Freeland's direction, went to Jack Kennedy, Barbara Leonard, Astrid Allwyn, Bradley Page and Halliwell Hobbes. The film's real star was cameraman Teddy Tetzlaff, whose aerial photography was terrific. (65 mins)

▷ Jack Holt (right) was in action again in **Man Against Woman**, this time playing a police detective much given to fisticuffs, and newcomer Lillian Miles (left) was the object of his affections. She played a torch singer in love with a good-looking crook (Gavin Gordon, centre), a fact that doesn't in the least bother our hero, who not only gets his woman in the end but also his man. The best performance in this indifferent narrative came from Walter Connolly as a gangster boss, with other roles assigned to Arthur Vinton, Emmett Corrigan, Clarence Muse, Harry Seymour and Jack LaRue. Busy Jo Swerling scripted it from a story by Keene Thompson, and the so-so direction was by Irving Cummings. (70 mins)

▽ Ladies' man Adolphe Menjou (left) abandoned love for crime detection in **Night Club Lady**, as a police commissioner out to discover who murdered tough nightclub hostess Mayo Methot (centre) – and, more intriguingly, how; for Methot had been given police protection ever since receiving a written warning that she won't live a minute past midnight on New Year's Eve. It turns out that the murder 'weapon' was a deadly scorpion, administered by Blanche Frederici who was posing as the victim's mother. Menjou performed with his usual aplomb, and Robert Riskin's screenplay (from a novel by Anthony Abbott) also furnished roles for Skeets Gallagher, Ruthelma Stevens (right), Gerald Fielding, Nay Pendleton and Albert Conti. Irving Cummings directed. (66 mins)

◁ There was no menace in **The Menace**, a bottom-of-the-bill adaptation by Dorothy Howell, Charles Logue and Roy Chanslor of Edgar Wallace's tale The Feathered Serpent. Indeed, the film was of interest only in that it featured Bette Davis (second left) in one of her earliest roles. She played Peggy, the fiancée of handsome Englishman Walter Byron who has been wrongly accused of murdering his father and sent to prison. The real culprit is his stepmother (Natalie Moorhead, left) who, in the way of such melodramas, wants her dead husband's estate all to herself. Escaping from prison, Byron takes a job on an oil-rig, where he has a nasty accident during which his face is badly burned. He has plastic surgery and then returns to England unrecognized, and ready to clear his name. Audiences didn't buy a line of it! Sam Nelson produced, Roy William Neill directed and the cast included top-billed H. B. Warner (centre) in the relatively small role of Tracey of Scotland Yard, William B. Davidson, Crauford Kent, Halliwell Hobbes, Charles Gerrard (right) and Murray Kinnell who, shortly after the film was completed, introduced Bette Davis to his friend George Arliss – which led to her being cast in The Man Who Played God (1932) and launched her career at Warner Bros. (64 mins)

▽ Following in the wake of the Jimmy Walker mayoral scandal in New York, **Night Mayor** was deemed by many to be a tasteless piece of headline exploitation whose central character, Mayor Bobby Kingston (Lee Tracy, left) was unashamedly modelled on the disgraced New York celebrity. As scripted by Gertrude Purcell from a story by Sam Marx, the film was basically a flashy vehicle for Tracy, who impersonated the flamboyant mayor most effectively. More interested in the high life than in his mayoral functions, Tracy does, however, manage to prevent one crime and to avoid a scandal by having his girlfriend (Evalyn Knapp) marry newspaperman Donald Dillaway. Director Ben Stoloff rounded up some reliable character actors to flesh out the wise-cracking, New York-orientated script, the best being Eugene Pallette (right) as an unscrupulous politician, and Vince Barnett as the mayor's bungling tailor. Other roles were allotted to Warren Hymer, Astrid Allwyn, Barbara Weeks and Gloria Shea. (65 mins)

▷ A hearts-and-flowers domestic drama owing a sizeable debt to *Abie's Irish Rose* (1929), **No Greater Love** was the lachrymose tale of a crippled orphaned Irish lass and the kindly Jewish delicatessen owner who, against much opposition, adopts her. Alexander Carr (left) played the deli man and Betty Jane Graham (centre) was his ward. Top-cast, though, was child star Dickie Moore (right), with other roles in Lou Breslow's Yiddish-influenced screenplay (story by Isadore Bernstein) going to Beryl Mercer, Hobart Bosworth, Mischa Auer (as a rabbi), Helen Jerome Eddy – and, in a bit part (though third-billed), Richard Bennett. Lewis Seiler directed. (59 mins)

▽ **Shopworn** lived up to its title in more ways than one. Starring Barbara Stanwyck (left) in a role rejected by the wise Lila Lee, it was the trite old story of a waitress from the wrong side of the tracks who falls in love with a man (Regis Toomey, right) way above her station. As befell Miss Stanwyck in *Ladies Of Leisure* (1930), her intended's mother (Clara Blandick) does everything she can to oppose the liaison – in this case even having Stanwyck framed and sent to a workhouse prison for three months. However, Stanwyck is a fighter, and on her release finds instant stardom in show business – as well as the social status she had always lacked. Blandick now withdraws her objections and the lovers are reunited. The End. A lacklustre belief-defying screenplay by Jo Swerling, Robert Riskin and Sarah Y. Mason (story by Mason) grounded all Stanwyck's efforts to turn the role into anything other than the shopworn thing it was, a situation exacerbated by Nick Grinde's makeshift direction. ZaSu Pitts and Lucien Littlefield headed a supporting cast that included Robert Alden, Oscar Apfel, Maude Turner Gordon and Albert Conti. (68 mins)

▷ It was one darn thing after another for Speed Morrow (William Collier Jr, centre), the hero of **Speed Demon** - a melodrama from scenarist Charles R. Condon. Playing a youthful mechanic, and a whizz behind the wheel of a racing car, Speed becomes the victim of a gangster rival on the track who, after unsuccessfully asking him to throw the race, gets him drunk. Speed is barred from racing, takes to booze, befriends a kid (Georgie Ernest, second left) from an orphanage, becomes a rum-runner and finally pulls himself together when Master Ernest is kidnapped. It was bilge from start to finish. Joan Marsh (second right) was the romantic interest (she and Speed become lighthouse keepers at the final fade), with other parts going to Frank Sheridan (right), Wade Boteler (left) and Wheeler Oakman. D. Ross Lederman directed. (71 mins)

▷ A drama with a football backdrop, **That's My Boy** starred a somewhat miscast Richard Cromwell (left) as a gridiron hero – who just about justifies his underweight appearance by being a canny runner. A sub-plot has him involved in a fake stock-selling scheme, the outcome of which could affect both his romance (with nonentity Dorothy Jordan, right) and career. It all worked out satisfactorily, of course – both on and off the field – and audiences went home happy. Well, some of them did. Mae Marsh played Cromwell's mother, with other roles under Roy William Neill's direction going to Arthur Stone (as his dad), Douglass Dumbrille, Lucien Littlefield and Leon Waycoft. Norman Krasna scripted from the novel by Francis Wallace. (71 mins)

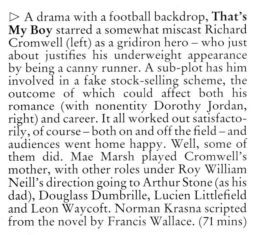

◁ Jack Holt (left) played a model father and a gentleman in **This Sporting Age**, the only girl in his life being his attractive daughter (Evalyn Knapp, right). She, in turn, is loved by decent Hardie Albright, though compromised by caddish Walter Byron. To avenge his daughter's betrayal, Holt engages Byron in a polo game that ends in the blackguard's death – an act of deliberate manslaughter by Holt. But Byron had it coming and no one complained. J. Farrell MacDonald, Ruth Weston, Nora Lane, Shirley Palmer and Hal Price backed up the rear, it was written by Dudley Nichols from a story by J. K. McGuiness, and directed by Andrew W. Bennison and A. F. Erickson. A fair-to-middling programmer. (71 mins)

△ **Vanity Street** was a tawdry little melodrama in which Charles Bickford (right, top-cast as a cop) rescues down-and-out Helen Chandler (left) from ruin, sets her up as a 'Follies' girl, then, after arresting her for a murder she did not commit, clears her name – and leads her to the altar. Forty-carat piffle. It was written by Gertrude Purcell from a story by Frank Cavett and Edwards Roberts, directed by Nicholas Grinde, and featured Mayo Methot, George Meeker, Arthur Hoyt, Raymond Hatton and Ruth Channing. (67 mins)

△ **Virtue**'s biggest virtue was the fact that it starred Carole Lombard (right) and Pat O'Brien (left). These two soon-to-be-stars brought a conviction it otherwise might not have had to the hackneyed tale of a prostitute and the man who marries and reforms her. Lombard was a girl of the streets, O'Brien a taxicab driver who makes an honest woman of her. The main plot contrivance in Robert Riskin's screenplay (from a story by Ethel Hill) found Lombard returning to a hotel of ill-repute to collect the $200 she once loaned to a girlfriend. Hubby O'Brien mistakenly

believes she has turned pro again and the situation is further complicated after Lombard is implicated in a murder and sent to jail. The last reel, however, saw virtue triumphant as O'Brien, believing in his wife's innocence, helps clear her of all charges. A better-than-average programmer, it also featured Ward Bond, Willard Robertson, Mayo Methot as a prostitute, Shirley Grey and Ed Le Saint. It was directed by the capable Ed Buzzell, who managed to wrest from Riskin's melodramatic screenplay all the action and suspense the plot could possibly yield. (68 mins)

▽ **War Correspondent** was a formula Jack Holt–Ralph Graves actioner with the two macho stars fighting over the same girl (Lila Lee, right) and with Graves (centre) getting her – even though Holt (left) proves to be the real hero of the story. Graves played a war correspondent while Holt was a mercenary or soldier of fortune. The finale finds them reconciled after being on the 'outs' for most of the running time, and taking on an entire army of Chinese bandits. The villain of the piece was Tetsu Komai as bandit-chief 'Fang', and the cast also included Victor Wong. It was written by Jo Swerling from a story by Keene Thompson, and directed by Paul Sloane off the assembly line. (76 mins)

△ The **Three Wise Girls** were Jean Harlow (left), Mae Clarke (right) and Marie Prevost. All from Hicksville, they decide to sample life in the big city (New York, where else?) – with varying degrees of success. Clarke is a kept woman in a Park Avenue apartment, Prevost addresses envelopes in an office, and Harlow becomes a model in a couturier store. Their romantic involvements made up the bulk of Agnes C. Johnson and Robert Riskin's fair-to-middling screenplay (from Wilson Collison's story *Blonde Baby*). When Harlow discovers her man is already married, she gives him the air and returns to Hicks-

ville. He divorces his wife and follows her to the country. Clarke commits suicide when her fellow tires of their romance, and Prevost finishes up with a lovable chauffeur. The three men were played by Walter Byron, Arthur Phelps and Andy Devine. With a tighter script and stronger performances this one might have been a contender, but under William Beaudine's routine direction it was a so-so morality tale. The really wise girl of the trio was Harlow, whose last film for Columbia this was. Sensing that her career was more or less on hold, she moved on to stardom at MGM. (67 mins)

◁ **Washington Merry Go Round** was a flag-waving political drama in which Lee Tracy (right), aided and abetted by elder statesman Walter Connolly (centre) and pretty Constance Cummings (left), exposes a group of corrupt politicians. The villain was Alan Dinehart as a traitor against the Republic and the evil genius behind a heinous catalogue of crooked deals. Workmanlike direction by James Cruze was not much help to a cast that also included Clarence Muse (as a black valet), Arthur Vinton, Frank Sheridan and Clay Clement. The story was the brainchild of the usually quality-conscious Maxwell Anderson, with journeyman Jo Swerling supplying the dialogue. (75 mins)

▽ A romantic melodrama of the type so popular in the early Twenties, **Air Hostess** starred Evalyn Knapp (centre) as – yes, an air hostess, who, after discovering her aviator husband (James Murray, right) in a compromising situation with seductive blonde Thelma Todd, boards a passenger train unaware that the locomotive is heading for destruction down a raging gulch. Repentent, Murray follows her in his plane, which he boldly crashes in front of the express just as it is on the verge of destruction. Emerging from the wreckage unscatched and unscratched, he wins back the love of Miss Knapp and all ends happily. Keene Thompson wrote it; Al Rogell directed, and it also featured Arthur Pierson (left), Jane Darwell, J. M. Kerrigan and Mike Donlin. (67 mins)

▽ Fay Wray (left) starred in **Ann Carver's Profession** and was monumentally miscast as a lady lawyer whose brilliance when it comes to legal procedure knows no peer. As a result of Ms Carver's success in her chosen profession, her husband (Gene Raymond, right) – an architect and not nearly as celebrated as his wife – is on a perpetual binge, as it is wife who pays all the bills. Tiring of architecture, he becomes a nightclub crooner, takes a liquor-imbibing lover (Claire Dodd) and is accused of murder when his mistress accidentally dies. Needless to say, the climax finds him being defended by his wife. It wasn't a bad idea – just a badly written one (by Robert Riskin), and it sank without trace, taking with it Arthur Pierson, Claude Gillingwater (as a crusty old judge), Frank Albertson and Frank Conroy. Edward Buzzell directed. (71 mins)

▽ An off-the-wall melodrama, **As The Devil Commands** was the convoluted story of a villainous lawyer (Neil Hamilton, right) who indulges in a spot of mercy killing, but not before persuading the elderly, terminally ill victim (Charles Sellon, left) to change his will in favour of the hero (Alan Dinehart) – thus making it appear that the hero was guilty of murder. Not only that, but the crooked lawyer then 'defends' the hero in so half-hearted a fashion that his client gets a life sentence. Blame the plot on Jo Swerling, the screenplay on Dan Nelson, and the heavy-handed direction on Roy William Neill. Mae Clarke, Charles Coleman and John Sheehan were also in it. (70 mins)

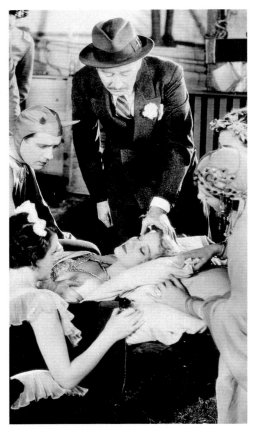

△ Adolphe Menjou (back) ran away with the acting honours in **Circus Queen Murder**, a big-tent thriller, in which he played a vacationing police commissioner who becomes involved in murder and mayhem as a travelling circus arrives for a date in a small town. Greta Nissen (centre) played Josie, the circus queen (who slips from a trapeze-perch with a poisoned arrow in her back) with other roles under Roy William Neill's nifty direction going to Ruthelma Stevens, Dwight Frye, Donald Cook (in hood), Harry Holman and George Rosener. Jo Swerling scripted it from the novel by Anthony Abbot. (63 mins)

▽ The sinking of a German U-boat, with $3,000,000 in gold bullion aboard, was the starting point for **Below The Sea**, a competent adventure which Al Rogell directed from a Jo Swerling screenplay, and which featured Fredrik Vogeding (right) as the U-boat's duplicitous commander determined to salvage the bullion from the sunken sub. Top-starred Ralph Bellamy, in a performance shy on personality, played a deep-sea-diving expert, who, for a share of the bullion, agrees to help Vogeding find the buried treasure. A Technicolor sequence showing the flora and fauna of the ocean-bed plus a sequence in which Bellamy grapples with a giant octopus were a couple of highlights in a film in need of all the help it could get. Fay Wray was the leading lady, and the cast was completed by Esther Howard, Trevor Bland, William J. Kelly and Paul Page. (78 mins)

▷ Frank Capra's only foray into the realms of the 'art movie' was **The Bitter Tea Of General Yen**, an exotic, romantic melodrama. It starred Barbara Stanwyck (left) as a strait-laced missionary from New England who, after arriving in Shanghai to marry missionary Gavin Gordon (a man she does not really love), is separated from him during a revolution of sorts and finds herself under the protection of Nils Asther (centre), an imposing Chinese warlord. Asther (General Yen) gradually falls in love with her and she with him, but, knowing that he will never be able to possess her, he drinks the bitter tea of poison – and dies. Edward Paramore's screenplay, from the novel by Grace Zaring Stone, provided Capra with the wherewithal to indulge in several set-pieces, the best being a lushly photographed (by Joseph Walker) dream sequence in which Stanwyck allows the general to make love to her; and an attack on Yen's gold-carrying freight train by a thousand enemy soldiers. Remarkable, too, was Capra's meticulous attention to the detail in his elaborate Oriental set-dressings. Unable to find a tall, overpowering Chinese

for the role of General Yen, Capra settled for exotic Swedish actor Asther who, with the generous assistance of the make-up department (they clipped his eyelashes and covered his upper eyelids with smooth, round false 'skins'), was made to look imposingly, mysteriously, Oriental. Not a great deal was required of Stanwyck as the American missionary – other than to provide a temperamental contrast between East and West. The acting honours went to Walter Connolly as Yen's Machiavellian financial adviser. The beautiful Toshia Mori (right) played Mah-Li, Yen's two-timing mistress and the architect of his downfall. Because of the film's hitherto taboo miscegenation theme **The Bitter Tea Of General Yen** wasn't served in any British cinema and, despite being respectfully reviewed by the critics, was a financial failure. It was, however, the film chosen to open the Radio City Music Hall in New York, and is still considered by Capra to be one of his 'pet' pictures. Other members of an excellent cast were Lucien Littlefield, Richard Loo and Clara Blandick. The producer was Walter Wanger. (87 mins)

△ Almost as perplexing as why it was called **Cocktail Hour** was why director Victor Schertzinger thought this flabby tale was worth filming. A successful commercial artist abandons her eminently suitable lover, takes a cruise to Europe and, on the voyage, falls for a smoothie who, she later learns, is already married. Bebe Daniels (right) played the artist itching for new experiences, relative newcomer Randolph Scott (left) was the man she jilted, and Sidney Blackmer the object of her ship-board romance. Clearly intended to appeal to sophisticates of all ages, the problem lay with the unsympathetic, rather common heroine and the fact that Scott, the man she finally returns to, is much too good for her. Muriel Kirkland had some amusing moments as a phony Russian pianist, and Marjorie Gateson was charming as Scott's agreeable mother. Schertzinger also supplied a ballad for Miss Daniels called 'Listen Heart Of Mine'. The film also found roles for Jessie Ralph, Barry Norton and George Nardelli. The original story on which it was based was by James K. McGuiness, and it was scripted by Gertrude Purcell and Richard Schayer. (73 mins)

▽ The **Child Of Manhattan** was Nancy Carroll (right), a dance-hall hostess who meets and falls in love with suave millionaire John Boles (centre). She becomes pregnant but the baby dies. Believing that Boles only married her out of sympathy, she heads for Mexico where, after getting a divorce, she decides to marry gringo Charles Jones (left). But Boles, who still loves her (and she him), follows her to Mexico, and saves her from marriage in the nick of time. Nothing, however, could save this melodramatic heap of nonsense, and the film sank under its own dead weight. Carroll over-acted, Boles did just the reverse, while Charles Jones – much better known to audiences as cowboy star Buck Jones – demonstrated that once a cowboy, always a cowboy. Astonishingly, the film was based on a play by Preston Sturges, and was indifferently adapted for the screen by Gertrude Purcell whose scenario provided supporting roles for Warburton Gamble, Jane Darwell, Clara Blandick, Luis Alberni, Gary Owen, Jessie Ralph, Tyler Brooke and, in a small role, Betty Grable. Edward Buzzell directed. (70 mins)

◁ Based on S. N. Behrman's disappointing Broadway play of 1931, which, in turn, was inspired by the true-life marriage between singer Libby Holman and tobacco tycoon Smith Reynolds, **Brief Moment** was the story of a nightclub singer (Carole Lombard, right) who, unable to tolerate her moneyed husband's dissipated existence, walks out on him. He reforms, however, and the final fade finds him and his forgiving wife re-united. Gene Raymond (left) played the wastrel husband with a mite more animation than Lombard (who had her name above the title on this one) brought to her part; but the combination of an indifferent screenplay (by Brian Marlow and Edith Fitzgerald), a series of stock characters, and David Burton's cliché-strewn direction turned *Brief Moment* into a non-starter. It also featured Monroe Owsley (in the role played on stage by the formidable Alexander Woolcott), Donald Cook, Arthur Hohl, Reginald Mason and Jameson Thomas. (69 mins)

△ There was minimal suspense in Lew Levenson's screenplay for **Dangerous Crossroads** (story by Horace McCoy), a mystery that featured Jackie Searle (centre) as the son of a detective who helps save his old man's job by apprehending a gang of freighttrain robbers. Diane Sinclair played his girlfriend, with other parts going to Chic Sale, Frank Albertson (right), Preston Foster, Niles, Welch and Eddie Kane. Lambert Hillyer directed. (62 mins)

△ A kind of *Grand Hotel* (MGM, 1932), but set in a boarding house, **East Of Fifth Avenue** was a modest drama that touched on the lives of several people – most notably those of an elderly couple, movingly played by Walter Connolly and Louise Carter, who decide to take their own lives. Willard Robertson played the doctor who defends their action to the other guests. There were romantic problems in the guise of Wallace Ford and Dorothy Tree, and several miscellaneous ones as enacted by Walter Byron (left – a lodger), Maude Eburne (right – the landlady), Mary Carlisle, Lucien Littlefield and Harry Holman. Jo Swerling wrote it, and Al Rogell directed. (74 mins)

▽ Cowboy Tim McCoy (centre) turned reporter for **Hold The Press**, a cliché-spattered thriller in which our hero's shoot-outs took place on rooftops rather than along the plains. Horace McCoy's script sent its star in search of murder evidence, as well as love. In the end, of course, he finds both. Shirley Grey was the romantic interest, with other parts under Phil Rosen's direction farmed out to Henry Wadsworth, Oscar Apfel, Wheeler Oakman (right), Samuel Hinds, Jack Long (left) and Joseph Crehan. (65 mins)

◁ The venerable May Robson (right) celebrated her golden jubilee as an actress in a delightful fantasy from the colourful pen of Damon Runyon called **Lady For A Day**. She played Apple Annie, a fruit pedlar in New York and the mother of a daughter she hasn't seen since childhood and who has lived most of her life in a European convent. In order not to disillusion the girl, Annie has regularly written to her on stationery belonging to a smart New York hotel, a deception she has underlined by leading her unsuspecting daughter to believe that the swanky hotel also happens to be her permanent residence. Runyon's plot moves into top gear when Robson receives a letter from Europe (delivered to her by an accommodating bellboy at the hotel) in which her daughter (Jean Parker) informs her of an impending trip to New York with her Spanish nobleman fiancé (Barry Norton) and would-be father-in-law (Walter Connolly). In order not to lose face, Annie enlists the assistance of Dave the Dude (Warren William, left), a superstitious gambler who never makes a wager without first buying one of Annie's apples, to help her find a way out of her predicament. He does so by persuading a friend to lend him his palatial residence for a day and all the trappings that go with it. Despite some near misses, the situation is saved. Annie (known to her daughter as Mrs E. Worthington Manville) becomes a lady for a day, and has the satisfaction of seeing the young lovers married. This wish-fulfilment Cinderella tale of immense charm and poignancy was engagingly directed by Frank Capra who, more than any other creative talent at the studio, would soon be responsible for bringing wealth and prestige to Columbia beyond even the dreams of Harry Cohn. Apart from May Robson (who was only offered the part when Cohn failed to secure the services of Marie Dressler from MGM) there were delightful performances from Guy Kibbee as Judge Blake and the reliable Walter Connolly as Count Romero, with frozen-faced Ned Sparks, and Nat Pendleton on equally good form. Runyon's story *Madame La Gimp* provided scenarist Robert Riskin with a solid narrative framework for some excellent dialogue – as well as an opportunity for him to write in a part for his girlfriend Glenda Farrell. (95 mins)

▷ Nat Pendleton (left), an Olympic wrestling champion in 1922, provided the story for, and starred in, **Deception**, a wrestling drama that spent most of its running-time in the ring. The remaining quarter was devoted to a plot involving 'Palooka' Pendleton, a footballer with aspirations to be a wrestler, proving his true worth to a syndicate who hitherto had written him off. An over-emotional Thelma Todd played the female lead; Leo Carrillo (right) was a crooked promoter. Also included: Dickie Moore, Barbara Weeks and Hans Steinke (centre). It was scripted by Harold Tarshis and directed, for less than it was worth, by Lew Seiler. Bryan Foy produced. (65 mins)

△ **A Man's Castle**, in this particular case, is a shanty in an area of New York known as 'Hoover Flats'. Inhabiting it is Spencer Tracy (right), a thoroughly resistible roughneck who, dressed in an evening suit whose shirt is an advertisement for a cigar, wanders around town until, one day, he meets derelict Loretta Young (left). He buys the homeless young woman a much-needed meal and takes her 'home' with him. Time passes, Miss Young falls pregnant and Tracy, though he has been having an affair with showgirl Glenda Farrell, commits a robbery to support Young and her soon-to-arrive baby. The robbery goes wrong and Tracy is injured. While he is recovering he realizes just how dependent he is on the loving Miss Young, and the film ends happily as the couple decide to start a new and better life together. Though **A Man's Castle** pre-dated the Hays Code by a year, it nonetheless underwent censorship problems in New York because of Young's out-of-wedlock pregnancy. With a snip-snip here and a snip-snip there, the guardians of the city's morality removed what was deemed offensive at the time without being able to save the film from the melodramatic sentimentality into which director Frank Borzage, working from a screenplay by Jo Swerling (from a play by Lawrence Hazard), plunged it. Both Tracy and Young would do better work than this; so would Glenda Farrell who walked and sounded just like Mae West. Walter Connolly was fine as a minister, Arthur Hohl played a heavy, and Marjorie Rambeau a drunk. (70 mins)

▽ Carole Lombard (left), fast approaching stardom, gave her best performance to date in **No More Orchids**, a romantic melodrama in which she played a poor-little-rich-girl who, to save her banker father (Walter Connolly, centre) from financial ruin, is forced to marry into royalty. The man she really desires (Lyle Talbot, right) is an impoverished commoner. In the end true love triumphs, but at far too high a price. In order to provide his daughter with the benefits of his life-insurance policy, Connolly deliberately crashes his plane and is killed. The bad guy was a miscast C. Aubrey Smith as Connolly's brother, an irascible old curmudgeon determined that his niece shall marry wealthy Prince Carlos (Jameson Thomas). The stately Louise Closser Hale played Lombard's booze-imbibing grandmother, with other roles under Walter Lang's efficient direction going to Allen Vincent, Ruthelma Stevens, Arthur Houseman and William V. Mong. It was written by Gertrude Purcell and Keene Thompson from the novel by Grace Perkins. (65 mins)

△ According to scenarists Edward Paramore and Seton I. Miller (working from an original story by Chester Erskine and Eugene Solow), the Wall Street crash was the result of a row between a husband his wife. At least, that's what **Master Of Men** would have you believe, espousing, as it does, the story of a steel-mill worker, who betters himself and becomes involved in the New York stock market. His wife disapproves, and gabs about her husband's activities to the wrong people with the result that the market collapses and he goes bankrupt – whereupon the couple make it up and lead a richer, albeit poorer, life in the country. The fanciful fiction starred Jack Holt (left) and Fay Wray (centre) as the couple in question, with Theodor von Eltz (right), Berton Churchill and, best of all, Walter Connolly as a wise old friend. The director was Lambert Hillyer. (65 mins)

△ **My Woman** was a backstage story designed for Wallace Ford (left). In Brian Marlowe's screenplay, Ford played a small-time song-and-dance man who allows success to go to his head and then eschews the homely but loving care of his self-effacing wife (Helen Twelvetrees, right) for a glitzier lifestyle in a swanky Park Avenue apartment. A swollen head came before a fall, and the finale found caddish husband and long-suffering wife reconciled. Director Victor Schertzinger was unable to circumvent the sheer familiarity of it all and – together with a cast that included Victor Jory (centre, as a radio network president), Warren Hymer, Raymond Brown, Hobart Cavanaugh and Charles Levison – floundered hopelessly. (76 mins)

▽ Mae Clarke (right) received top billing in **Parole Girl** and played a young woman whose involvement with a confidence trickster leads to a prison sentence when a 'scam' on a local store goes wrong. After being paroled for heroically fighting a fire in the prison shop (which she started!) she heads straight for the store manager (Ralph Bellamy, left) who could have saved her from jail had he refused to press charges. Though revenge is her motivation, she soon falls in love with him, despite the fact that he is already married. Marie Prevost played Bellamy's wife, with other roles in this Edward Cline-directed programmer going to Hale Hamilton and Ferdinand Gottschalk. (67 mins)

△ **Obey The Law** gave Leo Carrillo (centre) top billing as an immigrant barber who, on becoming a citizen of the USA, fights corruption in the guise of a tenement boss (Henry Clive) out to control the local vote. Carrillo's performance was fine in this otherwise mediocre drama, written by Arthur Caesar (story by Harry Sauber) and directed by Benjamin Stoloff. Also cast: Dickie Moore, Lois Wilson (right), Eddie Garr (left), Gino Corrado and Ward Bond. (64 mins)

▽ Tim McCoy (centre) swapped his saddle for a police car in **Police Car 17** - a 'Western' except that it was about cops and robbers rather than cowboys and Indians. Automobiles replaced horses in the film's several chases and, as the hero rounded up the bad guys and came to the rescue of heroine Evalyn Knapp (right), McCoy fans left the theatre satisfied – even though what they paid to see was over in under an hour. Wallis Clark, Ward Bond and Harold Huber (left) were also in it, and it was written and directed by Lambert Hillyer. (57 mins)

◁ Basically a two-reeler stretched way beyond its material worth, **So This Is Africa** was a Robert Woolsey (second right)–Bert Wheeler (left) vehicle in which they starred as a pair of lion-tamers who, for no discernible reason in Norman Krasna's 'original' screenplay, fetch up in Africa as stars of a movie whose extras are a group of wild, Amazonian women. To escape the amorous attention of their cast, Messrs W & W dress up in drag, but to little effect. A vulgar brew devoid even of good, honest, vulgar laughs, it was directed in nondescript fashion by Edward Cline, and featured Raquel Torres, Esther Muir, Berton Churchill, Henry Armetta and Spencer Charters. (61 mins)

△ Regis Toomey (right) played a border patrol cop-cum-stunt flier in **Soldiers Of The Storm**, a doggedly routine adventure yarn in which our hero apprehends, on behalf of the US government, a band of smugglers and is rewarded with the love of pretty Anita Page (centre). Aimed mainly at kids of 13 and under, it was crassly scripted by Charles Condon and Horace McCoy from a story by Thomson Burtis, directed with an underlying sense of *déjà vu* by D. Ross Lederman, and featured Barbara Weeks, Robert Ellis, Wheeler Oakman, George Cooper (left) and Dewey Robinson. (68 mins)

▽ Regis Toomey (illustrated) and Evelyn Knapp played lovers in **State Trooper**, a grim little melodrama in the course of which Toomey – the chief of police at Knapp's father's oil refinery – unravels a dangerous plot involving the refinery's crooked general manager (Walter McGrail) who has sold out to the opposition. Stuart Anthony cobbled it together from a story by Lambert Hillyer, D. Ross Lederman directed, and the cast included Raymond Hatton, Matthew Betz and Edwin Maxwell. (62 mins)

◁ **When Strangers Marry** was a passable Jack Holt (right) romantic melodrama in which the studio's favourite hero this time found himself building a railroad in the Malay straits – and married to bored socialite Lilian Bond (left). Attempting to break up both Holt's marriage and his career is bad guy Arthur Vinton, whom Miss Bond shoots in the end. Barbara Barondess played Vinton's mistress, and the cast included Ward Bond, Gustav Von Seyffertitz and Paul Porcasi. Clarence Badger directed from a script by James Kevin McGuiness and a story by Maximilian Foster. (65 mins)

△ Versatile Willard Mack wrote, directed and starred in **What Price Innocence?** in which he played a kindly doctor who makes house calls and is especially interested in the sexual education of the children he helped bring into the world. One such 'child' is 17-year-old Ruth (Jean Parker, right) whose high-school romance with an older boy ends in her suicide when her mother resolutely refuses to enlighten her on the facts of life. A curiosity with no commercial appeal, the film featured Minna Gombell as Parker's mother, as well as Bryant Washburn, Ben Alexander, Beatrice Banyard, Louise Beavers (left) and a young Betty Grable. (64 mins)

▽ Rough and ready Jack Holt (right) was the rugged, ruthless hero of **The Woman I Stole**, and the woman he stole was Fay Wray (left), wife of his best friend (Donald Cook, centre) an oil-company manager in Morocco. Not only is Cook aware of his wife's perfidy, but he also believes Holt is out to ruin him financially. Not so. The truth is, Holt is really an undercover agent who prevents villainous Noah Beery from appropriating Cook's oil concern for himself. As for the woman Holt stole – he gives her back in the end, but Cook (who has made it up with Holt) doesn't want any part of her. Such was life on the North African oilfields. Loosely adapted by Jo Swerling from Joseph Hergesheimer's novel *Tampico*, the film was niftily directed by Irving Cummings with a cast that also included Raquel Torres, Edwin Maxwell and Charles Browne. (70 mins)

△ **The Wrecker** was a soggy melodrama in which Jack Holt (right) starred as a building-demolition man whose own marriage comes under the wrecker's ball when he discovers his wife (Genevieve Tobin, left) has been unfaithful with pal Sidney Blackmer (centre). After disappearing on an alcoholic bender, he returns just in time to see his unfaithful spouse and her lover buried under rubble as a result of a convenient earthquake. Nothing earth-shaking, though, about Jo Swerling's script (story by Albert Rogell, who also directed), nor the supporting performances of George E. Stone, Ward Bond, Irene White, Russell Waddle and, as a black chauffeur, Clarence Muse. (72 mins)

▽ Clearly made for the undiscerning movie-goer, **Above The Clouds** was a potentially exciting little actioner that needed a much sharper script than the one provided by Albert de Mond (story by George B. Seitz). All about newsreel cameramen and the competitive world they inhabit, it starred Robert Armstrong as 'Scoop', a drunken cameraman whose irresponsible behaviour results in his young assistant losing his job. However, the assistant, appealingly played by Richard Cromwell (left), is given a chance to prove himself. This he does, much to Armstrong's annoyance – for not only does he eventually get Armstrong's job, but also the girl (Dorothy Wilson, right). Edmund Breese overacted shamefully as the boss-man, and the cast included Morgan Wallace, Dorothy Revier and Bessie Barriscale. (68 mins)

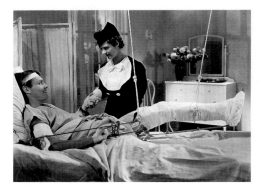

▽ Ambulance chases featured prominently in **Against The Law** in which Western star Johnny Mack Brown (right) played a busy ambulance driver who sacrifices all for an intern buddy involved with the local underworld. What there was of the plot went into top-gear with the death of the intern at the hands of the mob – and Johnny's ultimate act of revenge. The female lead was Sally Blane (left) with Arthur Hohl and George Meeker padding out the cast for director Lambert Hillyer. Harold Shumate provided both the story and the screenplay. (61 mins)

▽ A tale of double murder and mayhem, told confusingly in flashback, **Before Midnight** was the one in which a victim is murdered at exactly one minute before midnight (a regular occurrence in this particular establishment), the only unusual thing being the presence, at the time, of a top city detective. Edward Arnold played one of the victims, Ralph Bellamy (right) the detective, and Claude Gillingwater the culprit. The distaff side was perfunctorily represented by June Collyer and Betty Blythe. Robert Quigley scripted it from his own story, and the director was Lambert Hillyer. (63 mins)

△ Voodoo and black magic were the subjects of **Black Moon,** a plot, in questionable taste, about a married woman's obsession with sacrificial ceremonies in the West Indies which make it necessary for her husband to shoot her, for she involves their infant daughter in the proceedings. Dorothy Burgess was the wife, Jack Holt (centre) the husband, and Fay Wray (left) a pretty secretary

◁ Cast, script, and direction were all well below par in **Behind The Evidence.** A shoddy excuse for a melodrama, it starred Norman Foster (right) as a reporter who, in the course of his duty, captures a big-time racketeer (Donald Cook) and gets the girl (Sheila Mannors, left). The plot and screenplay were perpetrated by Harold Shumate, and the direction by Lambert Hillyer. Also cast: Geneva Mitchell, Samuel S. Hinds and Frank Darien. (70 mins)

△ A typical Tim McCoy (right) actioner, **Beyond The Law** cast him as a railroad policeman who, charmed by leading lady Shirley Grey (left), agrees to clear her ex-con father's name of a murder he did not commit. Addison Richards played the ex-con. Harold Shumate wrote it, and the director was D. Ross Lederman. (58 mins)

whom Holt finally ensnares and takes back to the States with him. All audiences took back with them was the memory of a programmer whose content all-too-quickly evaporated. Cora Sue Collins (right), Arnold Korff, Clarence Muse and Lumsden Hare filled out the cast for director Roy William Neill. It was scripted by Wells Root from a magazine story by Clements Ripley. (68 mins)

△ A domestic drama aimed at the family trade, **Blind Date** (GB: **Her Sacrifice**) wended its familiar, albeit agreeable way through the by-ways of a routine plot by Vida Hurst (screenplay by Ethel Hill) that charted the fortunes (or lack of them) of the Taylor family – an average bunch comprising out-of-work Pa (Spencer Charters), homely Ma (Jane Darwell, front), young brother Freddy (Mickey Rooney) and elder sister (and breadwinner) Kitty (top-starred Ann Sothern, second left). Story, such as it was, pivoted on Kitt's twin romances with a likeable garage man (Paul Kelly, left), and the well-to-do son of a department-store owner (Neil Hamilton). After an abortive marriage to the former, she settles for the latter. It was pleasant-enough entertainment which also found room for Theodore Newton (second right) and Geneva Mitchell (right), and included a very engaging performance from a young Mickey Rooney. Roy William Neill directed. (71 mins)

▽ A sort of *Grand Hotel* (MGM, 1932) of the ocean waves, **The Captain Hates The Sea** was set on board a ship whose skipper, Walter Connolly – tired of a never-ending routine in which he is expected to mingle with the passengers and show concern over their romances, their intrigues and their problems – understandably wants to leave the briny well behind him and return to the life of a land-lubber. The kind of passengers he is trying to avoid, but cannot, are people like Schulte (Victor McLaglen, right) a private detective; Mrs Magruder and Danny Checkitt (Alison Skipworth and Fred Keating), a pair of petty crooks; and Steve Bramley (John Gilbert, left), an alcoholic hoping to dry out. Wallace Smith's screenplay – which also offered Leon Errol several opportunities to provide light relief – was an episodic affair (in the style of *Grand Hotel*) and, at its best, merely serviceable. Because so many of the cast (Gilbert, McLaglen, Connolly, Errol and Walter Catlett) were, in real life, extremely heavy drinkers – as, indeed, was the film's director, Lewis Milestone – the production went way over budget, causing an anxious Harry Cohn to cable Milestone that 'the cost is staggering!' 'So is the cast' was Milestone's reply. The film, when it was finally completed, opened to mixed reviews, and despite the added presence of such scene-stealing players as Wynne Gibson (centre), Donald Meek, Arthur Treacher and Akim Tamiroff, floated indifferently by. (80 mins)

△ Jack Holt (right) played a crooked lawyer and Jean Arthur (centre) an office assistant who sets out to expose him but finishes up as his Mrs. That was the romantic gist of **The Defense Rests,** a fast-paced comedy of sorts in which both top-starred players were miscast, as was Arthur Hohl as a district attorney. Other roles were shared between Nat Pendleton (left – as a bodyguard), Raymond Walburn, Harold Huber, Robert Gleckler, Raymond Hatton, Shirley Grey and Vivian Oakland. Jo Swerling scripted and Lambert Hillyer directed. Diverting enough – but no fireworks. (70 mins)

▽ **The Crime Of Helen Stanley** was that she didn't read the script before giving her name to this preposterous thriller. Set in a film studio and involving the murder of an actress, the crime was solved by detective Ralph Bellamy (right) who discovers that the murder weapon was a camera containing a pistol programmed to fire after a number of turns. The brain-child of Charles R. Condon, who devised the story (Harold Shumate scripted), it also featured Shirley Grey, Gail Patrick (left), Kane Richmond, Bradley Page, Vincent Sherman and Ward Bond (centre). D. Ross Lederman directed. (58 mins)

◁ Based on a magazine story by Valentine Williams and Dorothy Rice Sims, and scripted by Ethel Hill and Dore Schary, **Fog** featured Reginald Denny as a most unconvincing villain responsible for a triple murder aboard an ocean liner. Menace, suspense and tension were kept to a minimum under Al Rogell's direction, with little in the way of performances from top-billed Donald Cook, Mary Brian, or Helen Freeman (front right) – the clairvoyant who forsees all the murders, including her own. (70 mins)

▽ In **Fury Of The Jungle,** three of the *dramatis personae* were eaten by crocodiles and two died in the jaws of a pair of jaguars. What killed the film stone dead, however, wasn't the shoddy special effects but a script by Ethel Hill and Dore Schary (story by Horace McCoy) that was hoarier than any of the animals on view. All about a small jungle village populated mainly by men and what happens to its inhabitants with the sudden arrival of a white woman and her sick brother, it was unabashed hokum which needed a cast far stronger than Donald Cook, Peggy Shannon (right), Alan Dinehart and Harold Huber (left) to get it off the ground. Only Dudley Digges as an inebriated doctor gave anything resembling a performance. The director was Roy William Neill. (55 mins)

▽ Ralph Bellamy (right), alias Inspector Trent, starred in **Girl In Danger** – though, in truth, it was audiences who were really in danger: of dying of boredom. The girl in question was Shirley Grey (left), who, in the course of Harold Shumate's screenplay, deliberately injects excitement in her life by joining forces with a notorious gangster in a jewel-raid, then agreeing to hide a stolen emerald in her luxurious apartment while the cops search for it. J. Carrol Naish, Charles Sabin and Arthur Hohl were also in the cast for director D. Ross Lederman. (57 mins)

▽ An abundance of plot involving Florence Rice (left) in her screen debut as the **Fugitive Lady** kept audiences from dozing. But it was heavy going, just the same, as Miss Rice, a fugitive from justice, is overtaken by her former bad companions after seeking refuge with a set of decent folk. Neil Hamilton played the young man to whom she becomes attached, and Donald Cook (right) appeared briefly as a well-bred thief. The lively cast also included William Demarest, Clara Blandick, Nella Walker, Wade Boteler and Rita La Roy. Al Rogell directed from a story and screenplay provided by Herbert Asbury and Fred Niblo Jr. (66 mins)

△ What director Frank Capra had cut his teeth on in *Platinum Blonde* (1931) he honed to perfection in **It Happened One Night.** The surprise hit of 1934 and the first of the great screwball comedies of the Thirties, the film gave Harry Cohn the one thing he'd wanted all his life: big-time status. It also firmly established Capra as a front-rank Oscar-winning director, and turned Clark Gable (right) into one of Hollywood's hottest male properties. The plot itself (scripted by Robert Riskin, and based on Samuel Hopkins Adams's story *Night Bus*) was a mere trifle. Gable played a hot-headed, frustrated newspaper reporter who, after being fired for drunkenness, finds himself sitting next to Claudette Colbert (left) on New York-bound bus. Colbert is the spoiled daughter of a millionaire (Walter Connolly) whose disapproval of the man (Jameson Thomas) she intends to marry has led to her running away from home. There is a $10,000 reward for her recovery, and it is not long before Gable recognizes the missing heiress and the meal ticket she is about to provide. Not only can he do with the reward money – but if he plays his cards right, there's a major scoop in it for him as well. In time, though, a romance develops between them and, after numerous plot complications, all of which rely on the freshness of the performances and Capra's masterful direction to camouflage their predictability – the inevitable happy ending was vouchsafed. From the outset, Harry Cohn had little faith in the property which he purchased for $5000 after Capra had read Adams's short story in *Cosmopolitan* magazine. In quick succession the leading roles were turned down by Robert Montgomery, Myrna Loy, Miriam Hopkins, Constance Bennett and Margaret Sullavan. Finally, Colbert agreed to play the heiress, but only if her fee was upped to $50,000 (twice as much as she was getting per picture at Paramount), and if the studio guaranteed that she would be required for no more than four weeks. Desperate for a leading lady, Cohn agreed to both conditions. As for Gable, he was acquired on loan-out from MGM, whose boss, Louis B. Mayer, considered the poverty-row assignment as a 'punishment' for Gable who, rather than start a new picture at MGM, had checked himself into hospital claiming he was overworked and needed a break. The Gable-Colbert chemistry ignited every scene they shared and was at its most potent in the famous 'walls of Jericho' sequence which took place in a motel cabin whose twin beds were separated by a rope over which a blanket was thrown. The scene was the sexiest in the film because of what *wasn't* shown; and, when Gable took off his shirt to reveal that he wasn't wearing a vest – he set a vestless trend among America's copy-cat males. The other memorable sequence – and one for the anthology books – was Colbert's unorthodox method of thumbing a ride by hitching her skirts – a scene she was, at first, reluctant to play. Though the box-office returns were, initially, unimpressive, word-of-mouth came to the film's rescue, as did its five Academy Awards. Playing supporting roles in the studio's most durable hit to date were Roscoe Karns, Henry Wadsworth, Claire McDowell, Alan Hale, Arthur Hoyt, Blanche Frederici and Ward Bond. Remade as *Eve Knew Her Apples* (1945) and *You Can't Run Away from It* (1956). (105 mins)

◁ Tim McCoy (right) and Lillian Bond (left) were **Hell Bent For Love.** He played a state trooper, she a night-club singer. The course of true love, however, was strewn with obstacles – mainly in the shape of bad-guy Bradly Page, Lilian's boss. As Page is in love with Lilian too, he sets out to stymie his rival – but to no avail. Rounding up a few former hoods (all of whom he once sent to jail), McCoy nails Page, as well as several rackets in which the latter was involved, such as horse-race fixing, jewel-store robbery and payroll holdups. It added up to pretty feeble entertainment, limply directed by D. Ross Lederman (from a story and screenplay by Harold Shumate) and featured Vincent Sherman, Lafe McKee, Harry C. Bradley and Wedgewood Newell. (65 mins)

▷ Audiences yawned throughout the antics of Robert Armstrong (centre) and Ann Sothern (left) in **The Hell Cat,** an antediluvian newspaper yarn in which he played a tough reporter and she a society woman masquerading as a lady journalist. The couple, initially at loggerheads, pool their respective talents to uncover a gang of racketeers who, it turns out, are using Sothern's father's yacht as a base. Benny Baker managed to snatch a few laughs from Fred Niblo Jr's dreary screenplay (story by Adele Buffington, additional dialogue by Joel Sayre), upstaging, in the process, a supporting cast that included Benny Bates, Minna Gombell (right), Purnell Pratt, Charles Wilson and J. Carrol Naish. Albert Rogell directed. (70 mins)

◁ Not since *Black Beauty* (Monogram, 1933) moistened the eyes of moviegoers had a horsey film played on the tear ducts as shamelessly as **Broadway Bill** (GB: **Strictly Confidential**). Directed by Frank Capra (straight from his triumph with *It Happened One Night*) with consummate skill, it starred Warner Baxter (right) as a harassed businessman who deserts the business world, as well as his unsympathetic wife (Helen Vinson), to become a racehorse owner. But Baxter is broke. Not only is he unable to pay the entry fee for the $25,000 handicap due to take place in a couple of days, but his horse, Broadway Bill, falls ill as a result of being kept in a leaky stable. No sooner does the horse recover than Baxter's jockey is 'fixed' by gamblers. To add to his woes, Baxter is unable to pay his horse's feed bill, and is jailed for having a spat with the local sheriff. Fortunately all resolves itself in time for the big race – which Broadway Bill wins. But the effort has been too much for the brave animal, who dies shortly afterwards. There's a happy ending, though, with Baxter finding loving care in the arms of Myrna Loy (left) – his wife's understanding, warm-hearted sister. Both Baxter and Loy did wonders with Robert Riskin's screenplay (from a story by newspaperman Mark Hellinger), and there were splendid performances, too, from Walter Connolly, Clarence Muse, Raymond Walburn and Lynne Overman. But the excellent cast notwithstanding, it was Capra's racy, pacey direction with its irresistible blend of pathos and comedy, that kept audiences involved – and caring. Remade by Paramount in 1951 as *Riding High*. (90 mins)

◁ The 'I'll' in **I'll Fix It** was Jack Holt (left), and what he fixed – or attempted to fix – was his adored young brother's place on the school football team. Trouble is, the kid's not much of a scholar, and his school teacher (Mona Barrie, right) refuses to let him play. Used to getting his way, arrogant Holt, the local Mr Bigwig, almost bites off more than he can chew when he takes on Barrie, who gives as good as she gets. It was written by Leonard Spiegelgass on an off day, scripted by Ethel Hill and Dorothy Howell, and featured Jimmie Butler as the kid brother, as well as Winnie Lightner and Ed Brophy. Roy William Neill directed. (68 mins)

▷ **Jealousy** starred George Murphy (front) as an insanely jealous boxer whose fiancée (Nancy Carroll, right) says she'll only marry him if he stops behaving so irrationally. He does. They marry. When, however, Murphy discovers her and her boss (Donald Cook) in a hotel room together, he goes beserk and kills the man. Carroll stands trial but, just as the verdict is about to be announced, Murphy admits to the murder and is sentenced to die in the electric chair. His last request is to ask the resident priest to count him out as if he were in the ring. On the count of nine a referee's voice interrupts the action and you realize it was all a dream. Or a nightmare, depending on how charitable you're feeling. So-so performances from Murphy, Carroll and Cook, a routine screenplay by William Moncure and Kubec Glasmon (story by Argyle Campbell), with direction (by Roy William Neill) on a par with the performances, added up to the kind of programmer no one need be jealous of. Raymond Walburn, Arthur Hohl and Inez Courtney were in it too. (66 mins)

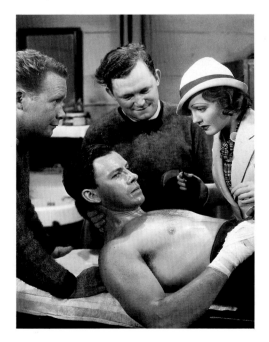

△ Though Carole Lombard (left) received top billing in **Lady By Choice,** the film was another showy vehicle for May Robson (right), after her triumph in Frank Capra's *Lady For A Day* (1933). Cast by director David Burton as an old bag-lady, this time Robson finds herself hired by fan-dancer Lombard as a surrogate mother for Mother's Day. Plot complications proliferated, but not before Robson, taking her 'mother' role seriously, persuades Lombard to give up fan-dancing for the nobler art of acting, and encourages her 'daughter's' romance with wealthy Roger Pryor. Working from an engaging screenplay by Jo Swerling (story by Dwight Taylor), Burton kept the sentimentality palatable. Robert North's production also gave employment to the excellent Walter Connolly as a night-court judge before whom Robson has appeared on several occasions, as well as to Arthur Hohl, Raymond Walburn (as Lombard's press agent) and James Burke. And, if you blinked, you'd miss Irishman Dennis O'Keefe as a dancing extra. (74 mins)

▽ **Among The Missing** rang the changes on the plot of *Lady By Choice* by having its elderly heroine temporarily usurp her wealthy background in order to take a job as a cook to an antique-dealer-cum-jewel-thief. An attempt to revitalize the career of Henrietta Crosman (centre, as the heroine), it needed a stronger plot than the one provided by Florence Wagner (in which Crosman helps regenerate a young jewel thief) and tighter direction than Al Rogell provided. Crosman went through her paces without distinction, being only as good as her material, and was supported by Richard Cromwell (right) as the young man in whom she takes an interest, Billie Seward (left), Ivan Simpson, Ben Taggert, Wade Boteler and Paul Hurst. Fred Niblo Jr. and Herbert Asbury provided the screenplay. (62 mins)

▽ The first film made by Columbia in Britain, **The Lady Is Willing** (based on a French farce by Louis Verneuil) boasted an all-British cast, though several of the technicians – including director Gilbert Miller – were recruited from America. Its star was the urbane Leslie Howard (right) who played an impoverished detective in the employ of three businessmen whose property shares have been misappropriated by swindler Cedric Hardwicke. In the course of bringing the reprobate to bay, Howard falls in love with the old man's charming wife, Binnie Barnes. Guy Bolton's screenplay kept the action light and fluffy, qualities not always replicated in Miller's direction. Also cast: Nigel Bruce, Nigel Playfair, Claud Allister and W. Graham Browne. (66 mins)

▽ Peppy newcomer Ann Sothern's (left) fourth film was a pleasant little musical called **Let's Fall In Love** whose pleasing score by Harold Arlen and Ted Kohler buttressed a backstage story in which film producer Gregory Ratoff falls victim to the temperament of a Swedish prima donna (Greta Meyer) and is forced to replace her. Enter Miss Sothern, a Brooklyn sideshow performer who happens to be around and, six weeks later, is passed off as a new discovery. While being groomed for stardom, Sothern falls in love with her good-looking director (Edmund Lowe, right) much to the chagrin of his fiancée (Miriam Jordan) who sets out to make trouble. But Herbert Fields' screenplay vouchsafed the obligatory happy ending, while at the same time providing parts for Tala Birrell, Arthur Jarrett and Marjorie Gateson. The good-natured direction was by David Burton. Remade in 1949 as *Slightly French*. (67 mins)

▷ A buddy-buddy movie, with Tim McCoy (right) and Ward Bond (left) as the inseparables, **A Man's Game** also found room for a spot of female interest – as provided by Evalyn Knapp (centre). She played an embezzling stenographer – protected by her two leading men, both of whom are firemen. The cast was completed by De Witt Jennings as the fire chief (and Bond's father). Harold Shumate provided both the story and screenplay, and it was directed from some ancient manual by D. Ross Lederman. (56 mins)

△ The illicit market in stolen furs, and the racketeers involved, formed the content of **The Lineup,** a crime drama that featured pretty Marion Nixon (illustrated) as a hatcheck girl framed by the bad guys, and top-starred William Gargan as the detective on the case who falls in love with her and clears her name. Comic relief was supplied by Paul Hurst as a bumbling detective who louses up everything he touches, with other roles under Howard Higgin's direction going to John Miljan, Harold Huber, Greta Meyer and Joseph Crehan. It was scripted, from his own story, by George Waggner. (64 mins)

△ In **Men Of The Night** – a programme-filler with no pretensions whatsoever – Bruce Cabot (right) played a Hollywood-based detective who falls in love with a girl he believes tipped off his plans to a gang of hold-up men. Well, did she or didn't she? That was the question, and it was answered by Lambert Hillyer doubling as writer and director on this inauspicious occasion. His cast included Judith Allen (second right), Ward Bond (left), Charles Sabin (second left), John Kelly and Arthur Rankin. (58 mins)

▽ The **Mills Of The Gods** ground slowly if this turgid family melodrama was anything to go by. Written by Garret Fort, it chronicled the travails of a game old girl (May Robson, right) who retires as the head of the Hastings Plow Works – only to see it slip rapidly into ruin. However, her ne'er-do-well son and daughter refuse to part with a cent of their £50 million trust fund to help save the business. In the end a workers' riot is avoided in the nick of time – and May returns with a bank loan to save the day. Fay Wray (centre), Victor Jory, Raymond Walburn (left), James Blakely and Mayo Nethot also appeared for director Roy William Neill. (66 mins)

△ Eight people receive a mysterious dinner invitation from an unknown host. On arriving at the appointed place, they learn, by radio, that **The Ninth Guest** is 'death' – and that one by one, they're all going to die. And, indeed, they do. Such was the creepy (albeit familiar) content of a play written by Owen Davis from the novel by Gene Bristow, and Garnett Weston's screen adaptation of it. The film featured Donald Cook, Genevieve Tobin (left), Hardie Albright (right), Edward Ellis, Edwin Maxwell, Vincent Barnett, Helen Flint, Samuel S. Hinds, Nella Walker and Sidney Bracey. A better-than-average mystery, it was competently directed by Roy William Neill, but could have done with a mite more humour – as Neil Simon proved in his re-working of the same idea, *Murder By Death* (1976). (65 mins)

▽ The marvellous Jean Arthur (right) brought a certain quality to **The Most Precious Thing In Life**, a lachrymose drama in which she mothers a child for upper-crust college student Donald Cook (left), only to be ejected from the family's bosom by Cook's parents who believe the girl has married well above her station. Twenty years pass; Arthur becomes a floor scrubber at the very college attended by her ex-husband and befriends a wealthy student – who turns out to be her son (he doesn't know this) – and saves the romance he is having with an indigent lass from going the same way as her own. Written by Ethel Hill and Dore Schary (from a story by Travis Ingham) and directed, unevenly, by Lambert Hillyer, it also featured Richard Cromwell, Anita Louise, Jane Darwell, Mary Forbes (centre front) and Paul Stanton (centre back). (67 mins)

△ **Name The Woman** wasn't a game show but a remake of a 1928 silent which, this time round, starred Richard Cromwell (right) as an incompetent newspaper reporter who inadvertently involves Arline Judge in a murder plot, then spends what's left of the running time trying to clear her name. A plodding screenplay by Fred Niblo Jr and Herbert Asbury, with direction to match by Albert Rogell, kept the dramatic temperature below normal. Also cast: Charles Wilson, Henry Kolker, Bradley Page, Purnell Pratt and Crane Wilbur. (60 mins)

▷ Based on Ferenc Molnar's autobiographical novel *The Paul Street Boys*, first seen as a German film in 1929, **No Greater Glory**, sensitively scripted by Jo Swerling, was a compelling portrait of the joy and the pain of childhood – as experienced by a frail lad whose happiest moment arrives when he is allowed to join a gang. What happens to the plucky youngster (who dies in the course of the film, but not before he proves his worth to all concerned) formed the touching content of this excellent, Frank Borzage-directed drama. George Breakston (front) played the youngster, Jimmy Butler (who, 11 years later died in World War II) was the gang leader, with other roles equally well taken by Jackie Searle, Frankie Darro, Donald Haines, Rolf Ernest, Julius Molnar, Ralph Morgan (right), Samuel S. Hinds, Lois Wilson (back left) and Egon Brecher. (78 mins)

▽ Based on a story by doctor-turned-novelist A.J. Cronin, scripted by Jo Swerling, and inspired, no doubt, by Sidney Kingsley's Broadway smash *Men In White* (1933), the clumsily titled **Once To Every Woman** was a drama with a hospital backdrop. The heart of the matter lay in the rivalry between Ralph Bellamy (left) as a young whizz-kid surgeon and Walter Connolly as his older mentor; but director Lambert Hillyer chose to concentrate instead on a trite romance between leading lady Fay Wray (right, as the hospital's head nurse) and a no-goodnik doctor in the guise of Walter Byron. In the end, though, it's Bellamy who wins Wray for himself. Also in this undistinguished effort were Mary Carlisle, J. Farrell MacDonald, Billie Seward and Georgia Caine. (70 mins)

◁ Victor Schertzinger combined his talent for song-writing as well as direction in **One Night Of Love** and, in the process, added another string to his versatile bow: that of star-maker. The star in question was Grace Moore (right), who made it to the screen via Broadway and the Metropolitan Opera. Her movie career, however, started badly. After appearing in *A Lady's Morals* (MGM, 1930) and *New Moon* (MGM, 1931) she developed a weight problem and MGM fired her. Three years later and many pounds slimmer, she was signed by Harry Cohn to a $25,000-a-picture deal after seeing her on Broadway in a revival of *The DuBarry* . The problem, now, was to find a suitable vehicle for her. It arrived in the shape of a simple Cinderella story about a young soprano's rise to operatic stardom. Moore, of course, was the soprano. Her teacher, and the man responsible for her success, was Tullio Carminati (left), while the American she met, and for whom she almost abandoned her career, was Lyle Talbot. Almost single-handedly *One Night Of Love* brought the hitherto rarefied world of opera down to a popular level and, against all the expectations of a worried Front Office in New York (the film had cost $200,000 to make), was an enormous smash. If the film made a star of Grace Moore, Miss Moore made a star out of the song 'Ciri-Biri-Bin', which was featured by Warner Bros. in *The Grace Moore Story* (1953) and by MGM in *Hit The Deck* (1955). The film's heavy operatic programme also featured extracts from *Madama Butterfly*, *Lucia Di Lammermoor* and *Carmen*. Harry Cohn personally took charge of the production, and, in minor roles, cast Mona Barrie, Jessie Ralph, Luis Alberni and Andres de Segurola. (84 mins)

▷ A jealous millionaire, whose wife has been having an affair with a prizefighter, murders both the pug and his manager. He is apprehended by the redoubtable Inspector Trent (Ralph Bellamy, right) – and that's all there was to **One Is Guilty**, a run-of-the-mill detective yarn from the typewriter of Harold Shumate, who provided both the plot and the screenplay. Lambert Hillyer was the director and his cast included Shirley Grey, Warren Hymer, Rita La Roy (left), J. Carroll Naish and Wheeler Oakman. (63 mins)

△ **The Party's Over** was an insubstantial domestic drama that starred Stuart Erwin (right) as a certified public accountant who decides he's had quite enough of his idle family sponging off him – and instigates a few changes. Those involved in Erwin's *volte face* included Ann Sothern (left), Arline Judge, Patsy Kelly, Catharine Doucet, Marjorie Lytell and Henry Travers. It was based on a play by Daniel Kusell, scripted by S. K. Lauren and directed with little, if any, distinction by Walter Lang. (68 mins)

◁ Mary Brian (left) and Bruce Cabot (right) made a pair of unarresting lovers – she a racketeer's sister, he the son of a detective – in **Shadows Of Sing Sing,** a thriller conceived at a turtle's pace by director Phil Rosen, and written without flair by Albert De Mond (story Katherine Scola and Doris Maloy). The couple's affair causes both families problems – climaxing in Cabot being framed, but being saved as a result of his father's access to departmental files. Harry Wood and Bradley Page gnashed the scenery as a pair of hoods, and the cast also included Grant Mitchell, Irving Bacon, Dewey Robinson and Fred Kelsey. (63 mins)

◁ The graceful Elissa Landi (left), the suave Joseph Schildkraut (right) and Frank (later Wizard of Oz) Morgan starred in **Sisters Under The Skin**, a familiar triangle drama whose story (by S.K. Lauren, screenplay by the ubiquitous Jo Swerling) found an older married man (Morgan) losing his young actress mistress (Landi) to a young bohemian composer (Schildkraut). And that, apart from a few glamorous trappings, was about the gist of it. Doris Lloyd played Morgan's put-upon wife and gave the best of a roster of very engaging performances. The supporting cast included Clara Blandick, Shirley Grey, Samuel S. Hinds and Henry Kolker. The glossy direction was by David Burton. (65 mins)

▷ Library footage of the racing tracks at Altoona, Providence, Utica, Elgin and Indianapolis was no substitute for a good, strong plot, as Tim McCoy (left) discovered in **Straightaway**, an enervating 'track' saga in which hero McCoy faced a murder trial should his kid brother win the big race. Sue Carol (right) was the leading lady in Lambert Hillyer's jerry-built screenplay, with other roles barely fleshed out by William Bakewell, Ward Bond, Lafe McKee, Francis McDonald and Samuel S. Hinds. Otto Brower directed. (58 mins)

▽ Coleen Moore (right) returned to the screen after a four-year absence in **Social Register**, playing a chorus girl whose romance with a society nob is frowned upon by the man's snobbish mother, who goes so far as to frame her. The film, which contained several songs by Con Conrad and Ford Dabney, was a complete waste of everyone's time – especially the audience's – and did nothing for Miss Moore's flagging career. Alexander Kirkland (left) was the prospective fiancé, Pauline Frederick played his disapproving mother, with other roles under Marshall Neilan's floundering direction going to Robert Benchley, Charles Winninger, Ross Alexander and Margaret Livingston. The complicated writing credits read thus: Story by John Emerson and Anita Loos, screenplay by Clara Beranger, additional dialogue by Grace Perkins, scenario by A. Creelman. (71 mins)

△ By unleashing a scenery-chewing John Barrymore (left) on the screen version of the frenetic Charles MacArthur–Ben Hecht Broadway hit **Twentieth Century** (which, in turn, was based on the play *Napoleon On Broadway* by Charles Bruce Milholland), producer-director Howard Hawks guaranteed audiences a roller-coaster ride between Chicago and New York as this celebrated screwball-comedy hit its energetic stride. Whereas the play on which it is based was set in its entirety on board the Twentieth Century (the famous train that took passengers from the Windy City to the Empire State), Messrs MacArthur and Hecht gave themselves more breathing space in their celluloid transfer; they opened out the narrative to show Barrymore's Svengali-like transformation of shop-girl Carole Lombard (right) into super-stardom on Broadway. The train was boarded only after Lombard (called Lily Garland) flees the maniacal stranglehold Barrymore (called Oscar Jaffe) has had on her career and on her emotions – and has left Broadway for Hollywood. Down and out and pursued by creditors, Barrymore is taking the Twentieth Century back to New York, hoping to revitalize his failing career,

when who should he meet on board but Lombard and her new football player fiancé Ralph Forbes (prosaically called George Smith). What follows is a sparring match *par excellence* in which Lombard proves the equal of the intimidating Barrymore – who is not only trying to wrench her away from her silly-ass lover, but desperately trying to convince her that she'd be perfect in the stage version he's preparing of *The Passion Play*. He succeeds on both counts. As the plot went into top gear, so did all the performances and the dialogue – which seemed, at the time, to be too sophisticated and show-biz-orientated. Barrymore's eccentric central performance (at one point he impersonated a camel) threatened, at times, to blow everyone off the screen, his tornado personality providing stiff competition for the seasoned likes of Walter Connolly as Lombard's manager and Roscoe Karns as her press-agent. Though Ralph Forbes as Lombard's college-type lover was woefully miscast, there were enjoyable performances from such stalwart supports as Etienne Girardot, Dale Fuller and, as a pair of bearded men anxious to appear in *The Passion Play*, Herman Bing and Lee Kohlmar. (91 mins)

◁ A domestic melodrama to the tune of hearts-and-flowers, **Whirlpool** was the story of a carnival owner (Jack Holt, third left) who receives a 20-year prison sentence for killing a man in a fight. While serving his sentence, Holt has his wife (Lila Lee) informed that he has committed suicide. Years later, after his release, he accidentally meets his daughter (Jean Arthur). So – does he keep his secret to himself or reveal his true identity to her and his wife (who, incidentally, has remarried)? The answer was duly supplied in Dorothy Howell and Ethel Hill's screenplay (story by Howard Emmett Rogers) – with tear-jerking results. Roy William Neill was the director, and the cast included Allen Jenkins (centre), Donald Cook, Rita La Roy (second left), John Miljan, Lila Lee (second right) and Ward Bond. (69 mins).

▽ A kidnapping, three plane crashes, several fist fights and the pilfering of vital plans were some of the familiar ingredients that went into **Speed Wings**, a Tim McCoy (centre) adventure that found the popular hero taking to the air for at least half the film's running time. Evalyn Knapp was the heroine, with William Bakewell, Vincent Sherman (later to become a director), Hooper Atchley and Ben Hewlett in support. Horace McCoy scripted from his own story, and the director was Otto Brower. (61 mins)

▽ The protean Frank Craven (left) scripted (from his stage play), starred in and directed **That's Gratitude** – a lame excuse for a farce in which he played a failed musical-comedy impresario who, as the story unfurls, befriends wealthy Arthur Byron, after which, with the help of a face specialist, he turns Byron's ugly daughter (Mary Carlisle) into a beauty. The result? Carlisle marries handsome tenor John Buckler (right). Helen Ware, Sheila Mannors (centre), Charles Sabin and Blythe Daley helped swell the meagre plot – but to little purpose. (67 mins)

▷ Another Tim McCoy (right) vehicle, **Voice In The Night** found the cowboy hero swapping his saddle for a telegraph pole as he single-handedly sees to it that, despite opposition, a line across Devil's Gulch is successfully stretched. Nothing else was stretched in this formula quickie – certainly not Harold Shumate's story or screenplay; nor Charles C. Coleman's straight-between-the-eyes direction. Billie Seward (centre) was the love interest, and the rest of the cast included Ward Bond (left), Joseph Crehan and Kane Richmond. (59 mins)

△ Walter Connolly (left), looking strikingly like the great Emil Jannings in *Sins of the Fathers* (Paramount, 1928), was the *raison d'être* for the pretentiously titled **Whom The Gods Destroy**. He played an imposing theatrical impresario who, to save his own skin when the ship on which he is a passenger goes down, dresses up in women's clothing to assure himself a place in one of the lifeboats. Assumed dead, and mourned at home as a hero, he decides he cannot reveal his true circumstances for fear of being branded a coward and bringing disgrace to his family. So he returns to New York incognito until the coincidence-prone screenplay (by Fred Niblo Jr and Sidney Buchman, from a story by Albert Dayson Terhume) contrives a meeting with his wife. Walter Lang's earnest direction failed to reconcile the implausible bits with the more truthful sections of the narrative, and was at its best in the depiction of the shipwreck that triggered the whole dilemma. Connolly's performance was impressive throughout, and there was good work, too, from Doris Kenyon as his wife. A very young Scotty Beckett (of the Our Gang series) played Connolly's son Jack at the age of four, while Macon Jones took over at the age of 14 and Robert Young (right) played him as an adult. (70 mins)

▽ Although the plot-line of **Air Hawks** (rival aviation companies competing for air-mail contracts) was pretty B-movie basic – involving, as it did, an infra-red death-ray device – director Albert Rogell nonetheless managed to generate excitement and suspense from Griffin Jay and Grace Neville's screenplay. The film top-starred Ralph Bellamy (left), and featured real-life aviator Wiley Post (right) as himself. Tala Birell provided female interest, and the cast included Douglass Dumbrille, Robert Allen, Billie Seward, Victor Kilian, Robert Middlemass, Geneva Michell, Wyrley Birch and Edward Van Sloan. (68 mins)

△ When reporter Lloyd Nolan (second right) is fired for spending more time with fiancée Nancy Carroll (right) than on his work, he attempts to win back his job by pursuing the murderer of the local district attorney on board an ocean liner. Not only does he get his man but a set of jewel thieves as well. Going along for this **Atlantic Adventure** were fiancée Carroll and photographer Harry Langdon. Also: Arthur Hohl (left), Robert Middlemass (second right), E. E. Clive, John Wray (centre) and Dwight Frye. Langdon, of course, provided the comic relief in the John T. Neville-Nat Dorfman screenplay (story by Diana Bourbon), and while he did so with his usual droll charm, it was sad to see him reduced to a programmer. Albert Rogell directedl (68 mins)

▽ **The Awakening Of Jim Burke** was an outdoor drama which pivoted on the attempts of Jack Holt (centre) to turn his sensitive, musician son (Jimmie Butler, left) into a he-man. He does this by removing the boy's violin. Young Butler does his best to be the kind of son his father wants and, in the last reel, wins back his fiddle by rescuing Holt from a bad accident. The sub-plot provided by Michael Simmons found good-gal Florence Rice and vamp Kathleen Burke (right) both after Holt – with, of course, the former winning out. Robert Middlemass, Wyrley Birch and Ralph M. Remley completed the cast, and the director of this passable programmer was Lambert Hillyer. (70 mins)

◁ Similar in mood (and, occasionally, plot) to *Atlantic Adventure*, **Public Menace**, another newspaper yarn, starred George Murphy (right). While tailing mobster Douglass Dumbrille aboard an ocean liner, Murphy neglects the job at hand when he becomes smitten with the ship's manicurist (top-billed Jean Arthur, centre) and is fired. Undaunted, he marries Miss Arthur who, after at first proving no help to him career-wise, saves his bacon by pointing him in the direction of Dumbrille. Slight and inconsequential, the film was saved from abject ordinariness by the potentially extraordinary Miss Arthur, who was still to find her best form. Erle C. Kenton's direction showed no real feeling for the world of tabloid journalism; while Ethel Hill and Lionel Houser's screenplay provided stereotypical roles for George McKay, Robert Middlemass, Victor Kilian and Charles C. Wilson. (72 mins)

△ Basically a Jack Holt-Ralph Graves melodrama, but with Edmund Lowe (left) in the Graves role, **The Best Man Wins** was a depressingly routine effort which starred the macho duo as deep-sea divers, one of whom (Lowe) loses an arm while saving his buddie's life and, rather than become a charity case, takes to crime. When, in time, Holt (centre) becomes a harbour policeman, a showdown between the two men becomes inevitable. The ending had Lowe drowning in a diving incident, thereby paving the way for Holt to get the girl they both fancied (Florence Rice). Bela Lugosi (right) was featured as the head of a crime syndicate. Ben G. Kohn provided the story, and it was adapted by Ethel Hill and Bruce Manning. Director: Erle Kenton. (75 mins)

◁ Lee Tracy (left) starred as a puppeteer in **Carnival,** whose screenplay (and story) by Robert Riskin combined equal portions of humour, schmaltz and melodrama. It turned out to be a pretty entertaining combination. The story began with the death of Tracy's wife in childbirth, and the suing for custody of the baby boy by Tracy's disapproving father-in-law. Tracy absconds with his son (called Poochy) and lies low for a couple of years; then, believing the coast to be clear, he joins his former assistant (Sally Eilers, right) and Jimmy Durante (centre) in a carnival act but finds the persistent grandfather is still on his heels. It is only after Eilers saves the infant Poochy in a circus fire that the near-sighted Tracy realizes what a perfect mother she'd make for his boy. Marriage also means the end of the custody battle, thus ensuring a hunky-dory fade-out for all concerned – except, of course, the grandfather. Riskin's screenplay was far less corny than his plot; and in the hands of director Walter Lang, who managed to tone down the usual high-octane performances of both Tracy and the great Durante, *Carnival* was worth paying money to see. Master Dickie Walters played Poochy, with other roles going to Thomas Jackson, Florence Rice, Fred Kelsey and, in her first credited role, Lucille Ball. (77 mins)

◁ Richard Arlen (left) played the titular hero of **Calling Of Dan Matthews** – a priest whose purpose in Dan Jarrett, Don Swift and Karl Brown's screenplay (from the novel by Harold Bell Wright) was to clean up a crooked amusement arcade owned by leading citizen Donald Cook, but run by vice operator Douglass Dumbrille. Charlotte Wynters (right) played Dumbrille's daughter (in love with Arlen), with other roles under Phil Rosen's journeyman direction going to Mary Kornman, Frederick Burton, Lee Morgan and Tommy Dugan. (67 mins)

▷ Despite the fact that **The Black Room** offered two Boris Karloffs (left) for the price of one, there was very little value for money on hand. Boris (billed, simply, as 'Karloff') played both Gregor and Anton, twin brothers, one good, the other evil. Needless to say, Arthur Strawn's predictable plot, which he scripted with Henry Meyers, had the latter eliminating the former, then paying for his wickedness by being hurled to his death courtesy of his dead brother's Great Dane. Roy William Neill's direction clearly aimed for Gothic horror with shots of ravens, graveyards, foreboding castles and shadows of cats – but nothing worked, except the expert double exposure featuring the two sides of Karloff. Marian Marsh (right), Robert Allen, Thurston Hall and Katherine De Mille were also featured. (75 mins)

▽ Not so much a whodunnit as a how-will-they-catch-him, **Case Of The Missing Man** starred Roger Pryor (centre left) as a reporter-cum-photographer who sets Lee Loeb and Harold Buchman's story and screenplay into motion when he inadvertently photographs a jewel robber emerging with his booty from a shop. Naturally, the thief wants to get hold of the film; and, naturally, Pryor wants to use the evidence against him. An entertaining resolution to the problem kept patrons happy. Joan Perry (the future Mrs Harry Cohn, centre right) provided the minor love-interest, Arthur Hohl played the chief heavy, with other parts under D. Ross Lederman's direction going to Thurston Hall, George McKay (right) and Tommy Dugan (second right). (58 mins)

△ **Champagne For Breakfast** was, as farces go, very flat. It starred Hardie Albright as an impecunious young attorney who falls in love with 'mad' Mary Carlisle (centre, top-starred) and finds himself acting as her legal adviser after the suicide of her father. The villain of the piece is the sinister Sidney Toler (right), a race-track tout and suitor of Ms Carlisle's sister (Lila Lee) who's out to appropriate the family estate for himself. Things got much worse before being satisfactorily resolved in the final moments of George Waggner's far-fetched screenplay (story by E. Morton Hough). Melville Brown directed, and the cast included Emerson Tracy, Joan Marsh, Natalie Morton and Bradley Page. (69 mins)

△ A flight between California and New York provided the setting for **Death Flies East,** a disaster movie that crashed in all departments. Florence Rice (left) played a nurse who, while on parole for a murder she did not commit, attempts to clear her name and bring the real culprit to trial. Conrad Nagel (right) was top-billed as a college instructor who, through the machinations of Philip Wylie's far-fetched plot (screenplay by Albert DeMond and Fred Niblo Jr), becomes involved in Ms Rice's plight. Raymond Walburn, Geneva Mitchell, Robert Allen, Oscar Apfel, Irene Franklin, and Adrian Rosley were some of the passengers on board. Phil Rosen directed. (65 mins)

▽ That notorious penal colony, Devil's Island, was the setting for **Escape From Devil's Island,** whose title said it all. Victor Jory (left) and Norman Foster (right) were the two convicts who embark on this particular escape and – had their dislike for one another not intruded at the last moment – they'd have got away with it too. Still, the steps leading up to their break-out were passably charted by director Albert Rogell and his scenarists (Earle Snell and Fred Niblo Jr; story by Fred De Gressac) and they provided roles for Stanley Andrews, Daniel Haynes, Herbert Heywood, Frank Lackteen (centre) and, as the female interest, second-billed Florence Rice. (64 mins)

△ Producer B. P. Schulberg hired Josef von Sternberg, a colleague from his Paramount days, to direct Dostoevsky's epic Russian novel **Crime And Punishment**. The result was a densely atmospheric, moodily photographed (by Lucien Ballard) melodrama which had some effective moments while never really entering the soul of the novel. Edward Arnold received top-billing as the wily Inspector Porfiry, though, not surprisingly, the dramatic impetus of the narrative was supplied by Peter Lorre (left) as the guilt-obsessed student Raskolnikov. Given the limitations imposed on him by S. K. Lauren and Joseph Anthony's psychologically impoverished screenplay, Lorre, oozing repugnance – yet at the same time eliciting sympathy – was mesmeric in the role, and his scenes with Arnold's Inspector positively crackled. There was a splendid cameo from the redoubtable English actress, Mrs Patrick Campbell, as Lorre's pawnbroker victim, passable performances from Tala Birell and Elizabeth Risdon, as Lorre's sister and mother, and a totally unconvincing one from a prettified Marian Marsh (right) as Sonya, the prostitute with whom Raskolnikov falls in love. As you'd expect from director von Sternberg, the film was brilliantly lit throughout and always cinematic. But, by the very nature of the complex material, it could not help but be an unsatisfying reduction of one of the greatest novels ever written. Also cast were Robert Allen as Dmitri, Douglass Dumbrille as Grilov, Gene Lockhart as Lushin and Charles Waldron as the university president. A week before the film opened in New York, a French version, with Harry Baur in the Lorre role, was released to generally favourable reviews. There were three Russian screen versions of the novel (in 1913, 1922, and 1926), and one from Pathé in 1917. It was remade in Sweden in 1958, by Allied Artists in 1959, who updated it and called it *Crime and Punishment USA* and, once again, by the Russians in 1975. (88 mins)

▽ I. A. R. Wylie's novel **A Feather In Her Hat,** whose theme was motherly love, came to the screen via a scenario by Lawrence Hazard. It starred Pauline Lord (centre) as a Cockney bookseller and Louis Hayward (left) as her illegitimate son. Because his mother is determined that her boy should be raised as a gentleman, she tells him, when he comes of age, that he isn't really her son, but the son of a famous actress (Billie Burke) who, years ago, had left him in her care. Hayward takes up residence in the madcap Burke home, writes a successful play (which his *real* mother helps finance) and, after he learns the truth about Miss Lord's sacrifice, falls in love with the well-spoken daughter of the Burke household (Wendy Barrie). Basil Rathbone (right) was second-billed as a well-born drunk to whom Miss Lord offers lodgings in the hope that something of his aristocratic mien will rub off on her son. Nydia Westman gave a touching performance as the boy's Cockney sweetheart (later jilted for the more personable Miss Barrie), with other roles in producer Everett Riskin's oh-so-very-English production going to Victor Varconi, David Niven, Thurston Hall and Nana Bryant. Alfred Santell directed. (72 mins)

▷ A very minor musical indeed, **The Girl Friend** top-billed delightful Ann Sothern (centre) with Jack Haley (second left) as her brother. All about an unproduced (and unproducable) play of Haley's finding success on Broadway, this amiable piece of escapism featured Roger Pryor (third right) as an actor who gets into hot water by pretending to be a producer, Victor Kilian (right), Ray Walker (second right) and Inez Courtney (left). Seymour Felix choreographed, Edward Buzzell directed and it was written by Gertrude Purcell and Benny Rubin from a story which, in turn, was written by Gene Towne and Graham Baker. (67 mins)

◁ Similar in content to *Gentlemen Are Born* (First National, 1934), and with faint echoes of King Vidor's vastly superior *The Crowd* (MGM, 1928), **I'll Love You Always** was a Depression-orientated story about a cocky engineer who marries a former actress and then cannot find employment. Sent to jail for larceny, he tells his wife that he is in Russia on a job. She, in turn, keeps from him the fact that she is going to have a baby. The final reel finds him paroled, thus paving the way for a happy clinch at the end. A lightweight and unsympathetic George Murphy (second left) didn't bring much conviction to the role of the engineer, though Nancy Carroll (second right) as his put-upon spouse was fine. If the Depression was the real villain of the piece, some of the blame must also go to scenarists Vera Caspary and Sidney Buchman, who based their familiar tale of woe on a story by Lawrence Hazard. Everett J. Riskin (Robert's brother) produced, Leo Bulgakov directed (most capably, given the indifferent material) and the supporting cast included Raymond Walburn, Jean Dixon, Arthur Hohl and Paul Harvey. (75 mins)

▷ A mind-bogglingly inept thriller, **Guard That Girl** starred a miscast Robert Allen (right) as a detective out to apprehend a crooked lawyer for the murder of an heiress (by bow and arrow) whose estate he then embezzles. The real hero, though, turns out to be Lobo, the dog – whose antics are responsible for sniffing out the villain. Florence Rice (left) played a secretary, badly – and the rest of the cast, including Ward Bond, Barbara Kent (centre), Arthur Hohl, Thurston Hall, Bert Roach and Nana Bryant, didn't fare much better. Lambert Hillyer directed from his own story and screenplay. (67 mins)

◁ The same team that brought you *I'll Love You Always* pooled their resources once again for **After The Dance**. A mild-mannered melodrama with two songs, it starred George Murphy (right) as an escaped convict who is befriended by cabaret dancer Nancy Carroll (left) and joins her act until her jealous ex-partner (Jack La Rue) informs on him. Murphy sang better than he acted, and danced better than he sang; but as this wasn't a full-blown musical, he wasn't called upon to do either often enough to make it count. Scenarists Harold Shumate and Bruce Manning couldn't do much with Harrison Jacobs' perfunctory plot; no-one could. Albertina Rasch (who was originally to have appeared in the film with her dancers) choreographed, and Leo Bulgakov directed. Helping to pad out the slender narrative in their respective ways were Thelma Todd, Arthur Hohl and Victor Kilian. (60 mins)

▷ In **Grand Exit**, Edmund Lowe (right) played a wise-cracking detective whose speciality is expensive cases for fire-insurance companies, and who, in the course of Bruce Manning and Lionel Hauser's screenplay (story by Gene Towne and Graham Baker) is himself suspected of arson. Just how Lowe (on top form) managed to track down the offending fire-bug was what the film was all about; and in the process it gave employment to Ann Sothern (left) as the romantic interest, Onslow Stevens (as Lowe's sidekick), and Robert Middlemass (as the fire-chief), as well as Guy Asher, Miki Morita, and Edward van Sloan. The director was Erle Kenton. One of the year's better Bs. (68 mins)

◁ **In Spite Of Danger** was an assembly-line action-melodrama – practically devoid of suspense – that starred Wallace Ford (centre) as a racing driver whose career is cut short by an accident. The girl in his life is waitress Marian Marsh. After going into the trucking business with her father, Ford discovers that his business rival just happens to be the man responsible for his accident on the track. Also cast: Arthur Hohl (right), Charles B. Middleton, Edward Le Saint, Richard Wessel and Charlie Grapewin (left). It was scripted by Anthony Coldeway and directed by Lambert Hillyer. (53 mins)

◁ The unshattering gist of **Let's Live Tonight** was that brothers Tullio Carminati (right) and Hugh Williams are both in love with Lilian Harvey (left). Carminati, the older of the siblings, gets her. A plot that might just have stood a chance had it furnished a small-scale musical relied, instead, on the leaden dialogue provided by Gene Markey (from a story by Bradley King). Further aggravating the situation was the miscasting of Harvey – who by this point in her career was no longer a convincing ingénue – and the almost total absence of anything resembling humour. Director Victor Schertzinger, stale from his triumphs in *One Night Of Love* (1934) and *Love Me Forever*, contributed one song: 'Love Passes By', sung by Carminati. A studio-bound Monte Carlo provided the bulk of the setting for producer Robert North's lustreless production. Also cast: Janet Beecher, Tala Birell and, for so-called comic relief, Luis Alberni. Arthur Treacher was in it too, playing a character called Ozzy Featherstone. (75 mins)

▽ The **Men Of The Hour** were newsreel cameramen Wallace Ford and Richard Cromwell (left), both of whom love leading lady Billie Seward (right). The paltry action supplied by scenarist Anthony Coldeway concerned Cromwell being in the right spot at the right time in order to photograph a murder, as a result of which his flagging reputation in the newsreel business was restored. Lambert Hillyer directed, and his cast included Jack LaRue, Wesley Barry, Charles Wilson and Pat O'Malley. (57 mins)

▽ Though the real villain of **One Way Ticket** was a banker (unseen, throughout) who ripped off his bank to the tune of $4,643.87, top-starred Lloyd Nolan (right) got all the blame. As an understandably angry victim of the robbery, Nolan decides to recoup his loss by robbing the bank himself; however, he's caught and sent to jail. Eventually he escapes from custody but, both inside and out, his life is no bed of roses – proving that for some, at any rate, crime does not pay. Peggy Conklin (left) provided a modicum of romance, and the rest of the cast included Walter Connolly, Edith Fellows, Gloria Shea, Nana Bryant, Thurston Hall, George McKay and Robert Middlemass. It was written (from a novel by Ethel Turner) by Vincent Lawrence, Joseph Anthony, Oliver H.P. Garret, and Grover Jones; unfortunately their screenplay did little to encourage belief in the proceedings. Herbert Biberman directed it and the producer was B. P. Schulberg. (66 mins)

△ After her triumph in *One Night Of Love* (1934), Grace Moore (centre) was immediately put to work in a big-budget musical and, courtesy of scenarists Jo Swerling and Sidney Buchman (working from a story by Victor Schertzinger), was top-billed in **Love Me Forever** (GB: **On Wings Of Song**). It was a musical concoction in which she became the opera-singing protégée of night-club owner-cum-hood Leo Carrillo (right) whose involvement with a bunch of rival mobsters kept what little plot there was simmering nicely. The film's full-throated climax found diva Moore warbling away in a production at the Metropolitan Opera House (financed by Carrillo) of Puccini's *La Bohème* in which all the acts were arbitrarily reversed, and in which she sang both Mimi and Musetta! It was Hollywood at its most philistine, but enjoyable just the same. Opera star Michael Bartlett played himself and gave his all in 'Your Tiny Hand Is Frozen'; with other roles going to Robert Allen (left) as Moore's romantic interest, Luis Alberni (second left) as Carrillo's stooge, as well as Spring Byington, Thurston Hall and Douglass Dumbrille. Director Schertzinger wasn't always able to bring off the awkward blend of grand opera and gangsterdom, but with his leading lady in particularly good voice throughout, who cared? (91 mins)

◁ Malicious gossip and the trouble it can cause was the subject of **Party Wire**, a small-scale comedy that starred Jean Arthur (centre) as the daughter of the town's most popular citizen (Charley Grapewin, left), and Victor Jory (right) as an eligible bachelor and dairy owner. When Arthur and Jory begin to take an interest in each other, local tongues wag – via a party line – in an attempt to end the romance. Helen Lowell, Robert Allen, Clara Blandick and Maude Eburne also had parts in Ethel Hill and John H. Lawson's screenplay (story by Bruce Manning). The film was directed, most enjoyably, by Erle Kenton. (70 mins)

▷ When Walter Connolly is nailed by the income-tax men for tax evasion, he accepts the resultant prison sentence as a much-needed respite from the spoiled, headline-making antics of his impossible family. While in prison he meets George Raft (left), a bootlegger who genuinely wants to tread the straight and narrow on his release. The two men strike up a friendship, and so impressed is Connolly with inmate Raft that he makes him executor of his will. Whereupon he promptly drops dead. **She Couldn't Take It** (GB: **Woman Tamer**), a screwball comedy with a touch of the crime thriller thrown in for added box-office, followed (with varying degrees of success) Raft about his executorial responsibilities, and showed how he tames Connolly's shrewish, but attractive young daughter – spiritedly played by Joan Bennett (right). Initially, Joan can't take it. In the end, though, and after a great deal of melodramatic high-jinks, macho Raft wins through, taming not only the lovely Joan, but her addlepated mother (Billie Burke) and brother (Lloyd Nolan) as well. Though the role hardly helped Raft extend his range, he gave his usual seamless performance by not seeming to perform at all. Oliver H. P. Garrett's screenplay (from a story by Gene Towne and Graham Baker) catered for a large supporting cast, including Wallace Ford, James Blakeley, Alan Mowbray, Donald Meek and Franklin Pangborn. B. P. Schulberg (who until 1932 had been production head of Paramount) produced, and it was niftily directed by the reliable Tay Garnett. (77 mins)

▽ A passable programmer that made the most of its limited production values, **Superspeed** starred Norman Foster (left) as a football hero who also happens to be the inventor of a 'superspeed' car formula. Out to sabotage the formula is bad guy Arthur Hohl, a car-plant manager. Of course, it all came right in the end, with our hero not only taking part in a climactic motorboat race, but having the choice of Florence Rice (right) and Mary Carlisle as the woman in his life. Charley Grapewin, Robert Middlemass and George McKay completed the cast for director Lambert Hillyer; and it was written, from his own story, by Harold Shumate. (53 mins)

△ The swellhead in **Swellhead** was Wallace Ford (right), the local 'home-run' king whose overweening ego is knocked out of him on the pitch when he's struck on the head by a speeding ball. And that was about all there was to it. Child star Dickie Moore was unfortunately forced to utter dialogue (by William Jacobs from a story by Gerald Beaumont) that was way beyond his years, and so was able to bring little conviction to his role. Others involved included Barbara Kent (left), J. Farrell MacDonald, Sammy Cohen, Bryant Washburn and Mike Donlin. Ben Stoloff directed. (63 mins)

△ **She Married Her Boss** was produced by Everett Riskin and directed with a glorious insouciance by Gregory La Cava – who took a truly shop-worn story (by Thyra Samter Winslow) and, with a great deal of seasoned help from scenarist Sidney Buchman, turned it into a sparkling comedy. It starred Claudette Colbert (centre) as an extremely bright young woman and the 'she' of the title, who, after landing her boss (Melvyn Douglas, left) and moving into the family home, discovers that not only has she to contend with an intolerable and unwelcoming sister-in-law (Katherine Alexander) – and with a venomous child (Edith Fellows being convincingly nasty) from a former marriage – but also with the fact that Douglas has married her more for her brains than her body. Undaunted, Colbert puts all that to rights. Just how she did so was what the film was all about. Helping to keep the mood bright and cheerful were Jean Dixon as Colbert's wisecracking best friend, Clara Kimball Young as a governess, Raymond Walburn (right) as a butler and the aforementioned Miss Fellows (the perfect antidote to Shirley Temple). Michael Bartlett was in it too, as a 'gay young blade'. (90 mins)

△ San Francisco's general strike of 1934 – depicted by newsreel footage – was the backdrop for **Together We Live**, written and directed by Willard Mack (right, who also starred in it) shortly before his death. Anti-red propaganda, it was also the story of a Civil War vet (Mack) who, after his two older boys take an interest in Communism, sets out to show them the error of their ways – which he does. Ben Lyon, Esther Ralston, Sheila Mannors, Wera Engles, Hobart Bosworth (left) and William V. Mong made little impression under Mack's direction, and the film came and went in a flash. (70 mins)

▷ Victor Jory (right) played an engineer in **Too Tough To Kill**, an action-melodrama which found him being sent to the southwest to investigate why the building of a tunnel is progressing so slowly. Using his fists to provide many of the answers, he proves himself unpopular with certain criminal elements in the construction crew, several of whom attempt to blow him up together with the tunnel. Romantic interest among these macho machinations was provided by Sally O'Neill as an unlikely girl reporter from Los Angeles who just happens to arrive at the site of the beleaguered tunnel. Thurston Hall, Johnny Arthur, Robert Gleckler, Robert Middlemass and Ward Bond (centre left) were also on hand; it was scripted by Lester Cole and J. Griffin Jay from a story by Robert D. Speers, and directed by D. Ross Lederman. (58 mins)

▽ The **Unknown Woman** in director Albert Rogell's film of the same name was Marian Marsh (left) – a federal agent whose identity wasn't revealed until the last reel. Racketeers featured prominently in Albert DeMond and Fred Niblo Jr's screenplay (story by W. Scott Darling); so did a miscast Richard Cromwell (centre) as a struggling young attorney whose fate is intertwined with Ms Marsh's. Henry Armetta supplied some comic relief as a fish-pedlar, Douglass Dumbrille was featured as a nightclub owner, and the cast also included Arthur Hohl, George McKay, Robert Middlemass and Richard Powell (right). (66 mins)

▽ **Unwelcome Stranger** was a welcome little programmer whose plot hinged on the superstition that Jack Holt (centre), a thoroughbred race-horse breeder, has about orphans. According to Holt they're bad news – which is bad news for young Jackie Searle (second left), an orphan who has turned up at the stock farm and is seeking a roof over his head. When, however, the youngster overhears a plot involving the fixing of an important race, he saves the day by riding Holt's horse in place of the duplicitous jockey, thus breaking the 'orphan' jinx and living happily ever after. Mona Barrie (second right) co-starred as Holt's warm-hearted wife, and the screenplay by Crane Wilbur (from a story by William Jacobs) called for contributions from Ralph Morgan, Bradley Page, Frankie Darro, Sam McDaniel (left) and Frank Orth. Phil Rosen directed. (65 mins)

▽ Director John Ford turned his considerable talents towards comedy in **The Whole Town's Talking** (GB: **Passport To Fame**), with exhilarating results. Equally successful were scenarists Robert Riskin and Jo Swerling, who took a tired old mistaken-identity plot (by W. R. Burnett) and with great ingenuity gave it a refreshing once-over. The story of a timid, white-collar clerk called Arthur Jones whose misfortune it is to be the spitting image of 'Killer' Mannion, a notorious gangster, it starred Edward G. Robinson (right) as both the innocent and the guilty parties, and a blonde Jean Arthur (left) as the

▽ **White Lies** featured Victor Jory (centre front) as a sartorially impeccable traffic cop with a taste for flowers and Chopin. He makes the mistake, however, of giving a ruthless newspaper publisher, top-billed Walter Connolly (second right), a ticket for a traffic offence, and is only saved from professional ruin by the publisher's sympathetic daughter (Fay Wray, third right) who lashes out at her father's abuse of his power. She is repaid by being arrested by Jory after being implicated in a murder. This time Connolly has his way and Jory is demoted. Down but not out, Jory now sets about discovering the real murderer and clearing Wray's name. A routine crime melodrama, it was written by Harold Shumate and directed by Leo Bulgakov. Also cast: Leslie Fenton (left, as the heavy), Irene Hervey, Robert Allen and William Demarest. (63 mins)

object of the clerk's unarticulated affection. The main plot point hinged on good-guy Robinson being given an identifying pass by the police, and bad-guy Robinson getting hold of it. The resultant confusion kept audiences chuckling away merrily – and also provided roles for Etienne Girardot as a fussy office manager, Edward Brophy as a frightened gangster, and Donald Meek. In addition, the cast included Arthur Hohl, Wallace Ford, Arthur Byron, Paul Harvey and J. Farrell MacDonald. The happy producer of this excellent combination of farce and melodrama was Lester Cowan. (95 mins)

1936

▽ Suspension of disbelief was a prerequisite for enjoying **Adventure In Manhattan**, a thoroughly implausible but mildly diverting frolic once again set against a backdrop of what Hollywood believed to be the newspaper world. The combined writing credits on this one (story by Joseph Krumgold 'suggested' by May Edington's *Purple And Fine Linen* and scripted by Sidney Buchman, Harry Sauber and Jack Kirkland) indicated something more substantial than the tale of a criminologist recruited on to the staff of a newspaper in order to apprehend a master burglar whose booty runs to art treasures and priceless gems. The twist is that the criminologist and the thief have similar tastes, and that the former can predict the latter's every move. This likeable film was greatly enhanced by the engaging performance of Joel McCrea (centre) as the criminologist, and by top-billed Jean Arthur (right) as an actress. As the burglar with impeccable taste, Reginald Owen (left) went in for a spot of scene-stealing as well, and comparative newcomer Thomas Mitchell splendidly threw his weight around as a managing editor. Also cast for director Edward Ludwig were Herman Bing, Victor Kilian and John Gallaudet. (73 mins)

◁ Though Melvyn Douglas (second right) and Mary Astor (second left) were the marquee names that advertised **And So They Were Married**, grand larceny was committed under their attractive noses by child stars Edith Fellows (left) and Jackie Moran (right). Douglas and Astor, a widower and widow, meet at a winter holiday resort and fall in love after taking an initial dislike to each other. Enter trouble in the guise of their respective offspring who do everything in their power to keep the couple apart. They succeed, then relent. Climax finds them staging a fake kidnap to bring the oldsters together again. The screenplay, written by Doris Anderson, Joseph Anthony and A. Laurie Brazee (story by Sarah Addington), wisely concentrated on the antics of the kids, and although master Jackie Moran's recurring stutter outstayed its welcome, they were the show and the show was them. Getting the occasional look-in were Donald Meek as an innkeeper, and a somewhat over-the-top Dorothy Stickney and Romaine Callender as the inn's entertainment directors. Douglas Scott did a bit of scene-pilfering too, as a sissy. Elliott Nugent directed. (72 mins)

▽ Paul Hurst played an early predecessor of Peter Sellers' Inspector Clouseau in **Blackmailer**, a farcical thriller in which he appeared as an inept police inspector assigned, in a blackmail case, to an equally inept amateur detective, played by William Gargan (right). Joseph Krumgold, Lee Loeb and Harold Buchman's screenplay aimed at a mixture of laughter and suspense and failed on both levels. It was loosely directed by Gordon Wiles with a cast that included Florence Rice (centre, as the romantic interest), H. B. Warner, Nana Bryant, George McKay (left), and, as a butler out to avenge his daughter's death, Wyrley Birch. (66 mins)

◁ A talkative thriller in which a moment's silence, every now and then, would have spoken far louder than scenarist Tom Van Dycke's words, **Alibi For Murder** was an assembly-line offering that starred William Gargan (left) as a Mr Wise-guy detective-cum-amateur broadcaster who sets the plot in motion when he witnesses the murder of a scientist (Egon Brecher, foreground). Marguerite Churchill (second left) played the murdered man's secretary (badly), with other roles going to Gene Morgan, John Gallaudet, Romaine Callender, Dwight Frye (right) and Wade Boteler. The director was D. Ross Lederman. (61 mins)

◁ **Counterfeit** was a crime thriller that just about passed muster. It starred Chester Morris (right) as an undercover T-man (Treasury Department Special Agent), who saves a Treasury Department bank-note engraver from the menacing activities of counterfeiter Lloyd Nolan (left). He also gets the girl (Margot Grahame, centre). It was written by William Rankin and Bruce Manning (from a story by Rankin), directed by Erle C. Kenton, produced by B. P. Schulberg, and featured Marian Marsh, Claude Gillingwater, George McKay and John Gallaudet. (73 mins)

▽ A quintessential 'woman's picture', **Craig's Wife**, first seen in 1926 as a Pulitzer Prize-winning Broadway play by George Kelly, came to the screen via Pathé in 1928 when the title role of the alienating Mrs Craig went to Irene Rich. It resurfaced when producer Edward Chodorov, working with scenarist Mary McCall Jr and director Dorothy Arzner, dusted the property off. This time round the talented Rosalind Russell (right) was cast in the celebrated role of a woman who is more interested in the well-being of her spotless home than in the human needs of the people around her – including her weak-willed husband (John Boles, left), whose love she trades for her security. Russell's embittered central performance turned a hitherto promising actress into a star and drew raves from the critics. As the husband, Boles made less of an impression; the scene in which he finally rebels over his icy wife's shrewish behaviour was, frankly, laughable. But there was excellent support from Alma Kruger as Boles's aunt, Jane Darwell as the Craig's housekeeper, Nydia Westman as a maid and Billie Burke as a flower-gathering neighbour unable to understand Mrs Craig's indifference towards her. Youthful interest was supplied by Dorothy Wilson and Robert Allen. Thomas Mitchell, Raymond Walburn, Elizabeth Risdon, Kathleen Burke and Frankie Vann completed the cast. It was remade in 1950 as *Harriet Craig* with Joan Crawford in the title role. (73 mins)

△ A respectable low-budget programmer, **Dangerous Intrigue** starred Ralph Bellamy (left) as a celebrated surgeon, who is rejected by his snobbish fiancée (Joan Perry) and suffers an attack of amnesia , in which condition he finds himself coming to the help of injured workers in a steel mill in Scranton, New Jersey. The heavy of the piece was Fred Kohler (right), whose murderous thoughts towards Bellamy are dramatically tempered when the latter saves the life of Kohler's son. Romance was supplied by Gloria Shea (centre) as a Polish girl Bellamy meets at the mill. Fredrik Vogeding, Edward Le Saint, George Billings and Boyd Irwin Sr were also in it, and it was directed by David Selman from a screenplay and story by Grace Neville and Harold Shumate respectively. (59 mins)

▷ Ann Sothern (left) and Bruce Cabot played husband and wife in **Don't Gamble With Love**, a modest programmer in which the birth of their first child prompts Cabot to give up his albeit 'straight' gambling house and enter a more salubrious business. Unfortunately, he's taken for a ride by his business associates whereupon he decides to turn crooked, much to his wife's disgust. She leaves him, opens a dress business of her own and returns only to save her man from the clutches of his murderous competitors – such was the story-line provided by Lee Loeb and Harold Buchman (who also scripted). The film employed the talents of Ian Keith as a racket attorney, Irving Pichel as a gambler, Elizabeth Risdon as a nursemaid, as well as Thurston Hall, the ubiquitous George McKay (right), Franklin Pangborn and, as the leading couple's baby (who never seemed to get any older), Master Richard Livernoin. The director was Dudley Murphy. (64 mins)

△ The fast-talking world of salesmen was highlighted in **Come Closer, Folks**, an implausible comedy in which top-starred James Dunn (right) works himself up from street salesman to important department store executive. The store's owner (Gene Lockhart, left) has a daughter (Marian Marsh, centre) – and with Dunn's success comes romance. Lee Loeb and Harold Buchman's unlikely screenplay, from an equally unlikely scenario by Aben Kandel, jeopardized the efforts of all concerned, though Herman Bing, as a merchant specialising in worthless goods, managed to make his eccentric presence felt. Less successful were George McKay, John Gallaudet, Gene Morgan and Wallis Clark. The over-employed D. Ross Lederman directed. (61 mins)

▷ Tall, rugged, square-jawed silent-movies action-man Richard Dix (right) played a test pilot in **Devil's Squadron**, an entertaining, well-made adventure, and spent much of his time testing new planes for Army use. A hazardous existence, to be sure – and one that supplied Howard J. Green, Bruce Manning and Lionel Houser's screenplay (from a story by Richard V. Grace) with most of its thrills. Somewhere in the middle of it all was the old chestnut about the disgraced airman (Dix) finally proving his worth, just one of the many clichés that didn't prevent this epic of the air from being one of the studio's better efforts. Karen Morley (left) played the daughter of an aircraft manufacturer (Boyd Irwin) who takes over the running of the plant when her father dies; with other roles going to Lloyd Nolan as one of her suitors (he's ousted by Dix), Gertrude Green and Gene Morgan. Erle C. Kenton directed. (80 mins)

▽ A down-and-out lawyer (Ralph Bellamy, left) is rescued from the gutter by hat-check girl Marguerite Churchill, and then comes to her defence in her **Final Hour** when she is charged with murder and larceny. Harold Shumate wrote this out-and-out loser, D. Ross Lederman directed, and the cast included John Gallaudet (right), George McKay, Elizabeth Risdon, Marc Lawrence (centre) and Lina Basquette. (57 mins)

▽ A frothy screwball comedy which benefited mightily from the casting of Herbert Marshall (left) and Jean Arthur (second left), **If You Could Only Cook** was the story of how Arthur (a homeless blonde) and Marshall (a millionaire automobile engineer), posing as a husband-and-wife team, find employment with gourmet mobster Leo Carrillo (right) in his imposing mansion. Howard J. Green and Gertrude Purcell's screenplay (from a story by F. Hugh Herbert) came up with some absurdly wacky flights of narrative fancy, providing in the process, nice parts for Lionel Stander (second right), Alan Edwards, Frieda Inescort, Gene Morgan and Ralf Harolde. It was produced by Everett Riskin and efficiently directed by William Seiter whose skilful juggling kept this far-fetched concoction lively. [When *If You Could Only Cook* opened in London, it was advertised as a Frank Capra production. It was nothing of the sort, and Capra, understandably, was furious with Harry Cohn who, hoping to cash in on the success of *It Happened One Night* (1934), had instigated the deception. Capra sued for libel and it wasn't until Cohn called on him personally – and promised to purchase the rights of the Kaufman and Hart smash *You Can't Take It With You* which Capra was anxious to direct, that the deplorable incident was finally resolved.] (70 mins)

△ **Lady From Nowhere** was a mediocre vehicle for Mary Astor (centre) who played a manicurist who is the only witness to a gang murder. Fearing for her life – and pursued both by the gangsters in question as well as the police – she flees to a small Connecticut town where, in order to escape detection, she poses as a runaway heiress. Very little in Ben J. Kohn's story (screenplay by Fred Niblo Jr, Arthur Strawn and Joseph Krumgold) convinced, though it did allow leading man Charles Quigley (left) a chance to ooze personality as a local newspaperman who believes Astor really is the missing heiress. Thurston Hall, Victor Kilian (right) and Spencer Charters were in it too, and it was directed by Gordon Wiles. (60 mins)

▷ The **Killer At Large** was a certain Mr Zero, played by Henry Brandon (centre front), who, after a modicum of mayhem, murder and robbery, is duly apprehended. This thankfully quite small helping of mish mash (almost too short to be a feature) starred Mary Brian (centre back) as an ineffectual store detective, Russell Hardie (fifth left) – momentarily suspected of being the culprit – as a jewellery store manager, Betty Compson as a shoplifter, George McKay (far left) as another inept detective, and Thurston Hall (second left). Harold Shumate scripted from a story by Carl Clausen, and it was directed by David Selman. (54 mins)

◁ After his ponderous attempt to turn Dostoevsky's *Crime And Punishment* into a film (1935), director Josef von Sternberg turned his attention to the world of operetta and in **The King Steps Out** seemed more at home in the court of Franz Josef of Austria than he did in the mind of guilt-ridden Russian student Raskolnikov. This slice of Viennese pastry top-starred Grace Moore (left) as a young lady who rescues her sister (Frieda Inescort) from an unwanted marriage to the emperor (Franchot Tone, right), only to marry the man herself. It was crammed full of good things, not least of which was Walter Connolly's robust performance as the King of Bavaria. Enjoyable, too, was Herman Bing as Pretzelberger (who else?), the owner of an establishment called 'The Golden Ox'. Indeed, all the supporting performances (Raymond Walburn, Victor Jory, Elizabeth Risdon, Nana Bryant and Thurston Hall) were a positive contribution to Sidney Buchman's well-turned libretto. Based on the play *Cissy*, by Gustav Hohn and Ernest Decsey, and on the operetta by Hubert and Ernst Marischka, it was produced by William Perlberg, had a score by Fritz Kreisler (borrowed from *Apple Blossoms*), and reworked lyrics by Dorothy Fields. (85 mins)

▷ **Lady Of Secrets** was a turgid melodrama in which Ruth Chatterton (left) played the lady of the title – her secret being that her so-called young sister isn't her sister at all but her daughter (Marian Marsh). It seems that her lover (Lloyd Nolan) was killed in the war and that his domineering father (Lionel Atwill, right) insisted that the child she was carrying at the time be reared as her sister rather than as a bastard. When the truth finally emerges, unpleasant Mr Atwill has her committed – but she escapes just in time to prevent her daughter from marrying a man she does not love (Otto Kruger). The dénouement finds Chatterton and Kruger romantically linked, and Marsh and Robert Allen similarly paired. Joseph Anthony and Zoë Akins's screenplay recounted the story (by Katherine Brush) largely in flashback, beginning in 1914 and ending in 1936. In neither period was Ms Chatterton convincing – blame for which could be laid squarely at Marion Gering's breast-beating direction and on the hearts-and-flowers scenario. It was produced by B. P. Schulberg whose cast was completed by Elizabeth Risdon, Nana Bryant and Esther Dale. (73 mins)

△ The studio paid four men to provide a story and scenario for **The Man Who Lived Twice**, then economized on the casting by having its star, Ralph Bellamy (left), play a dual role. When we first see him he is a vicious and ugly murderer on the run who, while taking refuge in a hospital, overhears a lecture being delivered by brain surgeon Thurston Hall, the gist of which is that it is possible to eliminate through brain surgery the more violent elements in mankind's make-up. After the lecture, Bellamy (alias Slick Rawley) confesses his crimes to Hall, and persuades him to perform an operation on him that will change both his physical appearance and his violent nature. The operation is a success, time passes and, under Hall's guidance, Bellamy – now James Blake – becomes an eminent medical scientist. But his voice, which remains unchanged after the operation, gives him away to the authorities, and Blake finds himself standing trial for the crimes of Slick Rawley. He's found guilty, but a last-minute reprieve frees him to marry Marian Marsh (right), the woman in his life. Stuff 'n' nonsense, of course, but with Bellamy giving audiences double their money's worth, Ben Pivar's taut little production – ably directed by Harry Lachman – was a minor crowd-pleaser. Isabel Jewell, Nana Bryant, Ward Bond, Henry Kolker and Willard Robertson helped flesh out the screenplay by Tom Van Dycke, Fred Niblo Jr and Arthur Strawn (story by Van Dycke and Henry Altimus.) It was remade in 1953 as *Man In The Dark*. (73 mins)

▽ The unmasking of a ruthless organization known as the **Legion Of Terror** (based on the topical Detroit Black Legion) was the subject-matter of Bert Granet's busy screenplay – in the course of which Bruce Cabot (right) and Crawford Weaver as a pair of coastal inspectors successfully bring the all-powerful outfit to justice. Charles Wilson played the leader of the legion – a man who sends bombs to Congressmen – with other roles under C. C. Coleman's workmanlike direction going to Ward Bond (left), John Hamilton, Arthur Loft and, as the love interest, Marguerite Churchill, whose brother (Bond) is a victim of the gang. (62 mins)

▽ A remake of Harold Bell Wright's novel – first seen as a film in 1924 (Sol Lesser Productions) – **Mine With The Iron Door**, again produced by Lesser, was the melodramatic story of an eccentric old villain (Henry B. Walthall) who not only attempts to keep a young prospector (Richard Arlen, right – top-starred) from finding some hidden treasure, but also stymies his romance with leading lady Cecilia Parker (left), whom he wants for himself. Comedy was supplied by Stanley Fields; Spencer Charters, Charles Wilson and Barbara Bedford were also in it, Don Swift and Daniel Jarrett scripted, and the director was David Howard. (64 mins)

◁ George Bancroft (right) returned to the screen after a two-year absence to play Captain Morgan, the rough-and-ready skipper of **Hell Ship Morgan**, a small schooner whose purpose is to supply a San Francisco cannery with all the fish it can handle. Harold Shumate's story and screenplay involved Bancroft's romance and abortive marriage to Ann Sothern (left), a down-and-out young woman who soon changes her romantic allegiance to Bancroft's chief mate, Victor Jory. After being maimed for life as a result of a hurricane, Bancroft drowns himself – thus leaving the way open for Jory and Sothern to pursue their affair without guilt. All three principals did well enough with the anaemic material – but the film was a programmer just the same. It was directed by D. Ross Lederman, and featured George Regas, Howard Hickman, Ralph Byrd and, as the comic-relief cook, Snowflake. (64 mins)

▷ A musical remake of *Matinee Idol* (1928), **The Music Goes 'Round** starred Harry Richman (centre) as the star of a musical comedy, who, while on a leave of absence from Broadway, encounters a troupe of untalented showboat players and takes them to New York. Without letting them in on the joke, he then features them in a new revue, hoping that their unintentionally funny act will bring the house down. Though the original idea was the brainchild of Robert Lord, on this uninspired occasion it was credited to Sidney Buchman with Jo Swerling supplying the forgettable dialogue. Rochelle Hudson was the female lead, with Douglass Dumbrille, Lionel Stander, Henry Mollison, Victor Kilian and Etienne Girardot in support. Victor Schertzinger, who wrote some of the songs, also directed. (80 mins)

▽ **Panic On The Air** starred a personable Lew Ayres (right) as a confident sports announcer with a penchant for scooping his media competitors – as well as the local police force – especially when it comes to headline-grabbing stories. One such story involved second-billed Florence Rice who, in attempting to retrieve some ransom money paid out by her father, inadvertently becomes involved in the murder of the kidnapper's husband. It's Ayres to the rescue, ably assisted by a workable Harold Shumate screenplay (story by Thodore S. Tinsley), a slick production by Ralph Cohn, direction to match by busy D. Ross L'ederman, and supporting performances from Benny Baker (left, comic relief), Edwin Maxwell, Charles Wilson, Wyrley Birch, Robert Emmett Keane, and Gene Morgan. (54 mins)

△ The first film in which Harry Cohn allowed his number-one money-making director to carry his name above the title, Frank Capra's **Mr Deeds Goes To Town** was quintessential 'Capra-corn' and, arguably, the film most closely associated with this remarkable director's little-man-against-the-world philosophy. Clarence Budington Kelland's custom-built story *Opera Hat*, scripted by the reliable Robert Riskin, offered a message that, in Capra's own words, was '. . . nothing earth-shaking. A simple, honest man, driven into a corner by predatory sophisticates, can, if he will, reach deep down into his God-given resources and come up with the necessary handfuls of courage, wit and love to triumph over his environment'. The 'simple honest man', in this case, was Longfellow Deeds, a tuba-playing hick from Vermont whose simple life undergoes a dramatic change when he inherits $20 million and leaves New England to take up residence in his benefactor's New York mansion. Pursued by a cynical newspaper editor who assigns Babe Bennett, a woman reporter, the task of ridiculing him in public, Deeds undergoes all manner of humiliations, not least of which is, unsurprisingly, falling in love with Babe who, against her nature, also falls in love with him. When Deeds learns that the object of his affection has made him the object of her scorn, he not only gives her up, but offers his vast fortune to any farmer in need of financial assistance. His opportunistic lawyer interprets this as a sign of insanity and recruits two elderly biddies from his hometown to testify that he has always been 'pixilated'. It is only when Babe admits her love for Deeds that he decides to fight the insane accusations. The heartwarming happily-ever-after ending found all of Deeds's priorities coming home to roost. There was never any question in Capra's mind as to who would be his Longfellow Deeds: his 'first, last and only' choice was Gary Cooper (right) for whom he was prepared to wait six months while the Paramount star fulfilled other contractual obligations. The role of Babe Bennett proved more troublesome. Capra wanted Jean Arthur. To the unsubtle Harry Cohn, Arthur was a 'no name' whose face was 'half angel and half horse'. The usually autocratic Cohn, however, knew better than to say no to one of the most successful directors in Hollywood's history. Jean Arthur (left) was cast, and a star was born. As was the case with Clark Gable and Claudette Colbert in *It Happened One Night* (1934), Cooper and Arthur were perfectly matched, their distinctive qualities effectively melding into an inseparable entity. Equally inspired was Capra's casting of the minor roles with George Bancroft, Lionel Stander, H. B. Warner, Raymond Walburn, Margaret Seddon, Margaret McWade and Douglass Dumbrille (as Deeds's conniving lawyer) all on tip-top form. (115 mins)

▽ Its well-known title song was the best thing about **Pennies From Heaven**. It starred Bing Crosby (centre, on loan from Paramount) as a singer with ambitions to strum a lute as a Venetian gondolier. Landing in prison on a phony smuggling rap, he promises one of the condemned inmates to call on the man's family as soon as he (Crosby) is released. The family turns out to be 10-year-old Edith Fellows (right) and her grandfather Donald Meek (second right). Crosby's involvement with the pair provided Jo Swerling (story by William Rankin) with the bones of his screenplay, though the onus was squarely on the stars involved to provide the flesh. Norman McLeod directed (lamely) for producer Emanuel Cohen, and in supporting roles cast Madge Evans (left), John Gallaudet, Tom Dugan, Nydia Westman and Nana Bryan. Also featured were Louis Armstrong and Lionel Hampton. (80 mins)

▽ It took five (count 'em) writers – Dale Van Every, Ethel Hill, Aben Kandel, Lynn Starling (story by Matt Taylor) – to produce **More Than A Secretary** which, it turned out, was little more than a routine office romance. Jean Arthur (left), the capable owner of a secretarial establishment, pays a visit to George Brent (right), the vegetarian publisher of a magazine called *Body And Brain*, to find out just why he is incapable of keeping a secretary for more than a few days at a time. In the course of her visit she is mistaken for a stenographer, decides she rather likes boss Brent, and stays on to revolutionize both the magazine and its editor. Far more

entertaining than the Brent-Arthur romance are the scenes involving newcomer Dorothea Kent as a dumb-blonde stenographer called Maizie whose mother once told her to take good care of her body as that's all she's got. Miss Kent provided the only gust of fresh air in a comedy that had, despite the presence of Jean Arthur, seen better days. As its leading man, George Brent was certainly no asset and, apart from Arthur and Kent, it was left to supporting players Ruth Donnelly, Lionel Stander, Reginald Denny and Charles Halton to draw attention away from the tedium of it all. Alfred E. Green directed for producer Everett Riskin. (80 mins)

△ **Shakedown**, a crime-melodrama, was of interest only in that it starred handsome Lew Ayres (centre). Otherwise it was a depressingly routine quickie about a young engineer (Ayres) who refuses to marry rich girl Joan Perry (right) until he can support her on his own. He starts working as a messenger in a telegraph company owned by Perry's father (Thurston Hall, left) in which capacity he foils a plot to kidnap his sweetheart. Grace Neville wrote the screenplay from a story by Harry Shipman, and it was directed by David Selman. The smaller roles featured Henry Mollison as Hall's treacherous aide, as well as Gene Morgan, Victor Kilian, John Gallaudet and George McKay. (55 mins)

▽ Charles Bickford (centre) played a snarling marine much given to fisticuffs and macho mannerisms in **Pride Of The Marines**, a paper-thin comedy whose humour was derived from a situation which, incongruously, found Bickford appropriating, and genuinely caring for, an orphan called Ulysses (Billy Burrud). A chance meeting with leading lady Florence Rice, however, results in young Ulysses' being legally adopted

by her when she decides to marry young Robert Allen. Exit Bickford, to an island in the Pacific – alone. Gerald Beaumont provided the story for Harold Shumate's patriotic screenplay which found roles for Thurston Hall, Ward Bond (second left), George McKay (left) and Joseph Sawyer (right). Director D. Ross Lederman used Burrud's presence as an excuse for a guided tour of a typical marine base. (64 mins)

△ Ralph Bellamy (left) and Fay Wray (centre) were romantically teamed in **Roaming Lady**, a yarn about a wealthy deb (Wray) and a dashing aviator (Bellamy). In Diana Bourbon and Bruce Manning's plot Wray stows away on a slow boat to China carrying her lover, as well as a shipment of bombs and machine-guns, and finds herself being held captive by some wily Orientals who will free her only if Bellamy agrees to pilot a plane for a group of Chinese bandits. It was scripted by Fred Niblo Jr and Earle Snell. Sid and Albert Rogell produced and directed, respectively, and the cast included Thurston Hall, Edward Gargan (right), Roger Imhof, Arthur Rankin and Paul Guilfoyle. (66 mins)

▷ As screwball comedies were finding their profitable way into neighbourhood cinemas with increasing regularity, producer Everett Riskin, whose screenwriter brother Robert was a pioneer of the genre with *It Happened One Night* (1934), bought a story by Mary McCarthy and hired Sidney Buchman to turn it into a wacky vehicle for the appealing Irene Dunne (left). The result was a frenetic little item called **Theodora Goes Wild** – and it was all about the adventures of a New England spinster who, after writing a racy *Peyton Place*-type best-seller, takes off for Manhattan. The proverbial 'fish out of water' Theodora goes wild after meeting personable Melvyn Douglas (right), the New York

sophisticate who illustrated her novel, and just what she did provided the bulk of the narrative. Richard Boleslawski's direction wasn't able to turn Miss Dunne into Jean Arthur (who would have been perfect in the role), but it managed to pile on the laughter despite the fact that much of the material was very silly. A fine supporting cast – including Spring Byington, Elizabeth Risdon and Margaret McWade (as members of a local literary society), Thomas Mitchell as the editor of a provincial paper, Robert Greig as a gouty uncle, Frederick Burton as a salesman and Thurston Hall and Nana Bryant as a publisher and his spouse – helped keep the zany goings on going on. (94 mins)

▷ The 'they' in **They Met In A Taxi** were Fay Wray (centre, sporting a mild British accent) and Chester Morris (right). He's a cab-driver, she's a mannequin accused of stealing a string of beads while modelling a wedding gown for a socialite bride-to-be. How hero Morris helps clear his sweetie's name provided the narrative content of Howard J. Green's screenplay (story by Octavus Roy Cohen) and parts for the excellent Lionel Stander, Raymond Walburn (left), Henry Mollison, Kenneth Harlan and Ward Bond. Green produced, and Alfred E. Green directed. It should have been more entertaining than it was. (70 mins)

△ Lyle Talbot (left) played a television pioneer in **Trapped By Television**, a melodrama which described the difficulties encountered by an ambitious inventor (Talbot) in marketing his new, up-to-date TV outfit. A gangster element intrudes when a bunch of crooks attempt to make a radio-station switch to TV at an exorbitant cost. Though offering little in the way of entertainment, the film retains a curiosity value for its early vision of a TV-dominated world. It was scripted by Lee Loeb and Harold Buchman from a story by Sherman Lowe and Al Martin, directed (flabbily) by Del Lord, and it top-starred Mary Astor (right), with Nat Pendleton, Joyce Compton and Thurston Hall in support. (64 mins)

▽ Silent melodrama was alive and kicking in **Tugboat Princess**, an old-fashioned yarn whose heroine was a 12-year-old orphan – played by the studio's resident Junior Miss, Edith Fellows. She's called Judy, and she lives on an ancient tugboat (called *Princess Judy*) with Captain Zack (Walter C. Kelly), who took her in after her parents died at sea. When Judy falls overboard and breaks her leg, Zack needs to find $1,000 to pay for her hospital bill. In desperation, he goes to an old rival (Clyde Cook) to borrow the money, and is given it on condition that Zack forfeits both his tugboat and his docking space if the loan isn't paid back by a certain date. In a race against time Zack endeavours to repay the loan – but his efforts are fraught with obstacles – not least of which was Robert Watson's hoary old screenplay (story by Dalton Trumbo and Isador Bernstein). It was directed by David Selman with a cast that included English actress Valerie Hobson (left, as a nurse), Lester Matthews (right) and Reginald Hincks. (66 mins)

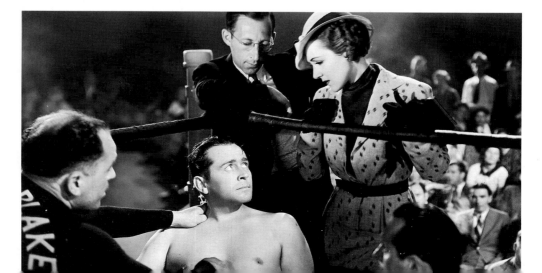

◁ An efficient crime thriller, **You May Be Next** (GB: **Panic On The Air**) featured Douglass Dumbrille (centre back) as a heavy whose scam is jamming local radio stations with high-frequency transmitters. He's a blackmailer, to boot, chief of whose innocent victims is nice-guy radio engineer Lloyd Nolan (right). Top-starred Ann Sothern (second left) was shown to excellent advantage as a roadhouse singer with other parts in Fred Niblo Jr and Ferdinand Reyher's screenplay (story by Reyher and Henry Wales) going to Berton Churchill, John Arledge (left), Nana Bryant, Robert Middlemass and George McKay. The nifty direction was by Albert Rogell. (66 mins)

▷ Though Tom Van Dycke provided both the story and the screenplay for **Two Fisted Gentleman**, his plot was so uncannily close to the one Robert Riskin devised for *The Big Timer* (1932) that he could easily have been sued for plagiarism. It is the story of a prizefighter (James Dunn, centre front) whose career, under the guidance of female promotor June Clayworth (right), hits the skids when he becomes involved with Muriel Evans and her society crowd. Director Gordon Wiles was unable to freshen up a tired old plot – and from the look of it all, didn't even try. Gene Morgan, Charles Lane (centre back), Paul Guilfoyle and Harry Taylor completed the cast. (64 mins)

▽ The Four Esquires and Deane Janis contributed a couple of musical numbers to **All-American Sweetheart** without making any appreciable difference to this wearisome campus caper starring Scott Colton who, in the last reel, and labouring against a couple of broken ribs, manages to win a climactic rowing race. Conflict asserted itself in the shape of Arthur Loft, a showboat-gambling racketeer who ensnares the crew's coxswain (Jimmy Eagles) into the rackets, and it's up to hero Colton to come to the lad's rescue. The Betty Co-Ed of the piece was Patricia Farr (right), with other roles under Lambert Hillyer's direction going to Gene Morgan, Joe Twerp, Louis Da Pron and Thurston Hall (left). It was written by Fred Niblo Jr, Grace Neville and Michael I. Simmons from a story by Robert E. Kent. (62 mins)

▷ **Counsel For Crime** starred Otto Kruger (right) as a crooked criminal lawyer who provides his clients with alibis prior to their committing crimes. Harold Shumate's story (screenplay by Fred Niblo Jr, Grace Neville, Lee Loeb and Harold Buchman) complicated the issue by providing Kruger with an upstanding lawyer son (Douglass Montgomery) who, predictably, faces his bent father in a climactic courtroom confrontation which results in Kruger receiving a 20-year prison sentence for murder. The cast also included Nana Bryant, Thurston Hall, Jacqueline Wells (later Julie Bishop). Gene Morgan, Marc Lawrence and Stanley Fields (left). The director was John Brahm. (61 mins)

△ Already seen as a play in 1922, as a silent comedy in 1925 and as an early talkie in 1929, **The Awful Truth** made its third celluloid appearance with Irene Dunne (left) and Cary Grant (right) in the roles played by Agnes Ayres and Warner Baxter in 1925 and Ina Claire and Henry Daniell in 1929. One of the classic screwball comedies of the Thirties, it was brilliantly directed by producer Leo McCarey from a sparkling screen play by Vina Delmar and performed to perfection by its two personable leads. A sophisticated examination of marital to-ing and fro-ing, it told the simple story of a happily married couple who decide to divorce on the grounds of (presumed) mutual infidelity. The problem is, who gets custody of their pooch Mr Smith (Asta of *The Thin Man*, MGM, 1934)? Dunne does – with Grant given visiting rights twice a month. Meanwhile, the couple go their separate ways. Dunne sees a handsome vocal coach (Alexander D'Arcy) as well as a Texan oil baron and part-time mother's boy (Ralph Bellamy, in a role originally written for Roland Young). Grant pursues an erstwhile relationship with nightclub singer Joyce Compton. Though physically separated, the ex-couple are still emotionally attached and both spend a great deal of time and energy looking for excuses and pretexts to come a-calling. You didn't have to be Nostradamus to know that, in the end, they'd both be back where they belong – in each other's arms. It was watching the inevitable take shape that provided so much of the pleasure being dispensed by all concerned. Though Grant, with his impeccable comic timing, was his usual suave self, doing nothing more or less than was expected from him on assignments of this lightweight nature (and for which he was paid $50,000), the real surprise was Irene Dunne who, although she showed intimations of it in *Theodora Goes Wild* (1936), emerged as a fully-fledged comedienne in this one. Indeed, so successful was the pairing of Dunne and Grant that the studio reteamed them in *Penny Serenade* (1941). They also appeared together for RKO in **My Favorite Wife** (1940). Leo McCarey's excellent supporting cast included Cecil Cunningham, Molly Lamont, Esther Dale, Robert Allen, Robert Warwick, Mary Forbes and Claude Allister. The film was remade as *Let's Do It Again* in 1953. (90 minutes)

◁ It is a measure of the phoney screenplay provided by Tom van Dycke (story by Harold Shumate) for **Counterfeit Lady** that no such lady existed – the titular heroine being a hard-working country girl who rewarded herself for her big-city industry by stealing a diamond worth $37,000 from a jewellery store. Thereafter she's pursued by a private detective, the cops, and associates of the put-upon jeweller. Joan Perry (centre) was the lady in question, Ralph Bellamy (left) the private eye, Douglass Dumbrille the heavy and George McKay played Bellamy's assistant. It was directed by D. Ross Lederman who seemed more concerned with details than the overall picture. (58 mins)

▽ Richard Dix (right) was the reluctant hero of **The Devil Is Driving**, an extended commercial against the evils of drunk drivers. He played a district attorney who agrees to take on the case of a friend's son accused of second-degree murder arising out of a drunk-driving crash. Dix succeeds in getting his guilty client acquitted – then spends what's left of the running time attempting to win back sympathy by coming down hard on drunk drivers. Joan Perry (left) played (unconvincingly) a newspaper reporter initially disgusted at Dix's taking on the rich man's case; Elisha Cook Jr was the snivelling runt Dix successfully defends, Harry Kolker the runt's father, with other roles going to Ann Rutherford, Ien (sic) Wulf, Nana Bryant, Walter Kingsford and Paul Harvey. Jo Milward and Richard Blake wrote it from a story by Lee Loeb and Harold Buchman, and the director was Harry Lachman. (69 mins)

△ Richard Dix (centre), Dolores Del Rio (left) and Chester Morris (right) were to be found cavorting on **Devil's Playground**, a romantic drama in which Dix played the US Navy's number one deep-sea diver, and Morris, his best pal, a submarine officer. In a story that was originally conceived for Jack Holt and Ralph Graves (*Submarine* in 1928), Dix marries a dance-hall hostess (Del Rio), who, while he is away at sea, 'puts the make' on Morris. He reciprocates, unaware that the woman he is dallying with is his best friend's wife. Dix says nix to his two-timing wife, gives her the air, then rushes off to save his buddy from a crippled submarine. No less a trio than Liam O'Flaherty, Jerome Chodorov and Dalton Trumbo (all of whom would graduate to worthier stuff) scripted it from a story by Norman Springer. It was directed by Erle Kenton, and featured studio regulars George McKay, John Gallaudet, Pierre Watkins and Ward Bond. (74 mins)

▷ Taxi warfare was the subject of **A Fight To The Finish**, and it starred Don Terry (right) as a tough-guy cabbie who, after being double-crossed by bad guy Ward Bond and serving time for manslaughter, gathers together his erstwhile colleagues and sets out to ruin Bond, now the superintendent of the city's biggest taxi fleet. Bond's comeuppance provided both the meat and the gravy of Harold Shumate's passable screenplay, with other roles assigned to Rosalind Keith (left, playing a nurse and providing the brief romantic interest), George McKay (as a pal of Terry's, and whose death cues in the 'fight to the finish'), Wade Boteler and Lucille Lund. Ralph Cohn produced, and the director was C. C. Coleman Jr. (58 mins)

△ **Find The Witness** was a manufactured title that bore no relevance to the programmer at hand and was symptomatic of a screenplay by Grace Neville and Fred Niblo Jr (story by Richard Sale) that didn't know where it was going – and couldn't have cared less. All about a Houdini-type magician who claims he couldn't possibly have murdered his wife as he was enclosed at the time, in a sealed box at the bottom of the sea, it starred Charles Quigley as a novice reporter who steals a march on the police by solving the crime himself. Henry Mollison was the magician, with other roles under David Selman's water-logged direction going to Rosalind Keith (left), Rita La Roy (right) and Wade Boteler. Ralph Cohn produced. (55 mins)

◁ **Criminals Of The Air** was an efficient programmer, efficiently directed by C. C. Colman whose most memorable moment featured brunette Rita Hayworth (right, no longer Cansino) in an exotic dance number for the benefit of male lead Charles Quigley (left – a cop masquerading as a pilot). The setting was a Mexican-type border town used by the criminals of the title to smuggle aliens into the USA. Hoping to get a good story out of this for her newspaper was top-starred Rosalind Keith. Owen Francis scripted from a yarn by Jack Cooper, and the cast was completed by John Gallaudet, Marc Lawrence (centre), Patricia Farr, John Hamilton and Russell Hicks – whose Mexican joint is the smuggler's hideaway. (61 mins)

▷ Even if admission had been free, **The Frame Up** would hardly have offered value for money. A warmed-over melodrama with a familiar race-track backdrop, it starred tough-guy Paul Kelly (centre) as a detective who, for the sake of his kidnapped girlfriend, agrees to a racketeer's scheme to swindle the track. How Kelly, a cop with both brains and brawn, finally gets the better of the baddies was the film's narrative gist – and its excuse for a fair amount of slightly less-than-spellbinding action. Jacqueline Wells (right) was the girl, Robert Emmett O'Connor the baddie and George McKay (left) the comic relief (in the guise of an assistant detective). Richard E. Wormster thought it up, Harold Shumate wrote it down, and it was directed by D. Ross Lederman. (59 mins)

◁ Another melodious vehicle for Grace Moore (right), **I'll Take Romance** took the easy way out where plot was concerned and concentrated, instead, on the vocalizing of its popular star. Selections from *Manon, La Traviata* and *Madama Butterfly* featured far more prominently than Stephen Morehouse Avery's minuscule tale of a prima donna who opts out of opening an opera season in Buenos Aires when a better offer arrives from Paris. Co-star Melvyn Douglas (centre), oozing charm and common sense, manages to persuade her to stick to her original engagement. George Oppenheimer and Jane Murfin's screenplay discreetly kept the narrative subservient to the musical interludes, while at the same time finding parts for a large supporting cast including Helen Westley, Stuart Erwin (left), Margaret Hamilton, Walter Kingsford, Richard Carle, Ferdinand Gottschalk, Greta Meyer, Franklin Pangborn, Albert Conti, John Gallaudet, and Adia Kuznetzoff. Everett Riskin produced, and it was directed for the piece of froth it was by Edward H. Griffith. (85 mins)

▽ Rita Hayworth (left) was third-billed as a member of a girl's soft-ball team in **Girls Can Play**, a painfully contrived thriller in which she was romantically paired with featured player John Gallaudet. The plot by Albert de Mond (screenplay and direction by Lambert Hillyer) had Gallaudet involved in selling illicit hooch on the one hand and running the girl's team on the other. A murder cues in the appearance of police officer Guinn 'Big Boy' Williams and top-starred Charles Quigley as a dim-witted cub reporter. Jacqueline Wells (right) received star billing as the team's ace player. Also cast: George McKay, Patricia Farr and Joseph Crehan. The producer was Ralph Cohn. (59 mins)

▽ **It Can't Last Forever** ran a little over an hour but, contrary to what its title proclaimed, it seemed like an eternity before Lee Loeb and Harry Buchman's banal and improbable screenplay had played its course. All about a theatrical agent and a newspaper sob-sister who become involved with a gang of crooks, its plot spiralled out of control in reel one and never ever regained its composure. Ralph Bellamy (left) starred as the theatrical agent, Betty Furness (right) was the lady reporter. Also: Raymond Walburn, Robert Armstrong, Thurston Hall, Ed Pawley, Wade Boteler and Charles Judels. Hamilton McFadden directed, and the producer was Harry I. Decker. The inclusion of a couple of songs didn't help. (68 mins)

◁ Borrowing money from loan sharks – and the consequences of not making the repayment – was the subject of **I Promise To Pay**, an exploitation quickie made to coincide with government legislation concerning the questionable practices of certain financial companies. It starred Chester Morris (right) as a decent family man who, to supplement his meagre salary of $27.50 a week, accepts a loan from crooked Leo Carrillo. Helen Mack played Morris's wife, Patsy O'Connor their oldest daughter, with other roles going to Thomas Mitchell, Thurston Hall, John Gallaudet, Mark Lawrence (left) and Wallis Clark. It was flatly written by Mary McCall Jr and Lionel Houser, and directed routinely by D. Ross Lederman. (68 mins)

▽ Rita Hayworth (left) received top-billing for the first time in her career in **The Shadow**, an otherwise unmemorable circus whodunnit. After the death of her father, Hayworth inherits his circus, together with debts totalling $60,000. The money is owed to a horse-rider (Donald Kike) in the show, a mean and unlovable man whose sudden murder triggers off the plot devised by Milton Raison (screenplay by Arthur T. Horman). As there are several people who would like to see Kike dead, the killer's identity is anybody's guess. Helping to solve the crime is Charles Quigley (right) as Hayworth's press agent. Marc Lawrence, Arthur Loft, Dick Curtis, Vernon Dent, Marjorie Main, Dwight Frye and Bess Flowers were also in it for producer Wallace MacDonald and the workaday direction was by Charles C. Colman. Remade as *Berserk* (1968). (59 mins)

△ Attactive Jean Parker (right) starred as a nursery-school teacher in **Life Begins With Love**, a romantic drama in which she was paired with a somewhat gormless Douglass Montgomery (left). The plot had Montgomery, as an heir to a fortune, pledging his wealth to charity while in a drunken stupor, then hiding out as a janitor in Ms Parker's school in order to avoid making good his pledge. Young Edith Fellows was prominently featured as an orphan with a lurid imagination, with other parts in Thomas Mitchell and Brown Holme's screenplay (story by Dorothy Bennett) going to Leona Maricle as a gold-digger, and Lumsden Hare as Montgomery's grandfather. Also: Minerva Urecal, Aubrey Mather, James Burke and little Scotty Beckett. The director was Raymond B. McCarey. (72 mins)

▽ What happened in **It Happened In Hollywood**, was that Richard Dix (second right) – playing a silent-screen cowboy star – found his voice unsuited to the talkies and his contract terminated. It's only after he shoots three bank-robbers and makes headline news that his old studio puts him back where he belongs – in the saddle, and in front of the cameras. Dix's leading lady, Fay Wray (centre), has a voice that *is* suitable for talkies, but she finds that, without Dix, she can no longer act with conviction. Myles Connolly provided the story-line, and it was scripted by Ethel Hill, Harvey Fergusson and Sam Fuller. Victor Kilian, Charlie Arnt, Franklin Pangborn (left), William B. Davidson (right) and young Billie Burrud were also featured; so were a handful of Chaplin, Mae West, Garbo, W. C. Fields and other lookalikes. Harry Lachman directed. (67 mins)

△ A Jack Holt (right) quickie, **North Of Nome** starred the hero of countless adventures – this time as a seal hunter who not only had to contend with a posse of seal-skin hijackers but with a company that claims they hold the rights to his hunting ground. Add to this a group of shipwrecked villains who fetch up on Holt's island hideaway and all the ingredients for a lower-case actioner soon become apparent – but not until the last 10 minutes – up to which point the film was just plain dull. Evelyn Venable (left) provided obligatory female interest, with Guinn Williams and John Miljan as a pair of heavies. Paul Hurst, Dorothy Appleby and Robert Gleckler were in it too. Albert De Mond scripted from a story by Houston Branch, and the director was William Nigh. (60 mins)

▷ **Let's Get Married** dropped off the studio's programmer assembly-line with a dull thud – despite the casting of Ida Lupino (right) Walter Connolly and Ralph Bellamy (left) who, together with fourth-billed Reginald Denny, did at least bring a zestful star presence to their under-characterized roles. Blame its failure on Ethel Hill's pedestrian screenplay (story by A. H. Z. Carr) which was powerless against a trite tale about the attempts of a politician (Connolly) to elevate daughter Lupino's ambitious suitor (Reginald Denny) into the higher echelons of politics. Denny is duly elected to Congress, but loses the girl to weatherman Bellamy. Raymond Walburn, Nana Bryant, Robert Allen, Eward McWade and Emmett Vogan also appeared for producer Everett Riskin and director Alfred E. Green. (68 mins)

△ They didn't come any more routine than **Motor Madness**, an action melodrama that introduced audiences to handsome new-comer Allen Brook (left), for whom the studio had great hopes. He played a struggling boat manufacturer who eschews a life of gangsterdom in time to win an important career-saving international cup race. The story followed a familiar course as signposted by scenarists Fred Niblo Jr and Grace Neville. There were no surprises, either, in D. Ross Lederman's direction, nor in the performances of Rosalind Keith (centre), Marc Lawrence, Richard Terry and J. M. Kerrigan (right). Production values were kept to a minimum, and it showed. (61 mins)

△ Richard Arlen (centre) and Fay Wray (second right) were romantically paired in **Murder In Greenwich Village**, a whodunnit whose title promised more than it delivered. Michael I. Simmons's screenplay, from a story by Robert T. Shannon, had Wray accused of a murder she didn't commit and Arlen, as a photographer, reluctantly ferreting out the culprit. Romance played a far greater part than mystery in this anorexic programmer (the victim's corpse was never seen), crime detection taking a decided backseat to Cupid. Albert Rogell directed a cast that also included Raymond Walburn (as Arlen's photographic model!), Wyn Cahoon, Scott Colton, Thurston Hall, Marc Lawrence (left), Gene Morgan and Leon Ames (right). (68 mins)

▽ Weighing in at $2 million – half the studio's annual budget – **Lost Horizon** put economy-conscious Columbia on a par with the Hollywood majors and was further indication of Harry Cohn's faith in his Midas man, Frank Capra, who'd discovered James Hilton's novel on a newsstand at Union Station. The book's Utopian theme of an earthly paradise where uncorrupted men lead un-corrupted lives, in marked contrast to the homespun, middle-class stories with which he had been occupying himself for the last few years, appealed to Capra enormously. The film came into being two years after Capra first read the book. Ronald Colman (left) was top-starred as Robert Conway, the esteemed British diplomat and historian who, together with the other five survivors of a plane crash in the Tibetan mountains, is introduced to the life-enhancing wonders of Shangri-La and its 'kindly' philosophy. Unlike Hilton's hero – whose lack of faith results in his rejection of the High Lama's request to take his place as leader of the lamasery – Capra's Conway returns to Shangri-La after leaving it with his weak-willed brother, and, eventually, emerges more of a hero than Hilton intended. Visually, the film, with its massive art-deco-inspired sets (by Stephen Goosson), was stunning. So, also, was Capra's attention to detail. To simulate the freezing conditions of a snow-bound Tibetan mountain-top, all the footage involving the

aircrash and the trek towards Shangri-La was filmed in a massive cold-storage warehouse. No dry ice was needed, therefore, to create the vapour that emerged from the actor's mouths. What audiences saw was the real thing. Authentic Tibetan musical instruments were rounded up from all over the world and, in order to simulate Tibetan yaks, Shetland ponies and yearling steers were covered in long hair. Unfortunately, not nearly enough attention went into Robert Riskin's screenplay. Colman's brother was unsympathetically played by John Howard (on floor); Edward Everett Horton (second right), as a fossil specialist, provided irritating light-relief; while fellow travellers Thomas Mitchell (second left), a swindler wanted by the police, and Isabel Jewell (right), a whore with tuberculosis, were two-dimensional. Also unsatisfactory was Colman's romance with Jane Wyatt, Shangri-La's resident beauty. Sam Jaffe (only 38 at the time) played the 250-year-old High Lama and, while on screen for only a few minutes, stole the show. Despite its narrative flaws, *Lost Horizon* captured the public's imagination. It received world-wide critical acclaim even though it barely recouped its heavy initial investment. Dimitri Tiomkin wrote the score, and the cast also included Margo, H. B. Warner (as Chang), Hugh Buckler and John Milton. Re-made in 1972 – but without the Capra magic. (118 mins)

◁ Jack Holt (left) and Mae Clarke (right) played rival news correspondents in **Trouble In Morocco**, an action melodrama whose other trouble spot was J. D. Newsom's feeble plot. Paul Franklin's screenplay was an honourable salvage job, but this tale of the two journalists' attempts to uncover an arms-smuggling syndicate along the Moroccan frontier was aimed very squarely at the bottom half of a double bill. The main thrust of the story found Holt, while gallivanting with an erstwhile New York gangster, winding up in the Foreign Legion and being mistaken for a gunman. Paul Hurst supplied the comedy relief, and the cast also included C. Henry Gordon, Harold Huber, Oscar Apfel, Bradley Page and Victor Varconi. Ernest B. Schoedsak directed and Larry Darmour produced. (62 mins)

▽ **Outlaws Of The Orient**, another Jack Holt (right) actioner, told the below par story of an oil driller (Holt) who, despatched to the Gobi oil fields, finds himself up against a ruthless protection racketeer (Harold Huber) as well as a rival oil company. Mae Clarke (left) co-starred as a book-keeper, and provided the only surprise twist in Charles Francis Royal and Paul Franklin's screenplay (story by Ralph Graves), by falling for Holt's brother (James Bush). Ray Walker, Joseph Crehan, Bernice (sometimes Beatrice) Roberts and Harry Worth completed the cast. It was directed by Ernest 'Shorty' Schoedsack. (61 mins)

▽ There were no surprises in **Parole Racket**. Resembling a Warner Bros. crime melodrama both in pace and content, it was the tired old story of a newspaper crime reporter (Paul Kelly, right) who pretends to be part of a mobster-controlled parole racket in order to gain the gang's confidence as well as all the evidence he needs to bring the criminals to trial. Kelly made the most of his showy role; Rosalind Keith (left) did the best she could as a girl reporter, Thurston Hall was Thurston Hall (as a city editor), while Gene Morgan and John Spacey convinced as the heavies. Harold Shumate wrote it and C. C. Coleman Jr directed. (62 mins)

△ An unsuccessful attempt to place the flagging career of George Bancroft (right) on a firmer footing, **Racketeers In Exile** was yet another variation on Sinclair Lewis's novel *Elmer Gantry*. The top-starred Bancroft played a one-time racketeer who forsakes organized crime for the commercial spoils of evangelism. Evelyn Venable was his leading lady, with other roles in Harry Sauber and Robert Shannon's screenplay (story by Sauber), going to Wynne Gibson (left), Marc Lawrence, John Gallaudet and George McKay. Erle C. Kenton's direction added nothing to the little there was. (60 mins)

▷ Ice hockey was **The Game That Kills**, the victim on this unmemorable occasion being the brother of top-starred Charles Quigley (second left) who was killed in a highly suspect rink accident. Skater Quigley decides to enter the game professionally in order to solve the riddle of his sibling's death. Rita Hayworth (second right), who at this stage of her career was undergoing electrolysis as part of a 'glamorization process', played the daughter of the team's trainer (J. Farrell MacDonald, centre). A fair amount of action kept Grace Neville and Fred Niblo Jr's screenplay (story by J. Benton Cheney) buoyant, and D. Ross Lederman's direction was always workmanlike. But the film went nowhere – except to the bottom half of a double bill. John Gallaudet, Arthur Loft and John Tyrell were also in the cast. (55 mins)

◁ A shameless attempt to cash in on the success of *Marked Woman* (Warner Bros., 1937), **Paid To Dance** was an inept rush job about racketeers who infiltrate the dance-hall-hostess game. State Investigator Don Terry sets out to ensnare the Mr Big of the organization, and does so by pretending to be one of the mob. Assisting Terry in his master scheme is dance hostess-cum-undercover agent Jacqueline Wells (third left) who also provided the love interest. Third lead was Rita Hayworth (right) who, in the supporting role of a dance-hall hostess, had little to contribute to the film; her appearance in this one was a decided come-down after her starring role in *The Game That Kills*. Story (by Leslie T. White) and screenplay (by Robert E. Kent) were dreadful; so was Charles C. Colman's direction. Ralph Cohn produced. Also cast: Arthur Loft, Paul Stanton, Paul Fix, Thurston Hall, John Gallaudet and Louise Stanley (third right). (55 mins)

▷ Undemanding fans of square-jawed Jack Holt (right) had no complaints about **Roaring Timber**, an old-fashioned melodrama which found its hero coming to the rescue of heroine Grace Bradley, whose late father (J. Farrell MacDonald) had left her his thriving lumber business. What Holt rescues her from is a pair of villainous employees (Charles Wilson and Willard Robertson) who attempt to do the dirty on her with regard to a major contract. Holt has interests of his own to look after as well, having once been the lumber magnate's right-hand man and who now finds himself being cheated of his dues. Ruth Donnelly, Raymond Hatton (left) and Ernest Wood also had parts in Robert James Cosgriff and Paul Franklin's formula screenplay (story by Cosgriff), and the director was Phil Rosen. (67 mins)

▽ John Boles (third right) was the only marquee name in **She Married An Artist**. He played a commercial artist who, together with his prize model (Frances Drake, second right), becomes a winning journalistic commodity. Though Bolt loves his model, he marries Luli Deste, an art-school crony from way-back and now a fashionable Paris couturier. He is soon made to see the error of his choice and, thanks to the good counsel offered by his sensible housekeeper (Helen Westley), ends up with Ms Drake. Jacqueline Wells had a four-line part, with other, more substantial roles going to Albert Van Dekker (later Albert Dekker, second left), Alexander D'Arcy and prissy Franklin Pangborn. Marion Gering directed from a screenplay by Delmer Daves and Gladys Lehman (story by Avery Strakosch) and it was produced by Sidney Buchman. (77 mins)

△ Don Terry (right) starred in **A Dangerous Adventure**, whose story by Owen Francis (screenplay by Francis and John Rathmell) bore more than just a passing resemblance to the plot of *Roaring Timber*. This time round it was Rosalind Keith (left) who found herself in charge of her late father's business, a steel mill. The heavies out to ruin both her and it were Russell Hicks and John Gallaudet. They hadn't, of course, bargained for the likes of Mr Terry who rights all wrongs and is more than useful in a romantic clinch. Nana Bryant played Ms Keith's aunt, and the cast also included Frank C. Wilson, Marc Lawrence and Joseph Sawyer. D. Ross Lederman directed. (58 mins)

▷ **Speed To Spare** was the one about two orphan brothers separated at birth who, sporting different names, are inadvertently thrown together by their mutual love of motor racing. When they first meet they are, of course, unaware that they're brothers. It is only towards the end, when the more egotistical and irresponsible of the siblings (Eddie Nugent, centre) kills a pal and almost kills his more agreeable brother (Charles Quigley) during a race, that all is revealed. Dorothy Wilson (left) played Quigley's sweetheart, and Patricia Farr (right), Gene Morgan and John Gallaudet were in it too. It was written by Bert Granet and Lambert Hillyer (the latter also directing). (60 mins)

◁ In **Trapped By G-Men**, (originally released as **River of Missing Men**), an FBI agent, posing as a criminal, infiltrates a gang of crooks and then brings them to justice. On this unmemorable occasion Jack Holt (left) was the intrepid lawman, C. Henry Gordon the big fish he's out to hook, and Wynne Gibson the love interest. Tom Kilp trick's screenplay from a story by Bernard McConnville, did nothing to disguise we antiquated nature of the material, and ill-served a cast that also included Jack La Rue (right) and Eleanor Stewart (centre). Lewis D. Collins directed. (65 mins)

▷ James Dunn (centre) continued to exploit his cinematic image as con-man *extraordinaire* in **Venus Makes Trouble**, a numbingly inept quickie that took less than an hour to show the rise-and-rise of this con-merchant from a small town in Pennsylvania to fame and fortune in New York where he becomes the city's number one merchandise promotions man. Just how he did it was never convincingly explained by Michael L. Simmons in the screenplay he fashioned from his own story. Patricia Ellis was Dunn's leading lady, with Gene Morgan, Thurston Hall, Beatrice Curtis and Donald Kirk also there for director Gordon Wiles. (58 mins)

◁ Dean Jagger (left) and Irene Hervey (right) played a pair of warring newspaper reporters in **Woman In Distress**, with May Robson (centre) as the woman in distress. And what she's distressed about, is the fact that a gang of art thieves is after a Rembrandt canvas in her possession. Hervey's involvement with the eccentric old biddy cues in a last-minute rescue bid by hero Jagger who, after a frantic race by plane and car, saves the Misses Hervey and Robson from a burning house. Even by formula standards the contents of Albert De Mond's screenplay (story by Edwin Olmstead) were old hat, a fact no one in a cast that included Douglass Dumbrille, George McKay, Gene Morgan and Paul Fix could camouflage. The director was Lynn Shores. (58 mins)

▽ Writer Robert Riskin provided the screenplay for, as well as directed, **When You're In Love** (GB: **For You Alone**), another vehicle for Grace Moore (centre), Columbia's operatic singing star. This time she played an Austrian diva who, in order to gain entrance to the USA after her visa expires in Mexico, enters into a marriage of convenience with artist Cary Grant (left). The main thrust of the slender but enjoyable plot (story by Ethel Hill and Cedric Worth) had a real love match developing between them. Catherine Doucet, Luis Alberni and Gerald Oliver Smith played Miss Moore's free-loading travelling companions. There was room in the script, too, for Emma Dunn, George Pearce, Aline MacMahon, Henry Stephenson and Thomas Mitchell. The musical programme was a bit of a mixed bag, with Jerome Kern and Dorothy Fields supplying two of the seven songs, including the hit 'One Song'. The other musical highlight had Moore changing pace to sing 'Minnie The Moocher'. Robert's brother Everett produced. (110 mins)

△ A straightforward, no-frills whodunnit, **Under Suspicion** was another Jack Holt (left) quickie in which the enduring hero was cast as the major stock-holder in a car factory, several of whose relatives and friends want to do away with him as he has promised his fortune not to them but to his faithful employees. It turns out it's his own attorney who's the guilty party. Katherine De Mille (right) made a few appearances as the token female lead, with other roles going to Luis Alberni, Rosalind Keith, Granville Bates (centre) and Robert Emmett Keane. It was written by Joseph Hoffman and Jefferson Parker from a story by Philip Wylie and directed by Lewis D. Collins. (61 mins)

◁ A weak remake of *Ladies Of Leisure* (1930), **Women Of Glamor** addressed itself to a triangle romance involving a gold-digger (Virginia Bruce, left), a socialite (Leona Maricle) and a wealthy artist (Melvyn Douglas, right). In the end, Bruce comes through and is paired off at the fade with Douglas – though it hasn't been easy, coming as she did from the wrong side of the tracks. Lending their talents to this undistinguished comedy-drama were Reginald Denny as a well-bred drunk, and Pert Kelton as a pert soubrette. It was directed by Gordon Wiles from a script by Lynn Starling and Mary McCall Jr from a story by Milton Herbert Gropper. (68 mins)

▷ C. Henry Gordon played a brutal officer in the Foreign Legion in **Adventure In Sahara**, a no-account actioner whose impoverished production values were reflected in Maxwell Shane's screenplay (story by Samuel Fuller) and D. Ross Lederman's direction. The brutal Gordon of the Foreign Legion is exiled to the desert at gun point, together with a few loyal supporters. Surviving the ordeal, he returns to wreak a terrible vengeance. Top-starred Paul Kelly (right) was the hero of the piece, Lorna Gray the token woman, with other roles farmed out to Robert Fiske, Marc Lawrence (left), Dick Curtis and Dwight Frye. (60 mins)

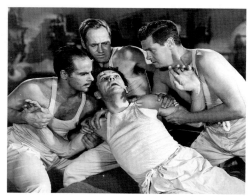

△ **City Streets** told the four-handkerchief story of a friendship between an orphan and her kindly benefactor. Edith Fellows (centre) was the orphan; Leo Carrillo (left) her benefactor. Together, they stole the show – not that there was all that much to steal. Basically a tug-of-war between Carrillo and the child-welfare authorities, the bargain-basement story (by I. Bernstein) had the benefit of a better-than-average screenplay by Fred Niblo Jr and Lou Breslow, with direction to match by Albert S. Rogell. Tommy Bond (right), Mary Gordon, Helen Jerome Eddy, Joseph King, Arthur Loft and Frank Sheridan were in it too. (68 mins)

◁ A shame-facedly 'schmalzy' melodrama, **Little Adventuress** was a vehicle for child star Edith Fellows (centre). In it she played an orphan (again!) who, after the death of her vaudevillian parents in an accident, moves to California together with her performing horse and wrangler Cliff Edwards (right). Young Edith enters the horse for a major race, rescues the animal from a burning barn, nurses it through a high fever – and wins the big race. Michael L. Simmons scripted it from a story he and Paul Jarrico wrote (but which, by now, must surely have been in the public domain), D. Ross Lederman directed, and the cast included Richard Fiske (left), Jacqueline Wells, Virginia Howell and Kenneth Harlan. Edwards sang one song with his ukelele. (60 mins)

▷ Although **Convicted** was the brain-child of Cornell (*Rear Window*) Woolrich (whose story *Face Work* provided the plot for Edgar Edwards's feeble screenplay), Kenneth J. Bishop's production, flabbily directed by Leon Barsha, had nothing to recommend it. Not even its leading lady, Rita Hayworth, added anything to this routine murder-mystery in which she plays a nightclub dancer whose brother (Edwards) is arrested for a murder he did not commit. Hayworth (right) and leading man Charles Quigley (centre) set out to solve the crime and in the process uncover seasoned screen killer Marc Lawrence. Also cast: George McKay, Doreen MacGregor (left), Bill Irving and Eddie Laughton. (50 mins)

◁ In **Crime Takes A Holiday**, Jack Holt (right) starred as a tough-guy district attorney who, prior to standing as a candidate for governor, knowingly convicts an innocent man in order to draw out the real culprit. Complications proliferate until Holt cleverly exposes smooth-talking Douglass Dumbrille via a phoney radio frame-up. It was written by scenarists Jefferson Parker, Henry Altimus and Charles Logue; it was directed by Lewis D. Collins, and also featured (unflatteringly) Marcia Ralston (centre) as a briefly-seen leading lady, Russell Hopton (left), Arthur Hohl and William Pawley. (59 mins)

▽ **Extortion** couldn't make up its mind whether it wanted to go for laughs or for thrills and, as a result, succeeded in being neither farce nor thriller. What it was, was a conveyor-belt whodunit involving the murder of an unpopular college proctor (Albert Van Dekker, centre). Suspects included physics professor Thurston Hall, his daughter (Mary Russell), the editor of the local campus paper (Scott Colton, left), J. Farrell MacDonald, and honours student Frank C. Wilson. Lambert Hillyer busily directed from a screenplay by Earl Felton. Also cast: Arthur Loft, Gene Morgan and Ann Doran (left). (57 mins)

▽ An aptly titled programmer, **Flight Into Nowhere** starred Jack Holt (right) as the head pilot of an American airline company about to open a service to the west coast of South America. Dick Purcell played his senior pilot, an irresponsible egotist who sets the plot whirling when a fuel shortage forces him to land a stolen plane in the middle of the jungle. Holt goes in search of his employee and finds him married to a native girl and pretending to be a descendant of a Peruvian Inca. The story was the brainchild of William Bloom and Clarence Jay Schneider (screenplay by Jefferson Parker and Gordon Rigby). Jacqueline Wells featured as Purcell's anxious sweetheart. Also cast: James Burke (centre), Karen Sorrell, Robert Fiske (left) and veteran Shakespearean actor Fritz Leiber. The director was Lewis D. Collins. (63 mins)

▷ Addison Richards, Jason Robards Sr, Charles D. Brown, Alexander D'Arcy, Hugh Sothern and Jacqueline Wells (right) supported top-starred Charles Farrell (left) in an inconsequential little sci-fi tale called **Flight To Fame**. Farrell played an air-force captain who has designed a plane of his own; Sothern was a World War I pilot with an electronic death-ray in tow. The plot hinged on the sabotage of one of Farrell's crucial test flights, and it provided Michael L. Simmons's screenplay with one or two pre-fabricated thrills. C. C. Coleman Jr directed. (67 mins)

△ Happily, there were no midnight feasts or pillow fights in **Girls' School**; it wasn't that kind of movie. Instead, it was a thoroughly refreshing little comedy, unpretentious, and totally bereft of the clichés so germane to the genre. The only thing wrong with it was its unimaginative title, which gave no indication at all of the delightful entertainment within. With the accent squarely on youth, scenarists Tess Slesinger and Richard Sherman delivered a screenplay (from a story by Slesinger) that eschewed plot for characterization and observation – the main narrative line revolving around a dormitory elopement. Anne Shirley and Nan Grey received top-billing together with Ralph Bellamy (right, whose appearance was limited to a handful of scenes at the close). Gloria Holden (left), Marjorie Main, Margaret Tallichet, Heather Thatcher (who delivers a three-minute lecture on charm), Kenneth Howell and Cecil Cunningham were also featured – and Noah Beery Jr appeared too briefly, in a small role as a plumber. It was directed by John Brahm with refreshing sensitivity and produced by Sam Marx. (71 mins)

△ **The Gladiator** was one of Joe E. Brown's best films, and an hilarious showcase for his particular brand of buffoonery. Written by Charles Meison and Arthur Sheekman from the novel by Philip Wylie, it was tailor-made for its star and generated nothing but laughter. Plot, such as it was, had Brown (centre) – through circumstances well beyond his control – winning $1,500 as a cinema giveaway prize, enlisting as a student at a college and being injected with a serum that turns him into the strongest man in the world. He even becomes a football hero in which guise he wins the love of leading lady June Travis. A wrestling match with 'Man Mountain' Dean (playing himself) was just one of the many comic highlights in David L. Loew's production – and it left Brown's fans limp with laughter. It was directed at a Mack Sennett-like pace by Edward Sedgwick and, in other roles, featured Dickie Moore, Lucien Littlefield and Ethel Wales. (70 mins)

△ When, in **Highway Patrol**, the harassed owner (Robert Middlemass) of a refinery becomes the victim of unscrupulous competitors who hi-jack his trucks and attempt to blow up his refinery, he seeks the help of tough-guy Robert Paige (right). It seems that the refinery's chief of police (Eddie Foster) and general manager (Arthur Loft) are the culprits as they've been working in cahoots with the boss's rivals. Jacqueline Wells (left) was the boss's daughter, and the cast was completed by Alan Bridge, George McKay, Eddie Laughton and Ann Doran. Robert E. Kent and Stuart Anthony scripted from a story by Lambert Hillyer. The solid direction was by C. C. Coleman Jr. (56 mins)

△ One of the several films inspired by the achievements of District Attorney Thomas E. Dewey, **I Am The Law** was a silly, albeit entertaining, crime melodrama which starred Edward G. Robinson (right) as a law professor-turned-special prosecutor who, against much opposition and more than a fair share of violent skulduggery, apprehends a group of mobsters. Jo Swerling's routine screenplay (story by Fred Allhof) offered Robinson a bespoke vehicle for his dynamic personality, and the result was a thriller that reached the home stretch purely on the star quality of its leading man. Barbara O'Neil was co-starred as Robinson's accommodating wife. John Beal (definitely over the top at times) played a corrupt civic leader, with other roles under Alexander Hall's unsubtle direction going to Wendy Barrie (left) as a gang moll, Otto Kruger (centre), and Marc Lawrence. The producer was Everett Riskin. (83 mins)

▽ First seen on Broadway in 1928, where it enjoyed a run of 230 performances, Philip Barry's *Holiday* reached the screen, via RKO, in 1930 (with Ann Harding, Mary Astor, Robert Ames, Edward Everett Horton and Hedda Hopper). The more successful remake of **Holiday** (GB: **Free To Live/Unconventional Linda**) starred Katharine Hepburn (left), Cary Grant (centre), Lew Ayres (second left), Doris Nolan (second right), Edward Everett Horton, Jean Dixon, Binnie Barnes, Henry Kolker (right) and Henry Daniell. It was directed by George Cukor from a screenplay by Donald Ogden Stewart and, all things considered, was one of the best, most stylish comedies of the year. It was about a cheerful but impecunious non-conformist (Grant) who becomes engaged to the socially prominent, rather snobby daughter (Nolan) of a millionaire banker (Henry Kolker) – only to discover that the girl he *really* loves is Nolan's unconventional sister (Hepburn). It was as simple as that but, in the sophisticated hands of Cukor, it emerged as a diamond-sharp comment on the values of the moneyed classes and delight-fully underlined Barry's point that the best things in life are beyond the reach of green-backs. Just watching Hepburn marshalling the courage to cut the gold-plated umbilical cord that tied her to her oppressive, gilded existence was worth an hour and a half of anyone's valuable time. As Hepburn's disillusioned brother, whose only escape from the monotony of his worthless existence is at the bottom of a bottle, Lew Ayres evoked much sympathy without inviting anyone to wallow in it; and, as Nick Potter, a fun-loving, down-to-earth married friend of Grant's, Edward Everett Horton (playing the same role as he did in the 1930 version) gave the best performance of his career. Unfortunately, despite the talent involved in it, the film didn't make money; and Harry Cohn, who originally wanted to cast Irene Dunne in the Hepburn role, but was talked out of it by Cukor, refused to employ Hepburn ever again. [In the New York production, Hepburn understudied leading lady Hope Williams without ever being given the chance to appear. She had to wait 10 years to make the role her own.] (93 mins)

△ Another in a seemingly never-ending chain of *Dead End*-inspired crime dramas, **Juvenile Court** combined some pretty juvenile performances with a juvenile screenplay (by Michael L. Simmons, Robert E. Kent and Henry Taylor), as it told the story of a slum kid (Frankie Darro) in trouble with the law, and the sympathetic sister (Rita Hayworth, left – who was rapidly becoming one of the studio's hardest working contract stars) who sets him straight. Paul Kelly (right) top-starred as public defender number one, Ralph Cohn produced, and it was directed by D. Ross Lederman whose cast included Hally Chester, Eddie Brian (centre), Don Latorre, David Gorcey and Dick Ellis. (60 mins)

▽ Audiences who responded favourably to the sight of an over-the-top Mischa Auer (left) playing matador to a cow doubtless enjoyed the rest of the shenanigans loosely packaged under the title **It's All Yours**. Critics and more demanding audiences, however, found it pretty resistible. All about a secretary (Madeleine Carroll, right) who inherits from her late boss a fortune that should, by rights, have passed on to his play-boy nephew (Francis Lederer), the plot (by Adelaide Heilbron, script by Mary McCall Jr) had Carroll swanning off to New York in order to spend some of her new-found wealth. She is followed by Lederer who, up till now, has shown no romantic interest in her at all – and it is only after her dalliance with the aristocratic Baron René de Montigny (Mischa Auer), an unscrupulous and penurious cad, that Lederer admits to being in love with her. Surprise, surprise! The leaden script was directed in kind by Elliott Nugent, whose cast was collectively devoid of the beguiling insouciance such trifles demand if they are to be succesful. It was produced by William Perlberg and, in smaller roles, featured Grace Bradley, Victor Kilian and George McKay. (80 mins)

▽ It wasn't only the lady who objected *vis à vis* **The Lady Objects**. Critics and discerning cinema-goers were equally put out by the film's lack of originality. The story of a successful college halfback (Lanny Ross, right) who, after marrying his campus sweetheart (Gloria Stuart, left) and setting himself up as a jobbing architect, is humiliated when his wife, now a criminal lawyer, becomes more successful than he does, it had very little going for it. Gladys Lehman and Charles Kenyon spiked their screenplay with a sub-plot involving the murder of a nightclub singer (Joan Marsh) for which Ross is blamed – but to no avail. The William Perlberg production, which featured songs by Oscar Hammerstein II, Milton Drake and Ben Oakland, had a cast that also included Roy Benson, Pierre Watkin, Robert Paige, Arthur Loft, Bess Flowers and Ann Doran. All in all, it was not one of the most commendable efforts of ace 'B' movie director Erle C. Kenton. (66 mins)

▷ The studio failed dismally to cash in on the current popularity of Universal's money-making thrush, Deanna Durbin, by casting Edith Fellows (right) in **Little Miss Roughneck**, complete with a big finish featuring an extract from *Rigoletto*. Fred Niblo Jr, Grace Neville and Michael L. Simmons's screenplay in which agent Scott Colton (left) finds himself resorting to a phony kidnap hoax in order to drum up interest in his hitherto rejected young would-be star (Fellows). Margaret Irving played Fellows's tiresome screen mom, and Jacqueline Wells her sister, with other roles in this no-go comedy taken by Leo Carrillo, Inez Palange, George McKay, Thurston Hall, Frank C. Wilson and John Gallaudet. The director was Aubrey Scotto. (64 mins)

△ **The Main Event** was quite untrue to its title, being a shoddily made, poorly acted programmer with no redeeming features whatsoever. It starred an under-cast Robert Paige as a detective involved in the case of a prize-fighter who engineers his own kidnapping on the eve of a big fight. Jacqueline Wells (second right) co-starred as the romantic interest, with other roles going to Arthur Loft, John Gallaudet, Thurston Hall, Gene Morgan, Dick Curtis (second left), Nick Copeland (left) and Lester Dorr (right). Lee Loeb scripted from a Harold Shumate story, Danny Dare directed, and Robert Cohn produced. (55 mins)

▷ Jack Holt (second right) fetched up as a prison warden-turned-reformatory superintendent in **Reformatory**, an elongated platitude in which he took on a group of tearaway kids, including Dead Ender Bobby Jordan, and, through kindness rather than cruelty, turned the place into the equivalent of a finishing school for boys. The 'original' screenplay was the work of Gordon Rigby, Lewis D. Collins directed for producer Larry Darmour, and the cast included Grant Mitchell (left), Tommy Bupp (right), Frankie Darro, Ward Bond (second left) and, as the resident psychiatrist, Charlotte Wynters, whose relationship with Holt never blossomed into romance. (61 mins)

▷ No one held the front page for **No Time To Marry**, another routine comedy which starred Richard Arlen (right) and Mary Astor (left) as reporters whose numerous assignments somehow always manage to keep them from plighting their troth to one another. When Astor finds the missing person Arlen has been looking for, she has to decide whether to keep the news to herself – and pull off a scoop – or tell her lover. The plot spiralled out of control at this point and, in its anything-goes approach to laughs, reunited a couple of goats and a missing heiress (Virginia Dale) to pad out the running time. Lionel Stander received third billing as the paper's resident photographer, with other roles under Harry Lachman's direction going to Thurston Hall as the paper's publisher, Marjorie Gateson as his wife, and Joseph Tozer (centre). It was based on Paul Gallico's story *Night Before Christmas* and scripted by Paul Jarrico. (63 mins)

◁ **Penitentiary**, a timely remake of *The Criminal Code* (1931) in that it coincided, more or less, with a real-life prison break from Alcatraz, followed the earlier film almost scene by scene and word for word. It had the same plot, the same characters, the same situations but, of course, a different cast. This time producer Robert North cast Walter Connolly in the role of district attorney-turned-prison warden. John Howard (centre right) was the convict whom Connolly, in his role as DA, sent to prison, and whom, as war-

◁ **Making The Headlines** originally released as **House of Mystery**, did no such thing. A below-par thriller, it starred Jack Holt (right) as a cop, transferred to a small town when his chief grows jealous of his success. Undaunted, Holt sets about solving a dual murder resulting from the unfavourable terms of a will. Craig Reynolds (left) was featured as a crime reporter, and Beverly Roberts (centre) was the beneficiary of the will. Also cast: Majorie Gateson, Dorothy Appleby, Gilbert Emery, and Tom Kennedy. Howard J. Green and Jefferson Parker were responsible for the story. The film was directed by Lewis D. Collins. (66 mins)

den, he meets again on the inside. Jean Parker was the warden's daughter who falls in love with Howard. John Brahm directed from Seton I. Miller and Fred Niblo Jr's screenplay (based on the stage play by Martin Flavin) and assigned the smaller roles in the familiar narrative to Robert Barrat, Marc Lawrence, Arthur Hohl (centre left), Dick Curtis, Paul Fix, Marjorie Main, John Gallaudet, Edward Van Sloan, Ann Doran, Ward Bond, James Flavin and Thurston Hall. It was remade in 1950, as *Convicted*. (74 mins)

△ A wearisome crime melodrama set against an American Legion convention, **Squadron of Honor** featured Thurston Hall as the Legion's leader, and the catalyst in Michael I. Simmons's screenplay (story by Martin Mooney). It seems that he's the victim of a phoney murder charge engineered by crooked armament man Robert Warwick. With rough-and-ready Don Terry (left) to the rescue, justice was seen to be served – and another hour or so bit the dust. Mary Russell (right) was second-billed as Warwick's secretary, with other roles falling to Arthur Loft, Marc Lawrence, Dick Curtis and George McKay. C. C. Coleman Jr directed. (65 mins)

▽ A lower-case *The Thin Man* (MGM, 1934) and none the worse for that, **There's Always A Woman** was a breezy comedy thriller. The fresh wind blowing through Gladys Lehman's somewhat cobwebby screenplay (story by Wilson Collison) was brought by the film's stars, Joan Blondell (third right) and Melvyn Douglas (centre). He played a down-at-heel gumshoe, she was his meddlesome wife (and amateur sleuth). Setting the fuse-paper of the plot alight was Mary Astor (right) who casually walks into Douglas's office and offers him a cool $300 to investigate a case which starts routinely enough, but ends as a double homicide. The script's tongue-in-cheek approach to the mayhem at hand kept audiences chuckling while, at the same time, managing to spoof the crime-melodrama genre. Responsible for this were the uncredited script contributions of Joel Sayre, Ralph Rapp and Morrie Ryskind. Blondell, who was especially delightful in the role, brought out the best in co-star Douglas, while director Alexander Hall brought out the best in Frances Drake, Jerome Cowan, Robert Paige and Thurston Hall (second left). The producer was William Perlberg. [As originally shot, the script contained a sizeable role for Rita Hayworth. When, however, it was decided that *There's Always A Woman* was to be the first of a series, the studio eliminated Hayworth's role rather than have a third major character who, like Blondell and Douglas, would be committed to the series. In the event, Blondell withdrew from the planned series, and all but 30 seconds of Hayworth's role landed on the cutting-room floor.] (81 mins)

△ Having produced *Harlem On The Prairie* (1937), the first all-black Western, producer Jed Buell came up with **The Terror Of Tiny Town**, the first all-midget Western. It was a cruel gimmick, most of whose jokes italicized the smallness of the cast (average height 3 feet 8 inches). Horses became Shetland ponies, bar-room swing doors were left unswung as the mini-cowboys entered underneath them, and hitching posts were always just out of reach. What might have worked in a 10-minute revue sketch outstayed its welcome despite a perfectly serviceable plot involving feuding families and ranch wars. Little Billy played the heavy and Billy Curtis (left) the good guy, with other roles among the cast of 60 going to pint-sized Yvonne Moray (right, as the love interest), Billy Platt, Johnny Bambary and Charles Becker. Sam Newfield directed this unfortunate curiosity, which was written by Fred Myton and Clarence Marks. (62 mins)

△ Jimmy Durante (left) received top-billing in **Start Cheering**, a cheerful campus musical in which he played a character called Willie Cumbatz. The plot, however, revolved around fourth-billed Charles Starrett (better known as the Durango Kid of countless Westerns) as a Hollywood matinee idol who eschews Tinsel Town for a quieter life on the campus. His manager (Walter Connolly) and sidekick (Durante), though, are unhappy at Starrett's defection and spend a great deal of time trying to get him in front of the cameras once again. Eugene Solow, Richard E. Wormser and Philip Rapp scripted this melange of music and comedy from a story by Corey Ford, finding appropriate moments in the tale for Louis Prima and His Band, Johnny Green and His Orchestra, Chaz Chase (whose specialty was eating cigarettes and cigarette boxes) and The Three Stooges to do their own thing. Joan Perry, Broderick Crawford, Gertrude Niesen (right), Dr Craig E. Earle (Professor Quiz), Hal LeRoy and Ernest Truex were in it too. Successfully balancing all the disparate elements in this enjoyable brew was director Albert S. Rogell. (78 mins)

▷ The conflict at the heart of **When G-Men Step In** was brought about by the seemingly opposed lifestyles of two brothers. Top-starred Don Terry (right) was head of a crooked syndicate involving charity swindles, bookmaking, counterfeit sweepstake tickets etc., while his brother – Robert Paige (left) – was a G-man. Romance took a back seat to racketeering in this one, with Jacqueline Wells (centre) the token woman in Arthur T. Horman and Robert C. Bennett's screenplay. It was produced by erstwhile actor Wallace MacDonald with a cast that included Gene Morgan, Paul Fix, Stanley Andrews, Edward Earle and Horace Mac-Mahon. C. C. Coleman Jr directed. (60 mins)

△ Though Rita Hayworth (centre), coiffed à la Hedy Lamarr, was the female lead in **Who Killed Gail Preston?**, viewers saw only about 20 minutes of the sultry beauty who, as the Gail Preston of the title, was shot while performing a song in a nightclub. So, whodunnit? Enter police inspector Don Terry. Miss Preston, it seems, was about as popular as a contagious disease, and there are at least eight possible suspects, one of whom (an uncredited Dwight Frye) makes a dramatic exit by jumping out of a fourth-floor window. Hayworth sang two songs – 'The Greatest Attraction In The World' and 'It's Twelve O'Clock And All Is Not Well'. Both were dubbed (by Gloria Franklin) and both were unmemorable. Indeed, Ralph Cohn's whole production was unmemorable. It was directed by Leon Barsha and written by Robert E. Kent and Henry Taylor (from Taylor's original screen story *Murder In Swingtime*). Also featured were Robert Paige (right), Wyn Cahoon, Gene Morgan, Marc Lawrence, Arthur Loft and John Gallaudet. (61 mins)

▽ Funny-man Joe E. Brown (left) and pretty Jane Wyman (centre) were teamed for **Wide Open Faces**, a laugh-sparse comedy which found several 'public enemies' taking up residence in a wayside inn reputed to house some missing loot. Running the inn were Wyman and her aunt (Alison Skipworth, right) with Lyda Roberti, Alan Baxter, Sidney Toler and Berton Churchill also on hand. However, hero Brown gets the crooks and the girl. Kurt Neumann directed from a screenplay by Earle Snell, Clarence Marks and Joe Bigelow and from a story by Richard Flournoy, with additional dialogue by Pat C. Flick. David L. Loew produced. (67 mins)

△ Blame for the awfulness of **Woman Against The World**, produced by Lew Golders and directed by David Selman, must fall squarely on the typewriter of scenarist Edgar Edwards whose story and screenplay were so congested it was difficult to tell who was doing what to whom, or why. Basically about a much-abused young mother (Alice Moore, left) who accidentally murders her aunt (Ethel Reese-Burns), the film followed the distraught mother through a prison sentence and her subsequent release, when she embarks on a harrowing search for the missing child (Sylvia Welsh). Ralph Forbes (right) was top-starred as an attorney who offers her his help, with other roles going to Collette Lyons and, in the small role of the heroine's husband (who dies early on), author Edwards. (66 mins)

▽ Frank Capra's sixth hit in a row was **You Can't Take It With You**. Scripted by Robert Riskin from the Kaufman-Hart Pulitzer Prize-winning Broadway smash, it was the middle-class comedy *par excellence*. Cohn paid a record sum of $200,000 (a record for Columbia, at any rate) to purchase for Capra a story about (in Capra's own words) 'a happy-go-lucky family of rebels, living in perfect concord, finding happiness in individual expression: doing the things they had always wanted to do, even though they did them badly'. The Vanderhof clan found the courage to do what most Americans secretly wished they could do: consign to oblivion the hammer blows of crisis headlines, Depression, wars, Hitler, Stalin, and, more important, to escape from the modern rat-race which pressured the average American into a lifetime of accumulating wealth and 'prestige'. Heading Kaufman and Hart's family of zany eccentrics was patriarch Lionel Barrymore, a wise old bird who, 35 years earlier, quit his job and never went back. Now he paints, and it doesn't worry him a jot that he's really not very good at it. His daughter (Spring Byington) was inspired to become a writer when someone delivered a typewriter to the Vanderhof home by mistake. Bying-

▽ **Women In Prison** starred Wyn Cahoon (centre right), who is framed by Arthur Loft on a manslaughter charge in order to give the latter an 'entrée' to the former's mother (Sarah Padden), who just so happens to be the warden of the prison to which Cahoon is sent. The reason is that one of the prison inmates is underworld floozie Mayo Methot (centre left), who double-crossed Loft in a hold-up and has failed to give him his share of the loot. Through Cahoon and her mother, Loft hopes to get even with Methot. It also starred Scott Colton in what must surely have been the smallest role ever offered a leading man with second billing and featured Ann Doran, Margaret Armstrong, John Tyrell and Bess Flowers. Saul Elkins scripted from a story by Mortimer Braus, and the director was Lambert Hillyer. (59 mins)

ton's hubbie (Samuel S. Hinds) is an explosives freak and spends most of his time in the basement perfecting a Roman Candle. Their daughter (Ann Miller, second right) is a mediocre ballet dancer whose teacher is an autocratic Russian called Kolenkhov (Mischa Auer, left); Miller's husband (Dub Taylor) is a xylophone player, while Barrymore's best friend (Donald Meek) invents toys and party masks. What little plot Messrs Kaufman and Hart devised, centred upon a romance between Barrymore's more 'normal' granddaughter (Jean Arthur, second left) and James Stewart (centre back), whose powerful businessman father (Edward Arnold, centre front) is her boss. A confrontation between the two very different families provided the narrative with its amusing climax, and, although at first the meeting between 'lion' Arnold and 'lamb' Barrymore is a disaster, the two men eventually settle their differences, paving the way for a joyously happy ending. The film, which Capra produced, also featured H. B. Warner, Halliwell Hobbes and Mary Forbes (front right). It was an expensive film (about $2 million) which couldn't recoup its production costs, but it garnered for its talented producer-director his third Best Director Oscar. (126 mins)

▽ Arthur T. Horman yanked out an old plot for his screenplay of **Behind Prison Gates** – the one in which an employee in the State Attorney's office spends time in prison posing as a con in order to ferret out some useful information: in this instance the whereabouts of stolen loot hidden by a pair of cop-killers. Brian Donlevy (right) starred as the tough would-be con; as he was hardly ever off the screen, he certainly justified his salary. Jacqueline Wells offered a mere whiff of romance towards the end. The cast was completed by Joseph Crehan as the warden, Paul Fix and George Lloyd (left) as the cop-killers, as well as Dick Curtis and Richard Fiske (centre). Charles Barton directed. (63 mins)

△ Comedian Joe E. Brown (left) didn't venture far from type in **Beware Spooks!** a formula farce which once again found him being proclaimed a hero in spite of himself. Based on an unproduced play by Richard Flournoy, and scripted by Flournoy, Albert Duffy and Brian Marlow, it featured its star as a dumb-cluck who is inducted into the police force in order to capture a notorious killer. Which he

does, eventually – and, of course, by accident while on his honeymoon. Mary Carlisle (left) played Brown's bride, Clarence Kolb was cast as the police commissioner, and Marc Lawrence, Don Beddoe and George J. Lewis were the crooks. Edward Sedgwick directed briskly – especially in an amusing haunted-house sequence. The producer was Robert Sparks. (65 mins)

▷ Counterfeit money was the subject of **Ouside The 3-Mile Limit** (GB: **Mutiny On The Seas**), another programmer quickie from the not-so-fertile imagination of scenarist Albert De Mond (story by De Mond and Eric Taylor). It starred Jack Holt as a G-man who, unbeknown to Eduardo Ciannelli, the owner of a palatial gambling ship, is quietly investigating the flood of counterfeit notes seeming to originate from on board. In his guise as a crew member Holt, together with fellow G-man Dick Purcell, sets out to nail Ciannelli and his crooked associates, in the process of which Purcell is murdered and the ship's crew mutiny. Justice inevitably prevails, thanks to leading-man Holt, with assistance from Irene Ware and Donald Briggs as a pair of crusading journalists. Harry Carey, Sig Rumann and Paul Fix were in it too. The director was Lewis D. Collins. (63 mins)

△ **Coast Guard** stretched the long arm of implausibility and coincidence to dislocation point in the tired telling of a tired plot involving the love of two men (Randolph Scott, right, and Ralph Bellamy) for the same girl (Frances Dee). Messrs Scott and Bellamy are coast guards, the former being the less worthy of the two. Dee chooses Scott, regrets it, and drops him again. It is only when he redeems himself by saving Bellamy, who has been lost in the Arctic, that the couple get together for the inevitable happy ending. Fred Kohlmar's production called on the services of director Edward Ludwig, writers Richard Maibaum, Albert Duffy and Harry Segall, and a cast that included hard-working Walter Connolly, Warren Hymer (left), Robert Middlemass, Stanley Andrews and Edmund MacDonald. (72 mins)

◁ What makes a killer? was the question posed in **Blind Alley**, a mildly diverting programmer in which ruthless killer Chester Morris (right), after a prison break, arrives at the home of Ralph Bellamy (left), a professor of psychology. Bellamy has some of the answers, as provided by scenarists Philip MacDonald, Michael Blankfort and Albert Duffy; they got them from the play by James Warwick on which their script was based. Charles Vidor's unhurried direction gave it all an appropriate 'gravitas' and coaxed good performances from a cast that also included Ann Dvorak, Joan Perry, Melville Cooper, Scotty Beckett, Ann Doran and Rose Stradner. Fred Kohlmar produced. Remade as *The Dark Past* (1948). (68 mins)

△ Walter Abel was the star of **First Offenders**, a low-budget programmer in which he played an idealistic district attorney who eschews public office in order to found a farm for wayward boys. Trouble in the shape of Johnny Downs (illustrated), whom Abel once sent to jail, provided the main narrative conflict in the screenplay Walter Wise carved out of J. Edward Slavin's original story. Romance was represented by Beverly Roberts and Iris Meredith. Also cast: Diana Lewis, John Hamilton, Forbes Murray, Pierre Watkin and John Tyrrell. The director was Frank McDonald. (63 mins)

△ The bad news was that **Homicide Bureau** was probably the worst film ever made by Rita Hayworth. The good news was that it was the last programmer she made for executive producer Irving Briskin's B-picture unit before the studio started grooming her for stardom. In it, she was miscast as a laboratory expert in the employ of a small-town police department. However, as romance was a very slim element in Earle Snell's screenplay, she had very little to do. The plot, such as it was, found perfunctory employment for Bruce Cabot (right) as a cop who doesn't care what methods he uses to stop gangsters making huge profits out of supplying scrap metal for some unnamed foreign power's war effort. Also cast in supporting roles were Marc Lawrence and Norman Willis as a pair of crooks, Richard Fiske, Moroni Olsen, Gene Morgan and Robert Paige (left). Jack Frier produced, and what passed for direction was credited to Charles C. Coleman. (58 mins)

▽ After appearing as an extra in *Prison Farm* (Paramount, 1938) and in a one-line bit in *Million Dollar Legs* (Paramount, 1938), newcomer William Holden (left) was chosen out of 65 candidates to re-create for the screen version of **Golden Boy** the role of Joe Bonaparte, which Luther Adler had created on the stage in the 1937 Group Theater Production of Clifford Odets' play. (Harry Cohn wanted John Garfield, but Jack Warner – to whom Garfield was contracted – said no.) The role of a sensitive young violinist who abandons music against his father's wishes for the easy money of the boxing ring was an actor's dream, and it offered Holden a golden opportunity to make that dream come true. However, had it not been for co-star Barbara Stanwyck (right, her first film for the studio since *The Bitter Tea Of General Yen* in 1933), who implored Harry Cohn not to replace Holden two weeks after shooting commenced, the role would have gone to someone else. Stanwyck's faith in the newcomer was justified, as indeed was the unselfish way in which she helped him prepare his scenes – and their work together was electric. She played Lorna Moon, an outwardly hard 'dame from Newark' who initially encourages Holden to stay the course in the ring until he becomes champ. It is only when she sees the rift his life as a prize-fighter has caused with his father (Lee J. Cobb) and realizes just how necessary music is in his life that she persuades him to throw in the towel, thus paving the way for a happy, optimistic ending. On stage both hero and heroine were killed in a car smash, an ending Cohn found unacceptable. For this reason Odets refused to adapt the play himself, and the task went instead to Lewis Meltzer, Daniel Taradash, Sarah Y. Mason and Victor Heerman. Apart from this fundamental change, and a reworking of the gangster character Fuseli (Joseph Calleia), the spirit – and often the letter – of the Broadway original remained intact. On those occasions when director Rouben Mamoulian did open it out, such as in his graphic depiction of a Madison Square Garden fight, and the poignant visit Holden makes to the dressing room of a black boxer he has killed in the ring, the film improved on the play. William Perlberg's high-grade production also featured Adolphe Menjou (centre) as Holden's opportunistic manager, as well as Sam Levene, Edward S. Brophy, Beatrice Blinn, William H. Strauss and Don Beddoe. (98 mins)

△ In **Fugitive At Large** Jack Holt (right) played an honest engineer – and a ruthless lookalike hold-up man. Bad-guy Holt has the bright idea of framing 'our hero' for a robbery he has staged. Also cast: Patricia Ellis, Stanley Fields, Arthur Hohl, Weldon Heyburn, Guinn Williams (left), Don Douglas and Leon Ames. Lewis D. Collins directed from a screenplay by Eric Taylor and Harvey Gates (story by Taylor). (66 mins)

△ **Hidden Power** had none. Another vehicle for Jack Holt (left), and one of his weakest, it miscast him as a research doctor out to perfect an antitoxin for severe burns. So involved is he in his work that his nagging wife (Gertrude Michael, second left) divorces him, taking their young son (Dickie Moore) with her to seek pastures new. The ending had Holt saving his own son's life with his new-found serum. Regis Toomey (right) played a laboratory assistant, Henry Kolker was the 'heavy', with other roles going to Henry Hayden, William B. Davidson (second right), Marilyn Knowlden and Holmes Herbert. It was written by Gordon Rigby and directed by Lewis D. Collins. (60 mins)

▽ Originally called *Good Girls Go To Paris, Too*, **Good Girls Go To Paris** had, at the insistence of the Hays Office whose job it was to protect America's morals, to drop that final 'Too'. Not that there was anything immoral about the content of Gladys Lehman and Ken Englund's frothy screenplay (from a story by Leonore Coffee and William Joyce Cowen), in which nobody, good or bad, goes to Paris at all. It starred Joan Blondell (left) as a campus waitress with only one ambition in life: to marry a rich man's son. In the event, she finishes up with top-starred Melvyn Douglas (right) as an English professor of Greek mythology. How and why formed the basis of this frenetic and wildly undisciplined farce whose entire cast, almost, gave the impression that they were being paid double to work twice as hard as was necessary. The worst offender was Walter Connolly as a disagreeable tycoon in whose household Miss Blondell stays. Alexander Hall directed the contrivance seemingly without pausing to take breath. The supporting players included Alan Curtis, Joan Perry, Isabel Jeans, Clarence Kolb, Howard Hickman and, doing virtual walk-ons, Dorothy Comingore, James Craig, Dave Willock and Robert Stirling. The producer was William Perlberg. (75 mins)

△ Mistaken identity and the problems faced by people struggling to prove their innocence when wrongly accused of a crime were the underlying themes of **Let Us Live**, tautly directed by John Brahm. It was based on a true incident in 1934 involving the wrongful arrest of two Boston cab drivers who, after being identified by seven out of eight members of an identity parade, were accused of murder and robbery. In real life the culprits were apprehended, as indeed they were in this re-telling of a similar tale. The fictional victims were Henry Fonda (right) and Alan Baxter, convicted for a murder they did not commit. Fonda's fiancée, Maureen O'Sullivan (left), canvassing aid from police lieutenant Ralph Bellamy, manages to save the men just an hour before they are due to be executed – the climax of a long and frustrating battle with an uncooperative legal system. The subject was by no means new to the literature of the stage or the screen; indeed, Fonda made two films with similar themes – *You Only Live Once* (1937) and Hitchcock's *The Wrong Man* (Warner Bros., 1956). Yet the excellence of the performances, combined with Brahm's intelligent direction and a well-structured screenplay by Anthony Veiller and Allen Rivkin (based on Joseph F. Dineen's book *Murder In Massachusetts*), resulted in a really worthwhile programmer. Stanley Ridges, Henry Kolker, Peter Lynn and George Douglas were also in it, and the producer was William Perlberg. (66 mins)

△ **Missing Daughters** starred Richard Arlen as a newspaper columnist who, together with Rochelle Hudson, the sister of one of the missing daughters of the title, infiltrates a gang operating a dance hall and employing hostesses recruited through phony talent agents. Marian Marsh (right) and Isabel Jewell (left) were also featured; so were Edward Raquello, Wade Boteler, Don Beddoe, Dick Wessell and Eddie Kane. It was written by Michael L. Simmons and George Bricker, produced by Larry Darmour, and directed by C. C. Coleman Jr. (63 mins)

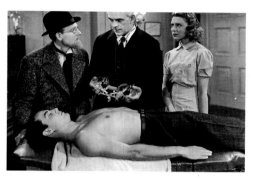

△ The two sides of Boris Karloff (centre back) were very much in evidence in **The Man They Could Not Hang**, a sci-fi programmer in which he first made his presence felt as a humanitarian doctor working on experiments that will restore life to the dead. About halfway through, after being arrested in the middle of such an operation, charged for murder and hanged, he is brought back to life by a trusted assistant, whereupon he turns decidedly nasty and sets about murdering the jury, the district attorney and the judge who sentenced him to the rope. Karl Brown invented the yarn and scripted it; Irving Briskin produced, Nick Grinde directed and the cast included Lorna Gray as Karloff's daughter, Robert Wilcox (centre front) as her newspaper boyfriend, as well as Roger Pryor, Don Beddoe, Ann Doran (right), and Byron Foulger (left). (64 mins)

▷ Fay Bainter (centre) ran away with whatever accolades were on offer for her delightful performance in **The Lady And The Mob** in which she played an aristocratic grande dame who, assisted by a colourful group of mobsters, transforms herself into a 'Miss Big' to take on the town's protection racket. For she is determined to defeat them, even if it means organizing a gang to 'protect' the 'protectors'. This tongue-in-cheek mayhem – whose screenplay by Richard Maibaum and Gertrude Purcell even found a spot for some timely pro-American sentiments – took flight immediately after the credit titles, gathered momentum thereafter, and raced home as a minor-league winner. Ida Lupino and Lee Bowman were the obligatory romantic leads, with other roles in Fred Kohlmar's production farmed out to Henry Armetta, Warren Hymer (right), Harold Huber, Forbes Murray and Joseph Sawyer (left) and Tom Dugan (fifth left). Ben Stoloff directed. (65 mins)

◁ Though not dissimilar in theme and content to RKO's *Flight From Glory*, made two years earlier, **Only Angels Have Wings**, produced and directed by Howard Hawks, who also supplied the story-line, was superior to the earlier Van Heflin-Chester Morris film. This was due to Hawks's superbly assured, always thrilling handling of the aerial sequences, and the chemistry engendered by leading players Cary Grant (centre), Jean Arthur (right), Richard Barthelmess and Rita Hayworth (left). The macho plot had Grant overseeing a broken-down air-mail and freight outfit in the wilds of Ecuador – or, to be more precise, a dot on the map called Barranca. It's dangerous work; not only are the planes at his disposal decrepit pieces of junk, but the hazardous weather conditions, combined with the treacherous mountain passes of Peru, call for pilots with a kamikaze streak. One such pilot is disgraced aviator Barthelmess (he once allowed a co-pilot to perish while he baled out to safety) who, to redeem himself, signs on with the intrepid Grant. Bringing more than a touch of glamour to the sleepy, one-saloon town of Barranca is a showgirl (Arthur) on her way to a nightclub engagement in Panama, and Barthelmess' beautiful wife (Hayworth) whom Hawks's story would have us believe was once an old flame of Grant's. Thus the scene was set for a cluster of romantic permutations and he-man heroics, all of which were milked to maximum cinematic effect by Hawks and his screenwriter Jules Furthman; the latter was given uncredited assistance by William Rankin and Eleanor Griffin. Particularly effective is an action sequence involving Barthelmess in the dangerous process of transporting nitroglycerine. Though for the most part the characterizations rarely went beyond those of pulp adventure fiction, Barthelmess eschewed all trappings of his former romantic screen image in his 'comeback' role, and managed to bring a certain complexity to the emotionally crippled, guilt-ridden aviator. The rest were on cliché territory but camouflaged the fact with star-quality. For the first time, Hayworth (looking great) acquired the image that would, from then on, be associated with her for the rest of her career; and although vulnerable Jean Arthur was hardly ideal casting as a showgirl from the school of hard knocks, her starry presence was enough to quell any such reservations. As the tough, flint-hearted hero, Grant (in a role better suited to Clark Gable) wasn't able to stop his intrinsic charm from getting in the character's way; but as the sign-posting of his Beatrice and Benedict-type romance with Arthur was writ large almost from the time of their first meeting – thus betraying his 'human' side early on – this didn't really matter. All the supporting performances, including Thomas Mitchell as Grant's faithful sidekick and Sig Rumann as the Dutchman, as well as Noah Beery Jr, James Millican, Allyn Joslyn, Victor Kilian, John Carroll and Donald Barry, were fine. The film, like *Mr Smith Goes To Washington*, brought financial glory to the studio, as well as critical hosannas. For the first time in its 12-year history, the Academy of Motion Picture Arts and Sciences included the art of special effects as a votable category, and nominated Roy Davidson and Edwin C. Hahn for their work on *Only Angels Have Wings*. The statuette, however, went to E. H. Hansen and Fred Sorsen for the effects they created for *The Rains Came* (20th Century-Fox). (121 mins)

◁ Alan Baxter (centre back, top-starred) played the son of a retired policeman in **My Son Is A Criminal**. His father (William Robertson) had always wanted him to follow in his footsteps but Baxter goes to the other extreme and, as the title revealed, became a criminal. The showdown in Arthur T. Horman's tepid screenplay had the father coming out of retirement and gunning down his son during a robbery attempt. Also cast: Jacqueline Wells, Joseph King, Eddie Laughton, Gordon Oliver (foreground) and John Tyrrell. C. C. Coleman Jr directed. (60 mins)

▷ Keye Luke (left) taking time off from his Charlie Chan capers, played a cameraman in **North Of Shanghai**. Luke, relative newcomer James Craig (right, another cameraman) and female lead Betty Furness (centre, a newspaper reporter) pool their respective resources to crack a spy ring north of Shanghai. And that's about all there was to Maurice Rapf and Harold Buchman's workaday story and screenplay which D. Ross Lederman directed. The cast also included Morgan Conway, Joseph Danning, Russell Hicks, Dorothy Gulliver and Honorable Wu. Who? (59 mins)

◁ Care, thought and effort clearly went into the making of **Outside These Walls**, a classy programmer whose underlying theme was the rehabilitation of convicts. It starred Michael Whalen (centre) as the editor of a prison newspaper who has difficulty finding a job after he is released from jail. Helped by a loan from the prison warden, he buys a small printing press and sets out to attack corrupt local politicians. When the warden loses his job, he joins forces with Whalen, runs for governor, and wins. Dolores Costello played (unconvincingly) the owner of a newspaper, and Virginia Weidler was excellent as Whalen's young daughter, with other roles in Harold Buchman's solid screenplay (story by Ferdinand Reyher) going to Don Beddoe, Selmer Jackson, Mary Forbes, Robert Emmett Keane and Pierre Watkin. Raymond B. McCarey directed. (60 mins)

▷ The **Parents On Trial** were Henry Kolker, Virginia Brissac and Nana Bryant; the kids in question: Jean Parker (left), Johnny Downs (second left), Noah Beery Jr (second right) and Linda Terry (right). The film asked the question whether parents are always responsible for how their children's lives develop – but failed to provide answers or insights. Blame this on the screenplay fashioned by J. Robert Bren, Gladys Atwater and Lambert Hillyer from Bren and Atwater's original story, and on Sam Nelson's uncaring direction. (58 mins)

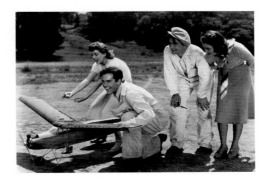

▽ Just as Gary Cooper was the 'first, last and only' choice for *Mr Deeds Goes To Town* (1936), so Jean Arthur, Cooper's co-star in that film, was the 'first, last and only' choice for the seen-it-all-before heroine of Frank Capra's masterpiece **Mr Smith Goes To Washington** – the last film he was to make for the studio. The eponymous hero was harder to cast, and the role eventually went to James Stewart (right) with whom Capra had never worked before. Stewart's 'callow, hayseed' idealist and Arthur's cynical, albeit golden-hearted, secretary were perfectly matched and both gave the performances of their careers to date. Stewart played Jefferson Smith, head of the Montana Boy Rangers and an expert on rocks and animals, who finds himself appointed as interim senator when the incumbent senator for Montana dies in office. The reason? Smith is so naive and so gullible, he'll do anything his idol, senior Senator Joseph Paine (Claude Rains, left), tells him to. And as Paine is presently involved in financing a new, albeit unnecessary, dam in the State – a crooked scheme designed to make all who partake in it rich – a 'safe' man in the Senate is absolutely vital. Just as Smith's predecessor in the 'little man' stakes, Mr Deeds, became an object of ridicule, so Smith finds himself labelled an 'incompetent clown'; and just as Deeds brought about a *volte face* in the attitude of the cynical woman in his life, so Mr Smith's refreshingly populist outlook ultimately wins the sympathy, the respect, and the love of Saunders, the Washington-based secretary assigned to him. How Smith finally managed to expose the graft and corruption inherent in the Senate and to clear his name after it is besmirched by the self-seeking Senator Paine formed the basis of Sidney Buchman's brilliant and emotionally-charged screenplay (in turn based on

Lewis R. Foster's book *The Gentleman From Montana*). The film's most stirring sequence involved Stewart in a 23-hour filibuster which left him, literally, hoarse from exhaustion. The effect was achieved by having Stewart swab his vocal chords with a mercury solution until the desired level of hoarseness was reached. Capra's obsession with detail and accuracy, and the results of days of painstaking research, were evident in the studio's recreation of the vast Senate chamber – a perfect replica (designed by Lionel Banks) of the real thing. Performed and directed with passion and emotional honesty, this ringing statement of America's democratic ideals was rapturously reviewed by many of America's heavyweight critics. However, at the time of its release in 1939, it also received a great deal of flak and vilification from several notable politicians (including Joseph P. Kennedy, then US Ambassador in London, who felt that the film would do 'inestimable harm to American prestige all over the world') and journalists, the gist of whose censure was that *Mr Smith Goes To Washington* ridiculed democracy. Arguably Capra's greatest achievement, the film was nominated for several Academy Awards but, unluckily, was up against *Gone With The Wind* (Selznick/MGM) which, with the exception of Robert Donat's Best Actor for *Goodbye, Mr Chips* (MGM), swept the board. Of the 186 impeccably cast supporting roles, the most memorable were Edward Arnold, Guy Kibbee, Thomas Mitchell, Eugene Pallette, Beulah Bondi, H. B. Warner, Astrid Allwyn, Ruth Donnelly, Grant Mitchell, Porter Hall, William Demarest and, as President of the Senate, veteran Western star Harry Carey. It was photographed by Joseph Walker and had a score by Dimitri Tiomkin. Capra also produced. (125 mins)

▽ A melodrama with a newspaper background, **Scandal Sheet** starred Otto Kruger (left) as a villainous tabloid editor who murders to protect his 'love child' (Edward Norris), a reporter on a rival newspaper, from being exposed as illegitimate. Also cast: Ona Munson as Kruger's mistress, Nedda Harrigan (right) as his ex-wife, as well as John Dilson, Don Beddoe, Eddie Laughton and Selmer Jackson. Nick Grinde directed from Joseph Carole's hokey screenplay. (66 mins)

▽ Having read the title, you didn't have to see the picture. For, in **Smashing The Spy Ring**, top-starred Ralph Bellamy, as a government spy-catcher, did just that. He was aided by Fay Wray (right) and Regis Toomey, and abetted by bad-guy Walter Kingsford as well as by scenarists Arthur T. Horman, Dorrell McGowan and Stuart E. McGowan (story by the McGowans) who, between them, didn't have an original thought in their heads. Ann Doran (left), Warren Hull, Forbes Murray and Lorna Gray were also featured, and the melodrama was directed by Christy Cabanne. (62 mins)

▽ In the **Strange Case Of Dr Meade** originally released as **Outside The Law** Jack Holt (left) played a New York doctor who, while vacationing in hillbilly country, comes across a so-called doctor (Paul Everton) and nurse (Beverly Roberts) who substitute herbs for medicine. When a typhoid epidemic is shrugged off by the country doc as a mere summer ailment, Holt swings into action to save lives. One of Holt's better efforts, it was scripted by Gordon Righy from a story he devised with Carlton Sand, directed by Lewis D. Collins, and featured Charles Middleton (right) and Arthur Aylesworth (centre). (66 mins)

▽ **There's That Woman Again**, as its title suggested, was a follow-up to the previous year's successful *There's Always A Woman* but without, alas, the delectable Joan Blondell as the interfering Sally Reardon. The role was played by Virginia Bruce (right) who did her best (and sometimes overdid her best) trying to re-create Blondell's charming daffiness. However, Melvyn Douglas (left) was again on hand to play sleuth Bill Reardon, and together he and his wife navigate their way through a couple of murders as they go after some stolen gems. The screenplay fashioned by Philip G. Epstein, James Edward Grant and Ken Englund (from a play by Gladys Lehman and Wilson Collison) was sardine-packed with clichés and inconsistencies which may, in part, have accounted for the disappointing box-office returns that found their way on to producer B. B. Kahane's desk. The director, once again, was Alexander Hall, whose cast included Margaret Lindsay and Stanley Ridges as the baddies, as well as Gordon Oliver, Tom Dugan, Don Beddoe and Jonathan Hale. (72 mins)

▷ **Those High Grey Walls** belong to a prison, one of whose inmates is a small-town doctor (Walter Connolly, third left) whose offence was to have removed a bullet from a boy he had helped bring into the world but who has since become an outlaw. Despite its prison locale Lewis Meltzer's screenplay, from a story by William A. Ullman Jr, eschewed the usual prison melodrama formula and concentrated instead on the conflict that develops between gentle Connolly and hard-hearted Onslow Stevens, the prison doctor, who resents the old man and prevents him from joining his medical staff. In time this issue is satisfactorily resolved, and the film ends with Connolly's eventual parole after a prison break in which he has mistakenly been implicated. B. B. Kulhane's serious-minded production offered little female interest – and no romantic interest at all, but Charles Vidor made the most of the material, and his direction – of a cast that included Paul Fix (third right), Bernard Nedell (as the heavy), Iris Meredith, Don Beddo (second left) Nicholas Soussanin and Oscar O'Shea – was never mawkish. (80 mins)

▽ **A Woman Is The Judge** was the one about a female judge who discovers that the girl on trial for murder is her very own daughter. It seems she hasn't seen her kid for at least 20 years – hence the mix-up. So, instead of sitting in judgement, mama steps down and becomes her daughter's attorney. Frieda Inescort (left), who played a female barrister in Republic's *Portia On Trial* (1937) reprised the role on this occasion;

▽ Jack Holt (centre) once again took to the skies in **Trapped In The Sky**, a passable aviation melodrama which found our busy hero in an equally busy plot involving secret agents, sabotage, and the invention of a noiseless plane. It was formula-fare to be sure, but confidently directed (by Lewis D. Collins) and tightly scripted (by Eric Taylor and Gordon Rigby from a story by Taylor). Larry Darmour produced, and his cast included Ralph Morgan, Paul Everton, Katherine De Mille, C. Henry Gordon, Sidney Blackmer, Ivan Lebedeff, Regis Toomey and Holmes Herbert. (61 mins)

while the original screenplay by Karl Brown went for its inspiration to Alexander Bisson's play Madame X (first seen as a Pathe Silent in 1916). Rochelle Hudson (right) was cast as the missing daughter (now a gangster's moll), with other roles under Nick Grinde's serviceable direction going to Otto Kruger, Mayo Methot, Arthur Loft, Gordon Oliver, Walter Fenner and Beryl Mercer. (61 mins)

△ In **Whispering Enemies**, the weapon used by rival cosmetic manufacturers to ruin their competitors was a malicious rumour concerning the product in question. With each company bad-mouthing the other, a state of war quickly existed – the opposing combatants being Jack Holt (left) and Dolores Costello (right) – each unaware of the other's identity. Larry Darmour's production, which didn't have very much spent on it, also featured Addison Richards, Joseph Crehan, Donald Briggs, Paul Everton and, in a non-comic role, Pert Kelton. Gordon Rigby and Tom Kilpatrick adapted it from a story by John Rawlins and Harold Tarshis, and Lewis D. Collins directed. (62 mins)

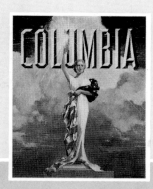

1940-1949

The need to provide escapist entertainment for a world plunged into war resulted in the Forties becoming the richest decade in Hollywood's history. Every studio flourished. Having, in the past, 'borrowed' stars (Claudette Colbert, Clark Gable and Irene Dunne) from other studios, or shared them (Cary Grant), Columbia now began to cultivate its own. Rita Hayworth was the studio's first superstar, and her most famous film for Columbia was *Gilda* (1946), one of the great *films noirs* of the Forties. Columbia's big money-makers of the decade included *Cover Girl* (1944), also with Hayworth, *A Song To Remember* (1944), *The Jolson Story* (1946), and *Jolson Sings Again* (1949).

1940

▽ The 'amazing' thing about **The Amazing Mr Williams** was that he preferred detecting to romance, even when the object of his mild affection was the sassy Joan Blondell (right). She played a mayor's secretary who, in the course of the Dwight Taylor-Sy Bartlett-Richard Maibaum screenplay, is frustrated by her inability to woo her man away from his sleuthing just long enough to make an honest husband out of him. Williams was played by the urbane Melvyn Douglas (left, seen here in drag). Both he and Blondell were far better than anything they were made to say or do. Ruth Donnelly played Blondell's room-mate, and John Wray a parolee innocent of the murder and robbery charges laid against him. Also cast: Clarence Kolb, Edward Brophy, Donald MacBride, Don Beddoe and Jonathan Hale. It was produced by Everett Riskin, and directed by journeyman Alexander Hall, who kept the proceedings light and airy. (80 mins)

▽ Humour and romance took back seats in **My Son Is Guilty** (GB: **Crime's End**), a grim-visaged programmer that featured veteran Harry Carey as a typically tough Hell's Kitchen by-the-book policeman, and Bruce Cabot (right) as the jailbird son he unsuccessfully tries to reform. Harry Shumate and Joseph Carole's screenplay (story by Karl Brown) focused mainly on the conflict between father and son and offered nothing new. Jacqueline Wells played the perfunctory love-interest, while Wynne Gibson (second right) repeated her familiar characterization as a gangster's moll. Don Beddoe (second left), John Tyrrell, Bruce Bennett (left), Dick Curtis (centre), Edgar Buchanan and a good-looking young newcomer called Glenn Ford were also cast. Charles Barton directed. (63 mins)

▽ An unsung artistic triumph and one of the year's best films (though less successful financially), **Angels Over Broadway**, produced and co-directed (with cameraman Lee Garmes) by Ben Hecht, was a minor masterpiece whose original screenplay (also by Hecht) was worthy of Damon Runyon at his best. Confined to three sets, and a time-span of just a few hours, it was the compact tale of a hapless little man (John Qualen) who has embezzled $3,000 from his business partner and has to return the money by morning – or find himself in police custody. He decides, instead, to take his own life, but is prevented from doing so by an alcoholic playwright (Thomas Mitchell) who devises a scheme involving cardsharps to win back the money. Hecht's brilliant screenplay – in which nothing was predictable – turned this simple story into a fascinating series of character studies, the most memorable being that of the all-observing playwright. Mitchell's performance was staggeringly good, and his delivery of some of Hecht's pithiest dialogue registered like a seismograph in the middle of an earthquake. The uniformly excellent cast included Douglas Fairbanks Jr (right) – who also co-produced – as a suave gambler out to fleece the minor-league Qualen, and Rita Hayworth (left) as his gorgeous girlfriend, together with George Watts, Ralph Theodore, Eddie Goster, Jock Roper and Constance Worth. Garmes' moody atmospheric photography contributed immeasurably to the overall effectiveness of the production, while the direction struck a nice balance between mordant humour, melodrama and tenderness. *Angels Over Broadway* was an uncharacteristic product to emerge from the studio at this particular time in that it was made completely free of front-office interference and was thus a uniquely Hechtian entertainment. (78 mins)

△ In **Before I Hang**, Boris Karloff (centre) played a doctor who holds firm to his belief that old age is a disease that can be cured. He is condemned to death for mercy-killing a pauper. While awaiting execution Karloff continues his experiment, aided by the prison doctor (Edward Van Sloan). By using the blood of a convicted killer, he concocts a serum which he then injects into his own bloodstream. The effect of this serum on Karloff is that it awakens in him a desire to kill. Needless to say, he indulges this desire to the full, his victims being the prison doctor, a prison trusty, a pianist and a politician. Evelyn Keyes (left) played Karloff's daughter with other roles in this fair-to-middling dollop of sci-fi going to a wooden Bruce Bennett (right), Ben Taggart, Pedro de Cordoba and Don Beddoe. Robert D. Andrews scripted from his and Karl Brown's story, Wallace MacDonald produced, and Nick Grinde directed. (62 mins)

▷ Weighing in at $2 million, **Arizona** was an epic Western about the pioneering days of Tucson, Arizona in the 1860s. Directed by Wesley Ruggles, a stickler for authenticity, the film looked good and had the right period 'feel' to it. What it needed, though, to elevate it to classic status, was a stronger plot; the one furnished by Clarence Budington Kelland, and scripted by Claude Binyon, being only serviceable. The story concerned the endeavours of Tucson's foremost female citizen – a hellion who is determined not to be exploited by the males in her one-horse town. She intends to get herself a ranch of her own. In this she's aided and abetted by a California-bound adventurer who not only comes to her rescue when the bad guys unleash a tribe of warring Apaches on the line she has established to Fort Yuma, but succeeds in softening her tomboy image and awakening romantic yearnings. Jean Arthur (right) played the pioneering woman (called Phoebe Titus) with spirited determination, while the role of her heroic knight in cowboy clobber (originally intended for Gary Cooper) went to William Holden. It wasn't the greatest pairing in screen history, but then neither was the teaming of Ruggles and Binyon. The strength of the film lay not in the contribution made by the plastic pawns of its meagre plot, but in the recreation of a pioneering community and its outback lifestyle. The film climaxed with a thrilling cattle stampede, a setpiece which, after two hours, arrived not a moment too soon. Warren William and Porter Hall (left) gave credible performances as the bad guys; Paul Harvey played Tucson's only storekeeper, and Edgar Buchanan was the town's venerable judge. Also cast: Regis Toomey, George Chandler, Byron Foulger, Paul Lopez, Griff Barnett and Patrick Moriarty. Wesley Ruggles also produced. (125 mins)

▷ Banal was the polite word for **Fugitive From A Prison Camp** originally released as Prison Camp, a humourless, dispiriting time-waster which starred Jack Holt (centre) as a humanitarian sheriff who puts first-time offenders to work on a major road-construction project, believing it will assist their moral rehabilitation. Minor love interest was supplied by Phillip Terry (centre right), as an innocent sent to prison – who is cleared, in the end, by Holt – and Marian Marsh. But who cared? Robert Barrat (third left) played a construction engineer, with other roles in Larry Darmour's penny-pinching production going to Dennis Moore, Ja La Rue and George Offerman Jr. Lewis D. Collins directed from a script and story by Albert DeMond and Stanley Roberts. (58 mins)

▷ Frieda Inescort played a lawyer (a role that kept coming her way) in **Convicted Woman**, a rampant melodrama set in a women's reformatory – with many of the attendant clichés of the genre intact. Top-starred Rochelle Hudson (face through doorhole, left) was cast as an unemployed victim of society, railroaded into the reformatory, Lola Lane (illustrated) appeared as a woman not destined to have a future away from prison bars, while June Lang was the obligatory in-house spy. The chief male role went to Glenn Ford as a reporter. Also cast: Iris Meredith, Lorna Gray, Esther Dale, William Farnum and Mary Field. Joseph Carole scripted (intelligently) from a story by Martin Mooney and Alex Gottlieb; Ralph Cohn produced, and capable Nick Grinde directed. (65 mins)

◁ Preston Foster, Ann Dvorak (left), Douglas Fowley, Wynne Gibson (right), Arthur Loft (centre), Bruce Bennett, Eddie Acuff and Bradley Page – troupers all of 'em – brought an air of professionalism to **Café Hostess** and just about managed to avoid tripping over the clichés that bedevilled Harold Shumate's crime-infested screenplay (story by Tay Garnett and Howard Higgin). A melodrama set in the unsavoury world of underground night-club owners, it told the tale of a brave sailor who rescues a singer from the murderous clutches of the club's owner and then falls in love with her. It was directed (from memory) by Sidney Salkow. The film also paraded under the title **Streets of Missing Women**. (65 mins)

▽ An amiable screwball comedy, **The Doctor Takes A Wife** top-starred Loretta Young (left) as a bachelor-girl-cum-authoress and a feminist to boot. Marriage is not for her, and she hates being dominated by males. Her co-star was Ray Milland (right) as a medical instructor hankering for a full-blown professorship (a role tailor-made for Cary Grant). A chance meeting and a publicity stunt find the couple mistaken for newlyweds – a deception Ms Young encourages, for she sees in the situation another best-seller. As for Milland, he gets his professorship because it is assumed he is now married. After moving into an apartment together and pretending to be man and wife – a move accompanied by the appropriate amount of bickering and arguing – the couple, predictably, find themselves falling in love for real, thereby guaranteeing a happy ending. An amusing screenplay by George Seaton and Ken Englund (story by Allen Leslie) kept it all light and undemanding, qualities echoed in the performances, and in Alexander Hall's up-tempo direction. Other roles in William Perlberg's production were filled by Reginald Gardiner, Gail Patrick, Edmund Gwenn (second left), Frank Sully, Natalie Moorhead (centre), Edward Van Sloan (second right) and Gordon Jones. (83 mins)

△ Just as *Girls Of The Road* (see below) focused on itinerant, derelict females, so **Girls Under 21** rang the changes (convincingly) on the familiar Dead End formula by featuring a collection of six girl delinquents who, as Jay Dratler and Fanya Foss's screenplay unfurls, see the error of their ways. Rochelle Hudson (centre) was top-starred as the wife of gangster Bruce Cabot (right), her purpose in the plot being to set a bad example to her sister (Tina Thayer) and her sister's easily-led friends. It is only after spending time in jail, and then being reformed by her ex-boyfriend (Paul Kelly, left), that Hudson realizes where she's gone wrong and tries to help her sister and her friends make a similar discovery. Ralph Cohn's absorbing production, which Max Nosseck directed, also featured Roberta Smith, Lois Verner, Beryl Vaughan and Joanne Tree. (64 mins)

▷ In **Babies For Sale** Glenn Ford (left) played a newspaper reporter who, despite being fired from his job, continues to investigate a case involving a crooked maternity-home doctor. It seems the medic persuades mothers to sign away their babies for adoption. Miles Mander played the scheming quack and Joseph Stetani an honest physician in the 'Mercy Shelter' setting where much of the story unfurls. (The roles should have been reversed.) Into the shelter comes leading lady Rochelle Hudson (second right), an abused wife about to give birth, with other roles going to Isabel Jewell (right), Georgia Caine, Eva Hyde and Selmer Jackson (second left). Robert D. Andrews provided the scenario from a story by Robert Chapin and Joseph Carole, and Charles Barton directed. (65 mins)

◁ The only novelty value to be found in **Girls Of The Road** was that it was girls rather than boys who were to be seen hoboing across the country sleeping rough, thumbing rides and dodging the cops. Otherwise it was just another variation on the theme of Depression derelicts in search of a job. Heading the predominantly female cast was Ann Dvorak (left) as a concerned, crusading governor's daughter, with Helen Mack (right), Lola Lane, Ann Doran, Marjorie Cooley, Mary Field, Mary Booth, Madelon Grayson, Grace Lenard and Evelyn Young as the objects of her concern. The men in Robert D. Andrews's original screenplay were represented by Bruce Bennett, Eddie Laughton, Don Beddoe and Howard Hickman. Nick Grinde directed. (61 mins)

◁ Ace reporter Hildy Johnson underwent a sex change in **His Girl Friday**, and although the name was retained, the 'he' of the famous Ben Hecht-Charles MacArthur Broadway smash hit *The Front Page* (United Artists, 1931) became a 'she'. After the role was turned down by Katharine Hepburn (whom Cohn never liked anyway), Irene Dunne (whom he did like), Jean Arthur, Margaret Sullavan, Claudette Colbert and Carole Lombard, it was pounced upon by Rosalind Russell (right), whose performace in *Craig's Wife* (1936) Cohn had greatly admired. Russell had done some good work at MGM (the studio to which she was contracted at the time), most notably in *The Women* (1938), but nothing in her career thus far prepared audiences for the energetic burst of comedic talent she displayed in this dazzling re-tread of a great original. Brilliantly responding to Howard Hawks' fast-paced, often frenetic direction with its over-lapping dialogue (a technique borrowed from Frank Capra's 1932 classic *American Madness*) and hard-sell approach to the narrative, she turned in a performance so germane to the plot that it was hard to believe Messrs Hecht and MacArthur hadn't written Hildy as a woman in the first place. With the authors' blessing, scriptwriter Charles Lederer added a romantic undercurrent to the text which allowed Cary Grant (left), as hard-boiled managing editor Walter Burns (the role had been played by Osgood Perkins on stage and Adolphe Menjou in the earlier film), the luxury of an understated love affair with his ace reporter, to whom he had once been married. A new twist to the plot had Grant's interest in her being rekindled after she hands in her notice in order to marry a stuffy insurance man (Ralph Bellamy). To delay her leaving, and in the hope that she'll change her mind, Grant assigns her to a major story involving an unhinged radical (John Qualen) whom the paper believes is innocent of the murder charge with which he has been saddled. In the end, Russell gets her scoop and Grant gets Russell. *En route* to this altogether satisfying conclusion, the narrative involved a colourful collection of miscellaneous characters, the most memorable being Mollie Malloy, the prostitute friend of the condemned man, played by Helen Mack (and by Mae Clarke in the 1931 film), and the effeminate poetry-writing reporter Bensinger (Ernest Truex, whose celluloid predecessor was the superior Edward Everett Horton). Others in this memorable Howard Hawks production were Porter Hall, Cliff Edwards, Gene Lockhart, Clarence Kolb, Roscoe Karns and Billy Gilbert. (92 mins)

▷ An escort service, thinly disguising such nefarious practices as fleecing drunks, blackmail and extortion, was at the centre of **Glamor For Sale** – a drama, daring for its time, which featured top-cast Anita Louise (right) as a 'good' girl inadvertently involved with 'bad' girl June MacCloy. Roger Pryor (left), second-billed as a policeman, helps (in the course of John Bright's screenplay) to rescue Louise from a life of crime and sin. Frances Robinson, Don Beddoe, Paul Fix, Arthur Loft and Veda Ann Borg were also involved. The direction was by D. Ross Lederman. (60 mins)

▷ If an indolent swagger and a thrust-out chin were the trademarks of fine acting, Jack Holt (left) would have been the best in the business. In **The Great Plane Robbery** he played an insurance investigator involved with a racketeer (Noel Madison) who has been released from prison just three months before the expiration of a $500,000 life policy. The plane on which Madison and Holt are travelling is hi-jacked, thus inconveniencing not only the leading man but a cast that also included Stanley Fields, Grancille Owen, Theodore Von Eltz, Hobert Cavanaugh, Milburn Stone, Paul Fix and leading lady Vicki Lester. Larry Darmour produced from Albert DeMond's screenplay (story by Harold Greene) and it was pasted together by director Lewis D. Collins. (55 mins)

▷ Costume drama and period re-creations were, on the whole, better left to studios such as MGM and 20th Century-Fox, though with producer-director Frank Lloyd's lavish **The Howards of Virginia** (GB: **The Tree of Liberty**), an elaborate saga set before and during the War of Independence, Columbia turned the clock back with impressive verisimilitude. The result was a film which took as its theme 'the clash of entrenched conservatism with the ferment of true democracy, out of which the American ideal rose', to quote a contemporary review. It was also about colonial oppression by the British – a theme which, at the outbreak of World War II, could not have been more untimely or less conducive to happy box-office returns. Against such well-documented historical events as the Stamp Act Riots, Valley Forge and the Boston Tea Party, Sidney Buchman's rambling and diffuse screenplay, using material drawn from the first half of Elizabeth Page's epic novel *The Tree of Liberty*, charted the romance between a Virginian backwoodsman (Cary Grant, centre right) and the daughter (Martha Scott, centre left) of a wealthy conservative reactionary (Cedric Hardwicke) who can tolerate neither change nor Thomas Jefferson (Richard Carlson). A clash of political interests provided the history lesson with its dramatic backbone, though it was hard to accept the suave, lightweight Grant (in a role tailor-made for Gary Cooper) as the burning embodiment of the democractic spirit. The rest of the performances, including the supporting contributions of Phil Taylor and Richard Alden (changed hereafter to Tom Drake) as Grant's sons, Elizabeth Risdon, Paul Kelly and Irving Bacon, were fine. Also cast: Alan Marshal, Ann Revere and Rita Quigley. Director Lloyd's eye for period detail was always impressive and his fervent commitment to his subject evident throughout but neither was sufficient to make the film compelling viewing. (116 mins)

▽ The French play *Liberté Provisoire* by Michel Duran (adapted by Sidney Howard) formed the basis for **He Stayed For Breakfast**, a sophisticated comedy not unlike Ernst Lubitsch's classic *Ninotchka* (MGM, 1939) in theme, though light years away from it in quality. It starred Melvyn Douglas (left) as a Communist agitator who shoots a banker in Paris and takes refuge in an apartment belonging to his victim's estranged wife – Loretta Young (centre). Before you can say Orchichornya, Melvyn has been so seduced by the gorgeous, negligée clad Loretta, a rabid capitalist, that he renounces his own political credo for a decadent life in the West. Scenarists P.J. Wolfson, Michael Fessier and

Ernest Vajda kept the action confined for the most part to Young's apartment, which may have kept the budget down, but ultimately engendered claustrophobia, especially during the several *longueurs* which even players as seasoned as Douglas and Young were unable to animate. Nor was the Alexander Hall touch the equivalent of the Lubitsch touch, and scenes that should have sparkled often fell flat. Still, B. P. Schulberg's good-looking production was not without its high-spots, one of them being Una O'Connor's (right) over-the-top performance as Miss Young's confused maid. The cast also included Alan Marshall, Eugene Pallette, Leonid Kinskey and Curt Bois. (86 mins)

◁ Paul Von Henried (left) (later Paul Henreid) played a Nazi spy in **Mad Men Of Europe**, (GB: **An Englishman's Home**) made by producer Neville E. Neville at the D and P Studios, in Denham, Pinewood. His mission: to install a sending-receiving radio set which will guide Nazi planes during bombing raids on London. This he does from the home of Mary Maguire (right), an English lass with whom he has fallen in love. Needless to say, in the final reel he pays for his treachery with his life – but not before saving the woman he loves from certain death in an air raid. Based on a stage play by Guy du Maurier, the screenplay was written by Ian Hay, Edward (Kismet) Knoblock and Dennis Wheatley. The direction was by Albert Courville. Also featured were Edmund Gwenn, Geoffrey Toone, Richard Ainley, Desmond Tester and Carl Jaffe. (73 mins)

△ **Island Of Doomed Men** starred Peter Lorre (left) as the brutal owner of Dead Man's Island, a hell-hole to which paroled prisoners are sent to mine diamonds. After murdering a Department of Justice agent sent to investigate conditions on the island, Lorre finds a new adversary in agent Robert Wilcox (centre), who has deliberately framed himself into a prison-sentence in order to expose Lorre's cruelty. Also cast: Rochelle Hudson (as Lorre's maltreated wife), George E. Stone, Don Beddoe, Kenneth McDonald and Charles Middleton (right). Charles Barton directed from an original screenplay by Robert D. Andrews. The producer was Wallace MacDonald. (68 mins)

▷ **The Lady In Question** was Rita Hayworth (left), who delivered her best, most solid screen performance to date. She played a French girl who stands trial for murder in a small town. Convinced of her innocence, juror Brian Aherne (centre), the bourgeois owner of a small bicycle shop, persuades the rest of the jury to acquit her. They do, whereupon Aherne, taking pity on the girl, invites her to move in with his wife (Irene Rich), son (Glenn Ford, right) and daughter (Evelyn Keyes), telling his family that she is the daughter of an old classmate of his. The plot thickens when Hayworth and Ford embark on what was to be the first of several screen romances, thereby necessitating her true background to be revealed. All ended happily, though, and producer B.B. Kahane found himself with a warm and winning domestic comedy on his hands. It was charmingly directed by Charles Vidor with a cast that included George Coulouris, Lloyd Corrigan, Edward Norris and Curt Bois. If the plot sounds familiar, it was, having been seen earlier in a French film called *Gribouille* (1937; USA: *Heart of Paris*). Michelle Morgan played the Hayworth role, and the Aherne character was created by the great Raimu. The original screenplay was by H.G. Lustig and Marcel Archard, and its English adaptation by Lewis Meltzer. (77 mins)

△ **Man With Nine Lives** (G.B: **Behind The Door**) starred Boris Karloff (shown with gun) as a crazy scientist whose unorthodox method of finding a cure for cancer is to freeze his patients and then perform experiments on them while they're in a state of suspended animation. Genuinely creepy and good of its type, the film featured Roger Pryor (centre right), Jo Ann Sayers (centre), with Stanley Brown, John Dilson, Hal Taliaferro (right), Byron Foulger (second left) and Charles Trowbridge. They were all upstaged by Karloff at his sinister best. Wallace MacDonald produced, Nick Grinde directed and the script was by Karl Brown from a story by Harold Shumate. (73 mins)

▽ Yet another melodrama with a prison backdrop, the portentously-titled **Men Without Souls** was a filler in which Glenn Ford (left) deliberately gets himself arrested in order to avenge the death of his father, killed by a vicious prison guard (Cy Kendall). Rochelle Hudson was Ford's inamorata, John Litel top-starred as the prison chaplain, Barton MacLane (right) played a tough old con and Don Beddoe was a warden. Not even journeyman director Nick Grinde could make much of a screenplay by Robert D. Andrews and Joseph Carole (story by Harvey Gates) which had little, except clichés, going for it. (62 mins)

◁ **Military Academy** was a solid little drama which focused on the rehabilitation of top-starred Tommy Kelly (second left) as a gangster's son who takes the rap in order to save his father's reputation, and Dead End recruit Bobby Jordan (right) as a big-headed athlete who needs straightening out. Jackie Searle was the young heavy, with Don Beddoe, David Holt (centre front) Jimmy Butler, Walter Tetley, Warren Ash, Earl Foxe and Joan Brodel (later Joan Leslie) completing the cast. It was written with a refreshing absence of sentimentality by Karl Brown and David Silverstein from a story by Richard English, and well directed D. Ross Lederman. (66 mins)

▷ Adapted by Doris Malloy from Walter White Jr's popular weekly radio programme of the same name, **Nobody's Children** was a lachrymose little number, set in an orphanage, which starred Edith Fellows (left) as a crippled thirteen-year-old and Billy Lee (right) as her nine-year-old brother. Because of her infirmity, young Edith isn't popular as an adoptee subject, a fact which affects her brother's chances too as he refuses to be separated from her. White Jr appeared as himself, with other roles under Charles Barton's so-so direction going to Georgia Caine, Lois Wilson, Ben Taggart and Mary Gordon. (64 mins)

▽ Rita Hayworth's (centre) first fully-fledged musical for the studio was **Music In My Heart**, a lightweight Irving Starr production in which she found herself loved by a newspaper publisher whom she bypasses for foreign singer Tony Martin (second right). Plot and screenplay by James Edward Grant (based on his story *Passport To Happiness*) centred on Martin's attempts to avoid deportation by appearing in a show with Hayworth. Bob Wright and Chet Forrest supplied the serviceable words and music, and the unremarkable direction was by Joseph Santley. Also cast: Edith Fellows (second left), Eric Blore, George Tobias, Joseph Crehan, George Humbert (left), Joey Ray, Don Beddoe and Andre Kostelanetz and his Orchestra. (69 mins)

◁ **Passport To Alcatraz** found Jack Holt (left) posing as a saboteur in order to ensnare a group of foreigners out to sabotage US explosive factories. Noah Beery Jr played Holt's assistant, Maxie Rosenbloom and C. Henry Gordon were the heavies and new studio 'discovery' Cecilia Callejo the 'pert ingénue'. Also cast: Guy Usher (right), Clay Clement, Ivan Lebedeff and Robert Fiske. It was directed by Lewis D. Collins from a screenplay by Albert DeMond. [When the film was shown in New York, its title was changed to **Passport To Hell**, and Holt was demoted from star billing to sharing a credit with Maxie Rosenbloom. The rest of the cast weren't even mentioned. Clearly New York knew something the rest of the country didn't.] (60 mins)

▷ **Scandal Sheet** starred Otto Kruger (second left) as a villainous tabloid editor who, in the course of Joseph Carole's hokey screenplay, is revealed as a murderer. The reason for his anti-social behaviour? To protect his illegitimate son (Edward Norris, left), a reporter on a rival newspaper, from the stigma of illegitimacy. A flat feature for the twinners, as the trade-paper *Variety* might have described it, it also featured Ona Munson (standing, centre) as Kruger's mistress and Nedda Harrigan as his ex-wife, as well as John Dilson, Don Beddoe, Eddie Laughton, Selmer Jackson and Frank M. Thomas (front right). Nick Grinde directed. (66 mins)

◁ **The Secret Seven** were a group of scientists dedicated to the idea of crime-busting through scientific methods. The 'mob' don't approve, and, in the course of this routine thriller written by Dean Jennings and Robert Tasker, they kidnap the daughter (Florence Rice) of the chief of police (Joseph Crehan) who happens to be working in league with The Seven. They hadn't reckoned on Bruce Bennett (centre), a reformed con and now a fully paid-up member of The Seven. It all worked out exactly as you knew it would, and provided work for Barton MacLane as the heavy, Joseph Downing, Howard Hickman, Edward Van Sloan, Don Beddoe and director James Moore. (62 mins)

◁ Banned by the Legion of Decency for its uninhibited approach to matters sexual, **This Thing Called Love** (G.B: **Married But Single**), a remake of Pathé's 1929 comedy, relied on the ingratiating personalities of its leading players – Rosalind Russell (left) and Melvyn Douglas (second left) – to keep its risqué content (risqué, that is, by 1940 standards) from offending the sensibilities of audiences weaned on milder fare. It was all about a married couple who've never quite managed to get their act – sex act – together. For the first three months of their marriage Russell insists on celibacy. Then, when she's finally ready to succumb to her deprived spouse, he contracts poison oak. Working from a breezy script by George Seaton and Ken Englund, director Alexander Hall whipped through the slender narrative at a cracking pace, making sure that his leading lady looked ravishing throughout and that the set-dressings were as sophisticated and stylish as the performances. To his credit, Hall managed to disguise the fact that his film was little more than a series of well-played farcical episodes. However, the observant will have noticed that a scene in which a Mexican fertility statue breaks into a smile, having frowned for most of the film, was also used by Hall in *The Doctor Takes A Wife*. Contributing to the fun were Binnie Barnes (right), Allyn Joslyn (second right), Gloria Dickson, Lee J. Cobb, Gloria Holden, Sig Arno and Don Beddoe. Producer William Perlberg took a stage play by Edwin Burke as his script material. (92 mins)

▷ Strictly for devoted Joe E. Brown (left) fans, **So You Won't Talk** was a hit-and-miss comedy with more misses than hits. In it Brown played a dual role: a mild-mannered book-reviewer-cum-novelist, and a con. The day on which Brown-the-reviewer is fired is also the day Brown-the-con is released from jail. The inevitable mix-up involving the lookalikes furnished scenarist Richard Flournoy with his narrative springboard. In the end, though, the situation – which wasn't great to begin with – certainly promised more than it delivered. Frances Robinson (right) was timid Brown's sweetheart, Vivienne Osborne the gangster's moll. The rest of the cast comprised Bernard Nedell, Tom Dugan, Dick Wessel and Anthony Warde. The direction was by Edward Sedgwick. (68 mins)

◁ **Too Many Husbands** was cast from strength (Jean Arthur, Fred MacMurray and Melvyn Douglas, seated left to right) and directed by the capable Wesley Ruggles from Claude Binyon's adaptation of a play by Somerset Maugham. However, although Ruggles' production tried desperately hard to be light and amusing, it provided far too few laughs. The plot went something like this: when MacMurray is reported drowned on a cruise, his widow (Arthur) marries publisher Douglas. A year later, MacMurray, after being washed up on a desert island, returns home to claim his wife. Both men attempt to get the better of the situation by wooing and flattering Arthur who, in turn, enjoys playing off one against the other before being forced by a judicial verdict to return to hubbie number one. Also cast: Harry Davenport (standing) as Arthur's father, Dorothy Peterson as a love-struck secretary, and Melville Cooper as a hatchet-faced butler. Edgar Buchanan and Tom Dugan completed the cast. Remade as *Three For The Show* (1955). (80 mins)

▽ Ingrid Bergman (left), on loan from David O. Selznick for whom she had made *Intermezzo* the previous year, looked radiant and behaved like a model of gentility and decorum in **Adam Had Four Sons**. She played French governess Emilie Gallatin, the heroine of Charles Bonner's novel *Legacy*, which centred on the to-ings and fro-ings of the all-American Stoddard family, from the first decade of this century until the outbreak of World War I. Gallatin is a governess to the household's four strapping sons, a position she holds until the death of Mrs Stoddard (Fay Wray) after which paterfamilias Adam Stoddard (Warner Baxter, right) suffers a financial setback and is forced to send her home. Ten years pass, during which Stoddard recoups his lost fortune and, with money no longer a problem, sends for spinster Bergman to resume her old chores as governess – despite the fact that his sons (Richard Denning, Johnny Downs, Robert Shaw and Charles Lind) are no longer in need of one. A sour note, however, enters the Stoddard household in the shape of bad girl Susan Hayward, who has recently married one of the Stoddard sons, and intends to take over the running of the household herself. A preponderance of plot (in which Bergman is prepared to sacrifice her own honour to save a scandal) ultimately brings the family saga to a satisfactory conclusion with Baxter and Bergman doing something they should have done much sooner – marrying each other. Basically little more than a soap-opera, it was the quintessential 'woman's picture', capably directed by Gregory Ratoff from a screenplay by William Hurlbut and Michael Blankfort. Helen Westley (as a dyspectic old maid), June Lockhart and Clarence Muse were in it too. The film was produced by Robert Sherwood (not the famous playwright), with Gordon S. Griffith as his associate. (108 mins)

△ The studio, it seemed, just couldn't leave the US Senate alone. After the previous year's *Mr Smith Goes To Washington*, which dared to suggest that some of the country's senators weren't entirely honest, **Adventure In Washington** turned the spotlight on the senators' page boys, and gave a thoroughly fictitious account of the things the lads got up to in that august assembly. The main plot thrust had page Gene Reynolds (as Marty Driscoll) selling senate secrets to a manipulating stockbroker, then being given a 'mock' trial by his fellow pages – who, after taking over the senatorial chambers, find him not guilty. If Washington was affronted by the activities of Mr Smith, heaven knows how they reacted to Master Driscoll! The quintessentially British Herbert Marshall (top-starred, left) was miscast as a US senator; nor did the romance that scenarists Lewis R. Foster and Arthur Caesar invented for him (with Virginia Bruce as a radio gossip, centre) ring true. Given that he began with two strikes against him – casting and script – there was little that either director Alfred E. Green or a supporting cast that included Samuel S. Hinds, Ralph Morgan, Vaughan Glaser, Charles Smith and Dickie Jones, could do to make this fanciful tale work. Charles R. Rogers produced. (82 mins)

△ Larry Parks made his screen debut in **Mystery Ship**. He played a G-man sharing a ship's hold with the most unappetizing bunch of criminals this side of the equator. They've been recruited from various penitentiaries, and are being deported to an unnamed country. Top-billed Paul Kelly (left), also a G-man, has the responsibility of ensuring that they all arrive at their unspecified destination in one piece. Lola Lane (right) co-starred as an ace girl-reporter who stows away to get the story. Other parts in this synthetic thriller were played by Trevor Bardette, Cy Kendall, Dwight Frye, Roger Imhof and Eddie Laughton. The script was by David Silverstein and Houston Branch from a story by Alex Gottlieb, the production by Jack Fier, and the direction by Lew Landers. (65 mins)

◁ **The Big Boss** dusted off plot number 745 to tell the stories of a pair of orphan brothers who are separated in childhood and meet again as adults. One of then (Otto Kruger, centre left) is a crooked politican, the other (John Litel) a crusading reform governor. The brothers ultimately recognize each other, and good triumphs over evil – as it always did in Hollywood movies of the Forties. Howard J. Green wrote this modest, well-made, competently acted programmer, Charles Barton directed and had a cast that included Gloria Dickson (centre) as a newspaper woman and Don Beddoe (second left) as a reporter. Wallace MacDonald produced. (70 mins)

△ **Escape To Glory** (also known as **Submarine Zone**), a melodrama made to cash in on the prevailing war in Europe, was the story of a group of diverse passengers who, while returning to America from England on a British freighter, learn that war has been declared. How the motley collection of travellers react to the news and, in time, contribute to the destruction of a Nazi U-boat, formed the often gripping content of the taut screenplay by P. J. Wolfson from a story by Sidney Biddell and Fredric Frank.

The *dramatis personae* included top-cast Pat O'Brien (second left) as an alcoholic layabout, John Halliday (centre) and Constance Bennett (third left) as a two-timing district attorney and his so-called 'secretary', Erwin Kaiser as a German doctor who sides with the enemy, Alan Baxter as a murderer on the loose, Marjorie Gateson as a flighty widow – plus Frank Sully (left), Francis Pierlot, Stanley Logan (right) and Jessie Busley. It was directed by John Brahm and produced by Sam Bischoff. (70 mins)

◁ **The Devil Commands** (aka **When The Devil Commands**) was probably the worst film that Boris Karloff (right) ever made. In it he played the proverbial mad scientist who invents a brain machine that allows him to communicate with his deceased wife – and then goes berserk. This unhappy statistic in the studio's long history of programmers was produced by Wallace MacDonald, written by Robert D. Andrews and Milton Gunzberg from a story by William Sloane, featured Richard Fiske, Amanda Duff, Anne Revere (left) and Ralph Penney, and was directed by Edward Dmytryk. (65 mins)

▽ About seventeen minutes before the final fade, Leif Erikson (left), the leading man in **Blonde From Singapore**, remarks: 'This is getting monotonous.' Critic as well as artist on this sorry occasion, his observation just about summed up the inept script George Brickner cobbled from Houston Branch's tired story. All about an air pilot (Erikson) who, together with his mechanic (Gordon Jones), goes pearl diving in order to finance the purchase of a plane and join the RAF in the Far East, it co-starred Florence Rice (right) as a former showgirl (as well as the love interest), and featured Don Beddoe, Alexander D'Arcy and Adele Rowland in support. Jack Fier produced, and the director – who would soon be doing far better work – was Edward Dmytryk. (67 mins)

▽ Penny Singleton got time off for good behaviour from her perennial role as Blondie to star in a minor-league musical called **Go West Young Lady**, which was spliced together by the same creative team responsible for the Blondie series. In a nutshell, it was all about a marshal (Glenn Ford, right) who rids a small town of an outlaw called Pecos Pete. Singleton and co-star Ann Miller (left) locked antlers (or the female equivalent) over Ford, the ensuing set-to being one of the few highlights, together with an all-too-brief dance number by Miss Miller, of an otherwise forgettable show. Robert Sparks produced, it was written by Richard Flournoy and Karen De Wolf and directed by Frank Strayer. Also cast: Charles Ruggles, Allen Jenkins, Jed Prouty and Onslow Stevens as well as The Foursome and Bob Willis and His Texas Playboys. The songs were by Sammy Cahn and Saul Chaplin. The choreography was by Louis Da Pron. (71 mins)

△ **The Face Behind The Mask** belonged to the unique Peter Lorre (right), here playing a Hungarian immigrant whose face was so badly burned in a rooming-house fire that he is forced to cover his scars with an equally hideous rubber mask. After turning to crime in order to finance his plastic surgery, Lorre becomes romantically involved with a blind girl (Evelyn Keyes, left). His happiness, however, is short-lived when she is killed in a car-bomb explosion meant for him. In the end he dies too. They didn't come more downbeat than this one, and it was no surprise that audiences wanted no part of it. All the same, it had some touching moments, and if only the screenplay by Allen Vincent and Paul Jar-

rico (based on a story by Arthur Levinson and a radio play by Thomas Edward O'Connell) wasn't crammed with 'silly dialogue' (Lorre's phrase), this could have been a deeply moving study of human suffering. What emerged, instead, was a half-baked piece of Grand Guignol. Director Robert Florey did the best he could in circumstances that brought him up against a 24-day shooting schedule, a poor script, and a leading man who turned with increasing frequency to alcohol and drugs throughout the filming. The producer was Wallace MacDonald, and the cast included Don Beddoe, John Tyrrell, Stanley Brown and a miscast George E. Stone as a kindly burglar. (69 mins)

▽ **The Great Swindle** was as welcome as hot chocolate in a heat-wave. It was Jack Holt's (left) last film for the studio and in it he once again played an insurance investigator. The plot hinged this time on arson, some incriminating photographs and the ultimate tracking down of the culprit. It was as thin as consomme, a fact that Larry Darmour's low-budget production did little to disguise. Albert DeMond wrote the screenplay from a story by Eric Taylor, providing parts for Jonathan Hale, Henry Kolker, Marjorie Reynolds (centre), Don Douglas (right), Sidney Blackmer and Douglas Fowley. Lewis D. Collins called the shots. (58 mins)

▽ Gridiron hero Tom Harmon (right, standing) – Michigan's All-American Back of 1940 – played himself in **Harmon Of Michigan**, though the film was in no way a biopic. A curiosity in which Harmon as Harmon was depicted in Howard J. Green's screenplay (story by Richard Goldstone, Stanley Rauh and Fredric Frank) as an unlikeable opportunist whose behaviour brings no credit to the game he represents, the film was a decided disappointment for fans of the game in general and Harmon in particular. Beginning with the football star's graduation from college and marriage (Anita Louise played his wife), we follow him through a couple of coaching jobs, one of which he leaves in mid-season in order to train an opposition college team. And as if that wasn't foul-play enough, he encourages his new team to beat their opponents by utilizing an illegal wedge formation. Also playing himself in this bizarre football drama was Harmon's Michigan team-mate Forest Evashevski, as well as Oscar O'Shea, Warren Ashe, Stanley Brown (centre, standing) Larry Parks and Lloyd Bridges. Wallace MacDonald produced and Charles Barton directed. (65 mins)

△ Jane Withers (left), on loan from 20th Century-Fox, starred in **Her First Beau**, a commendable light-entertainment package of puppy love in which she and top-billed Jackie Cooper (right) played adolescent sweethearts. When Jackie begins to take her for granted, Jane succumbs to the flirtatious charms of William Tracy, only to become disillusioned and return to Jackie. Gladys Lehman and Karen De Wolf's screenplay (story by Florence Ryerson) also produced good roles for Josephine Hutchinson, Martha O'Driscoll and Jonathan Hale. Third-billed Edith Fellows made a brief appearance, and the cast included Edgar Buchanan, Una O'Connor, Kenneth Howell and Addison Richards. The producer was B. B. Kahane and the director Theodore Reed. (76 mins)

△ Fantasy ran riot, but in the most beguiling way, in **Here Comes Mr Jordan**, a classy production from Everett Riskin, and the brainchild of Harry Segall from whose play Sidney Buchman and Seton I. Miller fashioned a plot-line more complicated than a Bach fugue. The gist of the proceedings concerned Robert Montgomery (centre, on loan from MGM) as a promising boxer-cum-saxophonist-cum-pilot who, after winning a fight, celebrates by taking his plane for a spin – and crashing. Surveying the catastrophe is Messenger 3014 (Edward Everett Horton, left) whose job it is to convey the dead boxer's spirit to celestial book-keeper Mr Jordan (Claude Rains, right). When, however, Horton arrives in Heaven, Rains is horrified to discover that Montgomery isn't on his list, and won't be for another 50 years! All that Rains can do to make amends for Horton's error is to find another body for Montgomery's soul to inhabit – which he does in the shape of a multi-millionaire who has been murdered in his bath by his evil wife (Rita Johnson) and scheming male secretary (John Emery). From this point onwards the fantasy spiralled dizzily into realms of inspired make-believe until it became the *reductio ad absurdum* of absurdity, but brilliantly so. The performances, for the most part, were well up to the quality of the script and to Alexander Hall's scintillating direction which miraculously always managed to make itself heard above the clatter of the busy plot's machinery. Montgomery, Rains and Horton were especially fine, and giving the performance of his career was James Gleason as Max Corkle, Montgomery's kindly albeit confused manager. Donald MacBride, Benny Rubin, Halliwell Hobbes, Bert Young, Ken Christy and Joseph Crehan were in it as well. So successful was the film that a musical sequel called *Down To Earth*, with Rita Hayworth, was made in 1948. The same material was reworked in 1978 as *Heaven Can Wait*. (93 mins)

▽ **Honolulu Lu** offered more plot than entertainment value for every yard of celluloid it consumed. Mistaken identity loomed large in Eliot Gibbons and Paul Yawitz's screenplay (story by Gibbons), with topstarred Lupe Velez (right) causing confusion by being nice-girl Consuelo one moment and burlesque-queen Lu the next. The narrative really hit the fan when, in both guises, she's entered in the Miss Honolulu beauty contest. Bruce Bennett played the sailor she loves, with other roles in Wallace MacDonald's production going to Leo Carrillo (left), Marjorie Gateson, Don Beddoe, Forrest Tucker, George McKay and Nina Campana. Charles Barton directed, and the songs for Miss Velez were provided by Sammy Cahn and Saul Chaplin. (72 mins)

▽ The only response to the information relayed in the title **I Was A Prisoner On Devil's Island** – was: so what? An over-ripe melodrama attached to a plot of brain-withering implausibility, it starred Donald Woods (left) as a first officer who accidentally kills his captain in a fight over wages and then finds himself on Devil's Island where he meets the girl (Sally Eilers, right) of his dreams. She's married to a crooked physician (Eduardo Ciannelli) who thinks nothing of selling medical supplies meant for the prisoners to opportunists on the mainland. Woods redeems himself, of course (but not, alas, the film), by rescuing those much-needed supplies and by braving a blinding snow-storm to do so. For good (bad?) measure, there was also a poorly-staged prison-break. Victor Kilian as a Foreign Legion war veteran, as well as Charles Halton, Dick Curtis and John Tyrrell were also featured in Wallace MacDonald's tacky production. The script was by Karl Brown from a story by Otto and Edgar Van Eyss. The director was Lew Landers. (71 mins)

△ Without wasting any time, producer Lester Cowan brought to the screen a very creditable version of Reginald Denham and Edward Percy's hit thriller **Ladies In Retirement**, which had opened on Broadway the previous year. Trailing in its wake all the Gothic trappings of a Victorian melodrama, and set in an isolated house on the Thames estuary, this was the suspense-filled tale of the tensions that develop between a retired actress (the matronly Isobel Elsom) and her housekeeper-cum-companion (a miscast Ida Lupino, right, in the role played on stage by Flora Robson) when the latter invites her two mentally deranged sisters (Elsa Lanchester and Edith Barrett) to the house for a visit. After a while the unsettling visitors outstay their welcome and are told to leave by the elderly, put-upon actress. To save her sisters from being institutionalized, the house-

keeper murders her employer and requisitions the house for herself. However, the unexpected arrival of Lupino's renegade nephew (Louis Hayward, left) puts paid to her plans, for he soon realizes what has happened and forces a confession out of her. Though it was difficult to feel sympathy for any of the leading characters, Charles Vidor's adroit direction made it easy to feel the rising tension in the household – and that, after all, was the main object of the exercise. The screenplay, by Denham and Garrett Fort, wisely resisted any temptation to 'open out' the action, keeping the narrative events in claustrophobic confinement. Evelyn Keyes played Lucy the maid, and the cast was completed by Emma Dunn and Queenie Leonard as a pair of nuns and Clyde Cook as the general dogsbody. Remade as *The Mad Room* (1960). (91 mins)

△ Based on Lady Eleanor Smith's novel *Ballerina*, **The Men In Her Life** was the tough tale of a woman's rise to stardom. Loretta Young (right) starred as a one-time circus performer transformed into a great ballerina through the tireless efforts of a stern ballet-master (Conrad Veidt). The trite screenplay by Frederick Kohner, Michael Wilson and Paul Trivers concentrated on their leading character's numerous romances – concluding with a tearful mother-daughter reunion in

New York. For most of the time Miss Young (right, patently miscast as a ballerina) occupied centre screen, thus reducing the men in her life – Veidt, Dean Jagger and John Shepperd (aka Shepperd Strudwick) – to cyphers. Producer-director Gregory Ratoff mounted it all handsomely enough, but ultimately choked on the mustiness of the material. Also cast: Eugenie Leontovich (left), Otto Kruger (centre), Paul Baratoff, Ann Todd and Billy Rayes. (89 mins)

▽ In **Naval Academy** three lads from vastly different backgrounds find themselves sharing a room. One is fresh from reform school, another is the spoiled son of wealthy parents, while the third comes from a family with a strong naval tradition. In time they all emerge as solid, upstanding members of the institution they represent – but not before undergoing several cliché-packed adventures as provided by Robert James Cosgriff whose story was scripted by David Silverstein and Gordon Rigby. Too familiar for words – especially those being uttered by Freddie Bartholomew (right), Jimmy Lydon (left) and Billy Cook as the trio of roommates – it was, frankly, a bore. Among the film's male *dramatis personae* were Pierre Watkin, Warren Ashe, James Butler, Joe Brown Jr, David Durand, Tommy Bupp, John Dilson and William Blees. Erle C. Kenton directed. (65 mins)

▽ **The Officer And The Lady** was as boring as its title suggested. Rochelle Hudson (left) starred as the daughter of a crippled ex-cop (Oscar O'Shea) whose disability makes her think twice about getting too romantically involved with leading man Bruce Bennett (centre) – another cop. She does, eventually – after he smashes a crime syndicate and rescues her and her father from an escaped convict (Sidney Blackmer). And that was about all there was to it. Lambert Hillyer and Joseph Hoffman scripted (story by Hillyer), gag-man Sam White made his debut directing, and Leon Barsha was the producer. Also cast: Roger Pryor (right), Richard Fiske and Tom Kennedy. (59 mins)

△ A more appropriate title for **Our Wife** would have been 'Our Husband'. The plot, which P. J. Wolfson cobbled out of a play by Lillian Day and Lyon Mearson, revolved around a battle royal between a fiancée (Ruth Hussey, right) and an ex-wife (Ellen Drew, left) for the love of a musician (Melvyn Douglas, centre). Hussey's the one who deserves him, having been responsible for drawing him out of the doldrums of divorce and inspiring him to write a trumpet concerto. In the end, she gets him, but not before enduring a series of entertaining cat-fights with her opportunistic rival, whose skulduggery she eventually uncovers. Apart from the worldly Mr Douglas – who was little more than a catalyst in the proceedings – the cast were not nearly accomplished enough to bring to froth of this kind the requisite lightness of touch, a quality also absent from producer John Stahl's heavy-weather direction. Also cast: Charles Coburn (as Hussey's father), John Hubbard, Harvey Stephens and Theresa Harris. (92 mins)

△ If you have tears, prepare to shed them now. That, at the very least, is the warning that the ads should have given to customers as they made their way to **Penny Serenade**. Generous supplies of paper handkerchiefs should also have been freely available. For George Stevens's production, which re-united Cary Grant (left) and Irene Dunne (right), was the weepiest weepie since *Madame X* (MGM, 1929). Grant starred as the publisher of a small, not-too-prosperous country newspaper; Dunne was his attractive wife. Their workaday trials and tribulations formed the undemanding content of Morrie Ryskind's sentimental screenplay (from a story by Martha Cheavens), which had as its saddest, most heartbreaking moment the death of their six-year-old adopted daughter. An unhappy period of adjustment followed by the couple's adoption of a two-year-old brought the story to a satisfactory conclusion. Whereas laughter was the main ingredient in the first Grant-Dunne encounter (*The Awful Truth*, 1937), tears were the first item on this particular agenda. Fortunately the two stars' innate skill combined with director George Stevens's restrained and tasteful direction to prevent what could so easily have been a mawkish and maudlin wallow. A fine cast included Beulah Bondi (as a common-sense orphanage matron), Edgar Buchanan (as a faithful family friend), Ann Doran, Eva Lee Kuney (as the adopted daughter) and Leonard Willey. (118 mins)

▽ **Phantom Submarine** was, on the one hand, the tale of a salvage ship's voyage to a Caribbean island in search of a sunken hulk containing a cache of gold, and, on the other, the routine story of a lady reporter (Anita Louise, second right) who, acting under instructions from the US Navy, temporarily leaves her newspaper in order to investigate the movements of a mysterious submarine cruising the Caribbean on a mission against the Panama Canal. Louise stows away on the salvage boat and in no time at all meets hero Bruce Bennett (second left), a diver who works overtime in Joseph Krumgold's screenplay (story by Augustus Muir) discovering the sunken treasure, ascertaining that the phantom sub has been laying mines, and proving that a diving suit he has invented is resistant to the severest water pressure. Oscar O'Shea (right) was cast as the ship's captain, Pedro De Cordoba played the heavy, with Victor Wong, John Tyrrell and Harry Strang in support. Ralph Cohn produced, and Charles Barton directed. (69 mins)

△ **The Richest Man In Town** was a sleep-inducing comedy that reverted to burlesque for some of its laughs and to Abbott and Costello for at least one of its routines. Frank Craven (right) and Edgar Buchanan (left) played a couple of small-towners forever feuding with one another, but basically friends. The friendship, however, is severely tested when Buchanan, the local newspaper publisher, writes an obituary of Craven, the banker. Also severely tested was the patience of the paying customer, who'd seen and heard it all before. Eileen O'Hearn, Roger Pryor, Tom Dugan and George McKay found themselves marooned in Jack Fier's aimless production which Fanya Foss and Jerry Sackheim scripted from a story by Sackheim. Charles Barton directed. (70 mins)

▽ The 'she' in **She Knew All The Answers** was pretty Joan Bennett (left), though precisely what the questions were remained a mystery. Joan played a chorus girl who is intent on marrying millionaire playboy John Hubbard. However, Joan's guardian – in the personable guise of Franchot Tone (right) – has other plans for her. A conservative broker and the very antithesis, personality-wise, of Hubbard, he successfully prevents the prospective union from reaching second base. With her eye still on money, Joan enters a brokerage firm in Wall Street where, surprise, surprise, she falls in love with her gentlemanly guardian. Playboy Hubbard nobly steps aside to allow true love to take its course. The End. The screenplay, presided over by Harry Segall, Kenneth Earl and Curtis Kenyon, did little to circumnavigate the clichés in Jane Allen's story and was not without its leaden stretches. However, it provided some bright moments too, and in the mouths of its attractive leading players, the dialogue often sounded amusing. Supporting roles were shared out between Eve Arden (centre), as a wise-cracking show-girl (what else?), William Tracy as an office 'gofer', Almira Sessions as a private secretary and Luis Alberni as a loony mouse exterminator, together with Grady Sutton and Thurston Hall. The producer was Charles E. Rogers and the director Richard Wallace. (84 mins)

△ **Sing For Your Supper** was an artless comedy (with two songs by Sammy Cahn and Saul Chaplin) about an impecunious band-leader (Charles 'Buddy' Rogers, right) whose dance hall is saved from closure by wealthy socialite Jinx Falkenburg (left). A cast that included among its ranks Eve Arden, Bert Gordon, Don Beddoe, Lloyd Bridges, and Larry Parks deserved better than the trash dished up by writer Harry Rebuas (Sauber), whose nothing-doing screenplay left director Charles Barton with egg all over his face. Leon Barsha produced. (66 mins)

▷ **The Story Pays Off** was an engaging Runyonesque concoction whose offputting title concealed a daft little programmer about likeable racketeers, chief of whom was Victor Jory as a tough beer-baron who inadvertently acquires a day nursery for children. Initially, the only appealing thing about this acquisition is that it is run by pretty Rochelle Hudson (right), to whom Jory soon becomes romantically attached. In the painless course of Fanya Foss and Aleen Leslie's original screenplay, Jory's involvement with the nursery brings about his reformation and, as the cherry on the top, he is made alderman of the city. Jory was splendid in the role and so was a scene-stealing Maxie Rosenbloom (left) as Brains Moran. Horace MacMahon and George McKay were a pair of mobsters, and the cast also included Ralf Harolde, Bonnie Irma Dane, Arthur Loft, and as a young Bowery tough, Danny Mummert. Lew Landers's direction made the most with the least, and generated some welcome laughter. (68 mins)

△ First the good news: **Sweetheart Of The Campus** (GB: **Broadway Ahead**) marked the return to the screen of Ruby Keeler (centre left) after a three-year absence. The bad news was that Ms Keeler had the misfortune to experience both her swansong to musicals and her last starring role in such an unmitigated dud. The story was about a stranded dance band that becomes involved with a run-down college in order to stimulate enrolment. Featured players were Ozzie Nelson (right foreground) and His Band, Harriet Hilliard (centre right), Gordon Oliver (centre), Don Beddoe, Charles Judels, Kathleen Howard (left foreground), Byron Foulger and The Four Spirits of Rhythm. The two spirits of prose who thought it up were Robert D. Andrews and Edmund Hartmann. The film was directed by Edward Dmytryk in an off moment. The choreography was by Louis Da Pron. (76 mins)

▽ After the studio's rather high-toned *Arizona* of the previous year, which did an almighty belly-flop at the box-office, along came **Texas**, an agreeable 'oater' which combined action and comedy in nicely balanced proportions. It starred William Holden (left) and Glenn Ford (centre) – two of the fastest-rising young leading men on the Columbia lot – who, at the kick-off to Horace McCoy, Lewis Meltzer and Michael Blankfort's easy-going screenplay, are Confederate veterans aimlessly wandering around Texas after the Civil War. In the course of the narrative they go their separate ways; Holden becomes a rustler and Ford an honest cowhand with rancher Joseph Crehan. Both men fall in love with the rancher's daughter Claire Trevor (right). The high point of the story was a cattle drive through the State of Texas, with Ford as overseer and Holden in charge of hijacking the herd. A last-minute switch in allegiance found Holden double-crossing gangleader Edgar Buchanan, and helping Ford with his cattle-drive. He pays for his defection with a bullet. Both leading men registered strongly with the public in this one – as did Buchanan as Doc Thorpe, a dentist-cum-rustler, the success of whose performance may have had something to do with the fact that in real life, he was a dentist before he became an actor. George Marshall's beautifully paced direction coaxed attention-drawing supporting performances from George Bancroft, Don Beddoe, Andrew Tombes, Addison Richards and Edmund MacDonald. Samuel Bischoff produced. (93 mins)

◁ **They Dare Not Love** was a portentous title that presaged a portentous contemporary drama set against the turbulent background of Hitler's invasion of Austria. While fleeing from the Nazis, top-starred – and woefully miscast – George Brent (centre, as a dispossessed Austrian prince) and leading lady Martha Scott (left) fall in love on a ship bound for America. Their romance is 'kiboshed' by Scott's father (Egon Brecher), after which the couple go their separate ways. He becomes a playboy, with Kay Linaker on his arm. Scott and her father open a Viennese restaurant and dedicate themselves to helping fellow refugees. At this point the plot moved into over-drive with Brent, high on the Nazi hit list, offering to sacrifice himself in exchange for the release of seven prisoners of war. The story's end saw the would-be lovers finally united in marriage. A stiff performance from Brent, exacerbated by James Whale's equally turgid direction, did not help Charles Bennett and Ernest Vajda's wooden screenplay (story by James Edward Grant). Indeed, Sam Bischoff's production was pretty heavy-going despite an entertainingly ripe performace from Paul Lukas as a villainous Gestapo chief. (75 mins)

▷ The **Three Girls About Town** were Joan Blondell (right), Binnie Barnes (left) and newcomer Janet Blair – sisters, all of them, whose misfortune it is to find a dead body in the hotel where the Misses Blondell and Barnes are employed. Reporter John Howard happens to be covering a labour convention on the premises at the time, and is recruited by the gals to help find out who-dunnit. Amiable nonsense, it was capably directed from Richard Carroll's meandering screenplay by Leigh Jason, and performed by all concerned with tongues lodged well in cheeks. Joining in the fun for producer Samuel Bischoff were Robert Benchley, Eric Blore (as a drunk), Hugh O'Connell (centre) and Una O'Connor. (71 mins)

◁ One of newspaper-magnate William Randolph Hearst's most popular comic-strips (created by Russ Westover) provided the inspiration for **Tillie The Toiler**, a remake of a 1927 MGM silent which starred Hearst's 'lady-friend' – Marion Davies. This version featured newcomer Kay Harris (centre) as the heroine, a stenographer in her boyfriend's office. After her incompetence all but ruins his business, she manages to redeem herself in time for a happy ending. William Tracy (right) was her leading man with George Watts (left), Daphne Pollard, Jack Arnold, Marjorie Reynolds, Franklin Pangborn and Ernest Truex in support. Though originally intended as the first of a series, poor critical reaction and even poorer box-office interest put paid to such an idea. Karen De Wolf and Francis Martin provided the screenplay (story by De Wolf), Robert Sparks produced, and Sidney Salkow directed. (67 mins)

▷ Russell Hayden (second right), better known for being a second lead in the studio's on-going series of Hopalong Cassidy Westerns, made it to leading-man status in **Two In A Taxi**, a seen-it-before programmer in which he played a taxi driver desperate to lay his hands on $300 for a down-payment on a gas station. The money – like the film's entertainment value – was hard to come by, as scenarists Howard J. Green, Morton Thompson and Malvin Wald palpably demonstrated. Anita Louise (right) played Hayden's sweetheart, with other roles in Irving Briskin's production going to Noah Beery as the hero's side-kick, and to Dick Purcell (centre) as the villain. Also cast: Chick Chandler (second left), Fay Helm (left), George Cleveland, Paul Porcasi and Frank Yaconelli. Robert Florey directed. (63 mins)

◁ Lodged somewhere in **Time Out For Rhythm** – between the tap dancing of Ann Miller (second right), the singing of Rudy Vallee (second left) and the guest appearances of The Three Stooges, Brenda and Cobina, Six Hits and A Miss, Eddie Durant's Rhumba Orchestra and Glen Gray and His Casa Loma Band – was the story of two warring theatrical agents. The plot was supplied by Edmund L. Hartmann and Bert Lawrence, who got it from a play by Alex Ruben, who got it from a story by Bert Granet. What none of them supplied was a magnifying glass to find it. Rosemary Lane, Allen Jenkins (left, as a character called Off-beat Davis), Joan Merrill (right), Richard Lane and Stanley Andrews were also cast for producer Irving Starr and director Sidney Salkow. LeRoy Prinz choreographed, and the score was by Sammy Cahn and Saul Chaplin. (74 mins)

▷ Three songs by Sammy Cahn and Saul Chaplin hardly buttressed the faltering plot of **Two Latins From Manhattan**. Inspired, no doubt, by Al Dubin and Harry Warren's song 'She's A Latin From Manhattan', a highlight of Warner Bros.'s *Go Into Your Dance* (1935), it was the story of a New York press agent's attempts to recruit two local stand-ins when the Cuban sister-act she has booked into the nightclub for which she works fails to materialize. Joan Davis (left) played the press agent; Jinx Falkenburg (second right) and Joan Woodbury (second left) were the substitute performers. Complications invaded Albert Duffy's screenplay when – you guessed it – the real Cuban ladies (Marquita Madero and Carmen Morales) eventually showed up. Fortunio Bonanova, Don Beddoe, Lloyd Bridges and Sig Arno (right) were also featured; Wallace MacDonald produced and it was directed by Charles Barton. (65 mins)

▽ After an absence of two years, Barbara Stanwyck (left) returned to the studio to make **You Belong To Me** (GB: **Good Morning, Doctor**) co-starring Henry Fonda (right) with whom she had successfully – and memorably – appeared in Preston Sturges's *The Lady Eve* (Paramount, 1941). Though not nearly as good as that classic comedy, Claude Binyon's screenplay (story by Dalton Trumbo), travelling a well-worn circuit, nonetheless gave them several opportunities to spark off each other. The uncluttered plot concerned a lady physician and the insane and unfounded jealousy experienced by her wealthy unemployed husband. There was little more to it than that though, under Wesley Ruggles's direction, it tripped along nicely. Ruggles, who also produced, cast Ruth Donnelly as a fast-talking nurse, Melville Cooper as a butler, Roger Clark as one of Miss Stanwyck's ex-suitors, and, best of all, Edgar Buchanan as a gardener given to philosophical musings. Remade in 1950 as *Emergency Wedding*. (93 mins)

▷ A variation on *Glamor For Sale* (1940), **Under Age** again exploited the female form in a serviceable quickie, directed by Edward Dmytryk, about a bunch of girls, fresh out of detention homes, who are forced to find jobs with a gang of ruthless hoods in establishments such as bent tourist camps, bar rooms and cafés. They're employed, of course, to lure suckers away from their money. In the end the theft of an $18,000 necklace from a wealthy client leads to the syndicate's demise. Nan Grey (centre) starred as one of the under-age girls and Tom Neal was the hero who helps smash the syndicate, with Mary Anderson (seated), Alan Baxter, Leona Maricle, Don Beddoe and Yolande Mollot (later Donlan – left) also featured. The screenplay was fashioned by Robert D. Andrews from Stanley Roberts's story. The producer was Ralph Cohn. (59 mins)

▽ After making three films away from her home base in 1941 – *The Strawberry Blonde* (Warner Bros.), *Affectionately Yours* (Warner Bros.) and *Blood and Sand* (20th Century-Fox) – Rita Hayworth (right) returned to Columbia a fully-fledged star, and was cast opposite Fred Astaire (left) in **You'll Never Get Rich** whose A-grade budget couldn't, alas, disguise its B-grade plot. All about a Broadway dance director (Astaire) who finds himself drafted into the US Army, it was a feeble excuse for a handful of Cole Porter numbers, none of which reached hit status because of the on-going ASCAP radio strike which limited their on-air exposure.

Removed from the burdensome plot, however, they stand up well and are much better than they seemed in the context of Michael Fessier and Ernest Pagano's screenplay. Hayworth and Astaire were magical – both singly and together – and received solid support from Robert Benchley as an amorous producer. John Hubbard provided the romantic complication, with other roles under Sidney Lanfield's no-more-than-serviceable direction going to Osa Massen, Frieda Inescort, Guinn Williams, Donald MacBride, Majorie Gateson and Ann Shoemaker. The choreography was by Robert Alton. Samuel Bischoff produced. (88 mins)

▷ Jack London's stirring story **The Adventures Of Martin Eden** deserved a more convincing screenplay than the one provided by W. L. River. Martin Eden is a sailor whose brutal treatment at the hands of the Bligh-like skipper of the 'hellship' on which he is serving prompts him to bring to public attention, through the publication of his memoirs, the seamen's unenviable lot. The eventual publication of the harrowing document results not only in bringing the brutal captain to justice, but in the freeing of a fellow sailor wrongly arrested for mutiny. B. P. Schulberg's well-intentioned production cast Glenn Ford (right) in the title role, Stuart Erwin as the wrongly arrested seaman, Ian MacDonald the sadistic skipper and Evelyn Keyes and Claire Trevor (left) the two women in the hero's life. Also cast: Dickie Moore, Frank Conroy and Rafaela Ottiano. Sidney Salkow was responsible for the routine direction. (87 mins)

▽ **The Boogie Man Will Get You** found Boris Karloff once again deploying his sinister persona to comic effect. This time he's a professor experimenting in a basement laboratory filled with test-tubes and other scientific impedimenta in the hope of producing a race of supermen. The premises (a run-down inn in New England) have just been sold to Larry Parks and Jeff Donnell, an unsuspecting divorced couple, whose discovery of a few corpses in the cellar sends Parks straight to Peter Lorre (centre), the local sheriff-cum-doctor. But far from arresting Karloff, Lorre – who sees in these experiments a chance of making untold personal wealth (and strength) for himself – decides to support rather than hinder the professor. Edwin Blum's familiar screenplay (story by Hal Timberg and Robert E. Hunt, adapted by Paul Gangelin) made full use of most of the clichés of the genre, but left Karloff and Lorre very much in command of the mayhem. An enthusiastic cast also included Maxie Rosenbloom (left), Maude Eburne, George McKay and Don Beddoe, director Lew Landers kept the fun fast and furious. The producer was Colbert Clark. (66 mins)

▽ Shy on marquee value, **Atlantic Convoy** was nonetheless, a gripping, well-made wartime adventure yarn dealing with sabotage off Iceland. Though Bruce Bennett (centre) received top-billing and played the captain of the air corps, Robert Lee Johnson's crisp little screenplay centred on third-billed John Beal as a US-patrol weather operator. The plot had Beal being suspected of spying for the Nazis. In the end, though, he proves himself as all-American as the next man by facilitating the sinking of a German spy-ship. Virginia Field (second left) played a nurse and Clifford Severn (right) cabin boy, with other parts in Colbert Clark's action-packed programmer going to Larry Parks (left), Stanley Brown, Lloyd Bridges (second right), Victor Kilian, Eddie Laughton and Hans Schumm. The fast-moving direction was by Lew Landers. (66 mins)

▷ In **Cadets On Parade**, Freddie Bartholomew (right) starred as a coward who, ashamed to face his father, runs away after being expelled from school. He takes up with young Jimmy Lydon (left), a newsboy, and the two become good friends. All goes well until Bartholomew's father posts a large reward for his son's return – a fact that does not go unnoticed by Lydon's unscrupulous, blackmailing old man. Howard J. Green wrote the screenplay from a story by Frank Fenton and Martha Barnett, Lew Landers directed for producer Wallace MacDonald, and the cast included Joseph Crehan, Raymond Hatton, Minna Gombell, Robert Warwick and Kenneth MacDonald. (66 mins)

▷ Though not funny enough to yank a tendon in your side, **Bedtime Story** was sufficiently amusing to keep audiences involved – including the more prurient viewers who, on the strength of the misleading title, might have expected something a little more risqué than the domestic bickerings of a successful playwright and his equally successful actress wife. After seven years of marriage she (Loretta Young, second right) wants to call showbiz life quits and live on a farm in Connecticut. He (Fredric March, left) will not hear of such a thing and continues to write plays in which she is expected to star. The result of these irreconcilable differences is that she walks out on him and into the arms of a starchy banker (Allyn Joslyn). In the end, though, March wins Young back – as you knew he would all along – and she appears in his next play – as you knew she would all along. A soufflé which, with, say, Cary Grant and Katharine Hepburn (or Jean Arthur, or Carole Lombard or Irene Dunne) might have risen higher, it nevertheless had its moments, the best of them being supplied by Robert Benchley (second left), Eve Arden, Helen Westley and Joyce Compton (right). Richard Flournoy scripted from a story by Horace Jackson and Grant Garrett. Alexander Hall directed it with an admirably deft touch, and B. P. Schulberg was in charge of the production. (83 mins)

▷ Joe E. Brown (right) played **The Daring Young Man**, another bespoke comedy strictly for fans of the wide-mouthed comedian. And what made him so daring in Karen De Wolf and Connie Lee's predictable screenplay was that, having been rejected by the draft, he apprehends a Nazi spy ring in New York and is proclaimed a hero. Marguerite Chapman (left), William Wright, Claire Dodd, Lloyd Bridges, Robert Middlemass, Minerva Urecal, Danny Mummert, Irving Bacon and Arthur Lake (on vacation from *Blondie*) lent moral support in featured roles, Frank Strayer directed, and Robert Sparks produced. (73 mins)

△ Plot No. 134 was hauled out for **Canal Zone**, in which know-it-all civilian flyer John Hubbard brings his irresponsible approach to aviation into war service – and makes himself thoroughly unpopular as a result. The finale finds him redeemed when he saves his instructor after a smash. Chester Morris (left, top-billed) was a pilot instructor concerned with ferrying bombs across the Atlantic; Harriet Hilliard (right) was his impatient sweetheart. Also cast: Larry Parks, Forrest Tucker (second right), Eddie Laughton, Lloyd Bridges (centre) and George McKay (second left). Lew Landers directed sluggishly from an equally sluggish screenplay by Robert Lee Johnson (story by Blaine Miller and Jean DuPont Miller). The producer was Colbert Clark. (79 mins)

▽ Filmed on location outside Vancouver Island in British Columbia, though actually set on the coast of Norway, **The Commandos Strike At Dawn** starred a restrained Paul Muni (centre) as a widower fisherman who falls in love with the daughter (Anna Lee) of a British admiral (Cedric Hardwicke, left). After the Nazi invasion of Norway, Lee and her father return to England and the Nazis occupy the village in which Muni lives with his daughter (Ann Carter), who is being held hostage. Escaping to England, Muni agrees to lead a commando raid on his village and destroy a German airfield, if the British promise to rescue his daughter. The film ends with the destruction of the airfield, the death of Muni in battle, and his daughter being rescued and taken to England by Lee. Lester Cowan's production was sensitively scripted by Irwin Shaw (from a story by C.S. Forester), solidly directed by John Farrow, and had fine supporting performances from Lillian Gish, Robert Coote (right), Ray Collins, Rosemary DeCamp, Richard Derr, Alexander Knox and Rod Cameron. It was a worthy contribution to the Cinema of World War II and a sensitive study of a nation under occupation. (100 mins)

▽ **Flight Lieutenant** was the one about the flyer (Pat O'Brien, right) whose negligence causes the death of his co-pilot. Disgraced, the surviving aviator attempts to find refuge from his guilt by exiling himself to Dutch Guiana where, for a while, he lives among the flotsam and jetsam of humanity. Glenn Ford (left) was cast as O'Brien's son, who just so happens to be in love with the daughter (Evelyn Keyes) of the dead pilot. O'Brien re-enlists as a private and in the final reel redeems himself by sacrificing his life in a test flight that should have been taken by his son. Michael Blankfort's screenplay (from a tired story by Richard Farrell and Betty Hopkins) was in no way able to animate the platitudes inherent in this seen-it-once-too-often melodrama. Sidney Salkow's enervating direction seemed equally afflicted by the triteness of it all, as did the two central performances. Also embroiled in B. P. Schulberg's hand-me-down production were Jonathan Hale, Minor Watson, Frank Puglia, Lloyd Bridges and Larry Parks. (80 mins)

△ A wearisome romantic comedy by Wallace MacDonald and journeyman Charles Barton, **Hello Annapolis** starred Tom Brown (centre) and Larry Parks as erstwhile high-school rivals who take their rivalry into a naval academy where they squabble over pretty Jean Parker (left). Thurston Hall, Phil Brown, Joseph Crehan, Herbert Rawlinson and Mae Busch were also cast. Donald Davis and Tom Reed scripted from a story by Reed. (62 mins)

◁ Ten years earlier Marlene Dietrich (centre right) had proved, in *Blonde Venus* (Paramount, 1932), that the role of mother-love wasn't beyond her sultry capabilities. In **The Lady Is Willing** she went down the same road all over again, but to (deservedly) less acclaim. Dietrich played an actress who finds an adorable one-year-old boy (David James) on Eighth Avenue. She embarks on a marriage of convenience to paediatrician Fred MacMurray (centre left) in order to adopt the child. Convenience turns to love, but not before MacMurray manages to cure the child of a potentially fatal attack of mastoiditis. Much obvious talent was invested in producer-director Mitchell Leisen's top-bracket production, but James Edward Grant and Albert McCleery's screenplay was unable to avoid the maudlin pitfalls inherent in the plot. A miscast Dietrich, who looked far too glamorous and sophisticated for the demands of the role, could do nothing to save the situation. Aline MacMahon, Stanley Ridges, Arline Judge, Roger Clark, Sterling Holloway and Marietta Canty supported. (93 mins)

▷ Maxie Rosenbloom (on horse) – he of the fractured English and the rapt dumb expression – received top-billing in **Harvard Here I Come** (a reworking of a short he made with a similar story line), and played himself in producer Wallace MacDonald's unsophisticated romp. 'Himself', in this instance, was a nightclub owner who enrols at Harvard. Hailed as the nearest thing to the missing link, he is signed up for $15,000 as a 'guinea pig' and given free room and board. The payoff has him dumbfounding students and professors alike. Enjoyable nonsense from start to finish, the film enlisted the talents of Arline Judge, Stanley Brown, Don Beddoe, Virginia Sale, Byron Foulger, Larry Parks and, as a co-ed who makes a play for the star, decorative Marie Wilson. Albert Duffy scripted it from a story by Karl Brown and the fast-paced direction was by Lew Landers. (64 mins)

▽ Described by one contemporary critic as 'an insult to American intelligence' and by another as 'one of the most explosive satires directed at the Nazi army that has come out of the studios', **The Wife Takes A Flyer** (GB: **A Yank In Dutch**) was a crude and unsubtle satire that attempted to debunk the Hitler régime in much the same way that Ernst Lubitsch did in the altogether more successful *To Be Or Not To Be* (United Artists) the same year. The wife was a Dutch woman (Joan Bennett, centre), and the flyer an Englishman (Franchot Tone, right) who takes refuge in Bennett's home after his plane is shot down over Nazi-occupied Holland. The plot (by Gina Kaus, screenplay by Kaus and Jay Dratler, with additional dialogue by Harry Segall) was bounced off the fact that

also billeted with Bennett is a Nazi major, played (or over-played) by Allyn Joslyn (left). In order to avoid being arrested, Tone is passed off as Bennett's mentally defective husband. After much farcical mileage has been drawn from Tone's disrespectful treatment of Joslyn, the flyer steals a German plane and flies to England with Miss Bennett in tow. Debunking Nazis was one thing; making idiots out of these dangerous thugs was quite another. In the end, producer B. P. Schulberg's film caricatured itself out of existence. Richard Wallace's direction applied the satire with far too heavy a hand – although Joslyn had some genuinely funny moments. The cast also included Cecil Cunningham, Roger Clark, Lloyd Corrigan and Lyle Lytell. (86 mins)

▽ Though **You Were Never Lovelier** – a far superior musical to *You'll Never Get Rich* (1941) – was set in Latin America, the only authentic Latin American in it was Xavier Cugat, who, with his celebrated Orchestra, provided some authentic music. But this was a minor criticism of a major entertainment that again teamed the incomparable Fred Astaire (left) with the luscious Rita Hayworth (right), who was reaching the peak of her powers. He played a nightclub dancer (from New York) with a passion for horse-racing; she was the aloof second daughter (of four) belonging to wealthy hotelier Adolphe Menjou, who is determined that his daughters will marry in the order of their ages. Astaire and Hayworth's on-off on-again relationship formed the slender content of Michael Fessier, Ernest Pagano and Delmer Daves's screenplay (story by Carlos Olivari and Sixto Pondal Rios), and provided choreographer Val Raset with a chance to take the two dancing stars through several bliss-making choreographic flights of fancy, the best being 'I'm Old Fashioned' and 'The Shorty George'. With the great Jerome Kern supplying one of his most melodious film scores (lyrics by Johnny Mercer) the film couldn't go wrong – and didn't. Leslie Brooks, Adele Mara, Larry Parks, Isobel Elsom, Gus Schilling and Barbara Brown completed the cast, with Nan Wynn dubbing Hayworth's vocals. The unobstrusive direction was by William A. Seiter. The lavish production was by Louis F. Edelman. (97 mins)

▽ Taking time off from her script chores on the *Blondie* series, Karen De Wolf remained on domestic terrain with **Meet The Stewarts**, whom she introduced to audiences as a pleasant, average Mr and Mrs America. She (Frances Dee, left) is rich; he (William Holden, right) isn't. Holden agrees to marry her on condition that she lives within the budget provided by his modest salary. At first all goes smoothly, but after successfully negotiating the financial hurdle of furnishing their new home, a massive bill from their country club turns the tables on their budget considerations – resulting in an almighty row and a separation. The rift and accompanying complications are only temporary, and, as this was a comedy rather than a drama, the handsome couple were reunited for the final fade. Miss De Wolf's screenplay (from a story by Elizabeth Dunn) never bit off more than her uncomplicated characters could chew or her audiences could digest, and it was breezily directed for producer Robert Sparks by Alfred E. Green. The cast also included Grant Mitchell, Marjorie Gateson, Anne Revere, Roger Clark, Danny Mummert, Don Beddoe, Ann Gillis, Margaret Hamilton and (as a pair of removal men) Edward Gargan and Tom Dugan. (72 mins)

▽ Mining disasters, Nazi agents, sabotage, gang murder and sibling rivalry were just a few of the ingredients Edward T. Lowe and Jack Roberts (story by Roberts and George Bricker) threw into an indifferent brew called **A Man's World**. It starred Marguerite Chapman (centre) as a nurse who is kidnapped after witnessing a murder in a hospital and sent to an unnamed country rich in the chromite deposits needed for national defence. There she meets William Wright (right) and his younger brother Larry Parks (left), the owners of a chromite mine, and becomes friendly with Parks but eventually falls for Wright. After her kidnappers are caught, she decides to remain in the unnamed country to nurse Wright, who has been injured in a mining accident. Wynne Gibson was featured as the owner of a honky-tonk saloon, with other parts under Charles Barton's direction going to Roger Pryor, Frank Sully, Ferris Taylor and Edward Van Sloan. Wallace MacDonald produced. (63 mins)

▽ Erstwhile model Jinx Falkenburg (centre) starred in **Lucky Legs** – as the recipient of a $1 million inheritance. The trouble is that racketeer Russell Hayden wants a bit of it too. Inconsequential to a fault, the film also featured Leslie Brooks (left), Kay Harris (right), Elizabeth Patterson, William Wright and Don Beddoe. It had a title song by Sammy Cahn and Saul Chaplin, was written by Stanley Rubin and Jack Hartfield, produced by Wallace MacDonald and directed by Charles Barton. (64 mins)

△ Usual espionage fare – **Underground Agent** starred Bruce Bennett (right) as a government agent out to prevent Nazi spies involved in a telephone tapping scheme from infiltrating a defence plant. To help him in his endeavours, Bennett invents an ingenious word scrambler which complicates life for the enemy and leads to the ultimate round-up of the spies. Leslie Brooks (left) assisted, and there was solid B-picture support from the reliable likes of Frank Albertson and George McKay. J. Robert Bren and Gladys Atwater wrote the screenplay, Sam White produced it, and Michael Gordon was the director. (67 mins)

△ A rowdy service caper, set at the time of Pearl Harbor, **Two Yanks In Trinidad** inducted hoodlums Pat O'Brien (left) and Brian Donlevy (right) into the US Army with mildly diverting results. Pat and Brian are partners in petty crime who fall out with one another. To escape the wrath of the latter, the former signs up for active service; so, eventually, do Donlevy and his two bodyguards, Frank Jenks and Frank Sully. A Nazi spy brings the two erstwhile partners together again to pool their talents, for their sense of patriotism far outweighs their sense of outrage. There was a fair amount of action in Sy Bartlett, Richard Carroll and Harry Segall's screenplay (story by Bartlett), and a generous quota of comedy – supplied, mainly, by Donlevy's wholesale disregard for army discipline. In the main, however, it was fomula film-making which the audience could take or leave with no harm done either way. Gregory Ratoff directed a cast that featured Janet Blair as a café entertainer (who sang a song called 'Trinidad' by Sammy Cahn and Saul Chaplin), as well as Donald MacBride as a tough top sergeant, John Emery, Veda Ann Borg and Clyde Fillmore. Samuel Bischoff produced. (84 mins)

▷ **The Man Who Returned To Life** squandered a passable idea on an indifferent screenplay, by Gordon Rigby (story by Samuel W. Taylor). A happily married man living in California has his composure understandably shattered when he reads that a man from his past is to be hanged for his murder. The events leading up to this news item are then boringly recalled in flashback. John Howard (left) starred as the man in the middle of it all, with other roles in Wallace MacDonald's production going to Lucille Fairbanks, Ruth Ford, Marcella Martin, Roger Clark (centre), Elizabeth Risdon and Clancy Cooper (right). Lew Landers directed. (61 mins)

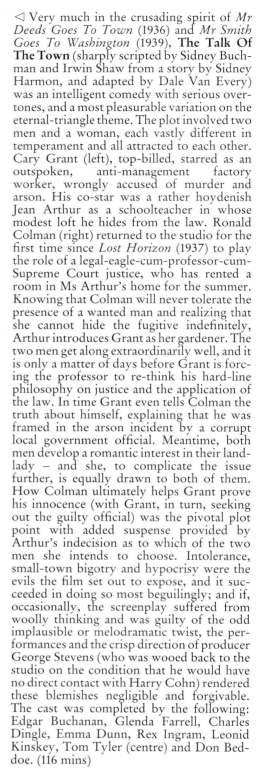

Very much in the crusading spirit of *Mr Deeds Goes To Town* (1936) and *Mr Smith Goes To Washington* (1939), **The Talk Of The Town** (sharply scripted by Sidney Buchman and Irwin Shaw from a story by Sidney Harmon, and adapted by Dale Van Every) was an intelligent comedy with serious overtones, and a most pleasurable variation on the eternal-triangle theme. The plot involved two men and a woman, each vastly different in temperament and all attracted to each other. Cary Grant (left), top-billed, starred as an outspoken, anti-management factory worker, wrongly accused of murder and arson. His co-star was a rather hoydenish Jean Arthur as a schoolteacher in whose modest loft he hides from the law. Ronald Colman (right) returned to the studio for the first time since *Lost Horizon* (1937) to play the role of a legal-eagle-cum-professor-cum-Supreme Court justice, who has rented a room in Ms Arthur's home for the summer. Knowing that Colman will never tolerate the presence of a wanted man and realizing that she cannot hide the fugitive indefinitely, Arthur introduces Grant as her gardener. The two men get along extraordinarily well, and it is only a matter of days before Grant is forcing the professor to re-think his hard-line philosophy on justice and the application of the law. In time Grant even tells Colman the truth about himself, explaining that he was framed in the arson incident by a corrupt local government official. Meantime, both men develop a romantic interest in their landlady – and she, to complicate the issue further, is equally drawn to both of them. How Colman ultimately helps Grant prove his innocence (with Grant, in turn, seeking out the guilty official) was the pivotal plot point with added suspense provided by Arthur's indecision as to which of the two men she intends to choose. Intolerance, small-town bigotry and hypocrisy were the evils the film set out to expose, and it succeeded in doing so most beguilingly; and if, occasionally, the screenplay suffered from woolly thinking and was guilty of the odd implausible or melodramatic twist, the performances and the crisp direction of producer George Stevens (who was wooed back to the studio on the condition that he would have no direct contact with Harry Cohn) rendered these blemishes negligible and forgivable. The cast was completed by the following: Edgar Buchanan, Glenda Farrell, Charles Dingle, Emma Dunn, Rex Ingram, Leonid Kinskey, Tom Tyler (centre) and Don Beddoe. (116 mins)

▽ 'When I want a sneak, I'll hire the best and get a Jap', quipped Joan Crawford (left) in **They All Kissed The Bride**, an entertaining 'woman's picture' equally enjoyed by men. Six months after Pearl Harbor was attacked, the line received the biggest laugh in the screenplay P.J. Wolfson fashioned from a story by Gina Kaus and Andrew P. Solt, which in turn was adapted by Solt and Henry Altimus. Today the line is merely offensive and is often removed from existing TV prints. What remains, however, is the fast-moving story of a career woman *par excellence* (Crawford) who, after inheriting her late father's mammoth trucking concern, successfully manages to sublimate all her womanly traits. A precursor of the superior *Mildred Pierce* (Warner Bros., 1945), the character played by Crawford was about as lovable as an angry porcupine, with no time for sentimentality and even less for marriage. Indeed, when marriage does intrude upon her day-to-day business, it isn't her own, but a marriage of convenience arranged by her for her sister

(Helen Parrish). It's at her sister's wedding reception, however, that she meets reporter Melvyn Douglas (right) and, for the first time in her life, goes weak at the knees (literally), a family trait indicating an interest in the opposite sex. The eventual taming of the shrew by Douglas was the red meat of this oft-told tale and how it was done provided some tailor-made moments to accommodate the temperaments of its two stars, as well as good parts for Billie Burke (as Crawford's flighty mother), Allen Jenkins, Andrew Tombes, Emory Parnell, Mary Treen, Nydia Westman, Roger Clark and Edward Gargan. Edward Kaufman's production was as adult as the Hays Code would allow at the time, and the unflagging direction was by Alexander Hall. [The Crawford role was orginally intended for Carole Lombard who, unfortunately, was tragically killed in a plane crash while returning from a war-bond rally. As a gesture to the memory of Miss Lombard, Crawford donated her entire salary for the film to various charities.] (86 mins)

▷ Jackie Gleason (centre) and Jack Durant conjured up shades of Abbott and Costello in **Tramp, Tramp, Tramp**, a really dire little comedy that, alas, bore no relation in quality to Harry Langdon's 1926 success of the same name for First National in which Frank Capra had had a hand. This one was about a couple of barbers who find themselves out of business when all their customers are drafted. After unsuccessfully trying to enlist, they form a home-guard which becomes a hideout for a gang of killers. Ho-hum. Florence Rice (right), Bruce Bennett, Hallene Hill, Billy Curtis, Mabel Todd and Forrest Tucker were also featured. The screenplay was by Ned Dandy (from a story by Shannon Day, Hal Braham and Marian Grant). Wallace MacDonald produced, and piloting the whole enterprise to disaster was director Charles Barton. (68 mins)

△ A comedy with four songs, **Sweetheart Of The Fleet** was a pleasant-enough quickie that starred Joan Davis (centre) as a publicist for an ad agency whose number-one client sponsors a show called 'A Blind Date With Romance'. The singers on the show are a pair called Brenda and Cobina (Blanche Stewart and Elvia Allman) whose unattractive looks make them naturals for radio but a no-no when it comes to live appearances. When called upon to 'unmask' Brenda and Cobina at a live United Service Organizations rally for the Navy, the resourceful Davis hires models Jinx Falkenburg (left) and Joan Woodbury (right) to mouth the words of the songs in front of the curtains while the ugly ducklings do the real singing off-stage. The Misses B and C agree to the deception in return for being supplied with a pair of sailor boyfriends. Such were the slender ingredients of Albert Duffy and Maurice Tombragel's screenplay (additional dialogue by Ned Dandy). Still, it was short and sweet, and under Charles Barton's efficient direction went down painlessly. Jack Fier's production also featured Tim Ryan, Robert Stevens, William Wright and George McKay. (65 mins)

▽ Because he's the smartest on-the-spot radio announcer in America, John Beal (right) is the arch enemy of saboteurs as well as a thorn in the side of the police and government agents. The uncovering of a group of fifth columnists was the main business in **Stand By All Networks**, screenplay by Maurice Tombragel, Doris Malloy, Robert Lee Johnson (story by Tombragel) and directed by Lew Landers. Florence Rice was top-starred, with other roles going to Margaret Hays and Alan Baxter. Jack Fier produced. (65 mins)

▽ Just as Tom Harmon played himself in *Harmon Of Michigan*, so football star Frankie Albert, Stanford's All-American Quarterback, played Frankie Albert (seated) in **The Spirit Of Stanford**. A wash-out in all departments, it was about an egotistical campus hero (Albert) who deserts his college in its hour of need to turn professional but, on learning that his roommate is dangerously ill, returns to win the big match for his school. Marguerite Chapman, Matt Willis, Shirley Patterson, Lloyd Bridges (centre back), Forrest Tucker (left), footballer Ernie Nevers and The Four Vagabonds were also in it. Howard J. Green, William Brent and Nick Lucats (story by Brent and Lucats) scripted, Sam White produced and Charles Barton directed. Dreadful. (74 mins)

△ You didn't have to be clairvoyant to predict that a film called **Shut My Big Mouth** was a vehicle for Joe E. Brown (right) – and, indeed, it was. Employing plot number 236 – about the timid nobody who arrives in a wild frontier town and eventually brings the bad guys to justice – Oliver Drake, Karen De Wolf and Francis Martin's screenplay (story by Drake) was etched in the kind of broad strokes so characteristic of its star's particular persona that Brown fans weren't disappointed. The supporting cast included Adele Mara, Victor Jory (left), Russell Simpson, Fritz Feld, Don Beddoe, Noble Johnson, Forrest Tucker (second right) and Lloyd Bridges (second left). Robert Sparks produced, and Charles Barton directed. (71 mins)

△ Undernourished, both in creative content and in budget, **Submarine Raider** was, at least, topical. The attack on Pearl Harbor was used to underpin a fictional yarn in which Marguerite Chapman (centre) survives hostile action by Japanese forces against the luxury yacht on which she is travelling. She's picked up by a US submarine that attempts to warn the American forces of the impending air strike on Pearl Harbor, but, of course, without success. Indeed, 'success' wasn't a word that could be applied to any aspect of this flung-together quickie. John Howard (left) starred as the sub commander, with other roles in Aubrey Wisberg's screenplay farmed out to Bruce Bennett (right), Warren Ashe, Larry Parks and Forrest Tucker. Lew Landers directed. (65 mins)

◁ Bruce Smith (centre), playing himself, starred in **Smith Of Minnesota**, a football film with a difference: there was no winning touchdown in the climactic final moments. Indeed, as scripted by Robert D. Andrews, the story-line has Columbia Studio signing Smith for a biopic of his career, then giving the assignment a top scenarist (Warren Ashe) on the proviso that the story they want from him is to be something different, and one that will reveal Smith to be a great American and a great personality. It's the scenarist's 'in-depth' probing of the gridiron's background that provided the film with its narrative content, as well as roles for Arline Judge (as a local reporter who helps Ashe meet the rest of the Smith family), Don Beddoe, Kay Harris and Robert Stevens. A passable programmer, it was produced by Jack Fier and directed by Lew Landers. (66 mins)

▽ Another cops and robbers melodrama, **Sabotage Squad** was tinged with topicality only in that it involved Nazi agents and American undercover men. It starred Bruce Bennett (left) as a would-be hero who slugs an Army physician for pronouncing him physically unfit to join up, and is sent to jail. His girlfriend (an insipid Kay Harris) uses her influence with a rival officer (Eddie Norris, right) to get him released. Only in the film's dying moments does Bennett become the hero his fans knew he was all along when he self-destructs (together with the chief Nazi agent) in a dynamite-filled truck headed for an aviation plant. Sidney Blackmer was the Nazi in question, with other roles in Bernice Petkere and Wallace Sullivan's screenplay going to Don Beddoe, John Tyrrell, George McKay and Robert Emmett Keane. Jack Fier produced and the direction was by Lew Landers. (60 mins)

▽ Female nurses who parachute into battle areas in order to minister to the wounded were the subject of **Parachute Nurse**, yet one more example of the studio's feminist approach to areas that hitherto had been male-dominated. Striking an early blow for Women's Lib were top-cast Marguerite Chapman (left), Kay Harris (right), Louise Albritton, Diedra Vale, Evelyn Wahl, Shirley Patterson, Eileen O'Hearn, Roma Aldrich, Marjorie Reardon and Catherine Craig. The men were represented by William Wright as the girls' instructor, Frank Sully and Forrest Tucker as lieutenants and Douglas Wood as a major. It was scripted by Rian James from a story by Elizabeth Meehan, produced by Wallace MacDonald, and directed by Charles Barton. (63 mins)

▽ The roistering, rollicking adventures of two Ohio girls newly arrived in New York's Greenwich village provided the content of **My Sister Eileen**, an all-out farce whose antics were first introduced in the pages of *The New Yorker* magazine. These stories (by Ruth McKenney) formed the basis of the Broadway play by Joseph Fields and Jerome Chodorov who imposed on them a shape and a structure which was retained, with minor variations and alterations, for the fun-filled screen version. Indeed, with the exception of a few 'opening out' sequences, the addition of a few gags and the deletion (for the benefit of the censors at the Hays Office) of the odd word here and there, the screenplay (by Fields and Chodorov) was as faithful to the original as the show's many admirers could have wished. The action was confined mainly to the two girls' basement apartment, with its foot-level view of the world above. The plot, such as it was, hinged on the to-ing and fro-ing of a number of colourful Village people whose paths cross those of the two heroines. For example, there is George Tobias (left) as a Greek landlord, Allyn Joslyn as a reporter, Donald MacBride as a pugnacious cop, Richard Quine as a drugstore clerk, Frank Sully as a janitor, Clyde Fillmore as a publisher, Gordon Jones as a pro footballer called 'The Wreck' (the latter two repeating their original Broadway assignments) and

▷ **Not A Ladies Man** was a predictable romance in which a youngster called 'Butch' Bruce (Douglas Croft, right) almost wrecks his divorced father's love-affair with a pretty schoolteacher (Fay Wray) when, motivated by jealousy, he tells her that his old man (Paul Kelly, left) is in love with someone else. Matters came right in the end, though, to vouchsafe for Rian James's undistinguished screenplay (story by Robert Hyde) the obligatory happy ending. Ruth Lee, Laurence Dixon, Mariette Canty and Don Beddoe were also in it. Leon Barsha produced, and the direction was by Lew Landers. (59 mins)

Jeff Donnell and Minna Phillips as a not-quite-married girl and her mother, who live upstairs. Eileen of the title, a would-be actress, and her sister Ruth Sherwood, an aspiring writer, were played by Janet Blair (centre) and the top-cast Rosalind Russell (right). Completing the cast were Elizabeth Patterson and Grant Mitchell (in the newly-written roles of the two girls' parents), and Brian Aherne as an editor who helps save Ruth from penury by buying her stories and falling in love with her. The Three Stooges were in it too (briefly) as a trio of workmen digging up the road to make way for a new subway. Max Gordon, who produced the show on Broadway (which starred Shirley Booth as Ruth) produced the movie version as well. The direction was by Alexander Hall, who wasn't always able to alleviate the claustrophobia engendered by confining most of the action to the basement apartment. No complaints, though, about Russell's beautifully timed central performance. The same material was recycled in 1953 as the Broadway musical *Wonderful Town* with music by Leonard Bernstein, lyrics by Betty Comden and Adolph Green and a libretto by Fields and Chodorov. In 1955 the studio commissioned an altogether different score from composers Jule Styne and Leo Robin, and musicalized the material under its original title. (97 mins)

▽ Both the leading characters – George Sanders (left) and Marguerite Chapman (right) – die in **Appointment In Berlin**; so does fourth-billed Gale Sondergaard as a British intelligence agent. A wartime melodrama unleavened by humour or, for that matter, suspense, it featured Sanders as a wing-commander in the RAF who is inducted into the British Secret Service, where, in the guise of a Lord Haw-Haw figure, he broadcasts seemingly anti-British propaganda which, in reality, contains coded messages of vital information. Horace McCoy and Michael Hogan's screenplay (story by B. P. Fineman) hardly stretched the languid talents of its leading man, any more than did Alfred E. Green's direction. Samuel Bischoff's production was, on the whole, an appointment not worth keeping. Also cast: Onslow Stevens (as a Nazi spy), Alan Napier, H P. Sanders and Don Douglas. (77 mins)

▽ 'Kvetch' is a Yiddish word which, loosely translated, means a pain in the neck. It describes perfectly the character played by Edward G. Robinson (right) in **Destroyer**, another wartime melodrama about ships and the men who sail in them. Robinson played a veteran World War I sailor who, after wangling a job as chief bosun on a destroyer called the *John Paul Jones*, sets out to alienate all and sundry – but especially Glenn Ford (left) as a laconic Chief Petty Officer – with his incessant talk of how much better things were done in the good old days. Indeed, Robinson is so unpopular that he is ousted from his position, and only in the last reel does he redeem himself, by saving the day when the destroyer goes into action against the Japanese in the Pacific. So much for the plot (by Frank Wead), which Wead, Lewis Meltzer and Borden Chase fashioned into a so-so screenplay. Meagre love interest was supplied by Marguerite Chapman (as Robinson's daughter) and the romance she has with the good-looking Glenn Ford. A clean-shaven Edgar Buchanan played a sailor, with Leo Gorcey, Regis Toomey, Ed Brophy, Warren Ashe, Craig Woods and Curt Bois completing the cast for producer Louis F. Edelman. The journeyman direction was by William A. Seiter. (97 mins)

◁ A lifeless programmer, **City Without Men** told the story of a group of women living in a boarding house adjacent to the prison where their men-folk are all serving time. Linda Darnell (centre) headed the cast for producer Samuel Bronston, with other roles under Sidney Salkow's listless direction going to Michael Duane, Sara Allgood (second left), Edgar Buchanan, Leslie Brooks, Glenda Farrell (second right), and Margaret Hamilton. The Budd Schulberg-Martin Berkeley story was scripted by W. L. River, George Sklar and Donald Davis. B. P. Schulberg produced. (75 mins)

◁ There were no dangerous blondes in **Dangerous Blondes**, a low-key thriller which used a come-hither title to conceal a *Thin Man*-inspired whodunnit set against a ritzy, high-society background. The mystery was duly solved by a writer of detective fiction who was an amateur sleuth. Allyn Joslyn (right) starred as the intrepid novelist who, with a little help from wife Evelyn Keyes (left), sets out to discover whether the owner of a photographic studio (Edmund Lowe, centre) murdered his wife (Ann Savage) or not. A tendency towards over-cuteness, in both the writing (screenplay by Richard Flournoy and Jack Henley) and direction (Leigh Jason), as well as in Joslyn's central performance, proved somewhat irksome, though, all things considered, the end result could have been a lot worse. Anita Louise, Frank Craven, Michael Duane, William Demarest, Hobart Cavanaugh, Frank Sully and Robert Stanford had featured roles in this Samuel Bischoff production. (81 mins)

▷ A no-holds-barred bar-room brawl, a thrilling wild horse stampede, and an exciting gunfight provided the action in **Desperadoes**, a big-budget Western and the studio's first venture into 3-colour Technicolor. For the rest, though, it was a formula horse-opera with all the usual ingredients of the genre left intact. Set in Utah in 1863, it starred Randolph Scott as the local sheriff and Glenn Ford (right) as a fugitive who wants to go straight. When a robbery and a couple of murders are pinned on Ford by the resident villains of the piece (Porter Hall and Bernard Nedell), Scott helps him escape. Ford soon returns to clear his name by smoking out the baddies. Robert Carson's anachronistic screenplay (there's a reference in it to Custer's Last Stand, which took place 13 years later!) from a story by Max Brand, was so cliché-logged it was difficult for the actors to make themselves heard above the rattle of the platitudes; and when they weren't being bogged down by the plot, they were being upstaged by the Technicolor. Still, there was enough action to keep the punters happy, and Charles Vidor's direction made the most of the familiar material at his disposal. Producer Harry Joe Brown's cast also included Evelyn Keyes (right, as Ford's romantic interest), Claire Trevor (as the owner of the town's hotel-cum-gambling-joint), Guinn Williams (as an outlaw pal of Ford's), Edgar Buchanan (as the droll postmaster, and the brains behind a gang of outlaws), and Raymond Walburn (as the judge). (85 mins)

▽ **Boy From Stalingrad** was a down-beat war drama in which a group of children, including a young English lad searching for the Nazi major who shot his father, attempt, with partial success, to hold a small Russian village against a German attack. Ferdinand Reyher wrote the screenplay from a story by Robert Arden and Robert Lee Johnson;

Colbert Clark produced, and Sidney Salkow directed. Apart from young Scotty Beckett (second left), the cast comprised unknowns, among them Bobby Samarzich (left), Conrad Binyon (third left), Mary Lou Harrington, Steven Muller (second right), Donald Mayo, John E. Wengraf (right) and Erik Rolf. (69 mins)

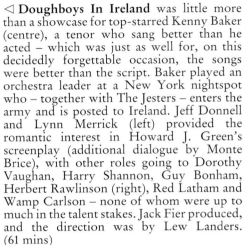

◁ **Doughboys In Ireland** was little more than a showcase for top-starred Kenny Baker (centre), a tenor who sang better than he acted – which was just as well for, on this decidedly forgettable occasion, the songs were better than the script. Baker played an orchestra leader at a New York nightspot who – together with The Jesters – enters the army and is posted to Ireland. Jeff Donnell and Lynn Merrick (left) provided the romantic interest in Howard J. Green's screenplay (additional dialogue by Monte Brice), with other roles going to Dorothy Vaughan, Harry Shannon, Guy Bonham, Herbert Rawlinson (right), Red Latham and Wamp Carlson – none of whom were up to much in the talent stakes. Jack Fier produced, and the direction was by Lew Landers. (61 mins)

△ An aura of artifice pervaded **First Comes Courage** which, like the previous year's *The Commandos Strike At Dawn*, was set on the Norwegian coast. Top-cast Merle Oberon (left) starred as a courageous Norwegian who befriends a Nazi major (Carl Esmond, right) not because she enjoys his company, but in order to ferret out of him vital military information which she dispatches to England via a doctor friend (Fritz Leiber). Complications ensue with the arrival of Brian Aherne as a British commando who, aware of what Oberon is doing, falls in love with her. Several plot contrivances later, Aherne tries to persuade Oberon to return to England with him, but feeling that her undercover work is not yet done, she refuses and they all live unhappily ever after. Neither Oberon nor Aherne brought even a smidgin of credibility to their ill-written roles (script by George Sklar, Lewis Meltzer and Melvin Levy from a story by Elliott Arnold) and, under Dorothy Arzner's earnest direction, made little impact. Harry Joe Brown's well-intentioned though lifeless production also featured Erville Alderson, Erik Rolf, Reinhold Schunzel and, as a nurse, Isobel Elsom. (86 mins)

▽ Jess Barker (right) had a pretty rough time in **Good Luck, Mr Yates**. As the titular hero, a lecturer in a military academy, he suffers the scorn of his students because he's not in uniform. The trouble is, he's been classified 4-F due to a pierced eardrum. Barker takes a job in a shipyard, pretends to his students that he's enlisted, and encourages them to write to him at camp. The letters are then forwarded to him by a soldier friend who is aware of the deception. Unfortunately, Barker's actions lead to the belief that he's a deserter. Not only that, but after having his ear treated by the heavily accented Albert Basserman, there's a rumour that he may be a Nazi spy! Lou Breslow and Adele Comandini's screenplay, from a fanciful story by Hal Smith and Sam Rudd, finally put things to rights by having our hero prove himself during a shipyard fire. Romantic interest was supplied by Claire Trevor (centre), with other parts going to Edgar Buchanan (left), Tom Neal, Tommy Cook, Frank Sully, Douglas Leavitt and, as a juvenile-delinquet cadet, Scotty Beckett. David Chakin produced, and Ray Enright directed, at far too slow a pace. (69 mins)

△ A spindly effort from all concerned, **Junior Army** was the one in which an aimless young drifter, with seemingly no potential, proves himself in a military academy by capturing a group of saboteurs about to make a getaway in a plane. Billy Halop (second left), once again reprising his Dead End characterization, played the hobo who makes good, though top-billing went to Freddie Bartholomew (centre) as an English refugee also at the academy. Bobby Jordan (left), Huntz Hall (right) and Billy Lechner played cadets, while the adults in Paul Gangelin's childish screenplay (story by Albert Bein) were represented by Boyd Davis, William Blees, Richard Noyes, Joseph Crehan and Don Beddoe. Colbert Clark produced and Lew Landers directed. (70 mins)

▷ **The Heat's On** (GB: **Tropicana**) was a decidedly tepid musical which lured a slimmed-down, but still curvaceous Mae West (right) back to the cameras after a three-year absence. She played a musical-comedy star caught at the centre of a feud between a pair of rival producers – Victor Moore (centre) and William Gaxton. Although the familiar West persona was still in evidence, scenarists Fitzroy Davis, George S. George and Fred Schiller failed to provide her with sufficient straw with which to make her verbal brick-bats. In the end, viewers were left with a feeble backstage plot, insecurely buttressed by several undistinguished production numbers (choreography by David Lichine). Alan Dinehart, Mary Roche (left), Almira Sessions and Lloyd Bridges were there to further the story, while providing the musical programme were Xavier Cugat and his Orchestra, vocalist Lina Romay and Hazel Scott. Gregory Ratoff directed for producer Milton Carter. (79 mins)

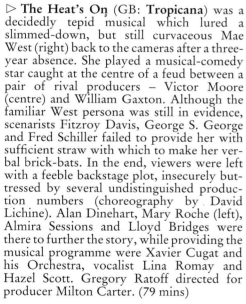

◁ Clarinettist Ted Lewis's catch-phrase **Is Everybody Happy?** provided the title for this corny-copia of songs (18 in all). While at an Army camp Lewis convinces a courting serviceman to marry immediately and not wait until the war is over. In flashback, Lewis tells the story of a pianist (Larry Parks) who, in World War I, had his hand damaged in the trenches but returned home to marry his sweetheart (Nan Wynn, left) and to take up the trumpet instead. It turns out that the couple at the centre of Lewis's tale are the serviceman's parents, who happen to be his best friends – though why the lad wasn't aware of all this was never explained in Monte Brice's warmed-over screenplay. Irving Briskin's production also featured Michael Duane (right), Lynn Merrick, Bob Haymes, Dick Winslow and Harry Barris. Charles Barton directed. (73 mins)

119

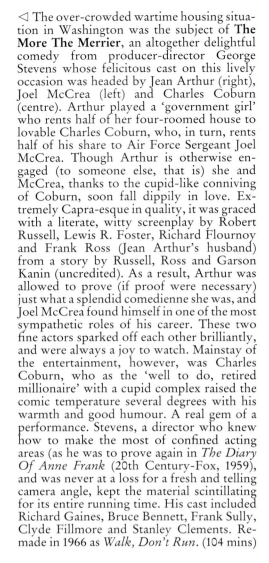

◁ The over-crowded wartime housing situation in Washington was the subject of **The More The Merrier**, an altogether delightful comedy from producer-director George Stevens whose felicitous cast on this lively occasion was headed by Jean Arthur (right), Joel McCrea (left) and Charles Coburn (centre). Arthur played a 'government girl' who rents half of her four-roomed house to lovable Charles Coburn, who, in turn, rents half of his share to Air Force Sergeant Joel McCrea. Though Arthur is otherwise engaged (to someone else, that is) she and McCrea, thanks to the cupid-like conniving of Coburn, soon fall dippily in love. Extremely Capra-esque in quality, it was graced with a literate, witty screenplay by Robert Russell, Lewis R. Foster, Richard Flournoy and Frank Ross (Jean Arthur's husband) from a story by Russell, Ross and Garson Kanin (uncredited). As a result, Arthur was allowed to prove (if proof were necessary) just what a splendid comedienne she was, and Joel McCrea found himself in one of the most sympathetic roles of his career. These two fine actors sparked off each other brilliantly, and were always a joy to watch. Mainstay of the entertainment, however, was Charles Coburn, who as the 'well to do, retired millionaire' with a cupid complex raised the comic temperature several degrees with his warmth and good humour. A real gem of a performance. Stevens, a director who knew how to make the most of confined acting areas (as he was to prove again in *The Diary Of Anne Frank* (20th Century-Fox, 1959), and was never at a loss for a fresh and telling camera angle, kept the material scintillating for its entire running time. His cast included Richard Gaines, Bruce Bennett, Frank Sully, Clyde Fillmore and Stanley Clements. Remade in 1966 as *Walk, Don't Run*. (104 mins)

◁ The efforts of a talented but unemployed young actor (Bert Gordon, centre) to find employment in his chosen profession was the subject of **Let's Have Fun**, a comedy of no particular merit that also featured Leonid Kinskey as Boris, an equally indigent producer-cum-choreographer. How the pair, aided by pretty agent Margaret Lindsay, finally find the success they've been looking for lay at the heart of Harry Sauber's routine screenplay. John Beal (right, arms folded), Sig Arno (left) and Dorothy Ann Seese were also in it, Jack Fier produced, and the director was Charles Barton. (63 mins)

▷ Scenarists Harry Sauber and Ned Dandy made it impossible to **Laugh Your Blues Away**, as they only wrote a trite little comedy (with songs by Larry Marks and Dick Charles). An inane non-starter about a once-wealthy dowager (Isobel Elsom) determined to marry her son (Douglas Drake, right) to the daughter (Phyllis Kennedy) of a wealthy Texan cattleman (Dick Elliott), it also starred Jinx Falkenburg (left) and Bert Gordon as a pair of out-of-work actors who agree to pose as Russian aristocrats in order to impress the cattleman. Their ploy also gave Gordon, a popular radio comedian of the period known as 'the mad Russian', a chance to reprise his well-known characterization on celluloid. No dice. Jack Fier produced and Charles Barton directed. (65 mins)

◁ In **Murder In Times Square**, John Litel played a doctor who, driven to murder through unrequited love, kills four people by stabbing them with a hypodermic needle containing snake venom. A pair of sub-plots involved the blackmail of an arrogant actor-cum-playwright – Edmund Lowe (centre left), top-starred – by a Times Square panhandler called Longacre Lil (Esther Dale), and a romance between Lowe and his press agent (Marguerite Chapman, right). Paul Gangalin's screenplay from a story by Stuart Palmer provided an hour or so of mild diversion. Also cast: Veda Ann Borg, Bruce Bennett (second right), William Wright and George McKay (third left). Colbert Clark produced, and Lew Landers's direction kept it buoyant. (65 mins)

▷ A backstage musical without a difference, **Something To Shout About** was a tired re-tread of *42nd Street* (Warner Bros., 1933) with Janet Blair (centre) in the Ruby Keeler role as the out-of-towner (this time it's Altoona) who finds everlasting Broadway stardom after replacing the untalented leading lady (Cobina Wright Jr) on the opening night. Momentarily underpinning the screenplay (which Lou Breslow, Edward Eliscu and George Owen carbon-copied from Fred Schiller's stencilled plot) were a few passable Cole Porter numbers, the best, by far, being 'You'd Be So Nice To Come Home To'. The art of the Hollywood musical wasn't advanced an iota by David Lichine's choreography, or producer Gregory Ratoff's pedestrian direction. An attractive cast that also included top-starred Don Ameche (left), as well as stalwarts Jack Oakie and William Gaxton, were hampered by the mediocrity of the material. Also cast: Veda Ann Borg, Hazel Scott (as herself), The Bricklayers, Teddy Wilson and his Band, and a newcomer called Lily Norwood (real name Tula Finklea) who'd soon become better known as Cyd Charisse. (88 mins)

◁ **A Night To Remember** was a film to forget. Following in the more successful footsteps of the previous year's *My Sister Eileen*, this comedy-thriller was also set in a Greenwich village basement, starred Brian Aherne (left), not as an editor this time, but as a writer, and also featured Jeff Donnell as the married occupant of an upstairs flat. Top-cast, though, was Loretta Young (right), who, concerned that hubbie Aherne only writes thrillers, persuades him to move into New York's Greenwich Village (No. 13, Gay Street, to be precise) in the hope that these more romantic surroundings will inspire him to write a love story for a change. When, however, the body of a dead man is found in their backyard, her best-laid plans go awry as Aherne hangs up his typewriter in order to indulge in a spot of amateur sleuthing. Helping to divert attention away from the rather mundane proceedings in the Richard Flournoy-Jack Henley screenplay (story by Kelley Roos) was a thoroughly professional cast that included Sidney Toler (taking time off from his Charlie Chan character) as a police inspector and Blanche Yurka as a nutty charwoman, as well as William Wright, Gale Sondergaard, Donald MacBride, Lee Patrick, Don Costello and Richard Gaines. One way or another, they were all more fun than the material on hand. The camerman was Joseph Walker and the flat direction was by Richard Wallace for producer Sam Bischoff. (92 mins)

▽ **No Place For A Lady** was no film for the connoisseur. A threadbare mystery which kept audiences wondering why they'd bothered to waste their time and money on it, it starred William Gargan (second right) as a detective who uncovers the mystery behind the slaying of a wealthy widow (Doris Lloyd). It seems the killer (Jerome Cowan, right) murdered the old broad for her collection of tyres! As motives went, this was definitely a 'first'. (Credit scenarist Eric Taylor for the topical idea.) Also cast: Margaret Lindsay (third left) as Gargan's fiancée, Dick Purcell (centre) Edward Norris (standing) and Thomas Jackson. Ralph Cohn produced and James Hogan directed. (66 mins)

◁ Bearing no relation to the studio's 1928 silent of the same name, **Power Of The Press** was a melodrama about an unscrupulous press baron (Otto Kruger, fourth left) who'll stop at nothing – including murder – to get his evil way. The good guy in Samuel Fuller's improbable yarn (screenplay by Robert D. Andrews) was Lee Tracy (centre left) as the managing editor of the newspaper owned by Kruger, while top-starred Guy Kibbee (third right) appeared as a typical country editor. Others involved in this slender melodrama were Gloria Dickson (centre right) as Tracy's loyal secretary and Victor Jory as a gunman, as well as Larry Parks, Rex Williams, Minor Watson, Don Beddoe (right) and Frank Sully (centre), Leon Barsha's production was directed by Lew Landers. (64 mins)

▽ Mistaken identity was the theme of Rex Taylor's story for **Redhead From Manhattan**. Lupe Velez (second left) stretched her range by playing twin sisters – Rita and Elaine. When sister Elaine, a Broadway star, comes down with a bout of marital difficulties, Rita switches places with her. The consequences of this move are mind-boggling. The story called for gangsters, the FBI, a producer with a dislike for married women in his shows, and a massive suspension of disbelief. Michael Duane (second right), Tim Ryan, Gerald Mohr and Lilian Yarbo were also featured; Wallace MacDonald produced, and Lew Landers directed. (63 mins)

▽ Deception ran rife throughout **She Has What It Takes**, a comedy with songs about a singer of no consequence (Jinx Falkenburg, second right) who pretends to be the daughter of a recently deceased stage star. Her reason? To hoodwink a Broadway producer into starring her in a show meant as a tribute to her supposed mother. Also cast: Joe King, Constance Worth, Alma Carroll (left), Ernie Adams (third left) and Tyler Brooke (right). Paul Yawitz wrote the screenplay from a story he devised with Robert Lee Johnson. Colbert Clark produced and Charles Barton directed. (66 mins)

▷ Despite its meagre budget ($40,000) and meagre plot (girl disc-jockey works on a radio show that caters to soldiers in a nearby army camp), **Reveille With Beverly** turned a handsome profit for the studio. No doubt responsible for this windfall was the one-song appearance of the country's favourite teen idol, Frank Sinatra. He sang Cole Porter's standard 'Night And Day' and had all the girls in the audiences swooning in the aisles. The musical programme also included contributions from The Mills Brothers, Bob Crosby, Freddie Slack, Duke Ellington and Count Basie and their Orchestras as well as the Radio Rogues. The 'rise and shine' disc jockey was top-billed Ann Miller (centre) whose tap shoes would be put to far better use when she left the studio for MGM. Also cast in Sam White's production were William Wright, Dick Purcell, Franklin Pangborn, Tim Ryan, Larry Parks and Adele Mara. Charles Barton directed. (78 mins)

△ Directed with sweaty realism by Zoltan Korda, **Sahara**, which was inspired by an incident in the 1937 Soviet film *Trinadstat* (*The Thirteen*), was far and away one of the best of the plethora of war films inundating the world's screens at that time. Written by Korda and John Howard Lawson, from a story by Philip MacDonald, and adapted by James O'Hanlon, the plot followed a group of six Allied Forces' stragglers plus a Sudanese soldier, an Italian prisoner-of-war and a downed Nazi pilot – all of them stranded in the desert after the fall of Tobruk in 1942. Attaching themselves to an American tank crew commanded by Sergeant Joe Gunn (Humphrey Bogart, second left), they head off into the desert until they reach an abandoned well where they eventually make a stand against a motorized Nazi battalion who are also heading for the precious water supply. Apart from the advancing Germans, Bogart and his assorted desert rats also have to face sand, heat and thirst, all of which take their toll as the story unfurls. Korda, for whom the desert was a home from home, made audiences experience the intense heat, the agony of thirst and the discomfort engendered by billowing sand, without recourse to cheap theatrical tricks or melodrama. His was an honest depiction of a real situation and if, in the end, the he-man heroics of Bogart brought to mind the gung-ho *Boy's Own* idealism of *The Lost Patrol* (RKO, 1934), the film's heart was definitely in the right place. Besides, Bogart was perfectly cast as Gunn, and defending himself (with the help of Patrick O'Moore, as his sole surviving tankman) against 500 or so Germans seemed the most natural thing in the world for him to do. Rex Ingram was featured as the Sudanese soldier, J. Carrol Naish as the Italian prisoner of war, and Kurt Kreuger as the captured Nazi pilot. Louis T. Mercier played a Frenchman, Bruce Bennett (left) and Dan Duryea were American tank crewmen, with other roles taken effectively by Lloyd Bridges, Richard Nugent (centre), Carl Harbord and Guy Kingsford. The only 'female' in the cast was Bogart's 28-ton tank, the *Luluhelle* which, next to Bogey himself, was the star of the show. The outstanding photography was the work of Rudolph Maté. Remade as *Last Of The Commanches* (1952). (95 mins)

▽ An unashamed re-working of the plot for *Two Latins From Manhattan* (1941), **Two Senoritas From Chicago** featured Jinx Falkenburg (right) and Ann Savage as a pair of actresses who, sporting phoney Portuguese accents, pass themselves off as the sisters of the authors of a discarded, Portuguese play and, as such, con their way into the two leading roles. Enter the real authors who sell the play to another producer. Such were the machinations of the Stanley Rubin-Maurice Tombragel screenplay (story by Steven Vas), which furnished a starring role for Joan Davis (second left) as a Chicago hotel refuse-sorter who just so happens to be a play agent on the side, and the person responsible for setting the plot in motion. Leslie Brooks (second right) and Ramsey Ames played a pair of hoofers who blow the gaff on the girls; Emory Parnell was a producer, with other parts going to Bob Haymes (left), Douglas Leavitt, Stanley Brown and Frank Sully. Wallace MacDonald produced and his director was Frank Woodruff. (63 mins)

△ Ann Miller (third right) starred in **What's Buzzin' Cousin?** a paltry excuse for a musical in which the long-legged tap-dance kid devoted her energies to refurbishing a hotel she has inherited in a ghost town. Assisting her were Eddie (Rochester) Anderson (kneeling), John Hubbard (second right), Leslie Brooks (left), Jeff Donnell (right), Carol Hughes, Theresa Harris (third left) and Roy Gordon. The screenplay was by Harry Sauber and John P. Medbury (story by Aben Kandel), the choreography by Nick Castle, the direction by Charles Barton, and the production by Jack Fier. (75 mins)

▷ Old codger Charles Coburn (right) was given star billing for the first time in **My Kingdom For A Cook**, a comedy which would definitely have benefited from a more seasoned script and a few hearty laughs. Coburn played Rudyard Morley, an eccentric ambassador from the court of St James, and a Shaw-like author, on a goodwill lecture trip to the USA. Unfortunately, his English cook has been unable to accompany him, and – being something of a gourmet – this upset becomes a major catastrophe; so much so, that he is forced to steal a cook of 18-years' duration from a New England socialite (Isobel Elsom). A romance between the socialite's son (an inexperienced Bill Carter) and Coburn's daughter (Marguerite Chapman, left) further complicated the undernourished screenplay by Harold Goldman, Andrew Solt, Joseph Hoffman, Jack Henley, story by Solt and Lili Hatvany. Edward Gargan, Mary Wickes, Almira Sessions (as the cook) and Eddy Waller also had parts in P. J. Wolfson's production. The director was Richard Wallace. (81 mins)

◁ The third pairing of Rosalind Russell (centre) and Brian Aherne (right), **What A Woman!** (GB: **The Beautiful Cheat**) told the (incredible) story of a powerful agent (Russell) and her burgeoning romance with a journalist (Aherne) who comes to interview her. The sub-plot involved Russell's attempts to persuade the author (Willard Parker second right) of a book she has recently sold to Hollywood to play the leading role in the film himself. As scripted by Therese Lewis and Barry Trivers (story by Erik Charell) it added up to precious little, though the spectacle of a somewhat mis-cast Aherne taming the over-confident career-woman Russell provided some amusing moments, and again allowed Russell to demonstrate that, as a comedienne, she was one of the very best in the business. The film was produced and directed by Irving Cummings with a cast that included Alan Dinehart (left), Edward Fielding, Ann Savage, Norma Varden (second left) Grady Sutton and, making her screen debut in a bit part, Shelley Winter (later Winters). (94 mins)

▷ Nina Foch received star billing in **Cry Of The Werewolf** and played Celeste, the gypsy daughter of a deceased New Orleans belle. The belle is now secretly entombed in a museum and fanatically guarded by Foch – who, it transpires, is a werewolf and will stop at nothing to protect the whereabouts of her dead mother (from whom she inherited the curse). Dreadfully old-hat, even by Forties programmer standards, it got by simply on the strength of Foch's performance – and nothing more. Griffin Jay and Charles O'Neal scripted it, with parts for Blanche Yurka, Stephen Crane, Osa Massen, Barton MacLane (centre), Ivan Triesault and Robert Williams (left); it was directed by Henry Levin with little flair, and produced on a B-minus budget by Wallace MacDonald. (63 mins)

△ **The Ghost That Walks Alone** starred Arthur Lake (second right) as a radio-station sound-effects man whose honeymoon takes a turn for the worse when he discovers a corpse in his hotel room. For the record, the screenplay was written by Clarence Upson Young from a story by Richard Shattuck. Jack Fier produced, Lew Landers directed, and the cast featured Janis Carter (right), Lynne Roberts, Frank Sully (third right), Warren Ashe (left), Barbara Brown (second left) and Arthur Space (third left). (63 mins)

▷ The studio's attempt to team Edmund Lowe (left) and Janis Carter (right) in answer to MGM's William Powell and Myrna Loy failed woefully – as lovers of the detective yarn discovered in **Girl In The Case**. Lowe played a lawyer with a penchant for lock-picking who finds himself involved with enemy agents after agreeing to open an old chest belonging to mysterious Robert Scott. Though director William Berke kept the action moving, he was under-serviced by scenarists Joseph Hoffman and Dorcas Cochran (story by Charles F. Royal) whose screenplay was deficient in humour. Sam White's production also featured Robert Williams, Richard Hale, Stanley Clements, Carole Matthews and Robert Scott. (65 mins)

▽ An enjoyable, light-headed, lightweight, low-budget comedy with songs, **Ever Since Venus** told the story of how lipstick manufacturer Ross Hunter (centre), with a little assistance from Hugh Herbert (second right) and Billy Gilbert (left), manages, after several trials and tribulations, to launch a new lipstick he has invented. About as taxing as 2+2, it added up to an agreeable entertainment that also featured (prominently) Ina Ray Hutton playing herself, Ann Savage, Glenda Farrell (right), Alan Mowbray, Marjorie Gateson, Thurston Hall, Fritz Feld (second left) and Dudley Dickerson. It was snappily directed by Arthur Dreifuss who also co-scripted with McElbert Moore. (74 mins)

▽ Ex-radio announcer Jim Bannon received top-billing for **Missing Juror**, a routine quickie that in no way disgraced its production team as it recounted the story of a phantom murderer who has, so far, eliminated six members of a jury responsible for sending a murderer to the chair. Bannon played a reporter who trails the remaining half-dozen jurors, and while in the process of uncovering the identity of the culprit unleashes the tale's twist ending. Janis Carter (left) played Bannon's sweetheart and Jean Stevens his secretary, with other roles in Wallace MacDonald's tidy little package going to George Macready (right), the studio's favourite heavy, Joseph Crehan, Carole Mathews and Mike Mazurki. Budd Boetticher directed from a screenplay by Charles O'Neal. (66 mins)

△ Ann Miller (right) starred in **Jam Session**, a B musical in which she played a country girl whose prize for winning a dance contest is a trip to Hollywood. In Tinsel Town she meets and falls in love with scriptwriter Jess Barker. So much for the thin skein of plot (by Harlan Ware and Patterson McNutt, screenplay by Manny Seff) on which was hung about a dozen musical numbers (staged by Stanley Donen), none of them particularly distinguished, an observation which might also be made of the supporting cast, who included Charles D. Brown, Eddie Kane, George Eldredge, Bill Shawn (left), Clarence Muse and Pauline Drake. Irving Briskin's production also featured several top orchestras under the direction of Louis Armstrong, Charlie Barnet, Jan Garber, Teddy Powell, Alvino Rey and Glen Gray – as well as The Pied Pipers and singer Nan Wynn. The director was Charles Barton. (78 minutes)

▷ In **The Impatient Years**, scenarist Virginia Van Upp made heavy weather of a situation in which a husband and wife, who've been married for eighteen months but have had to endure an enforced separation because of the war, find, on the husband's return, that their marriage may have been a dreadful mistake. True, the couple in question married after a hasty four-day courtship. But the reticence, the suspicion and the embarrassment displayed by both parties (especially the wife) were hard to accept. Throughout the film there was the nagging belief that, in real life, it would all have been so different; and that the situation could so easily have been remedied with a mixture of compassion, understanding and commonsense. The difficult period of adjustment men and women had to face at the war's end would receive its definitive expression in William Wyler's masterly *The Best Years Of Our Lives* (Goldwyn, 1946). This attempt to deal with a similar subject irritated more than it entertained. Jean Arthur (right) starred as the wife, and was far too intelligent an actress to make believable her confusion, while Lee Bowman (centre) as her returning husband was simply pathetic. Charles Coburn (left) was cast as Arthur's sympathetic father, with other roles in producer-director Irving Cummings' disappointing comedy going to Edgar Buchanan, Charley Grapewin, Phil Brown, Harry Davenport and Jane Darwell. Co-producer Van Upp ensured a happy ending through a ploy whereby the estranged couple re-live their honeymoon in an attempt to kindle the old romantic spark. A visit from the stork helped as well. (91 mins)

◁ Top-starred Joan Davis (right) played a song-plugger in **Kansas City Kitty**, a meagre excuse for a musical in which she's tricked into purchasing a music-publishing house, one of whose composers immediately saddles her with a plagiarism suit. Seems that his song 'Kansas City Kitty' wasn't written by the cowboy whose name is on it, but by himself. Matt Willis (left) as the aggrieved composer, with Bob Crosby, Jane Frazee, Erik Rolf, Tim Ryan and Robert Emmett Keane also featured. The screenplay was written by Manny Seff who couldn't have burned up too many brain-cells in the process. Ted Richmond produced, and Del Lord directed. (72 mins)

▷ Judy Canova (second left) returned to the sticks for her familiar hayseed characterization in **Louisiana Hayride** – a laugh-sparse farce, with a couple of songs, in which she played a film-struck hick who, in the course of Paul Yawitz's screenplay (story by Yawitz and Manny Seff), gets the better of a pair of con-men (Richard Lane, left; and George McKay). The bad guys, it seems, have appropriated some of the fortune she's accrued as a result of an oil discovery on her farm. Ross Hunter (later to become a successful producer at Universal) co-starred, with other parts in producer-director Charles Barton's opus going to Lloyd Bridges, Matt Willis (second right), Minerva Urecal, Hobart Cavanaugh (right) and Eddie Kane. (67 mins)

△ **Meet Miss Bobby Socks** bored the pants off its punters for just over an hour as it charted the rise to mega-popularity of a crooner shortly after he returns to civvies from the war. Bob Crosby (right) was what all the fuss was about – and he was aided in his endeavours by Lynn Merrick, Louise Erickson (left), Howard Barnes and Robert White. Ted Richmond's indigent production hardly bankrupted the studio; it was directed by Glenn Tryon and written by Muriel Roy Bolton. They didn't come much worse than this. (68 mins)

▽ Based on a long-running play by K. B. Colvan and Doris Culvan, **Hey, Rookie** recounted the efforts of an enlisted producer to produce an army show on a shoestring budget of $209. The producer in question was Larry Parks. Ann Miller (illustrated) co-starred as Parks' former leading lady; Joe Besser (top-starred) and Jimmy Little provided (ad nauseam) the 'comic' relief, with other roles in producer Irving Briskin's modestly diverting musical shared out among Joe Sawyer, Selmer Jackson, Larry Thompson, Barbara Brown, Charles Trowbridge, and Charles Wilson. Helping to make Parks' musical staging a success was choreographer Val Raset. [In the dance sequence 'Streamlined Sheiks', Ms Miller set the world record of 550 taps per minute.] Apart from Ms Miller, the song and dance talent was supplied by Hi Lo Jack And A Dame, The Condos Brothers, The Vagabonds, The Johnson Brothers, Judy Clark And The Solid Senders, and Bob Evans. Jack Gilford was in it too. The screenplay was written by Henry Myers, Edward Eliscu and Jay Gorney. Charles Barton directed. (71 mins)

◁ With so many leading men actively involved in the war effort, the studio had the happy notion of concocting a thriller which gave the distaff side a chance to take centre screen. The diverting result was **Nine Girls**. Set in a small Californian sorority college, headed by Ann Harding, the plot revolved around the murder of Anita Louise – one of the nastiest broads on the campus. Several of her colleagues had good reason to do away with her – specially Nina Foch, who has been threatened with blackmail, and Evelyn Keyes (left), whose brother's legal problems the hateful Ms Louise has promised to expose. So, whodunnit? All was duly revealed in the pithy screenplay by Blondie regulars Connie Lee and Karen De Wolf – but not before a good (and suspenseful) time was had by all. The female side of the cast was completed by Jinx Falkenburg (right), Leslie Brooks, Lynn Merrick (doing a great imitation of Katharine Hepburn), Jeff Donnell, Shirley Mills, Shelley Winter and Marcia Mae Jones. The men were represented by reliable William Demarest, Willard Robertson, Lester Matthews and Grady Sutton. Burt Kelly produced and the neat direction was by Leigh Jason. (78 mins)

△ Director André de Toth's sombre and anguished **None Shall Escape** was a virulent condemnation of Nazi ideology in which top-starred Alexander Knox (second left), as a Reich commander, was made to symbolize all that was evil in Hitler's brutal régime. Using a lengthy flashback to trace the rise of Knox's Nazism, Lester Cole's intelligent screenplay (from a story by Alfred Neuman and Joseph Thau) depicted Knox as an embittered, crippled German soldier who, after World War I, resumes his post as a teacher in a small Polish village near the German border. After losing the love of his fiancée because of his vengeful ideology, and violating one of his girl students, he is forced to leave the village, whereupon he joins the Nazi party. After the invasion of Poland and the outbreak of World War II, Knox returns to the same village of his youth in order to vent his wrathful spleen on the villagers, all of whom he considers 'idiots'. This searing, serious-minded drama also starred Marsha Hunt (wearing headscarf) as Knox's fiancée, and in smaller roles featured Henry Travers, Erik Rolf, Richard Crane (third left), Dorothy Morris (lying down), Ruth Nelson, Kurt Kreuger (left), and, as a rabbi, the excellent Richard Hale. The producer was Samuel Bischoff. (85 mins)

△ **Once Upon A Time** was the story of a dancing caterpillar. Based on a radio play called *My Client Curly* by Norman Corwin, from an idea by Lucille Fletcher Herrmann, and written for the screen by Lewis Meltzer and Oscar Saul (adaptation by Irving Fineman), this disastrous fantasy starred Cary Grant (centre) as a failed Broadway producer who, learning of the existence of a dancing caterpillar (whose speciality is 'Yes Sir, That's My Baby') owned by youngster Ted Donaldson (right), acquires the miraculous insect with a view to exploiting its commercial worth. When Walt Disney offers him $100,000 for it, he knows he's on to something big. What little drama there was revolved around the young lad's heartbreak at the disappearance of his pet caterpillar. A happy ending eventually found the caterpillar turning into a butterfly, and Grant finding recompense in the arms of Janet Blair (left), Donaldson's pretty sister. As the pivotal caterpillar was never seen, the vote for the most cringe-making performance of the year went, instead, to young master Donaldson. Also cast: James Gleason as Grant's right-hand man, Howard Freeman, William Demarest, Art Baker and Paul Stanton. Alexander Hall directed and Louis Edelman produced. (89 mins)

▽ Edward G. Robinson (right) – best known for his tough-guy roles – was cast against type in **Mr Winkle Goes To War** (GB: **Arms And The Woman**). The routine plot offered little more than the edifying sight of a 44-year-old, hen-pecked milquetoast being inducted into the Army and, against all the odds (and in defiance of credibility), leaving it a hero when, in the South Pacific, he drives a bulldozer at a fox-hole concealing a nest of Japs. Audiences able to accept Robinson as a meek bank-clerk-turned-war-hero doubtless enjoyed it all. Those who couldn't, didn't. Ruth Warrick was cast as his mean wife. Young Ted Donaldson (so objectionable in *Once Upon A Time*) was fine as an orphan whom Robinson befriends, with other roles under Alfred E. Green's stolid direction divided between Bob Haymes, Richard Lane and Robert Armstrong (all as soldiers), Richard Gaines, Walter Baldwin, Art Smith and Ann Shoemaker. The rather stale screenplay was the work of Waldo Salt, George Corey and Louis Solomon, from the novel by Theodore Pratt. Jack Moss's production used stock footage of the Pacific Islands Invasion to supply some action. (78 mins).

1944

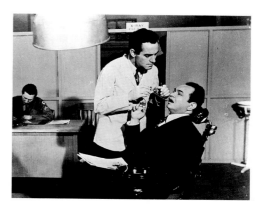

▽ Master racketeer Matt Benson (Torn Neal, centre) was the chief character in **The Racket Man**, a melodrama based on a story by Casey Robinson, and first seen in 1931 as *The Last Parade*. Basically the yarn of a hood who makes good after being inducted into the Army and where his commanding officer orders him to wage undercover war against black marketeers, it was scripted to formula by Paul Yawitz and Howard Green, produced by Wallace MacDonald, and directed for the programmer it was by D. Ross Lederman. Tom Neal almost achieved the impossible in producing a performance that was even more wooden than his dialogue. Jeanne Bates played Neal's love interest, with Hugh Beaumont, Larry Parks, Douglas Fowley, Clarence Muse, Mary Gordon, Anthony Caruso (left) and Warren Ashe also cast. Strictly forgettable. (65 mins)

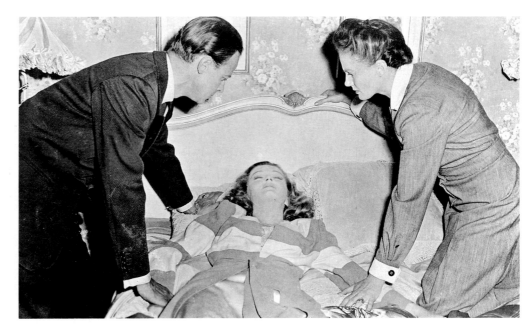

▷ As Universal owned the Dracula copyright, Griffin Jay's screenplay for **Return Of The Vampire** (from an idea by Kurt Neumann) was unable to refer to Bram Stoker's creation (again played by Bela Lugosi) by name. Instead, the nocturnal count was renamed Armand Tessla, a vampire who, disturbed by World War II bombs, shakes off the cobwebs from his crypt and, in company with a werewolf (Matt Willis), goes in search of fresh young blood. Though his nemesis is the proprietor (Frieda Inescort, right) of a nearby asylum, it's werewolf Willis who finally puts paid to Tessla's antisocial behaviour by plunging a dreaded crucifix into his heart. The vampire's climactic deterioration was, under Lew Landers's graphic direction, considered unpalatable by the British Board of Censors who excised the scene from United Kingdom prints. Nina Foch (centre) here made her debut, and Roland Varno and Miles Mander were also in it. The effective, genuinely scary production was overseered by producer Sam White. (69 mins)

▷ Though Arthur Lake (seated), taking time off from his Dagwood chores, Bob Haymes and Lewis Wilson (as marines) were the three leading men in **Sailor's Holiday**, the real star of this lightweight, thin-as-air comedy was Columbia studios, a tour of whose backlot was the highlight of the show. The plot was a mere trifle in which two of the three marines break off their engagements after being charmed by other women. Jane Lawrence and Shelley Winter were the gals in Manny Seff's screenplay, with Edmund MacDonald, Pat O'Malley, Herbert Rawlinson and Buddy Yarus in support. Wallace MacDonald produced, and it was directed for the chore it was by William Berke. (60 mins)

◁ A fist-flying espionage melodrama, **Secret Command**, written by Roy Chanslor and based on a story called *The Saboteurs* by John and Ward Hawkins, starred Pat O'Brien (right) – whose company, Torneen, also produced – as Irishman Sam Gallagher, a member of the FBI who, on learning that the Nazis plan to sabotage a West Coast shipyard, gets himself a job there in order to ferret out as much information as he can. O'Brien is provided with a 'wife' (Carole Landis, centre) and two ready-made children, as well as a house near the shipyard. Not surprisingly, O'Brien's brother (Chester Morris) finds the whole thing extremely suspicious ... Of course, the film ends with O'Brien's marriage of convenience turning into the real thing. The lusty hokum was directed with the accent on action by Irishman Edward Sutherland, and the predominantly Irish cast included Ruth Warrick (left), Barton MacLane, Tom Tully, Wallace Ford, Howard Freeman, Matt McHugh and Frank Sully. Not a great day for the Irish, but a good one. (82 mins)

◁ Director William Castle's fourth feature film was **She's A Soldier Too** – yet another undistinguished wartime drama in which a soldier (Lloyd Bridges, second right) enlists the aid of a female cab-driver (Nina Foch, left) to help him find the son he left behind years ago. Beulah Bondi (second left), Nina Foch and Jess Barker starred, and the film, written by Melvin Levy (story by Hal Smith), also featured Percy Kilbride, Ida Moore (right), Erik Rolf, Jeanne Bates, and Shelley Winter. Wallace MacDonald produced. (67 mins)

1944

▷ Writer Sidney Buchman dusted over the treatment Frank Capra had written for his proposed life of Chopin, and emerged with **A Song To Remember**, the studio's third venture into Technicolor – and a box-office blockbuster. Though Buchman's scenario (which contained more than its fair share of howlers) bore as little resemblance to the truth as did subsequent Hollywood biopics on the lives of Cole Porter, Jerome Kern, Rodgers and Hart and Sigmund Romberg (the list was endless) – it was crafted for maximum entertainment value, and, under Charles Vidor's schmaltzy direction, it delivered the goods. Music and plot shared equal billing in producer Louis F. Edelman's scheme of things. The music was adapted by Miklos Rozsa and played by José Iturbi; the plot acted out by a cast headed by Cornel Wilde (left) as Poland's greatest composer, Paul Muni (right) – way over the top – as his music professor, Merle Oberon (centre) as the alluring George Sand, and Stephen Bekassy as Liszt – with Nina Foch, George Coulouris, Sig Arno, Howard Freeman and George Macready in support. (113 mins)

▽ Time, thought, and money were three ingredients absent from **Soul Of A Monster**, a horror entry which on a scale of one to ten did well to register a two. Rose Hobart starred as a ghoulish hypnotist whose supernatural powers save a dying doctor (George Macready, right) – but at a terrible price: he is kept alive solely to perform a few of her evil deeds under hypnosis. How he is eventually saved from a fate worse than death (though nothing could save him from the fate of the film) was described in Edward Dein's soggy screenplay. Ted Richmond produced, Will Jason directed and the cast also included Jim Bannon (left), Jeanne Bates, Erik Rolf (left) and Ernest Hilliard. (61 mins)

▽ There were no real stars in **Stars On Parade**, even though its flimsy plot found room to showcase the musical talents of The King Cole Trio, The Chords, The Ben Carter Choir and tenor Danny O'Neill. Another 'Hey, kids, let's put on a show' effort, it featured Larry Parks (left) and Lynn Merrick (right) as two Hollywood hopefuls out to convince some producers in Los Angeles that there's a great deal of talent in their own backyard just waiting to be discovered. Monte Brice wrote it, Lew Landers directed and the producer was Wallace MacDonald. Also cast: Ray Walker, Jeff Donnell, Robert Williams and Selmer Jackson. (63 mins)

◁ Following their successful teaming in *Dangerous Blondes* (1943), Evelyn Keyes (centre) and Allyn Joslyn (right) starred in **The Strange Affair**, yet another variation on the mystery-writer-turned-real-life-sleuth theme. Instead of being a writer, though, Joslyn is the creator of comic-strip thrillers – who, away from the drawing board, enjoys his role as amateur detective. Keyes played his wife. The plot hinged on the case of fundraiser Erwin Kalser who drops dead at a banquet. Joslyn's investigations point to homicide by poisoning, and, much to the annoyance of the police, he proves to be correct. Oscar Saul, Eve Greene and Jerome Odlum wrote it (from a story by Saul), and crammed a fair amount of honest laughter into the dishonest goings-on. Alfred E. Green's direction, like everything else in sight, was best taken with a sizeable pinch of salt. Producer Burt Kelly's cast included Edgar Buchanan, Marguerite Chapman, Nina Foch, Hugo Haas, Shemp Howard and Frank Jenks (left). (78 mins)

▽ Crooner Bob Haymes was top-billed in **Swing Out The Blues**, an energetic lower-case musical, and was referred to in the script as 'the poor man's Sinatra'. Maybe, but he sang well and provided the perfect foil for The Vagabonds (the poor man's Ritz Brothers?). The plot had the latter trying to prevent the former from breaking up their partnership when Haymes and socialite Lynn Merrick (left) plan to marry. Enter complica-tions in the form of Janis Carter, The Vaga-bonds' agent who tries to stop the wedding from taking place. Tim Ryan, Joyce Comp-ton, Arthur Q. Bryan, John Eldridge (second left), Dick Elliott (second right) and Kathleen Howard (right) were also featured in Sam White's jolly little production; Dorcas Cochran wrote the screenplay from a story by Doris Malloy. The direction was by vet-eran Mal St Clair. (73 mins)

▽ The Officer Candidate School of the Anti-Aircraft Artillery Command at Camp Davis, North Carolina, was the setting of **There's Something About A Soldier**, a docu-drama that followed the fortunes of five cadets at the school. In between being made privy to the rigorous training programme undertaken on the premises, a plot of sorts (courtesy of Horace McCoy and Barry Trivers, who also supplied the screenplay) intruded, and it concerned a know-it-all novice who, through the good counselling of a girl and a North African campaign veteran, finally turns into a decent and responsible human being. Tom Neal (centre right) was the boy, Evelyn Keyes the girl and Bruce Bennett (right, foreground) the vet. Also cast: John Hubbard (centre, back turned), Lewis Wilson (left foreground), Robert Stanford, Jeff Donnell, Frank Sully and Jonathan Hale. The Samuel Bischoff production was direct-ed by Alfred E. Green. (81 mins)

◁ Wartime propaganda, but reduced to pro-grammer proportions, **They Live In Fear** starred Otto Kruger as a refugee from Nazi oppression whose concern for the safety of the family he left behind in Germany was the chief item on Michael L. Simmons and Sam Ornitz's screenplay (story by Wilfred Pettit). Jack Fier's production comprised a cast of relative unknowns: Clifford Severn, Pat Par-rish, Jimmy Carpenter, Erwin Kalser, Fre-deric Brum (right), Danny Jackson, to name a few. The director was Josef Berne. There was no mileage in it at all. (65 mins)

◁ After appearing together in *Love Affair* (RKO, 1939) and *When Tomorrow Comes* (Universal, 1939), Irene Dunne (second left) and Charles Boyer (left) were together again in **Together Again**. It was an unashamedly romantic comedy in which she played the mayor of a small Vermont town (her late hus-band was once mayor there), and he a New York sculptor. While making a statue of her husband, he falls in love with her – and, eventually, she with him. The course of their love, however, ran anything but smoothly, as Virginia Van Upp and F. Hugh Herbert's witty screenplay entertainingly demon-strated. Van Upp, who also produced, assem-bled a top-notch supporting cast, which included Charles Coburn as Dunne's lovable father-in-law, who again played cupid, this time in her affair with Boyer. There were two absolutely splendid performances from Mona Freeman (second right) as Dunne's teenage daughter (who mistakenly believes Boyer is in love with her rather than her mother), and from newcomer Jerome Court-land (right) as her teenage sweetheart. A gan-gling, gauche youth with an innate flair for comedy, Courtland was seen at his hilarious best in a sequence in which Miss Dunne makes a playful play for him. Charles Vidor's top-notch direction kept it moving at a spark-ling pace, and in the smaller roles drew convincing performances from Elizabeth Patterson, Charles Dingle, Walter Baldwin, Fern Emmett and Frank Puglia. (93 mins)

◁ Sammy Cahn and Jule Styne supplied the songs for **Carolina Blues**, the most memorable of which was 'There Goes That Song Again'. It starred Kay Kyser (left) as a bandleader out to raise money to build a cruiser through a series of war-bond rallies. Ann Miller (right) played a dancer who finds employment with Kyser; so was Victor Moore who played Miller's father, as well as five other members of the same family (male and female). The brainchild of M. M. Musselman and Kenneth Earl (screenplay by Joseph Hoffman and Al Martin), the fragile plot was bolstered by the guest appearances of the incomparable Nicholas Brothers, The Cristianis, The Layson Brothers, and the Four Step Brothers. The Kyser regulars included vocalist Georgia Carroll, Harry Babbitt, and the painfully unfunny Ish Kabibble. Sammy Lee was in charge of the choreography, Sam Bischoff produced and the direction was by Leigh Jason. (81 mins)

1944

▽ Radio comedienne Joan Davis (illustrated) pulled a lot of funny faces in **Beautiful But Broke** but to little avail. Another musical with a wartime setting, its pinprick of a plot found Davis taking over the running of a theatrical agency specializing in big bands when her boss is recruited into the service. Because of the shortage of available male talent, she forms an all-girl band – whom she leaves stranded in a Nevada war-plant community. Jane Frazee, on loan from Universal, was in it too – so were John Hubbard, Judy Clark, Bob Haymes, Danny Mummert and Byron Foulger. The screenplay was by Monte Brice from a story by Arthur Houseman (adaptation by Manny Seff). Irving Briskin produced, and Charles Barton directed with minimal enthusiasm. (74 mins)

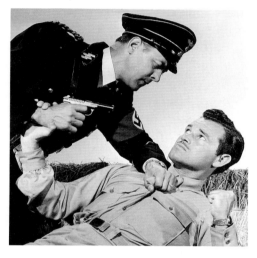

△ Though Ann Savage and Tom Neal (right), as a student nurse and an army sergeant respectively, received top billing in **The Unwritten Code**, the plot devised by Charles Kenyon and Robert Wilmot (screenplay by Kenyon and Leslie T. White) favoured Roland Varno (left). Varno played (believe it or not) a Nazi officer who gains entry into the USA by taking on the identity of a British officer he has killed. His purpose? To help German prisoners escape by pretending to be a wounded ally. Nothing in the script rang remotely true, a fact producer Sam White's stalwart cast were unable to camouflage. They included: Mary Currier, Bobby Larson and Howard Freeman. Herman Rotsten directed. (61 mins)

▽ Although John Carradine (right), as a Nazi general, received top-billing in **The Black Parachute**, the star of the show was Larry Parks (left) as an American who, disguised as a Nazi colonel, parachutes into an un-named country in order to rescue its king and government from Nazi oppression. Osa Massen (centre) played a German spy and Jonathan Hale was the captive king, with other roles in Jack Fier's production going to Jeanne Bates, Ivan Triesault, Trevor Bardette and Art Smith. Clarence Upson Young wrote the screenplay from a tall story by Paul Gangelin. Lew Landers directed. (68 mins)

▷ Patriotism ran riot in **U-Boat Prisoner**, a heap of chauvinistic flag-waving of which only Senator McCarthy would have approved. Based on the derring-do exploits of seaman Archie Gibbs (who provided scenarist Aubrey Wisberg with the story-line), it starred Bruce Bennett (centre) as Gibbs and told the far-fetched story of a merchant seaman (Bennett) who, after changing identity with a Nazi spy, is picked up by a Nazi sub. Thereupon, pretending to be a German, he contrives a series of situations which culminate in the sub being sunk by an American destroyer. Also mixed up in this mindless farrago were Erik Rolf, John Abbot, John Wengraf (left), Robert Williams (second left) and Egon Brecher. The all-male cast was directed by Lew Landers. The producer was Wallace MacDonald. (65 mins)

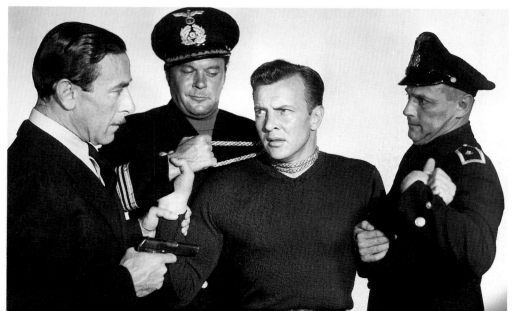

▽ The studio's second Technicolor production was the big-budget musical **Cover Girl**, designed as a showcase for the gorgeous Rita Hayworth (centre). Produced by composer Arthur Schwartz, it went into production without a leading man as there was no one under contract talented enough for the assignment. Only one man, Schwartz felt, would be suitable: Gene Kelly (right). Harry Cohn, however, was outraged at the mere thought, dismissing the dancer as a 'tough Irishman' who was 'far too short'. Schwartz, however, was undeterred, and signed Kelly as a loan-out from MGM. When he broke the news to Cohn, the mogul put his arms around him, and said 'Thank God' – as well he might. Although Rita was the cover girl of the title around whom the plot pivoted, the film remains memorable for the innovative dance numbers (such as the 'alter ego' routine) Kelly choreographed with his assistant Stanley Donen. *Cover Girl*'s plot was nothing to shout about. It was the conventional story of a Brooklyn nightclub dancer (Hayworth) who deserts her lover (Kelly) for the heady glamour of show business, only to return to him when she learns that money and glamour aren't everything. The tale unfolds against a series of flashbacks, set at the turn of the century, in which Rita's famous grandmother (also played by Hayworth) was shown to have followed a similar course. With a stunning score by Jerome Kern and Ira Gershwin (the most memorable number being 'Long Ago And Far Away'), some first-rate dancing by the two stars (Hayworth's vocals were dubbed by Martha Mears), glorious Technicolor photography and a supporting cast that included Eve Arden, Phil Silvers (left), Lee Bowman, Otto Kruger, Jinx Falkenburg, Leslie Brooks, Jess Barker, Thurston Hall and The Cover Girls, Schwartz's lavish production couldn't help registering strongly and was an enormous smash. It brought Hayworth mega-star status, and established Kelly as the most exciting male dancer since Fred Astaire, a fact which did not exactly go unnoticed at MGM where his star potential had not yet been recognized. Val Raset and Seymour Felix co-choreographed, Virginia Van Upp, Marion Parsonnet and Paul Gangelin (story by Erwin Gelsey) wrote the screenplay and the lush direction was by Charles Vidor. (105 mins)

△ Based on Kressmann Taylor's epistolary story, **Address Unknown** starred Paul Lukas (centre) as a German-American art dealer who returns to Germany at the outbreak of World War II, adopts the Nazi philosophy, refuses to protect his son's fiancée whom he has brought to Germany with him, and ultimately falls victim to the Gestapo himself. Peter Van Eyck played Lukas' son (who remains in America to run the family business) and K. T. Stevens (right) his would-be daughter-in-law, with other parts in Herbert Dalmas's ponderous, heavy-going screenplay shared by Morris Carnovsky, Mady Christians (left), Emory Parnell, Mary Young and Frank Faylen. William Cameron Menzies was responsible for both the production and the (plodding) direction. (80 mins)

△ Even actors far, far better than Tom Neal (right) and Ann Savage (centre) wouldn't have stood a chance with the screenplay flung together by Griffin Jay and Leslie T. White for **Two Man Submarine**. A pathetic time-filler about the efforts of the Japanese and the Nazis to steal the secrets of a penicillin drug from American researchers on a Pacific island, it gave B pictures a bad name and brought out the worst in J. Carroll Naish, Robert Williams, Abner Biberman (left) and George Lynn, all of whom were featured in Jack Fier's stale production. The director was Lew Landers. (62 mins)

1945

▽ Radio comedian Fred Brady (second right) made an inauspicious screen debut in **Dancing In Manhattan**, a tepid comedy, with a few songs, about a trucker (Brady) who finds $5,000, and, together with his girlfriend (Jeff Donnell, right) blows it. Later in Erna Lazarus's pale excuse for a screenplay, Brady traps a blackmailer who, it turns out, extorted from one of his victims the $5,000 that Brady and his girlfriend have spent. All ends happily. Also cast: William Wright (left) Ann Savage (second left) and Cy Kendall. Wallace MacDonald produced and the hapless director was Henry Levin. (60 mins)

▽ Lynn Merrick (centre) was the **Blonde From Brooklyn**, an unknown singer who sets Erna Lazarus's off-the-peg screenplay in motion when, together with song-and-dance man Robert Stanton (left, formerly Bob Haymes, brother of crooner Dick), she dons a Deep South accent and pretends to hail from the land of cotton. Complication begat complication, but it all worked out in the end – with the duo succeeding without recourse to deception. Thurston Hall (right) played a bogus Southern colonel, with other roles in Ted Richmond's okay little musical programmer going to Mary Treen, Walter Soderling, Arthur Loft and Byron Foulger. The director was Del Lord. (65 mins)

▽ **Eadie Was A Lady** leading a life of unblemished respectability by day, while at night she performed in a burlesque show. That was the main plot point in Monte Brice's screenplay, which gave its star, Ann Miller (illustrated), and choreographer, Jack Cole, a few energetic moments on the dance floor. Joe Besser co-starred as a comedian-turned-schoolteacher; while the romance was supplied by clubowner William Wright. Jeff Donnell, Jimmy Little, Marion Martin and Kathleen Howard were also featured; so was Tom Dugan, and Hal McIntyre and His Orchestra. Michael Kraike produced and Arthur Dreifuss directed. (67 mins)

▽ A filmed version of a 1943 play by Janet and Phillip Stevenson (based, in turn, on a Russian original by Ilya Vershinin and Mikhail Ruderman), **Counter-Attack** (GB: **One Against Seven**) was yet another drama with a wartime setting. This time, though, the 'action' took place not on a battlefield but in the subterranean cellar of a factory on the eastern front. Trapped inside the cellar by bomb debris are a Russian soldier (Paul Muni, left) and his co-guerrilla (Marguerite Chapman) as well as seven Nazi soldiers they are holding captive. Using psychological tactics, Muni attempts to draw out information from his quarry, and it was the will-he-or-won't-he aspect of the situation that producer director Zoltan Korda, working from a first-rate screenplay by John Howard Lawson, milked to greatest effect. With the action confined to the cellar for most of the film's duration, dialogue and performances had to be good to avoid stagnation. Muni's central performance was riveting and compelled audience attention. There were some effective histrionics from Ms Chapman, and convincing character studies from Larry Parks (seen briefly), Philip van Zandt, George Macready, Roman Bohnen, Harro Meller (centre), Erik Rolf, Ludwig Donath and Rudolph Anders. (90 mins)

▷ A far-fetched, undistinguished programmer from director Budd Boetticher, **Escape In The Fog** starred Nina Foch (right) as a Navy nurse who, while resting at a little inn near San Francisco and recuperating from nervous shock, has a nightmare in which she sees a man about to be murdered. The man in her dream turns out to be a guest at the inn (William Wright) who is shortly to embark, in his capacity as Officer of Psychological Warfare, on a dangerous mission; and before the film is over she has saved him from a real-life murder. Otto Kruger (left) played a German spy called Schiller, and the cast also included Konstantin Shayne, Ivan Triesault and Ernie Adams. Aubrey Wisberg scripted, and the producer was Wallace MacDonald. (60 mins)

▽ A comedy with four songs appliquéd on to its meagre plot, **Eve Knew Her Apples** starred Ann Miller (left) as a radio singer who, on a vacation from her manager and her press-agent, falls in love with reporter William Wright (right). There wasn't much more to E. Edwin Moran's screenplay than that – and pretty feeble it was too. Robert Williams, Ray Walker, Charles D. Brown, John Eldredge and Eddie Bruce completed the cast for producer Wallace MacDonald. The director was Will Jason. A weak remake of *It Happened One Night* (1934). (64 mins)

◁ A musical B – with a vengeance! – **The Gay Senorita** featured Jim Bannon as a property developer out to turn the Mexican section of a Californian town into a factory site. Love – in the shape of Jinx Falkenburg (right) – intrudes on his plans, and the Latin American community is saved from progress. This exercise in Good Neighbour relations was produced by Jay Gorney, directed by Arthur Dreifuss, written by Edward Eliscu (story by J. Robert Bren) and also featured Steve Cochran (centre), Corinna Mura, Isabelita (left) and Thurston Hall. (69 mins)

△ Gene Stratton Porter's soapie novel *A Girl of the Limberlost* came to the screen for the second time (the first being in 1934 when it was made by Monogram) with its title fractionally altered to **The Girl Of The Limberlost**. The story, however, remained unchanged and told of the hatred a mother feels towards her child whom she blames for the death of her husband. Just *why* the child was blamed, and *how* the husband died were questions answered by Erna Lazarus's screenplay, which involved Ruth Nelson (left, as the mother) and Dorinda Clifton (right) as the daughter. Loren Tindall, Gloria Holden, Ernest Cossart, Vanessa Brown and James Bell were also in producer Alexis Thurn-Taxis's overheated melodrama. Mel Ferrer directed. (60 mins)

▷ Alexander Dumas' *Companions of Jehu* was the inspiration for **The Fighting Guardsman**, a Robin Hood-type yarn, set during the reign of Louis XVI and involving one Baron Francois de Sainte Hermaine – also known as Roland (Willard Parker, right) – who, beneath his aristocratic exterior, is a revolutionary at heart robbing the King's tax collectors in order to pay the poor. It takes the arrival of the French Revolution to smooth the passage of his romance with well-born Amelie de Montreval (Anita Louise). Henry Levin directed at a bracing pace, but was restricted from achieving anything really special by Michael Kraike's budget-conscious production. Franz Spencer and Edward Dein's screenplay gave employment to Lloyd Corrigan as Louis XVI, and Janis Carter as his mistress, as well as to Edgar Buchanan, George Macready, John Loder (left) and Elisabeth Risdon. (84 mins)

◁ **Let's Go Steady** was a passable B movie which featured crooner Jackie Moran (centre back), eccentric dancer June Preisser (second right), mimic Jimmy Lloyd (second left) and singer Mel Tormé (right). Having been conned by a phoney New York publisher, the quartet arrive in the big city to promote their songs themselves. Apart from the inevitable romance that intruded, mainly involving pretty Pat Parrish (left), the screenplay – fashioned by Erna Lazarus from William B. Sackheim's story – provided little else by way of plot. Tormé penned three of the featured numbers for producer Ted Richmond, and it was directed by Del Lord with a cast that also included Arnold Stang (centre front), Skinnay Ennis, William Moss and Byron Foulger. (60 mins)

▷ F. Hugh Herbert adapted (without too many changes) his successful Broadway comedy **Kiss And Tell** as a vehicle for the teen-aged Shirley Temple (right). Although the quality of the former child star's performance divided the critics, it certainly did no damage to the flimsy tale of a young girl and the havoc she causes when she pretends to be pregnant in order to protect her secretly married brother, who's in the army. Jerome Courtland (left) played Shirley's hapless young boyfriend, Walter Abel and Katharine Alexander (centre) were her confused parents and (in the role played on stage first by Richard Widmark, then by Kirk Douglas) Scott Elliott was the brother at the root of all the problems. George Abbott produced (as he had done on Broadway) Sol C. Siegel was the associate producer, and it was directed by Richard Wallace. The splendid cast also included Robert Benchley, Porter Hall, Tom Tully, Darryl Hickman, Edna Holland and Virginia Welles. (90 mins)

△ Director Joseph H. Lewis entered the black and white world of *film noir* with **My Name Is Julia Ross**, a stylish, low-budget (albeit far-fetched) thriller based on Anthony Gilbert's novel *The Woman In Red*. Set in England, it told the story of a young woman (Nina Foch – in her first starring role) who is hired by the elderly Mrs Hughs (Dame May Whitty, left) as a private secretary. What she doesn't know at the time is that her employer is in cahoots with her evil son (George Macready, right) to implement a diabolical scheme in which innocent Miss Foch is to be murdered in such a way as to make her death appear like suicide. The whys and wherefores of the plot were well taken care of by Muriel Roy Bolton, whose screenplay created roles for Roland Varno, Anita Bolster, Doris Lloyd, Leonard Mudie and Queenie Leonard. Wallace MacDonald produced. [In 1987 the same material as reworked by director Arthur Penn as *Dead Of Winter* (MGM).] (64 mins)

◁ In 1944 Ruth Gordon wrote her first play, **Over 21**, as a vehicle for her own flibbertigibbet, highly individual image. It came to the screen, via producer Sidney Buchman (who also adapted Miss Gordon's screenplay), with Irene Dunne (left) in the Gordon role. Dunne plays a successful authoress who, together with her editor husband (Alexander Knox), moves to a small town near an army base, at which point middle-aged hubbie decides to acquire some first-hand knowledge of the war by joining the officer-candidate school. Dunne gave a most commendable impression of Ruth Gordon playing Irene Dunne. It was certainly an enjoyable performance – though, in the end, it lacked genuine eccentricity. Nor, alas, was she helped by her co-star, Alexander Knox, who was almost as dull on this occasion as he was playing President Wilson in *Wilson* (20th Century-Fox, 1944). The acting honours went, as they so often did, to scene-stealing Charles Coburn (right) as a grumpy publisher who wants Knox to return to his old job. Wartime housing shortages and wartime compromises were subjects touched upon in Miss Gordon's slender comedy – with nothing new being said about either. And the fact that most of the action was confined (as in the stage play) to a single set, focused attention on the miscasting of the film's two principals. Still, director Charles Vidor made the most of what he had, and kept the laughs flowing. His cast also included Jeff Donnell, Loren Tindall, Lee Patrick, Phil Brown, Cora Witherspoon and Charles Evans. (104 mins)

▷ It took just over an hour for Lynn Merrick (left) to decide that, all things considered, she wanted serviceman Ross Hunter (right) as her guy and civilian George Meeker to remain her pal in **A Guy, A Gal, And A Pal**. Ted Donaldson (centre) played chaperone to the lovers, and the cast – for the record – included Jack Norton, Will Stanton and Sam McDaniel. Monte Brice's screenplay (story by Gerald Drayson Adams) was, like Budd Boetticher's soporific direction, of no consequence whatsoever. The same could be said of Wallace MacDonald's instantly evaporating production. (62 mins)

▽ Fred MacMurray (left) played a dual role in **Pardon My Past**, a deft little mistaken-identity comedy from the typewriters of Earl Felton and Karl Lamb (story by Patterson McNutt and Harlan Ware). First seen as Eddie York, a discharged GI *en route* to Wisconsin with buddy William Demarest (right) to start a mink farm, MacMurray is soon mistaken by gambler Akim Tamiroff for Francis Pemberton, a wastrel playboy who owes him money. Naturally the more York tries to prove his innocence, the more involved he becomes. As with most mistaken-identity yarns, complication begat complication – but it all came right in the end, with the worthier of the two MacMurrays even getting the girl (Marguerite Chapman, centre). Adding considerably to the enjoyment of the nonsense was a supporting cast that included Rita Johnson, Harry Davenport and Douglass Dumbrille. Leslie Fenton produced and directed (most efficiently). (88 mins)

△ A blatant piece of anti-Japanese propaganda, **Prison Ship** was set aboard a Jap tanker carrying prisoners from a Pacific island to Tokyo. The nasty Nips are using the ship as a decoy for Yankee submarines – a fact to which its prisoners take exception, and revolt. Among the revolting were top-billed Nina Foch (right) and Robert Lowery (centre), while also sailing in the hold of producer Alexis Thurn-Taxis's trite little melodrama were Richard Loo (left), Ludwig Donath, Robert Scott, Barry Bernard, Erik Rolf and Coulter Irwin. Arthur Dreifuss directed from a screenplay by Josef Mischel and Ben Markson. (60 mins)

▷ The plot of **Rhythm Roundup**, a backwoods musical from producer Colbert Clark, centred on a member of the rowdy Hoosier Hotshots inheriting a hotel in Arizona, but having to find $146 in back taxes before he can receive the deed to the property. There is a further complication in the shape of leading-man Ken Curtis (centre), the rightful owner of the hotel. Charles Marion's screenplay (story by Louise Rousseau) attempted (unsuccessfully) to give this shadow of a plot some substance, and relied on all the help it could get from a cast that included Cheryl Walker (centre left), Guinn Williams (extreme right), Raymond Hatton (second right), Victor Potel, The Pied Pipers and Bob Wills and his Texas Playboys. The director was Vernon Keays. (66 mins)

◁ Chester Morris (centre) and Victor McLaglen (left) starred (in roles that would once have been given to Jack Holt and Ralph Graves) in **Rough, Tough And Ready** (GB: **Men Of The Deep**), a comedy set against a wartime back-drop in which Morris (as part of the film's running gag) two-times buddy McLaglen by stealing his girl (Jean Rogers, right). It is only when, during combat near a South Pacific island, the former saves the latter's life, that all is forgiven. No one, however, could forgive producer Alexis Thurn-Taxis's makeshift production, or the script (by Edward T. Lowe) that went with it. Del Lord directed a cast that also included Veda Ann Borg, Amelita Ward, Robert Williams and John Tyrrell. (66 mins)

▷ Larry Parks (illustrated) and Jeanne Bates received top-billing in **Sergeant Mike** and found themselves upstaged by a couple of canines called Mike and Pearl – there was a kid in it too, eight-year-old Larry Joe Olsen, thus completing the actor's nightmare of working with kids and animals. Designed for the under twelves, it was the tale of a hard-boiled machine-gun operator (Parks) who finds himself assigned to the Canine Corps where he is detailed to train pooches for war work. Robert Lee Johnson's cute screenplay showed the hounds in action and tugged at the heart-strings in the process. Loren Tindall, Jim Bannon, Richard Powers and Eddie Acuff were also featured in Jack Fier's calculating production. The director was Henry Levin. (60 mins)

△ Aspiring to the lowest rung on the musical totem-poll, **She's A Sweetheart** was a plastic entertainment that featured an over-the-top Jane Darwell as the proprietor of a house she makes over into a night canteen for servicemen on short-time passes. Entertainment is supplied; and there's romance on tap as well. Jane Frazee and Larry Parks starred, with Nina Foch (right), Ross Hunter (left), Jimmy Lloyd, Loren Tindall and Carole Mathews in it too. Ted Richmond was in charge of the routine production; Del Lord the direction and Muriel Ray Bolton the screenplay. (69 mins)

▽ **SNAFU** (Situation Normal – All Fouled Up) (GB: **Welcome Home**) first surfaced as a stage play in 1944. Its authors Louis Solomon and Harold Buchman adapted it to the screen with fair-to-middling results. It concerned the difficulties experienced by a 15-year-old soldier when he returns to civilian life after his parents succeed in having him honourably discharged. The story suffered at the hands of producer-director Jack Moss, whose sluggish approach to the material, plus the miscasting of Robert Benchley (left) – one of whose last films this was before his untimely death in 1945 – and Vera Vague (right) as the young soldier's parents. Fortunately, the catalyst himself – young Conrad Janis – was first-class, and a scene in which he attempts to explain to his father the facts of life as taught to him in the army was the best thing in a comedy whose subject promised much more than it delivered. Nanette Parks, Janis Wilson, Jimmy Lloyd, Enid Markey (centre) and Eva Puig made little impact in supporting roles. (82 mins)

◁ The best thing to emerge from **Tahiti Nights** was Mitchell Parrish and Rene Touzet's catchy song 'Let Me Love You Tonight'. For the rest it was an average programmer musical about an American bandleader – Dave O'Brien (centre) – who, soon after he arrives on a Tahitian Island, finds himself about to be betrothed to the princess of a local tribe. Jinx Falkenburg played the princess, with Mary Treen, Carole Mathews, Florence Bates, Cy Kendall and Pedro de Cordoba in attendance. Also featured were The Vagabonds. Sam White produced, Lillie Hayward scripted, and the direction was by Will Jason. (63 mins)

◁ There wasn't a great deal to say for – or against – **Ten Cents A Dance**. It was a comedy, with songs, about a pair of dance hostesses – Jane Frazee (second right) and Joan Woodbury (right) – who attempt unsuccessfully, on henchman John Calvert's (standing) behalf, to lure a pair of GIs, Jimmy Lloyd (second left) and Robert Scott (left), who are out on a 36-hour pass, into a crooked card game. Instead, the four of them become romantically paired, with Woodbury falling for Scott – he keeping under wraps the fact that he's heir to a fortune. Will Jason directed for producer Michael Kraike, from a screenplay by Morton Grant. The cast included George McKay, Edward Hyams, Dorothea Kent and Carole Mathews. (60 mins)

◁ After the success of the previous year's *Cover Girl*, in which Rita Hayworth proved such a knockout in glorious Technicolor, the studio put her before the colour cameras once again – in **Tonight And Every Night**. The title of this entertaining musical reflected the policy of London's intimate Windmill Theatre, where the action was set, and whose proud boast was that it kept open throughout the war. Though called the Music Box in the film, the establishment employing the services of Hayworth (right) and Janet Blair (second right) was clearly modelled on the Windmill, just as the indefatigable owner of the place – played by Florence Bates (left), was, to some degree, modelled on the formidable Sheila Van Damm. Choreographer Jack Cole's lavish production numbers, however, made quite sure that fact and fantasy were kept light years apart for never, ever, could they have fitted on to that tiny stage off London's Shaftesbury Avenue! Lesser Samuels and Abem Finkel's screenplay, based on Lesley Storm's play *Heart Of A City*, romantically paired Hayworth with pilot Lee Bowman and Blair with dancer Marc Platt (second left) – though, in the end, Hayworth rejects her suitor's offer of marriage in order to continue entertaining the troops at the Music Box. The Platt-Blair romance also ends in tears – for they're killed in an air-raid. It was never maudlin, though – thanks to producer-director Victor Saville's sure-footed direction, and an agreeable score by Sammy Cahn and Jule Styne. Val Raset shared the choreography chores with Cole, and the cast was completed by Leslie Brooks (third left), Professor Lamberti, Dusty Anderson, Stephen Crane, Jim Bannon, Ernest Cossart, Patrick O'Brien and Gavin Muir. Hayworth's vocals were dubbed by Martha Mears. (92 mins)

▷ A colourful and – thanks to Phil Silvers (left) – often very funny spoof of the Arabian Nights, **A Thousand And One Nights** starred Cornel Wilde (right) as Aladdin, and Adele Jergens as the sultan's daughter he longs to marry. He's hindered in his attempts at wedlock by pretty Evelyn Keyes as the red-headed genie of the lamp. Wilfrid H. Pettitt, Richard English and Jack Henley's screenplay (story by Pettitt) featured Silvers as the hero's anachronistic side-kick, and Rex Ingram played a giant genie – as he had in Alexander Korda's *The Thief Of Baghdad* (London Films, 1940). Other parts under Alfred E. Green's tongue-in-cheek direction went to Dusty Anderson, Dennis Hoey, Philip Van Zandt, Gus Schilling, Nestor Paiva and, as a handmaiden, Shelley Winter (later Winters). It was produced (in Technicolor) by Sam Bischoff. (92 mins)

◁ 'Physician heal thyself' was the message embedded in **Youth On Trial**, an efficient programmer from producer Ted Richmond. The 'physician' in this instance was a judge (Mary Currier) assigned to the adolescents' court. She discovers, as Michael Jacoby's screenplay gathered momentum, that her very own daughter (Cora Sue Collins, top-starred) is one of the young offenders arrested in a raid on a roadhouse of ill-repute. David Reed (centre) was second-billed as the high-school delinquent, with other roles under Budd Boetticher's direction falling to Eric Sinclair (left), Georgia Bayes, Robert Williams (right), John Calvert, Joseph Crehan and Edwin Stanley. (59 mins)

▽ **The Bandit Of Sherwood Forest** could just as easily have been called Son Of Robin Hood, for that's precisely who its handsome hero was. Known as Robert of Nottingham, he takes on the mantle of his elderly father (Russell Hicks) some 20 years after the signing of the Magna Carta at a time when all was not so merry in Merrie England. The Magna Carta has been revoked, and the dastardly William of Pembroke (Henry Daniell) is plotting the murder of boy-king Henry III with a view to usurping the throne. Enter Little John (Ray Teal), Friar Tuck (Edgar Buchanan) and Allan-A-Dale (Leslie Denison) who, under Robin's brave heir (Cornel Wilde, right), restore law and order to the tyrannized land. Robert's reward? The hand in marriage of Lady Catherine Maitland (Anita Louise, left). Beautifully photographed in Technicolor, Leonard S. Picker and Clifford Sanforth's good-looking production also engaged the services of bad guy George Macready, John Abbott (as Will Scarlet), Lloyd Corrigan (the Sheriff of Nottingham), Eva Moore and Ian Wolfe – all of whom responded vigorously to Wilfrid H. Pettitt and Mervin Levy's screenplay (story by Pettitt and Paul A. Castleton from the latter's novel *Son Of Robin Hood*). George Sherman and Henry Levin directed with immense panache. (83 mins)

▷ Harry J. Essex's play *Corpus Delicti* formed the basis of **Dangerous Business**, a crime time-filler that starred Forrest Tucker (second left) and Gerald Mohr as a pair of attorneys who come to the aid of a company president falsely accused of embezzlement. Gus Schilling (right), Shemp Howard, Lynn Merrick (centre right), Frank Sully, Cora Witherspoon (left) Matt Willis (centred) Thurston Hall helped pad out Hal Smith's screenplay; Ted Richmond produced and the director was D. Ross Lederman. (59 mins)

▽ There was nothing at all gallant about **Gallant Journey**, a maudlin and mawkish biopic of John J. Montgomery. Who? A not unreasonable question. He was the man who, in 1883, became the first man ever to make a successful flight in a glider. His story ended in tears when vertigo caused his premature demise. What caused the premature demise of William Wellman's obvious labour of love (for he produced, directed and co-wrote it with Byron Morgan) was a stodgy, ill-constructed, anachronistic screenplay, an impossibly inert central performance from Glenn Ford (right), and other performances from Janet Blair (left, as his lady love), Charlie Ruggles, Henry Travers, Jimmy Lloyd, Charles Kemper and Arthur Shields that were, to say the least, indifferent. The film crashed both artistically and at the box-office. (86 mins)

▽ In **The Gentleman Misbehaves**, Robert Stanton (left) played a Broadway producer who turns to marriage in order to inject much-needed funds into his production. When that doesn't provide the resources he needs, he enlists the help of a gambler. Such was the wafer-thin content of Robert Wyler and Richard Weill's screenplay (story by Wyler and John B. Clymer), which made no demands on a cast that included Osa Massen (right), Hillary Brooke, Frank Sully, Sheldon Leonard and Shemp Howard. Alexis Thurn-Taxis produced and George Sherman directed. (70 mins)

 'A slow, opaque, unexciting film' was how the critic of the venerable *New York Times* described **Gilda**, one of the most commercially successful movies of the year – and a sizeable money-earner for the studio. 'Boring and slightly confusing' said the *New York Herald Tribune*. 'High-class trash' snorted the *Daily News*. Over 40 years later, despite the critical brick-bats hurled at the time, it remains one of the great *films noirs* of the Forties, a triumph of chemistry over plot-line. True, the story *is* confusing, the central character's motivations ambiguous and the morals of its heroine decidedly dubious. But in the grey, black-and-white world of *film noir*, these flaws became virtues. *Gilda's* initial detractors also overlooked (or were unaffected by) the heady sexual sparks the film's two stars – Rita Hayworth (illustrated) and Glenn Ford, last seen together in *The Lady In Question* (1940) – struck off one another. Hayworth's sensual, exotic beauty, allied to an amoral life-style and an enigmatic temperament, contrasted dramatically with Ford's explosive, angry personality and petulant behaviour. The result was instant combustion whenever they shared the same frame. Set against a backdrop of high-life and low characters in Buenos Aires, the plot found Hayworth married to a wealthy club-owner (George Macready). After what looks to be little more than a common male pickup, Macready offers down-and-out gambler Ford a job in his club. Ford accepts and, by the long arm of coincidence, it turns out that he and Hayworth were once lovers – a fact Ford conceals from his benefactor. Just why the relationship between Ford and Hayworth soured, or the reasons for the deeply-felt grudge he continues to hold against her, were never fully explained. Nor did much elucidation come from a sub-plot involving Macready's nefarious underworld activities with a mysterious cartel. What counted was the extraordinary atmosphere director Charles Vidor managed to evoke from the disparate elements in the plot (including a sinister homosexual undercurrent between Ford and Macready, never stated but clearly felt), and the performances he coaxed out of all three of his leads. Hayworth was especially magnificent. Whether delivering lines like 'If I'd been a ranch they'd have called me the Bar Nothing . . .' or giving her classic renditions of Doris Fisher and Allan Roberts's 'Amado Mio' and 'Put The Blame On Mame', the latter strikingly delivered in a strapless black Jean Louis creation, and stunningly photographed by Rudolph Maté, she not only exuded star-quality, but became the embodiment of the Forties 'love goddess'. Little wonder that soon after the film's release Hayworth found herself the world's most photographed superstar, whose likeness adorned the first atom bomb to be dropped in peacetime. *Gilda's* screenplay, written by Marion Parsonnet, was based on Jo Eisinger's adaptation of an original story by E. A. Ellington. Virginia Van Upp was in charge of the big-budget production, and her cast was completed by Joseph Calleia, Steven Geray, Joseph Sawyer, Gerald Mohr, Robert Scott, Ludwig Donath, Ruth Roman and Don Douglas. Morris Stoloff and Marlin Skilers were in charge of the musical direction. [Though Hayworth's vocals were dubbed by Anita Ellis, she can be heard singing in her own voice, and accompanying herself on the guitar, in a short reprise of 'Put The Blame On Mame'.] (110 mins)

◁ Two Judy Canovas for the price of one was the best that **Hit The Hay** could offer. Playing an operatic diva from the Ozarks who can sing but can't act – as well as an actress who can't sing but knows her way around a stage – Canova (second left) had a field day doing her eccentric thing. Whether audiences had as much fun as the hillbilly star they paid to see was open to doubt. The best thing about this amiable, though singularly undistinguished romp was Canova's burlesque of Rossini's 'William Tell' – retitled 'Tillie Tell'. Her leading man was Ross Hunter (right), who would soon be better known as a successful producer, with other parts in Ted Richmond's raucous production going to Fortunio Bonanova (left), Doris Merrick (second right), Gloria Holden, Francis Pierlot and Grady Sutton. Del Lord directed from a screenplay by Richard Wells and Charles R. Marion. (75 mins)

◁ One of the few entertainers idolized by Harry Cohn was Al Jolson – a love affair that began years earlier when Cohn was still a song-plugger. So, when columnist Sidney Skolsky suggested that the studio mount a full-scale biopic of the great entertainer, Cohn agreed. (The project was first offered to Jack Warner at Warner Bros. but was rejected.) Sidney Buchman was hired to work on an adaptation of **The Jolson Story** with Stephen Longstreet, Harry Chandler and Andrew Solt scripting. It was produced by Skolsky and directed by Alfred E. Green who turned every single one of the film's galloping clichés into gold. *The Jolson Story*, lavishly budgeted at $2.8 million, performed cartwheels at the box-office to the tune of $8 million – the biggest-grossing film in Columbia's history thus far. After James Cagney (who in 1943 had so charismatically brought to life the legendary George M. Cohan in Warner Bros.'s *Yankee Doodle Dandy*) turned down the pivotal role of Jolson, the part was offered to Danny Thomas – on condition that he did something to reduce the size of his nose. Thomas refused, and José Ferrer and Richard Conte were then considered. In the end the part went to contract player Larry Parks (foreground) who had worked steadily at the studio for the past five years but without making much impact. Parks did a truly magnificent job, not only of miming to the tracks Jolson had specially recorded for the film, but in the way he combined the star's legendary arrogance with his equally legendary vitality. If it takes a star to play a star – Parks certainly had what it took, and just as the phenomenal, runaway success of *The Jolson Story* revitalized its subject's flagging career, it turned Parks into a major Hollywood name. Playing opposite him was Evelyn Keyes – as Jolson's first wife Ruby Keeler (called Julie Benson in the film). In this highly fictionalized account of the crooner's rise to fame and fortune, William Demarest was third-billed as Steve Martin, Jolson's life-long friend and mentor. Scotty Beckett played Jolson as a youngster still known as Asa Yoelson. Ludwig Donath and Tamara Shayne were Cantor and Mrs Yoelson, and John Alexander played minstrelman Lew Dockstader, with other roles in Skolsky's irresistible Technicolor production going to Ernest Cossart, Ann E. Todd, Edwin Maxwell (as Oscar Hammerstein), Emmett Vogan and William Forrest. Jack Cole choreographed, Saul Chaplin and Morris Stoloff were in charge of the Oscar-winning musical arrangements, and the musical numbers were directed by Joseph H. Lewis. (128 mins)

◁ So bad it was almost good, **Betty Co-Ed** blew the lid off sorority snobbery and completely detonated itself in the process. It starred Jean Porter (illustrated) as a carnival singer who gains admission to a posh college under the misapprehension that she's from a well-bred Virginia family. Shirley Mills co-starred as an absolutely vile sorority president out to make Miss P's life a misery, with other parts under Arthur Dreifuss's unsubtle direction going to William Mason, Rosemary La Planche, Kay Morley, Jackie Moran and Edward Van Sloan. The best moment was Porter reprising Allan Roberts and Doris Fisher's 'Put The Blame On Mame' from *Gilda*. Hayworth did it better. The screenplay was written by Dreifuss and George H. Plympton. (68 mins)

▷ The breezily titled **It's Great To Be Young** was a talent-sparse musical about the efforts of a stage-struck group of ex-GIs whose borscht-circuit show catches the eye of a Broadway producer – and presto! Fame at last! Allan Roberts and Doris Fisher's score was about as fresh as the plot it embellished; and the performances – from Leslie Brooks (right), Jimmy Lloyd (back to camera), Jeff Donnell (centre, standing), Robert Stanton (second left), Frank Orth, Jack Williams (second right), Ann Codee, Jack Fina, Grady Sutton and Milton DeLugg and His Swing Wing – were mediocre in the extreme. Ted Richmond produced, Jack Henley wrote the screenplay (story by Karen De Wolf) and the director was Del Lord. (69 mins)

▽ In **Meet Me On Broadway**, leading man Fred Brady played an arrogant director who is reduced to staging a small-scale show at a country club with a group of amateurs. He then falls in love with his leading lady Marjorie Reynolds (right) who turns out to be the daughter of the club's owner. End of plot, courtesy of George Brecker and Jack Henley (story by Brecker). Allen Roberts and Doris Fisher supplied some songs, and Billy Daniels did the choreography. The direction was by Leigh Jason for producer Burt Kelly. Also cast: Jinx Falkenburg, Spring Byington, Loren Tindall, Gene Lockhart, Allen Jenkins, Nita Berber (left) and Gloria Patrice (centre). (77 mins)

△ Phillips H. Lord's popular radio show **Mr District Attorney** provided the inspiration for this lukewarm thriller. The DA in question was the personable Adolphe Menjou (right) who, in the story contrived by Sidney Marshall (screenplay by Ben Markson), has an assistant Dennis O'Keefe (left), who is blinded by love for no-good gold-digger Marguerite Chapman. Indeed, O'Keefe openly resents his boss's interference in his burgeoning romance. It's only when Miss Chapman, who has already eliminated two men so far, is about to add O'Keefe to her list, that he realizes just *how* blind he's been. The rather muddy screenplay gave employment to Michael O'Shea as the DA's wise-cracking investigator, as well as to George Coulouris, Jeff Donnell, Steven Geray, Ralph Morgan and John Kellogg. Robert B. Sinclair directed for producer Samuel Bischoff. (81 mins)

▽ **The Man Who Dared** was George Macready (left), and what he dared (in his capacity as a crusading newspaper reporter) was to expose the judicial system's concept of 'circumstantial evidence'. In order to do this, he pretends to be the prime suspect in a murder case. An entertaining thriller, it was well assembled by John Sturges, here making his directorial debut, and well played by a cast that included Leslie Brooks, Forrest Tucker (right), Charles D. Brown, Warren Mills, Richard Hale and Charles Evans. The screenplay was by Edward Bock and Malcolm Boylan (story by Maxwell Shane and Alex Gottlieb), and it was produced by Leonard S. Picker. (66 mins)

△ **Night Editor** was an inept cop drama in which top-starred William Gargan (right) as an inebriated police lieutenant jeopardizes his marriage to Jeff Donnell by having an affair with wealthy socialite Janis Carter (left). It's only when a man is convicted of a crime he didn't commit that Gargan redeems himself by tracking down the guilty party. Stuff 'n' nonsense, it was written by Hal Smith from a story by Scott Littleton (in turn based on the radio programme of the same name). The producer was Ted Richmond and the director Henry Levin. Also cast: Coulter Irwin, Charles D. Brown, Paul E. Burns, Harry Shannon, Frank Wilcox and Robert Stevens. (65 mins)

▷ A blurred, over-extended screenplay (by Joseph Hoffman and Jack Henley, story by Lester Lee and Larry Marks), plus a conspicuous absence of star names, undercut **One Way To Love**. A comedy, with more than a passing resemblance to the studio's far superior *Twentieth Century* (1934), it concerned the break-up of a pair of radio writers, and their agent's attempts – rattling across country aboard the 20th Century – to reunite the team. Willard Parker (right) and Chester Morris played the scribes, Marguerite Chapman (left) and Janis Carter their girlfriends. Hugh Herbert appeared as an escaped lunatic posing as a millionaire, and Jerome Cowan as the sponsor of a radio show. It turns out that Cowan is the loony and Herbert the millionaire. Dusty Anderson, Irving Bacon, Roscoe Karns, Frank Sully, Frank Jenks and Lewis Russell completed the cast for producer Burt Kelly. Directing to the best of the screenplay's faltering ability was Ray Enright. (83 mins)

△ **Out Of The Depths** was a submarine drama which found scenarists Martin Berkeley and Ted Thomas (story by Aubrey Wisberg) out of their depths in the telling of a flag-waving tale involving an American sub, a Japanese aircraft carrier and the foiling of a kamikaze attack by the latter on the former. The all-male cast kicked off with Jim Bannon (right) and Ross Hunter (left), who were followed by Ken Curtis, Loren Tindall, Robert Scott, Frank Sully, George Khan (centre) and Coulter Irwin. Director D. Ross Lederman botched the climactic sequence showing the sub ramming the carrier – and Wallace MacDonald's production sank with all hands on deck. (61 mins)

▽ Children and animals were the prime ingredients in **Personality Kid**, a minor entry aimed strictly at minors. Although it top-starred Anita Louise and Michael Duane (left), young Ted Donaldson (centre) was prominently featured as a youngster determined to keep a burro for a pet. Duane played the kid's older brother – a would-be commercial photographer locked into a compromise job in a soap factory. The threads of Lewis Helmar Herman and William B. Sackheim's screenplay (story by Cromwell MacKechnie) came together when Duane wins a photographic contest with pictures he's taken of his brother's pet donkey. Barbara Brown (right), Bobby Larson and Oscar O'Shea were also in it; Wallace MacDonald produced, and director George Sherman successfully managed to keep the 'corn' quota lower than might be expected. (62 mins)

◁ Some better-than-average production values in producer Phil L. Ryan's **Perilous Holiday** couldn't disguise the fact that the product he was selling was a very ordinary secret-agent melodrama with a Mexico City backdrop. Top-starred Pat O'Brien (left) played a treasury-agent detective out to curtail the activities of counterfeiters Alan Hale (second right) and Edgar Buchanan. Ruth Warrick (second left) – in her best role since *Citizen Kane* (RKO, 1941) – also has a vested interest in the mob's apprehension: Hale, it appears, murdered her father. Leading man and leading lady become romantically entwined and, after initially mistrusting each other's motives, bring the baddies to heel. Audrey Long, Willard Robertson, Eduardo Ciannelli, Minna Gombell, Jay Novello and Eddie LeBaron and his Orchestra were worked into Ray Chanslor's over-long screenplay (story by Robert Carson). The director was Edward H. Griffith. (90 mins)

▷ Following in the well-worn and well-documented tradition of the brothers James and Younger were the brothers Dembrow and their pappy Kirk. These fictional bad guys of the West fetched up in Technicolor, and in all their ornery glory, in **Renegades**, a standard Western elevated to the top half of a double bill solely by virtue of its colour. Story-wise, though, it was as old as the hills in which it all took place and involved the courageous attempts of good-guy Willard Parker (left), a doctor by profession, to see that the renegade Dembrow clan bite the proverbial dust in the last reel – which, to a man (or skunk), they do. The plot also found Doc Parker in love with beautiful Evelyn Keyes (right) who, perversely, prefers a more exciting life with Ben Dembrow (Larry Parks, centre). But Melvin Levy and Francis Edwards Faragoh's screenplay (story by Harold Shumate) made sure that, come the final fade-out, she's seen the error of her choice. George Sherman's direction successfully camouflaged the triteness of the storyline by keeping the action simmering throughout in a series of shoot-outs and chases. In addition to the scene-pilfering Edgar Buchanan as old man Dembrow, and Parks as his son Ben, the other members of the clan were Jim Bannon and Forrest Tucker as Ben's two brothers, and Virginia Brissac as Sarah Dembrow. Other roles in producer Michael Kraike's colourful horse opera were allotted to Ludwig Donath, Frank Sully, Willard Robertson and Addison Richards. (67 mins)

▷ In **The Return Of Monte Cristo**, Alexandre Dumas's glamorous hero, Edmond Dantès, was again played by Louis Hayward (left). George Bruce and Alfred Neuman's screenplay (story by Curt Siodmak and Arnold Phillips) found Hayward, this time round, as the Count's grandson who, aided by a series of cunning disguises, tracks down the villains who had framed him, robbed him of his fortune and dispatched him to Devil's Island (whence he escaped with fellow inmate Steven Geray). The Edward Small–Grant Whytock production turned the familiar unfurling of events to entertaining advantage, courtesy of adroit direction by Henry Levin who bulldozed his way through the cliché-infested narrative with appropriate *brio*. He was considerably helped by a well-seasoned cast that included Barbara Britton (right), Ray Collins, George Macready, Una O'Connor, Henry Stephenson, Ludwig Donath and Ivan Triesault. (92 mins)

◁ Anita Louise (right), Lloyd Corrigan (left) and Michael Duane starred in **Shadowed**, a listless murder melodrama about a manufacturer of agricultural implements who risks his all to stop the crooked activities of a group of counterfeiters whose stolen engraving plates have come into his possession. Producer John Haggott's programmer had little going for it, especially not Brenda Weisberg's screenplay (story by Julian Harmon), nor John Sturges's direction, and audiences left the cinema under-nourished. Also cast: Robert Scott, Doris Houck, Helen Koford (later Terry Moore) and Wilton Graff. (70 mins)

◁ **Alias Mr Twilight** was a no-account melodrama in which Lloyd Corrigan (left), a counterfeiter (and the affable grandfather of a six-year-old orphan), pulls off one last big job ($1 million in counterfeit notes) in which he deliberately implicates his granddaughter's hateful aunt Elizabeth (Rosalind Ivan). The film ends with both the old scoundrel and the obnoxious aunt going to jail, and with the little orphan (Gigi Perreau) being taken care of by Trudy Marshall and her policeman boyfriend Michael Duane (right). The kind of vehicle that might have been better serviced by Shirley Temple in the Thirties, it was scripted by Brenda Weisberg from a story by Arthur E. Orloff (additional dialogue by Malcolm Stuart Boylan), produced by John Haggott, and directed by John Sturges. Also cast: Jeff York, Peter Brocco and Torben Meyer. (71 mins)

▽ It took five people to think up the minute plot for **She Wouldn't Say Yes**; scenarists Virginia Van Upp (who also produced), John Jacoby, Sarett Tobias, Laslo Gorog and William Thiele, the latter two supplying the story. Rosalind Russell (left) starred as a psychiatrist who ardently believes one should keep one's emotions under control; Lee Bowman (right) was a cartoonist whose most successful comic creation, a character called 'Nixie', is of the opposite opinion. The couple meet when he slams a door in her face, and, despite their diametrically opposed views, an uphill romance ensues. As talented as Miss Russell was, even she was unable to make such a trite, predictable script sparkle, and the comedy sank without trace. Charles Winninger played her doctor father, with other roles under Alexander Hall's uninspired direction being farmed out to Adele Jergens, Harry Davenport, Sara Haden and Percy Kilbride. (87 mins)

△ Ellen Drew (right) starred in **Sing While You Dance**, a so-what? musical in which she clawed her way along Tin Pan Alley by persuading the widow of a deceased composer to allow some of his compositions to be given a commercial once-over. Robert Stanton (left) was second-billed as an amateur composer, with other roles in Leon Barsha's production going to Ethel Griffies (as the widow), Andrew Tombes, Edwin Cooper, and Robert Stevens. Robert Stephen Brode wrote the screenplay from a story by Lorraine Edwards. The director was D. Ross Lederman. (88 mins)

▷ Only the most die-hard fans of the noisome Judy Canova (second left) could take comfort from **Singin' In The Corn** (GB: **Give And Take**), a risible little musical in which its star played a carnival mind-reader who stands to inherit a relative's estate on condition that a ghost town, which once belonged to the Indians, be returned to its rightful owners. Allen Jenkins (second right), Guinn Williams, Charles Halton, Alan Bridge, Frances Rey (left), Nick Thompson (right) and The Singing Indian Braves lent their talents to an enterprise from which no one emerged with credit – and that included producer Ted Richmond, director Del Lord, and writers Isobel Dawn and Monte Rice (story by Richard Weil). (64 mins)

◁ Behind the pretentiously titled **So Dark The Night** lurked a dreary psychological thriller that numbered among its thrills no fewer than four murders. They were all perpetrated by a schizophrenic Parisian police inspector who is Mr Normal by day but a cold-blooded killer at night. The plot by Aubrey Wisberg (screenplay by Martin Berkeley and Dwight Babcock) had the inspector (Steven Geray, left) tracking down the murderer of his country-girl fiancée (Micheline Cheirel, second left) on their wedding night – only to discover that the culprit is . . . you guessed it, himself. Eugene Borden (third right), Ann Codee (second right), Egon Brecher, Helen Freeman and Theodore Gottlieb wrestled gamefully with French accents – and lost (apart from Codee). Ted Richmond produced and the director was Joseph H. Lewis. (71 mins)

▷ Jinx Falkenburg (left) sang four songs in **Talk About A Lady** – and inherited a nightclub and $1 million. Conflict reared its head in the shape of Trudy Marshall, a socialite who believes the inheritance should have been hers. How Jinx coped with this situation was dealt with by scenarists Richard Weil and Ted Thomas (story by Robert E. Andrews and Barry Trivers) in routine fashion. The

film was produced by Michael Kraike, directed by George Sherman, and featured Forrest Tucker, funnyman Joe Besser, Richard Lane, Jimmy Little, Frank Sully, Jack Davis and Stan Kenton (right) and His Orchestra. (71 mins)

◁ There was nothing wrong with **Tars And Spars** that an overhauled screenplay and half a dozen good tunes couldn't have remedied. In the conspicuous absence of both, it was a tired, run-down coast-guard romance which paired Janet Blair (second right) and Alfred Drake (second left), the latter as a seaman mistakenly labelled a hero. For Drake, fresh from his Broadway triumph in Rodgers and Hammerstein's *Oklahoma!* (1944) this, his movie debut, was quite a let-down. All, however, wasn't entirely lost. In *his* movie debut, comedian Sid Caesar (left) scored strongly in several specialties, and dancer Marc Platt appeared for choreographer Jack Cole in a plot-enhancing (if not life-enhancing) ballet. Jeff Donnell (right) also featured. The below-par songs were by Sammy Cahn and Jule Styne, the screenplay was by John Jacoby, Sarett Tobias and Decla Dunning (story by Barry Trivers), Milton Bren produced, and Alfred E. Green directed. (86 mins)

▷ Keenan Wynn starred as a Broadway producer whose main concern in **The Thrill Of Brazil** (screenplay concocted by Allen Rivkin, Harry Clork and Devery Freeman) was to prevent his ex-wife (Evelyn Keyes, left) from marrying toothpaste magnate Allyn Joslyn. There was nothing at all sparkling about the outcome of this *His Girl Friday* plot retread, except the tap-dancing of Ann Miller (centre right) who played a nightclub entertainer in love with Wynn. Latin-American singer Tito Guizar was in it, as were the dance team of Veloz and Yolanda. Nick Castle, Jack Cole and Eugene Loring shared the choreography for producer Sidney Biddell, the underlying score was by Doris Fisher and Allan Roberts, and this pleasant-enough romance was directed by S. Sylvan Simon for the time-filler it was. (91 mins)

◁ Lee Bowman (right) starred in **The Walls Came Tumbling Down** as a Broadway gossip columnist determined to discover who murdered an elderly priest friend of his – and why. The police think it's suicide – but Bowman has other ideas, and, in the course of proving himself right, becomes involved with a beautiful Boston socialite (Marguerite Chapman), an eccentric art dealer (J. Edward Bromberg) and a crooked lawyer (Edgar Buchanan). The killer turns out to be George Macready, and the motive a pair of Bibles and a painting of the tumbling walls of Jericho. Also involved were Lee Patrick, Jonathan Hale (left, as a police captain), Elizabeth Risdon (centre), Miles Mander and Moroni Olsen. Wilfrid H. Pettitt's screenplay (from the novel by Jo Eisinger) kept interest simmering. Directing with competence but not much distinction was Lothar Mendes, for producer Albert J. Cohen. (81 mins)

▽ A king-size suspension of disbelief was the pre-requisite for **Blind Spot**, a thriller that starred Chester Morris (left) as an impecunious thriller writer whose tight-fisted publisher, Smith, is murdered shortly after he refuses to re-negotiate Morris's contract. It seems the method of the murder coincides precisely with a plot-line he outlined to Smith in the presence of a financially more successful author, and for which he was paid a mere $20. Not a great deal of mystery or suspense attached itself to Martin Goldsmith's screenplay (story by Harry Perowne), even though its unravelling, under Robert Gordon's direction, proved moderately diverting. Constance Dowling (right), Sid Tomack, Steven Geray, James Bell and Paul E. Burns filled out the cast for producer Ted Richmond. (74 mins)

▽ Leslie Brooks (left) and Jimmy Lloyd (right) played sweethearts in **Cigarette Girl** – a poor excuse for a musical in which both pretend to be people they ain't. She claims to be a Broadway star; he an oil baron. As the story (by Edward Huebsch) unfurled to the accompaniment of a few Allan Fisher-Doris Roberts songs, scenarist Henry K. Moritz waved his not-so-magic wand over the proceedings, in the process of which Brooks did, indeed, land a part in a Broadway musical, and Lloyd became a tycoon. That, as they say, is show business. Producer William Bloom's cast included Ludwig Donath, Doris Colleen and Howard Freeman as well as Russ Morgan and His Orchestra. The director of this no-account nonsense was Gunther V. Fritsch. (74 mins)

▽ When a Hollywood actress (Adele Jergens) receives a box containing a corpse, newspaper reporter George Brent (centre) together with rival reporter Joan Blondell (right) set about solving the mystery of who sent the body. George Bricker and Dwight Babcock's screenplay for **The Corpse Came COD**, based on the novel by Jimmy Starr, wisely refused to take itself seriously and, with tongue well in cheek, the authors offered a lightweight brew that tempered its three murders with a fair amount of chuckles. The Hollywood locale, seen at its best in a chase sequence, was a bonus for star-struck cineastes. But, in the end, though Samuel Bischoff's production was passable entertainment, its old-hat plot tried the patience of even the most avid devotees of the genre – Henry Levin's direction added nothing new to the familiar material, and a cast that included Jim Bannon (as the heavy), John Berks (left), Fred Sears, William Trenk, Grant Mitchell, Una O'Connor, Marvin Miller and (briefly) Leslie Brooks went through their paces as if by rote. (86 mins)

△ Not unlike the superior *The Maltese Falcon* (Warner Bros., 1941) in atmosphere, **Dead Reckoning** again found Humphrey Bogart (left) – on loan from Warner Bros. – attempting to unravel the death of a friend and, in the process, becoming involved with a dame whose activities are decidedly suspicious. The friend in question is an Army buddy who mysteriously disappears in Philadelphia while *en route* to Washington where both he and Bogey are to receive a Congressional Medal for bravery. It turns out that the missing hero (William Prince) was a convicted killer who enlisted under an alias. Two days after his disappearance, he is killed. 'When a guy's pal is killed, he ought to do something about it', Bogey wryly observed in a line from *The Maltese Falcon* – and do something about it he certainly did. Just what, formed the basis of the often violent screenplay Oliver H. P. Garrett and Steve Fisher fashioned from the Gerald Adams-Sidney Bidwell scenario, which was an adaptation of a story by Allen Rivkin. Though Bogart was cast to perfection as the returning paratrooper who encounters some heavy-duty resistence from bad guys Morris Carnovsky and Marvin Miller, co-star Lizabeth Scott (right) – as a nightclub singer and girlfriend of the dead man – wore a permanently blank expression on her face. Sidney Bidwell's taut melodrama was given the full *film noir* treatment by director John Cromwell, whose cast was completed by Charles Cane, Wallace Ford, James Bell, George Chandler, William Forrest and Ruby Dandridge. Miss Scott sang one song, the appropriately titled 'Either It's Love Or It Isn't'. (100 mins)

▽ Very much a down-market *Double Indemnity* (Paramount, 1944), **Framed** (GB: **Paula**) was the *noir*-ish story of a greedy girl (Janis Carter, right) who, anxious to lay her hands on $250,000, schemes with a devious banker (Barry Sullivan) to commit the perfect theft from his bank. The scheme involved a 'fall guy' on whom the theft would be blamed, but who would be unable to attest his innocence due to his being killed in a car smash. The twist in Ben Maddow's screenplay (story by Jack Patrick) was that Carter falls in love with fall-guy Glenn Ford (second right), and kills Sullivan instead. Ford sees through her though, and turns her in. The End. Richard Wallace's brisk direction made it look a lot fresher than it was. Jules Schermer was the producer. The cast included Edgar Buchanan, Karen Morley, Jim Bannon and Sid Tomack. (81 mins)

△ There was no marquee value whatsoever in **Devil Ship**, a minor-league time-waster about the adventures of a tuna-ship skipper whose purpose in Lawrence Edmund Taylor's 'original' screenplay was to taxi prisoners to Alcatraz Island in the San Francisco Bay. A few storms, a shipwreck and a couple of fist-fights padded out the narrative, but to little effect. Richard Lane (second left) was the skipper and Louise Campbell a widow he has his eye on, with other parts going to William Bishop (right), Damian O'Flynn, Barbara Slater (left), Anthony Caruso (second right), Marc Krah and child actor Myrna Liles. Martin Mooney produced and Lew Landers directed. (61 mins)

▷ **Down To Earth**, an opulent Technicolor musical, was pre-sold from the start. Using the character of Mr Jordan from *Here Comes Mr Jordan* (1941) – played, this time, not by Claude Rains but by Roland Culver, and reuniting, from the same film, James Gleason and Edward Everett Horton as Broadway agent Max Corkle and Messenger 7013 respectively – the studio returned to the world of fantasy and as an added bonus, top-cast Rita Hayworth (center), as Terpsichore, the Greek goddess of the dance. Her function in Edwin Blum and Don Hartman's none-too-convincing screenplay was to return to Earth disguised as a showgirl in order to prevent a successful Broadway producer from producing a musical that lampoons the muses. With said producer played by Larry Parks, in his first film since *The Jolson Story* (1946), the studio was guaranteed a hit. And so it proved; despite the fact that Doris Fisher and Allan Roberts's score was anything but memorable. More successful was Jack Cole's choreography, which amusingly caricatured classical dance while making sure never to stray very far from Hollywood *kitsch*. Hayworth looked sensational and under Alexander Hall's direction successfully drew attention away from the whimsical plot. Hartman produced, Hayworth's vocals were dubbed by the useful Anita Ellis, and the supporting cast included Marc Platt (as principal dancer), Adele Jergens, (right) George Macreay and William Frawley. (101 mins)

◁ The lure of Broadway and its effect on a zither-plucking singer from the wilds of Tennessee was the subject of **Glamor Girl**, a musical designed to showcase Susan Reed as the thrush whose arrival – thanks to talent scout Virginia Grey (left) – in Gotham hardly takes the town by storm. It was also a showcase for drummer Gene Krupa whose 'Gene's Boogie' was the only excitement in a show desperately in need of some. Michael Duane (centre) appeared as Miss Grey's partner (together they start their own company to promote the unappreciated talent of Miss Reed) with other roles in the M. Coates Webster–Lee Gold screenplay going to Jimmy Lloyd (right), Jack Leonard, Pierre Watkin and Eugene Borden. Sam Katzman produced and Arthur Dreifuss directed. (68 mins)

△ A good idea in search of a better script, **The Guilt Of Janet Ames** was a psychological drama with fantasy overtones which starred Rosalind Russell (centre) as the confused widow of a World War II soldier who heroically threw himself on a grenade in order to save the lives of five of his comrades. The narrative thrust of Louella MacFarlane, Allen Rivkin and Devery Freeman's screenplay, based on a story by Lenore Coffee, had Russell attempting to discover whether any of the men her husband saved were worthy of the sacrifice. Incapacitated after an accident, Russell experiences a fit of hysterical paralysis and finds herself unable to walk. Co-star Melvyn Douglas (right) was one of the five men saved by her brave husband and, though suffering from guilt himself, manages to help Russell out of her mental fixation through hypnosis, under which she confronts the remaining four men her husband saved. It was either a ludicrous con, or a fascinating exercise in psychology, enjoyment of it depending on the viewer's own state of mind. Certainly a tighter, more convincing screenplay would have helped matters considerably. No producer credit was given, but it was directed by Henry Levin, whose cast included Betsy Blair, Victoria Horne (left), Nina Foch, Charles Cane and, best of all, Sid Caesar who, as one of the comrades, comically satirized the whole screen genre of the psychological drama – of which *The Guilt Of Janet Ames* was a good example. (81 mins)

▽ The 'affairs' in **Her Husband's Affairs** were not extra-marital dalliances, but involved a screwball business venture undertaken by husband and wife Franchot Tone (third right) and Lucille Ball (second right) with zany inventor Mikhail Rasumny (third left), whose latest product is a miraculous potion (a by-product of embalming fluid) capable of doing everything from growing hair to preserving flowers. The screenplay by Ben Hecht and Charles Lederer pivoted on Tone's attempts to market the product to an important industrialist (Gene Lockhart, right) – and the problems posed by Ball trying to help. The proceedings were rather innocuous, but not unenjoyable. Under S. Sylvan Simon's bouncy direction the cast, which included Edward Everett Horton (left), Jonathan Hale (second left), Nana Bryant, Paul Stanton, Mabel Paige and Frank Mayo, seemed to have a lot of fun (sometimes more than the audience). Raphael Hakim was billed as associate producer in this Cornell production. (84 mins)

◁ Not to be confused with the 20th Century-Fox film of the same title (a 1938 vehicle for Shirley Temple), **Little Miss Broadway** stretched credibility to breaking point as it told the story of a girl who mistakenly believes that her only living relatives are madly wealthy socialites. They're nothing of the sort but, not to disappoint the Little Miss of the title, a group of colourful actors move into a Long Island mansion owned by a thief who's currently doing time and put on a very convincing show of being to the manor born. Miss Broadway (Jean Porter, on piano), is duly impressed, so is her fiancé (John Shelton). Needless to say, complications follow – but not to anyone's detriment. Ruth Donnelly, Edward Gargan, Charles Jordan and Vince Barnett were the well-meaning relatives. The director was Arthur Dreifuss, and the screenplay was by Dreifuss, Victor McLeod and Betty Wright. Also cast: Doris Colleen, Douglas Wood, Milton Kibbee and Jerry Wald And His Orchestra. Sam Katzman produced. (70 mins)

▷ A thoroughly respectable thriller, produced and directed by S. Sylvan Simon (for Cornell Pictures) and written by Roy Higgins from his novel *The Double Take*, **I Love Trouble** starred Franchot Tone (right) as a private eye whose latest assignment had him uncovering some background information on a politician's wife. Tom Powers played the politician in need of the answers, Lynn Merrick the wife in question. The distaff side was also represented (most attractively) by Janet Blair, Janis Carter and Adele Jergens, all of whom lent decorative support to a cast that included Steven Geray and John Ireland (as the bad guys), Sid Tomack, Donald Curtis, Eduardo Ciannelli and Raymond Burr. Glenda Farrell (left) – welcome back, Glenda! – was in it too, as Tone's secretary. Most agreeable. (93 mins)

▷ In *Lady In The Dark* (Paramount, 1943) Ginger Rogers (illustrated) underwent psychiatric treatment because of the problems she was having with men. In **It Had To Be You** she hadn't been entirely cured of her mental ailment, having stood up three men at the altar – and being on the brink of doing the same to groom number four. Suddenly, into her life comes an American Red Indian in the Caucasian shape of Cornel Wilde. It turns out that Wilde isn't really an Indian at all, but only exists as one in Miss Rogers's fervid imagination (her first sweetheart had been a six-year-old dressed in Indian gear). The kinder of the comedy's critics euphemistically labelled it 'screwball' – the more honest simply dismissed it as 'inane' and 'asinine'. Audiences simply dismissed it. It was produced by Don Hartman, who also supplied the story-line with Allen Boretz, and directed by Hartman and Rudolph Maté – the latter also serving as cameraman. Their cast, on this inauspicious occasion, included Percy Waram and Spring Byington as Miss Rogers's understandably perplexed parents, with other roles in the Norman Panama-Melvin Frank screenplay going to Thurston Hall, Charles Evans, William Bevan and Frank Orth. (98 mins)

▽ For his first directorial assignment, Robert Rossen entered the twilight world of *film noir* with **Johnny O'Clock**, a gritty thriller which cashed in on the new screen persona created by its leading man, Dick Powell (left), in *Murder My Sweet* (RKO, 1944). Powell played the partner of Thomas Gomez, the Mr Big of an underworld gambling establishment, one of whose hat-check girls (Nina Foch) is murdered together with a crooked cop. The plot (by Milton Holmes, screenplay by Rossen) was nudged into motion when Powell becomes involved with the murdered girl's show-girl sister (Evelyn Keyes). Together they set out to discover just

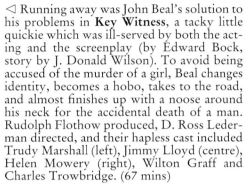

◁ Running away was John Beal's solution to his problems in **Key Witness**, a tacky little quickie which was ill-served by both the acting and the screenplay (by Edward Bock, story by J. Donald Wilson). To avoid being accused of the murder of a girl, Beal changes identity, becomes a hobo, takes to the road, and almost finishes up with a noose around his neck for the accidental death of a man. Rudolph Flothow produced, D. Ross Lederman directed, and their hapless cast included Trudy Marshall (left), Jimmy Lloyd (centre), Helen Mowery (right), Wilton Graff and Charles Trowbridge. (67 mins)

who killed her and why. This was easier said than done, and as the plot unfolds and becomes increasingly convoluted, Powell finds himself caught between Gomez and police detective Lee J. Cobb. Rossen's screenplay was an almost perfect parody of the genre, its echoes of Raymond Chandler emerging loud and clear not only in the dialogue but in the numerous plot contortions. The boldest bit of scripting involved Gomez's sadistic treatment of his wife, Ellen Drew (right). Producer Edward G. Nealis's cast included John Kellogg, Jim Bannon, Mabel Paige, Phil Brown and relative newcomer Jeff Chandler. (95 mins)

△ Gene Stratton Porter's novel **Keeper Of The Bees**, adapted by Ralph Rose Jr and scripted by Lawrence E. Watkin and Malcolm Stuart Boylan, came to the screen via producer John Haggott and director John Sturges with all its homeliness intact. It starred Michael Duane (left) as the embittered young New York artist who runs away from a wife he no longer loves and a career he believes has soured on him and takes a job in an apiary owned by ailing bee-keeper Henry Davenport (right). There he befriends a 12-year-old orphan (Jo Ann Marlowe) and falls in love with pretty Gloria Henry, an employee in an orphanage run by mean-spirited Jane Darwell. After some obligatory romantic complications, the couple marry when Duane's divorce comes through, adopt little Miss Marlowe, and live happily ever after. (68 mins)

▷ A reworking of James Fenimore Cooper's *The Last of the Mohicans*, and aimed largely at the kiddie-brigade, **Last Of The Redmen** was a serviceable adventure. It starred Jon Hall (centre front), whose purpose in Herbert Dalmas and George H. Plympton's screenplay-by-numbers was to escort three youngsters – Evelyn Ankers, Julie Bishop (second left) and Buzz Henry (right) – through perilous Indian territory at the behest of their father a British general (Guy Hedlund). Photographed in Vitacolor, it was produced by Sam Katzman and directed by George Sherman. Also cast: Michael O'Shea (centre back, as Hawk-Eye), Buster Crabbe and Rick Vallin (left). (78 mins)

△ Crusty Harry Davenport (left) played a Deep South colonel with a predilection for horse racing in **Sport Of Kings**, a slow-paced, flatly scripted (by Edward Huebsch, story by Gordon Grand) programmer that barely reached the starting post. The plot was set in motion when two Northerners – Paul Campbell (right) and Mark Dennis (centre) – receive Davenport's Kentucky plantation in settlement of a gambling debt. Initial anti-Yankee prejudice contrives to make the new owners' lives a misery. However, all is resolved when a scheme is devised to allow the colonel to believe he was left a trust fund as part of the settlement, and the Yankees enter a horse of the colonel's in a big race which, needless to say, it wins. Gloria Henry was the female lead. The cast, under Robert Gordon's tired direction, was completed by Harry Cheshire, Clinton Rosemond, Louis Mason, Oscar O'Shea and Ernest Anderson. The producer was William Bloom. (67 mins)

▽ Zane Grey's novel *Twin Sombreros* was the inspiration behind **Gunfighters** (GB: **The Assassin**) which, despite its pretty Cinecolor, engendered little more than a paralysing sense of *déjà vu*. It starred tough-guy Randolph Scott (right), the fastest shot in the West, whose purpose in Alan Le May's familiar screenplay is to cut down to size a corrupt cattle baron (Griff Barnett) who, in the time-honored way, is doing his level best to see that the county's smaller ranches don't get a look in. The baron has two pretty twin daughters: one of them isn't to be trusted at all, but the other's a fine upstanding lass. They were played by Barbara Britton and Dorothy Hart (second right) respectively. Harry Joe Brown's good-looking production assembled a reliable cast, including Bruce Cabot (left), Charley Grapewin, Steven Geray, Forrest Tucker and Grant Withers (second left), all of whom gave no more and no less than the undemanding script demanded. The same observation applies to director George Waggner. (87 mins)

◁ Doris Fisher, Allan Roberts, Saul Chaplin, Dorothy Fields and Jimmy McHugh supplied the songs for **Two Blondes And A Redhead**, a so-so musical that starred Jean Porter (centre front) as a society girl who plays hookey from her exclusive girls' school in order to appear in a Broadway chorus. When the show closes, she invites fellow show-girls June Preisser (front right) and Judy Clark (front left) back home with her – a move that cues in whatever 'action' Victor McLeod and James Brewer's screenplay (story by Harry Rebuas) had supplied by way of plot, which wasn't much. Jimmy Lloyd played a rich boy masquerading as a servant, with other parts going to Rick Vallin, Douglas Wood, Charles Smith and Tony Pastor (front, second right) and His Orchestra. Sam Katzman produced, and Arthur Dreifuss directed. (69 mins)

1947

▷ A mindless campus comedy, **Sweet Gene-vieve** starred Jean Porter (second left) as an ace basketball player, who, apart from winning the big game for Franklin High (thereby ensuring the building of a new gymnasium) as well as the affections of the college's most popular boy (Jimmy Lydon, left), finds herself involved with a pair of racketeers, as well as a sub-plot in which she mistakenly assumes that her father is being blackmailed by the college secretary. This juvenile concoction was the brainchild of Jameson Brewer and Arthur Dreifuss, whose undergraduate screenplay also found parts for Gloria Marlen (second right), Ralph Hodges (right), Lucien Littlefield, Tom Batten, Kirk Allen and Al Donahue and His Orchestra. Sam Katzman produced and Arthur Dreifuss directed. (68 mins)

◁ **Millie's Daughter**, a mother-daughter melodrama whose screenplay by Edward Huebsch (from the novel by Donald Henderson Clarke) was reminiscent of silent-screen weepies, told the tale of a woman who makes considerable personal sacrifices to ensure that her daughter is not corrupted by the desire for easy money, as she herself had been in her youth. Gladys George (left) played the mother (scraping a living by organizing functions for Palm Beach socialites), and Gay Nelson (right) was her 18-year-old daughter, who is forced to live a dreary existence with austere relatives in Boston in order to keep her share of an inheritance. Director Sidney Salkow's cast also included Paul Campbell, Ruth Donnelly, Norma Varden, Arthur Space, Nana Bryant and Ethel Griffies. The producer was William Bloom. (74 mins)

▽ Not even glorious Technicolor could dazzle audiences into forgetting that **The Swordsman** trod the same footpath taken by the studio the previous year in *The Bandit Of Sherwood Forest*, or that the 'original' screenplay provided by Wilfrid H. Pettitt was anything more than Romeo and Juliet transplanted to the banks and braes of Scotland. Narrative conflict came in the shape of an all-out feud between the MacArdens and the Glowans – which was tough for Alexander MacArden and Barbara Glowan (Larry Parks and Ellen Drew) who, despite their families' ingrained hatred of each other, are lovers. It all came right in the end, of course, but not before a certain amount of blood was spilled in the name of honour. Larry Parks (left) was embarrassingly miscast as the hero; so was Marc Platt as his adversary. The juiciest performance was George Macready's (right) as the villainous, hate-stirring Robert Glowan. Good support, too, came from Edgar Buchanan, Holmes Herbert and William Bevan. In a cast that also included Ray Collins, Michael Duane, Nedrick Young, Robert Shayne and Lumsden Hare, Ellen Drew was conspicuous by the fact that she was the only woman with a speaking role in Burt Kelly's macho production. The corny direction was by Joseph H. Lewis. (81 mins)

△ A comedy with a few songs, **When A Girl's Beautiful** starred Marc Platt as a promotions man in a model agency who submits a composite photograph of the perfect model; this then lands him with the job of finding a girl to fit the picture. It was a pleasant enough idea that went awry in Brenda Weisberg's routine screenplay (story by Henry K. Moritz) and in Frank McDonald's equally mundane direction. Lack of star power didn't help either. Also cast: Adele Jergens, Patricia White (right), Stephen Dunne, Steven Geray (left), Mona Barrie, Jack Leonard and Paul Harvey. The producer was Wallace MacDonald. (68 mins)

1948

▽ Warner Baxter (right) played a supposedly 'dead' man in **The Gentleman From Nowhere**. He is resuscitated, so to speak, when, after becoming involved in a warehouse robbery, an insurance detective spots him and is struck by his physical similarity to the deceased. Baxter initially resorted to deception after being implicated in a crime he did not commit, and he spends the major part of Edward Anhalt's screenplay trying to clear his name. Fay Baker (left) played Baxter's wife and Luis Van Rooten the insurance detective. Also cast: Wilton Graff, Charles Lane, Grandon Rhodes, Noel Madison, Pierre Watkin, Robert Emmett Keane and Victoria Horne. The proceedings were directed by William Castle for producer Rudolph Flothow. (65 mins)

△ Very loosely based on Robert Louis Stevenson's romantic adventure of the same name, **The Black Arrow** (GB: **The Black Arrow Strikes**) employed battleaxes, crossbows, bows and arrows and swords and daggers in the telling of this knights-in-armour tale of a handsome hero who, on returning from Germany after the Thirty Years War (1618-48), learns that his wicked uncle has murdered his father, seized the House of York, and executed the innocent Lord of the House of Lancaster. This will never do – and our hero, in the personable shape of Louis Hayward (left), sets about righting the wrongs as perpetrated by arch villain George Macready (who else?). He is rewarded for his efforts by winning the maidenly hand of Janet Blair (right) – the daughter of the slain Lancastrian. Indeed, love and war were the twin themes of the screenplay fashioned by Richard Schayer, David P. Sheppard and Thomas Seller from Stevenson's original. Gordon Douglas's direction didn't spare the clichés, and, given the familiar nature of the material, was none the worse for that. Edward Small produced and his cast included Edgar Buchanan, Rhys Williams, Walter Kingsford, Lowell Gilmore, Halliwell Hobbes and Paul Cavanaugh. (76 mins)

▽ A leaping frog and a clever canine came close to upstaging top-starred Edgar Buchanan (left) in **The Best Man Wins**, an adaptation, by Edward Huebsch, of Mark Twain's *The Jumping Frog Of Calaveras County*. Buchanan played an itinerant gambler, who returns home after a long absence to discover that his wife (Anna Lee, second left) has divorced him and is about to marry another man (Robert Shayne, right). Through the good services of his supportive young son (Gary Gray, second right), Buchanan and wife are reconciled, and the family live happily ever after. Director John Sturges made the most of this simple tale, as did producer Ted Richmond, whose resourceful handling of the modest budget gave the impression that more was spent on it than was actually the case. Hobart Cavanaugh, Stanley Andrews, George Lynn and Bill Sheffield were in it too. (78 mins)

▷ A facile psychological thriller that was a remake of the studio's *Blind Alley* (1939), **The Dark Past** starred William Holden (centre) as a killer with an Oedipus complex who escapes from prison, and in the company of his sweetheart Nina Foch (right) plus two accomplices (Berry Kroeger and Robert Osterloh), seeks refuge in a lakeside cabin presently inhabited by pipe-smoking psychiatrist Lee J. Cobb (left), as well as by Lois Maxwell, Bobby Hyatt, Wilton Graff and Adele Jergens. In no time at all Cobb is analysing Holden – who, as soon as he realizes the root of his problems, shows no resistance and willingly allows himself to be taken into care. Holden and Cobb worked well together, but the sheer predictability of the material (it was written by Philip MacDonald, Michael Blankfort, Albert Duffy, Malvin Wald and Oscar Saul from the play *Blind Alley* by James Warwick) robbed the film of any surprises. Buddly Adler produced, and the competent direction was by Rudolph Maté. (75 mins)

▷ More or less an extended slapstick commercial for Fuller brushes, **The Fuller Brush Man** (GB: **That Mad Mr Jones**) starred Red Skelton (sitting down), on loan from MGM, as a timid street cleaner who becomes a brush salesman to impress girlfriend Janet Blair (horizontal). So much for the first half. It was in the second half, however, that Frank Tashlin and Devery Freeman's screenplay (based on a story by Roy Huggins) really took off, with Skelton being wrongly accused of a society murder (the murder instrument was, needless to say, a Fuller brush). How Skelton, aided and abetted by Blair, finally tracks down the real culprits, involved a Sennett-like chase and a hilarious finale in a war-surplus warehouse. Skelton fans had a field-day and, in one sequence, a bonus in the shape of the nasty little 'Junior' character whom Skelton had created in his popular radio show. S. Sylvan Simon's direction more than kept pace with the frenetic plot. Edward Small's production found employment for Don McGuire, Hillary Brooke, Adele Jergens, Ross Ford, Trudy Marshall and Nicholas Joy. (92 mins)

◁ **Coroner's Creek** starred Randolph Scott (left) as an avenging gunman whose sole mission (in the screenplay Kenneth Gamet adapted from the novel by Luke Short) it was to track down the villainous skunk (George Macready) responsible for an Indian raid on a stagecoach and the subsequent theft of a sizeable payroll. Ray Enright directed with the accent squarely on violence, the best example of his no-punches-pulled approach being a painful encounter between Scott and Macready's henchman, Forrest Tucker. Other roles in Harry Joe Brown's Cinecolor production went to Marguerite Chapman, Sally Eilers, Edgar Buchanan (centre) as the sheriff, Wallace Ford, William Bishop (right), Joe Sawyer, Lee Bennett, Douglas Fowley and Barbara Reed. (89 mins)

▷ Real-life disc jockeys Jack Eigen, Dave Garroway and Peter Potter were featured in **I Surrender Dear**, a formula musical whose plot pivoted on a career switch made by leading man David Street (right). He changes from being an orchestra leader to a disc jockey, thereby easing his girlfriend's father out of a job. However, it all worked out right in the end. Gloria Jean (left) was the girlfriend, Robert Emmett Keane her father. Don McGuire, Alice Tyrrell, Douglas Wood and Byron Foulger were also in it; M. Coates Webster wrote the screenplay, with additional dialogue provided by Hans Collins; Sam Katzman produced (and borrowed Allan Roberts and Doris Fisher's song 'Amado Mio' from *Gilda*, 1946), and Arthur Dreifuss directed. (67 mins)

◁ A really lamentable musical, **Ladies Of The Chorus** was distinguished only by the fact that it offered Marilyn Monroe (left) her second screen role – as a leggy burlesque chorus girl who, like her mother (Adele Jergens) before her, has fallen in love with a man (Rand Brooks, right) way out of her class. Monroe did well enough by Harry Sauber and Joseph Carole's excuse for a screenplay without, for an instant, revealing even a smidgin of the star quality she would later exude. For the record, the film also featured Nana Bryant, Eddie Garr, Steven Geray and Bill Edwards. Harry H. Romm produced, and the direction was by Phil Karlson. (59 mins)

◁ **The Lady From Shanghai** was a stylishly photographed failure that was nonetheless full of wonderful moments. It starred Orson Welles (left, who also produced and directed it, and wrote the screenplay, based on Sherwood King's novel *Before I Die*). Welles played an Irish seaman, Everett Sloane was the wealthy owner of a luxury yacht whose crew Welles joins, Rita Hayworth (right) played Sloane's blonde, bobbed and beautiful wife, and Glenn Anders was the wealthy man's demented lawyer partner. The plot centred on Welles' passionate desire for Hayworth, which leads him to agree to participate in the phoney murder of Anders, only to find that the killing is for real. There was atmosphere a-plenty in Welles' handling of his ill-resolved clumsily-plotted material – especially in a climactic chase inside the Mandarin Theater in San Francisco's Chinatown, where a group of Chinese actors are in the midst of an Oriental drama; and, even more strikingly, in a sequence in an amusement arcade's hall of mirrors. Both scenes bore the hallmarks of a great director working at full tilt, and it was to be regretted that the same flair and sheer cinematic virtuosity were absent from so much of his screenplay. Still, for all its obvious flaws, it remains not what Welles unfairly claimed it to be ('an experiment in what *not* to do') but an effective, moody piece of *film noir* that was never boring, despite the confusing plot elements. The cast was completed by Ted de Corsia, Erskine Sanford, Gus Schilling, Carl Frank, Louis Merrill and Evelyn Ellis. The cinematographer was Charles Lawton Jr. [Hayworth was in the throes of divorcing Orson Welles during the shooting of the film, and only agreed to take the role (which was originally intended for Ida Lupino) in the hope that her daughter Rebecca would benefit financially from it as Welles had agreed to waive his actor's salary for a percentage of the gross. Welles, however, was in debt to Harry Cohn to the tune of $60,000 – a loan for an unsuccessful stage venture – and the money that he expected to make was not realized. *The Lady From Shanghai* was Hayworth's last film for the studio under her existing contract; and by the time the film was released some 15 months after production was completed, she had already formed Beckworth, her own production company.] (86 mins)

 1948

▷ Four thrilling swordfights, glorious Cinecolor and Larry Parks (left) in fine swashbuckling form were a few of the pluses that helped **Gallant Blade** add up to an engaging period adventure – the period being the seventeenth century. Playing fast and loose with history, Walter Ferris and Morton Grant's screenplay, with additional dialogue by Wilfrid H. Pettitt, from a story by Ted Thomas and Edward Dein, homed in on a struggle between the noble General Cadeau (George Macready in a sympathetic role, for a change) and the scheming Marshal of France (Victor Jory) who is hell-bent on provoking a war with Spain. Marguerite Chapman (right) played Jory's espionage agent, Larry Parks was Macready's loyal supporter (and the object of Chapman's affections, which are reciprocated by Parks) with other parts going to Edith King, Michael Duane and Onslow Stevens. Irving Starr's handsome production broke no new ground in the genre, but, under Henry Levin's direction, saw to it that familiarity did not, on this occasion, breed contempt. (81 mins)

▽ A programmer with a prize-fighter for a hero, **Leather Gloves** (GB: **Loser Takes All**) was a middle-of-the-road drama which starred Cameron Mitchell (left) as a light-heavyweight boxer whose role in Brown Holmes's neat little screenplay (from a *Saturday Evening Post* story by Richard English) was to improve the lives of several small town folk with whom he comes into contact in the course of a single week. And, indeed, the only life that remains unchanged is his own – for, in the end, he doesn't even get the girl (Virginia Grey, right). The film was produced and directed by Richard Quine and William Asher with a cast that included Jane Nigh, Sam Levene, Henry O'Neill and Blake Edwards. (75 mins)

△ Based on a 1926 Broadway play by Charles MacArthur and Edward Sheldon, **Lulu Belle** (played by Dorothy Lamour, centre) underwent a change of profession in Benedict Borgeaus's tepid musical-drama – from prostitute to saloon chanteuse. Everett Freeman's script (with additional dialogue by Karl Lamb) employed a flashback to tell of the heroine's numerous romantic liaisons, which included attorney George Montgomery, prizefighter Gregg McClure, the fighter's manager Albert Dekker, and railroad baron Otto Kruger (left) who takes her from New Orleans to stardom on Broadway. Lulu's reward for a life of promiscuity is a bullet – at which point Freeman's screenplay became something of a whodunnit. Leslie Fenton's direction was no better than his material, nor was he able to do much with a cast that included Addison Richards, Glenda Farrell (right), Charlotte Winters, William Haade and Clancy Cooper. (86 mins)

▷ After her blonde bob in *The Lady From Shanghai*, Rita Hayworth (right) once again became a tawny temptress in **The Loves Of Carmen**, produced and directed by Charles Vidor for Hayworth's Beckworth Corporation. As the heroine of Prosper Mérimée's famous tale of passion and death, she cut a dramatic swathe through the flak engendered by Helen Deutsch's uninspiring screenplay, and made an eye-catching impact in the role she was born to play. She miscalculated, however, in the casting of Glenn Ford (left) as Don José – a monumental error from which the film never fully recovered. Nor was the music by Mario Castelnuovo-Tedesco an adequate replacement for the more familiar Bizet melodies so inextricably linked with the tragedy of Carmen. Still, with Technicolor coming to the rescue on more than one occasion, and with Hayworth's ravishing looks ravishingly photographed by William Snyder, this lavish $2.5 million production was quite an eye-full. Hayworth's father, Eduardo Cansino, assisted Robert Sidney in choreographing two sultry dance numbers for his daughter; her uncle José appeared as a dancer, while her brother Vernon surfaced in a bit part as an extra. The film's exteriors were shot on Mount Whitney and its environs in California. If the landscapes bore little resemblance to those of Seville, who noticed, and who cared? Also cast: Ron Randell, Victor Jory, Luther Adler, Arnold Moss, Joseph Buloff and Margaret Wycherly as the old gypsy crone who predicts the heroine's death at the hands of her lover. [This was the twentieth screen version of Mérimée's tragedy, the first being a Spanish version made in 1910. To date there have been five further versions: *Carmen Jones* (20th Century-Fox, 1954), *Carmen Baby* (1967), Carlos Saura's flamenco *Carmen* (Orion, 1982), Jean-Luc Godard's *Prénom Carmen* (Sara Films/Films A2/JLG Films, 1983), and Francesco Rosi's *Carmen* (Gaumont, 1984).] (99 mins)

▷ The **Manhattan Angel** in the musical of the same name was Gloria Jean (centre). What made her so special, in the screenplay Albert Derr fashioned from a story he devised with George H. Plympton, was that she outfaced formidable resistance from an unpleasant bachelor tycoon (Thurston Hall) in order to save a youth centre in New York from being replaced by a factory. The failure of the script to provide freshness and/or regular servings of humour rendered the proceedings all too trite and predictable for comfort. Ross Ford, Patricia White, Alice Tyrrell, Benny Baker, Russell Hicks (right), Fay Baker (left), Jimmy Lloyd and Leonard Sues were in it too, Sam Katzman produced and, as was usual with films of this sort, Arthur Dreifuss directed. (67 mins)

▽ In **Port Said**, Gloria Henry (right) played both a good gal and a bad gal – and wasn't particularly convincing in either guise. All about the efforts of a father (Edgar Barrier) to track down the Fascist murderer of his wife, it emerged under Reginald LeBorg's direction as a ponderous cloak-and-dagger melodrama whose exotic Egyptian backdrop added nothing to the entertainment value in Wallace MacDonald's lack-lustre production. It was scripted by Brenda Weisberg from a story by Louis Pollock and also featured William Bishop (left), Steven Geray, Richard Hale, Ian MacDonald, Blanche Zohar and Jay Novello. (66 mins)

△ Not a great deal of plot attached itself to **Mary Lou**, which was just as well as the little there was hardly demanded an encore. All about a pair of rival singers bickering over the use of the name Mary Lou, it starred Joan Barton (centre, as an air hostess fired for soothing her passengers with a song) and Abigail Adams as her rival. Also working for producer Sam Katzman and director Arthur Dreifuss were Robert Lowery (right), Glenda Farrell (the lady on the left), Frank Jenks (centre left), Emmett Vogan, Pierre Watkin, Frankie Carle (third right) and His Orchestra, Thelma White, Charles Jordan, Les Turner and Chester Clute. It was written by M. Coates Webster – probably on the back of a napkin over breakfast. (65 mins)

▽ Cinecolor came to the aid of **The Prince Of Thieves**, another variation on the Robin Hood legend. In it Jon Hall (second left) played Robin, whose main concern in Maurice Tombragel and Charles H. Schneer's corny screenplay was to ensure that Lady Christabel (Adele Jergens) marries the man of her choice (Michael Duane) rather than the man (Gavin Muir) to whom she has been pledged by her father. Alan Mowbray played Friar Tuck (broadly), and Patricia Morison (second right) was Lady Marian, with other roles under Howard Bretherton's flaccid direction going to H. B. Warner (left), Lowell Gilmore, Walter Sande (Little John), Syd Salor (Will Scarlet) and Belle Mitchell (right). Sam Katzman produced. (71 mins)

▽ **The Mating Of Millie** was a bright albeit predictable comedy in which Evelyn Keyes (front left), as a smart career woman, decides she wants to adopt a baby. Trouble is, she's not married and, legally, needs a spouse if the adoption papers are to go through. Enter Glenn Ford (right), a rather charmless oaf who volunteers to coach Miss Keyes in the ways of ensnaring a man. Needless to say, the man she ensnares is him. Louella MacFarlane and St Clair McKelway wrote the screenplay from a story by Adele Commandini, Henry Levin directed, and Casey Robinson produced. The cast included Ron Randell, Willard Parker, Virginia Hunter, Jimmy Hunt and Mabel Paige. No world-beater, but agreeable just the same. (86 mins)

◁ **Racing Luck** was a youthful comedy about a brother and sister who, after being orphaned, have nothing in the world but their late father's debts and two race-horses: Charm Boy and Flasher. However, the problem is that the former won't move on to the track unless the latter is entered in the same race. Using this slender plot point, scenarists Joseph Carole, Al Martin and Harvey Gates emerged with a wafer-thin entertainment that starred Gloria Henry (right) and Stanley Clements (centre) as the brother and sister, and also featured David Bruce (left), Paula Raymond, Harry Cheshire and Dooley Wilson. William Berke directed for producer Sam Katzman. (66 mins)

▽ 'A pleasant and refreshing variation on an old theme' is how a contemporary critic described **Relentless**, and he was spot on. The old theme was that of a cowboy (Robert Young, left) who becomes an outlaw for a while in order to track down the man who alone can clear him of a murder charge, and it was rendered refreshing by Young's always credible and sympathetic performance as the wronged buckaroo. Winston Miller's screenplay (from a story by Kenneth Perkins) kept the romance (as supplied by Marguerite Chapman, right) subservient to the action (as supplied by bad-guy Barton MacLane), while Edward Cronjager's Technicolor lensing assured that the whole production looked gorgeous. Akim Tamiroff was effective as a saloonkeeper prepared to hide Young for a fee of half a gold mine, with other parts in Eugene B. Rodney's production going to Willard Parker as a thwarted sheriff, as well as to Mike Mazurki, Robert Barrat, Clem Bevans and Frank Fenton. Director George Sherman kept the clichés to a minimum. (91 mins)

△ The studio clearly had great faith in **The Return Of October** (GB: **A Date With Destiny**) for, although its subject hardly cried out for costly Technicolor, that was precisely what it got. A fantasy which recalled *Here Comes Mr Jordan* (1941) and *My Brother Talks To Horses* (MGM, 1946), it managed to keep whimsy at bay while telling the decidedly whimsical story of a young woman (relative newcomer Terry Moore, left) whose late uncle Willie James Gleason, briefly seen) is re-incarnated as a thoroughbred horse. At least, as far as Miss Moore is concerned, he is. The horse's name is October. As a ruse to obtain her estate, Miss Moore is tried for insanity, and becomes the subject of a book written by a diffident psychologist with whom she falls in love. Glenn Ford (right) was top-billed as the psychologist, with other roles under Joseph H. Lewis's lighthearted, admirably restrained direction falling to Albert Sharpe, Dame May Whitty, Henry O'Neill, Frederic Tozere, Samuel S. Hinds, Nana Bryant, Lloyd Corrigan and Gus Schilling. Norman Panama and Melvin Frank' screenplay (story by Connie Lee and Karen De Wolf) kept the potentially indigestible material digestible; and it was produced by Rudolph Maté. It may not have been art, but it was good fun. (87 mins)

▽ A mélange of comedy, romance, and music – though undistinguished in all areas – **Rose Of Santa Rosa** pivoted on a mistaken-identity ploy involving happy-go-lucky Fortunio Bonanova and one Dolores de Garfias (Patricia White, right) whom he has never met but whom his father has arranged for him to marry. Barry Shipman's story and screenplay found the ugliest of the Hoosier Hotshots (Hezzy) impersonating Bonanova in the hope that Dolores will be put off and hence turn him down. Eduardo Noriega (left), Eduardo Ciannelli, Ann Codee and Douglas Fowley also had parts in director Ray Nazarro's mish-mash; so did The Philharmonica Trio, as well as Aaron Gonzales and his Orchestra. (65 mins)

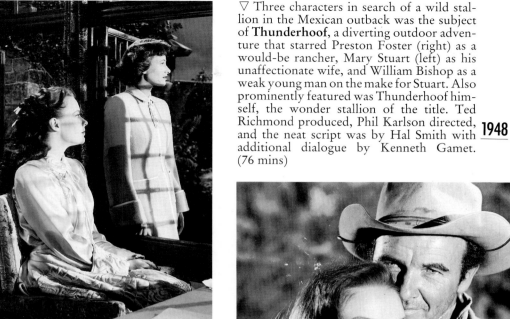

△ The film that marked the return of Susan Peters (left) to the screen (in a wheelchair) after being crippled in a hunting accident, was **The Sign Of The Ram**, a slow-moving domestic melodrama in which she played a rather malignant invalid wife and step-mother who, being born under the troublesome sign of the ram, causes all kinds of havoc in the house she shares with her good-natured husband (Alexander Knox) and her three grown-up foster children (Peggy Ann Garner, Allene Roberts and Ross Ford). In the end, after alienating those closest to her, she wheels herself off a cliff and into the sea. So-so performances, to a bogus screenplay (by Charles Bennett from the novel by Margaret Ferguson) and unhelpful direction from John Sturges added up to a mediocre 'women's picture'. It was produced by Irving Cummings Jr whose cast included Phyllis Thaxter (right), Ron Randell and Dame May Whitty. (84 mins)

▽ Three characters in search of a wild stallion in the Mexican outback was the subject of **Thunderhoof**, a diverting outdoor adventure that starred Preston Foster (right) as a would-be rancher, Mary Stuart (left) as his unaffectionate wife, and William Bishop as a weak young man on the make for Stuart. Also prominently featured was Thunderhoof himself, the wonder stallion of the title. Ted Richmond produced, Phil Karlson directed, and the neat script was by Hal Smith with additional dialogue by Kenneth Gamet. (76 mins)

◁ Opium-smuggling was the subject of Sidney Buchman's $2 million production **To The Ends Of The Earth** which encountered some heavy-duty opposition from the Production Code Administration. In the event, the PCA had no cause for alarm, as the end result was an action-packed melodrama that in no way glamorized the world it set out to expose. It starred Dick Powell (right) as an intrepid Treasury agent who travels to the ends of the earth (actually Shanghai, Egypt, Cuba and New Jersey) in order to track down an international group of fanatics whose aim it is to take over the universe through the large-scale infiltration of dope. It was the type of plot that Ian Fleming's 007 would happily have nipped in the bud, and, indeed, might be seen as a forerunner of the kind of 'global' adventure in which James Bond would, a couple of decades later, so profitably thrive. The complicated screenplay, with its numerous plot contortions, was the work of Jay Richard Kennedy; the no-nonsense direction was by Robert Stevenson, and the cast included Signe Hasso, Maylia, Ludwig Donath, Vladimir Sokoloff (centre), Edgar Barrier, John Hoyt, Marcel Journet, Fritz Lerber, Vernon Steele and, playing himself, Commissioner Harry J. Anslinger of the Treasury Department from whom Powell received his instructions. (104 mins)

▽ **Triple Threat** was precisely that: it was indifferently directed (by Jean Yarbrough), flatly scripted (by Joseph Carole) and listlessly performed by a cast that included Richard Crane (front left), Gloria Henry, John Litel (centre front), Pat Phelan (front right) and Joseph Crehan. It called into play plot number 125 – the one about the big-headed amateur gridiron hero who's cut down to size when he turns professional, and redeems himself during the climactic match at the end etc. etc. A team of well known contemporary football stars made brief appearances – but to no avail. This one was a stinker – in triplicate. (71 mins)

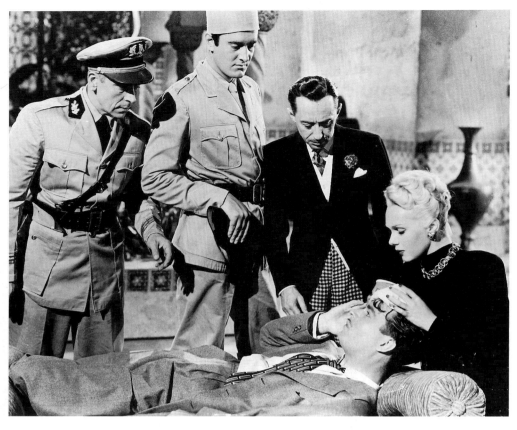

△ An action-filled melodrama whose screenplay by Irwin Franklin was as basic as a punch on the jaw, **The Woman From Tangier** starred Adele Jergens (right) as a café singer who, in tandem with leading man Stephen Dunne (lying down) – an insurance investigator – helps an investigation involving a double murder and the theft of $50,000 from a ship in Tangier harbour. Also cast in Martin Mooney's well-paced production were Ian McDonald, as a gangster, Denis Green, as a British ship's captain, Ivan Triesault (left) and Curt Bois (second right). Harold Daniels directed. (66 mins)

▷ Louis Hayward (centre) starred as a Scotland Yard investigator, and Dennis O'Keefe (left) as an FBI agent in **Walk A Crooked Mile**, a documentary-style espionage thriller that purported to give the layman a working knowledge of the methods employed by both Scotland Yard and the FBI in smoking out Communist infiltrators. Onslow Stevens was the villain of the piece, and played the Mr Big of an international spy ring whose purpose in George Bruce's screenplay (story by Bertram Millhauser) was to prise out of prominent nuclear scientists secret information about the A-bomb. Grant Whytock's production (for Edward Small), which also employed the talents of Carl Esmond, Raymond Burr, Louise Albritton (right), Art Baker and Lowell Gilmore, was best taken with a lot more than just a pinch of salt, even though Gordon Douglas's direction played it for real. (91 mins)

◁ 'Inspired' by Henry W. Longfellow's poem, and suggested by an Edward Huebsch story, **The Wreck Of The Hesperus** was a maritime melodrama that starred Willard Parker (left) as an embittered captain who joins forces, in 1830, with a wealthy Bostonian ship salvager (Edgar Buchanan), unaware that his employer deliberately wrecks ships by placing lanterns along false channels. Buchanan's eventual and inevitable comeuppance occupied scenarist Aubrey Wisberg as well as a cast that included Patricia White (second left, the romantic interest), Holmes Herbert, Wilton Graff, Boyd Davis, Jeff Corey (third left), Paul Campbell, and Paul E. Burns (right). Wallace MacDonald produced and John Hoffman directed. (70 mins)

▽ **Air Hostess**, by scenarists Robert Libott and Frank Burt, story by Louise Rousseau (no connection with *Air Hostess*, 1933) followed the lives of three air stewardesses and what made them want to fly. Producer Wallace MacDonald's cast, which included Gloria Henry (second right), Ross Ford (second left), Audrey Long (right), Marjorie Lord, Barbara Billingsley (left), William Wright, Ann Doran, Olive Deering and veteran Leatrice Joy, helped give it credence; so did director Lew Landers. (60 mins)

▽ Robert Penn Warren's Pulitzer Prize-winning novel **All The King's Men**, inspired by the sensational political career of Huey Long, came to the screen in a brilliant, no-punches-pulled adaptation of the book by Robert Rossen who brought the film in for under $1 million, and whose own salary for writing, producing and directing was a mere $25,000. It was the story of a backwoods would-be politico who ruthlessly exploits the gullibility and lemming-like mindlessness of the masses while at the same time receiving a massage for his massive ego as he systematically elevates himself to the powerful office of governor of an unnamed Southern state. The rise and fall of the main character, Willie Stark, is seen through the eyes of a newspaperman (John Ireland, centre) and was recounted though a mixture of psychological insight and melodrama. For the all-important role of Stark, Harry Cohn originally wanted Spencer Tracy but Rossen hoped to make an impact with a leading man less well-known and chose Broderick Crawford (right) instead. It was an inspired choice, for Crawford had all the charisma and histrionics necessary to convince audiences of his potent powers of persuasion when it came to manipulating the mob and getting his own way – regardless of the means. Also effectively cast were Joanne Dru as Ireland's cultured sweetheart (and a victim of Crawford's magnetism), John Derek (left) as Crawford's adopted son, Anne Seymour as Mrs Stark and, best of all the supporting performers, Mercedes McCambridge as Crawford's mistress-cum-secretary. There was fine work, too, from Ralph Dumke, Raymond Greenleaf and Walter Burke. Indeed, the entire cast responded marvellously to Rossen's trenchant, sure-footed, documentary-style approach to the material; and if the domestic sequences involving the protagonist's effect on those nearest and dearest to him didn't have quite the same impact as the sequences involving large-scale mob hysteria and violence, it hardly spoiled what was one of the most convincing indictments of political chicanery ever made. It was photographed by Burnett Guffey. (109 mins)

▽ The confusion caused when a recent divorcee (Barbara Hale, left) discovers, while *en route* to the altar to marry hubbie number two (Robert Hutton), that she's pregnant from hubbie number one (Robert Young, right), formed the rather feeble basis of **And Baby Makes Three.** It might just as easily have been called Three Characters in Search of a Couple of Laughs for, as scripted by Lou Breslow and Joseph Hoffman, there were precious few in evidence. The plot pivoted on Young's refusal to give Hale custody of the unborn child. All was resolved to everyone's satisfaction (except, possibly, the audience's) when Hale discovers that she isn't pregnant after all, and still loves husband number one. Janis Carter, Billie Burke, Nicholas Joy, Lloyd Corrigan, Howland Chamberlin and Melville Cooper also had parts in Robert Lord's Santana Production, and it was directed for the tosh it was by Henry Levin. (83 mins)

▽ Though the Broadway stage version of Philip Yordan's **Anna Lucasta** was performed by an all-black cast in 1944, the play was originally about an avaricious Polish family in Pennsylvania. For the screen adaptation, Yordan, working with playwright Arthur Laurents, reverted to his original concept, and the all-black cast was replaced by an all-white one with Paulette Goddard (centre) as the heroine. The seamy plot, which somehow managed to circumvent Production Code restrictions, told how Anna, the youngest of the Lucasta clan, was thrown out of her home by her drunken father Joe (Oscar Homolka) for kissing a man in the carriage room. Driven to prostitution on the Brooklyn waterfront, Anna is recalled home when her domineering brother-in-law Frank (Broderick Crawford) sees a chance to make some easy money by marrying her off to a young would-be farmer (William Bishop) with $4,000 to his name. Anna, however, foils her family's greedy plans by falling in love with Bishop and preventing Crawford from laying his hands on the loot. Though not nearly as pungent as the stage version it still emerged as solid 'adult' entertainment with more than its fair share of laughs. It was directed by Irving Rapper who, having had to contend not only with a wordy screenplay but a leading lady better known for her glamorous looks than her acting ability, did all he could to bring this somewhat sordid tale to life. It was produced by Yordan (for Security Pictures), and also featured Will Geer as a sympathetic barman, John Ireland (right), Mary Wickes, James Brown (left) Gale Page, James Stewart and Dennie Moore. The film was remade by United Artists in 1958 with Eartha Kitt and Sammy Davis Jr. (86 mins)

▽ In **Bodyhold** Willard Parker (left, top-starred) played a plumber with a penchant for wrestling. Conveniently, while on a repair job for a wrestling promoter (Roy Roberts), he talks his way into a trial bout and is taken on to replace dethroned Gordon Jones who had the temerity to ask his boss for a better percentage deal. How Parker coped with the conniving promotor formed the content of George Bricker's well-structured screenplay. Lola Albright, Hillary Brooke, Allen Jenkins, Sammy Menacker, Frank Sully and John Dehner were also in it, Rudolph Flothow produced, and Seymour Friedman directed. (63 mins)

▽ San Francisco's Chinatown was the colourful setting of **Chinatown At Midnight**, a routine thriller involving a search for a killer. It starred Hurd Hatfield (right) – last seen, to any effect, in MGM's 1945 drama *The Picture Of Dorian Gray* – as the villain on the loose, and Tom Powers as the police captain on his trail. Ray Walker and Charles Russell appeared as police aides, Jacqueline de Witt was one of Hatfield's victims, with other parts in Sam Katzman's serviceable production taken by Jean Willes, Maylia (left), Ross Elliott, Benson Fong, Barbara Jean Wong and Victor Sen Yeng. Seymour Friedman directed. The script was by Robert Libott and Frank Burt. (67 mins)

◁ **Holiday In Havana** was a small-scale musical with a Latin-American beat to its six musical interludes. Plot-wise, however, the rhythms of Robert Lees, Frederick I. Rinaldo and Karen De Wolf's screenplay (story by Morton Grant) were far less seductive, involving, as they did, a hackneyed romance between a Cuban bandleader (Desi Arnaz, centre) and a dancer (Mary Hatcher). A few hitches in their love-affair were resolved in time for them to take first prize at the Havana Festival. Ted Richmond's production recruited Ann Doran, Steven Geray, Minerva Urecal, Sig Arno, Ray Walker and Tito Renaldo for supporting roles. The director was Jean Yarbrough. (70 mins)

▷ Randolph Scott (left) played an outlaw in **The Doolins Of Oklahoma** (GB: **The Great Manhunt**), a modest Western from producer Harry Joe Brown, directed by Gordon Douglas, that rode the same sagebrush trail as did the brothers James, Younger and Dalton. The Doolins, headed by Scott, comprise half a dozen outlaws who take to their saddles after a US marshal kills two of Scott's buddies. Kenneth Gamet's screenplay hardly extended the frontiers of the Western, but was content to re-work all the main elements of the genre to watchable effect. It even managed a bit of humour on occasion. Charles Kemper, John Ireland, Frank Fenton (right), Robert Barrat and Jock Mahoney played members of the Doolin gang; Virginia Huston supplied some love interest as the daughter of a respected deacon (Griff Barnett), Dona Drake (second left) caused some diverting chaos, while Louise Allbritton fetched up as the owner of the dance-hall hotel used by the Doolins as a hide-out. They were all upstaged by Noah Beery Jr (second right) as an ex-con. (90 mins)

△ An under-acting George Raft (right) played an ex-con turned good guy in **Johnny Allegro** (GB: **Hounded**), a diverting crime melodrama which found the laconic star in the pay of the US government's Treasury Department. His job? To smoke out the Mr Big (George Macready, left) behind a counterfeit money operation. Posing as a fugitive from justice, Raft is taken in by Macready, and Macready (for a while, at least) is taken in by Raft. Macready's wife (Nina Foch, centre), meanwhile, has taken a shine to Raft, who lets her in on his plans to bring her husband to justice. But, as Macready's home is an island in the Caribbean, this is easier said than done. In a plot point reminiscent of *The Most Dangerous Game* (RKO, 1932), Raft learns that his host enjoys hunting down his guests with silver-tipped arrows – a fate which would most certainly have been his had the Feds, led by Treasury agent Will Geer, not arrived in the nick of time. It was all too far-fetched for words – especially scenarists Karen De Wolf and Guy Endore's words (story by James Edward Grant) – but it was fun while it lasted, and gave Macready yet another opportunity to ooze menace as the colourful, classical music-loving heavy of the piece. The rest of the cast, including Gloria Henry, Ivan Triesault and Harry Antrim, made little impact under Ted Tetzlaff's routine direction. The producer was Irving Starr. (80 mins)

▽ **Kazan** was not a biopic of Elia Kazan, the celebrated Broadway and Hollywood director, but the old-fashioned story of man's inhumanity to animals. The four-legged victim was a dog (called Kazan) who, after falling into the cruel hands of Joe Sawyer and Roman Bohnen and being trained as a pit fighter, is rescued by wildlife expert (and top-starred) Stephen Dunne (illustrated). Arthur A. Ross's screenplay, from the novel by James Oliver Curwood, held few surprises, even for unsophisticated kiddies. Will Jason directed, Lois Maxwell, George Cleveland, Ray Teal and Loren Gage completed the cast, and it was produced by Robert Cohn. The film was a remake of a 1921 Selig Production. (65 mins)

▽ Though not in the same league as *The Treasure Of The Sierra Madre* (Warner Bros., 1948), **Lust For Gold** was another adventure-drama that anatomized man's greed for hidden treasure – especially gold. The Lost Dutchman Gold Mine in Arizona was the name of the quarry, and its yield to anyone lucky enough to find it was $20 million worth of high-grade gold ore. In flashback we learn about the mine's original discovery a century before by Dutchman Jacob Walz (Glenn Ford, left) who, in his selfish quest to keep its yield to himself, murders both the woman he loves (Ida Lupino, right) and her husband (Gig Young) as soon as he realizes that they, too, have designs on the gold. Ford, in turn, pays with his own life in an earthquake. Back in the present we follow the fortunes of Barry Storm (William Prince) who, like Ford before him, is intent on finding the lost treasure which he knows to be situated some 26 miles east of Phoenix. He, too, is doomed to failure – and death. A straightforward adventure yarn, it was written by Ted Sherdeman and Richard English from the novel *Thunder God's Gold* by Barry Storm, and produced and directed by S. Sylvan Simon with a cast that included Edgar Buchanan, Will Geer, Paul Ford, Jay Silverheels, Eddie Waller and Will Wright. It was photographed in sepia. (90 mins)

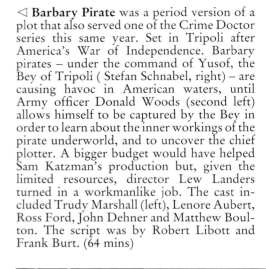

◁ **Barbary Pirate** was a period version of a plot that also served one of the Crime Doctor series this same year. Set in Tripoli after America's War of Independence. Barbary pirates – under the command of Yusof, the Bey of Tripoli (Stefan Schnabel, right) – are causing havoc in American waters, until Army officer Donald Woods (second left) allows himself to be captured by the Bey in order to learn about the inner workings of the pirate underworld, and to uncover the chief plotter. A bigger budget would have helped Sam Katzman's production but, given the limited resources, director Lew Landers turned in a workmanlike job. The cast included Trudy Marshall (left), Lenore Aubert, Ross Ford, John Dehner and Matthew Boulton. The script was by Robert Libott and Frank Burt. (64 mins)

▽ In the obtusely titled **Knock On Any Door**, Humphrey Bogart (second left), in his own Santana Production (producer Robert Lord), retraced certain sociological steps he had previously (and to better effect) taken in *Dead End* (United Artists, 1937) and *Crime School* (Warner Bros., 1938). The film's message was that a bad social environment is the breeding ground for delinquency, and it pointed an accusatory finger at society. The premise was demonstrated through a series of flashbacks in which the living conditions of a young man accused of murdering a police-man become, in lawyer Bogart's court-room defence of the lad, the chief culprit of the piece. As in most court-room dramas, the material was often compulsive. But scenarists Daniel Taradash and John Monks Jr, work-ing from a novel by Willard Motley, did their cause no good by loading the argument so heavily against society – a miscalculation further compounded by the sympathetic casting of handsome John Derek (back right) as the accused. In the end, although the cross-questioning of seasoned prosecutor George Macready (left) exacted a full confession from the defendant, as a result of which the lad is sent to the electric chair, no doubts were left in audiences' minds that boys like Derek were the innocent victims of an uncaring society. The message was unequivocally echoed in Nicholas Ray's equally loaded direction. Allene Roberts was cast as Derek's wife (driven to suicide), with other parts going to Susan Perry, Mickey Knox, Barry Kelly (back – the judge), Cara Williams, Jimmy Conlin and Sumner Williams. Though John Derek had the showier of the two leading male roles, Bogart was the film's centre of gravity and, as the axe-grinding lawyer – himself a skid-row graduate – almost made you believe the sociological clap-trap the script had him espouse. (98 mins)

△ It came as no surprise to anyone that the studio should choose to follow *The Jolson Story* (1946), the most successful movie in its history so far, with a sequel. The result was **Jolson Sings Again**, and it literally began where the earlier film left off. With Larry Parks (right) reprising his impact-making performance as the legendary crooner, pro-ducer Sidney Buchman clearly hoped his sub-ject's on-going story would help swell the studio's coffers once more. It did – to the happy tune of $5.5 million, making it the biggest-grossing film of 1949. However, the red-meat of the Jolson saga had already been devoured by audiences in Part One – and all that was left second time around, were scraps of plot involving the singer's work in a series of army-camp shows, the removal of a lung, and marriage to his second wife (played by Barbara Hale, left). Spicing it up and helping to make the most of the least were a handful of Jolson standards, to which Parks mimed just as convincingly as he had done three years earlier. One novelty sequence showed Parks the actor shaking hands with Parks (as Jolson) – but apart from that, Buchman's screenplay was severely stretched to find something compelling to say that hadn't been better said in the first film. William Demar-est, Ludwig Donath, Tamara Shayne and Bill Goodwin reprised the roles they created in *The Jolson Story*, with other parts under Henry Levin's uninspired direction going to Myron McCormick, Eric Wilton and Robert Emmett Keane. The music direction was in the capable hands of Morris Stoloff and George Duning. (96 mins)

▷ Though Glenn Ford (second right) received top billing in **The Man From Colorado**, the real hero of this Technicolor oater was second-billed William Holden (second left) by virtue of the fact that he was by far the nicer of the two men. In this early example of the 'psychological' Western, Ford, a Civil War colonel, is so scarred by his experiences in battle that death has become a way of life for him, even in peace-time. In other words, he can't get enough killing. Holden, a long-time pal of Ford's, realizes what is happening and becomes his marshal in order to keep an eye on him after Ford is appointed a judge in Colorado. But he is powerless to curb the blood lust that characterizes everything the disturbed judge does. In the end, the two men face each other not as friends, but as deadly adversaries. Ellen Drew was cast as Ford's wife, with other roles in Jules Shermer's production divided between Ray Collins (left), Edgar Buchanan, Jerome Courtland, James Millican, Jim Bannon (right) Craig Reynolds (centre back) and William 'Bill' Phillips. Robert D. Andrews and Ben Maddow wrote the screenplay from a story by Borden Chase, their purpose, no doubt, being to draw parallels between the psychological traumas suffered by Ford and by the home-bound veterans of the recent world war. The director was Henry Levin who, despite the film's 'serious' theme, did not ignore the conditional histrionics of the genre. (99 mins)

◁ Uneasily cast Marsha Hunt (right) starred in and as **Mary Ryan, Detective**, an inconsequential thriller that utilized plot number 234 – the one about the sleuth who deliberately serves a jail sentence in order to obtain some vital 'inside' information. In this instance, Miss Mary is after a notorious fence. John Litel (left) co-starred as a police captain, with other parts in Rudolph Flothow's indifferent production going to June Vincent, Harry Shannon, William 'Bill' Phillips, Katharine Warren, Victoria Horne and John Dehner. Director Abby Berlin gave as good as he got; and what he got was a routine, thoroughly undistinguished screenplay from Harry Fried. (68 mins)

△ In **Make Believe Ballroom** the music of Frankie Laine, The King Cole Trio, Charlie Barnet, Jimmy Dorsey, Gene Krupa, Pee Wee Hunt, Kay Starr, The Sportsmen, Jack Smith, and Toni Harper spoke louder than Albert Duffy and Karen De Wolf's words (in turn based on the radio programmes of Al Jarvis and Martin Block). All about a couple of carhops (Jerome Courtland, third right, and Virginia Welles, fourth right) who enter a radio quiz show, fall in love, and win the top prize, it was produced by Ted Richmond, directed by Joseph Santley and also featured the non-musical talents of Ruth Warrick, Ron Randell, Adele Jergens, disc jockey Al Jarvis (playing himself), Paul Harvey, Louis Jean Heydt and Frank Orth. (78 mins)

△ Audiences who'd paid good money to see **The Mutineers** might easily have been excused for indulging in a spot of mutinous behaviour themselves. So paltry were the entertainment rations being offered by producer Sam Katzman that the appetites of even the most uncritical of spectators can hardly have been appeased. The plot had a group of gun-runners and counterfeiters commandeering a freighter after murdering the honest skipper (Lyle Talbot), imprisoning the sailors in the hold, then heading for Marseille. Top-starred Jon Hall (left) heroically saves the day, releases the captured crew and turns the tables on the heavies. Yawn yawn. George Reeves was the chief crook, and Adele Jergens (right) his man-loving moll, with other roles under Jean Yarbrough's direction going to Noel Cravat, Don C. Harvey, Matt Willis, Tom Kennedy and Pat Gleason. (60 mins)

▷ Glenn Ford (right) starred in **Mr Soft Touch** (GB: **House Of Settlement**) an unconvincing drama, directed by Henry Levin and Gordon Douglas, and produced by Milton Holmes who also supplied the storyline for scenarist Orin Jannings. The plot went something like this: a hunted gambler (Ford) takes refuge in a settlement house after robbing a gambling joint of money he considers to be rightfully his. In charge of the settlement house is a social worker (Evelyn Keyes, left) who, after mistakenly believing Ford to be a wife-beater, falls in love with him. Being the soft touch the title proclaims him to be, Ford henceforth devotes his energies to helping the needy. An interesting supporting cast that included John Ireland, Beulah Bondi, Percy Kilbride, Clara Blandick and Ted de Corsia momentarily brightened a pretty dull movie. (92 mins)

△ Nat Perrin, Devery Freeman and Frank Tashlin, working from a story by Freeman, turned in a tailor-made screenplay for the zany talents of their star Lucille Ball (right). They called it **Miss Grant Takes Richmond** (GB: **Innocence Is Bliss**), and although it was no blockbuster, or, for that matter, a constant laugh-machine, it kept the punters amused. Ball played a dumb-blonde secretary hired by a bookie syndicate to 'front' their activities in a phoney real-estate office. Her boss was William Holden (centre, showing a nice flair for comedy) who, when Ball, unaware of what's really going on, actually becomes involved with the plight of a few homeless people, finds himself promoting a low-cost housing scheme. S. Sylvan Simon's lightweight, undemanding production made good use of Frank McHugh, James Gleason (left), Janis Carter and Gloria Henry in supporting roles. Lloyd Bacon directed with a great deal of innocent charm. (87 mins)

▽ Yet another prison-break drama, **Prison Warden** was an undistinguished effort that starred Warner Baxter (left) as a public-health official who becomes the warden of a prison deeply in need of a few reforms. In the course of implementing them, a sub-plot intruded involving his wife (a miscast Anna Lee, right) and the affair she is having with forger Harlan Warde – an inmate, and her personal chauffeur. Scenes of prison brutality spiced up Eric Taylor's platitudinous screenplay – but not enough to keep audiences involved. James Flavin, Charles Cane, Reginald Sheffield and Harry Antrim also had roles in Rudolph Flothow's production. The director was Seymour Friedman. (60 mins)

◁ **The Reckless Moment** in the screenplay Henry Garson and R. W. Soderborg adapted from Elizabeth Sanxay Holding's novel *The Blank Wall* occurs when leading lady Joan Bennett (right), oblivious of the consequences, removes the body of a man she believes her daughter (Geraldine Brooks) has murdered, and deposits it on an island where she hopes it will never be found. Her daughter is, it transpires, innocent (the man was accidentally killed in a fall) and the body *is* found by blackmailer James Mason (left) who demands $5,000 for his silence. From this point on nothing that occurred in Walter Wanger's production was even barely credible. But, with director Max Ophuls working wonders with the silly material, not to mention Mason's oily charm and the appealing quality exuded by the lovely Joan Bennett – this rather amoral melodrama was better than it ought to have been. The cast was completed by Henry O'Neill, Shepperd Strudwick, David Blair, Roy Roberts and Francis Williams. (81 mins)

▷ A wordy period adventure set during the Napoleonic wars, **The Secret Of St Ives**, from a story by Robert Louis Stevenson,(scripted by Eric Taylor), starred Richard Ney (right) as a blue-blooded Frenchie who, after being captured by the British, escapes to London from Edinburgh Castle in the company of his pretty English fiancée (Vanessa Brown). More action and fewer words might have raised the dramatic temperature of Rudolph Flothow's ambitious programmer several notches and kept the punters' minds off the triteness of the plot. Henry Daniell played a villainous English officer, while Aubrey Mather and Douglas Walton provided a sub-plot of sorts by attempting to do the hero out of his rightful inheritance. Also cast: Edgar Barrier, Luis Van Rooten, John Dehner and Paul Marion. Philip Rosen directed. (75 mins)

◁ Minor-league *film noir*, **Shockproof**, written by Samuel Fuller and Helen Deutsch (who co-produced it with S. Sylvan Simon), told of the tribulations faced by Patricia Knight (right) who, after serving five years for murder, is paroled into the care of officer Cornel Wilde (left). (In 'real life', Ms Knight was Mrs Wilde at that time.) Wilde, who is hoping to better himself career-wise, gives Knight a job caring for his blind mother (Esther Minciotti) though he probably would never have done so had he realized the complications (including marriage to her) that thereby ensue. A phony ending robbed the film of any impact it might have had; but until the final reel, and under Douglas Sirk's compulsively watchable direction, it was OK. John Baragrey (as Knight's former lover), Howard St John, Russell Collins and Charles Bates were in it too. (79 mins)

▽ Dorothy Lamour (centre), *sans* sarong, starred in **Slightly French**, a remake of *Let's Fall In Love* (1934). She played a cooch dancer who, through the Professor Higgins-like attention of film director Don Ameche (right), is successfully passed off as a classy French actress. It was hardly the stuff of which classics are made, but Lamour was in good form, and there were passable supporting performances from Janis Carter, Willard Parker (left) and Adele Jergens – and some attractive songs by Harold Arlen and Ted Koehler, and Allan Roberts and Doris Fisher. Add to that a slick, thoroughly professional job of direction by Douglas Sirk, and Karen De Wolf's screenplay (story by Herbert Fields) was more than given its due. Irving Starr produced. (80 mins)

▽ The Hoosier Hot Shots – all four of 'em – featured prominently in **Song Of Idaho**, a comedy with songs about a hillbilly radio crooner (Kirby Grant, top-starred, right) who has to please his sponsor's tearaway young son (Tommy Ivo) if he's to have his contract renewed. Corn for the cornbelt, but moderately entertaining, it gave employment to June Vincent (left) as a programme analyst (also the love interest), Dorothy Vaughn, Emory Parnell and Eddie Acuff, as well as The Sunshine Boys, The Sunshine Girls, and The Starlighters. Colbert Clarke's production was directed by Ray Nazarro from a screenplay by Barry Shipman. (67 mins)

▷ Joan Davis (right) starred in and as the **Travelling Saleswoman**, a really enervating comedy (with two songs), which found her going West in order to promote her father's ailing soap-factory. Part of her baggage included Andy Devine (left) – her 'intended'. Howard Dimsdale's patchy screenplay involved heroine Davis in, among other things, an Indian uprising – but the laughs were few and very far between. Shapely Adele Jergens played a saloon gal, Joe Sawyer was the heavy and Chief Thundercloud a hostile Indian chief. Tony Owen produced and Charles F. Riesner directed. (74 mins)

▷ The studio backlot served (not very convincingly) as an Indian jungle in **Song Of India**, a for-children-only tale of an exotic prince (Turhan Bey, left) and princess (Gail Russell) who embark on a game-hunting expedition only to discover, via jungle-boy Sabu (right), that for each animal that dies so must a human. In the plodding course of Art Arthur and Kenneth Perkins's screenplay (story by Jerome Adlum), Sabu took more than just a passing fancy to Russell, and, in a big finish, was given some timely assistance by a wounded tiger in eliminating the unwanted Mr Bey. Produced and directed by Albert S. Rogell and photographed in a sepia tint throughout, *Song Of India* (with music by Alexander Lazlo based on themes by Rimsky-Korsakov) wasn't much to sing about. The undistinguished supporting cast included Anthony Caruso, Aminta Dyne, Fritz Leiber and Trevor Bardette. (77 mins)

◁ As producer (with Robert Lord) of **Tokyo Joe**, a kind of oriental *Casablanca* (Warner Bros., 1943) but without any of that classic's haunting atmosphere, Humphrey Bogart (right) – who also starred – had only himself to blame for the beat-up screenplay, his own sour contribution to it, and the general tone of mawkishness that permeated Stuart Heisler's cliché-infested direction. What was clearly intended as a typical Bogart thriller emerged as little more than a Bogart parody – and it sank with very little trace. In this second of the four films made by his own company, Santana, and released by Columbia (Columbia eventually bought Santana), he played an expatriate American who, after the war, returns to Tokyo only to learn that his wife (Florence Marly, left), whom he believed to be dead, is alive and kicking and married to a shady albeit successful lawyer (Alexander Knox, centre). Serving notice on Marly and Knox that he intends to win back the former at the expense of the latter, he becomes involved with the sinister head of the Japanese secret service (welcome back, Sessue Hayakawa!) who threatens to make public Marly's wartime propaganda broadcasts unless Bogart agrees to smuggle a trio of notorious war criminals back into Japan. He also threatens the life of Bogart's daughter. So it goes and so it went. As Cyril Hume and Bertram Millhauser's confused screenplay, adapted by Walter Doniger from a story by Steve Fisher, tied itself into knots, Bogart's performance grew more and more dyspeptic until, in the end, it was difficult to care who did what to whom or why. 'These Foolish Things' was the appropriately titled theme song. Also cast: Jerome Courtland, Gordon Jones, Teru Shimada, Hideo Mori, Charles Meredith and Rhys Williams. (87 mins)

◁ Screwball comedy was alive and kicking again in **Tell It To The Judge**, a Buddy Adler production which top-cast Rosalind Russell (centre) as a would-be Federal Court judge whose ex-husband (Robert Cummings, left) wants her back. Seems the cause of the split-up was dumb-blonde Marie McDonald who kept popping up at the most untimely moments throughout Devery Freeman's uncomplicated screenplay. A good cast, bolstered by Gig Young (centre right) as a playboy, as well as Harry Davenport, Fay Baker, Katherine Warren, Douglass Dumbrille, Thurston Hall and Louise Beavers, helped it bounce along, as did Norman Foster's direction. (87 mins)

▽ Director John Sturges's first Western, **The Walking Hills** was a solidly crafted programmer that followed a group of treasure hunters looking for buried gold in Death Valley. Tension among the hopefuls supplied scenarists Alan Le May and Virginia Roddick with narrative conflict, and performance opportunities for Randolph Scott (back right), Ella Raines (centre front), William Bishop (right), Edgar Buchanan (left of post), Arthur Kennedy, John Ireland (in front of Scott), Russell Collins, Jerome Courtland (centre back) and Josh White. The modest but entertaining production was the responsibility of Harry Joe Brown. (78 mins)

△ Al Capone's arrest for tax evasion was the inspiration behind **The Undercover Man**, a crime thriller in which Glenn Ford (left) starred as a Treasury Department employee out to nab a character referred to only as the 'Big Fellow' (Ken Harvey), who owes more than $3 million in back taxes – though, in fact, his crimes go way beyond that. In an attempt to retrieve the dough, Ford, together with his partner (James Whitmore, back right), journeys to Chicago. Needless to say, the 'Big Fellow' has other ideas. There weren't, alas, many ideas in the Sidney Boehm, Marvin Wald, Jerry Rubin screenplay (from Frank J. Wilson's article 'Undercover Man: He Trapped Capone') that hadn't already been seen on screen; though, under Joseph H. Lewis's sturdy direction, what there was came together neatly. Nina Foch (second left, as Ford's wife), Barry Kelley, David Wolfe, Frank Tweddell, Howard St John, Angela Clarke, Kay Medford, Leo Penn (third left), James Whitmore (third right) and Esther Minciotti (right) were part of the large cast assembled by producer Robert Rossen. (85 mins)

◁ Robert Sylvester's novel Rough Sketch was the inspiration behind **We Were Strangers** in which a group of revolutionaries attempt to overthrow the dictatorial regime of President Machado in Cuba, 1933. It starred John Garfield (right) as a Cuban-born American who returns to the Caribbean island to help a group of insurrectionists successfully carry out an elaborate plot in which top government officials will be eliminated when explosives planted in a tunnel underneath a cemetery are detonated at a state funeral. The plan goes wrong when the family of the dead politician makes a last-minute change to the arrangements, as a result of which Garfield is killed in a clash with the police. All, however, is not lost, and the film ends with the sound of gunfire in the background to indicate that the sought-after revolution has taken place regardless. As directed by John Huston (who also co-produced) and who had recently completed work on *The Treasure Of The Sierra Madre* (Warner Bros., 1948), it was an earnest, sombre and serious-minded piece of film-making whose meticulous regard for detail in the central tunnelling operation focused attention on specifics at the expense of the story's broader political implications. The script Huston fashioned with Peter Viertel often had a sub-Hemingway ring to it, and the romance invented for Garfield and top-billed Jennifer Jones (left) was perfunctory. Though Jones wasn't able to do much with the material, far more was achieved by the excellent Pedro Armendariz as the chief of police and Gilbert Roland as a Cuban labourer. There was good work, too, from Wally Cassell, David Bond, Jose Perez, Morris Ankrum and an almost unrecognizable Ramon Novarro as a fast-talking rebel chief. It was produced by S. P. Eagle – Sam Spiegel. (106 mins)

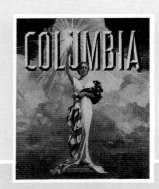

1950-1959

Cinema attendances had dropped drastically by 1950 – largely because of the burgeoning popularity of television. To compete, the cinemas had to offer ticket buyers something they couldn't see on the small screen – CinemaScope, Cinerama, 3-D, and 'adult' dramas considered unsuitable for family viewing. Columbia produced a number of excellent dramas, such as *From Here To Eternity* (1953) and *On The Waterfront* (1954), plus some fine comedies, many of which featured the studio's brightest new star – Judy Holliday. But despite the studio's box-office and artistic successes, profit margins were narrow, and, with the deaths of Jack Cohn in 1956 and his brother Harry two years later, Columbia went into the red. An era was over.

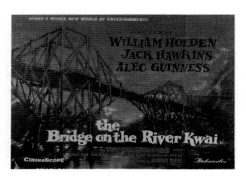

△ Which is more important – a career or a marriage? That was the question asked in **Beauty On Parade**. The answer, it transpired, was the former. An erstwhile beauty queen (Ruth Warrick) who has relinquished her career for domesticity, tries to ensure that her daughter (Lola Albright, right) doesn't make the same mistake. Robert Hutton was top-starred as a newsman (and Ms Albright's sweetheart), with other parts in this so-so drama going to John Ridgely (left, as Albright's father), Hillary Brooke, Wally Vernon, Frank Sully and Jimmy Lloyd. It was written by Arthur E. Orloff and George Bricker (story by Orloff), and directed by Lew Landers for producer Wallace MacDonald. (66mins)

△ Producer Hunt Stromberg's tough little melodrama **Between Midnight And Dawn** starred Mark Stevens (right) and Edmond O'Brien (left) as patrol-car cops. They arrest gangster Donald Buka who then breaks jail and kills Stevens, whereupon O'Brien sets out to avenge his buddy's death and bring the criminal to justice. The distaff side was represented by Gale Storm (centre), who is loved by both Stevens and O'Brien, and by Gale Robbins, the bad guy's nightclub-singer girlfriend. Also cast in Eugene Ling's tough-guy screenplay (story by Gerald Drayson Adams and Leo Katcher) were Anthony Ross, Ronald Winters and Philip Van Zandt. Gordon Douglas directed. (89 mins)

▽ Harry Cohn paid $1 million for the screen rights to Garson Kanin's hit Broadway comedy **Born Yesterday**, then balked at the idea of having its star, Judy Holliday (left), whom he called 'that fat Jewish broad' recreate the role of Billie Dawn on celluloid. After seeing her in *Adam's Rib* (MGM, 1949), however, he changed his mind and a new Hollywood star was born. Holliday (who originally replaced Jean Arthur prior to the Broadway opening of the play) was quite superb as the 'dumb broad' ex-showgirl, and turned in a performance that mingled laughter and pathos in equal portions. When Paul Douglas – who created (on Broadway) the role of Harry Brock, the uncouth junk-merchant who hires a liberal writer to tutor Billie in the social and intellectual graces – turned down the movie version, believing that the Holliday role had been built up at the expense of his own, the part went to Broderick Crawford (centre). Crawford defused whatever humour there was in the role and played Brock as a relentlessly cruel, totally selfish profiteer without a trace of humanity. This bold and disagreeable interpretation contrasted well with Holliday's vulnerability, so when, in the end, he received his come-uppance, the moment was that much sweeter. As the writer who takes Holliday on a guided tour of Washington, inculcates in her an appreciation of some of the finer things in life, then falls in love with her, director George Cukor (to perfection) William Holden (right). Holden's sensitivity in the role blended well with Holliday's warmth and their on-screen love-affair was one of the joys of the cinema year. After ditching the screenplay that Julius and Philip Epstein cobbled out of Kanin's play, Cohn persuaded Kanin to work on the adaptation himself. Kanin agreed, though the official screen credit went to Albert Mannheimer. In charge of the day-to-day production chores was S. Sylvan Simon, whose cast for this miraculous and enduring comedy was completed by Larry Oliver as a congressman, Howard St John as the inebriated lawyer who uses legal chicanery to further Crawford's nefarious schemes, and Frank Otto as a stooge. Cukor's unobtrusive direction brought out the very best in his cast and, without in any way reducing the comedy, heightened the play's social implications. *Born Yesterday* was simply terrific and a heartening throwback to the golden days of Capra and Hawks. (103 mins)

◁ The cargo in **Cargo To Capetown** comprised, for the most part, clichés and platitudes. A routine melodrama set aboard a battered oil tanker, the human cargo was represented by skipper John Ireland, his chief-engineer pal Broderick Crawford, and Ellen Drew, the girl they both love and over whom they come to blows. A violent storm and a shipboard fire supplied the rest of the action in producer Lionel Houser's been-there-before screenplay. Earl McAvoy's direction managed, somehow, to keep it afloat. Also cast: Edgar Buchanan as a ship's mate, Ted de Corsia as an untrustworthy sailor and Robert Espinoza as a Javanese mess boy. (80 mins)

171

▽ **Chain Gang** was the one about the crusading newspaperman who becomes a chain-gang guard in order to expose the brutality meted out towards prisoners. A fair amount of action swelled Howard J. Green's otherwise routine script and the climax, while predictable, carried a degree of tension. Douglas Kennedy (left) was top-cast as the hero and Marjorie Lord as his fiancée (and the stepdaughter of Thurston Hall, the baddie). Also cast: Emory Parnell, William Tannen, William Phillips (right), and Frank Wilcox (as Hall's henchmen), Harry Cheshire, and Don Harvey. Lew Landers directed for producer Sam Katzman. (70 mins)

▽ **Convicted** was a relentlessly routine prison melodrama which reworked Martin Flavin's play *The Criminal Code* (first seen as a film in 1931, then remade once again as *Penitentiary* in 1938). Top-cast Glenn Ford (right) kills a man in a bar-room brawl and is convicted of manslaughter. This time round Broderick Crawford (left) played the convicting district-attorney-turned-prison-warden whose daughter (Dorothy Malone) becomes the object of Ford's romantic attentions. Over-familiarity with the predictable material robbed Jerry Bresler's production of any surprise value, an observation that applied equally to Henry Levin's serviceable direction. The screenplay was the work of William Bowers, Fred Niblo Jr and Seton I. Miller. Also cast: Millard Mitchell as Malloby, a con who kills for revenge, Carl Benton Reid, Frank Faylen, Will Geer, Henry O'Neill, Martha Stewart, Douglas Kennedy and Ed Begley. (89 mins)

▷ When a naval officer at a torpedo plant is killed, naval commander Willard Parker (centre right) is called in to replace the dead man, knowing that the victim's widow (Audrey Long) is a foreign agent. Such was the basic set-up for **David Harding, Counterspy** – an espionage melodrama based on a radio programme by Phillips H. Lord, and scripted by Clint Johnston and Tom Reed. Harding himself was played by Howard St John (centre left), with other roles in director Ray Nazarro's modest, and modestly successful effort going to Raymond Greenleaf, Harlan Warde, John Dehner, Anthony Jochim and Jock O'Mahoney (later Jock Mahoney). The producer was Milton Feldman. (70 mins)

▽ A lack-lustre remake of *You Belong To Me* (1941), **Emergency Wedding** reteamed Larry Parks (centre) and Barbara Hale (left) after their success in *Jolson Sings Again* (1949). He is a millionaire playboy, she is a respected doctor, but his jealousy where her male patients are concerned all but wrecks their marriage, and, two-thirds of the way in, the comedy turns serious. The film's happy ending is vouchsafed when Parks decides to build a hospital for refugee doctors and so re-

◁ **Customs Agent** was the one about the intrepid undercover man who involves himself in dope-smuggling in order to track down a syndicate of streptomycin thieves. He does. The End. William Eythe (left) was the hero; an under-employed Marjorie Reynolds (right) played the female lead, with Griff Barnett and Howard St John as the heavies. Jim Backus was in it too (as a customs man). The cast also included Robert Shayne, Denver Pyle and John Doucette. Rudolph Flothow produced from a screenplay by Robert S. Hughes and Malcolm Stuart Boylan (story by Hal Smith), and the director was Seymour Friedman. (71 mins)

gains the respect of his wife. Nat Perrin and Claude Binyon's screenplay (story by Dalton Trumbo) brought nothing new to the material, and the same could be said of Edward Buzzell's direction. Perrin produced and cast, in supporting roles, Willard Parker (right) as one of Ms Hale's would-be suitors, Una Merkel as a nurse, Alan Reed as a barber and Jim Backus as a drunk. Also present were Irving Bacon, Don Beddoe and Eduard Franz. (78 mins)

▷ Childish was the word for **The Counterspy Meets Scotland Yard** in which super federal-sleuth Howard St John (left), the head of America's counterspy division, investigates the mysterious death of one of his agents. Based on Phillips H. Lord's radio programme *Counterspy*, it was scripted by Harold R. Greene, from his own story, and Seymour Friedman directed for producer Wallace MacDonald. Also cast: Amanda Blake, Ron Randell (second left), June Vincent, Fred Sears, John Dehner, Rick Vallin and Lewis Martin. (67 mins)

▽ In **Father Is A Bachelor**, a decidedly lukewarm comedy from the typewriters of Aleen Leslie and James Edward Grant (story by Grant), William Holden played an out-of-work doctor who is adopted by five moppets for whom he cooks, sews and chops wood. After initially ignoring the advances of the local village beauty (Coleen Gray) the finale finds him succumbing to her charms and living happily ever after. S. Sylvan Simon produced, Norman Foster directed, and the hapless cast included Mary Jane Saunders (left), Charles Winninger, Stuart Erwin, Clinton Sundberg, Gary Gray, Billy Gray, Lloyd Corrigan and Sig Rumann. (83 mins)

▽ **The Flying Missile** was a war drama that addressed itself to the subject of guided missiles. The protagonist was Glenn Ford (right), a submarine commander who is convinced that these weapons can be successfully launched from an undersea craft. His problem, in Richard English and James Gunn's screenplay (from a story by Harvey S. Haislip and N. Richard Nash), was how to prove his theory to the powers-that-be in a short space of time. After a stint at the US Naval Air Test Missile Centre at Point Mugu in California (plus a few plot complications), he does. Documentary footage gave the tale some contemporary validity – but Jerry Bresler's production couldn't, in the end, disguise the fact that it was little more than a *Boy's Own* adventure yarn with a typical *Boy's Own* hero. In this respect Glenn Ford fitted the bill admirably, but was given little support either from director Henry Levin or a cast that included Viveca Lindfors (left, as the token woman), Carl Benton Reid, Joe Sawyer, John Qualen, Anthony Ross, Harry Shannon, Ross Ford and crusty old Henry O'Neill as an admiral. (91 mins)

△ The studio continued to plunder the picaresque roles that had made Errol Flynn famous at Warner Bros. in the Thirties with **Fortunes Of Captain Blood** – though 'misfortunes' might have been a more appropriate label to pin onto Michael Hogan, Robert Libott and Frank Burt's enervating adaptation of Rafael Sabatini's stirring adventure. Louis Hayward (left) played the dashing Irish physician who turned pirate after being expelled from England and aiding a wounded political enemy. His adversary, the evil Marquis de Riconete was played by – you guessed it, George Macready. The script concentrated on the former's ability to outwit the latter which, under Gordon Douglas's routine direction, was demonstrated with monotonous regularity. Patricia Medina played Isabelita, the hissable marquis's niece, with other character roles in Harry Joe Brown's stencilled production allotted to Alfonso Bedoya, Dona Drake (right), Lowell Gilmore, Wilton Graff, Curt Bois and Lumsden Hare. (90 mins)

△ Melodrama ran haywire in **Frightened City** in which Evelyn Keyes (right) had, for a change, a full-throttle dramatic role that allowed her to run the gamut of emotions from the coolly confident to the desperate. She played a woman who smuggles valuable diamonds into the USA from Havana only to find that she has brought to New York not only gems but a virulent, contagious disease. Furthermore, she's been deserted by her husband (Charles Korvin, left) who has transferred his affections to her sister (Lola Albright) – but not for long. Korvin soon deserts Albright who commits suicide as a result. The film ends with Korvin falling to his death from a high ledge and Keyes giving the police details of her personal contacts so that potential victims of the disease she is carrying can be immunized. Nothing, however, could immunize audiences from the dross that Robert Cohn produced and Earl McEvoy directed. Also cast: William Bishop, Dorothy Malone, Barry Kelley, Carl Benton Reid, and Whit Bissell. It was written by Harry Essex from a *Cosmopolitan* magazine article by Milton Lehman. (75 mins)

▽ Just as *The Fuller Brush Man* (1948) was a tailor-made vehicle for the zany antics of its star Red Skelton, so **The Fuller Brush Girl** (GB: **The Affairs Of Sally**) was a piece of bespoke slapstick cut to suit Lucille Ball's (left) comedic measurements to perfection. As a door-to-door salesgirl who becomes involved in a murder, Ball, who'd like nothing better than to settle down with her dim-witted boyfriend (Eddie Albert, right), is sent off in all directions and undergoes all manner of indignities (including doing a striptease in a burlesque show) as she desperately tries to avoid the pursuing cops. Confusion begat confusion in Frank Tashlin's Keystone Kop-inspired screenplay, with Jerome Cowan, Carl Benton Reid, Gale Robbins, Lee Patrick, Jeff Donnell, John Litel and, in a brief unbilled appearance, Red Skelton all, in their various ways, adding to the mayhem. Veteran Lloyd Bacon's direction aimed for slapstick laughs - and got 'em. (87 mins)

▽ A programmer from producer Wallace MacDonald, **Girl's School** starred Joyce Reynolds (right) as the recipient of a $30,000 bequest left to her by her late father – a gambler. Fearing that her old man's crooked associate will claim some of the cash for himself, she hides out in a girls' school run by Thurston Hall and Julia Dean. In the end the money is returned to the person that the gambler-father won it from, and, at the fade-out, Ms Reynolds finds true love in the arms of Ross Ford (left), a gas-station operator. Lew Landers directed Brenda Weisberg's perfunctory screenplay (story by Jack Henley), and his cast included Laura Elliott as a bitchy classmate, Leslie Banning, Joyce Otis and Louise Beavers. (61 mins)

▽ A companion piece to *The Fuller Brush Man* (1948), **The Good Humor Man** was a slapstick romp, many of whose sight-gags paid homage to the great days of the Mack Sennett two-reeler. Jack Carson (left) starred as an inept ice-cream vendor who inadvertently finds himself the patsy in a payroll holdup. He's wanted both by the police and a gang of crooks, but is saved in the nick of time by a group of kids belonging to the Captain Marvel Club. Indeed, kids were the film's most appreciative audiences, though adults with a penchant for the wilder forms of slapstick found much to enjoy in it as well. It was scripted by the inventive Frank Tashlin (from Roy Huggins's *Saturday Evening Post* story *Appointment With Fear*), directed by Lloyd Bacon with a faultless sense of knockabout timing, and also featured Lola Albright (centre) as Carson's girlfriend, Jean Wallace (right), George Reeves, Peter Miles and Frank Ferguson. (80 mins)

▽ The cockeyed wonder in **He's A Cockeyed Wonder** was Mickey Rooney (centre), an orange-packer who can't seem to do anything right. He's loved by Terry Moore (right) but hated by her father (William Demarest). However, after inheriting an estate owned by his late magician uncle, he redeems himself by apprehending a trio of payroll robbers – Douglas Fowley (left), Mike Mazurki (second left) and Bill Phillips (second right). Rooney did the best he could with Jack Henley's demanding screenplay (demanding in the sense that it require its participants to go beyond the call of duty to bring it to life), and even managed to wheeze out of it the odd laugh or two. But it was sad seeing this versatile star being misused in a vehicles so unworthy of his extraordinary talent. Peter Godfrey directed for producer Rudolph Flothow. (76 mins)

▷ 'An over-dressed clothes horse without character or sex' was a contemporary verdict on the performance of Joan Crawford (right) in **Harriet Craig**, a remake of George Kelly's stage play last seen as *Craig's Wife*, a vehicle for Rosalind Russell in 1936. To be sure, it was not one of the year's more subtle offerings but, in her first film for the studio, Crawford brought to the selfish and tyrannical Mrs Craig a psychotic undertone and such a sense of downright nastiness that she compelled audiences' attention by being the woman you loved to hate. Kelly's familiar story of a bitch-wife who worships the security provided by her home at the expense of her husband in particular and humans in general was dusted off by scenarists Ann Froelick and James Gunn, whose 'psychological' approach to the material resulted in a screenplay far wordier than its more successful predecessor. The dramatic temperature, which Crawford tried so hard to raise every time she appeared, was sabotaged by Wendell Corey (left) as her weak-willed husband who, far from inducing sympathy for his sad plight, deserved everything he got. Vincent Sherman's direction was on the dull side and left all the histrionics to the film's exhibitionistic leading lady. William Dozier's production also featured Allyn Joslyn, William Bishop, K.T. Stevens, Raymond Greenleaf, Viola Roache, and, in a small but showy part, Lucille Watson. (93 mins)

△ After the failure of *Tokyo Joe* (1949), Humphrey Bogart and his Santana Production Company made an impressive return to form with **In A Lonely Place**, a superior, sometimes enigmatic melodrama in which Bogart (second right) played a neurotic, deeply disturbed Hollywood screenwriter wrongly accused of murdering a hatcheck girl. Even when his sexy neighbour (seductively played by Gloria Grahame, right) provides him with a name-cleansing alibi, policeman Brub Nicholai (Frank Lovejoy, left), an erstwhile wartime buddy of Bogart's, remains unconvinced. Despite the pressures brought to bear by the situation, Bogart and Grahame manage a romance, but it's detonated by his quick temper, and the film ends with the writer winning his innocence and losing the girl. Andrew Solt's screenplay, from Edmund H. North's adaptation of Dorothy B. Hughes's story, concentrated on the honest resolution of the plot and on the creation of believable characters; apart from the convincingly drawn central roles of Bogart and Grahame, the secondary parts were endowed with flesh and blood too. Particularly effective was the character of Charlie Waterman – played by Robert Warwick – a brandy-sodden old ham whom Bogart protects from himself; Warwick here gave the most memorable performance. There was excellent work, too, from Art Smith, Carl Benton Reid, Jeff Donnell (second left) and Morris Ankrum. Nicholas Ray brought together plot and character in several bold directorial strokes and was very much at home with *film noir* material like this. (92 mins)

▽ A minor league comedy, **Kill The Umpire** starred a grimacing William Bendix (front left) as a baseball fanatic who simply can't hold down a job during the baseball season. So, to keep his wife (Una Merkel) and children (Gloria Henry and Connie Marshall) from giving him the air, he enrols at an umpire school. What befalls our hapless hero once he takes to the pitch as a fully-fledged umpire provided scenarist Frank Tashlin with the main narrative thrust of his screenplay plus the opportunity to work in several sight gags and situations *à la* Keystone Kops. Controversial calls seemed to be Bendix's undoing – one of which provided director Lloyd Bacon with the comedy's central setpiece. John Beck's modest little production pleased both baseball fans and lovers of slapstick – and provided secondary roles for Ray Collins, Richard Taylor, William Frawley (third right), Tom D'Andrea (centre) and Alan Hale Jr. (77 mins)

▽ A Technicolor adventure pitched at audiences with a mental age of about ten, **Last Of The Buccaneers** starred Paul Henreid (right) as the Gulf of Mexico's fabulous pirate Jean Lafitte. Every cliché known to the swashbuckling genre was aired afresh in Robert E. Kent's action-filled screenplay – and, as our hero not only wins the day against the Spanish, but also leading lady Karin Booth's heart, no platitude was left unturned. It was produced by Sam Katzman, directed from memory by Lew Landers and featured Jack Oakie as Henreid's comic side-kick; as well as Mary Anderson, John Dehner and Edgar Barrier (left). (78 mins)

▷ Plot number 56 was dusted off for **Military Academy**, the oh-so-familiar story of four juvenile delinquents – Stanley Clements (on his back) Myron Welton, Gene Collins, and Leon Tyler – who eventually become worthwhile young citizens after being sent by a judge (John R. Hamilton) to a tough academy rather than a reform school. James Millican played a school counsellor who is rescued from a tough spot by the querulous quartet, with other roles in the all-male cast going to James Seay, William Johnstone, Dick Jones, Buddy Swan and Conrad Binyon. The formula screenplay was by Howard J. Green, Wallace MacDonald produced, and it was directed by D. Ross Lederman. (64 mins)

▽ Randolph Scott (centre) was **The Nevadan** (GB: **The Man From Nevada**), an undercover US Marshall on the lookout for bad guy Forrest Tucker (right) and the quarter of a million dollar's worth of gold he has misappropriated. George Macready as a no-good rancher also has his beady eye on the booty. The main business in George W. George and George F. Slavin's screenplay (additional dialogue by Rowland Brown) was to see that neither of the heavies kept the dough. Dorothy Malone as Macready's

daughter provided the romantic interest by falling for Scott, and he for her – and, in common with the Nevadan landscapes, looked lovely in Cinecolor. There were two excellent supporting performances from Jeff Corey and Frank Faylen as a pair of gold-lusting brothers, and some competently drawn stereotypes from Charles Halton left), Tom Powers, Jock O'Mahoney and Stanley Andrews. Harry Joe Brown was the producer. The film was directed by Gordon Douglas most enjoyably. (80 mins)

▷ The luminous Margaret Sullavan (centre) returned to the screen after an unconscionably long absence of seven years to appear in **No Sad Songs For Me**, a five-star weepie in which she played a wife and mother who is told by her doctor that she is dying of cancer and has only six months to live. She conceals the news from husband Wendell Corey (left) and daughter Natalie Wood (right), and even encourages the flirtation Corey is enjoying with another woman (Viveca Lindfors). The combination of Sullavan's superbly unsentimental performance and a screenplay (by Howard Koch) that miraculously managed to avoid all the pitfalls in the Ruth Southard novel from whence it came, eliminated all traces of mawkishness from the potentially maudlin material. The result was a quality 'woman's picture' that left both men and women alike with the proverbial lump in their throats. Rudolph Maté directed with admirable discretion, and the splendid supporting cast included John McIntire (as the doctor), Ann Doran, Richard Quine, Jeanette Nolan, Dorothy Tree and Raymond Greenleaf. The producer was Buddy Adler. [Sadly, Sullavan's return to the screen was brief, for this was her last film.] (89 mins)

▷ Melodrama – not quite of the vintage variety but passable – reared its exciting head in **Revenue Agent** in which top-starred Douglas Kennedy (right) as an employee of the Bureau of Internal Revenue, becomes involved in a murder case as well as a million-dollar tax dodge. Employing a documentary approach to much of the footage, director Lew Landers added a veneer of realism to a routine yarn, and drew okay performances from a cast that included Jean Willes (left), Onslow Stevens, William 'Bill' Phillips, Lyle Talbot, Ray Walker, David Bruce and Rick Vallin. It was written by William Sackheim and Arthur A. Ross, and the producer was Sam Katzman. (71 mins)

△ Jon Hall (right) took to exotic Pacific islands like Columbia took to programmers, and in **On The Isle Of Samoa** he played a money-loving thief who crash-lands on Samoa with the strong-box he's stolen from his gambling partner. It takes a volcanic eruption and the love of native islander Susan Cabot (left) to make our hero realize that there's more to life than a healthy bank-balance. Brenda Weisberg and Harold R. Greene scripted this escapist romance from a story by Joseph Santley; it was directed by William Berke, and featured Raymond Greenleaf as a shipwrecked missionary, as well as Henry Marco, Al Kikume, Rosa Turich and Jacqueline De Wit. (65 mins)

▽ A crime-melodrama whose timely release (it coincided with a nation-wide bookmaking exposé in the US press) generated better box-office returns than it otherwise might have, **711 Ocean Drive** starred Edmond O'Brien (centre) as a telephone repair-man whose intricate knowledge of electronics brings him into profitable contact with a bookmaking establishment run by Barry Kelley. O'Brien is persuaded to devise a wire system that will furnish Kelley with the results of races being held in various tracks across the country. Richard English and Francis Swan's screenplay gradually sucked O'Brien deeper and deeper into crime – which in this instance certainly didn't pay, as the hero loses his life in a climactic Hoover Dam chase sequence. The strong cast included Otto Kruger (as the Mr Big of a large bookie syndicate in the East), Joanne Dru (left) as Kruger's wife and the object of O'Brien's affections, and Howard St John as a police detective. Also cast: Don Porter (right), Sammy White, Bert Freed and Dorothy Patrick. Joseph H. Newman's direction kept the proceedings fast and snappy. The producer was Frank N. Seltzer. (102 mins)

△ **Rogues Of Sherwood Forest** again featured the son of Robin Hood. As played by the good-looking John Derek (centre left) with all the Technicolor swat and buckle the role demanded, Robin Snr would certainly have had no qualms about the family name and occupation falling into disrepute. Like his dad before him, Robin Jr robs the rich to help the poor and is instrumental in getting the villainous King John (played with requisite malignance by George Macready) to sign the Magna Carta. George Bruce's screenplay (story by Ralph Bettinson) added nothing new to a legend that had been better handled in the superior Errol Flynn version for Warner Bros. (1938); but under Gordon Douglas's full-blooded and picturesque direction the cast – Diana Lynn as Lady Marianne, Alan Hale (centre) as Little John, Paul Cavanagh as Sir Giles, Lowell Gilmore as the Count of Flanders, Billy House (second left) as Friar Tuck, Lester Matthews (centre right) as Alan-a-Dale, and William Bevan (second right) as Will Scarlet – gave their all. Fred M. Packard produced. (80 mins)

△ Robert Cummings (left) starred in **The Petty Girl** (GB: **Girl Of The Year**) a lively little musical, in which he played a calendar artist who falls for a prudish college professor (Joan Caulfield, right). His persistence in matters romantic results in her dismissal, after which she agrees to pose for him. Marriage soon follows and the couple live happily ever after. Such was the frayed content of producer Nat Perrin's untaxing screenplay, which provided work for Audrey Long (as Cummings's pushy sponsor), Melville Cooper, Mary Wickes, Frank Orth, John Ridgely, and, best of all, Elsa Lanchester. Tippi Hedren, making her screen debut, appeared in a production number as, appropriately, an ice-box. Harold Arlen and Johnny Mercer supplied the pleasant score. It was photographed in Technicolor and directed by Henry Levin. (87 mins)

◁ Coasting on a meagre budget, Milton Feldman's production of **Rookie Fireman** concentrated on the tribulations of ex-seaman Bill Williams (centre right) who enters the fire-fighting business during a dock strike. Barton MacLane co-starred as the martinet fire-chief whom he ultimately befriends, and Marjorie Reynolds as the waitress whom he ultimately marries. Gloria Henry (centre), Richard Quine, John Ridgely, Frank Sully (centre left) and Richard Benedict were also cast. Jerry Sackheim wrote it from a story by Harry Field. The neat direction was by Seymour Friedman. (63 mins)

▽ Filmed largely on location at the Nevada state penitentiary, **State Penitentiary** was an efficient, fast-paced programmer that starred Warner Baxter (left) as an airplane engineer wrongly imprisoned for embezzling $400,000. How, after escaping, he and his wife (Karin Booth) finally run the real culprit to ground provided Henry E. Helseth with his story-line (screenplay by Howard J. Green, Frank Burt and Robert Libott). Second-billed Onslow Stevens (centre) played a government agent, with other roles shared by Robert Shayne, Richard Benedict (right), Brett King, Rick Vallin and Leo T. Cleary. It was a Sam Katzman production, directed by Lew Landers. (66 mins)

△ Released in sepia, **The Tougher They Come** was an actioner *sans* action set in the Pacific North West. It starred Wayne Morris (centre) and Preston Foster (left) as buddies whose lives change not a little when Foster inherits a lumber camp. Foster's good fortune also results in the gold-digging Kay Buckley (right) finally accepting his proposal of marriage. The heavy of the piece was William Bishop, the camp's foreman, secretly in the employ of a combine out to sabotage the logging operation. It was flatly scripted by George Bricker, directed by Ray Nazarro, and also featured Frank McHugh (as the camp's cook), Gloria Henry, Mary Castle, Joseph Crehan and Frank O'Connor. Wallace MacDonald produced. (69 mins)

▽ Cinecolor failed to give **The Texan Meets Calamity Jane** the lease-of-life it required, and writer-producer-director Ande Lamb's dreary romantic Western bit the proverbial dust. The plot involved the attempts of a Texan lawyer to help Calamity Jane repossess her South Dakota gambling hall. Evelyn Ankers (right) starred as the titular heroine, and James Ellison (left) as the lawyer. Also featured were Lee 'Lasses' White, Ruth Whitney, Jack Ingram (as the heavy) and Frank Pharr. (71 mins)

◁ The **Tyrant Of The Sea** was Rhys Williams (right), an iron-willed captain whose stern handling of his men ultimately leads to mutiny. A costume drama set in 1803, during the Napoleonic Wars, it also involved a mini-romance between the captain's daughter (Valentine Perkins) and one of Williams's officers (Ron Randell, left). The film's only set-piece, a sea battle between English and French forces, was routine, to say the least. Robert Libott and Frank Burt wrote the screenplay, Sam Katzman was the producer, and Lew Landers directed. Also cast: Doris Lloyd, Lester Matthews and Harry Cording. (70 mins)

▽ **When You're Smiling** was a musical in search of a decent plot – without which it served merely as an excuse for a series of musical numbers involving Frankie Laine, Bob Crosby, The Mills Brothers, The Modernaires, Kay Starr and Billy Daniels. The meagre narrative line was provided by Karen De Wolf and John R. Roberts, and involved the attempts of Jerome Courtland (right), as a singer from Texas , to learn the music business. He does, and with the help of pretty Lola Albright (left) wins a recording contract. Jerome Cowan, Margo Woods, Collette Lyons and Jimmy Lloyd were also in it; the producer was Jonie Taps and the director Joseph Santley. (75 mins)

▽ As the dignified dean of a New England girl's college, Rosalind Russell (right) allowed some pretty undignified things to happen to her in **A Woman Of Distinction**, a screwball comedy that brought her together with Ray Milland (left) as a visiting British professor of astronomy. Russell, who is very anti-marriage and leadenly unromantic, becomes the victim of a press-agent's enthusiasm when she and the professor read about their 'affair' in a newspaper which, of course, turns out to be a prelude to the real thing. Edmund Gwenn (centre) played Russell's match-making father, with other roles assigned to Janis Carter, Mary Jane Saunders, Francis Lederer and Jerome Courtland. Charles Hoffman wrote the screenplay from a story by Hugo Butler and Ian McClellan Hunter. The film was produced by Buddy Adler, and directed at a frenetic pace by Edward Buzzell. Unutterable drivel – but fun in parts. (85 mins)

▽ Outlaw-turned-Oklahoma lawyer Al Jennings was still alive when **Al Jennings of Oklahoma** was made from the book he wrote with Will Irwin, which could explain the virtual whitewash his crimes were given at the end of George Bricker's action-filled screenplay. True, Jennings did serve five years in prison for a holdup that went wrong – but, by and large, Rudolph Flothow's Technicolor production glorified rather than censured its colourful subject. Dan Duryea (second right) was cast as Al, Dick Foran was his brother Frank, Gale Storm (third right) was the faithful woman in Al's life, Stanley Andrews (right) a railroad detective and Guinn Williams an outlaw. Ray Nazarro's direction took full advantage of the film's picturesque backdrops without contributing a single new idea in the unfurling of the fanciful narrative. Also cast: Raymond Greenleaf (second left), Charles Meredith (judge at rear), John Ridgely, James Millican, Harry Shannon, John Dehner, Helen Brown and Louis Jean Heydt (left). (77 mins)

▽ **The Barefoot Mailman** stinted both on laughs and action as it told the story of a con-man (Robert Cummings, left) who joins mailman Jerome Courtland (right) and leading lady Terry Moore (centre) on a hazardous journey, by foot, from Palm Beach to Miami in order to avoid the law. (This was, in fact, the first postal route across Florida.) Adding to the danger of the trek is beachcomber John Russell, the chief heavy of the piece. Based on Theodore Pratt's novel (set in Florida in the 1880s), and scripted by James Gunn and Francis Swann, Robert Cohn's production (in SuperCinecolor) promised more than it delivered. Earl McEvoy directed, and his cast included Will Geer, Arthur Shields, Trevor Bardette and Arthur Space. (81 mins)

▷ Wayne Morris (second right) and Preston Foster (right) – the Ralph Graves and Jack Holt of the early Fifties – starred in **The Big Gusher** as a pair of oilfield workers who become involved in a wildcat oil operation with oldtimer Paul E. Burns (left). Also in on the act is scheming Dorothy Patrick (second left) who, together with oil-supply dealer Emmett Vogan, hopes to take over the oil-field. Instead, she falls in love with Foster. Action was top of producer Wallace MacDonald's agenda and was given plenty of play in the scenario fashioned by Daniel B. Ullman from Harold R. Greene's story. Lew Landers directed, and his cast also included Eddie Parker and Fred Sears. A better-than-average programmer. (68 mins)

△ Tom Lea's novel **The Brave Bulls** came to the screen with its integrity intact. Given the restrictions imposed on producer-director Robert Rossen by the Production Code authorities regarding the portrayal of bull-fighting on the screen, one can only marvel at the accuracy with which he caught the horror and the excitement of this most controversial of sports. As in the novel on which it was based, 'fear' was another ingredient in this drama of the bullring; for it is fear, and the confusion that lurks in the mind of its protagonist, Luis Bello (Mel Ferrer, right) that gave the film its special resonance. The story of a Mexican peasant who rises to eminence and idol-status in the arena, it veered off into areas of psychological trauma after the hero's loved one (Miroslava) is killed in a car accident. The tragedy unleashes in the bull-fighter's mind all sorts of anguishes and insecurities and, initially, a loss of courage. How he regains that courage provided Rossen and scenarist John Bright with a stirring climax to a stirring drama. Floyd Crosby and James Wong Howe's camerawork vividly captured the atmosphere of Lea's best-seller, with an equally atmospheric music-score. Mel Ferrer, as the matador, gave one of the best performances of his up-and-down career; Anthony Quinn (left) was superb as his cunning manager; and Eugene Iglesias, as Ferrer's younger brother, and José Torvay, as the tight-fisted impressario of the small-town bull plaza, were both excellent. Unfortunately **The Brave Bulls** never fully found favour with the public as a result of the McCarthy witch-hunts, one of whose victims was Rossen. Another sad note was struck with the suicide, shortly after the film's completion, of the beautiful Miroslava. (106 mins)

△ Made with the co-operation of *True Story* magazine, **Chain Of Circumstance** was a woebegone little tear-jerker about a happily married couple whose lives are almost ruined by an unhappy chain of circumstances. First they lose the baby they are expecting, then, after adopting a child, they find themselves involved in the theft of an antique ring and the suicide of its owner. They are blameless, of course, but it takes a last-minute witness to prove their innocence. Richard Grayson (right) and Margaret Field (left) played the hapless young couple, while other non-marquee names in Wallace MacDonald's production included Marta Mitrovich, Harold J. Kennedy, Helen Wallace and Connie Gilchrist. David Lang wrote it and Will Jason directed. (68 mins)

△ Jon Hall (left) starred in **China Corsair**, a fast-paced, albeit familiar adventure whose setting – as in most films starring Hall – was a remote island. This time it's off the China coast and, apart from being the natural habitat of exotic Lisa Ferraday (right), as a Eurasian, it was the address out of which Ernest Borgnine (in his film debut) – as a double-crossing villain interested in getting his hands on a collection of priceless jade antiques – operated. Hall (playing an unemployed ship's engineer) shared Miss Ferraday with Ron Randell, her British sweetheart (who makes off with the coveted jade collection). It all ended in tears with Ferraday dying in Hall's arms. Harold R. Greene wrote the screenplay, Ray Nazarro directed, and Rudolph Flothow produced. Also cast: Douglas Kennedy, John Dehner, Marya Marco and Philip Ahn. (76 mins)

▽ Arthur Miller's devastating drama **Death Of A Salesman**, which won both the Pulitzer Prize and the Drama Critics Award when it opened on Broadway in 1949, took to the screen brilliantly and powerfully under the guidance of director Laslo Benedek (Elia Kazan had directed the play). The ultimate statement concerning the pursuit of The American Dream and the success ethic, it starred in its film adaptation Fredric March (left) – in the role played on stage by Lee J. Cobb – as Willy Loman, Miller's 63 year-old travelling salesman 'riding on a smile and a shoe-shine'. A man obsessed with the notion of being 'well-liked' (as opposed to just being liked), he has spent 34 years on the road with nothing to show for it except self-deception and despair. In the end this irritating mediocrity is so haunted by the realization that he has spent his life motivated by false values and unfulfilled dreams that he commits suicide. The inability of his put-upon, long-suffering wife to cry at his grave is an unbearably poignant reinforcement of Loman's ultimate comment on himself. Though the action takes place over a mere two days it was inter-cut by flashbacks over a twenty-year period; a process fluidly and naturally accomplished in Benedek's faithful screen version. Indeed, these transitions, which were 'filmic' in nature, seemed far more natural in the cinema than they had on stage. As Loman's wife Linda, Mildred Dunnock (right) repeated the superb performance she gave on Broadway; so did Cameron Mitchell as her son Happy. Other hold-overs from the Broadway production (which ran 742 performances), were Howard Smith as Willy's friend Charley, and Don Keefer as Charley's successful son Bernard. The part of Loman's older son, Biff (played on stage by Arthur Kennedy) was given to newcomer Kevin McCarthy. The cast was completed by Royal Beal (as Ben), Jesse White (as Stanley), Claire Carleton (as Miss Francis), David Alpert, Elizabeth Fraser and Patricia Walker. A Stanley Kramer production, it was scripted with immense fidelity to the original by Stanley Roberts, and marvellously photographed by Frank F. Planer. (115 mins)

◁ **Criminal Lawyer** was a modest programmer in which Pat O'Brien (left) starred as an attorney with aspirations to become a judge. Trouble is, he's not all that honest – and thinks nothing of fixing juries and indulging in other shady goings-on to further his ends. Failing to get the Bar Association's endorsement, he hits the bottle with alarming frequency. But he pulls himself together in order to handle a couple of big cases, thereby redeeming himself and finally winning over the confidence of the Association. O'Brien turned in an excellent performance and made the most of Harold R. Greene's efficient screenplay. Jane Wyatt (right) played his right-hand gal, with other parts in Rudolph Flothow's low-budget melodrama going to Carl Benton Reid, Jerome Cowan, Mary Castle, Robert Shayne and Mike Mazurki. The director was Seymour Friedman (73 mins)

▷ The family secret in **The Family Secret** belonged to John Derek, (right), who confided it to his respected attorney-father (Lee J. Cobb, left). In an act of self-defence, Derek had killed his best friend. The act went unwitnessed and Derek fled the scene of the crime. Cobb feels his son should go to the police; his wife (Erin O'Brien-Moore) believes otherwise, especially as the police have no clues as to whodunnit. The plot went into overtime when an innocent man is apprehended, and Cobb takes the accused man's case. This Santana Production (with Robert Lord as producer) was a potentially good idea that went awry in the talkative screenplay by Francis Cockrell and Andrew Solt, from a story by Marie Baumer and James Cavanagh. Henry Levin's direction failed to bring the plot to life, and the performances, with the exception of Cobb's, weren't much help either. The cast included Jody Lawrance (as Derek's sweetheart), Santos Ortega, Carl Benton Reid and veteran Henry O'Neill. (85 mins)

◁ Billy Brown (front right), a member of that famous basketball team the Harlem Globetrotters, played a fictional character in a well-made sports entry called, quite simply, **Harlem Globetrotters**. He's a college athlete who joins the team for commercial reasons rather than for the sheer love of the sport – but a few personal setbacks plus the love of a good woman (Dorothy Dandridge) soon help him change his unattractive ways. There wasn't much more to co-producer Alfred Palca's screenplay than that, but in its modest way it worked well – both on and off the court. The basketball sequences were directed by Will Jason; the narrative sequences by Phil Brown. Thomas Gomez (centre) played real-life team manager Abe Saperstein, with other roles going to Bill Walker, Angela Clarke, Peter Thompson, Steve Roberts, Peter Virgo and Ray Walker. The producer was Buddy Adler. (75 mins)

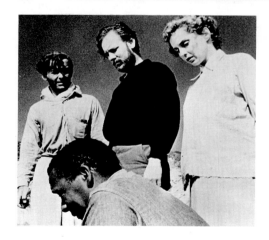

▷ An espionage actioner set in the Orient, **Flame Of Stamboul** was a cliché-encrusted melodrama redolent of dozens of back-alley yarns – most of which were usually to be found skulking in the lower half of a double-bill. Daniel B. Ullman's screenplay-by-numbers dealt with a high-powered international crook and his attempts to lay his hands on documents concerning the future of the Suez Canal. George Zucco played the criminal and Richard Denning (centre) the US intelligent agent who is tailing him. Lisa Ferraday played a belly dancer, with other roles in Wallace MacDonald's production going to Norman Lloyd, Nestor Paiva and Donald Randolph. The director was Ray Nazarro. (68 mins)

△ Arch Oboler's **Five** was the sombre story of the last five survivors of an atomic holocaust. Alone in a dead world, the cheerless quintet live in a mountain-top lodge and comprise a spiritual young man (William Phipps, centre back), a pregnant young woman (Susan Douglas, right), a mountain-climbing 'heavy' (James Anderson, left), the sole surviving black man (Charles Lampkin, foreground), and a dying bank teller (Earl Lee). In the course of Oboler's unimaginative screenplay, all die except Phipps and Douglas (who become lovers). Only a few genuinely eerie moments bolstered the static narrative line. Directed by Oboler. (93 mins)

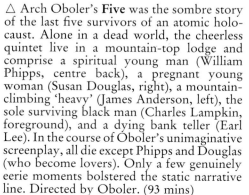

◁ Child-star Margaret O'Brien (front right) made an awkward transition to love-struck teenager in **Her First Romance**. Albert Mannheimer's script, from a story by Herman Wouk, found O'Brien robbing her father's safe of $25 so that her young sweetheart (Allen Martin Jr, front left) can finance his business. Together with the $25, O'Brien takes a document which is vital to her father's company, but of course it all comes right in the end. Other roles under Seymour Friedman's direction went to Arthur Space, Ann Doran, Jimmy Hunt, Sharyn Moffett, Lloyd Corrigan (centre left), Elinor Donahue and Susan Stevens. (72 mins)

△ The explorer Ponce De Leon's search for the elusive Fountain Of Youth was the 'inspiration' behind **Hurricane Island**, a swashbuckling period adventure, written by David Matthews, that starred Jon Hall (right) as a Spanish captain, Marie Windsor (left) as a lady pirate, and featured Edgar Barrier as Ponce. A gang of cut-throats and a band of outlawed Indians were thrown in to impede Messrs Hall and Barrier's explorations – but they receive their just deserts in a climactic hurricane wished upon them by Indian princess Okhala (Jo Gilbert). Though filmed in SuperCinecolor, there was little that was colourful about Sam Katzman's budget-conscious production, or Lew Landers's direction. Also cast: Marc Lawrence, Romo Vincent, Karen Randle, and Rick Vallin. (71 mins)

▽ Director Joseph Losey's remake of Fritz Lang's 1931 German classic, **M** relocated the gruesome story of a child murderer to California, and cast David Wayne (centre) – an actor whose talents had hitherto been confined to musicals and light comedies – in the leading role. Though Wayne was by no means as effective as his predecessor Peter Lorre, by toning down the histrionics and the more overtly grotesque appearance of the 'schizophrenic with paranoic tendencies', he instantly eliminated some of the more obvious comparisons with Lorre's unique interpretation. His was a quieter, less flashy performance which sacrificed none of the tortured emotions of the man within.

Norman Reilly Raine and Leo Katcher's screenplay more or less maintained the structure of the original German version (which director Fritz Lang wrote with Thea von Harbou from an article by Egon Jacobson) in which, for selfish reasons, the criminal underworld, led by Martin Gabel, are just as anxious to apprehend the murderer as are police officials Howard da Silva and Steve Brodie. The harrowing production was supervised by Seymour Nebenzal (who also produced the 1931 original), and the cast – who responded marvellously to Losey's atmospheric direction – included Luther Adler, Glenn Anders, Norman Lloyd, Walter Burke and Raymond Burr. (88 mins)

△ Dick Turpin's historic 200-mile ride from St Albans to York in 18th-century England provided the setting and plot of **The Lady And The Bandit** (GB: **Dick Turpin's Ride**), a romantic adventure that starred Louis Hayward (left) as highwayman Dick and Patricia Medina (right) as his wife. Tom Tully played Tom King, Dick's sidekick, Alan Mowbray was the treacherous Lord Willoughby, with other roles in producer Harry Joe Brown's swashbuckler going to John Williams, Suzanne Dalbert, Malu Gatica, Lumsden Hare and Ivan Triesault. It was written by Robert Libott and Frank Burt from a story by Jack De Witt and Duncan Renaldo which, in turn, was based on Alfred Noyes's poem 'Dick Turpin's Ride'. Ralph Murphy directed. (79 mins)

▽ Technicolor and Yosemite National Park (standing in for rural England in the reign of Charles II) came to the rescue of **Lorna Doone**, but they arrived a couple of decades too late. For this 'freely adapted' version of Richard D. Blackmore's classic revenge novel had nothing new to offer bored audiences. The tale of an arrogant family who receive their come-uppance at the hands of a group of oppressed villagers under the leadership of Richard Greene (centre) – its old age showed in every creaky scene. Barbara Hale was top-cast as the titular heroine (who turns out not to be a Doone after all, and therefore worthy of Greene's hand in marriage) – but her performance, together with her leading man's, was as *papier-mâché* as the sets. William Bishop (left), as Carver Doone, supplied a welcome dollop of animation as the arch villain of the piece, and there was a spirited performance from Sean McClory (fourth left) as Charleworth Doone. The rest of the cast – including Carl Benton Reid (second left), Ron Randell (third left), Onslow Stevens (right) and Lester Matthews were powerless against the crushing banality of Jesse Lasky Jr and Richard Schayer's screenplay (adapted by George Bruce). Edward Small produced, and the rough-and-tumble direction was by Phil Karlson. (82 mins)

△ Harry Cohn hoped Lucille Ball (left) would turn down the script he sent her of **The Magic Carpet**, thereby breaking her contract and saving the studio the $85,000 she was still owed for the last of a three-picture deal. Ball, however, wouldn't play ball. She accepted the non-role of Princess Narah (she was pregnant at the time) and was happy to allow John Agar (right) as the handsome Scarlet Falcon (son of the late Caliph of Baghdad) to marry Patricia Medina. The usual Arabian-nights brew of exotic romance and intrigue informed producer Sam Katzman's SuperCinecolor production. It was written by David Mathews, directed by Lew Landers and featured, in support, Gregory Gay as the usurping Caliph, George Tobias, Raymond Burr and Rick Vallin. (82 mins)

▷ Made in Austria, **The Magic Face** was a preposterous drama that, at best, might be excused as a jape for April Fool's. However, as the film was released in October 1951, this could not apply. It was the story of Janus The Great, a small-time vaudevillian who is thrown into jail after Hitler steals his wife, escapes by impersonating the warden, then, in another impersonation, becomes Hitler's valet – after which he kills the Führer and takes his place for the duration of the war. It was written in all seriousness by Mort Briskin and Robert Smith (who also produced). Frank Tuttle directed, and the generally reliable Luther Adler (right) starred as both Janus The Great and Hitler. Patricia Knight (left) played Janus's wife, with other roles in this tasteless farrago going to Ilka Windish, Heinz Moog, Peter Preses and, as himself, William L. Shirer. (88 mins)

▽ Western fans had nothing to complain about with **Man In The Saddle** (GB: **The Outcast**), a Randolph Scott horse-opera, photographed, in Technicolor, in the High Sierras. For Kenneth Gamet's screenplay, based on a novel by Ernest Haycox, allowed Scott (illustrated) to do everything he did best – including a spectacular fist-fight with gunslinger John Russell. Scott played a small-time rancher who, in the early stages of the film, loses his girl (Joan Leslie) to big-time rancher Alexander Knox. Leslie pays for choosing money instead of love by finishing up a widow while Scott finds romance in the arms of pretty schoolmistress Ellen Drew. There wasn't a great deal more to the Randolph Scott-Harry Joe Brown production than that, but it looked good, never insulted the intelligence, and was agreeably well acted by all the leads. The supporting cast included Richard Rober, Alfonso Bedoya, Guinn Williams, Clem Bevans, Cameron Mitchell, Don Beddoe, James Kirkwood and Frank Sully. The title tune was supplied by Tennessee Ernie. The director was André de Toth. (87 mins)

△ John Derek (left) made a dashing hero in the Technicolorful **Mask Of The Avenger**. He played a Monte Cristo-esque character called Captain Renato Dimorna who, in the funfilled course of Jesse Lasky Jr's screenplay (adapted by Ralph Bettinson and Philip MacDonald), played an aristocrat in the Italy of 1848. The plot had him donning a disguise in order to avenge the murder of his father at the hands of evil Anthony Quinn (centre). Sword fights, scaling castle walls and helping to keep the fires of romance blazing brightly were all in a day's (and night's) work for hero Derek, and he sailed through the assignment (and the clichés) with *brio* to spare. His inamorata was the ineffectual Jody Lawrance (right), with other roles in Hunt Stromberg's good-looking production going to Arnold Moss, Eugene Iglesias and Dickie LeRoy. Phil Karlson directed. (83 mins)

▷ **The Mob** (GB: **Remember That Face**) was a thoroughly professional cops-and-robbers melodrama that benefited from a taut and exciting screenplay (by William Bowers based on a magazine serial by Ferguson Findley) and from the central performance of Broderick Crawford (right). As a cop who poses as a hood in order to overthrow a gang of racketeers, Crawford brought the full weight of his personality to bear on familiar material, and, under Robert Parrish's no-frills direction, helped give producer Jerry Bresler one of the better crime pictures of the year. Also cast: Betty Buehler, Richard Kiley, Otto Hulett, Matt Crowley, Neville Brand, Ernest Borgnine (left, in his third film), Charles Buchinsky (later Bronson – his third film, too) and Walter Klavun. (87 mins)

△ Mickey Rooney, that little man with enormous talent, made his directorial debut in **My True Story** – and came a cropper. A flaccid melodrama with a no-name cast, it was the story of a convicted jewel thief (Helen Walker, right), who, after being sprung from prison by gang-chief Wilton Graff, is expected to assist in the heist of a priceless perfume oil owned by super-rich recluse Elisabeth Risdon. Like the film, however, the plan goes wrong. Willard Parker (left) played a policeman who helps foil Graff's scheme, with other roles assigned to Emory Parnell, Aldo DaRe (later Ray), and Ivan Triesault. The screenplay was provided by Howard J. Green and Brown Holmes from a story by Margit Mantica. Milton Feldman was the producer. (67 mins)

▽ A chase sequence climaxing on top of a massive shipyard crane provided the only moments of genuine excitement in **Never Trust A Gambler**, an action-melodrama from producers Louis B. Appleton Jr and Monty Shaff. The man being chased was Dane Clark (left), a murderer on the run. Cathy O'Donnell (right) played his ex-wife (with whom he seeks refuge) who falls in love with Tom Drake, the homicide officer in charge of the investigation. Also cast: Jeff Corey, Myrna Dell and Rhys Williams. Jesse Lasky Jr and Jerome Odlum scripted from the latter's story. The director was Ralph Murphy. (76 mins)

△ Hugo Haas co-produced (with Edgar E. Walden), co-wrote (with Arnold Phillips, from the novel by Joseph Kopta), directed and starred in **Pickup**, a drama whose limited budget was resourcefully deployed. Haas (left) played a widowed, middle-aged railway despatcher in a tiny, whistle-stop town who has the misfortune to meet a luscious blonde floozy (Beverly Michaels, right). Michaels quickly discovers that the rather colourless widower has a nest-egg of $7,300 – and marries him. Complications set in when old Haas suffers a bout of deafness enabling Michaels to start an affair with her husband's young assistant (Allan Nixon, centre). An automobile accident restores the railwayman's hearing, though, and it's exit wifie. Haas made a meal of the cuckolded spouse, but – with minimal back-up from Michaels (who looked good, but wasn't much of an actress), and an indifferent cast that also included Howard Chamberlin, Jo Carroll Dennison, Mark Lowell and Art Lewis – much of *Pickup* was a let-down. (76 mins)

▽ American band singer Frances Langford (left) and her duo (guitarist Tony Romano and comedian Ben Lessey) fetched up as 'greasepaint soldiers' for the USO (United Service Organization) in **Purple Heart Diary** (GB: **No Time For Tears**) and, in the course of William Sackheim's screenplay (based, allegedly, on Ms Langford's syndicated newspaper column), played Cupid to an amputee (Brett King) and a nurse (Aline Towne). Ms Langford also sang several songs, on her own as well as with Romano and Lessey. It was all as inconsequential as a yawn and certainly did nothing to stretch the frontiers of the Hollywood musical, except, possibly, backwards. Judd Holdren (centre), Warren Mills, Larry Stewart and Joel Marston were also in it; Sam Katzman produced, and Richard Quine directed. It was released as a sepia print. (73 mins)

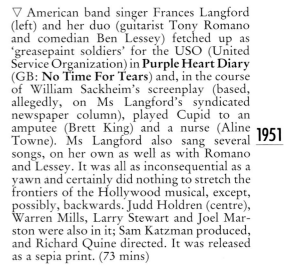

◁ In **Saturday's Hero** (GB: **Idols In The Dust**) college athletics competed with college education, and the former won. A cynical exposé of the emphasis placed on sport rather than on study, this angry drama starred John Derek (right) as a high-school hero who, anxious to rise above his modest Polish-immigrant background, wins a scholarship to an elite Southern university where he hopes to divide his time equally between socializing, studying, and sport. The possessor of more brawn than brain, he is soon being exploited by his gridiron coaches (Otto Hulett and Don Gibson) as well as a self-promoting wealthy college alumnus (Sidney Blackmer) who sees football as big business and Derek as a means of making him rich. When, however, Derek injures himself and is unable to perform on the football field, he is dropped by Blackmer (though not by Blackmer's niece, Donna Reed), and is made to realize that on the field he was a star – though off it he's nothing. Undaunted, Derek continues his studies by night and takes a job during the day. A far cry from the rah-rah campus comedies and musicals of the Thirties and Forties, *Saturday's Hero* was a cynical, well-written drama (by Millard Lampell and Sidney Buchman, based on Lampell's novel *The Hero*) dealing with a subject that is still topical today. It was directed by David Miller who was equally comfortable on or off the football field, and also featured Alexander Knox as Derek's English professor and faculty adviser, Elliott Lewis (as a sportswriter), as well as Aldo DaRe (later Aldo Ray), Alvin Baidock, Wilbur Robertson, Charles Mercer Barnes and Bill Martin. A Sidney Budhman production, it was produced by Buddy Adler. (109 mins)

▽ Another Randolph Scott western, **Santa Fe** was the story of the four Canfield brothers, three of whom – Jerome Courtland (left), Peter Thompson (centre left) and John Archer (centre right) – leave the south at the end of the Civil War and split with the fourth Canfield (Scott, second right) after the latter decides to take a job (and Yankee pay) with the Santa Fe railroad. While Scott leads an honest, hard-working life as a railroad pioneer, his brethren turn bad. They all get their just deserts in the end, but not before a lot of prairie dust has been kicked up in producer Harry Joe Brown's Technicolor oater into which director Irving Pichel packed as much action as Kenneth Gamet's screenplay (story by Louis Stevens and the novel by James Marshall) could comfortably contain. Janis Carter (right) played Scott's girl, with other roles going to Warner Anderson, Allene Roberts (second left) and Jock O'Mahoney. (85 mins)

▽ There was no producer's credit on **The Son Of Dr Jekyll** and the final results of this programmer horror certainly reflected the lack of any definite viewpoint. A hodge-podge that recycled the basic Jekyll and Hyde plot, it starred Louis Hayward (left) as the eponymous son of the old scientist-turned-monster, whose chief purpose in Mortimer Braus and Jack Pollexfen's screenplay was to convince one and all – but especially Alexander Knox (right) the evil and conniving trustee of Hayward's estate – that his father wasn't a monster at all, but a serious scientist devoted to the welfare of humanity. Oh yeah? It was directed by Seymour Friedman for the shlock-horror it was, but much helped by a cast that included Jody Lawrance (centre, the love interest), Lester Matthews, Gavin Muir, Paul Cavanagh, Rhys Williams and Doris Lloyd. (76 mins)

◁ **Smuggler's Gold** was a thoroughly professional little programmer whose director, William Berke, stirred its melodramatic ingredients with a sure hand and added just the right amount of action and suspense. Working from a screenplay by Daniel Ullman (story by Al Martin), Berke made the most of a story about how a deep-sea diver (Cameron Mitchell, right) discovers that smuggling is rife in his waters when he finds himself recovering some gold that the local fishing-boat operator (Carl Benton Reid) has thrown overboard. To further complicate matters, smuggler Reid is the uncle of Mitchell's fiancée (Amanda Blake, centre). The Coast Guard are alerted in the nick of time, thus ensuring that justice takes its inevitable course. Milton Feldman produced and his cast included Peter Thompson, Bill Phillips and William Forrest. (64 mins)

▽ If TV was a threat to the industry in the early Fifties, you'd never have known it from **Sunny Side Of The Street**, a weakling of a musical (in SuperCinecolor) which emerged as a commercial for TV itself. The plot concerned singer Jerome Courtland's attempts to break into TV with the help of Frankie Laine (left) and Billy Daniels (who played themselves) – and, finally, Audrey Long – whose father turns out to be a top TV sponsor. Some agreeable songs came to the rescue of Lee Loeb's nothing screenplay (story by Harold Conrad); it was produced by Jonie Taps, directed by Richard Quine, and featured Terry Moore (right), Toni Arden, Dick Wesson and Lynn Bari. (71 mins)

▷ Joseph Kessel's novel *Coup De Grâce* surfaced as **Sirocco**, a Santana Production which provided co-producer Humphrey Bogart (left) with another grim-visaged, somewhat charmless character to add to his impressive repertoire. This time he played Harry Smith, the simplicity of whose name belied his complex activities. For Harry is an American gunrunner in French-occupied Damascus in 1925, whose purpose is to supply arms and ammunition to the Emir of Syria (Onslow Stevens). The job of nobbling such gunrunners falls to Colonel Feroud (Lee J. Cobb, right) who, in the course of A.I. Bezzerides and Hans Jacoby's screenplay, has several reasons for wanting Smith out of the way – not the least of them being the American's successful wooing of his (Cobb's) seductive Egyptian mistress (Marta Toren). The mechanical working out of a complex plot resulted in a pretty absurd dénouement which neither the heavyweight presence of Bogart nor the efforts of gifted director Curtis Bernhardt and ace photographer Burnett Guffey could mitigate. There were some amusing supporting performances in the Bogart-Robert Lord production, especially from Everett Sloane as a general, Zero Mostel as an out-sized Armenian spy and Nick Dennis as Bogart's flunky. (97 mins)

▷ **Storm Over Tibet** was a storm in a teacup about a pilot (Rex Reason, right) who steals a mask from a sacred Tibetan temple only to discover that the wretched thing is cursed. How else could he explain the mysterious death-crash of a fellow flier (Myron Healy) in the Tibetan mountainside? Reason returns to the USA and marries the dead flier's widow (Diana Douglas, left). Together they return to the Himalayas on a UNESCO expedition in search of peace of mind. It was written by Ivan Tors and Sam Meyer, produced by Tors and Laslo Benedek and directed by Andrew Marton, and featured Robert Karnes, Strother Martin, and Harold Fong. (87 mins)

▽ Burt Lancaster (left) and producer Harold Hecht (from Norma Productions) were clearly in a lighthearted mood when they conceived the desert romp that was **Ten Tall Men**. A humorous spoof on tits-and-sand epics with a screenplay by Roland Kibbee and Frank Davis (story by Willis Goldbeck, who also directed, and James Warner Bellah), it contained every cliché known to that noble genre. Lancaster top-starred as a sergeant in the Foreign Legion who learns of a Riff invasion. He sets out with nine volunteers to quell the attack – and succeeds admirably. Just how the ten tall men went about their business kept audiences chuckling, and a cast that included Gilbert Roland, Kieron Moore, George Tobias and John Dehner (as fellow legionnaires) gainfully employed. Also cast: Jody Lawrance (right), Mike Mazurki, Gerald Mohr (centre), Ian Macdonald, and Mari Blanchard as the daughter of a sheikh whom the men kidnap as part of their plan. Goldbeck's direction kept it light and inconsequential, and it all looked splendid in Technicolor. (97 mins)

▽ **Two Of A Kind** had the sort of plot-line that wouldn't disgrace a glossy night-time soap opera. Alexander Knox (right), an attorney for a wealthy old couple, working with Lizabeth Scott (centre) and carnival card-sharp Edmond O'Brien (left), decides to fleece his clients (Griff Barnett and Virginia Brissac) of some $10 million by having O'Brien impersonate the couple's son (missing since the age of two). All proceeds according to plan until Barnett refuses to change his will. Knox tries to eliminate O'Brien, after which the latter confesses everything to the old man, who says he knew what was happening all along, and only allowed the deception to continue as it gave his wife pleasure. The final reel shows Knox being run out of town and O'Brien and Scott – two of a kind – deciding they're made for each other. This abject poppycock was written by Lawrence Kimble and James Gunn from a story by James Edward Grant, produced by William Dozier, and directed by Henry Levin. Completing the cast were Terry Moore, Robert Anderson, J.M. Kerrigan, Claire Carleton and Louis Jean Heydt. (75 mins)

▷ The short but eventful life of Rodolpho Alfonzo Raffaelo Pierre, Filibert Guglielmi di Valentina d'Antonguolla – better known to his fans as **Valentino** – came to the screen as a Technicolor biopic (from producer Edward Small) that played fast and loose with the truth, and was as fanciful and as absurdly romantic as any of the films in which the great lover himself appeared. Anthony Dexter (right), chosen from over 2,000 actors who auditioned for the role, played the matinee idol; the best that could be said of his performance was that, in appearance at any rate, he was not that dissimilar to the real McCoy. If Valentino was, in essence, a parody of smouldering romance, Dexter was a parody of a parody, but with none of the real star's charisma. George Bruce's screenplay began with Valentino on a freight ship to America. It charted his romance with an incognito actress (Eleanor Parker, left) as well as his rise to success after a stint as a dishwasher and dance host, his rejection of Parker, and his marriage to another actress (Patricia Medina); and ended with his untimely death in 1926. Simulated sequences from *The Sheik* (Paramount 1921), *Blood And Sand* (Paramount, 1922), *The Sainted Devil* (Paramount, 1924) and *The Eagle* (United Artists, 1925) were interspersed with much fictitious nonsense and, in the end, very little of the mystery of the star's private life was unravelled. Lewis Allen's direction made no attempt at veracity, which would not, anyway, have been possible given the liberties taken in a screenplay that contained such lines as: 'Love is a language spoken by the heart, not the tongue'. Also cast: Richard Carlson, Joseph Calleia, Dona Drake, Lloyd Gough and Otto Kruger. [In 1977 Ken Russell directed Rudolph Nureyev as Valentino for United Artists.] (103 mins)

△ The idea of a union leader who finds himself in the management's seat – and wants to do right both by employer and employee was the subject of **Whistle At Eaton Falls** (GB: **Richer Than The Earth**), a semi-documentary that starred Lloyd Bridges (centre) as a union leader who is made president (by Dorothy Gish) of the town's plastic plant when its owner (Gish's husband) dies in a plane crash. The problems of divided loyalties provided the fulcrum on which Lemist Esler and Virginia Shaler's screenplay ('developed from the research of J. Sterling Livingston') swung – but at over an hour and a half, the film and its issues couldn't sustain sufficient dramatic momentum. Louis de Rochemont (the producer of *The March Of Time* series) produced it on location in Eaton Falls, it was directed with a heavy hand by Robert Siodmak, and also featured Anne Seymour (left), Diana Douglas (right), Carleton Carpenter, Murray Hamilton, James Westerfield, Lenore Lonegan, Ernest Borgnine and Anne Francis. (94 mins)

▽ **A Yank In Korea** was a tired World War II battle drama in which Lon McCallister (second left) starred as a mechanically-minded young man who enlists on his wedding day. He wastes no time in proving himself a hero, then suffers a decline in popularity when his carelessness endangers his platoon. Needless to say he redeems himself (by destroying an enemy ammunition dump), and the film ends when, on his return to the USA, he reads a moving letter written by his sergeant buddy (who has been killed in action) to his (the sergeant's) two children. McCallister and Bill Phillips (crouching) as the sergeant did the best they could with William Sackheim's *déjà vu* screenplay (story by Leo Lieberman), but the rest of the cast, including Brett King (left), Larry Stewart (right), William Tannen, Tommy Farrell and Norman Wayne were merely stereotypes. Sam Katzman produced, and the workaday direction was by Lew Landers. (73 mins)

▽ Rita Hayworth's return to the screen after an absence of four years was described by one contemporary critic at the time as 'an occurrence almost as momentous as the birth of a new camel at the zoo.' If the return was momentous, the vehicle that once again brought her to the attention of her fans was an old jalopy, called **Affair in Trinidad**, which had the kind of plot that the studio's B-picture department had so successfully employed throughout the Thirties and Forties. Rita (left) was cast as a dancer who, at the cost of damaging her relationship with leading man Glenn Ford (right), secretly agrees to work in cahoots with the police in an attempt to extract information from a gang of international spies. It took four established writers – scenarists Oscar Saul and James Gunn working from a story by Virginia Van Upp and Berne Giler – to think it all up, though, judging from the tremendous script problems that threatened to jeopardize the entire production, another four were needed to make it work in front of the camera. Still, there was much that was salvageable. Hayworth looked simply gorgeous in the gowns Jean Louis created for her, and had her redblooded, male admirers drooling over her sexy rendition of Lester Lee and Bob Russell's 'Trinidad Lady' and 'I've Been Kissed Before', her vocals being dubbed by Jo Ann Greer. Dancer Valerie Bettis (who also appeared) was in charge of the choreography. Attempting to give the kiss of life to the atrophied dialogue was a cast that included Alexander Scourby as the hissable villain of the affair, Torin Thatcher as a cop, as well as Howard Wendell, Karel Stepanek, George Voskovec, Steven Geray, Walter Kohler and Juanita Moore. Producer Vincent Sherman directed for Hayworth's Beckworth Production Company and such was the tremendous drawing power of the film's leading lady that, despite the poor notices, it was one of the top grossing pictures of 1952, outstripping *Gilda* (1946) at the box-office by over a million dollars, and proving all over again that a star is a star is a star. (98 mins)

▽ **Boots Malone** was an honest-to-goodness race-track melodrama that starred William Holden (left) as the Boots of the title. The neatly structured screenplay by producer Milton Holmes had Boots, a down-on-his-luck jockey's agent, taking under his wing a wealthy, albeit neglected kid (Johnny Stewart, right, making his debut), and with the help of an elderly horse-trainer (Basil Ruysdael) and an untried nag, turning him into a prize jockey. *En route* there were complications – such as the kid's mother's refusal to allow her son to make his riding debut, and Boots' attempts to talk his protegé into losing a race for reasons involving a gambling syndicate. But it all came right in the end and audiences went home with a satisfied glow on their faces. William Dieterle's direction smoothly incorporated into the narrative some informative details about the process involved in training jockeys, and, as most of the film was shot on location at existing race-tracks, an authentic 'feel' permeated the action. A Sidney Buchman Enterprises production, the film also featured Stanley Clements, Carl Benton Reid, Ed Begley, Hugh Sanders, Henry Morgan, Anna Lee and Anthony Caruso. (103 mins)

△ Paris and Budapest provided the settings for the intrigue-laden thriller **Assignment Paris**. Based on a *Saturday Evening Post* story called *Trial By Terror* (written by Paul and Pauline Gallico and scripted by William Bowers from an adaptation by Walter Goetz and Jack Palmer White), it starred Dana Andrews (left) as a no-nonsense reporter working under editor George Sanders (right) in the Paris office of the *New York Herald Tribune*. Also on the staff is woman reporter Marta Toren (centre), who has just returned from Budapest with a story she has been unable to substantiate about a plot between the country's puppet dictator and Tito. When the bureau's Budapest correspondent is taken ill, Andrews is sent out to take his place, at which point in the far-fetched yarn (allegedly based on the true-life experiences of Robert A. Vogeler) Andrews becomes involved in Communist activities and is arrested as a spy. How he eventually finds his freedom provided producers Samuel Marx and Jerry Bresler with the climax to their tired melodrama. It was competently directed by Robert Parrish and the cast included Audrey Totter (as a fashion editor once in love with Sanders), Sandro Giglio, Donald Randolph, Herbert Berghof and Ben Astar. (84 mins)

▽ Two Anthony Dexters for the price of one was hardly the cinema-going world's great bargain, but that was the special offer in **The Brigand**, a swashbuckling programmer, in Technicolor. Dexter (left) played a soldier, who, when his king is wounded in an assassination attempt, stands in for him – much to the chagrin of the villainous Anthony Quinn (centre) who wants the throne for himself, and who hunts out the real monarch's hiding place. 'Inspired' by an Alexandre Dumas story, it was written by Jesse Lasky Jr from a treatment by George Bruce, and also starred Jody Lawrance as the female interest, with other roles under Phil Karlson's direction going to Gale Robbins, Carl Benton Reid, Ron Randell (second right), Fay Roope, Carleton Young (right), Lester Matthews, Walter Kingsford and Holmes Herbert. There was no producer's credit as the production was originally to have been overseered by Edward Small – who left Columbia for United Artists. (93 mins)

▽ Fact took a back-seat in **California Conquest**, a Technicolor Western in which the United States, Mexico, and Russia fought for possession of California. No prizes for guessing the winner – though in Robert E. Kent's wildly inaccurate screenplay, anything could have happened. Cornel Wilde (left) played Don Arturo Bordega, the leader of a group of Spanish Californians who would prefer to see their territory in the hands of the Americans; while the villain of the piece was John Dehner, a landowner who has his own greedy reasons for wanting California to go to the Russians. Just how this proposed Russian take-over was eventually thwarted provided director Lew Landers with several action sequences, one of which included a raid on a gun shop owned by the heroine Teresa Wright (right) and her father (Hank Patterson). It was produced by Sam Katzman and featured Alfonso Bedoya, Lisa Ferraday and Eugene Iglesias. (78 mins)

▽ Rafael Sabatini's novel *Captain Blood Returns* provided the story-line for **Captain Pirate**, a wordy swashbuckler in the timeworn tradition which starred Louis Hayward (left) as Peter Blood. Retired from medicine, and living peacefully and comfortably in the West Indies, he's galvanized into action when he learns that he is being falsely accused of piracy on the high seas. The villain of the piece is John Sutton, who has been using Blood's name while perpetrating raids on several coastal towns. Harry Joe Brown's Technicolor production called for more action than scenarists Robert Libott, Frank Burt and John Meredyth Lucas provided, but, generally, as period adventures went, this was par-for-the-course. Patricia Medina (right) co-starred as Hayward's loving fiancée, with other roles under Ralph Murphy's direction assigned to Charles Irwin, George Givot, Rex Evans, Ted de Corsia, and, for a musical interlude, singer-guitarist Malu Gatica. (85 mins)

△ Eclectic producer Stanley Kramer turned his attentions to a musical, and with **The 5,000 Fingers of Dr T** emerged with a minor surrealist triumph. The story of a youngster (Tommy Rettig) who'd rather be playing baseball than practising the piano for his music teacher, Dr Terwilliker (Hans Conried, left), it entered the realms of fantasy via a dream sequence in which Master Rettig found himself re-located to a nightmarish underworld where the sinister Dr T runs a piano school for 500 boys, and maintains a dungeon housing anyone silly enough to play a musical instrument other than a piano. A bizarre ballet performed by these recalcitrant miscreants (effectively choreographed by Eugene Loring), was the undoubted highlight of a film that might best be described as one of a kind. It was written by Ted Geisel (better known as Dr Seuss) and Allan Scott, directed by Rod Rowland, photographed (in Technicolor) by Franz Planer, imaginatively designed by Rudolph Sternad and had music by Frederick Hollander. The cast included Peter Lind Hayes (right), Mary Healy, John Heasley, Robert Heasley, Noel Cravat and Henry Kulky. (89 mins)

△ Domestic comedy was very much alive and kicking in **The First Time**, a chronicle of the trials of a young married couple experiencing the joys of their first baby. Robert Cummings (left) and Barbara Hale (right) were the couple joining the nappy brigade; Bill Goodwin and Jeff Donnell were their next-door neighbours, Carl Benton Reid, Mona Barrie and Kathleen Comegys the proud grandparents, and Cora Witherspoon the nurse. Paul Harvey and Bea Benaderet further filled out the cast. The screenplay was written by Jean Rouverol, Hugo Butler, Frank Tashlin (who also directed) and Dane Lussier (story by Rouverol and Butler), one of whom had the neat notion of letting baby do the bridging narration. The producer was Harold Hecht. (89 mins)

▽ Real-life husband and wife Rex Harrison (left) and Lilli Palmer (right), who comprised the entire cast of **The Fourposter**, were a mite too sophisticated and worldly for the couple created by Jan de Hartog in his stage-play of the same name. Nearer the mark were Jessica Tandy and Hume Cronyn (another real-life couple) who successfully essayed the roles in the 1951 Broadway production which ran for 632 performances. (The original London production, in 1950, starred Michael Dennison and Dulcie Gray, who were also married to each other). Harrison and Palmer's particular personalities sat less well than they might have on de Hartog's unashamedly sentimental chronicle, with the result that the film never quite caught fire. Beginning in 1890 and moving through 45 years of married life – from the threshold to the grave – the main plot points embraced the husband's successful attempts to fulfil his promise as a writer; the lives of the couple's children, including the death of a son in World War I and various romantic escapades, and, finally, the couple's own demises. Throughout it all, the fourposter-bed loomed large as a symbol of married life as, indeed, did the bedroom itself – from whence the 'action' never ventured. Producer Stanley Kramer's screen transfer interrupted the play's seven boudoir scenes with snippets of animation (provided by UPA) as a means of bridging the time gaps – a clever ploy to draw attention away from the claustrophobic two-character, one-set nature of the piece. De Hartog's original London version of the play was used by scenarist Allan Scott in his adaptation, the major change in the two versions being the more sentimental ending, retained for the film version. Irving Reis's direction, considering the limitations imposed on him both by the confinement of the set and the basic miscasting, managed to convey the essence of this gentle and human comedy of married life. Though completed in 1951, the film was withheld for release until the Cronyns had completed their run on Broadway. A musical version of the same material, called *I Do! I Do!* opened on Broadway in 1966 where it had a successful run of 560 performances. It starred Mary Martin and Robert Preston who were *not* married to one another in real life. (103 mins)

▷ After a happy run of 614 performances on Broadway, Samuel Taylor's **The Happy Time** (a variation on a theme first explored by Eugene O'Neill in his play *Ah Wilderness*) came to the screen via producer Stanley Kramer, and with a cast headed by Charles Boyer (left), Louis Jourdan, Marsha Hunt (right), Kurt Kasznar, Linda Christian and Bobby Driscoll. All about the growing pains of a French-Canadian lad (Driscoll), the movie version retained the play's major incidents *vis à vis* the Bonnard household but, alas, without the charm. Indeed, director Richard Fleischer took a sledgehammer to his delicate subject, and there was a leering, prurient quality to most of the performances. It was, however, adroitly scripted by Earl Felton from Taylor's stage adaptation of Robert Fontaine's novel, with supporting parts for Marcel Dalio (as Grandpère Bonnard), Jeanette Nolan and Jack Raine. (93 mins)

▽ Much more care than was usual went into Randolph Scott and Harry Joe Brown's handsome Technicolor Western, **Hangman's Knot**, and quite a lot of thought into director Roy Huggins's plausible screenplay which set its plot in Nevada in 1865. Co-producer Scott (left) starred as Matt Stewart, the leader of a small Confederate band, who, after ambushing a Union gold train and killing a dozen or so men, learns that the war between the North and South has been over for a month. This news presents Scott with something of a problem, for he and his men are now guilty of murder and felony. Just how he solved this problem, and disposed of the gold, was the subject of Huggins's exciting tale, and it provided roles for Donna Reed (right) as an ex-Union army nurse, Claude Jarman Jr as Scott's last remaining soldier, Frank Faylen as a brave 'Reb', Lee Marvin (centre) as a vicious killer, as well as Jeanette Nolan, Richard Denning, Clem Bevans, Ray Teal, Guinn Williams and veteran Monte Blue. (80 mins)

◁ The sight of top-starred Joan Davis (this was her last movie) masquerading as a harem dancer wasn't exactly worth the price of admission, but at least it was one of the better moments in **Harem Girl**, a comedy that redefined the word 'forced'. Davis (illustrated), who played a secretary-cum-companion to the exotic Princess Shareen (an unexotic Peggie Castle), foils the plot in the course of Edward Bernds and Elwood Ullman's screenplay (story by Bernds), in which a wicked sheikh (Donald Randolph) attempts to dispose of the princess in order to lay his hands on the country's oil reserves. Arthur Blake, Paul Marion, Henry Brandon, Minerva Urecal, John Dehner, Peter Brocco and Wilson Millar also appeared in producer Wallace MacDonald's low-ranking effort, and director was Edward Bernds. (70 mins)

▽ Frank Yerby's novel **The Golden Hawk** came to the screen in luscious Technicolor and with all its piratical clichés in full sail. An unconvincing Sterling Hayden (centre left) starred as Kit Gerardo, a gentleman pirate steeped in swash and buckle; with Rhonda Fleming as a lady pirate called Rogue, but actually a wellbred plantation owner in disguise. The plot had France and Spain fighting it out in the blue waters of the Caribbean in the 17th century, during which time Hayden rescues Fleming from Spanish blackguard Luis de Toro (John Sutton, centre right). Not a great deal in Robert E. Kent's picturesque screenplay made much sense, and everyone involved in it, including producer Sam Katzman, director Sidney Salkow and supporting players Helena Carter, Paul Cavanagh (left), Michael Ansara, and Raymond Hatton (second right), finished up in Davy Jones's locker. (83 mins)

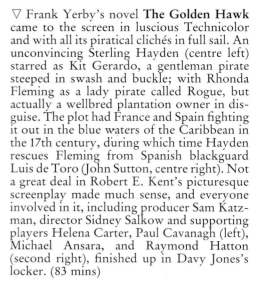

▽ **Invasion USA** was a propagandistic piece of flim-flam which found America under atomic attack by an unnamed (but clearly Soviet) enemy. Hostilities begin in Alaska and continue in Washington DC and New York. The country's factories are seized, and Boulder Dam blown to smithereens. In the end, though, it turns out that none of these calamities occurred, and that a group of men and women in a New York bar had been hypnotized by a TV magician into believing they had. What scenarist Robert Smith (who produced with Albert Zugsmith) was saying, was that it *could* happen, and that Americans had better prepare for the fateful day. The 'human' interest in this prophetic drama was supplied by Gerald Mohr (second right) as a TV reporter, Peggie Castle (second left) as a debutante, Dan O'Herlihy as the mass hypnotist, as well as Robert Bice, Erik Blythe, Wade Crosby and Tom Kennedy. Alfred E. Green directed, and relied heavily on stock wartime footage supplied by the Atomic Energy Commission. Effective but crude. (73 mins)

▽ Cavalrymen clashed with Red Indians in **Last of the Comanches** (GB: **The Sabre And The Arrow**), a relentlessly familiar horse-opera dominated by Technicolor and the formidable presence of Broderick Crawford (right). Crawford played a cavalry sergeant whose task it is to lead the five survivors of an Indian attack on a 100 mile trek across the desert. The cavalrymen are joined by several members of a stage coach, including a murder suspect and a young Indian who leads the desperate, thirst-crazed bunch to an abandoned mission where most of the action eventually takes place. Sounds familiar? Well it was, being a loose remake of *Sahara* (1943). But then nothing in Kenneth Gamet's anachronistic screenplay could even remotely be called original. Stereotyped characters rubbed shoulders with a stereotyped plot, and the results were dispiriting. Also caught up in the proceedings were Barbara Hale (left), as one of the stage-coach passengers, Johnny Stewart (as the young Indian) as well as Lloyd Bridges, Mickey Shaughnessy, George Matthews and Hugh Sanders. The stolid direction was by André de Toth. The producer was Buddy Adler. (85 mins)

▽ **Last Train From Bombay** attempted to be an action melodrama as it told the wearisome story of an American diplomat who, in strife-ridden India, not only proves himself innocent of the murder of a former army buddy (Douglas R. Kennedy), but saves the country from civil war when he prevents the destruction of a train carrying an Indian prince and his daughter. Jon Hall (left) was the dashing hero, with Christine Larson and Lisa Ferraday (right) in support. Also cast: Michael Fox, Donna Martell and Matthew Boulton. It was written by Robert Libott, directed by Fred F. Sears and produced by Sam Katzman. (73 mins)

△ After her triumph in *Born Yesterday* (1950), Judy Holliday returned to the screen in **The Marrying Kind**, a domestic comedy (by Ruth Gordon and Garson Kanin) tailor-made to suit her particular talents. It was the bitter-sweet story of a marriage and the problems that so often turn wedded bliss into wedded hiss. Her co-star was Aldo Ray and, when we first meet the couple, they're in the throes of getting a divorce. Listening patiently to their tales of woe is a sympathetic divorce-court judge (silent-screen star Madge Kennedy). In flashback, we retrace the high-spots and low-spots of their life together, starting with their meeting in Central Park. He's a post-office worker, she's an ex-secretary and it's love at first sight. We follow them to the altar, then into their first home, eavesdrop on their petty domestic spats, are present at the birth of their children, and witness the tragic death, by drowning, of one of them. We're even in at the kill for the split-up. Both parties give their versions of these events, and one of the joys of the witty screenplay was seeing how these versions differed. In the end, having talked through their marital problems, the couple are reunited for a happy fade-out. Both Holliday and Ray's particular vocal eccentricities were heard to humorous effect throughout, with director George Cukor discreetly preventing their larger-than-life personalities from drawing attention away from the simple story. Also taking a ride on this entertaining marital see-saw were Sheila Bond, John Alexander, Rex Williams, Phyllis Povah, Peggy Cass, and Mickey Shaughnessy. The producer was Bert Granet. (92 mins)

△ Donald Powell Wilson's book **My Six Convicts**, which related the experiences of a prison psychologist, came to the screen under the aegis of producer Stanley Kramer (and associates Edna and Edward Anhalt) and was a prison film with a difference. The difference being that its screenplay, by Michael Blankfort, combined intelligence and humour in probing the psyches of the six criminals on whom the action focused. Eschewing melodrama for genuine character development, the film offered a series of well-observed case-histories all of which were socially relevant. John Beal played the newly-installed prison psychologist, and his subjects were Millard Mitchell (right), a safe cracker, Gilbert Roland (centre), a mobster, Marshall Thompson, an alcoholic, Alf Kjellin (left, formerly Christopher Kent), a holdup man, Henry Morgan, a psychopathic killer, and Jay Adler, an embezzler. In a cast that also included Fay Roope as the warden, Regis Toomey, Carleton Young, John Marley, Russ Conway, Byron Foulger, and, in a small part, Charles Buchinski (later Bronson), the acting honours went to Mitchell and Roland with Beal and Kjellin close behind them. The director was Hugo Fregonese. Much of the film was shot at the newly refurbished San Quentin prison (called Harbour State prison in the film), with real prisoners being used as extras. (104 mins)

▽ Carson McCullers's haunting **The Member of the Wedding**, first written as a novella in 1946, then as a Broadway play in 1950 (it ran for 501 performances), came to the screen with its original stars – Ethel Waters (right), Julie Harris and Brandon de Wilde – with Fred Zinnemann directing, and in an adaptation by Edna and Edward Anhalt that paid homage to the play by sticking closely to it. Julie Harris starred as Frankie Addams, a lonely, adolescent tomboy who, at the age of 12, longs for companionship but has to make do with the company of the family cook (Ethel Waters) – called Berenice Sadie Brown – and her bespectacled, seven-year-old cousin, called John Henry (de Wilde). When her older brother Jarvis (Arthur Franz) and his sweetheart Janice (Nancy Gates) marry and go on their honeymoon, Frankie decides she'd like to be a 'member' of that honeymoon and go along with them. She is prevented from doing so by her widowed father (William Hansen) and is heart-broken when bride and groom leave without her. But by the end of the play (and the film), Frankie has found a few friends of her own age, John

Henry has died – and Berenice is left alone with her memories. If this extraordinary and beautiful piece of work seemed to go nowhere – it didn't have to. For it was there already – at the very centre of the human condition. No American author understood adolescence and the problems of growing-up and loneliness better than Carson McCullers, and *The Member of the Wedding* contained some of her wisest, most lyrical writing. Apart from some minor 'opening out', and the inclusion of a scene from the novella in which Frankie runs away from home and pays a nocturnal visit to a seedy downtown nightspot, the film confined itself to Berenice's kitchen and took the same tender route as the play. In McCullers' own words, the subject concerned itself 'with the weight of time, the hazard of human existence, bolts of chance'. Zinnemann made the most of his confined acting areas, and drew from all three of his principals memorable performances – though, at times, the 27 year-old Julie Harris wasn't always able, in close-up, to camouflage her age. The producer was Stanley Kramer. (88 mins)

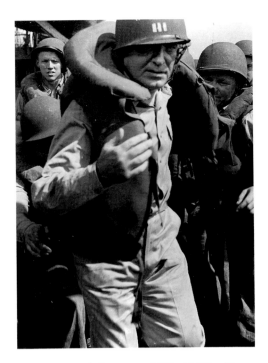

△ Some stock footage of World War II sea and air battles momentarily injected interest into **Okinawa** – a dreary effort with an invisible plot and a set of stock characters endlessly spouting trite sentiments. Set on a destroyer and involving a gun crew, it starred Pat O'Brien (centre), as the ship's no-nonsense commander, Cameron Mitchell as a powder man with a heart of 40 carat gold, Richard Denning as a likeable lieutenant, Rhys Williams as an old veteran, Richard Benedict as a girl-crazy stoker, and Jim Dobson as a homesick youngster. Scenarists Jameson Brewer and Arthur Ross (story by Ross) made it difficult for audiences to give a damn about any of them, and Leigh Jason's sluggish direction didn't help. The producer was Wallace MacDonald. (67 mins)

◁ Loretta Young (second left) was perfectly cast as **Paula** (GB: **The Silent Voice**), the heroine of a tear-jerking soap-opera that bore her name. The story by Larry Marcus (screenplay by James Poe and William Sackheim) focused on the attempts of Ms Young to teach the young victim (Tommy Rettig) of a hit-and-run driver to talk. What the kid doesn't know is that Young was responsible for the accident. When, eventually, the truth emerges, his only motivation for wanting to talk again is to expose her. In the interests of a happy ending, he changes his mind – and audiences filed out of the cinema with lumps in their throats. Also cast were Kent Smith (left) as Young's college-professor husband, Alexander Knox (right), Otto Hulett, Will Wright and Raymond Greenleaf (second right). Buddy Adler produced, and it was tastefully directed, with suds in his eyes, by Rudolph Maté. (80 mins).

△ **The Pathfinder** (from the novel by James Fenimore Cooper) starred George Montgomery (second left) as the eponymous hero, Helena Carter (left) as his inamorata, and Jay Silverheels (second right) as a helpful Mohican. The story had scout Montgomery and Carter (posing as a Frenchie) being sent by the British to a French stronghold in order to ferret out the plans behind France's intention of taking control of the Great Lakes. Our heroes are rumbled by renegade Bruce Lester – but saved from the firing squad by the timely arrival of the British army. Not bad of its type – it featured Walter Kingsford (right) as a British colonel, Steven Bekassy as a French commandant, Rodd Redwing as a hostile Chief Arrowhead, and Elena Verdugo as an Indian princess married to white man Lester. It was scripted by Robert E. Kent for producer Sam Katzman. The director was Sidney Salkow. Technicolor. (78 mins)

▽ Technicolor and a handful of good tunes came to the rescue of **Rainbow 'Round My Shoulder**. Although it starred Frankie Laine (centre) and Billy Daniels, it was actually the story of a young girl (Charlotte Austin) who, against the wishes of her grandmother (Ida Moore), craves to become a movie star. By mistake she is auditioned by the head of the studio's music department (Arthur Franz, left) for the leading role in Laine's new musical. A tour of Columbia's back lot was a bonus in this agreeable, small-scale offering which Richard Quine directed from the workable screenplay he wrote with Blake Edwards. Lee Scott choreographed the unambitious numbers, and the producer was Jonie Taps. Also in the cast was Barbara Whiting (right). (78 mins)

△ Stock footage of Eskimos at work, at play, and coping with an ice break-up and a marauding bear failed to rescue **Red Snow**, a routine programmer whose plot found the US Air Force sending Eskimo soldiers home in order to investigate strange phenomena on the Russian side of the Bering Strait. They discover that the commies are developing a new top-secret weapon. Guy Madison (left) was top-cast as a US flier, Ray Mala played an Eskimo soldier, Carole Mathews (right) was his wife, with other roles in Boris L. Petroff's production going to Gloria Saunders, Robert Peyton, John Bryant and Richard Vath. Tom Hubbard and Orville H. Hampton wrote it from a story by Robert Peters, William Shaw narrated, and the direction was by Petroff and Harry S. Franklin. (74 mins)

▷ It was only a matter of time before the studio turned its attentions to the Bible and Rita Hayworth (right) to the custom-built role of **Salome**. Producer Buddy Adler, for Beckworth Productions, brought both subject and star together. The result bore about as much resemblance to the Biblical facts as a comic-book does to literature. With De Mille's Biblical spectaculars, over at Paramount, the Scriptures did at least take a back seat in favour of entertainment. As directed by William Dieterle, however, the famous tale of the beautiful temptress who danced for King Herod in return for the head of John the Baptist was a high-toned non-starter in which Salome, as a result of her love-affair with Commander Claudius (Stewart Granger), is dancing to *save* the Baptist's head. In scenarist Harry Kleiner's re-write of the Holy Book (story by Jesse Lasky Jr), it's Salome's mum who demands, and receives, the prophet's head – thus exonerating the leading lady from any unsociable behaviour. True, Salome's alluring Dance of the Seven Veils, choreographed by Valerie Bettis, was expertly performed and strikingly photographed, and both Charles Laughton (left) and Judith Anderson as Mr and Mrs Herod chewed up and then spat out Kleiner's deadly dialogue with an enthusiasm verging on desperation. The rest of the cast, though – including Sir Cedric Hardwicke as Caesar Tiberius, Alan Badel as John the Baptist, Basil Sydney as Pontius Pilate, and the great Yiddish actor Maurice Schwartz as Ezra – were, alas, more circumspect. Hayworth brought nothing to the part except her looks, while Stewart Granger was positively soporific. Daniele Amfitheatrof provided the music to which Salome danced, and Jean Louis the veils. It was photographed in Technicolor by Charles Lang. [Previous Salomes from the silent era included Theda Bara and Nazimova. Both were more fun to watch.] (102 mins)

▽ A hard-boiled newspaper editor (Broderick Crawford) whose own culpability in a double murder provided his paper with a lurid front-page story was the germ of a good idea behind Edward Small's melodrama **Scandal Sheet** (GB: **The Dark Page**) – but it was too small a germ. What it needed, but lacked, was a credible script. The one provided by Ted Sherdeman, Eugene Ling and James Poe from Samuel Fuller's novel *The Dark Page* simply wouldn't wash. Busy John Derek (right) co-starred as a star-reporter-cum-sleuth who eventually pins the murders on his own editor, Donna Reed (left) was a reporter who disapproved of Crawford's recourse to sensational journalism as a circulation builder, with other roles under Phil Karlson's so-so direction going to Rosemary DeCamp, Henry O'Neill, Henry Morgan and James Millican. (82 mins)

▽ Actor Arthur Franz (left) wasn't able to convey convincingly the dark underside of a mentally disturbed mind or the psychotic forces that turn an outwardly normal-looking man into a random killer of brunettes. As a result, **The Sniper**, an intelligent melodrama whose screenplay by Harry Brown (from a story by associate producers Edward and Edna Anhalt) which told the tale of a psychopathic lady-killer on the rampage in San Francisco, was never as convincing as it might have been. It asked more questions than it managed to answer, and emerged, under Edward Dmytryk's direction, as a tense police hunt rather than a psychological study of a man who takes a carbine to four hapless female victims. Ideally, it should have been both. Adolphe Menjou played a police lieutenant, Marie Windsor (right), as a saloon pianist, was the sniper's first victim, Marlo Dwyer the second, Richard Kiley was a police psychiatrist, with other excellent performances turned in by Mabel Paige, Geraldine Carr, Gerald Mohr, Frank Faylen, Ralph Peters and Sidney Miller. The producer was Stanley Kramer. (87 mins)

▽ Mickey Rooney (right) starred in **Sound Off**, a pleasant enough comedy with music in which he played a nightclub singer who suddenly finds himself in the army. Blake Edwards and Richard Quine's screenplay concentrated on milking situations rather than on inventing plot – with Rooney involved in one scrape after another before being dispatched abroad to entertain the troops. Anne James, Sammy White (left), John Archer, Gordon Jones and Arthur Space were in it too; Jonie Taps produced, and it was brightly directed (in Super-Cinecolor) by Richard Quine. (83 mins)

▽ That one-man band, Hugo Haas (right), wrote, produced, directed and starred in **Strange Fascination**, a down-beat, humourless drama in which he played a concert pianist whose good fortune changes as soon as he marries blonde dancer Cleo Moore (left). His career goes to the dogs, his wealthy sponsor (Mona Barrie) loses interest in him, penury descends like a black cloud and, to make matters worse, Ms Moore leaves him for a younger man. The final blow comes when, after injuring his hand, the insurance company refuses him compensation. The film ends with Haas giving a one-hand concert in a Bowery backroom. Human disintegration was the theme – and it kept audiences away in droves. Rick Vallin, Karen Sharpe, Marc Krah and Genevieve Aumont were in it too. (80 mins)

△ Based on a *Reader's Digest* article by J. Edgar Hoover, **Walk East On Beacon** (GB: **The Crime Of The Century**), was a piece of blatant FBI propaganda which claimed to probe deeply into 'the Red Menace'. It starred George Murphy (centre), whose purpose in the script written by Leo Rosten, Virginia Shaler, Emmett Murphy and Leonard Heidemann was to trace the whereabouts of a Soviet spy (Ernest Graves) who, after failing to secure some valuable information, has been replaced by Karel Stepanek and sent away on a Polish ship. It was produced by Louis de Rochemont in his usual pseudo-documentary style, directed by Alfred Werker at a cracking pace, and boasted a fine cast that included Finlay Currie as a refugee scientist, Virginia Gilmore, Peter Capell (who later turned into director George Roy Hill) and Bruno Wick. (98 mins)

▷ Another costume spoof from producer Sam Katzman, **Thief of Damascus** went back to the year AD 642 for its story-line, and to well before the flood for the manner of its telling. Paul Henreid (left) starred as Abu Andar in this Arabian Nights rip-off, and his duty in Robert E. Kent's leaden screenplay was to save Damascus from being plundered by invaders. Helping him were Aladdin (Robert Clary, second right), Sinbad the Sailor (Lon Chaney Jr, second left), Ali Baba (Philip Van Zandt) and the talkative Sheherazade (Jeff Donnell). Accuracy was hardly the first item on Katzman's agenda (was it ever?), the emphasis being on Technicolor escapism at any cost. The anachronistic direction was by Will Jason. (78 mins)

◁ Producer Sam Katzman's **Target Hong Kong** had pace on its side which was just as well, for plot-wise it stretched credibility to breaking point. All about the attempts of an American mercenary to prevent British Hong Kong from falling into the hands of Red leader Ben Astar it starred Richard Denning (second left) as the hero, Nancy Gates as his love-interest, and Michael Pate (left) and Henry Kulks (right) as two of his pals. Soo Yong played a pirate called Lao Shan, with other roles going to Philip Ahn (second right) and Victor Sen Young. Herbert Purdum wrote the screenplay from his own story. The director was Fred F. Sears. (72 mins)

◁ John Archer (centre right) and Douglas Dick (centre left) were the heroes of **A Yank In Indochina**, a melodrama of no distinction whatsoever from producer Sam Katzman. They played a pair of buddies who operate an air-freight line in Indochina, and who, after detonating a plane belonging to Red Chinese guerilla Harold Fong, escort Jean Willes (behind boy) and Maura Murphy through treacherous jungle terrain to safety. Blame the bilge on scenarist Samuel Newman whose screenplay gave director Wallace A. Grissell very little to work with. (67 mins)

▽ There was action in abundance (and much of it pretty gruesome, too) in **Ambush At Tomahawk Gap**, a violent Western which began with the prison release of four men – John Derek (centre), John Hodiak (left), David Brian and Ray Teal, each of whom has served a five-year sentence for a holdup. Seems, though, that Hodiak was innocent, but had to serve time anyway when the rest of the gang claimed he was the fourth man. The *real* fourth man, it turns out, escaped with the loot and has buried it in the ghost town of Tomahawk Gap. The story (screenplay by David Lang) found its stride as the quartet set off in search of their buried treasure. They're hindered in their endeavours by some troublesome Apaches who suddenly swoop down on the group and indulge in a spot of scalping. It is at this point in producer Wallace MacDonald's Technicolor epic that things turn decidedly nasty. Fred F. Sears's direction didn't spare the horses, nor a cast that included Maria Elena Marques (right), John Qualen, Otto Hulett and, as the sheriff, Trevor Bardette. (73 mins)

△ Charlton Heston (left) and Lizabeth Scott (right) were not only **Bad For Each Other** but fatal for audiences. The predictable bilge in which they starred featured Heston as an army doctor, who, after returning from Korea, cannot decide whether to put his Hippocratic oath to the service of a small mining community or to Pittsburgh's café society. Under the heady influence of Scott – as a wealthy mine-owner's daughter – he chooses money over integrity, but soon rues his decision. A pit disaster for which his services are desperately needed brings him to his senses, and, after jettisoning Scott, he walks off into the proverbial sunset with nurse Dianne Foster whose trenchant values are just what he has been looking for. Irving Rapper directed it for the women's magazine story it was, drawing few, if any perks, from a cast that included Mildred Dunnock as Heston's unsmiling mother, Arthur Franz, Ray Collins, Marjorie Rambeau, Lester Matthews and Rhys Williams. The screenplay was by Irving Wallace and Horace McCoy from the latter's story. The producer was William Fadiman. (83 mins)

△ If producer Jonie Taps's Technicolor musical **All Ashore** reminded one of *On The Town* (MGM, 1949) it was because its plot involved three sailors on shore leave and the three girls they meet while pretending to be entertainers. That, unfortunately, was where the similarity ended. Mickey Rooney (left), Dick Haymes (right), and Ray McDonald were a likeable enough trio, ditto Peggy Ryan, Jody Lawrance (centre) and Barbara Bates as the lasses in their lives. Rooney upstaged them all, which only made one wish that he had had better material than that supplied him by Richard Quine and Blake Edwards. Quine also directed. (80 mins)

◁ Fritz Lang returned to the world of *film noir* in **The Big Heat**, a melodrama of 'dice, vice and corruption' (as the ads proclaimed) that was largely shot in studio interiors and which potently conveyed a world of sordid brutality. Glenn Ford starred as a rogue homicide cop who takes the law into his own hands when he sets out to smash a vicious crime syndicate and find out who planted the car bomb that killed his wife (Jocelyn Brando). Sidney Boehm's tight, taut screenplay, based on a *Saturday Evening Post* serial by William P. McGivern, was awash with violence. Although much of the blood-letting took place off-screen, one of the film's most shockingly memorable sequences showed Gloria Grahame (left), as a gangster's moll, being disfigured by her sadistic, jealous boyfriend (Lee Marvin, right) when he throws a pot of scalding coffee into her face. Grahame gets her revenge on her so-called lover when she repeats the gesture in his darkened apartment. Ford's main prey, as the sleazy narrative unfurled, was Alexander Scourby (centre), head of a corrupt gambling syndicate. Watching the hero and the villain play cat and mouse under Lang's suspenseful direction kept audiences on the edge of their seats. Robert Arthur's tip-top production, which emerged as one of the most powerful statements on postwar urban crime of the Fifties, recruited an excellent supporting cast including Jeanette Nolan, Peter Whitney, Willis Bouchey, Robert Burton, Adam Williams, Howard Wendell and Carolyn Jones. Charles Lang's fine camerawork contributed immensely to the overall *noir* atmosphere of this impressive thriller. (89 mins)

▽ The good looks of both Jean-Pierre Aumont (left) and Paulette Goddard (right) – plus Technicolor – were the major ingredients of producer Sam Katzman's **Charge Of The Lancers**, thus proving that beauty is only skin deep. For underneath the cosmeticized flourish of William Castle's direction, there lay exposed a trite yarn, set in the Crimean War, which recounted the success of the British at Sebastopol. Aumont played an Allied captain, Goddard a gypsy romantically involved with him. How the pair contrived to be captured by the Russians as a prelude to some heavy-duty spying activities formed the kernel of Robert E. Kent's screenplay, and provided roles for Richard Stapley, Karin Booth, Charles Irwin, Ben Astar and Lester Matthews. (73 mins)

▽ **China Venture**, a mild programmer, was of interest only in that it was directed by Don Siegel, who'd go on to better things than this. All about a US Naval Intelligence mission at the end of World War II, it starred Edmond O'Brien (right) as a marine captain who, with the help of naval officer Barry Sullivan (left), kidnaps a Japanese admiral (Philip Ahn) from the China coast and takes him for questioning by top intelligence officials. What little conflict existed in the screenplay that George Worthing Yates and Richard Collins wrote from the story by producer Anson Bond centred on O'Brien's resentment of the younger Sullivan. Siegel's direction made no impact whatsoever on the trite yarn, nor did a cast which included Jocelyn Brando, Leo Gordon, Richard Loo and Dayton Lummis. (83 mins)

△ Ten songs, Technicolor and the vocalizing of Dick Haymes (right) and Billy Daniels added up to an agreeable little low-budget musical called **Cruisin' Down The River**. The plot was a trifle about a New York night-club crooner (Haymes) who, on inheriting a riverboat from his grandfather, also inherits the old man's feud with Cecil Kellaway. Peace is eventually restored, with the help of Audrey Totter, thus cueing in the happy ending. Richard Quine directed and co-scripted (with Blake Edwards), Jonie Taps produced and Lee Scott choreographed. Also cast: Connie Russell (left), Douglas Fowley, Larry Blake, Johnny Downs, Byron Foulger and, as themselves, the Bell Sisters. (79 mins)

▷ Produced by Jerry Thomas for Border Productions and purchased by the studio for distribution, **Combat Squad** was a programmer that used the Korean war as its backdrop. John Ireland (right) starred as a flinty combat sergeant and Lon McCallister (back left) as a frightened rookie under his protection. As Ireland's GI platoon experiences several skirmishes with the enemy, McCallister eventually loses his fear of fighting, and proves himself a hero in battle. Wyatt Ordung's formula screenplay also provided parts for veteran George E. Stone (centre), Hal March (front left), Norman Leavitt (back right), Myron Healey (front right) and Don Haggerty. Female relief was supplied by Jill Hollingsworth, Linda Danson, Neva Gilbert and Eileen Howe – all as USO entertainers. Cy Roth directed. (72 mins)

▽ Following in Jeff Chandler's footsteps at Universal, John Hodiak (right) starred as Apache chief Cochise in **Conquest Of Cochise**. Robert Stack (left) co-starred as an American major whose troops are protecting the Mexicans. Cochise wants peace but the Comanches (with whom he has joined forces against the Mexicans) want war. This was the conflict in Arthur Lewis and DeVallon Scott's screenplay, which was resolved by the arrival of the cavalry who, together with the Apaches, finally oust the Comanches. Technicolor slightly brightened a dull plot, though Sam Katzman's production never escaped being a routine oater. William Castle directed a cast that also included Joy Page, Rico Alaniz, Carol Thurston, John Crawford, and Rodd Redwing. (70 mins)

◁ Larry Brown's 1945 Broadway play *A Sound Of Hunting* (which ran a mere 23 performances) was bought by Stanley Kramer Productions and came to the screen as **Eight Iron Men**. A rag-bag platoon of war-weary American soldiers is holed up in a bombed-out Italian town. The men talk about this, that and the other – but mainly about rescuing a buddy who has been pinned down in a nearby shell-hole by an enemy machine-gun. Towards the end of the film, one of the soldiers actually attempts to do something about his trapped comrade and succeeds, only to discover that the guy hadn't been pinned down at all, but was having a quiet snooze. A who-cares? plot in a so-what? production, it starred Bonar Colleano (as the talkative hero of the platoon), Arthur Franz, Lee Marvin (right), Nick Dennis, Richard Kiley (left), James Griffith, Dick Moore, George Cooper, Barney Phillips and, as the only female in the cast, Mary Castle. Edward Dmytryk directed from Brown's own adaptation. Why? (80 mins)

◁ The behind-the-scenes shenanigans that went into the making of **From Here To Eternity** were almost as dramatic as the contents of James Jones's foul-mouthed best-seller about life in an army base at Pearl Harbor just before America entered World War II. Having paid $82,000 for the film rights, Harry Cohn made quite sure that the screenplay fashioned from the sprawling 860-page novel retained the book's raw, almost unfilmable elements, but without offending either the army or Hollywood's hyper-sensitive Production Code. Finally, when Daniel Taradash presented him with a scenario he felt was both workable and true to the spirit of the novel, casting reared its awesome head. For the central role of Robert E. Prewitt, a bugler who boxes (or vice versa), Cohn wanted either John Derek or Aldo Ray, both under contract to the studio. Director Fred Zinnemann rebelled: either the role went to Montgomery Clift (centre), or they'd have to find another director. Cohn capitulated and Clift was signed for $150,000. Zinnemann originally cast Eli Wallach in the role of the tough, wise-cracking Angelo Maggio, but Wallach backed out after being offered a part in Elia Kazan's Broadway production of *Camino Real* by Tennessee Williams. The part eventually went to Frank Sinatra (right), whose career at this point had hit the skids. Although deeply in debt, Sinatra offered to do the role for nothing. Cohn didn't want to know initially, and only after Ava Gardner made a personal plea on her husband's behalf did the reluctant mogul agree to test the erstwhile heart-throb. The test impressed Zinnemann and Sinatra's flagging career was spectacularly relaunched for a mere $8,000 in a great comeback performance. The part of the compassionate Sergeant Milton Warden was originally offered to Edmond O'Brien. Burt Lancaster's sudden availability, however, put paid to that and Lancaster's services were secured for $120,000. There were problems with the women as well. When Joan Crawford, who was originally cast as the neglected Karen Holmes, learned that her wardrobe was bereft of shoulder pads, she said 'no'. The career-enhancing role went to Deborah Kerr, whose outwardly cool and sedate English manner intensified the shockwaves that rippled through the cinemas of the world when she and Lancaster took to the beach for one of the screen's most famous love scenes. Even Donna Reed, in the role of Alma Lorene, a hostess at the New Congress Club, wasn't Zinnemann's first choice. He wanted Julie Harris. But Cohn considered her too homely after the box-office failure of *The Member Of The Wedding* (1952). Having won his battle over Clift, Zinnemann didn't push his luck, and Reed it was. The final line-up for Buddy Adler's memorable production could not have been improved upon. It included Philip Ober as the sadistic and insecure Captain Dana Holmes, Ernest Borgnine as the vicious stockade bully 'Fatso' Judson, Jack Warden as Corporal Buckley, Micky Shaughnessy as Sergeant Leva – as well as Harry Bellaver, George Reeves, John Dennis and Tim Ryan. The result was a haunting, hard-hitting drama that captured the imagination of the ticket-buying public to the tune of $18 million world-wide. The only sad note was the failure of the Motion Picture Academy of Arts and Sciences to award three-time nominee Clift with an Oscar for the finest performance of his career. (118 mins)

◁ Stock World War II footage marginally buttressed the sleepy story of **El Alamein**, a routine actioner from Wallace MacDonald. Told in flashback, it starred Scott Brady (left) as a civilian who becomes involved in a skirmish at an oasis, while delivering tanks to the British Army. However, the oasis is, in fact, a supply dump for Rommel's Afrika Korps tanks. Herbert Purdum and George Worthing Yates scripted (story by Purdum), Fred F. Sears directed, and the cast included Edward Ashley (centre), Robin Hughes (right), Rita Moreno, Peter Brocco and Michael Pate. Dreary. (66 mins)

▽ Technicolor and 3-D momentarily bolstered the tired plot of **Fort Ti**, an outdoor adventure set in the 1700s and all about the efforts of Ranger George Montgomery (right), working with the British, to oust the French from Fort Ticonderoga. Scenarist Robert E. Kent threw every cliché he could think of into his story-line, and director William Castle threw it back into the audience via tumbling bodies, flaming arrows and airborne bats. Joan Vohs (left) appeared as a girl suspected of being a French spy, with other roles in Sam Katzman's weary production going to Irving Bacon, James Seay, Ben Astar and Phyllis Fowler. (73 mins)

△ India in 1760 was the setting for **Flame Of Calcutta**, more period action from Sam Katzman whose production values, on this Technicolorful occasion, alternated between battle and harem sequences. Denise Darcel (centre), who had more shape to her than Robert E. Kent's screenplay (story by Sol Shor), starred as the daughter of a slain government official, out to wage war against a treacherous usurper (George Keymas, right). She's abetted in her efforts by British Army captain Patric Knowles, (left), with whom, of course, she falls in love. Paul Cavanagh, Joseph Mell, Gregory Gaye and Leonard Penn were also featured: so were specialty dancers Sujata and Asoka. The director was Seymour Friedman. (70 mins)

▷ Italian heart-throb Vittorio Gassman (left) received top-billing in **The Glass Wall**, and played a European who has jumped ship in an effort to gain entry into America. Landing in New York, he is helped in his desperate efforts by a young woman (Gloria Grahame, right) who has seen better days, and a jazz musician (Jerry Paris), the latter being fully acquainted with Gassman's pro-Allied underground activities during the war. Basically a protracted chase between the hero and the immigration authorities (led by Douglas Spencer), it was written by producers Ivan Tors and Maxwell Shane, directed by Shane, and had a cast that included Ann Robinson, Robin Raymond, Elizabeth Slifer and Richard Reeves. (78 mins)

△ The use of library wartime footage gave producer Sam Katzman's **The 49th Man** a documentary-like feel to it, but it was still just a low-budget programmer which starred John Ireland (left) as a US Security Investigation Division agent who smells a rat when his tips about the transportation of atomic devices into the USA are written off by the Navy and the SID as 'war game exercises'. How Ireland uncovers a group of spies responsible for duping his superiors was the main business of Harry Essex's serviceable screenplay (story by Ivan Tors). It was directed by a budget-conscious Fred F. Sears, and also featured Richard Denning, Suzanne Dalbert, Robert C. Foulk and Mike Connors (right). (73 mins)

◁ A Western, filmed in 3-D and Technicolor, **Gun Fury** starred Rock Hudson (centre) and Donna Reed (third left) as newlyweds travelling West. In the course of Roy Huggins and Irving Wallace's par-for-the-course screenplay (based on the novel *Ten Against Caesar* by Kathleen B. George and Robert A. Granger), Reed is kidnapped by the psychotic leader (Phil Carey, right) of a gang of outlaws – whom, of course, Hudson is now forced to pursue ... with drastic consequences. Director Raoul Walsh gave the material much more than it deserved and drew from Carey a really mesmeric performance. The producer was Lewis J. Rachmil. Also cast: Roberta Haynes, Leo Gordon (second left) and Lee Marvin. (83 mins)

▽ Kirk Douglas (left) gave a powerful performance in producer Stanley Kramer's **The Juggler**. He played a Jewish vaudevillian who, after being incarcerated in a Nazi concentration camp during the war, emigrates to Israel where he hopes to begin a new life. Neurotic about authority and confinement and still bleeding mentally from his experiences in the death camp, he is given to violent fits, and when asked by an Israeli policeman for his identification papers, smashes the man in the face. Believing the policeman to be dead, he flees across the country. In what was basically an extended chase, Douglas meets a young orphan (Joey Walsh) whom he befriends and teaches to juggle, as well as a beautiful girl called Ya'El (Milly Vitale) with whom he falls in love. The film ends with Douglas realizing he needs

help and giving himself up to the authorities. As scripted by Michael Blankfort, from his novel, viewers were left in no doubt that in time the juggler would find his peace of mind, and that he would settle down happily with Ms Vitale. Underlining the main narrative thrust was an inspirational picture of a brave, hard-working people building up a country of their own. Edward Dmytryk's direction concentrated on maintaining narrative tension and the development of character. He wasn't able to do much with the inexperienced Miss Vitale, but drew super performances from his star and from Joey Walsh. Paul Stewart was cast as the detective on Douglas's trail, with other roles going to Alf Kjellin, Beverly Washburn, Charles Lane, Oskar Karlweis and Richard Benedict (right). The film was shot in Israel. (84 mins)

△ Flash-backs and flash-forwards needlessly complicated **The Last Posse**, a small-scale Western about a posse of basically honest citizens, who, after tracking down the trio of outlaws responsible for robbing a wealthy cattle baron, decide to keep the booty themselves. Sheriff Broderick Crawford (left), the leader of the posse, is mortally wounded in the course of the raid and unaware that the recovered cash has not been returned to its rightful owner. Honest Crawford is expected to die at any moment and, as far as the greedy men comprising his posse are concerned, the sooner the better. Director Alfred Werker, working from a screenplay by Seymour and Connie Lee Bennett and Kenneth Gamet (story by the Bennetts) packed as much action as he could into the yarn, and drew convincing performances from Crawford, John Derek (second left), Charles Bickford (centre), Wanda Hendrix, Warner Anderson, Henry Hull, Tom Powers (right), Raymond Greenleaf and Skip Homeier (second right). Harry Joe Brown produced. (73 mins)

△ A re-make, with songs, of the studio's 1937 comedy *The Awful Truth*, **Let's Do It Again** – photographed in Technicolor – starred Jane Wyman (centre) as an erstwhile musical comedy star and Ray Milland (left) as a successful playwright. After claiming to be on a business trip but, in fact, enjoying a binge, Milland falls out of favour with Wyman who decides to teach her spouse a lesson by embarking on an innocent flirtation with bachelor Tom Helmore. Her scheme, however, misfires and the couple are divorced. Their eventual reconciliation was unconscionably prolonged in the screenplay written by Mary Loos and Richard Sale (from the play by Arthur Richman), during which time Aldo Ray (right) as an Alaskan millionaire got a chance to woo Miss W. Lester Lee and Ned Washington supplied the film's seven songs, the choreography was shared between Valerie Bettis, who also appeared, and Lee Scott; and it was directed for producer Oscar Saul by Alexander Hall, who hadn't made a film for the studio since the 1947 musical *Down To Earth*. Also cast: Leon Ames, Karin Booth, Mary Treen and Richard Wessel. (94 mins)

▽ Rita Hayworth (left) followed in the legendary footsteps of Jeanne Eagels, Gloria Swanson and Joan Crawford to portray **Miss Sadie Thompson** in Jerry Wald's Beckworth Production of the famous Somerset Maugham story *Rain*. Though sanitized in accordance with Hays Office requirements – with 3-D and Technicolor plus a couple of songs – Maugham's steamy story of sex, sin and salvation still packed quite a wallop. Updated to take place after World War II, Harry Kleiner's screenplay, based on the 1922 stage play by John Colton, transformed Sadie from a self-confessed whore to a free-and-easy singer in a Honolulu bawdy house. Another major change took place in the all-important character of Alfred Davidson. In Wald's version he was no longer an ordained cleric but a mere member of the missionary board. This switch definitely softened the impact of his liaison with Sadie, and left José Ferrer as Davidson (a role originally intended for Henry Fonda) with little to sink his scenery-chewing teeth into. As scripted by Kleiner, Sadie is chased out of Honolulu by the loathsome Davidson, and fetches up on board a ship bound for New Caledonia. During the voyage the ship is quarantined at an island occupied by marines – one of whom (Aldo Ray, right) falls for her, and she for him. There's a happy ending, but not before Sadie falls under the spell of Davidson's anti-sin campaign, and is raped by the reformer who, in turn, commits suicide. In one of the very best performances of her career, the beautiful and provocative Hayworth gave her all to the demanding role, and danced up a storm in Lester Lee and Ned Washington's 'The Heat Is On' and 'Blue Pacific Blues' (choreography by Lee Scott, with Hayworth's vocals being dubbed by Jo Ann Greer). Curtis Bernhardt directed with an appropriately sultry touch. Also cast: Russell Collins, Diosa Costello, Harry Bellaver, Peggy Converse and Charles Buchinsky (Bronson). (90 mins)

△ Little more than a compendium of wartime platitudes, **Mission Over Korea** was also an inept programmer which starred John Hodiak (centre), as the captain of an army observation plane, and John Derek (right) as the rookie he commands. Given the two characters' very different approaches to discipline, the script fashioned by Jesse Lasky Jr, Eugene Ling and Martin M. Goldsmith (story by Richard Tregaskis) was clearly meant to contrast two generations of Americans fighting for the same cause. All that emerged, however, was a tedious clash of personalities. Stock footage of Korean combat underlined the meagreness of producer Robert Cohn's budget, as well as the phoniness of director Fred F. Sears's efforts in the studio. Audrey Totter, Maureen O'Sullivan (left), Harvey Lembeck and Richard Erdman completed the cast. (85 mins)

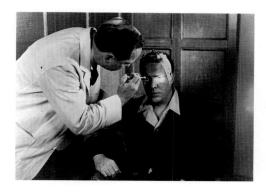

△ Photographed in sepia tints and in 3-D, **Man In The Dark** was nevertheless a thoroughly conventional melodrama (indeed, a remake of *The Man Who Lived Twice*, 1936). Edmond O'Brien (right) is a former criminal who undergoes brain surgery to rid him of his anti-social tendancies, but in the process loses his memory. He then meets up with three former partners in crime (Horace McMahon, Nick Dennis and Ted de Corsia) who try (pretty violently) to 'persuade' him to remember where he hid $13,000 from the payroll holdup they pulled before his 'conversion'. The money turns out to be in the check-room of an amusement park – the garish setting for the film's second half. Audrey Totter, Dayton Lummis and Dan Riss were, together with the rest of the cast, just as two-dimensional in 3-D, an observation that applied equally to George Bricker and Jack Leonard's screenplay (story by Tom van Dycke and Henry Altimus), and to Lew Landers's direction. The producer was Wallace MacDonald. (70 mins)

▷ Holding one's nose was the best way to endure **One Girl's Confession**, a 22-carat stinker from Hugo Haas (left), who wrote, produced and directed it. All about the tribulations undergone by leading lady Cleo Moore (right, who steals $25,000, hides it, confesses to the crime, then goes to jail) it had about as much entertainment value as walking uphill. Glenn Langan, as a mackerel fisherman, played Moore's love interest, with other parts taken by Ellen Stansbury, Anthony Jochim and Russ Conway. Haas was in it too – as the owner of a harbour café-bar. (73 mins)

▽ A British entry from producers Irving Allen and Albert R. Broccoli, **Paratrooper** (GB: **The Red Beret**) starred Alan Ladd (left) as a guilt-ridden US Army officer who – after inadvertently causing the death of a friend by ordering him to bail out of a crashing plane – enlists in a British paratrooper training camp pretending to be a Canadian. How he learns, once again, to face responsibility was the subject of Richard Maibaum and Frank S. Nugent's somewhat fanciful screenplay. Ladd, under Terence Young's stiff-upper-lip direction, did no more and no less than was expected of him in such circumstances, and received moderate support from Britishers Harry Andrews, Susan Stephen, Leo Genn (right), Donald Houston, Anthony Bushell, Patrick Doonan, Stanley Baker and Lana Morris. It was photographed in Technicolor for Warwick Productions. (88 mins)

▷ A distaff version of 20th Century-Fox's 1942 success *Tales Of Manhattan*, **Paris Model** re-cycled a beautiful gown, known as 'Nude At Midnight' through four separate skeins of plot. In the first, which takes place in Paris, it is purchased by Eva Gabor (left) who wants to make an impression on the Maharajah of Kim-Kepore (Tom Conway, right). In the second, the dress has been illegally copied for sale in America, where it is bought by Paulette Goddard to impress her lawyer-boss (Leif Erickson). Unfortunately, though, Erickson's wife (Gloria Christian) has precisely the same idea. Story number three found Marilyn Maxwell using the gown to seduce her retiring employer (Cecil Kellaway) into appointing her husband (Robert Bice) as the new president. Kellaway's wife (Florence Bates), however, wears the pants in this particular family, and gives the job to the firm's book-keeper. The final segment, which took place at Romanoff's restaurant, simply found Barbara Lawrence using the gown as a come-on to cue her longtime boyfriend (Robert Hutton) into proposing marriage. The best that could, in the end, be said of Albert Zugsmith's production, was that it was mildly diverting in parts. Robert Smith wrote the screenplay which was directed, by Alfred E. Green. (81 mins)

△ John Derek (second left) traversed some pretty well-worn territory in **Prince Of Pirates**, a tired old costume drama (set in the 16th century) which once again allowed its star to pretend he was Douglas Fairbanks Sr. This time he played Prince Roland, who, in a mythical European country, leads a band of volunteers against the tyranny of his older brother Stephan (Whitfield Connor). After encountering the usual obstacles rounded up by scenarists John O'Dea and Samuel Newman (story by William Copeland and Herbert Kline), Derek saw that justice prevailed and was rewarded for his efforts with the beauteous Barbara Rush (second right). The film was produced (in Technicolor) by Sam Katzman, and directed (mechanically) by Sidney Salkow. Carla Balenda, Edgar Barrier (right), Robert Shayne and Harry Lauter (left), supported. (78 mins)

◁ The real **Prisoners Of The Casbah** were audiences who found themselves paying good money to see a good cast – Gloria Grahame (centre right), Cesar Romero, Turhan Bey (centre left) – in a thoroughly lousy effort from producer Sam Katzman. Bey was the unlikely hero, Grahame the wooden princess he woos, and Romero the villain. No amount of Technicolor could camouflage the sheer lack of colour in DeVallon Scott's screenplay, or the see-through direction by the aptly named Richard Bare. For the record, the cast also included Nestor Paiva (on ground), Paul E. Newlan, Lucille Barkley and Philip Van Zandt. (78 mins)

▽ Arson, larceny, murder and alcoholism were some of the condiments producers Aubrey Wisberg and Jack Pollexfen used to spice up a tawdry little melodrama called **Problem Girls**. Set in a private school for mentally deranged girls, it starred Ross Elliott as a psychology instructor who soon discovers that all is not well on the premises. It seems that the school's owner (Helen Walker, right), in cahoots with its athletic director (James Seay), is drugging pretty Susan Morrow (left) and passing her off as an oil heiress. Their reasons were the mainstay of the story-line, but not reason enough for audiences to spend time in their anti-social company. E. A. Dupont directed, and his cast included Anthony Jochim, Marjorie Stapp, Roy Regnier, Eileen Stevens and Tom Charlesworth. (70 mins)

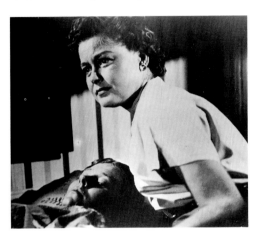

▽ Producer Sam Katzman not only distorted history in his Technicolor production of **Serpent Of The Nile**, but was guilty of some flagrant mis-casting. Rhonda Fleming (centre, in gowns by Jean Louis) played Cleopatra, third-billed Raymond Burr (right) was Mark Antony, and William Lundigan (left) carried the onus of the film's romantic element as Burr's lieutenant, Lucilius. In the screenplay fashioned by Robert E. Kent from his own story, and in sets borrowed from *Salome*, the ambitious Queen of Egypt plots Anthony's murder as a means of securing the throne of Rome for herself. She is prevented from doing so by Lundigan, who brings the Roman legions into Alexandria, vanquishes the Egyptians, and is responsible for Ms Fleming's death by suicide. Kent's script was constructed from the same wooden substance out of which all the performances were built, and, unlike Cleo's burnished barge (at least in the Shakespeare version), sank without trace. Also cast: Jean Byron, Michael Ansara, Michael Fox, and, as a 'golden girl', Julie Newmeyer (later Newmar). The director was William Castle. (81 mins)

▽ Sam Katzman's production team moved out of Rome and Egypt (or, to be more precise, on to another part of the studio back lot) for **Siren Of Bagdad**, a jokey 'tits and sand' actioner that starred Paul Henreid (second left) as Kazah, an itinerant magician playing one-night stands in and around Bagdad. What happens when a gang of marauders kidnaps his scantily-clad dancing girls and relocates them in an already well-stocked harem belonging to the Sultan El Malid (Charlie Lung), was the *raison d'être* of the story and screenplay Robert E. Kent provided by connecting the dotted lines of a familiar Hollywood blueprint. Patricia Medina (left) co-starred as the lovely Zendi, Michael Fox was her deposed sultan father, with other roles shared by Hans Conried (second right), Laurette Luez, Anne Dore, George Keymas (right) and Vivian Mason. Richard Quine directed with little distinction – though the script did contain one well-executed 'in' joke that featured Henreid (in an exotic replay from *Now Voyager*, Warner Bros., 1942) lighting two hookahs (instead of cigarettes) for one of his harem playmates. Technicolor. (72 mins)

△ Randolph Scott fans had a field day with **The Stranger Wore A Gun**, a 3-D Western, in Technicolor, in which they could almost touch their gun-toting hero as he turned from bad to good in Kenneth Gamet's achingly familiar screenplay, adapted from John M. Cunningham's novel *Yankee Gold*. After serving as a spy for the notorious Quantrill, Scott (right), moves to Prescott, Arizona, where he joins forces with the villainous George Macready (left) to get his hands on some gold shipments. At this point Scott decides to play it straight and sets Macready against bandit Alfonso Bedoya. The finale found Scott and Macready shooting it out in a burning saloon, after which the hero rides off with faithful Claire Trevor, much to the disappointment of Joan Weldon who also loves the guy. Lester H. White's 3-D photography hurled as much merchandise into audience's laps – including gobs of tobacco juice – that the scene decorators could provide, but, when all was said and done, nothing was memorable about the Randolph Scott-Harry Joe Brown production. André de Toth directed a cast that included Lee Marvin and Ernest Borgnine (as heavies), Pierre Watkin, Joseph Vitale and Clem Bevans. (82 mins)

▽ Producer Sam Katzman traversed Cecil B. De Mille territory with **Slaves of Babylon**, a Biblical drama about the overthrow of Babylon and the freeing of the Israelite slaves. Only two things were missing: De Mille's budget and his flair. Richard Conte (left) played Nahum, the Israelite who acts as the agent of the prophet Daniel, Yiddish actor Maurice Schwartz was Daniel, Linda Christian (right) played a Princess, Michael Ansara was Belshazzar, Leslie Bradley portrayed Nebuchadnezzar, with other roles going to Ruth Storey, John Crawford, Terence Kilburn, Ric Roman and Robert Griffin. Julie Newmayer had a spot in it too, as a specialty dancer. The film was photographed in Technicolor, had a story and screenplay by DeVallon Scott, and was directed by William Castle. (81 mins)

△ Inspired by an incident in 1947 when a group of 4,000 motorcyclists celebrated the Fourth of July by invading the small Californian town of Hollister, producer Stanley Kramer's powerful **The Wild One** was not only the first of a long-running series of 'biker' or 'road' films, but one of the first of the 'generation gap' dramas that would find its fullest expression in anti-hero James Dean's performance in *Rebel Without A Cause* (Warner Bros. 1955). After its brilliant opening sequence, in which a gang of leather-clad motorcyclists invade the peace and quiet of Wrightsville, the film, under Laslo Benedek's screw-turning direction, concentrated on the anti-social behaviour of the nomadic men in black (called 'The Black Rebels'), the most vicious of them being Marlon Brando (centre) as Johnny and Lee Marvin as Chino. However, in the course of John Paxton's screenplay (story by Frank Rooney), Brando's romantic encounter with Mary Murphy, the daughter of the town's ineffectual cop, (Robert Keith), brings out the contradictory nature of his personality – and, in a sell-out ending, reveals him to be a creature not totally devoid of sensitivity. Brando managed to bring into focus these two diverse elements of the character in a performance that was an extraordinary *tour de force*. Marvin had his moments, too, but there weren't enough of them as he more or less disappeared from view after the commencement of Brando's romance with Murphy. Also in the cast of this important, trail-blazing film (which was banned in Great Britain for 14 years on the grounds that it would incite British teenagers to acts of violence) were Jay C. Flippen, Peggy Maley, Hugh Sanders, Ray Teal, John Brown and Will Wright. (79 mins)

▽ **Bait** was the fourth film Hugo Haas produced, directed and starred in for Robert Erlik Productions, and which the studio released. Athough on this occasion he didn't write the screenplay (it was scripted by Samuel W. Taylor), he did provide some additional dialogue. The result was a sordid melodrama set in the mountains of northern California. Haas (behind) played an eccentric gold prospector who, with the aid of partner John Agar (front) – and after a 20-year search – finds a 'lost' gold mine. Greed intervenes, and the bulk of the film concerned Haas's abortive attempt to murder Agar. Cleo Moore starred as Haas's waitress-wife, with other roles going to Emmett Lynn, Bruno Ve Sota, Jan Englund, George Keymas and, as a kind of devil-figure in the film's bizarre prologue, Sir Cedric Hardwicke. (79 mins)

▽ Producer Bryan Foy's **The Bamboo Prison** was set in a North Korean prison camp. It starred Robert Francis (right) as an American prisoner-cum-intelligence-officer who feigns an interest in Communism in order to ferret out information that might be useful to the impending Panmunjon peace negotiations. Brian Keith co-starred as a spy in cahoots with Francis, and the only female in the cast was Dianne Foster (left) as the wife of an American traitor. The taut screenplay was by Edwin Blum and Jack DeWitt (story by DeWitt), and Lewis Seiler directed it without undue sensationalism. The cast also featured Jerome Courtland, Earle Hyman, Jack Kelly, King Donovan, Keye Luke, Dick Jones, Pepe Hern, Leo Gordon and, as a phony priest, E. G. Marshall. (79 mins)

◁ A comic-strip Western transplanted, say, from Dodge City to Camelot, and with knights in armour subbing for cowboys in stetsons, **The Black Knight** was an enjoyable Technicolor romp, filmed in England and Spain, which starred an athletic Alan Ladd (illustrated) in the third of his ventures with Warwick Productions. He played a sword-maker called John who is driven to prove how heroic he is after being wrongly accused of cowardice. Ladd disguises himself as a black knight and foils a dastardly attempt by the Saracens to dethrone King Arthur and massacre his army. His reward? A knighthood and the hand of the beauteous Lady Linet (Patricia Medina). As scripted by Alec Coppel the action was fast and furious, leaving little time to mull over the cardboard characterizations or the familiar direction (by Tay Garnett). Peter Cushing made a splendid arch villain, Patrick Troughton had fun with King Mark of Cornwall, Harry Andrews and André Morell inspired confidence as Ladd's faithful friends, and Anthony Bushell was a suitably regal King Arthur. (85 mins)

△ Scenarist Stanley Roberts's inevitable 'opening out' of Herman Wouk's gripping stage adaptation of his Pulitzer Prize-winning novel **The Caine Mutiny** dissipated some of the sustained tension of the play, and gained little by showing scenes that were later described in the naval courtroom. Nevertheless, the movie version benefited from a handful of powerful performances, and from some pulse-quickening direction by Edward Dmytryk. As in the play (called *The Caine Mutiny Court-Martial*), the main thrust of the narrative concerned the proceedings against Lieutenant Maryk (Van Johnson, second right), accused of forcibly relieving Captain Queeg (Humphrey Bogart, right, in the role played on Broadway and the West End by Lloyd Nolan) of command during a typhoon in the Pacific. The man stirring up all the trouble is the perfidious Captain Keefer (Fred MacMurray, left). Defence attorney Lt Barney Greenwald (José Ferrer in the role played on stage by Henry Fonda) reveals Queeg's incompetence and petty tyrannies, and eventually exposes the captain's character in a chilling portrait of mental disintegration. Maryk is acquitted. It wasn't a good idea to include in the screen version the novel's love interest (May Wynn and Robert Frances, second left); nor did Technicolor contribute much to the court-martial proceedings. The strength of Stanley Kramer's successful production, lay less in its approach to the material than in the performances (especially by Bogart and MacMurray) of a cast that also included Tom Tully, E. G. Marshall, Arthur Franz, Lee Marvin, Warner Anderson and Claude Akins. (123 mins)

▽ **A Bullet Is Waiting** was a verbose non-starter, set on an isolated sheep-ranch somewhere along the Californian coast. It starred Jean Simmons (below) as the lonely daughter of an Oxford don (Brian Aherne) bored to distraction so many thousands of miles away from home. Romance enters her life when a handsome prisoner (Rory Calhoun, above), and his vindictive sheriff escort (Stephen McNally) crash the plane taking them to Utah, and are forced to hole up with father and daughter. Simmons takes a shine to Calhoun, whom she believes is innocent of the crime of murder, and after a great deal of talk (supplied by Thames Williamson and Casey Robinson from a story by Robinson), the quartet head for Utah where, it is implied, Calhoun will be given a fair trial. There was nothing fair about the trial audiences were put through watching it all. The film was produced, in Technicolor, by Howard Welsch and directed by John Farrow. (83 mins)

▽ Atomic zombies, capable of causing havoc when let loose, provided **Creature With The Atomic Brain** with its shock-horror gimmick. Though the zombies are the brain-children of Professor Gregory Gaye (left), they're being used as weapons of revenge by Michael Granger (right), a deported mobster out to destroy the men who convicted him. Richard Denning (centre) starred as the head of the Police Laboratories and S. John Launer was his sidekick. Angela Stevens, Linda Bennett, Tristram Coffin, Harry Lauter and Larry Blake were also featured. The screenplay was by Curt Siodmak, and Edward L. Cahn directed for Sam Katzman's Clover Productions. (69 mins)

△ A wildly contrived tale of revenge that stretched the elasticity of belief to snapping point, **The Crooked Web** was the story of a wealthy father's efforts to bring to justice the man who killed, some eight years previously, his GI son in Berlin. The elaborate scheme concocted by undercover agents Mari Blanchard and Richard Denning (right) occupied most of the running time in Lou Breslow's far-fetched screenplay – and was not, in any way, to be taken seriously. Top-cast Frank Lovejoy (left), the owner of a drive-in restaurant, was the killer, with other roles going to John Mylong, Harry Lauter, Steven Ritch and Louis Merrill. Sam Katzman produced for Clover Productions, and Nathan Juran directed. (77 mins)

▷ Mickey Rooney (right) gave an 'A' performance in **Drive A Crooked Road**, despite a 'B' script by scenarist Blake Edwards and adaptor and director Richard Quine (from the story by James Benson) that was strewn with platitudes. He played a shy, lonely little guy whose passion is cars and who dreams about becoming a racing-driver in Europe. His dreams turn to nightmares, however, after he is shamefully used by Dianne Foster in a scheme involving a bank robbery in Palm Springs. Rooney's purpose is to drive the getaway car for hoods Kevin McCarthy (left) and Jack Kelly (centre) – but it all goes wrong and, in a downbeat ending, Rooney and Foster are left to face the music. Producer Jonie Taps's doggedly routine programmer also featured Harry Landers, Jerry Paris, Paul Picerni and Dick Crockett. (83 mins)

▽ A climactic volcanic eruption and a hurricane, lasting about three minutes, was the only action on hand in **Drums Of Tahiti**, a talkative bore whose relentless tedium was not obviated by 3-D or Technicolor. Set in 1877, and all about an American who purchases a bride in San Francisco in order to hide the fact that he is a gun smuggler, it starred Dennis O'Keefe (right) and Patricia Medina (left) – both of whom were powerless against the banalities of Douglas Heyes and Robert E. Kent's screenplay (story by Kent). Francis L. Sullivan played Tahiti's police prefect, and the cast also included George Keymas, Sylvia Lewis, Cicely Browne and Raymond Lawrence. The producer was Sam Katzman, and the director William Castle. (73 mins)

◁ A miscast Maureen O'Hara (centre) starred as a Mata Hari-type secret agent in **Fire Over Africa**, a Tangier-based adventure, independently produced by Mike Frankovich and Richard Sale, and distributed by the studio. Her leading man was Macdonald Carey (left) who, despite being shot in the head and in the chest (twice), nonetheless manages, together with Ms O'Hara, to uncover a dangerous smuggling ring in Tangier. There were some pretty Technicolor shots of the exotic locale, though the ear was less well served by Robert Westerby's screenplay. Binnie Barnes played the tough but likeable owner of a local gambling dive, with other roles under Richard Sale's workaday direction going to Guy Middleton, Hugh McDermott, James Lilburn, Harry Lane, Leonard Sachs and Ferdy Mayne (right). (84 mins)

△ Alan Ladd's second British-made film was **Hell Below Zero**, a murder-melodrama which took to the high seas in a screenplay by Alec Coppel and Max Trell from Hammond Innes's novel *The White South*. Ladd (right) played a seaman adventurer who signs on as first-mate to a British whaler in order to help leading lady Joan Tetzel (left) uncover the truth about her husband's mysterious death. Reports suggest that the deceased man committed suicide in the Antarctic by jumping overboard. The question to which the scenarists addressed themselves was: did he jump – or was he pushed? Helping to conceal the truth was bad-guy Stanley Baker, a skipper who hadn't reckoned on the ingenuity of leading man Ladd. An all-British supporting cast, including Basil Sydney (another heavy in the piece), Joseph Tomelty, Niall MacGinnis and Jill Bennett (as a female whaling captain) did their best to pump adrenalin into both the script and Mark Robson's enervating direction – but weren't able to elevate this Warwick Production (in Technicolor) beyond the level of routine. (90 mins)

▽ **Human Desire**, scripted by Alfred Hayes from the novel by Emile Zola, was a ponderous, self-consciously 'arty' affair, directed by Fritz Lang and starring Glenn Ford (right) as a train driver, Gloria Grahame (left) as the married slut who makes a play for him, and Broderick Crawford as Grahame's insanely jealous husband. Together they comprised an unappetizing trio who not only seemed to get on each other's nerves, but on the nerves of the audience as well. Lewis J. Rachmil's low-key production also featured Edgar Buchanan, Kathleen Case, Peggy Maley and Diane DeLaire. [The French director Jean Renoir first filmed Zola's story in 1938 as *La Bête Humaine* (USA: *The Human Beast*; GB: *Judas Was A Woman*).] (90 mins)

△ It took a quintet of writers – Robert E. Kent and Samuel J. Jacoby (story), and Jesse Lasky Jr, DeVallon Scott and Douglas Heyes (scenarists), to bring to the screen **The Iron Glove** – an 18th-century costume actioner in which the Scottish Prince James Stuart attempts to seize the throne from England's George I. Otto Waldis played the English monarch and Richard Stapley was his would-be successor. Top-billing went to Robert Stack (illustrated) as a dashing swashbuckler who not only rescues Stapley's pretty bride-to-be (Ursula Thiess) but ultimately wins the lady for himself. Lots of swordplay characterized Sam Katzman's good-looking Technicolor production, and the overall results, under William Castle's well-paced direction, were better than average. Also cast: Charles Irwin, Alan Hale Jr, Leslie Bradley and Louis D. Merrill. (77 mins)

◁ Originally called A Name For Herself, but retitled **It Should Happen To You**, this thoroughbred comedy from the stable of Messrs Kanin and Cukor was a winner all the way. It starred Judy Holliday (left) as a model-cum-small-town-nobody who arrives in New York hoping to become a somebody. The city, she quickly discovers, isn't exactly holding its breath for her, and, in order to make an impact, she alights on the ingenious idea of hiring a bill-board in Columbus Circle and blazoning her name – Gladys Glover – across it. One billboard leads to another and it doesn't take too long before curiosity gets the better of resident New Yorkers and sets the whole town talking. Kanin's screenplay really took off when a wealthy soap-manufacturer (Peter Lawford, right) – while trying to buy Gladys's choice Columbus Circle advertising site – falls in love with her. Gladys, meantime, has been enjoying a romance of sorts with a maker of 16mm documentary films, one of whose quirkier notions is to record the bumpy progress of their affair on film. Making his movie debut, Jack Lemmon, a TV recruit, brought his delightfully idiosyncratic personality to bear on the role of the small-time cameraman, and his scenes with the equally idiosyncratic Holliday were pure joy. Each complimented the other, while director George Cukor complimented them both by concentrating the full weight of his talent on drawing performances from them that remain as fresh today as they were 35 years ago. Garson Kanin's racy and satirical screenplay hasn't dated either, and producer Fred Kohlmar's film remains a comedy classic. Completing the cast were Michael O'Shea, Vaughn Taylor, Connie Gilchrist, Walter Klavun, Whit Bissell and Arthur Gilmore. (86 mins)

△ Not a great deal of plot attached itself to **Phffft!** a situation comedy designed to show off the proven talents of Judy Holliday (left) and Jack Lemmon (right). He's a successful attorney, she's a writer of soap-operas. After a briefly successful marriage they have an unsuccessful divorce. She has a flirtation with bachelor Jack Carson, he has a dalliance with sexy Kim Novak. Tired of filing separate tax returns, they get together again – as, of course, you knew they would all along. Adapted by George Axelrod from an unproduced play of his, and performed for much, much more than it was worth by Holliday and Lemmon, the film emerged as a lightweight, often very funny marital caper. Luella Gear, Donald Randolph, Donald Curtis, Arny Freeman, Merry Anders and Eddie Searless completed the cast for producer Fred Kohlmar, and it was directed at a fair pace by Mark Robson. (91 mins)

▷ **The Mad Magician** shared many ingredients with *The House Of Wax* (Warner Bros., 1953). Both dollops of 3-D horror were produced by Bryan Foy, both starred Vincent Price, and both were scripted by Crane Wilbur and photographed by Bert Glennon. However, this later venture left much to be desired. In it Price played a crazy illusionist who kills three people before finally perishing himself. Mary Murphy was his unsuspecting assistant, and glamorous Eva Gabor his ex-wife. Also cast: John Emery, Donald Randolph, Lenita Lane, Patrick O'Neal and Jay Novello. The director was John Brahm. (72 mins)

▽ When Marlon Brando (second left) vacillated over accepting Elia Kazan's offer to appear in **On The Waterfront**, written by Budd Schulberg, the role was offered to Frank Sinatra, who was now a 'hot' property after his success in *From Here To Eternity* (1953). Sinatra accepted. Then so did Brando. Kazan stuck to his first choice – wisely, as it turned out. Brando was magnificent as Terry Malloy, an uneducated, inarticulate, confused ex-boxer and denizen of the waterfront, who finds a way through his confusion – with the help of a good woman and a tough, no-nonsense priest – to eschew his amoral life-style and realize his potential as a decent human being with love rather than hate in his heart. His was a great performance that did not, however, exist in isolation. Equally fine were Lee J. Cobb as Johnny Friendly, the unscrupulous, all-powerful, thoroughly corrupt labour boss, Karl Malden (left) as Father Barry, the crusading Catholic priest who successfully helps to bring an end to Cobb's domination of crooked and violent waterfront politics; Rod Steiger as Brando's 'educated' brother and one of Cobb's henchmen; as well as newcomer Eva Marie Saint (second right) as Brando's refreshingly wholesome girl and the sister of one of Cobb's victims.

Schulberg's screenplay, inspired by a series of Pulitzer Prize-winning newspaper articles by Malcolm Johnson, was a *tour de force* that managed to be both poetic and brutally realistic. His dialogue, especially as delivered by Brando, turned inarticulacy into an art form, and created a tone-of-voice that has often been imitated and parodied, but rarely equalled. The film, shot entirely on location in Hoboken, New Jersey (though the actual locale was never identified), was brilliantly directed by Kazan. Working with such heavyweight Actors Studio alumnae as Brando, Steiger and Malden, Kazan was very much in his element, and on turf that suited his own crusading temperament. The film was a perfect marriage of cast, director and writer, and was furnished with a compelling score by Leonard Bernstein. The producer was Sam Spiegel, who took on the production after it was turned down by every major Hollywood studio, including, initially, Columbia. The heartening box-office returns topped $9.5 million world-wide. Also cast: Leif Erickson, James Westerfield, Tony Galento, Tami Mauriello, John Hamilton, John Heldabrand, Martin Balsam, Pat Henning, Fred Gwynne, Rudy Bond and Don Blackman. (108 mins)

△ In **The Miami Story**, Barry Sullivan (right), as a reformed gangster-turned-detective, poses as a rival Cuban racketeer in order to nail syndicate chief Luther Adler. The plot was as basic as that, but tautly scripted by Robert E. Kent, and tightly directed by Fred F. Sears. The result was a fast-paced crime melodrama that also benefited from producer Sam Katzman's 'documentary' approach to the material, and the convincing performances of the two male leads. Also cast: Adele Jergens, Beverly Garland (left, as Jergens's sister, and the object of Sullivan's affections), George E. Stone, Dan Riss and Damian O'Flynn. The weakest performance was third-billed John Baer's as Adler's 'pretty boy' henchman. (75 mins)

△ In **Pushover**, Kim Novak (right), whom the studio was grooming as a second Marilyn Monroe (they could have had the original had Harry Cohn not dropped her contract), played a role not unlike Barbara Stanwyck's in the far-superior *Double Indemnity* (Paramount, 1944). She was a ruthless moll who persuades plain-clothes detective Fred MacMurray (left, in a role similar to the one *he* played opposite Stanwyck) to do away with gangster lover (Paul Richards), presently on the lam with a bank-heist haul of $200,000 and to split the cash between them. He does, is caught, and they all live miserably ever after. It was crisply directed by Richard Quine from a script by Roy Huggins (based on stories by Thomas Walsh and William S. Ballinger), and produced by Jules Schermer for Philip A. Waxman Productions. A first-rate supporting cast included Phil Carey, Dorothy Malone and E. G. Marshall. (88 mins)

▽ Action and a fair share of laughs mingled to entertaining effect in **A Prize Of Gold**, directed by Mark Robson and produced by Irving Allen, Albert R. Broccoli and Phil C. Samuel for Warwick Productions. It starred Richard Widmark (right) as a US Army sergeant who, in the course of Robert Buckner and John Paxton's screenplay (from a novel by Max Catto), hijacks a shipment of gold that's being sent from England to Germany in order to help refugee Mai Zetterling repatriate a group of war orphans from Europe to Brazil. Donald Wolfit, Joseph Tomelty, Nigel Patrick and George Cole (left) were also involved in the hijacking, the latter two Englishmen taking responsibility for landing the plane on an abandoned airstrip. Andrew Ray, Karel Stepanek, Robert Ayres and Eric Pohlmann were also cast, and it was photographed in Technicolor. (98 mins)

▽ Producer Sam Katzman went back in time to the 13th century for **The Saracen Blade**, a Technicolor swashbuckler that wasn't too proud to feature black-and-white stock footage of a castle being attacked. Budget considerations aside, director William Castle's action-packed adventure went at a terrific lick as it told the story of a commoner who has devoted his life to avenging the death of his father at the hands of a wicked count and his son. Ricardo Montalban (left) played the avenging hero, Michael Ansara was the Count, and Rick Jason (right) the son. Betta St John appeared as the lovely Iolanthe, wife of Jason but loved by Montalban, with other roles farmed out to Carolyn Jones as the evil blonde Montalban marries as part of his revenge scheme, Whitfield Connor, Edgar Barrier, Nelson Leigh, and Frank Pulaski. It was written by DeVallon Scott and George Worthing Yates from a novel by Frank Yerby. (77 mins)

△ An off-beat Western involving a fair amount of mob psychology and an illegitimate baby, **Three Hours To Kill** starred Dana Andrews (right) as a fugitive who is run out of town after being nearly lynched for the murder of a man he did not kill. He returns, bearing the mental and physical scars of his experience, determined to clear his name. The would-be lynchers, fearing that Andrews will exact some kind of revenge for their previous anti-social behaviour, sets out to get him before he gets them. Donna Reed (centre) co-starred as the girl Andrews left behind and who, after falling pregnant by him, marries another man when she learns of her condition. Pretty Diane Foster (left) was the girl Andrews takes away with him after the real killer has been identified and dealt with. Produced, in Technicolor, by Harry Joe Brown, the film was directed by Alfred Werker from a screenplay provided by Richard Alan Simmons and Roy Huggins (that was based on a story by Alex Gottlieb). The supporting roles featured, among others, Stephen Elliott, Richard Coogan, Laurence Hugo, James Westerfield, Richard Webb and Carolyn Jones. (77 mins)

△ Barbara Stanwyck (second left) returned to the studio after an absence of 13 years to star in **The Violent Men**, a CinemaScope Western, in Technicolor. She played the grasping, two-timing wife of an equally disagreeable cattle baron (Edward G. Robinson, left) who, together with Brian Keith (third left), her husband's brother (and the man with whom she's having an affair), comes to a violent end. Hero of the piece was solid Glenn Ford (right), a pacifist who nonetheless decides to indulge in a spot of guerilla warfare against the land-grabbing Robinson.

Two spectacular ranch fires, a horse stampede and an ambush helped bolster the screenplay Harry Kleiner had fashioned from a novel by David Hamilton, and there could be no underestimating the value of both Stanwyck and Robinson to Lewis J. Rachmil's production. Under Rudolph Maté's direction, they helped turn a routine Western into a fairly good one. Also cast: Dianne Foster as Robinson's disgusted daughter, May Wynn, Warner Anderson, Basil Ruysdael, Richard Jaeckel, Willis Bouchey, James Westerfield and Lita Milan. (95 mins)

1955

▽ Operation 'Cockleshell' was set up, during World War II, to destroy German shipping in Bordeaux harbour. Eight men of the Royal Marines paddled four canoes into enemy waters and planted limpet mines on the Nazi vessels. Two men survived, two were killed in a getaway attempt, and the remaining four were executed as saboteurs. Producers Irving Allen and Albert R. Broccoli, for Warwick Films, brought the incident excitingly to life in **Cockleshell Heroes** directed by José Ferrer (front), who also starred. Trevor Howard (second back), Victor Maddern, Anthony Newley (second front), David Lodge (back), Peter Arne (second back), Karel Stepanek and Dora Bryan were also featured, and screenplay was by Bryan Forbes and Richard Maibaum (from the story by George Kent). Filmed in CinemaScope and Technicolor. (97 mins)

▷ Although Frankie Laine (right) received top-billing in **Bring Your Smile Along**, and, indeed, warbled his way through several assorted songs, the plot devised by Blake Edwards and Richard Quine (script by Edwards) centred on a New England schoolteacher (Constance Towers, left, in her debut performance) forsaking her small-town biology-lecturer fiancé (William Leslie) for fame and fortune as a lyricist in New York. After forming a partnership with composer Keefe Brasselle, she pens hit after hit, all of them recorded by popular Mr Laine. It was diverting in a familiar kind of way, and thoroughly professional. Edwards also directed (his debut) for producer Jonie Taps. His supporting cast included Lucy Marlow, Mario Siletti, Ida Smeraldo, Ruth Warren and Jack Albertson. Technicolor. (83 mins)

▽ The changing social order in the post-Civil War South was the theme of **Count Three And Pray**. The plot that underpinned it featured Van Heflin (centre) as an ornery dude who not only fought for the North but has a decided predilection for wild women and hard liquor. Peacetime changes him though, and Herb Meadow's screenplay turned him into a reformed man preaching the Gospel and dedicated to rebuilding the local church. The opposition engendered by these activities furnished the film with its conflict and also gave Heflin a chance to dominate the action with his fists. His co-star was Joanne Woodward (left), a hillbilly whose Cinderella-like transformation leads the way to romance. It added up to passable entertainment, aided by a strong supporting cast that included Phil Carey, Jean Willes (as a prostitute), Myron Healey, Nancy Kulp, James Griffith, Allison Hayes (right), Richard Webb, Kathryn Givney and Robert Burton. A Copa Production for Ted Richmond and Tyrone Power, it was photographed in CinemaScope and Technicolor, and directed by George Sherman. (102 mins)

▽ **Cell 2455, Death Row** was the biopic of condemned rapist Caryl Chessman and as scripted by Jack DeWitt from Chessman's own book, barely scratched the surface of its subject's personality. Motivation wasn't what motivated Wallace MacDonald's production, and the result was simply a bald narrative depicting a senseless life of crime. William Campbell (second left) portrayed Chessman as an adult; Robert Campbell played him as a boy. The rest of the cast under Fred F. Sears's direction included Marian Carr, Kathryn Grant, Harvey Stephens, Vince Edwards (left), Allen Nourse and Diane De Laire. (77 mins)

▷ Paul Stewart played a mobster in **Chicago Syndicate**, while top-billed Dennis O'Keefe (centre) starred as a smart accountant who gains Stewart's confidence and then nails him after discovering the source of his crooked income. A routine crime melodrama, written by Joseph Hoffman from a story by William Sackheim (which made pivotal use of a piece of micro-film), it also featured bandleader Xavier Cugat and his wife Abbe Lane, Allison Hayes, Dick Cutting, and Chris Alcaide. Fred F. Sears directed for Sam Katzman's Clover Productions. (84 mins)

◁ Lenore Coffee's screenplay from Graham Greene's novel **The End Of The Affair** was in no way able to reconcile the theme, so intricately explored in the book, of religious faith versus sexual longing. The result was a tedious drama which found Deborah Kerr as the unfaithful wife of civil servant Peter Cushing, vacillating between her love for a miscast Van Johnson (left), with whom she has been enjoying an illicit wartime romance, and, ultimately, her love of God. Kerr's dilemma is finally resolved when she catches a cold and dies. John Mills (right) played a sprightly private-eye called Albert Parkis (and sniffed out all the best reviews), with other roles under Edward Dmytryk's earnest though unenlightening direction going to Stephen Murray, Nora Swinburne, Charles Goldner, Michael Goodliffe and Joyce Carey. The film was produced, in Britain, by David E. Rose. (107 mins)

▷ Unfortunately technicolor did very little to alleviate the tedium engendered by **Footsteps In The Fog**, a British-made melodrama that starred real-life husband and wife Stewart Granger (left), and Jean Simmons (right). The screenplay by Lenore Coffee and Dorothy Reid had Stewart poisoning his wife then being blackmailed by his maid (Simmons) after which she becomes his housekeeper as well as his next target. However, due to a heavy fog (mainly in the script), Granger kills the wrong woman. Simmons's false testimony results in an acquittal for her would-be slayer who, in the final reel, conveniently poisons himself. Granger gave a good impression of a somnambulist, and Simmons was ineffectual. Director Arthur Lubin's all-British supporting cast included Bill Travers, Finlay Currie, Ronald Squire, Belinda Lee and William Hartnell. It was a Mike Frankovich-Maxwell Setton production. (90 mins)

▽ Louisiana in 1820 was the setting of **Duel On The Mississippi**, a romantic actioner, in Technicolor, whose story and screenplay (by Gerald Drayson Adams) dealt with a series of plantation raids perpetrated by vicious bayou killers. Promoting the raids is Patricia Medina, a lowly Creole gambling-ship owner vengefully aware of her 'inferiority' to Southern aristocracy. Top-starred Lex Barker (left) played the son of aristocrat John Dehner, with other roles going to Craig Stevens, Warren Stevens (right), Ian Keith, Chris Alcaide, John Mansfield and Celia Lovsky. Keeping it all simmering nicely was director William Castle for Sam Katzman's Clover Productions. (72 mins)

△ The **Five Against The House** were Guy Madison (right), Kim Novak (second left), Brian Keith (second right), Alvy Moore, and Kerwin Mathews. The house they're against is Harold's Club in Reno. What begins as a jape ends as a reality when a heist – planned by Mathews but disapproved of by Madison – goes ahead, with disastrous results. Character and plot, and the tensions generated by both, were expertly juggled by writers Sterling Silliphant, John Barnwell (both of whom also produced for Dayle Productions) and William Bowers, working from a *Good Housekeeping* story by Jack Finney. They emerged with a gripping little thriller. The nifty direction was by Phil Karlson, who, when it came to laying on the suspense, didn't miss a trick. (82 mins)

△ Independently produced by Wray Davis, and purchased outright by the studio, **Hell's Horizon** starred John Ireland (right) as an unlikeable Korean War bomber pilot, who, together with co-pilot Bill Williams (centre), sets out from Okinawa to bomb a strategic bridge over the Yalu River. He does, then returns to base and crash-lands on an empty tank. The End. It was perfunctorily written and directed by Tom Gries, and featured Marla English as the obligatory love interest, Larry Pennell (left), William Schallert, Paul Levitt and John Murphy. (78 mins)

▷ Corruption in the United Auto Workers Union was the subject of **Inside Detroit**, another melodrama from Sam Katzman's Clover Productions. It starred Dennis O'Keefe as an honest union leader and Pat O'Brien (right) as a former union-man-turned-racketeer about to be released from prison after a five-year sentence. Robert E. Kent and James B. Gordon's screenplay concentrated on O'Brien's unsuccessful attempts to use the union for his own nefarious ends. It gave employment to Tina Carver (as O'Brien's mistress as well as his partner in a call-girl operation), Margaret Field, Mark Damon (left), Larry Blake, and Ken Christy. Fred F. Sears directed. (80 mins)

◁ A horrific marine monster, created by special-effects wizard Ray Harryhausen, was the real star of **It Came From Beneath The Sea** – an enjoyable wadge of hokum which always upstaged its flesh-and-blood stars, Kenneth Tobey (right) and Faith Domergue (centre). Driven into the Pacific by H-bomb explosions off the Marshall Islands, the giant octopus was the *raison d'être* of this passable sci-fi adventure, and allowed scenarists George Worthing Yates and Hal Smith (story by Yates) to create several tense situations as the creature demolished everything in its path. It was neatly directed by Robert Gordon with a cast that included Donald Curtis (left), Ian Keith and Dean Maddox Jr. But it was the monster that audiences wanted to see, and they weren't disappointed. The movie was produced by Charles H. Schneer for Clover Productions. (79 mins)

▽ In **Joe Macbeth** scenarist Philip Yordan took the bare outlines of Shakespeare's Scottish tragedy, and turned it into a dreadful underworld melodrama. Paul Douglas (centre) and Ruth Roman starred as the anti-social Macbeths, Banquo (re-christened Banky) was played by English (South African-born) actor Sidney James, his son (called Lennie) by Bonar Colleano (left), McDuff by Nicholas Stuart (top right), with other distinctly un-Shakespearean types – in the hands of Grégoire Aslan (as The Duke), Robert Arden (second top right), Minerva Pious, Harry Green and Bill Nagy (right). The film was produced in England and directed by Ken Hughes. (90 mins)

1955

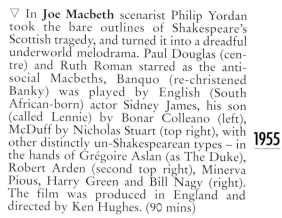

▷ Nice cast – Victor Mature (second left), Guy Madison (second right), Robert Preston (left), Anne Bancroft, James Whitmore (right) – shame about the script. That's the kindest that could be said for **The Last Frontier**, a numbingly familiar Western about a trio of fur trappers and their set-to with the Injuns. Meanwhile, back at the fort – run by a demented Preston – there's trouble when the macho Mature falls for Preston's wife Bancroft. Philip Yordan and Russell S. Hughes's screenplay, based on Richard Emery Roberts's novel *The Gilded Rooster*, came to a predictable conclusion with a climactic shoot-out in which Preston is killed, thus alleviating Bancroft of any bad conscience she may have had in responding to Mature's romantic overtures. William Fadiman's CinemaScope production was photographed in murky Technicolor, and directed for the elongated cliché it was by Anthony Mann. Also cast: Russell Collins, Peter Whitney and Pat Hogan. (97 mins)

◁ **A Lawless Street** once again found Randolph Scott (left) in the familiar role of marshal. This time his determination to rid Medicine Bend of its undesirable elements turns him into a one-man killing machine – much to the disapproval of wife Angela Lansbury (right). The predictable finale found Scott's law-enhancing efforts paying dividends and the film ended with him exchanging his badge and his gun for a life of domesticity. The bad guys in producer Harry Joe Brown's Scott-Brown Technicolor Western were Michael Pate, Warner Anderson and John Emery – with other roles under Joseph H. Lewis's direction farmed out to Jean Parker, Wallace Ford, James Bell, Ruth Donnelly, Don Megowan, Jeanette Nolan and Peter Ortiz. (78 mins)

▽ Director John Ford's **The Long Gray Line** took James Hilton's schoolmaster, Mr Chips, and relocated him at West Point. For Hilton's fictional account of a dedicated schoolteacher was closely echoed by the real-life saga of Marty Maher – an Irishman who spent fifty years of his life as an athletics instructor at West Point Military Academy. Both men married charismatic women: both men's wives lost babies in childbirth, and both, at different times in their lives, lost their wives. Edward Hope's warm and often tear-stained screenplay, based on the biography Maher wrote in collaboration with Nardi R. Campion, provided Tyrone Power (right), as Maher, with one of the meatiest, most challenging roles of his career. Like Robert Donat in *Goodbye Mr Chips* (MGM, 1939) Power gave the performance of his career. Maureen O'Hara (second right) played his wife Mary, with other roles under Ford's emotionally charged (though never mawkish) direction going to Donald Crisp (excellent) as Maher's father, Robert Francis as a second-generation cadet befriended by Maher and his wife, Ward Bond as the Academy's Master of the Sword, Phil Carey as General Dotson and Harry Carey Jr as cadet Dwight Eisenhower. Also cast: Betsy Palmer (centre), William Leslie (second left), Patrick Wayne (left), Sean McClory, Peter Graves and Milburn Stone. The film was stunningly photographed by Charles Lawton Jr in CinemaScope and Technicolor, and produced on location by Robert Arthur, whose $2 million production yielded happy box-office returns of $15 million. (135 mins)

△ **The Man From Laramie**, one of the best Westerns of the year, brought to an end a cycle of outdoor actioners – such as *Winchester '73* (Universal-International, 1950), *Bend Of The River* (Universal-International, 1952) and *The Naked Spur* (MGM, 1953) – on which James Stewart (foreground) collaborated with director Anthony Mann. Obsession was the underlying theme of their fifth successful movie, and it manifested itself in the character of Will Lockhart (Stewart), who leaves his home in Laramie, Wyoming, to seek out the men responsible for selling automatic rifles to the Apaches, thereby precipitating his brother's death. Stewart's obsession brings him into violent contact with a megalomaniac rancher (Donald Crisp) and his two sons, one of them psychotic (Alex Nicol, fourth right) and the other adopted (Arthur Kennedy). Stewart's concern over his brother's death, and Crisp's concern over which of his sons should inherit his ranch, were the twin narrative threads that scenarists Philip Yordan and Frank Burt (working from a *Saturday Evening Post* story by Thomas T. Flynn) wove into their intelligent and absorbing screenplay. William Goetz's good-looking production, in CinemaScope and Technicolor, also featured Cathy O'Donnell, Wallace Ford (second right), Jack Elam, John War Eagle, Boyd Stockman (third left) and James Millican. (102 mins)

▽ A kind of On the New Orleans Waterfront, **New Orleans Uncensored** took a quasi-documentary approach to its waterlogged material, even though there was nothing realistic about Orville H. Hampton and Lewis Meltzer's tired old screenplay (story by Hampton). Set, for the most part, along the New Orleans docks, it told the familiar story of a racketeer (Michael Ansara) who pollutes the dockside air with graft, corruption and crooked dealings. His strong-arm tactics are, eventually, brought to an end by hero Arthur Franz (left), a navy veteran who finds employment on the docks. Beverly Garland and Helene Stanton (right) provided female interest, with other roles under William Castle's so-so direction going to Stacy Harris, Mike Mazurki, William Henry, and Michael Granger. The producer was Sam Katzman. (76 mins)

◁ A musical re-make of the studio's 1942 success, **My Sister Eileen** recycled the same material from Joseph Fields and Jerome Chodorov's durable comedy. It starred Betty Garrett (centre) and Janet Leigh (right) as Ruth McKenney and her pretty sister Eileen. Once again it was set in a Greenwich Village basement apartment, with the fast-rising Jack Lemmon (left) co-starred as a magazine publisher who gives Ruth her big chance to become a writer. Kurt Kasznar, Tommy Rall, Dick York, Barbara Brown and Horace McMahon were in it too; the score was by Jule Styne and Leo Robin and the choreography by Bob Fosse, who also appeared. If, in the end, Fred Kohlmar's Technicolor production, scripted by Blake Edwards and Richard Quine and directed by Quine, didn't have quite the freshness of its Broadway counterpart, there were still lots of goodies on offer. (108 mins)

▽ **Picnic**, William Inge's Pulitzer Prize-winning Broadway hit, which enjoyed a 477-performance run at New York's Music Box Theatre, came to the screen via its original director, Joshua Logan, and in a finely wrought screenplay, by Daniel Taradash, that allowed Inge's moving drama to speak for itself. Set in a sleepy Kansas town one warm, Labor Day morning, **Picnic** focused on the impact made by a muscle-flexing vagrant whose presence (especially at the annual picnic) causes a fair amount of emotional havoc among the local womenfolk. By the time he leaves the following day he has broken the heart of an ugly-duckling tomboy (a miscast Susan Strasberg, left), has driven a frustrated school-mistress (Rosalind Russell) into talking her reluctant boyfriend (Arthur O'Connell) into marriage, and persuaded the town's local beauty (Kim Novak, centre) to abandon her fiancé (Cliff Robertson) and run away with him. Though William Holden was a bit too old for the part of the itinerant charmer, he was sufficiently well directed by Logan (making an impressive screen debut) to overcome an absence of raw sexuality, and his sultry, suggestive come-hither dance with the voluptuous Miss Novak was certainly memorable. In general, Logan's handling of the picnic sequences was masterly, and he drew fine supporting performances from Betty Field (right) as Novak's mother, Verna Felton and Reta Shaw. Rosalind Russell, in the role played on Broadway by Eileen Heckart, offered a touching study of sexual frustration; while O'Connell (repeating his stage performance) was excellent as the show's 'comic' relief. Fred Kohlmar's production, in CinemaScope and Technicolor, grossed $6.3 million. (115 mins)

△ Joan Crawford (right) turned herself into something resembling a human chainsaw in **Queen Bee**, an over-the-top (if not over-the-hill) drama which found the scenery-demolishing Ms Crawford demolishing a few lives in the process as well. Written by Ranald MacDougall from a novel by Edna Lee, its evil, power-crazed heroine cut a ruinous swathe through the Phillips family, turning the Southern mansion in which it was set into a cold-comfort heartbreak house. The victims of her hatred are Barry Sullivan (centre front), her bitter, alcoholic husband, and Sullivan's sister (Betsy Palmer, centre back) who is driven to suicide after her chances of marriage to John Ireland, a former lover of Crawford's, are wrecked. Ireland gets his revenge when Crawford is killed in a deliberately planned car smash which releases the hapless Sullivan from his misery and allows him to marry pretty Lucy Marlow (left). MacDougall directed a cast that also included William Leslie, Fay Wray, Katherine Anderson and Tim Hovey. The overwrought production was the responsibility of Jerry Wald. (94 mins)

▷ A combination of *Blind Alley* (1939) and Joseph Hayes's Broadway chiller *The Desperate Hours*, **The Night Holds Terror** was based on a real-life incident and piled tension upon tension as it told the story of a trio of hoodlums who terrorize a family. Vince Edwards (left), John Cassavetes, and David Cross (centre) played the villains; Jack Kelly (right), Hildy Parks, Charles Herbert and Nancy Dee Zane were their victims. It was written, produced and directed by Andrew Stone who did creditable jobs in all three capacities. The smaller roles featured Jack Kruschen, Edward Marr, Joyce McCluskey and Jonathan Hale. All the performances were first-rate. (85 mins)

△ After turning the clock back to the 13th century for *The Saracen Blade* (1954), producer Sam Katzman, fast becoming the poor man's Cecil B. De Mille, turned to the 16th century for **Pirates Of Tripoli**. This Technicolor swashbuckler, rich in colourful scenery, starred Paul Henreid (left) as the titular hero and Patricia Medina (centre) as a princess who seeks out his help when her kingdom is overrun by the evil John Miljan. Henreid saves the day, with Medina his romantic *coup d'état*. Allen March wrote it, Felix Feist directed, and the cast included Paul Newland, Mark Hanna, Jean Del Val (right), Lillian Bond, Mel Welles, William Fawcett and Louis G. Mercier. (70 mins)

△ Juvenile delinquency was the exploitable subject of **Teenage Crime Wave**, a youth-orientated melodrama with no names to its credit, and not a great deal of entertainment value either. The exaggerated title led audiences to expect a criminal epidemic when, in reality, all they got was an isolated case in which a trigger-happy teenager (Tommy Cook, centre), kills a sheriff while springing his moll (Mollie McCart) from a reformatory station wagon. The repercussions of the killing formed the basis of Harry Esse and Ray Buffum's screenplay (story by Buffum), which provided work for Sue England, Frank Griffin, James Bell, Kay Riehl and Larry Blake. A Clover Production, it was directed by Fred F. Sears. (77 mins)

△ **Ten Wanted Men** was a pretty conventional oater in which Randolph Scott (centre) – for his own Scott-Brown Productions – cast himself as a law-abiding rancher whose rivalry with gun-toting bad-guy Richard Boone supplied the conflict in the screenplay Kenneth Gamet chiselled out of a story by Irving Ravetch and Harriet Frank Jr. A climactic fight between the two adversaries brought the story to its logical (and predictable) conclusion, with the vigilant among audiences noticing Scott's obvious stand-in during the more energetic action sequences. Jocelyn Brando was cast as a widow-woman in love with the hero, with other roles under Bruce Humberstone's middle-of-the-road direction going to Skip Homeier (right), Alfonso Bedoya, Donna Martell, Clem Bevans, Minor Watson (second left), Lester Matthews, Tom Powers, Dennis Weaver (seated), and Lee Van Cleef. (80 mins)

▽ The Roman Catholic Legion of Decency condemned **Three For The Show**, a flashy Technicolor musical, in CinemaScope, for its flippant approach to the taboo subject of polygamy. A tuneful remake of *Too Many Husbands* (1940), it starred Betty Grable (centre) as a showgirl who is understandably dismayed when she discovers that she is married to two men: Gower Champion (right) *and* Jack Lemmon (left). The innocent reasons for this complication were breezily explained in the screenplay written by Edward Hope and Leonard Stern (from Somerset Maugham's play *Home And Beauty*). The successful resolution of her problem is aided by Marge Champion (as a dancer) who is ready and willing to accept whichever hubbie Grable decides to discard. Jack Cole's choreography enlivened the proceedings considerably; so did a score with contributions by the Gershwins and Hoagy Carmichael. Jonie Taps produced, H.C. Potter directed and the cast included Myron McCormick, Paul Harvey, Robert Bice and Hal K. Dawson. (93 mins)

▽ Aldo Ray (right) starred as Hugh O'Reilly, a Jap-hating sergeant of the 27th Infantry Regiment (the Wolfhounds) who visits Japan in 1949 and undergoes a change of heart when he sees for himself the appalling conditions endured by the inhabitants of a Japanese orphanage. The melting of Ray was the subject of **Three Stripes In The Sun** (G.B: **The Gentle Sergeant**), a romantic drama which introduced to American audiences Mitsuko Kimura as the hero's love-interest. Phil Carey, Dick York (left), Chuck Connors, Camille Janclaire and Henry Okawa were also featured in Fred Kohlmar's heart-warming production, which was caringly directed by Richard Murphy from his own screenplay (based on E. J. Kahn's *New Yorker* article 'The Gentle Wolfhound' and adapted by Albert Duffy). (93 mins)

△ Playwright Leonard Kantor's *Dead Pigeon*, which had a 21-performance run on Broadway in 1953, came to the screen via producer Lewis J. Rachmil as a vehicle for Ginger Rogers (right). Retitled **Tight Spot**, it told the story of a brassy blonde (Rogers) who is temporarily released from a four-year prison rap in order to testify against a notorious gangster (Lorne Greene). Keeping her company in a plush hotel are attorney Edward G. Robinson (left), detective Brian Keith (centre), and matron Katharine Anderson. William Bowers's screenplay provided director Phil Karlson with enough raw tension and a few nice twists on which to go to work – and he did, to maximum effect. Rogers and Robinson were terrific together and did wonders to draw attention away from the fact that much of the writing was verbose, and that most of the action took place in one room. Also cast: Lucy Marlow, Allen Nourse, Peter Leeds, Doyle O'Dell and Eve McVeagh. (95 mins)

△ Among the inmates of **Women's Prison** were Phyllis Thaxter, guilty of manslaughter in a car accident, Audrey Totter (centre, standing), arrested for possessing a gun, and Jan Sterling (second right), convicted for forgery. Cleo Moore (seated, back left) and Vivian Marshall were inside too – all under the unhelpful supervision of Ida Lupino (left), who hates women who have had more success with the opposite sex than she has. Crane Wilbur and Jack DeWitt's screenplay was unrelieved by humour, but it did give its predominantly female cast a chance to shine. Howard Duff played an amiable prison doctor, with other roles in Bryan Foy's production going to Warren Stevens, Barry Kelley, Gertrude Michael and Mae Clarke. Lewis Seiler directed. (80 mins)

1956

▷ Joan Crawford (right) went through the agonies of the damned in **Autumn Leaves**, a psychological melodrama in which she played an ageing spinster, who, in the autumn of her years, is lucky enough to marry a good-looking younger man (Cliff Robertson, left). Then, quite unexpectedly, her husband's father (Lorne Greene) shows up with his wife (Vera Miles) and all hell breaks loose. It seems that Robertson was once married to his step-mother and caught her and his father in a compromising position. This traumatic encounter resulted in Robertson flipping his lid and becoming psychotic. The sudden re-appearance of these ghosts from his past turns him violent and he is institutionalized. But, by the end of Jack Jevne, Lewis Meltzer and Robert Blees's screenplay, whatever demons he took with him to the sanitarium have been exorcised and he emerges happy, healthy, and very much in love with Miss Crawford. Owing more to over-the-top theatrics than to psychology, William Goetz's production, under Robert Aldrich's sledgehammer direction, piled on the anguish, a situation of which its volatile leading lady took unrestrained advantage. The supporting cast included Ruth Donnelly, Selmer Jackson, Maxine Cooper, Shepperd Strudwick and Leonard Mudie, and the title song was sung twice – once at the beginning and once at the end – by Nat King Cole. (107 mins)

△ The first ever Rock 'n' Roll movie, **Rock Around The Clock** literally had its enthusiastic young audiences dancing in the aisles to the seductive beat provided by Bill Haley and His Comets (illustrated). Though the plot was a mere trifle involving deejay Alan Freed's discovery of the legendary rock band in a mountain village and promoting them in New York – what counted most on this occasion was the music, and there was an abundance of that – including such 40-carat hits as 'See You Later, Alligator', 'Razzle Dazzle' and the title tune – all of them written by Haley. Also contributing their talents to this pop-pourri were The Platters, Tony Martinez and His Band, Frankie Bell and His Bellboys, as well as Johnny Johnston, Alix Talton, Lisa Gaye, John Archer and Henry Slate. Robert E. Kent and James B. Gordon wrote the screenplay, Sam Katzman produced, and Fred F. Sears directed. (77 mins)

▷ Richard Conte (right) starred as Eddie, one of **The Brothers Rico**, who once worked for syndicate boss Sid Kubick (Larry Goates) but has gone straight. However, brothers Johnny (James Darren, right) and Gino (Paul Picerni) are still in the racket. Eddie is warned by Kubik that Johnny and Gino have been 'marked' by a rival mob, but realizes – too late – that it's Kubik who wants them dead. Phil Karlson directed this brutal, no-hope story (based on *Les Frères Rico* by Georges Simenon; screenplay by Lewis Meltzer and Ben Perry) whose bleakness was superbly caught by Burnett Guffey's camera. Also cast: Dianne Foster, Kathryn Grant (centre), Argentina Brunetti and Lamont Johnson. Lewis J. Rachmil produced. (81 mins)

◁ Producer Sam Katzman (for Clover Productions) and his scenarist James B. Gordon made very little attempt to disguise the fact that the smidgin of plot they cobbled together for **Cha-Cha-Cha Boom!** was little more than a peg on which to hang no fewer than sixteen musical numbers. With the music of Perez Prado, the Mary Kaye Trio, Helen Grayco (right), Sylvia Lewis, Dante De Paulo as well as the bands of Luis Arcaraz and Manny Lopez, the story of a disc jockey's attempts to recruit new talent from Cuba for his own recording company was of secondary importance. Steve Dunne played the disc jockey, Alix Talton was a rival talent scout (and the romantic interest), with the comedy relief going to José Gonzales Gonzales (left). Fred F. Sears directed, and the musical numbers were staged and created by Earl Barton. (78 mins)

▷ Life aboard an aircraft carrier was the subject of **Battle Stations**, a stereotypical World War II drama which relied on large chunks of stock footage to convey a documentary-like sense of verisimilitude. Seemingly unaware that a good plot usually helped the story along, Crane Wilbur's screenplay (story by Ben Finney) concentrated, instead, on the participating characters, chief among whom was John Lund as a chaplain newly assigned to the vessel. Richard Boone played the captain, William Bendix (centre right) the chief bos'un, Keefe Brasselle a cocky sailor, and William Leslie a young pilot about to experience the joys of fatherhood for the first time. The highlight of the film was a guided tour, from stem-to-stern, of the carrier in question. Lewis Seiler directed (flatly), Bryan Foy produced, and the cast included John Craven, James Lydon, Claude Akins, George O'Hanlon and Eddie Foy III. (81 mins)

▽ Ray Harryhausen supplied the superb stop-motion special effects for **Earth Vs The Flying Saucers**, a budget-conscious science-fiction entry that was anything but earth-shattering. All about a group of ancient humanoids who have been using their flying saucers to knock artificial satellites out of the sky in a bid to take over planet Earth, it starred Hugh Marlowe (right) as a space-exploration scientist and the hero of the piece. Putting his honeymoon on hold for the moment, he devises a weapon that neutralizes the magnetic anti-gravity equipment on the aliens' saucers. The plot was as simple as that. Joan Taylor (left) was Marlowe's bride, with other roles going to Donald Curtis, Morris Ankrum, John Zaremba and the voice of Paul Frees. The screenplay was written by George Worthing Yates and Raymond T. Marcus from a story by Curt Siodmak, suggested, in turn, by Major Donald E. Keyhoe's tale of *Flying Saucers From Outer Space*. The director was Fred F. Sears and the producer Charles H. Schneer. (82 mins)

▽ Lachrymose was the word for **The Eddy Duchin Story**, a tear-inducing biopic of the famous pianist-cum-bandleader whose catalogue of personal tragedies was sufficient to give Job a run for his money. Tyrone Power (left) starred as Eddy (with Carmen Cavallaro subbing for him on the keyboard), Kim Novak (right) played his wife Marjorie (who died shortly after the birth of their son), Rex Thompson was the son, and Victoria Shaw an English girl called Chiquita, with whom he falls in love. Also in the cast were James Whitmore, Mickey Maga, Shepperd Strudwick, Frieda Inescort, Gloria Holden, Larry Keating and John Mylong. It was written by Samuel Taylor from a story by Leo Latcher, produced by Jerry Wald (in CinemaScope and Technicolor) and directed by veteran music-man George Sidney. The musical sound-track, which featured almost 30 golden-oldies, was in the capable hands of Morris Stoloff. (123 mins)

△ A spoof gangster comedy with two songs (sung by Frankie Laine, left) and a mini production number, **He Laughed Last** was good, clean fun, and entertaining too. Told in flashback (and narrated by nightclub owner Laine), it was the story of a singer-dancer who, sometime during the Twenties, inherits the crooked empire of an underworld Mr Big (Alan Reed). The recipient of this windfall is Lucy Marlow (third left) and she's tickled pink. Not so her policeman boyfriend (Richard Long). As directed by Blake Edwards from a screenplay he co-authored with Richard Quine, it breezed along enjoyably enough and kept undemanding customers happy. It was photographed in Technicolor, featured Anthony Dexter (as a dancing gigolo), Jesse White, Florenz Ames, and Henry Slate, and was produced by Jonie Taps. (76 mins)

◁ Produced in England by Warwick Films, **The Gamma People** was a dreadful sci-fi effort in which Walter Rilla played a mad scientist who, in the mythical state of Gudavia, is conducting experiments which, if successful, will turn ordinary children into geniuses. However, in order to achieve this he is bombarding them with harmful gamma rays. He's deflected in his evil course by reporter Paul Douglas (left) and Leslie Phillips. Nothing worked in producer John Gossage's feeble effort, and *The Gamma People* came and went with indecent haste. Gossage scripted with director John Gilling (story by Louis Pollock) and the cast included Eva Bartok, Philip Leaver (right), Martin Miller, Pauline Drewett, Rosalie Crutchley, and Leonard Sachs. (78 mins)

△ Judy Holliday (left) was, literally, **Full Of Life** in director Richard Quine's domestic comedy of the same name. Just days away from becoming a mother for the first time, she has to endure the irritating, albeit well-intentioned interference in her affairs of hubby Richard Conte's (right) oversized, wine-imbibing father. Played by Metropolitan Opera bass Salvatore Baccaloni (in his screen debut), Papa Rocco – as he is known – is initially called in to fix a hole in the floor. He decides to build an oversized fireplace for the expectant couple, not to mention attempts to convert his daughter-in-law to Catholicism. In short, he becomes a king-sized pain in the neck whose insensitivity was the driving force behind John Fante's spasmodically amusing screenplay (from his own novel). Baccaloni's assertive performance dwarfed even the talented Miss Holliday and Fred Kohlmar's production never quite recovered from it. Esther Minciotti played Mama Rocco, with other roles in this comedy of diminishing returns going to Joe de Santis, Penny Santon, Arthur Lovejoy, Trudy Marshall and Eleanor Audley. (91 mins)

△ Producer Philip Yordan eschewed CinemaScope and Technicolor in favour of old-fashioned, hard-hitting black and white to bring Budd Schulberg's powerful exposé of the boxing racket – **The Harder They Fall** – to the screen. Loosely based on the treatment meted out to heavyweight boxer Primo Carnera some twenty years earlier, Schulberg's story concerned a gentle giant from South America called Toro Moreno (Mike Lane) whose brawny outward appearance belied the fact that, once in the ring, he couldn't fight his way out of an argument. Exploiting the behemoth's impressive physical attributes (though keeping his inability to box a guarded secret), fight promoter Nick Benko (Rod Steiger, right) working in cahoots with sports writer Eddie Willis (Humphrey Bogart, second left, in his last film) embarks on a promotional campaign for their pugilistic wash-out that culminates, after a winning series of arranged fights across the country, in a for-real championship bout in New York. Believing his own publicity, Moreno enters the ring confident that he can beat champion Buddy Brannen (Max Baer). He is, however, in for a cruel and painful awakening as Brannen, in one of the most brutal fight sequences ever filmed, pulverizes his ineffectual opponent. The film ends with Moreno being sent back to the pampas with $49 (his payment after expenses), and with sports-writer Willis's cumulative disgust with the corrupt underbelly of the fight game manifesting itself in the shape of a virulent exposé for 'every bum who ever got his brains knocked loose in the ring'. Very much in the tradition of the handful of impressive, realistic, no-punches-pulled, socially aware, black-and-white dramas of the Fifties, *The Harder They Fall*, trenchantly scripted by producer Yordan from Schulberg's novel, moved at a dizzying pace. It combined humour with pathos and revealed the malignancy at the core of the fight world through characterization and narrative without ever preaching. Mark Robson's direction was superb, and drew from Bogart and Steiger two sharply defined, unforgettable performances. Jan Sterling (second right) was splendid as Bogart's wife. Also cast: Jersey Joe Walcott, Edward Andrews, Harold J. Stone, Carlos Montalban, Herbert Faye, Nehemiah Persoff (left) and Pat Comisky. (109 mins)

▽ **Hot Blood** coursed through the veins of Jane Russell (right) and Cornel Wilde (left) in director Nicholas Ray's colourful mishmash. The good-looking couple played gypsies in Los Angeles doomed to a pre-arranged marriage. At first wedding bells couldn't be further from either of their thoughts – but, as Jesse Lasky Jr's screenplay (story by Jean Evans) unfurled to the accompaniment of a couple of songs, the pair fall in love for real. Luther Adler (right) co-starred as Wilde's brother, with other roles in Howard Welsch and Harry Tatelman's CinemaScope and Technicolor production going to Joseph Calleia (second left), Mikhail Rasumny, Nina Koshetz and Helen Westcott. (85 mins)

▽ In **The Houston Story** Gene Barry (centre) starred as an enterprising oilman who decides to steal gasoline from his competitors. 'Syndicate' assistance is sought and is given in the portly shape of Edward Arnold (left) plus top-man John Zaremba. Things get out of hand when Barry's waitress girlfriend (Jeanne Cooper) tips-off the cops. Also cast for Sam Katzman's Clover Productions were Barbara Hale (second billed), Paul Richards, Frank Jenks and Chris Alcaide. Story and script were by James B. Gordon and the director was William Castle. (79 mins)

▽ The Grand Teton country in Wyoming provided the colourful backdrop (seen to excellent advantage in CinemaScope and Technicolor) for **Jubal**, a steamy Western which top-starred Glenn Ford (right) as an itinerant cowpoke who sets the plot in motion when he takes a job on a cattle-ranch owned by Ernest Borgnine (left). The catalyst of the drama, however, was Valerie French (centre), Borgnine's amoral wife. Though French has been hitting the hay with cowpoke Rod Steiger, she turns her affections to the innocent Mr Ford, the consequence of which is Borgnine's death after Ford kills him in self-defence. The film's Mr Bad Guy, though, is Steiger who sets out to hang Ford and brutally rape Miss French. He fails with the former, but has his way with Borgnine's widow – who, in the course of the screenplay fashioned by director Delmer Daves and Russell S. Hughes from Paul I. Wellman's novel *Jubal Troop* – pays for her infidelity with her life. The film ended with Ford in the welcoming arms of religious Felicia Farr. Though Steiger turned in the most high-profile performance of all, there was good work from Ford, Borgnine and the women in their lives; as well as from Basil Ruysdael, Noah Beery Jr, Charles Bronson, John Dierkes and Jack Elam. The producer was William Fadiman. (100 mins)

▽ That fine actor, Edward Arnold, suffered a fatal heart attack while making **Miami Exposé** and it is to be regretted that his final film appearance wasn't a worthier memorial to his talents. Instead, it was a thoroughly routine melodrama along the lines of *The Houston Story* (1955) and *The Miami Story* (1955) in which top-starred Lee J. Cobb, as a cop, investigates an all-out battle for the Florida gambling franchise between mobsters Michael Granger (left) and Alan Napier. Arnold played a blackmailing lobbyist, and Patricia Medina (right) a gangster's moll on the run. Story and script were by James B. Gordon, Sam Katzman produced for Clover Productions, and Fred F. Sears directed a cast that featured Harry Lauter, Chris Alcaide and Barry L. Connors. (73 mins)

▽ A small slice of suspense and a large chunk of inevitability were the chief ingredients of **Nightfall**, a low-budget thriller in which husky-voiced Aldo Ray (right) had the devil of a time proving himself innocent of murdering his hunting companion and of taking part in a bank raid. The culprits, in fact, were Brian Keith and Rudy Bond who have carelessly mislaid the ill-gotten loot, and are convinced Ray knows where it is. It won't be giving too much away to relate that in the end the money is found, the criminals apprehended, and Ray cleared of all charges. The familiar storyline notwithstanding, Sterling Silliphant's screenplay (from the novel by David Goodis) capitalized on the basic situation; so did Jacques Tourneur's direction. Ted Richmond's Copa production also starred Anne Bancroft (left) as a model who falls for Ray; with Jocelyn Brando, James Gregory, Frank Albertson and George Cisar in it too. (78 mins)

▽ The studio's British-based Warwick Productions turned out, in CinemaScope and Technicolor, a 'family entertainment' called **Odongo** which was set on an animal farm in Kenya. It starred Macdonald Carey (left) as a hunter who offers his valuable menagerie to circuses and zoos. Also on hand was beautiful redhead Rhonda Fleming (right), as an unlikely vet. They were both well and truly upstaged by jaw-snapping crocodiles, a charging rhino and blaring elephants – as well as by a black boy called Juma. There was also a scene-stealing chimp in director John Gilling's seen-it-all-before screenplay so, one way or another, the principals barely got a look-in. Eleanor Summerfield, Francis De Wolf, Errol John, and Leonard Sachs (centre) were also cast. (85 mins)

△ Hugo Haas's favourite leading lady, Cleo Moore (left), received star-billing in **Over-Exposed**, a tepid melodrama that charted the career of a Little Miss Nobody to top commercial photographer. *En route* she meets an alcoholic cameraman (Raymond Greenleaf) who teaches her the tricks of the trade, a handsome reporter (Richard Crenna, right) who woos and wins her, and a society matron (Isobel Elsom) who takes an interest in her career. James Gunn and Gil Orlovitz's screenplay (story by Richard Sale and Mary Loos) provided parts for James O'Rear as a Broadway columnist, Donald Randolph as a nightclub owner and Dayton Lummis as a 'front man' for the mob. Shirley Thomas was in there too. They all acted Ms Moore off the screen, which, given her own limitations and the limitations of the screenplay, wasn't difficult. The producer was Lewis J. Rachmil and the director Lewis Seiler. (80 mins)

△ Originally made for TV (and does it show!), **Ride The High Iron** underwent a change of direction and was given a theatrical release instead. Clearly too bad even for TV, it made no impact whatsoever on the big screen and quickly disappeared. A soap-opera about the attempts of an indigent son of an immigrant railroad worker to better himself, it starred Don Taylor (centre) as the man on the make, and Raymond Burr (right) as a high-powered public-relations man who has never been accepted into polite society but whose main job is to keep his clients' more irresponsible antics out of the papers. Sally Forrest played the poor little rich girl Taylor falls for when he is given a job by Burr. Milton Gelman wrote it, William Self produced, Don Weis directed, and the hapless cast included Lisa Golm, Otto Waldis, Nestor Paiva, and Mae Clarke. (73 mins)

▽ Poor Phil Carey (right). As American pilot Rip Reardon, the hero of the British-made **Port Afrique**, he returns to his home in Morocco after the end of World War II to discover that not only has his wife been murdered (the police claim it was suicide, though Carey knows better), but that his business partner (Dennis Price) has done the dirty on him. His plantation is no longer a going concern and, to add to his miseries, a valuable diamond necklace that belonged to his wife is missing. His peace of mind is further disturbed by the nagging suspicion that his wife's killer has to be either Price, or James Hayter, a nightclub owner. Or could it be Pier Angeli (centre) – a nightclub singer who had been his wife's house-guest? In the end, of course, all was revealed, but through such an enervating narrative process (screenplay by Frank Partos and John Cresswell) that it was hard to care one way or another whodunnit, or why. The film was produced (in Technicolor) by David Rose, sluggishly directed by Rudolph Maté, and, in smaller roles, featured Eugene Deckers (as the police chief), Rachel Gurney, Anthony Newley and Christopher Lee. (90 mins)

▽ **Reprisal!** was the one about a half-breed (Guy Madison, left) who – after buying a piece of land on which to raise cattle for prime beef, and hoping for a quiet, peaceful life – finds himself the butt of the three Shipley brothers (Michael Pate, Edward Platt and Wayne Mallory) who still believe that the only good Injun is a dead one. A feud develops between the two parties, ending with the eventual deaths of the anti-social Shipleys. Felicia Farr, as the daughter of land-agent Robert Burton, supplied the romantic interest in Lewis J. Rachmill's Technicolor production, with other roles going to Kathryn Grant (right), Otto Hulett, Ralph Moody, Frank de Cova, and Paul McGuire. David P. Harmon, Ralph Hayes and David Dortort scripted from a screen-story by Harmon which, in turn, was based on a novel by Arthur Gordon. The film was directed at a cracking pace by George Sherman. (74 mins)

△ Although *Rock Around The Clock* was a box-office hit, the critics hated it. Sam Katzman promptly remounted the rockin' reel bandwagon, and, with a very modest budget, produced the aptly named rebuke – **Don't Knock The Rock**, a compendium of sixteen rock 'n' roll numbers performed by Bill Haley and His Comets (illustrated), The Treniers, Little Richard, and Dave Appell and his Applejacks, and which included such hits as 'Tutti Frutti' and 'Long Tall Sally'. The film had a minimal plot which centred on the efforts of top rock 'n' roll artist Alan Dale to win over some stuffy old reactionaries to the new music. He does this by making them remember their own youth – when the Black Bottom and the Charleston were all the rage. Robert E. Kent and James B. Gordon provided the unobtrusive screenplay, Fred F. Sears directed, and the cast included Patricia Hardy, Fay Baker, Jana Lund, Gail Ganley, and Pierre Watkin. (85 mins)

▽ The jungles of Africa as depicted in **Safari** looked great in CinemaScope and Technicolor, even though the plot devised by Robert Buckner (screenplay by Anthony Veiller) was far too tiny to sit well on the cavernous big screen. All about a white hunter (Victor Mature, right) seeking vengeance for the death of his young son at the hands of the deadly Mau Mau, it introduced a sub-plot in the shape of millionaire Ronald Culver (left) who, together with his wife (Janet Leigh, centre), arrives in Africa to hunt lion and seeks out Mature to be their guide and leader. By the time the hunt is over, Mature has not only found the killers of his son, but has managed to woo Leigh away from hubby Culver. Such was the predictable, *déjà vu* content of this Warwick Production which was produced on location in Africa by Adrian D. Worker for Irving Allen and Albert R. Broccoli. Director Terence Young kept the action simmering, and his cast included John Justin, Liam Redmond and Earl Cameron. (90 mins)

△ James Darren (left) made a big impact in his first film, **Rumble On The Docks**. He played the head of a rough, tough juvenile gang which becomes involved in the labour problems of Manhattan longshoremen. Michael Granger co-starred as a mean-minded mobster and union chief who takes Darren under his wing, with other roles going to newcomer Laurie Carroll (as the romantic interest) and Edgar Barrier as Darren's bitter father. Also cast: Angela Stevens, Timothy Carey, David Bond, Celia Lovsky, Jerry Janger and Robert Blake (right). The producer was Sam Katzman; Lou Morheim and Jack DeWitt wrote it (from the novel by Frank Paley), and the director was Fred F. Sears. Not at all bad of its type. (84 mins)

▽ A makeshift story-line (by Glendon F. Swarthout) and a wordy screenplay (by Peter Packer) provided Randolph Scott (centre) with obstacles he was unable to surmount in **7th Cavalry**. He played a man branded a coward for not taking part in Custer's catastrophic 'last stand', and spent the bulk of producer Harry Joe Brown's Technicolor Western proving his accusers wrong. What little action there was, was only unleashed in the last fifteen minutes or so – which was too late. Barbara Hale was the female lead, with other parts under Joseph H. Lewis's direction going to Jay C. Flippen (left), Jeaneatte Nolan, Frank Faylen (right), Leo Gordon, Denver Pyle, Harry Carey Jr, and Michael Pate. (76 mins)

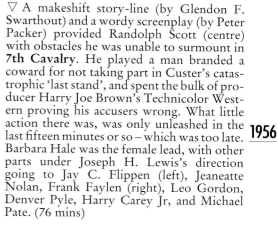

△ Though the elderly Josephine Hull scored a personal triumph on Broadway in the Howard Teichmann-George S. Kaufman comedy **The Solid Gold Cadillac**, the role was originally conceived for a younger woman. Producer Fred Kohlmar's screen version therefore cast comedienne Judy Holliday (right), added a love interest, and emerged with a winner. The pleasure-providing story of a small stockholder who brings a massive company to its knees after attending a stockholders' meeting and asking the Chairman of the Board a few embarrassing questions, it was, in a word, delightful. As was the case in the long-running play, Abe Burrows's adaptation pitted the individual against the corporation with hilarious, heartwarming results and as heroine Laura Partridge, Holliday notched up yet one more triumph. She was ably supported by Paul Douglas (left) whose efforts to re-establish himself in the company he had founded (but whose Board members treacherously stabbed him in the back) provided the film with its entertaining sub-plot. Fred Clark, John Williams, Hiram Sherman and Ray Collins were cast as the grim-visaged representatives of big business, with other roles under Richard Quine's nifty direction going to Neva Patterson, Ralph Dumke, Arthur O'Connell, Richard Deacon, and, heard but not seen, George Burns. The show's title referred to the car of the leading lady's dreams – and in the final scene (shot in Technicolor), Miss Holliday not only discovers that some dreams do come true, but is romantically linked with Douglas, who, once again, is running the company he created. In other words, the proverbial happy ending – with a vengeance! (99 mins)

△ The storm at the centre of **Storm Center** was the refusal of widowed librarian Bette Davis (right) to remove from the shelves of her library a book called *The Communist Dream*. Her refusal to bend to the headline-grabbing will of councilman Brian Keith results in her dismissal, and in her being branded a 'Red'. It is only when a young lad, under the influence of his bigoted father, burns down the library that the locals realize the error of their ways (and how easily children are influenced by the narrow-mindedness of their parents), and Davis's good name is restored – together with the promise of getting her job back when the new library is built. In the wake of the crushing McCarthy witch-hunts which devastated Hollywood a few years earlier, producer Julian Blaustein's film on the theme of civil liberties was to be welcomed, but the script fashioned by director Daniel Taradash and Elick Moll was more moral tract than pulse-quickening drama, and not even the committed central performance of Bette Davis could disguise this fact. Kim Hunter was featured as Brian Keith's fiancée, with other parts going to Paul Kelly (second left) as a City Council Member very much on Miss Davis's side, Joe Mantell as a gossip-monger, Kevin Coughlin (left) as his fire-raising son and Edward Plath (second right). (86 mins)

△ **Suicide Mission**, a semi-documentary acquired by Warwick Productions and distributed by Columbia, was the story of a group of brave Norwegians in the Shetland Islands who, during World War II, and under the direction of the British Royal Navy, regularly crossed the North Sea in midwinter to ferry arms, explosives and agents into their Nazi-held homeland. It featured several of the men actually involved (including Norwegian captain Leif Larsen, second right), as well as actors Michael Aldredge (left), Atle Larsen (second left), Per Christensen (right), T. W. Southam and Oscar Egede Nissen. Producer-director Michael Forlong also co-wrote the screenplay with David Howarth and Sidney Cole from Howarth's book *The Shetland Bus*. (69 mins)

216

▽ Claude Binyon and Robert Riskin, working from the latter's screenplay of the 1934 hit *It Happened One Night*, updated Samuel Hopkins Adams's original story about a runaway heiress and the reporter she meets on a cross-country bus trip, left gaps in the narrative for a few songs and a ballet, and called it **You Can't Run Away From It**. It starred June Allyson (left) and Jack Lemmon (right) in the roles created by Claudette Colbert and Clark Gable, with Charles Bickford as Allyson's distraught father. Though not nearly as good as the original, it passed the time agreeably enough. Paul Gilbert, Jim Backus, Stubby Kaye and Allyn Joslyn also featured in director Dick Powell's CinemaScope and Technicolor production. The songs were by Johnny Mercer and Gene De Paul. (95 mins)

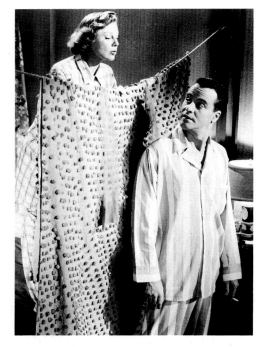

▽ With **Uranium Boom**, the studio stepped back a few decades to the days of Jack Holt and Ralph Graves. Dennis Morgan (left) and William Talman were the hero-buddies on this occasion, and the girl they break up over was Patricia Medina (right). When they're not vying for the heroine's favours, they're prospecting for uranium in the Colorado wastelands. The little bit of plot that attached itself to George F. Slavin, George W. George and Norman Rechtin's screenplay concerned the efforts of Talman (the loser in love) to render Morgan bankrupt. When, however, Talman realizes that Medina really does prefer Morgan, he relents and makes it up with his erstwhile buddy in time for the final fade. Sam Katzman produced for Clover Productions. William Castle directed a cast that included Tina Carver, Philip Van Zandt, Bill Henry and Gregg Barton. (66 mins)

△ A throwback to Universal in the Thirties – with Steven Ritch (right) subbing for Lon Chaney Jr – **The Werewolf** was a tired little would-be shocker that merely numbed the senses with over-familiarity. It was all about an accident victim (Ritch) who, while unconscious, is injected (by scientists Harry Lauter and George M. Lynn) with a serum intended to cure radiation poisoning, but which turns him into a werewolf. Robert E. Kent and James B. Gordon's screenplay focused on the consequences of the experiment – but to little, if any, effect. Don Megowan, Joyce Holden, Eleanore Tanin and Kim Charney were part of the no-name cast; Sam Katzman produced, and Fred F. Sears directed with no conviction whatsoever. (78 mins)

△ A tits-and-sand opus produced for Warwick Productions by Irving Allen and Albert R. Broccoli, **Zarak** was an exotic, if undeniably trite, mélange of action and romance which found both its stars – Victor Mature (right) and Anita Ekberg (left) – in roles tailor-made to guy their own screen images. All about an Afghan outlaw (Mature) who, in the service of Richard Maibaum's sand-encrusted screenplay (story by A. J. Bevan), saves the life of a British major (Michael Wilding) at the cost of his own – it filled its one-dimensional plot with two-dimensional characters. Bonar Colleano, Finlay Currie, Bernard Miles, Frederick Valk, Eunice Gayson, Peter Illing, Patrick McGoohan and Oscar Quitak were some of the British actors on hand in this Moroccan-made cliché. Terence Young directed with the accent on action. CinemaScope, Technicolor and a colourful and rousing score by William Alwyn didn't help. (94 mins)

▽ Recalling Alfred Hitchcock's *Lifeboat* (Fox, 1944) and the sinking of the *Titanic*, **Abandon Ship!** (GB: **Seven Waves Away**) – set mainly in a lifeboat equipped to carry 14 people, but overloaded with 27 survivors of an ocean liner wrecked by an iceberg – was a gripping drama that starred Tyrone Power (left), Lloyd Nolan and Mai Zetterling (right). Power played a man with life-and-death authority over the mass of humanity under his command. He had the grim task in director Richard Sale's unsentimental screenplay of deciding which of his passengers were to remain in the lifeboat and which were to be thrown overboard, for without this cruel process of elimination all 27 survivors would surely die. First to go were the injured and the useless – such as an ageing opera star, a playboy and a playwright. Power's orders are carried out at gunpoint, thus raising the dramatic temperature of the story and several moral issues. Lloyd Nolan played a ship's engineer, Mai Zetterling was a nurse, with other roles in producer Ted Richmond's first British production going to James Hayter (as a Cockney cook), Marie Lohr (the opera diva), Stephen Boyd (as a junior officer) as well as Moira Lister, Moultrie Kelsall, Noel Willman and Gordon Jackson. The story was based on fact, being inspired by a similar tragic incident that occurred in 1841 when a US freighter travelling from Liverpool to Philadelphia struck an iceberg and split in two. As the freighter was not equipped to carry passengers, there were only two small lifeboats on board. (98 mins)

▷ **The Burglar** was a low-budget thriller which starred Jayne Mansfield (left) as the glamorous assistant of a jewel thief (Dan Duryea (right) with designs on a necklace belonging to spiritualist Phoebe Mackay. It was a sorry attempt at a *film noir* which, plot and performance-wise, barely made the grade. David Goodis wrote the screenplay from his own novel, Paul Wendkos directed for producer Louis W. Kellman, and the cast included Martha Vickers, Peter Capell, Mickey Shaughnessy and Wendell Phillips. (90 mins)

△ Never one to ignore a fad, producer Sam Katzman, for Clover Productions, smartly hopped on to the calypso bandwagon with **Calypso Heat Wave**. Aimed almost exclusively at the teenage market, it was a low-powered contrivance that starred Johnny Desmond in his film debut as a calypso idol who becomes so disgusted with crooked jukebox czar Michael Granger when the latter attempts to muscle in on the good fortunes of Disco Records, that he leaves the company. Whereupon the firm goes broke, whereupon Granger exits, whereupon Desmond returns, whereupon everyone lives happily ever after. Working from a story by Orville H. Hampton, scenarist David Chandler didn't have to burn up too much midnight oil to keep the plot simmering – especially as Katzman's package offered more music than words. Merry Anders, Maya Angelou, Meg Myles, and Paul Langton were also featured; so was Joel Grey, who played an errand boy and was given a dance solo choreographed by Josephine Earl. Other musical talents: The Hi-Los, The Treniers, The Tarriers (who included Alan Arkin), and Mac Niles and The Calypsonians. Fred F. Sears directed. (86 mins)

△ The futility of war was the underlying theme of **The Bridge On The River Kwai**, Sam Spiegel's impressive $3 million production filmed on location in the jungles and mountains of Ceylon. However, Pierre Boulle's novel, and the screenplay fashioned from it (by blacklisted Carl Foreman and Michael Wilson – uncredited), centred on the clash of wills between a martinet, strictly-by-the-book British colonel and the equally duty-bound Japanese commander in whose Burmese prison-camp he is ensconced. Alec Guinness (illustrated) was cast (quite brilliantly) as the colonel, and Sessue Hayakawa – once a star of American silent films – was just as impressive in the role of his Japanese overseer. The story told by Boulle (and based on fact) concerned Hayakawa's insistence that officers as well as privates must take part in building a massive bridge across the River Kwai. At first Guinness manages to withstand all manner of torture and physical degradation rather than agree. In time, however, he cracks, and, rationalizing that British soldiers can achieve the impossible, agrees to undertake the construction of the bridge. What begins as a challenge ends as an obsession, blinding him to the fact that he has created the wherewithal for the Japanese to move vital troop trains from one strategic point to another. The film's memorable climax finds Guinness completely off his rocker, oblivious that he is fighting a war, and intent only on seeing that no harm befalls his masterpiece. Though Guinness dominated the action whenever he appeared, top-billing went to William Holden as an American sailor who, after escaping from Hayakawa's camp, makes his way to Australia where, pretending to be an officer, he informs Jack Hawkins (as Major Warden), of Guinness's bridge-building activities. Together with a sabotage unit, Holden returns to the Burmese jungle in time to facilitate the climactic destruction of the pivotal bridge. The film was directed by David Lean whose strong cinematic eye and ability to tell a story for maximum impact were here demonstrated to perfection; and it was strikingly well performed by a cast that also included James Donald, Geoffrey Horne, André Morell and Peter Williams, and stunningly photographed (in Technicolor) by Jack Hildyard. *The Bridge On The River Kwai* was an artistic as well as commercial triumph that grossed over $30 million. (161 mins)

◁ Realism was the key-note in **The Garment Jungle**, a tough, hard-hitting drama inspired by Lester Velie's articles in the *Reader's Digest* concerning labour warfare within the garment district of New York. The film starred Lee J. Cobb (right) as a dress manufacturer who for years has been his own boss without 'union interference'. He has slept easily at nights because of the protection money he has paid, and only begins to question his wisdom when he learns that the protection purchased has resulted in the murders of his partner and of a union official. In time, it leads to a third murder – his own. Kerwin Mathews (left) co-starred as Cobb's son, a Korean war veteran opposed to his father's anti-union thinking; with Richard Boone as the killer-heavy to whom Cobb had been paying $2,000 a week for protection. Robert Loggia and Gia Scala were both well cast as a couple of union newlyweds; and there was fine support, too, from Valerie French as the woman in Cobb's life and Joseph Wiseman as a union weakling. Also cast for producer Harry Kleiner were Harold J. Stone, Adam Williams, Wesley Addy, Willis Bouchey and Celia Lovsky. It was written by Kleiner, and tautly directed by Vincent Sherman, who replaced Robert Aldrich a week before shooting was due to be completed, but who then worked a further 16 days on the production. (88 mins)

△ Singer Johnny Desmond (left) in his second screen appearance, starred in **Escape From San Quentin**, a prison melodrama of no distinction whatsoever. Together with hardened cons Richard Devon (right) and Roy Engel, he escapes from prison and, in time, is duly recaptured – but not before singing a song of his own composing called 'Lonely Lament' and romancing Merry Anders, whose sister (Peggy Maley) is married to him but is suing for divorce. Sam Katzman produced for Clover Productions. It was written by Raymond T. Marcus, directed by Fred F. Sears, and also featured William Bryant, Ken Christy, Larry Blake, and Don Devlin. (81 mins)

▽ With the dissolution of her marriage to crooner Dick Haymes and of her Beckworth Production Company, Rita Hayworth (second left) returned to the screen after a four-year absence to appear as a shady lady in Irving Allen and Albert R. Broccoli's CinemaScope and Technicolor production, for Warwick Films, of **Fire Down Below**. Her leading men were Jack Lemmon (left) and Robert Mitchum (right) and, indeed, the first half of director Robert Parrish's lively melodrama smouldered as Messrs Lemmon and Mitchum both vied for her affections. Jealousy, sexual passion and a host of other emotions to which the flesh is heir formed the steamy content of Irwin Shaw's screenplay (from Max Catto's novel of the same name), though the second half of the film – which found Lemmon trapped in the hold of a Greek freighter after it collides with a heavier vessel – drew attention away from the romantic triangle and to Lemmon's desperate plight. This shift was a pity, as the exploration of the basic relationships between the three stars was far more explosive than anything that occurred to them individually. Hayworth obliged with a credible performance as well as a sultry, exotic dance; while Lemmon and Mitchum, though hardly extending the frontiers of dramatic art, were suitably virile throughout. Also cast: Bonar Colleano as a US Navy lieutenant, as well as Herbert Lom, Bernard Lee, Peter Illing, Joan Miller, Anthony Newley (second right), Lionel Murton (centre), Eric Pohlmann and, best of all, Edric Connor as a West Indian sailor. The 'Stretch' Cox Troupe did an extraordinary limbo dance, and Lemmon provided the film's harmonica theme. (116 mins)

△ Arguably the worst sci-fi ever to emerge from a major studio, **The Giant Claw** was about a monstrous extraterrestrial bird that causes havoc on planet Earth. Able to avoid detection by use of a radar-resistant shield, the creature goes along its destructive path, undaunted even by a train, which it picks up in its giant beak and disposes of. Scientists Jeff Morrow (centre), Mara Corday and Morris Ankrum (left) finally get the better of the monster – but it's a near thing. Samuel Newman and Paul Gangelin wrote it, Fred F. Sears directed, Sam Katzman produced (for Clover Productions) and the cast included Louis D. Merrill, Edgar Barrier (right), Robert Shayne, and Morgan Jones. (76 mins)

△ A rather dark Western starring Randolph Scott (centre), **Decision At Sundown** told the tale of a mysterious gunman (Scott) who rides into the town of Sundown one day, and, in the course of 24 hours, makes sure that the local bad-guy (John Carroll), is driven out for good. Seems that years ago, the creep was responsible for stealing Scott's wife – the galling factor being that his victim was a willing agent. Director Budd Boetticher was here working from a serviceable screenplay by Charles Lang Jr (story by Vernon L. Fluharty). It was produced by Harry Joe Brown for Scott-Brown Productions and featured Karen Steele, Valerie French, Noah Beery Jr (right), John Litel, John Archer (left) and Andrew Duggan. Technicolor. (77 mins)

▽ Guy Madison (centre) brought a virile presence to **The Hard Man**, a Technicolor Western in which he played a deputy sheriff at odds with a wealthy rancher (Lorne Greene, left). Complications insinuated themselves mainly in the shape of the rancher's wife (Valerie French, right) who wants Madison to eliminate her husband. Helen Ainsworth's production was par for the prairie course, as were Leo Katcher's screenplay (from his novel) and George Sherman's direction. Also cast: Barry Atwater, Robert Burton, and Rudy Bond. (80 mins)

▽ **Hellcats Of The Navy** starred Ronald Reagan (left) as a World War II submarine commander who is forced to leave a frogman behind when interrupted by an enemy vessel while in the process of retrieving a Japanese mine. Lieutenant Commander Arthur Franz is of the mistaken opinion that Reagan deliberately abandoned his colleague for personal reasons – but, of course, this wasn't the case at all as the screenplay by David Lang and Raymond Marcus, based on the novel by Charles A. Lockwood and Hans Christian Adamson, eventually made all too clear. The love interest was supplied by Nancy Davis (right – already Mrs Nancy Reagan), with other roles in Charles H. Schneer's routine production handled by Robert Arthur, William Leslie, William Phillips, Harry Lauter and Selmer Jackson. The director was Nathan Juran. (81 mins)

△ Kim Novak (right) lacked the dramatic equipment to star as **Jeanne Eagels** in producer-director George Sidney's appalling biopic of the celebrated Broadway actress who, in 1922, made her name playing Sadie Thompson in Somerset Maugham's *Rain*. And, even if she had had the necessary skills, the screenplay by Daniel Fuchs, Sonya Levien and John Fante (story by Fuchs) would most certainly have scuppered her efforts. Little more than a mawkish soap-opera, it traced Miss Eagels's rags-to-riches-to-liquor-to-narcotics story (with a divorce thrown in for good measure), never once managing, either through the script or Novak's central performance, to convince audiences that the story was worth telling in the first place. The single sequence showing Novak/Eagels in a scene from *Rain* was, frankly, ludicrous and wouldn't have passed muster in a touring company; neither would the performance of Jeff Chandler as a carnival operator who offers Eagels a job on the midway as a cooch-dancer. Agnes Moorehead was Agnes Moorehead (left) as Eagels's dramatic coach ('This girl has talent!' she says, managing, somehow, to keep a straight face), with other roles in what was little more than the vaporizing of a screen-writer's brain going to Charles Drake as a footballer, Larry Gates as a producer, as well as to Virginia Grey, Gene Lockhart, Joe de Santis and Murray Hamilton. The curious disclaimer at the start of the film that 'All events in this photoplay are based on fact and fiction' was indicative of the whole, muddleheaded enterprise. (108 mins)

△ **How To Murder A Rich Uncle** traversed Ealing comedy territory as it told the amusing tale of an indigent British nobleman's attempts to kill off his wealthy Canadian uncle in order to pay his debts. Nigel Patrick (left) starred as the impoverished Brit, while Charles Coburn (right) was his targeted relative. Patrick also directed (most ably) and his cast included Wendy Hiller, Katie Johnson, Anthony Newley, Athene Seyler, Kenneth Fortescue, and an early screen appearance by Michael Caine. John Paxton (who also produced for Warwick) wrote the screenplay from the French comedy *Il Faut Tuer Julie* by Didier Daix. Top-notch entertainment all round. CinemaScope. (79 mins)

▽ **High Flight** was low on entertainment value. A programmer about the routine training of RAF cadets, this British-made drama for producers Irving Allen and Albert R. Broccoli starred Ray Milland (left) as a wing commander who undergoes a personality clash with cadet Kenneth Haigh, whose squadron-leader father was killed during World War II while trying to save Milland. In the course of Joseph Landon and Kenneth Hughes' second-hand screenplay (from a story by Jack Davies), Milland gets to save Haigh – so the score is even and an understanding between the two men struck. Some good aerial photography was about the best on offer in this predictable little effort, and justified the use of CinemaScope. It was sluggishly directed by John Gilling with an all-British cast that included Bernard Lee, Anthony Newley (right), Kenneth Fortescue, Sean Kelly, Leslie Phillips, Helen Cherry, Kynaston Reeves, John Le Mesurier, Jan Brooks and Richard Wattis. (83 mins)

▽ **The Man Who Turned To Stone** was the story of a group of ageless scientists, who, for the last couple of centuries, have managed to keep young and healthy by tapping the life force of women. The process, however, demands a constant supply of girls, so the scientists have set themselves up as the heads of a women's reformatory. It's only when the institution's young and observant welfare worker notices the unusually high death rate among the inmates, that she smells the proverbial rat. Charlotte Austin played the welfare worker, with Victor Jory (second left), top-billed, as one of the scientists. Sam Katzman produced the hokum; Leslie Kardos directed it from a screenplay by Raymond T. Marcus, and the cast included Ann Doran (left), William Hudson (right), Paul Cavanagh (second right), Tina Carver, and Jean Willes. (71 mins)

▽ Rebellious youth reared its ugly head in the shape of Robert Vaughn (centre) who, in **No Time To Be Young**, an unappealing little melodrama produced by Wallace MacDonald, emerged as the anti-hero's anti-hero. He played a college drop-out, who, in an attempt to avoid the draft, schemes to hold up a supermarket with two of his buddies, both of whom have troubles of their own. His plan goes wrong – and the consequences, like the film itself, are dire. Roger Smith (left) and Tom Pittman (right) were his companions in crime, the women in their lives were Merry Anders, Kathy Nolan and, as Vaughn's un-appealing mother, Sarah Selby. John McPartland and Raphael Hayes scripted from the former's story, and the director was David Lowell Rich. (81 mins)

△ As there was nothing in producer Jed Harris's hilarious **Operation Mad Ball** that remotely resembled recognizable human behaviour, it was totally appropriate that the characters invented by Harris, Arthur Carter and Blake Edwards (from a play by Carter) were an assemblage of caricatures. Let loose in a welter of rib-tickling sight gags, the dramatis personae kept the comic temperature of the story well above normal – and clearly enjoyed themselves. Set in France, and involving an army medical unit (a forerunner of *M.A.S.H*?), it was all about a ball being planned by a group of enlisted men, and their efforts to keep the fact a secret from an ambitious, obnoxious busy-body officer. The inventive private behind the scheme was Jack Lemmon (left), while his adversary was TV comedian Ernie Kovacs (right), making a high-profile big-screen debut. Also contri-

buting to the fun, albeit in a brief cameo appearance, was Mickey Rooney as a hepcat transportation sergeant who manages to whisk an entire battalion out of Le Havre before you could say Le Havre. Another comic highlight was generated by William Hickey who, as Lemmon's mortuary assistant, drew one of the biggest laughs in the show doing a double-take after seeing a cadaver move. Dick York was terrific as Kovacs' hatchet-faced clerk-corporal, and there was good work, too, from Arthur O'Connell as the colonel in charge of the medical unit, and Kathryn Grant (centre) as a nurse-cum-dietician caught in the conflict between the privates and the officer class. Also cast: James Darren, Roger Smith and L. Q. Jones. The film was exhilaratingly directed at the pace of an animated cartoon by Richard Quine. (105 mins)

▽ After the studio's enormous success with *Cover Girl* in 1944, Harry Cohn purchased the rights of the 1940 Broadway musical **Pal Joey** which had a score by Richard Rodgers and Lorenz Hart, and a book by John O'Hara (based on his *New Yorker* stories). The original Joey was Gene Kelly, and, understandably, Cohn was eager that he should repeat his extraordinary characterization of O'Hara's irredeemable, womanizing heel on film. His co-star, of course, would be Rita Hayworth, thus re-uniting the *Cover Girl* team in a vehicle guaranteed to show off their talents to maximum effect. But Louis B. Mayer, to whom Kelly was under contract at MGM, demanded more money for his popular male star's second loan-out to the studio than Cohn was prepared to pay, and the project was put on hold. 17 years later it came to the screen – not with Gene Kelly, but with his buddy Frank Sinatra (front left), whose production company, Essex, together with George Sidney, produced it with Fred Kohlmar. Hayworth eventually got to play the role of Vera Simpson, Joey's spouse; ironically, she was better equipped to handle it

now than she would have been in 1944. Though the passage of time in no way softened the show's hard edges, Hollywood's Production Code did, and, even in 1957, the screen version of O'Hara's sleazy tale underwent a certain amount of sanitizing. The Hayworth character – married in the Broadway show – was now a widow, many of Hart's off-colour lyrics were reworked, and half the original score dropped completely. The opportunistic Joey was more hero than heel, and generally far more likeable than he was ever intended to be. Still, with a score that included such hardy perennials as 'Bewitched, Bothered and Bewildered', 'I Could Write A Book', 'My Funny Valentine', 'Zip' and 'The Lady Is A Tramp' there was cause for optimism. Kim Novak (right) co-starred as the 'mouse' in the chorus for whom Joey has the hots, with other roles in Dorothy Kingsley's unremarkable screenplay going to Bobby Sherwood, Hank Henry and Barbara Nichols (seated, left). It was directed by George Sidney, choreographed by Hermes Pan, and photographed in Technicolor by Rudolph Maté. (112 mins)

△ A fast-moving action melodrama, **Pickup Alley** (GB: **Interpol**), filmed in CinemaScope – but in gritty black-and-white, starred Victor Mature (right) as a member of the FBI's narcotics bureau, who, working in tandem with Interpol, sets out to apprehend a gang of dope peddlers. Mature is particularly interested in bringing their leader (Trevor Howard, left) to justice, for it was Howard who strangled his (Mature's) sister to death. Beginning in London, taking in the back alleys of Rome and Athens and finishing up in New York, John Paxton's screenplay relied heavily on the inner workings of Interpol to tell his story, and provided solid roles for Anita Ekberg (as Howard's sexy courier) and Bonar Colleano as a police informer. Also cast: André Morell, Martin Benson, Peter Illing, singer Yana and Sidney James. An Irving Allen-Albert R. Broccoli production for Warwick, it was directed by John Gilling.

(92 mins)

△ Nicholas Monsarrat's best-selling novel **The Story Of Esther Costello** came to the screen with all the vices of the original intact, and with several virtues of its own. The story of Esther was that she was rescued from a miserable existence as a blind, deaf and dumb girl by an American socialite, was schooled in braille, and then exploited by her saviour's estranged husband who capitalizes on her remarkable progress by organizing an international promotional tour for her. Not only that, he rapes the young woman, as a result of which her faculties are restored to her. Horrified at what her husband has done, the socialite deliberately drives her car into a tree, killing both herself and her spouse, and leaving Esther in the capable hands of a reporter who has fallen in love with her. That scenarist Charles Kaufman actually managed to inject credibility into this arrant nonsense was an

accomplishment not to be underestimated; nor was the contribution of its excellent cast. Joan Crawford (right) was a modicum more restrained than usual as the American benefactress, Rossano Brazzi was her disreputable husband, newcomer Heather Sears (left) was especially touching and vulnerable as Esther, and Lee Patterson was the friendly reporter in whose care she is left. Director David Miller adopted an almost documentary-like approach in the scenes involving Esther's learning to communicate with the outside world, and successfully steered the maudlin narrative through one potentially sticky situation after another. His fine cast also included Ron Randell, Fay Compton, John Loder, Denis Ò'Dea, Sidney James, Bessie Love, Megs Jenkins and Andrew Cruickshank. It was a Romulus Production, filmed in Britain. (104 mins)

▽ Calder Willingham's novel *End As A Man*, which, under the same title, surfaced as a Broadway play in 1953, came to the screen called **The Strange One** (in Britain it retained its original title) and, although scripted by Willingham, included changes that were not always for the better. Basically about paranoia in a Southern military academy, it starred Ben Gazzara (left), in the role he created on stage, as a student-leader who abuses the powerful hold he has over some of the younger students in the school. The play's strong homosexual element – as represented in the film by Paul E. Richards and Arthur Storch (right) – fell foul of the Production Code Administration, and three minutes were excised from the release print. The screen version added a woman to the cast – Julie Wilson as a prostitute out to corrupt one of the boys – as well as a cop-out ending in which mischief-maker Gazzara, rather than receiving his come-uppance at the hands of the academy's authorities, is run out of school by a group of vigilantes. Sam Spiegel produced for Horizon Productions, and first-timer Jack Garfein was the director. Also cast: George Peppard (debut), Pat Hingle, Larry Gates, Mark Richman, Geoffrey Horne and James Olson. (97 mins)

△ When the young son of a policeman, Jerry Mathers, witnesses a murder and the kidnapping of his mother by a trio of delinquents, he goes into shock and is unable to give the cops any information about the incident. How, through methodical police sleuthing, the crime is eventually solved, formed the absorbing content of **The Shadow On The Window**, a neat little melodrama from producer Jonie Taps. Phil Carey and Betty Garrett (left) starred as the boy's parents, with other roles in Leo Townsend and David P. Harmon's screenplay (story by John Ward Hawkins) going to John Barrymore Jr (second left), Corey Allen, and Gerald Sarricini as the three thugs, as well as Sam Gilman, Rusty Lane, Ainslee Pryor and Paul Picerni. The director was William Asher. (73 mins)

▽ Bearing more than just a passing resemblance to *High Noon* (United Artists, 1952), **3.10 To Yuma** was the story of an ordinary, peace-loving cowboy (Van Heflin, right) whose sense of morality imbues in him the courage to stand up to a ruthless law-breaker (Glenn Ford, left). How Heflin – a rancher devastated by drought and desperately in need of the reward money being offered for Ford's delivery to the state prison in Yuma – goes about apprehending the bandit formed the tightly-knit content of Halsted Welles's screenplay (story by Elmore Leonard). As in *High Noon*, the climax found him facing his adversary alone, his supporters having either deserted him or having been killed by Ford

and his outlaws. Confining most of the action to a hotel room, and relying heavily on close-ups to convey tension and atmosphere, director Delmer Daves resourcefully recycled some of the genre's most durable themes, and coaxed out of Heflin his finest screen performance to date. Ford also managed to turn the bad-guy into more than just a conventional Western villain, and it wasn't his fault that Welles's script let him down in the final moments of the film. Also cast – for producer David Heilweil – were Leora Dana as Heflin's understanding wife, and Felicia Farr as the town's pretty barmaid, plus Henry Jones, Richard Jaeckel, Robert Emhardt and Sheridan Comerate. (92 mins)

▽ Burt Kennedy's screenplay for the mystifyingly titled **The Tall 'T'** (story by Elmore Leonard) did its best to circumnavigate the clichés to which most Westerns starring Randolph Scott were prone, and partially succeeded with a suspense-making yarn in which rancher Scott (centre), together with newlyweds Maureen O'Sullivan (left) and cowardly John Hubbard are captured by a trio of killers led by Richard Boone (right). How the laconic Scott finally outsmarts his deadly captors (and wins the heart of Miss O'Sullivan whose husband is conveniently laid to rest by the heavies) formed the better-than-average content of this better-than-average Technicolor horse-opera. A Randolph Scott-Harry Joe Brown production, it was tightly directed by Budd Boetticher, and featured Skip Homeier and Henry Silva as Boone's thuggish henchmen, as well as Arthur Hunnicutt, Robert Burton, Robert Anderson and Fred E. Sherman. (78 mins)

▽ The assassination of real-life newspaperman Manuel Acosta Mesa in Tijuana provided producer Sam Katzman with the inspiration for **The Tijuana Story**. It was inspiration, too, to cast the charismatic Rodolfo Acosta as Mesa. At which point inspiration ran out, being replaced, instead, by routine programmer film-making. Robert Blake played Acosta's son who, in the course of Lou Morheim's rather plodding screenplay, brings the leaders of a narcotics ring to justice after his crusading father falls victim to the ring's Mr Big (Paul Newlan). A love affair between Acosta's secretary (Joy Stoner, right) and another of the mob's casualties (James Darren, left) padded out the proceedings, but to little effect. Also cast: Robert McQueeney, Jean Willes, George E. Stone, Michael Fox and Rick Vallin. The director was Leslie Kardos. (72 mins)

▽ **20 Million Miles To Earth** was the one about a small alien creature (from Venus) who, overnight, grows into a humungous monster that destroys everything in its path. Rome was the setting of much of the action in Bob Williams and Christopher Knopf's screenplay and story respectively, with the Coliseum providing the climax to the hostilities. Ray Harryhausen's special effects (particularly a fight to the death between the creature and an elephant in the streets of Rome) were, once again, an asset to Charles H. Schneer's production, upstaging, as they usually did, the flesh-and-blood contributions of the cast. William Hopper (centre) starred as the only survivor of a crashed rocket-ship, with other roles under Nathan Juran's direction taken by Joan Taylor (left), Frank Puglia, John Zaremba, and Thomas B. Henry. (84 mins)

▷ Anti-Communist propaganda in the wake of the McCarthy witch-hunts (and dressed up as sci-fi), **The 27th Day** was the story of an alien (Arnold Moss) who, because his own planet is dying, comes to Earth where he gives to each of five humans from five different countries an out-of-space capsule. These kill instantly on being opened but they lose their power after 27 days. One of the bearers is summoned to the Kremlin by a wicked Soviet leader (Stefan Schnabel), who sees the capsules as a means of destroying the West, thus keeping Communism safe for the Soviets. In the end the USSR is wiped off the face of planet Earth while the aliens take up residence on the globe. John Mantley scripted it from his novel, William Asher directed (capably), Helen Ainsworth produced, and the film starred Gene Barry (right) and George Voskovec (as two recipients of the capsule). Also cast: Valerie French (left) and Ralph Clanton. (75 mins)

◁ A low-budget drama adroitly scripted by Richard Jessup from his own novel (*The Cunning And The Haunted*) and observantly directed by Alfred L. Werker, **The Young Don't Cry** starred Sal Mineo (left) as a young man who sets out to 'find' himself during his last year of schooling at a Georgia orphanage. He does, through a series of incidents, one of which involves his helping to facilitate the escape of chain-gang convict James Whitmore. Mineo was fine as the confused youngster coming to grips with manhood. There was a good performance, too, from J. Carrol Naish (right) as a brutal prison warden. Also cast: Gene Lyons, Paul Carr, Thomas Carlin, Leigh Whipper and Stefan Gierasch. Philip A Waxman produced. (89 mins)

△ The **Zombies Of Mora Tau** (GB: **The Dead That Walk**) were a group of living-dead sailors, turned into their present state years ago when they attempted to loot an African idol of its diamond treasure. The treasure now lies buried at the depths of the ocean, and it is up to the zombies in question to see that no one else goes diving for it. Enter Gregg Palmer and Joel Ashley as the leaders of a new expedition in search of the swag – and, in tandem with them, George Plympton's workable plot (screenplay by Raymond T. Marcus). Allison Hayes (centre), Autumn Russell, Morris Ankrum and Marjorie Eaton were also in Sam Katzman's effective Clover Production. The director was Edward L. Cahn. (68 mins)

▽ John Van Druten's 1950 Broadway play **Bell, Book And Candle** enjoyed a modest run of 233 performances; the chief reasons for spending time and money on it were its stars – Lilli Palmer and Rex Harrison. Van Druten's feather-light tale of a contemporary Manhattan witch with a penchant for making men love her, but who loses her powers of sorcery the moment she loves them back, was a one-joke charade that, on the stage at any rate, was buttressed by two superb comic performances. For its screen incarnation, producer Julian Blaustein, for Phoenix Productions, cast over-cool Kim Novak (right) in the Palmer role – with nebulous results. He was better served by James Stewart as a publisher with whom she falls in love, and Jack Lemmon (centre) as her warlock brother. But without the solid central support the material needed, the film simply didn't bewitch. James Wong Howe's lush Technicolor photography and Cary Odell's art direction more than made up for Miss Novak's lack of sparkle, but, in the end, their work drew attention away from the plot, which further reduced the impact of Daniel Taradash's screenplay. The supporting cast included Hermione Gingold and Elsa Lanchester (left) as a couple of dotty witches (no complaints there), Ernie Kovacs as a hard-drinking author and The Brothers Condoli – as well as Janice Rule, Philippe Clay and Bek Nelson. The flashy direction was by Richard Quine. (106 mins)

▽ **Buchanan Rides Alone**, from the Harry Joe Brown-Randolph Scott stable, was based on Jonas Ward's novel *The Name's Buchanan*. Charles Lang's screenplay featured Scott (left) as a taciturn figure who, while journeying from Mexico to his home in Texas, unwittingly becomes involved in the goings-on of a frontier border town in general, and with a young Mexican (Manuel Rojas) in particular. When Rojas does away with the town's bully, he and Scott are sent to jail whereupon, as the script unfurls, Scott begins to play off various members of the town's First Family against each other, climaxing in an exciting shoot-out. Budd Boetlicher drew creditable performances from a cast that also included Craig Stevens (right), Barry Kelly, Tol Avery, L. Q. Jones, Robert Anderson, Joe De Santis, Nacho Galindo and William Leslie. It was photographed in Columbia Color. (89 mins)

△ Four-time Oscar-winner John Ford underwent a change of scenery from Death Valley to cosmopolitan London for **Gideon Of Scotland Yard** (GB: **Gideon's Day**), a light-hearted look at a day in the life of a CID chief inspector. The titular hero was Jack Hawkins, and, in the course of an ordinary working day, scenarist T. E. B. Clarke (who scripted *The Blue Lamp* for Ealing in 1950) had him accusing one of his sergeants of taking bribes (after which the hapless sergeant is killed by a hit-and-run pay-snatch driver), coping with a maniac killer from Manchester, and counting the costs of a grisly safe robbery. Nor were things all that quiet on the domestic front. Hawkins forgets to buy some salmon, and is too late to attend his daughter's first concert. What could, in lesser hands, have so easily become trite and predictable, emerged, under Ford's winning direction, as a satisfyingly unified piece of story-telling. Credit, too, must go to Jack Hawkins's (left) central performance, Clarke's dyed-in-the-wool screenplay, and the stalwart support from the likes of Andrew Ray as a zealous young policeman, Cyril Cusack as a Cockney informer, Maureen Potter as Cusack's gin-imbibing wife, Frank Lawton, Derek Bond and John Loder as officers, Jack Watling as a vicar, and Anna Massey as Hawkins's young daughter. Also cast: Dianne Foster (right), Anna Lee, James Hayter, Ronald Howard, Howard Marion-Crawford and Laurence Naismith. The film was produced, in Technicolor, by Ford and Michael Killanin. (91 mins)

▷ Otto Preminger's young protegé, Jean Seberg (left), whom he cast to little effect in his disastrous production of *Saint Joan* (United Artists, 1957), surfaced in yet another Preminger no-no – **Bonjour Tristesse**. The results of this vapid and shallow film version of Françoise Sagan's vapid and shallow novel were dire, with producer-director Preminger proving himself as ill at ease with Sagan as he had, the previous year, with George Bernard Shaw. Seberg played a 17-year-old who recalls, in flashback, life with her father, a charming roué (David Niven) directly responsible for the suicide of a beautiful but repressed woman (Deborah Kerr, right) to whom he promises marriage in order to bed her, then promptly embarks on

an affair with sexy Mylene Demongeot. What, basically, should have been a haunting 'mood' piece, was turned into a high-voltage 'woman's picture' with a travelogue approach to the picturesque French Riviera, a situation which Arthur Laurents's literally unspeakable screenplay did little to alleviate. With the exception of Miss Kerr who did give something approaching a performance, the casting was wretched. It included Geoffrey Horne, Juliette Greco, Walter Chiari, Martita Hunt, David Oxley, Jean Kent and Roland Culver. It was photographed in CinemaScope and Technicolor except for sequences in a Paris bistro, which went into black-and-white. The clever titles were by Saul Bass. (94 mins)

223

▽ Darren McGavin (right), star of TV's popular Mike Hammer series, starred in **The Case Against Brooklyn**, a tough and gritty melodrama based on truth and all about the hold a group of corrupt bookmakers have on a fear-ridden portion of the police force. McGavin played a newly-graduated under-cover cop out to smash the bookies' hold on his colleagues, and did so with a fair amount of conviction. Maggie Hayes (left), whose husband was a victim of the syndicate, became McGavin's romantic *vis à vis*, with other roles under Paul Wendkos's no-punches-pulled direction assigned to Warren Stevens, Peggy McCay, Tol Avery, Emile Meyer, Nestor Paiva, Brian Hutton and, in a small part, veteran character-actress Cheerio Meredith. It was scripted by Raymond T. Marcus from a story by Daniel B. Ullman, which, in turn, was based on an article in *True Magazine* by Ed Reid. The producer was Charles H. Schneer. (82 mins)

▽ An altogether superior addition to the horror genre, **Curse Of The Demon** (GB: **Night Of The Demon**), filmed in England, starred Dana Andrews (right) as an American psychologist who, while on a fleeting visit to Britain in order to investigate a dabbler in the occult (Niall MacGinnis), is forced to view the world of black magic and its exponents in a somewhat less cynical light than before. Charles Bennett and Hal E. Chester's genuinely creepy screenplay (story by Montague R. James) involved the mysterious killing of a doctor by some other-worldly creature, as well as a piece of parchment containing runic symbols. Hypnotism, seances, and mysterious forces also played a part in producer Chester's neat little effort which director Jacques Tourneur (no slouch in this particular genre) tied up into a horror package that somehow never insulted the intelligence. Peggy Cummins co-starred (most attractively), as the niece of the dead doctor (Maurice Denham), with other parts going to Athene Seyler, Liam Redmond (left), Reginald Beckwith, and Ewan Roberts. (82 mins – GB version 95 mins)

▽ Though Edmund H. North's screenplay for the Phoenix Production of **Cowboy** (based on Frank Harris's *My Reminiscences As A Cowboy*) set out to de-glamorize the myth of the old West, a hard-core vein of nostalgia coursed through it – with entertaining results. Glenn Ford (left) and Jack Lemmon (centre) co-starred, the former as a tough, no-nonsense trail boss, the latter as a tenderfoot Chicago hotel clerk for whom the lure of the West is a great deal stronger than his own constitution. Eager to leave the plush confines of the hotel for the romance of the wide-open spaces, Lemmon, in return for

lending Ford some money, is allowed to accompany the trail boss and his men on a 3000-mile cattle drive during the bumpy course of which he discovers that being a cowboy isn't nearly as romantic as he thought. Lemmon's ultimate education by way of hard-knocks, cattle stampedes and the endurance of gruelling physical conditions was at the heart of director Delmer Daves's salty, albeit episodic, adventure. Also featured were beautiful Anna Kashfi as the daughter of a Mexican cattle baron, Brian Donlevy (second right) as a disillusioned gunslinger and Dick York and Richard Jaeckel (right). (92 mins)

▽ Though Kim Stanley (right) didn't quite have the body for a Hollywood sex-pot, she was a fine enough actress to convey the loneliness and the anguish of Paddy Chayefsky's **The Goddess**. Divided into three distinct parts – Portrait Of A Young Girl, Portrait Of A Young Woman, and Portrait Of A Goddess – producer Milton Perlman's touching drama was the story of Emily Ann Faulkner, an unloved child of the Depression who dreams of becoming a famous movie-star. The daughter of a woman who had no time for her, the film traced her gradual rise to stardom (as Rita Shawn), probing, *en route*, her wretchedly unhappy private life – for, never having received love, Rita is incapable of giving it. *The Goddess* was not so much a

film about Hollywood, but about the turmoil created in the mind of a vulnerable, star-struck young woman, desperately seeking to find, in fame, the recognition denied her in childhood. It was a tragic, heart-breaking story, sensitively directed by John Cromwell, compassionately scripted by Chayefsky, and, quite apart from Stanley, convincingly acted by a dedicated supporting cast, best of whom was Betty Lou Holland as Stanley's pitiful mother. Steve Hill and Lloyd Bridges (left) played husbands number one and two, with other roles going to Joan Copeland and Gerald Hiken as Stanley's aunt and uncle, and Elizabeth Wilson as her secretary-cum-nurse. The effective score was provided by Virgil Thompson. (104 mins)

▽ A no-hoper which the studio sat on for six months after its completion, **Ghost Of The China Sea** was a dud from producer-writer Charles B. Griffith. It was set during World War II and starred David Brian (front right) as the skipper of a run-down boat (nicknamed the USS *Frankenstein*) fleeing from the Japanese. With no food, no oil, no gas, no weapons (and no script) Brian and his men were definitely in trouble. Help, in the shape of the British, was at hand and all ended happily. A cast of unknowns – including Lynn Bernay (centre back), Jonathan Haze (left), Norman Wright (lying down), and Harry Chang (back right) hardly lit up the marquees; nor was there much joy from Fred F Sears's direction. (73 mins)

△ The chief strength of scenarist Frank Nugent's screenplay for **Gunman's Walk** was the conflict created in the three central characters. Basically a generation-gap story (by Rick Hardman) with a Western background, it told of a father (Van Heflin, left) and his two sons – Tab Hunter (centre) and James Darren (right) – and how all three coped with the changing times in the West. A rancher who believes in law and order through guns, Heflin has been unable to adapt to progress, and encourages Hunter to emulate him in his outmoded outlook. Darren, on the other hand, has been more or less left to his own devices and consequently emerges as the better-adjusted of the boys – his brother having turned bad in a misguided attempt to impress his father. Director Phil Karlson skilfully juggled the tensions inherent in the behaviour of his central trio and drew from his three stars well-rounded, and clearly differentiated performances. Kathryn Grant featured, too, as a half-Indian girl, her role serving to offer an honest insight into the discriminatory treatment of Red Indians by the whites. Also featured in this Technicolor and CinemaScope production by Fred Kohlmar were Mickey Shaughnessy, Robert F. Simon, Edward Platt, Ray Teal and Paul Birch. (95 mins)

▽ There was a TV-sit-com 'feel' to the screenplay Bud Grossman fashioned for **Going Steady** (story by Grossman and Sumner A. Long) – but that didn't prevent Sam Katzman's modest Clover Production from being a jolly little entertainment aimed at both parents and their teenage offspring. All about a secret marriage between high-school seniors Molly Bee (centre) and Alan Reed Jr (right) – and the complications arising out of a pregnancy, the film featured Irene Hervey and Bill Goodwin (left) as Ms Dee's parents, as well as Ken Miller, Susan Easter, Linda Watkins and Byron Foulger. Fred F. Sears called the shots. (82 mins)

△ Jan de Hartog's novel *Stella* came to the screen as one of Carl Forman's Open Road Productions, and was retitled **The Key**. Part action-melodrama, part romance, it was, under Carol Reed's sure-footed direction, a classy job of film-making. As scripted by Forman it skilfully reconciled the he-man heroics with the story's more tender aspects, and emerged very much as a man's film that women could enjoy – or vice versa. Set during World War II, it starred William Holden (right) and Trevor Howard as tug commanders engaged in convoy rescue duty; and an enigmatic Sophia Loren (left) as a landlady *extraordinaire* whose apartment (and all that goes with it, including herself) she willingly shares with the skipper of the moment. Her erstwhile fiancé, we learn, was a tug skipper who was killed on the eve of their wedding. Ever since, she has passed the key of her apartment on to his successor – identifying them with her dead would-be husband. After Howard's death, the key is passed to Holden, with whom she genuinely falls in love, thus, for the first time, obliterating the memory of the man she was going to marry. Believing that he, too, will be killed in a dangerous mission, Holden passes on the key to *his* successor. He survives the mission, and his lack of faith is interpreted by Loren as a betrayal – paving the way for an unhappy ending. All three stars gave exemplary performances, and there was excellent backing from an all-British supporting cast that included Oscar Homolka and Kieron Moore as a pair of tug skippers, Bernard Lee as a shore-based naval officer and Noel Purcell as a disreputable porter in a disreputable waterfront hotel. It was photographed in CinemaScope and black-and-white. (134 mins)

◁ Twenty-eight years after making his motion-picture debut in John Ford's *Up The River* (Fox, 1930) Spencer Tracy (centre) was working once again for the veteran director in **The Last Hurrah** – an intelligent, heart-warming drama based on Edwin O'Connor's best-seller of the same name. Tracy played Frank Skeffington, an Irish-American mayoral candidate of an Eastern city (presumably Boston). A loner by nature, and with his heart very much in the right place, Skeffington decides to stand for office one more time, and the processes by which he attempts to outwit his opponents – such as John Carradine, the editor of a local paper, and Basil Rathbone, a powerful banker (who refuses Tracy a loan for the city's new housing project) – was the stuff of Frank Nugent's effective, though occasionally long-winded, screenplay. Jeffrey Hunter co-starred as Tracy's idealistic nephew, a newspaper reporter who believes his uncle possesses genuine greatness, and who faithfully records his 'last hurrah'. The chief woman's role went to Dianne Foster as Hunter's perky wife, with other parts in a uniformly first-rate cast going to Edward Brophy, Pat O'Brien (back left), Donald Crisp, James Gleason, Willis Bouchey, Ricardo Cortez (second right), Wallace Ford and Frank McHugh. John Ford also produced. (121 mins)

▷ Columbia Color did nothing for **Good Day For A Hanging**, though the central performances of Fred MacMurray (centre, in hat) as a marshal, and Robert Vaughn (in headband) as a sympathetic (albeit psycopathic) killer did. Daniel B. Ullman and Maurice Zimm's screenplay, from a story by John Reese, concentrated mainly on MacMurray's efforts to prove his charismatic young captive guilty of murder – which eventually, against much opposition, he does. The no-name supporting cast recruited by producer Charles H. Schneer included Maggie Hayes, James Drury, Wendell Holmes, Kathryn Card and Denver Pyle (left). Nathan Juran directed. (85 mins)

▽ Producer Jaime Del Valle's **The Line-Up** was little more than a routine melodrama involving a narcotics gang who plant heroin on unsuspecting travellers abroad, then collect the stuff on their return to California. The leader of the gang was Eli Wallach (left), whose retinue included Robert Keith (second right) and Richard Jaeckel (right). The film was directed by Don Siegel and scripted by Sterling Silliphant (based on the TV series 'The Line-Up' by Lawrence L. Klee), both of whom should have known better. Also cast: Warner Anderson, Mary LaRoche (second left), Cheryl Callaway (third left) and William Leslie. (85 mins)

▽ Singer Julius La Rosa (left) made his screen debut for producer-director Harry Foster in **Let's Rock!** (aka **Keep It Cool!**) – playing a ballad singer who, after initially refusing to go rock 'n' roll, literally changes his tune. And that's about all there was to Hal Hackady's uncluttered screenplay. More important was the plethora of featured songs, and they were supplied not only by La Rosa but by Roy Hamilton and The Cues, Danny and The Juniors (who sang 'At The Hop'), The Royal Teens, Della Reese ('Lonelyville'), Paul Anka ('Waiting There For You'), and The Tyrones ('Blast-off'). Also cast: Phyllis Newman, Conrad Janis, Joy Harman (right) and, as himself, Wink Martindale. (78 mins)

△ Vince Edwards (left) starred as a paid killer in **Murder By Contract**. The woman he's paid to kill is wealthy Caprice Toriel, who's about to testify against Edwards's mobster employer. After two unsuccessful attempts, he gains entry to her palatial manor, tries to garrot her, fails, and is himself killed by the police. Such was the slender content of Ben Simcoe's screenplay which, under Irving Lerner's direction, nonetheless piled on the suspense. Phillip Pine (right) and Herschel Bernardi (centre) played Edwards's confederates, and producer Leon Chooluck's cast also included Michael Granger and Cathy Browne. (80 mins)

▽ Romance teenage-style was the chief commodity on offer in **Life Begins At 17**, which starred Mark Damon as a personable youngster who, in order to land a date with pretty Dorothy Johnson, embarks on a convoluted piece of subterfuge that involves dating Dorothy's ugly-duckling young sister (Luana Anders, right). When Miss Anders duly discovers Damon's not very chivalrous ploy, she pretends to be pregnant by him. The switcheroo in Richard Baer's unlikely screenplay had Damon actually falling for the off-beat charms of Luana, leaving Dorothy free to pursue her affair with long-standing boyfriend Edward Byrnes (left). Hugh Sanders and Ann Doran played the sisters' parents, with other parts going to Cathy O'Neill, George Eldredge, Tommy Ivo and Bob Dennis. Sam Katzman produced, and Arthur Dreifuss directed. (74 mins)

△ A psychological thriller with bizarre overtones, **Screaming Mimi** was a curiosity from producer Harry Joe Brown that starred Anita Ekberg (centre) as a stripper in a club owned by Gypsy Rose Lee and called the 'El Madhouse'. After being attacked in her shower by a knife-wielding maniac (a sequence that predated Hitchcock's *Psycho* (Paramount) by a couple of years), she seeks the help of psychiatrist Harry Townes (right). Meanwhile, a local newspaper man (Phil Carey, left) learns about the attack and, after linking it with several similar cases, decides to take matters into his own hands, with interesting results. Linda Cherney, Romney Brent, Alan Gifford and Red Norvo were also featured, Robert Blees wrote the screenplay from a book by Fredrick Brown and director was Gerd Oswald. (79 mins)

▽ With 20 musical numbers on offer, producer Harry Romm's **Senior Prom** wasn't so much a feature as a series of musical shorts loosely pasted together with a semblance of a boy-meets-girl plot. First the plot: singer Jill Corey (left) falls for wealthy fellow student Tom Laughlin. However, she changes her mind and settles for the indigent Paul Hampton (centre). As for the music – it was provided by the aforementioned Ms Corey (five songs), Louis Prima, Keely Smith, Sam Butera and The Witnesses, Mitch Miller, Connee Boswell, Bob Crosby, Toni Arden, and Freddie Martin and His Orchestra. Also featured were Frieda Inescort (as Corey's mum), Jimmie Komack (right), Barbara Bostock, Selene Walters and emcee Ed Sullivan. Hal Hackady wrote the screenplay and, with Don Gohman, the songs, and the director was David Lowell Rich. (82 mins)

1958

▷ Danny Kaye (centre) made an impressive, albeit uncharacteristic, debut at Columbia playing S. L. Jacobowsky, the wily Jewish hero of Franz Werfel and S. N. Behrman's Broadway comedy, *Jacobowsky And The Colonel*, now called **Me And The Colonel**. The film's setting, like the play's, was France in 1940, during the German occupation. Jacobowsky and an anti-semitic Polish colonel (Curt Jurgens, left), pool their resources (the former has a car and gasoline) and flee Paris together. Their flight from the Nazis is complicated by the colonel's stubborn insistence that his mistress (Nicole Maurey) travel with them. S. N. Behrman's screenplay, which he wrote with George Froeschel, was concerned with the attempts made by this variegated trio to reconcile their outlooks on life, and was the *raison d'être* of the story. The arrogant colonel ('one of the finest minds of the 15th century') has a penchant for turning everything he touches into trouble, and it is left to the resourceful little Jew to extricate the trio from one scrape after another. A hit of the 1944-45 Broadway season, the play was a thought-provoking comedy, which, despite a plot redolent of dozens of wartime B pictures, was a whoop of joy for the indomitability of the human spirit. The same quality was captured in director Peter Glenville's light-hearted approach to the material, though Jurgens' performance was more of a caricature than that of a rounded, believable human being. A Court – Goetz Production, it also featured Akim Tamiroff (right) as the colonel's broadly comic aide, Martita Hunt as a nun, as well as Françoise Rosay, Lilliane Montevecchi, Alexander Scourby, Celia Lovsky and Ludwig Stossel. (105 mins)

△ Though Kerwin Mathews (illustrated) received top-billing as Sinbad in **The Seventh Voyage Of Sinbad**, and Torin Thatcher was also very much in evidence as his adversary the evil magician Sokurah – once again the real hero of this action-packed fantasy was Ray Harryhausen and his effective Dynamation process. Without the genuinely frightening assortment of monsters (not to mention vultures and skeletons) that besets Sinbad in his efforts to find a piece of egg belonging to a Roc bird – without which his sweetheart, Kathryn Grant (right), is doomed to spend the rest of her life no bigger than Tom Thumb – this Morningside Production would barely have justified its existence. Harryhausen's stop-motion gallery of grotesques produced queues around the box-offices of the world, as kids as well as parents gleefully responded to his evil creations. The special effects upstaged a cast that also included Richard Ever, Alec Mango, Danny Green and Harold Kasket. It was produced by Charles H. Schneer (in Technicolor), written by Kenneth Kolb and directed by Nathan Juran. (89 mins)

△ Clichéd situations and stereotypical characters turned **Tank Force** (GB: **No Time To Die**) into a no-go area. Produced by Irving Allen and Albert R. Broccoli for Warwick, not even such visual aids as Technicolor and CinemaScope could render digestible this story of a group of five men who escape from a desert prison-camp, only to be pursued by the Nazis. Victor Mature (right) starred as a Yankee sergeant (whose torture at the hands of the Arabs was nothing compared to the torture suffered by audiences at the hands of scenarists Richard Maibaum and Terence Young, the latter also sadistically in charge of the direction). Leo Genn, Anthony Newley, Bonar Colleano and Sean Kelly completed the quintet, with other roles in this expendable effort going to Luciana Paluzzi, Kenneth Fortescue, Anne Aubrey, George Coulouris, David Lodge (left) and Alfred Burke. (103 mins)

▷ Producer Charles H. Schneer's **Tarawa Beachhead** was an intelligent, well-made World War II programmer dealing with marine combat in the Pacific. Top-starred Kerwin Mathews (left) was cast as an idealistic young marine who happens to witness the murder, in combat, of a fellow marine. Responsible for the killing is Mathews's commanding officer (Ray Danton, right) who, as Richard Alan Simmons's screenplay unfurls, finds himself thrown into Mathews's company. Simmons gave his story an enigmatic resolution which added to the overall effectiveness of the piece. Julie Adams (third left) and Karen Sharpe (second left) provided the romantic interest, and the cast, for director Paul Wendkos, included Onslow Stevens, Russell Thorsen, Eddie Ryder and John Baer. (77 mins)

▽ Based on newspaper articles by Santa Ana reporter Pat Michaels, **The True Story Of Lynn Stuart** shaped up well as an attention-holding melodrama – handled in semi-documentary fashion – about a local housewife (Betsy Palmer, right) who volunteers her services to help smoke out a syndicate of dope-pushers after her nephew, under the influence of drugs, is killed in a car crash. Jack Lord (left) co-starred as a womanizing pusher, and supporting roles were filled by Barry Atwater, Kim Spalding, Karl Lukas, and Casey Walters. John H. Kneubuhl's screenplay was a bit on the talky side, but like practically everything else in Bryan Foy's production, got its message across. The director was Lewis Seiler. (76 mins)

◁ Though some of the courtroom proceedings in **The World Was His Jury** were light years away from reality, scenarist Herbert Abbott Spiro nonetheless managed to concoct a gripping yarn involving a case of criminal negligence. The defendant is Robert McQueeney (right), the captain of a luxury liner, whose vessel sank with a loss of 162 lives off the coast of New Jersey. Though his defence attorney, Edmond O'Brien (left), has very little evidence to suggest that his client isn't guilty, skilful examination of witnesses soon reveals that the real culprit was McQueeney's jealous second-in-command (Paul Birch). Mona Freeman played O'Brien's wife and Karin Booth was McQueeney's wife, with other parts in Sam Katzman's production going to John Berardino (centre), Dick Cutting, Harvey Stephens, and Carlos Romero. Fred F. Sears directed. (82 mins)

△ **Crash Landing** was a budget re-tread of Warner Bros's. *The High And The Mighty* (1954). It assembled a diverse group of passengers on board a trans-Atlantic flight and chronicled their reactions to the news that the plane was in serious trouble. Gary Merrill (centre) starred as the martinet pilot, Nancy Davis (Mrs Ronald Reagan, left) was his wife, Kim Charney (right) their young son. On board, the passengers included a retired businessman (Lewis Martin), a schoolteacher (Irene Hervey), a bullying tycoon (Richard Keith), the tycoon's mild associate (Hal Torrey), a Portuguese grandmother (Celia Lovsky), a Greek Orthodox priest (Frederich Ledebur), two chorus girls (Joan Bradshaw and Brandy Bryan) and Uncle Tom Cobbleigh and all. Fred Freiberger wrote it, Sam Katzman produced for Clover Productions, and the direction was by journeyman Fred F. Sears who died shortly after the film's completion. (76 mins)

1959

▽ **Anatomy Of A Murder**, directed by Otto Preminger for Carlyle Productions, remains unsurpassed for the accuracy and detail it brought to bear during the lengthy hearing of a single case. An army lieutenant (Ben Gazzara, left) is accused of murdering the bartender who raped and beat up his wife (Lee Remick). At first, defence lawyer James Stewart (right) refuses to take the case. He then sees it as a challenge, and agrees. The prosecutor is George C. Scott and the cat-and-mouse games played by the two men during the trial allowed both Stewart and Scott equal time to act each other off the screen. There was no clear winner and the result was a draw. Though Wendell Mayes's screenplay – based on a novel by John Traver (Judge John D. Voelker) – was certainly mindful of all the suspense-making elements that go into the manufacture of the-court-case-as-entertainment, he concentrated, equally, on the development of the characters. The result was a riveting legal tussle as

well as an absorbing psychological drama whose protagonists were far more complex than anything to be found in an ordinary, run-of-the-mill courtroom melodrama. A genuine sense of mystery surrounded the accused (which Gazzara's excellent performance strongly emphasized); nor was there anything cut-and-dried about the character of his wife. Indeed, the numerous undercurrents that ebbed and flowed as the case unfolded more than justified the film's unusually generous running time. The supporting cast was first rate and included Arthur O'Connell as Stewart's alcoholic researcher friend, Eve Arden as his wise-cracking secretary, Kathryn Grant as a friend of the murdered man, and Joseph N. Welch (a real-life Boston attorney-turned-actor) as the presiding judge. Preminger's direction went all-out for realism and, aided by Sam Leavitt's *film noir*-ish black-and-white photography, achieved it. Duke Ellington provided the score. (160 mins)

◁ The only difference between the Indians who featured so prominently in **The Bandit Of Zhobe** and those usually pursued by the hero across the American mid-West was that Zhobe's variety was from India – Victorian India, to be precise. Otherwise, this Warwick Production, in CinemaScope and Eastman Color, was an 'Eastern' which top-starred a somewhat over-the-hill Victor Mature (right) as an Indian leader who mistakenly believes that his family was killed by the British. Director John Gilling's screenplay, based on a story by Richard Maibaum, left no cliché untrammelled as it worked towards a satisfactory conclusion, and although there was plenty of action on hand, all of it was numbingly familiar. The same applied to the supporting performances – including those by a clownish Anthony Newley, Anne Aubrey (as the obligatory female interest), Norman Wooland, Dermot Walsh, Walter Gotell, Sean Kelly (left), Dennis Shaw and Murray Nash. (80 mins)

▷ Producer Leon Chooluck, director Irving Lerner and star Vince Edwards (illustrated) teamed up for a second time in **City Of Fear**, a tense albeit modest melodrama (written by Steven Ritch and Robert Dillon) in which Edwards played an escaped convict on the run with what he believes to be a metal cylinder containing pure heroin (and hence worth a fortune). What, in fact, the cylinder contains is radioactive Cobalt 60 – as lethal a substance as any known to mankind. Unless the police wrest it from him – and soon – the consequences could, of course, be disastrous. Patricia Blair played Edwards's sweetheart, with other roles going to John Archer, Steven Ritch, Kelly Thordsen and Lyle Talbot. No world-beater, but above average for its type. (75 mins)

△ An extremely dour Cliff Robertson (left) starred as a submarine captain in Charles Schneer's Morningside Production **Battle Of The Coral Sea**. Concentrating more on what happened before the decisive battle in the Pacific (which altered the course of the war) than on the battle itself (for which stock footage and miniatures were used), the narrative followed the crew of the sub as they return to port, are captured, and flung into a Japanese prison. With the help of a Eurasian girl (Gia Scala), three of the officers escape on a Jap torpedo boat in time to provide the Navy with the vital information it needs to demolish the enemy. San Diego and the San Fernando Valley stood in for the South Pacific, and considering the tightness of the budget, the production values were pretty good. Unfortunately the material was decidedly old-hat – a fact that the cast – including Teru Shimada, Patricia Cutts, Gene Blakely, Rian Garrick and L. Q. Jones (right) – could do little to disguise. It was written by Daniel Ullman and Stephen Kandel (story by Kandel), and the routine direction was by Paul Wendkos. (86 mins)

229

▽ In **The Crimson Kimono** director Samuel Fuller buttressed a routine murder investigation with an inter-racial love affair. Glenn Corbett and James Shigeta (right) starred as officers in the Los Angeles Homicide Squad who have been buddies ever since the Korean War (in which they both fought). During the investigation of a murdered stripper (Gloria Pall) both men meet and fall in love with a beautiful artist (Victoria Shaw, left). She falls for Shigeta – much to Corbett's anger. Shigeta believes that the reason for his friend's 'disgust' is that he, an Oriental, is having an affair with a white woman – but, in effect, it is nothing of the sort. Corbett is simply jealous to have lost the woman he loves to another – regardless of race. However, the main thrust of producer-director Fuller's screenplay concentrated on the murder – and, despite one mismatching of scenes, the tension was cumulative and generally well-sustained. Also cast: Anna Lee, Paul Dubov, Jaclynne Greene and Neyle Morrow. (81 mins)

▽ Fred MacMurray (left) starred as a bank robber in **Face Of A Fugitive**, a down-beat Western in which he is accused of killing a deputy sheriff. The real culprit, however, is MacMurray's brother – who dies early on in David T. Chantler and Daniel B. Ullman's leisurely screenplay. Changing his name, MacMurray makes for a town in which he is not known, and promptly falls in love with the deputy sheriff's sister (Dorothy Green). While rescuing the young sheriff (Lin McCarthy) from death, MacMurray facilitates his own capture, and the film's climax finds him being defended in court by McCarthy, who also happens to be a lawyer. As all this action took place in the course of a single day, there was little room for character development which wasn't too damaging to Charles Schneer's Morningside Production given that there wasn't much character to develop anyway. An exciting chase in the film's final minutes provided director Paul Wendkos with some much-needed action. James Coburn (right) gave a stand-out performance in a supporting cast that included Alan Baxter, Myrna Fahey and Francis De Sales. It was photographed in Eastmancolor. (80 mins)

△ **The Flying Fontaines** were circus aerialists around whom Sam Katzman's pacey circus melodrama revolved. Michael Callan (holding net) top-starred as the star of the troupe who, returning to the circus after a two-year stint in the army, discovers that his girl (Joan Evans, third right) has married the troupe's catcher. Furthermore his father refuses to recommend him for a place in one of the acts until he achieves his pre-war excellence. Callan's ensuing problems, both romantic and professional, formed the basis of Don Mullaly and Lee Erwin's atmospheric screenplay, and gained momentum under George Sherman's efficient direction. Evy Norlund (centre) co-starred as a romantic complication, with other roles in the Eastmancolor production going to Rian Garrick (lying flat), Joe DeSantis (behind net), Roger Perry and John van Dreelen (front right). (73 mins)

△ Not surprisingly, music spoke louder than words in **The Gene Krupa Story** (GB: **Drum Crazy**), a biopic of the great jazz drummer. Sal Mineo (left) played the titular hero (with Krupa lending a hand on the drums), and although he breezed through the film's early sequences, was never very convincing as the older, alcohol-imbibing, marijuana-smoking musician. The oft-told tale of an idealistic youngster who eschews a conventional background (in this case, the priesthood) for a crack at the big-time in show business, it focused on both the triumphs and the tribulations of its subject – a man who was often down but never out. Susan Kohner was cast as Krupa's girl-next-door sweetheart, James Darren was his best friend. Also cast: Susan Oliver (right), Yvonne Craig, Lawrence Dobkin, Celia Lovsky, and, playing themselves, Red Nichols, Anita O'Day and Buddy Lester. Orin Jannings wrote it, Don Weis directed and Philip A. Waxman was the producer (102 mins)

▽ Sandra Dee (right) started out in the successful teen-comedy **Gidget** as a kid who, at first, lacks the wherewithal to turn the boys on. However, it's only a matter of time before she has attracted the beefy attentions of James Darren and Cliff Robertson (left). The agony and the ecstasy of young love was explored with pleasing, entertaining results in Gabrielle Upton's screenplay (from the novel by Frederick Kohner). Paul Wendkos glossily directed for producer Lewis J. Rachmil, and a top-drawer supporting cast included Arthur O'Connell, Mary La Roche, Jo Morrow, Joby Baker, Tom Laughlin, Sue George, Robert Ellis, Yvonne Craig, Patti Kane and Doug McClure. It was filmed in CinemaScope and Eastmancolor, and featured three songs by Patti Washington and Fred Karger. *Gidget* was popular enough to spawn various sequels in the sixties – though without Sandra Dee. (95 mins)

▽ In **Forbidden Island**, Jon Hall (centre) once again found himself in his favourite locale – a forbidden island. He's a peacetime frogman whose purpose in writer-producer-director Charles B. Griffith's blood-shot screenplay is to dive for an emerald lost in a shipwreck. The man who hires him to do so is John Farrow (left), the villain of the piece – and the victim of his own treachery. Nan Adams (right) co-starred as Hall's romantic interest (and Farrow's pretended wife). Also cast: Greigh Phillips, Jonathan Haze, Dave 'Howdy' Peters, and Tookie Evans. It was filmed (in Technicolor) on location in Hawaii and Florida. (66 mins)

△ The rejuvenation of The Three Stooges via TV resulted in **Have Rocket, Will Travel** – a low-budget comedy aimed exclusively at the young 'uns. A *mélange* of sight gags and special effects (such as talking unicorns and flame-throwing giant spiders), its plot found handymen Moe Howard, Larry Fine and Joe de Rita (replacing Shemp Howard) trapped in a rocket that has been programmed for Venus. As the first earthly representatives on that planet, The Three Stooges (illustrated) undergo several hair-raising adventures, all of which – in Raphael Hayes' screenplay – incorporated the usual Stooges 'shtick'. There was nothing out of this world, however, about the redundant romantic sub-plot involving Anna-Lisa and Bob Colbert. Completing the cast was Jerome Cowan. Harry Romm produced, and the director was David Lowell Rich. (76 mins)

△ A low-budget musical intended to showcase the talents of Louis Prima (left) and Keely Smith (right), **Hey Boy! Hey Girl!** was an undemanding entertainment that featured Ms Smith as a church go-between who persuades Prima to appear in a parish benefit. The couple fall in love and live happily ever after. Raphael Hayes and James West's screenplay, though light on plot, was well-crafted *vis-à-vis* its accommodation of the musical programme, and provided roles for James Gregory (as a priest), Henry Slate, Kim Charney, and Barbara Heller. Sam Butera and The Witnesses were in it too. The producer was Harry Romm, and the director David Lowell Rich. (83 mins)

▽ What happened to Jane in **It Happened To Jane** was that she became involved in a lengthy legal battle with a railroad chairman and 'the meanest man in the world'. Jane, played by Doris Day (left), is a New England lobster dealer, and when a shipment of lobsters she is expecting is ruined in transit as a result of the railroad's tardiness, she hires lawyer Jack Lemmon (right) and successfully wins her action against Ernie Kovacs, the railroad chairman. Day, however, has underestimated the true nastiness of her adversary, who counterattacks by suspending the train service to her local town – an action which makes her extremely unpopular with the locals. Though Norman Katkov's screenplay (story by Katkov and Max Wilk) had some amusing moments – most of them in the film's funny first half – and although all three central performances were fine, the film, which was originally to have been called 'That Jane From Maine', failed to find a public and lost money. Even a later change of title to *Twinkle And Shine* failed to do just that at the box-office. It was produced and directed by Richard Quine, photographed in Eastmancolor, and, in supporting roles featured Teddy Rooney and Gina Gillespie as Miss Day's two kids, as well as Steve Forrest (centre), Mary Wickes, Parker Fennelly, Russ Brown, Philip Coolidge and John Cecil Holm. Doris Day sang two songs – the title number and 'Be Prepared'. (100 mins)

◁ Elvis Presley's army call-up provided **Idol On Parade** (GB: **Idle On Parade**) with a certain topicality. It starred Anthony Newley (left) as a rock-'n'-roll singer who is called up for National Service, and, in lieu of plot, offered a series of corn-fed army gags involving the comic talents of William Bendix (right), as a loud-mouthed sergeant, Lionel Jeffries (as a fuss-pot adjutant) and Sidney James as Newley's agent. Also cast: Anne Aubrey, David Lodge, Dilys Laye, William Kendall, Bernie Winters and Harry Fowler. John Antrobus scripted from a novel by William Camp, John Gilling directed, and Harold Huth produced, in CinemaScope, for Warwick Productions. (88 mins)

▽ Several members of the Warwick stock company fetched up in **In The Nick**, a small-scale comedy about prison life. Director Ken Hughes also wrote the screenplay, from a story by Frank Norman – himself an ex-con. All about a quartet of toughies and their experiences in a 'progressive' prison (ie one without bars), it starred James Booth (right), Derren Nesbitt, Bernie Winters and Al Mulock as the four inmates, with a miscast Anthony Newley (left, top-starred) playing a serious-minded psychologist. Harry Andrews was in fine form as a prison warder. Female interest was supplied by Anne Aubrey, whose chief contribution was a strip-tease act in a nightclub. Also cast: Niall McGinnis, Ian Hendry, Barry Keegan and Victor Brooks. A Harold Huth production, it was filmed in CinemaScope. (105 mins)

▽ A lively musical programmer from producer Sam Katzman, **Juke Box Rhythm** once again shoe-horned a full musical programme into a pin-prick of a plot. It starred Jo Morrow and Jack Jones (right) – she as a European princess in New York to purchase her coronation wardrobe, he as a young singer determined that the clothes order goes to an unknown designer (Hans Conried, left) and former junk man. On to this meagre narrative (story by Lou Morheim, script by Mary McCall Jr and Earl Baldwin) were appliquéd songs and musical numbers (choreographed by Hal Belfer) by the aforementioned Mr Jones, as well as by The Earl Grant Trio, The Nitwits, The Treniers, and Johnny Otis. Frieda Inescort played Ms Morrow's aunt, and the cast also included Brian Donlevy, Karin Booth, Marjorie Reynolds, Edgar Barrier, Fritz Feld and, as himself, George Jessel. The director was Arthur Dreifuss. (82 mins)

△ Paul Muni (left) returned to the screen after an absence of 13 years to star in **The Last Angry Man**. He played Dr Sam Abelman, a dedicated Jewish doctor, who, for the past 45 years, has worked out of a small clinic in a slum-infested area of Brooklyn. As in Gerald Green's best-selling novel on which the screenplay was based, the story accelerated when a TV producer (David Wayne) reads an article written by Muni's nephew (Joby Baker) and decides to do a programme on the good doctor himself. At first Muni will have nothing to do with network TV, and it is only after a colleague of his (Luther Adler, right) persuades him that by taking part in the show he will be giving himself an opportunity to express his views on the hypocrisy of the medical profession, that Muni reluctantly agrees. On the night of the telecast, one of Muni's patients (Billy Dee Williams) is arrested for car theft, and Muni, believing that it is more important to be at the side of

the troubled young man than to appear on TV, walks out on the show. Muni dies of a heart attack while in the police station. Dedicated to some of life's more sterling values, such as honesty, decency and charity (while, at the same time, taking a few swipes at the medical profession and commercial TV), the film, scripted by Green from an adaptation by Richard Murphy) was unashamedly sentimental. However, it benefited immeasurably from Muni's powerful central performance which over-rode some of the flaws in Daniel Mann's occasionally awkward direction. There were excellent performances from a fine supporting cast including Nancy R. Pollock as Muni's devoted wife and Betsy Palmer as Wayne's wife, as well as from Joanna Moore, Claudia McNeil, Robert F. Simon and Dan Tobin. It was photographed (much of it on location in Brooklyn) by James Wong Howe, and produced by Fred Kohlmar. (100 mins)

▽ Producers Harold Huth, Albert R. Broccoli and Irving Allen – for Warwick – scoured Europe for pretty locations with which to boost their make-shift, totally forgettable cops 'n' robbers melodrama **The Man Inside**. Nigel Patrick appeared as a clerk-turned-jewel thief, Jack Palance (right) was top-billed as a vapid detective who trails his English quarry in and out of New York, Lisbon, Madrid, Paris and London, and Anita Ekberg (left) went along for the ride as the true owner of the stolen gem. John Gilling's screenplay (which he co-scripted with David Shaw from a novel by M. E. Chaber) was as listless as his direction, and, apart from the urbane Mr Patrick and Anthony Newley as a Spanish cab-driver, the performances were on a par with the whole wasted enterprise. Also cast: Bonar Colleano (whose last role this was before his death in a car crash), Sean Kelly, Sidney James, Donald Pleasence, Eric Pohlmann and Anne Aubrey. It was filmed in CinemaScope. (97 mins)

△ The only unusual thing about **The Last Blitzkrieg**, a predictable World War II actioner, was that its star, all-American boy-next-door Van Johnson (right), played a German spy-cum-saboteur who has infiltrated American lines. Audiences who believed that would believe anything! Of course, as Lou Morheim's screenplay unspooled, Johnson discovers that the Nazis are a pretty resistible lot, a realization that dawns after his Yankee buddies Larry Storch and Dick York are ordered to be shot in cold blood by a German officer. Kerwin Matthews (left), Lise Bourdin, Hans Brents van den Berg and Leon Askin comprised the unmemorable supporting company; Arthur Dreifuss directed (or, what passed for direction) for producer Sam Katzman. (85 mins)

▽ Paddy Chayefsky was right up there with Carson McCullers, William Inge and Tennessee Williams when it came to writing about the pain of loneliness, and **Middle Of The Night** proved it. First seen as a TV play with E. G. Marshall and Eva Marie Saint in 1954, then, two years later, as a Broadway play with Edward G. Robinson and Gena Rowlands, the film version starred Fredric March (left) and Kim Novak (right). March played a 53-year-old widowed clothing manufacturer who happens to fall in love with one of his employees – a girl (Novak) 30 years his junior. As the romance blossoms and March experiences happiness for the first time in years, his family resents the intrusion of the young newcomer and do their best to end the romance. Not only that, but the difference in the couple's ages attracts adverse comment and is a further blight to the fulfilment of their happiness. Undaunted, and amidst much opposition, the couple persevere, and the film ends with their impending marriage. Whether, in the long run, the relationship will prove to be successful was left an open question. By toning down some of

the play's Jewishness (as typified in the casting of March), an essential element had been excised from the screen version which robbed the family scenes of their ethnic power and seemed to work against the grain of much of Chayefsky's writing. Furthermore, March lacked the charisma of Edward G. Robinson, making it difficult to see what a cool beauty like Novak would have seen in him – especially given how unwelcome she was made to feel by his thoroughly disagreeable family. Still, whether ideally cast or not, March was always worth watching, and, consummate professional that he was, brought heavyweight conviction to Chayefsky's realistic dialogue. Novak, working well for director Delbert Mann, actually managed a semblance of a performance, and there was excellent work from Joan Copeland (playwright Arthur Miller's sister) as March's selfish daughter, Albert Dekker as March's unhappy partner, Glenda Farrell as Novak's mother, as well as from Lee Grant, Martin Balsam, Lee Philips, Betty Walker and Edith Meiser. The producer was George Justin for Sudan Productions. (117 mins)

△ The star of 53 one-reeler cartoons over a period of 11 years, the nearsighted Mr Magoo (on carpet) was elevated to feature-film status in **1001 Arabian Nights**. Whisked to Baghdad aboard a magic carpet, and with a cat he thinks is a dog for companionship, the myopic McGoo encounters good and evil as the familiar tales – originally told by Scheherazade – weave their magic all over again. Admirers of UPA's approach to animation doubtless found much to enjoy in this colourful reworking of the story of Aladdin and his lamp; lovers of the lusher, Disney approach to cartoons were wise to stay away. Czenzi Ormonde scripted it from a story by Dick Shaw, Dick Kinney, Leo Salkin, Pete Burness, Lew Keller, Ed Nofziger, Ted Allan, and Margaret Schneider. The film was produced (in Eastmancolor) by Stephen Bosustow, directed by Jack Kinney and featured a fine cast of voices – including those of Jim Backus (as Magoo), Kathryn Grant, Dwayne Hickman, Hans Conried, Herschel Bernardi, Alan Reed, Daws Butler and the Clark Sisters. (76 mins)

▽ **Porgy And Bess**, the last film to be produced by 75-year-old Sam Goldwyn, did not quite manage to do justice to the spirit of George and Ira Gershwin and DuBose Heyward's masterpiece. Sidney Poitier (right), vocals dubbed by Robert McFerrin, and Dorothy Dandridge, vocals dubbed by Adele Addison starred as Porgy and Bess and their performances reeked more of Hollywood than Catfish Row. It was left to Brock Peters as Crown and Sammy Davis Jr as Sporting Life to bring it conviction. By employing playwright N. Richard Nash to write a screenplay in place of Heyward's original libretto (based on the play *Porgy*, which Heyward wrote with his wife Dorothy), producer Goldwyn turned a folk opera into another Hollywood musical, a fact that Otto Preminger's uninspired direction underlined. (Rouben Mamoulian, the director of the original stage version, was Goldwyn's first choice, but after eight months of pre-production work, he was replaced when he and Goldwyn failed to agree on several matters of artistic policy.) The film was choreographed by Hermes Pan, photographed in Technicolor and Todd-AO by Leon Shamroy (the budget exceeded $6.5 million, much of that going on an impressive hurricane), and, in featured roles, boasted a cast that included Diahann Carroll (as Clara), Pearl Bailey (left, as Maria), Ruth Attaway (Serena) as well as Clarence Muse, Leslie Scott, Everdinne Wilson, Joel Fluellen and Earl Jackson. André Previn and Ken Darby combined forces to mastermind the musical direction. (138 mins)

◁ Tennessee Williams's off-Broadway success **Suddenly Last Summer**, a one-act play which shared a bill with another short piece, *Something Unspoken*, reached the screen in an atmospheric version, scripted by Williams and Gore Vidal. Their screenplay extended the play's original running time but, while being rife with symbolism, diluted the work's twin themes of cannibalism and homosexuality. The story revolved around the painstaking attempts of a brain surgeon (Montgomery Clift) to discover just what happened to Sebastian Venable, poet and dilettante, during a trip abroad taken in the company of his attractive cousin Catherine (Elizabeth Taylor, illustrated); and why Catherine's aunt (Katharine Hepburn), a wealthy Louisiana dowager, is insisting that her niece have a lobotomy. What was vividly spelled out in the play was merely hinted at in the film, and the result was a steamy melodrama that never quite had the courage of its author's convictions. The performances, though, were splendid. Top-billed Elizabeth Taylor convincingly conveyed the trauma and confusion of the 'used' Catherine; Montgomery Clift gave an intensely 'passive' albeit sympathetic interpretation as the surgeon, while Katharine Hepburn was her formidable self as the redoubtable Mrs Venable, a desperate woman afraid to face the truth about her son or his appalling death. Mercedes McCambridge and Gary Raymond were cast as Catherine's mother and brother, with other roles going to Albert Dekker, Mavis Villiers and Patricia Marmont. Joseph L. Mankiewicz directed with a moody sense of doom and foreboding, and Sam Spiegel was the producer. The film was shot at Shepperton Studios in England, and grossed nearly $2 million. (112 mins)

▽ Showman William Castle introduced an early form of Sensurround (he hooked up vibrating motors to the backs of the cinema seats) in **The Tingler**, an enjoyable piece of hokum which starred Vincent Price (left) as a scientist who discovers that fear actually 'grows' inside people into a scaly little monster that 'tingles' up and down the spine, and that when someone dies of fright it's because 'the tingler' has broken their spine. However, he also discovers that the monster can be effectively destroyed by screaming. This knowledge comes into the hands of an unloving husband who promptly starts devising 'horror' situations to scare his deaf-mute wife to death. 'Scream for her!' Castle encouraged his audiences. However, one of 'the tinglers' is already loose in the cinema . . . At this point the Sensurround vibrators were switched on – and the audience nearly screamed themselves to death. How this deadly creature is isolated and dealt with formed the crux of the narrative, and provided horror addicts with one of the better examples of the genre. Apart from Price, the film featured Judith Evelyn, Darryl Hickman (right), Patricia Cutts, Pamela Lincoln and Philip Coolidge. Castle produced and directed – most effectively – from a screenplay by Robb White. (80 mins)

▽ **The Legend Of Tom Dooley** was a downbeat entertainment, not without quality, that took its inspiration from the popular Tom Dooley song (sung in the film by The Kingston Trio). Taking the theme of the song, writer-producer Stan Shpetner's screenplay concentrated on three young Confederate soldiers – Michael Landon (right), Richard Rust (left) and Dee Pollock – who, after ambushing a Yankee stagecoach and killing a couple of Union soldiers, learn that the war is over, and that, in effect, they're guilty of murder. Jo Morrow, Jack Hogan, Ken Lynch, Howard Wright, Ralph Moody, John Clift and Cheerio Meredith were also cast, and the director was Ted Post. Believable, and involving. (79 mins)

▽ War came under satirical attack in **The Mouse That Roared**, a diverting farce in which the Grand Duchy of Grand Fenwick (the smallest country in the world) decides to declare war on the USA when Fenwick's wine industry (its only durable export) is overtaken by the vineyards of California. The resulting battle finds the Fenwickians being mistaken for Martians – and in possession of a deadly Q-bomb. It was an enjoyable piece of mickey-taking (although its resolution failed to match the film's inspired first half) whose *raison d'être* was the casting of Peter Sellers in three roles. Sellers played the Prime Minister of Grand Fenwick, the dotty Grand Duchess of same, and the Hereditary Field Marshal and Grand Constable who leads the attack on the States. He was brilliant in all three incarnations, and shamefully upscreened a supporting cast that included David Kossoff as the bomb's inventor, Jean Seberg (as Kossoff's daughter), William Hartnell, Leo McKern, Harold Kasket, Monty Landis and Timothy Bateson. Roger MacDougall and Stanley Mann wrote the screenplay from the novel by Leonard Wibberley, Jon Pennington and Walter Shenson produced and Jack Arnold directed. The witty credit titles were by Maurice Binder and included an unexpected joke at the Columbia logo's expense. It was photographed in Eastmancolor. A sequel, *The Mouse On The Moon*, followed in 1963. (83 mins)

▽ A tensile and often hard-hitting screenplay by Burt Kennedy did wonders for **Ride Lonesome**, a Budd Boetticher-directed Western which starred Randolph Scott (right), for his Ranown Productions, as a taciturn bounty hunter on the trail of giggling killer James Best (left). Intent on rescuing Best from Scott (right) is his brother, Lee Van Cleef. Conflict and sub-plots abounded, all of them tightly interwoven into the fabric of the piece by scenarist Kennedy, and kept under suspense-making control by Boetticher. Also in the cast were Karen Steele (second left), James Coburn, Pernell Roberts (second right), Dyke Johnson, and Boyd Stockman. It was filmed in CinemaScope and Pathé's Eastmancolor. (74 mins)

▽ **They Came To Cordura** was an often harrowing action drama that questioned the nature of courage. Scripted by director Robert Rossen and Ivan Moffat from a novel by Glendon Swarthout, the film starred Gary Cooper (right) as a US Army officer detailed to lead back to Texas five Medal of Honor candidates from the front line of the punitive 1916 war with Pancho Villa. Cooper, who has been made Awards Officer, is interested in the 'heroes' under his command, believing them to possess qualities he lacks. But as the lengthy trek gets underway, the hardships his men are forced to endure bring out the worst in them – and the best in himself, thus questioning the whole notion of what makes a hero. Van Heflin, Tab Hunter, Richard Conte, Michael Callan and Dick York were the quintet, and Rita Hayworth (left) played the daughter of a disgraced US senator. Hayworth was clearly happy to forego glamour if it meant a juicy acting role, and her work under Rossen's spiky direction was among the best of her career. Cooper, who was, in truth far too old for the central role of Major Thomas Thorn, nonetheless managed to bring a characteristic sense of strength and dignity to the part, as well as an authority not always in evidence among his co-stars. Robert Keith, Carlos Romero, James Bannon and Edward Platt were also featured in William Goetz's CinemaScope and Eastmancolor production. (123 mins)

△ What does a man do with a 30-foot bride? The question was asked and answered in **The 30 Foot Bride Of Candy Rock**, a fantasy distinguished only by the fact that it was Lou Costello's last film. Costello (left) appeared without Abbott, which had the same effect as applauding with one hand, and played a rubbish collector in the town of Candy Rock. Blessed with a photographic memory, he's a self-taught scientist as well as an inventor – his most impressive creation being a robot of sorts called Max. What happens to the pair of them, once leading lady Dorothy Provine (right) inexplicably grows to be 30 foot in height, formed the contents of Rowland Barber and Arthur Ross's screenplay (story by Lawrence L. Goldman) and provided work for Gale Gordon, Jimmy Conlin, Charles Lane, Robert Burton and Will Wright. It was a DRB Production, in 'Wonderama and Mattascope'. The director was Sidney Miller. (75 mins)

△ Originally intended for release by Disney's Buena Vista Productions, **The Young Land**, made in 1957, finally came to the screen via Columbia and directed by Ted Tetzlaff. Set in California in 1848, it centred on the murder of a Mexican by an American (Dennis Hopper). In the ensuing court case, justice itself, as well as Hopper, is on trial. The case is considered something of a test, and is watched with great interest by the Spanish-speaking citizens of the new state. In the course of Norman Shannon Hall's inept, albeit well-intentioned, screenplay (story by John Reese), Hopper is duly found guilty, given a 20-year sentence, and told never to carry a weapon again. Pat Wayne (right, son of John) played the sheriff and received star billing, Yvonne Craig (left) was his romantic interest, and Dan O'Herlihy played the judge. The film was produced, in Technicolor, by Patrick Ford (son of director John) for C. V. Whitney Productions. *The Young Land* was the third and final Whitney production to deal with America's history, the other two being *The Searchers* (Warner Bros., 1956) and *The Missouri Traveller* (Buena Vista, 1958). (92 mins)

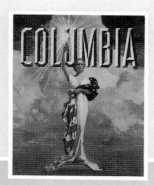

1960-1969

In the Sixties, all the big Hollywood studios began to lose their corporate identities. More and more independent producers rented space on the Columbia lot – the most successful being Sam Spiegel, whose *Lawrence Of Arabia* (1962) brought profit as well as prestige to the studio. In 1965, Columbia opened its own production offices in 'Swinging London' – the fruits of which included *A Man For All Seasons* (1966), *To Sir With Love* (1967) and *Oliver!* (1968). Columbia's most successful film in the Sixties was, however, the American-made *Guess Who's Coming To Dinner* (1967) – the most profitable movie in the studio's history thus far.

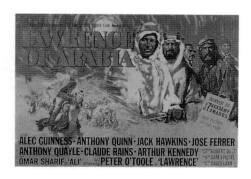

▷ If racial prejudice was the subject of **All The Young Men**, its object was to bury audiences up to their elbows in every narrative ploy ever inflicted on a wilting story-line. Though Alan Ladd (right) was top-cast in Hall Bartlett's potty production, it was Sidney Poitier (left) around whom the action pivoted. He played a black novice sergeant left in command of a handful of men defending a strategic Korean farmhouse against enemy attack. Chief opponent of the black man's command is Ladd, who feels *he* should have been given the position; so does Paul Richards, a dyed-in-the-wool Southern bigot. Writer-director Bartlett's screenplay paved the way for a reconciliation of sorts by having Poitier give Ladd his blood in a vital transfusion. Other cast members included James Darren (centre, as a likeable Mr Nice Guy), Ingemar Johansson (as a Swede who should have stuck to boxing), Mario Alcalde (as an American Red Indian who supports Poitier) and Mort Sahl (as a comedian who lightens the atmosphere by going into his routines). (86 mins)

▽ A much slighter version of the *Blackboard Jungle* (MGM, 1955) theme, **Because They're Young** starred Dick Clark as a compassionate new teacher who doesn't quite realize what he is undertaking when he becomes involved in the lives of some of his students. A showcase for some of the studio's younger talent, the film featured Doug

McClure (second right), Michael Callan, Warren Berlinger, Tuesday Weld, Roberta Shore and Victoria Shaw, with guest appearances by James Darren, Duane Eddy and The Rebels. It was scripted by James Gunn from John Farris's book *Harrison High*, and directed, with little evidence of flair, by Paul Wendkos Jerry. Bresler produced. (97 mins)

◁ The old-fashioned, middle-budget Western was becoming a rarity by the beginning of the Sixties, and **Comanche Station**, an excellent example of the genre, proved to be the last film director Budd Boetticher would make for Randolph Scott (illustrated) and Harry Joe Brown's Ranown Productions. Enhancing all the solid production values – including CinemaScope and Eastmancolor – Burt Kennedy's screenplay focused attention on the tribulations of loner Scott whose purpose is to return Miss Nancy Gates, captured by Comanches, to her settler husband. Accompanying Scott on this mission are Claude Akins, Skip Homeier and Richard Rust, a disreputable trio who, in the course of the tale, give Scott as much trouble as the surrounding Comanches. Also cast: Rand Brooks, Dyke Johnson, Foster Hood and Joe Molina. (74 mins)

△ The wide open spaces of the Grand Canyon provided the picturesque backdrop to **Edge Of Eternity**, a Don Siegel-directed actioner with a climax – a cable-car brawl involving top-billed Cornel Wilde (illustrated) and Mickey Shaughnessy (with female lead Victoria Shaw in attendance as well) – that went some considerable distance to compensate for the mundanities of Knut Swenson and Richard Collins' screenplay (story by Swenson and Ben Markson). Wilde played a deputy sheriff out to find the murderer of a gold-mine executive who was killed after discovering that his stolen gold was being sold in Mexico for $50 an ounce instead of the usual $35 it would fetch in the USA. The culprit turns out to be Shaughnessy. A Thunderbird (Kendrick Sweet) Production, it featured Edgar Buchanan, Rian Garrick, and Jack Elam; and was photographed in Pathé's Eastmancolor. (81 mins)

△ **The Enemy General** was a thoroughly undistinguished B movie which starred Van Johnson (second right) as an American (masquerading as a Frenchman) in the Maquis underground during World War II. The screenplay by Dan Pepper and Burt Picard (story by Pepper) traded in irony, as it called on Johnson to assist in the escape to London of the heinous Nazi general (John Van Dreelen) responsible for the murder, in cold blood, of Johnson's fiancée (Dany Carrel, second left), as well as 11 innocent French hostages. The villainous Van Dreelen has bought his escape with the promise of some vital information for the Allies. However, it soon becomes clear that he has been indulging in a counter-espionage plot – at which point Johnson, unhappy at having to assist the enemy in the first place, disposes of him. Jean-Pierre Aumont (right) co-starred, with other parts in Sam Katzman's tired production going to Françoise Prévost, Hubert Noël (left), Jacques Marin, Gérard Landry, Edward Fleming, Paul Bonifas and Paul Miller. The director was George Sherman. (75 mins)

▷ Having once made on-screen love to Greta Garbo, Vivien Leigh and Elizabeth Taylor, Robert Taylor (right) found himself in somewhat reduced circumstances in **Killers Of Kilimanjaro** – his leading lady on this inauspicious occasion being Anne Aubrey (left). Traversing territory mined by deadly platitudes and numbing clichés, he played a safari leader who braves charging rhinos, hungry crocodiles and greedy cannibals in order to lay the foundations for the first East African railway. The script was the work of John Gilling (screen story by Richard Maibaum and Cyril Hume from the book *African Bush Adventures* by J.A. Hunter and Dan P. Mannix), it was directed by Richard Thorpe, and featured Anthony Newley (centre) as Taylor's sidekick, Grégoire Aslan, Allan Cuthbertson, John Dimech and Donald Pleasence. It was produced, in CinemaScope and Technicolor, by John R. Sloan for Warwick Productions. (91 mins)

▷ Part musical, part comedy, part crime-melodrama, **Jazz Boat** was a mish-mash from producers Irving Allen and Albert R. Broccoli (for Warwick Productions) that unsuccessfully attempted to cash in on the then current British youth-cult rage. Top-billed Anthony Newley (second left) played a youngster who inadvertently finds himself involved in a robbery after bragging to a group of teenage hoodlums that he is a big-time crook. None of it made any sense and the film came and went with indecent haste. Anne Aubrey was the 'heroine', Lionel Jeffries played a sadistic cop, James Booth (right) was a young heavy, with other arts under Ken Hughes's bleary direction going to Joyce Blair, David Lodge, Bernie Winters (3rd left), Al Mulock (left) and Leo McKern. It was scripted by Hughes and John Antrobus, and photographed in CinemaScope. (96 mins)

◁ Is genius sufficient justification for a man to turn his back on accepted ethical codes of behaviour and morals? That was an issue scenarist Jay Dratler (working from a story by George Froeschel, U. Wolter and H.W. John) raised, rather fuzzily, in **I Aim At The Stars**, a biopic of Nazi scientist Wernher von Braun. The film also attempted to deal with the fact that the inventor of the Nazis' deadly V-2 rocket was warmly welcomed in America and given US citizenship. As perceived by Dratler, von Braun was an apolitical creature whose only dream in life was to create rockets that explored the mysteries of outer-space – but who, because of his extraordinary talent, was forced to ply his skills in the service of Hitler. Curt Jurgens (illustrated) as von Braun communicated precious little of the man's character, and meticulously avoided taking sides. Herbert Lom was cast as the scientist's chief aide, and Gia Scala was Lom's secretary. Between them they provided the film with its romantic interest, and a modicum of intrigue – Scala also being a British spy. Victoria Shaw appeared as von Braun's fiancée, and James Daly as a major embittered by the death of his wife and child in a V-2 attack on London. Charles H. Schneer produced, and it was directed by J. Lee Thompson. (106 mins)

▽ Shelley Winters (centre) packed a powerhouse performance into **Let No Man Write My Epitaph**, a decidedly downbeat drama which Robert Presnell Jr scripted from novelist William Motley's trenchant look at life in the slums of Chicago's South Side (a follow-on from Motley's earlier novel which had already been seen on screen as *Knock On Any Door*, 1949). Winters played Nellie Romano, widow of a hood who went to the electric chair, and mother of a young son (James Darren, right) who dreams of becoming a concert pianist, and whom she is determined to see remains unaffected by the squalor of their surroundings. The fact that she is a dope addict (thanks to mobster Ricardo Montalban) complicates matters, and leads to a climactic scene (and one of the best in the film) during which mother and son have an ugly showdown over her reliance on drugs. An ending which smacked more of wish-fulfilment than of reality, and direction by Philip Leacock which needed to be far tauter than it was, robbed the film of much potential impact. Burl Ives (centre) received top-billing as the endearing Judge Bruce Mallory Sullivan, Jean Seberg made a brief appearance as Darren's romantic interest, Philip Ober featured as her father, and there was an appearance from Ella Fitzgerald who not only sang Jimmy McHugh and Ned Washington's 'Reach For Tomorrow' but was also given a chance to do a spot of acting. The producer was Boris D. Kaplan. (105 mins)

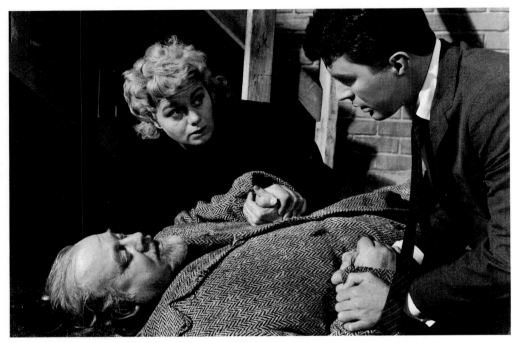

△ James Stewart's name above the title wasn't a sufficient box-office draw for **The Mountain Road** to lead to glory, either commercially or artistically. Stewart (centre) played Major Baldwin, US Army officer in charge of a small demolitions team in the Chinese backwoods during the last stages of World War II. His purpose? To block the path of advancing Japanese, none of whom is ever seen in the film. Stewart's dislike of his Chinese colleagues and his eventual capitulation (inspired by a Chinese war-widow) underpinned what was an average actioner, spasmodically involving events with a wartime flavour. There was a sensitive performance from Lisa Lu as the widow who manages to instil in Stewart a certain compassion; and a fine one from Glenn Corbett as a China-loving GI. William Goetz's production also featured Henry Morgan, Frank Silvera, James Best and Rudy Bond. The screenplay was written by Alfred Hayes from a novel by Theodore White and directed by Daniel Mann. (102 mins)

▽ In **Man On A String** (GB: **Confessions Of A Counterspy**) Ernest Borgnine (illustrated) played Boris Mitrov, a Moscow-born American citizen, who, between stints as a successful Hollywood producer, is a Soviet spy. When, however, his activities are tumbled by the US Central Bureau of Intelligence, he changes his allegiance and finds himself in Moscow spying on the Russians – while under surveillance from both sides. Taking a documentary-like approach to the subject of espionage, director André de Toth brought a hard-edged sense of reality to the proceedings and moved his protagonists at such a pace there was hardly time for the platitudes in John Kafka and Virginia Shaler's screenplay to sink in. The screenplay was adapted in part from the book *Ten Years A Counterspy* by Boris Morros and Charles Samuels, which was based on Morros's own espionage activities. Location shooting in Berlin, Moscow and New York also helped offset some basic cloak-and-dagger melodramatics. Kerwin Mathews co-starred as an FBI friend of Borgnine's, with other roles assigned to Colleen Dewhurst, Alexander Scourby and Ed Prentiss as a trio of cell leaders whose 'triangle situation' provided the film with its romantic sub-plot. The producer was Louis de Rochemont. (92 mins)

△ Made for a mere $73,000 by the McLendon Company Radio station in Dallas, and picked up by Columbia for national distribution, **My Dog Buddy** was a quintessential kiddies' melodrama about a boy, a dog, and their enforced separation occasioned by the death of the boy's parents in a car accident... a case of boy meets dog, boy loses dog, and, finally boy finds dog – or, rather, dog finds boy. Buddy was played by canine star London, the boy he goes in search of was Travis Lemmond (illustrated), with other parts in the Gordon McLendon production going to Ken Curtis, Ken Knox, James H. Foster, Jane Murchison and Bob Thompson. It was written and directed by Ray Kellogg whose tendency to cram the film full of extraneous gimmicks and superfluous narrative was a decided minus factor. (76 mins)

▷ The screen version of Harry Kurnitz's Broadway hit, **Once More With Feeling** was relocated from America to Europe. Otherwise, this tall story about a disagreeable orchestra conductor and his fed-up-to-the-gills wife followed the guidelines of the original. Yul Brynner (right) was cast as the conductor; and Kay Kendall (left, who died three months after the film was completed) was his wife. The plot revolved around Kendall's decision to leave her husband for physicist Geoffrey Toone. Nothing unusual in that – except that Brynner and Kendall aren't legally wed. And, in order not to create a scandal, they have to marry before they can obtain a divorce. Needless to say, in the few days the couple spend together while waiting to be properly married, they discover they don't want a divorce after all. Kurnitz's witty one-liners frequently came to the rescue of this featherweight plot; so did the presence of Gregory Ratoff as Brynner's agent. But there was little that either the script or Stanley Donen's direction (more concerned with the way the show looked than sounded) could do about the basic unlikeability projected by Brynner, or the disagreeable tantrum-throwing behaviour of the usually delectable Miss Kendall. Donen also produced. It was photographed in Technicolor – and had main titles by Maurice Binder that were cleverer than Kurnitz's screenplay. Also cast: Maxwell Shaw, Mervyn Johns, Martin Benson and Harry Lockhart. (92 mins)

◁ **Pepe** was a catastrophe that weighed in at over three hours. Its painfully protracted story followed the tribulations of a Mexican peasant (Mexican superstar Cantinflas, illustrated), who, after spending years training and grooming a white stallion, is distraught when he discovers that the horse has been sold to a Hollywood director (Dan Dailey). What happens after the peasant goes to California and persuades the director to allow him to take care of the horse was of little consequence to lovers of good movie musicals. For the record, though, the film featured the talents of Shirley Jones, Matt Mattox, Ernie Kovacs, William Demarest, Carlos Montalban, Vicki Trickett, as well as guest appearances by Carlos Rivas, Joey Bishop, Michael Callan, Bing Crosby, Zsa Zsa Gabor, Maurice Chevalier, Charles Coburn, Richard Conte, Bobby Darin, Sammy Davis Jr, Hedda Hopper, Greer Garson, Peter Lawford, Janet Leigh, Jack Lemmon, Jay North, Kim Novak, André Previn, Donna Reed, Debbie Reynolds, Edward G. Robinson, Cesar Romero, Frank Sinatra, Billie Burke and the voice of Judy Garland. Of course, if you blinked, you missed 'em. The director was George Sidney, who compounded the felony by producing as well. It was written by Dorothy Kingsley and Claude Binyon, from a story by Leonard Spigelgass and Sonya Levien, which, in turn, was based on the play *Broadway Magic* by Ladislas Bus-Fekete. It was filmed in Panavision (with special sequences in CinemaScope) and Eastmancolor. (195 mins)

▷ The hot-house world of international espionage was the target which Graham Greene so successfully and humorously demolished in his novel **Our Man In Havana**; and, in its film incarnation, under the meticulous aim of director Carol Reed, a bullseye was struck once again. The deliciously droll story of a mild-mannered vacuum-cleaner salesman in Havana who, in order to find the financial wherewithal to send his daughter to a Swiss finishing school, becomes a member of the British secret service, it starred Alec Guinness (centre) as the unlikely spy and Burl Ives (right) as one of his victims. The nub of the plot found Guinness, in his efforts to keep his job, being forced to invent a totally fictitious espionage network. The reports of his activities are taken so seriously by MI5 that they send out two assistants to help him complete his work. In time, of course, these deceits spiral out of control with tragic results, and the film's second half is couched in a darker, more sombre mood than the first. There was total consistency, however, in all the central performances, with the acting honours going to Noël Coward (left) as the boss of a Caribbean network who, in one of the best scenes in the film, recruits Guinness into the seedy world of espionage. Ralph Richardson was in top form as Coward's London-based boss, and there was excellent work from Paul Rogers, Grégoire Aslan, Duncan Macrae, Maxine Audley and Ferdy Mayne. Jo Morrow was adequate as Guinness's daughter, Maureen O'Hara looked attractive as the girl sent out to help Guinness, and Ernie Kovacs displayed a more serious side as a ruthless Cuban police officer. Carol Reed also produced (in CinemaScope) and Graham Greene provided the script. (111 mins)

◁ Dirk Bogarde (centre) played composer-pianist Franz Liszt in **Song Without End** and adequately went through the Hollywood-biopic motions of agonizing over whether to concentrate on being a virtuoso pianist, or devote his talents to composition. The women in his life were Capucine as Princess Carolyne (whom he adores but who proves to be unattainable), and Genevieve Page as the Countess Marie. Katherine Squire played his mother Anna. It was unalloyed kitsch from start to finish, redeemed only by Jorge Bolet's piano playing (as Liszt) and some fairly hefty 'bleeding chunks' of music. Patricia Morison was cast as George Sand, Alex Davion as Chopin, Lyndon Brook as Wagner, Ivan Desny as Prince Nicholas, with other roles in Oscar Millar's fanciful screenplay assigned to Martita Hunt, Lou Jacobi and Marcel Dalio. The film was begun by director Charles Vidor, and, after Vidor's death, completed by George Cukor. It was filmed in CinemaScope and Eastmancolor by James Wong Howe and produced by William Goetz. (145 mins)

▷ A splicing together of ten Three Stooges shorts, with linking material by ventriloquist Paul Winchell (illustrated) and The Marquis Chimps, **Stop! Look! And Laugh!** was aimed squarely at the children's market, and, as such, didn't disappoint. With Moe and Curly Howard and Larry Fine as the knock-about trio, producer Harry Romm was guaranteed his fair share of laughs, and, considering how little it all cost to put together, some nifty box-office profits as well. Most of the original sequences were directed by Jules White, plus one by Edward Bernds, one by Charley Chase and one by Del Lord. (76 mins)

◁ Producer-director Stanley Donen laid a king-sized egg with **Surprise Package**, a witless comedy (based on a book by Art Buchwald) which not even gagster Harry Kurnitz salvaged with his laugh-sparse screenplay. All about an American hoodlum who tries to steal an exiled king's crown from a Mediterranean island, it starred an unfunny Yul Brynner (right) as the gangster, an even less funny Mitzi Gaynor (centre) as his girlfriend, and, unfunniest of all, Noël Coward (left) as the King. Bill Nagy, Lionel Murton, Barry Foster, Eric Pohlmann, George Coulouris, 'Man Mountain' Dean and Warren Mitchell appeared in support (of what?), and the title tune was penned by Sammy Cahn and James Van Heusen. (100 mins)

▽ Infidelity reared its troublesome, albeit popular, head in **Strangers When We Meet**, a glossy soap-opera set among the well-heeled of suburban Los Angeles, and involving a mid-life crisis that afflicts a successful architect (Kirk Douglas, left) who falls out of love with his personable wife (Barbara Rush). When, one day, Douglas meets Kim Novak (right) and learns that her husband (John Bryant) has lost interest in her sexually (a likely story), he decides to have an affair with her himself. Evan Hunter's screenplay (based on his best-selling novel) made quite sure, though, that the romance was doomed, and the film ended with both Douglas and Novak back with their respective spouses. Embroidering this emotional blood-bath was a comic sub-plot involving Ernie Kovacs as a successful author (and womanizer) who has commissioned Douglas to build him a dream hilltop home. Shown from conception to completion, the construction of the house served almost as a running gag; and the Misses Novak and Rush's good looks notwithstanding, the finished edifice stole the film. Walter Matthau was also sub-contracted to add texture to the plot – as a lecherous neighbour who makes advances to Ms Rush as soon as he learns of her husband's infidelity with Novak. Though Hunter's dialogue was a cut above the *Dynasty* or *Dallas* breed, it was hardly insightful, and merely provided its stars with a chance to prove how adept they were at making verbal bricks out of straw. A Bryna-Quine Production, in CinemaScope and Eastmancolor, it was directed by Richard Quine. Also cast: Virginia Bruce, Kent Smith, Helen Gallagher, Roberta Shore, Nancy Kovack and Paul Picerni. (117 mins)

△ William Castle – producer, director and showman – revived the haunted-house genre with **13 Ghosts** and, just to add novelty value to the proceedings, provided viewers with a 'ghost viewer' or visual aid that (through a process glorified by Castle with the name Illusion-O) allowed them to see the ghosts on the screen – or not, as their temperaments dictated. It was an amusing and original gimmick and the only reason for enduring an otherwise silly tale about a well-adjusted but indigent family of four who take up residence in a haunted house, whose 12 ghosts are out to recruit the thirteenth. Rob White wrote it, and the cast included Donald Woods (left), Charles Herbert, Jo Morrow, Martin Milner, Rosemary De Camp (right) and Margaret Hamilton. It was filmed in black and white except for the credit titles and the sequences involving the 'ghost viewers'. (85 mins)

▽ Producer Charles H. Schneer took several diabolical liberties with Jonathan Swift's swingeing four-part satire, *Gulliver's Travels*, but did so in the name of wholesome family entertainment. The result of his tampering was **The Three Worlds of Gulliver** which gave top-billing to Kerwin Mathews (illustrated) as Gulliver, but whose stars were Ray Harryhausen and Bernard Herrmann: Harryhausen for his eye-catching Superdynamation effects (in Eastmancolor); and Herrmann for his rousing score. Arthur Ross and director Jack Sher's screenplay concentrated, understandably, on the episodes involving the Brobdingnagians and the Lilliputians; and despite obvious simplifications, the film managed, nonetheless, to convey something of the book's satire. The predominantly English cast included Lee Patterson, Grégoire Aslan, Jo Morrow, Basil Sydney, Peter Bull, Charles Lloyd Pack and, as Gulliver's girl, June Thorburn. (98 mins)

△ A lightweight dollop of sci-fi, **12 To The Moon** despatched a dozen passengers of both sexes and several nationalities to the moon. They find the moonlings, a peace-loving mob, wanting nothing to do with their out-of-space visitors. And in the circumstances, who can blame them? Heading the expedition was earthling Ken Clark, with Tom Conway (as a Russian), John Wengraf (the son of a Nazi), Richard Weber (an Israeli scientist whose parents were killed by Nazi Wengraf), Anna-Lisa (left, a Swedish research chemist), Tema Bey (a Turkish biologist and the object of Anna-Lisa's affections), veteran Francis X. Bushman (as the director of the entire project) and Philip Baird going along for the ride. It was written by DeWitt Bodeen from a story by producer Fred Gebhardt, and directed by David Bradley. (74 mins)

◁ Norman Krasna's knockabout farce *Who Was That Lady I Saw You With?* – a moderate Broadway success (208 performances) in the 1958 season – came to the screen with its title truncated to **Who Was That Lady?** It also lost quite a few laughs *en route* for director George Sidney who, with the blessing of producer-scenarist Krasna, knocked it around, until it emerged as less of a farce and more of a romantic comedy. It was all about an assistant chemistry professor (Tony Curtis, left) at Columbia (the university, not the studio) whose wife (Janet Leigh, centre) catches him kissing one of his pretty young students, and threatens to divorce him. In desperation Curtis consults a TV writer-friend (Dean Martin, right) for advice. Martin suggests that Curtis tell his wife that he's really an FBI undercover agent, and was only kissing the student-suspect-spy in the line of duty. Well, one thing leads to another and the plot (and all who sailed within it) spiralled out of control when Messrs Curtis and Martin found themselves involved with real FBI agents, real spies and real broads. All three leading players (under Sidney's guidance) did more than justice to the contrivance, and it certainly wasn't their fault if, in the end, the material simply was not funny enough. James Whitmore was prominently featured as a Federal agent and drew some of the biggest laughs without even opening his mouth. Also cast: John McIntire, Barbara Nichols, Larry Keating, Larry Storch, Simon Oakland and Joi Lansing. It was an Ansark-George Sidney Production. (116 mins)

▽ What happens when four members of a naval photographic unit, on leave in Japan after a Korean combat mission, misinterpret the civilized services rendered by four very proper geisha girls, formed the less-than-hilarious content of **Cry For Happy**. A romantic comedy whose fade-out, predictably, saw two of the men safely married to two of the girls, with the remaining couples well on the way, its familiar contrivances engendered an agonizing tedium as audiences impatiently waited for the inevitable happy ending. Glenn Ford (right), Donald O'Connor (left), James Shigeta and Chet Douglas were cast as the American sailors; Miiko Taka, Miyoshi Umeki, Michi Kobi and Tsuruko Kobayashi were the geishas. Director George Marshall did a stalwart job attempting to draw laughter from situations that didn't warrant any; it was scripted by Irving Brecher from a novel by George Campbell, and produced, in CinemaScope and Eastmancolor, by William Goetz. Dispiriting was the word for it all. (110 mins)

△ Deborah Walley (left) made her debut in **Gidget Goes Hawaiian**, replacing Sandra Dee as the cutesy-cutesy teenage heroine who in the inaugural offering (*Gidget*, 1959) lost her heart to handsome James Darren (right). Mr Darren featured prominently in the further adventures of Gidget – but this time in sun-drenched Hawaii, where he isn't the only male with designs on the appealing nymphet. Ruth Brooks Flippen's screenplay, based on characters created by Frederick Kohner, needed all the help it could get and benefited considerably from the adult presence of Carl Reiner, Peggy Cass, Eddie Foy Jr and Jeff Donnell – all of whom were far more appealing than any of the kids on display, including Miss Walley. It was produced by Jerry Bresler, breezily directed by Paul Wendkos, and filmed in Eastmancolor. Also featured: Vicki Trickett as Gidget's jealous rival, dancer Michael Callan, Joby Baker, Don Edmonds and Bart Patton. (101 mins)

◁ A volcanic island in the South Seas (though actually Hawaii) was the colourful and exotic setting of **The Devil At Four O'Clock**, a high-octane adventure in which a priest, accompanied by a trio of escaped convicts, heroically saves the lives of a number of children in a mountainside leper colony when the island is devastated by a volcano. A grim-faced Spencer Tracy (left) played the priest; while Frank Sinatra (right), Grégoire Aslan and Bernie Hamilton were the convicts. All four leading actors did wonders with the screenplay fashioned by Liam O'Brien from the novel by Max Catto. Barbara Luna was Sinatra's romantic *vis-à-vis*, with other roles in the physically impressive Fred Kohlmar–Mervyn LeRoy production going to Kerwin Mathews as the missionary about to replace Tracy on the island, Alexander Scourby as the governor of the island, Jean-Pierre Aumont as the pilot of the plane carrying the three convicts, and Martin Brandt as a doctor. LeRoy directed it, and it was filmed in Eastmancolor. (125 mins)

▷ **Everything's Ducky** was the asinine tale of a pair of simple-minded seamen – Mickey Rooney (left) and Buddy Hackett (right) – who befriend a duck. Not just any old duck, but a talking duck and the proud possessor of a formula vital to the successful launching of a naval satellite programme. Aimed at the mental age of backward ten-year-olds, it squandered the comic talents of its two leading men. John Fenton Murray and Benedict Freedman wrote it, Don Taylor directed, and it was produced by Red Doff with a cast that included Jackie Cooper (as a psychiatrist), vocalist Joanie Sommers, Roland Winters, Gene Blakely, Gordon Jones and Richard Deacon. And, as the voice of the duck, Walker Edmiston. (80 mins)

▷ A bloody hand-to-hand skirmish between the good guys and the Nazis, an enormous tidal wave, and scenes of heart-stopping tension as our heroes brace the elements whilst scaling a treacherous sea-facing cliff; these were just some of the exciting ingredients that went into **The Guns of Navarone**, an adventure-filled blockbuster, written by Carl Foreman from the best-seller by Alistair MacLean, and directed with cliff-hanging suspense by J. Lee Thompson, who filmed most of it on Rhodes, in the Aegean Sea. Basically the story of a handful of assorted Allied saboteurs whose brief it is to infiltrate an impregnable Nazi-held Greek island and blow up a pair of large, radar-controlled guns, it concentrated on action at the expense of characterization – which, given the excellence of the cast, was a pity. Still, on this occasion, the stunts spoke louder than Foreman's words; and if there wasn't any real acting to behold, the starry likes of Gregory Peck (right), as the leader of the undertaking, Anthony Quinn (left) as a Greek resistance fighter, and David Niven as a British dynamite expert – not to mention Stanley Baker, Anthony Quayle and James Darren - certainly did no harm to the box-office. The obligatory female interest was supplied, albeit perfunctorily, by Irene Papas and Gia Scala, and the cast also included James Robertson Justice, Richard Harris, Bryan Forbes, Alan Cuthbertson, Michael Trubshawe, Percy Herbert and Tutte Lemkow. An Open Road Production, it was filmed in CinemaScope and Eastmancolor. (157 mins)

△ The obligatory gimmick devised by producer-director William Castle for **Homicidal** occurred five minutes before the end of the film when a title announcing 'Fright Break' interrupted the action. What this meant was that the audience had 45 seconds to decide whether they wanted to leave the cinema and claim a refund, or see the film through to the end. The wise ones chose to be paid back in full. What they missed was a *Psycho*-inspired climax that raised more laughter than chills. The plot – about a nurse (Jean Arless) and the weird household she oversees – was written by Robb White, and the hapless cast included Glenn Corbett, Eugenie Leontovich, Patricia Breslin (illustrated), Alan Bunce and James Westerfield. (87 mins)

▷ John Chandler (left) starred as **Mad Dog Coll**, one of the most notorious underworld killers in the Twenties. As an exercise in screen brutality and gratuitous violence, it passed muster. But as an accurate biopic of a vicious gangster and an insight into the criminal mentality, producer Edward Schreiber's screenplay (based on material by Leo Lieberman) didn't touch first base. Loosely following Coll's career from an unhappy childhood to his violent death at the age of 23, the film attempted to recreate its blood-stained milieu as forcefully as Warner Bros. had done in the Thirties. Unfortunately, Chandler was no Cagney (nor Raft, nor Robinson, nor Bogart) and nothing seen nor heard in the film remotely resembled a social conscience. Here was blood-letting for the sake of a fast buck. Also cast: Neil Nephew as Coll's chief aide, Jerry Orbach, Joy Harmon, Telly Savalas, Kay Doubleday (right), Vincent Gardenia, Brooke Hayward (daughter of actress Margaret Sullavan and producer Leland Hayward) and Gene Hackman (in his first bit part). The director was Burt Balaban. (88 mins)

◁ The idea of a man whose face is permanently locked into a grin was hardly new to movies, having been brilliantly, and movingly, handled by director Paul Leni in *The Man Who Laughs* (Universal, 1928). William Castle picked up on it over thirty years later in **Mr Sardonicus**, the story of a wealthy baron (Guy Rolfe, illustrated), who, while searching for a lottery ticket, uncovers his father's corpse and finds himself unable to wipe off the shocked grimace which came over his face when the corpse moved. It was left to Ronald Lewis, a celebrated neurosurgeon and erstwhile lover of Rolfe's wife (Audrey Dalton) to find a solution to the problem. Not nearly as horrific as it could have been, it benefited from a full-blown performance from Oscar Homolka as Sardonicus's sinister servant, and a typical Castle gimmick in which audiences were asked to judge, shortly before the end of the film, whether or not they felt Sardonicus had suffered enough. It was scripted by Ray Russell from his own *Playboy* story and produced by Castle – who also directed. The cast included Vladimir Sokoloff, Erika Peters and Tina Woodward. (89 mins)

▽ Ron Randell (left) was **The Most Dangerous Man Alive**, and the reason for this was that, while on the run for a crime he did not commit, he wanders into a desert test site, becomes exposed to the rays of Cobalt element X and is promptly turned into steel, in which guise he sets about wreaking a horrible vengeance on the men who framed him. Directed by veteran Allan Dwan (a sad end to a distinguished career, and produced by Benedict Bogeaus, it also featured Debra Paget (right), Elain Stewart, Anthony Caruso, Gregg Palmer, Morris Ankrum and Tudor Owen. Their own steely determination not to be fazed by James Leicester and Philip Rock's screen lay (based on the story *The Steel Monster* by Rock and Michael Pate) was the only commendable thing in a virtually unreleasable disaster. (82 mins)

△ Composer Bernard Herrmann and special-effects wizard Ray Harryhausen were, once again, the stars of a Columbia fantasy. **Mysterious Island** was an entertaining though clumsily plotted re-working by scenarists John Prebble, Daniel Ullman and Crane Wilbur of Jules Verne's novel of the same name (already filmed by MGM in 1929 – and made again in 1941 and 1951). It told the tale of a group of Union soldiers, plus one Confederate deserter, who, after making a daring balloon escape from a Confederate jail, fetch up on an island inhabited by outsized bees and behemoth crabs. It was spirited balderdash that utilized the flesh-and-blood talents of Michael Craig, Joan Greenwood, Michael Callan, Gary Merrill, Herbert Lom (as Captain Nemo), Beth Rogan, Percy Herbert, Dan Jackson and Nigel Green. Cy Endfield directed with tongue well in cheek, and it was produced (in Technicolor) by Charles H. Schneer. (100 mins)

▽ Winner of the New York Drama Critics Award for the best play of 1959, **A Raisin In The Sun** was written by Lorraine Hansberry who, at the age of 29, became the first black woman ever to have a play produced on Broadway – where it ran for 530 performances. Producers David Susskind and Philip Rose had the good sense not to tamper with the basic structure of the play even if it meant emerging with little more than a filmed record of the original production. With the exception of a few scenes which scenarist Hansberry relocated in a neighbourhood bar, most of the 'action' took place in a small, sunless Chicago apartment in the City's all-black South Side. Director Daniel Petrie nevertheless found enough invention and movement in his camera set-ups to make a virtue (and plot point) of the claustrophobic setting. Hansberry's story was about a hardworking black family's attempts to move out of their stifling environment and into a more salubrious white area. The son of the family (Sidney Poitier, right) takes the $10,000 life-insurance money that his mother (Claudia McNeil, second right) receives on the death of her husband, and invests it unwisely in a liquor store. When his partner absconds with the proceeds, the family see their dreams of a better life disappearing, but decide to move to a new neighbourhood just the same. Though they have lost their fortune they still have their pride, and the film, like the play, ended in a burst of optimism. Seven members of the Broadway production were recruited to repeat their roles on celluloid, including Poitier, Ruby Dee (centre) as his hard-working wife, Diana Sands (left) as his sister, and, best of all, Claudia McNeil as Mrs Lena Younger, the family matriarch, who had all the best and wisest lines. Louis (later Lou) Gossett, Ivan Dixon and John Fiedler, as the one obligatory white man (and the least successful characterization), also made the transfer from stage to screen. (127 mins)

△ Ernie Kovacs' (left) last film, **Sail A Crooked Ship**, was an uneven comedy in which he played an incompetent burglar who becomes the captain of the barely seaworthy freighter he and his crooked crew boarded in order to escape from Boston to New York after a bank heist. Everything, including the film, went desperately awry, and there was nothing that its cast, including Robert Wagner (second right), and Dolores Hart (right), Frank Gorshin (back left), Carolyn Jones, Frankie Avalon, Jesse White (back right) and Harvey Lembeck, could do to salvage it. It was scripted by Ruth Brooks Flippen and Bruce Geller from a novel by Nathaniel Benchley, produced by Philip Barry Jr, and directed by Irving Brecher. (88 mins)

◁ An unashamed update of *Rock Around The Clock* (1956), **Twist Around The Clock** used a simple story of a rock 'n' roll manager's attempts to popularize The Twist as a springboard for an album-full of currently popular songs. John Cronin played the manager, though the names that young audiences everywhere paid good money to see and hear were Chubby Checker, Dion and the Belmonts (illustrated), Vicki Spencer, The Marcels, and Clay Cole – all of whom played themselves. Also cast: Mary Mitchell and Maura McGiveney. It was produced by Sam Katzman, written by James B. Gordon, and directed by Oscar Rudolph. (86 mins)

▷ The two in **Two Rode Together** were James Stewart (second left) and Richard Widmark (centre). Stewart, making his first appearance in a John Ford-directed movie, convincingly played a cynical, mercenary sheriff of a small town whose salary is boosted by a 10-per-cent bonus for condoning illicit activity among the locals. Widmark, an upstanding cavalry officer, approaches Stewart to help him retrieve from the Comanches a group of kidnapped children whose parents – after several years of unallayed anxiety – want them back. Stewart agrees on condition he is paid $500 for each hostage recovered. A basically disagreeable Western which found director Ford in a sour mood and actor Stewart deliberately playing against type, it was not without its *longueurs*, many of them supplied by scenarist Frank Nugent (working from Will Cook's novel *Comanche Captives*). Shirley Jones and Widmark were involved in a romantic sub-plot, with other parts in Stan Shpetner's Eastmancolor production going to Linda Cristal as a Mexican woman forced into squawdom by warrior Woody Strode (left), Andy Devine, John McIntire, Paul Birch, Willis Bouchey, Henry Brandon, Harry Carey Jr, Olive Carey, and veteran Mae Marsh as an elderly captive of the Comanches. (108 mins)

▽ A conventional crime melodrama with a strong revenge theme, **Underworld USA** was raised several notches above the norm thanks to direction by Samuel Fuller that made every shot count. A master at creating intensity and suspense by cunning camera placement, Fuller drew maximum impact from the story of a hate-infected ex-convict who as a child witnessed the brutal murder of his father, and who ever since has been consumed with the need to seek vengeance. Cliff Robertson (right) starred as the man with a mission, the successful completion of which was the motivating factor in the script Fuller fashioned from a series of *Saturday Evening Post* articles by Joseph F. Dineen. Representing the criminal element were Paul Dubov, Robert Emhardt, Richard Rust, Gerald Milton and Alan Gruener; while the distaff side included Dolores Dorn (left) as Robertson's romantic interest, and singer Beatrice Kay as a compassionate mother figure. Also featured were Larry Gates, David Kent, Tina Rome and Sally Mills. It was produced by Fuller for Globe Enterprises. (98 mins)

▷ Though director Edward Bernds's screenplay for **Valley Of The Dragons** (story by Donald Zimbalist) was based on Jules Verne's *Career Of A Comet*, the film it brought to mind was United Artists' 1940 romp *One Million BC/Cave Man* (GB: *Man And His Mate*), an altogether superior example of the genre. Aimed more at the young 'uns than their parents, the tale's heroes (Cesare Danova (left) and Sean McClory), a pair of 19th-century duellists, are wafted, in a wind storm, onto a passing comet, whence they are transported to a land populated by mastodons, plateosaurs and dinosaurs as well as an assortment of anti-social neanderthal cavemen. The story ends with Messrs Danova and McClory falling in love with girls from rival tribes and eventually bringing peace to the prehistoric community. Joan Staley (right), Danielle De Metz and Gil Perkins were also in it for producer Byron Roberts. (79 mins)

△ Set aboard the USS *Echo*, **The Wackiest Ship In The Army** was, for most of its running time, a light-hearted naval romp requisitioned, almost in toto, by Jack Lemmon (left). As the skipper of an obsolete vessel commissioned to transport an Australian coast-watcher (Chips Rafferty) through treacherous waters to a Japanese-occupied zone, Lemmon was in dazzling comic form. Irreverently scripted by Richard Murphy, from a screen story by Herbert Margolis and William Raynor (and a story by Herbert Carlson), and with direction (also by Murphy) that neatly combined farce and action, the end result was a bracingly enjoyable caper (filmed in Hawaii in CinemaScope and Eastmancolor) that also showed off a cast which included John Lund, Ricky Nelson as a young ensign, Tom Tully, Joby Baker, Patricia Driscoll, Richard Anderson, Alvy Moore, Joe Gallison, Walter Berlinger and Teru Shimada. The producer was Fred Kohlmar. Later a TV series. (99 mins)

1962

▽ Not since Mr Smith went to Washington, and took the lid off some shady goings-on among the political denizens of Capitol Hill, had skullduggery in the US government been so mercilessly (and often meretriciously) exposed as in Otto Preminger's lengthy screen version of Allen Drury's best-seller *Advise And Consent*. Revolving around the appointment of Henry Fonda to the powerful position of Secretary of State, Wendell Mayes's screenplay divided itself between those members of the senate who are for the appointment, and those who are against it. Standing for the former is Walter Pidgeon, while Charles Laughton (right), a Southerner, represents the latter. Also against Fonda's appointment is a bigoted, McCarthyesque villain (George Grizzard) who sets the film's most powerful sub-plot in motion by raking up the homosexual past of a freshman senator (Don Murray, left) whose vote in support of Fonda's nomination is vital to the success of the campaign. Even though, in the end, democracy triumphs over political corruption, the picture painted by Preminger and Hayes of big-time party politics was considered too 'sensational' and 'loaded' by many patriotic Americans (and critics); and although the performances were admired, the content was not. Completing the cast were Gene Tierney (after a long absence from the screen) as a Washington hostess, Peter Lawford as a playboy senator, Franchot Tone as the ailing President as well as Inga Swensen, Lew Ayres, Burgess Meredith, and Paul Ford. It was filmed in black-and-white and Panavision. (140 mins)

△ Anthony Quinn (left) starred in and as **Barabbas**, the thief-cum-murderer who was released from prison and replaced – in jail and on the cross – by Jesus Christ. Christopher Fry's screenplay, based on a novel by Pär Lagerkvist, concentrated on Barabbas's troublesome conscience and his desire to discover something about Christ's faith. It was a lengthy (and futile) process, during which Barabbas seeks out Christ's disciples, suffers the death (by stoning) of Rachel (Silvana Mangano), the woman he loves, and is arrested and sentenced to a life of torment in Sicily's sulphur mines where he lingers until a mine collapses. Together with Sahak (Vittorio Gassman, right), the only other survivor of the mine disaster, Barabbas is transferred to gladiator school. In the end he too is crucified – for having helped set fire to Rome. Fry's lengthy screenplay was underpinned by several spectacular set pieces – including the mine collapse and the burning of Rome. And although it moved fluently from plot point to plot point, it was undercut by too many characterizations that were either indifferent (such as Mangano's Rachel) or caricatures (such as Jack Palance's sadistic gladiator). Arthur Kennedy played Pilate, Harry Andrews was St Peter, Michael Gwynn was Lazarus, and Roy Mangano (way down on the cast list) was Jesus Christ. Other roles under Richard Fleischer's somewhat stolid direction went to Katy Jurado, Valentina Cortese, Ernest Borgnine and Laurence Payne. It was produced by Dino De Laurentiis and filmed, in Italy, in Technicolor and Technirama 70. (144 mins)

△ Though billed as a 'guest star', Polly Bergen (right) appeared in and as **Belle Sommers**, a singer who, in the course of Richard Alan Simmons's wretched screenplay, attempts to divest herself of her gangster-syndicate past and make it as a nightclub performer. David Janssen (left) played her press agent, with other parts in this low-budget drama going to Carroll O'Connor and Joan Staley. The film ran barely over an hour – and the best thing in it was Bergen's singing of Harold Arlen's beautiful 'I Had Myself A True Love'. For the rest, Belle Sommers was definitely not here to stay. Elliot Silverstein directed and William Sackheim produced. (62 mins)

△ The problem faced by producer Sam Katzman with **Don't Knock The Twist** was how to develop a plot without detracting from the main purpose of the undertaking – which was to feature as many songs as was possible without giving audiences the impression they were attending a filmed rock concert. The solution was found by scenarist James B. Gordon, who invented a story about a TV special involving The Twist (and some nonsense about a summer camp for orphans) that was all but invisible. Chubby Checker (left), Vic Dana, Linda Scott (second right), The Carroll Brothers and the Dovells featured as themselves, with other parts under Oscar Rudolph's unobtrusive direction going to Gene Chandler (second left), Lang Jeffries (right), Mari Blanchard, and Georgine Darcy. (86 mins)

▷ A Western, but translated to the South African veldt circa 1862, **The Hellions** starred Richard Todd (left) as an upstanding police sergeant in the Transvaal whose unenviable job it was to apprehend the murderous 'hellion' Luke Billings (Lionel Jeffries, 3rd left) and his four thuggish sons. How he managed to eliminate the Billings gang, with the eventual help of some local townsfolk, starting with storekeeper Jamie Uys, formed the violent content of the over-emphasized screenplay which Harold Swanton, Patrick Kirwan and Harold Huth fashioned from a story by Swanton. Directed (by Ken Annakin) and performed in italics throughout, it finished up as a parody of a tired genre. Anne Aubrey was the female lead, with other roles in this Irving Allen-Jamie Uys-Harold Huth production going to Marty Wild, James Booth, Al Mulock, Colin Blakely, Bill Brewer, Ronald Fraser and Zena Walker. It was photographed in Technirama. (80 mins)

▽ Peter Shaffer's West End and Broadway success, **Five Finger Exercise**, was a sensitive and powerful domestic drama in which the corrosive effects of an insensitive father and an intellectual poseur of a mother take on tragic consequences for their offspring, and for the young German tutor lodging with them. Relocated from England to California, palpably miscast, and with its original running time greatly reduced, producer Frederick Brisson's inept screen version was a travesty of Shaffer's fine first play. The film was unbalanced by an out-of-character performance from Rosalind Russell (right) as the mother – and poor-to-indifferent ones from Jack Hawkins as her husband, Richard Beymer as her 'mother's boy' son, Annette Gorman as her troubled daughter, and Maximilian Schell (left) as the confused German tutor. It was clumsily scripted by Frances Goodrich and Albert Hackett, clodhoppingly directed by Daniel Mann, and proved to be a disaster that, deservedly, sank without trace. (108 mins)

◁ Not satisfied with a fairly straightforward 'war of attrition' plot – in which a pretty bank clerk is forced to embezzle $100,000 in order to stay alive – director Blake Edwards (who also produced) gussied up **Experiment In Terror** (GB: **The Grip Of Fear**) with far too many arty, self-conscious, cutely angled shots for his picture's good. The end result was less an experiment in terror than an experiment in lily-gilding. Lee Remick was cast as the put-upon bank clerk, Stefanie Powers was her sister (also threatened) and, topping the cast, Glenn Ford (illustrated) was the reassuring FBI agent to whom she goes for protection. All three leading players delivered the goods – despite Edwards's directorial pyrotechnics. The supporting cast also included Roy Poole, Ned Glass, Patricia Huston, Ross Martin, Anita Loo, Al Avalon and Sidney Miller. It was written by Mildred and Gordon Gordon from their novel *Operation Terror*, and photographed mainly on location in San Francisco, the story's setting. (123 mins)

△ Little more than a TV soap opera, **The Interns** followed the lives and loves of four medical students. Cliff Robertson (centre left) falls for beautiful, pregnant and unwed model Suzy Parker, sacrificing his career to secure (unsuccessfully) an abortion for her. James MacArthur, who has the hots for young nurse Stefanie Powers, becomes an obstetrician, then turns Robertson in to the authorities. Michael Callan is having affairs with socialite Anne Helm as well as nurse Katharine Bard, while Nick Adams is in love with a dying patient. Walter Newman and director David Swift's trashy screenplay, from the best-seller by Richard Frede, furnished a sequel (*The New Interns*, 1964) and a TV series, and also gave employment to Haya Harareet (centre right), Buddy Ebsen, Telly Savalas, Kay Stevens and Connie Gilchrist. Robert Cohn produced. (130 mins)

△ Though **Lawrence Of Arabia** was a small, shy and physically unprepossessing man, Peter O'Toole (right), who played him in Sam Spiegel and David Lean's epic desert adventure, was tall, dashing and every inch the traditional Hollywood matinee idol. O'Toole was also an extremely fine actor at that point in his promising career, and under director Lean's guidance, he delivered a charismatic performance. If there was something unspoken, mysterious and unexplained about Lawrence the philosopher, the activities of Lawrence the man of action were brought graphically and stirringly to life in Robert Bolt's screenplay (based on Lawrence's own *The Seven Pillars Of Wisdom*, adapted by Bolt and an uncredited Michael Wilson) and in David Lean's thrilling handling of the narrative. Commencing with Lawrence's death in a motorcycle accident along an English country lane in May 1935, and flashing back to British Headquarters in the Cairo of World War I, the film followed its hero's military career (with emphasis on the horrific battles he fought) from the unification of warring Arab tribes (in order to promote a successful Arab rebellion against the Turks) to the sad dissolution, years later, of the Arab Council in Damascus. As effective as Lean's epic handling of the action sequences were the film's more intimate episodes which yielded moments of intense drama – none more powerful than Lawrence's capture by the Turks and his eventual rape by the brutal Turkish Bey (José Ferrer). The film's visual splendour (it was photographed by F.A. Young in Super Panavision 70 and Technicolor) was complemented by some superb individual performances – notably Alec Guinness's Prince Feisal, Anthony Quinn's Auda Abu Tayi (left), Omar Sharif's Sherif Ali Ibn El Kharish, Jack Hawkins's General Allenby, Anthony Quayle's Colonel Harry Brighton, Claude Raines's Mr Dryden, Donald Wolfit's General Murray, and Arthur Kennedy's Jackson Bentley, a character based on journalist and commentator Lowell Thomas. Also in the cast were Howard Marion Crawford, Kenneth Fortescue, Norman Rossington and Zia Mohyeddin. A quarter of a century later, *Lawrence Of Arabia* (made at the vast cost of $13 million – easily Columbia's most expensive film till then) remains one of the finest, most intelligent and consistently stimulating adventure epics of all time. [After its initial showing, the film was cut to 202 mins and then to 187 mins to satisfy exhibitors. Archivist-producer Robert A. Harris embarked on the daunting job of reconstruction in 1986, and the restored original received a Gala Premiere at the Cannes Film Festival in 1989.] (222 mins)

△ Jack Lemmon (right) teamed up with Kim Novak (left) and director Richard Quine again in **The Notorious Landlady**, a diverting caper in which he played an American diplomat who rents a room from landlady Novak, while under surveillance by Scotland Yard for the suspected murder of her husband. Novak and Lemmon begin a romance of sorts when the missing husband (Maxwell Reed) unexpectedly surfaces, only to be shot (in self-defence) by his wife. At this point the screenplay (which Larry Gelbart and Blake Edwards wrote from a short story by Margery Sharp) moved into top gear as Novak faces a murder trial. A climactic chase sequence brought the agreeable mayhem to a satisfactory conclusion. As usual it was left to Lemmon to milk most of the laughs – and, as usual, he did – most engagingly. Quine's direction drew attention-getting performances from third-billed Fred Astaire as Lemmon's employer, and from Estelle Winwood, Lionel Jeffries, Philippa Bevans and Henry Daniell. The producer was Fred Kohlmar. (127 mins)

▽ Yankee superstars Mickey Mantle (right) and Roger Maris (second right) made token appearances in **Safe At Home**, a film for junior audiences about a young braggart (Bryan Russell, second left) who claims that he and his father are intimate buddies with Messrs Mantle and Maris, and then has to make good his boast. Unashamedly sentimental, it was scripted by Robert Dillon from a story by Tom Naud and Steve Ritch, directed by Walter Doniger with a treacly touch, produced by Naud, and featured William Frawley (left) as a lovable albeit irascible coach, Patricia Barry and Don Collier, as well as moppets Flip Mark, Scott Lane and Chris Hughes. (84 mins)

▽ Rod Serling's highly acclaimed TV play **Requiem For A Heavyweight** (GB: **Blood Money**) moved from the small screen to the big screen with Anthony Quinn (centre) top-starred in the pivotal role of Mountain Rivera, an inarticulate boxer – complete with broken nose and cauliflower ears – who, after 111 wins in the ring, is little more than a punched-out wreck with nothing to show for his life. Jackie Gleason (right) played the fighter's ruthless manager who, despite his devotion to the pug, cannot help exploiting him and thus robbing him of his dignity. Mickey Rooney (left) was cast as Quinn's sympathetic, innately sad trainer, and Julie Harris was an employment counsellor who determines to meet the challenge of finding Quinn a job in the real world. All four performances were excellent (with Rooney in top form in a card-playing scene) and contributed substantially to the overall impact of Serling's grittily written, if occasionally clumsily plotted, exposé of the sleazy underbelly of professional boxing. Though not as good as *Body And Soul* (United Artists, 1947) or *The Harder They Fall* (1956), the film was well directed by Ralph Nelson, here making his feature-film debut. It was produced by David Susskind, and featured, in smaller roles, Stan Adams, Madame Spivy and Herbie Faye, together with Cassius Clay (aka Muhammad Ali), Jack Dempsey and Paolo Rossi. (85 mins)

▷ Screen slapstick was alive and kicking in **The Three Stooges In Orbit**, a dose of unbridled finger-poking and head-banging as Moe (centre), Larry (left) and Curly Joe (right) locked antlers with Martian agents and an inventor for possession of a piece of military apparatus with the combined functions of a sub, a tank and a rocket. It was aimed at 'youthful' audiences – and found its mark. Carol Christensen, Emil Sitka, George N. Neise, Nestor Paiva and Norman Leavitt were also caught up in the nonsense (written by Elwood Ullman from a story by producer Norman Maurer), and it was directed by Edward Bernds. (87 mins)

▷ In **The Three Stooges Meet Hercules**, the next of the wacky trio's outings, Moe Howard (right), Larry Fine (front) and Joe De Rita (back) take a time-machine trip to Ithaca, Greece in 961 BC, where, dressed in obligatory sandals and togas, they not only meet Hercules (Samson Burke, left), but a pair of Siamese-twin cyclops (Mike and Marlin McKeever). Producer Norman Maurer, mindful of the audience to whom he was catering, made sure Elwood Ullman's screenplay was full of the usual slapstick shtick to which the hapless trio were prone; and it was directed by Edward Bernds. Also in the cast were: Vicki Trickett, Quinn Redeker, George N. Neise and Emil Sitka. (89 mins)

▽ A ship-board romance between twister Joey Dee (right) and Jeri Lynne Fraser (centre) provided the puny narrative for **Two Tickets To Paris**, an appalling showcase for the limited talents of Dee and The Starliters. Dee performed 7 of the 14 featured numbers. Kay Medford (left) was cast as a chaperone, Gary Crosby was along for the ride (and made the occasional pass at Miss Fraser); so were Charles Nelson Reilly, Lisa James, Richard Dickens and Nina Page. Harry Romm produced, Hal Hackady wrote it, and it was directed by Greg Garrison. (78 mins)

▽ Photographed in 'Fantascope', **The Underwater City** was a soggy sci-fi melodrama about man's first attempt to establish a suburban paradise on the ocean floor. There was little more to Owen Harris's mouldy screenplay than that, and even less to the waterlogged performances of William Lundigan (right), Julie Adams (left), Roy Roberts, Carl Benton Reid, Chet Douglas, Paul Dubov and Karen Norris. Alex Gordon produced, Frank McDonald directed, and, although filmed in Eastmancolor, it was released in black and white. (78 mins)

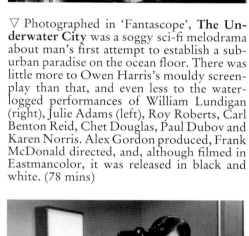

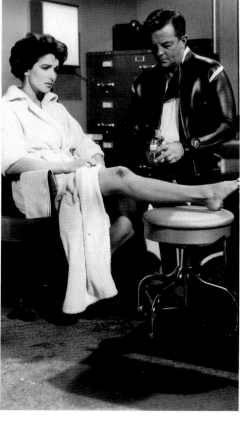

△ Why would five overprivileged teenagers, without reason or motivation, brutally beat up a rocket engineer, and almost leave him for dead? That was the question asked by scenarists Bernard C. Schoenfeld and Robert Presnell Jr (working from Leigh Brackett's novel *The Tiger Among Us*) in **13 West Street**, an intriguing little melodrama. Alas, no answer was forthcoming. Alan Ladd (centre) starred as the angry victim, and Rod Steiger was the police officer in charge of the case. When Steiger fails to bring the young men to justice, Ladd sets out to finish off the job himself, at which point the film turned into a one-man crusade and the working out of an obsession. Though Ladd is beaten up a second time, and his wife (Dolores Dorn) threatened, he continues his pursuit of his assailants until he is successful. Villain of the piece turns out to be Michael Callan, the group's paranoid leader, whom Ladd, in a climactic confrontation, just stops short of killing. As the screenplay failed to provide a satisfactory sociological explanation for Callan's anti-social behaviour, this Ladd Enterprise Production (producer William Bloom) emerged, in the end, as little more than a thriller whose aim was to exploit the currently popular youth market with yet one more violent excursion into teenage delinquency. Ladd, Steiger and Callan gave three finely delineated, strikingly contrasted performances, and there was good work, too, from Kenneth MacKenna, Margaret Hayes, Stanley Adams, Chris Robinson and Jeanne Cooper. Philip Leacock directed. Pity there was so little point to it. (80 mins)

▷ Just as producer Charles K. Feldman didn't quite have the courage of Tennessee Williams's convictions in the screen version of *A Streetcar Named Desire* (Warner Bros. 1951) and eliminated all references to homosexuality, so, in **Walk On The Wild Side** he diluted the material's twin themes of prostitution and lesbianism. What survived from Nelson Algren's novel (screenplay by John Fante and Edmund Morris) was the story of a tart with a heart of gold (or ice, as she was played by the glacial Capucine, right), rescued from a New Orleans 'doll's house' – and from its over-affectionate madame (Barbara Stanwyck) – by a Texas drifter (Laurence Harvey, left). It was as 'adult' as the funny papers, and just as convincing. Production values included terrific opening credits that were designed by Saul Bass and set to a throbbing background score by Elmer Bernstein; a title song by Bernstein and Mack David; and a supporting cast that featured Jane Fonda, Anne Baxter, Joanna Moore, Richard Rust and Karl Swenson. Edward Dmytryk directed. (114 mins)

△ Set in 1943, against a backdrop of English B-17 bombing raids on Germany, **The War Lover** was a psychological action-drama that focused on pilot Steve McQueen (right), whose aggressive love of war and all its masculine accoutrements was little more than a cover-up for a psychopathic inability to form normal, lasting relationships with the opposite sex. As scripted by Howard Koch from the novel by John Hersey, the eponymous hero remained stubbornly undefined and undelineated and emerged as a cantankerous pain in the neck who thinks nothing of stealing co-pilot Robert Wagner's (left) girlfriend (Shirley Anne Field). The aerial sequences and bombing raids were far more convincing than the private dramas on hand, and were the sole sources of excitement in an otherwise ponderous effort. Gary Cockrell, Michael Crawford and Jerry Stovin offered valuable support; it was produced by Arthur Hornblow Jr, and the director was Philip Leacock. (105 mins)

▷ A routine Western from producer Sam Katzman, **The Wild Westerners**, set in Montana in 1864, told of the hardships encountered by US marshals as they attempt to transport shipments of gold to the East in order to help the Unionists. James Philbrook starred as Marshal Jim McDowell, and, between coping with warring Red Indians and troublesome, gold-hungry outlaws, he has an involvement with Nancy Kovack. However, after tricking him into marriage, she soon proves herself worthy of his respect and his affection. Guy Mitchell (illustrated) was cast as the heavy (and all but stroked a black moustache to convey villainy), Duane Eddy was equally unsubtle as a deranged deputy marshal, with other roles under Oscar Rudolph's direction going to Hugh Sanders, Elizabeth MacRae, Marshall Reed, Nestor Paiva and Harry Lauter. It was written by Gerald Drayson Adams, and photographed in Eastmancolor. (70 mins)

△ Producer-director William Castle moved out of the realms of horror and into fantasy farce with **Zotz!** whose level of fun was aimed squarely at the 10-15 age group. All about an ancient coin which enables its owner to inflict pain at the pointing of an index finger, reduce movement to slow-motion at the mere mention of the word 'zotz', or eliminate chosen victims by indulging in a combination of both, it starred TV-recruit Tom Poston (right) as an absent-minded professor in possession of the magic coin. Ray Russell's screenplay, based on a novel by Walter Karig, put Poston through several adventures – two of which involved the Pentagon and a group of Communist agents. Castle's direction made few demands on a cast that included Julia Meade, Jim Backus, Fred Clark, Mike Nazurki (left), and veterans Cecil Kellaway and Margaret Dumont. (85 mins)

△ The Cardinal, produced and directed by Otto Preminger and scripted by Robert Dozier from the 1950 novel by Henry Morton Robinson, followed the trials, tribulations and faith-testing of a man of God (Tom Tryon, left) who, over a 22-year period, rises from a lowly curate in Boston to the preeminence of a Carinal of the Catholic Church. Georgia racists, Austrian Nazis and a recalcitrant sister (Carol Lynley, right) who has a jewish fiancé (John Saxon) are just some of the problems he has to face following his ordination in 1917. With the help of an elderly Cardinal (John Huston) in Boston and a tired old priest (Burgess Meredith) who reveal to him the true meaning of faith and spirituality, Tryon finally passes muster. However, it was heavy going – for him and for the paying customers. The physical aspects of Preminger's elaborate production, set in Rome, Vienna and Boston, were far more impressive than the verbal ones. Apart from Huston and Meredith, who at least provided the narrative with a core of authenticity, the supporting performances were resolutely perfunctory – a few notable exceptions being Raf Vallone as a benevolent Roman prelate, Josef Meinrad as Cardinal Innitzer, and Ossie Davis as a black Georgia priest and victim of the Ku Klux Klan. It was photographed in Technicolor. (175 mins)

△ Charlton Heston (right) starred in **Diamond Head**, a steamy melodrama set in Hawaii, in which he played a powerfully wealthy pineapple plantation landowner and a bigoted bully who, despite the fact that he himself has a Chinese mistress (France Nuyen), flatly refuses to allow his young sister (Yvette Mimieux, centre) to marry a good-looking, full-blooded Hawaiian (James Darren). When Heston accidentally stabs Darren to death, Miss Mimieux, undaunted, moves on to Darren's equally attractive half-brother (George Chakiris, left). The screenplay Marguerite Roberts fashioned from Peter Gilman's novel begat futher complications when Heston's mistress becomes pregnant – even though she coveniently dies in childbirth. Jerry Bresler's production – shot in Hawaii, in Panavision and Eastmancolor – looked far better than it sounded. If nothing else, it did bring Aline MacMahon back to the screen in the featured role of Darren's Hawaiian mother. Also in the cast were: Elizabeth Allen, Vaughn Taylor, Marc Marno, Philip Ahn and Harold Fong. The sluggish direction was by Guy Green. (107 mins)

△ Inspired by the brouhaha caused when Elvis Presley was drafted into the US Army, composers Charles Strouse and Lee Adams, working with book-writer Michael Stewart, surfaced with a Broadway sleeper called Bye Bye Birdie that took New York by storm and ran a healthy 603 performances. Three years later it was purchased by producer Fred Kohlmar for the screen, and, with its title, most of its songs, and its story more or less intact, emerged as the best musical of the year – not that it had much competition. Presley became Conrad Birdie (Jesse Pearson), a rock singer whose imminent induction into the army isn't just a blow for his millions of fans, but is especially bad news to songwriter Albert Peterson (Dick Van Dyke) who has written the title song for Birdie's latest movie. If Birdie is drafted, the movie won't get made, and Albert will lose out on the royalties, a situation that will prevent him from turning his back on his possessive mother (Maureen Stapleton) in order to marry his secretary, Rose (Janet Leigh). It's Rose, though, who comes up with a solution to the pressing problem: she persuades Albert to write a song for Birdie called 'One More Kiss', which he does, and which is duly performed by a fan of Birdie's called Kim AcAfee (Ann-Margret, left) on the Ed Sullivan Show. Plot-wise the show was no world-beater, but Irving Brecher's bouncy screenplay provided a solid-enough springboard for its handful of catchy tunes; and, with Onna White's choreography constantly keeping the score on the move, lovers of the genre found no cause for complaint. Ann-Margret's was the standout performance, but there was solid support from Bobby Rydell (right), Paul Lynde, Mary LaRoche, Michael Evans and Robert Paige. It was filmed in Panavision and Technicolor, and directed by veteran George Sidney. (120 mins)

▽ The third and feeblest of the Gidget series starred Cindy Carol (left) as the titular heroine, and, in company with her long-standing boyfriend James Darren (right), it took her to Italy for **Gidget Goes To Rome** in which she and Darren change partners in the Eternal City before reuniting for the final fade. In what basically appeared to be an excuse for some pretty travelogue shots of Rome, Ruth Brooks Flippen and Katherine and Dale Eunson's screenplay disappeared up its own slender narrative, leaving the caracters created by Frederick Kohner with nothing to do and even less to say. Others involved in this waste of Eastmancolor stock were Jessie Royce Landis, Cesare Danova, Danielle de Metz, Joby Baker, Trudi Ames, Jeff Donnell, and Lisa Gastoni. Jerry Bresler produced, and it was directed by Paul Wendkos. (103 mins)

△ Billy Wilder's The Apartment (United Artists 1959) found Jack Lemmon loaning his apartment to numerous executives in his office to use for illicit sexual assignations. In the inferior **Under the Yum-Yum Tree**, based on Lawrence Roman's hit Broadway play, Lemmon rents apartments to attractive single women, all of whom he views as potential sexual conquests for himself. Unaware that pretty Carol Lynley's boyfriend (Dean Jones) has moved in with her in order that they might test their compatibility, Lemmon (right) makes a play for her with, alas, less than hilarious consequences. As a sheep in wolf's clothing Lemmon, playing against type, made a convincing cad, but there was no sparkle in the screenplay devised by Roman and David Swift (who also directed) and the film failed to match the success of the play. Edie Adams co-stared as Lynley's marriage counsellor aunt, with Robert Lansing as a professor and her lover, while Imogen Coca and Paul Lynde played a pair of custodians. Frederick Brisson produced. (110 mins.)

△ Three million dollars were spent on **Jason And The Argonauts**, mainly on Ray Harryhausen's Dynamation 90 special effects – and it was not difficult to see where the money went. In this lively and imaginative re-telling of the Greek myth wherein intrepid Jason, aboard the Argos, braves all manner of dangers in his undivided quest for the Golden Fleece, Harryhausen was called on to create an animated version of Talos, the bronze god; bat-winged Harpies; a menacing seven-headed Hydra; an assorted selection of belligerent skeletons – not to mention the Argos itself, as well as the dangerous rock-infested route it takes in search of the mythical fleece. Todd Armstrong (left) was cast as the fearless

Jason, and Nancy Kovack was Medea. Miss Kovack was certainly pretty to look at, and even coped well with the dialogue Jan Read and Beverly Cross wrote for her. But to boast – as a studio hand-out unblushingly did – that her performance followed in the footsteps of Maria Callas, a renowned operatic Medea, was tantamount to entering the fantasy realms in which the film was set! Gary Raymond, Laurence Naismith, Niall McGinnis, Michael Gwynn, Douglas Wilmer, Jack Gwillim, Honor Blackman and Andrew Faulds comprised the predominantly British supporting cast. It was produced (in Technicolor) by Charles H. Schneer, and directed by Don Chaffey. (104 mins)

▽ Producer-director William Castle came a cropper with **13 Frightened Girls**, an unmitigated disaster about a cutesy-cutesy teenage girl (Kathy Dunn, left) who, after falling for a member of the Counter Intelligence Agency (Murray Hamilton), helps him uncover the activities of an international spy ring, and provides him with information concerning a 'Red' agent. Robert Dillon's jerry-built scenario (story by Otis Guernsey Jr) had a low credibility threshold, and ceased to sustain interest shortly after the completion of the credit titles. Joyce Taylor, Hugh Marlowe, Khigh Dhiegh, Lynne Sue Moon, Charlie Briggs and Norma Varden were also featured, and it was filmed in Eastmancolor. (89 mins)

▽ Danny Kaye's ability to move mountains and indifferent properties deserted him in **The Man From The Diners' Club**, a slapstick commercial for that plastic institution in which Kaye (illustrated) played a timid, browbeaten employee whose function it is to vet suitable candidates for acceptance to its ranks. The screenplay by William Peter Blatty (of *Exorcist* fame), from a story by Blatty and John Fenton Murray, hits its improbable stride when Kaye agrees to the application of a bankrupt mobster (Telly Savalas), presently on bail awaiting trial for tax evasion. The fact that both Kaye and Savalas have left feet an inch longer than their right proves a crucial plot point in the climactic winding up of the frenetic narrative. A sequence in which Kaye finds himself pretending to be a masseur in a gym, and another in which he takes on a group of beatnik intellectuals, offered smatterings of vintage Kaye – but, for the rest, it was an effortful contrivance that strained for laughs and wasted the considerable talents of its versatile star. Savalas made a meal of the heavy, and there was passable support from Everett Sloane, Martha Hyer, Cara Williams, Howard Caine, Kay Stevens, George Kennedy, Jay Novello and, as a beatnik, Harry Dean Stanton. It was directed by Frank Tashlin with the emphasis on sight gags, and produced by Bill Bloom. (96 mins)

△ Carl Foreman's mocking anti-war film **The Victors** emerged as a kaleidoscopic mish-mash which mingled poor taste with gross sentimentality as it followed the exploits of a squad of US riflemen from Sicily through the invasion of France to war's end. If its main theme was that war is hell and nobody wins, it was equally obsessed with the romantic encounters snatched by its protagonists – much of the battle seemingly fought in bed, and between the sexes. Thus GI Vincent Edwards finds comfort in the arms of Rosanna Schiaffino, even though both love their respective spouses. Sergeant Eli Wallach grabs a *soupçon* of romance with frightened French widow Jeanne Moreau in a bombed-out villa, while all-American boy George Hamilton (left) becomes involved with Belgian violinist Romy Schneider (second left) only to discover that she's a prostitute (and schizophrenic, to boot). Finally, Corporal George Peppard (right) has

an affair with a black-marketeer (Melina Mercouri). And just to spice things up there's a male prostitute (Joel Flateau) who offers his services to the uninterested Messrs Peppard and Hamilton. But the most memorable scene in the film was the execution, by firing squad and on a snowy Christmas Eve, of a deserter. Staged to the ironic accompaniment of Frank Sinatra singing 'Have Yourself A Merry Little Christmas', then segueing into 'Hark The Herald Angels Sing', it demonstrated the film's theme to gruesome, chilling effect. Written, produced and directed (in Panavision) by Foreman (from the book *The Human Kind* by Alexander Baron), *The Victors* suffered from an indifferent screenplay, top-heavy direction, and uninteresting performances. Also cast: Elke Sommer, James Mitchum, Tutte Lemkow, Maurice Ronet, Senta Berger, Michael Callan (second right), Peter Fonda, Mervyn Johns and Albert Finney. (172 mins)

▽ Set some 20 years after the Spanish Civil War, **Behold A Pale Horse**, an arty, allegorical drama that marked the return (after a four-year absence), of producer-director Fred Zinnemann, told of a bitter vendetta between an elderly Loyalist hero (Gregory Peck, centre), now a part-time bandit living in reduced circumstances in the French city of Pau, and a crude and arrogant captain of the Civil Guard (Anthony Quinn, left) who lives across the border in San Martin. Though geographically separated, the two men continue to wage a private war against each other which ends when Peck, despite being warned, falls for a trap set by his deadly adversary. Based on a novel by Emeric Pressburger called *Killing A Mouse On Sunday* and scripted by J.P. Miller, the film failed to ignite, largely as a result of Zinnemann's inability to create a genuine dramatic conflict between his antagonists or to maintain tension or interest in the narrative. He and his scenarist simply failed to make audiences care, and this proved fatal. Though Peck was somewhat miscast as a Spaniard, Quinn was in fine form; so was Omar Sharif (right) as a young priest with divided loyalties, and Raymond Pellegrin as the traitor who lures Peck into the fateful trap set by Quinn. In smaller roles there was good work, too, from Paolo Stoppa, Mildred Dunnock, Daniela Rocca, Christian Marquand and Rosalie Crutchley. (119 mins)

▽ The not-so-hypothetical prospect of nuclear annihilation provided the satiric content of Stanley Kubrick's jet-black comedy **Dr Strangelove, Or: How I Learned To Stop Worrying And Love The Bomb.** The questions asked by Kubrick, Terry Southern and Peter George in their screenplay (based on George's novel *Red Alert*) was what would happen if an insane Communist-hating US Army General, fearful that the 'Reds' are fluoridating our drinking water in order to pollute our bodily fluids, initiated a B-52 attack on the Soviet Union? And what would happen if the General commited suicide before deciphering the code that could recall the bombers? Furthermore, what would happen if the Russians themselves had their own doomsday device – a weapon with the power to eliminate the entire planet? In an attempt to arrive at the inevitable answers, Kubrick created a frighteningly comic gallery of grotesque incompetents whose titanic ineptitude tickled the funny bone while, at the same time, tingling the spine and raising the hair on the back of one's neck. A monu-mental sick joke whose tone was best illustrated by having Vera Lynn sing 'We'll Meet Again, Don't Know Where, Don't Know When . . .' as the bomb finally drops on Russia, it was (and remains) the most chilling anti-nuclear statement ever made. In his portrayal of the bald President Muffley of the USA, his technical expert Dr Strangelove and the sensible British Officer Group Captain Lionel Mandrake, Peter Sellers (illustrated) contributed three more brilliant characterizations to his collection. George C. Scott was scarifying as Air Force General Buck Turgidson, while Sterling Hayden – as the lunatic Jack D. Ripper whose obsession brings the world to an end – found just the right balance between caricature and credibility. Slim Pickens played Major 'King' Kong, and provided the film with its most memorable image when, in the climactic final moments, he hurtles to his destruction astride the atomic bomb. Also cast: Keenan Wynn, Peter Bull, Tracy Reed, James Earl Jones, Jack Creley, Shane Rimmer, Frank Berry and Glenn Beck. (93 mins)

▽ India in the 1880s provided the setting for **East Of Sudan**, a gung-ho adventure (using stock footage from Alexander Korda's 1939 *The Four Feathers*) which recounted the efforts of the British (led by General Gordon) to stop the Sudanese Moslems from slave trading. Anthony Quayle (centre) starred as an army trooper, Derek Fowlds (left) was his greenhorn lieutenant, while Sylvia Syms (right, as a governess) and Jenny Agutter (as her charge) found themselves being led to Khartoum in the company of the two men after the sacking of Batash. Danger in the form of wild animals, hostile terrain and Moslems kept scenarist Jud Kinberg's screenplay alive (only just), though the focal point of the yarn centred around the increasingly hostile relationship between Quayle and Fowlds. It was directed by Nathan Juran, produced by Charles H. Schneer in Techniscope and Technicolor, and featured Johnny Sekka, Harold Coyne, Desmond Davis and Derek Blomfield. (85 mins)

▷ Covering almost precisely the same territory as *Dr Strangelove, Or: How I Learned To Stop Worrying And Love The Bomb*, **Fail Safe** was another anti-nuclear statement – but without the laughs. And, unlike the Kubrick film, it was the vulnerability of machines rather than the lunacy of men that set the plot in motion. The machine in question was a sophisticated mechanism housed in the Omaha Headquarters of the Strategic Air Command. It malfunctions and sends out a message to a flight of loaded bombers in Alaska to head for Moscow where they are to discharge their deadly cargo. The balance of the screenplay, fashioned by Walter Bernstein from the novel by Eugene Burdick and Harvey Wheeler, dealt with the frenzied efforts of all concerned – including the President of the USA – to prevent a global holocaust. Though an element of science-fiction was apparent in director Sidney Lumet's suspenseful handling of the material, there was no denying the serious intention behind the enterprise, or the wholehearted dedication to the project by a cast that included Henry Fonda (as the President), Dan O'Herlihy (left), Walter Matthau (right), Frank Overton, Edward Binns, Fritz Weaver, Larry Hagman, William Hansen, Russell Collins and Russell Hardie. The producer was Max E. Youngstein. Because of the striking similarity between *Fail Safe* and *Dr Strangelove*, and the fact that the latter was released several months earlier, Lumet's film, despite (or because of?) the earnestness of its approach, failed to find the audience it deserved. (112 mins)

▽ A wacky comedy, and a bespoke vehicle for the zany talents of Jack Lemmon (right), **Good Neighbor Sam**, despite loose threads and some decidedly lenient plotting, came up trumps. All about a happily married advertising agent (Lemmon) who, to help a female neighbour (Romy Schneider, left), poses as her husband in order to fulfil the terms of a legacy in which she stands to inherit $15 million, it spiralled out of control as James Fritzell, Everett Greenbaum and producer-director David Swift's screenplay (from the novel by Jack Finney) piled complication upon complication. Chief of these 'complications' was Edward G. Robinson as one of Lemmon's more difficult clients in the agency. Awash with moral rectitude, Robinson believes implicitly in the sanctity of marriage. Thus, when Lemmon introduces Schneider to him as his wife, it is a deception that has to be maintained, regardless of the acute inconvenience to all concerned. Swift's direction – and the central performances from Lemmon and Schneider (making her first film in Hollywood) – helped camouflage the fissures in the plot, and kept the arrant nonsense bright and cheerful. Also cast were Michael Connors as Schneider's ex-husband, Edward Andrews as Lemmon's boss, Joyce Jameson as a hooker and Dorothy Provine (centre) as Lemmon's real wife. It was photographed in Eastmancolor. (130 mins)

△ A diverting update of H.G. Wells's novel, **First Men In The Moon** relied heavily on Ray Harryhausen's Dynamation for its visual effects as it described how, in 1899, an aspiring playwright (Edward Judd, left), his fiancée (Martha Hyer) and an eccentric professor (Lionel Jeffries, right) arrive on the moon almost by accident and encounter all kinds of dangers – from Selenites (dwarfs dwelling under the moon's surface) to oversized moon-cows. Charles H. Schneer's production, in Panavision and Technicolor, was clearly aimed at the matinee brigade, though fathers with a touch of the schoolboy in them enjoyed it too. It was written by Nigel Kneale and Jan Read, directed by Nathan Juran, and, in smaller roles, featured Eric Chitty, Betty McDowall, Miles Malleson and Gladys Henson. (102 mins)

◁ Five new songs, several secondary characters and a full-length story-line were the 'come on' attractions of **Hey There, It's Yogi Bear**, an animated feature from producer-directors Hanna and Barbera, who also wrote it with Warren Foster. Aimed squarely at the 10-and-unders (or the 'popsicle brigade', to quote a contemporary reviewer), its plot concerned itself with Yogi's on-going battle of wits with Ranger Smith of Jellystone Park, and traced the progress of the love-affair he has with high-wire performer Cindy Bear. It was all told through the voices of Mel Blanc, J. Pat O'Malley, Julie Bennett, Daws Butler and Dan Messick. At nearly 90 minutes, the film overextended itself but, given the paucity of full-length animated features in the mid-Sixties, its novelty value saw it through. (89 mins)

△ A 'problem' drama, set in a private mental hospital and involving a romance of sorts between an occupational therapist and a beautiful girl patient, **Lilith** starred handsome Warren Beatty (left) as the therapist and Jean Seberg (right) as the object of his affections. Wealthy, schizophrenic and unusually intelligent, Seberg is also pursued by an older woman patient (Anne Meacham), and by a disturbed Peter Fonda – who, eventually, commits suicide. As producer-director Robert Rossen's enigmatic screenplay (from the novel by J.R. Salamanca) was extremely unforthcoming (the hero and heroine, for example, barely strung two sentences together at a time), it became increasingly difficult to know what he was on about, or what point he was trying to make. The result was a moody, atmospheric, self-consciously arty, decidedly downbeat psychological melodrama that asked many more questions about its protagonists than it attempted to answer. Kim Hunter was featured as the head of the institution, and the supporting cast included James Patterson, Jessica Walter, Gene Hackman, Robert Reilly, René Auberjonois and Lucy Smith. (110 mins)

▷ Richard Widmark (right) and Sidney Poitier played adversaries in **The Long Ships**, a colourful, often unintentionally hilarious adventure spectacle that looked better than it sounded, and was more of a feast for the eye than the brain. Widmark received top-billing as Rolfe, a Viking adventurer; Poitier was cast as El Mansuh – leader of the Moors. Both were after the legendary Golden Bell, whose contents contained 'half the gold in the world'. Berkely Mather and Beverley Cross's screenplay (from the novel by Frans Bengtsson) was blood-spattered and violent, a fact emphasized by Jack Cardiff whose unsqueamish direction was aimed at audiences with strong constitutions. The supporting cast included Russ Tamblyn (left) as Widmark's athletic sidekick, Rosanna Schiaffino as Poitier's wife, Oscar Homolka as a boozy ship-builder, Clifford Evans as King Harald, and Lionel Jeffries as a black eunuch called Aziz. Also cast: Edward Judd, Jeanne Moody, Colin Blakely and Gordon Jackson. A Warwick-Avala (Irving Allen) Production, it was photographed in Technirama-70 and Technicolor by master cameraman Christopher Challis. *The Long Ships* made no impression on the world's box-offices and recorded a sizeable loss. (124 mins)

▽ Soap opera of the medical kind masqueraded as high drama in **The New Interns**, a sequel to the studio's successful 1962 offering, *The Interns*. Pitched at a temperature way above 100°F, this delirious and feverish saga about doctors, nurses and patients repeated the original formula as it focused on the lives of several assorted members of the profession. Audiences followed, for example, the lighthearted involvement between the zany, womanizing Dr Michael Callan (right) and nurse Barbara Eden. On a more 'serious' note, they became privy to the problems of obstetrician Dean Jones (centre) and nurse Stefanie Powers (left) whose marriage is threatened by the former's sterility. A third sub-plot – and undoubtedly the 'heaviest' – found ex-hood George Segal (in his first featured role), now a qualified surgeon, having to perform an operation on the thug who raped his girlfriend, Inger Stevens. Though hardly contributing to realism in the cinema, Robert Cohn's glossy production, scripted by Wilton Schiller and based on characters created by Richard Frede in his novel *The Interns*, was the movie equivalent of junk food. It filled a gap without providing much nutritional content. Despite the choppiness of the narrative line, director John Rich somehow kept it all glued together. Telly Savalas was featured as the hospital's head of administration, with other roles going to Kay Stevens, Jimmy Mathers, George Furth and Lee Patrick. (122 mins)

△ Patricia Neal (right) starred in the mystifyingly titled **Psyche 59** as a woman blinded in a fall during pregnancy. She is married to London businessman Curt Jurgens (left), has two children, as well as the affection of a faithful family friend (Ian Bannen). Enter her sister – played by Samantha Eggar – and her dark world becomes even darker. It seems that the reason for Miss Neal's traumatic fall is that she caught sister Samantha and hubby in a compromising situation and has 'blacked out' the memory ever since. Julian Halevy's screenplay (from a novel by Françoise de Ligneris) restores Miss Neal's sight to her, and one of the first things she sees is . . . sister Samantha and hubby in a compromising situation. This time, however, she continues to feign blindness as she attempts to come to grips with her husband's infidelity. A psychological melodrama, it was self-consciously directed by Alexander Singer with a mistaken emphasis on 'art' rather than on 'craft'. The result was an over-pretentious mixture whose characters were far too 'complex' for the basically simple tale being told. Padding out the cast for producer Philip Hazelton were Beatrix Lehmann (as Patricia Neal's grandmother), Elspeth March, Sandra Lee and Shelley Crowhurst. (94 mins)

△ In the film of Penelope Mortimer's domestic novel **The Pumpkin Eater**, Anne Bancroft (left) fecund, twice-married mother who decides to leave her second husband for a promising screen-writer (Peter Finch, right), only to discover that, as success overtakes him, their marriage is more hiss than bliss. Finch's infidelities, and his unwillingness to conform to the kind of domesticity in which she thrives, lead to her having a breakdown shortly after the birth of her seventh child. Bancroft's reluctant acceptance of her unhappy lot, as well as her coming to terms not only with her own character but her husband's, gave scenarist Harold Pinter's screenplay its painful bite and dramatic thrust. Rarely had the problem of marital conflict been so truthfully examined or so ruthlessly exposed. Bancroft's performance – delivered in an impeccable English accent – was extra-ordinary for the range of moods and emotions it encompassed in the space of a couple of hours, and was rewarded with a Best Actress citation at the Cannes Film Festival. Finch was equally impressive, and there was a splendid cameo from James Mason as a deeply cynical, embittered cuckold. Also helping to underpin this probing anatomy of a breakdown were Cedric Hardwicke as Bancroft's father, Richard Johnson as her second husband, as well as Yootha Joyce, Eric Porter, Rosalind Atkinson, Maggie Smith, Frances White, Alan Webb and Janine Gray. It was produced by James Woolf and directed by Jack Clayton (for Romulus Productions) – with sometimes too much emphasis on the arty jump-cut or arresting camera angle. Material as fundamentally honest as this was hardly in need of distracting visual embellishment. (118 mins)

◁ An old-fashioned horse-opera that arrived a couple of decades too late, **The Quick Gun** starred Audie Murphy (right) as a gunslinger on his way back to the home he left after killing the son of a no-good rancher in a duel. *En route* he is approached by a gang of desperadoes who seek his help in robbing the local bank. Murphy not only refuses, but proceeds to help Sheriff James Best protect the town from the in-coming outlaws. Best is killed in the fray, and the film ends with Murphy taking his place. Photographed in Techniscope and Technicolor, and with Merry Anders (left) providing the romantic interest, it passed the time agreeably enough, and, as Westerns went, was par for the well-worn course. It was scripted by Robert E. Kent from a story by Steve Fisher, and featured Ted de Corsia as the 'heavy', with other parts in Grant Whytock's Admiral Pictures Production going to Walter Sande, Rex Holman, Charles Meredith, Frank Ferguson and Mort Mills. Sidney Salkow directed. (89 mins)

▽ The Oahu Islands in Hawaii provided the colourful setting for **Ride The Wild Surf** in which only the most vigilant of viewers could have detected a plot. For those who couldn't, it was the tale of a group of surfers – led by Fabian (left), Tab Hunter and Peter Brown (right) – who compete for the title 'king of the mountain': in other words, to see who can stay upright the longest. The handsome trio were paired off with Shelley Fabares, Susan Hart and Barbara Eden – but romance was a mere side-line. The heart of producers Jo and Art Napoleon's youth-orientated biking and muscle parade was where the surf was. The Napoleons wrote it, and it was directed by Don Taylor with a cast that also included Anthony Hayes, James Mitchum, and Catherine McLeod. It was photographed in Eastmancolor. (101 mins)

◁ The heroine of **Strait Jacket** was an axe-murderess. Such a character was dough in the hands of Joan Crawford (left), and she kneaded it with all the over-the-top zest she could. The story of William Castle's tawdry little shocker, from the pen of Robert Bloch (who also wrote *Psycho*, Paramount 1960) began with Miss Crawford administering 40 blows apiece to her husband and his lover, and ended some twenty years later when, after she is released from jail, three further murders in similar vein immediately follow. However, these are the work of her daughter (Diane Baker), who at the age of three witnessed her mother's anti-social behaviour with the axe. Other roles under Castle's direction went to Leif Erickson, Howard St John, John Anthony Hayes, Rochelle Hudson and George Kennedy (right). Castle also produced. (93 mins)

▽ The character played by Steve McQueen (right) in the Alan Pakula-Robert Mulligan Production **Baby The Rain Must Fall** was a question mark wrapped up in an enigma. A rockabilly singer recently paroled for knifing a man, McQueen joins his wife (Lee Remick, left) and four-year-old daughter (appealing Kimberley Block) in a small southern Texas town, and proceeds to spend his days doing odd jobs and his nights singing at a local saloon. As Remick does her wifely best to regenerate her unhappy and troubled spouse, he becomes increasingly obsessed with the elderly dictatorial spinster (Georgia Simmons) who raised him – and when the old martinet finally croaks, McQueen loses his marbles, turns violent again, and is thrown back into the slammer. But as scenarist Horton Foote, working from his play *The Travelling Lady*, chose not to reveal to audiences McQueen's tormented past and tortured personality, it was difficult for them to feel sympathy for a character who came across as little more than a brooding boor. A downbeat, understated performance from Lee Remick added to the general mystification under Mulligan's equally low-key direction. Others caught up in Foote's enclosed little drama were Don Murray as a deputy sheriff and boyhood friend of McQueen's (a nothing part), Paul Fix, Josephine Hitchinson, Ruth White and Zamah Cunningham. The catchy title song was by Elmer Bernstein. (93 mins)

△ History took a back seat in **Arizona Raiders**, an Audie Murphy (illustrated) Western in which the star played a young Confederate who, together with his buddy Ben Cooper, joins guerilla Quantrill shortly after the Civil War. Apprehended by Buster Crabbe and his Union Soldiers, they are sentenced to 20 years hard labour, but are offered an unconditional pardon by Crabbe if they agree to co-operate in tracking down a group of former Quantrill killers who have been causing havoc in the territory. Written by Alex Gottlieb, and Mary and Willard Willingham (story by Frank Gruber and Richard Schayer), it contained enough gunplay to keep Audie's fans happy, and it looked good in Techniscope and Technicolor. Michael Dante was prominently featured as the leader of the bad guys, with other roles under William Witney's indifferent direction going to Gloria Talbot, Ray Stricklyn, George Keymas and Fred Krone. It was a Grant Whytock Production. (90 mins)

◁ The peace-time monitoring of Russian submarine movements by US destroyers was the subject of **The Bedford Incident**, a highly-strung, somewhat fanciful adventure, set aboard the USS *Bedford*. Captain of the newly launched destroyer was Richard Widmark (left), obsessed with hunting down a particular Soviet submarine regardless of the great risks involved. His salty character comes into conflict with a smart-aleck journalist (Sidney Poitier, right) who is there to cover the trip for a magazine, as well as Martin Balsam as a World War II reserve medic back on active duty. James MacArthur played a young ensign who accidentally fires off an atomic weapon, and Eric Portman was on hand as a former Nazi submarine captain-turned-NATO-consultant. Though director James B. Harris managed to capture the claustrophobia of the confined setting and maintained dramatic tension throughout, he was unable to bring a sense of verisimilitude to James Poe's often unlikely dialogue, or to some of the wildly exaggerated incidents that periodically occurred on board ship. The film was based on a novel by Mark Rascovich, produced by Harris and Widmark for Bedford Productions, and also featured Wally Cox, Michael Kane, Phil Brown, Donald Sutherland and Brian Davies. (102 mins)

▽ There was plenty of bull in **Love Has Many Faces**, not least of which was the one that gored heroine Lana Turner (left) in the final reel. This glossy rubbish, set in Acapulco and Mexico (its glitzy milieu created by scenarist Marguerite Roberts), found Turner as a millionairess married to erstwhile beach-bum Cliff Robertson. He loves Turner's money far more than he loves her, and begins a romance with new arrival Stefanie Powers – in town to investigate the suicide of her fiancé – while Turner turns her attention to bullfighter Jaime Bravo. Meanwhile, back at the merry-go-round, gigolo Hugh O'Brian (right) can't make up his mind whether he wants Ruth Roman, another wealthy American, or Miss Turner. So it goes – and so it went. Turner looked ravishing in one Edith Head creation after another; Acapulco looked a dream as photographed by Joseph Ruttenberg in Eastmancolor – but the script, the performances, and the direction, by Alexander Singer, lacked credibility. Jerry Bresler produced, and his cast included Virginia Grey, Ron Husmann, Enrique Lucero and Carlos Montalban. (104 mins)

▽ The cavalry clashed with the Indians – Sam Peckinpah-style – in **Major Dundee**, a rugged, often violent Western in which Union Officer Charlton Heston (left), together with a motley collection of misfits, pursues a renegade tribe of Apaches into Mexico in order to rescue three kidnapped white children and to avenge an Apache attack on an army outpost. As scripted by Harry Julian Fink, Oscar Saul and director Peckinpah (story by Fink), a plethora of sub-plots drew attention away from the central narrative thus slowing down the pace and damaging the continuity. Like the cavalry itself, the action sequences came to the rescue of the plot on more than one occasion; but, at over two hours, the film was not without its

▽ A self-consciously arty excursion into paranoia, **Mickey One** was the story of a nightclub singer (Warren Beatty, illustrated) in Chicago, who, believing the mob are after him for non-payment of gambling debts, flees his sleazy, dissipated existence, and, in an effort to bury his past, destroys all personal documents and assumes the identity of a Pole enigmatically called Mickey One. After sleeping rough and taking a job hauling garbage, the smell of greasepaint and the roar of applause tempt him back to his former existence. He cannot, however, eliminate the demons that haunt him – or his involvement with 'the mob' – and the film ends with him facing a bleak future, if, indeed, there is a future for him to face. Confusing and

longueurs. Charlton Heston, looking like something carved into Mount Rushmore, was the titular hero; Irish actor Richard Harris co-starred as a rebel captain, James Coburn was an Indian scout, Jim Hutton a young lieutenant, Michael Anderson Jr a bugler and sole survivor of the Apache massacre, Mario Adorf was a sergeant, Brock Peters a black trooper, and Senta Berger (right, the obligatory love-interest) the widow of a Mexican doctor. Others in the cast included Warren Oates, Slim Pickens, Ben Johnson and L.Q. Jones. The film was strikingly photographed in Panavision and Eastmancolor by Sam Leavitt, rousingly scored by Daniele Amfitheatrof, and produced by Jerry Bresler. (134 mins)

weighed down with symbolism, *Mickey One*, written by Alan M. Surgal, might, at best, be called an ambitious disaster in which Warren Beatty failed to come to grips with the complex character he was portraying. A disagreeable heel given to bouts of irrationality and violence, it was hard to decipher just what made him tick. Alexandra Stewart fared better as the girl who loved him, and there was an intriguing performance from Hurd Hatfield as a nightclub owner with an insidious homosexual hold on Beatty. Franchot Tone appeared as a big-time gambler, with other roles under Arthur Penn's obfuscating direction going to Jeff Corey, Kamatari Fujiwara and, as Mickey's agent, Teddy Hart. Penn also produced. (93 mins)

△ A slapstick Western spoof, and, in some respects a forerunner of Mel Brooks' superior *Blazing Saddles* (Warner Bros. 1974) **Outlaws Is Coming** (GB: **Three Stooges Meet The Gunslinger**) starred, for the last time, Stooges Larry Fine (left), Moe Howard (right) and Joe De Rita (centre) who, after being fired from the Preservation of Wildlife Society, travel to Wyoming where they become involved in a battle between gunslingers and an Indian tribe. Elwood Ullman's anarchic screenplay (story by producer-director Norman Maurer) dragged in every mythic bad guy known to the West – including Jesse James, Billy the Kid, Johnny Ringo, The Dalton gang and Cole Younger, a few good guys (Wyatt Earp, Bat Masterson and Wild Bill Hickok), and a few celebrated womenfolk, such as Annie Oakley (Nancy Kovack) and Belle Starr. Extremely funny in parts, it was one of the trio's better efforts and a fitting finale to their knockabout careers. Adam West, Mort Mills, Don Lamond, Rex Holman and Emil Sitka contributed to the horseplay. (88 mins)

▷ A kind of *Grand Hotel* (MGM, 1932) of the ocean waves, **Ship of Fools**, hewn from the massive 1962 best-seller by Katherine Anne Porter, employed the classic, time-worn formula of bringing together, in an enclosed space, a diverse group of characters, and then jump-cutting from story to story in order to make some penetrating (or simply entertaining) statement about the human condition. The 'fools' contained on this voyage – which takes place in 1932 on a German passenger ship travelling from Vera Cruz, Mexico to Bremerhaven in Germany – included José Ferrer as a loud-mouthed anti-Semite, Lee Marvin (left) as a baseball player, George Segal and Elizabeth Ashley as a pair of warring young lovers, Simone Signoret as a declining Spanish countess, José Greco as the leader of a troupe of energetic Spanish dancers, and, most memorable of all, Vivien Leigh (right, in her last movie) as a fast-fading American divorcée. To Oskar Werner went the pivotal role of the ship's sad and disillusioned doctor – a symbol, almost, of the well-bred German intellectuals that Hitler's Nazis were systematically ousting from power. His brief affair with Signoret's countess was just one of the film's many highlights. Other memorable scenes included Vivien Leigh dancing the charleston, and deliberately smearing her make-up. Memorable, too, was Michael Dunn's performance as Glocken, the dwarf. Indeed, Abby Mann's screenplay illuminated so many aspects of human character and was so richly textured that there wasn't a dull moment in nearly two and a half hours of screen time. It was produced and superbly directed by Stanley Kramer. (148 mins)

▽ Producer-director Richard Quine adopted a semi-documentary-like approach for **Synanon** (GB: **Get Off My Back**) a grim, hard-hitting drama about drug addiction inspired by the rehabilitation work being carried out by Charles E. Dederich in Synanon House on the Santa Monica beach-front. By mixing actual case-histories with fiction, scenarists Ian Bernard and S. Lee Pogostin (story by Pogostin and Barry Oringer) emerged with a plot-line involving the arrival at Synanon of an ex-con drug addict (Alex Cord) and the affair he has with a former prostitute (Stella Stevens) now assigned to oversee his recovery. Fellow inmate Chuck

Connors (left), jealous of the relationship, forces the couple to seek privacy away from Synanon, and it is in a sleazy hotel room that Cord, not yet recovered from his addiction, overdoses and dies, leaving Stevens to continue with her therapy alone. Richard Conte and Eartha Kitt (right) played real-life characters Reid Kimball and Betty Coleman, both attached to Synanon House in an executive capacity, while Dederich, who founded the home in 1958, was convincingly played by Edmond O'Brien. Also cast: Barbara Luna, Alejandro Rey, Richard Evans, Gregory Morton, Larry Kert and Bernie Hamilton. (105 mins)

◁ A characterless teenage musical jamboree, **Winter A Go-Go** was about a group of kids in search of a venue for their music-making. A ski-lodge inherited by leading man William Wellman Jr (son of the famous director) came to the rescue and cued in some action sequences on the slopes. James Stacy, Beverly Adams, Anthony Hayes, Jill Donahue, Tom Nardini, Duke Hobbie and Julie Parrish were on hand to help pad out Bob Kanter's meagre screenplay (story by producer Reno Carrell), while the Nooney Rickett Four, The Astronauts, Joni Lyman and The Reflections were called upon to supply the music. Richard Benedict directed, and it was photographed in Pathé Color. (87 mins)

△ Audiences with a low threshold of endurance found nought for their comfort in **You Must Be Joking**, a relentlessly middle-of-the-road British slapstick jape whose indiscriminate screenplay by Alan Hackney (story by Hackney and Michael Winner, who also directed) made no attempt to separate the good jokes (of which there were some) from the bad (of which there were many). Following the pattern of a treasure hunt, the story involved a 48-hour army-initiation test dreamed up by Terry-Thomas, an eccentric psychiatrist, during which time the five competing soldiers were ordered to find a rare breed of rose, an electric hare from a dog-track, a mascot from the bonnet of a Rolls-Royce, a set of plaster flying ducks, a lock of hair and a signed photo of a well-known Continental singer, and last, but by no means least, Lloyds of London's celebrated Lutine Bell. Taking part in the test were guards officer Denholm Elliott, Scottish sergeant Lionel Jeffries (right), American lieutenant Michael Callan, as well as Lee Montague and Bernard Cribbins. Also cast for producer Charles H. Schneer were Gabriella Licudi, Patricia Viterbo and hardy perennials Wilfrid Hyde-White, James Robertson Justice, Richard Wattis, James Villiers, Irene Handl, Norman Vaughan, David Jacobs and Clive Dunn. (99 mins)

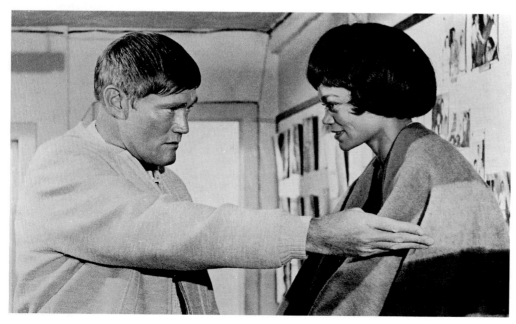

▽ Allegedly based on a true Civil War incident, **Alvarez Kelly** starred William Holden (right) as a Mexican-Irish war profiteer and cattleman who plays the North and the South off against each other as he sells both sides cattle. Richard Widmark (left) was second-billed as a one-eyed Confederate officer, who, in the course of Franklin Coen and Elliot Arnold's uninspired screenplay, kidnaps Holden and forces him to teach his troops how to handle cattle. Holden's revenge is to help Widmark's fiancée (Janice Rule) escape to New York, and into the arms of sea captain Roger C. Carmel. The conflict between the two leading men was the only dramatically viable element in an otherwise routine, often confused actioner. Sol C. Siegel's production looked good in Panavision and Technicolor, and featured Victoria Shaw, Patrick O'Neal, Richard Rush, Arthur Franz and Harry Carey Jr. The uneven direction was by Edward Dmytryk. (110 mins)

▷ In **Birds Do It** Soupy Sales (right) played Melvin Byrd, a 'miniscule molecular particle surveillance monitor' (or, in other words, a janitor), hired by the government to make sure that their missiles remain dust-free. Counter-agent Tab Hunter, however, has sabotage on his mind and sets out to undermine the hero. Arnie Kogen and Art Arthur's screenplay (story by Leonard Kaufman) wasn't exactly bursting with ideas, though the film's big set-piece, which found Byrd 'negatively ionized' and flying his way around Florida, was moderately amusing. Arthur O'Connell played a wacky scientist, Beverly Adams was his daughter, Edward Andrews was a general and Doris Dowling a Congresswoman. Ivan Tors produced (in Pathé Color), and it was directed by Andrew Marton. (95 mins)

△ Joy Adamson's best-seller **Born Free** came to the screen in a faithful and loving adaptation by Gerald L.C. Copley and with real-life husband-and-wife team Virginia McKenna (left) and Bill Travers (right) in the roles of Joy and George Adamson. A moving wild-life documentary-drama, shot entirely in East Africa, the film showed how Joy – the wife of a game warden in Kenya – raised a wild lion cub called Elsa to maturity, then re-educated her so that she could, eventually, return to the wild from whence she originally came. If the animal sequences upstaged the human activity, blame must go to trainer and supervisor Peter Whitehead for 'coaching' his four-legged cast with such skill and dexterity. Director James Hill kept the moving narrative free from bathos – and if this true-story had the occasional sentimental streak running through it, it was never actually cloying. An Open Road-High Road production, filmed in Technicolor and Panavision for executive producer Carl Foreman and producers Sam Jaffe and Paul Radin, the film also featured Geoffrey Keen as an amiable government commissioner who finally persuades the Adamsons that Elsa should either be set free or confined to a zoo, Peter Lukoye as Elsa's 'nursemaid', and Omar Chambati, Bill Godden and Bryan Epsom. The popular title song was written by John Barry and Don Black. The sequel, *Living Free*, appeared in 1972. (95 mins)

△ **The Chase** – director Arthur Penn's steamy and violent descent into small-town corruption – purported to say something significant about civil rights, but submerged its intentions in a welter of torrid, Peyton Place-like incidents, each more unedifying than the last. As the sheriff of a small Texas town seemingly populated by bigots, racists, thugs, nymphomaniacs and religious fanatics, top-starred Marlon Brando (left) sets out to apprehend a fugitive (Robert Redford, right) who is returning to town in order to see his wife (Jane Fonda). What should, ordinarily, have been a pretty routine assignment turns into a nightmare as some of the more corrupt local inhabitants decide to do the sheriff's job for him. Given the paucity of Redford's role in the general scheme of Lillian Hellman's fervid screenplay (from the novel and 1952 play by Horton Foote), the good-looking actor (whose fourth film this was) nonetheless managed to establish his presence with more conviction on this occasion than did the far more experienced Brando, E.G. Marshall as the town's powerful oil baron and banker, James Fox as Marshall's son, Janice Rule as the man-crazy wife, or Angie Dickinson as Brando's spouse. Also featured in Sam Spiegel's unsympathetic Panavision and Technicolor Horizon production were Miriam Hopkins, Martha Hyer, Robert Duvall, Henry Hull, Diana Hyland and Richard Bradford. (138 mins)

▽ James Coburn (left) brought a certain suave charm and authority to **Dead Heat On A Merry-Go-Round**, in which, having been paroled after an affair with an attractive prison psychiatrist (Marian Moses) he sets out to rob a bank at Los Angeles's International Airport, planning the heist to coincide with the arrival of a Russian premier. Unfortunately, writer-director Bernard Girard's screenplay was too episodic to create ongoing narrative tension and the film only partially fulfilled its potential. Camilla Sparv (right) played Coburn's bride-cum-innocent-accomplice, and Aldo Ray was in there pitching as one of his confederates in crime. Robert Webber was a government official in charge of the security arrangements concerning the visit of the Soviet official, with other roles in the Carter De Haven-Bernard Girard Production going to Rose Marie, Todd Armstrong, Severn Darden and Harrison Ford (in his film debut). It was photographed in Eastmancolor. (107 mins)

▽ Algeria's struggle for independence provided the action-filled background to **Lost Command**, a routine, albeit well-made, war drama which centred on the activities of a group of intrepid French paratroopers. A gruff Anthony Quinn (second left) starred as a Basque peasant who, through nothing but his own determination, becomes a lieutenant-colonel; Alain Delon played a disenchanted writer-cum-parachutist, a heavily-made-up George Segal (right) was an Arab officer whose family has been decimated by the Algerian revolt; Maurice Ronet (left) was a

brutal and sadistic soldier, Claudia Cardinale looked ravishing as Segal's sister and Delon's lover, while Michele Morgan was equally decorative as Quinn's romantic interest and support. Action spoke louder than words in Nelson Gidding's terse screenplay (from the novel *The Centurions* by Jean Larteguy) and the panoramic battle sequences, under Mark Robson's visually striking direction, were thrilling. Robson also produced, and it was filmed in Panavision and Pathé Color. The excellent score was by Franz Waxman. (129 mins)

▽ An exhilarating comedy of questionable morals, and set in the London of the Swinging Sixties, **Georgy Girl** gave Lynn Redgrave above-the-title billing as a dumpy plain-Jane sharing a slovenly flat with a brittle, sexually attractive, decidedly promiscuous Charlotte Rampling. As Margaret Forster and Peter Nichols' lively screenplay (from Forster's novel) unfurled, ugly-duckling Redgrave becomes a surrogate mother when Rampling disowns her new-born baby. She then falls in love with the baby's father (Alan Bates) but ultimately chooses to make a life with her parents' middle-aged employer (James Mason, left) – who agrees to adopt Rampling's unwanted offspring. Basically a

vehicle for the talented Miss Redgrave (and extremely good she was in it, too), the film was also an accurate reflection of the values that informed the Swinging Sixties. It marked an impressive directorial debut by Silvio Narizzano (hitherto a TV director), who kept some potentially dicey material bright, if not always light. The cast also included Bill Owen (right), Rachel Kempson (Redgrave's real-life mother), Clare Kelly, Denise Coffey and Dandy Nichols. An Everglades Production, it was produced by Otto Plaschkes and Robert A. Goldston. The title song, which became an enormous hit, was written by Tom Springfield and Jim Dale, and sung by The Seekers. (100 mins)

△ ABC-TV's successful cartoon series, 'The Flintstones', was elevated to feature-film status with **A Man Called Flintstone**, a full-length animated caper that spoofed the 'special agent' genre and drew much of its fun from placing its prehistoric characters in contemporary settings. The plot by Harvey Bullock and Ray Allen (with additional story material by producer-directors Joseph Barbera and William Hanna) found Fred Flintstone (illustrated) becoming involved in espionage and, together with his wife Wilma and neighbours Barney and Betty Rubble, setting off to Paris where he encounters the villainous Green Goose. Flintstone is mistaken for a secret agent, and is pursued by SMISH agents. The voices of Alan Reed as Flintstone and Mel Blanc as Barney were heard; there were six songs by John McCarthy and Doug Goodwin, and it was photographed in Eastmancolor. (90 mins)

▷ Robert Bolt's international stage success **A Man For All Seasons** came to the screen via producer-director Fred Zinnemann in boldly naturalistic settings and with the character of the Common Man completely eliminated. The result was a worthy and wordy slice of British history, impeccably acted by its fine cast – and, as scripted by Bolt from his play, literate, graceful and blazingly intelligent. The plot centred on Sir Thomas More's refusal to play yes man to King Henry VIII in the matter of his monarch's willingness to defy the Church and marry Anne Boleyn. The film allowed Paul Scofield (right) the opportunity to repeat his stage performance as More and he did so with consummate brilliance. More's stubbornness, his spiritual convictions, his conscience and his intellect were superbly conveyed by the remarkable Scofield whose charisma and presence compelled attention, even during the film's several lengthy theological discourses. An extrovert Robert Shaw (left), full of bluff and bark, played Henry VIII, Leo McKern was a roundly malevolent Thomas Cromwell, Orson Welles a vile Cardinal Wolsey, and John Hurt an ambitious, sycophantic Rich – the Judas who betrays More. Wendy Hiller played More's no-nonsense, matter-of-fact wife, Susannah York his affectionate daughter and Colin Blakely his servant Matthew. Nigel Davenport was the Duke of Norfolk, Corin Redgrave played William Roper and Yootha Joyce played Averil Machin. It was photographed in Technicolor by Ted Moore. (120 mins)

△ A feeble sequel to *The Silencers* (1965) – see following page – and an even feebler recycling of some leftover 007 plot-points, **Murderer's Row** again starred Dean Martin (right) as Matt Helm, this time rescuing a kidnapped scientist (Richard Eastham) from a mechanized gadget-infested island. The island's overseer is a villainous Karl Malden who plans to destroy Washington with a perilous ray. Ann-Margret (left) played Malden's sexy daughter, with Camilla Sparv, Beverly Adams, James Gregory, Tom Reese and Duke Howard along for the ride. It was written by Herbert Baker (from the novel by Donald Hamilton), produced in Technicolor by Meadway-Claude (Irving Allen) Productions, and directed by Henry Levin. (108 mins)

▷ The Mexican-US border in 1917 provided the setting for **The Professionals**, a strongly cast action-melodrama, written, produced and directed by Richard Brooks from the novel *A Mule For the Marquesa* by Frank O'Rourke. Played out against some stunning scenic backdrops, it was the story of a quartet of professional gunfighters – Burt Lancaster (right), Lee Marvin (left), Robert Ryan and Woody Strode – hired by tycoon Ralph Bellamy to cross the border into Mexico in order to rescue his wife (Claudia Cardinale) from kidnapper Jack Palance. There were few surprises *en route*, but, given the heavyweight roster of stars on hand, plus Brooks's efficient direction (more reliable, on this occasion, than his screenplay), his Technicolor and Panavision production kept one's interest simmering. (117 mins)

◁ TV star Chuck Connors (illustrated), fresh from his 'Branded' small-screen series, starred in **Ride Beyond Vengeance**, an adaptation by Andrew J. Fenady of Al Dewlen's novel *The Night Of The Tiger*. Produced by Fenady and TV's Mark Goodson and Bill Todman, the film betrayed its TV ancestry in all but the excessive and often gratuitous violence it employed to soup up a revenge tale. It told (in a confusing double-flashback) of how Connors, a trader in buffalo skins, returns home and is branded by an alcohol-sodden Claude Akins and a sado-masochistic Bill Bixby. The remainder of this Western was devoted to Connor's vengeance-seeking activities, before he finally becomes reconciled with his wife (Kathryn Hays, making her debut). Despite an interesting cast that included Michael Rennie (as a banker), Joan Blondell, Gloria Grahame, Gary Merrill, Paul Fix, Arthur O'Connell, Ruth Warrick, Buddy Baer and Frank Gorshin, the ride was definitely not worth taking. It was directed by Bernard McEveety, and photographed in Pathé Color. (100 mins)

▽ In a decidedly tongue-in-cheek attempt to out-Bond 007, producer Irving Allen commissioned Oscar Saul to cobble together two Matt Helm adventures – by Donald Hamilton – and called them collectively, if somewhat inappropriately, **The Silencers**. The result was a noisy, colourful, gadget-filled, girl-infested secret-agent melodrama that succeeded (to the tune of a healthy profit) in spoofing the genre while at the same time offering viewers a lightweight alternative to Sean Connery in the personable shape of Dean Martin (right, as Matt Helm). All about Helm's attempts to prevent a global catastrophe when Chinese agent Tung-Tze

(Victor Buono, left) diverts a US missile into the New Mexican desert, the film was directed by Phil Karlson with the emphasis squarely on action and romance, and performed by a bevy of pulchritude headed by Stella Stevens (centre), Daliah Lavi, Nancy Kovack, Cyd Charisse, and, as the immortal Lovey Kravezit, Beverly Adams. Apart from the aforementioned Dean Martin, the ladies in the audience were catered for by Arthur O'Connell, Robert Webb and James Gregory. It was filmed in Pathé Color, and spawned several successful sequels: *Murderer's Row* (1966), *The Ambushers* (1967) and *The Wrecking Crew* (1969). (103 mins)

▽ How do you solve a problem like May Clancy? A hoydenish scamp in an American convent, May thinks nothing of substituting bath salts for sugar, covering a classmate's face in plaster, or smoking in the basement. In **The Trouble With Angels**, the 'problem', in the appealing guise of Hayley Mills (centre), was efficiently dealt with and solved by Mother Superior Rosalind Russell (right), who, after three years of patient and subtle guidance, manages to turn the little devil into a little angel intent on becoming a nun herself. Harmless, and cheerfully predictable, the film also featured June Harding (left, in her film debut) as Miss Mills' shy and sensitive best friend, Binnie Barnes (her first screen appearance in 12 years) as a nun in charge of the local band, as well as Camilla Sparv, Marge Redmond, Mary Wickes, Dolores Sutton, Margalo Gilmore and Portia Nelson. Gypsy Rose Lee and Kent Smith featured briefly, and Jim Hutton (unbilled) appeared in a cameo. It was written by Blanche Hanalis from Jane Trahey's novel *Life With Mother Superior*, directed without a great deal of sparkle by Ida Lupino, and produced in Pathé Color by William Frye. *Where Angels Go, Trouble Follows* followed in 1968. (111 mins)

▽ Jerry Lewis (left), as a one-man band, beat his personal drum to little effect in **Three On A Couch**, which he produced, directed and starred in as an artist engaged to a pretty psychiatrist (Janet Leigh). The plot revolved around Lewis's being offered a scholarship to Paris, but he won't accept it unless his fiancée accompanies him. She, however, is in the middle of treating three women patients with 'men' trouble and can't leave until they are cured. So what does Jerry do? He decides to cure them himself, which he does by donning a series of disguises and wooing the first (Gila Golan), as a wealthy ranch owner, the second (Leslie Parrish, right), as an athlete, and the third (Mary Ann Mobley) as an effeminate zoologist. He even gets into drag when pretending to be the latter's old-maid sister Heather. Four Jerry Lewis's for the price of one might be construed as value for money, depending on one's response to Mr Lewis. For all but his most ardent fans, though, there was little in *Three On A Couch* (apart from the germ of an idea) to tickle the funny-bone. It was written by Bob Ross and Samuel A. Taylor from a story by Arne Sultan and Marvin Worth, photographed in Pathé Color, and also featured James Best, Kathleen Freeman, Buddy Lester, Fritz Feld and Renzo Cesna. (109 mins)

▽ An effervescent re-make of *The More The Merrier* (1943), **Walk Don't Run** was set during the 1964 Olympics, and starred Cary Grant (right) in the role played by Charles Coburn, Jim Hutton (left) in the role played by Joel McCrea and Samantha Eggar (centre) in the role played by Jean Arthur. As in the original Robert Russell-Frank Ross story (screenplay by Sol Saks), the plot had Grant, as an English industrialist temporarily lodging in Miss Eggar's apartment, this time around in crowded Tokyo not Washington DC, and playing cupid when he takes it on himself to offer accommodation to US Olympic athlete Jim Hutton (left). Though Miss Eggar already has a fiancée – a stuffy

embassy official (John Standing, far right) she and Hutton, after becoming involved in a 'phoney' marriage, pledge their respective troths for real. Though Eggar was no match for the delectable Jean Arthur in the original version, Messrs Grant (in his last film) and Hutton shaped up extremely well – and, aided by some eye-catching location shots of Tokyo (in Panavision and Technicolor), almost managed to obliterate memories of their beguiling predecessors in the roles. A Granley Company Presentation of a Sol C. Siegel production, it was directed by veteran Charles Walters and, in smaller roles, featured Miiko Taka, Ted Hartley, Ben Astar and George Takei. (114 mins)

△ The third, and feeblest, of the Matt Helm series, **The Ambushers** offered yet another rehash of James Bond leftovers, with decidedly unappetizing results. Set in and around picturesque Acapulco, it again starred Dean Martin (right) as Helm. In the screenplay devised by Herbert Baker from a book by Donald Hamilton, Matt curtails the villainous activities of bad-guy Albert Salmi, who, in addition to having abducted pretty Janice Rule (left), has stolen a flying saucer belonging to the US government. Senta Berger, James Gregory, Kurt Kasznar and Beverly Adams were also featured in producer Irving Allen's Meadway-Claude Technicolor production, and it was flaccidly directed by Henry Levin. (101 mins)

▽ Jerry Lewis (illustrated) produced, directed, co-wrote (with Bill Richmond, who provided the story) and starred in **The Big Mouth**, his thirty-sixth feature. As an eccentric fisherman who lands a frogman with a map showing the whereabouts of sunken treasure, Lewis went through several well-worn routines in the service of this extended chase comedy, some of them very funny, some of them plain juvenile. The usual Lewis 'shtick' buttressed what was basically a running gag (ie the use of disguises to give a pair of pursuing gangsters the slip), and kids everywhere lapped it up. Lewis took time off from being chased (as well as chaste) to have a mini-romance with Susan Bay, an airline stewardess who comes to his rescue. Buddy Lester, Del Moore, Paul Lambert, Jeannine Riley, Harold J. Stone and Frank DeVol were in it too, and it was photographed in Pathé Color. (107 mins)

▽ Ian Fleming's **Casino Royale** retained nothing but its title in this spoof of the successful James Bond industry. Though the book was the first of the Bond thrillers to appear in print, the film chose to feature 007 as an ageing agent who comes out of retirement in order to curtail the deadly activities of SMERSH. Frankly, it was a self-indulgent mess – an inferior Monty Python sketch stretched way beyond its limits, and, financially speaking, a disaster. Much of the loot was spent by producers Charles K. Feldman and Jerry Bresler on acquiring some of the best talent the world of movies had to offer – both in front of and behind the camera, but to little avail. A preponderance of star names does not necessarily a great movie make, and the likes of Peter Sellers, Orson Welles, Woody Allen, Deborah Kerr, William Holden, John Huston, Peter O'Toole, Jean-Paul Belmondo and, as James Bond, David Niven (left), could not save this hapless and misguided enterprise. Also in the cast were: Ursula Andress, Joanna Pettet, Daliah Lavi, Kurt Kasznar, George Raft, Richard Wattis, Ronnie Corbett, Anna Quayle, Jacqueline Bisset, Bernard Cribbins, Derek Nimmo and Barbara Bouchet (right). It was directed en masse by John Huston, Kenneth Hughes, Robert Parrish, Richard Jalmadge, Val Guest and Joseph McGrath and written by Wolf Mankowitz, John Law and Michael Sayers (with uncredited assistance from Billy Wilder, Val Guest, Joseph Heller, Ben Hecht and Terry Southern). It was photographed by John Wilcox, Jack Hilyard and Nicolas Roeg in Panavision and Technicolor and had a score by Burt Bacharach. An object lesson in how to get the least out of the most – it was a top-heavy dud from which none of the participants emerged with any credit. (131 mins)

△ After so many fanciful, high-gloss, high-tech excursions into the 007-Matt Helm world of espionage and counter-espionage, it was refreshing to touch base with reality in **The Deadly Affair**, a thriller, intelligently scripted by Paul Dehn and based on John Le Carré's first novel *Call For The Dead*, which went all out to place the shabby existence of spies and secret agents into a context that was anything but glamorous. Starring James Mason as Charles Dobbs, a British Home Office 'control' agent, the story followed Mason's attempts to unravel the mystery behind the supposed suicide of Samuel Fennen (Robert Flemyng), a top Foreign Office official. Helping him in his inquiries are Inspector Mendel (Harry Andrews), a retired police inspector, and Appleby (Kenneth Haigh), a young colleague in his office. As the plot thickens, Dobbs' private life comes under scrutiny too, and, with an unfaithful wife (Harriet Andersson) to add to his problems, is definitely found wanting. The film's exciting climax involved London's Royal Shakespeare Company in a stage performance of Marlowe's Edward II with David Warner as the tragic king. Simone Signoret (left) was second-billed as Elsa Fennen, the widow of the deceased official – and gave a touching performance as a woman who suffered a great deal at the hands of the Nazis. Mason himself was superb as Dobbs and there was good work, too, from Maximilian Schell (right), Lynn Redgrave, Roy Kinnear, Max Adrian and Corin Redgrave – all in minor roles. Producer Sidney Lumet's direction, despite a certain harshness in the cutting, built to a suitable climax and gleaned as much atmosphere as it could from the story's often bleak milieu. (107 mins)

▽ Satire and sophisticated comedy jostled gently in **Divorce American Style**, which took an irreverent though unflinching look at the consequences of broken homes *vis-à-vis* the kids as well as the crippling financial burden of alimony payments, etc. Central to Norman Lear's screenplay (story by Robert Kaufman) was a *nouveau-riche* Los Angeles couple – played by Dick Van Dyke (left) and Debbie Reynolds (right) – who, after 17 years of marriage, decide, having consulted marriage counsellor Martin Gabel, to call it quits. Thereafter much of the narrative centres on Van Dyke's efforts to maintain a decent lifestyle on what's left after regular alimony obligations. Also paying alimony was Jason Robards, whose divorce from Jean Simmons has put him through a similar financial

▽ After their 1966 appearance for the Oxford University Dramatic Society in Marlowe's rarely performed **Dr Faustus**, Richard Burton (left) and Elizabeth Taylor (right) decided to capture the occasion for posterity by recording their performances on film. The result was a decided oddity – directed by Burton and Nevill Coghill – with Burton as the titular hero and Taylor as a ravishing Helen of Troy. The familiar story of a medieval doctor's attempts to master all human knowledge by selling his soul to the Devil, it had some visually striking moments and a handful of passable performances from a cast comprised of amateur members of the OUDS. The indulgence was produced by Burton and Richard McWhorter and photographed in Technicolor. (92 mins)

mangle. Helping to pad out the Bud Yorkin-Norman Lear Production were Van Johnson as a Southern Californian used-car salesman, hypnotist Pat Collins (playing herself), Joe Flynn as a man who believes having sex without love isn't cheating, Emmaline Henry as Joe's wife, Lee Grant as a hooker, Shelley Berman and Dick Gautier as a pair of lawyers, Tom Bosley as a thrice-married man, and John J. Anthony (a real-life marriage counsellor) as a judge. By and large, the film had some trenchant things to say about divorce American-style and, despite an unconvincing sit-com performance from Dick Van Dyke, director Yorkin said them with a workable combination of humour and pathos. It was photographed in Technicolor. (109 mins)

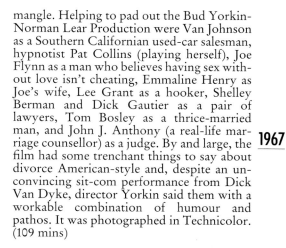

△ **Enter Laughing** (a Broadway hit by Joseph Stein) was based on Carl Reiner's autobiographical novel about a Brooklyn delivery boy's initiation into show business. Sadly, it came to the screen in a limp, clapped-out version for which Reiner, as producer and director of the disappointing transfer, had no-one to blame but himself. The main casualty was the pivotal casting of the young hero. On stage the character was played by Alan Arkin. On screen the plum role went to newcomer Reni Santoni, a recruit from TV's Merv Griffin Show, who was simply not up to the comic demands of the material. It was left, therefore, to the more experienced likes of José Ferrer, as an ageing ham who operates a run-down 'free theatre', David Opatoshu and Shelley Winters as Santoni's stock Jewish parents, Jack Gilford as his uncomprehending employer – as well as Elaine May (illustrated), Nancy Kovack, Don Rickles, Michael J. Pollard (who was in the stage play) and Richard Deacon to milk whatever laughs they could from Stein and Reiner's sporadically funny screenplay. A Carl Reiner-Joseph Stein production, it had a score by Quincy Jones, and was photographed in Pathé Color. (112 mins)

▷ After quelling a rebellion started by Corporal Kenneth Tobey, brave Captain Audie Murphy (right), all on his own, takes on the Apaches, led by Cochise (Michael Keep), and defeats them. Such was **40 Guns To Apache Pass**, a relentlessly routine Western (in Pathé Color) that also featured Michael Burns, Laraine Stephens (left), Robert Brubaker, Michael Blodgett and Kay Stewart. It was written by Mary and Willard Willingham, produced by Grant Whytock, and directed by William Witney. (95 mins)

△ Spencer Tracy (centre) appeared as the father of a would-be bride in Stanley Kramer's **Guess Who's Coming To Dinner**, a black-and-white comedy, in Technicolor, in which he played a prominent San Francisco liberal confronted with a daughter (Katharine Houghton) who, after a ten-day romance, announces her intention of marrying a black man. Fortunately, he not only has the looks of Sidney Poitier (left), he also happens to be charming, handsome, articulate and a Nobel Prize contender. In a variation of the Abie's Irish Rose theme, both families in question are somewhat taken aback by their offspring's sudden marital plans, though Katharine Hepburn (right) as the mother of the would-be bride (in reality Hepburn is Houghton's aunt), and another blue-stocking liberal, adjusts to the idea in no time flat and becomes positively enthusiastic. Old man Tracy, despite his liberal viewpoint, takes a bit more persuading – his doubts having less to do with his prospective son-in-law's colour than the haste in which it has all happened. Equally concerned are Poitier's parents (Beah Richards and Roy E. Glenn Sr) – especially his father. In the end, though, they capitulate and another blow for interracial marriage is forcibly struck. Despite its sanitized, glossy, over-sweetened soap-opera approach to certain aspects of race relations, and the air of unreality and almost make-believe that permeated the production, scenarist William Rose, whose screenplay was as pithy and glamorous as the milieu in which it all took place, surfaced with an irresistible blend of social comment and sophisticated drawing-room comedy. The production (which was the studio's biggest success of the Sixties) benefited, too, from Kramer's smooth-as-silk direction and from attractive performances by an attractive cast. Cecil Kellaway played a family friend, Isabel Sanford was the white family's disapproving black maid, and Alexandra Hay played Hepburn's business partner. Kramer produced, and the stylish wardrobe was provided by Jean Louis. (108 mins)

△ Richard Brooks's screen version of Truman Capote's 'factional' best-seller, **In Cold Blood**, never made it clear just who the real victims of this appalling story were: the four innocent members of the Clutter family brutally murdered in cold blood in Holcomb, Kansas, 1959, or ex-convicts Richard Hickock and Perry Smith their slayers. For, as delineated by Brooks, Messrs Hickock and Smith were victims too – of the gross inhumanity they experienced while awaiting execution in the Kansas State Penitentiary. In the main, though, the film was an absorbing anatomy of a senseless murder which continually addressed itself to the question of why the crime was committed in the first place. The first 35 minutes served as an introduction to the two criminals and took them to the scene of their crime; the next hour or so showed them on the run, climaxing with their capture in Las Vegas; an 18-minute flashback described the circum-

▽ **The Happening** achieved a dogged sameness of effect from a desperate attempt to be different. A pot-pourri of black comedy, slapstick farce, pop culture and Beach Boy shenanigans, it juggled satire with melodrama, and pathos with laughs as it lurched from one cinematic style to another without much rhyme or reason. Debauched youngsters George Maharis, Michael Parks, Robert Walker Jr and Faye Dunaway (debut), kidnap Mafioso Anthony Quinn (illustrated) in Miami; but when they ransom him off for $200,000 nobody wants him back. At this point Quinn, giving an excellent impression of Zorba the Greek, takes over his own kidnapping (the film's only promising idea) and, after making a few threatening phone-calls, manages to raise the ransom to $3 million. The kidnappers collect the cash without drawing the attention of the FBI, only to discover that the bills are marked, and, like their lives (as well as the life of the so-called victim), worthless. Quinn burns the loot and casually leaves. As directed by Elliott Silverstein, the film's diverse elements failed to gel into a cohesive whole, and the end result was more wild than wacky. Milton Berle played Quinn's partner (and provided whatever laughs were to be excavated from Frank R. Pierson, James Buchanan and Ronald Austin's screenplay – story by Buchanan and Austin), Martha Hyer was Quinn's wife, and Oscar Homolka a Mafia big-wig. Jud Kinberg produced for Spiegel-Horizon, Jud Kinberg Productions, and it was photographed in Pathé Color. (101 mins)

stances leading up to the actual murder; and the final 23 minutes told of their trial, unsuccessful appeal, and ultimate execution. Former child-actor and serial-star Robert Blake (left) starred as the fantasy-prone Perry Smith, and Scott Wilson played Hickock, a man living with a grudge against society and a fear of his own sexual impotence. There was excellent work, too, from John Forsythe (right) as one of the investigators, Paul Stewart as a journalist, Jeff Corey and Charles McGraw as Smith and Hickock's respective fathers, Teddy Eccles and Raymond Hatton as hitch-hikers, Will Geer as the prosecutor, Sheldon Allman as a clergyman, and Don Sollors as a salesman. Also cast: John Gallaudet, Jim Lentz, Gerald S. O'Loughlin, and James Flavin. It was written, produced and directed by Brooks, photographed in Panavision and black-and-white by Conrad Hall, and had an effective background score by Quincy Jones. (133 mins)

▽ A thoroughly inept, if not downright embarrassing, spy-spoof from producer Dino De Laurentiis, **Kiss The Girls And Make Them Die** starred Raf Vallone as a loony industrialist and womanizer who sets out to sterilize the world – excepting himself. In other words, it is his wish to become the only progenitor left on planet Earth. This arrant nonsense was the brain-child of Dino Maiuri, who scripted it with Jack Pulman, and it gave top-billing to Michael Connors (right) and Dorothy Provine (left) as undercover agents. Terry-Thomas was wasted in a dual role – and the cast also included Margaret Lee, Nicoletta Machiavelli, Beverly Adams and Jack Gwillim. Henry Levin directed. (105 mins)

▽ It wasn't always easy to tell – from Hal Collins and Arthur Dreifuss's screenplay – whether the Haight-Ashbury hippie movement, which featured prominently in Sam Katzman's confused production **The Love-Ins**, was being ridiculed or taken seriously. The film starred Richard Todd (left) as a university professor who, after resigning his position in protest over the expulsion (for publishing an underground newspaper) of two of his students, becomes something of a hippie cult-figure himself. It all ended in tears, though, when – after seducing student Susan Olivier (right) – he is killed by her boyfriend (James MacArthur). Straining at the leash to be 'hip', the film espoused the use of LSD and took snide digs at such middle-class symbols as the police, university presidents and bourgeois parents. It was directed by Arthur Dreifuss, photographed in Pathé Color, and featured Mark Goddard, Carol Booth, Marc Cavell, Janee Michelle and Ronnie Eckstein. (85 mins)

△ Is the murder of an individual any less reprehensible than the wholesale slaughter of thousands? – was the question obliquely posed in the Sam Spiegel-Anatole Litvak Horizon-Filmsonor Production, **The Night Of The Generals**, an earnest, sometimes ponderous wartime drama that began in Nazi-occupied Warsaw in 1942. A prostitute has been brutally murdered, the only clue to her attacker being that her killer wore the uniform of a Nazi general. Armed with this information, a major in charge of Military Intelligence (Omar Sharif) narrows the suspects down to a possible three. Is it Donald Pleasence, a cold and cynical authoritarian? Is it Charles Gray, a henpecked weakling? Or is it ruthless disciplinarian Peter O'Toole (right)? It turns out to be O'Toole, who, while on a sightseeing tour of Paris, murders a second prostitute. But Joseph Kessel and Paul Dehn's screenplay, from the novel by Hans Helmut Kirst, was not content with simply being a whodunnit; it made lengthy forays into other areas – one of them being the romance between an orderly (Tom Courtenay, left) and a general's daughter (Joanna Pettet), another being an elaborate plot to assassinate Hitler. In the end, the film bit off more than audiences could chew and sprawled out of control. Peter O'Toole's performance as the murderer certainly drew attention to itself without being particularly convincing; Courtenay was fine as the orderly (a pacifist musician out of place in the theatre of war); Omar Sharif was Omar Sharif as the sleuthing major, while Donald Pleasence and Charles Gray both made convincing Nazis. Philippe Noiret was excellent as a French Resistance worker, and there was adequate support from a cast that included Coral Browne, John Gregson, Nigel Stock, Juliette Greco, Gordon Jackson, Harry Andrews and, as Field Marshal Rommel, Christopher Plummer. It was directed by Anatole Litvak, who was unable to sustain interest in the elaborate narrative – or only sporadically – and lavishly photographed in Panavision and Technicolor. (148 mins)

▽ Murray Schisgal's long-running play **Luv** (901 performances on Broadway) was a surreal spoof on the theme of the eternal romantic triangle that also took a few satirical jabs at such dearly-cherished avant-garde themes as alienation, despair, frustration and mangled relationships. It starred Alan Arkin, Eli Wallach and Anne Jackson, was set entirely in the middle of the Brooklyn Bridge (from which one of the characters attempts suicide), and had a madcap sophistication to it that captured the imagination of New York neurotics. For the movie version (which retained the plot of a former classmate preventing the suicide of his friend, then palming his wife off on to him so that he can marry someone else), Jack Lemmon (centre) was cast as the potential suicide, Peter Falk (left) as his erstwhile mate, and Elaine May (right) as the woman in the middle. Elliot Baker's screenplay was not courageous enough to confine itself to the play's single setting, new characters were introduced, and the end result was a self-conscious, often irritating farce that brought out the worst mannerisms in its cast and jettisoned the sheer zaniness of the original production. It was produced by Martin Manulis in Pathé Color, and, in the lesser roles, featured Nina Wayne, Eddie Mayehoff (as a lawyer), Paul Hartman, Harrison Ford and Severn Darden. It was the work of British director Clive Donner who showed little evidence of belief in, or understanding of, the property. (93 mins)

▽ Having indulged in several whopping marital spats as the hero and heroine of *Who's Afraid Of Virginia Woolf?* (Warner Bros., 1966), Elizabeth Taylor (right) and Richard Burton (left) offered few surprises as the equally bellicose Katharina and Petrucchio in Franco Zeffirelli's lusty production of **The Taming Of The Shrew**. The question on everyone's lips wasn't whether Taylor was physically right for the role (which she quite clearly was), but whether she could handle the bard's poetry. Never having played Shakespeare before, the words did not, alas, fall trippingly from her tongue, but stridently and hysterically – which, though justified in the film's first half, was less convincing in the play's more tender moments. But then poetry and language were not among the first items on Zeffirelli's agenda. More concerned with the glorious way the production looked, he relied on the Taylor-Burton charisma (and the undoubted star-quality they exuded) to carry them through Shakespeare's knockabout comedy rather than on a well-modulated delivery of the text. The end result was definitely not for purists. Resembling, at times, an opera without the music, it was, in the end, a good-looking, fun-filled, over-the-top romp in which its two super-stars were clearly having a great time of it. The rest of the performances, with the exception of the excellent Michael Hordern as Katharina's father Baptista, were fair-to-middling, with Cyril Cusack as Grumio, Alfred Lynch as Tranio, Alan Webb as Gremio, Victor Spinetti as Hortensio, Michael York as Lucentio, and Natasha Pyne as Bianca. A Royal Films International-FAI Production, produced by the Burtons, it was adapted by Paul Dehn, Suso Cecchi D'Amico and Zeffirelli, and photographed in Technicolor and Panavision by Oswald Morris. (122 mins)

▷ If real-life husband and wife team Eli Wallach (left) and Anne Jackson (right) missed out on recreating their original stage performances in the film version of Murray Schisgal's *Luv*, the same author offered them the opportunity to repeat the much-praised performances they gave in his one-act play *The Tiger* which came to the screen as **The Tiger Makes Out**. A piece of screwball social satire depicting the frustrations of an ordinary New York mailman, it starred Wallach as the mailman, who, angry at life in general and his eccentric landlords (as well as the housing authorities) in particular, decides to assert himself by kidnapping a suburban housewife (Jackson). She, too, it turns out, isn't wild about her lot, and, although he holds her captive in his apartment, the couple strike up a genuine relationship – which ends with her inevitable return to her husband (Bob Dishy). As scripted by Schisgal, various aspects of urban existence come under some zany sociological scrutiny – though the film, as a whole, in no way benefited from the expansion it underwent in its transfer from stage to celluloid. Wallach and Jackson were fine as the protagonists, and there was good support from Ruth White and Roland Wood as Wallach's landlords, as well as from Sudie Bond, David Doyle, David Burns, Bibi Osterwald, Elizabeth Wilson, Jack Fletcher, Kim August (as a female impersonator), John Ryan, Charles Nelson Reilly, Mariclare Costello, Oren Stevens, Rae Allen, Remak Ramsay, James Luisi, Sherman Raskin, and, in the part of a beatnik, newcomer Dustin Hoffman. The film was produced (in Pathé Color) by George Justin, and directed by Arthur Hiller. (94 mins)

△ A variation on the *League of Gentlemen* (Allied Film Makers, 1961) theme, in which experts are recruited to ensure the success of a heist, **Who's Minding The Mint?** was a zany comedy from the Three Stooges' producer Norman Maurer. All about a clerk who works in the mint in Washington DC and who accidentally destroys $50,000 in banknotes, it focused on the attempts of said clerk (Jim Hutton, left) to sneak back into the building at the dead of night, and replace the lost money by running off a further 50 grand on the mint's presses. Just how he goes about his task – with the help of money-cutter

△ Having first become involved with the teaching profession as a student in *Blackboard Jungle* (MGM, 1955), Sidney Poitier (centre) returned for a second helping of teacher-pupil bonding – this time as a teacher – in the enjoyable **To Sir With Love**. The setting of the first film was a school in a rough, tough New York slum area, but this time round it was an altogether less menacing establishment near the London docks. Indeed, *To Sir With Love* had little of the earlier movie's punch-in-the-gut impact, even though, at one point, Poitier does actually biff recalcitrant student Christian Roberts in the belly just to show him who's boss. In all, though, the screenplay which producer-director James Clavell adapted from the novel by E.R. Braithwaite was a pretty soft-centred vehicle for the personable Mr Poitier and belonged more to the wish-fulfilment Forties than the tell-it-as-it-is Sixties. All about Poitier's successful attempts to turn his initially reluctant pupils into decent, caring, responsible and well-mannered members of society, its heart was in the right place – but at the wrong time. Also in the cast were pretty Judy Geeson as a student with a crush on Poitier, Suzy Kendall, Faith Brook and Geoffrey Bayldon as teachers, Ann Bell as a glamorous mother and pop-singer Lulu (right), who sang the film's popular title song (by Don Black and Marc London). Despite its bland flavour (or, perhaps, because of it), *To Sir With Love* became the seventh top-grossing film of the year. (104 mins)

Dorothy Provine (second left, also the romantic interest), retired mint-employee Walter Brennan (second right), safecracker Jack Gilford, pawnbroker Milton Berle (centre), sewer-expert Joey Bishop (third right), boat-builder Victor Buono (right), truck-operator Bob Denver and lookout-man (who can't speak English) Jamie Farr – provided the comedy content of R.S. Allen and Harvey Bullock's light-hearted screenplay. Under Howard Morris's well-paced direction, the top-notch cast delivered the goods, and a jolly time was had by all. It was filmed in Pathé Color. (98 mins)

1968

▽ The Allied landings in January 1944 at the little village of Anzio, 30 miles south of Rome and 55 miles behind enemy lines, was the subject of producer Dino De Laurentiis's noisy actioner, **Anzio** (GB: **The Battle For Anzio**). As scripted by Harry A.L. Craig from the novel by Wynford Vaughan-Thomas, historical fact gave way to Hollywood B-picture conventions as a sniper with a deadly aim (Wolf Hillinger) picked off most of the cast as they returned to the Allied beachhead. Survivors at the final fade were Robert Mitchum (centre), a wise-guy newspaper reporter, and Earl Holliman. Others involved in this historical farrago included Arthur Kennedy as a timid general who fails to capitalize on the Allies' initial advantage at Anzio, Robert Ryan as his commanding general, and Peter Falk (right) as a no-nonsense corporal. An inappropriately romantic theme song was sung by Jack Jones over the sound-track and added nothing to the atmosphere of war-torn Italy being evoked by director Edward Dmytryk. It was filmed in Panavision and Technicolor. Also cast: Mark Damon, Reni Santoni (left), Joseph Walsh, Thomas Hunter, Giancarlo Giannini, Anthony Steel and Patrick Magee. (117 mins)

△ Euphemistically speaking, **Assignment 'K'** was a mundane minor spy thriller, totally bereft of originality and suspense. The film expended time and energy on an anorexic plot about a British agent (Stephen Boyd, left) who makes the unsettling discovery that his girl-friend (Camilla Sparv, right) is a German agent. Third-billed Michael Redgrave, as Boyd's sole contact, had precisely two scenes, with other roles in Ben Arbeid and Maurice Foster's Gildor Production going to Leo McKern (as the heavy), Robert Hoffman, Jeremy Kemp, Jane Merrow, John Alderton and David Healy. It was sluggishly directed by Val Guest – who also wrote the screenplay, with Foster and William Strutton, from Hartley Howard's novel *Department K* – and filmed in Techniscope and Technicolor on location in London, Munich, and Kitzbuhel in Austria. (96 mins)

▽ Though the day-to-day routine of circus folk was well-documented in **Berserk!** (a remake of *The Shadow*, 1937), the main purpose of Aben Kandel and Herman Cohen's screenplay was to shovel as many shock-horror sequences as it could into audiences' laps – and, of course, to create a chewable role for its star – Miss Joan Crawford (centre). Dressed in leotards, red jacket and top hat, Crawford was at her imperious best as the circus's owner and ringmaster – an iceberg of a character who takes in her stride a series of grisly murders. A high-wire performer is garrotted on his own rope, a tightrope artist plunges to his death on a sea of bayonets, and the show's manager (Michael Gough) is spiked through the head. To help find out whodunnit, the services of Scotland Yard superintendent Robert Hardy (left) are enlisted and, in the end, all is surprisingly revealed. Ty Hardin (right) was second-billed as a romantic lead for Crawford, with other parts going to Judy Geeson (as Crawford's daughter), Diana Dors, Geoffrey Keen, Sydney Tafler, George Claydon and Philip Madoc. A Herman Cohen-Robert Stern Production, it was directed – efficiently – by Jim O'Connolly, and photographed in Technicolor. (96 mins)

▽ **Corruption** was a ghoulish programmer, produced by Peter Newbrook for Titan Film Distributors, in which proverbial mad doctor Peter Cushing (centre) spent a great deal of his time and energy murdering innocent women in order to transplant their glands into the disfigured face of his wife (Sue Lloyd), an erstwhile model. The failure of scenarists Donald and Derek Ford to create even halfway-believable characters robbed the film of any suspense it might possibly have generated, and the end result was a seen-it-all-before mish-mash, photographed in a process called Perfect Color, which director Robert Hartford-Davis was totally unable to animate. Also cast: Noel Trevarthen, Kate O'Mara, David Lodge, Anthony Booth (left) and Wendy Vernals. (90 mins)

▽ A limp-wristed espionage thriller, **A Dandy In Aspic**, starred an inert Laurence Harvey (centre) as a double agent (a fact known to all but his boss, British Intelligence Official Harry Andrews) who is ordered to eliminate his Soviet counterpart – ie, the Soviet-spy half of himself. Tom Courtenay (right) co-starred as Harvey's ill-wishing partner in the assignment, Mia Farrow (left) was the plot's perfunctory love-interest, Peter Cook another of Harvey's partners, Lionel Stander a Russian spy, and Per Oscarsson a drug addict. It was scripted by Derek Marlowe from his own novel, and produced and directed by Anthony Mann who died shortly before shooting was completed. Harvey took over the directorial chores – but by then the damage had already been done. It was photographed on location in London and West Berlin by Christopher Challis in Panavision and Technicolor. (107 mins)

▽ Advertised as a treat for the 'very rich, very beautiful, very hip, elaborately over-sexed, tuned in, turned on, and bored to death' **Duffy** was a relentlessly 'with-it' psychedelic thriller whose self-conscious attempts to 'swing' failed dismally. Buried underneath an overtly trendy approach to film-making was the potentially engaging story of a ruthless British banker (James Mason) whose two sons (James Fox and John Alderton), by different mothers, plan to rob him of the several million dollars he is transferring from Tangiers to Marseilles. Together with Fox's beautiful mistress (Susannah York, left), the brothers enlist the help of an exiled American criminal (and ageing hippie) living in Tangier – called Duffy (James Coburn, right). Lethargy set in from this point onwards as Donald Cammell and Harry Joe Brown Jr's screenplay (story by Cammell, Brown and Pierre de la Salle) proceeded to trade unremittingly in bluff and double-bluff. A Martin Manulis Production, it was directed by Robert Parrish as a cross between an elaborate commercial for hippie-dom and an exotic travelogue. (101 mins)

▷ Jerry Lewis (left) played a Walter Mitty-ish dreamer in **Don't Raise The Bridge, Lower The River**, an intermittently amusing spy-spoof, shot in England for producer Walter Shenson. Scripted by Max Wilk from his novel, it was the tale of an American wheeler-dealer's attempts to regain the love of his estranged wife (Jacqueline Pearce, right) through an outlandish scheme involving the sale of stolen oil-drilling plans to the Arabs. As confusion begat confusion, so the law of diminishing returns applied, and the end result was a laugh-sparse farce which left its talented star with sweat all over his face. Gap-toothed Terry-Thomas co-starred as Lewis's accomplice in the scheme, with other roles under Jerry Paris's uninspired direction going to Bernard Cribbins, Patricia Routledge, Nicholas Parsons, Michael Bates and John Bluthal. It was photographed by Otto Heller in Technicolor. (99 mins)

◁ **For Singles Only** was a total non-event, set in a southern California singles complex. It attempted, with the help of several songs, to be a tribute to free-wheeling youth, but finished up a view of the under-thirties scene as observed through the out-of-touch eyes of its middle-aged producer (Sam Katzman) and middle-aged director (Arthur Dreifuss). John Saxon (right) received star-billing, and Dreifuss and Hal Collins's inanity-ridden screenplay (story by Arthur Hoerl and Albert Derr) had him betting two buddies that before the week is out he'll have bedded shapely Mary Ann Mobley (left) – nicknamed 'Ironsides'. Lana Wood played a rape victim, Milton Berle appeared as the social director of the apartment complex, with other roles going to Mark Richman, Ann Elder, Chris Noel, Marty Ingels and Hortense Petra. It was filmed in Pathé Color. (91 mins)

▷ After enjoying a run of 1,348 performances on Broadway, the Jule Styne-Bob Merrill-Isobel Lennart musical **Funny Girl**, a biography of comedienne Fanny Brice, came to the screen via producer Ray Stark (the husband of Fanny Brice's daughter) and director William Wyler, with its star Barbra Streisand (illustrated) repeating the sensational, award-winning performance she gave on Broadway and in London's West End. The centrifugal force behind the whole enterprise, Streisand injected a charge of adrenalin into every scene in which she appeared, and single-handedly turned a compendium of backstage musical clichés into a warm and winning personal drama. True, she had some excellent Styne-Merrill songs (including 'People', 'Don't Rain On My Parade' and 'I'm The Greatest Star') to fall back on, as well as the perennially popular 'My Man', but not a great deal of support from Lennart's screenplay, which, although an improvement on the stage show, bogged down in the film's wordy second half. Nor was she helped by a mis-cast Omar Sharif as Nicky Arnstein, the handsome gambler she marries – and the man responsible for most of her unhappiness. As Streisand was the entire show, and the entire show was Streisand, there were few opportunities for the supporting cast – including Anne Francis as a backstage chum and Walter Pidgeon as Florenz Ziegfeld – to shine. Kay Medford as Streisand's mother was luckier and, despite the upstaging activities of her on-screen daughter, managed to make her presence felt. Both Wyler's direction and Herbert Ross's choreography emphasized their star's special comedic abilities, though, in the film's latter half, Streisand proved just as capable in her more dramatic moments as she was in her funny ones. The film, which cost a mammoth $10 million, was photographed by Harry Stradling in Panavision 70 and Technicolor, and turned out to be the studio's second-biggest grosser of the decade. The cast also included Lee Allen, Mae Questel, Gerald Mohr, Frank Faylen, Mitti Lawrence, Gertrude Flynn, Penny Santon and John Harmon. Streisand starred again in the sequel, *Funny Lady* (1975). (151 mins)

▽ Confusing, inept, and who needs it? That was the consensus of opinion for **Hammerhead**, another dreary Technicolor excursion into the world of international espionage that starred Vince Edwards (right, TV's hospital-series star Ben Casey) as a secret agent out to apprehend master criminal Peter Vaughan, a pornographer in pursuit of vital defence secrets. Produced in England by Irving Allen, directed by David Miller, scripted by William Bast and Herbert Baker, and with a cast that also included Judy Geeson, Beverly Adams (left), Diana Dors, Michael Bates, Patrick Cargill, Kenneth Cope, Kathleen Byron and George Pravda, it added nothing to a tired, well-worn genre. (99 mins)

▽ TV's The Monkees made their big-screen debut in **Head**, a virtually plotless psychedelic romp whose free-wheeling approach to its material resulted in a collage of this and that, most of it unrelated, all of it surreal. It was written by producers Bob Rafelson and Jack Nicholson, whose screenplay had the synthetic quartet jumping off the Golden Gate Bridge and performing water ballets in San Francisco Bay, satirizing TV blurbs and the Late Show, staging an assault on a Coca-Cola machine and appearing as dandruff in guest-star Victor Mature's hair. None of it made any sense, but then it was never meant to. The cinematic equivalent of an LSD trip, it was photographed in splashy Technicolor, artily rather than artfully directed by Rafelson, and featured Annette Funicello, Timothy Carey, Logan Ramsay, female impersonator T.C. Jones and, in small roles, Teri Garr and Nicholson himself. Representing the Monkees were Peter Tork (left), Davy Jones, Mickey Dolenz (centre) and Michael Nesmith (right). (85 mins)

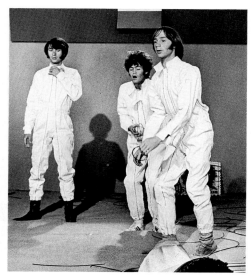

△ Stanley Shapiro, who wrote a slew of movies for Rock Hudson and Doris Day over at Universal, proved he hadn't lost his commercial touch with his screenplay for **How To Save A Marriage ... And Ruin Your Life**. This passed the time agreeably enough as it described how a dedicated bachelor-lawyer (Dean Martin, right) goes about saving the marriage of his best friend (Eli Wallach). What he does is to seduce Wallach's mistress, thus removing her from his pal's life. Unfortunately, Martin incorrectly assumes that the girl in question is Wallach's pretty secretary (Stella Stevens, left) when all the time it's his next-door neighbour (Anne Jackson). Shapiro, who also produced, emerged with a glossy comedy which, under Fielder Cook's gag-infested direction, settled for a steady quota of laughs and a handful of sprightly comic performances. Betty Field, Jack Albertson, Katharine Bard, Woodrow Parfrey and George Furth were also in it, and Mack David provided a pleasant enough over-the-title song called 'The Winds Of Change', sung by The Ray Coniff Singers. It was filmed in Panavision and Pathé Color, and had a score by Michel Legrand. (102 mins)

△ A story filmed first by Universal as *When Tomorrow Comes* (1939), and remade by that studio as *Interlude* (1957), surfaced again as **Interlude** – this 1968 version from producer David Deutsch. It starred Oskar Werner (right) as an international orchestra conductor (married to Virginia Maskell), and Barbara Ferris (left) as the journalist with whom he has an on-off-on-again affair. Music by Rachmaninoff, Beethoven, Tchaikovsky, Brahms, Dvorak and Mozart contributed to the lush romantic mood of the piece, and there were enjoyable supporting performances from Donald Sutherland, Nora Swinburne, Alan Webb and John Cleese. It was written by Lee Langley and Hugh Leonard, beautifully photographed in Technicolor by Gerry Fisher and directed without undue sentimentality by Kevin Billington for Domino Productions. (113 mins)

▽ **The Swimmer**, based on a *New Yorker* short story by John Cheever, and adapted for the screen by Eleanor Perry, was a mystifying enigma which, with great originality, set out to piece together some fragments of a man's life during the course of a single summer's afternoon. A resident of Westport, Connecticut, Burt Lancaster (illustrated), dressed only in his swimming trunks, and finding himself a few miles away from his own home, decides to swim back via the homes of several of his friends and acquaintances. The owner of each of the pools into which he dives has, in some way or another, touched upon his life, or he on theirs; and as he begins his journey home he is made to feel welcome in some, unwelcome in others. As the marathon suburban swim gets underway, various details about the swimmer's past life emerge. However, too many vital questions remained unanswered, and too many knotted threads were left untied and dangling. Just as a drowning man is said to see his life passing before him, so too do the swimmer's encounters, on this macabre occasion, convey a sense of a life having been passed through, albeit none too fruitfully. Those involved included Janet Landgard, Janice Rule, Tony Bickley, Marge Champion, Nancy Cushman, Bill Fiore, Kim Hunter, Diana Van Der Vlis, Richard McMurray, Joan Rivers, Louise Troy, Jan Miner, Cornelia Otis Skinner, Dolph Sweet and John Garfield Jr. Taking a chance with the risky material were producers Frank Perry and Roger Lewis, and it was directed by Perry (with uncredited assistance from Sidney Pollack). However, without the participation of Burt Lancaster, who brought a sensitivity as well as a strong physical presence to the role, the film would have been even more of a box-office flop than it was. It was photographed in Technicolor, and had a score by newcomer Marvin Hamlisch. (94 mins)

▽ John Woolf's Romulus Production **Oliver!** was a brash, colourful and boundlessly energetic expansion of Lionel Bart's popular stage musical based on the novel by Charles Dickens. In spite of the limitations imposed on this famous plot by the conventions of a musical libretto, Vernon Harris nevertheless managed to convey a Dickensian mood through his screenplay. Trying equally hard to keep a semblance of conviction in the proceedings was director Carol Reed, whose biggest problem was retaining the intimacy of the story while filling the Panavision screen with movement and activity. This aspect of the production was largely the province of choreographer Onna White whose routines filled the frame with wildly energetic hordes of dancers. Ron Moody (centre), repeating his celebrated stage interpretation of Fagin ('You've Got To Pick A Pocket Or Two'), received top billing and gave the performance of his career. Shani Wallis was Nancy, Oliver Reed (right) played Bill Sikes, Harry Secombe was Mr Bumble, Hugh Griffith the Magistrate, Jack Wild the Artful Dodger, Peggy Mount was Widow Corney, Leonard Rossiter was Mr Sowerberry, Joseph O'Connor was Mr Brownlow, Hylda Baker played Mrs Sowerberry and newcomer Mark Lester (second right) played Master Oliver Twist. Also cast: Sheila White, Kenneth Cranham, Megs Jenkins, Wensley Pithey, James Hayter, Fred Emney and John Bascombe. It was photographed, in Technicolor, by Oswald Morris, and the impressive recreations of Dickensian London were the work of designer John Box and art director Terence Marsh, whose elaborate sets accounted for much of the film's $10 million budget. The music director was John Green. *Oliver!* was a healthy box-office success and it remains a lasting favourite. (146 mins)

◁ A violent, often ugly, Western, **A Time For Killing** (GB: **The Long Ride Home**) was begun by director Roger Corman and completed by Phil Karlson. It starred George Hamilton as a Confederate major who, in the closing days of the Civil War, escapes from a Union prison camp in Utah; Glenn Ford (right, top-billed) was the captain sent to pursue him. The bitter confrontation between the two men – exacerbated when Hamilton rapes Ford's wife (Inger Stevens) – was the mainstay of Halsted Welles's tough screenplay (from a novel by Nelson and Shirley Wolford), which did well by its protagonists but undersold its secondary characters. Shot on location in Pathé Color and Panavision in Utah's spectacular Zion National Park, the film was produced by Harry Joe Brown, and featured Paul Petersen, Max Baer Jr, Todd Armstrong, Timothy Carey, Kenneth Tobey (left), and, in minor roles, Harrison Ford and Dean Stanton (now Harry Dean Stanton). (83 mins)

▽ A low-budget compendium of horror, **Torture Garden**, written by Robert Bloch and directed by Freddie Francis, featured Burgess Meredith (right) as a carnival barker whose specialty is giving his customers a peek at the future. In the first of four separate episodes, a playboy (Michael Bryant) turns murderer in order that a satanic cat can eat his victim's heads. The second part featured Beverly Adams as a would-be movie star who, in order to achieve her ambition, becomes a 'living-doll' as a means of retaining her beauty. The third (and least effective) segment involved the girl friend (Barbara Ewing) of a concert pianist who is murdered by his piano which contains the spirit of his jealous mother. The final espisode featured top-billed Jack Palance (left) as a collector of Edgar Allan Poe memorabilia who, after murdering fellow collector Peter Cushing in order to acquire some valuable Poe manuscripts, comes face to face with Poe himself. Based on Bloch's short stories 'Enoch', 'Terror Over Hollywood', 'Mr Steinway' and 'The Man Who Collected Poe' – the film was, at best, a mild curiosity which was ultimately sabotaged by the unevenness of the material. The cast also included Michael Ripper, and it was produced, in Technicolor, by Max J. Rosenberg and Milton Subotsky for Amicus Productions. (92 mins)

△ A sequel to the studio's successful 1966 entry *The Trouble With Angels*, **Where Angels Go . . . Trouble Follows** again starred Rosalind Russell (right) as the mother superior of a girl's school, Binnie Barnes and Mary Wickes as teachers, and had a screenplay by Blanche Hanalis (based on characters created by Jane Trahey). This story also had Stella Stevens as a young nun with a far less conservative outlook on her faith than that of Russell. Unfortunately, although scenarist Hanalis provided herself with a springboard for an interesting confrontation between the old and the new in the Catholic Church, the subject was only superficially touched upon. Of more importance to the enterprise was the plot, which manifested itself in the shape of a cross-country 'inter-faith' youth rally from Pennsylvania to California. The misadventures *en route* of the schoolgirls (a night at a boys' school, an encounter with a trio of Hell's Angels, etc) provided the red meat of the comedy, with relentlessly predictable results. Russell, as usual, was always watchable – and there were amusing contributions from Milton Berle as a film-director whose big chase scene is being sabotaged by Russell's busload of girls and nuns, and from Arthur Godfrey as a bishop, Van Johnson (left) as a priest in charge of a boys' school, Robert Taylor as a rancher, and William Lundigan as the father of one of the students. Also in the cast were Dolores Sutton, Susan Saint James and Barbara Hunter. A William Frye Production, it was directed by Disney director James Neilson, and photographed in Pathé Color. (93 mins)

△ As co-author, with director Joseph McGrath and John Wells, of **30 Is A Dangerous Age, Cynthia**, diminutive funny-man Dudley Moore (illustrated) handed himself a massive showcase. It was a one-joke affair in which he sets out, before the arrival of his thirtieth birthday, (a) to be married, and (b) to have the musical comedy he has just written performed. Just how he goes about achieving these ambitions was described in a wildly slapstick, anything-goes fashion, much of it extremely funny, much of it not. Fortunately, the good outweighed the bad, and with an excellent supporting company – including Eddie Foy Jr, Suzy Kendall, John Bird, Duncan MacRae, Patricia Routledge, Peter Bayliss, John Wells, Harry Towb, Jonathan Routh, Ted Dicks, Nicky Henson, Frank Thornton, Derek Farr and Micheal MacLiammoir – to inject their particular comic skills into the script, there was plenty of nonsense and merriment afoot for fans of irreverent British humour. It was produced by Walter Shenson and directed by Joseph McGrath with a nice sense of the improbable. The score was composed and conducted by Dudley Moore and performed by The Dudley Moore Trio. It was photographed in Technicolor. (85 mins)

△ Australia's Great Barrier Reef looked marvellous in Panavision and Technicolor, and provided the picturesque setting for **Age Of Consent**. The film starred James Mason (right) as a famous Australian painter who, disenchanted with life in New York, takes up residence on an island on the reef. His neighbours there include a spinster of independent means (Antonia Katsaros), a gin-soaked harridan (Neva Carr-Glyn) and her sexy young granddaughter (Helen Mirren, left, making her screen debut). Apart from Mason's growing attraction for Mirren, the screenplay by Peter Yeldham (from the novel by Norman Lindsay) concentrated on the shady activities of a drifter friend (Jack MacGowran) of Mason's and of the dishonest exploits of Ms Carr-Glyn who accidentally falls to her death during a cliff-top struggle. And that was about the sum of it. Director Michael Powell, who also co-produced it with Mason for Nautilus Productions, brought a modicum of charm to the slender tale, and, from his principals at any rate, drew passable performances. But in general it was not a particularly well-made effort – nor was it especially entertaining. Also cast: Michael Boddy, Frank Thring, Harold Hopkins, Slim Da Gray and Clarissa Kaye (Mrs James Mason in real life). (98 mins)

▽ Wife-swapping and extra-marital sexual relations were the related subjects of **Bob And Carol And Ted And Alice**, a liberated comedy which rang a few risqué changes on the less prurient on-screen relationships between Irene Dunne and Cary Grant, and William Powell and Myrna Loy. Taking his cue from the sexual revolution of the Swinging Sixties, director Paul Mazursky (debut), who co-wrote the screenplay with Larry Tucker, set out to examine changing sexual values in general – and in southern California in particular. The result was a basically old-fashioned domestic comedy unencumbered by censorship restrictions and pre-conceived notions of propriety. It put a toe into the inviting waters of the cinema's new permissiveness, and, to judge from the film's success at the box-office, the water felt fine. Robert Culp (second right) and Natalie Wood (second left) starred as a married couple who, after a session with an EST-type encounter group (in which they undergo some kind of emotional growth), relate their experiences to Elliott Gould (left) and Dyan Cannon (right), a more conventional couple. Culp tells Wood that he has had an affair with another woman, a fact which the liberated Miss Wood not only willingly accepts but which she shares with Gould and Cannon. In no time at all they, too, are experimenting with different partners – and when the four of them take a trip to Las Vegas together, the inevitable bout of wife-swapping is suggested. A disappointing cop-out ending, however, found the four friends unable to go through with it, leaving audiences to interpret their 'fidelity' any way they wished. Until this point, the film – beautifully performed by all four leading players – was a definite breakthrough, and as much a watershed comedy in its own right as was Otto Preminger's *The Moon Is Blue* (United Artists, 1953). A Frankovich Production that had excellent results at the box-office, it was produced by Larry Tucker, photographed in Technicolor, and also featured Horst Ebersberg, Lee Bergere and Donald F. Muhich. (104 mins)

◁ Giggling Goldie Hawn (left), one of the stars of Rowan and Martin's TV 'Laugh-In', made a delectable big-screen debut in **Cactus Flower**, producer Mike Frankovich's disappointing celluloid re-working of the long-running Broadway hit. She played a Greenwich Village kook and the object of bachelor dentist Walter Matthau's (second left) desire. Ingrid Bergman (right) was cast as Matthau's plain-Jane assistant, who, in the course of the screenplay I.A.L. Diamond expanded from the play by Abe Burrows (in turn an adaptation from the original French version by Barillet and Gredy), emerged from her chrysalis and, despite the younger competition, finally found herself paired off with her employer. There wasn't a great deal more to the content than that, a fact Diamond's surprisingly lack-lustre script failed to camouflage. Nor was director Gene Saks able to bring much of a bloom to the well-worn material. Bergman's basic sophistication and Matthau's lack of it made their ultimate pairing appear far-fetched and served only to draw attention to the mechanical contrivance of the plot. Still, there was always Goldie to keep one's flagging spirits buoyant – so all was not lost. Rick Lenz, Jack Weston (second right), Vito Scotti, Eve Bruce, Irwin Charone and veteran Irene Harvey (welcome back, Irene!) completed the cast. It was filmed in Technicolor. (103 mins)

▷ The treatment of displaced persons in Austria, 1945, was the subject of **Before Winter Comes,** a rather muddle-headed drama, directed with no discernible style by journeyman J. Lee Thompson and with David Niven (right) top-cast as a quintessentially English major assigned to running a camp for the human flotsam and jetsam washed up by the war. Helping him decide which of the DPs should be handed over to the Americans and which to the Russians was Topol (centre, the Israeli actor, Chaim Topol, making his US screen debut), one of the DPs himself, but a wizard with languages and a magician in the art of survival. Topol energized his way through the film in a performance of decided star quality. In the end though, Andrew Sinclair's rather bland screenplay (from a *New Yorker* short story by Frederick L. Keefe called 'The Interpreter') defeated his efforts as well as those of John Hurt (left, as a young lieutenant), Anna Karina (as both Niven and Topol's love-interest) and Ori Levy (as a Soviet officer). Robert Emmett Ginna's Windward Production (in Technicolor) also featured Anthony Quayle, John Collin, George Innes and Hugh Futcher; and the Zorba-inspired score was the work of Ron Grainer. (107 mins)

▽ A homage to silent comedy, **The Comic,** written, produced and directed by Carl Reiner, starred Dick Van Dyke (right) as a deceased silent-movie comic who, from a supine position in his coffin, narrates (in flashback) his autobiography. As Billy Bright, he emerges as an amalgam of several silent funny men (Stan Laurel, Buster Keaton and Harry Langdon), not only in style, but also in the content of their lives. The overall picture created was of an overweening womanizing egotist and habitual drunk whom Hollywood and a fickle public quickly forgot in the twilight of his career. After a brief comeback engineered by Steve Allen (playing himself), Billy marries a floozie (Nina Wayne, left) in hospital, and expires in the process. Material as *déjà vu* as this required a far stronger screenplay than the protracted rag-bag of clichés supplied by Reiner, and needed tighter and more individual direction. Far more successfully cast than leading man Van Dyke as Mickey Rooney as a ham comedian called Cockeye. Rooney was much the best thing in Reiner and co-scenarist Aaron Rubin's Pathé Color production, and he should have played the Van Dyke role himself. Michele Lee was second-billed as an Dyke's long-suffering wife, and the cast also included Cornel Wilde, Pert Kelton (her last film appearance), Barbara Heller, Ed Peck, Jay Novello, Jeannine Riley, Fritz Feld – and, as an agent, Carl Reiner. (95 mins)

△ Set in the Ardennes forest in the winter of 1944, and involving eight 'walking-wounded misfits from the American army', it was difficult to tell from Daniel Taradash and David Rayfiel's screenplay of **Castle Keep** (from the novel by William Eastlake) just whether the film was pro- or anti-war. Complicating matters further was the fact that fantasy and reality were constantly bumping into each other in a story that had the 'walking misfits', led by a one-eyed Burt Lancaster (left), occupying an art-infested Belgian castle owned by an impotent count (Jean-Pierre Aumont), and attempting, unsuccessfully, to hold it against a German onslaught. Pretentious in the extreme, it was confusingly directed by Sydney Pollack, who, in his one concession to commercialism and the box-office, staged an all-out climactic battle sequence between the Yanks and the advancing Bosch that was, to be fair, spectacular. The fact that it belonged in an altogether different film was another matter entirely. As well as the aforementioned Lancaster, the cast included Patrick O'Neal (right) as a captain whose special interest is 12th-century ivory miniatures, Al Freeman Jr as a would-be novelist (and the author's mouthpiece), and Peter Falk, Tony Bill and James Patterson as GIs. Also: Astrid Heeren, Bruce Dern and Scott Wilson. A Martin Ransohoff-John Calley Production, it was photographed in Panavision and Technicolor by Henri Decaë, and had a score by Michel Legrand. (106 mins)

▽ A violent, revenge-orientated Western, **The Desperados,** set just after the Civil War, starred an almost parodic Jack Palance (illustrated) as a Southern guerilla masquerading as a Confederate commander. After the death of his wife, Palance embarks on an orgy of rape, plunder and murder in cahoots with his Quantrill-like three sons (George Maharis, Christian Roberts and Vince Edwards) which takes them from one small border town to another. Tiring, however, of this life of crime, Edwards (top-billed) breaks away and, under an assumed name, travels to Texas with his wife (Sylvia Syms). Six years later the now-respectable breakaway is reunited with his unreformed family – with bloody consequences all round. Also cast for producer Irving Allen were Neville Brand, Kenneth Cope, John Paul and Kate O'Mara. It was written by Walter Brough from a story by Clarke Reynolds and, although episodic in nature, it cohered under Henry Levin's workmanlike direction. It was photographed in Technicolor. (90 mins)

◁ The best thing that could be said for Tony Richardon's bowdlerized version of Shakespeare's **Hamlet** was that it was so heavily cut it ran less than two hours. (By comparison, the 1948 Laurence Olivier production, presented by Two Cities, ran 153 minutes, despite heavy textual editing in that version as well.) Shot largely in close-ups against backdrops that were murky or dark or both, little sense of court-life at Elsinore emerged, with the result that the play seemed suspended in an ill-defined vacuum. As a record of the recent stage performance of Nicol Williamson (left), Neil Hardey's production was woefully inadequate (though whether Williamson's working-class, unpoetic Hamlet should have been recorded at all remains debatable). Furthermore, little was gained by Gordon Jackson's uncharismatic Horatio or Marianne Faithfull's picture-postcard Ophelia (right). Mark Dignam played Polonius, Anthony Hopkins was Claudius, Judy Parfit was Gertrude, Michael Pennington was Laertes, Ben Aris and Clive Graham were Rosencrantz and Guildenstern, John Carney was the Player King, and Peter Gale played Osric. It was photographed by Gerry Fisher in Technicolor (though you'd never have guessed it) and was a Filmways Presentation of a Woodfall Production. (119 mins)

▽ A landmark 'road' movie that spawned a plethora of inferior variations, **Easy Rider** was a low-budget bonanza whose episodic narrative chronicled the search for freedom by two bike-riding drop-outs as they journey between California and New Orleans. The film caught the imagination of America's hippie-orientated, pot-smoking, LSD-imbibing youth – as well as sober film critics from Cannes to Katmandu. Written by Dennis Hopper (left), Peter Fonda and Terry Southern, its story looked at the largely unbridgeable gap between conformists and non-conformists – each group posing a threat to the other. If it preached anything, it was the doctrine of 'doing one's own thing', and if its free-wheeling, open-ended structure concealed a message, it was the impossibility of doing that 'thing' in what used to be 'a fine country'. Hopper, making an impressive directorial debut, also appeared in it, together with Fonda (they played the two bikers), though the acting honours undoubtedly went to Jack Nicholson as an alcoholic young lawyer from a respectable family whom the bikers meet in a small Southern jail, and whom he helps spring before joining them on their liberating journey. Looking decidedly old on the back of Fonda's motor-cycle, Nicholson nonetheless emerged as the most liberated spirit in the film, and the scene in which he describes how the Venutians have conquered the world was an undoubted highlight. The unexpectedly violent ending, in which both Hopper and Fonda are senselessly shot by a passing trucker, brought a memorable film to a powerful and unforgettable conclusion. A Pando Co-Raybert Production, it also featured Antonio Mendoza, Phil Spector, Mac Mashourian, Robert Walker Jr, Luana Anders, Karen Black and Warren Finnerty. It was dazzlingly photographed in Technicolor by Laszlo Kovacs, with music provided by Steppenwolf, The Byrds, The Holy Modal Rounders, The Band, The Jimi Hendrix Experience, Little Eva and The Electric Prunes. The film was made – at least partially in 16mm – for a mere $375,000; and given that its box-office returns were the studio's fourth highest of the decade, an awful lot of profit money went back into the company coffers. (94 mins)

△ **Hook, Line and Sinker** was a fair-to-middling Jerry Lewis (right) vehicle in which he played a family man whose doctor (Peter Lawford, centre) informs him one day that he has only a short while to live. On the advice of his wife (Anne Francis), Lewis takes off on a credit-card spree, only to learn (in Lisbon) that his electro-cardiograph had been incorrectly diagnosed, and that he is 100 per cent healthy. So much for the good news. The bad news is that he has, to date, clocked up over $100,000 in credit-card charges. Lawford persuades him that the only solution would be for him to 'die' in order for his wife to inherit the insurance money, and that he and his family can then disappear abroad. What Lewis doesn't know, however, is that the whole thing is a ploy to enable Lawford and Francis to run off – with the money – themselves. A few isolated routines – such as Lewis attempting to light a cigarette on a dance floor, or trying to shave in spite of family interference – momentarily perked up Rod Amateau's screenplay (story by Amateau and David Davis); but only the most dedicated of Lewis junkies could respond unequivocally to its lack of originality. Lewis produced (in Technicolor), George Marshall directed, and the cast included Pedro Gonzalez, Jimmy Miller and Jennifer Edwards. (91 mins)

△ An abundance of first-rate British talent was squandered on David Deutsch's frantically busy Domino production of **Lock Up Your Daughters,** a handsomely mounted, relentlessly inert transfer from the stage of the Lionel Bart-Laurie Johnson-Bernard Miles musical which opened London's Mermaid Theatre, and enjoyed a long and profitable run there. Adapted for the screen by Keith Waterhouse and Willis Hall, this tuneful reworking of Henry Fielding's bawdy play *Rape Upon Rape* and John Vanbrugh's equally risqué *The Relapse* made little impact in the cinema, and its story of three wanton lasses and the three sailors they pursue was lost in an avalanche of vulgar posturings and a confusion of styles. Director Peter Coe was not up to the task of rendering frantic eighteenth-century shenanigans cinematic, and did no service to a cast that included Christopher Plummer as the deliciously ripe Lord Foppington, Susannah York as Hilaret, Glynis Johns (centre) as Mrs Squeezum, Ian Bannen (left) as Ramble and Tom Bell (right) as Shaftoe. Also cast: Jim Dale, Elaine Taylor, Kathleen Harrison, Roy Kinnear, Georgia Brown, Vanessa Howard, Roy Dotrice, Peter Bull, Fenella Fielding, Fred Emney, Arthur Mullard and Patricia Routledge. It was photographed in Technicolor. (102 mins)

▽ Treachery, family feuds, blood-spattered massacres, stage-coach holdups, murder most foul, saloon brawls most brutal as well as scalpings – these were just a handful of the elements that producer Charles Schneer brewed up in **Land Raiders**, a Western written by Ken Pettus and directed by Nathan Juran. It starred Telly Savalas (illustrated) as an Apache-hating, greed-obsessed land-owner intent on claiming territory that rightfully belongs to the Indians. Savalas's eventual come-uppance arrives in the shape of a gory Apache uprising as well as a climactic showdown between him and his younger brother (George Maharis) with whom he has been feuding. Arlene Dahl played Savalas's placatory wife, with other roles going to Janet Landgard as Maharis's love-interest, Jocelyn Lane, George Coulouris, Guy Rolfe, Marcella St Amant and Paul Picerni. It was photographed in Technicolor. (101 mins)

▽ The fourth and worst of the Matt Helm thrillers, **The Wrecking Crew** offered tired actors, tired gags, tired gadgets and a tired old plot involving the hijacking of a billion dollars worth of gold bullion and the global financial holocaust that will result therefrom. A decidedly worse-for-wear Dean Martin (right) again starred as agent Helm; Elke Sommer, Nancy Kwan and (best of all) Sharon Tate (left) represented the distaff side; the heavy of the piece was Nigel Green; and the cast for producer Irving Allen (for Meadway-Claude Productions) also included Tina Louise and John Larch. It was written by William McGivern from a novel by David Hamilton and directed (in Technicolor) by Phil Karlson. (105 mins)

△ **MacKenna's Gold** was a disaster which began with top-starred Gregory Peck (right) being handed a map by a dying Indian detailing the whereabouts of a mythical 'valley of gold', and ended with an avalanche effectively sealing off the mouth of the canyon leading to the hidden bounty. In between, Peck, on his way to the treasure, encounters newspaper editor Lee J. Cobb, preacher Raymond Massey, arch-rival and Mexican bandit Omar Sharif (left), as well as Telly Savalas, Camilla Sparv, Keenan Wynn, Julie Newmar, Ted Cassidy, Burgess Meredith, Anthony Quayle, Edward G. Robinson, Eli Wallach, and Eduardo Ciannelli. An excellent cast, to be sure, but powerless against the clichéd inanities of co-producer (with Dmitri Tiomkin) Carl Foreman's screenplay (based on the novel by Will Henry) of which not even Victor Jory's narration could make much sense. It was flabbily directed by J. Lee Thompson, photographed in Technicolor and 70mm Super Panavision and had an insistent score by Quincy Jones. (128 mins)

1969

◁ Waris Hussein, hitherto a TV director, took naturally, and impressively, to the world of feature films with **Thank You All Very Much** (GB: **A Touch Of Love**). It starred Sandy Dennis (right) as an independent graduate student who falls pregnant as a result of being seduced by a TV announcer (Ian McKellen, left). Against the advice of her friends she decides to have the baby – without telling either her parents, or the baby's father. An off-beat, understated drama that relied heavily on Dennis's central performance for its impact (and on Hussein's subtle, unobtrusive, but always telling direction), it also featured Eleanor Bron, John Standing, Michael Coles, Rachel Kempson, Margaret Tyzack and Maurice Denham. It was scripted by Margaret Drabble (from her novel *The Millstone*), produced by Max J. Rosenberg and Milton Subotsky, and photographed in Eastmancolor. (106 mins)

◁ The US Justice system, no less, came under close (and often compelling) scrutiny in **Pendulum**, an absorbing melodrama which addressed itself to the question of whether the law over-protects criminals, and whether a person is innocent until proved guilty – or vice versa. It starred George Peppard (illustrated) as a tough Washington DC police captain who arrests a psychotic rapist (Robert F. Lyons) only to learn that his prize catch is being released on a legal technicality. To add injury to insult, Peppard is next suspected of murdering both his unfaithful wife (Jean Seberg) and her lover (Harry Lewis). How he sets about proving his innocence as well as nailing – once and for all – the aforementioned rapist, formed the intelligent content of producer Stanley Niss's screenplay. The film was directed, somewhat leadenly at times, by TV recruit George Schaefer (making his big-screen debut) and photographed in Technicolor. Richard Kiley played the civil libertarian who first acts as Lyons's defence attorney, and is then hired by Peppard to defend him; Charles McGraw, Frank Marth and Dana Elcar appeared as Peppard's police colleagues, and the cast also included Madeleine Sherwood, Marj Dusay, Paul McGrath and Stewart Moss. (101 mins)

▽ The contours that separate science-fiction from science-fact were effectively blurred in **Marooned**, a beautifully-mounted, well-cast, high-tension drama in which three astronauts – Gene Hackman (illustrated), Richard Crenna and James Franciscus – on an extended space mission find themselves free-floating in space when the lunar rocket designed to project them back to Earth fails to fire. Director John Sturges, working from a taut, cliff-hanging screenplay by Mayo Simon (based on a novel by Martin Caidin), brought a documentary-like verisimilitude to the situation, and relentlessly extracted from it all the in-built suspense he could. The result was an edge-of-the-seat adventure, without the benefit of a music score, that packed quite an emotional wallop as well. Gregory Peck was top-cast as the Houston-based Commander in charge of ground operations (and had the unenviable task of suggesting that one of the men commit suicide to conserve oxygen), David Janssen was the senior astronaut in charge of an eleventh-hour rescue bid, while the three wives who agonized at home were Lee Grant, Nancy Kovack and Mariette Hartley. A Mike Frankovich-John Sturges Production, it was filmed in Technicolor and Panavision. (131 mins)

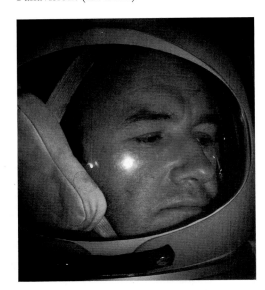

◁ A family film *par excellence*, **Run Wild, Run Free** was all about the regeneration of a mute, psychosomatic, 10-year-old boy who, through his love for a splendid white colt – and the patience and understanding shown toward his predicament by a retired colonel – regains his power to speak and to communicate. Shot on location in rugged Dartmoor, the film featured an excellent British cast with John Mills (left) as the colonel, Mark Lester (centre) – fresh from his success in *Oliver!* (1968) – as the mute, Sylvia Syms and Gordon Jackson as the boy's uncomprehending parents, Fiona Fullerton (right) as the young girl who befriends him, and Bernard Miles as the girl's farmer-uncle. David Rook's screenplay, from his novel *The White Colt*, never patronized the young audience for whom the film was clearly intended. It managed at all times to avoid mawkish sentimentality, and, under Richard C. Sarafian's direction, offered a 20-minute climactic sequence (in which the colt is rescued from a bog) that was in the very best tradition of edge-of-seat movie cliff-hangers. The film was produced by John Danischewsky for Irving Allen Productions and photographed in Technicolor. (100 mins)

△ As a ruthless violent Irishman who bull-dozes his way out of his lower-class Liver-pudlian background and into the world of big business in London, Nicol Williamson (right) – in **The Reckoning** – was mesmeric. He was also charmless and unlikeable – qual-ities which rarely, in a leading man, pave the way to box-office success. He played Michael Marler, a man so consumed by ambition that his private life has, as a result, suffered. Mar-ried to a wealthy woman (Ann Bell) with whom he has little in common, he is peren-nially morose and unhappy. News from Liverpool – that his father is critically ill fol-lowing a beating-up by a Teddy-boy – does nothing to improve his state of mind. He rushes up to Liverpool to see his father but arrives too late. Williamson decides to spend a few hours in his old stamping ground before returning to London – which he does, with

disquieting results. Far from mellowing him, the tragedy of his father's killing makes him even more ruthless – as John McGrath's cyn-ical, uncompromising screenplay (from Patrick Hall's novel *The Harp That Once*) unflinchingly revealed. Similarly, director Jack Gold pulled no punches in the telling of this unsavoury story, and he drew first-rate performances not only from his bullish pro-tagonist, but also from a cast that included Paul Rogers as Williamson's business super-ior, Zena Walker as a secretary, Rachel Roberts (left) – whom Williamson picks up at a wrestling match and takes to bed), as well as Gwen Nelson, Lilita De Barros, Tom Kem-pinski (later to become a successful play-wright), Douglas Wilmer, Kenneth Hendel and Barbara Ewing. It was photographed in Technicolor by Geoffrey Unsworth and pro-duced by Ronald Shedlo. (109 mins)

◁ **Otley** (Tom Courtenay, right) is an English 'yob' whose simple, uncluttered life revolves around girls, soccer, and bacon sandwiches – not necessarily in that order. So when one morning he awakes to discover he is wanted for the murder of a friend, he is, not surprisingly, baffled, bothered, and bewil-dered. Furthermore, he is not at all bewitched by attractive Romy Schneider (left) and her cohorts, who then unceremoniously kidnap him, believing him to be a spy in possession of valuable government information, and beat him up when he fails to tell them what they want to know. Courtenay's bafflement grows in tandem with the grotesque Kaf-kaesque nightmare he is having, and, by the end, it was often difficult to decipher from director Dick Clement's screenplay (which he wrote with Ian La Frenais from the novel by Martin Waddell) just who was doing what to whom and why. As the fashionable, Swinging Sixties anti-hero, Courtenay gave his all (which wasn't really enough) in the company of a fine English supporting cast which featured Alan Badel (as an upper-class government official), James Villiers (as a defecting spy), Freddie Jones (as a gay agent), as well as Leonard Rossiter, James Bolam, Fiona Lewis, James Cossins and Ronald Lacey. It was produced by Bruce Cohn Cur-tis (in Perfect Pathé Color and with Carl Foreman as executive producer), the high-light of whose production was a car chase Courtenay finds himself unexpectedly in-volved during his driving test. (90 mins)

△ A retread of *Ladies in Retirement* (1941), **The Mad Room** moved out of rural England and into scenic Vancouver Island to tell the familiar story of what happened to a wealthy widow (Shelley Winters, right) when the mentally deranged young brother (Michael Burns) and sister (Barbara Sammeth) of her companion (Stella Stevens) take up residence in the Winters household after being dis-charged from a mental institution. Under Bernard Girard's tension-building direction it worked well enough, with Miss Winters in fine form as the rich widow who becomes a knifing victim shortly after the arrival of the anti-social siblings. Skip Ward (right) played the Winters' stepson and Stevens' lover, with other parts in Norman Maurer's (Pathé Color) production going to Carol Cole, Sev-ern Darden and Beverly Garland. It was writ-ten by Girard and A. Z. Martin, based on the play by Reginald Denham and Edward Percy, and the Forties screenplay by Denham and Garrett Fort. (93 mins)

▽ **The Virgin Soldiers** followed the tried and tested formula in which a group of raw army recruits undergo their basic training to the obligatory accompaniment of the three B's (booze, brawls and birds). It chronicled – with much humour but little of the irony in-herent in the novel by Leslie Thomas on which it was based – the National Service tribulations of a group of youngsters prior to their being sent to South-East Asia in the Fifties. Those who survived returned not as boys but as men. Chief among these recruits was Hywel Bennett (second right), a sensitive army clerk desperate to lose his virginity and prove his manhood. He gets his chance with a Singapore hooker called Juicy Lucy (Tsai Chin) though the real object of his affection is Lynn Redgrave (left), the rather sulky schoolmistress-daughter of Sergeant Major Nigel Patrick. The rest of the lads were repre-

sented by Jack Cosmo, Ray Holder, Riggs O'Hara, Christopher Timothy, Don Haw-kins, Geoffrey Hughes, Gregory Phillips and Wayne Sleep. An ambushed train sequence in which many of the men are killed provided this humorous, sympathetic and, in the main, unsentimental tragicomedy with its climax. The cast included Nigel Davenport as the tough old sergeant, Jack Shepherd as the resi-dent coward, Michael Gwynn (an over-the-top caricature as a colonel) and Rachel Kemp-son as the wife of Nigel Patrick. It was scripted by John Hopkins, adapted by John McGrath, with extra dialogue by Ian La Fre-nais, and directed by John Dexter. It was photographed in Technicolor by Ken Hig-gins and produced for Carl Foreman Produc-tions by Ned Sherrin and Leslie Gilliat. *Stand Up Virgin Soldiers* (Warner Bros.) followed in 1977. (96 mins)

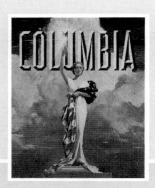

1970-1979

In the Seventies' contemporary American society came under close scrutiny in such Columbia films as *Five Easy Pieces* (1970) and *Getting Straight* (1970). But between 1971 and 1974 the studio found itself in the financial doldrums and was saved from bankruptcy only by the huge box-office returns of producer Ray Stark's *The Way We Were* (1973) and *For Pete's Sake* (1974), both of which starred Barbra Streisand. In 1973, with the arrival of Alan Hirschfield and David Begelman, the studio embarked on the most profitable period in its history – the biggest money-makers of the decade being *Close Encounters Of The Third Kind* (1977) and *Kramer Vs Kramer* (1979).

▽ Janice Elliot's gracefully written novel **The Buttercup Chain** allowed, in its transfer to the screen, for a great deal of emotional flagellation as four decidedly intense young people become deeply involved with each other while travelling through Spain, England and Sweden. Hywel Bennett and Jane Asher are first cousins (born, on the same day, of twin sisters) whose incestuous feelings for one another are consuming them with guilt; while Sven-Bertil Taube (right), a Swedish architectural student, and Leigh Taylor Young (left), an attractive, extrovert young American, meet, marry, and lose a child. Totally confined to their own emotional hothouses, the quartet of inseparable friends-cum-lovers allow no outside interference to redress the precarious balance of their lives, with one exception: a generous, middle-aged millionaire – beautifully realized by Clive Revill – whose attraction to Taylor Young is made manifest by the handsome picnic hampers and gifts he periodically delivers to the four young people. In the end, though, the points Peter Draper's screenplay was trying to make about emotional dependency remained unclear. It was atmospherically directed by Robert Ellis Miller, who also produced for Whitney-Waddilove Productions. Others in the small cast were Roy Dotrice, Michael Elphick, Jonathan Burn, Yutte Stensgaard, Susan Baker and Jennifer Baker. (95 mins)

▽ A lavish, full-blown, very expensive biopic of Oliver Cromwell, but without the irreverent dash that director Michael Curtiz and Warner Bros. might have brought to it in the Thirties, **Cromwell** was a worthy enterprise that looked good in Geoffrey Unsworth's Technicolor and Panavision photography but had a pedestrian and prosaic ring to it. Beginning in 1640 and covering 13 key years in the life of the famous Anglican puritan whose twin purpose was to wipe out corruption in England and to see that his country remained untouched by Catholicism, it starred a hoarse Richard Harris (right) as Cromwell and Alec Guinness (left) as Charles I, Cromwell's weak-willed adversary. The large, and largely impressive cast offered, in Madame Tussaud fashion, Robert Morley as the Earl of Manchester, Dorothy Tutin as Charles's Catholic Queen, Frank Finlay as John Carter, Patrick Wymark as the Earl of Strafford, Patrick Magee as Hugh Peters, Charles Gray as Lord Essex, Michael Jayston as Henry Ireton, Richard Gornish as Oliver Cromwell II, and an early appearance by Timothy Dalton. It was scripted by director Ken Hughes (research consultant was Ronald Harwood) as earnestly as it was directed, and revolved around the English persecution of the Irish Catholics, the impending advance on England by a Scottish army, and the injustices perpetrated by the King's court while raising money for the Scottish war. Parliament was rallied by Cromwell with the resultant clash between the Roundheads and the Cavaliers. The history lesson was given under the aegis of producer Irving Allen, but it wasn't a lesson that audiences wanted to learn. (139 mins)

◁ A tedious spy drama with barely a redeeming feature, **The Executioner** starred George Peppard (right) as a British (though American-raised) undercover agent who, during most of Jack Pulman's puzzling screenplay (from a story by Gordon McDonell) is determined to prove to his superiors (Charles Gray and Nigel Patrick) that Keith Michell, a former associate of his, is a double agent. As directed by Sam Wanamaker it was slow moving in the extreme and wasted the talents of a competent British cast that included infrequent appearances by Joan Collins (left) as Michell's wife and Judy Geeson as Peppard's girlfriend, Oscar Homolka as a defected Russian agent, Alexander Scourby as CIA sleuth, as well as Peter Bull, George Baker and Ernest Clark. It was produced by Charles H. Schneer. (111 mins)

△ That hardy perennial of movies and literature, a man's search for his identity, was the subject of Bob Rafelson's 'road' drama, **Five Easy Pieces**. The searcher was Jack Nicholson (illustrated) who, when first encountered, is an oil-rigger out of kilter with his environment. It turns out, though, that he is really the concert-pianist-cum-intellectual son of an aristocratic family from Puget Sound, Washington. When Nicholson learns from his sister (Lois Smith), also a pianist, that their father (William Challee) has suffered two strokes, he heads for home in the company of his pregnant bimbo-like girlfriend (Karen Black). For Nicholson, however, home is not where the heart is, and, after a mild sexual encounter with the fiancée (Susan Anspach) of his violinist-brother (Ralph Waite), he abandons Miss Black, his car and his worldly possessions, and continues his search for a meaning to his life by hopping a truck bound for Alaska. A curiously unsettling film, it was held together by Nicholson's restless energy, as well as by truthful supporting performances from a cast that included Helena Kallianiotes as a disgruntled hitchhiker, Toni Basil, Billie Green Bush, Fannie Flagg and, in a small role, Sally Ann Struthers (who would later drop the Ann). The funniest scene in the film had Nicholson becoming involved in a heated *contretemps* with diner waitress Lorna Thayer who refuses to 'hold' the chicken in his order of 'a chicken salad on toast'. Rafelson's uncluttered tell-it-as-it-is direction was greatly enhanced by Laszlo Kovacs's gentle, unflamboyant photography which captured all the subtle beauty of the Pacific Northwest. A BBS Production, it was produced by Rafelson and Richard Wechsler, and was written by Adrien Joyce (real name Carol Eastman) from her own story. (96 mins)

▷ A cop-out ending added a frustratingly inconclusive note to **Fragment of Fear,** which, for most of its running time, was an intriguing thriller that not only asked 'whodunnit?' but also 'why was it done?'. The victim was a briefly-seen Flora Robson, who has been strangled to death in Pompeii. David Hemmings (right), as her reformed drug-addict nephew, sets out to apprehend his aunt's murderer and to discover why a harmless old lady should have met such a violent death. However, he never does; he has a nervous breakdown instead. Paul Dehn's screenplay, from the novel by John Bingham, was a labyrinth of intrigue in which it was often difficult to decide what was actually happening and what were merely fragments of Hemmings's imagination. Richard C. Sarafian's direction kept matters deliberately vague, but drew solid performances not only from his leading man, but from a cast that also included Wilfrid Hyde-White, Daniel Massey, Roland Culver, Adolfo Celi, Mona Washbourne, Patricia Hayes, Zakes Mokae, and, as Hemmings's girlfriend, his real-life wife, Gayle Hunnicutt (left). The producer was John R. Sloan. (95 mins)

△ At the time of its release **Getting Straight** seemed to be making a profound statement about contemporary America, the generation gap, and the nervy climate of student unrest and rebellion that was ripping through the country's campuses. It was a receptacle into which scenarist Bob Kaufman (working from a novel by Ken Kolb) poured all the scorn, the rage and the frustration that the Viet Nam generation felt for the mindless foolishness of those either too old to have taken part in the war, or too young to have understood its senseless waste. Though the passing of time may have diluted its impact and rendered it dated, there was no under-cutting the dynamic central performance of Elliott Gould (left) around whom the film pivoted. As a womanizing Viet Nam veteran who returns to university to obtain a degree in education and who becomes involved in the campus activities that helped define the latter half of the Sixties, he was superb. Also making an impact (for the first time in her career so far) was Candice Bergen (right) as the student lover with whom he shared some tastefully directed, albeit passionate, love scenes. Kaufman's episodic screenplay also found room for Robert F. Lyons, Jeannie Berlin (Elaine May's daughter), Max Julien and Jenny Sullivan (Barry Sullivan's daughter) as a cross-section of students, as well as Jeff Corey, Cecil Kellaway, Leonard Stone, Jon Lormer and William Bramley as the college staff. They, too, provided a comprehensive cross-section of differing values and mores. Also cast: John Rubinstein, Richard Anders, Brenda Sykes, Gregory Sierra, Billie Bird and Harrison Ford. The film was produced and directed by Richard Rush. (126 mins)

▽ **Husbands,** indulgently directed by John Cassavetes from his own, largely improvised screenplay, was a protracted, virtually plotless wallow about male bonding and the onslaught of middle-age. Three buddies, Harry (Ben Gazzara, right), Archie (Peter Falk, centre) and Gus (Cassavetes, left), all of them married, attend the funeral of the fourth member of their group (David Rowlands) – a coronary victim, and realize that there but for the grace of God, it could have been any one of them. They are so shaken up by their friend's premature death, they go on an extended four-day bender that takes them from their Long Island residences to New York and London. They drink heavily, sleep on the subway, talk a lot, play basketball, pick up girls, vomit, talk some more, and constantly indulge in affectionate horseplay. Finally Gus and Archie decide to go home, where, apart from their wives, they have 'three garages and five kids' between them. However, Harry, the broodiest of the trio, remains in London. Though the camaraderie (and frustration) of the three men during their four-day odyssey was brilliantly captured by Cassavetes, the film's excessive length and the lack of a sustaining narrative resulted in diminishing dramatic returns. More might have been achieved with less indulgence. All the performances were excellent, especially newcomer Jenny Runacre as Cassavetes's neurotic English pick-up. Al Ruban and Sam Shaw's production also featured Jenny Lee Wright, Noelle Kao, Leola Harlow, Meta Shaw, John Kullers and Dolores Delmar. (138 mins)

▽ That old Broadway chestnut, the family squabble – so beloved of American playwrights from Eugene O'Neill (who inherited it from Strindberg), through Arthur Miller to Robert Anderson – surfaced, with a vengeance, in Anderson's unsuccessful, quasi-autobiographical stage play **I Never Sang For My Father** which had a loss-making run of 124 performances in 1964. The story of a 40-year-old professor who tries in vain to establish a bond between himself and his selfish, cantankerous old father, the film starred Gene Hackman (left) as the son and Melvyn Douglas (right) as the father (on stage the roles were taken by Hal Holbrook and Alan Webb), with Dorothy Stickney as Douglas's ailing wife and Estelle Parsons as the daughter he disowns for marrying a Jew. Though Anderson's screenplay managed on occasion to ventilate the stage play, producer-director Gilbert Cates was unable to disguise the work's origins and the end result was a distended, rather stagey character-study of two opposing wills. There was no diminishing the impact, though, of the two central performances. Hackman and Douglas tore into this familiar, oft-told tale with the relish of actors who know a potential Academy Award-winning role when they see one, and together brought a moving conviction to their series of painful confrontations. Also in it were Elizabeth Hubbard (as a divorced doctor whom Hackman hopes to marry), Lovelady Powell, Daniel Keyes, Conrad Bain and Jon Richards. (92 mins)

▽ Director John Frankenheimer did an excellent job evoking the look and 'feel' of the Tennessee backwoods in **I Walk The Line,** but wasn't able to pummel life into the screenplay which Alvin Sargent fashioned from Madison Jones's novel *An Exile*. A folk ballad told to the accompaniment of five Johnny Cash songs, it was the downbeat story of a Southern sheriff's infatuation with an amorous and amoral moonshiner's young daughter, and the tragic consequences of that infatuation. Gregory Peck (front), essentially 'a good man', played the smitten sheriff, Tuesday Weld (back) was the sensual object of his affections, Ralph Meeker was her father, and Estelle Parsons played Peck's confused wife. Also in the cast were Charles Durning as Peck's deputy, and Lonny Chapman as a bawdy federal agent. The producer was Harold D. Cohen. (96 mins)

▷ At the age of 68, veteran director William Wyler made **The Liberation of L. B. Jones**. It was his last film and definitely not one of his best. Moving into the realm of 'contemporary' subjects, Wyler's swansong turned out to be a platitudinous melodrama involving racism and Southern bigotry. It told the story of a wealthy black undertaker from Somerset, Tennessee (Roscoe Lee Browne, right) who not only has to contend with an unfaithful wife (Lola Falana), but is arrested under false pretences, shot, and castrated. His death is finally avenged by an angry young black (Yaphet Kotto), who pushes his killer, a crooked cop (Arch Johnson), into a harvester. Despite being the titular hero of the piece, Browne received third billing to top-starred Lee J. Cobb who played a powerful Southern lawyer unduly given to compromise (not one of his more subtle performances), and Anthony Zerbe as the white policeman with whom Browne's wife is having an affair. Lee Majors, Barbara Hershey, Chill Wills and Zara Cully were also featured in Ronald Lubin's production, which was scripted by Stirling Silliphant and Jesse Hill Ford from the latter's novel *The Liberation of Lord Byron Jones*. (102 mins)

△ The frustration and the futility of Cold War espionage, so potently captured by John Le Carré in his novel **The Looking Glass War,** was somewhat underplayed in producer John Box's youth-orientated screen version. Christopher Jones was miscast as a ship-jumping Pole recruited by Ralph Richardson (right) and Paul Rogers (centre) of British Intelligence to acquire some graphs of a new rocket in East Germany; Susan George played his pregnant girlfriend, and Pia Degermark was the more mature and worldly woman who enters his life in East Germany. Anthony Hopkins (left) was also prominently featured as a young undercover agent and Ray McAnally, Anna Massey and Robert Urquart were in it, too. It was written and directed by Frank R. Pierson with a certain flair but without much dramatic consistency, and, although well-made, left a flat and stale impression. (108 mins)

▽ A harassed George Segal (left) dominated **Loving,** director Irvin Kershner's fashionable comedy about the success ethic. He played a talented commercial artist in the bewildering process of juggling the component parts of his busy life. Married to pretty Eva Marie Saint (right) and living in the chic confines of Westport, Connecticut, he has a mistress (Janis Young) in New York whom he is in danger of losing, is about to buy a new house, and is a hair's-breadth away from acquiring a profitable new account. Just how Segal coped with the day-to-day realities of his demanding schedule, as well as remaining a good husband and father, and a responsible breadwinner, and satisfying his extra-marital sexual drives, formed the well-observed, though uneven, content of the screenplay Don Devlin shaped from a novel by J. M. Ryan. The film's most impressive set-piece was saved till the end when, at a large cocktail party in Fairfield County, Segal disappears into a children's playroom with the nymphomaniac wife (Nancie Phillips) of his neighbour (David Doyle), only to have their sexual tussle relayed to the assembled guests – including his wife – on closed-circuit TV. Sterling Hayden was featured as a self-made industrialist. Keenan Wynn played Segal's agent, and Sherry Lansing (centre, later to become production head of 20th Century-Fox for a year) had a small role as a sexpot. But it was Segal's film and he inhabited it completely. It was produced by scenarist Devlin and Raymond Wagner. (89 mins)

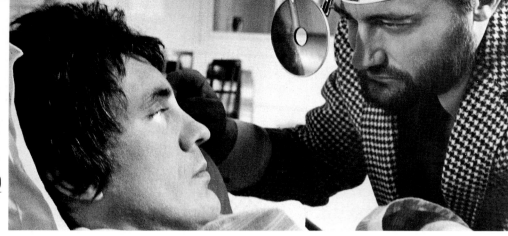

▽ The very kind of affectation that had its title reduced to lower-case informed practically all of **riverrun.** Sarah and Dan – Louise Ober (centre) and Mark Jenkins (left) – leave the student rat race to find peace of mind (as vegetarians, naturally) on a picturesque sheep ranch a couple of hours out of San Francisco. Their idyll is punctured by the arrival of Sarah's father Jeffries (John McLiam, right) and the conflict that develops between them passed for plot. It was written, directed and photographed by John Korty whose work in all three capacities left much to be desired. Stephen Schmidt produced. (95 mins)

△ Sporting a story-line (by John Hale and Edward Simpson from the novel by Charles Eric Maine) straight out of a sci-fi programmer from the Thirties or Forties, but given serious, A-picture consideration by producers Max J. Rosenberg and Milton Subotsky for Abicus Productions, **The Mind of Mr Soames** was engaging hokum – thanks, largely, to a touching central performance by Terence Stamp (left, which was not unlike the one given by Cliff Robertson in the similarly-themed *Charly*, CRC, 1968). Stamp played John Soames who, since the day of his birth, has lived in a coma. After 30 years he emerges from sleep, having had the brain of an infant transplanted into his skull by American surgeon Robert Vaughn (right). As Stamp undergoes a rigorous programme to cram 30 years of experience into his new brain in just a matter of weeks, a clash of ideologies develops between Vaughn, who believes his patient should be treated with loving care, and Nigel Davenport, the head of the institution, who is of the opinion that a martinet approach is what is called for. Stamp literally runs away from the issue, but finds the outside world too hostile to handle, and, in front of a live TV audience, kills Vaughn, his Frankenstein. Christian Roberts played a hard-boiled TV director and Donal Donnelly was a kindly doctor, with other roles under Alan Cooke's restrained direction going to Norman Jones, Dan Jackson, Vickery Turner and Judy Parfitt. (97 mins)

▷ Refined was hardly the word for **The Owl And The Pussycat,** a loud-mouthed transfer of Bill Manhoff's bawdy 1964 Broadway comedy which came to the screen via producer Ray Stark and with Barbra Streisand (front, her first non-singing role) in the part played on stage by black actress Diana Sands. Buck Henry's adaptation eliminated all references to colour, and, with George Segal (back) as Streisand's leading man (Alan Alda did it on stage), the film became a typical Brooklyn-Bronx comedy about an endearing Jewish kook and the nebbish intellectual with whom she falls in love and whom she draws out of his shell. Streisand played Doris, a casual hooker ('I may be a prostitute, but I'm not promiscuous') who forms an on-off-on-again relationship with her neighbour, would-be author and bookstore clerk Felix (Segal), after he reports her soliciting activities to their landlord (Jacques Sandulescu) and has her evicted. Plot-wise not a great deal happened, and the comic mileage Herbert Ross clocked up in this, his second feature film as fully-fledged director, relied heavily on Manhoff's raunchy, 'R' rated dialogue, and on the interplay (or foreplay, on this occasion) between his two stars. Confidently treading the deep waters of situation comedy, Streisand was more than a match for Manhoff's risqué material and didn't have to burst into song to re-establish her star quality. With or without vocalizing, she was a natural comedienne and brought to the role her special magic. Segal, an old-hand at the comedy of fluster, was equally at home with his sexually awakened character (and his co-star's special brand of zaniness), and together they helped a rather flimsy vehicle gross a splendid profit. The rest of the cast didn't get much of a look in, but, for the record, they included Robert Klein, Allen Garfield, Roz Kelly, Jack Manning, Grace Carney and Barbara Anson. The film's photography was begun by Harry Stradling, who died during its making, and was completed by Andrew Laszlo. (98 mins)

▽ Having, in the past, addressed himself to some of the world's most important issues – such as nuclear annihilation, the Nazi holocaust, and racial discrimination – Stanley Kramer boarded the student-revolution band-wagon in **RPM** (Revolutions Per Minute) and fell off with a resounding thud. A woefully miscast Anthony Quinn (left) starred as an anti-Establishment college professor, who, after the forced resignation of the college's president (John Zaremba), takes his place and is faced with answering a list of 12 demands put to him by a group of student radicals. When a deadlock in their negotiations is reached and the students threaten to destroy the college's recently-acquired $2 million computer, laid-back Quinn has no choice but to call in the cops, a move which totally undermines his popularity with the students who humiliate him with a series of insults. Ann-Margret (right) played Quinn's graduate-student mistress and evinced more sex appeal than conviction, with other roles going to Gary Lockwood as a student radical, and Graham Jarvis as the chief of police. Kramer produced and directed from a script by Erich (*Love Story*) Segal and, if his heart *was* in it, the film clearly suffered a thrombosis. (92 mins)

▽ The heroine of Kingsley Amis's 1960 novel **Take A Girl Like You** was a 20-year-old school-mistress determined, until her wedding night at any rate, to hold on to her virginity. Why? asks Oliver Reed as her would-be lover. 'Because' replies Miss Hayley Mills (right). The more determined and obsessed Reed becomes with taking from Hayley that which does not belong to him, the more infuriatingly stubborn she becomes, and his desires remain unfulfilled by the final fade. George Melly's screenplay hinted at a sexual liaison between Mills and a cynical, extremely wealthy playboy (Noel Harrison, centre, son of Rex) but their relationship, and hence perhaps a possible explanation of her attitude, was never made clear. And that was about all there was to producer Hal Chester's liberated battle of the sexes – a war which, on this occasion, was hardly worth the fight. John Bird (left) and Sheila Hancock appeared as the heroine's incompatible landlords, cute Aimi MacDonald played a sexy blonde TV model, and Ronald Lacey was Reed's Scottish room-mate. The film was directed by a debut-making Jonathan Miller with competence rather than flair. (101 mins)

▷ Considered bold for its time (for both its plot and its dialogue), **There's A Girl In My Soup** was a breezy sex-comedy, cast from strength, with Peter Sellers (right) as a lecherous TV gourmet and Goldie Hawn (left) as his latest 'bit on the side'. After he attempts to seduce her in an apartment designed for just that purpose, and reminiscent of the ones used in *Under The Yum Yum Tree* (1963) and *Lover Come Back* (Universal, 1961), she simply suggests they sleep with each other. They do, she moves in with him, they take a holiday in the South of France, tour the *château* country together, and return to London. Sellers asks for her hand in marriage, she refuses (claiming still to be in love with erstwhile boyfriend Nicky Henson) and moves out. Sellers is temporarily distraught but soon pulls himself together when a pretty young secretary enters his life. Though no world-beater on any level, it was continuously diverting, thanks, mainly, to its two stars. Like the play that preceded it, it was just the job for the tired businessman; clearly there were enough of those around for John Boulting and Mike Frankovich's production to be a solid financial success. Tony Britton excelled in the featured role of Sellers' confidant and publisher, with other roles under Roy Boulting's direction going to John Comer (as Sellers' envious doorman), Diana Dors (as the doorman's shrewish wife), Gabrielle Drake and Ruth Trouncer. It was written by Terence Frisby (based on his play, the Broadway production of which featured Gig Young and Barbara Ferris), with additional dialogue by Peter Kortner. (94 mins)

△ A really dreadful love affair involving a mature couple and set against the picturesque backdrop of the Smoky Mountains, **A Walk In The Spring Rain** was every bit as sudsy as its hearts-and-flowers title suggested. It starred a middle-aged Ingrid Bergman (right) as the happily married but bored wife of an equally bored university professor (Fritz Weaver). While on a campus sabbatical in the Tennessee mountain country, she meets and falls in love with local man Anthony Quinn (left) here playing a life-enhancing, Zorba-like mountaineer. The whole notion was, frankly, preposterous, and was further aggravated by the casting of Virginia Gregg as Quinn's nag of a wife, and Tom Fielding as Quinn's method-actorish son. Also in the cast for producer Stirling Silliphant (who scripted it from the novella by Rachel Maddux) were Katherine Crawford (as Bergman's selfish daughter) and Mitchell Silberman as Crawford's young son. The dreary direction was by Guy Green. (98 mins)

▽ Basically a revue-sketch involving a single, solitary gag, **Watermelon Man** stretched itself way beyond endurance as it described the cliché plight of a white, middle-class, married suburbanite who, due to some biological mishap, turns black overnight. Just as when Gregory Peck took on the mantle of a Jew way back in 1947 in *Gentleman's Agreement* (20th Century-Fox) in order to experience anti-semitism first hand, so the hero of Herman Raucher's well-intentioned but half-baked screenplay learns the meaning of racial prejudice head-on. It wasn't a bad idea – just not very original; and, as it lacked a brilliantly witty and satirical script, it was unable to survive its inflated running time. The hapless hero was played by black actor Godfrey Cambridge (right, who, before the biological accident had to 'white' up), Estelle Parsons (left) was his feckless wife, with other roles going to Howard Caine, D'Urville Martin, Kay Kimberley, and, in his 301st film, veteran black actor Mantan Moreland. A John B. Bennett Production, it was directed by Melvin Van Peebles. (100 mins)

▽ Tony Curtis (right) played the fool to Charles Bronson's (left) leer in **You Can't Win 'Em All** which, as one contemporary wag noted at the time, was both a title as well as a dismissal of this Gene Corman-produced potboiler. Messrs C & B were cast as a pair of bungling adventurers who, at the time of the collapse of the Ottoman Empire in the Turkey of the Twenties, became involved in a series of guerilla intrigues. One Turkey begat another as the desperately unentertaining farrago – which also featured Michèle Mercier as the sex interest – fell apart at the seams. Peter Collinson directed (badly), and the cast was completed by Patrick Magee, Fikret Hakan, Grégoire Aslan and Tony Bonner. It was written by Leo V. Gordon, who also appeared in it – as a character called Bolek. (95 mins)

▽ Lovers of movie trivia may be interested to learn that the Convent of the Sacred Heart on New York's East 9th Street was the building used to represent the plush Manhattan apartment house that Sean Connery (illustrated), in cahoots with a group of cohorts, systematically burglarized in Sidney Lumet's riveting surveillance caper, **The Anderson Tapes.** Based on the novel by Lawrence Sanders, though by no means faithful to its complexities and convolutions, Frank Pierson's screenplay added quite a bit of humour to the intriguing tale of an ex-con (Connery) who finds backing for his heist by mobster Alan King, but is unaware that his every move is being monitored by the FBI, the IRS, the NYPD and a surveillance organization known as the POM (Peace of Mind). Though Connery's cool, cat-like presence dominated the action, there were good performances from a large supporting cast including Dyan Cannon as a high-priced hooker, Stan Gottlieb, Ralph Meeker, newcomer Christopher Walken, Garrett Morris, Val Avery, Margaret Hamilton, and, as one of Connery's assistants, a swishy Martin Balsam as a stereotypical gay antique dealer. Balsam, in the showiest role, made a meal of the part, doubtless offending, in the process, gay activists sensitive to the caricaturing of elderly queens. The film was directed with awesome professionalism by Sidney Lumet, scored by Quincy Jones, and produced by Robert M. Weitman. (98 mins)

△ **Brother John** was a whimsical disaster in which Sidney Poitier (illustrated) played a sartorially elegant messenger of God who returns to his home town in Hackley, Alabama – ostensibly for a family funeral – is suspected by the locals of being up to no good, and imprisoned. Who Poitier was and what his purpose was in returning was never made clear in Ernest Kinoy's mystical screenplay, nor in James Goldstone's unfocused direction. If Joel Glickman's production was intended to be a doomsday parable of sorts, it failed. Will Geer played the town doctor, Bradford Dillman was his ambitious son, Beverly Todd provided the romantic interest, and the cast also included Raymond Bieri, Warren J. Kemmerling and Lincoln Kilpatrick. (94 mins)

△ Message-bringer-cum-director Stanley Kramer turned himself into Western Union for **Bless The Beasts And Children**, a drama, ostensibly for children, in which a simple plot was wrapped in layers of social significance. It was the story of a group of six wealthy misfit kids – losers, all of them – who, while spending time at a riding camp, are horrified to witness the destruction of a herd of buffalo. When they learn that even more of the animals are destined for the slaughterhouse, they set out, by foot, on a horse and in a stolen truck, to save them. *En route*, and in flashback, we learn something about each of the kids' backgrounds – how one is ignored by his father, how another is over-protected, how sibling rivalry has come between two brothers – and it takes no perspicacity to realize that the kids, too, are an endangered species in need of protection. The standout performance – in a cast of unknowns including Barry Robbins, Miles Chapin, Darel Glasser, Bob Kramer, Marc Vahanian, Jesse White, Ken Swofford and Dave Ketchum – was Bill Mumy (centre) as the laconic leader of the group. It was written by Mac Benoff from the novel by Glendon Swarthout, and produced by Stanley Kramer. [Barry DeVorzon and Perry Botkin's music for this film became very popular, and was retitled 'Nadia's Theme' and 'The Young And The Restless' theme.] (109 mins)

△ A small-scale horror curiosity that wielded a certain fascination, **The Brotherhood Of Satan** concerned a coven of witches operating in a small Southwestern town. According to William Welch's uneven screenplay (story by Sean MacGregor) an all-important 13th child is required for the diabolical coven to infiltrate the young 'uns bodies, thereby assuring for themselves immortality. Enter child number 13 (Geri Reischl), the daughter of a vacationing couple who mysteriously find they are unable to leave the town . . . A handful of good ideas offset Bernard McEveety's indifferent direction, and aficionados of the genre didn't go home entirely unrewarded. Strother Martin (left) was top-cast, with other roles going to Charles Bateman, Anna Capri, Charles Robinson, and L. Q. Jones and Alvy Moore (who both also produced). (92 mins)

△ The sexual shenanigans of doctors and their wives was the subject of **Doctors' Wives**, a soapy drama – directed by George Schaefer – which took a prurient look at the sexual underbelly of the medical profession. Based on a novel by Frank G. Slaughter, Daniel Taradash's screenplay was a shoddy affair that began with the murder of an over-sexed wife (Dyan Cannon, on screen for a mere eight minutes) by her doctor husband (John Colicos), and ended with practically everyone in the cast having had everyone else. And to prove it was all about doctors and not, say, lawyers, there were scenes of open-heart surgery as well. The sexual pairings in Mike Frankovich's synthetic production involved Richard Crenna (left) and Janice Rule (right), with Diana Sands as Crenna's black mistress, Gene Hackman and Rachel Roberts (the latter having also had a one-night stand with Miss Cannon), Carroll O'Connor and Cara Williams, and Anthony Costello and Kristina Holland who enjoys tape-recording her most intimate experiences. Also in it were Ralph Bellamy as Cannon's father, Richard Anderson as a district attorney, and Scott Brady as a cop. (102 mins)

▷ Nudity (both male and female), four-letter words and heavy-duty love-making were some of the permissive items in Jack Nicholson's directorial debut, **Drive, He Said**, another anti-war campus caper that at least had the courage of its dated convictions. Nicholson's sense of commitment to his subject was never in doubt; all the film needed was a less diffuse screenplay (by Nicholson and Jeremy Larner, based on Larner's Delta Prize novel) and a more appealing hero. The one audiences were saddled with was William Tepper as a confused basketball jock who, in his own words, feels 'disconnected'. As the film unspools, disillusion sets in. The college professor's wife (Karen Black, right), with whom Tepper is in love, is pregnant and not in love with him, his room-mate (Michael Margotta, left) feigns insanity to avoid the draft and then really does go mad, and even basketball, his great passion in life, isn't what it used to be. It turns out, too, that Tepper is a Greek major and has a mind as well as a body – a fact not revealed until late in the film. But by then it's too late. For, although central to the scheme of things, Tepper is never as interesting as some of the supporting characters with whom he comes into contact – such as his quirky aforementioned room-mate, his sex-loving girlfriend, or her professor-husband (Robert Towne). Nicholson's easy-going directorial approach was in keeping with the material, and, judging from the performances, he was good with actors too. It was produced by Nicholson, Steve Blauner and Bert Schneider for BBS Productions, and the cast also included Bruce Dern, Henry Jaglom, Mike Warren and June Fairchild. (95 mins)

▽ **Flight Of The Doves** was that rare cinematic phenomenon, a 'family' film which, indeed, every member of the family – from eight to eighty – could enjoy. Filmed entirely on location in Ireland by producer-director Ralph Nelson, it re-teamed Ron Moody – and Jack Wild (left) of *Oliver!* fame in the suspenseful, often humorous tale of a pair of runaway kids (Wild and newcomer Helen Raye) fleeing a cruel stepfather (William Rushton) and searching for their kindly grandmother (Dorothy McGuire) 'somewhere' in Ireland. More dangerous, though, than Rushton, is the children's uncle (Ron Moody), a failed actor who stands to inherit their fortune should the children not survive. Nelson's handling of the breathless chase sequences generated genuine tension, and, with Moody popping up in several unrecognizable disguises, a satisfying blend of fun and excitement was guaranteed. Stanley Holloway played a judge, singer Dana was featured as a tinker-girl, and Noel Purcell (right) surfaced as an Irish rabbi! It was written by Nelson and Frank Gabrielson from the book by Walter Macken, beautifully photographed by Harry Waxman, and included several songs by Roy Budd. (101 mins)

△ In **Dollars** (GB:**The Heist**), superstars Warren Beatty (right) and Goldie Hawn (left) both took on the mantle of Robin Hood as they set out to fleece the criminally over-privileged (drug dealers, racketeers, gamblers, etc) of $1 million from a safe-deposit vault in Hamburg. He's a security expert, she's a hooker. Together they made a dynamite combination at the box-office from Hamburg to Harare and left producer Mike Frankovich with a smile on his face. Director Richard Brooks's screenplay was climaxed by an over-extended chase which found Beatty trapped on thin ice. Everything else about the caper, though, was on solid ground – including a serviceable supporting cast comprising Gert Frobe, Robert Webber, Scott Brady and Arthur Brauss. (119 mins)

▷ James Stewart (illustrated), complete with white hair, moustache and removable glass eye, starred in **Fools' Parade** (GB: **Dynamite Man From Glory Jail**) – his 75th film. The year is 1935, and Stewart is a newly released prisoner who, after serving a 40-year sentence, wants nothing more than to claim the $25,000 waiting for him in a local bank. Together with two other convicts freshly out of West Virginia State Penitentiary (Strother Martin and Kurt Russell), he intends to open a store. Unfortunately, the no-good president of the bank (David Huddleston) has a mind to keep the money for himself, and hires a corrupt prison guard (George Kennedy) to kill Stewart and his buddies. Just how the trio outwit their brutal overseer formed the tension-building content of James Lee Barrett's screenplay (from the novel by Davis Grubb). Anne Baxter played the madame of a run-down riverboat bordello, with other roles under Andrew McLaglen's uneven (often static) direction going to William Windom, Mike Kellin, Kathy Cannon, Morgan Paul and Robert Donner. Barrett and McLaglen produced. (97 mins)

◁ Director John Frankenheimer's obsession with the macho male – who, through a mixture of pride and vanity, pushes himself beyond endurance – was demonstrated, once again, in **The Horsemen.** If racing and sky-diving were the subjects of Frankenheimer's *Grand Prix* (MGM, 1966) and *The Gypsy Moths* (MGM, 1969) respectively, the sport featured in *The Horsemen* was buzkashi, a gruesome variation of polo, played with the head of a decapitated calf. Omar Sharif (right) is the son of an Afghan sheik who has a violent collision during such a game, is humiliated, and, with his wounded leg in plaster, travels home by a difficult mountain route accompanied by a treacherous servant (David De) and an 'untouchable' girl (Leigh Taylor-Young) out to fleece him. In a remote mountain village in Afghanistan, Sharif has his leg amputated at the knee, and spends the remainder of the film training rigorously in order to re-establish his macho image as the greatest horseman in the land – which, of course, he does. If Dalton Trumbo's worthy screenplay (based on the novel by Joseph Kessel) didn't offer much to nurture the intellect, it was full of local colour – all of it beautifully captured in Claude Renoir's SuperPanavision photography. Jack Palance (left) played Sharif's chieftain father, with other roles in John Frankenheimer and Edward Lewis's epic Eastern going to Peter Jeffrey, Mohammed Shamsi, George Murcell and Eric Pohlmann. (105 mins)

△ Cliff Robertson (right) wrote, produced, directed and starred in **J. W. Coop** and achieved distinction in all four categories, bringing to life this simple, quirky, often elegiac story of a rodeo man, who, after spending nine years in jail for passing a bad cheque and then beating up a sheriff, rejoins the circuit, has an affair with an ecology-minded hippie (Cristina Ferrare, left) and takes part in the Oklahoma City rodeo championship. The film's minimal narrative was clearly of secondary interest to Robertson who was more occupied with capturing on film the effects that those nine years have had on his protagonist – both privately and professionally – and this was splendidly achieved in terms of his performance and in his sensitive, beautifully observed writing and direction. Geraldine Page was second-billed as Robertson's deranged, evangelism-obsessed mother, and though her role was brief, this incomparable actress made it memorable. Also cast: R. G. and R. L. Armstrong, John Crawford, Wade Crosby, Marjorie Durant Dye and Paul Harper. (112 mins)

△ Style and content clashed head-on in Lester M. Goldsmith's production of **Happy Birthday Wanda June.** The basic problem was that Kurt Vonnegut's screenplay (based on his off-Broadway play) – which was about man's fear of death and the modern world's need for heroes who do not kill – remained rooted in the theatre and nothing that director Mark Robson did with the material camouflaged this fact. The result was an uneasy hybrid whose artificial style seemed inflated on the big screen. Taking a swipe at the macho Hemingway-type hero, Vonnegut contrived a comedy about a big-game hunter (Rod Steiger, left) who, having been lost in the wilds of the Amazon for eight years, returns to civilization to find that his third wife (Susannah York, right), a car-hop bimbo has, in his absence, educated herself out of his league, and is in the process of choosing either a pacifist violin-playing doctor (George Grizzard) or a vacuum-cleaner salesman (Don Murray) as her new lover. Vonnegut's aromatic dialogue was full of laugh lines which were well delivered by Steven Paul as Steiger's son, William Hickey as his private-helicopter pilot, Louis Turrene as a German pilot killed by Steiger, and Pamela Saunders as one of Steiger's erstwhile lovers. (These, and several other members of the cast, appeared in the original off-Broadway production.) (105 mins)

▷ In his second feature film, **The Last Picture Show,** Peter Bogdanovich, its director, looked back not only with fond nostalgia but with a profound sense of loss at the small, dilapidated town of Anarene, Texas in 1951. The entry of Anarene into the second half of the century was inevitably characterized by the growth of TV as a popular entertainment and the resultant closure of the Royale Theatre, the town's only movie-house. Against a meticulously observed background of small-town life, Bogdanovich brilliantly, and evocatively, re-created the look and the feel of backwoods Fifties as he vividly brought to life the characters created by Larry McMurtry in his compelling novel. Timothy Bottoms (left) played Sonny Crawford, the high-school senior and football captain through whose eyes the changing urban landscape is perceived, and whose gradual maturation from boyhood to manhood was part of the film's *raison d'être.* Jeff Bridges (right) was cast as Duane Jackson, Sonny's best friend, and Cloris Leachman was the sexy middle-aged wife of the school's basketball coach (Bill Thurman) who initiates Sonny into adult sex. A stunningly attractive Cybill Shepherd (her debut) was perfectly used as the man-eating Jacy Farrow, the richest, and most spoilt girl in town, and the excellent Ellen Burstyn was her frustrated, conniving mother. Ben Johnson (in a homage, of sorts, to John Ford, one of Bogdanovich's heroes) gave the best, most moving performance of all as Sam The Lion, a surrogate father to the town's youngsters, and the owner of the local pool room and 'picture show'. Also cast were Sam Bottoms as the retarded Billy, Eileen Brennan as a waitress, Sharon Taggart as Bottoms's first girlfriend, and Randy Quaid, Clu Gulager, Joe Heathcock and Barc Doyle. Robert Surtees's sharp, black-and-white photography added immeasurably to the period verisimilitude of the piece; the screenplay was the work of McMurtry and Bogdanovich; and it was produced by Stephen J. Friedman for BBS Productions, for whom it grossed a healthy profit. (118 mins)

△ A really dreadful Western, **The Last Rebel,** made in Italy and Spain, starred New York Jets quarterback Joe Namath (right) as a Confederate soldier, who, in southwest Missouri in 1865, continues the war with second-billed Jack Elam, a pal-turned-enemy. As adept at romance as he is with a gun, Namath wins the heart of the local madam (Victoria George) – but hardly the admiration of the paying customers, as acting was clearly not his thing. Woody Strode (left) was featured as a black man whom Messrs Namath and Elam rescue from a lynching, with other roles under Denys McCoy's non-direction going to Ty Hardin, Renato Romano and Marina Coffa. Warren Kiefer wrote it, and it was produced by Larry G. Spangler. (90 mins)

△ As critic Kenneth Tynan once observed, there are good films and bad films, good bad films, and bad good films. **The Love Machine** was a bad bad film and not nearly as trashily entertaining as the Jacqueline Susann novel from which it was culled. All about the rise (to network programme controller) and fall of a flint-hearted TV newscaster whose basic rottenness eventually ousts him from the network he had been hoping to take over, it starred an inadequate and ineffectual John Phillip Law as the heel. Robert Ryan was cast as his boss, Jackie Cooper as a network president, Greg Mullavey as his twitchy assistant, Shecky Greene, Gene Baylos and Ben Lessy as saloon comics, William Roerick as a corporate lawyer, David Hemmings (right) as an outrageously camp photographer, Clinton Greyn as his pal, Jodi Wexler as an adoring lover of Law (and over whom she commits suicide), Sharon Farrell as another of the 'hero's' long-suffering admirers and, as Ryan's beddable wife, Dyan Cannon (left) – whose main purpose in the sudsy narrative was to use her influence and her feminine wiles, to make sure that good-looking Law succeeds all the way to the top. It was written by Samuel Taylor, with his tongue not nearly enough in his cheek, and directed with the same restraint by Jack Haley Jr. Mike Frankovich produced (108 mins)

▽ Following in the wake of the gruesome murder of his wife, Sharon Tate, Roman Polanski, as if indulging in some kind of deeply personal act of exorcism, chose Shakespeare's violent **Macbeth** as his next film and didn't spare the gore. What the film lost in individual performances it almost compensated for in the sweaty realism of its medieval settings and in the earthiness of its staging. The film's theme, the passing of the crown ('the golden round') from one recipient to another, was graphically pursued, and it was to be regretted that the lightweight casting of Jon Finch (right) and Francesca Annis (left) as the anti-social Macbeths undermined much of the drama. (Tuesday Weld was originally slated for Lady Macbeth but withdrew when she learned that Polanski intended her to do the sleep-walking scene in the nude.) More successfully cast were Martin Shaw as Banquo, Nicholas Selby as Duncan, John Stride as Ross (the real villain of the piece), Stephen Chase as Malcolm, Terence Bayler as Macduff and, as the three witches, Elsie Taylor, Maisie MacFarquhar and Noelle Rimmington. The screenplay was fashioned by Polanski and Kenneth Tynan, and it was produced by Andrew Braunsberg for Playboy Enterprises. Because of the nudity and the violence, the film received an X-rated certificate and was a box-office bomb. (140 mins)

▽ Though not exactly a Spaghetti Western, **A Man Called Sledge,** (filmed in Italy and produced by Dino De Laurentiis), had the look and feel of one – despite its predominantly American cast. A downbeat, blood-spattered tale whose moral might have been that man cannot live by gold alone (though he could certainly die by it), it starred James Garner (right) and Dennis Weaver (centre) as a pair of ruthless, amoral baddies who spend their time in director Vic Morrow's screenplay (which he co-scripted with Frank Kowalski), breaking into a maximum-security prison in which half a million dollars' worth of gold-dust is being kept. With the gold safely in their possession, Garner and his men slowly begin to fall out over how the bounty should be divided, and shoot it out in a climactic showdown during a religious procession in a small Mexican town. Morrow, usually to be found playing a baddy himself, here made one of his occasional forays into film directing, and kept the action brisk and tense. His cast included Claude Akins (left), John Marley, Laura Antonelli, Wade Preston and Ken Clark. (93 mins)

▽ The fall of the Romanov Empire, no less, was the subject of Sam Spiegel and Franklin Schaffner's production **Nicholas And Alexandra** which, while epic in intent, was unable to confine two decades of extraordinary history into a three-hour drama. It came to life only in fits and starts and, although it ravished the eye, demanded little from the brain. However, on the plus side, it was well researched, meticulously mounted and, for the most part, historically accurate. And if James Goldman's screenplay (based on the book by Robert K. Massie), with additional dialogue by Edward Bond, lacked the narrative sweep of some of the cinema's great epics, it rarely offended the ear with the kind of mundane inanities so dear to the genre. It also offered two walloping central roles which Michael Jayston (left, as Nicholas) and Janet Suzman (right, as Alexandra) greedily devoured. Naturally, the character of Rasputin, the mad monk, was also a prominent feature of the story, and, in the flamboyant hands of Tom Baker, the madman flared into life. The rest of the supporting-cast were less well served by their material and emerged wax-like from the large and unwieldy canvas. They included Roderic Noble as Alexis, Fiona Fullerton as Anastasia, Lynne Frederick as Tatiana, Ania Marson as Olga, Harry Andrews as the Grand Duke Nicholas, Irene Worth as the Queen Mother Marie Fedorovna, Jack Hawkins as Count Fredericks, Timothy West as Dr Botkin, Laurence Olivier as Count Witte, Eric Porter as Stolypin, Michael Redgrave as Sazonov and John McEnery as Kerensky. The rest of the large cast comprised a veritable 'Who's Who' in British films and theatre. It was filmed in Yugoslavia and Spain (in Panavision) by Freddie Young, and had a score by Richard Rodney Bennett. Unfortunately, box-office returns didn't cover its $11 million costs. (183 mins)

△ Arriving on the scene about a year too late, **The Pursuit Of Happiness,** produced by TV talk-show host David Susskind, was about a post-revolutionary New York college dropout, Michael Sarrazin (left), who, having accidentally run over an elderly woman in a rain storm, lands up in prison for refusing, in court, to co-operate with 'the Establishment'. While in prison he becomes involved in a knifing, and, with only a week of his sentence to serve, escapes to Canada with girlfriend Barbara Hershey (right). Adroitly scripted by John Boothe and George L. Sherman from the novel by Thomas Rogers, this earnest view of youthful disillusionment provided meaty roles for a supporting cast that included E. G. Marshall as a reactionary lawyer, David Doyle as a bent politician, comedian Robert Klein as a hippie, Arthur Hill as Sarrazin's millionaire father (a social drop-out himself), and Ruth White (her last film) as Sarazzin's grandmother. Also: Sada Thompson, Barnard Hughes, Peter White and William Devane. The caring direction was by Robert Mulligan. (93 mins)

△ The sight of Orson Welles occupying a bench in Central Park, and, in the guise of a magician, attempting the disappearance of a llama, was the best thing on offer in **A Safe Place,** a decidedly unsafe first feature from writer-director Henry Jaglom who, happily, would make far better films than this. A fantasy that looked as though it had been spliced together by an editor with St Vitus Dance, it purported, by jump-cutting from the past to the present, and then into the future and back again, to inhabit the psyche of a beautiful young woman (Tuesday Weld, left – photographed in countless close-ups) about whom one learned very little except that she was clearly a bit of a 'case'. Jack Nicholson (right) fetched up as one of her randy lovers, Gwen Welles, as a hippie with troubles of her own, was given an indulgent soliloquy. Philip Proctor, Dov Lawrence, Fanny Birkenmier, Rhonda Alfaro and Sylvia Zapp filled out the cast for producer Bert Schneider's BBS Production. (94 mins)

▽ A really creepy thriller that owed its central idea to Frederick Knott's *Wait Until Dark* (Warner Bros., 1967), **See No Evil** (GB: **Blind Terror**) was the suspense-filled story of a young woman (Mia Farrow, illustrated) blinded in a horse-riding accident who, while convalescing in a mansion belonging to her uncle (Robin Bailey), is terrorized by a psychopath (Paul Nicholas, whose face isn't revealed until the climax) after he enters the mansion and murders her uncle, her aunt (Dorothy Alison) and her cousin (Diane Grayson). How Farrow managed to save her own skin was revealed, amid much tension, in Brian Clemens' taut little screenplay with which director Richard Fleischer did wonders. The cast was completed by Brian Rawlinson and Norman Eshley (as Farrow's fiancé), and it was produced by Martin Ransohoff and Leslie Linder for Filmways Productions. (87 mins)

▽ Frederic Raphael's adaptation of **A Severed Head,** based on the novel by Iris Murdoch and the play Murdoch wrote in collaboration with J. B. Priestley, emerged as a vacuous, empty-headed comedy parading as a sophisticated sexual romp. It starred Ian Holm as a wine-taster whose wife, Lee Remick (right), falls in love with Richard Attenborough (left), a psychologist who happens to be sexually involved with his half-sister, Claire Bloom. And that's just for starters. A sexual roundelay, in which various couplings and permutations are tried and discarded, formed the risqué content of the film, but, as directed by Dick Clement and performed by a cast whose chemistry never seemed to jell, it was a dull, flat, and unprofitable experience for all concerned – including the audience. Jennie Linden, Clive Revill, Rosamund Greenwood, Constance Lorne, Robert Gillespie and Katharine Parr were also in the cast for producers Jerry Gershwin, Elliott Kastner and Alan Ladd Jr. (98 mins)

▽ The generation gap, as represented by Jack Warden and his aimless college drop-out son (Michael Douglas, centre), was effectively explored in **Summertree** in which Douglas, against his father's wishes, unsuccessfully sets out to dodge the draft – and is killed in Viet Nam. Barbara Bel Geddes played his sympathetic mother, Brenda Vaccaro (left), his married girlfriend, and Kirk Callaway (right) an unhappy young black boy (who did not appear in the Ron Cowen play on which Stephen Yafa and Edward Hume based their screenplay) whom Douglas befriends. Anthony Newley's direction didn't go nearly as far as it might have with the material, and the result was a respectable drama that could easily have been a TV movie of the week. It was produced by Kirk Douglas for Bryna Productions. (89 mins)

△ In bringing the sordid facts of mass-murderer John Reginald Christie to the screen, director Richard Fleischer adopted the same unhistrionic approach he took in telling the story of Albert de Salvo, *The Boston Strangler* (20th Century-Fox, 1968). Indeed, there was almost a documentary-like precision to the Martin Ransohoff-Leslie Linder production that kept audiences one step removed from the terrible events being described. As all students of criminology know, Christie (Richard Attenborough, left) was a sexually repressed madman, living at **Ten Rillington Place,** who committed seven murders between 1944 and 1950. Among his victims were his own wife – and also the wife of the simple-minded Timothy Evans (John Hurt), a crime for which Evans, on perjured testimony from Christie, was hanged. When, through a series of grisly circumstances, the truth about Christie finally emerged, Evans was given a posthumous pardon. As for Christie himself, he was executed on July 15, 1953. Working from a screenplay by Clive Exton (and a book by Ludovic Kennedy) that underplayed Evans's simple-mindedness, John Hurt gave a deeply affecting performance which consistently upstaged Attenborough's suitably prissy Christie. Judy Geeson (right) was cast as Evans's wife Beryl, Pat Heywood was Mrs Christie, with other parts under Fleischer's restrained guidance going to Isobel Black, Phyllis MacMahon, Ray Barron, André Morrell, Geoffrey Chater and Douglas Blackwell. (111 mins)

◁ **Welcome To The Club** was a mega-bomb, set in Hiroshima, and all about the attempts of an American Quaker (Brian Foley, right) who, while billeted to an officer's club in 1945, has a devil of a time bucking prejudice as he unsuccessfully attempts to introduce a black singing combo into the all-white quarters. He is no more successful in persuading his sister back home to date a black friend. A crassly exploitative 'comedy' with barely a laugh to its bad name, it was ineptly directed by Walter Shenson, who also produced it with Leon Becker, and scripted by Clement Biddle Wood from his novel. Jack Warden (left) was the only name in a cast that included Andy Jarrell, Francesca Tu, Al Mancini, David Toguri, Art Wallace and Marsha Hunt. (88 mins)

▷ You either responded to the zany, anarchic, surreal, illogical, non-sequiturs as perpetrated by the Monty Python comedy team, or you did not. Enlightened folk who did, had a great time with **And Now For Something Completely Different**, a selection of well-loved sketches from Python's long-running TV series – some very good, some good, some not so good – all of them, regardless of quality, bearing the madcap, imprimatur of their risk-taking creators. Whether comparing American foreign policy to toothpaste, or indulging in more obvious humour – such as a clever send-up of a TV series called 'Blackmail', – the Python team were always uniquely themselves, that is (from left to right) Eric Idle, Graham Chapman, Michael Palin, John Cleese, Terry Jones and Terry Gilliam. They all contributed to the conception and screenplay. Ian Mac-Naughton directed, Gilliam was in charge of the cheeky animation, and it was a Kettledrum-Python Production for Playboy. Also in the cast were Carol Cleveland and Connie Booth. (88 mins).

▽ Maybe the fact that **Black Gunn** was produced and directed by white Englishmen was why its overall view of black-white race relations was so far off the mark. Whatever the reason, it was a shoddily made, gratuitously violent piece of black exploitation. It starred Jim Brown (right) as a well-to-do nightclub owner, who, after his militant black-power-orientated brother (Herbert Jefferson Jr) is rubbed out by a white man (Martin Landau) while robbing his bookie joint, stalks the killer with vengeance in mind. Nothing about the John Heyman-Norman Priggen Champion Production was worth recommending – least of all the passé screenplay provided by Franklin Coen which, in turn, was based on a screenplay by Robert Shearer and an idea by Robert Hartford-Davis, who also directed. Also cast: Brenda Sykes (left), Luciana Paluzzi, Vida Blue, Stephen McNally, Keefe Brasselle and Timothy Brown. (94 mins)

◁ Having created the Western's first black hero in Ralph Nelson's *Duel At Diablo* (United Artists, 1966), Sidney Poitier (right) filled the plains with black men in **Buck And The Preacher**, an amiable Western which he starred in and directed. He played a former Union cavalryman-turned-trail-guide who, when the film opens, is seen protecting former slaves, heading west, from white labour recruiters. Enter Harry Belafonte (left) as a tooth-stained con-man pretending to be a preacher, and the mood lightened as he and Poitier join forces to defeat white villain Cameron Mitchell. As an exercise in providing black youngsters with a pair of black heroes to root for, it served its purpose. But as quality Westerns go – forget it. Ruby Dee played Poitier's 'woman' and Julie Robinson (Mrs Belafonte in real-life), was an Indian maid. It was produced by Joel Glickman, written by Ernest Kinoy (story by Kinoy and Drake Walker) and also featured Denny Miller, Enrique Lucero and Nita Talbot. (102 mins)

△ **Butterflies Are Free** by Leonard Gershe was a 'heartwarming' Broadway comedy *par excellence* with all the quintessential ingredients for box-office success. Without ever insulting the intelligence, it managed, nonetheless, to be cloyingly sentimental and offered tailor-made opportunities for a handful of personable stars to twinkle brightly. Producer Mike Frankovich's glossy film version, a box-office winner, appealed enormously to the saccharine brigade, and starred Edward Albert (right, son of Eddie Albert) as a handsome young man attempting to overcome the handicap of blindness in a San Francisco garret, and Goldie Hawn (left) as a kooky kid-next-door who falls in love with him. Eileen Heckart played his possessive suburban mother, and Michael Glaser appeared briefly as a 'hip' stage director. All were exceedingly good and brought a ring of conviction to Gershe's cunningly manipulative screenplay. It was efficiently directed by Milton Katselas, and had a title song by Stephen Schwartz. (109 mins)

▷ Kris Kristofferson (left) made his screen debut in **Cisco Pike** as a rock singer who, after being released from prison for drug-dealing, is blackmailed by bent cop Gene Hackman into selling $10,000 worth of marijuana in 53 hours. Why? Because Hackman is underpaid and could do with the cash. Also in the cast were Karen Black (right) as Kristofferson's likeable girl, Harry Dean Stanton as his erstwhile partner, Joy Bang and a pregnant Viva as cruising partners, Antonio Fargas as a dealer, Douglas Sham as a rock star, and Roscoe Lee Browne. But as written and directed by Bill L. Norton, the film emerged as an aimless bore that showed none of its performers to best advantage. The producer was Gerald Ayres. (94 mins)

▽ On the stage, some of the pain expressed by Peter Nichols in his play **A Day In The Death Of Joe Egg** was ameliorated by an almost Brechtian, 'alienation' technique; for the leading players talked directly to the audience or indulged in burlesque-type joke-telling and song-and-dance routines to the accompaniment of an on-stage musical combo. In director Peter Medak's film version, naturalism was introduced, resulting in a harrowing drama about the dissolution of a marriage due to the problems of having to bring up a ten year-old spastic daughter (a virtual 'living parsnip') called Joe. Alan Bates (left) played Bri, a schoolteacher attempting to anaesthetize his despair through humour, and Janet Suzman (right) was his long-suffering wife Sheila. Both performances projected a deep-rooted pain and anguish which was harder to take on screen than it was in the theatre. Nichols's screenplay also found roles for Joan Hickson (excellent as Suzman's relentlessly middle-class mother), Peter Bowles and Sheila Gish as a social-climbing husband and wife, as well as for Murray Melvin, Fanny Carby and Elizabeth Robillard. It was produced by David Deutsch for Domino Productions. (106 mins)

▽ In **Dirty Little Billy** Michael J. Pollard (left), who first came to prominence as C.W. Moss in *Bonnie and Clyde* (Warner Bros., 1967), played Billy Bonney – a lad who was later to become Billy the Kid. Basically about the formative years of a mentally deficient psychopath who – in later years – would develop into a classic Western hoodlum, Charles Moss and Stan Dragoti's screenplay defused the mythic and romantic elements of their tale and emerged with a truly gritty, unalluring look at the way things out West really were. Dragoti's direction was unadorned by pretty images, and the performances by Lee Purcell, Richard Evans (right), Charles Aidman, Alex Wilson and Dran Hamilton were suitably trenchant. Jack L. Warner produced. (100 mins)

◁ John Huston's first American film since *The Misfits* (United Artists, 1961) was **Fat City**, a downbeat, off-beat drama that focused, in general, on the flotsam and jetsam of a small western town (actually Stockton, California), and in particular, on the (unsuccessful) efforts of a down-at-heel boxer (Stacy Keach, left) to re-establish himself as a fighter. It was also concerned with Jeff Bridges (right), another would-be boxer (and failure) who befriends Keach, and with Susan Tyrell, an alcoholic living with a black man and still coming to grips with a society unsympathetic towards inter-racial relationships. Huston's compassion for the underdogs of society, for the lonely, the dispossessed, the eccentrics, and the misfits was unsentimentally articulated and vividly fleshed out by all the principal players, as well as by Candy Clark, Nicholas Colasanto, Art Aragon, and Curtis Cokes. It was written by Leonard Gardner (from his own novel) and if the screenplay didn't seem to go anywhere, it didn't have to; it was there already, at the very heart of the human condition. Huston and Ray Stark produced. (96 mins)

▷ Though made in 1970, **Glass Houses** wasn't released until after Jennifer O'Neill (left) had appeared in Howard Hawks's *Rio Lobo* (Cinema Center, 1970) and the extremely popular *Summer of '42* (Warner Bros., 1971), thus providing *Glass Houses* with an unexpected drawcard. She played the mistress of a bored Los Angeles businessman (Bernard Barrow, right) whose own daughter (Deidre Lenihan) is secretly in love with him.

Barrow's wife (Ann Summers) is having an affair with a novelist. At the same time, Barrow's business partner (Philip Pine), is sleeping with Ms Lenihan who, accidentally on purpose, arranges for her and Pine to join Barrow and O'Neill at a weekend encounter group. Though Alexander Singer's swinging screenplay offered a scenario more suited to a porno movie, the film took a wryly observed poke at a libidinous group of middle-class nonentities. Singer directed, and drew surprisingly convincing performances from his largely unknown cast. The producer was George Folsey Jr. (103 mins)

△ There was something genuinely touching about a British film-maker's attempt to recapture an aspect of American movie mythology without betraying his English roots – and at the same time to turn back the clock while remaining firmly in the present. That's what director Stephen Frears, working with scenarist Neville Smith, did in **Gumshoe**, an affectionate homage to the likes of Chandler's Marlowe and Hammett's Spade, but set in contemporary Liverpool. The film starred Albert Finney (right) as a bingo-caller who, bored with his mundane existence, takes out a newspaper ad offering his services as a private detective. There's an immediate response, and, in no time at all, Finney, alias Eddie Ginley, finds himself involved in a series of plots and counterplots involving murder, kidnapping and gun and drug smuggling. In the process of anglicizing the genre, Frears managed to de-glamourize the mystique of the 'private eye' while paying tribute to it. The result was a thriller that resonated on several levels, and which gave Finney a marvellous opportunity to prove once again just how fine an actor he is. There was excellent support, too, from Billie Whitelaw, Frank Finlay, Janice Rule (left), Carolyn Seymour, Fulton Mackay, Billy Dean, Maureen Lipman and, as 'the fat man', George Silver. It was produced by Michael Medwin for Memorial Films and had an effective score by Andrew Lloyd Webber.

(88 mins)

▽ The usually reliable Robert Altman aberrated with **Images**, a pretentious, self-conscious and largely incomprehensible potpourri of trendy cinematic techniques that purported, in a series of eye-catching but mind-numbing images, to chart the breakdown of a schizophrenic housewife-cum-children's-author (Susannah York, right) who, in an idyllic country retreat, has to cope with hallucinations involving a dead lover (Marcel Bozzuffi) and an artist friend (Hugh Millais, left). Poor Miss York, poor René Auberjonois, who played her husband, and poor audiences, having to suffer with them both. It was written by Altman (based on Susannah York's story *In Search of Unicorns*), stunningly photographed by Vilmos Zsigmond, and produced by Tommy Thompson for Hemdale. (100 mins)

△ Jacob Brackman's needlessly repetitive screenplay, and direction by Bob Rafelson that pretentiously juggled fantasy and reality in an all-out attempt to be different, made it difficult to warm to any of the characters in **The King Of Marvin Gardens**. Though the film was not without its moments, the overall impression it left was bleak and hollow. Jack Nicholson (right) starred as an FM disc jockey in Philadelphia who, instead of playing music, talks for hours on end about the things he and his older brother (Bruce Dern, centre) got up to as kids. He has nicknamed Dern 'King of Marvin Gardens', Marvin Gardens being both a property on the American Monopoly board and a place in Atlantic City. Atlantic City happens to be where Dern is shacked up with erstwhile beauty queen Ellen Burstyn (left) and her step-daughter (Julia Anne Robinson). He works for the boss of a black crime syndicate ('Scatman' Crothers), and aims, with Crothers's money, to buy an island to which he and Nicholson can retire. It's a pipe dream that leads to tragedy. At its best, the film had an enigmatic, quite haunting quality to it; at its worst it dragged. Rafelson produced, Laszlo Kovacs' photography brought out the most depressing aspects of Atlantic City (before its recent reconstruction), and the supporting cast included Charles Lavine, Arnold Williams, John Ryan and Josh Mostel (son of Zero). (103 mins)

▷ Six years after *Born Free* took the world's box-offices by storm came its sequel, **Living Free**, with pretty Susan Hampshire (illustrated) and manly Nigel Davenport (as the Adamsons) in roles originally occupied by Virginia McKenna and Bill Travers. As the childless couple in charge of lioness Elsa's three baby cubs, the newcomers were as charming and as efficient as their predecessors. True, the film they carried didn't have the freshness of the original, but it made for more than passable family entertainment. Wolfgang Suschitzky's African wild-life photography was captivating and, despite a certain tedium engendered by Millard Kaufman's cosy screenplay, there was much to enjoy. Jack Couffer directed a cast that included Geoffrey Keen, Edward Judd, Peter Lukoye and Shane De Louvre, and it was produced by Paul Radin for Carl Foreman's Open Road/High Road Productions. (90 mins)

△ Possibly the silliest, most tasteless movie of the year, **Pope Joan**, also known as **The Devil's Imposter**, was inspired by a legend that a woman held the papal throne between Leo IV and Benedict III. Deciding not to opt for a straight account (or biopic) of Pope Joan, as the woman was called, producer Kurt Unger, working with writer John Briley, settled instead for a format in which a 20th-century small-time evangelist imagines herself to be the mythical Joan, thereby allowing the film to indulge in a series of long-range flashbacks as the modern-day Joan time-warps herself back (disguised as a man) to the Middle Ages in order to prove how similar her own circumstances were to those of her historical (or, in this case, hysterical) counterpart. It was all too ridiculous to endure, and shamelessly squandered the luminous talents of its star, Liv Ullmann (left), as Joan, as well as those of Olivia de Havilland (as a medieval Mother Superior), Lesley-Anne Down, Keir Dullea, Robert Beatty, Jeremy Kemp, Maximilian Schell (right), Franco Nero, Natasa Nicolescu, Patrick Magee, Nigel Havers and, as Pope Leo, Trevor Howard. The hapless director was Michael Anderson. (132 mins)

△ **The New Centurions** (GB: **Precinct 45: Los Angeles Police**), based on the novel by real-life cop Joseph Wambaugh but substantially altered and restructured by Stirling Silliphant for the movie, was in several respects a forerunner of the popular long-running TV series *Hill Street Blues*; indeed, James Sikking, one of that series's regulars, appeared as a sergeant in it. All about life (and death) in the Los Angeles Police Department, it starred George C. Scott (back) as an old die-hard who plays it as dirty as his sense of survival dictates, and Stacy Keach as a rookie working towards a law degree. As Keach and Scott's friendship develops, so does the former's interest in police work – so much so that he neglects his law studies and loses his wife (Jane Alexander, front). It all ends in tears with Keach on his deathbed – after a silly mistake while on the job. Basically an old-fashioned B picture masquerading as a high-octane 'A', it boasted a terrific performance from Scott who, unfortunately, disappeared from the screen for too large a chunk of the movie. It was produced by Irwin Winkler and Robert Chartoff, directed by Richard Fleischer, and, in smaller roles, featured Scott Wilson, Rosalind Cash, Eric Estrada and Clifton James. (102 mins)

▽ The momentous, epoch-making events that led to the historic signing of the Declaration of Independence in Philadelphia were the subject of **1776**, a long-running (1,217 performances) Broadway smash that came to the screen via producer Jack L. Warner and its original director, Peter Hunt. The story (script by Peter Stone from his original libretto) revolved around the efforts of John Adams to break down the opposition to Independence, an issue primarily revolving around free status versus slave states. William Daniels (left) repeated the role of John Adams that he created on the stage, with other Broadway hold-overs including David Ford as John Hancock, Howard da Silva (right) as Benjamin Franklin, Ken Howard as Thomas Jefferson, Roy Poole as Stephen Hopkins, Ron Holgate as Richard Henry Lee, and Virginia Vestoff as Abigail Adams. Newcomers to the cast included Blythe Danner (centre), Donald Madden, Rex Robbins and Peter Forster. Unfortunately, what worked on stage didn't succeed on screen; the charm and originality that the Broadway show possessed were lost on the Panavision screen, and the film had a self-congratulatory, almost pompous air to it. The music and lyrics were by Sherman Edwards. (141 mins)

◁ Like *Gumshoe*, **Shamus** remained in the present while harking back to the world of Philip Marlowe in *The Big Sleep* (Warner Bros., 1946), a film Barry Beckerman often aped in his screenplay. But whether this homage, rooted as it was in Seventies violence, was meant to be tongue-in-cheek, or taken seriously, remained an open question. Burt Reynolds (front) played, in his best Bogart manner (and with a few laughs thrown in), the shamus (a word first coined in *The Big Sleep*, and a derivation of the Yiddish word 'shammes', meaning synagogue sexton) who accepts wealthy diamond merchant Ron Weyand's offer of $10,000 to track down some stolen gems. That was the springboard for Beckerman's tale of intrigue and counter-intrigue, and it gave Reynolds an opportunity to prove that, on occasion, he could be a lot better than his material. Dyan Cannon (back), as a social butterfly, stridently played the female lead, with other roles under Buzz Kulik's undecided direction going to John Ryan, Joe Santos, Giorgio Tozzi, Larry Block and, as a girl in a bookstore not unlike the one featured in *The Big Sleep*, Kay Frye. Robert M. Weitman produced, the music was by Jerry Goldsmith, and it was photographed, largely on location, in New York. (98 mins)

▷ Hollywood's first cinematic encounter with the women's liberation movement was **Stand Up And Be Counted**, whose tepid approach to its subject made it difficult to decide whether it was a comedy-drama or a dramatic comedy. Either way it merely skirted the issue as it showed the effects of the movement on several women in the Denver area. A miscast Jacqueline Bisset starred as a fashion journalist dispatched to Denver to cover the scene for her magazine; Lee Purcell played her younger sister, a feminist who draws up a contract to have a baby; Stella Stevens (illustrated) was the sex-hungry wife of a lingerie tycoon (Hector Elizondo) and Loretta Swit played the wife of an ad man (Steve Lawrence), a woman who, apart from bringing up four kids, is seeking an identity of her own in the fashion business. Playwright Bernard Slade's screenplay, though not without its amusing moments, never gave the impression that it was fully committed to its subject. The same might be said for Jackie Cooper's direction (an uninspired debut). The film was produced by Mike Frankovich, the face of whose wife, Binnie Barnes, was featured on a mock dollar bill during a demonstration sequence. Also cast: Gary Lockwood, Anne Francine, Madlyn Rhue, Alex Wilson, Michael Ansara and Joyce Brothers. (99 mins)

△ **To Find A Man** (aka **Sex And The Teenager**) was a modest and (artistically speaking) modestly successful drama that explored the nature of contemporary teenage relationships . . . platonic, that is. It starred Pamela Sue Martin (right) as Rosalind, a spoiled, vacuous brat who, while on vacation in New York from her Catholic school, confides in Andy (Darren O'Connor) her friend and neighbour, that she is pregnant. How Andy, a precocious, extremely bright chemistry student (albeit sexually naïve) coped with the situation, and Rosalind's response, provided Arnold Schulman's screenplay (from the novel by S.J. Wilson) with its *raison d'être*. Phyllis Newman and Lloyd Bridges (left) played Rosalind's parents, Tom Bosley was a pharmacist and Tom Ewell an abortionist. The film was produced by Irving Pincus for Rastar Productions, and decently directed by Buzz Kulik. (90 mins)

▽ Elizabeth Taylor (left) gave a barnstorming performance in **X, Y and Zee** (GB: **Zee And Co**) which made her histrionics in *Who's Afraid Of Virginia Woolf?* (Warner Bros., 1966) look positively vapid. She played the loud, coarse, obnoxious wife of architect Michael Caine, and her shrewish behaviour sends him into the arms of Susannah York, a boutique owner very different in looks and personality from the vulgar Miss T. Needless to say Caine's infidelity brings out the worst in his wife, and, after hurling abuse and throwing garbage cans at York's bedroom window, she attempts suicide. When that doesn't work, the unstoppable Liz, having heard about a lesbian indiscretion perpetrated by Miss York eons ago, jumps into bed with her rival, claiming victory over her unfaithful spouse, and daring him to join them in a *ménage à trois*. Whatever deeper purpose the formidably intelligent Edna O'Brien attached to her screenplay (and there must have been one) remained obscured under Brian G. Hutton's indulgent direction. York and Caine did the best they could against the devouring onslaught of Taylor; and there was a fine supporting performance by Margaret Leighton. Also momentarily drawing attention away from the central trio were John Standing, Mary Larkin, and Michael Cashman. The film was produced by Elliot Kastner and Alan Ladd Jr (line producer Jay Kanter). (110 mins)

▽ The story goes that Winston Churchill was so enamoured of Carl Foreman's production of *The Guns of Navarone* (1961) that he suggested his own autobiography (*My Early Life: A Roving Commission*) as suitable material for Foreman to turn into a screen biography. The result was **Young Winston**, a serviceable, if uninspired peek at the great statesman's formative years – from the age of seven to twenty-seven. These were the Victorian years, beginning with young Winston's enrolment in public school and ending with his impressive plea to the House of Commons for a reasonable fiscal policy. In between, the story encapsulated the arrogant, ambitious young man's involvement as a war correspondent on the Northwest Frontier, in the Sudan, and in South Africa during the bitter Boer War. It also found time to outline the love-hate relationship Churchill had with his father ('You're my greatest disappointment!' chanted Lord Randolph in the guise of Robert Shaw), and the coolly indifferent one he had with his socializing American mother, Jennie Jerome (Anne Bancroft). Young Winston's 'alienation' from his family, was, claimed Foreman's episodic screenplay, what ultimately motivated him into leadership. Three actors took on the mantle of the young hero: Russell Lewis played him at the age of seven, Michael Anderson at the age of 13, and, from the age of 17 for the next 10 years the task went to Simon Ward (illustrated) – who did a very creditable job. Indeed, most of the performances, including John Mills's Kitchener, Lawrence Naismith's Lord Salisbury, William Dexter's Arthur Balfour and Anthony Hopkins's Lloyd George, rose above both their indifferent material – and direction, by Richard Attenborough, that was coldly impersonal. Also cast: Raymond Huntley, Pat Heywood, Robert Hardy, Colin Blakely, Jack Hawkins, Ian Holm, Edward Woodward, Robert Flemyng, Patrick Magee, Jane Seymour, Dinsdale Landen and Willoughby Gray. Foreman and Attenborough produced. (157 mins)

1973

▽ Pierre Barillet and Jean-Pierre Gredy's **Forty Carats**, produced on Broadway by David Merrick in a version by Jay Presson Allen, underwent further changes at the hands of Leonard Gershe for its screen incarnation, and the result was a frivolous comedy, usually described as 'undemanding', whose only demand was that you accepted a miscast Liv Ullmann (right) as a glamorous, fortyish divorcée adept at the whys-and-wherefores of light, romantic flim-flam. (The role was originally played in New York by the enchanting Julie Harris.) Among the many qualities of Sweden's favourite actress are not to be found enchantment and lightness of touch, a fact from which the film never fully recovered. The story couldn't have been simpler. While holidaying in Greece, Ullmann, a successful real-estate agent in Manhattan, meets and falls in love with 20-year-old Edward Albert (left), who since last seen in the same production team's *Butterflies Are Free* (1972), has, happily, regained his sight. Her passions are requited and, after convincing herself that the differences in their ages shouldn't interfere with their future happiness, she agrees to become his wife. A sub-plot involved the romance of her daughter (Deborah Raffin, second left) with an older man (Billy Green Bush), but proved to be mere padding in the general scheme of things. Gene Kelly surfaced as Ullmann's ex-husband, and Binnie Barnes (second right) was her mother (she and Kelly got to do a brief dance together in a disco). Completing the cast for producer Mike Frankovich was Nancy Walker (very funny), Don Porter, Rosemary Murphy and Natalie Schaefer. It was directed for the fluff it was by Milton Katselas. (108 mins)

△ A thoroughly engaging musical that owed a great deal more to show-biz know-how than to the New Testament, **Godspell** transformed Jesus into a flower child, and relocated him to Manhattan. The result was an energetic, fun-filled celebration – not so much of religion, but of youth – which its youthful and talented cast, especially Victor Garber (illustrated, clad in sweatshirt and overalls) as Jesus and David Haskell as Judas, sold for all it was worth. Indeed, the film featured the entire original off-Broadway cast, which included Jerry Sroka, Lynne Thigpen, Katie Hanley, Robin Lamont, Gilmer McCormick, Joanne Jones, Merrell Jackson and Jeffrey Mylett. It was zestfully directed by David Greene, who co-wrote it with John-Michael Tebelak, and had a score by Stephen Schwartz, whose best number was the hit 'Day by Day'. Sam Beyes choreographed, and it was produced by Edgar Lansbury. (103 mins)

△ Though director Alan Bridges adopted too leisurely a pace to tell novelist L.P. Hartley's class-conscious story **The Hireling** (screenplay by Wolf Mankowitz), he cast it to perfection. Sarah Miles (right) played Lady Franklin who, after suffering a mild breakdown following the death of her husband, journeys back to Bath in a hired limousine chauffered by Robert Shaw (left). She is so taken with her driver that she arranges several more outings with him, in the course of which he falls in love with her. It is a doomed romance, however, for, as Lady Franklin returns to normal health, class rears its ugly head and she makes it quite clear that their relationship cannot continue. A sad little tale, played out against a class-ridden backdrop of England in 1923, it lacked the impact of the same author's *The Go-Between* (1970) due largely to Mankowitz's sometimes bloodless screenplay which needed some Lawrentian passion in order fully to engage audiences' emotions. It was produced by Ben Arbeid, and featured Peter Egan, Elizabeth Sellars, Caroline Mortimer, Patrick Lawrence and Petra Markham. (95 mins)

▽ Producer Ross Hunter laid a gargantuan egg with **Lost Horizon**, a stultifyingly boring musical re-make of the celebrated 1937 Capra classic about a group of passengers who survive an aircrash in the Tibetan mountains and find their Shangri-La. Nothing about the film worked: not Larry Kramer's screenplay (based on James Hilton's best-seller and a screenplay by Robert Riskin), Charles Jarrott's elephantine direction, Hermes Pan's coy choreography, Burt Bacharach and Hal David's forgettable score, nor a cast that included Peter Finch (left, in the Ronald Colman role), Liv Ullmann (right), Sally Kellerman, George Kennedy, Michael York, Bobby Van, John Gielgud, Olivia Hussey and, as the High Lama, Charles Boyer. The film weighed in at $7 million – and lost all of it. (150 mins)

△ Producer-director Stanley Kramer's cliché-strewn **Oklahoma Crude** was a throwback (but not quite as likeable) to the type of macho adventure yarn in which Clark Gable used to appear over at MGM (such as *Boom Town*, 1940). The Gable character in Kramer's retread was played by a boozy George C. Scott (left), whose purpose in Marc Norman's hokey screenplay was not only to tame the man-hating Faye Dunaway (right) – a mean-spirited, small-time wildcatter – but to help her derrick bring forth a gusher. He succeeded on both counts and managed, despite the crudeness of his characterization, to give a pretty good performance as well. John Mills (centre, in a typical Frank Morgan role) played Dunaway's estranged father who, after years of neglecting his daughter, returns to help her and is unceremoniously sent on his way. Rafael Campos was an Indian employed by Dunaway, and the villain of the piece was Jack Palance – head of an oil-trust that wants to appropriate Dunaway's land. Whichever way you cut it, *Oklahoma Crude* was a potboiler – but with Kramer at its helm, not without some enjoyable moments. Trouble was, there weren't enough of them. (108 mins)

▷ In **Love And Pain And The Whole Damned Thing**, Maggie Smith (left) and Timothy Bottoms (right) meet 'cute' when he inadvertently squirts mouth-freshener in her face on a Spanish bus. The embarrassment is compounded when she then sits on one of his chocolate bars. It's a prologue to a rather touching, often tender, love affair. She's fortyish and a spinster; he's a confused, asthmatic college student. She's taking a break from a pair of demanding aunts; he from a formidable Pulitzer-prize-winning father and a sister who makes her own cellos. Clearly they're destined for each other, and, as their romance burgeons, all is well with Alvin Sargent's engrossing screenplay. There's a catch to their happiness, though. Maggie, it turns out, has only a short while to live. It's a revelation from which the film and its audiences never recovered. Still, in this instance, a good half of a half-good film was better than a totally bad one, and with Smith and Bottoms in fine form, only the churlish complained. It was produced and directed (sensitively) by Alan J. Pakula, and also featured Emiliano Redondo (as a lecherous Spanish duke with an eye for Ms Smith), Charles Baxter, Margaret Modin and May Heatherly. (110 mins)

◁ Strange, *Psycho*-like goings on in a gloomy Gothic mansion were provided by scenarists Edward Hume and Lewis John Carlino (from Stanton Forbes' novel *Go To Thy Deathbed*) in **A Reflection Of Fear** (aka **Labyrinth**), all related to the bizarre, antisocial behaviour of Sondra Locke (centre) who, confined to the mansion by her grandmother (Signe Hasso), has turned an androgynous doll (Aaron) into her best friend. All it takes to send young Sondra on a stomach-churning killing spree is the unexpected arrival of her father (Robert Shaw, right) in the company of his mistress (Sally Kellerman, left). It seems that Sondra is really a boy – brought up as a girl by a mother (Mary Ure) with a pathological hatred of men – and her sexual confusion is the cause of her unbalanced state of mind. Given the potential talent both in front of and behind the cameras (the film was shot by the excellent Laszlo Kovacs), the end result was tepid, to say the least, with only the disturbed Ms Locke making any attempt to give a performance. William A. Fraker's self-consciously 'atmospheric', symbol-laden direction didn't help either. The cast, for producer Howard B. Jaffe, included Mitchell Ryan, Gordon Anderson, Victoria Risk, Leonard John Crofoot and Gordon DeVol. (90 mins)

▷ Either by accident or by design, Michael Winner's **The Stone Killer** was a homage to the gangster flicks of the Thirties and, quite apart from its parodic elements, was pretty entertaining in its own right. A rather contrived plot found a vengeful Martin Balsam recruiting a group of highly-skilled Viet Nam War veterans to help him eliminate all those responsible, way back in 1931, for a shoot-out that resulted in the introduction of non-Sicilian elements into organized crime. Top-billed Charles Bronson (left) is the 'stone man', a cop whose job it is to unravel the mysteries that have alerted the the Los Angeles Police Station that something is afoot. Though Gerald Wilson's screenplay (from the book *A Complete State Of Death* by John Gardner) wasn't exactly wall-to-wall with fresh ideas, it effectively recycled those it had – a nice touch being that Bronson and Balsam never get to meet. Winner's raw, vulgar vitality was a plus factor on this occasion, and his handling of the obligatory car-chase sequence was first-rate. Winner produced (with Dino De Laurentiis as executive producer), and cast supporting all the violence on this occasion included David Sheiner, Norman Fell, Ralph Waite, Stuart Margolin and, as a bisexual, spaced-out jazz musician-cum-hood, Paul Koslo. (95 mins)

△ Stewart Stern's screenplay for **Summer Wishes, Winter Dreams** made a sincere attempt to come to grip's with the onset of middle-age and approaching mortality as experienced by a bored housewife and grandmother whose life undergoes an emotional crisis with the sudden death of her mother (Sylvia Sidney in her first film for 17 years). The trouble was that Joanne Woodward (left) as the woman in question was a bit of a 'kvetch' whose grumpy aggressiveness, while perfectly understandable in her menopausal circumstances, hardly made for edifying entertainment. Her sympathetic husband was played by Martin Balsam (right), an occulist, who, after 24 years of marriage, leads an equally uneventful, routine existence. Stern's screenplay took them both to Europe for a holiday and, in one of the most touching scenes in the film, Balsam returns to Bastogne where, 28 years earlier in World War II, he experienced the only real drama his life was to know. For the most part, director Gilbert Cates successfully negotiated the emotional highs and lows the narrative provided though, in the end, the emptiness of his protagonists' unimportant lives was self-defeating. Ron Rickards played their estranged, homosexual son and Dori Brenner was their daughter, with other roles in this Rastar-Gilbert Cates Production (produced by Jack Brodsky) going to Win Forman, Tresa Hughes and Peter Marklin. (87 mins)

▽ At the time of its initial release, **The Way We Were** brought out the barracuda in most of the major critics. And did the public take one bit of notice? No; the film did extremely well at the box-office, produced a hit-song (score by Marvin Hamlisch, lyrics by Marilyn Bergman and Alan Bergman) of humungous proportions, and started a run on paper handkerchiefs. Maybe it was the film's tear-stained final scene that did it; maybe it was the chemistry between its two superstars, Barbra Streisand (right) and Robert Redford (left); maybe it was the nostalgia in which it so shamelessly traded; maybe it was Arthur Laurents' bitter-sweet plot; or maybe it was all those things put together. Whatever it was, the viewing public from Aachen to Zanzibar lapped it up and swallowed it whole. Streisand played Katie Morosky, a young Communist activist who, on a college campus, meets Hubbell Gardiner, a blonde, god-like politically uninvolved WASP and would-be writer who is so handsome she dubs him 'America the beautiful'. Years pass, they meet again, fall in love, marry and settle in Hollywood where he becomes a screenwriter and she, predictably, finds herself involved in the McCarthy witchhunts. The basic differences in their ideologies bring their marriage to an end, and the film closes, years later, with the two of them meeting, quite by chance, outside the Plaza Hotel in New York. Though married to other people, the're still in love – a fact neither can disguise but equally, neither can do anything about. Soapy it might have been, but the suds – as applied by its two stars – were of the highest quality. Furthermore, the combined skills of the behind-the-scenes team of craftsmen – especially Harry Stradling Jr's classy photography and Sidney Pollack's direction – were just what the material required. Professionalism was the key word of Ray Stark's production, and it paid off handsomely. Also cast: Bradford Dillman as a college chum of Redford's, Lois Chiles as Dillman's gorgeous wife, Viveca Lindfors as a Hollywood literary light, Patrick O'Neal as a director, Allyn Ann McLerie as an agent, and Herb Edelman as a radio producer. (118 mins)

△ **Buster And Billie** didn't bear close examination. On the surface, though, and before it turned nasty, it was a pleasant enough slice of youthful nostalgia, set in Georgia in 1948. Its two principal characters were Billie (Joan Goodfellow, right), the local good time girl, and Buster (Jan-Michael Vincent, left), a high-school senior – and the best-looking, most popular guy in town. While the rest of his mates are content with the sexual largesse offered by Billie, Buster has a girlfriend (pretty Pamela Sue Martin) all his own. The trouble is, she won't let him go the whole way, a state of affairs which, in a moment of frustration, leads Buster into the accommodating arms of Billie. And that's when it all happened. Buster fell for Billie hard enough to want to marry her, and was driven to murder after several of his buddies raped and killed her. All very unfortunate – both for the characters concerned as well as for audiences who, until violence reared its head, were having a pretty good time. Blame for this must be laid at the typewriter of Ron Turbeville (story by Turbeville and Ron Baron). Ron Silverman produced, Daniel Petrie directed, and the cast also included Clifton James, Robert Englund, Jessie Lee Fulton, J.B. Joiner and Dell C. Payne. (98 mins)

△ Compulsive gambling was the subject of **California Split**, and it brought together Elliott Gould (left) and George Segal (right) as a pair of compulsive gamblers who meet in a Los Angeles poker bar and, because of their mutual addiction, become buddies. Gould is a small-time, devil-may-care bettor – the easy-come, easy-go type. Segal takes it more seriously. A magazine editor separated from his wife, he's up to his neck in debt, and, as the film unspools, he takes a wrecking ball to his life as he prepares to sell everything he owns in order to finance a poker game in Reno. Both men gave sharply delineated per-formances and punched home the message in Joseph Walsh's observant, often humorous, screenplay – that, in the league of full-time gambling, winning can be almost as bad as losing. It was directed by Robert Altman in a fine return to form, and excellently per-formed by a supporting cast that included Ann Prentiss and Gwen Welles as happy hookers, Bert Remsen as a transvestite, Barbara Ruick, Barbara London and Barbara Colby as a barmaid, a horseplayer and a spaced-out receptionist respectively, and Joseph Walsh. Altman and Walsh produced (108 mins)

◁ It wasn't only the bats that got into one's hair in **Chosen Survivors**. How about the script (by H.B. Cross and Joe Reb Moffly, story by Cross) and the TV-orientated direction by Sutton Roley? All about 11 people carefully hand-picked by the US government in an underground survival experiment, it featured top-billed Jackie Cooper as a boozy businessman, Diana Muldaur (centre) as a congresswoman, Alex Cord (left) as a novelist, Lincoln Kilpatrick as a (token) black athlete, Bradford Dillman (right) as the demented official who thought up the whole experiment, Barbara Babcok as the group's doctor (whose misfortune it is to be half-heartedly raped by Cooper), and Richard Jaeckel as an officer who is sent along to see that nothing goes wrong. It does, of course. It seems that someone forgot to close an electrical vent, and before anyone can say 'disaster', the the place is inundated with hundreds of killer bats. Catastrophe begat catastrophe, the biggest one being the film itself. Leon Benson produced. (99 mins)

◁ The amorous sexual adventures of a Cockney window cleaner provided the far from edifying content of **Confessions Of A Window Cleaner**, a leery, prurient British farce that squandered the talents of Anthony Booth, Linda Hayden, Sheila White, Dandy Nichols, John Le Mesurier and Joan Hickson. Robin Askwith (illustrated) played the randy young apprentice – with all the charm of a piranha. It was written by Christopher Wood and director Val Guest (from the book by Timothy Lea, who was a window-washer in real life), and produced by Greg Smith. Best forgotten. (90 mins)

△ Producer Dino De Laurentiis wasted no time in dishing up, to an indifferent world, a biography of Mafia mobster Joe Gallo, who was gunned down on April 7, 1972 at a clam house in Little Italy. He called it **Crazy Joe** (Gallo's nickname), and cast a slobbish Peter Boyle (illustrated) as the monster with intellectual pretensions. The whole enterprise had a makeshift, exploitative feel to it, which the performances of Paula Prentiss (as Boyle's personable wife), Eli Wallach (as Don Vittorio), Rip Torn (as Boyle's brother) Henry Winkler (as a moustachioed hoodlum) and veteran Luther Adler served only to underline. Lewis John Carlino scripted it from a story by Nicholas Gage, and it was directed by Carlo Lizzani. (100 mins)

▽ A raucous, vulgar, old-fashioned knockabout farce designed specifically for the comedic talents of Barbra Streisand (right), **For Pete's Sake** gave Streisand a role whose screwball potential she gloriously realized, and kept her fans chuckling. She played the wife of a Brooklyn taxi-driver (Michael Sarrazin, left), who, in order to finance her husband's return to college, borrows money to invest in pork-belly futures. She then spends the majority of the film's running time trying to find a way to pay back the loan. The story was straight out of a Blondie and Dagwood situation comedy but, as scripted by such talented die-hards as Stanley Shapiro and Maurice Richlin, emerged fresh as a daisy and twice as exhilarating. Estelle Parsons played a thoroughly disagreeable sister-in-law, Molly Picon was a cosy Jewish madam called Mrs Cherry, and Heywood Hale Broun played a Brooklyn judge. It was produced by Martin Erlichman and Shapiro for Rastar Productions, and directed, at the speed of light, by Peter Yates. (90 mins)

△ A classic morality tale with good overcoming evil (though not without a struggle), **The Golden Voyage Of Sinbad** once again called into service Ray Harryhausen's special effects as it told the tale of Sinbad's quest over land and sea for a legendary gold tablet that guarantees eternal wealth and power to its possessor. Also in pursuit of the trinket was one Koura (Tom Baker) the demonic baddie of the piece. John Phillip Law (centre) took on the well-worn mantle of Sinbad, with other roles in Charles H. Schneer's youth-orientated production going to Caroline Munro (left), Douglas Wilmer, Martin Shaw, Grégoire Aslan and Kurt Christian. As usual, though, it was Harryhausen's Dynamation that was the true star of the show. Gordon Hessler directed from a hoary screenplay ('He who walks on fire will burn his feet. . .') by Brian Clemens, and there was an outstanding score by Miklos Rozsa. (105 mins)

▽ Brotherly love was a prominent feature of **The Gravy Train** (aka **The Dion Brothers**), violence another. A better-than-average crime melodrama, it starred Stacy Keach (left) and Frederic Forrest (right) as West Virginia coal-mining brothers who decide to board the gravy train by forsaking a menial, honest existence for armed robbery. Working in cahoots with gang-leader Barry Primus, they successfully pull off a job, after which Primus skips town with the goods, leaving the brothers, plus innocent klutz Denny Miller, to shoot it out with the law. Miller is killed and the brothers now begin a search for Primus – starting with the mobster's girl (Margot Kidder). A building in the process of being demolished by a wrecking ball provided the bloody climax to director Jack Starrett's passable actioner. The screenplay (which occasionally suffered from preachiness), was the work of Bill Kerby and David Whitney (a pseudonym for director Terrence Malick), and the film was produced by Jonathan T. Taplin. (94 mins)

◁ **The Last Detail,** written, with a generous quota of four-letter words, by Robert Towne (from the novel by Darryl Ponicsan), and strikingly directed by Hal Ashby, was a gritty comedy that took a long and lingering look at life in the military and didn't like what it saw. It starred Jack Nicholson (left) as a 20-year navy man who, together with sailor Otis Young (right), is detailed to escort 18 year-old Randy Quaid (centre) from their base in West Virginia to a Massachusetts prison. Quaid's offence was stealing the proceeds of a polio charity-box for which he received the unreasonable sentence of eight years in the brig. The brunt of the screenplay rested squarely with Nicholson who, in the course of the week-long journey, is determined, come what may, to show his unfortunate young prisoner a good time. With no last-minute reprieve for Quaid (who at least gets to lose his virginity), the film ended on a sad and sombre note, qualities echoed in Ashby's direction, in the bleached look of Michael Chapman's photography, and in Nicholson's angry, compassionate and humorous central performance. As for Quaid, without betraying a trace of self-pity or sentimentality, he always managed to make palpable the pain he was feeling. There were fine performances from Clifton James as the chief Master-at-Arms, Luana Anders, Carol Kane (as a prostitute), and Michael Moriarty. The producer was Gerald Ayres. (103 mins)

▽ Following the same path taken by Michael Winner in *Death Wish* (Paramount, 1974) but with none of that film's gratuitous violence or crass commercialism, **Law And Disorder** starred Carroll O'Connor (left) as a cab driver and Ernest Borgnine (right) as a hairdresser, who, unhappy with the rising crime-rate in their Lower East Side housing project take matters into their own hands and form a vigilante group. However, unlike Mr Bronson, hero of Winner's film, they do not succeed due to the sheer complexity of the problems they face and the fact that, thankfully, they're not Mr Bronson. By alternating comedy with seriousness, the screenplay, which the film's Czech director Ivan Passer co-wrote with William Richert and Kenneth Harris Fishman, blurred its intentions, and it wasn't always clear just what response its creators intended. Still, its heart was clearly in the right place and the problems inherent in big-city living came across loud and clear. Both men were splendid in their vigilante roles, and there was a fine performance, too, from Karen Black as Borgnine's vulgar beautician assistant. Also cast: Ann Wedgeworth, Anita Dangler and Leslie Ackerman. William Richert produced. (103 mins)

△ Set in Texas, and covering 20 years (1925-45) in the lives of its protagonists, **Lovin' Molly** told of a salty farm woman (Blythe Danner, left) and the two friends (Beau Bridges and Anthony Perkins, right) who share a lifelong love for her. However, director Sidney Lumet totally betrayed Larry McMurtry's novel *Leaving Cheyenne* on which it was based (screenplay by Stephen Friedman), and was as phoney as the ageing make-up worn by all three participants in the *ménage à trois*. Danner gamely attempted to make of Molly a livin', breathin' liberated woman, but Lumet's direction and the lines she had to utter ('my menfolk began rising with the moon...') defeated her. Edward Binns, Susan Sarandon, Conrad Fowkes, Claude Traverse and John Henry Faulk were in it too, and it was produced by Friedman. (98 mins)

▽ After making an uncredited appearance in Woody Allen's *Bananas* (United Artists, 1971) Sylvester Stallone (left) became a leading man in **The Lords Of Flatbush**, a low-budget, nostalgic, youth-orientated wallow set in Brooklyn in 1957 and involving a tough, but basically harmless street gang whose name gave the film its title. Stallone, a pigeon fancier, is a member of the gang; so is Perry King. Both have girlfriends. King's is Susie (later Susan) Blakeley, the daughter of an army colonel who finds his advances immature and dumps him; Stallone's is Maria Smith (right), whom he marries. Other members of the gang included Henry Winkler who, together with Armand Assante, Ray Sharkey and Dolph Sweet, would, like Stallone, all go on to bigger and better things. Paul Mace, Renee Paris, Paul Jabara (who with Paul Nicholas and Joe Brooks provided the music), Bruce Reed and Frank Steifel were in it too, it was produced by Stephen F. Verona, directed (with a genuine feeling for Fifties Brooklyn), by Verona, and Martin Davidson, and written by Verona, Davidson and Gayle Gleckler. (86 mins)

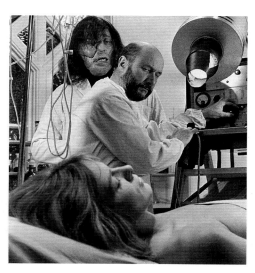

△ **The Mutations** was a grotesque dabble in horror sci-fi that starred Donald Pleasence (right) as a mad scientist whose crazy purpose in producer Robert Weinbach and Edward Mann's screenplay was to cross a plant with an animal in order to develop a new species. Tom Baker (left) played his assistant, and roamed the country kidnapping human guineapigs for his master's experiments. The unfortunate rejects were then donated to midget Michael Dunn for exhibition at his circus side-show. Brad Harris, Julie Ege (front), Scott Anthony and Jill Haworth fetched up in it too, and it was directed by Jack Cardiff who photographed *The Red Shoes* (The Archers, 1948), directed *Sons And Lovers* (20th Century-Fox, 1960), and should have known better. (91 mins)

▷ Frederick Forsyth's best-selling novel **The Odessa File** was hardly the nail-biting experience its producer, John Woolf, intended it to be. Blame this on the obvious and irrefutable fact that there was no way that Jon Voight (left), its hero (and the film's star), was about to be bumped off. Turning himself into a Houdini of narrow escapes, Voight, who was hardly off-screen, successfully outmanoeuvred his adversaries to tell the tale (set in 1963) of a group of former SS men (called Odessa) who, equipped with new identities, are building long-range rockets in the hope of reducing Israel to ashes. How Voight, a German journalist in pursuit of a Nazi war criminal, infiltrates these boys in the Bund, and survives, was entertainingly described in the screenplay Kenneth Ross and George Markstein cobbled out of Forsyth's novel. The film gave employment to Maximilian Schell (right) as an erstwhile concentration camp butcher, Derek Jacobi as a printer, Mary Tamm as Voight's girl, and Maria Schell (in a cameo) as Voight's mother – and to Klaus Lowitsch, Peter Jeffrey and Noel Willman. Ronald Neame directed it with the kind of anonymous professionalism associated with him, and the score was by Andrew Lloyd Webber. (128 mins)

△ **The Take** had nothing to give. A routine police melodrama of the type found nightly on network TV, it was the yawningly familiar story of a black cop (Billy Dee Williams, front left)) who busts syndicates in order to finance, with the cooked loot, business investments of his own. Sorrell Booke played his bent manager, Vic Morrow was an underworld ringleader, Frankie Avalon (seen only in three scenes) was a stoolie, Eddie Albert (left) was second-billed as Williams's put-upon chief, with other roles in Howard Brandy's production going to Tracy Reed, Albert Salmi and James Luisi. It was written (with a fairly hefty seasoning of profanities) by Del Reisman and Franklin Coen from G. F. Newman's novel *Sir You Bastard*, and directed – with the accent on fist fights, shoot-outs and the obligatory car chase – by Robert Hartford-Davis. (91 mins)

▷ Cheap and nasty were euphemisms for **Open Season**. A low-budget exploitationer from its talentless director Peter Collinson and 'inspired' by *The Most Dangerous Game* (RKO, 1932), it starred Peter Fonda (left), John Phillip Law (second right) and Richard Lynch (centre) as a trio of amoral hunters who kidnap innocent people to act as their servants, then mercilessly stalk them to death. Apart from the paying customers, Cornelia Sharpe (second left) and Albert Mendoza (right) were the victims on this shoddy occasion, so was William Holden who also made a brief cameo appearance. With the exception of Lynch, all the performances were as wretched as David Osborne and Liz Charles-Williams's screenplay. José S. Vicuna produced. (103 mins)

▽ A black *Bonnie And Clyde* (Warner Bros. 1967), **Thomasine And Bushrod**, set in the southwest between 1911 and 1915, was the fictional story of a pair of black bank robbers who shared the spoils of their life of crime with needy Indians, Mexicans and poor-whites. They had a love affair, were pursued by sheriff George Murdock – and that was about all there was to it. The charismatic criminals were marvellously played by Max Julien (right, as Bushrod), who wrote and co-produced it with Harvey Bernhard, and Vonetta McGee (left, as Thomasine). It was a solid piece of film-making that broke no new ground, but was efficiently and professionally directed by Gordon Parks Jr. Glynn Turman, Juanita Moore, Joel Fluellen, Jackson D. Kane and Bud Conlan were also featured, and it was beautifully photographed by Lucien Ballard. (93 mins)

1975

▽ A black *Romeo And Juliet* in which a Harlem boy falls in love with a Puerto Rican girl, **Aaron Loves Angela** did at least have a happy ending. It also had Kevin Hooks (right) and Irene Cara (left) as the star-crossed lovers, and a pretty beguiling pair they made. As was the case with their Veronese counterparts, the course of true love was paved with obstacles – in this instance a motley collection of pimps, prostitutes, dope dealers and white racketeers. Their love, however, conquered all – except, perhaps, audience indifference. For the film came and went in a flash. Gerald Sanford wrote it, Gordon Parks Jr directed, Robert J. Anderson produced, and the cast included Leonard Pinkey (as Hooks' best friend), Moses Gunn, Ernestine Jackson and Robert Hooks. The music was by José Feliciano. (99 mins)

△ An assorted collection of Western stereotypes fetched up in **Bite The Bullet**, a moderately enjoyable time-passer from writer-director Richard Brooks who chose a 700-mile cross-country endurance horseback race to reveal his variegated dramatis personae. They included top-billed Gene Hackman (left), Candice Bergen, James Coburn (right), Ben Johnson, Ian Bannen, Jan-Michael Vincent, Paul Stewart and Robert Donner.

◁ A trashy youth-orientated melodrama that combined romance and nostalgia, **Aloha, Bobby And Rose**'s thin little plot showed all the strains of having been on a severe diet. Paul Le Mat (left) played a motor mechanic, and Dianne Hull (right) a car-wash attendant. They become involved in a liquor-store robbery during which a clerk is shot dead, and spend the rest of the film on the run in Mexico and Los Angeles. It was written and directed by Floyd Mutrux, jazzily photographed by William A. Fraker, and produced by Fouad Said. The cast included Tim McIntire, Leigh French, Noble Willingham, Robert Carradine and Martine Bartlett. Condolences all round. (88 mins)

After a leisurely paced build-up, the race began in earnest – and lasted the better part of an hour and a half. Interest rested solely on one's involvement with the characters none of whom, like the material itself, was particularly original or compelling. Brooks produced, Alex North provided the music, and the excellent location photography in Nevada, Colorado and New Mexico was the work of Harry Stradling Jr. (131 mins)

◁ Buried somewhere in the morass of **The Black Bird** was a terrific idea – for a revue sketch. It went something like this: Sam Spade's son has inherited his father's agency. The location is the same as it was in the Hammett original – except that the neighbourhood is now black and rundown. Sam Spade has a secretary. She's a bit of a ditz called Effie. Stashed away in a filing cabinet is the Maltese Falcon which, it just so happens, is being sought by a man in an opera-cape who offers Sam $300 for it – then dies. Not wanting to get involved (that's the type of private eye he is) Spade Jr tries to pawn the troublesome bird but is offered only $14.50 for it – at which point, he decides to take the case. Four Hawaiian thugs, a Nazi midget, and a beautiful woman are all after the falcon, and their pursuit of the bird should have provided the film with most of its fun. In the end, though, audiences were left with several characters in search of not only falcon but also a plot. The film's opening credits aped those of the original 1941 Warner Bros. classic – but there, alas, similarities ended (except that Lee Patrick and Elisha Cook Jr reprised their roles of Effie and Wilmer). George Segal (right) played young Spade, Stéphane Audran (left) was the chic romantic interest, with other roles under David Giler's well-intentioned but uninventive direction going to Lionel Stander, Felix Silla, Signe Hasso and John Abbott. Giler wrote it from a story by Don M. Mankiewicz and Gordon Cotler, and it was produced by Michael Levee and Lou Lombardo with Segal as executive producer. (98 mins)

△ **Breakout** was a dispiriting actioner that starred Charles Bronson (right) as an aviator whose purpose in Howard B. Kreitsek, Marc Norman and Elliot Baker's mouldy screenplay (from a novel by Warren Hinckle, William Turner and Eliot Asinof) was to rescue Robert Duvall (centre) from a Mexican prison after being framed by his father-in-law (John Huston). Jill Ireland played Duvall's wife, with other roles in Robert Chartoff and Irwin Winkler's production going to Randy Quaid (left), Sheree North and Alejandro Rey. Tom Gries directed. Talk about waste! (96 mins)

▽ An authentic 1920s period feel pervaded **The Fortune**, a black farce from producers Mike Nichols and Don Devlin that teamed two megastars – Jack Nicholson (third left) and Warren Beatty (second right) – with talented Stockard Channing, and chivalrously allowed the lady to run off with all the acting honours. Nicholson and Beatty played a pair of con artists who kidnap heiress Channing; then, on learning that she has been disinherited, spend the last half of the film trying to do her in. What the film needed in order to make it work were the comic personas of, say, Terry-Thomas, Alec Guinness, Peter Sellers or Alastair Sim (and, as the victim, Margaret Rutherford) – ie the cast of a British Ealing Comedy. What it got instead were two Hollywood heart-throbs, neither of whose forte was outlandish farce. The result was a rather raucous, self-indulgent romp with a handful of intermittently funny moments – most of them belonging to the quirky Miss Channing. Florence Stanley played an interfering landlady, Richard Shull a detective, Tom Newman a barber, John Fiedler a photographer and Scatman Crothers a fisherman. It was scripted by Adrien Joyce and directed by Mike Nichols with, one sensed, more than a touch of desperation. (88 mins)

▽ After the runway success of *Funny Girl* (1968), it was inevitable that the studio would want a sequel. The result was **Funny Lady**, a sort of Fanny Sings Again which took up the Fanny Brice story after Nicky Arnstein's exit, and continued to show how the great comedienne had no luck with her love life by chronicling her unhappy marriage (on the rebound) to showman Billy Rose. The Fanny lady was, of course, Barbra Streisand (left). James Caan was cast as Rose (who in real-life was pint-sized, and towered *under* his famous wife), with Omar Sharif (right) reprising his role as gambler Arnstein. Also in the cast were Roddy McDowall, Ben Vereen, Carol Welles, Larry Gates and Heidi O'Rourke. The film's first quarter, which hilariously described the trials and tribulations of an Atlantic City try-out of a new revue, promised far more than the rest of the film delivered. Betty Walberg choreographed, and the musical director was Peter Matz. It was written by Arnold Schulman and Jay Presson Allen (story by Schulman), directed by Herbert Ross, and produced – very profitably – by Ray Stark. (136 mins)

▽ **Hard Times** (GB: **The Streetfighter**) wasn't a film version of Charles Dickens's celebrated novel but a modestly entertaining 'fight' film evocatively set in the Thirties. It had nothing to do with professional boxing, none of it took place in a conventional ring, and the leading character was never referred to as 'kid'. His name is Chaney (Charles Bronson, right), and he is a peripatetic streetfighter who uses his bare knuckles rather than gloves. He makes his living taking on all comers and, in the story that Bryan Gindorff and Bruce Henstell had to tell (screenplay by Gindorff, Henstell and director Walter Hill), so impresses fight-promoter James Coburn (left), that Coburn takes him on for a series of illegal bouts, one of which is with a shaven-headed behemoth. Coburn gambles away his winnings, finds himself indebted to the Mob and is hauled out of his financial troubles by Bronson in a climactic final fight, after which the laconic hero leaves town as mysteriously as he arrived in it. In his first directorial effort, Hill expertly exploited the qualities endemic to his two leading men, and, with the help of art director Trevor Williams, lovingly and painstakingly created the look and the feel of the period in which it all took place. Bronson (who was 54 at the time), gave one of his best performances to date, ditto Coburn. Jill Ireland (Mrs Bronson in real-life) provided minimal female interest as Bronson's fling, Strother Martin appeared in the role of a dope-addicted unlicensed doctor attached to Coburn, Maggie Blye was Coburn's girl, and Michael McGuire played a big-time gambler. The producer was Lawrence Gordon. (92 mins)

▽ **Harry And Walter Go To New York** was a spectacularly awful comedy in which James Caan (left, as Harry) and Elliott Gould (right, as Walter), starred as a pair of mediocre vaudevillians who, in the New York of 1892, are thrown into jail for petty theft. Inside, they meet international safecracker Michael Caine (centre back) whom they partner in a major bank heist. Diane Keaton (front) could wring no laughs from her role as the editor of a radical underground newspaper who is in on the heist. John Byrum and Robert Kaufman's stultifyingly wasteful screen play also found roles for Charles Durning, Lesley Ann Warren, Val Avery, Jack Gilford, Dennis Dugan and Carol Kane. Mark Rydell directed, and Don Devlin and Harry Gittes produced. In the words of a reviewer of the day, 'strictly for those who'll laugh at anything'. (120 mins)

△ Ira Levin's creepy novel **The Stepford Wives** was turned into a rather under-paced movie by scenarist William Goldman and director Bryan Forbes. Set in the small, peaceful town of Stepford, Connecticut (but shot in Westport), it was a male chauvinist's fantasy about a group of model housewives, all of whom rejoice in their unswerving dedication to their husbands and the meticulous upkeep of their homes. As it turns out, they're robotic replicas of themselves. Just what has happened to their real selves was the mystery underpinning the tale. Katharine Ross (centre front) was top-starred as the latest recruit to the town of Stepford, Peter Masterson was her husband, with other roles going to Paula Prentiss (centre back), Nanette Newman (second right, Mrs Bryan Forbes in real life), Tina Louise, Carol Rossen, William Prince and, as the town's most important citizen – and the owner of a mysterious men's club – Patrick O'Neal. Edgar J. Scherick produced, and with 20 minutes cut from the first ponderous hour, he may have had a contender on his hands. (In 1980 there followed a TV movie called *Revenge Of The Stepford Wives*.) (114 mins)

▽ Though **Shampoo** was set on the day Richard Nixon became President of the USA, the politics involved in Hal Ashby's often venomous satire on the shallowness of the wealthy Beverly Hills set was purely sexual. Lampooning his own sexually voracious image far more successfully than he would do 12 years later in *Ishtar*, Warren Beatty (illustrated) – who produced and co-wrote the screenplay with Robert Towne – played randy George Roundy, a high-class ladies' hairdresser who rings the changes on that allegedly campy profession by sleeping with practically every one of his clients – including Lee Grant (whose husband, Jack Warden, thinks he's gay), Julie Christie, Goldie Hawn and, as Grant's nymphettish daughter, Carrie Fisher (her debut). In the end though, disillusion with his (and his clients') lives takes its toll as Beatty realizes that, apart from his sexual prowess and its resultant conquests, his life is empty and meaningless. Beatty brought a jaded conviction to the role, and gave the bravest performance of his career. All the women were fine, especially Carrie Fisher as the outspoken mouth-piece of liberated youth, and there was excellent support from Jay Robinson, George Furth, Brad Dexter and, as a producer, William Castle. *Shampoo* was one of the hits that confirmed Columbia's rising profitability in the mid-Seventies. (109 mins)

▽ A trucker's lot is not a happy one. At least not for Jan-Michael Vincent (right), the good-looking hero of **White Line Fever**, a stylish action-drama about the hazards of earning an honest buck in a business dominated, it would appear from Ken Friedman and Jonathan Kaplan's convincing screenplay, by graft and corruption. After refusing to accept contraband cigarettes as part of his cargo, Vincent finds himself blacklisted, then beaten up, shot at, framed for murder, and, together with his pregnant wife (Kay Lenz, left), nearly burned alive. In the end, he and some of his supporters actually manage to eliminate some of the baddies and organize a states-wide trucker's strike. Although this represented a victory of sorts, it was by no means a finite solution. Kaplan's emotionally charged direction kept the workable material simmering and drew sharply etched performances not only from his principals, but also from Slim Pickens, L.Q. Jones, Don Porter, Sam Laws, Johnny Ray McGhee and Leigh French. It was produced by John Kemeny. (89 mins)

△ A decent, middle-of-the-road drama with decent, homespun Norman Rockwell values, **Baby Blue Marine** was the story of a young man (Jan-Michael Vincent, illustrated) who, in 1943, is rejected from a Marine Corps boot camp for not shaping up (hard to believe, given Vincent's physical attributes), and, while returning to St Louis, finds himself in a small California town where he masquerades as a hero (shades of Preston Sturges's *Hail The Conquering Hero*, Paramount, 1944). How, through the love of one of the town's families, Vincent is eventually turned into the kind of man he never thought he could be, was the stuff of Stanford Whitmore's Rockwell-inspired screenplay, which, under John Hancock's direction, seemed unbelievable. Glynnis O'Connor was cast as the girl who falls in love with Vincent; Bert Remsen and Katherine Helmond were her kindly parents, Art Lund played a neighbour who sees in Vincent his dead son, while Richard Gere, in an early screen appearance, played a drinking buddy of the hero who agrees to swap his Marine Corps Raider uniform for his chum's light-blue fatigues (hence the title), a move which allows Vincent to bring a touch of authenticity to his 'hero' masquerade. The producers were Aaron Spelling and Leonard Goldberg. (90 mins)

▷ Filmed in and around Lagos, Nigeria, **Countdown At Kusini** was a humourless adventure melodrama set against a backdrop of an emerging African nation and was all about the attempts of a multi-national corporation to remove a black revolutionary leader (Ossie Davis, left). Romance wasn't overlooked, and it arrived in the shape of a woman dedicated to the revolution (Ruby Dee), and a jazz pianist (Greg Morris). It was written by Davis and producer Ladi Ladebo (based on a story by John Storm Roberts), directed by Davis, and also featured Tom Aldredge, Michael Ebert and Thomas Baptiste. The effective African music score was by Manu Dibango. The film went all out to be serious about African politics, as well as entertaining; it was neither. (99 mins)

▽ **Drive-In**, aimed squarely at the youth market, was two movies wrapped up into one; or, if you like, its own double feature. One half of the film concerned the amorous antics in a drive-in theatre in Texas of local beauty Lisa Lemole (left), who's in the process of dropping big-wig gangleader Billy Milliken in favour of the sexually naïve Glenn Morshower (right); the other half was a deliciously humorous send-up of the whole disaster-movie genre. The film the kids are watching at the drive-in is called 'Disaster '76' – about a 747 that crashes into a burning building. Not only that but there's an earthquake which results in a dam break which results in a tidal wave which results in a passenger ship being overturned! Alex Rose and Tamara Asseyev's production mined maximum laughter from a minimal budget; while Rod Amateau's direction drew engaging performances from a cast comprised largely of unknowns. Apart from the above-mentioned trio they included Gary Cavagnaro, Trey Wilson, Gordon Hurst, Louis Zito, Linda Lorimer, Kent Perkins and Ashley Cox. It was written by Bob Peete. (96 mins)

◁ **The Front** was a serious comedy that used as its springboard the shameful McCarthy witch-hunts of the late Forties and Fifties during which time the lives and livelihoods of scores of creative artists in the movie and TV industry were effectively truncated. It starred Woody Allen (right) as a 'nebbish'; an amateur book-maker who 'lucks out' when he agrees to 'front' for a group of blacklisted writers by putting his name to their scripts. Against a not-so-funny background of duplicity, blackmail and tragedy, the rise and fall (through greed) of the central character was compulsively charted in Walter Bernstein's intelligent screenplay. Zero Mostel (left) played a blacklisted comedian called Hecky Brown whose career ends in suicide after he has been reduced to playing the Catskills for a fraction of his regular fee; with other roles under Martin Ritt's sure-footed direction going to Herschel Bernardi as a TV producer, Andrea Marcovicci as a story editor (and Allen's love interest), Michael Murphy as a high-school friend of Allen's, and Lloyd Gough and David Margulies as blacklisted writers. Ritt also produced. For many involved with *The Front*, the film was a re-enactment of their own history: Ritt, Bernstein, Mostel, Bernardi, Gough and Joshua Shelley – another member of the cast – had all been blacklisted as a result of the McCarthy witch-hunts. (94 mins)

309

▷ Whether the idea belonged to producer Ray Stark or scenarist Neil Simon, it was, either way, an out and out winner. For **Murder By Death** brought together, under one Gothic roof, the vaguely disguised likes of Hercule Poirot, Miss Marple, Nick and Nora Charles, Charlie Chan and Sam Spade. No, it wasn't a detective's convention – but a dinner party, organized by the diabolical Lionel Twain, an eccentric millionaire, who back in the Thirties was arrested for smuggling white Americans into Mexico to pick melons. He has invited to his forbidding mansion the world's leading literary sleuths in order to eliminate them. Aiding and abetting him in his wicked plan are a blind butler and a deaf-and-dumb maid. Truman Capote (making a belated movie debut) lispingly played Twain, Alec Guinness was the butler (called Bensonmum) and Nancy Walker (who had one truly hysterical moment as she emitted a silent scream) was the maid. Portly James Coco (left) was Milo Perrier, sleazy Peter Falk (fourth left) was Sam Diamond, scatty Elsa Lanchester (fourth right) played Jessica Marple, a slit-eyed Peter Sellers (third right) did his Oriental bit as Sidney Wong, while urbane David Niven (second right) and Maggie Smith (right) played Dick and Dora Charles. The cast also featured Estelle Winwood (centre back) and Eileen Brennan (third left). A complementary combination of Simon's laugh-a-line script and Robert Moore's light-hearted direction (his debut in movies) kept audiences in stitches, especially fans of Agatha Christie, Earl Derr Biggers, Raymond Chandler and Dashiell Hammett. *Murder by Death* was unalloyed joy from start to finish. (94 mins)

△ The pioneering days of moving pictures when struggling independent film-makers had to face the wrath of the powerful Motion Picture Patents Company, or Trust, as it was called, was the promising subject of **Nickelodeon**, a noisy, frenetic comedy from director Peter Bogdanovich. It starred Ryan O'Neal (second right) as an incompetent lawyer, who suddenly finds himself directing movies, and Burt Reynolds (third left) as a rodeo rider-turned-leading man. After a frivolous, slapstick-orientated first half, the film struck a more serious note as it followed the chequered (and separate) careers of its two protagonists prior to an obligatory happy ending. The script Bogdanovich wrote with W.D. Richter was as strident as his direction and did nothing for his two leading men nor for a cast that also included Tatum O'Neal (left, as a thoroughly resistible brat), Brian Keith (as a producer), Stella Stevens (right), John Ritter, Jane Hitchcock, Harry Carey Jr, James Best, George Gaynes and M. Emmet Walsh. The producers were Irwin Winkler and Robert Chartoff. (121 mins)

▽ Brian De Palma's **Obsession**, generally considered to be a homage to Alfred Hitchcock, relied less on the maestro's style than on the plot he used for his classic thriller *Vertigo* (Paramount, 1958) – a film obsessed with obsession. De Palma's film was the story of a New Orleans businessman (Cliff Robertson, left) who, in 1948, marries beautiful Genevieve Bujold, right). After a party celebrating their tenth wedding anniversary, Bujold and their daughter (Wanda Blackman) are kidnapped, and, one is led to believe, murdered when the ransom payment backfires. Almost 20 years later, Robertson, obsessed with guilt over his family's demise, is on a business trip in Italy when, in a church, one day, he meets a young Italian woman who is the image of his deceased wife. And, just as James Stewart did *vis à vis* Kim Novak in *Vertigo*, Robertson sets about making the Italianate Bujold over in his late wife's image. A surprise twist in Paul Schrader's not very logical screenplay (story by Schrader and De Palma) supplied some of the answers. John Lithgow, making an impressive screen debut, played a friend and business partner of Robertson's, with Sylvia Kuumba Williams, Patrick McNamara and Stanley J. Reyes in it too. Bernard Herrmann provided the over-emphatic score and it was produced by George Litto and Harry N. Blum. The film was a solid box-office success. (98 mins)

△ The idea behind James Goldman's screenplay for **Robin And Marian** was to re-unite the two legendary lovers 20 years after their first clinch. Thus Robin (Sean Connery, left), on his return to Sherwood Forest after a lengthy Crusade in the Holy Lands, has a grey beard, is less agile and, where combat is concerned, less motivated. Marian – Audrey Hepburn (right) in her first film since *Wait Until Dark*, Warner Bros., 1967 – is visibly less radiant, too, having attempted suicide after Robin's abandonment of her for the Crusades. She has taken herself to a nunnery and is now its Mother Superior. The love affair that is rekindled between the two of them was the most moving element in a plot that ended with a climactic confrontation between Robin and the Sheriff of Nottingham

▷ The ubiquitous Jan-Michael Vincent (right) received top-billing in a low-budget potboiler called **Shadow Of The Hawk**. He played the grandson of medicine man Chief Dan George (centre), who, in the course of the screenplay (Norman Thaddeus Vane and Herbert J. Wright wrote it, and Vane, Peter Jensen and Lynette Cahill provided the story) is sought out by his grandfather to help ward off evil spirits emanating from a sorceress called Dsonoqua (Marianne Jones). This load of old Sitting Bull was produced by John Kemeny and directed by George McCowan. The cast also featured Marilyn Hassett (left) and Pia Shandei. (92 mins)

(Robert Shaw) in which Robin is badly wounded. To spare him suffering, he is poisoned by Marian, who then poisons herself. Despite much of the humour invested in it by director Richard Lester, there was a mellowness and a sadness about this tale of middle-aged romance which remained in the memory long after the mechanics of the narrative had disappeared. Richard Harris played a demented King Richard, Nicol Williamson was uncomfortably cast as Little John, and Denholm Elliott was under-used as Will Scarlett. Kenneth Haigh played Sir Ranulf, Ronnie Barker was Friar Tuck, and the cast also featured Ian Holm as the evil King John. It was produced by Denis O'Dell (with Ray Stark and Richard Shepherd as executive producers). (106 mins)

▽ Psychotics or psycopaths do not, as a rule, make compelling screen heroes. It takes a great actor to compel undivided attention with aberrant behaviour. Robert De Niro (illustrated) does it in Martin Scorsese's **Taxi Driver**, a brilliant but flinch-making look at the slimy underbelly of humanity. Set in a New York populated almost in its entirety by pimps, prostitutes, killers and a ripe assortment of human garbage, the film featured De Niro as Travis Bickle, a moralistic Viet Nam veteran who is now a cabbie, and who keeps a diary, pops pills, swigs peach brandy and, for relaxation, goes to porn movies. A loner, and very much a part of the landscape he despises, De Niro has a growing need to be someone and 'do something' and this leads him to plan a political assassination. When that goes wrong, he decides to clean up the sordid milieu in which he operates and to liberate a 14-year-old prostitute (Jodie Foster) from her lover-pimp (Harvey Keitel) and his assistant (Murray Moston) by killing both men. He thus becomes what he has always wanted to become: a media hero, if only for a day. Having worked his frustrations out of his system, he returns to his dreary routine. Clearly, though, his insane foray into murder is not a one-off aberration, and the film left audiences wondering how long it would be before Travis Bickle blows his cool again. The nasty taste it left in audiences' mouths was put there by Paul Schrader's obscenity-splattered screenplay and by Scorsese's uncompromising depiction of sex and violence (though by toning down the blood hues in the more violent sequences from red to a brownish tint, Scorsese made sure the film escaped the 'X' rating it deserved). It was De Niro's astonishingly charismatic, undeniably hypnotic performance that allowed us to savour the taste without rejecting it as unswallowable. With a lesser actor at the wheel, *Taxi Driver* would have been unthinkable. Cybill Shepherd was second-billed as an intelligent senator's assistant (whom De Niro discovers to be way out of his league), Peter Boyle was his best pal, and Steve Prince the man who supplies him with guns. Scorsese appeared in it too; as a deranged passenger in De Niro's cab whose wife is living with another man. The brilliant score was the work of Bernard Herrmann (who died the day after he completed it), and the film was produced by Michael Phillips and Julia Phillips. (113 mins)

△ **Bobby Deerfield** was an incredibly silly romantic drama of the type Warner Bros. did so much better with George Brent and Bette Davis (or Stanwyck, or Crawford) back in the Forties. In a blatant, full-frontal attack on the tear-ducts, it told the hearts-and-flowers story of an unlikeable and uninteresting international racing driver (Al Pacino, left) who, while investigating an accident in which a colleague was killed, has the misfortune to meet the lovely Marthe Keller (right) in an expensive Swiss clinic. It's a misfortune in that Miss K, with whom he naturally falls head-over-heels in love, has a mysterious, unnamed terminal illness – probably cancer or leukemia, because chemotherapy has resulted in handfuls of her hair falling out. Like the film, she, too, dies. The high-grade mush was the work of Sydney Pollack, who produced and directed it, and Alvin Sargent, who scripted it from a novel by Erich Maria Remarque called *Heaven Has No Favourites*. The Swiss Alps, Bellagio, Florence and Paris provided the travel-brochure backdrop to the doomed romance, and completely upstaged a little-known supporting cast that included Anny Duperey, Walter McGinn, Romolo Valli, Stephan Meldegg and Jaime Sanchez. The pretty photography was by Henri Decaë. (124 mins)

▽ Steven Spielberg, who has gone on record saying that the movies he enjoys making are big-budget retreads of the programmers and potboilers he enjoyed watching as a kid, impressively demonstrated this in his breathtaking re-working of a typical Fifties excursion into inter-galactic sci-fi, **Close Encounters Of The Third Kind**. Using a mind-bending range of space-age hardware as well as all the latest equipment in sophisticated movie technology, his film was a dazzling cinematic adventure that stimulated the retina without ever numbing the brain. It was an awesome piece of film-making that could be both looked at and thought about with equal fascination. The story, such as it was, involved the sighting of a UFO by Richard Dreyfuss (illustrated) during a blackout in the small town of Muncie, Indiana. Two other people, that same dark night, have close encounters with the aliens: Melinda Dillon, and her four-year-old son Cary Guffery. The effect the sightings have on the three of them – especially Dreyfuss, who becomes so obsessed by what he has seen that his marriage begins to crumble – was the springboard for a story that ended over two hours later, and which was memorably climaxed by a sequence in which an alien spacecraft, peopled by childlike creatures, actually makes a peaceful landing. Stanley Kubrick's *2001: A Space Odyssey* (MGM, 1968) notwithstanding, the cinema of sci-fi had experienced nothing more profoundly moving than this remarkable 'close encounter' between earthlings and visitors from another galaxy. French film-maker François Truffaut played an important part in Spielberg's screenplay, as a French scientist conversing through interpreter Bob Balaban, with the film's other key role going to Teri Garr as Dreyfuss's wife. J. Patrick McNamara, Warren Kemmerling, Roberts Blossom, Philip Dodds, Shawn Bishop, Adrienne Campbell and Justin Dreyfuss were also cast. The special effects were the work of Roy Arbograst, Gregory Jein, Douglas Trumbull and Matthew and Richard Yuricich; John Williams provided the music; and the film was produced by Julia Phillips and Michael Phillips at a cost of $20 million. The film grossed a mammoth $116.4 million at the box-office in its initial release, and a further $11.8 million in the expanded 1980 version – dubbed The Special Edition. (135 mins)

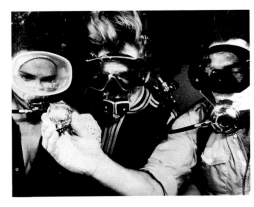

△ **The Deep** was a shallow adventure, based on Peter Benchley's equally shallow novel, that starred sexy Jacqueline Bisset (left) and hunky Nick Nolte (centre) as a pair of deep-sea divers who discover a cache of drugs (morphine) while exploring the depths of the Bermuda waters. Though the stuff has been refrigerated at the bottom of the sea for some time, it is nonetheless hot. So hot, in fact, that a group of lecherous, thoroughly despicable villains, led by Louis Gossett (later Lou Gossett Jr), will do anything to get their hands on it. Little more than a *Boy's Own* adventure tarted up out of all proportion to its worth, it was scripted by Benchley and Tracy Keenan Wynn, produced by Peter Guber and, in smaller roles, featured Eli Wallach (as a beach bum), Robert Tessier, Earl Maynard and Dick Anthony Williams. They were all upstaged by a giant moray eel. Topping the cast was Robert Shaw who, in a blatant reprise of his *Jaws* (Universal, 1975) characterization, played a grisly scuba diver. The best thing about the film was the wet T-shirt worn by Bisset. It was the only thing that clung. Peter Yates directed. Despite its impoverished content, the film was a box office hit. (124 mins)

▽ A mind-blowingly awful melodrama that traded in violence, **The Farmer** starred Gary Conway (left) as a much-decorated soldier who, after returning to his run-down Georgia farm at the end of World War II, accepts a contract from mobster Michael Dante to eliminate a few hoods, the proceeds of which will help restore his property to its former glory. In the course of this junk-fest, Dante is blinded by acid, Conway's girl (Angel Tompkins, right) is anally raped while a third victim (Ken Renard) is burned alive. It took four untalented scenarists (George Fargo, Janice Colson-Dodge, Patrick Regan and John Carmody) to think it up; David Berlatsky directed it, and leading-man Conway produced. (97 mins)

▷ Middle-class American affluence, wrong-headed values, and the lengths to which some people will go to maintain both, was the fun-filled content of **Fun With Dick And Jane**. Dick was George Segal (left), Jane was Jane Fonda (right), an upwardly mobile young couple whose world comes crashing down when Segal loses his job as a Los Angeles aerospace engineer and finds himself with a half-finished swimming pool and $72,000 in debt. In order to alleviate their financial crisis, they decide to take to crime – armed robbery, actually, with hilarious results. The David Giler-Jerry Belson-Mordecai Richler screenplay asked audiences to condemn the values by which the couple live, while at the same time manipulating them into total acceptance of those values. It was a commercially motivated, cunning piece of double-think that, given the beguiling personalities of its two stars, worked like a charm: a perfect case of having one's cake and eating it. Both Segal and Fonda handled the comedy terrifically and there was a peach of a performance, in the plum role of Segal's boozy employer, by Ed McMahon. Director Ted Kotcheff brought just the right touch to it all. His supporting cast included Dick Gautier and Hank Garcia, and the film was produced by Peter Bart and Max Palevsky. (95 mins)

◁ As was the case with the preceding two Charles H. Schneer–Ray Harryhausen 'Sinbad' collaborations, it was Harryhausen's Dynamation process – this time involving such wonders as animated skeletons, a giant bee, a king-sized walrus and a sabre-toothed tiger – that captured the attention and the imagination of the young audiences at which **Sinbad And The Eye Of The Tiger** was aimed. For the rest it was a poorly scripted (by Beverley Cross from a story by Cross and Harryhausen) adventure yarn which found Sinbad (Patrick Wayne, son of John) on a quest to free a Prince (Damien Thomas) from the spell of an evil sorceress (Margaret Whiting). Taryn Power (daughter of Tyrone) and Jane Seymour added a touch of pulchritude to the proceedings, and the cast under Sam Wanamaker's unobtrusive direction also included Kurt Christian, Nadim Sawaiha, Bruno Barnabe and Bernard Kay. (112 mins)

▽ Joseph Brooks wrote, produced, and directed **You Light Up My Life**, as well as composed, arranged and conducted its score. A low-budget drama about the attempts of a comedian's show-biz-orientated daughter to find her own identity – both privately and professionally – it starred an appealing Didi Conn (illustrated) as the daughter, Joe Silver as her funny-man pop, Stephen Nathan as the self-absorbed tennis coach she's about to marry (unhappily, no doubt), and Michael Zaslow as a movie director who, for a while, at any rate, lights up her life. Miss Conn was a delight who lit up the film, and she brought genuine pathos to what could so easily have been a cloying and over-sentimentalised experience. Five songs were featured, including Joseph Brooks's title song, which became a hit. (90 mins)

△ Just as Audie Murphy played himself in *To Hell And Back* (Universal, 1955), as did Douglas Corrigan in *The Flying Irishman* (RKO, 1939), so Muhammad Ali (illustrated) brought his special brand of charisma to the screen in **The Greatest**, an old-fashioned biopic that didn't delve too deeply and was satisfied simply to recreate some highspots. A PR job, almost, it began with the young Cassius Clay (Phillip 'Chip' McAllister) returning to Louisville from Rome (where he won an Olympic medal) and, despite his success (or, because of it), encountering serious discrimination. More determined than ever to make an impact on a white world, Clay turns professional, at which point Muhammad Ali stepped into his own shoes and remained in them for the rest of the film. What followed was a superficial (but enjoyable) recap of his life, covering his friendship with Malcolm X (James Earl Jones), his conversion to the Muslim religion, his fight successes, his refusal to be inducted into the US Army, his victorious Supreme Court hearings and his triumph over George Foreman in Zaire. Malcolm X mysteriously vanished half-way through; and there was no mention at all of Ali's first wife. In other words, a typical Hollywood biopic. Annazette Chase played Ali's second wife Belinda, with other roles in the Ring Lardner Jr screenplay (based on *The Greatest: My Own Story* by Ali and Richard Durham) going to Ernest Borgnine and John Marley as his trainer and his doctor, Roger E. Mosley as Sonny Liston, Robert Duvall (a cameo bit), Paul Winfield, David Huddleston, Ben Johnson and Dina Merrill. It was produced by John Marshall, and directed by Tom Gries (who died shortly afterwards). (114 mins)

▽ Singer Buddy Holly died in a plane-crash, together with The Big Bopper and Richie Valens, in 1959. The story of his short but impressive career was movingly told in **The Buddy Holly Story** and benefited immeasurably from the marvellous central casting of Gary Busey (illustrated) as the gangling, galvanic, bespectacled rock star. Don Stroud played drummer Jesse, Charles Martin Smith portrayed bassist Ray Bob (of The Crickets) and both did their own music-making, just as Busey did his own singing of Buddy Holly's songs. Bill Jordan, Maria Richwine, Conrad Janis and Albert Popwell were also featured in Robert Gittler's affectionate screenplay (story by Alan Swyer), and it was sensitively directed by Steve Rash and produced by Fred Bauer. (113 mins)

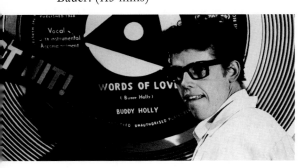

▽ Neil Simon scored a movie hat-trick with *Murder by Death* (1976), *The Cheap Detective* (see next page) and **California Suite** – an adaptation of a quartet of one-act plays (all set in the Beverly Hills Hotel) which had been presented, under the same title, on Broadway in 1976. Apart from the casting, the main difference between the two versions was that, for the screen, Simon interlocked the four separate stories so that they ran into a seamless, laugh-drenched whole. In a cast as near perfection as you could hope to find on either side of the Atlantic, Maggie Smith (right) and Michael Caine (left) played an English actress and her gay antique-dealer husband who are in Los Angeles to attend the Oscar ceremony for which she has been nominated as Best Actress; Jane Fonda and Alan Alda (both terrific), played a divorced couple concerned about the future of their daughter; Walter Matthau and Elaine May, as husband and wife, added a touch of bedroom farce as the former is forced to explain to the latter his one-night involvement with a hooker, while Richard Pryor and Bill Cosby, together with Gloria Gifford and Sheila Frazier as their wives, find themselves on a vacation in which everything goes wrong. Under Herbert Ross's sharp, observant, well-paced direction it added up to block-buster entertainment that skilfully combined humour and pathos – which only in the Pryor-Cosby segment, slipped, momentarily, into caricature. Producer was Ray Stark. (103 mins)

△ A ghetto dope-peddler turned hero (Stan Shaw, right), a hippie (Craig Wasson, left), a ladies-man from Brooklyn (Michael Lembeck) a sensitive diarist (James Canning) and an athlete-turned-junkie (Andrew Stevens, centre): those were **The Boys In Company C**, a forerunner of Stanley Kubrick's superior *Full Metal Jacket* (Warner Bros., 1987). Though the setting of director Sidney Furie's familiar boot-camp-to-battleground story was Viet Nam in 1967, given the number of clichés that played leapfrog over one other, the screenplay Furie wrote with Rick Natkin could have been set in World War II or even Korea. The situations were as stereotyped as the characters, with the result that Andre Morgan's production contributed nothing to the theatre of war that hadn't been encountered many times before in Hollywood's past. Scott Hylands, James Whitmore Jr, Noble Willingham, and Lee Ermey were also featured. (125 mins)

▽ A good-natured, thoroughly agreeable family film that might almost be described as a thoroughbred, **Casey's Shadow** was the story of a Cajun, tobacco-chewing horse-trainer (the great Walter Matthau, left) who not only has to cope with training quarter horses on a run-down Louisiana farm, but also with raising, single-handedly, three sons – Andrew A. Rubin, Stephen Burns (right) and Michael Hershewe. The fulcrum on which Carol Sobieski's enjoyably predictable screenplay (based on the story *Ruidoso* by John McPhee) pivoted was the rich quarter-horse race at New Mexico's Ruidoso track in which Matthau has entered a two-year-old called Casey's Shadow, named after his youngest son. Murray Hamilton and Robert Webber were featured as a pair of baddies, and Alexis Smith was second-billed as a wealthy and humorous owner of quarter horses. It was engagingly directed by Martin Ritt, who co-produced it with Ray Stark. (116 mins)

▷ Those hardy perennials of the detective genre, *The Big Sleep* (Warner Bros., 1946) and *The Maltese Falcon* (Warner Bros., 1941), plus more than a soupçon of *Casablanca* (Warner Bros., 1943), were the inspiration behind Neil Simon's story of **The Cheap Detective**, an expensive *hommage* to Humphrey Bogart and the type of flicks Bogey made during the Forties. Peter Falk (right) played Bogey (known in the film as Lou Peckinpaugh), who this time finds himself enmeshed in a complicated plot involving a set of diamond eggs – originally found by a group of Albanian fishermen in China, Mongolia and Tibet circa 1853 – which are sought after by a dozen or so recognizable Hollywood characters. These characters included Marsha Mason (left, as a hard-boiled Gladys George type), Madeleine Kahn (the Mary Astor role), Dom De Luise (an oversized Peter Lorre), John Houseman (Sydney Greenstreet to the life) and Eileen Brennan (not very successful, alas, as Lauren Bacall). Also: Stockard Channing (as Falk's Girl Friday), Ann-Margret (Claire Trevor), Sid Caesar (Miles Mander), James Coco, Louise Fletcher, Fernando Lamas, Phil Silvers, Paul Williams, Abe Vigoda, Scatman Crothers, Vic Tayback and Nicol Williamson. The film was set in San Francisco in 1939, and while not all the elements in Simon's screenplay hit their mark, there were enough highspots to light up half a dozen comedies. A pity, though, that producer Ray Stark didn't film it in black and white, thereby adding pictorial authenticity to the parody. Wayne Fitzgerald's witty titles set the mood for the caper, it was directed by Robert Moore, and grossed a splendid profit. (92 mins)

△ **If Ever I See You Again**, produced, directed, starred in and co-written (with Martin Davidson) by Joe (*You Light Up My Life*, 1977) Brooks, took a gentle – but protracted well past the point of overkill – swipe at the world of advertising jingles and TV commercials. The plot has Brooks (right) playing an insufferably egotistical writer of jingles. He tracks down a former girlfriend (Shelley Hack, left) who had jilted him 12 years ago, in order to impress her with his new-found fame and fortune. Also cast: Jimmy Breslin, Kenny Karen, Jerry Keller and George Plimpton. (105 mins)

▽ Turkey itself was the chief villain in Alan Parker's **Midnight Express**. The country emerged as a cesspool whose inhabitants were either evil, corrupt, incompetent, or sadistic: 'a nation of pigs' as its leading character, Billy Hayes, refers to it in the course of the film. Based on Hayes's own less brutal, less racist account of his incarceration in a Turkish prison for attempting to smuggle two kilos of hashish out of the country, and which he wrote with William Hoffer, Oliver Stone's screenplay repeatedly went for the jugular where brutality and violence were concerned. The result was a harrowing, sadistic melodrama whose most excessive and flinch-making scene showed young Hayes biting out the tongue of one of his money-hoarding fellow prisoners. Brad Davis (right) played the unfortunate Billy, a psychotic Randy Quaid was a fellow convict, Irene Miracle was Billy's girl, Mike Kellin (left) his father, John Hurt a drug addict, Norbert Weisser the obligatory gay inmate, Paul Smith the number-one guard and torturer, and Bo Hopkins a sympathetic investigator. There was no question that Alan Parker's loaded direction engaged one's emotions, but in a shamefully manipulative way. Not a pleasant film, but commercially a very successful one from producers Alan Marshall and David Puttnam. (120 mins)

△ A trendy, chic, though undeniably seedy, occult thriller, **The Eyes of Laura Mars** starred Faye Dunaway (illustrated) as a rather kinky fashion photographer who suddenly turns psychic and, in a series of graphic visions, sees several of her friends and associates being gruesomely murdered. Assigned to the strange case is Tommy Lee Jones, a police lieutenant who soon becomes an integral part of the on-going mystery. René Auberjonois played Dunaway's resistible manager, Raul Julia her ex-husband, and Brad Dourif her bedraggled chauffeur. Set against a photogenic backdrop of New York and its beautiful people, the film's stylish outward appearance went far to disguise its hollow centre, though nothing could save its dénouement from being plain stupid. Blame this on John Carpenter and David Zelag Goodman's screenplay (story by Carpenter). Jon Peters produced, Irvin Kershner directed (flashily), and the cast also included Frank Adonis, Lisa Taylor, Darlanne Flugel, Rose Gregorio, Bill Boggs and Steve Marachuk. (104 mins)

◁ A throwback to countless thrillers of the Thirties and Forties in which an innocent party is accused of a crime he or she did not commit, then spends the rest of the film clearing his or her name (and, in the process, apprehending the real culprit), **Somebody Killed Her Husband** was a creaky old thing that starred Farrah Fawcett-Majors (right) as an unhappily married blonde, who, while shopping in Macy's one-day, meets toy clerk Jeff Bridges (left). It's love at first sight, though it runs anything but smoothly after the couple discover Farrah's husband (Laurence Guittard) in his East Side apartment with a kitchen knife embedded in his back. When Jeff and Farrah are blamed – for this and three other similar-looking murders – they turn sleuth and, almost an hour an a half later, the crimes are solved to everyone's satisfaction. Tammy Grimes, John Wood and Beeson Carroll played the three further victims in Reginald Rose's arthritic screenplay; Lamont Johnson directed it, and the producer was Martin Poll. (96 mins)

▷ Alan Rudolph, whose *Welcome To L.A.* (United Artists, 1976) became something of a cult film, followed that rather pretentious look at a group of Los Angeles weirdos with **Remember My Name**, 'a contemporary blues fable' that looked quite striking (it was photographed by Tak Fujimoto) but which maddeningly obfuscated a simple story. It starred Geraldine Chaplin (left) as a woman who, having just completed a 12-year jail sentence for murdering her husband's lover, tracks down the husband (Anthony Perkins, right) and his new wife (Berry Berenson – Perkins's real-life wife – making her screen debut). Her revenge consists of hurling rocks through their window when they're making love and digging up their marigolds. She also takes a job at a local five-and-dime store (managed by Jeff Goldblum), terrorizing his lady store clerk (Alfre Woodard). Chaplin finds accommodation in a decrepit apartment block managed by Moses Gunn – with whom she has a short affair. What the film was saying (its message being telegraphed via background TV flashes of a calamitous earthquake) was that both Man and nature are in a mess. Rudolph scripted it, and it was produced for Lion's Gate Films by Robert Altman who engaged 83-year-old Alberta Hunter to supply the score – and to enrich the soundtrack with her striking blues vocals. Also featured: Timothy Thomerson. All the performances were first rate. (95 mins)

▽ Ivan Passer's **The Silver Bears** was a dreary, laugh-rationed comedy about mobster Martin Balsam who, with the help of Michael Caine (left), buys a Swiss bank in order to launder illegal profits. In the process he and his crooked associates become involved in the silver market, a silver mine in Iran, and an avaricious Californian bank. Peter Stone's screenplay-by-numbers (based on a novel by Paul Erdman) dissipated the talents of Balsam and Caine, as well as a cast that included sexy Cybill Shepherd (right), gorgeous Stéphane Audran, handsome Louis Jourdan and an interesting-looking David Warner. Also Tom Smothers, Charles Gray, Joss Ackland and Jeremy Clyde. Alex Winitsky and Arlene Sellers produced. (113 mins)

△ Chuck Vennera's amusing parody of Gene Kelly in a parking-lot dance routine was the best thing in **Thank God It's Friday**, an unsubtle and not very successful attempt to cash in on the runaway success of *Saturday Night Fever* (Paramount, 1977). Set during the course of a Friday night at a Hollywood disco (called The Zoo), the film's narrative attached itself to the goings-on of a handful of the establishment's performers and clientele – culminating in a dance contest – and provided a flimsy excuse for yet one more disco-orientated album. Robert Klane directed it from a screenplay by Barry Armyan Bernstein, Rob Cohen produced, and the cast included Donna Summer, Valerie Landsburg, Terri Nunn, Ray Vitte, Mark Lonow, Andrea Howard, and Debra Winger and Jeff Goldblum (right) – who'd both go on to far, far better things – Paul Jabara, and The Commodores (as themselves). (89 mins)

▷ A co-production between Columbia and 20th Century-Fox, **All That Jazz** was the first musical to address itself seriously to the subject of death. It was also the not-so-loosely autobiographical story of director-choreographer Bob Fosse who, seven years after directing the film, died of a heart-attack – just as his central character (played by Roy Scheider, left) does in the film. Thus, Fosse's warning to himself turned into tragic reality – a fact that makes his extraordinary film almost unbearably painful to watch today. Not that it was all that digestible at the time. Full of indulgent, typically Fosse-like excesses, it was the first truly adult backstage musical to emerge from the Hollywood dream factory, with grotesque nightmares and open-heart surgery taking the place of musical escapism. Leland Palmer was cast as Scheider's wife (based on Fosse's wife Gwen Verdon), his daughter was played by Erzsebet Foldi, and his mistress by Ann Reinking (right). Cliff Gorman was a 'Lenny'-type stand-up comedian, with other roles going to Ben Vereen (as an unctuous TV host), Jessica Lange (as Death) and John Lithgow. Fosse's choreography was superb and the excellent screenplay, by Fosse and producer Robert Alan Arthur was, for once, no mere appendage to the musical numbers. The musical director was Ralph Burns. (123 mins)

△ According to director William Richert's eccentric black comedy **The American Success Company**, the way to succeed in the world today is to become a crook – which is precisely what a mild-mannered Jeff Bridges (left), the son of a tough credit-card tycoon (Ned Beatty), is required to do in the screenplay handed him by Richert and Larry Cohen (story by Cohen). He even hires an experienced hooker (Bianca Jagger, right) to teach him how to satisfy his oversexed wife (Belinda Bauer). Bridges' reconstitution from near-nebbish to powerful lover was the film's *raison d'être* and under Richert's stylish direction it added up to an entertaining, latter-day fantasy. Steven Keats, John Glover, Mascha Gonska and Michael Durrell also had featured roles, and Maurice Jarre provided the score. The film was twice re-edited and reissued: as **American Success** in 1981, and **Success** in 1983. (94 mins)

▽ Corruption in the American judicial system, and its effect on a sensitive lawyer (Al Pacino, left) was the subject of **... And Justice For All**, a muddle-headed drama that seemed to be saying that if the system wasn't so tragic it would be funny; or, conversely, that if it wasn't so funny, it would be tragic. It was hard to tell from Valerie Curtin and Barry Levinson's screenplay, which was a series of sub-plots involving various aspects of the legal profession, the human detritus it spews up, as well as the dilemmas and decisions its practitioners are heir to every moment of their working day. The film also featured Jack Warden as a judge, Jeffrey Tambor as Pacino's suicidal partner, a pre-*Dynasty* John Forsythe (right) as an implacable judge, Robert Christian as a black transvestite, Thomas Waites as an innocent victim, Christine Lahti as a pretty lawyer, Lee Strasberg as Pacino's senile grandfather and Sam Levene as the grandfather's best friend. As for Pacino himself, his performance began on such a note of pitched tension that there was no room for development. Norman Jewison's direction didn't quite know what tone of voice to adopt, hence the film's confusion of purpose. It was produced by Jewison and Patrick Palmer. (120 mins)

△ It was no secret that Neil Simon's Broadway play **Chapter Two** was a semi-autobiographical drama (with lots of laughs, of course) in which the world's most successful playwright attempted to exorcise something of the guilt he felt when, after the death of his much-loved first wife, he married actress Marsha Mason. Just how, after a great deal of soul- and heart-searching, as well as a fair amount of suffering (not only his own), he was able to face the new relationship in his life without recourse to depression was what *Chapter Two* was all about. On the stage the emphasis was on Simon's own character, renamed George Schneider. In the film it veered towards his second wife, called Jennie MacLaine, and played wonderfully well by Marsha Mason (right) herself. The result was an always watchable, generally enjoyable romantic drama that told audiences more about her than about him. Simon, alias Schneider, was played by James Caan (left), an actor well-versed in the ways of looking hurt, troubled and introspective; and if, in the end, his character remained slightly out of focus, the fault lay not in the performance but in the screenplay which stated rather than probed. Joseph Bologna played Leo Schneider, George's loud-mouthed, advice-giving brother, with other roles under Robert Moore's solid, if uninspired, direction going to Valerie Harper as Mason's best friend, Judy Farrell, Debra Mooney and Isabel Cooley. Marvin Hamlisch wrote the soupy score and Ray Stark produced. (124 mins)

▽ **The China Syndrome** was a timely reminder that in a nuclear world there is no room for human error. Made seven years before Chernobyl, it was the fearful story of an impending global disaster resulting from a malfunction in a nuclear-energy plant in Southern California that could easily have resulted in a 'meltdown' (known as the China Syndrome) which, in turn, could possibly have led to the destruction of the planet. The film starred Jane Fonda (right) – in an excellent performance – as Kimberly Wells, a bright and ambitious TV news reporter who, while on an assignment to the power plant with photographer Michael Douglas (centre), witnesses what the company's public relations man euphemistically refers to as 'a routine turbine trip'. Fonda soon learns that what is really happening is a control-room crisis (surreptitiously photographed by Douglas) – involving supervisor Jack Lemmon (left) – and that she is onto something both literally and figuratively explosive. The development of the crisis and its ultimate resolution (in which the film's hitherto anti-nuclear stance was, surprisingly, toned down) generated edge-of-the-seat tension. A truly terrifying thriller, it was written by Mike Gray, T.S. Cook and James Bridges, tautly directed by Bridges and especially well acted by all three of its principals. Michael Douglas produced, and his cast was augmented by Scott Brady, James Hampton, Peter Donat, Wilford Brimley and Richard Herd. A potential nuclear disaster at the Three Mile Island plant shortly after the film's release gave it a topicality that added millions of dollars to its box-office take. (122 mins)

△ In **Fast Break** TV's Gabriel Kaplan (centre) made his big-screen debut. He played a New York delicatessen clerk who abandons his attractive wife (Randee Heller) to take up a basketball-coaching job in an obscure college in Nevada, and, after recruiting some players from New York's streets, turns a ragbag team into winners. Very reminiscent of *The Bad News Bears* (Paramount, 1976), but a lot more refined, it coasted along amiably enough, and unashamedly wallowed in its wall-to-wall clichés. But it could have (and should have) been made for TV. Harold Sylvester, Mike Warren, Bernard King, Reb Brown, Mavis Washington and Bert Remsen were also in it; Sandor Stern scripted from a story by Marc Kaplan, Jack Smight directed, and it was produced by Stephen Friedman. (117 mins)

▷ Robert Redford (illustrated) and Jane Fonda, having worked together twice before – in *The Chase* (1966) and *Barefoot In The Park* (Paramount 1967) – were teamed by producer Ray Stark for a third time in **The Electric Horseman**, a co-production with Universal Pictures. Though drawing its romantic inspiration from the Capraesque comedies of the Thirties, it told the contemporary story of a five-time rodeo champion (Redford) whose present pitch is selling cereal for a massive food conglomerate. Tired of making humiliating special appearances at supermarket launches, etc, he takes off into the desert with a tranquillized $12-million show-horse with whom he is expected to appear in a Las Vegas stage revue. He is pursued by reporter Fonda (with whom he falls in love) and, after giving the horse, called Rising Star, its freedom (a gesture which causes the sales of his cereal food to rise spectacularly), returns a hero. Unfortunately Robert Garland's talky and diffuse script (based on a screenplay by Garland and Paul Gaer and a story by Shelly Burton) made the least of the most, and did not fully exploit the several opportunities it had for taking a few hardhitting punches at the dehumanizing world of conglomerates. Potentially, the sub-text was all there. A pity that the script and Sydney Pollack's direction failed to take advantage of it. No complaints, though, about the two central performances – which were excellent – or the work of a cast that also included John Saxon as the dollar-grasping head of the company for whom Redford works, Alan Arbus, Wilford Brimley, Willie Nelson, and Timothy Scott. Valerie Perrine was in it, too, in a bit part. (120 mins)

△ Re-visiting literary legends well past their prime (the idea behind *Robin And Marian*, 1976), was the theme of **The Fifth Musketeer** whose dramatis personae included Dumas's swashbuckling Aramis (Lloyd Bridges), Porthos (Alan Hale Jr), Athos (José Ferrer) and D'Artagnan (Cornel Wilde) as middle-aged men. The fifth musketeer was Rex Harrison, as Colbert. Apart from this moderately amusing notion, the film was, basically, a re-make of *The Man In The Iron Mask* with Beau Bridges (right) playing both King Louis XIV and his incarcerated twin brother Philippe. Bridges wasn't nearly as effective in the role as Louis Hayward had been in Edward Small's celebrated 1939 version for United Artists, but then neither was anything, nor anyone else in this yawn-provoking re-tread. The stellar cast also included Sylvia Kristel as the virginal Infanta of Spain, Olivia de Havilland as Queen Anne, Helmut Dantine as the Spanish Ambassador, an overdressed Ursula Andress (left) as Madame de la Vallière, and, best of all, Ian McShane as the villain Fouquet. Ken Annakin directed; Ted Richmond produced and it was written by David Ambrose from a screenplay by George Bruce and the novel by Alexander Dumas. (103 mins)

▽ By using out-takes from Chuck Norris's *Return Of The Dragon* (Golden Harvest, 1974), as well as a Bruce Lee double and all the unfinished footage of Lee's last film (during the making of which he had died), producer Raymond Chow surfaced with **Game Of Death**, an enterprising, albeit abortive, attempt to cash in on the Kung Fu star's popularity by cobbling bits and pieces together in the hope that the finished product would resemble an on-going story. It didn't, and the so-called plot in which Lee (left) and his double attempt to smash a crime syndicate was a confusing mess. Jan Spears cut his screenplay according to what was available footage-wise, and Robert Clouse directed in a similar vein. The cast included Lee, Gig Young, Dean Jagger, Hugh O'Brian, Colleen Camp and Chuck Norris. (102 mins)

▽ After meeting 'cute' while running for the same bus in wartime London, Harrison Ford (left) and Lesley-Anne Down (right) fall passionately in love, despite the unimportant fact that she's already married to a British Intelligence officer (Christopher Plummer), and has a precocious eight-year-old daughter (Patsy Kensit). Thus the scene was set for **Hanover Street**, a zillionth carbon copy of *Brief Encounter* (Cineguild, 1945), for which John Barry provided a far less effective score than did Rachmaninov. Though aiming for the tear-ducts, writer-director Peter Hyams hit the funny-bone instead, and the result, almost, was a comic parody of every doomed wartime romance ever made. Paul N. Lazarus III produced, and his cast also included a pipe-smoking Alec McCowen, Max Wall, Shane Rimmer, Richard Masur and Michael Sacks. (109 mins)

△ Paul Schrader's **Hardcore** (GB: **The Hardcore Life**) dealt (on the surface, at any rate) with the taboo subject of pornography and (as did the same director's screenplay for *Taxi Driver*, 1976) with some of the less savoury aspects of human behaviour. The story of a Calvinist mid-Western businessman's search for his missing teenage daughter (whom he has good reason to believe has become involved in the making of porno movies), the film's fascination derived not from its sleazy and unedifying narrative, but from what the search revealed about the character of the father himself. A self-denying George C. Scott (illustrated) played the father, while Peter Boyle was the man he hires to help him find his child. Both actors were mesmeric, and brought to Schrader's boldly chilling screenplay a sub-text without which the film would have been mere exploitation. Season Hubley played a prostitute desperate for affection, with other roles assigned to Dick Sargent, Leonard Gaines, David Nichols, Gary Rand Graham, and Larry Block. The brave producer was Buzz Feitshans. (105 mins)

△ An agreeable and engaging comedy from Dom De Luise (illustrated), who starred in it as well as making his directorial debut with it, **Hot Stuff** hit on the hoary notion of having a group of likeable Miami cops going into business as fences in order to hook the bad guys red-handed. Assisting De Luise were Suzanne Pleshette, Jerry Reed, and Luis Avalos – all of them thoroughly decent cops. Even the villains weren't too nasty on this occasion – and they included Marc Lawrence (as a Miami godfather) and Pat McCormick. A Rastar-Mort Engelberg Production, it also featured Ossie Davis, as well as Carol, Peter, and David De Luise as Dom's wife and kids. Michael Kane and Donald E. Westlake scripted. (103 mins)

▽ Had it been made in the Forties, **Ice Castles** would undoubtedly have surfaced as a Sonja Henie musical. Alas, it was no such treat, but a rather dewy-eyed romantic drama of courage and endurance (directed by Donald Wrye) which starred Lynn-Holly Johnson (left) as an Iowa farm girl and a skater with Olympic potential. Thanks to the efforts of ice-rink operator Colleen Dewhurst and Olympic coach Jennifer Warren, Ms Johnson is propelled into instant stardom. Then tragedy. A freak accident partially blinds her, and the bulk of Donald Wrye and Gary L. Baim's half-baked screenplay (story by Baim) concerned itself with her recovery. Largely responsible for Lynn-Holly's mental and physical regeneration was her boyfriend Robby Benson (right) who, together with her father (Tom Skerritt), helps her rejoin the human race in an inspiring, albeit predictable, finish. Though John Kemeny's good-looking production had all the potential for a full-blown, lump-in-the-throat weepie, it was sabotaged by its screenplay. The score was by Marvin Hamlisch and it was far more impassioned than anything vouchsafed either in the performances or the dialogue. (113 mins)

△ In **Just You And Me, Kid**, a laugh-sparse comedy written by Oliver Hailey and Leonard Stern from a story by Tom Lazarus, 83-year-old George Burns (right) played an ex-vaudevillian who has the good-fortune to discover a naked, worldly-wise young person (Brooke Shields, left) in the trunk of his vintage car. It seems she's on the run from dope-pusher William Russ, to whom she owes $20,000, and has no place to go. Neither does the plot. And while it's always a pleasure to spend time in Burns's urbane company, on this occasion it was a pleasure one could have foregone. Burl Ives played a victim of catatonia (a condition he clearly passed on to director Leonard Stern), Lorraine Gary was Burns's daughter, with other roles in Irving Fein and Jerome M. Zeitman's dispiriting production going to Nicolas Coster, Keye Luke, John Schuck, Andrea Howard and, as a pair of Burns's card-playing cronies, Ray Bolger and Leon Ames. (93 mins)

▽ The dissolution of a family and its painful aftermath was the subject of **Kramer Vs Kramer**, an intelligently written, beautifully observed drama which was also about coping, and compromise. It starred Dustin Hoffman (left) as a successful art director in an advertising agency who, when we first meet him, is on top of the world. He has a lovely wife (Meryl Streep, right) and a delightful young son (Justin Henry), enough money to enjoy a luxurious Manhattan East-side existence, and a career that is definitely going places. Then, on the day before he is expected to deliver a major new ad campaign, his wife walks out on him leaving young Master Justin in his care. The reversal in Hoffman's fortunes and the growing relationship that develops between him and his son underpinned Robert Benton's marvellous screenplay (from the book by Avery Corman). And although one's initial sympathy was clearly directed towards Hoffman, at no point was Streep made to be the villain of the piece. Indeed, during the heart-tugging custody case that climaxes the film (and in which Streep is the successful contender), no sides were taken – and this made the outcome that much more painful for audiences to endure. Though the story-line undeniably bore the traces of a quintessential Forties weepie, Stanley R. Jaffe's production was a Class 'A' effort which under Benton's silky-smooth direction was never allowed to descend into mawkishness. As the troubled mother, Streep (in a relatively small role), gave the best performance of her career – up till then – and served notice, once and for all, that a star was in the ascendant. In addition, there were fine performances from Jane Alexander as a friend of the couple who changes allegiances, Howard Duff as Hoffman's lawyer, George Coe as his boss, and JoBeth Williams as Hoffman's one-night stand. The box-office grosses were phenomenal, making the film one of the year's biggest hits. (105 mins)

△ Yet another romance was launched as a result of a 'meeting cute' situation in **Lost And Found**. A skiing accident played cupid to Glenda Jackson (right) and George Segal (left) who, at a French ski-resort, collide into each other and break each other's legs. She's an intelligent Brit, he's a 'lovable' college professor (and widower). They fall in love, marry and return to the USA where Jackson settles down as an average college professor's wife. The couple bicker a great deal (the spectre of Segal's deceased first wife looming large in their arguments), and what little plot there was addressed itself to the question of whether Segal or his best friend (John Cunningham) will gain tenure at the college. Though the chemistry between Segal and Jackson that turned *A Touch Of Class* (Avco, 1973) into such a hit was still very much in evidence, Melvin Frank and Jack Rose's screenplay was nowhere as good as the one they provided for the pair first time out, and the result was a pleasant enough romantic comedy that relied solely on the personalities of its two stars. Maureen Stapleton played a typical Jewish mother, Hollis McLaren was Segal's assistant, and Paul Sorvino a wise-guy cabbie. It was produced and directed by Melvin Frank. (106 mins)

△ A bad screenplay, performances and direction to match, and some really feeble special effects were the main ingredients of **Nightwing**. All about killer bats on the rampage, it starred David Warner (right) as a creepy English rodent-destroyer out to seek a terrible revenge on the creatures for eating up his father. Nick Mancuso (left) and Stephen Macht were a couple of Native Americans also involved with the batty bats. Kathryn Harrold, Strother Martin and Ben Piazza had featured roles in the screenplay, which Steve Shagan, Bud Shrake and Martin Cruz Smith wrote from the latter's novel; it was produced by Martin Ransohoff and directed by Arthur Hiller. (103 mins)

▽ On this occasion a good cast and good production values were no guarantee of a good film, and **The Ravagers** turned out to be just one more nuclear-aftermath action drama. It starred Richard Harris (right) as the inhabitant of a deserted steel mill whose purpose in Donald S. Sanford's screenplay (based on the novel *Path To Savagery* by Robert Edmond Alter) was to avenge the death of his wife (Alana Hamilton) at the brutal hands of the Ravagers, led by Anthony James. Once Hamilton was out of the way, Ann Turkel (left) entered the picture as Harris's latest bed-mate; with other roles under Richard Compton's botched direction going to a daffy Art Carney as the guardsman at a missile base, Ernest Borgnine as a benevolent dictator, as well as Woody Strode and Seymour Cassell. It was produced by John W. Hyde. (91 mins)

△ Though by no means a disgrace to its many spine-chilling predecessors, **When A Stranger Calls** had far too many plausibility gaps in it to be taken in any way other than for the creepy hokum it was. Yet another variation on that gilt-edged horror ploy of the baby-sitter who's being terrorized by threatening phone calls and stalked in a lonely house by a crazed killer, the film starred Carol Kane (illustrated), Charles Durning, Colleen Dewhurst and Tony Beckley. Steve Feke and Fred Walton's screenplay (based on an earlier short film called *The Sitter*) had Kane being pursued by killer Beckley, first when she's a teenage baby-sitter and then, several years later, as a wife with kids of her own. Durning played a cop obsessed with the idea of nailing the culprit, and Dewhurst a boozy barfly whom the killer also stalks. It was produced by Doug Chapin and Feke and directed by Walton with a cast that also included Rachel Roberts, Rutanya Alda and Ron O'Neal. (97 mins)

▽ **Skatetown USA**, the first of the roller-disco comedies, was a piece of juvenile escapism in which Greg Bradford (right), as the good guy, takes on Patrick Swayze (left – his film debut) as the leather-clad bad guy, in a roller-skating contest. Scott Baio (second left) was top-starred. Also cast: Ron Pallio (second right), Ruth Buzzi, Maureen McCormick (centre), Dave Mason, Billy Barty – and Dorothy Stratten, the Playboy Playmate whose murder formed the basis of *Star 80* (Warner Bros., 1983). It was written by Nick Castle from a story he worked up with producers William A. Levey and Lorin Dreyfuss. Levey also directed. (98 mins)

▽ Mark Medoff's gripping, pulse-quickening off-Broadway melodrama **When You Comin' Back Red Ryder?** came to the screen in an elaborated-upon version (by the playwright) that failed to deliver the kick-in-the-guts it had done on stage. It was set, for most of the time, in a small-town southwestern diner whose staff and customers are being terrorized by a sadistic thug and his hippie moll, and starred Marjoe Gortner (right) as the thug, and Candy Clark as his moll. Their victims were Pat Hingle (left) as a crippled motel keeper, Stephanie Faracy (excellent) as a plump waitress, Peter Firth as an edgy punk, and Hal Linden and Lee Grant as a bickering city couple. On stage, at least, the sadistic games perpetrated by Gortner on this hapless bunch provided the narrative content of the piece with a genuine sense of menace and claustrophobia. On screen, however, much of the tension seemed to evaporate. Nor did the need to provide a hero for the movie version help matters. Still, it was, by and large, effectively performed, with Gortner's powerful central performance a definite asset. A Melvin Simon Production, it was produced by Gortner and directed by Milton Katselas. (118 mins)

△ Kirk Douglas (left) played the villain in **The Villain** (aka **Cactus Jack**), a soggy Western spoof of sagebrush stereotypes in which his frequent attempts to abduct luscious Ann-Margret (centre) are foiled by beefy Arnold Schwarzenegger (right). Described, at the time, as a live-action Road Runner cartoon, it was a series of sight-gags in desperate need of a serviceable plot, and it squandered the talents of a good cast that also included Paul Lynde (as a fey Indian chief) and, in cameo roles, Ruth Buzzi (from TV's Laugh In), Jack Elam and Strother Martin. Robert G. Kane wrote it. Mort Engelberg produced for Rastar-Engelberg Productions, and it was directed by Hal Needham. (93 mins)

1980-1988

The Eighties was the decade in which the studio produced the two biggest-grossing movies in its entire history – *Tootsie* (1982) and *Ghostbusters* (1984). Quality-wise, though, it was not a particularly distinguished ten years. Corporate upheavals and several changes in management resulted in the lack of a definable production policy, the studio's most honoured films – *Ghandi* (1982) and *The Last Emperor* (1987) – both having originated through independent production companies. Though *Stir Crazy* (1981) and *Karate Kid II* (1986) were massive earners, Columbia's track record during the latter half of the decade – financially as well as artistically – was disappointing.

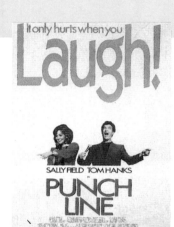

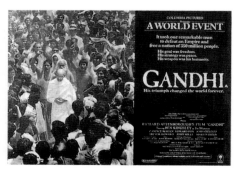

1980

▽ In 1949 Jean Simmons and Donald Houston starred in **The Blue Lagoon** as the victims of a shipwreck who grow up in each other's company on a romantic desert island. Thirty-one years later producer-director Randal Kleiser remade their story, but with Brooke Shields (left) and handsome newcomer Christopher Atkins (right) as the children of nature. The result was a visually stunning commercial for the natural life in which, taking full advantage of the cinema's new permissiveness, there was a great deal of sex talk and nudity. The fact that Shields insisted on a double to take her place whenever the script called for her to appear naked (usually underwater) was of no consequence. Managing to be both explicit and coy at the same time, the film concerned itself with the young couple's sexual awakening and the inevitable consequences thereof. It couldn't be taken seriously, and was probably never meant to be. Its chief virtues were the attractiveness of its two young players, Nestor Almendros's gorgeous Fiji-based photography, and the underwater sequences (for which the photographers were Ron Taylor and Valerie Taylor). Douglas Day Stewart's screenplay (from the novel by Henry Devere Stacpoole) left much to be desired, and, like Kleiser's direction, lacked narrative excitement. Though basically a two-hander, Leo McKern, William Daniels, Elva Josephson and Glenn Kohan were in it too. Audiences responded to it to the hearty tune of $43.6 million at the box-office. (102 mins)

▽ The idea of an individual outwitting the mob is hardly new to the cinema, but in **Gloria** it was refreshingly reworked by writer-director John Cassavetes into a full-blown vehicle for his real-life wife, Gena Rowlands (right). She played a one-time gangster's moll who, in middle-age, wants nothing more than to be left alone with her cat and to get on with her uncomplicated life. But that's not to be. While borrowing some coffee from a Puerto Rican friend she inadvertently becomes involved in a Mafia stake-out and, instead of the coffee, finds herself in possession of a little Puerto Rican lad (John Adames, left) whose family has been murdered by the mob. She's also in possession of a notebook – owned by the kid's book-keeper father (Buck Henry) – whose contents detail certain financial transactions that could be embarrassing to the Mafia. What follows is an extended chase as Rowlands and her young charge attempt to make their way to Pittsburgh. Cassavetes's sub-text centred on the relationship that developed between his odd couple, and it was in this area that the heart of the film beat strongest. Being a Cassavetes production, it was totally devoid of sentimentality and had an unreal 'feel' to its characters which served either to undermine or enhance the film's worth, depending on one's response to this director's work in general. Certainly, there was nothing mundane about it. Good supporting performances came from Julie Carmen, Tony Knesich, Gregory Cleghorne, Lupe Garnica and Tom Noonan were fine. The producer was Sam Shaw. (123 mins)

▽ **Foolin' Around** was the one about the country-bumpkin who, uninvited, finds himself hobnobbing among the local moneyed set and stealing a pretty young WASP heiress from under the nose of her dim-witted, sartorially elegant fiancé. Gary Busey was the goofily persistent intruder, Annette O'Toole the object of his affections and John Calvin her fiancé. They were all out-acted, though, by Cloris Leachman (right) as O'Toole's status-conscious mother. Eddie Albert played O'Toole's grandfather (another stock character), with other roles in Arnold Kopelson's no-account production going to Tony Randall (left), Michael Talbott, Shirley Kane and W. H. Macy. It was written by Mike Kane and David Swift (story by Swift) and directed, messily, by Richard T. Heffron. (101 mins)

△ A tasteless rip-off of *American Graffiti* (Universal, 1973), **The Hollywood Knights** was a raucous non-starter whose funniest moment had four members of a fraternity urinating into a punch bowl. Set on Hallo-ween night in 1965, it divided itself into several sub-plots in order to disguise the feebleness of a story-line which involved a group of teenagers taking revenge on the elders of Beverly Hills for closing down the suburb's only drive-in eatery. It starred, among others, Tony Danza (in his feature-film debut), Michelle Pfeiffer, Fran Drescher, Leigh French, Randy Gornel and Robert Wuhl. It was written and directed by Floyd Mutrux (story by Mutrux, William Tennant and producer Richard Lederer), and featured songs by The Beach Boys. (91 mins)

▽ The cut-throat world of international piano competitions provided the quasi-intellectual backdrop for **The Competition**, a high-octane soap opera set at a music competition in San Francisco and involving the romance and rivalry between Richard Dreyfuss (left) and Amy Irving (right) – two of the competitors. Case-histories of a handful of the other finalists were perfunctorily dealt with in Joel Oliansky's plebian screenplay (from a story by Oliansky and William Sackheim). These included Ty Henderson as a wealthy black contender who practises in the nude, Vickie Kriegler as a Russian prodigy undergoing a crisis of confidence as a result of her teacher's defection to the West, and Joseph Cali as a young, middle-class Italian student who seeks publicity by pretending to have been reared in the slums. It was the Dreyfuss-Irving romance that occupied most of the screen-time, though, and pretty phony it turned out to be. Indeed, not much of William Sackheim's glossy production could be taken without a generous pinch of the proverbial salt. Dreyfuss was marginally less arrogant than usual as the ageing 'wunderkind', Irving was Irving, and, as Irving's over-the-top teacher, Lee Remick shamefully pilfered every scene that she was in. A Rastar-William Sackheim production, it was Oliansky's directorial debut and also featured Sam Wanamaker, Adam Stern, Bea Silvern and Philip Sterling. The musical direction was by Lalo Schifrin. (129 mins)

△ Charlton Heston (left) and Brian Keith (right) starred as a pair of ageing fur-trappers in **The Mountain Men**, a blood-drenched Western-*manqué* that was crude and pointless in the extreme. It was a crass excuse to pit a 'vanishing breed' against the Indians, and the film's several gruesome hand-to-hand battles between these two groups was its *raison d'être*. What little plot there was (courtesy of Chuck's son Fraser Clarke Heston, who scripted) involved the runaway wife (Victoria Racimo) of brutal Blackfoot Heavy Eagle (played by Stephen Macht) and the protection she seeks from Messrs Heston and Keith against her pursuing husband. John Glover, Seymour Cassel and David Ackroyd were also featured; Richard Lang directed and it was produced by Martin Shafer and Andrew Scheinman. (102 mins)

▽ An overwhelming triumph of style over content, **It's My Turn** was a gem. It combined a witty, intelligent screenplay, delightfully real performances, and direction by Claudia Weill which matched the quality displayed by both script and cast. It starred Jill Clayburgh (left) as a mathematics professor, Charles Grodin as the Chicago real-estate developer with whom she lives, and Michael Douglas (right) as an ex-baseball player whose mother (Beverly Garland) is about to marry Clayburgh's father (Steven Hill) in New York. While in the Big Apple to attend the wedding, Clayburgh and Douglas meet, fall in love and have an affair. The outcome of this situation wasn't so interesting, but the 'getting there' provided all three principals with marvellous opportunities to display their skills. Eleanor Bergstein wrote the screenplay, Martin Elfand produced for Rastar-Elfand Productions, and the cast also featured Teresa Baxter, Joan Copeland, John Gabriel, Charles Kimbrough and Diane Wiest (in her film debut). (91 mins)

△ Thirty cars were wrecked in the service of **Night Of The Juggler**, a zestfully directed (by Robert Butler) albeit hollow thriller set in and around New York and involving the kidnapping of a former policeman's daughter. The fact that the daughter (Abby Bluestone) has been mistaken by her abductor (Cliff Gorman) for someone else, was of little consolation to the girl's father (top-starred James Brolin, centre) who is determined to get her back. It turns out that Gorman is a psychotic racist out to revenge the deterioration of the Bronx neighbourhood in which he was raised. Just what writers Bill Norton Sr and Rick Natkin and producer Jay Weston were out to revenge by foisting this claptrap on innocent and unsuspecting audiences was never revealed. Completing the cast were Julie Carmen, Richard Castellano, Linda G. Miller, Barton Heyman, Dan Hedaya and Mandy Patinkin, who would soon become a star on Broadway. (100 mins)

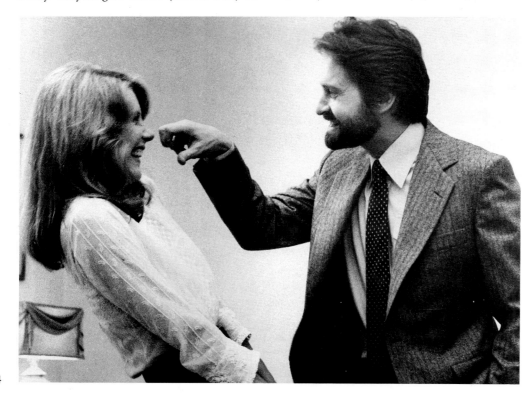

▽ **Seems Like Old Times** took an affectionate look at some of the screwball comedies of the Thirties, liked what it saw, and paid homage to them in a plot of inspired idiocy. The brainchild of Neil Simon, master-craftsman and king of the one-liners, it starred Goldie Hawn (second right) as a liberal lawyer whose home is a welcoming repository for waifs and strays of both the human and animal kind, Charles Grodin (right) as her husband (a nerdish district attorney), and Chevy Chase (third right) as the ex-husband who re-enters her life while fleeing from the cops. Needless to say Hawn and her ex reawaken in each other the passion they once felt, and the film (largely a showcase for Chase's particular brand of comic 'shtick') ended with the hapless Grodin out on his ear. It was all good, clean, gag-infested fun and directed that way by TV-recruit Jay Sandrich, here making an impressive feature debut. Harold Gould (left), George Grizzard, Robert Guillaume and Yvonne Wilder also contributed to the laughs and it was produced by Ray Stark to the healthy box-office tune of $38.2 million. (102 mins)

△ 'It's a dog-eats-dog world' was the message of **Used Cars**, a cynical farce that aimed a few blows at the American way of life in general and used-car dealers in particular. In a dual role, Jack Warden (right) played Roy and Luke Fuchs, brothers and business-rivals who own second-hand automobile shops across the street from one another. Roy is the more successful of the two, and, when his brother dies, Luke's partners (Gerrit Graham and Frank McRae) in cahoots with operator Kurt Russell (left) hide the fact from Roy to prevent him from inheriting the property. How they go about putting the run-down business back on its feet provided the film with its best moments. Unfortunately, there were too few of them and an air of tired over-familiarity prevailed. Deborah Harmon played the daughter of the deceased Fuchs, with other parts under Robert Zemeckis's one-note direction going to Joseph P. Flaherty, David L. Lander, Michael McKean and Michael Talbott. Bob Gale produced and also scripted with Zemeckis, and the executive producers were Steven Spielberg and John Milius. (113 mins)

▽ A tender, though at times antiseptic drama based on Lena Canada's book *To Elvis With Love*, **Touched By Love**, scripted by Hesper Anderson, was the real-life story of how nurse Canada (Deborah Raffin, left) newly arrived in a school for cerebral-palsied children in Calgary, Alberta, takes a special shine to little Karen (Diane Lane, right) whom she teaches to write. As a result, Karen embarks on a life-enhancing correspondence with Elvis Presley. Gus Trikonis's direction was undemonstrative to the point of blandness, a quality equally evident in most of the central performances. The film took no risks, either, with its subject matter, and emerged as a decent, well-intentioned human drama that, somehow, should have been much more involving. Michael Learned, John Amos, Cristina Raines, Mary Wickes, Clu Gulager and (most noteably) Clive Shalom as 'Topper' were also featured in Michael Viner's production; and the romantic score, interspersed with Presley's 'Love Me Tender', was by John Barry. (95 mins)

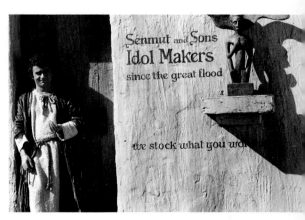

△ Not to mince words, **Wholly Moses!** was a 40-carat stinker. It was a biblical spoof about a character called Herschel who, as a baby, was hidden in the same bulrushes as the infant Moses. Grown-up Herschel marries Moses' sister-in-law – and then he overhears the Lord's instructions from the burning bush and mistakenly believes they were meant for his ears.... It was cringingly embarrassing from start to finish and savaged the talents of James Coco, Jack Gilford, Richard Pryor, Madeline Kahn, John Houseman, John Ritter, Laraine Newman, Paul Sand and Dom DeLuise. Top-billed Dudley Moore (illustrated) played Herschel and was excruciatingly unfunny. Guy Thomas wrote it, Gary Weis directed and Freddie Fields produced. Shame on them. (109 mins)

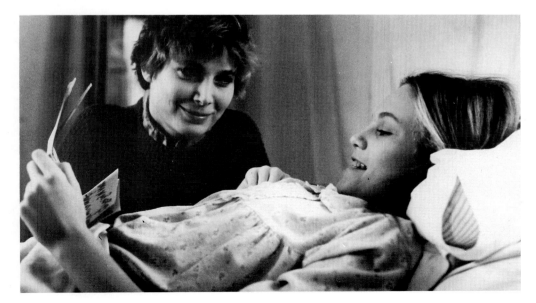

▷ An emotionally charged newspaper 'exposé' drama in the best tradition of *Five Star Final* (Warner Bros., 1931), **Absence Of Malice** was a sincere and serious-minded attempt to illustrate the suffering caused by unscrupulous reporting. It starred Paul Newman (left) as the son of a deceased mobster who, though totally uninvolved in crime, becomes the subject of an investigation concerning the disappearance of a labour leader. He is implicated in the disappearance of the missing man by reporter Sally Field (right), whose journalistic probings result in the suicide of innocent Melinda Dillon. A less complicated story-line and screenplay than the one provided by Kurt Luedtke might have resulted in the film packing greater punch. In this instance, more definitely meant less. Still, it was never dull, and provided its two leading players with meaty roles. It was produced and directed by Sydney Pollack and in secondary parts featured Luther Adler (as Newman's unsavoury uncle), Bob Balaban (as a federal investigator), John Harkins (as the paper's attorney) as well as Barry Primus, Josef Sommer, Don Hood and Wilford Brimley. Box-office gross to date is over $40.9 million. (116 mins)

▷ There were six murders in **Happy Birthday To Me**, a shlock-horror thriller that didn't gel. The first was a common-and-garden throat slashing, the second and third were ordinary stabbings, the murder weapon in the fourth was a fire poker, in the fifth the victim was crushed by barbells, and in the sixth skewered. All victims were friends of leading lady Melissa Sue Anderson (left), who thinks she, herself, might be the killer. Glenn Ford (right), her psychiatrist, thinks otherwise. Anyway, who cares? Certainly not scenarists John Saxton, Peter Jobin and Timothy Bond (story by Saxton), to judge from the quality of their screenplay. Tracy Bregman, Lawrence Dane, Jack Blum, Matt Craven, Lenore Zann, David Eisner and Lisa Langlois were in it; John Dunning and André Link produced; and the director was J. Lee Thompson. (108 mins)

△ Using an animation technique that owed little to Walt Disney, Ralph Bakshi, in **American Pop**, attempted to chart the history of popular American music from its beginnings in blues and jazz to rock 'n' roll and its discordant offspring. It was an ambitious subject that Disney and his crew would have taken in their stride. Lacking Walt's imagination (or any recognizable point of view *vis-à-vis* the subject), Bakshi's attempt was doomed to failure – and fail it did. Ronni Kern scripted, Bakshi directed, Martin Ransohoff produced and the voices heard on the sound-track included those of Ron Thompson, Marya Small, Jerry Holland, Lisa Jane Persky, Jeffrey Lippa and Roz Kelly. (97 mins)

◁ Science fiction, sword-and-sorcery, violence, sex and humour – even the drug culture – were featured, in varying degrees, in **Heavy Metal**, an animated feature that took its title from the adult fantasy magazine. Of the six segments that comprised the film, one involving an unheroic cab-driver in a futuristic New York, and another in which a young bookworm is transformed into an intergalactic stud, were the best. The others, including an Alien-type yarn of doomed B-17 pilots, a 'Hulk'-type comedy take-off, and a fantasy in which a Pentagon secretary is abducted by a flying saucer, had less of an edge to them, but benefited from some striking animation. The film was produced by Ivan Reitman, directed by Gerald Potterton, and written by Dan Goldberg and Len Blum based on original art and stories by Richard Corben, Angus McKie, Dan O'Bannon, Thomas Warkentin and Berni Wrightson. The sound-track voices included those of Roger Bumpass, Jackie Burroughs, Harold Ramis, John Candy, Joe Flaherty, Don Francks, Martin Lavut and Eugene Levy. (91 mins)

▷ **Neighbors** was the John Belushi-Dan Aykroyd show, with the famous 'Saturday Night Live' team swapping personas for this bizarre excursion into the outer-reaches of manic comedy. In his final film, Belushi (right) played a suburbanite, who, with his wife (Kathryn Walker, left), leads a staid, un-eventful life. But that all changes with the arrival of Aykroyd (second right) and his spouse (Cathy Moriarty, centre), their new neighbours. A dyed-blonde nut, Aykroyd makes a frontal attack on Belushi's values, and in no time at all has taken over his car, his bank account, his house and even his family. Aykroyd's insane behaviour triggers off a like response from the hitherto tranquil Belushi, and the two neighbours soon in-dulge in a series of way-out 'getting even' schemes, ending with Belushi's total trans-formation from suburban bore to liberated madman. Just what point scenarist Larry Gelbart (working from Thomas Berger's novel) was trying to make (if any) remained obscure. There was nothing vague, though, about the laughs his screenplay induced, nor the ample opportunities it provided its two leading men to spark each other. All the same, it was a box-office disappointment, having failed to attract its potential audience – even after Belushi's death a few months subse-quent to its release. It was produced by Richard D. Zanuck and David Brown, and directed by John G. Avildsen. (94 mins)

▽ There was an improvisational air to much of the dialogue spouted by both Gene Wilder (right) and Richard Pryor (centre) in **Stir Crazy**, a frenetic prison-farce designed to juxtapose the very different comic talents of its two stars. Both losers – Wilder is a would-be playwright, and Pryor a would-be actor – they decide to try California after making no headway in New York. In Arizona, however, they're arrested for a rob-bery they didn't commit, and are given 120 years in the slammer. How they manage to outwit their wardens, guards and fellow pris-oners – one of whom (Erland Van Lidth de Jeude) is a crazed killer, another (Georg Stan-ford Brown) a lisping gay – was the main con-cern of Bruce Jay Friedman's screenplay, which Messrs Wilder and Pryor merely used as a springboard for doing their own thing. Director Sidney Poitier seemed merely to point the camera in the direction of his stars – with erratic results. Hannah Weinstein pro-duced, and the cast also included JoBeth Williams, Miguelangel Suarez, Craig T. Nelson and Lewis Van Bergen (left). The happy box-office gross was in excess of $101.3. (Later a brief TV series.) (111 mins)

▷ **Cheech And Chong's Nice Dreams**, the anarchic street-comic duo's third outing, was another spaced-out commercial for the freaked-out life, with pot replacing plot, and gutter-talk subbing for dialogue. This one featured Stacy Keach as a cop on their trail, but he too is suffering from reefer-madness. Richard 'Cheech' Marin (right) and Thomas Chong (left) were the stars, a cast of un-knowns (Evelyn Guerrero, Paul Reubens (aka Pee-Wee Herman – in his film debut), Michael Masters, Jeff Pomerantz, James Faracci) supported, Howard Brown pro-duced and it was directed by Mr. Chong, who also wrote the screenplay with Mr. Cheech. Strictly for fans and devotees – of whom there were many, to judge from the film's robust $35.5 million gross at the North American box-office. (88 mins)

▽ Nobody's perfect, and nobody expects perfection, but in a film billed as a comedy, it isn't being unreasonable to expect a laugh or two. No such luck with **Nobody's Perfekt**. It was a dire farrago in which Gabe Kaplan (left) played a retard, Alex Karras (right) was a mother's boy and Robert Klein (centre) re-joiced in the role of a schizo who can't make up his mind whether he's Bette Davis or James Cagney. They drive their car into a pothole and spend most of their time devising ways to get themselves reimbursed. Banal wasn't the word for it, and it had no business being inflicted on an unsuspecting public. Tony Kenrick wrote the screenplay from his novel *Two For The Price Of One*, Mort En-gelberg produced for Rastar Productions, and actor-improvisor Peter Bonerz was (in a decidedly inauspicious debut) the director. Also cast: Susan Clark, Paul Stewart, Alex Rocco, Arthur Rosenberg and Bonerz him-self. (96 mins)

▽ A re-working of his flop stage play *The Gingerbread Lady*, **Only When I Laugh** (GB: **It Hurts Only When I Laugh**) may not have been vintage Neil Simon, but it contained more good lines in it per minute than most comedies do in an hour. Not that there was all that much to laugh about, mind you. The story of a divorced actress (allegedly inspired by Judy Garland) who has just been released from a drying-out programme in hospital, it starred Marsha Mason (right) as the actress and Kristy McNichol as her teen-aged daughter. The restructuring of their decimated relationship was Simon's main narrative concern, and he handled it with sensitivity, insight, and, of course, humour.

Though much of what mother-and-daughter had to say to each other was witty in itself, the 'light-relief' was heavyweight funny-man James Coco (left) as a failed gay actor, as well as Joan Hackett as Mason's brittle-tongued best girlfriend. Their respective characters were perfect outlets for Simon's celebrated one-liners. David Dukes was cast as Mason's former lover, a playwright who has written a play with which he hopes she'll make her Broadway comeback, with other roles under Glenn Jordan's serviceable direction going to John Bennett Perry, Guy Boyd, Ed Moore and Byron Webster. It was produced by Neil Simon and Roger M. Rothstein and grossed $26.9 million. (120 mins)

△ There was something decidedly Woody Allen-ish about **Modern Romance**, a comedy of neuroses about a film editor unable to live with the girl he loves, yet equally unable to live without her. Written and directed by Albert Brooks (left), who also occupied the central role, the film put its leading man through a mangle of hell, romantically speaking, as it charted the on-again, off-again nature of his relationship with Kathryn Harrold (right). At the same time it offered a fascinating backstage peek at the world of movie-making, and allowed audiences to follow, step by step, the editing of a shlock science-fiction epic on which the protagonist is working. A delightful, funny and undervalued piece of work, it also featured George Kennedy, Tyann Means, Bruno Kirby, Jane Hallaren, Karen Chandler and Dennis Kort – plus real-life director James L. Brooks (playing a director). Andrew Scheinman and Martin Shafer produced. (93 mins)

▷ The army in peacetime was the satirical target of **Stripes**, replete with foul language, nudity and a general lack of refinement in keeping with its subject. It starred Bill Murray (right) who, as one of life's losers, falls for the recruiting commercials and, together with buddy Harold Ramis, joins a misfit platoon supervised by an uncompromisingly tough drill sergeant (Warren Oates). The screenplay by Len Blum, Dan Goldberg and Harold Ramis was fun, though hardly of the good, clean variety, and it took our heroes to Italy, West Germany and communist Czechoslovakia, where a mistaken alarm almost starts World War III. John Candy was prominently featured as a fat guy who joins the Army to lose weight; with other parts going to Sean Young, P. J. Soles (left), John Larroquette, John Voldstadt, John Diehl, Lance LeGault, Roberta Leighton, Joe Flaherty and Dave Thomas. Ivan Reitman and Dan Goldberg produced, and Reitman directed. His ingenuous combination of humour and tastelessness resulted in a box-office gross of nearly $85.3 million. (106 mins)

1982

▽ Filmed on the last two nights of his Palladium concerts in LA, **Richard Pryor Live On The Sunset Strip** was simply a record of his dazzling one-man show, the memorable centre-piece of which was his harrowing (and yet very funny) description of the freebase explosion that almost ended his life. A routine on racism and a discussion on the differences between animals in a zoo and animals in their natural habitat also revealed Pryor (illustrated) at his best, and, although the language employed throughout was characteristically raunchy, the general tone of the concert was mellower and less cynical than his fans had come to expect. It was written and produced by Pryor for Rastar Productions, and directed by Joe Layton. The box-office gross ($35 million) attested to the star's enormous popularity. (82 mins)

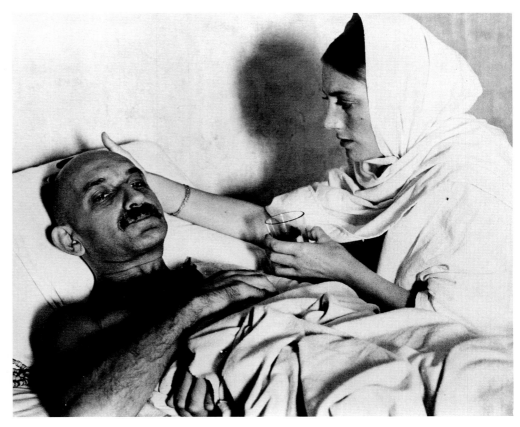

▷ A suspense comedy directed by Sidney Poitier that was neither suspenseful nor funny, **Hanky Panky** starred a characteristically frenetic Gene Wilder (centre) as a Chicago architect who is inadvertently plunged into a web of intrigue and murder. Evoking the type of sinister situations in which Bob Hope often found himself (but not nearly as enjoyably), writers Henry Rosenbaum and David Taylor seemed to run out of steam from reel one. The result was a protracted bore in which even an *hommage à* Hitchcock – with Wilder being pursued by helicopter in the desert – fell flat. Gilda Radner (left) and Kathleen Quinlan provided female relief, with other parts in Martin Ransohoff's damp-squib production going to Richard Widmark, Robert Prosky, Josef Sommer and Johnny Sekka. (105 mins)

△ From the moment he was kicked off a whites-only train in South Africa in 1893 at the age of 24, and thus experienced the evils of apartheid for the very first time, lawyer Mohandas Karamchand Gandhi realized that the main purpose in his life was to obtain – through non-violent means – peace and dignity for mankind, regardless of race, colour or creed. His struggle to achieve this aim formed the basis of Richard Attenborough's epic biopic **Gandhi**, a labour of love on which the director had worked for 10 years. The result was a sprawling, somewhat antiseptic piece of screen hagiography whose screenplay by John Briley set out to capture the 'spirit' of the man and the times in which he functioned, rather than to provide a detailed description of the historic events as they occurred year by year. As in most screen biographies (even the bad ones, and *Gandhi* was by no means bad, just disappointing), the major characters and events concerning its subject were all there – including the massacre of more than 1,500 Indian men, women and children by native soldiers under Brigadier Dyer in Jallianwalla Bagh. Attenborough's handling of this brutal sequence, and his organization of the crowd scenes at Gandhi's funeral, was always assured if impersonal, a criticism that might easily be levelled at the film as a whole. The chief glory of the expensive enterprise was Ben Kingsley's (left) monumental performance as the saintly hero. From the aforementioned early scene in which he is thrown off the train in South Africa, to his death by assassination (at the age of 78) in 1948, Kingley's physically accurate portrayal provided the film with its centre of gravity. The rest of the cast were merely waxwork appendages; they included Edward Fox as General Dyer, John Gielgud as Lord Irwin, Candice Bergen as Margaret Bourke-White, Trevor Howard as Judge Broomfield, John Mills as The Viceroy, Martin Sheen as Walker, Rohini Hattangady as Kasturba Gandhi, Saeed Jaffrey as Sardar Patel, Ian Charleson as Charlie Andrews, and Athol Fugard as General Smuts. Ravi Shankar and George Fenton supplied the music, and Attenborough produced for Indo-British Films, in association with Goldcrest Films International, the National Film Development Corporation of India, and International Film Investors. (188 mins)

▷ Costing over $40 million, the lavish screen version of the Broadway blockbuster **Annie** had nothing going for it – and, as a result, went nowhere. An inflated, over-produced behemoth of a show, it substituted production values for entertainment. Furthermore, it employed a director (John Huston) whose work on the film indicated that he had never directed a musical before (unless you count the first 15 minutes of *Moulin Rouge*, Romulus, 1952), and also that he had no feeling for the genre whatsoever. A catalogue of squandered opportunities, it wasted the considerable talents of the unmusical Albert Finney miscast as 'Daddy' Warbucks, Carol Burnett (left) as Miss Hannigan, Bernadette Peters (right) as Lily, Tim Curry (centre) as Rooster and especially Ann Reinking as Grace. Newcomer Aileen Quinn played the coveted central role with a commendable lack of precocity, and it was hardly her fault that the production surrounding her just sat there like a piece of expensive upholstered furniture. Chief villain of the piece was editor Michael A. Stevenson whose insensitive, uncinematic piecing together of Arlene Phillips's uninspired choreography totally defused the musical 'feel' of the original. True, a handful of the Charles Strouse-Martin Charnin numbers survived unscathed, but that was due to the talents of the performers rather than the way the material had been assembled. Having paid $9.5 million for the rights of the show, Carol Sobieski worked from the book by Thomas Meehan, which was based on the 'Little Orphan Annie' comic strip by Harold Gray, and in the process of opening it out for the big screen dissipated whatever charm the flimsy material possessed on Broadway. The producer of this wasted opportunity was Ray Stark, and, despite box-office grosses of $60 million, *Annie* has yet to earn enough to cover its expensive budget. (130 mins)

△ An interesting (and, at $27 million, expensive) failure, **One From The Heart** was a top-heavy romantic musical, set in a studio-constructed Las Vegas, whose failure brought to an end director Francis Coppola's dream of running his own (Zoetrope) studio. The story told of a couple – Frederic Forrest (right) and Teri Garr – who decide to put their affair on hold while they experiment (unsuccessfully) with other partners – he with Nastassia Kinski (left), she with Raul Julia. Yet this featherlight plot was the victim of an over-elaborate production that choked the life out of the story's human values. With so much technology to gawp at, it was hard to care one way or another about the human element, and the film, understandably, failed to find an audience. It was scripted by Coppola and Armyan Bernstein (story by Bernstein), produced by Bernstein, Gray Frederickson and Fred Roos, and also featured Lainie Kazan, Harry Dean Stanton, Allen Goorwitz and Jeff Hamlin. The music and lyrics were by Tom Waits. (107 mins)

◁ **Silent Rage** was exploitation run rampant. It starred Chuck Norris (left) as a karate-kicking sheriff on the lookout for a crazy killer (Brian Libby) who also happens to be indestructible, thanks to the efforts of three doctors who are trying out a new formula on him. Best seen under the influence of a soft drug or a hard drink, the film nevertheless found a willing market and turned a decent profit for producer Anthony B. Unger. The unintentionally hilarious screenplay was the work of Joseph Fraley, and the director was Michael Miller. Also cast: Ron Silver, Steven Keats, Toni Kalem (right), Stephen Furst and William Finley. (100 mins)

△ Paul Mazursky's modern-day reworking of Shakespeare's **Tempest** was an acquired taste, and, judging from the disappointing box-office returns, not enough people acquired it. Those who did, though, had a pretty good time. John Cassavetes (right) starred as Phillip (Prospero), a New York architect married to actress Gena Rowlands. A mid-life crisis forces him to re-examine his high-pressured existence and he takes off for Greece with his virginal daughter Miranda (Molly Ringwald, left, making her debut) where he meets a roaming singer (Susan Sarandon, centre) with whom he has a celibate love affair. The trip takes in an idyllic island inhabited by a goatherd called Kali-banos (Raul Julia), at which point fantasy intruded and paved the way for a happy ending that saw Cassavetes and Rowlands reunited as they attempt to start life afresh in Manhattan. The film was full of unexpected delights (such as Liza Minnelli singing 'New York, New York' as a chorus-line of goats perform a production number!) and, in the main, beautifully performed and photographed (by Don McAlpine). Mazursky, who produced, directed and also appeared in a cameo role as Rowlands's producer, co-wrote the screenplay with Leon Capetanos. Also cast: Vittorio Gassman, Sam Robards, Paul Stewart, Jackie Gayle and Anthony Holland. (140 mins)

▷ **Tootsie** was a brilliant comedy about sexual identity as well as a sharply observed satire on various aspects of show business – from unemployment to the 'catastrophe of success' (a phrase coined by Tennessee Williams). It starred Dustin Hoffman (right) as an out-of-work actor with an 'attitude' problem, who, in a moment of desperation, 'drags up' in order to audition for the role of a 'mature' woman in a daytime soap-opera. Pretending to be Dorothy Michaels, he reads for the part, gets it, becomes an overnight star, and falls for his leading lady (Jessica Lange). The complications inherent in maintaining his female identity were resourcefully (and hilariously) exploited in the screenplay provided by Larry Gelbart and Murray Schisgal (story by Gelbart and Don McGuire, with uncredited script assistance from Elaine May) with every potential laugh-situation mined for maximum mirth. Apart from Hoffman, whose triumph in creating a totally believable character in Dorothy (rather than a caricature) was the film's greatest achievement, there were terrific performances, too, from the aforementioned Ms Lange, from Dabney Coleman as Dorothy's director, Charles Durning as Lange's father (who falls for Dorothy), Bill Murray as Hoffman's best friend, George Gaynes as the soap-opera's leading man, and Teri Garr as Hoffman's neurotic girlfriend. Director Sydney Pollack (left) played Hoffman's agent, and the cast further included Geena Davis, Doris Belack, Lynne Thigpen, Ronald L. Schwary, Debra Mooney and Amy Lawrence. *Tootsie* was a box-office (as well as critical) smash to the tune of $177.2 million (it cost $25 million). It was produced by Pollack and Dick Richards, and, among its many pleasures, yielded a hit song, 'It Might Be You' by Alan Bergman, Marilyn Bergman and Dave Grusin, sung by Stephen Bishop. (116 mins)

▷ Two Cheech and Chongs for the price of one was even more than their most devoted fans could take, and **Things Are Tough All Over**, the duo's fourth big-screen outing, was a box-office dud. Richard 'Cheech' Marin (left) and Tommy Chong (right) played a pair of Arab bigwigs as well as the two buffoons they hire to chauffeur a limousine full of money from Chicago to Las Vegas. The sight of Cheech and Chong in drag was the best the duo's flaccid screenplay had to offer by way of laughs. It was produced by Howard Brown with a directive that the scenario for this usually stoned couple's antics be drug-free, which it was, and directed by Thomas K. Avildsen, with a cast that also included Rikki Marin and Shelby Fiddis (Mrs Cheech and Chong in real-life) and Michael Aragon. (90 mins)

△ A mawkish, doggedly unfunny re-make of *Le Jouet* (1976), **The Toy** told the story of the spoiled-brat son of a millionaire who gets his father to buy him a human toy as a gift. Dad obliges, and through the good services and understanding of his acquisition, father and son come to a much better appreciation of each other, while, at the same time, the kid is taught that friendship cannot be bought but has to be earned. Richard Pryor (left) played 'the toy', Jackie Gleason (right) was his purchaser, and the resistible recipient was Scott Schwartz. Carol Sobieski's screenplay, based on a scenario by Frances Veber, was singularly laugh-sparse and relied entirely on the antics of leading-man Pryor to provide the occasional chuckle. Phil Feldman produced, Richard Donner directed, and the cast included Ned Beatty, Teresa Ganzel, and Wilfrid Hyde-White as the butler Gleason wins in a billiards match. In this case quantity had little to do with quality for the film grossed $50.1 million. (99 mins)

△ **Wrong Is Right** (GB: **The Man With The Deadly Lens**) was a cry of anguish from writer-producer-director Richard Brooks, who – using Sean Connery (left) as a peripatetic global TV commentator with total access to the world's leaders – had some pretty harsh things to say about the world in general and America in particular. The FBI, Presidents Nixon, Carter and Reagan, the Arabs, the oil crisis, terrorism, mankind's lack of moral standards, the rejection of the eternal verities, and the CIA (the real villain of the piece) were all targets for Brooks's wrath. What it all added up to was a deeply personal melange of stylistic confusion that baffled far more than it enlightened. George Grizzard, Robert Conrad, Katharine Ross, G. D. Spradlin, John Saxon, Henry Silva, Leslie Nielsen, Robert Webber, Rosalind Cash, Hardy Kruger, Dean Stockwell, Jennifer Jason Leigh and Ron Moody were all part of the cast. (117 mins)

1983

▷ Just as writer-director John Sayles had done in *The Return of the Secaucus Seven* (1980), director and co-writer (with Barbara Benedek) Lawrence Kasdan brought together, in **The Big Chill**, a group of college friends, all of whom have known each other since the Sixties, in order to reassess their lives and careers. The setting was the beautiful seaside home of happily married Glenn Close (right) and Kevin Kline (left), the occasion the suicide of one of their number. Attending the weekend wake were Tom Berenger as a well-known TV personality, recently divorced, Jeff Goldblum as a sexually over-active wise-guy writer for *People* magazine, William Hurt as an injured Viet Nam veteran, Mary Kay Place as a career woman desperately seeking a private life, and JoBeth Williams as a grass widow for the duration of the weekend as her husband returns home to their two kids soon after arriving. Having dispensed with the obligatory period of grieving for their dead friend, the group indulge in a great deal of retrospective talk in an effort to understand the present, with some even plotting their future. Kasdan and Benedek's screenplay didn't delve much below the surface of things, but was written with enough perspicacity about upwardly mobile people in their thirties to keep that particular group in a constant state of relating! It was beautifully (and convincingly) acted by every member of the cast, including Meg Tilly as the deceased's young girlfriend whose unemotional response to her lover's suicide is of concern to the rest of the group. It was directed by Kasdan with exemplary restraint, and profitably produced by Michael Shamberg. (103 mins)

▽ A cross between a beach-party movie and *Where The Boys Are* (MGM, 1960), **Spring Break** was a youth-orientated romp set in Fort Lauderdale with sex the chief item on producer-director Sean S. Cunningham's menu. Unfortunately, David Smilow's screenplay didn't have the courage of Cunningham's convictions and the result was a rather prurient piece of exploitation that promised much more than it delivered. As sex was talked about a lot more than indulged in, it was left to a rheumatic plot about the comings and goings of four room-mates (one of whom is having problems with a wealthy but decidedly unpleasant stepfather) to buttress the jaded enterprise. David Knell, Steve Bassett, Perry Lang, and Paul Land, were the adventurous quartet, with Corinne Alphen, Jayne Modean and Donald Symington bringing up the rear. (101 mins)

△ Action, not so pure and never simple, was the keynote of **Blue Thunder**, a barnstorming thriller, set in Los Angeles and featuring Roy Scheider (illustrated) and Malcolm McDowell – though the real star of the show was the high-tech helicopter that gave the film its name. Brought to LA as a deterrent against terrorist activity during the 1984 Olympics, the helicopter is equipped with microphones so sensitive it can pick up sounds behind walls as well as being fitted with extraordinarily sophisticated zoom lenses, and a 'whisper mode' that allows it to

travel silently. The script (by Dan O'Bannon and Don Jakoby) had McDowell attempting to sabotage the chopper, and Scheider – as a Viet Nam veteran – making quite sure he doesn't. Also involved were Candy Clark (as Scheider's girlfriend), Warren Oates (as Scheider's boss), Daniel Stern and Paul Roebling. John Badham's speedy direction allowed no time to realize just how implausible it all was; and it was produced with no expense spared on the gadgetry ($22 million) by Gordon Carroll for Rastar Productions. A TV series followed. (108 mins)

▽ Owing less to Walt Disney's Herbie, that lovable Volkswagen with a mind of its own, than to films such as *The Car* (Universal, 1977) and Steven Spielberg's TV movie *Duel* (1971), **Christine** was created by horror-novelist Stephen King, and filmed by horror-director John Carpenter. As scripted by Bill Phillips, it was the taut tale of a 1950s Plymouth – called Christine – which, after being bought by a misfit student (Keith Gordon, left) and refurbished, takes on human characteristics. Unlike Herbie, though, Christine is a thoroughly nasty piece of work who exacts revenge on everyone who treated her owner badly at school, and then gets even more possessive and goes after Gordon's girlfriend (Alexandra Paul, right). John Stockwell played Gordon's best friend, the baddies were William Ostrander, Malcolm Danare and Stuart Charno, with Robert Prosky (as a cantankerous garage owner), Harry Dean Stanton (wasted in a nothing part) and Christine Belford also in it for producer Richard Kobritz. (110 mins)

◁ With more than just a passing nod in the direction of *Star Wars* (20th Century-Fox, 1977), *Excalibur* (Warner Bros., 1981), *The Adventures Of Robin Hood* (Warner Bros. 1938), *The Thing* (RKO, 1951), *E.T.* (Universal, 1982) and *Raiders Of The Lost Ark* (Paramount, 1981), **Krull** was an expensive ($27 million) fantasy with no personality (or ideas) of its own. The age-old story of a young prince who, before rescuing a beautiful bride from the clutches of a Beast, has to prove himself by passing a series of dangerous tests, it starred Ken Marshall (left) as the heroic young Prince, Lysette Anthony (right) as his would-be bride and Freddie Jones as a Ben Obi-Wan Kenobi-like character who leads Marshall to a magical, spinning boomerang called a 'glaive' as important to the plot as Excalibur was to King Arthur. Francesca Annis, Alun Armstrong, David Battley and Bernard Bresslaw were also featured in Ted Mann and Ron Silverman's high-tech production which was directed with no trace of originality by Peter Yates, and written in a similarly impoverished vein by Stanford Sherman. Box-office returns pronounced it a failure. (117 mins)

▷ The tacky world of a World War II touring theatre was evocatively recreated by playwright Ronald Harwood in his West End and Broadway hit **The Dresser**. That same world was vividly and atmospherically brought to life on the screen by director Peter Yates who was helped, in no small measure, by Albert Finney (right) and Tom Courtenay (left), his two leading men. Finney played an elderly actor-manager (based on Sir Donald Wolfit with whom Harwood once worked) called 'Sir', and Courtenay was Norman, his gay, long-standing, long-suffering dresser. The complex relationship between the two men, set against a typical makeshift production of *King Lear* ('Sir's 227th performance in the title role) provided the piece with its centrifugal force – as well as two meaty roles which both protagonists hungrily devoured. Finney's autocratic, egomaniacal, bombastic 'ham' contrasted most effectively with the cynical subservience of his dresser, and the result was mesmeric. Edward Fox was excellently cast as a fellow-actor resentful of Finney's dominance in the company, Cathryn Harrison (grand-daughter of Rex) played an eager young assistant, Eileen Atkins was the stage manager, and Zena Walker featured prominently as Finney's wife-cum-leading lady. Lockwood West played an ageing Fool to Finney's Lear, and the cast also included Michael Gough, Betty Marsden and Sheila Reid. Harwood's screenplay did little (apart from some minor 'opening out') to disguise the work's stage origins and the result was wordy and claustrophobic on too many occasions. In this instance, though, it wasn't the play but the players that were the thing – and, performance wise, the film (produced by Yates and Harwood) could not be faulted. (118 mins)

▽ **The Man Who Loved Women** was an irredeemably awful remake of François Truffaut's *L'Homme Qui Aimait Les Femmes* (1977), which wasn't all that good to begin with. It starred Burt Reynolds (right) as a successful sculptor living in Los Angeles who, because he's an inveterate womanizer, pays a visit to psychiatrist Julie Andrews (left), with whom, of course, he falls madly in love, and she with him. Told in flashback, and narrated by Andrews at Reynolds's funeral, it featured Kim Basinger (as one of Reynolds's kinky conquests), as well as Marilu Henner, Cynthia Sikes, Jennifer Edwards, Sela Ward, Ben Powers, Ellen Bauer, Barry Corbin and Denise Crosby. Blake Edwards wrote the screenplay with Milton Wexler and Geoffrey Edwards produced it with Tony Adams, and directed it all on his own. The film cost $15 million to make, and only grossed $10.9 million at the box-office. In every respect a disaster. (110 mins)

▷ Guaranteed (because of its foul language) never to be shown on network TV, **Richard Pryor . . . Here And Now** was the fourth of the outspoken comedian's one-man shows and, like its predecessors, was a *tour de force*. With such subjects as sex, drugs, marriage, drinking, and racism forming the basis of his material, there was never a dull moment – nor a dishonest one. Based on his own observations and experiences, Pryor's routines never pulled their punches, and although what he had to say about himself in particular and life in general was less introspective than before, it was just as revealing and the laughs just as plentiful. Pryor (illustrated) was responsible for the script and the direction. Bob Parkinson and Andy Friendly were the producers. (94 mins)

△ Originality was hardly the keynote of **Spacehunter: Adventures In The Forbidden Zone**, a sci-fi adventure, in 3-D, that starred Peter Strauss (left) as a galactic salvage captain who, together with 'tagalong tomboy' Molly Ringwald (right), sets off in search of three girls whose space ship has crashed on a long-forgotten, plague-ridden planet called Terra Eleven. The girls are being held by a cyborg called 'Overdog' McNabb, and, before Strauss can rescue them, he has to navigate his way around some decidedly inhospitable mutants and monsters, all heightened by the use of 3-D effects. Ernie Hudson, Andrea Marcovicci and Beeson Carroll were also featured. The screenplay was by David Preston, Edith Rey, Dan Goldberg, and Len Blum (story by Stewart Harding and Jean Lafleur), Don Carmody, André Link and John Dunning produced, with Lamont Johnson directing and a full-blooded score from Elmer Bernstein. (90 mins)

▽ The only things that survived **The Survivors** were a witty opening sequence in which executive Robin Williams (left) is fired by a parrot because his boss finds the whole business of dismissing his employees stressful; and Walter Matthau's (right) performance as an erstwhile gas-station owner whose business was blown up. The two men meet in an unemployment line, witness a robbery, and thus find themselves on the hit list of mob hitman Jerry Reed. As an example of how to make bricks with straw, Matthau (who replaced Joseph Bologna a couple of weeks after shooting commenced) was worth his weight in diamonds – but even he couldn't buck Michael Leeson's tepid screenplay or direction by Michael Ritchie that failed to generate laughter. William Sackheim produced for Rastar Productions and the cast included James Wainwright, Kristen Vigard, Annie McEnroe and Anne Pitoniak. (102 mins)

1984

▷ If certain elements in producer-director Brian De Palma's **Body Double** had a feeling of *déjà vu* about them, that was because, both in style and in content, he had liberally borrowed a handful of memorable moments from Alfred Hitchcock's *Rear Window* (Paramount, 1954) and *Vertigo* (Paramount, 1958). Another *hommage* to the master of suspense, but far nastier than anything 'Hitch' foisted on his public, *Body Double* was the story of an out-of-work movie actor who, while taking refuge from his unemployment in the hill-top home of a friend, falls in love with a beautiful woman whom he first encounters (via a telescope) doing a striptease in a house across the way. Through the same telescope, the actor sees the woman being murdered with a power drill, but because no body has been found, the police do not believe his story. How, eventually, the culprit is unmasked, provided De Palma and Robert J. Avrech (story by De Palma) with a sleazy, highly improbable scenario which simply did not add up. Craig Wasson (left) was top-cast as the actor, Gregg Henry was the fellow-actor whose home Wasson borrows, Deborah Shelton the unfortunate girl in the telescope and Melanie Griffith (right, daughter of actress Tippi Hedren) a porno actress hired to be Ms Shelton's 'body double'. Also cast: Guy Boyd (as the disbelieving policeman), Dennis Franz, David Haskell and Rebecca Stanley. De Palma's effective placement of the camera was no recompense for the crassness of his narrative style; nor could it disguise the inherent ugliness or exploitative quality of the material. Audiences everywhere thought so too, and this $19 million production recouped only $9 million of its costs from the box-office. (109 mins)

▽ Originally conceived as a vehicle for Dan Aykroyd and John Belushi, but recast after the latter's death in 1982 with Aykroyd (left) and Bill Murray (centre), **Ghostbusters** was an amiably diverting comedy that relied more on special effects for its laughs than on the screenplay by Aykroyd and Harold Ramis. However, the idea of a trio of ghostcatchers who round up a network of ghosts in a Manhattan apartment block greatly appealed to the imagination of the ticket-buying public, and director Ivan Reitman's $32 million production showed box-office grosses in excess of $221 million, making it not only the biggest money-spinner in the studio's history, and also one of the biggest in motion-picture history. (Ray Parker Jr's gleefully bouncy title tune was a hit in its own right.) Harold Ramis (right) co-starred as the trio's technical expert, and they were soon joined in their endeavours by Ernie Hudson, with other roles going to Sigourney Weaver and Rick Moranis as two inhabitants of the ghost-infested apartment block. Annie Potts, William Atherton, David Margulies and Steven Tash were also in it, though they, like the stars, were subservient to Richard Edlund's visual effects, without which *Ghostbusters* would have been little more than a retread of Paramount's *The Ghost Breakers* (1940) with Bob Hope – but not as funny. (107 mins)

▽ A luke-warm re-make of *Out Of The Past* (GB: *Build My Gallows High*, RKO 1947), **Against All Odds** went back to the *film noir* thrillers of the Forties to tell the contemporary story of an obsessive love two men (Jeff Bridges and James Woods) have for the same woman (Rachel Ward, right). Bridges (left) is a professional footballer with a shoulder injury that's threatening to curtail his career; Woods is a small-time Los Angeles bookie-cum-nightclub owner. Daniel Mainwaring's plot (scripted by Eric Hughes) was set in motion after Ward stabs Woods and flies the coop. Woods sends Bridges to Mexico to find her – which he does, and falls in love with her with dramatic consequences for all concerned. Jane Greer (who played Ward's role in the 1947 film) was featured as Ward's mother (and the owner of Bridges's ex-football team), Richard Widmark was Greer's newly-married real-estate husband, and Alex Karras a football buddy of Bridges' sent by Woods to Mexico to see what's going on between Bridges and Ward. An exciting carchase on Sunset Boulevard brought the film to its climax but failed to resolve the plot as neatly as in the earlier version. Director Taylor Hackford co-produced with William S. Gilmore, and the cast included Dorian Harewood, Swoosie Kurtz, Saul Rubinek, Pat Corley and Bill McKinney. The film also featured Phil Collins' wistful opening melody 'Take A Look At Me Now' – a 'singles chart' hit. (128 mins)

▽ Director John G. Avildsen surfaced with **The Karate Kid**, a family film through this tale of the triumph of the under-dog. Ralph Macchio (illustrated) starred as Daniel, a likeable kid from New Jersey who, together with his mother (Randee Heller), relocates from the East Coast to Southern California where he immediately encounters hostility from his new classmates. He's also having problems with a would-be new girlfriend (Elisabeth Shue). Daniel's life changes, however, with the appearance of Mr Miyagi (Noriyuki 'Pat' Morita), an enigmatic maintenance man who teaches Daniel how to defend himself through karate. After instilling in him the notion that karate is a discipline of the spirit, not a means of revenge, Mr Miyagi puts Daniel through a rigorous training period, climaxed by the Valles Karate Championships. It was a simple, but infallible scenario (courtesy of Robert Mark Kamen) and Avildsen mined it for all it was worth – which, in terms of dollars at the box-office, was considerable. Macchio made an appealing young hero, but it was Morita who stole the show – and most of the good notices. The scene in which he takes on a group of Daniel's adversaries and single-handedly karate-chops them into submission was, like most of Jerry Weintraub's production, a real crowd-pleaser. Further enhancing the cast of this profitable (it grossed $90.9 million) sleeper were Martin Kove, William Zabka, Ron Thomas and Rob Garrison. (126 mins)

▽ When a trio of lecherous, middle-aged Lotharios fail to make it sexually with a bunch of bathing beauties known, collectively, as **Hardbodies**, they decide to hire a beach house as well as a well-known local stud to help them score. And that was all there was to Steve Green, Eric Alter and director Mark Griffiths's puerile story-line. Sorrells Pickard, Gary Wood and Michael Rapport played the overgrown schoolboys, Grant Cramer (centre) was the stud, Teal Roberts his girlfriend, with other roles in Jeff Begun and Ken Dalton's production (which was originally made for Cable TV but also had a short theatrical release) going to Roberta Collins, Cindy Silver and Courtney Gaines. (88 mins)

△ After his appalling *The Man Who Loved Women* (1983), Blake Edwards made an excellent return to form with **Micki And Maude**, a well-structured farce in which top-cast Dudley Moore, as the host of a TV show, has the bad sense to impregnate both his attorney wife Micki (Ann Reinking) and mistress Maude (Amy Irving) at the same time. Nine months later they're both about to pop in the same maternity hospital – a situation which leaves Moore frantically dividing his time between the two women, neither of whom knows of the other's existence. A somewhat weak resolution robbed Jonathan Reynolds's otherwise ingenious screenplay of classic status, but not enough to spoil the on-going fun. It was directed by Edwards with a sure-footed farcical touch, and convincingly performed by its three principals and also by a cast that included Richard Mulligan as Moore's best friend and George Gaynes and Wallace Shawn as the Misses Reinking and Irving's obstetricians. Lu Leonard was funny as a heavyweight nurse, and the cast was completed by John Pleshette, Priscilla Pointer, Robert Symonds, George Coe, and, as Irving's intimidating wrestler father, H. B. Haggerty. The producer was Tony Adams. (118 mins)

△ Robin Williams (left) had his best role to date in **Moscow On The Hudson**, an affectionate comedy from producer-director Paul Mazursky in which he played a Russian saxophonist who defects while on a circus tour in the USA. Basically a springboard from which to make some observations and comparisons between life in the USSR and a freer existence in the USA, Mazursky's screenplay, written with Leon Capetanos, was strong on characterization though short on plot. Williams took full advantage of his 'alien abroad' role, which, as fans of his TV series 'Mork And Mindy' would know, was hardly new to this talented actor. Cleavant Derricks played a black security guard who gives Williams sanctuary in his home in Harlem, Maria Conchita Alonso (right) was his Italian girlfriend (who helps him receive official US status), and Alejandro Rey played an immigration attorney, with other roles going to Savely Kramarov, Elya Baskin, and Oleg Rudnik. (115 mins)

△ **No Small Affair** was no big deal. Originally begun in 1981 with Matthew Broderick and Sally Field in the leads, and with Martin Ritt directing, the film was closed down ten days into production due to Ritt's illness. It re-surfaced three years later with Broderick lookalike Jon Cryer (right) and Demi Moore (left) as the leads, and with Jerry Schatzberg directing. The project, however, was still the brainchild of producer William Sackheim, though the original scriptwriter (Craig Bolotin) had been replaced by Charles Bolt and Terence Mulcahy. In the circumstances, this to-ing and fro-ing hardly seemed worth it. The story of a 16-year-old photographer (Cryer) who helps singer Moore on her way to a successful career in Los Angeles by plastering her photograph on 175 San Francisco taxi-cabs, it had a few pleasant moments but not much more. Ann Wedgeworth and Jeffrey Tambor were cast as Cryer's mother and her ex-hippie boyfriend, Peter Frechette played Cryer's brother, and Elizabeth Daily and George Wendt were in it too. Though it wasn't a musical, the soundtrack boasted no fewer than 14 tunes by Rupert Holmes. (102 mins)

▽ Just as Italy served to unleash some dormant English passions in Lucy Honeychurch in *A Room With A View* (Merchant-Ivory, 1986), so India, in **A Passage To India**, brought the repressed Adela Quested (Judy Davis) face to face with her sexuality. The theme of the Englishman (or woman) abroad, and the consequences thereof, was a favourite of novelist E. M. Forster, and, in David Lean's leisurely, visually splendid recreation of (arguably) Forster's finest novel, it was most effectively dramatized. Though Ms Davis (an Australian actress) was possibly too contemporary both in her manner and her appearance to convince as an innocent young girl from England who, after an unexplained incident in the Marabar caves, accuses a young Indian doctor (Victor Banerjee, centre) of rape, the quality of Lean's screenplay (from the Forster novel and the play by Santha Rami Rau) helped camouflage this fact. Nothing, though, could camouflage the fact that Alec Guinness (as the sage Godbole) was a white man in brown-face, and, understandably, this off-beat casting raised a few eyebrows in 1984. There were no complaints, though, about Peggy Ashcroft as Mrs Moore, Davis's companion-cum-chaperone – whose performance, though not entirely faithful to Forster, was superb. James Fox was excellent as a pro-Indian medic; so was Banerjee as a well-educated Indian with British sensibilities. Nigel Havers, Richard Wilson, Antonia Pemberton, Michael Culver, Art Malik, Saeed Jaffrey, Clive Swift, Anne Firbank, Roshan Seth and Sandra Hotz were also in the cast. It was produced by John Brabourne and Richard Goodwin, edited by Lean and photographed beautifully by Ernest Day. Sadly, although receiving warm critical acclaim and many Oscar nominations, the film was slow to recover its $16 million production costs. (163 mins)

△ Bill Murray (illustrated) agreed to make the phenomenally successful *Ghostbusters* (1984) on condition that the studio allowed him to co-script and star in a remake of Somerset Maugham's **The Razor's Edge**, first seen as a vehicle for Tyrone Power (20th Century-Fox, 1946). It was a classic case of the clown wanting to play Hamlet. Murray, however, was simply not up to the demands of the role of Larry Darrell – the well-to-do lad from Illinois who finds spiritual redemption in the Himalayas, but is unable to save the life of the prostitute Sophie (Theresa Russell) whom he meets in Paris, and with whom he falls in love – and both he and the film failed miserably. Denholm Elliott played the worldly Elliott Templeton, and, if he wasn't nearly as effective in the role as his predecessor Clifton Webb, it was because in the remake the character was greatly reduced in importance. Catherine Hicks, James Keach, Peter Vaughan, Brian Doyle-Murray (Bill's real-life brother), Stephen Davies and Saeed Jaffrey were also cast; it was produced by Robert P. Marcucci and Harry Benn, and directed with anything but a razor's edge by co-scripter John Byrum. (128 mins)

▷ Producer-director Norman Jewison returned to the USA's steamy south (the setting for one of his very best films, *In The Heat Of The Night*, United Artists, 1967) with **A Soldier's Story**, a powerful and dramatic thriller which not only explored racial tensions between white and black, but, more interestingly and compellingly, examined fundamental differences between black and black. The setting was a black army base at Fort Neal, Louisiana towards the end of World War II. The action was triggered by the murder, one night, of Sergeant Waters (Adolph Caesar), a tough, no-nonsense manager of the base's black baseball team. Enter Captain Davenport (Howard E. Rollins Jr, left, top-starred) as a proud black army attorney sent to the base to investigate the murder. In a series of flashbacks, during which Rollins interviews several team members, all of whom offer revealing insights into the 'negro' experience, the events leading to Caesar's death are probed until the mystery is finally unravelled. Based on the Negro Ensemble Company's 1981 stage production in New York (which won a Pulitzer Prize for its author, Charles Fuller) and featuring several members of the original cast, the film, scripted by Fuller, was less a thriller than a profound examination of the black psyche. The fact that it worked on both levels was a testimony to its author's skill and to the unflinching honesty of Jewison's direction. All the performances were spot-on, including Denzel Washington's as a militant private and Larry Riley's as a complacent ballplayer-cum-country-singer who is content, in an Uncle Tom sort of way, with his downtrodden lot. Also cast: Dennis Lipscombe, Art Evans, David Alan Grier (right), Wings Hauser and Patti LaBelle. Jewison co-produced with Ronald L. Schwary and Patrick Palmer. (101 mins)

△ Based on S. M. Eiger and Will Eisner's comic-strip books, **Sheena, Queen Of The Jungle** (GB: **Sheena**), shot entirely on location in Kenya, was a campy concoction with a comic potential that director John Guillermin completely failed to realize. It was the unlikely story of a beautiful woman (Tanya Roberts, illustrated), raised by a remote and noble tribe, who has to save her stepmother (Elizabeth of Toro) from a trumped-up murder charge – in which task she is aided by a TV producer (Ted Wass). Even the sight of Miss Roberts in the altogether wasn't enough of a come-on for the studio to recoup much more than a quarter of it's $26 million investment. Paul Aratow produced, David Newman and Lorenzo Semple Jr scripted it from a story by Newman and Leslie Stevens, and the cast included Trevor Thomas, Donovan Scott, France Zobda, Clifton Jones and John Forgeham. (117 mins)

▽ Audiences who sought out plausibility and logic in **Starman** left the cinema disappointed. Those more generously disposed to its easy-going charm and the derivativeness of Bruce A. Evans and Raynold Gideon's screenplay had a far better time. Borrowing liberally from *E.T.* (Universal, 1982) and *Close Encounters Of The Third Kind* (1977), the plot had starman Jeff Bridges (right) arriving from an alien planet, transforming his shape into human form and embarking on an earthly romance with Karen Allen (left) – whose late husband he is made to resemble. As the story unfurled, Bridges was pursued by Richard Jaeckel of the State Department, as well as by a kindly, well-intentioned scientist (Charles Martin Smith). The finale has the Starman returning in a mother-ship to whence he came. Basically a touching love story in sci-fi clothing, it was well-directed by John Carpenter who, happily, refused to allow the special-effects department to overwhelm the simple story with obtrusive machinery. The producers were Michael Douglas and Larry J. Franco, and the cast also included Robert Phalen and Tony Edwards. *Starman* later became a TV series. (115 mins)

1985

△ A visually stunning evocation of Universal's 1935 horror classic *The Bride of Frankenstein*, but with little menace or suspense, **The Bride**, directed by Franc Roddam, was a disappointing re-make of the James Whale classic that split, amoeba-like, into two separate stories. One of them involved the romance between Frankenstein (Sting, left) and his beautiful new creation Eva (Jennifer Beals, right); the other the male-bonding (*à la* Lenny and George in Steinbeck's *Of Mice And Men*, United Artists, 1939) between Frankenstein's monster (Clancy Brown) and an amiable dwarf (David Rappaport). The latter section of Lloyd Fonvielle's screenplay (based on the Mary Shelley novel) was the more effective of the two and, artistically at any rate, Victor Drai's production might have been more successful had it jettisoned the Sting-Beals romance in its entirety and just retained the touching monster-dwarf relationship. A kind of Pygmalion meets Beauty and the Beast, it also featured Anthony Higgins, Geraldine Page, Alexei Sayle, Phil Daniels, Veruschka, Quentin Crisp, Cary Elwes, Tim Spall and Ken Campbell. The music was by Maurice Jarre. The film cost $14 million, but only grossed $4.2 million at the box-office. (119 mins)

▷ **Fast Forward** was a tired re-play of the kind of musical (such as MGM's *Strike Up The Band*, 1940) in which a group of talented kids buck all the odds by making it big in the business. In John Patrick Veitch's now-you-see-it-now-you-don't production, eight teenagers from a racially mixed high school in Ohio decide to audition for a show called The Big Showdown in New York, and, after finding themselves stranded in the Big Apple when their only contact dies, they meet all the predictable challenges of the city, audition, and, of course, win the contest. Though there was some outstanding dancing on view (choreography by Rick Attwell), the acting wasn't up to much; neither was Richard Wesley's routine screenplay (story by Timothy March). Sidney Poitier's direction kept it wholesome, which, alas, was all that could be said for it. Apart from veteran Irene Worth as a retired talent manager who comes out of the woodwork to help the octet on its way, the cast was composed largely of unknowns. They included John Scott Clough, Don Franklin (centre), Tamara Mark, Tracy Silver, Gretchen F. Palmer (second right), Monique Cintron (second left), Debra Varnado (right), Noel Conlon, Cindy McGee (left) and Karen Kopins. (110 mins)

▽ **Fright Night** deserved its surprise success, for it managed to spoof the vampire genre without sacrificing the 'chill' factor. It starred Chris Sarandon (left) as a vampire who takes up residence next door to teenager William Ragsdale, and pivoted on Ragsdale's awareness of his new neighbour's proclivities and on his attempts to convince a played-out horror-movie star (Roddy McDowall, right) to help him do something about the newcomer. A neat script (and debut direction) by Tom Holland, some excellent special effects by Richard Edlund, plus a clutch of splendid performances from a young and enthusiastic cast added up to a spine-chillingly effective dollop of horror that was refreshingly free of gratuitous nastiness. Amanda Bearse co-starred as Ragsdale's girlfriend, and the cast was completed by Stephen Geoffreys, Jonathan Stark, Dorothy Fielding, Art J. Evans and Stewart Stern. The producer was Herb Jaffe. (106 mins)

◁ A handsomely mounted thriller, stylishly directed and convincingly performed, **Jagged Edge** was a welcome return to the *film noir* genre and kept audiences guessing all the way to the ambiguous final scene. It starred Jeff Bridges (left) as a tough, often insensitive newspaper editor accused of the brutal murder of his attractive wife (Maria Mayenzet). Divorcée Glenn Close (right) is hired to defend him, and her adversary in the case is Peter Coyote, an unscrupulous public prosecutor for whom she once worked. As Joe Eszterhas's tautly written screenplay moved into second gear, Close and Bridges begin an affair even though all the evidence being gathered together by Close's anti-Establishment legman (Robert Loggia) suggests that Bridges is, indeed, guilty of murder. Close, Bridges and Loggia were simply terrific together and brought a pulsing conviction to the narrative. The producer was Martin Ransohoff. The cast also included Leigh Taylor-Young, John Dehner, Karen Austin, Guy Boyd, Marshall Colt and Louis Giambalvo. The skilled direction was by Richard Marquand. (108 mins)

△ There were a lot more questions than answers in **Agnes Of God**, a Patrick Palmer-Norman Jewison Production of John Pielmeier's religious re-tread of Peter Shaffer's *Equus* (United Artists, 1977). A Broadway success in 1982 (with a cast of three), it was expanded by Pielmeier for the screen, and, in the process, he forfeited some of the intensity that made the stage presentation so much more compelling (though just as spurious). Jane Fonda (right) starred as a chain-smoking court-appointed analyst sent to a cloistered convent to investigate the strange case of Meg Tilly (Sister Agnes of the title), a young nun whose newborn baby is found strangled. It's up to Fonda to decide whodunnit, and to determine whether Agnes (who cannot recall the child's conception) is a saint or an insane murderer. Anne Bancroft (left) co-starred as the mercurial Mother Superior, a married woman, with children, who turned to religion late in life. Anne Pitoniak played Fonda's mother, and the script was stretched to include Winston Rekert (as a detective), Gratien Gelinas, Guy Hoffman, Gabriel Arcand, Françoise Faucher, Jacques Tourangeau and Janine Fluet – to name but a few. Jewison's direction wasn't able to fill the gaping fissures in the narrative, but he did draw some fine performances from his leading trio, and was particularly successful with Tilly who truly did navigate the emotions from A to Z. A curiosity, and, like the play, not to be taken seriously. (98 mins)

◁ **The New Kids** were a brother (Shannon Presby, right) and sister (Lori Loughlin, left), who, in the course of Stephen Gyllenhaal's no-go screenplay (story by Gyllenhaal and Brian Taggert), were terrorized by James Spader and his repellent band of bullies. Spader gets his comeuppance, of course, but only diehards of the horror genre remained in the cinema long enough to see in what form. John Philbin, Eric Stoltz, David H. MacDonald, Vincent Grant, Theron Montgomery and Eddie Jones were also featured in this cheesy Sean S. Cunningham-Andrew Fogelson Production; Cunningham also doubled as director. (90 mins)

△ Sally Field (left) and director Martin Ritt teamed up for the third time for the making of **Murphy's Romance**, an enjoyable, low-profile romantic drama on which Field served as executive producer (for Fogwood Films), and starred as a divorcée with a 12-year-old son (Corey Haim) who starts a fresh life for herself by arriving at a small Arizona town with a view to setting up as a horse-trainer. An unwanted visit from ex-husband Brian Kerwin doesn't prevent her from pursuing a relationship with James Garner (centre), the town's rugged pharmacist, who proposes marriage at the film's end. It couldn't have been simpler or more effective, thanks (largely) to Garner's charismatic performance (the best of his career), and Harriet Frank Jr and Irving Ravetch's leisurely, beautifully observed screenplay. Fields was her usual spunky self, and the rest of the fine cast included Dennis Burkley, Georgann Johnson, Dortha Duckworth, Michael Prokopuk, Billy Ray Sharkey, Michael Crabtree and Anna Levine. It was gloriously photographed by William A. Fraker, and the producer was Laura Ziskin. (107 mins)

▷ Aaron Latham and James Bridges's screenplay for **Perfect** followed a reporter (John Travolta) as he covers two 'hot' stories for *Rolling Stone* magazine. Once concerns a wealthy businessman (Kenneth Welsh), arrested on drugs charges, who grants Travolta an 'exclusive' on condition that he doesn't give the interview tapes to either his editor or the police. The other scoop is about a health club which Travolta believes is nothing more than a singles bar. Aerobics instructor Jamie Lee Curtis (illustrated) only grants him an interview on being assured that he is doing a glowing report of her club. The result of all this is that 'good-guy' Travolta is prepared to go to jail (and does) for refusing to relinquish the tapes, while 'muck-raking' Travolta thinks nothing of lying to Curtis (with whom he is now having an affair) and writing a headlining story that's insensitive and damaging to the lives of people 'implicated', in it. Both *Rolling Stone* and its editor, Jann Wenner (who depicts himself in the film) emerged from all this as pretty unscrupulous. *Perfect* was glossily directed by Bridges, and featured Laraine Newman, Marilu Henner, Mathew Reed, John Napier-ala, Stephan Gierasch, Anne De Silvo and Tom Schiller. (115 mins)

▽ If *Heaven's Gate* (United Artists, 1980) was, literally, the Western to end all Westerns, **Silverado** was a last-gasp attempt to revive the genre. That it cost far too much money, was far too noisy and failed to find a willing audience, was surely the final nail in the coffin of the legendary West. It was a story of four stereotypical oater heroes – Kevin Kline (right), Kevin Costner, Scott Glenn (left) and Danny Glover – bearing names like Paden and Emmett and Jake and Mal, who team up in order to rid the town of Silverado of its evil sheriff (Brian Dennehy) and his cohorts. However, Lawrence and Mark Kasdan's violent screenplay complicated matters with the motivations all four of its heroes have for wanting to be part of the clean-up. Instead of adding depth and texture to the throw-away narrative, this merely slowed it down. Lawrence Kasdan's expressive production, which he also directed, wasn't particularly well cast, and a desperate feeling of contrivance and *déjà vu* ran through it. Rosanna Arquette, John Cleese, Jeff Goldblum and Linda Hunt provided tongue-in-cheek support. (132 mins)

△ In **Sylvester**, a kind of *National Velvet* (MGM, 1944) revisited, Melissa Gilbert (right – in her feature-film debut) followed in the footsteps of young Elizabeth Taylor as she broke in a wild horse (called Sylvester, after her favourite actor, Stallone) and, with the help of grizzled old Richard Farnsworth, won an all-important horse-show. Well-scripted by Carol Sobieski and competently directed by Tim Hunter, Martin Jurow's production (for Rastar) was an old-fashioned, nicely acted family story which had a longer life on video release than it did in the cinema. Also cast: Michael Schoeffling (left), Constance Towers, Pete Kowanko, Yankton Hatten and Shane Serwin. (103 mins)

△ **The Slugger's Wife** was that rarity of the cinema: a Neil Simon dud. All about the turbulent relationship between an ace baseball player for the Atlanta Braves and a rock singer he meets at a local club, it starred Michael O'Keefe as the 'slugger' and Rebecca De Mornay (illustrated) as the woman in his life. The indifferent audience response to their romance was the fault of Simon's sniggering, well-below-par screenplay and an insistent rock score (aimed squarely at the record-buying youth market) that overloaded every frame in Ray Stark's no-no production. Director Hal Ashby struck out with the material (who could blame him?), leaving a cast that included Martin Ritt (as O'Keefe's caring manager), Randy Quaid and Cleavant Derricks (as fellow players), Lisa Langlois, Loudon Wainwright III and Georgann Johnson to salvage what they could from the mess – which wasn't much. (105 mins)

▽ Ballet-dancer Mikhail Baryshnikov (right) was given his first starring film role in **White Nights**, directed by Taylor Hackford. In this hokey, but not unentertaining, musical drama he played a Russian defector who, while on a dance tour of Europe, crash-lands in Siberia and finds himself back in the country he risked everything to flee. Naturally, the KGB are delighted to have the world-famous dancer back on Russian soil and do their best to have him remain. In order to achieve this, a KGB official (played by director Jerzy Skolimowski) has Baryshnikov billeted with an American tap dancer (Gregory Hines), who defected behind the Iron Curtain during the Viet Nam war, in the hope that the American will persuade the Russian to remain in the old country. Just the reverse happens and the two men, aided by Baryshnikov's former lover (Helen Mirren), plan an elaborate escape back to the USA.

▽ A glossy, vacuous offering from director Joel Schumacher (who also wrote the screenplay, with Carl Kurlander), **St. Elmo's Fire** was a 'group' drama that followed the comings and goings of a batch of graduates from Georgetown University. A showcase for some of the up-and-coming young stars of the 'Brat Pack', it starred Emilio Estevez (centre) as a law student in love with Jenny Wright, Rob Lowe (left) as a no-goodnik married to a girl he made pregnant but doesn't love, Judd Nelson (second right) as a philanderer who's having a relationship with Ally Sheedy (second left), Mare Winningham (third right) as a social-worker virgin burdened with overbearing parents and in love with Lowe, Demi Moore (third left) as a cocaine-snorting high-flyer, and Andrew McCarthy (right) as an obituary writer who hankers for bigger and better things. Their individual stories were inter-cut to little purpose thanks to the feebleness of both script and direction. However, the film found its audience and grossed $37.8 million at the box-office. Martin Balsam was in it, too, and the producer was Lauren Shuler. (110 mins)

Just how this was achieved provided the screenplay (by James Goldman and Eric Hughes) with its extremely far-fetched climax. Before the great escape, however, both Baryshnikov and Hines were given several opportunities to strut their stuff and they did so (especially Baryshnikov in Roland Petit's 'Le Jeune Homme et la Mort') most effectively. Beautiful Isabella Rossellini (left) was featured as Hines's wife, while Geraldine Page brought her usual stamp of authority to the role of Baryshnikov's aggressive agent. John Glover, Stefan Gryff, Shane Rimmer and William Hootkins were there too, Twyla Tharp choreographed it and Lionel Richie sang 'Say You Say Me'. Hackford's and William S. Gilmore's production made quite sure that every element vital to box-office success was abundantly in evidence, and the film more than covered its substantial costs. (136 mins)

1986

▽ Unadulterated desperation was the keynote of **Armed And Dangerous** – a comedy-thriller short on comedy and even shorter on thrills. It starred John Candy (centre) as a former police officer sacked from the force after being framed, and Eugene Levy (left) as an erstwhile attorney disbarred for incompetence. They become security guards for a company owned by Kenneth McMillan, and are soon involved in the machinations of

union mobster Robert Loggia. Mark L. Lester's frantic direction was more of a hindrance than a help to Harold Ramis and Peter Torokvei's groping screenplay (story by Brian Grazer, Ramis, and James Keach) which needed all the help it could get. Grazer and Keach produced, and their cast included Meg Ryan, Brion James, Jonathan Banks, Don Stroud, Larry Hankin, Stacy Keach Sr, and Steve Railsback. (88 mins)

◁ A sequel to *The Care Bears Movie* (Goldwyn, 1985), **Care Bears Movie II: A New Generation** was a full-length animated feature, aimed at the under-sixes, which followed the antics of True Heart Bear (centre back) and his friend Noble Heart Horse (left) whose nemesis, Dark Heart, is up to no good in a summer camp. The fair-to-middling animation was the responsibility of Charles Bonifacio, it was written by Peter Sauder, produced by Michael Hirsh, Patrick Loubert and Clive A. Smith and directed by Dale Schott. The songs, by Dean Parks and Carol Parks, were performed by Stephen Bishop, Debbie Allen and various members of the Parks family. The film featured the voices of Maxine Miller, Pam Hyatt, Hadley Kay, Cree Summer Francks, Alyson Court and Michael Fantini. (77 mins)

▽ Alan Arkin and Peter Falk (who had appeared together in Warner Bros.'s *The In-Laws* in 1979), starred in **Big Trouble**, an unsuccessful variation on the *Double Indemnity* (Paramount, 1944) theme. Scripted by Warren Bogle (aka Andrew Bergman), it centred on the attempts of lovely Beverly D'Angelo (left) and insurance man Arkin (right) to kill-off the former's husband (Falk, centre). John Cassavetes directed and, although one or two cherishable moments were salvaged from the

performances and the screenplay, the emphasis was misguidedly focused on characterization rather than on plot. The project, in big trouble from the start, sank with very little trace, taking with it Valerie Curtin as Falk's wife, Steve Alterman, Jerry Pavlon, and Paul La Greca as their triplet sons (musical geniuses hoping to go to Yale), as well as Charles Durning, Paul Dooley, and Robert Stack. An uncredited Michael Lobell produced. (93 mins)

△ An affectionate tribute to the blues, **Crossroads** was a mystical, highly individual drama that flopped abysmally but nonetheless had some good things in it. Ralph Macchio (left), exchanging karate-chops for a guitar, played a musical prodigy and Julliard scholar whose passion is the Mississippi blues and whose mission it is to track down a forgotten song written 50 years earlier by his hero Robert Johnson (Tom Russ). Macchio's search for that song takes him to the South, where in the company of Joe Seneca (right), as a cranky, superstitious old blues-singer friend of Johnson's (and a man who has sold his soul to the Devil), he undergoes a crash-course in maturity. Seneca (in a role similar to the one played by Noriyuki Morika in *The Karate Kid*, 1984) was superb as the jazz man, and his scenes with Macchio – beautifully written by white blues-singer John Fusco – were memorable. Though Macchio had lessons in guitar-playing, and looked convincing throughout, his music-making was provided by Ry Cooder (as was the film's excellent score). Jami Gertz was third-billed as an ambitious young runaway with dance aspirations (and Macchio's romantic interest). The cast also included Joe Morton, Robert Judd, Steve Vai, Dennis Lipscomb, Harry Carey Jr, John Hancock, Allan Arbus, and Gretchen Palmer. Mark Carliner produced and Walter Hill directed. (96 mins)

▽ Of the two score and more movies with which Blake Edwards had hitherto been associated, **A Fine Mess** was one of the most dispiriting. Inspired by Laurel and Hardy's classic 1932 three-reeler, *The Music Box*, the film was a misguided homage to the era of slapstick comedy. With homages such as this, however, Hollywood history was in dire danger of being misrepresented. All about a movie-extra (Ted Danson, left) who, while working on location at a racetrack, overhears a plot being hatched by Richard Mulligan and Stuart Margolin to dope a horse, the film was an extended chase as bad guy Paul Sorvino sets his hoods on both Danson and Howie Mandel (right) – as a rollerskating cashop – both of whom are trying to cash in on their inside information. Mistaking speed for pace, Edwards' direction could only be described as frantic. Edwards wrote the screenplay, Tony Adams produced, and the cast included Maria Conchita Alonso, Jennifer Edwards, Rick Ducommun, Keye Luke, Ed Herlihy and Walter Charles. Henry Mancini provided the score, and there were 12 featured songs. (88 mins)

△ Following the runaway success of *The Karate Kid* (1984), a sequel was not only inevitable but made sound commercial sense. **The Karate Kid: Part II** re-teamed Ralph Macchio (right) and Noriyuki 'Pat' Morita (left) and began exactly where its predecessor had ended – in the parking lot of the venue where Macchio had won his climactic showdown. After being pounced on by Martin Kove (who had coached Macchio's opponent in the big bout), and successfully karate-chopping the bully into submission, Morita and Macchio travel to Okinawa where the former's elderly father is dying. There they are immediately plunged into an adventure involving Morita's childhood sweetheart (Nobu McCarthy) and Danny Kamekona, an erstwhile rival of Morita's, as well as Kamekona's American-orientated nephew Yuji Okumoto. Nothing that happened in Robert Mark Kamen's screenplay was as compelling as even the dullest moment in the earlier film, and an air of makeshift contrivance permeated Jerry Weintraub's crassly-conceived $14 million sequel. All the same, the public swallowed it whole and it pulled in $115.1 million – even more than its predecessor. It was directed by John G. Avildsen, who wasn't able to make much of the second-hand material, and featured Tamlyn Tomita, Pat E. Johnson, Bruce Malmuth, Eddie Smith and Garth Johnson. (113 mins)

▽ Richard Pryor (right) co-wrote, produced, directed and starred in **Jo Jo Dancer, Your Life Is Calling**, a largely autobiographical piece which began with the comedian's near-fatal accident during a free-basing experiment, then flashed back to his youth, and thereafter moved forward in chronological sequence as it followed his rise to stardom via several marriages and the drug scene. Scoey Mitchell and Diahnne Abbott played Pryor's parents, E'lon Cox was Pryor as a 7-year-old with other roles going to jazz singer Carmen McRae (as Pryor's grandmother), Billy Eckstine (as a night-club singer), Fay Hauser, Barbara Williams, Debbie Allen (left) and Tanya Boyd (as Pryor's wives) as well as Paula Kelly, Wings Hauser, Michael Ironside, Michael Genovese and Virginia Capers. The foul-mouthed script by Pryor, Rocco Urbisci and Paul Mooney fell short of what it should have been – as, indeed, did the film as a whole. (97 mins)

△ More of a promo-film to hype the album it spawned than a satisfying cinematic experience, **Quicksilver** was the flashily-told tale of a young stock trader who, after a bad day on the market – during which he manages to lose a fortune for his company as well as his parents' savings – abandons Yuppiedom, shaves off his moustache and takes a job as a bicycle courier. It is while rubbing shoulders with several ethnic minorities and experiencing the underbelly of life that our hero matures and, with a newfound understanding of the world, returns to his former existence a better and wiser man. Good-looking Kevin Bacon (right) starred as the Yuppie-courier, Jami Gertz was a dope-runner, Paul Rodriguez (left) an ambitious Mexican, Rudy Ramos a drug dealer and Larry Fishburne an angry young black. Also cast: Andrew Smith, Gerald S. O'Loughlin and Louis Anderson. Both the screenplay and the direction, by Tom Donnelly, patronized the minority groups with whom Bacon comes into contact. The producers were Michael Rachmil and Daniel Melnick. The film was a box-office dud, so was the album. (101 mins)

△ A mind-blowingly moronic thriller aimed at the teen-market, and missing by several light-years, **Out Of Bounds** starred Anthony Michael Hall (right) as an Iowa farmboy whose visit to an older brother (Kevin McCorkle) in Los Angeles begins badly when he inadvertently mistakes a duffel-bag containing 10 kilos of heroin for his own and becomes implicated in the murder of his brother and sister-in-law (Linda Shayne). Nothing in Tony Kayden's ill-conceived screenplay made much sense, and, under Richard Tuggle's inept direction, the film was a bomb of megaton proportions. Charles Fries and Mike Rosenfeld were the hapless producers. The cast included Jenny Wright (left), Jeff Kober (the rightful owner of the heroin-filled duffel-bag), Glynn Turman, Raymond J. Barry, Pepe Serna, Meatloaf and Michelle Little. (93 mins)

▷ A beautifully wrought comedy about adolescence and adolescent friendships, **Stand By Me** (based on Stephen King's story *The Body* and scripted by Raynold Gideon and Bruce A. Evans) was set in 1959 and involved a quartet of 12-year-olds. Wil Wheaton (right) was top-starred as the smartest of the lads and a boy with literary pretensions (his mature self was played by Richard Dreyfuss who also served as the narrator), River Phoenix (left) was the group's older leader, Corey Feldman took the role of the most macho and complex of the four, and Jerry O'Connell played the klutzy fat kid who sets the plot in motion when he mentions to his three friends that he knows where they can find a dead body. As they set out on their adventure, we learn about their respective backgrounds; and are made privy to the secrets and fears of youngsters on the brink of manhood. The only jarring note was the preponderance of bad language (much of it out of place in 1959). The main performances were a delight and the supporting performances first class. Among the latter were Kiefer Sutherland (son of Donald), Casey Siemaszko, Gary Riley, Bradley Gregg, Jason Oliver and Marshall Bell. Rob Reiner's direction was characterized by many illuminating little touches. Produced by Andrew Scheinman, Evans and Gideon on a relatively inexpensive budget of $8 million, the film has grossed $55.6 million to date. All-in-all the best film about adolescence since *Summer Of '42* (Warner Bros., 1971). (87 mins)

▷ An old-fashioned romance of the type on which Hollywood thrived for most of its history, **Violets Are Blue** was the hearts-and-flowers story of a doomed love affair between Kevin Kline (left) and Sissy Spacek (right), youthful lovers whom time and circumstances have contrived to separate. When, 15 years after their first meeting, their paths cross once again, he is the owner of a local newspaper, married (to Bonnie Bedelia) and the father of an adolescent son (Jim Standiford). She, on the other hand, is single and a successful, high-powered, globe-hopping photo-journalist. While on vacation to see her parents (John Kellogg and Augusta Dabney) Spacek becomes involved with Kline all over again (both emotionally and professionally) but, despite their plans to do a major story on the children of Lebanon together, Kline ultimately declines and dutifully returns to his hearth and home. Naomi Foner wrote the screenplay, Jack Fisk directed, and Marykay Powell produced for Rastar Productions. Kline and Spacek (Mrs Fisk in real life) were never convincing in their respective roles, and their on-screen affair, like the film itself, was perfunctory, to say the least. (88 mins)

◁ **Stewardess School** was a cretinously unfunny formula farce about a pair of incompetent student pilots who enrol in a stewardess school as a means of seeing, more easily, all the beauties of the world. The cast included (back row – left to right) Vicki Frederick, Donald Most and Brett Cullen (the pilots), Rob Pulsen, Sandahl Bergman and (front row – left to right) Julia Montgomery, Corinne Bohrer, Mary Cadorette, Judy Landers and Wendie Jo Sperber. The prurient script was by Ken Blancato (who also directed), and the producer was Phil Feldman. (84 mins)

△ In **Happy New Year**, Peter Falk (right) – giving the performance of his career in some wonderfully convincing disguises – and Charles Durning played a pair of suave thieves-cum-con-men who plan to clean-out Palm Beach's top-priced jewellery store. The film was inspired by Claude Lelouch's *Le Bonne Année* (France, 1973), and Lelouche himself appeared in a cameo role in director John G. Avildsen's version. Although there were some watchable moments in the screenplay Nancy Dowd (here called Warren Lane) fashioned from the original Lelouch, the love-angle – involving Australian actress Wendy Hughes (left), in her first American film – plus the film's resolution, were tepid, to say the least. Tom Courtenay led the supporting cast (most effectively) as a rather effete and smarmy jewellery-store manager, with other roles in Jerry Weintraub's loss-making production going to Joan Copeland, Tracy Brooks Swope, Daniel Gerroll and Bruce Malmuth. (85 mins)

△ In 1949, a struggling New York writer called Helene Hanff began a formal correspondence with antiquarian book-dealer Frank Doel at **84 Charing Cross Road**. As long sought-after volumes of Hazlitt, Landor and Newman made their way from London to Manhattan – to the delight of the Anglophile Miss Hanff – her letters became less formal and a friendship developed between the two correspondents (as well as with Doel's wife, and various members of the book-store's staff) · that would, in time, become the basis of a best-selling book, a successful stage play, and the film of the book and the play. Though those trans-Atlantic missives endured for 20 years, by 1969, when Hanff had finally saved up enough money to pay her first-ever visit to her beloved England, Doel had died and 84 Charing Cross Road was up for sale. An extraordinary and touching 'romance', it came to the screen via producer Geoffrey Helman for Mel Brooks's Brooksfilm as a 'gift' from Brooks to his wife Anne Bancroft (illustrated), who, as the big hearted and enthusiastic Miss Hanff, was absolutely splendid. Anthony Hopkins was excellent as the bemused Frank Doel, Judi Dench played his wife Nora, with other roles under David Jones's nostalgia-orientated direction going to Jan De Baer, Maurice Denham, Eleanor David and Mercedes Ruehl. It was adapted from James Roose-Evans's play and Miss Hanff's book by Hugh Whitemore. Sadly (though inevitably), this off-beat charmer failed to find an audience. (99 mins)

◁ An ambitious but unworldly youngster from the sticks makes it big in **The Big Town** (Chicago), then pays for his success through a series of belittling events. It starred Matt Dillon (left) as an uncannily talented 'arm' (or dice thrower) who, after leaving his widowed mother and travelling to Chicago, is employed as a freelance craps shooter by club-owner Bruce Dern. Dillon's way with a pair of dice is truly awesome and after taking gambler Tommy Lee Jones's Gem Club to the brink of bankruptcy (and bedding Jones's wife Diane Lane, right) he finds himself framed for cheating. As scripted by Robert Roy Pool from the novel *The Arm* by Clark Howard, the narrative and its resolution held few surprises – of which the same could be said for Dillon's humourless performance. Lee Grant was featured as Dern's wife, with Tom Skerritt, Suzy Amis, David Marshall Grant, Don Francks and Del Close also cast by producer Martin Ransohoff. The director was Ben Bolt (son of playwright Robert Bolt) who did the best he could with the material, but whose best, on this occasion, wasn't good enough. (110 mins)

△ Remember all those 'Road To' comedies with Bob Hope, Bing Crosby and Dorothy Lamour made by Paramount throughout the Forties? Well, writer-director Elaine May didn't, not if **Ishtar**, which was clearly modelled on them, was anything to go by. The cinematic equivalent of the Chernobyl disaster, it was a $43 million melt-down which, overnight, destroyed the credibility of Ms May, who also directed it, and that of Warren Beatty (right) and Dustin Hoffman (left) the film's two powerhouse male stars. Beatty, an actor as renowned for his artistic accomplishments as for his Casanova-like exploits, cast himself, on this occasion, as a 'nebbish' ignorant of the ways of seduction. Pintsized Hoffman, an actor not exactly famous

for his sex-appeal, played Beatty's 'irresistible' side-kick. The entire misguided enterprise failed to yield a solitary smile, let alone a laugh. The couple played a pair of groan-makingly awful New York song writers whose long-suffering agent (Jack Weston) finds them a nightclub engagement in Marrakesh. Once there, they become embroiled in revolutionary events so excruciatingly laboured, inept and unfunny that even seeing, on this occasion, was not believing. The emphatically un-Dorothy Lamour-like Isabelle Adjani was the female lead, with other roles in producer Beatty's catastrophe going to Charles Grodin, Tess Harper, Carol Kane, David Margulies and Rose Arrick. Least said, soonest mended. (107 mins)

◁ **Housekeeping**, written and directed by Bill Forsyth (from the novel by Marilynne Robinson), was the story of two young girls (Sara Walker and Andrea Burchill, right) who move in with their eccentric aunt (Christine Lahti, left) in Montana after the death of their mother (Margot Pinvidic). As the girls grow older, they become critical of their aunt's slovenly housekeeping; the house is a repository for discarded newspapers and tin-cans. Miss Burchill is so sensitive as to what people may think of her domestic environment that she runs away from home and is adopted by one of her teachers. When the authorities threaten to remove the remaining niece on the grounds that her aunt is an unfit guardian, the Misses Walker and Lahti (who have become increasingly dependent on each other), being unable to clear the parlour of its accumulated junk, set fire to the house and boldly leave town via a railway bridge no-one has ever walked across before. In *Housekeeping* the surface charm and quirkiness that characterizes much of director Forsyth's work was, once again, in evidence, though this time filtered through a context that was real and increasingly sad. All the performances, including those of Anne Pitoniak, Barbara Reese, Bill Smillie and Wayne Robson, glowed under Forsyth's observant direction. The film was photographed by Michael Coulter with a refreshingly un-American approach to the landscape; and produced by Robert F. Colesberry. (116 mins)

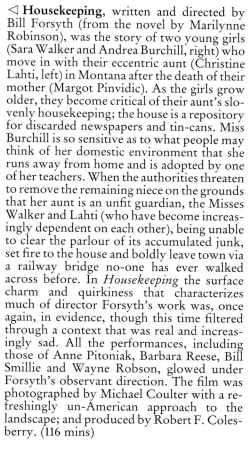

△ John Boorman's **Hope And Glory** was Britain's answer to Woody Allen's *Radio Days* (Orion, 1987). Both films saw the early Forties through the eyes of future film makers; both were narrated; both involved large, working-class families; both were imbued with a bitter-sweet nostalgia; both were autobiographical; and both, to varying degrees, featured the radio or 'wireless'. In Allen's film, the radio was a magic box that brought glamour into his family's home; in Boorman's it was a prophet of doom announcing the commencement of war. As it turned out, war was the villain of the piece, separating families, disrupting lives, destroying property and killing neighbours and friends. The heroes were the Londoners who faced such chaos with courage and fortitude. Yet, as interpreted by the fledgling Boorman (a delightfully unassuming performance from Sebastian Rice-Edwards, second left), war was also a pretty exciting adventure with

secret-society meetings in bombed-out houses, phantom airships, 'fireworks' nearly every night, thrilling air-raids, bomb-sites rich in shrapnel, and an idyllic summer spent with grand-parents Ian Bannen (centre) and Annie Leon (third left) in their Thames-side house outside London. Though short on plot there was no rationing of incident, and with Boorman's probing eye alert to every telling detail, his lovely and lovable film offered a beguilingly nostalgic wallow for those who actually lived through the war years. And for those who didn't, he provided an evocative taste of what it must have been like. Sarah Miles (left) and David Hayman were cast as young Boorman's parents, with other roles going to Geraldine Muir (right), Sammi Davis (second right), Derrick O'Connor, Susan Wooldridge, Jean-Marc Barr, Jill Baker, Amelda Brown and Katrine and Charley Boorman. Boorman produced, and also scripted. (112 mins)

△ Teenage Mexican fruit-picker Richard Valenzuela had both a dream and a recurring nightmare. His dream was of becoming a rock singer; his nightmare – of being killed in a plane crash. Both would come true. Valenzuela, whose professional name was Ritchie Valens, was the first Mexican to escape the slums and make an impact in the gringo-dominated world of rock'n'roll. How he did it was told in **La Bamba**, a captivating, though conventional, Hollywood biopic that managed to reproduce the sound of an era. Though looking nothing like the real-life Valens (and with his vocals dubbed by David Hidalgo of the popular Latin rock group Los Lobos), newcomer Lou Diamond Phillips (left) was utterly convincing as the 17-year-old who recorded three hits ('Come On Let's Go', 'Donna', and 'La Bamba') in his eight months as a professional singer, and who was killed with Buddy Holly and The Big Bopper when their plane crashed on the way back from a gig. Esai Morales (right) was cast as Ritchie's resentful brother Bob, Rosana De Soto was his mother Connie, with other roles under writer Luis Valdez's direction going to Elisabeth Peña, Joe Pantoliano, Danielle von Zerneck, Rick Dees, Marshall Crenshaw (as Buddy Holly), Stephen Lee (The Big Bopper) and Howard Huntsberry. This affectionate tribute was produced by Taylor Hackford and Bill Borden. (108 mins)

▽ Filmed almost entirely in China and on locations hitherto out of bounds to film makers (such as The Forbidden City), Bernardo Bertolucci's **The Last Emperor** was an ambitious, albeit disappointing, biopic of Pu Yi, the last emperor of China who, in 1908 at the age of three, became the 'Lord Of Ten Thousand Years'. When, three years later, China became a republic and 3,000 years of imperial rule was brought to an end with the forced abdication of Pu Yi, the strange isolated medieval life he was living in The Forbidden City hardly changed at all. He was still treated as a god, and grew up surrounded by high consorts, courtiers, and over 1,500 eunuchs. He was free to do anything he chose, except set foot outside the palace. Reality entered this unreal world in the shape of a Scottish tutor called Sir Reginald Johnston who played an important part in educating the young man in Western ways, although not sufficiently well to prevent Pu Yi from taking two wives for himself at the age of 18. Pu Yi was expelled from The Forbidden City in 1924, after Peking was captured by a republican warlord, and, aided by his tutor, went to Tientsin where he led the life of a 'western' playboy. Pu Yi's nightmare began in 1932 when he made the great mistake of accepting Japan's invitation to become the puppet emperor of the new state of Manchu-

kuo. He died in 1967 having spent ten years in a Communist jail before returning to Peking where he became a gardener in the Botanical Gardens. The momentous turns in Pu Yi's eventful life were contained by Bertolucci (who co-wrote the indifferent screenplay with Mark Peploe) in just over 2½ hours of screen time. The end result was often congested and, given the numbers of flashbacks, confusing. Questions were raised that were never answered and, because structurally the film was an unsatisfying sprawl, much of it, despite its spectacle and ritual, was, frankly, a bore. The adult Pu Yi was played by John Lone whose ageing process wasn't all that convincing; and Peter O'Toole was eccentrically cast as his accent-fluctuating Scottish tutor. Richard Vuu, Tijger Tsou and Wu Tao played Pu at the ages of 3, 8 and 15 respectively, Joan Chen played the Empress Wan Jung, with other roles going to Ying Ruocheng as China's Deputy Minister of Culture, Ryuichi Sakamoto as Amakasu, head of the Japanese Secret Service, Wu Jun Mei as Wen Hsiu, Pu Yi's second wife and consort, and Maggie Han as Eastern Jewel, a Japanese spy who has a lesbian relationship with the Empress and turns her into an opium addict. The film was produced by Jeremy Thomas and marvellously photographed by Vittorio Storaro. (162 mins)

△ **White Mischief**, based on the book of the same name by James Fox, was the true story of an unsolved murder which took place in Kenya in 1940. The *dramatis personae* of the intriguing case were Sir John 'Jock' Delves Broughton (Joss Ackland), a middle-aged English aristocrat-cum-gambler; his beautiful wife Diana (Greta Scacchi, right) who was 30 years his junior (and with whom he made a pact which enabled either of them to take other sexual partners), and the handsome, womanizing, twice-married Josslyn Hay, 22nd Earl of Erroll (Charles Dance). With Jock's promise to pay her £5,000 a year for seven years, Diana and Hay embark on a serious affair – much to the embarrassment of Jock, and the consternation of Lady Delamere (Susan Fleetwood), the mayoress of Nairobi and one of Hay's former lovers. Also put out by the affair is the unstable Alice de Janze (Sarah Miles), another of the Earl's former playmates. The day after an uneasy confrontation between husband, wife and lover – Hay is found shot dead in his car. So, whodunnit? All the evidence points, of course, to Jock, but, despite having burned some vital evidence, he is acquitted. Shortly after, de Janze commits suicide, Diana takes her leave of Jock, Jock shoots Diana's dog, then, finally, turns the gun on himself. The film ends with news that Diana has married the reclusive Gilbert Colville (John Hurt), the richest man in Kenya. Given the fascination of the crime itself, the hedonistic atmosphere of well-to-do Brits hibernating in Kenya during the war, and the lurid sexual hanky-panky that seemed almost to be a way of life, the potential for a meaty melodrama with all the stops pulled out was great. But what emerged under Michael Radford's direction (of the screenplay he co-authored with Jonathan Gems) was a run-of-the-mill thriller, set against some pretty African backdrops. The film was produced by Simon Perry with the participation of Curzon Film Distributors, the BBC, Nelson Entertainment, Goldcrest, and Power Tower Investments, and also featured Geraldine Chaplin (left), Ray McAnally, Trevor Howard (in his last screen appearance), Hugh Grant, Murray Head and Alan Dobie. (107 mins)

▷ Arguably the worst 'A' film in the studio's history – including *Ishtar* – **Leonard Part 6**, starring Bill Cosby (right), who also produced from his own story, was yet another spoof on the James Bond-Matt Helm spy yarns so popular in the Sixties. This one featured Leonard (Cosby) as a former secret agent (and a multi-millionaire) who's forced out of retirement to track down the murderer of eight CIA operatives. They're all victims, it would appear, of the bizarre Medusa (Gloria Foster) whose demented mission in life is to encourage the entire animal kingdom to take its revenge on mankind for eons of maltreatment. Add to this a sub-plot involving

Leonard's attempts to reactivate a dormant marriage, and another sub-sub-plot in which Leonard does his best to prevent his daughter from marrying a man three times her age, and you have – precisely nothing. Though Jonathan Reynolds scripted and Paul Weiland directed, blame for this vanity production has to be shouldered by its star – who should have known better. Also cast: Tom Courtenay as Leonard's butler, Pat Colbert (left) as his wife, Victoria Rowell as his daughter, Joe Don Baker, Moses Gunn as his boss – and, as herself, Jane Fonda, who appeared briefly in one of her videotape workout sessions. (85 mins)

▽ Director Ridley Scott and his cameraman Steven Poster brought a flashy eye to **Someone To Watch Over Me**, a glossy, highly entertaining romantic thriller, set in New York, in which a happily married police detective from Queens finds his life undergoing some dramatic and un-called for changes when he is assigned to protect an elegant Upper East Side material witness (living in a $3 million apartment) from being murdered. Tom Berenger (left) starred as the confused, *simpatico* cop; and relative newcomers Lorraine Bracco and Mimi Rogers (right) were prominently featured as Berenger's ex-cop wife (Bracco) and the wealthy witness with whom he falls in love (Rogers). More the story of a burgeoning romance between two people from vastly different social backgrounds than a fully-fledged thriller (the latter elements in Howard Franklin's screenplay being rife with implausibilities), its centre of gravity was the relationship between the three protagonists (two of whom never meet) rather than the simple plot which brought them together; and it was the tender, 'human' side of the drama that made the greater impact. From the opening panoramic shots of New York at dusk, through to its tense, albeit far-fetched finale, the film was a visual treat whose good looks came to the rescue of the routine material on more than one occasion. The wide range of music used throughout was another plus factor; so was the quality of the lead performances. It was produced by Thierry de Ganay and Harold Schneider, designed by Jim Bissell, and also featured John Rubenstein (in the thankless role of Ms Rogers's stuffed-shirt boyfriend), Jerry Orbach (as one of the homicide squad), Andreas Katsulas, Tony Di Benedetto, James Moriarty, Mark Moses and Daniel Hugh Kelly. (106 mins)

▽ **Roxanne** was *Cyrano de Bergerac* in modern dress with actor-scenarist Steve Martin (right) redefining Edmond Rostand's durable hero for contemporary audiences in the guise of C. D. Bales, a fire chief in Nelson, Washington State. C. D. falls in love with beautiful astrologer Roxanne Kowalski (Daryl Hannah, left), but is afraid to make advances due to the undue length of his nose. Instead, he agrees to woo her by proxy for his beefy but intellectually thick colleague Chris (Rick Rossovich). Martin's screenplay had Chris subsequently falling for waitress Sandy (Shandra Beri), and Roxanne's best friend Dixie (Shelley Duvall wasted in an unworthy role) telling her chum all about the deception that had been played on her. The film ended with Roxanne, after angrily rejecting C. D., admitting her love for him. As directed by Fred Schepisi and performed (most delightfully) by Martin, the Michael Rachmil–Daniel Melnick production was a charmer that reinforced Martin's status as one of the best comedians in motion pictures – or anywhere. Also cast: John Kapelos, Fred Willard, Max Alexander, Michael J. Pollard and Matt Lattanzi. (107 mins)

▽ After squandering a good deal of his time (and goodwill) on mechanical comedies such as *The Man Who Loved Women* (1983) and *A Fine Mess* (1986), Blake Edwards turned to more personal matters in **'That's Life'**, a trenchant comedy with serious overtones about encroaching old age. Filmed in Edwards's Malibu home, it starred Jack Lemmon (left) as a successful Californian architect and Julie Andrews (right) – Mrs Blake Edwards – as his affectionate, supportive wife. As he is about to turn 60, Lemmon comes down with a severe attack of male menopause, while Andrews, unbeknown to the rest of her family, is anxiously awaiting the results of tests she has had for suspected cancer. As if this were not enough, one of their daughters (Jennifer Edwards) is seven months pregnant and feels her husband (Matt Lattanzi) is more interested in other women than he is in her; while another daughter (Kate Walton – Ms Andrews real-life daughter) is nursing the wounds caused by the break-up of a long-standing relationship. As for their son Josh (Chris Lemmon), he's just brought home yet another brainless bimbo. It all comes to a head when the chaotic family, each with their own selfish problems, gathers to celebrate Lemmon's sixtieth birthday. Though occasionally over-indulgent, it was a sincere attempt to say something meaningful about family relationships, and for most of the time it rang true. Other roles went to Sally Kellerman (as a scatterbrained neighbour), Robert Loggia, Rob Knepper, Cynthia Sikes, Dana Sparks, Felicia Farr (Mrs Jack Lemmon) and Jordan Christopher. The screenplay was by Edwards and Milton Wexler, the production was by Tony Adams, and the score by Henry Mancini. (102 mins)

△ Shot on location on the McCloud River in California, on the Ottawa River in northern Ontario, and in the South and North Islands of New Zealand, **White Water Summer** was a 'rite of passage' adventure in which an extremely bright and personable youngster from New York (Sean Astin, right) finds himself, one summer, setting out reluctantly for the Sierra wilderness with a group of boys. The main purpose of Manya Starr and Ernest Kinoy's screenplay was to pit young Astin against the forces of nature and also against his overzealous counsellor (Kevin Bacon, left, top-starred). John Alcott's photography (especially the spectacular waterfall sequences) was the real star of a film that had nothing new to say on the subject of adolescents confronting their inner selves; it was produced by Mark Tarlov, directed by Jeff Bleckner, and also featured Jonathan Ward, K. C. Martel, Matt Adler, Caroline McWilliams, Charles Siebert, and Joseph Passerelli. (90 mins)

▷ The only vibes produced by **Vibes** were bad ones. As if wilfully setting out to prove that a comedy need not be funny, scenarists Lowell Ganz and Babaloo Mandel constructed a series of leaden circumstances involving a pair of mismatched psychics who fall in love (predictably) while on a mysterious trek in the mountains of Ecuador. He – played by Jeff Goldblum (right) in his best Mr. Nebbish Nice Guy manner – is an expert in antiquities (as well as a 'psychometrist', ie a man who, just by holding an object in his hands, can give you its provenance). She – played by Cyndi Lauper (left) – is a man-seeking beautician with a gift for astral projection. In the company of Peter Falk (centre), as a conniving opportunist, Julian Sands, as an expert in psychic research, and Googy Gress, as another psychic weirdo – they discover a lost civilization which has a powerful, untouched source of energy at its core. Nothing, however, in director Ken Kwapis's scheme of things worked, and Deborah Blum and Tony Ganz's production didn't need a psychometrist to predict its doom. The executive producers were Ron Howard and Brian Grazer. The cast also included Michael Lerner, Ramon Bieri, Ronald G. Joseph, Bill McCutcheon, and Elizabeth Peña. (95 mins)

▽ **Vice Versa** was one of several role-reversal comedies released in 1988. But, given the popularity of the subject, producers Dick Clements and Ian La Frenais were neither inventive nor funny enough, for their script just didn't gel. The story told of a busy Chicago Executive Vice-President who changes places with his neglected 11-year-old son after inadvertantly acquiring an ancient, mystical skull while on a business trip to Bangkok – but the results of this switch were far from hilarious. By failing to avoid the obvious clichés germane to the basic idea, Clements and La Frenais simply saddled audiences with a caper that even juveniles were bound to find juvenile. Judge Reinhold (right) and Fred Savage (left) starred as father and 11-year-old son respectivley, and did their best with the hokey material. Brian Gilbert's sit-com-like direction severely rationed laughter and involvement. Swoosie Kurtz and Corinne Bohrer were the women in the lives of the leading men, with other roles going to Jane Kaczmarek, David Proval, William Prince, Gloria Gifford, Beverly Archer, Harry Murphy and Kevin O'Rourke. (98 mins)

▽ The message behind writer-director David Seltzer's astringent comedy **Punchline** – that comedy is no laughing matter – is hardly new but, as punched home by Sally Field and Tom Hanks, it reverberated long and loudly. Field (left) played Lilah Krystick, a New Jersey housewife and mother of three who has attempted for over three months to make her mark as a stand-up comic in an intimate New York nightclub called The Gas Station. Despite the chaos and disruption her 'public' life is causing in her private life, Lilah is convinced she's a funny lady – so much so that she's prepared to spend all her 'cookie jar' money on inferior gags from a professional gag peddler. An inauspicious meeting with a student called Steven Gold (Hanks, right) changes her life. Steve is a medical student by day and a would-be comedian by night. The star attraction at The Gas Station, he's a genuinely funny man whose obsession to be even funnier finally results in his flunking out of medical school. Drawn to Lilah – in whom he recognizes talent – he slowly helps her shape an entirely new, much funnier, more appropriate act while she, in turn, helps him keep the particles of his own lonely, somewhat tortured life from disintegrating completely. Their mutual dependence on one another – climaxing in an all-important, career-boosting TV contest at the club – gave the film its emotional mileage as well as its heart and soul. Field and Hanks were brilliant in their roles, and if, in the end, their two chosen acts at the club weren't really as funny as the judge's reactions indicated, blame their material rather than them. In the main, though, Seltzer's screenplay was spot-on, both in its handling of the personal aspects of his protagonists' lives and in its dissection of the not-so-funny world of the would-be comic. John Goodman was excellent as Lilah's mundane insurance salesman husband; so was Mark Rydell as Romeo, The Gas Station's opportunistic owner and Master of Ceremonies. Kim Greist and Paul Mazursky were in it too. Also cast: Pam Matteson, George Michael McGrath, Taylor Negron, Barry Neikrug, Angel Salazar, Damon Wayans, Joycee Katz and Mac Robbins as some of The Gas Station's team of regulars. Daniel Melnick and Michael Rachmil produced. (122 mins)

△ **Stars And Bars** starred Daniel Day Lewis (right) as a British art dealer who has recently come to live in New York. It told of his attempts to cope with Loomis Gage (played by Harry Dean Stanton), the eccentric Deep South owner of a desirable Renoir, and Loomis's decidedly weird Georgia family. Sadly, the script (by William Boyd from his own novel) wasn't nearly inventive enough in its handling of many stock situations; nor was the direction (by Pat O'Connor) sufficiently imaginative to salvage the platitudes. In the face of such adversity, therefore, Day Lewis certainly earned the praise lavished on his performance by critics otherwise indifferent to the film. Laurie Metcalf appeared as Melissa, his fiancée (and his boss's daughter), Martha Plimpton was Melissa's wilful daughter, and Joan Cusack (left) played a dynamic New York businesswoman who pursues Day Lewis with determination. Also cast were Glenne Headly, Will Patton, Maury Chaykin, Matthew Cowles, Kent Broadhurst, Keith David, Spalding Gray and Dierdre O'Connell. The producer was Sandy Lieberson. (94 mins)

1989

▽ James Woods' intense, deeply committed performance in **True Believer** worked wonders in elevating him from supporting player to star. He played a once respected attorney who, during the ideological sixties and seventies, was closely associated with cases involving civil rights. Reaganite disillusion, however, has reduced him to a pot-smoking shyster living in a sleazy Greenwich Village tenement, and only too happy to defend drug-dealers. Two occurrences help steer him in the direction of his more noble self: the appearance of an enthusiastic young Midwestern attorney (Robert Downey Jr, illustrated), fresh out of law school, who arrives in New York to become his clerk; and a request made to him by a Korean mother (Misan Kim) to defend her son (Yuki Okumoto, seated) who is currently awaiting trial for killing a racist convict in a jailhouse incident. At Downey's urging Woods takes the case, but not before Wesley Strick's convoluted, often implausible screenplay puts him through a narrative mangle involving fascistic cons, crooked cops and duplicitous prosecutors. Margaret Colin was featured as a private investigator who, despite some flirtatious banter, provides platonic female interest, with other parts under Joseph Ruben's direction going to Kurtwood Smith (as a self-righteous DA), Tom Bower, Miguel Fernandes and Charles Hallahan. Walter F. Parkes and Lawrence Lasker produced. (103 mins)

△ Special effects and a bravura, larger-than-life central performance by John Neville (second right) came to the rescue of **The Adventures Of Baron Munchausen**. The third in Monty Python director Terry Gilliam's trilogy of fantasies after *Time Bandits* (Handmade Films, 1981) and *Brazil* (Universal, 1985), *Munchausen*, set in the 'Late 18th century, The Age of Reason, Wednesday', begins as the Turks are about to invade a walled city. In what remains of the local theatre, a hammy impresario (Bill Paterson) and his troupe are presenting the legendary exploits of the famous story-teller Baron Karl Friedrich Hieronymous von Munchausen (1720–1797) when the performance is interrupted by the real Baron, who, together with his servants Berthold (Eric Idle, second from left), the fastest man alive, the marksman Adolphus (Charles McKeown, left) and Gustavus, a dwarf with gale-force lungs (Jack Purvis, front), embarks on the authentic story of his life. As a cinematic project, it was perfect for Gilliam. His imagination, aided and abetted by Richard Conway and the Peerless Camera Company Ltd, cameraman Giuseppe Rotunno, and production designer Dante Ferretti, was given full reign in one set-piece after another. The visual surprises included a hot-air balloon made from the panties of the Baron's many female admirers, a trip to the moon, a visit to the belly of a sea-monster, a detached, talking head and Idle's race with a bullet. Sarah Polley appeared as the Baron's travelling companion, Oliver Reed and Uma Thurman played Vulcan and Venus, an uncredited Robin Williams materialised as the King of the Moon with Valentina Cortese as his queen, with other roles going to Winston Dennis (right), Jonathan Pryce, Alison Steadman and Sting. They were, however, all upscreened by the cinematic wizardry which helped catapult the budget to $41 million. It was produced by Thomas Schuhly and Ray Cooper, and written by Charles McKeowan and Terry Gilliam, from stories by Rudolph Erich Raspe. (126 mins)

▷ Loosely based on the 1984 murder of Solidarity supporter Father Jerzy Popieluszko, **To Kill A Priest**, directed by Agnieszka Holland, had all the potential for a powerful, socio-political thriller, but squandered it on a screenplay by Holland and Jean-Yves Pitoun that raised more issues than it addressed. The film starred Christopher Lambert as charismatic Polish priest Father Alek who, in Warsaw, 1981, confronts the full might of the Communist Party in his determined and fearless fight for freedom. His opponent is Stefan (Ed Harris, right), a committed Communist who, pretending to be a parishioner, infiltrates Father Alek's church as a prologue to murdering him. If good intentions alone could make a good film, *To Kill A Priest* would have been a winner, but nothing coalesced – despite an excellent supporting cast that included Joanne Whalley, Joss Ackland (left), David Suchet, Tim Roth, Timothy Spall, Pete Postlethwaite and Cheri Lunghi. The film was produced by Jean-Pierre Alessandri. (117 mins)

▽ Five years after *Ghostbusters* proved such a smash with both audiences and critics, came the much vaunted and anticipated sequel, **Ghostbusters II**, only this time without creating the same critical and financial furore. Set in a Manhattan as yet untouched by the clean-up, feel-good, almost suburban hand of Mayor Giuliani, much of the crazy plot devised by Harold Ramis and Dan Aykroyd had to do with the negative energy festering in the city's environs and caused by the frustrations of angry New Yorkers. The visible manifestation of these bad vibes is a river of evil pink slime that runs through an abandoned subway tunnel and to which the ghostbusters – Bill Murray (left), Dan Aykroyd (centre), Harold Ramis (right) and Ernie Hudson – all in desperate need of a juicy assignment – turn their attentions. The plot also involved Sigourney Weaver as an unmarried mother whose baby is a potential victim of the nameless evil that has befallen Gotham. On hand, too, was an eastern European art historian (Peter MacNicol) who is possessed by someone or something called Vigo (Wilhelm Von Homburg) in a painting he's restoring. The film's special effects – courtesy of Industrial Light and Magic – plus some amusing dialogue, helped to paper over the cracks in the preposterous plot; so did most of the performers, including Rick Moranis as the ghostbusters' lawyer (in the first film he was their wimpish accountant) and Annie Potts as his token love interest. Cameo appearances were provided by Judy Ovitz, Cheech Marin, Janet Margolin and Ben Stein; it was directed with noise and pace by Ivan Reitman who also produced. (102 mins)

▷ Though Ralph Macchio (centre) was 27 when, for the third time, he undertook the role of Daniel in **The Karate Kid III**, he just about managed to get away with playing 17 – a year older than he was meant to be in *The Karate Kid II* (1986). But on the evidence of Robert Mark Kamen's truly sluggish screenplay, the kid was hardly any wiser. Third time round the plot found bad guy-cum-karate-master Martin L. Kove, whose martial arts institution is in deep decline, still smarting from the humiliation he suffered at the hands of Miyagi (Noriyuki 'Pat' Morita, right) in the first film in the series (1984) and accepting the offer of a wealthy former Vietnam buddy (Thomas Ian Griffith) to seek vengeance on his behalf. Daniel, meanwhile, has helped Miyagi finance a bonsai tree nursery with what should have been his college tuition fees, only to see it trashed by a group of thugs who want to force Daniel to defend his All-Valley Karate Tournament title. Producer John G. Avildsen's direction-by-numbers was unable to alleviate Macchio's persistent whine throughout, or to draw from Morita anything other than the engaging benevolence he displayed with such sage-like observations as 'life is like a bonsai tree'. Robyn Liveley (left), Sean Kanan, Jonathan Avildsen and Christopher Paul Ford completed the cast. (111 mins).

▽ The culture clash between China and New York's Chinatown, and the generation gap between young and old Chinese-Americans was the subject of director Wayne Wang's charming comedy **Eat A Bowl Of Tea**. After a voice-over reminding audiences that, until the end of World War II, women from China were not allowed entry into the U.S., the film begins, in 1949, with Wah Gay (Victor Wong) the owner of a New York gambling club, sending his soldier son Ben Loy (Russell Wong, right) to Hong Kong to marry Mei Oi (Cora Miao, left) the daughter of his best friend. They fall in love at first sight, marry as planned, then return to America where their problems begin. Ben Loy finds that coping with marriage while running the restaurant his father has given him as a wedding present puts too much pressure on him and ruins his sex life. Mei Oi, who is no blushing Oriental violet, takes a secret lover called Ah Song (Eric Tsiang Chi Wai) and falls pregnant – much

to the fury of Wah Gay who, in the film's funniest moment, chases Ah Song with an axe. Wang's familiarity with his characters and their lifestyles manifested itself in every scene, and the late 1940s atmosphere was beautifully evoked in an appropriate choice of period songs on the sound-track, as well as in clips from films such as Orson Welles' *The Lady from Shanghai* (1948). An American Playhouse Theatrical Films production, it was written by Judith Rascoe from Louis Chu's 1961 novel and produced by Tom Sternberg. (102 mins)

△ Sean Penn, Hollywood's Mr. Nasty and Michael J. Fox, the industry's small but perfectly formed Mr Nice, pooled their talents in Brian De Palma's **Casualties Of War**. It was type-casting with a vengeance, but it worked. Penn (right) played a foul-mouthed battle-scarred sergeant, Fox (left) was the squad's 'cherry' (newcomer). One look at them side by side instantly dispelled all notions of peaceful co-existence. If conflict is the essence of drama, it reared its inflamed head when Penn is detailed to take his men on a long-distance reconnaisance mission. To enliven the dangerous trek, and in a gesture of contempt for the Vietnamese, he kidnaps a young girl (Thuy Thu Le, centre) from her village and takes her along for the sexual gratification of his men. Predictably, Fox is appalled at his sergeant's behaviour ('we're supposed to *help* these people!' he cries) and refuses to take his turn in line. Indeed, he is so horrified at the outrage perpetrated on the innocent girl, that he tries to help her escape. But it is not to be and she is brutally murdered. Unwilling to allow what has happened to go unreported, Fox now finds himself in a war not only against the unseen enemy, but also against his own men. Though De Palma used the central rape scene as a metaphor for America's involvement in Vietnam, there was no escaping his characteristic knife-turning approach to the material. Similarly, his handling of the hapless girl's harrowing death left a decidedly nasty taste. With the rape and the murder out of the way and the squad safely returned

to base, De Palma seemed to lose interest in what was left of the plot. An attempt on Fox's life and his uncharacteristic revenge-taking never reaches the authorities, while the film's penultimate scene – a trial resulting from the rape and murder – was over almost before it began. David Rabe's tough and sinewy screenplay (from an article by Daniel Lang) framed the action in a flashback – with Fox, from the safety of a subway train, going back to the past to relive the whole traumatic experience. This device not only robbed the film of some of its tension (audiences knew from the outset that the hero survived), but cued in a reassuring ending that was out of place. The performances, though, were full of conviction, Penn's frighteningly so; and the cumulative effect of De Palma's sledgehammer approach was not without its desired effect. But as a statement on the dehumanising things men do in war, and the dehumanising things war does to men, *Casualties Of War* was far from definitive. It was produced by Art Linson, shot in Thailand, and its cast included Don Harvey, John C. Reilly, John Leguizamo, Erik King and Jack Gwaltney. (113 mins)

△ **The Big Picture** was a small, inexpensive and adroitly-made look at the problems that face a young graduate (Kevin Bacon, left) from a Los Angeles film school. If, as it has been noted, L.A. is a state of mind rather than a city, that mind, when it comes to the movie industry, works in mysterious ways – as debut director Christopher Guest's satirical comedy – and the screenplay he wrote with Michael Varhol and Michael McKean (story by Varhol) – was at pains to illustrate. Success, how to get it, what to do with it, and how to keep it, were just some of the problems faced by fledgling director Bacon who quickly discovers that in L.A. the key to celebrity is never to return calls. Bacon gave his most convincing performance to date, his best work manifesting itself in his reactions to the boggling stupidity of his peers, most notably J.T. Walsh's high-powered studio executive. Delightful stuff, with excellent performances, too, from Emily Longstreth as Bacon's ex-girlfriend, Teri Hatcher as his current fling, and an unbilled Martin Short as his eccentric agent. Also cast: Jennifer Jason Leigh (right), Michael McKean, Dan Schneider and Jason Gould, with appearances by Don Franklin, Fran Drescher, Eddie Albert, June Lockhart, Stephen Collins, Roddy McDowall, John Cleese and Elliot Gould. An Aspen Film Society production, it was produced by Michael Varhol. (99 mins)

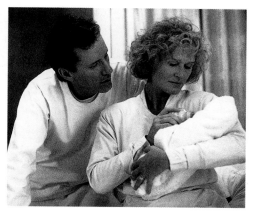

△ An absence of nuance and motivation characterised **Old Gringo**, a tedious, initially incomprehensible adaptation of Carlos Fuentes' novel *Gringo Viejo* that relied, with varying degrees of success, on its star casting rather than on its screenplay (by Aida Bortnik and Luis Penzo, who also directed). Jane Fonda (left) top-starred as Harriet Winslow, a virgin schoolteacher from Washington D.C. who, in order to escape a dreary existence and her father's high expectations of her, travels to revolutionary Mexico in 1913. There she meets Tomas Arroyo (Jimmy Smits), a smouldering young general attached to Pancho Villa's army, and 'old gringo' Ambrose Bierce (Gregory Peck, right), a scabrously witty journalist seeking to end his days away from hearth and home in the pursuit of adventure. Inevitably, a romantic triangle linking the protagonists insinuated itself at the expense of the novel's more serious-minded themes such as the nature of loss, destiny and courage. And while there was no denying the impressive physical attributes of Lois Bonfiglio's troubled, $24 million production – especially Felix Monti's ravishing photography – Puenzo's cosmetic job was a major disappointment to the novel's many admirers. Though Fonda was miscast as Harriet Winslow, her basic intelligence and feistiness, and her obvious commitment to the role, always made her watchable, especially in her suggestive love scene with TV star Smits who brought real presence to his performance. But it was Peck (in a role originally offered to Burt Lancaster) who had all the best lines and whose years of experience as a Hollywood icon gave all his scenes that extra, much-needed edge. Ann Pitoniak appeared as Fonda's mother, and the large, predominantly Mexican cast included Patricio Contreras, Gabriele Roel, Sergio Calderon, Pedro Armendariz Jr and Pedro Damian. (119 mins)

△ What could so easily have been little more than a handful of maudlin episodes in a long-running soap-opera was, in **Immediate Family**, transformed into a high-quality drama by a sensitive, beautifully observed screenplay, excellent direction and performances that were a credit to the profession. Glenn Close (right) and James Woods (left) starred as the Spectors, a middle-class family who, after 13 years of a happy but childless marriage, decide to adopt. The couple on whom they have set their sights are the Moores (Mary Stuart Masterson and Kevin Dillon), young, working-class newlyweds soon to have their first, and unwanted, baby. The Spector's lawyer (Linda Darlow) suggests that Lucy Moore move in with the adoptive parents as a getting-to-know-you exercise prior to the baby's birth, which she does. It all works out well in the initial stages, but in the course of Lucy's pregnancy complications, as they say, ensue ... By avoiding undue sentimentality, writer Barbara Benedek managed, most effectively, to plumb the heart of an emotionally charged matter with a seriousness of purpose that was echoed in Jonathan Kaplan's restrained direction. And while all the performances were excellent, the glue that held it all together was provided by Mary Stuart Masterson whose combination of strength, guile and charm was a winner all the way. Jane Greer was featured as Woods' mother, with other roles in Sarah Pillsbury and Midge Sanford's classy production (for executive producer Lawrence Kasdan) going to Jessica James, Mimi Kennedy, Charles Levin and Harrison Mohr. (95 mins)

▽ Though party-mad chorus girls, clandestine crap games, prohibition hooch and an inventory of colourful and colourfully named characters attested to the fact that **Bloodhounds of Broadway** was Damon Runyon territory writ large, the essential charm, wit and pathos that had defined better Runyon screen adaptations such as *Little Miss Marker* (Paramount, 1934), its remake *Sorrowful Jones* (Paramount, 1949) and, best of all, Frank Loesser and Abe Burrows' 1950 Broadway smash *Guys and Dolls*, was singularly missing. Based on four Runyon short stories and set on Broadway on New Year's Eve in 1928, the film, which was produced, directed and co-scripted (with Colman deKay) by Howard Brookner – who, sadly, died before the film's release – had pace and plot a-plenty, but failed to deliver a knock-out punch. The first and best of the yarns featured Madonna (below) as Hortense Hathaway, a nightclub singer in love with Feet Samuels (Randy Quaid), a gambler who has mortgaged his feet to pay off a gaming debt; the second found socialite Harriet McKayle (Julie Hagerty) inviting a bunch of mobsters to jazz up her New Year's Eve party in her swanky Park Avenue apartment. In the third episode Matt Dillon, as an unlucky punter called Regret, becomes a murder suspect; while the last (and least) of the segments found Rutger Hauer (as The Brain) being driven around town with a knife in his stomach as he seeks out one of his ex-girlfriends to help save his life. Notwithstanding the effectiveness of Madonna and Quaid, the four plots (or subplots) didn't add up to much and the film came and went unceremoniously. Ethan Phillips, Jennifer Grey, Esai Morales and Anita Morris were also cast, and it was narrated à la Walter Winchell by Josef Sommer as a newspaper reporter called Waldo Winchester. (101 mins)

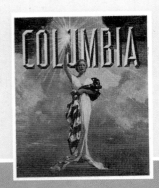

1990-1998

In September 1989, the Japanese electronics giant Sony purchased Columbia Pictures Industries. Under Mark Canton whose early successes at Columbia-TriStar included *Sleepless in Seattle* (1993), *Philadelphia* (1993), *Legends Of The Fall* (1994) and *To Die For* (1995), the latter released in Britain by Rank, the future looked bright. In October 1996 John Calley was appointed President and Chief Operating Officer of Sony Pictures Entertainment. His Columbia-TriStar successes have included *Jerry Maguire* (1996), *As Good As It Gets* (1997) and *Air Force One* (1997), a Buena Vista release in Britain. It was under Calley's guidance that Columbia, in its 75th anniversary year, was looking forward to many happy box-office returns.

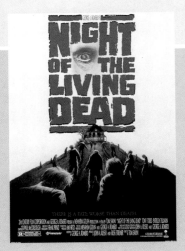

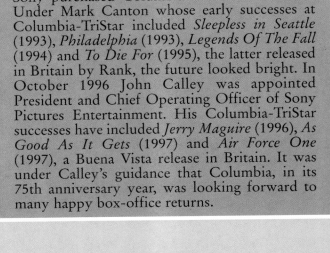

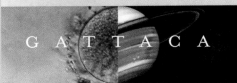

1990

▽ In director Tony Scott's **Revenge** Kevin Costner played a macho gringo who goes out of his way to look for trouble and finds it in the grizzled shape of Anthony Quinn – a ruthless, Mexican Mr. Big who invites Costner (left), a retired naval pilot, to visit him in his luxurious estate in Puerto Vallarta. Costner accepts, moves into an attractive beach cabana and, to while away the time, plays the odd game of tennis. Then he makes the mistake of allowing himself to be seduced by Quinn's beautiful wife Miryea (Madeleine Stowe), at which point the proverbial manure hits the air-conditioning. Unaware that her phone is tapped, Miryea misguidedly plots to deceive her husband with an elaborate lie involving a weekend in Miami. She and Costner are duly discovered *in flagrante*, the bloody aftermath of which leaves his face looking as though it has been through a food processor. Costner is left for dead while his lover is despatched to a local whorehouse – a punishment befitting her crime. Nursed back to health by a Mexican witch and a tubercular Mexican cowboy, Costner changes his Mr. Nice Guy image and, with revenge on his mind, turns into a ruthless killer. Clearly aware that Jim Harrison and Jeffrey Fiskin's screenplay was little more than ham dressed up as mutton, director Scott wisely opted to accoutre this elongated cliché in visuals of stunning beauty, courtesy of cinematographer Jeffrey Kimball. The more far-fetched the plot, the more fetching the landscape. Sally Kirkland appeared, all too briefly, alas, as an ageing rock singer and refreshingly aerated the claustrophobic atmosphere of it all; and there was a memorable moment, too, in which Costner makes lemonade, then love, as if the one were a natural extension of the other. Apart from that, and the sight of Quinn (right) trying to hide a spreading midriff as he discreetly surfaces from a swimming pool, Revenge, produced by Hunt Lowry and Stanley Rubin, wasn't worth the taking. (124 mins)

△ Is there life after death, and, if so, what form does it take? Continuing Hollywood's preoccupation with such questions, was Joel Schumacher's **Flatliners**, an often provocative drama that bordered on sci-fi and in which a group of medical students embark on a Twilight Zone-type experiment in the hope of reaching the other side and returning to tell the tale. Initiating the project is Kiefer Sutherland(left), an ambitious, self-seeking student who visualises his face on the cover of *Time* magazine. Working with fellow students Kevin Bacon (second left), Oliver Platt (right), Julia Roberts (second right) and a womanising William Baldwin (centre), Sutherland anaesthetises himself to the point where his heart stops and the ECG monitor indicating his vital signs shows nothing but flat lines – hence the title. About 90 seconds after being clinically dead he is successfully revived. Other members of the group continue the experiment, each 'dying' for longer periods than the last. What is initially revealed is a series of isolated visions, from picture-postcard landscapes (Sutherland) and erotic fantasies (Baldwin), to alpine peaks (Bacon), but it is the side-effects, however, that turn out to be disturbing. Sins from their pasts return to haunt them. Sutherland, for example, was a schoolboy bully whose main victim, killed as a result of harassment, materialises to inflict some grievous bodily harm on him; while the womanising Baldwin cannot escape the collective wrath of his discarded conquests. Given the quasimetaphysical nature of the subject, these individual visions and their consequences seemed trivial. The film's repetitive structure (it was written by Peter Filardi) became predictable, and its biblical message – atone for one's sins, and always do unto others, etc etc – was hardly in keeping with Filardi's original central idea. Schumacher kept it watchable, underplayed its manifold absurdities, and drew excellent performances from his attractive young cast. A Stonebridge Entertainment production, it was produced by Michael Douglas and Rick Bieber, with Scott Rudin, Michael Rachmil and Peter Filardi as executive producers. (111 mins)

▷ Absolutely irresistible, **Postcards From The Edge** came complete with two whopping star roles, a super-charged screenplay, direction that never missed a trick, a couple of terrific songs, and a fail-safe, mother-daughter relationship with which many women easily and readily identified. Nor did it matter much that the mother and daughter were based on Debbie Reynolds and Carrie Fisher. The heart of this largely autobiographical Hollywood story beat to the familiar rhythms of the terrible things parents and their offspring say to each other in the name of love. Written by Ms Fisher from her bestseller, it was, on face value, about a young actress' attempts to rebuild her life after a near-fatal drug-overdose and a brief stint in a rehabilitation centre. In other words, an everyday Hollywood tale. What, however, gave it its resonance and appeal had less to do with the daughter's triumph of won't over will, but her no-holds-barred relationship with her mother. Mother (played by Shirley MacLaine, right) is Doris Mann, a shamelessly self-absorbed superstar who, like her daughter Suzanne (Meryl Streep, left) operates better in public than in private. She drinks a little too much, has an infuriating habit of never listening when spoken to, and invariably makes herself the centre of everyone's gravity. Not that Suzanne is a whole lot better. Jealous of her mother's celebrity and ashamed of her own irresponsible behaviour, she emerges from the drug clinic as flip and frivolous – the kind of person for whom the easy put-down is a defence mechanism against her confused emotions and thoughts. The sight and sound of Doris' superego crashing head-on with her defensive, more fragile daughter – and both living to tell the tale – was the film's chief pleasure. It also provided its stars with roles to kill for. MacLaine gave yet another fearless performance, entirely eschewing personal vanity in the looks department and inhabiting the role completely. Whether busting a gut singing Stephen Sondheim's great ode to endurance, 'I'm Still Here' from *Follies*, or spitting venom at her shell-shocked daughter, she was always in total command of Fisher's scorching, shrewd and often hysterically funny screenplay. Less convincing was Meryl Streep who, despite giving a technically flawless performance, was miscast as the vulnerable, drug-addicted Suzanne. Dennis Quaid was fine as a womanising producer, ditto the always reliable Gene Hackman as a director. The real director, Mike Nichols, who imparted a glossy finish to an enjoyably seductive high-class soap. It was produced by Nichols and John Calley and prominently featured Richard Dreyfuss (as a doctor who rescues Streep from a drug overdose), Rob Reiner, veteran Mary Wickes, Conrad Bain, Annette Bening, Simon Callow, Gary Morton and Dana Ivey. (101 mins)

▽ Oliver Sacks' 1973 book **Awakenings** offered a remarkable series of case histories involving a group of profoundly catatonic mental patients in a Bronx neurological hospital. Victims of a sleeping sickness epidemic in the 1920s, they existed for 40 years or more, dead to the world but inwardly alive. In 1969 Dr Sacks, experimenting with a new drug called L-Dopa, managed to 'awaken' his group of the 'living dead' all of whom briefly but miraculously erupted into life. How they adjusted to the world around them and faced the reality of their lost years was moving beyond words. So was Sacks' description of the drug's unpredictable side-effects and his patients' gradual return to limbo. For director Penny Marshall's screen version, scripted by Steven Zaillian, Sacks was fictionalised into Dr Malcom Sayer, played by Robin Williams (right) as a shy, somewhat awkward loner. Like his patients, Sayer lives in a world of his own, and through his experiments, awakens not only a certain Leonard Lowe (Robert De Niro, left) after a 30-year sleep, but awakens himself to the possibilities of a richer, more emotionally rewarding life with a member of the opposite sex (Julie Kavner). Given the narrower vision and sentimental edge brought to the film, it was tastefully directed by Marshall who told a remarkable story with clarity, conviction and a discreet use of symbolism. Less convincing, though, were the two central performances. Keeping his instinctive exuberance under control, though not without a certain amount of visible effort, Williams reverted to the mode of his *Dead Poets Society* (Touchstone, 1989); while De Niro was never really able to divorce the character he played from the high-profile star playing him. Completing the cast for producers Walter F. Parkes and Lawrence Lasker were Ruth Nelson, Penelope Ann Miller, John Heard and Alice Drummond. (121 mins) .

▷ **Forbidden Dance**, a low-budget attempt to cash in on the popular lambada dance craze, was a piece of low-octane fun, with some enjoyable dancing, that starred Laura Herring as Nisa, the princess of a Brazilian tribe who makes a pilgrimage to Los Angeles in order to try and stop an American company from destroying her rain-forest home. Accompanying her is shaman Joa (Sid Haig) who uses black magic to further the cause, but only gets himself arrested. Nisa, after getting a job as a servant in Beverly Hills, becomes involved with Jason (Jeff James, illustrated centre, with Herring) who has seen her dance. Leaving domestic service she fetches up as a dancer in a tacky club called Xstasy, pursued there by the besotted Jason with whom, after several meandering plot turns, she finishes up in a dance contest. And lest anyone came away from it all with the notion that what they witnessed was a mindless mini-musical, writers Roy Langsdon and John Platt (from a story by Joseph Goldman) made sure their plot, quite apart from dealing with the central issue of the environment and its preservation, touched on such topics as safe sex, immigration difficulties, racism and the homeless. Richard Lynch was the user-unfriendly bad guy out to destroy the rain forests, with other parts under Greydon Clark's anything-but-subtle direction going to Barbara Brighton, Angela Moya, Miranda Garrison, Shannon Farnon and Kid Creole and the Coconuts, who provided the soundtrack album. Marc S. Fisher and Richard L. Albert produced. (94 mins)

▷ There can be no question that without George Romero's original **Night of the Living Dead** (Continental, 1968), cult monsters such as Jason in the *Friday 13th* series or Freddy Kreuger of Elm Street would not have flourished for as long as they did. Produced for a mere $200,000, Romero's

genuinely frightening little chiller became a cult classic and, as such, should have been left in peace to consolidate its reputation rather than provide the basis of comparison for a more expensive but far less effective remake. Faithfully following the original narrative (by Romero and John A. Russo) in which a group of seven people, while trapped in a remote farmhouse, spend their time fighting off an endless succession of walking corpses, Romero's retread added little to the original's squeal appeal. This time the film was shot in colour, which diminished rather than enhanced the overall effect; the zombies (created by Everett Burrell and John Vulich) were a tad more elaborate than their predecessors (but not more frightening), and the character of Barbara, who in the original was reduced to a state of permanent catatonia after a close encounter with a ghoul, was now made of sterner stuff. For the rest it was the formula as before but without the impact. It was directed without distinction by Tom Savini, a well-respected make-up artist specialising in horror, and featured Tony Todd, Patricia Tallman (as Barbara), Tom Towles, McKee Anderson, William Butler, Katie Finnerman, Bill Mosley, Heather Mazur, David Butler and Zachary Mott. John A. Russo and Ross Streiner produced. (96 mins)

△ If the greatness of a play (or opera) can be measured against its ability to survive and/or inspire an endless number of updates and interpretations, then Shakespeare's *Macbeth* is pretty close to the top of the pile. Age cannot wither its plot, nor custom stale the infinite variety of the many versions it has spawned – **Men Of Respect** being just one more not particularly distinguished example. Instead of 11th-century Scotland, the setting was a storm-struck 20th-century New York. Macbeth became Michael Battaglia (John Turturro), a lower-case hit-man whose boss is mafia big shot Charlie D'Amico (Rod Steiger). The anti-social Lady Macbeth resurfaced as Ruthie (Katherine Borowitz, illustrated with Turturro), while Banquo became Bankie Como (Dennis Farina). Macduff was Duffy (Peter Boyle), Mel and Don (Stanley Tucci and Carl Capotorto) were the murdered Malcolm and Donalbain, while the witches turned into a fortune-teller called Lucia (Lilia Skala). Though William Reilly's screenplay stuck pretty closely to Shakespeare's play in structure and plot, Reilly the director was unable to bring verisimilitude to the finished product. An air of contrivance seeped through the proceedings, robbing the adaptation of any credibility. The producer was Ephraim Horowitz. (107 mins)

▷ Twenty-three-year-old writer/director John Singleton made an impressive debut with **Boyz 'N The Hood**, a disturbing but accurate chronicle of the problems – mainly violent – faced by youngsters living in a black community in south-central Los Angeles. Beginning in 1984, then jumping seven years to 1991, the $6 million production, while embracing a diverse cross-section of ethnic types, focused on the lives of three boys and the roles played by their parents – and violence – throughout their teens. The most interesting of the group is Tre Styles (Cuba Gooding Jr, left), a bright though moody kid who, when we first meet him at the age of ten, leaves the care of his devoted mother (Angela Bassett) and moves in with Furious (Larry Fishburne, centre), his equally devoted father. Furious is determined to do the right thing by his only son and see that the boy grows up a credit to the community. At high school Tre's best friend is Ricky Baker (Morris Chestnut), a would-be football player who has already become a father. Completing the trio is Doughboy, Ricky's foul-mouthed half-brother (rapper Ice Cube, right) a scowling thug destined for a life of crime. To illustrate an opening credit claiming that one in 21 black males will end up murdered, Singleton succeeded in painting a convincing picture of a milieu in which the sounds of overhead surveillance helicopters, blaring police sirens and the echo of gun-shots are an everyday part of the environment. Not surprisingly, sex and violence were the prime topics of conversation in an urban hell whose moral and social centre of gravity no longer exist. Nia Long played Brandi, Doughboy's sensible girlfriend, with other roles under Singleton's confident and assured direction going to Tyra Ferrell, Meta King, Whitman Mayo and, as Tre, Doughboy and Ricky at age ten, Desi Arnez Hines II, Baha Jackson and Donovan McCrary. The producer was Steve Nicolaides. (111 mins)

▽ A truly tedious addition to the teen market, **Return To The Blue Lagoon** was a pointless sequel to *The Blue Lagoon* (1980) which, in turn, was a remake of the superior 1949 British film with the same title. Latest casting had Russian super-model Milla Jovovich (right) and TV hunk Brian Krause (left) fetching up, through circumstances too incredible for intelligent appraisal, on the very same island first inhabited by Donald Houston and Jean Simmons, then by Christopher Atkins and Brooke Shields. And just as their illustrious and equally attractive predecessors did before them, they grow up together, experiencing the joys of sex – and, in this latest outing, marriage before sex. Skirmishes with sharks and greedy cannibals did little to ginger up the screenplay Leslie Stevens and Doug Day Stewart devised from H. DeVere Stacpoole's novel *The Garden of God*, and the only things the film had going for it were the physical attributes of its two young stars and the eye-catching beauty of its exotic location – Taveuni in the Fiji archipelago. Lisa Pelikan played Ms Jovovich's mother, Courtney Phillips and Garette Patrick Ratcliff appeared as Jovovich and Krause's younger selves, with other roles in Randal Kleiser's hokey production going to Emma James, Jackson Barton, Nana Coburn, Brian Blane and Peter Hehir. It was directed by TV stalwart William Graham (100 mins)

◁ Who needs men? This was the question at the heart of **Mortal Thoughts**, a buddy-buddy thriller with *noir*-ish overtones. Its protagonists are two childhood girl-friends (Demi Moore, right and Glenne Headly, left) who run a beauty salon in New Jersey called Clip 'n' Dye, and whose respective spouses (John Pankow and Bruce Willis) are enough to give heterosexuality a bad name. Pankow is a loutish salesman, Willis an abusive thug. When Headly can take her husband's despicable behaviour no more, she murders him at a local carnival with a box-cutter. Attempting, via flashback, to get the truth, the whole truth and nothing but from Headly is Detective Harvey Keitel, in whose interrogation room much of the film takes place. As directed by Alan Rudolph, from a screenplay by William Reilly and Claude Kerven, it had its moments – the best of them occurring before Willis' demise. Occasional instances of over-direction intruded, no doubt in an attempt to compensate for the workaday plot. But the acting was good, especially from Headly and Moore, whose relationship was the film's most interesting and best explored element. The producers were John Fielder and Mark Tarlov. (104 mins)

357

△ A curious comedy-drama whose awkward combination of the cute and the ghoulish made for unsettling entertainment, **My Girl** top-starred Dan Aykroyd as a jokey mortician and the widower father of Vada (Anna Chlumsky, right) – an exceptionally bright ten-year-old who enrols in a poetry course run by teacher Griffin Dunne on whom she has a crush. Joining Aykroyd in his funeral home is hippie cosmetologist Jamie Lee Curtis, who's been hired to apply make-up to the corpses in her care, and who soon makes a play for the boss. Also in the cast, though by no means the star of the show, was Macaulay Culkin (left), fresh from his triumph in *Home Alone* (20th Century-Fox, 1990). He played Thomas J. Sennett, Vada's neighbour and the current boy in her life. The film's barrage of pre-publicity made major issues of the youngster's first screen kiss, as well as the fact that he is stung to death by bees. Parents who found themselves and/or their kids surprised and traumatised by this unlikely turn of events clearly never read the papers. Basically a rites-of-passage, coming-of-age story in which Vada emerged as the film's engaging heroine, *My Girl*, directed with a bold callousness of tone by Howard Zieff, and scripted in similar vein by Laurice Elehwany, appealed to some and repelled others. Young Anna Chlumsky's enchanting performance, however, made it consistently watchable. Richard Masur, Ann Nelson, Peter Michael Goetz and Jane Hallaren completed the cast for producer Brian Grazer. (102 mins)

△ The first Western film ever made inside the Kremlin and in KGB headquarters, **The Inner Circle**, directed by Andrei Konchalovsky (his first in Russia for 12 years) and based on truth, was the story of Ivan Sanshin (Tom Hulce), a subservient projectionist who is summoned, to project a film for Stalin in his private screening room in Moscow in 1939. After successfully completing the task (the movie was *The Great Waltz*, MGM, 1938), he is offered the job permanently with the proviso that he tell no one about it. Overjoyed, he gratefully accepts. Ivan's wife (Lolita Davidovich), meanwhile – much to her husband's displeasure – is obsessed with the orphaned daughter of a Jewish family who have been evicted from their home and condemned as enemies of the state. Though muddled both in its intention and its execution as well as in its uneasy shifts from comedy to pathos, the picture it conveyed of life in Stalinist Russia which, while by no means definitive, was generally compelling. Though it was difficult to warm to Hulce's character or to become involved in his far from satisfactory marriage, both he and Davidovich (both illustrated) were convincingly cast, as was Bob Hoskins as brutal KGB chief Lavrenti Beria who sexually forces himself on Davidovich during a trip to the Ural Mountains with Stalin and his entourage. Stalin was played forcefully by Aleksandr Zbruyev, with other roles going to Bess Meyer, Fydor Chaliapin Jr, Oleg Tabakov and Aleksandr Garin. The film was scripted by Konchalovsky and Anatoly Usov and produced by Claudio Bonivento. (137 mins)

△ Pat Conroy's sprawling 1986 novel, **The Prince Of Tides**, came to the screen pared of many of its excesses and, instead of giving equal time to all the members of the dysfunctional Wingo family, made the burgeoning relationship between Tom Wingo (Nick Nolte) and smart New York psychiatrist Susan Lowenstein (Barbra Streisand, illustrated with Nolte, who also directed) the main focus of the film. Narrated by Tom, and intercutting between past and present by means of flashbacks, the story he tells is of his poor, South Carolina tidewater family and the devastating effect of his abusive father (Brad Sullivan) and Southern belle mother (Kate Nelligan) on him and his siblings. The family has been so physically and emotionally mauled by a past incident as to mentally unhinge Tom's traumatised twin sister Savannah (Melinda Dillon). When Savannah, a poet living in Greenwich Village, again attempts suicide, Tom comes to New York at the request of Lowenstein, the girl's analyst. Though Tom's own life is on the verge of collapse – he's an unemployed high-school teacher and football coach, married with three children – he seeks refuge from his personal pain in humorous put-downs of himself. His meeting with Dr Lowenstein proves as much to his advantage as to his ailing sister's, for, in the six weeks he spends in Manhattan talking to her about their turbulent childhoods, the closeted demons suppressed by his whole family come tumbling out. Breaking the patient-doctor code of ethics, Tom and Lowenstein (who's unhappily married to an arrogant, unfaithful, concert violinist) embark on a romantic relationship, in the course of which Tom is able to help her seriously withdrawn son Bernard (Jason Gould) by becoming his personal football coach – a gesture which is helpful to both men. Despite all the misery experienced by the protagonists, the film ends happily, with the put-upon Bernard regaining his self-esteem, Lowenstein deciding to ditch her impossible spouse, Savannah on the mend and Tom, his confidence fully restored, returning to South Carolina and his wife (Blythe Danner) and able, in the film's last line, to say: 'I'm a teacher, a coach and a well-loved man.' Soap to be sure, but as scripted by Conroy and Becky Johnston and marvellously acted by Nolte, high-class soap – an uplifting, thoroughly entertaining romantic drama that certainly distilled the essence of the bestseller on which it was based. Though Streisand the actress made sure, via flattering close-ups and lingering shots of her shapely legs and fashionably manicured fingernails, that she always looked as good as the camera would allow (and why not?), Streisand the director recognised that the film wasn't really the psychoanalyst's story, but Tom's, a fact reflected in Nolte's top billing and the director's attention to detail in shaping his well-rounded performance. There was excellent work, too, from Kate Nelligan as Lila Wingo Newbury, Tom's strong-willed, long-suffering mother who becomes a grandiose patron of society; and from Brad Sullivan as her surly shrimp-boat captain husband. Also in it for producers Streisand and Andrew Karsch were George Carlin, Maggie Collier, Lindsay Wray and Brandlyn Whitaker. The lush music score and photography were by James Newton Howard and Stephen Goldblatt respectively. (135 mins)

▽ Violence and action are, of course, a frequent winning combination – at least as far as the box office is concerned. However, despite liberal lashings of both, as well as some obligatory sex and drug activity, **Stone Cold** left audiences precisely that. An old-fashioned actioner in which a cop (Brian Bosworth, right) infiltrates a white supremacist group of bikers known as The Brotherhood, it recycled practically every cliché the movies have perpetrated since Edwin S. Porter's *The Great Train Robbery* in 1903. And the miscasting of the rather prissy, leather-clad Bosworth as a macho biker, made it even more difficult to engage with Walter Doniger's seen-it-all-before screenplay. Despite its slam-bang action sequences, the film was a bomb. Lance Henriksen, William Forsyth, Arabella Holzbog, Sam McMurray and Richard Gant were also in it for producers Mace Neufeld and Yoram Ben-Ami. (90 mins)

▽ The impossibility of returning to the past was one of the themes explored in **Falling From Grace**, written by Larry McMurtry and directed by John Mellencamp, an erstwhile rock performer. Mellencamp (below) also starred, as easygoing country and western singer Bud Parks who, together with his beautiful Californian wife Alice (Mariel Hemingway, below) returns to his midwestern chicken farm in Doak City, Indianapolis to celebrate the 80th birthday of his grandfather (Dub Taylor). But the news on the home front isn't good. A disease is decimating the area's chicken population, while, on a more personal level Bud learns that P.J. (Kay Lenz), an erstwhile high-school girl friend, is having a sexual relationship with Speck (Claude Akins), his randy old father, despite the fact that she's married to Speck's son Parker (Brent Huff). Undeterred, Bud rekindles his own romance with P.J. who, though treating it as a mere fling, cannot convince Bud to do likewise, as a result of which his marriage to Alice begins to unravel. Though filmed in Mellencamp's hometown of Seymour, Indianapolis, in plot and characterisation the material traversed typical McMurtry territory, especially in the assertive P.J., a creation reminiscent of Ellen Burstyn's Lois Fallow in the *The Last Picture Show* (1971). Lenz was especially good in the role, and there were fine performances, too, from Deirdre O'Connell as Bud's sister, and from Larry Crane as Ramey, Bud's half-brother and confidante. Mellencamp's familiarity with the locale and material was in evidence throughout, and in his handling of the actors, including himself, he never put a foot wrong. Harry Sandler produced. (100 mins)

△ Child abuse and suicide were just two of several indigestible ingredients that went into **Radio Flyer**, a film about childhood and childhood fantasies, as seen through the eyes of Bobby and Mike (Joseph Mazzello, right, and Elijah Wood, centre, both of whom were excellent), two young brothers who live in northern California with their waitress mother (Lorraine Bracco, left) and abusive, drunken stepfather known as the King (Alec Baldwin). Bobby is particularly vulnerable to the King's ill treatment of him and, since he and his brother feel unable to confide in their hard-working mother, they retreat into a fantasy world in which Bobby hopes to turn his Radio Flyer wagon into an aeroplane in order to escape from the King's physical abuse. He does, but with tragic consequences. What should, and could, have been a deeply affecting mood-and-memory piece that probed the mysterious world of childhood with all its hopes and fears, became, under Richard Donner's top-heavy direction, a rather bleak and cumbersome mix of melodrama and fantasy. Though seen predominantly from the children's point of view, the film was narrated by an unbilled Tom Hanks (as the grown-up Mike), who is telling the story of his childhood to his own children. ('History,' he says somewhat cryptically, 'is all in the mind of the teller. Truth is in the telling.'). As the bullying stepfather, Alec Baldwin, who appeared either in shadow, from the waist down or in acute angles, and whose abuse of the kids took place off-screen, was only allowed a single dimension in which to work; ditto Ms Bracco, whose character as developed (or under-developed) by writer David Mickey Evans made little impact. Evans, originally slated to direct, was fired soon after starting the film in 1990 and was replaced; so was Rosanna Arquette, originally cast as the mother. *Radio Flyer* was produced by Donner and Lauren Shuler, and featured John Heard, Sean Baca, Robert Munic and, as the promoter of a Wild West show, Ben Johnson who was wasted in a nothing role. (113 mins)

▽ A buddy-buddy movie, in which one of the buddies (James Marshall, right) is white and the other (Cuba Gooding Jr, left) black, **Gladiators** was also formula film-making at its most predictable and manipulative. Racial tension in a Chicago high school and the sleazy world of illicit, underground boxing bouts provided the backdrop to a narrative in which Marshall and Gooding Jr are paired in a climactic match arranged by businessman Brian Dennehy, the unscrupulous villain of the piece. When the buddies refuse to treat each other as human punch-bags, Dennehy himself takes on Marshall, despite the latter being younger and fitter. Trailing *Karate Kid* overtones (it was co-scripted by Robert Lyle Kessler and Robert Mark Kamen from a story by Ddjorje Milicevic), the film was clearly aimed at teenagers but failed to offer them anything by way of novelty. Robert Loggia appeared as a fight promoter, John Heard as Marshall's debt-plagued father, Ossie Davis as a veteran boxing trainer, Francesca D. Roberts as a schoolteacher and Cara Buono as Marshall's statutory love interest. Rowdy Herrington directed as if by rote, and it was produced by Frank Price and Steve Roth. (98 mins)

△ Although the major baseball leagues never had to shut down through loss of manpower during World War II, Philip K. Wrigley of the Chicago Cubs formed a non-profit All-American Girls Professional Baseball League which continued drawing crowds until it disbanded in 1954. This was the inspiration for **A League Of Their Own**, a terrific comedy from the writing team of Lowell Ganz and Babaloo Mandel and director Penny Marshall. It starred Tom Hanks (left) who, like Robert De Niro in *Raging Bull* (United Artists, 1980), put on weight for his role as tobacco-chewing Jimmy Dugan, a former major league superstar whose career was hi-jacked by booze and an ailing knee. Dugan is reluctant to take on the job of coach to the girls at the Rockford Peaches club during their first turbulent season: a team that includes ace hitter and catcher Geena Davis (right), her younger sister Lori Petty, centre-field's Madonna, Rosie O'Donnell and Megan Cavanagh – winners all the way. Not only are the girls expected to excel on the playing field, but in order to dispel nasty rumours concerning their 'masculinisation', they're obliged to attend a kind of charm school to hone up on deportment, make-up, and all the other niceties associated with perfect young ladies. Ganz and Mandel's script was a joy. It never sacrificed characterisation for quick one-liners (of which there were plenty) and allowed an exceptionally fine cast, especially Hanks and Petty, to glow. The producers were Robert Greenhut and Elliott Abbott. (128 mins)

▽ Comedy and action didn't always coalesce in **Mo' Money**, nor was its plot as solid as it might have been. But that didn't prevent it playing like a breeze and increasing the popularity of its talented star, Damon Wayans, (right) who wrote it and was the film's executive producer. He played Johnny Stewart, a Brooklyner who, in order to be near beautiful Amber Evans (Stacey Dash), gives up his job in a bookshop and takes up employment in the mail-room of the credit card company for which she works. In cahoots with his brother Seymour (his real-life brother Marlon Wayans, left), Johnny devises a scam involving uncancelled credit cards in order to go on a shopping spree in the hope of impressing Amber. Unfortunately, his own little scam is soon tied into a larger one operating out of the same company. It involves murder, and is organised by villainous John Diehl, a company executive whose henchman Johnny is forced to become. All of which gave Damon Wayans ample opportunity to demonstrate what a fine mimic he was. Whether taking off a white personnel officer, a junkie, a pedantic black executive or a gay man having a spat with his lover (played by Marlon), he was very funny indeed. Unfortunately, Peter Macdonald's direction didn't quite have Wayans' inventive spark and wasn't able to decide whether to concentrate on action or on laughs. Still, *Mo' Money* was enjoyable hokum whose supporting roles featured Joe Santos as a cop hoping to steer the Stewart boys clear of crime, Harry J. Lennix, Mark Beltzman and Almayvonne. The producer was Michael Rachmil. (89 mins)

◁ Top-billing went to Tom Cruise (illustrated) on **A Few Good Men**, but pilfering the glory from under his nose was Jack Nicholson who, although he had only three scenes in director Rob Reiner's superbly entertaining courtroom drama, proverbially chewed up the scenery in all of them. He played Col. Nathan Jessep, a tough officer in the US Marine corps who, in the film's climactic show-down faces defence lawyer Lt. J.G. Kaffee (Cruise) in a murder case involving Pfc Downey and Lance Corporal Dawson (James Marshall and Wolfgang Bodison), two marines who have been accused of murdering private Santiago (Michael DeLorenzo) at the Guatanamo Bay Cuba naval base. The defendants claim they were ordered by their superiors to perform a 'Code Red' – a form of hazing – after Santiago threatened to tell the authorities that Dawson fired illegally at a Cuban watchtower. Though Santiago's death was officially registered as accidental, a poisoned rag had been stuffed down his throat prior to his mouth being taped. Downey and Dawson insist that they were ordered to eliminate Santiago by Lieut. Jonathan Kendrick

▽ **Sleepwalkers**, scripted by Stephen King, was a pretty routine job of work and a minor variation on the Dracula theme. An added ingredient was incest, with a mother (Alice Krige, right) and son (Brian Krause), when not making love, taking unhealthy bites out of beautiful young virgins. The only thing they seem to fear are cats. The story took place in the sleepy town of Travis, Ind., where Krause enrols as a 'transfer student' in the local school. After brutally murdering his interfering teacher he date-rapes Madchen Amick (left) in a cemetery. It was directed by Mick Garris whose reliance on the occasional shock effect was no substitute for real tension; and, apart from calling on the guest services of Stephen King himself as well as Joe Dante, John Landis, Clive Barker and Tobe Hooper, the movie featured Jim Haynie, Cindy Pickett, Ron Perlman and Lyman Ward. Mark Victor, Mark Grace and Nabeel Zahid produced. (91 mins)

(Kiefer Sutherland). As the commander of the marines stationed at Guatanamo Bay, Jessep takes the witness stand to deny Kiefer's involvement in the case. The confrontation, in which it would appear that Jessep is about to swallow Kaffee whole, does not, of course, happen that way, and in the best courtroom tradition, the bully is ultimately bullied. *A Few Good Men* was originally a successful Broadway play, running for 449 performances in 1989. It was written by Aaron Sorkin, whose own screen adaptation managed to open events up without losing any of the basic tension achieved on stage. Demi Moore co-starred opposite Cruise as his co-counsel and the first person to realise a Marine conspiracy is a-foot; while completing the team for the defence was Kevin Pollak as their research partner. Kevin Bacon was featured as the prosecuting attorney, with other roles under Reiner's scalpel-sharp direction going to J.T. Walsh, Christopher Guest, J.A. Preston, and Matt Craving. All were first rate. The film was produced by Reiner, David Brown and Andrew Scheinman for Columbia Pictures and Castle Rock Entertainment. (138 mins)

△ With its echoes of *Fatal Attraction* (Paramount, 1987), and *The Hand That Rocks The Cradle* (Interscape Communications, 1992), a nod in the direction of *Rosemary's Baby* (Paramount, 1968) and *The Tenant* (Paramount, 1976), and a backward glance at Ingmar Bergman's *Persona* (1966), **Single White Female**, produced and directed by Barbet Schroeder, shaped up as a chillingly effective psychological thriller that never insulted the intelligence. Written by Don Roos from the novel *SWF Seeks Same* by John Lutz, it starred Bridget Fonda (right) as a forceful, bright Manhattanite with her own computer company who lives in a desirable Upper West Side apartment. After breaking up with her boyfriend (Steven Weber), she advertises for a flatmate and finds the perfect candidate – or so she thinks – in the shape of Jennifer Jason Leigh (left). A self-effacing bookstore assistant, Leigh also happens to be an extremely fine cook, an expert house cleaner and a most considerate companion who is, simply, too good to be true. When, one day, she arrives home from the beauty parlour with her hair dyed the same colour as Fonda's and wearing it in exactly the same style, notice is definitively served that all is far from well – indeed Leigh, it transpires, is a psychotic killer. Schroeder's direction, light and unassuming at the film's start, gradually tightened its grip until the suspense became almost too much to bear. It was also extremely sexy. Leigh, Fonda and Weber made a formidable trio, with other roles going to Peter Friedman as a gay neighbour and Stephen Tobolowsky. Familiar material, to be sure, but deftly handled. (107 mins)

▷ **Hero** (GB: **Accidental Hero**) was a concept movie whose pitch went something like this: on a dark and stormy night, Bernie Laplante (Dustin Hoffman, right), an unappealing small-time hood and a failure in both his private and professional lives, comes across a crashed commercial airliner and, on an uncharacteristic impulse, enters the wrecked plane and saves a few lives. His work completed, he leaves before the police and firefighters arrive. No one sees him, no one knows who he is. A reward of a million dollars is offered to 'the Angel of Flight 104' as the unknown hero is dubbed, and it is claimed not by Bernie, but by handsome Vietnam vet John Bubber, with whom Bernie hitched a ride shortly after his anonymous rescue mission. How the rightful hero finally comes to be recognised was the film's gravitational pull, and it focused on the attempts of an ambitious TV reporter called Gayle Gayley (Geena Davis)

△ Like the Sorcerer's Apprentice gone wild in a world of high-tech, state-of-the-art movie magic, and with ear-shattering Dolby Surround-sound relentlessly blasting away at one's eardrums, Francis Ford Coppola unleashed an avalanche of sights and sounds to assault the senses in **Bram Stoker's Dracula**. A fervid, deliciously, extravagantly over-the-top interpretation of Stoker's enduring 1897 epistolary novel, it eschewed the more conventional 1927 Hamilton Deane-John Balderston version of events – which spawned the celebrated Tod Browning 1931 film starring Bela Lugosi (and a plethora of sequels, remakes, updates and variations therefrom) – and went right back to Stoker's original intentions. James V. Hart's screenplay began with a prologue in which Dracula's origins as the 15th-century king, Vlad the Impaler, are explained. Having been duped into believing that Vlad had been killed in battle, his beloved Elisabetta ended her own life rather than live without him, whereupon the enraged monarch renounced his allegiance to God and commenced his never-ending reign of evil. Centuries later Vlad, now Count Dracula (Gary Oldman) fetches up in Transylvania where he plays host to real-estate agent Jonathan Harker (Keanu Reeves) who's brokering a property deal for him in London. Harker, subsequently held hostage, ends up as fodder for the Count's three greedy concubines, while the scheming Count himself turns his attentions to his personal invasion of Britain. Though Coppola's imagination was always in full throttle, the familiar Dracula tale unfurled

– one of the people Bernie saved without her having managed to get a good look at him – to locate him. Complications ensue when Gayley, believing Bubber to be her saviour, falls in love with him. Top-starred Hoffman reverted to his Ratso Rizzo character in *Midnight Cowboy* (United Artists, 1966), although a good 20 years older, and Andy Garcia was cast as the matinee-idol hero that Gayle Gayley and all of America embraces. It was written by David Webb Peoples from a story by producer Laura Ziskin and directed by Stephen Frears in rambling, unfocused mode, its contours blurred, and with Garcia's character too under-developed to command attention. Hoffman mumbled irritatingly and characteristically throughout most of his scenes, leaving the acting honours to Geena Davis, whose ace-reporter role managed to make some pertinent comments about the media. Joan Cusack was fine as Hoffman's

with all Stoker's characters in tow. Winona Ryder (left) played Mina, Harker's fiancee and the object of the Count's desire; her friend Lucy was played by Sadie Frost, and Lucy's fiancé Lord Arthur Holmwood by Cary Elwes. Richard E. Grant was Dr Jack Seward and Anthony Hopkins was cast as the Dutch doctor-cum-metaphysician Abraham Van Helsing. Hart's screenplay dispelled the notion that vampires are functional only after sunset and can't abide bright light; and made the point that the Holy Cross is about as effective at repelling the evil creatures as a sharp slap on the wrist. Oldman (right) as Dracula, complete with Romanian accent, appeared in several guises – bloodless host, hairy incubus, the Devil, a wolf, a lizard, a bat, fog – and had make-up artist Michele Burke and brilliant costume designer Eiko Ishioka to thank for the visual concept on which he based his sophisticated performance. Equally impressive were Thomas Sanders' designs and Michael Ballhaus' photography, as well as the many stunning photographic tricks from Fantasy II Film Effects. Coppola's risk-taking direction, with its bold cross-cutting, dissolves and superimpositions, resulted in a boggling cinematic adventure which, in keeping with the times and the subject matter, evoked the spectre of AIDS in its references to infected blood and the plague. An American Zoetrope/Osiris Films production, it was produced by Coppola, Fred Fuchs and Charles Mulvehill, with Michael Apted and Robert O'Connor as executive producers. (123 mins)

bemused ex-wife, her real-life sister Susie Cusack was equally good as Hoffman's public defender, with other roles going to Kevin J. O'Connor, Maury Chaykin, Stephen Tobolowsky and an uncredited, bald Chevy Chase as Davis' assignment editor. (116 mins)

▽ Jean-Claude Van Damme (illustrated) went back to the past for **Nowhere To Run**, an old-fashioned actioner that blended melodrama with elements of the western – neither genre winning through. He played a wrongly accused bank-robber who, after a jail-break hides out, together with the stolen booty, in a farm belonging to a beautiful widow (Rosanna Arquette) and her two children (Kieran Culkin and Tiffany Taubman). In return for her hospitality, she gets to play a nude love scene with him, and he saves her and her brood from the clutches of a nasty real-estate developer (Joss Ackland) and his henchman (Ted Levine). Though Van Damme (who at one point is seen skinny-dipping) abandoned his familiar trade-mark kickboxing technique for more Westernised forms of self-defence, the opposition on this occasion was hardly worth the effort. Anthony Starke and Edward Blatchford completed the cast, it was directed with no sense of style or purpose by Robert Harmon, scripted by a trio of writers (Joe Eszterhas, Leslie Boehm and Randy Feldman) who should have known better (story by Eszterhas and Richard Marquand), and produced by Craig Baumgarten and Gary Adelson. (94 mins)

▷ Bad taste for the sake of bad taste was about all that **Hexed** had to offer. A spoof whose target was female slasher movies such as *Fatal Attraction* (Paramount, 1987) and *Basic Instinct* (Carolco-Tri-Star, 1992), it starred Arye Gross, as a 30-year-old hotel desk clerk who, to add a dash of piquancy to his dreary existence, fantasises to his co-workers about his extraordinarily colourful past. Fantasy becomes reality, though, with the appearance of a drop-dead gorgeous French model (American Claudia Christian, right, with Gross) with whom Gross sets himself up on a date by impersonating a man who just happens to be blackmailing her. Gross soon finds out that

△ 'What would you do,' asks Bill Murray in Groundhog Day, 'if you were stuck in one place and everything was exactly the same, and nothing that you did mattered?' In this engagingly original, well executed fantasy, Murray played an arrogant, self-satisfied TV weatherman who, after insulting practically all his colleagues as well as everyone else with whom he comes into contact, inexplicably finds himself having to re-live, over and over again, one February 2nd (Groundhog Day) in the town of Punxsutawney, Pa. The day into which Murray has been time-locked begins at 6 a.m. with Sonny and Cher singing 'I Got You, Babe' and continues until turn-in time, in the course of which Murray gets to replay the same daily events with unfailing regularity until he realises the folly of his anti-social ways and is transformed from resistible cynic to a lovable, caring member of society. A feel-good comedy the great Frank Capra might have been proud to make, **Groundhog Day**, scripted for giggles and smiles rather than guffaws by Danny Rubin and director Harold Ramis (story by

his luscious date is, in fact, a psychotic killer who's spent six years in a mental institution. Undaunted, the shnook falls in love with her while she, in the meantime, continues her murderous little ways. Hexed by a lack of talent both in front of and behind the camera, and with only the occasional moment of vulgar humour coming to the surface in writer-director Alan Spencer's foul-mouthed screenplay – usually at the expense of the cops – the film failed to find an audience and suffered a hasty demise. Adrienne Shelly, Ray Baker, R. Lee Ermey and Norman Fell were in it too, and it was produced by Marc S. Fischer and Louis G. Friedman. (90 mins)

Rubin), was consistently inventive and entertaining and gave Bill Murray (left) a chance to prove, in a Scrooge-like transformation, that he could be equally effective as both the man you love to hate and Mr Nice Guy. Andie MacDowell (right) charmingly co-starred as Murray's producer and, ultimately, love interest, with other parts under Ramis' exuberant direction going to Stephen Tobolowsky (excellent as Murray's long-time-no-see ex-schoolmate), Chris Elliott, Brian Doyle-Murray, Marita Geraghty and Angela Paton. Director Ramis was in it too, as a neurologist, and co-produced with Trevor Albert. (103 mins)

▽ In writer-producer-director Paul Mazursky's **The Pickle** top-billed Danny Aiello (left) played Harry Stone, a middle-aged director whose once illustrious career is on the skids. A recent string of flops, culminating in his latest project – a sci-fi extravaganza about a giant pickle grown by a bunch of farm kids – has done terrible things to his blood pressure and depressed the hell out of him. 'I didn't make a movie,' he bemoans to his long-time agent (Jerry Stiller, right), 'I committed a crime.' Demeaned and dispirited, he checks in at New York's Plaza Hotel and has to cope not only with the prospect of the movie's upcoming sneak preview, but with an ex-wife (Dyan Cannon), his very young French girlfriend (Clotilde Coureau), his rehabilitated drug-addict son (Chris Penn), his mother (Shelley Winters) and the production head of his studio (Barry Miller). Paul Mazursky appeared as a boyhood friend-cum-projectionist who will be screening the sneak preview of 'The Pickle', with other roles going to Ally Sheedy (as the star of the film-within-the-film), Rebecca Miller, Jodi Long, Stephen Tobolowsky and, in cameo bits, Spalding Gray, Little Richard, Griffin Dunne, Isabella Rossellini and Dudley Moore. To judge from the number of punters who paid good money to see it, the film, which took several mean-spirited swipes at the people who run the studios, was of interest only to people who run the studios. (103 mins)

▷ Weighing in at around $126 million, **The Last Action Hero** was a humungous parody of state-of-the-art, special effects-driven actioners in which the on-screen merchandise is blown to smithereens every couple of minutes; it was also a parody of Arnold Schwarzenegger (right), the show's star and executive producer. The cinematic equivalent of taking a wrecking ball to a peanut, the film set out to dissect (and lampoon) the nature of cartoon-type screen violence by confronting action-movie hero Jack Slater (Schwarzenegger) with real-life violence. Although not without its wry moments, the movie's confused premise and a screenplay by Shane Black and David Arnot, from a story by Zak Penn and Adam Leff (a definite case of too many cooks), lacked definition of purpose. The film didn't know what it wanted to be or where it wanted to go. Underlying the narrative was an 11-year-old boy (Austin O'Brien) whose devotion to Jack Slater (he has seen his latest movie 37 times) pays dividends when he literally finds himself inside a Slater movie, accompanying his hero in a 1966 Pontiac convertible as they're pursued by the bad guys. Because Master O'Brien has seen the film so many times, he's able to tip Slater off about what's coming next, thus allowing the last action hero to stay one jump ahead of the plot. It was a cute idea, but not cleverly enough developed, and because

▷ Though playwright Neil Simon made the obligatory attempts to open out his award-winning 1991 Broadway hit **Lost In Yonkers**, and even added one major character not in the original play, director Martha Coolidge wasn't able to disguise the theatrical origins of its confined setting – a Brooklyn candy-store and the apartment above it. The action of Simon's moving domestic comedy-drama takes place in 1942, and centres on a martinet grandmother Kurnitz (Irene Worth) who has to cope with her backward 36-year-old daughter Bella (Mercedes Ruehl). In addition, she has been asked by her son Eddie (Jack Laufer) to look after Jay and Arty, his two teenaged boys (Brad Stoll, left and Mike Damons, right), while he travels south in the hope of earning some money to pay off a loan shark. How the youngsters cope in their new environment, which is made a mite more colourful by the presence of their Uncle Louie (Richard Dreyfuss), a small-time hood lying low from a gangster called Hollywood Harry (Robert Guy Miranda), gave Simon's story its comic pulse; while the fortunes of Bella, and the romance she has with the correspondingly gauche Johnny (David Strathairn), an usher at the local cinema she regularly attends, provided its emotional kick. Though Simon imposed a happy – or, at any rate, more positive – ending on the movie (in which Bella finds the courage to leave her stentorian mother), the mood and the humour of the play were faithfully retained. Worth and Ruehl, repeating their Tony Award-winning performances, were chilling and heart-breaking respectively; Stoll and Damons were charmingly funny, Dreyfuss (in the role played on stage by Kevin Spacey) gave a pretty good imitation of a whirlwind, while Strathairn as Johnny – a character talked about but not seen in the play – was excellent. Susan Merson completed the cast. It was evocatively designed by David Chapman, and produced by Ray Stark. (112 mins)

so much of the action took place in a movie-within-a-movie, it was difficult to get involved with the plot-within-the-plot, or any of its characters. Anything goes and everything went, including credibility. There were some arcane references to movies and moviemaking, and some in-jokes beyond the comprehension of the hordes of young Schwarzenegger fans at whom the film was aimed. With its blurred paramaters, big-budget, seen-it-all-before chases, wild and woolly shoot-outs and ultra noisy sound-track, *The Last Action Hero* was the perfect recipe for a headache. Arnie playing Arnie hardly extended his acting range; and young Austin O'Brien's Hollywood kid was a mite too knowing to warm to. Which left the acting honours to a truly impressive supporting cast that included F. Murray Abraham, Art Carney, Charles Dance (as yet another British villain), Frank McRae, Robert Prosky, Anthony Quinn, Mercedes Ruehl, Ian McKellen, Joan Plowright and Tina Turner. In addition there were cameos from Keith Barish, Jim Belushi, Chevy Chase, Chris Connelly, Karen Duffy, Larry Ferguson, Maria Shriver, Sharon Stone, Jean-Claude Van Damme, Melvin Van Peebles and Damon Wayans. John McTiernan directed it as a series of action set-pieces rather than as a coherent whole, and co-produced with Steve Roth. (130 mins)

▽ Sublimely efficient, high-gloss, high-tech, high-satisfaction entertainment, **In The Line Of Fire** was that *rara avis* of the industry: an adult suspense thriller whose plot made sense, rarely defied logic, kept audiences gripped, and doggedly refused to insult the intelligence. It starred Clint Eastwood (below), on the very top of his form, as Frank Horrigan, a fifty-something, piano-playing Secret Service agent whose commitment to his job has cost him his marriage. Thirty years earlier Horrigan had been a member of the Secret Service group assigned to protecting President Kennedy in Dallas. His failure, that fateful November day, to save the President's life, has haunted him ever since and when, in the course of a routine investigation, he comes across a man obsessed with presidential assassinations, danger warnings begin to sound – not, it transpires, without reason. The suspect (John Malkovich), whose name is Mitch Leary, starts calling Horrigan at all hours to tell him about his plans to eliminate the current President. It's terrible news, but it gives Horrigan a chance to redeem himself three decades later. How he does so formed the basis of Jeff Maguire's taut, beautifully structured screenplay, in the course of which Horrigan gets to have a brief affair with an attractive, much younger agent (Rene Russo) who is also attached to the President's security team. Though Eastwood, by now a dab hand at roles which required him to age gracefully and attractively, brought his uniquely masculine brand of magic to Horrigan, the showier of the two main men's roles went to Malkovich whose reptilian cool and manic sense of evil was compulsively watchable. They made a formidable duo, playing cat and mouse games that were the mainstay of the movie. *In The Line Of Fire* was directed by Germany's Wolfgang Petersen with a sure sense of where the story was going and how best to get it there; and also featured Dylan McDermott, Gary Cole, Fred Dalton Thompson, John Mahoney, Jim Curley and John Heard. A Columbia-Castle Rock presentation, it was produced by Jeff Apple. (128 mins)

△ **Poetic Justice**, writer-director John Singleton's eagerly awaited follow up to *Boyz 'N The Hood* (1991) was a disappointing mish-mash. Part drama, part romantic comedy, it dealt with a young girl from South Central Los Angeles called Justice (Janet Jackson, right) who eventually comes to terms with the traumatic loss of her boyfriend – murdered by gang members at a drive-in movie – first, through the poetry she writes and, eventually, through the love of Lucky, a mailman, played by Tupac Shakur (left). Initially hostile to Lucky, who once made a pass at her, Justice gradually changes her mind and soon recognises the guy as a kindred spirit. Her change of heart takes place during a trip from L.A. to Oakland, San Francisco in the company of her gullible, kind-hearted best friend Iesha (Regina King) and Iesha's current, quick-tempered boyfriend Chicago (Joe Torry) who works with Lucky in the post office. It was the 'road' element of Singleton's second feature that justified its existence – the best sequences being the quartet's visit to an African fair and their gate-crashing of a family reunion. For the rest *Poetic Justice*, which laboured heavily under the burden of having Justice's poetry read over the soundtrack (and which in reality was the work of poet Maya Angelou), didn't quite know where it wanted to be and floundered in its own lack of direction. Also cast were Tyra Ferrell, Roger Guenveur Smith, Q-Tip, Tone Loc, Miki Howard, Keith Washington, Maya Angelou and, most memorably, Billy Zane and Lori Petty as the stars of the drive-in movie Justice and her boyfriend are watching before he is murdered. It was produced by Steve Nicolaides. (110 mins)

△ The facts behind **El Mariachi** were as remarkable as the finished product itself. It was made by a 24-year-old Mexican-American called Robert Rodriguez who'd been making movies since he was 13. It cost $7000, a large chunk of which came from the $3000 the young would-be director earned for his services as a guinea pig in a research hospital. The shooting schedule – on location in Mexico – was two weeks, and although the film was initially intended for release in the Spanish home-video market, it was picked up by Columbia, had some cosmetic post-production work done to it, and was entered at the Sundance Festival where it won the audience prize. A kind of *noir* Western, its feeling for both genres attested to its young film-maker's awareness of and affection for certain age-old Hollywood traditions in much the same way that Sergio Leone's more lavishly produced Spaghetti Westerns had revealed a pre-digested feel for its familiar material. The story was simple. El Mariachi, an unemployed singer/guitarist (Carlos Gallardo, illustrated) arrives at a small Mexican town and is mistaken for hitman Azul (Reinol Martinez) who has just broken out of jail and is on the vengeance trail of a drug-dealer called Moco (Peter Marquardt). Moco's henchmen, meanwhile, are out to get Azul. As El Mariachi and Azul both wear black and both carry guitar cases, they're easily mistaken for one another, thus cueing in the well-worn mistaken identity ploy. Romantic interest was supplied by Consuelo Gomez as Domino, the owner of a local tavern whose initial suspicion of the musician melts after he convinces her that he is innocent, then charms her with his singing. Though, inevitably, the film betrayed its humble origins in the often crude way it looked and sounded, *El Mariachi* was, nonetheless, a rough diamond that instantly attested to its director's cinematic skills and his sure-fire ability to tell a story. Rodriguez also wrote the screenplay, received an editor's credit, and co-produced it with Carlos Gallardo. As an example of how to make the most with the least, the film – its technical shortcomings notwithstanding – was a minor miracle. (84 mins)

▽ Period detail and the accurate evocation of aristocratic, class-conscious England in the late 1930s were high on the list of accomplishments by the Merchant Ivory team who brought Kazuo Ishiguro's distinguished 1989 Booker Prize-winning novel **The Remains of the Day** to the screen. And, as in Edith Wharton's *The Age of Innocence*, the two central characters were not destined to spend the rest of their lives together, despite the deep friendship each felt for the other. Though largely related in flashback through narrated letters, the film began with Stevens (Anthony Hopkins, left), an elderly butler at Darlington Hall, journeying across country to pay a visit to Miss Kenton (Emma Thompson, right), a former housekeeper who, 20 years earlier, was employed by the recently deceased Lord Darlington (James Fox, perfectly cast). The new owner of Darlington Hall is ex-congressman Lewis (Christopher Reeve), a wealthy American who had known the stately home and its owner in their heyday. Lewis has retained Stevens' services and it is during the old butler's visit to Miss Kenton, whom he is hoping to persuade to return to her old position at Darlington Hall, that Stevens relives the formative years of his life in service. Actively against any emotional attachments between members of his staff, he does nothing to encourage (beyond friendship) the interest shown in his well-being by the pretty and efficient Miss Kenton, the new housekeeper, who is clearly falling in love with him. Rather than allow romance to fill his leisure hours, he relaxes, instead, with a penny-dreadful novel and a cigar. In time, this rigidity of resolve proves to be one of the two greatest regrets of his life; the other is the realisation that his beloved and respected employer was a Nazi sympathiser. Stevens' sombre reflections on these two aspects of life at Darlington Hall in the late 1930s, provides the food for thought that occupies him on his emotional cross-country visit, and Anthony Hopkins was superb in conveying their sad legacy. Nor did he put a foot wrong in portraying Stevens' unwavering, unquestioning dedication to his position. It was a marvellously controlled performance, whose solid depiction of a man's slavish and unyielding sense of duty ultimately made it difficult to see just what it was that the fun-loving and life-enhancing Miss Kenton actually found to love in him. Emma Thompson, also giving the performance of her life, breezed through stuffy Darlington Hall like a breath of fresh air. James Ivory directed from Ruth Prawer Jhabvala's magnificent screenplay, with exemplary fidelity to the novel and a strong supporting cast that featured Peter Vaughan, Hugh Grant and Tim Piggot-Smith. Mike Nichols, John Calley and Ismail Merchant produced. (134 mins)

△ It was not at all surprising that Martin Scorsese's **The Age Of Innocence** gave screen credit to the people responsible for the table decorations, the general etiquette and the food that was served throughout the director's luxurious treatment of Edith Wharton's Pulitzer Prize-winning 1921 novel of the same name. The meticulous attention to period detail (New York in 1870) – from place settings, cigar trimmers and fabrics, to the furniture, the floral arrangements and the paintings – was one of the many pleasures in this sumptuous recreation of a world long gone. Remaining remarkably faithful to the book Scorsese, who co-wrote the screenplay with erstwhile film critic Jay Cocks, made sure that all the important narrative twists and turns of Wharton's society-driven plot were intact while nonetheless focusing on the novel's three central characters. Michelle Pfeiffer played Ellen Olenska, a stunningly beautiful American woman who, after a lengthy sojourn in Europe, where she was rumoured to have enjoyed a romantic liaison with her male secretary, returns to New York to divorce her womanising husband, a Polish Count. It's a decision that does not go down well with the conservative society in which she moves, and it falls to Newland Archer (Daniel Day-Lewis), a wealthy young lawyer engaged to the eminently suitable May Welland (Winona Ryder), to persuade the Countess Olenska that divorce will lead to her social ostracisation. As it is she's already considered something of a loose woman but, as she and Archer continue to meet on the increasingly flimsy grounds of legal business, they fall in love – a hopeless passion that, if pursued further, will ruin both their reputations. Accepting that the affair is doomed, Newland marries May, who is steelier and more manipulative than one might have

◁ Jason Priestley (centre), of TV's *Beverly Hills 90210*, made his feature debut in **Calendar Girl**, in which he starred as a rebellious young man whose pubescent initiation into sex via images of Marilyn Monroe culminates with a trip from his dreary hometown in Nevada to Hollywood, where he and two of his mates (Jerry O'Connell, right and Gabriel Olds, left) – driving a blue Galaxy 500 convertible – hope to meet the famous screen icon herself. The time is 1962, just after Monroe has been fired from *Something's Got To Give* (20th Century-Fox), and after arriving in Los Angeles, the boys crash down in a bachelor pad belonging to Priestley's ageing hipster-cum-actor uncle (Joe Pantoliano). Up to this point the film, directed by first-timer John Whitesell, had its fair share of laughs and kept interest simmering. It was in the latter stages of the story – when the boys actually get to meet Monroe (Stephanie Anderson,, that the film loses its way. Priestley's good looks were an obvious plus for the teen market at which the film was aimed; but the only performances really worth watching were provided by Stephen Tobolowsky and Kurt Fuller as a pair of thuggish repo men for whom Priestley once worked, and whose convertible blue car he has borrowed without asking. It was written by Paul W. Shapiro, and produced by Debbie Robbins and Gary Marsh with Penny Marshall and Elliott Abbott as executive producers for Parkway Productions. (90 mins)

imagined, while Ellen returns to Europe. In a moving epilogue, which takes place 20 years later, Newland's son (Robert Sean Leonard) persuades his father to pay a visit to Ellen, who is living in Paris. Newland agrees, but gets no further than the sidewalk outside her apartment before changing his mind. A far cry from the modern, violent New York of several previous Scorsese films, *The Age Of Innocence* nevertheless found its director successfully facing the challenge of a necessarily different approach with his customary flair and cinematic brilliance. And if, at times, the film had a too studied, almost academic and even airless quality that duplicated the formal tone of the society under observation, its elegance and sense of style won through. Both Day-Lewis (left) and Ryder (right) were excellent in roles that, by definition, were fairly subdued, which left the way open for Michelle Pfeiffer, in more extrovert mode, to radiate as Ellen. The supporting cast included many English actors, notably Miriam Margolyes who was superb as May's autocratic, overbearing grandmother Mrs. Manson Mingott, Richard E. Grant, Alec McCowen, Sian Phillips, Michael Gough, Norman Lloyd and Jonathan Pryce, alongside Americans Carolyn Farina, Alexis Smith, Mary Beth Hurt and Geraldine Chaplin. It was narrated by Joanne Woodward. Michael Ballhaus was the cinematographer, Dante Ferretti was responsible for the production design, Speed Hopkins and Jean-Michel Hugon for the art direction, Robert J. Franco for the set decorations and Gabriella Pescucci for the costumes. The music was by Elmer Bernstein and the film was produced – at a cost of $40 million – for Cappa/De Fina Productions by Barbara De Fina. (136 mins) .

△ Beginning with a well-staged car chase, and ending with an exciting boat chase, **Striking Distance** (originally called *Three Rivers*) was a violent, routine actioner that starred Bruce Willis (right) as an alcoholic cop trailing a serial killer. Having alienated himself from the other members of his department for accusing a colleague of excessive violence, Willis' troubles continue with the murder of his cop father (John Mahoney) and, finally, with being turfed out of the force for insisting that a derelict arrested as the killer is the wrong man. Two years later, Willis is working for Pittsburgh's River rescue team. With his sympathetic new partner Sarah Jessica Parker, he sets out to track down his father's killer, who strikes again. This time, though, the victims are all women associated with Willis. Director Rowdy Herrington's far-fetched screenplay, written with Martin Kaplan, was more convoluted than his in-your-face direction, but the action was what the star's die-hard fans wanted and they weren't disappointed. Dennis Farina was Willis' unsupportive cop uncle, with Tom Sizemore, Robert Pastorelli (left), Brian James and Timothy Busfield also cast. An Arnon Milchan Production, it was produced by Milchan, Tony Thomopoulos and Hunt Lowry. (101 mins)

△ In attempting to revitalise a genre whose hey-day had come and gone during Hollywood's golden years, director George Hill offered audiences **Geronimo: An American Legend**, a Western that inverted many of the genre's traditional elements and which, most notably, was characterised by an absence of heroes at the final fade. In shifting the emphasis from gung-ho histrionics to a truthful, unheroic reconstruction of the events relating to the Apaches between 1885 and 1886, Hill's earnest efforts to be fair both to the warring Chiricahua

▽ Death, a subject already explored by writer Bruce Joel Rubin in *Ghost* (Paramount, 1990) and *Jacob's Ladder* (Tri-Star/Carolco, 1990), was again the first item on his agenda in **My Life**, a five-handkerchief weepie with which he made his directorial debut. Its central character was a workaholic publicity director called Bob Jones (Michael Keaton, below) who learns that he has terminal, inoperable cancer. The timing could not be worse. His wife Gail (Nicole Kidman, below) is pregnant with their first child (a son) and, in all likelihood, Bob will be dead before the baby is born. So what he does is make a home video for his unborn son in which he gives the boy a few pointers about growing up. The video is also a resolution of his own life since, in the course of making it, he is able to come to terms with his past (especially his rejected Ukrainian-American parents) and with his own childhood. Despite the potential grimness of the material, it wasn't until the last half hour or so that Rubin's film, which had hitherto managed to retain a sunny disposition, took on a darker, more sombre hue, its laughter turning to tears. Keaton, in one of his better performances, was adept at both the humour and the tragedy inherent in the role; and there was a touching performance from Nicole Kidman, fast proving herself more than just a pretty face. Haing S. Ngor was effective as an Asian faith-healer who helps Bob confront his roots, with other roles going to Michael Constantine as Bob's alienated father, Rebecca Schull as his mother, Bradley Whitford, Toni Sawyer, Romy Rosemont, Lee Garlington and Queen Latifah. Director Rubin wasn't always able to control the gamut of different moods and emotions thrown up by the script but did well enough. Rubin, Jerry Zucker and Hunt Lowry produced. (114 mins)

braves and the U.S. army resulted in a sober-minded epic that was, for all its good intentions, never as gripping as it should have been. Though Geronimo's name appeared in the film's title, the story was, in fact, told from the viewpoint of a rookie cavalry officer called Britton Davis (Matt Damon), whose 1929 book *The Truth About Geronimo* painted a far more savage portrait of his subject than was evident in the film. Davis, straight out of West Point, serves under Lt. Col. Gatewood (Jason Patric, top-starred), a Virginian ex-Confederate who, following a skirmish between the Chiricahua Apaches and the cavalry, escorts Geronimo, a man he knows and respects, to Brig. Gen. Crook (Gene Hackman, right). A liberal player in the Indian situation, Crook pronounces the Indian Wars at an end and resettles Geronimo in a farming reservation in Arizona. For a while all is quiet on the western front, but the fragile peace is soon shattered when an army party led by veteran Indian scout Al Sieber (Robert Duvall, left) mistakenly kills an Apache medicine man (Pato Hoffmann). Geronimo and his followers quit the reservation and head for Mexico – murder and destruction their vengeful purpose. The army has no choice but to counter attack, and when Gen. Crook

fails to persuade Geronimo to surrender, he is relieved of his position and replaced by Gen. Nelson Miles (Kevin Tighe) who, unlike his tolerant predecessor, has no compunction in wiping the troublesome Apaches off the face of the earth. As narrated by young Davis, there were no real heroes and no real villains to praise or castigate. The events and characters were imbued with certain ambiguities that made for a more complex overview of the situation and of the men who shaped it. The film had its fair share of massacres, Indian raids, cavalry skirmishes and most of the other elements germane to Westerns, but it also invited audiences to think about the events depicted rather than simply respond to them emotionally. With the possible exception of Robert Duvall, there were no stand-out performances – just competent ones that more than fulfilled the unflashy demands of John Milius and Larry Gross' screenplay (story by Milius). Completing the bill for producers Walter Hill and Neil Canton were Rodney A. Grant, Steve Reevis, Carlos Palomino and Victor Aaron. It was stunningly photographed by Lloyd Ahearn in Moab, Utah, on locations used many times over, and in very different circumstances, by the great John Ford. (115 mins)

△ Originally conceived and filmed as a musical but re-edited – minus most of the songs and dances after unfavourable audience reactions at previews – **I'll Do Anything** revealed the scars of its drastic surgery. In his first film as writer, producer (with Polly Platt) and director since 1987, James L. Brooks' mild satire on the movie industry attempted, with only a modicum of success, to knit together three plot strands of varying quality. Plot number one was about Matt Hobbs (Nick Nolte, right) an out-of-work actor who, after his wife (Tracey Ullman) is sent to jail, is saddled with their impossible six-year-old daughter (Whittni Wright, left). Attempting to eke out a living, Matt takes a job as chauffeur to Burke Adler (Albert Brooks), a self-absorbed producer, thus cueing in the film's second plot when he becomes romantically involved with Burke's insecure script reader (Joely Richardson). Burke, meanwhile, is having a fling with a divorced market-researcher (Julie Kavner), thus providing the third strand of plot. There were some terrific moments but the fair share of one-liners and satiric observations had limited audience appeal, and the film suffered irreparably from the damage inflicted on it in the editing room. Nolte was never able to get a handle on his role, and wasn't much helped by Ms Whittni Wright whose adorable looks belied the unpleasant moppet beneath. (115 mins)

▷ Aimed essentially at the teen market, and with a refreshing absence of gratuitous violence, **Blankman** was an over-the-top comic caper. Rich in Rube Goldberg-type gadgetry, its superhero Darryl Walker (Damon Wayans, right) was an enthusiastic young inventor who doubles as self-appointed crimebuster Blankman in the fictional town of Metro, Illinois. Wayans' screenplay, based on his own story and written with J.F. Lawton, kicked in when, after a local police strike, the inefficient crusader, wearing a cape made from an old housedress that once belonged to his grandmother, comes to the rescue of Mayor Harris (Christopher Lawford) who is being held hostage by mobster Michael Minelli (Jon Polito). Blankman

△ Unlike the majority of sequels, **My Girl 2** made a genuine attempt to take its young heroine of *My Girl* (1991), a $120 million box-office grosser, a couple of stages further along the path to adulthood. Beginning two years after the first film, Vada Sultenfuss (Anna Chlumsky, centre), now 13 years old, still lives in Madison, PA. with her stepmother Shelly (Jamie Lee Curtis, right), now pregnant, and father (Dan Aykroyd, left). But where Madison had been the focal point of the first film, 1970s L.A. featured prominently in the sequel, for it is here that Vada goes, as part of a school project, to learn more about her mother, who died in labour. In the process, Vada makes the acquaintance of a cop (Keone Young), an ailing poet (Aubrey Morris) and an egocentric film director (Richard Beymer). She also learns that her mother was married once before and, after meeting Maggie's ex-husband (John David Souther), is shown a home-movie of her in the film's most affecting scene. Aykroyd and Curtis occupied barely a third of the film's running-time, allowing Miss Chlumsky to run away with the acting honours. It was directed (as was the first) by Howard Zieff and scripted by Janet Kovalci. Brian Grazer produced. (99 mins)

▷ An expensive ($70 million) horror flick with a touch of class, **Wolf**, directed by Mike Nichols from a screenplay by Jim Harrison and Wesley Strick, had a terrific beginning before settling into conventional movie lycanthropy in its less compelling second half. Jack Nicholson (right) starred as Will Randall, a worldly, civilised editor-in-chief for a publishing house who, while driving in Vermont one snowy night, hits a wolf. Mistakenly believing the animal to be dead, he touches it and is bitten on the hand. It's nothing serious, and he travels back to New York more concerned with the prospect of losing his job in the wake of a takeover by billionaire tycoon Raymond Alden (Christopher Plummer). His concern is not

not only gets the baddies in the end, but also wins the heart of attractive Kimberley Jonz (Robin Givens), a TV reporter whose accounts of Blankman's various escapades help turn him into a national celebrity. Manically directed by Mike Binder with far too much emphasis on slapstick, the film was good-natured enough and had its heart in all the right places but held little interest for adults. Basically a showcase for its enterprising and very appealing young star, *Blankman* also featured David Alan Grier (left) as Wayans' protective brother Kevin, Lynne Thigpen as his grandmother and Jason Alexander as an unsavoury newspaperman. The producers were Eric L. Gold and C.O. Erickson. (92 mins)

misplaced: at a formal dinner party given by Alden Will is duly fired but he gets to meet Alden's beautiful daughter Laura (Michelle Pfeiffer, left) with whom he begins an affair. However, strange things start happening to him, beginning with a thick growth of hair surrounding the bite on his hand. There's also a definite, youthful surge in his energy level and a heightened awareness in his sensory powers – all of which helps him in his schemes against the duplicitous Stewart Swinton (James Spader, excellent), a former protégé of his who has replaced him as editor-in-chief. So far so good. Unfortunately, this interesting take on the werewolf legend wasn't sustained as, little by little, Will succumbs to the burgeoning wolf in him and, at full moon, commits some grisly acts of violence on both animals and human beings. A pity, for up to this point *Wolf* was a sophisticated mix of horror and satire which, while paying homage to the werewolf genre, also took some enjoyable swipes at the wolf-eat-wolf world of publishing. Nicholson gave his subtlest performance in some while, though he had to work hard to make his personality felt through Rick Baker's werewolf wizardry and special effects. Michelle Pfeiffer did the best she could with the underwritten role of Laura, whose romance with Nicholson was the film's least successful element. Nor was there much meat for Kate Nelligan, as Nicholson's wife, to sink her teeth into. Strong supporting performances came from Eileen Atkins, David Hyde Pierce, Ron Rifkin, Prunella Scales, Richard Jenkins and Om Puri. Douglas Wick produced. (125 mins)

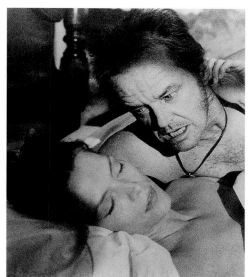

△ In **The Next Karate Kid**, the latest (and last) instalment of the long-running series, Ralph Macchio was replaced as Mr. Miyagi's star pupil by Julie Pierce (Hilary Swank, right), a 17-year-old with attitude who, after the death of her parents in a car crash, is taken up by the platitude-sprouting Miyagi (Noriyuki 'Pat' Morita, left). By pic's end she's every bit as effective with a karate chop as her illustrious predecessor, and, after coming to terms with her parents' tragic death, even gets a chance – on prom night – to see off the school bullyboy (Michael Cavalieri) who's been trying to have his way with her. Though not as violent as the earlier films in the series ('Fighting not good,' observes Miyagi somewhat late in the day. 'Someone always get hurt'), there were sufficient karate demonstrations to keep die-hard fans happy but not enough action to tempt many new recruits. Constance Towers played Julie's grandmother, with other roles going to Chris Conrad and Arsenio Trinidad. Jerry Weintraub produced, it was written by Mark Lee, and the director was Christopher Cain. (104 mins)

△ Written and directed by Darnell Martin, the first black female to work in this dual capacity for a major Hollywood studio, **I Like It Like That** starred Lauren Velez (centre) as Lisette Linares, a struggling Bronx N.Y. housewife, and mother of three unmanageable kids who is forced to get a job in order to raise bail when her macho Latino husband Chino (Jon Seda, right) is arrested for stealing a stereo. Though it's a modelling job she's really after, Lisette settles for work as an assistant to Stephen Price (Griffin Dunne), an executive in a record company specialising in Hispanic music. After carefully establishing the Linares milieu – with its snooping, interfering neighbours, etc – Martin's incident-heavy screenplay went into chaotic overdrive when rumours about an affair Lisette is having with her employer

reach Chino, who, after his release from jail, decides to have a revenge affair of his own with a local siren called Magdalena (Lisa Vidal). Complications begat complications, but it all ended happily. Though humour was not always Ms Martin's strong point, the film had several witty lines, most of them uttered by its heroine Lisette who, as played by Ms Velez, was something of a one-woman life-force. And although the script wasn't without its cliches or its ethnic and sexual stereotypes – notably Rita Moreno as Lisette's raucous mother-in-law and Jesse Borrego as Alexis, Chino's trans-sexual brother – Martin made sure that they weren't fatal. Thomas Melly, Desiree Cassado and Isaiah Garcia completed the cast for producers Ann Carli and Lane Janger. (105 mins)

△ Filmed five times previously between 1917 and 1978, **Little Women** proved its durability yet again in a lavish version directed by Australian Gillian Armstrong. By highlighting such feminist issues as women's suffrage and the difficulty for women in asserting themselves or their opinions in the male-dominated society of the times – issues which the earlier versions by and large avoided – Armstrong made sure that her film, while never forfeiting the period flavour of Louisa May Alcott's famous 1868 novel (screenplay by Robin Swicord), would resonate in the 1990s. Her canny casting was spot-on for contemporary moviegoers, with Winona Ryder's Jo March (standing left) the perfect role model for present-day teenage girls. It was an enchanting performance, matched in quality by Trini Alvarado's Meg (standing centre back), Kirsten Dunst (2nd right) and Samantha Mathis as the younger and older Amy, Claire Danes as Beth (seated left) and Susan Sarandon (right) as the girls' fount-of-love mother 'Marmee', as Mrs. March is fondly called. As in the novel the male characters featured less prominently, but were solidly portrayed by Christian Bale as Laurie, the loving friend and neighbour whom Jo rejects, Gabriel Byrne as Friedrich Bhaer, the German philosophy professor with whom she quotes Whitman and has an immediate rapport, Eric Stoltz as the impoverished tutor who finds happiness with Meg, John Neville as Laurie's wealthy grandfather, veteran Mary Wickes as the family's formidable Aunt March and Matthew Walker as the March paterfamilias – away from home most of the time, fighting in the Union Army. Alcott's nostalgic world of Concord, New England, during and after the Civil War, was atmospherically evoked in Richard St. John Harrison's handsome set designs, Colleen Atwood's costumes and Geoffrey Simpson's cinematography. The producer was Denise Di Novi. (115 mins)

▽ With *City Slickers* (Castle Rock) having grossed $123.8 million on its initial release in 1991, a sequel was inevitable. What was less easy to predict was that **City Slickers II: The Legend of Curly's Gold**, would continue to excavate laughs from a comedy-patch whose potential, one might justifiably have thought, had been well and truly ploughed. The intent was precisely the same as the previous film: to relocate a trio of city slickers to the Wild West for some adventure and male bonding. The plot kicked in a year after Mitch Roberts (Crystal, below), the programme controller of a Manhattan radio station, 'found his smile' while participating in a cattle drive. The smile, however, has soured. It's Mitch's fortieth birthday; he's about to fire his pal Phil (Daniel Stern) from the sales department; Glen (Jon Lovitz), his worthless scrounger of a brother whose only redeeming feature is his photographic memory, has arrived unexpectedly for a visit; and, as a topper, he cannot get the image of his mentor Curly (Jack Palance), who died on the trail, out of his mind. While casually adjusting the stetson Curly left him, Mitch unexpectedly finds a map of hidden treasure in the hat's lining. Using this as the perfect excuse to exit the big city and its attendant woes, he providentially sets out, together with Phil and Glen, for the Nevada desert and a possible $20 million worth of gold. Also along for a ride that deliciously parodied every movie cliché concerning the search for hidden gold – as well as offering a few neat twists of its own – were Duke Washburn (Jack Palance) who, after initially being mistaken for Curly's ghost, turns out to be his twin brother. Thus was the scene emphatically set for a re-run of the original *City Slickers*. But, as he'd already 'found his smile' in the first film, Crystal had nowhere to go with his performance other than to crack wise at every possible opportunity. Which he did most effectively. But with the comic momentum of the original missing, director Paul Weiland and the rest of his cast, including Patricia Wettig as Crystal's wife, found themselves in the recycling business. A Castle-Rock-Columbia Production, it was produced by Peter Schindler, with Crystal as executive. (116 mins).

△ Based on Ann M. Martin's successful series of pubertal books, **The Baby-Sitters Club** made very little impact in its transition from page to screen, due largely to a screenplay, by Dalene Young, that didn't really find enough unusual situations for its young protagonists. All about the attempts of group leader Kristy Brewer (Schuyler Fisk, right) to open a summer camp for her charges, what little conflict there was pivoted on neighbour Ellen Burstyn's objection to the noise, and on the sudden appearance of Kristy's estranged father Patrick (Peter Horton), who shows up in the ficticious town of Stoneybrook hoping to land a job on the local newspaper. Patrick makes his daughter promise not to tell her mother (Brooke Adams) that he's in town – a promise she keeps, but with great difficulty. Several inconsequential sub-plots later the film arrived at its sunny conclusion, much in the method of a TV sitcom. Average kiddies' fare nonetheless offered an engagingly spunky central performance from Miss Fisk – the real-life daughter of Sissy Spacek and Jack Fisk. Also cast: Bre Blair, Christian Oliver, Rachel Leigh Cook, Larissa Oleynik, Tricia Joe, Stacey Linn Ramsower, Zelda Harris and Bruce Davison. It was directed by Melanie Mayron for producers Jane Startz and Peter O. Almond. (94 mins)

▽ If ever a film underlined the fact that less is more, and vice versa, it was **Desperado**, Robert Rodriguez's sequel and/or follow up to *El Mariachi* (1993), his promising debut film which he made for just $7000. The new one, weighing in at $7million was hardly a thousand times better. With a budget that made it possible for Rodriguez to have almost everything that money could buy, the one thing it couldn't buy, and which had made *El Mariachi* such a breeze, was inspiration. It began promisingly enough, though. In a Mexican cantina, an unnamed gringo (Steve Buscemi) tells the establishment's sleazy clientele that he has just witnessed a bloodbath perpetrated by a mysterious stranger at a nearby bar, and that the stranger, on the trail of a man called Bucho (Joaquim de Almeida), is headed their way. The stranger, it transpires, is the guitar-strumming El Mariachi – this time played by charismatic Antonio Banderas (illustrated) who, carrying a guitar case filled with guns, has been wandering round the country looking to avenge the murder of the woman he loved – an event from the earlier film restaged in flashback. The ensuing cat and mouse game as El Mariachi and Bucho stalk one another, piled violence upon violence until the body-count hit three figures. Rodriguez, who wrote, edited, directed and produced (with Bill Borden), made no attempt at characterising his vengeance-seeking hero, the only motive for his (and the film's) existence being to invent variations on the single theme of how a lone gunman can outwit his adversaries. Salma Hayek co-starred as a local beauty with whom Banderas enjoys a romantic dalliance; Cheech Marin played a bartender, with other roles going to Carlos Gallardo (who starred in *El Mariachi*) Albert Michel Jr, and Quentin Tarantino, who told an elaborate toilet joke. (103 mins)

△ From successful Jerry Bruckheimer and Don Simpson, the begetters of *Beverly Hills Cop* (Paramount, 1984) and *Top Gun* (Paramount, 1986), **Bad Boys** starred Martin Lawrence (left) and Will Smith (right) as Marcus Burnett and Mike Lowry, longtime buddies-cum-partners in Miami's undercover police force. Like the film itself, their personalities comprised an amalgam of instantly recognisable clichès, with married Marcus, the zanier of the two, constantly frustrated by the lack of quality time he's able to devote to his wife (Theresa Randle) and three kids. Mike, in contrast, is one laid-back dude whom an inheritance has allowed to live the rich life – ritzy apartment, great clothes, lots of women and a Porsche. The plot (story by George Gello, screenplay by Michael Barrie, Jim Mulholland and Doug Richardson) kicked in when the Force's evidence room is robbed of the $100 million worth of heroin Mike and Marcus confiscated in a major drug bust. Given 72 hours to solve the case before the F.B.I. take over, the boys get on the job, their prime suspect being a crooked ex-cop. The only area of originality found Marcus being forced to pretend he's Mike in order to nail the culprit. As in most Bruckheimer/Simpson productions it was the action sequences the producers spent money on and the punters paid to see. It was directed with flair and confidence by first-timer Michael Bay. Tea Leoni was featured in support with Mary Helgenberger, Nestor Serrano and Joe Pantoliano also cast. (118 mins)

△ Going back to the days of silent movies for its opening series of title cards, and to the Hollywood of *The Adventures Of Robin Hood* (Warner Bros. 1938) for its narrative approach, **First Knight** was an efficient, generally entertaining albeit old-fashioned swashbuckler that somehow seemed to have passed its sell-by date in 1995. Sean Connery, who did not appear for the first half hour or so, top-starred as a dignified, soft-spoken King Arthur opposite a preening Richard Gere (right), Errol Flynn-like except that his Lancelot sported an American accent the size of Camelot. The Lady Guinevere, who both men love, was Julia Ormond (left), whose excellent performance made it clear just what it was that Arthur and his reluctant American knight saw in her. For the rest, William

Nicholson's screenplay, based on a story line he fashioned with Lorne Cameron and David Hoselton, relied mainly on the power of the original Arthurian legend to keep it simmering, even throwing in a *Raiders Of The Lost Ark* (Paramount, 1981) rescue involving Lancelot and Guinevere after she is abducted by the evil Malagant (Ben Cross, the latest in a line of ever-popular English movie villains) and incarcerated in his subterranean hideaway. John Gielgud, 91 years young, was cast as Oswald, Guinevere's sage-like confidante, with other parts going to Liam Cunningham as Sir Agravaine, Christopher Villiers as Sir Kay, Valentine Pelka as Sir Patrise, Colin McCormack as Sir Mador and Ralph Ineson as Ralf. Jerry Zucker directed and produced with Hunt Lowry. (132 mins)

369

1995

△ Racial tension, campus politics, higher education, sexual identity, and tolerance (or the lack of it) were just a handful of the themes John Singleton interwove and attempted to address, with varying degrees of success, in his third feature, **Higher Learning**. Set in a fictitious university, and concerned with a brand new intake of freshmen, the film, after presenting an initial overview of about a dozen characters, exchanged the general for the particular and focused on just three. Omar Epps (right) played Malik Williams, an athlete valued more for sporting than academic prowess; Kristy Swanson was Kristen Connor, a none-too-bright beauty who, after getting drunk and date-raped, has a crisis of sexual identity. The third was Remy (Michael Rapaport), a social reject from Idaho who, threatened by the university's many minority groups, falls in with a bunch of campus neo-Nazis headed by Scott Moss (Cole Hauser). It is Remy who fuels the last act of Singleton's screenplay when, to prove his commitment to his Aryan supremacists, he kills Malik's girlfriend (Tyra Banks). Though Singleton's concern with ethnic divergence was evident throughout, the one character who refuses to make distinctions between colour groups is Professor Phipps (Laurence Fishburne, left) whose take on racism and bigotry might well echo the film's message – 'unlearn'. The characters, however, were one-dimensional and unengaging, among them Ice Cube as a sixth-former with attitude, Bradford English, Regina King, Busta Rhymez, Jay Ferguson and Andrew Bryniaski. It was produced by Singleton and Paul Hall for New Deal Productions. (127 mins)

▷ Contributing in no small measure to the continuing global rediscovery and love affair with novelist Jane Austen, was **Sense and Sensibility**, directed by the Taiwanese Ang Lee. It followed in the path of *Clueless* (Paramount, a successful update of *Emma*), an outstanding TV mini-series of *Pride and Prejudice* and a stunning version of *Persuasion* (BBC Films), making 1995 a bumper year for this most precious of British writers. Though not as satirical as the novel (Austen's first), screenwriter Emma Thompson's witty and intelligent adaptation managed to remain true to the spirit of the original while at the same time giving it a contemporary resonance that was echoed in all the central performances. Thompson (second right) starred as sensible Elinor Dashwood who, together with her mother (Gemma Jones) and two sisters (Kate Winslet, left and Emilie Francois, centre), are left more or less penniless when their stepbrother John (James Fleet) inherits the family estate after Mr Dashwood's death. Bullied by his self-seeking wife Fanny (Harriet Walter), John, despite his late father's wishes, forces them to take up lodgings in a small cottage on the estate of their cousin, Sir John Middleton (Robert Hardy). Thus the scene is set for all three of the Dashwood sisters, in true Austen fashion, to find eligible husbands. Their suitors included the romantically handsome John Willoughby (Greg Wise, right), the dull but decent Edward Ferrars (Hugh Grant) and the brooding Col. Brandon (Alan Rickman). Austen's filmed novels provide some of Britain's best actors with a chance to shine in vividly etched roles; here they included Elizabeth Spriggs, Imelda Staunton, Hugh Laurie, Tom Wilkinson, Oliver Ford Davies and Richard Lumsden. Luciana Arrighi's production design and Jenny Beavan's costumes added immeasurably to Lee's meticulous recreation of the manners and mores of British period society. Lindsay Doran produced and the executive producer for Mirage Productions was Sydney Pollack. (135 mins)

◁ Little more than an excuse to re-team Wesley Snipes (left) with Woody Harrelson (right) after their 1992 hit *White Men Can't Jump* (20th Century-Fox), **Money Train** was a routine comedy-caper whose main visual joke was pairing its stars as foster brothers. They're New York City Transit cops whose duties range from apprehending pickpockets to pursuing a mad fire-raiser around the subway system. Though an aspect of Doug Richardson and David Loughery's screenplay involved Harrelson owing money to the mob as a result of a high-stakes poker game, the main business found him, against the wishes of Snipes, planning to rob a subway car (called the money train) that collects the subway's takings every day. Sibling rivalry also intruded in the shape of Grace (Jennifer Lopez), their new partner whom they both fancy. An implausible, poorly constructed plot, abetted by equally inane characterisations, left audiences with little to respond to other than the charismatic Snipes, the film's saving grace. Robert Blake, Chris Cooper and Joe Grifasi also appeared, Joseph Ruben directed, and the producers were Jon Peters and Neil Canton. (110 mins)

△ That faithful old movie cliché – an innocent caught in a nightmare world over which he/she has no control – had, over the years, been put to brilliant use by its chief exponent, Alfred Hitchcock. It was recycled in a high-tech, state-of-the-art context in **The Net**, an edge-of-the-seat thriller whose many plot contrivances and implausibilities were, happily, no obstacle to enjoyment. It starred Sandra Bullock (left) as Angela Bennett, a housebound computer nerd who, though based in Venice, California, works for a large computer company in San Francisco. Just before setting off on her first holiday in years, she receives a new Internet programme from a colleague which is so powerful that, if abused, could cause havoc in Wall Street, shut down airports, and provide access to highly confidential government files. After some decidedly unnerving occurrences, including a brief holiday affair in Mexico with a handsome Englishman (Jeremy Northam, right) who turns out to be more interested in her explosive diskette than in her, it becomes clear that the inventor of the programme is determined to get it back. The first thing that happens is that Angela loses her identity. Her picture I.D., fingerprints and social security number are transferred and she no longer exists, replaced by 'Ruth Marx', a woman wanted for prostitution and drug dealing. How the vulnerable Angela eventually reverts back to her true identity and nails the villains provided the juicy red meat of John Brancato and Michael Ferris' gripping if hardly credible screenplay. Irwin Winkler's direction, kept the suspense simmering, but glueing it together was the excellent Ms Bullock, whose sheer likeability made it difficult not to root for her all the way. Diane Baker gave a cameo as her Altzheimer-sticken mother, Dennis Miller her former lover, with other parts going to Wendy Gazelle, Ken Howard and Ray McKinnon. Winkler and Rob Cowan produced. (112 mins)

1996

▽ Resorting once again to playing twin brothers, as he had in *Double Impact* (1991) Jean-Claude Van Damme (below), starred in **Maximum Risk**, another brainless actioner in which karate kicks spoke louder and more effectively than words – especially those scripted by Larry Ferguson. The twin brothers this time were Mikhail and Alain who, after being separated at birth because their mother (Stephane Audran) could not afford to support them both, grew up to lead very different lives, each unaware of the other's existence. Mikhail becomes involved with the Russian Mafiosi and the F.B.I. in New York while Alain becomes a cop in Nice. When Mikhail is killed in Nice's old city in the opening shoot-out-cum-car-chase and is mistaken for his twin brother, Alain realises there is something fishy afoot, visits his mother, and learns the truth about his sibling. Determined to avenge his brother's death, he travels first to Paris, then to a largely unrecognisable New York (the exteriors were filmed in Toronto and Pittsburgh) before finally returning to Nice to complete the job. Love interest was supplied by Natasha Henstridge, who quickly shifts her allegiance from Mikhail to Alain after the former's death, though sex was merely a by-product of a story whose raison *d'être* was to see just how many fights and chases could be crammed into about an hour and a half's running time. Van Damme wasn't required to do much more than act with his fists and feet (his expression never changed once throughout), the villains were a bunch of cliché baddies and the plot mindlessly preposterous. Still, as directed by Hong Kong's Ringo Lam with the accent squarely on action, Van Damme addicts were not disappointed. Zach Grenier, Frank Senger and Paul Ben-Victor were in it too; and it was produced by Moshe Diamant. (97 mins)

△ An enchanting family-cum-animal picture from director Carroll Ballard, who made *The Black Stallion* (United Artists, 1979), **Fly Away Home** was the absorbing story of a 13-year-old girl who rears a bunch of orphan goslings, then teaches them how to fly. After the death of her mother in a car crash, Amy Alden (Anna Paquin, above), an only child, leaves New Zealand and takes up residence in Ontario, Canada with her estranged father Thomas (Jeff Daniels), whom she has not seen since she was three. An eccentric sculptor and inventor, Thomas is powerless to assuage his daughter's loneliness and grief, but just as the situation is looking hopeless, Amy discovers 16 goose-eggs that have been turfed out of their nest by some ruthless property developers and, playing Mother Goose, nurtures them until they eventually hatch. However, since geese, as Amy learns, 'imprint' on the first living creature they see, it becomes her responsibility to teach them to fly so that they can migrate South during the cold winter months. Just how, with the help of her equally enthusiastic father, she does so, formed the basis of this warm-hearted odyssey, in which young Amy has to learn how to fly herself. Scripted by Robert Rodat and Vince McKewan from Bill Lishman's autobiography, and ravishingly photographed by Caleb Deschanel, the aerial sequences provided genuine goose-bumps as they followed Amy and her charges on their epic 500-mile journey to North Carolina. Things were less inspirational on ground level, notably the writers' attempts to inject conflict into the story with a pair of obligatory baddies, a minor blemish in an appealing wild-life adventure that left audiences glowing. Ballad's skill in working with animals and children was always evident, and Anna Paquin, so good in Jane Campion's *The Piano* (Miramax, 1993), again proved her worth. Also cast: Dana Delany, Terry Kinney, Holter Graham and Jeremy Ratchford, for producers John Veitch and Carol Baum. (107 mins)

▷ Low-key charm and zany poignancy seeped through **Bottle Rocket**, a strangely affecting little film directed by Wes Anderson, that defied categorisation. First made as a 13-minute black-and-white short and seen at both the USA Film Festival in Dallas and the Sundance Festival, it was brought to the attention of producers Barbara Boyle, Polly Platt and James L. Brooks, whose Gracie Films provided the modest financial wherewithal to develop the mini scenario into a feature-length film. The result was a generous-spirited little gem about three friends from Dallas, Texas who, to add a touch of zest to their basically wasteful lives, decide to go on a robbing spree. Anthony (Luke Wilson, left), after a short stay in a mental institution for 'exhaustion', is joined by the vaguely dysfunctional, criminally motivated Dignan (Owen Wilson, centre) as well as by wealthy Bob (Robert Musgrave, right). The favourable perception they have of their criminal skills bears no truth to the reality of the situation, which is that they're incompetent losers. While hiding in an out-of-town motel, Anthony falls in love with Inez (Lumi Cavazos), the motel's Paraguayan maid who can't speak English. Their affair results in the three rookie robbers splitting after Anthony gives Inez the stolen money from the bookstore. Back in Dallas, however, the trio patch up their differences

and agree to a factory heist masterminded by a local big-wig (James Caan). Needless to say, the heist goes wrong, resulting in the feckless Dignan being jailed for two years. The script, by director Anderson and Owen C. Wilson, was stronger on dialogue than on plot, and allowed its protagonists, despite their criminal leanings, to insinuate themselves into the audience's good books through what they said rather than what they did. The performances were first rate, notably from a touching, understated Ms. Cavazos and a characteristically ballsy Caan. Also cast: Andrew Wilson, Teddy Wilson, Jim Ponds. (95 mins)

371

△ With a salary tag of $20 million for his work on **The Cable Guy**, Jim Carrey (left) became one of the highest paid movie stars in the world. And was he happy? Well, not if his bilious, misogynistic, mean-spirited performance as a cable-television repair man who develops an unhealthy obsession with one of his clients was anything to go by. The client was Matthew Broderick (right), an architect who, after getting the heave-ho from his girlfriend (Leslie Mann), moves into a new apartment. After his television equipment is hooked up by Carrey, who goes on to inform him 'I can be your best friend or your worst enemy,' Broderick makes the mistake of befriending the manic mechanic. In what was basically a series of loosely interwoven incidents and sketches, Lou Holtz Jr's unpleasant screenplay, with its occasional

barbs at TV culture, went to great lengths to illustrate how Carrey, after showing signs of being homosexually attracted to Broderick, sets out systematically to destroy him. The fact that Broderick, for the most part, allows this to happen, did little to win audience sympathy for his nightmarish plight. Saddled, therefore, with a pair of the most alienating protagonists imaginable – one of whom was repellent and revolting, the other an ineffectual nerd – the film had nowhere to go but down. Brief appearances by George Segal, Diane Baker, Eric Roberts and Janeane Garofalo offered scant respite from the terminally glum proceedings. It was directed as a series of over-the-top revue sketches by Ben Stiller; and the producers were Andrew Licht, Jeffrey A. Mueller and Judd Apatow. (95 mins)

△ With echoes of the 1989 independently made *Heathers* still reverberating in the ether, producer Douglas Wick's **The Craft**, like the earlier film, alighted on the idea of a quartet of high-school she-monsters causing havoc and mayhem to anyone who crosses their vengeful paths. Collectively known as 'the bitches of Eastwick' this particular coven was led by reckless Fairuza Balk (centre) and includ-

ed Neve Campbell (left), who suffers from burn scars on her back, Rachel True (being levitated), a black victim of racism, and newcomer Robin Tunney (right), whose mother died in childbirth and was also a witch. After initially applying their sinister craft to themselves by way of cosmetically improving certain aspects of their appearances, they use their powers to inflict damage on enemies such as snooty Christine Taylor, whose insulting remarks about the colour of Ms. True's skin have to be paid for. And when the local high-school Lothario (Skeet Ulrich) plays fast and loose with Tunney's reputation, she casts a spell on him that forever puts him in thrall to her. Things, however, become decidedly nasty when the girls turn the dark side of their powers onto each other, evoking horrors that certainly put the special effects department to the test. Though quite creepy as occult melodramas go, *The Craft*, scripted by Peter Filardi and Andrew Fleming (who also directed), managed to fill most of the requirements of the genre without adding anything new or startling to it. (100 mins)

▽ Filmed over a three-week period in Super-16 mm at a cost of $2.4 million, and financed to the tune of $200,000 to $300,000 apiece by a group of 15 African Americans, including Wesley Snipes, Danny Glover, Robert Guillaume, Will Smith and Spike Lee, who also directed, **Get On The Bus** was an exhilarating commemoration of the 16 October 1995 Million Man March in Washington D.C. Though modest in budget, there was nothing small about its heart and soul or its treatment of the many issues concerning the contemporary black experience. Essentially a joyous, often very funny celebration of black male camaraderie, the screenplay by Reggie Rock Blythewood (another of the film's financiers) was set for the most part on a cross-country bus whose organiser George (Charles S. Dutton) is taking 15 passengers from South Central L.A. to the March in D.C. Socially, culturally, politically, economically and sexually the group represented a cross-section of the black community and included Flip (Andre Braugher), a self-absorbed would-be actor; Gary (Roger Guenveur Smith), a light-skinned cop whose father was murdered by a black man; Jamal (Gabriel Casseus), a recent convert to Islam; Xavier (Hill Harper), a film student recording the outing on videotape; Randall (Harry Lennix) and Kyle (Isaiah Washington), a gay couple about to split up; Evan Thomas (Thomas Jefferson Byrd) and his son Junior (DeAundre Bonds) who are literally shackled together by a 72-hour court order, and Jeremiah (Ossie Davis), who's just been laid off his factory job, is suffering from a heart ailment and plays an African drum. When an accident delays the ride, a replacement vehicle arrives with a white driver (Richard Belzer), a Jew who takes exception to the fact that the march has been organised by the Nation of Islam leader, Louis Farrakhan. He abandons the trip mid-way, leaving George to take the wheel. As the journey progresses the passengers discuss such topics as economic problems, sexual preferences, family relationships, women and infidelity. What little – and largely cosmetic – plot there was included the bus being searched for drugs by a white Tennessee state trooper (Randy Quaid), the pickup of a wealthy black car dealer (Wendell Pierce) whose abusive disapproval of 'niggers' who lay their problems squarely at the white man's feet results in his forcible ejection from the bus; and Jeremiah's inevitable heart-attack, which leaves him in a coma. The film's far-ranging issues, and the way they were expressed, was what mattered, and in this respect Lee's film was an unqualified success. The producers were Reuben Cannon, Bill Borden and Barry Rosenbush. (122 mins)

▽ After Harold Ramis' *Groundhog Day* (1993) came the same director's potentially intriguing though rather less successful **Multiplicity**, a dollop of wish-fulfilment sci-fi, which he wrote with Chris Miller, Mary Hale, Lowell Ganz, and Babaloo Mandel from a story by Miller. Predicated on the notion that life would be a lot easier if we could clone ourselves, thus allowing our responsibilities to be shared between several copies of ourselves, the film starred Michael Keaton (all characters below) as Doug Kinney, a married man employed in a senior position with a construction firm. Given added responsibilities without benefit of a rise, Doug finds he has no leisure time at all. It's all work and no play – until he meets Dr Leeds (Harris Yulin) who has learned how to clone himself, thus allowing for a situation in which he can be in two places at the same time. Intrigued, Doug allows himself to be cloned not once, but three times, leading to several farcical cross-over situations. These though, were never an adequate substitute for plot, which was noticeably lacking. Still, Keaton was given a great chance to demonstrate his ingenuity and provided his fans with four Keatons for the price of one. Andie MacDowell played Keaton's wife, with Richard Masur, Ann Cusack and Eugene Levy also cast. It was produced by Ramis and Trevor Albert. (117 mins)

◁ Writer Ted Tally, who adapted Thomas Harris' *The Silence of the Lambs* (Orion, 1991), was offered a million dollars to do the same for George Dawes Green's **The Juror**, even though Green's bestseller already read like a movie treatment from its very first page. The film starred Demi Moore (illustrated) as an artist and single mother who is summoned for jury duty on a Mob-related murder trial. Pressure is put on her to sway the other eleven members of the jury to find in favour of the defendant. Helping to see that she does so was smoothy Alec Baldwin, who initially wins her over with his charm then turns nasty, bugging her house and threatening her son. Terrified of what may happen, Moore takes off for Guatemala. Until that point, however, the movie was a taut, intelligent psychological thriller that gave Baldwin ample opportunity to imprint a chillingly effective ruthless charm on the proceedings. Moore was convincing in a role that catered to her trademark brand of feistiness, with other roles under Brian Gibson's direction going to Joseph Gordon-Levitt as Moore's equally feisty son, Anne Heche as her best friend, and James Gandolfini as one of Baldwin's criminal associates. Also cast: Lindsay Crouse, Tony LoBianco, Michael Constantine and Matt Craven. The producers were Irwin Winkler and Rob Cowan. (116 mins)

▽ In his first film for seven years, director Milos Forman chose as his subject pornographer Larry Flynt, the founder of *Hustler* magazine. Freedom of speech was the issue at the heart of **The People Vs. Larry Flynt**, but by using Flynt as a means of showing just how important that freedom is to the American Constitution, Forman and his writers Scott Alexander and Larry Karaszewski, turned a physically unprepossessing vulgarian into an eccentric maverick. And, as played by Woody Harrelson (right), a man not without a certain charm, and even likeable. While omitting some of the details of Flynt's private life (e.g. his four marriages), the film could not be accused of stinting on plot. Beginning in 1952 with a scene in Kentucky showing the young Larry, a grade-school dropout, peddling moonshine, the narrative moved to the early 1970s when Flynt ran a dreary strip-club in Cincinnati. His first foray into print was a newsletter that featured far more explicit photographs than anything to be found in *Playboy* and *Penthouse*; shortly after, it grew into a fully-fledged magazine called *Hustler*, and Flynt hit the jackpot with the publication of *paparazzi* photographs of Jacqueline Onassis. Working with his wife Althea (Courtney Love, left), a bisexual former stripper, Flynt daringly expanded the paramaters of bad taste, flourished as a result, and quickly became a millionaire. A backlash endemic to American Reaganite conservatism at the end of the 1970s led to a series of obscenity lawsuits, culminating in Flynt's well-documented appearance in the U.S. Supreme Court after publishing a piece in which 'Moral Majority' leader Jerry Falwell was shown having sex with his mother in an outhouse. The First Amendment was upheld and Falwell lost the case. Meanwhile, Flynt, to everyone's amazement, became a born-again Christian after meeting evangelist Ruth Carter Stapleton, a calling he abandoned shortly after being paralysed from the waist down by a sniper's bullet. While Flynt found himself addicted to pain-killers, Althea became hooked on heroin and died of AIDS in 1984. Though there was nothing attractive about Flynt's life-style, Forman managed to make an absorbing narrative out of the potentially repellent material and Flynt emerged as a flawed hero. The best performance, though, was from Courtney Love, who made Althea the only character it was possible genuinely to care about. Joining a cast that included Edward Norton, James Cromwell and Crispin Glover, were non-actors such as political consultant James Carville, as an anti-obscenity prosecutor, Donna Hanover, the wife of New York's Mayor Giuliani, as Stapleton, and law professor Burt Neuborne as Falwell's attorney. Also in it, as a judge, was Larry Flynt himself. Oliver Stone, Janet Yang and Michael Hausman produced. (130 mins)

△ A big-screen vehicle for small-screen star Matthew Perry (Chandler Bing in *Friends*, right), **Fools Rush In** was a wishy-washy romantic fantasy in which Perry played Alex Whitman, an on-site construction manager who has been temporarily posted from Manhattan to Las Vegas to oversee the building of a discotheque. Standing outside the lavatory of a Mexican cantina one day, he and a Mexican girl called Isabel Fuentes (Salma Hayek) 'meet cute' and pop into bed, as a result of which she falls pregnant. The ensuing trials and tribulations of the situation – involving a great deal of soul-searching and an on-off-on-again marriage prior to the baby being born – occupied much of a screenplay (by Katherine Reback, story by Reback and John Taylor) that merely skirted such issues as cultural incompatibility and unplanned pregnancies

and which, even at its best, never approached the skill, charm or invention of a *Friends* episode, despite the general sitcom feel of the script. And while Mexico's Salma Hayek made an attractive and often appealing leading lady, for whose predicament one felt a certain concern, Perry emerged as a charmless weak-willed nebbish it was difficult to like. More damaging, though, was the lack of chemistry between the couple – a fact director Andy Tennant was powerless to disguise. Jill Clayburgh appeared as Alex's WASP New York mother, John Bennett Perry was his father, and other parts went to Jon Tenney (left), Carlos Gomez, Thomas Milian, Siobhan Fallon and Stanley DeSantis. The producer was Doug Draizin. (106 mins)

▽ The reverse of a buddy-buddy story, **The Devil's Own** starred Harrison Ford (left) and Brad Pitt (right) – both heroes in the context of the plot – who become mortal adversaries. Pitt played an Irish Catholic who, 20 years after seeing his father shot by the British Army, has become a wanted IRA operative. To avoid arrest after ambushing a posse of British soldiers, he travels to America with one purpose in mind: to bring back to Ireland stinger missiles. Top-starred Harrison Ford was the scrupulously honest New York police sergeant in whose Staten Island home Pitt, pretending to be a construction worker, takes up lodgings and, against his better judgement, becomes a family friend. Working secretly with an old friend (Paul Ronan), Pitt purchases a boat that will eventually take them – and the missiles – back to Ireland. But it does not work out that way and the doomed mission ends with Pitt being shot by Ford. Written by David Aaron Cohen, Vincent Patrick and Kevin Jarre (from a story by Jarre), *The Devil's Own* was a serious-minded attempt to examine aspects of Northern Ireland's problems from an IRA viewpoint, and through characters that attempted to be more than just walking stereotypes. It also made an effort to pose interesting moral questions about friendship and betrayal. Yet, despite the potential box-office clout of its two male stars, there was no

hero in this particular scenario that audiences could comfortably root for. Also, there were some glaring gaps in the fabric of the narrative which, at times, strained credibility. (Precisely where did the money come from to buy the missiles?). Still, Harrison and Pitt (whose Irish accent was most convincing) worked well together and brought charisma to a grim subject. The solid, no-frills direction was by Alan J. Pakula, whose cast also included George Hearn as a New York judge-cum-undercover IRA spy, Treat Williams as a vicious businessman with whom Pitt has to deal in purchasing the missiles, Ruben Blades as a cop, Margaret Colin as Ford's wife and Ashley Carin and Kelly Singer as his two teenage daughters. It was produced by Lawrence Gordon and Robert F. Colesberry. (107 mins)

▽ Hong Kong director Tsui Hark made a noisy entry into the Hollywood mainstream with **Double Team**, an all-shouting, all-shooting, all-brawling vehicle for Jean-Claude Van Damme (left) which led with its fists and feet rather than its brains. Van Damme starred as an anti-terrorist covert action operative who, after failing to nail an international crime baron called Stavros (Mickey Rourke), is sent to The Colony – a safe island retreat for intelligence agents whose elimination would not be in the organisation's best interests. Though the island is seemingly escape-proof Van Damme, of course, escapes – via a supply boat – and lands up in the South of France where he is apprehended by Stavros' goons. How he finally kicked, shot and punched his way out of trouble provided director Hark with countless opportunities to increase the body count, and to stage a climactic shoot-out in the Colosseum in Rome. Basketball star Dennis Rodman (right) co-starred as an arms expert (and provided what little humour there was), with other roles going to Paul Freeman, Valeria Cavalli, Jay Benedict, Joelle Devaux-Vullion and, as Van Damme's pregnant wife, Natacha Lindinger. It was written by Don Jakoby and Paul Mones (story by Jakoby) – who also served as the producing team. (90 mins)

▽ **Anaconda** employed up-to-the-minute computer-generated effects and high-tech animatronics to scare the life out of audiences, but director Luis Llosa and writers Hans Bauer, Jim Cash and Jack Epps Jr went back to *The Creature from the Black Lagoon* (Universal, 1954) and, even earlier, *King Kong* (RKO, 1933) for their inspiration. In the earlier film a movie producer sets off on a boat to make a film on a remote island – with devastating consequences; in *Anaconda* a team of documentary film-makers set off on a boat to make a film about a mysterious Amazonian tribe – with devastating consequences. In Merian C. Cooper and Ernest B. Schoedsack's classic, the crew were terrorised by a giant gorilla; in Llosa's adventure it was a giant anaconda that did the mischief. Determined to capture the mighty reptile for financial gain is a Paraguayan poacher (Jon Voight) who joins the film-makers after his boat is damaged. When the crew's anthropologist (Eric Stoltz) is stung by a wasp and retires to his sick-bed, and the Captain (Vincent Castellanos) is eaten by the anaconda, Voight takes over, making it clear that nothing will prevent him capturing the giant snake. But the anaconda, like King Kong, will not be tamed, and the unleashing of its anger at being stalked formed the backbone of the film. Some compensation for an undernourished script that, at one point, kept Stoltz off the screen for about half an hour and made no attempt at characterisation, were the special effects. These, and Voight's Brando-esque performance, more or less kept interest afloat. The rest of the cast, including Jennifer Lopez (left), sank without trace. The casualties included Ice Cube (right) as the crew's cameraman, Jonathan Hyde as its English narrator, Kari Wuhrer, and Owen Wilson. Verna Harrah, Carole Little and Leonard Rabinowitz produced. (90 mins)

▷ Based on the true story of Trudy Lintz, a wealthy and highly eccentric animal-lover from Brooklyn who, in the late 1920s and early 1930s filled her mansion with a collection of chimpanzees she dressed as humans, shared her meals with and took to the cinema, **Buddy** was a fair-to-middling family orientated film that took Lintz's obsession with primates even further. Hearing that a baby gorilla at a local zoo is pining to death for its mother, she rescues him, names him Buddy and, against all perceived wisdom, successfully bonds with him. As a result she is invited to present her primate menagerie at the 1933 Chicago International Exposition. They're a hit but Buddy escapes and causes mayhem among the terrified crowds. Back in Brooklyn the beast no longer prepared to tolerate captivity, goes wild and

△ Elbowing out Steven Spielberg's *Jurassic Park: The Lost World* (Universal) as the hit of the 1997 summer blockbusters, **Men In Black** more than justified its success through its refreshing combination of wit, intelligence, humour and excitement – qualities absent from Hollywood's recent crop of science fiction offerings. To have all those particular attributes in a single bumper attraction was little short of a miracle. Story-wise, the eponymous men in black are members of an ultra-secret society whose function is to monitor the to-ings and fro-ings of extra-terrestrials on earth. Not only that, but to make quite sure that anyone who may have witnessed alien activity has his or her memory of the incident irrevocably removed. When Agent K (Tommy Lee Jones, left) seeks a new partner, he appoaches New York cop James Edwards (Will Smith, right), who recently had a close encounter with an alien. Together the pair head upstate to check out an unauthorised crash-landing on a farm, in the course of which they uncover evidence that a 'bug' has landed and is wandering around disguised as the farm's owner. Using this off-beat development as a springboard and working from a story, 'The Men in

destroys several rooms in the Lintz residence. Trudy reluctantly places him in a zoo with several other gorillas. Written and directed by Caroline Thompson from a story she devised with William Joyce, from the book *Animals Are My Hobby* by Gertrude Davies Lintz, *Buddy* was too short on plot and documentary content to succeed either with children or adults, and relied too much on Jim Henson's Creature Shop animatronics. Rene Russo (right) as Trudy Lintz laughed and giggled a great deal and was given no opportunity to develop anything that approached a believable character; ditto Robbie Coltrane as her doctor husband. Alan Cumming featured as the Lintzs' faithful assistant, and Irma P. Hall as their long-suffering cook. Steve Nicolaides and Fred Fuchs produced. (84 mins)

Black' by Lowell Cunningham, screenwriter/writer Ed Solomon came up with a beautifully constructed, vastly entertaining plot. Soloman made sure that he endowed his characters – even the aliens – with convincing flesh and blood qualities, and that he put them through a series of highly original situations designed to test the ingenuity and imagination of the film's crack special effects team. In addition the script was meaty enough to allow Tommy Lee Jones and Will Smith to spark off one another, which they most effectively did. Indeed, not since Butch and Sundance bonded back in 1969 had the movies thrown up so entertaining a pair of on-screen buddies. The female of the species was represented by Linda Fiorentino as a medical examiner, with other roles under Barry Sonnenfeld's confident direction going to Vincent D'Onofrio, Rip Torn, Tony Shalhoub, Siobhan Fallon, Mike Nussbaum and Jon Gries. The special effects originated out of Industrial Light and Magic; Thomas Duffield was responsible for the striking art direction, and the producers were Walter F. Parkes and Laurie MacDonald, with Steven Spielberg as executive producer for Amblin Entertainment. (98 mins)

△ Four floundering characters very much in search of a plot – that was the gist of **Booty Call**, an unstructured, often offensive series of gags devoted to gender wars and sex in the permissive society. Substituting raunchy dialogue for raunchy action, and with an unhealthy reliance on ethnic and sexual stereotypes to keep the fragile edifice afloat, screenwriter Takashi Bufford paired two couples – Tommy Davidson and Tamala Jones (right); and Jamie Foxx and Vivica A. Fox (left) – on a double date. Condoms featured prominently in the creative team's scheme of things (not any old condoms, but the disease-preventing latex variety); and what action there was involved Davidson being shot in the leg by a cab driver who mistakenly believes he is about to be robbed. Complications, as they say, ensue when Davidson is refused hospital admission for not having his insurance card to hand. As Foxx, the star of television's *Living Color* series, is also a mimic by reputation, there's even a scene in which his girlfriend cues in a series of impressions of Jesse Jackson, Mike Tyson and Bill Cosby by telling her beau she gets really turned on by men who impersonate celebrities. Little more than fodder for the mentally challenged, *Booty Call* also featured Scott La Rose, Ric Young, Gedde Watanabe and Art Malik; it was directed by Jeff Pollack and produced by John Morrissey for Turman/Morrissey Productions. (79 mins)

△ Alicia Silverstone, fresh from her success in *Clueless* (Paramount, 1995), starred in **Excess Baggage** as a disagreeable, whisky-guzzling, cigarette-smoking teenager who, rightly believing that her mega-rich father (Jack Thompson) prefers his money to her, fakes her own kidnapping and demands a million-dollar ransom. Her scheme, however, goes awry when the car in which she hides is stolen by a young car thief (Benicio Del Toro) and driven to a warehouse where the rest of his stolen cars are kept. Initially hostile to her unwitting kidnapper, Silverstone soon finds herself attracted to him, and before the screenplay by Max D. Adams, Dick Clement and Ian La Frenais arrived at its climactic showdown, love was definitely in the air. Christopher Walken (left) made a major contribution to the proceedings as Thompson's business associate, whose job it is to rescue Silverstone (right) from her kidnapper, with other roles farmed out to Harry Connick Jr, Nicholas Turturro, Michael Bowen, Sally Kirkland, Leland Orser and Robert Wisden. However, the combination of Silverstone's unyielding petulance throughout, and Del Toro's robotic, zombie-like performance as the thief (who turns out to be a really nice guy), hardly made movie heaven, and as directed by Marco Brambilla and produced (for Silverstone's company, First Kiss) by Bill Borden and Carolyn Kessler, failed to find an audience. (98 mins)

▷ With cloning fast moving away from science fiction and into science fact, **Gattaca** was a timely drama, set in the 'not-too-distant future' which introduced a refreshingly plausible note into a genre more often associated with intergalactic space travel and star wars than with genetic manipulation. Gattaca's class system, as represented by writer-director Andrew Niccol, was divided not between the haves and have nots, but between the 'valids' and 'invalids'. The 'valids' are a patrician breed whose genes have been worked on at birth to eliminate undesirable mental and physical defects; while the 'invalids' are specimens obliged to live with the imperfect genes with which they were born. Called 'de-gene-rates', 'invalids' are destined to a life of menial chores and sub-servience and denied certain privileged activities. Such an 'invalid' is Vincent (Ethan Hawke, right) who, frustrated by his station in life, devises a daring scheme to change identities with a *bona fide* 'valid' willing to go along with the deception. Just such a person is Jerome (Jude Law, left), a clinically depressed alcoholic left paralysed from the waist down after a suicide attempt. Just how Vincent implements the deception – and the ultimate consequences of his illegal actions – made for a gripping cinematic experience whose rather bleak, futuristic atmosphere was wonderfully evoked by Sarah Knowles' cold, clinical designs. The intensity of the strange, dependent relationship between the two protagonists was convincingly conveyed by both Hawke and Law, though second-billed Uma Thurman, Vincent's love-interest, was wasted in an unfulfilling role. Better served by the script were Alan Arkin as an inspector and Elias Koteas as a supervisor. Gore Vidal played a Gattaca flight director, with other parts going to Ernest Borgnine, Loren Dean, Tony Shalhoub, Xander Berkeley and Jayne Brook. It was produced by Danny DeVito, Stacey Sher and Michael Shamberg. (112 mins)

△ Though set in Manhattan, **Replacement Killers** was, in essence, style and content, a Hong Kong-type thriller from executive producers John Woo and Terence Chang. Asian action-man Chow Yun-Fat (left), whose first American movie this was, top-starred as John Lee, a hired gunman in the employ of Manhattan-based crime chief Terence Wei (Kenneth Tsang). Lee's latest assignment is to murder the seven-year-old son of a cop (Michael Rooker) in retaliation for the death of Wei's own drug-dealing son, who was killed by the cop in a botched drug operation. Though Lee is a cold-blooded assassin, he cannot bring himself to shoot an innocent child, and his last-minute crisis of conscience puts not only his own life in danger from Wei and his 'replacement killers', but also the lives of his mother and sister who live in Shanghai. Needing a phony passport to return to China, Lee is put in touch with master forger Meg Coburn (Mira Sorvino, right). Wei's henchmen, however, follow him to Coburn's premises, and after a noisy shoot-out Coburn and Lee escape. What follows is an extended chase through New York as Lee and Coburn attempt to keep one step ahead of their pursuers. Very predictable, very formulaic, and directed by Antoine Fuqua without an original thought or shot, the film was just one more yawning statistic in a very tired genre. Jurgen Prochnow, Till Schweiger and Randall Duk Kim were in it too; it was written by Ken Sanzel, and produced by Brad Grey and Bernie Brillstein. (86 mins)

▽ A woman's film – big time! – **Stepmom** was also a manipulative four-Kleenex weepie that mercilessly wrung the emotional withers as it told the story of two strongly independent, albeit very different women who start off as enemies and end up as friends. Isabel (Julia Roberts, left) is an ambitious, successful fashion photographer; Jackie (Susan Sarandon, right) once had a career in publishing but gave it all up to be a wife and mother. Her 13-year marriage to lawyer Luke Harrison (Ed Harris) is, however, over. Ed is in love with Isabel, who, as a result, is not only the recipient of Jackie's undisguised animosity but is also having a hard time with Jackie's two precocious children – 12-year-old Anna (Jena Malone), and seven-year-old Ben (Liam Aiken). Taking her cue from her mother, Anna is particularly vile to Isabel, who is genuinely trying her very best to be an accommodating stepmom. When, about halfway through the film, Jackie discovers that she has terminal cancer, screenwriters Gigi Levangie, Jessie Nelson, Steven Rogers, Karen Leigh Hopkins and Ron Bass (story by Levangie) embark on an emotional roller-coaster ride that culminates, on Christmas day, with the dying Jackie separately and tearfully confronting her two children with the fact of her imminent death. The only good news is that, in the tragic circumstances, Jackie finally comes to realise just what a good stepmom Isabel will be to her kids. Indeed, she's almost too good for credibility. Though for much of the film's running time Isabel is treated like dirt by both Jackie and Anna, she swallows the rudeness and the insults whole. She's even prepared to jeopardise

her career by leaving assignments early in order to fetch the ungrateful brats from school whenever Jackie is unable to do so herself. Jackie, meantime, is so unpleasant that, until the best written scene in the film – in which she confides to Isabel over lunch that she has cancer – her character is in serious danger of alienating audiences past the point of no return. Fortunately Sarandon's terrific performance managed to keep the overt bitchiness in check, ultimately making it impossible not to be affected by her situation. In the less rewarding role of Isabel, Roberts was called on to do little more than spread a warm glow over the proceedings, which aided and abetted by her radiant smile, she does. As for Ed Harris as Luke, it was not his fault that he contributed little to the proceedings other than a certain masculine irritation at his wife and children's initial unwillingness to accept his pretty young lover. The quintet of writers were simply unable to give him an interesting life of his own, all their creative juices flowing, instead, in the direction of the two women. Jena Malone had the difficult task of making the spoilt, far-too-knowing Anna into something other than a monster who should have been strangled in her crib; while young master Aikens was always likeable as the more pliable Ben. Completing the cast for director Chris Columbus – whose direction was squarely focused on the tear-duct factor – were Lynn Whitfield, Mary Louise Wilson, Darrell Larson and Andre Blake. A Wendy Finerman-1492 production, *Stepmom* was produced by Finerman, Columbus, Mark Radcliffe and Michael Barnathan. (130 mins)

△ State-of-the-art technology was put to predictably gruesome use in **John Carpenter's Vampires**, an imaginative variation on a well-worked theme that starred James Woods (centre) as vampire slayer Jack Crow. Leading a contingent of fearless mercenaries known as Team Crow in a long and ongoing war against the undead, Crow and his partner Tony Montoya (Daniel Baldwin) are the only survivors following a bloody encounter with Master Vampire Valek (Thomas Ian Griffith). After a search lasting several centuries, Valek has tracked down an elusive mediaeval cross that will provide him and all other vampires with a major breakthrough in their life (or death) style – the ability to walk in the daylight. Valek's centuries in the darkness have fuelled his determination to find the cross and destroy Crow, his greatest adversary. The climactic clash between the forces of good and evil is suitably violent, yet somehow not nearly as effective as the film's tense opening scene depicting Crow and his team staking out an isolated vampire lair somewhere in New Mexico. Sheryl Lee appeared as a prostitute out of whose neck Valek has taken a substantial bite, and who, in turn, develops a psychic link with the Master Vampire; other roles in Don Jakoby's gory screenplay (from a novel by John Steakly) were filled by Maximilian Schell and Tim Guinee as priests – the former working in cahoots with Valek, the latter on the side of Woods. A Storm King production presented by Columbia and Largo Entertainment, it was produced by Sandy King. (108 mins)

▽ In *The Shining* (Warner Bros., 1980) a visitor-free hotel in an out-of-season ski resort gave novelist Stephen King ample opportunity to prove just how menacing such a setting could be. Unfortunately, what worked so well for King and director Stanley Kubrick emerged as little more than a series of schlock-horror clichés in **I Still Know What You Did Last Summer**. Set for the most part in a deserted Bahamian resort on the eve of the hurricane season, the movie involved four teenagers and a murderer with a hook where his right hand should have been. *I Still Know … was* a hokey sequel to *I Know What You Did Last Summer* (1997). The gist of the plot in that one had pretty Julie James (Jennifer Love Hewitt, left) spending a harrowing summer dealing with the brutal murders of several high-school friends, while wondering whether or not she herself killed a fisherman named Ben Willis. Seems she didn't. The vengeful Willis has tracked down Julie to the Bahamas where she is spending the Fourth of July weekend with her best friend Karla (Brandy, right), winner of the all-expenses-paid-holiday for four sponsored by a radio station back home. Accompanying the girls are Karla's randy lover Tyrell (Mekhi Phifer) and Julie's adoring classmate Will (Matthew Settle). Integral to the plot is the fact that Will is only there because Julie's long-standing boyfriend Ray (Eddie Prinze Jr) couldn't get away from work. For the first half hour or so, writer Trey Calloway and director Danny Cannon's attempts to create tension by involving Julie in a series of tense situations which, with the exception of a cat jumping out of a closet and scaring everyone half to death, all ended in anti-climax. Almost every cliché germane to the slasher genre was employed, and when things *did* finally beginning happening to the quartet of teenagers, the gore quotient went too far over the top to make for genuine suspense. It was the formula as before with nothing fresh added. The film's final shot indicates that a sequel to the sequel might be on the cards – a horrifying thought that wilfully ignores the law of diminishing returns. Bill Cobbs, Jeffrey Combs, Jennifer Esposito, Jack Black and John Hawkes completed the cast for producers Neil H. Moritz, Erik Feig, Stokely Chaffin and William S. Beasley, in association with Mandalay Entertainment. (96 mins)

▽ **Can't Hardly Wait** painted a dispiriting picture of contemporary youth as it brought together a cross-section of graduates from Huntington Hills High at a party being thrown by one of their number (Michelle Brookhurst) whose parents are conveniently away. While Ms Brookhurst spends the evening appalled at the damage being done to her house, the majority of the partygoers – self-styled Lotharios, bimbos, computer geeks, show-offs, prom queens, would-be musicians, extroverts, introverts, and a variety of teenage flotsam and jetsam it would be hard to imagine graduating from kindergarten let alone high school – are either drinking themselves comatose, trying to get laid or indulging in a combination of both. After a confusing start in which it was difficult to tell who was after whom, the film began to get a grip on itself by narrowing its focus to a handful of characters. Chief among these were Amanda (Jennifer Love Hewitt, right) and Preston (Ethan Embry, left). She's just been ditched from a four-year relationship with an arrogant self-serving stud (Peter Facinelli) who wants a clean slate to pursue other women in college; Preston's been carrying a torch for Amanda ever since he laid eyes on her four years earlier. So – will he or won't he find the courage to hand her the love-letter he's written now that she's no longer attached? Much more interesting was the relationship that develops between Denise (Lauren Ambrose) and her childhood friend Kenny (Seth Green) when they find themselves trapped in an upstairs bathroom for an hour or so and have sex. Narratively speaking, that was about it. Occasional flashes of well-observed writing penetrated the conversational murk, but for the most part the film painted an irritating and depressing picture of modern American youth and the mindless things that motivate them. It was co-written and directed by Deborah Kaplan and Harry Elfont whose low opinion of the species in question was little short of insulting. Indeed, the only refreshing aspect of their film was its cast – a group of talented youngsters who included Charlie Korsmo, Alexander Martin and, playing an older student who attempts to disillusion a girl-crazy youth by warning him not to expect too much when he gets to college, Erik Palladino. 'Guys like us,' says the older and wiser Palladino, 'are a dime a dozen.' Jenno Topping and Betty Thomas produced. (98 mins)

FILMS RELEASED BY COLUMBIA IN THE U.S. BUT NOT IN THE U.K.

In the last decade, due to a complicated pattern of distribution deals, Columbia, in common with most Hollywood majors, had release rights on certain titles for the U.S. but not the U.K. In this book, such films only qualify as main entries when released by Columbia in the U.K. Thus, Columbia's association with Castle Rock Entertainment is of particular significance. Columbia owned one third of Castle Rock, founded in 1987 by director Rob Reiner and executives Alan Horn, Glenn Padnick, Andrew Scheinman and Martin Schafer. The company made many major hits, released by Columbia under a distribution deal that applied only in the U.S. and are listed here.

1989

Physical Evidence
Dir: Michael Crichton; stars: Burt Reynolds, Theresa Russell, Ned Beatty
(Albacore Productions)

Winter People
Dir: Ted Kotcheff; stars: Kurt Russell, Kelly McGillis, Lloyd Bridges
(Castle Rock)

When Harry Met Sally
Dir: Rob Reiner; stars: Billy Crystal, Meg Ryan, Carrie Fisher, Bruno Kirby
(Castle Rock)

Me and Him
Dir: Doris Dörrie; stars: Griffin Dunne, Ellen Greene, Kelly Bishop
(Neue Constantin Film)

Welcome Home
Dir: Franklin J. Schaffner; stars: Kris Kristofferson, JoBeth Williams, Sam Waterston, Brian Keith
(Albacore Productions)

1990

The Gods Must Be Crazy II
Dir: Jamie Uys; stars N'xau, Lena Farugia, Hans Strydom
(A Boet-Troski Production, Fox)

Lord of the Flies
Dir: Harry Hook; stars: Balthazar Getty, Chris Furrh, Danuel Pipoly
(Castle Rock)

Texasville
Dir: Peter Bogdanovich; stars: Jeff Bridges, Cybill Shepherd, Annie Potts, Timothy Bottoms, Cloris Leachman, Randy Quaid

(Nelson Films)
Fifth Monkey, The
Dir: Eric Rochat; stars: Ben Kingsley, Mika Lins, Vera Fischer
(21st Century Film Corporation)

Sprit of '76, The
Dir: Lucas Reiner; stars: David Cassidy, Olivia d'Abo, Geoff Hoyle, Leif Garrett
(Castle Rock)

Sibling Rivalry
Dir: Carl Reiner; stars: Kirstie Alley, Bill Pullman, Carrie Fisher, Jami Gertz, Scott Bakula, Sam Elliott
(Castle Rock)

Misery
Dir: Rob Reiner; stars: James Caan, Kathy Bates
(Castle Rock)

1991

City Slickers
Dir: Ron Underwood; stars: Billy Crystal, Daniel Stern, Bruno Kirby, Jack Palance, Helen Slater
(Castle Rock)

Above *Texasville* (1990), with, left to right, Cybill Shpherd, Jeff Bridges and Annie Potts

Late For Dinner
Dir: W.D. Richter; stars: Brian Wimmer, Peter Berg, Marcia Gay Harden, Peter Gallagher
(Castle Rock)

Taking of Beverly Hills, The
Dir: Sidney J. Furie; stars: Ken Wahl, Matt Frewer, Harley Jane Kozak
(Castle Rock)

Below: *Winter People* (1989), with left to right Kurt Russell, Kelly McGillis and Lloyd Bridges

Above *A River Runs Through It* (1992), with, left to right, Craig Sheffer, Brad Pitt and Tom Skerritt

1992

Under Suspicion
Dir: Simon Moore; stars: Liam Neeson, Laura San Giacomo, Kenneth Cranham
(LWT-Rank)

Year of the Comet
Dir: Peter Yates; stars: Penelope Ann Miller, Timothy Daly, Louis Jourdan
(Castle Rock)

Honeymoon In Vegas
Dir: Andrew Bergman; stars: James Caan, Nicolas Cage, Sarah Jessica Parker, Pat Morita
(Castle Rock-New Line Cinema-First Independent)

Mr. Saturday Night
Dir: Billy Crystal; stars: Billy Crystal, David Paymer, Julie Warner, Helen Hunt, Ron Silver
(Castle Rock-First Independent)

Hard Promises
Dir: Martin Davidson; stars: Sissy Spacek, William Petersen, Brian Kerwin, Mare Winningham
(Stone Group Pictures)

A River Runs Through It
Dir: Robert Redford; stars: Craig Sheffer, Brad Pitt, Tom Skerritt, Brenda Blethyn, Emily Lloyd
(Allied Filmmakers-Guild)
Academy Award Nominations: Screenplay Based on Material from Another Medium: Richard Friedenberg; Music (Original Score): Mark Isham

1993

Needful Things
Dir: Fraser C. Heston; stars: Ed Harris, Max Von Sydow, Bonnie Bedelia, J.T. Walsh
(Castle Rock-New Line-Rank)

Malice
Dir: Harold Becker; stars: Alec Baldwin, Nicole Kidman, Bill Pullman, Bebe Neuwirth
(Castle Rock-New Line-Rank)

My Life
Dir: Bruce Joel Rubin; stars: Michael Keaton, Nicole Kidman, Bradley Whitford
(Capella Films-Guild)

Amos & Andrew
Dir: E. Max Frye; stars: Nicolas Cage, Samuel L. Jackson, Dabney Coleman, Brad Dourif
(Castle Rock)

Josh & S.A.M
Dir: Billy Weber; stars: Jacob Tierney, Noah Fleiss, Martha Plimpton, Stephen Tobolowsky, Joan Allen, Chris Penn
(Gaumont)

1994

North
Dir: Rob Reiner; stars: Elijah Wood, Jon Lovitz, Jason Alexander, Alan Arkin, Dan Aykroyd, Kathy Bates
(Castle Rock-New Line-Rank)

Little Big League
Dir: Andrew Sheinman; stars: Luke Edwards, Timothy Busfield, John Ashton
(Castle Rock-Rank)

The Shawshank Redemption
Dir: Frank Darabont; stars: Tim Robbins, Morgan Freeman, Bob Gunton
(Castle Rock-Rank)
Academy Award Nominations: Best Picture: Niki Marvin; Best Actor: Morgan Freeman; Best Screenplay Based on Material from Another Medium: Frank Darabont; Cinematography: Roger Deakins; Film Editing: Richard Francis-Bruce; Music (Original Score): Thomas Newman; Sound: Willie Burton, Robert J. Litt, Elliot Tyson, Michael Herbick

The Road to Wellville
Dir: Alan Parker; stars: Anthony Hopkins, Bridget Fonda, Matthew Broderick, John Cusack
(Beacon/Dirty Hands-Entertainment)

Immortal Beloved
Dir: Bernard Rose; stars: Gary Oldman, Jeroen Krabbé, Isabella Rossellini
(Majestic Films/Icon-Entertainment)

Professional, The
Dir: Luc Besson; stars: Jean Reno, Gary Oldman, Natalie Portman, Danny Aiello
(Les Films du Dauphin)

1995

The American President
Dir: Rob Reiner; stars: Michael Douglas, Annette Bening, Martin Sheen, David Paymer
(Universal/Castle Rock/ Wildwood Enterprises UIP)
Academy Award Nomination: Music (Original Musical or Comedy Score): Marc Shaiman

Before Sunrise
Dir: Richard Linklater; stars: Ethan Hawke, Julie Delpy, Erni Mangold
(Castle Rock/Detour Film/Filmhaus Wien-Rank)

Beyond Rangoon
Dir: John Boorman; stars: Patricia Arquette, Frances McDormand, Spalding Gray
(Castle Rock-Rank)

Dolores Claiborne
Dir: Taylor Hackford; stars: Kathy Bates, Jennifer Jason Leigh, David Strathairn, Judy Parfitt
(Castle Rock-Rank)

Above Nicole Kidman (left) in *To Die For* (1995)

Dracula: Dead and Loving It
Dir: Mel Brooks; stars: Leslie Nielsen, Peter MacNicol, Steven Weber, Amy Yasbeck, Lysette Anthony, Harvey Korman
(Castle Rock-Gaumont-Brooks Films-Polygram)

Forget Paris
Dir: Billy Crystal; stars: Billy Crystal, Debra Winger, Joe Mantegna, Cynthia Stevenson
(Castle Rock/Face-Rank)

Othello
Dir: Oliver Parker; stars: Laurence Fishburne, Irene Jacob, Kenneth Branagh
(Castle Rock/Dakota Films/Imminent Films-Rank)

The Run of the Country
Dir: Peter Yates; stars: Albert Finney, Matt Keeslar, Victoria Smurfit
(Castle Rock-Channel Four-One Two Nine-Rank)

To Die For
Dir: Gus Van Sant; stars: Nicole Kidman, Matt Dillon, Casey Affleck, Illeana Douglas
(Rank)

For Better Or Worse
Dir: Jason Alexander; stars: Jason Alexander, Lolita Davidovich, James Woods, Joe Mantegna
(Castle Rock)

1996

City Hall
Dir: Harold Becker; stars: Al Pacino, John Cusack, Bridget Fonda, Danny Aiello, Martin Landau, David Paymer, Anthony Franciosa
(Castle Rock-Rank)

Alaska
Dir: Fraser C. Heston; stars: Thora Birch, Vincent Kartheiser, Charlton Heston, Dirk Benedict
(Castle Rock-Rank-Castle Rock-Turner)

Extreme Measures
Dir: Michael Apted; stars: Hugh Grant, Gene Hackman, Sarah Jessica Parker, David Morse
(Castle Rock/Simian Films-Rank-Castle Rock/Turner)

Ghosts of Mississippi (a.k.a. Ghosts from the Past)
Dir: Rob Reiner; stars: Alec Baldwin, Whoopi Goldberg, James Woods, Craig T. Nelson, Diane Ladd
(Castle Rock-Rank)

Hamlet
Dir: Kenneth Branagh; stars: Kenneth Branagh, Julie Christie, Billy Crystal, Gerard Depardieu, Charlton Heston, Derek Jacobi, Jack Lemmon, Rufus Sewell, Robin Williams, Kate Winslet, John Gielgud, John Mills, Brian Blessed, Richard Briers, Reece Dinsdale, Ken Dodd, Rosemary Harris, Judi Dench, Ian McElhinney
(Castle Rock-Rank-Castle Rock-Turner)
Academy Award Nominations: Screenplay Based on Material From Another Medium: Kenneth Branagh; Art Direction: Tim Harvey; Costume Design: Alex Byrne; Music (Original Dramatic Score) Patrick Doyle

Lone Star
Dir: John Sayles; stars: Ron Canada, Chris Cooper, Kris Kristofferson, Frances McDormand, Clifton James
(Castle Rock/Rio Dulce-Rank-Castle Rock-Turner)

Some Mother's Son
Dir: Terry George; stars: Helen Mirren, Fionnula Flanagan, Aidan Gillen
(Castle Rock/Hell's Kitchen-Rank/Castle Rock/Turner)

The Spitfire Grill
Dir: Lee David; stars: Ellen Burstyn, Marcia Gay Harden, Will Patton
(Castle Rock/Gregory Productions/Mendocino Corp/ Rank/Castle Rock-Turner)

Striptease
Dir: Andrew Bergman; stars: Demi Moore; Armand Assante, Burt Reynolds, Ving Rhames, Paul Guilfoyle
(Castle Rock-Rank-Castle Rock/Turner)

1997

Absolute Power
Dir: Clint Eastwood; stars: Clint Eastwood, Gene Hackman, Ed Harris, Laura Linney, Judy Davis, Scott Glenn
(Castle Rock/Malpaso-Rank-Castle Rock/Turner)

Air Force One
Dir: Wolfgang Petersen; stars: Harrison Ford, Gary Oldman, Wendy Crewson, Paul Guilfoyle
(Buena Vista)
Academy Award Nominations: Film Editing: Richard Francis-Bruce; Sound: Paul Massie, Rick Kline, D.M. Hemphill, Keith Wester

The Fifth Element
Dir: Luc Besson; stars: Bruce Willis, Gary Oldman, Ian Holm, Milla Jovovich, Luke Perry
(Gaumont-Guild)
Academy Award Nomination: Sound Effects Editing: Mark Mangini

I Know What You Did Last Summer
Dir: Jim Gillespie; stars: Jennifer Love Hewitt, Sarah Michelle Gellar, Anne Heche
(Entertainment)

Spice World
Dir:Bob Spiers; stars: The Spice Girls, Richard E. Grant, Alan Cumming, Roger Moore
(Polygram)

Wind in the Willows, The
Dir: Terry Jones; stars: Terry Jones, Eric Idle, Steve Coogan, John Cleese, Michael Palin
(Allied Filmmakers)

1998

Zero Effect
Dir: Jake Kasdan; stars: Bill Pullman, Ben Stiller, Ryan O'Neal
(Warner Bros.)

Palmetto
Dir: Volker Schlöndorff; stars: Woody Harrelson, Elisabeth Shue, Gina Gershon
(Warner Bros.)

Wild Things
Dir: John McNaughton; stars: Kevin Bacon, Matt Dillon, Neve Campbell, Theresa Russell
(Entertainment)

My Giant
Dir: Michael Lehmann; stars: Billy Crystal, Gheorghe Muresan, Kathleen Quinlan
(Warner Bros.)

Sour Grapes
Dir: Larry David; stars: Steven Weber, Craig Bierko, Matt Keeslar
(Warner Bros.)

Les Misérables
Dir: Bille August: stars: Liam Neeson, Geoffrey Rush, Uma Thurman, Claire Danes
(Warner Bros.)

Dance With Me
Dir: Randa Haines; stars: Vanessa L. Williams, Chayanne, Kris Kristofferson, Joan Plowright

Shadrach
Dir: Susanna Styron; stars: Harvey Keitel, Andy MacDowell, John Franklin Sawyer, Martin Sheen (Tidewater Pictures)

Below: Harrison Ford (centre) in *Air Force One* (1997)

SERIALS

The Hollywood serial – those weekly, cliffhanging doses of derring-do, mystery, murder, and mayhem – reached its peak in the Forties. Its chief purveyors were Universal, Republic and Columbia who, between them, churned out no fewer than 192 titles between 1929 and 1956 when the genre finally died a natural death.

Designed specifically to lure patrons into the movie-houses of the world each week, these serials were, without exception, low-budget productions in which the script, the performances and the direction counted for very little. The essential ingredients of success were action, thrills and the ingenuity with which the makers contrived the hero or heroine's escape from the multiple disasters that closed each week's episode. The widely-read sci-fi comic-strips of the day gave many of the best serials their heroes: for Columbia the most notable of these were Batman and Robin, Brick Bradford, Captain Marvel, The Phantom, and Superman – who made his first screen appearance in 1948. Western shoot-outs, steamy jungle dramas, pirate adventures on the high seas and convoluted espionage plots were popular too. Columbia had most of the top serial actors on its lists at one time or another, including Buster Crabbe, Kane Richmond, Robert Lowery and Tom Tyler.

After World War II, a combination of TV, the ever-increasing costs of movie production, and the changing habits of America's cinema-going public saw a decline in the number of serials. Universal shut down its serial unit as early as 1946, and Republic followed suit in 1955. Columbia held out until 1956, and then brought the curtain down on an era with *Blazing The Overland Trail*.

1937
Jungle Menace
15 episodes. Frank Buck, John St Polis. Dir: George Melford, Harry Fraser. Rubber-plantation melodrama.
The Mysterious Pilot
15 episodes. Frank Hawks, Dorothy Sebastian. Dir: Spencer G. Bennet. Murder in the Canadian wilds.

1938
The Great Adventures of Wild Bill Hickok
15 episodes. Gordon Elliott, Carol Wayne. Dir: Mack V. Wright, Sam Nelson. Marshal Hickok outsmarts the Phantom Raiders.
The Secret Of Treasure Island
15 episodes. Don Terry, Gwen Gaze. Dir: Elmer Clifton. Caribbean-island treasure hunt.
The Spider's Web
15 episodes. Warren Hull, Iris Meredith. Dir: Ray Talor. One man's fight against terrorist gang.

1939
Flying G-Men
15 episodes. Robert Paige, Robert Fisk. Dir: Ray Taylor. G-Men versus enemy spies.

Mandrake The Magician
12 episodes. Warren Hull, Doris Weston. Dir: Sam Nelson, Norman Deming. Magician outsmarts master villain and his gang.
Overland With Kit Carson
15 episodes. Bill Elliott, Iris Meredith. Dir: Sam Nelson, Norman Deming. Carsons end Black Raiders' reign of terror in the West.

1940
Deadwood Dick
15 episodes. Don Douglas, Lorna Gray. Dir: James W. Horne. Robin Hood of the plains takes on masked gang leader.
The Green Archer
15 episodes. Victor Jory, Iris Meredith. Dir: James W. Horne. Mysterious hero solves murder mystery.
The Shadow
15 episodes. Victor Jory, Veda Ann Borg. Dir: James W. Horne. Criminologist risks life to defeat underworld mastermind.
Terry And The Pirates
15 episodes. William Tracy, Granville Owen. Dir: James W. Horne. Terry and his pals defeat Fang and the Tiger Men.

1941
Holt Of The Secret Service
15 episodes. Jack Holt, Evelyn Brent. Dir: James W. Horne. Detective versus counterfeiters.
The Iron Claw
15 episodes. Charles Quigley, Walter Sande. Dir: James W. Horne. Infamous Iron Claw unmasked.
The Spider Returns
15 episodes. Warren Hull, Mary Ainslee. Dir: James W. Horne. The Spider outwits gang of saboteurs.
White Eagle
15 episodes. Buck Jones, Raymond Hatton. Dir: James W. Horne. Outlaws frame Indian tribe for their dastardly deeds.

1942
Captain Midnight
15 episodes. Dave O'Brien, Dorothy Short. Dir: James W. Horne. Famous aviator smashes sabotage ring.
Perils Of The Royal Mounted
15 episodes. Robert Stevens, Kenneth MacDonald. Dir: James W. Horne. The Mounties get their men.
The Secret Code
15 episodes. Paul Kelly, Anne Nagel. Dir: Spencer G. Bennet. Police lieutenant defeats enemy agents.
The Valley Of Vanishing Men
15 episodes. Bill Elliott, Slim Summerville. Dir: Spencer Bennet. Western prospectors free slave labourers from gold mine.

1943
Batman
15 episodes. Lewis Wilson, Douglas Croft. Dir: Lambert Hillyer. Masked crime-fighter destroys murder ring.
The Phantom
15 episodes. Tom Tyler, Kenneth MacDonald. Dir: B. Reeves Eason. Another masked hero – in a jungle adventure.

1944
Black Arrow
15 episodes. Robert Scott, Adele Jergens. Dir: B. Reeves Eason. Carpetbaggers frame Navajo chief's son for murder.

Above: *Jungle Menace* (1937)

The Desert Hawk
15 episodes. Gilbert Roland, Mona Maris. Dir: B. Reeves Eason. Desert Prince fights for his throne.

1945
Brenda Starr, Reporter
13 episodes. Joan Woodbury, Kane Richmond. Dir: Wallace F. Fox. Million-dollar payroll robbery.
Jungle Raiders
15 episodes. Kane Richmond, Eddie Quillan. Dir: Lesley Selander. Jungle doctor makes deadly enemy of village priestess.
The Monster And The Ape
15 episodes. Robert Lowery, George Macready. Dir: Howard Bretherton. Trained ape foils theft of amazing robot.
Who's Guilty?
15 episodes. Robert Kent, Amelita Ward. Dir: Wallace Grisell. Multiple murder attempts in spooky house.

1946
Chick Carter, Detective
15 episodes. Lyle Talbot, Douglas Fowley. Dir: Derwin Abrahams. Intrepid detective on trail of stolen Blue Diamond.
Hop Harrigan
15 episodes. William Blakewell, Jennifer Holt. Dir: Derwin Abrahams. Triumph over villainous inventor of secret weapons.
Son Of The Guardsman
15 episodes. Robert Shaw, Daun Kennedy. Dir: Derwin Abrahams. Medieval hero defies robber-baron.

1947
Brick Bradford
15 episodes. Kane Richmond, Rick Vallin. Dir: Spencer G.Bennet. The evil rulers of the Moon are after Earth's Interceptor Ray.
Jack Armstrong
15 episodes. John Hart, Rosemary La Planche. Dir: Wallace W. Fox. Crime-busters find themselves on an enchanted island.
The Sea Hound
15 episodes. Buster Crabbe, Jimmy Lloyd. Dir: Walter B. Easson, Mark Wright. Captain of schooner up against a ruthless sea-robber.
The Vigilante
15 episodes. Ralph Byrd, Ramsay Ames. Dir: Wallas W. Fox. Western movie star is really government undercover agent.

1948
Congo Bill
15 episodes. Don McGuire, Cleo Moore. Dir: Spencer G. Bennet and Thomas Carr. Wild animal trainer in adventure with circus heiress.

Above: *Batman And Robin (1949)*

Superman
15 episodes. Kirk Alyn, Noel Neill. Dir: Spencer G. Bennet and Thomas Carr. Clark Kent pits his strength against the Spider Lady.

Tex Granger
15 episodes. Robert Kellard, Peggy Stewart. Dir: Derwin Abrahams. The masked Midnight Rider of the Plains saves Western town.

1949

Adventures Of Sir Galahad
15 episodes. George Reeves, Charles King. Dir: Spencer G. Bennet. Sir Galahad seeks Excalibur.

Batman And Robin
15 episodes. Robert Lowery, John Duncan. Dir: Spencer G. Bennet. The superhero and his pal triumph over the evil Wizard.

Bruce Gentry, Daredevil Of The Skies
15 episodes. Tom Neal, Judy Clark. Dir: Spencer G. Bennet and Thomas Carr. Fight for control of deadly secret weapon.

1950

Atom Man Vs Superman
15 episodes. Kirk Alyn, Noel Neill. Dir: Spencer G. Bennet. Arch enemy Luthor sets out to make Kryptonite, so as to destroy Superman.

Cody Of The Pony Express
15 episodes. Jock O'Mahoney, Dickie Moore. Dir: Spencer G. Bennet. Respectable lawyer turns out to be masterminding outlaw raids on stagecoaches.

Pirates Of The High Seas
15 episodes. Buster Crabbe, Lois Hail. Dir: Spencer G. Bennet and Thomas Carr. Ocean traffic under attack from phantom pirate ship.

1951

Captain Video
15 episodes. Judd Holdren, Larry Stewart. Dir: Spencer G. Bennet and Wallace Grissell. Sci-fi battles on the planet Atoma.

Mysterious Island
15 episodes. Richard Crane, Marshall Reed. Dir: Spencer G. Bennet. Civil War castaways in sci-fi adventure.

Roar Of The Iron Horse
15 episodes. Jock O'Mahoney, Virginia Herrick. Dir: Spencer G. Bennet and Thomas Carr. Western railroad drama.

1952

Blackhawk
15 episodes. Kirk Alyn, Carol Forman. Dir: Spencer G. Bennet. Saboteurs brought to justice by freedom fighters.

King Of The Kongo
15 episodes. Buster Crabbe, Gloria Dee. Dir: Spencer G. Bennet and Wallace Grissell. Hero battles subversive jungle activities.

Son Of Geronimo
15 episodes. Clayton Moore, Bud Osborne. Dir: Spencer G. Bennet. The Apaches help white settlers defeat outlaws.

1953

The Great Adventures Of Captain Kidd
15 episodes. Richard Crane, Dave Bruce. Dir: Derwin Abbe (Abrahams) and Charles Gould. Pirate or patriot?

The Lost Planet
15 episodes. Judd Holdren, Vivian Mason. Dir: Spencer G. Bennet. Invaders from planet Ergro.

1954

Gunfighter Of The Northwest
15 episodes. Jack Mahoney (earlier Jock O'Mahoney), Clayton Moore. Dir: Spencer G. Bennet. The Mounties to the rescue.

Riding With Buffalo Bill
15 episodes. Marshall Reed, Rick Vallin. Dir: Spencer G. Bennett. Indian Scout saves settlers from outlaws.

1955

Adventures Of Captain Africa
15 episodes. John Hart, Rick Vallin. Dir: Spencer G. Bennet. Jungle adventure helps deposed caliph regain throne.

1956

Blazing The Overland Trail
15 episodes. Lee Roberts, Dennis Moore. Dir: Spencer G. Bennet. Wagon-train Western.

Perils Of The Wilderness
15 episodes. Dennis Moore, Richard Emory. Dir: Spencer G. Bennet. The Mounties versus the ruthless Randall gang.The Forties

Below: *Superman (1948)*

The Forties equivalent of episodic TV was the film series. All the major studios produced them, and although their budgets were usually modest – falling as they did into the B-feature or 'programmer' category their entertainment value is not to be underestimated. Indeed, for many movie buffs these series offerings are often of more interest for what they reveal about the 'look' of a studio's product than the A-feature they usually accompanied.

Though no masterpieces emerged, Columbia's Blondie, Jungle Jim, the Lone Wolf (etc) entries were an integral part of the studio's bread-and-butter output and, because they cost so little to make, usually showed a profit.

BLONDIE

Chic Young's famous syndicated comic strip made the transfer from pen and ink to celluloid in a long and popular series – starring Penny Singleton as Blondie – that remained faithful in spirit to Young's much-loved, all-American family with its all-American middle-class values. Arthur Lake as Blondie's husband Dagwood, Larry Simms as Baby Dumpling (who grew into the name Alexander) and Marjorie Kent as little Cookie – a later happy event – completed the Bumitead family line-up. Jonathan Hale played Dagwood's boss in the early films, with Jerome Cowan taking over in 1947; Danny Mummert joined the regular cast from film four onwards as Alvin the postman. Daisy the dog played Daisy the dog.

1938

Blondie
This engaging start to the series fades in on the eve of the Bumsteads' fifth wedding anniversary – but the happy occasion is marred by Dagwood's having involved himself in a scheme that promises financial ruin. However, Blondie seizes on an unexpected stroke of luck and puts the family back on its financial feet again. Also cast: Gene Lockhart, Ann Doran. Dir: Frank Strayer. Prod: Robert Sparks. (68 mins)

1939

Blondie Meets The Boss
In which many of the gags seen in the first of the series were recycled as Blondie becomes the family breadwinner while her husband is away on a fishing jaunt. Dir: Frank Strayer. Prod: Robert Sparks. (75 mins)

Blondie Takes A Vacation
At a mountain-lake resort; the Bumstead family encounter some heavy-duty skulduggery – as well as an elderly couple whose life-savings would almost certainly have been lost were it not for Dagwood's timely intervention. Also cast: Donald McBride, Thomas W. Ross, Elizabeth Dunne. Dir: Frank Strayer. Prod: Robert Sparks. (68 mins)

Blondie Brings Up Baby
While Dagwood is having problems with his boss, Baby Dumpling is enrolled at school – and then goes missing. Also cast: Olin Howland, Fay Helm, Peggy Ann Garner. Dir: Frank Strayer. Prod: Robert Sparks. (67 mins)

1940
Blondie On A Budget
After starring in the big-budget and prestigious Only Angels Have Wings, Rita Hayworth's career suffered a momentary setback when she was cast as one of Dagwood's old flames. Also cast: Don Bed-doe, John Qualen. Dir: Frank Strayer. Prod: Robert Sparks. (72 mins)

Blondie Has Servant Trouble
This good excuse for another 'haunted house' comedy found the Bumsteads moving into an old dark house at the suggestion of Dagwood's boss. Also cast: Esther Dale, Arthur Hohl. Dir: Frank Strayer. Prod: Robert Sparks. (69 mins)

Blondie Plays Cupid
The usual Bumstead routines were routinely aired as Blondie assists in the elopement of a romantic young couple. Also cast: Glenn Ford and Luana Walters (as the lovers), Irving Bacon. Dir: Frank Strayer. Prod: Robert Sparks. (67 mins)

1941
Blondie Goes Latin (GB: Conga Swing)
The eighth entry in the series had half a dozen songs stitched on to a plot that found the Bum- steads all at sea (literally) while en route to South America with Dagwood's ailing boss. Also cast: Irving Bacon, Ruth Terry. Dir: Frank Strayer. Prod: Robert Sparks. (70 mins)

Blondie In Society (GB: Henpecked)
In which Dagwood acquires a Great Dane and Blondie enters it for a dog show. Par-for-the-course. Also cast: Douglas Frawley, Edgar Kennedy. Dir: Frank Strayer. Prod: Robert Sparks. (77 mins)

1942
Blondie Goes To College (GB: The Boss Said 'No')
Ma and Pa Bumstead decide to enrol at college while Baby Dumpling is sent to a military academy in a time-worn formula addition to the series. Also cast: Janet Blair, Adela Mara, Larry Parks, Lloyd Bridges. Dir: Frank Strayer. Prod: Robert Sparks. (74 mins)

Blondie's Blessed Event
A new character was added to the regular cast in the shape of Cookie Bumstead and with her arrival came both joy and chaos. Also cast: Hans Conried, Mary Wickes. Dir: Frank Strayer. Prod: Robert Sparks. (69 mins)

Blondie For Victory (GB: Troubles Through Billets)
When Blondie organizes her neighbours into the Housewives of America, Dagwood – bored with domestic duties – joins the US Army. One of the series' strongest entries. Also cast: Majelle White (as Cookie), Stuart Erwin. Dir: Frank Strayer Prod: Robert Sparks. (72 mins)

1943
It's A Great Life
Dagwood confuses 'house' with 'horse' and buys the latter instead of the former – with tedious consequences. Also cast: Marjorie Ann Mutchie (as Cookie from here on), Hugh Herbert, Irving Bacon. Dir, prod: Frank Strayer. (68 mins)

Footlight Glamour
Dagwood's involvement in the building of a new war-plant is nearly frustrated when Blondie produces a play. A dreary addition enlivened by the laughter milked from the play-within-the-film sequence. Also cast: Thurston Hall, Ann Savage. Dir, prod: Frank Strayer. (68 mins)

1945
Leave It To Blondie
Blondie, Dagwood and Dagwood's boss all enter a song-writing competition, not because they have any desire to break into Tin Pan Alley – but because they all need the money. Also cast: Marjorie Weaver, Eula Morgan. Dir: Abby Berlin. Prod: Burt Kelly. (74 mins)

1946
Blondie Knows Best
Dagwood is up to his neck in trouble, when he ineptly impersonates his boss – but is saved from terminal disaster in the nick of time. Also cast: Marjorie Kent, Shemp Howard, Stephen Gerzy. Dir: Abby Berlin. Prod: Burt Kelly. (69 mins)

Life With Blondie
Daisy the dog comes into her own when she is elected by the Navy as their favourite pin-up and takes over as the family breadwinner. Also cast: Ernest Truex, Veda Ann Borg. Dir, prod: Burt Kelly. (69 mins)

Blondie's Lucky Day
Dagwood is left in charge of the office and, when things go wrong, he sets up on his own with an ex-WAC architect. Also cast: Frank Jenks, Paul Harvey. Dir: Abby Berlin. Prod: Burt Kelly. (70 mins)

1947
Blondie's Holiday
Dagwood acquires a new boss in the shape of Jerome Cowan and tries to please his temperamental new employer – with disastrous results. Also cast: Sid Tomack, Bobby Larson, Grant Mitchell. Dir: Abby Berlin. Prod: Burt Kelly. (61 mins)

Blondie's Big Moment (GB: Bundle Of Trouble)
The usual comic strip characters were given ample opportunity to do their familiar thing when Blon-die has the chance to become a star. Also cast: Anita Louise. Dir: Abby Berlin. Prod: Burt Kelly. (69 mins)

Blondie In The Dough
Blondie has a windfall, during the course of which the series finally began to show wrinkles and go grey at the edges. Also cast: Hugh Herbert, Clarence Kolb. Dir: Abby Berlin. Prod: Burt Kelly. (69 mins)

Blondie's Anniversary
The slender gist of which involved Blondie finding a watch that she erroneously believes to be an anniversary present from Dagwood. Also cast: Grant Mitchell, Adele Jergens. Dir: Abby Berlin. Prod: Burt Kelly.

1948
Blondie's Reward
Dagwood falls foul of his boss when he takes an option on the wrong property and then socks the son-in-law of a prospective client. Also cast: Gay Nelson, Ross Rord. Dir: Abby Berlin. Prod: Burt Kelly. (65 mins)

Blondie's Secret
A series of mishaps prevents the Bumsteads taking their holiday. One of the weakest. Also cast: Frank Orth, Thurston Hall. Dir: Edward Bernds. Prod: Burt Kelly. (68 mins)

1949
Blondie's Big Deal (GB: The Big Deal)
This story of an experimental inflammable paint invented by Dagwood was a mite more entertaining than some of its recent predecessors. Also cast: Alan Dinehart III. Dir: Edward Bernds. Prod: Ted Richmond. (66 mins)

Blondie Hits The Jackpot (GB: Hitting The Jackpot)
A really feeble entry in which Dagwood blows a construction deal and finds himself in a labour gang. Also cast: Lloyd Corrigan, James Flavin. Dir: Edward Bernds. Prod: Ted Richmond. (66 mins)

Blondie's Hero
Dagwood inadvertently joins up for the Army and Blondie goes along for the ride. Also cast: William Frawley, Joe Sawyer. Dir: Edward Bernds. Prod: Ted Richmond. (67 mins)

1950
Beware Of Blondie
The last of the popular long-running series saw Dagwood sowing confusion as he temporarily takes over his boss's business. Also cast: Adele Jer-gens, Dick Wessel, Emory Parnell. Dir: Edward Bernds. Prod: Milton Feldman. (66 mins)

JUNGLE JIM

Johnny Weissmuller's well-worn – but still highly popular – Tarzan persona joined forces with the newspaper-cartoon character of Jungle Jim in this adventure series for junior audiences. The plot formula always had Jungle Jim (assisted by wonder ape Tamba) rescuing a heroine embroiled in a bizarre storyline – some of them bizarre enough to be collector's items. The last three entries, while not strictly Jungle Jims, trod the same well-worn path with Johnny Weissmuller in the lead. All were produced by Sam Katzman.

1948
Jungle Jim
A leopard, a bon, and a sea serpent prove no match for Jungle Jim when he heads a safari in search of hidden treasure – as well as a witch-doctor's serum against infantile paralysis. Also cast: Virginia Grey, George Reeves, Lita Baron. Dir: William Berke. (71 mins)

1949
The Lost Tribe
The inhabitants of a hidden city deep in the heart df Africa try to prevent a group of outsiders from pilfering the colony of its riches. Par for the jungle course. Also cast: Joseph Vitale, Myrna Dell, Ralph Dunn. Dir: Willam Berke. (72 mins)

1950
Captive Girl
Jungle Jim goes in search of a leopard goddess who never travels without her symbolic jungle cat and who is also being hunted by an evil medicine man with a terrible secret. Also cast: Anita Lhoest (the swimmer), John Dehner, Rick Vallin. Dir: William Berke. (73 mins)

Mark Of The Gorilla
In this far-fetched screen play, Jungle Jim sets out to expose Brandt, a fake doctor (Onslow Stevens) who is looking for gold hidden by the Nazis in a game reserve. Also cast: Trudy Marshall, Suzanne Dalbert. Dir: William Berke. (68 mins)

Pygmy Island
Marauding elephants, hungry crocodiles and a gorilla gone ape are among the hazards when Jungle Jim tries to save a local company from falling into the hands of enemy agents. Also cast: Ann Savage, David Bruce, Steven Geray. Dir: William Berke. (69 mins)

1951
Fury Of The Congo
While preventing a gang of smugglers from laying their hands on a strange narcotics plant, Jungle Jim has a few minor thrills and chills in coping with sandstorms, giant spiders, ferocious leopards as well as some two-legged villains. Also cast: Sherry Moreland, William Henry, Lyle Talbot. Dir: William Berke. (69 mins)

Jungle Manhunt
Professional football star Bob Waterfield joined Johnny Weissmuller in this feeble entry in which Waterfield disappears into the jungle on a routine flight in his army plane. Also cast: Sheila Ryan, Lyle Talbot. Dir: Lew Landers. (66 mins)

1952
Jungle Jim In The Forbidden Land
The usual set of two and four-legged hazards beset Jungle Jim as he leads an anthropologist (Angela Greene) to a land inhabited by giants. Also cast: Lester Matthews, William Tannen, Jean Willes. Dir: Lew Landers. (64 mins)

Voodoo Tiger
Iri this moribund jungle caper, Jungle Jim single handedly routs a group of American hoods as well as a bunch of African headhunters in his search for a Nazi officer and hidden art treasures. Also cast: Jean Byron, James Seay, Charles Horvath. Dir: Spencer G. Bennet. (67 mins)

1953
Killer Ape
More talk than action characterized this adventure in which Jungle Jim apprehends a bunch of crooks working on a drug that renders docile anyone who takes it. Also cast: Carol Thurston, Max Palmer. Dir: Spencer G. Bennet. (68 mins)

Below: Jungle Jim

Savage Mutiny
Jungle Jim is given the job of relocating a tribe of natives from their West African island prior to a series of atom bomb tests. Also cast: Angela Stevens, Lester Matthews, Nelson Leigh. Dir: Spencer G. Bennet. (72 mins)

Valley Of The Headhunters
This time Jungle Jim, as intrepid as ever, helps a government representative negotiate mineral rights in a rich valley – against the wishes of bad guys Robert Foulk and Joseph Allen Jr. No prizes or uessing the outcome. Also cast: Christine Larson, Steven Ritch. Dir: William Berke. (67 mins)

1954
Jungle Man-Eaters
Jungle Jim gets involved in the diamond business when smuggler Gregory Gaye threatens the stability of the world's diamond market after a massive jewel strike in the middle of the jungle. Also cast: Karin Booth, Richard Stapley. Dir: Lee Sholem. (67 mins)

Cannibal Attack
After the studio turned over its Jungle Jim rights to its TV subsidiary, Screen Gems, Johnny Weiss-muller starred in another jungle adventure about the mysterious disappearance of cobalt from a crocodile-infested river. Also cast: Judy Walsh, David Bruce, Charles Evans. Dir: Lee Sholem. (69 mins)

1955
Jungle Moon Men
Inspired by H. Rider Haggard's She, this jungle adventure had Weissmuller (now called Johnny, rather than Jungle Jim) encountering a high priestess (Helene Stanton) who has discovered the secret of eternal life. Also cast: Jean Byron, Bill Henry, Myron Healey. Dir: Charles S. Gould. (69 mins)

Devil Goddess
This low-octane adventure had Johnny Weissmuller guiding a girl and her professor father through treacherous African jungle in search of a self-styled white 'god'. Also cast: Angela Stevens, Selmer Jackson, Kimba the chimp. Released in a sepia print. Dir: Spencer G. Bennet. (70 mins).

THE LONE WOLF

Michael Lanyard, alias the Lone Wolf, is a gentleman jewel thief often to be found solving rather than committing crimes. The series, based on thriller-writer Louis Joseph Vance's characters, wound its way through eighteen films and six changes of principal actor.

1926
The Lone Wolf Returns
Bert Lytell was the screen's first Lone Wolf in this crime melodrama about a stolen necklace. Also cast: Billie Dove, Freeman Wood, Gwendolyn Lee. Dir: Ralph Ince.

1927
Alias The Lone Wolf
A woman asks Michael Lanyard (Bert Lytell) to smuggle some jewels through customs for her in this shipboard mystery. Also cast: Lois Wilson, William V. Mong. Dir: Edward H. Griffith.

1929
The Lone Wolf's Daughter
A pair of international thieves force Lanyard (Bert Lytell) to open a safe by threatening to expose his criminal past. Lanyard forestalls them and saves the valuables. Also cast: Gertrude Olmstead, Lilyan Tashman. Dir: Albert S. Rogell.

1930
The Last Of The Lone Wolf
Bert Lytell continued as the Lone Wolf in this Dumas-style story of royalty – the first of the series to have a soundtrack. Also cast: Alfred Hickman, Maryland Morne, Otto Matieson. Dir: Richard Boleslawsky. (70 mins)

1936
The Lone Wolf Returns
A moderately involving mystery in which Michael Lanyard, played by Melvyn Douglas, is on the trail of yet another jewel thief. Also cast: Douglass Dumbrille (as his sinister adversary), Gail Patrick, Tala Birell. Dir: Roy William Neill. (68 mins)

1938
Lone Wolf In Paris
Francis Lederer took over as Michael Lanyard in this fast-paced thriller involving a mission to recover a cache of crown jewels from Grand Duke Walter Kingsford. Also cast: Frances Drake, Olaf Hytten, Leona Maricle. Dir: Albert S. Rogell. (67 mins)

1939
The Lone Wolf Spy Hunt
(GB: The Lone Wolf's Daughter)
In the first of nine appearances as the Lone Wolf, Warren William found himself dealing with a ruthless bunch of £nternational spies. A neat blend of comedy and thrills. Also cast: Ida Lupino, Rita Hayworth, Ralph Morgan. Dir: Peter Godfrey. Prod: Joseph Sistrom. (69 mins)

1940
Lone Wolf Meets A Lady
Michael Lanyard (Warren William) comes to the aid of a young society woman (Jean Muir) whose $000,000 necklace is stolen on the eve of her wedding in this capably scripted (by John Larkin) thriller. Also cast: Warren Hull, Victor Jory, Eric Blore (as Jamison, the butler), Thurston Hall (as Inspector Crane). Dir: Sidney Salkow. Prod: Ralph Cohn. (70 mins)

The Lone Wolf Strikes
A neat and nifty quickie that never overreached its modest expectations saw Michael Lanyard (Warren William) come out of retirement to tackle yet another jewel thief. Also cast: Astrid Allwyn, Alan Baxter, Eric Blore. Dir: Sidney Salkow. Prod: Fred Kohlmar. (66 mins)

1941
The Lone Wolf Keeps A Date
This routine addition to the series found the Lone Wolf (Warren William) in Florida assisting Frances Robinson to recover her stolen money. Also cast: Bruce Bennett, Eric Blore, Thurston Hall. Dir: Sidney Salkow. Prod: Ralph Cohn. (66 mins)

The Lone Wolf Takes A Chance
A murder followed by the theft of a set of valuable engraving plates triggered off this formula thriller. Cast: Warren William, June Storey, Heniy Wilcoxon, Eric Blore, Thurston Hall. Dir: Sidney Salkow. Prod: Ralph Cohn. (76 mins)

Secrets Of The Lone Wolf (GB: Secrets)
One of the sturdier entries in the series, it departed from the usual formula by allowing Eric Blore to be mistaken for the Lone Wolf. Also cast: Warren William, Ruth Ford, Roger Clark, Thurston Hall. Dir: Edward Dmytryk. Prod: Jack Fier. (62 mins)

1942
Counter Espionage
A passable melodrama in which the worldly detective (Warren William) sets aside a case in blitz-torn London in order to outsmart a group of Nazi spies. Also cast: Eric Blore, Hillary Brooke, Thurston Hall. Dir: Edward Dmytryk. Prod: Wallace McDonald. (71 mins)

1943
Passport To Suez
Michael Lanyard (Warren William) is once again suspected of skulduggery, this time in Egypt. An absurdly complicated climax threw John Stone's screenplay out of kilter. Also cast: Eric Blore, Robert Stanford, Ann Savage, Lloyd Bridges. Dir: André de Toth. Prod: Wallace MacDonald. (72 mins)

One Dangerous Night
A passable entry in which the Lone Wolf (Warren William) discovers the body of a playboy-cum-blackmailer who has been murdered just as he was about to marry for the fourth time. Also cast: Marguerite Chapman, Eric Blore, Mona Barrie. Dir: Michael Gordon. Prod: David Chatkin. (77 mins)

1946
The Notorious Lone Wolf
Gerald Mohr replaced Warren Williams as Michael Lanyard in this agreeable yarn about a museum jewel heist. Also cast: Eric Blore, Janis Carter, John Abbott. Dir: D. Ross Lederman. Prod: Ted Richmond. (64 mins)

1947
The Lone Wolf In London
This fragile whodunnit found reformed jewel thief Michael Lanyard (played here by the uncharismatic Gerald Mohr) once again suspected of a crime he did not commit. Also cast: Eric Blore (who stole the show), Evelyn Ankers, Queenie Leonard. Dir: Leslie Goodwins. (64 mins)

The Lone Wolf In Mexico
Michael Lanyard's south-of-the-border activities involved him in bringing to justice a band of diamond smugglers: not very different from The Lone Wolf In London, Paris or Havana. Cast: Gerald Mohr, Sheila Ryan, Eric Blore, Jacqueline de Wit. Dir: D. Ross Lederman. Prod: Sanford Cummings. (69 mins)

1949
The Lone Wolf And His Lady
Ron Randell took over the lead in this familiar but competently directed thriller whose totally unremarkable plot found Michael Lanyard wrongly accused of stealing a famous diamond. Also cast: Alan Mowbray, William Frawley, Douglass Dumbrille. Dir: John Hoffman. Prod: Rudolph Flothow. (60 mins)

BOSTON BLACKIE

Chester Norris took on the role of Boston Blackie, a reformed crook turned sleuth – who has to spend most of his time proving to the law that he's innocent of the crimes he's investigating. Others with regular roles in the series, and based on characters created by Jack Boyle, included George F. Stone as the Runt, Blackie's dim-witted sidekick and the comic relief, Richard Lane as the ineffectual Inspector Faraday, always suspecting Blackie of murder, and Lloyd Corrigan Blackie's millionaire pal.

1941
Meet Boston Blackie
A risible start to the series which failed to establish Blackie's credentials, and in which he uncovers an international spy ring whilst proving himself innocent of murder. Also cast: Rochelle Hudson, Charles Wagenheim, Constance Worth. Dir: Robert Florey. Prod: Ralph Cohn. (61 mins)

Confessions Of Boston Blackie
Lightning-paced direction adroitly skipped over all the unnecessary details of a plot that found Boston Blackie on the lookout for a valuable sculpture stolen from a damsel (Harriet Hillard) in desperate need of the money she would have raised From its sale. Also cast: Joan Woodbury, Walter Sande. Dir: Edward Dmytryk. Prod: William Berke. (60 mins)

1942
Alias Boston Blackie (GB: Bulldog Jack)
Blackie sets out – in this carbon copy of his previous adventures – to free a prisoner (Larry Parks) by apprehending the real culprit. Also cast: Adele Mara, Walter Sande, Lloyd Bridges. Dir: Lew Landers. Prod: Wallace MacDonald. (67 mins)

Boston Blackie Goes To Hollywood (GB: Blackie Goes To Hollywood)
A routine, none-too-imaginative quickie which sent Blackie west to seek out the fabulous Monterey Diamond. Also cast: Forrest Tucker, William Wright, Constance Worth. Dir: Michael Gordon. Prod: Wallace MacDonald. (68 mins)

1943
The Chance Of A Lifetime
A neat little thriller in which Blackie sponsors the parole of a group of hardened cons so they may take up wartime employment in a tool manufacturing workshop owned by his millionaire friend (Lloyd Corrigan). Complications, as they say, ensue. Also cast: Erik Rolfe, Jeanne Bates. Dir: William Castle (his first feature). Prod: Wallace MacDonald. (66 mins)

After Midnight With Boston Blackie
Not one of the better entries in the series, this formula thriller found Blackie once again arrested for a murder he did not commit. Also cast: Walter Baldwin, Ann Savage, Cy Kendall. Dir: Lew Landers. Prod: Sam White. (64 mins)

1944
One Mysterious Night
Another routine whodunnit in which Boston Blackie is corralled into service by the police in order to help them find a valuable stolen diamond. Also cast: Janis Carter, William Wright, Robert Williams. Dir: Budd Boetticher. Prod: Ted Richmond. (61 mins)

Above: Boston Blackie

1945
Boston Blackie Booked On Suspicion (GB: Blackie Booked On Suspicion)
A plot gone berserk has Blackie helping a friend by pretending to be an auctioneer – but then, after inadvertently selling a fake first edition, becoming suspect number one in a murder case. Also cast: Lynne Merrick, Frank Sully, Steve Cochran. Dir: Arthur Dreifuss. Prod: Michael Kraike. (66 mins)

Boston Blackie's Rendezvous (GB: Blackie's Rendezvous)
A better-than-usual entry which centred on a killer (Steve Cochran) who breaks out of an asylum and, while pretending to be Blackie, embarks on a strangling spree. Also cast: Nina Foch, Frank Sully. Dir: Arthur Dreifuss. Prod: Alexis Thurn-Taxis. (64 mins)

1946
Boston Blackie And The Law (GB: Blackie And The Law)
Murder rears its head when a girl in a woman's penitentiary uses Blackie's celebrated magic show to escape. How Blackie sees to it that justice prevails was a yawnsome business. Also cast: Trudy Marshall, Constance Dowling, Frank Sully. Dir: D. Ross Lederman. Prod: Ted Richmond. (69 mins)

A Close Call For Boston Blackie
One of the sturdier entries in the series, this one saw Blackie charmingly and cunningly proving to Inspector Faraday that be's been framed for murder. Also cast: Lynn Merrick, Frank Sully, Claire Carlton. Dir: Lew Landers. Prod: Frank Stone. (68 mins)

The Phantom Thief
Blackie is suspected of murder when he becomes embroiled in spiritualism and seances while attempting to locate the usual stolen gems. Also cast: Jeff Donnell, Frank Sully, Dusty Anderson. Dir: D. Ross Lederman. Prod: John Stone. (65 mins)

1948
Boston Blackie's Chinese Adventure
Blackie and the Runt (played this time by Sid Tomack) are mistaken for homicidal maniacs when they are seen leaving a Chinese laundry in which the proprietor has just been murdered. A purely formula entry. Also cast: Maylia, Don McGuire, Joan Woodburt. Dir: Seymour Friedman. Prod: Rudolph Flothow. (59 mins)

Trapped by Boston Blackie
The last of the series made do with a threadbare plot about a missing pearl necklace which Blackie is suspected of stealing. Also cast: June Vincent, Patricia White, Edward Norris, Frank Sully. Dir: Seymour Friedman. Prod: Rudolph Flothow. (67 mins)

CRIME DOCTOR

Based on the popular CBS radio show created by Max Marcin, this series cast Warner Baxter as Dr Robert Ordway who – after a blow on the head – turns from being a criminal mastermind into a celebrated psychiatrist and infallible solver of crime. All but the first in the series were produced by Rudolph Flothow.

1943
Crime Doctor
A badly wounded man with amnesia is brought to a hospital. The staff christen him Ordway and help him build a new life as a psychiatrist and criminologist. Then one day a woman prisoner recognizes him and reveals that Dr Ordway – the Crime Doctor – has his own criminal past. Also cast: Margaret Lindsay, John Litel. Dir: Michael Gordon. Prod: Ralph Cohn. (66 mins)

Crime Doctor's Strangest Case
Dr Ordway examines mysterious death by poisoning) of a retired estate agent. Lynn Merrick, Lloyd Bridges. Dir: Eugene J. Forde. (68 mins)

1944
Shadows In The Night
The Crime Doctor investigates the case of an heiress (Nina Foch) being haunted into madness by one of her party of house-guests. Also cast: George Zucco, Minor Watson. Dir: Eugene J. Forde. (67 mins)

1945
The Crime Doctor's Courage
Dr Ordway solves a murder which might have been the work of a novelist, a pair of Spanish dancers, a fortune-teller and a young man of serious disposition. Also cast: Hillary Brooke, Jerome Cowan. Dir: George Sherman. (70 mins)

The Crime Doctor's Warning
The Crime Doctor has to prove that a series of murders is not the work of art dealer Miles Mander. Also cast: John Litel, Dusty Anderson. Dir: William Castle. (69 mins)

Below: The Crime Doctor

1946
Crime Doctor's Manhunt
While investigating the murder of a young man, Dr Ordway discovers that the boy's deceased fiancée had a troublesome twin sister who now appears, in the guise of her dead sister, to be murdering people. But which twin is really dead? Ellen Drew played both of them. Also cast: William Frawley, Frank Sully. Dir: William Castle. (64 mins)

Just Before Dawn
Ordway finds himself on a search for a mad psychopath (Martin Kosleck) whose murder methods are highly inventive. Also cast: Adelle Roberts, Mona Barrie. Dir: William Castle. (65 mins)

1947
The Millerson Case
(aka The Crime Doctor's Vacation)
Crime Doctor Ordway springs into action when he discovers that a typhoid epidemic is being used as a cover for the murder of a country doctor (Griff Barnett) in the Blue Ridge Mountains of Virginia. Also cast: Nancy Saunders, Clem Bevans. Dir: George Archainbaud. (72 mins)

1947
The Crime Doctor's Gamble
Ordway is on holiday in Paris – but finds his interest turning from the Louvre and the Folies Bergéres to a young Frenchman who's been accused of murdering his father. Also cast: Micheline Cheirel, Roger Dann. Dir: William Castle. (65 mins)

Crime Doctor's Diary
Ordway helps a man (Stephen Dunne) who has been framed for arson and murder (of George Meeker), and unveils the real culprit (Lois Maxwell). Also cast: Adele Jergens. Dir: Seymour Friedman. (61 mins)

ELLERY QUEEN

Following on from two Republic films of the Thirties, Manfred B. Lee and Frederic Dannay's famous sleuth, the debonair Ellery Queen, returned to the screen in a series which was, in the main, unworthy of him. Ralph Bellamy played the eponymous gumshoe in the first four films, then William Gargan took over for the next three. Margaret Lindsay appeared regularly as his secretary Nikki, with Charley Grapewin as Inspector Queen – his celebrated father – and James Burke as the inspector's dim-witted aide The series was scripted by Eric Taylor, directed by James Hogan (except this first, by Kurt Neumann) and produced by Larry Darmour (except the last, by Ralph Cohn).

Below: Ellery Queen

1940
Ellery Queen, Master Detective
The sudden death of a millionaire health freak (Fred Niblo) was the mystery to be unravelled by Queen (Bellamy) in this lacklustre opener to the series. Also cast: Michael Whalen, Marsha Hunt. (58 mins)

1941
Ellery Queen's Penthouse Mystery
A marginal improvement on the first in the series, though still no masterpiece, this yarn saw Inspector Queen investigating the murder of a Chinese vaudeville performer-cum-jewel smuggler (Anna May Wong) – with the expert help of talented son Ellery (Bellamy). Also cast: Eduardo Ciannelli, Frank Albertson. (69 mins)

Ellery Queen And The Perfect Crime
A feeble tale in which Queen (Bellamy) uncovers the killer of a utilities promoter who earns his living (and, ultimately, his death) by selling crooked stock. Also cast: Spring Byington, H. B. Warner, Douglass Dumbrille.(67mins)

Ellery Queen And The Murder Ring
A tired formula whodunnit had Queen (Bellamy) solving three murders in a hospital while being stalked by heavies Paul Hurst and Tom Dugan. Also cast: Mona Barrie. (70 mins)

1942
A Close Call For Ellery Queen
A deftly scripted thriller in which Ellery Queen (Gargan) finds himself involved in the murders that result from the efforts of a wealthy retired businessman (Ralph Morgan) to trace his three daughters in order to transfer his estate to them a move not appreciated by his ex-partners. Also cast: Kay Linaker. (65 mins)

Desperate Chance For Ellery Queen
A lifeless screenplay had Queen (Gargan) hired by a woman (Charlotte Wynters) to search for her missing husband – and finding several dead bodies along the way. Also cast: John Litel, Lillian Bond. (70 mins)

1943
Enemy Agents Meet Ellery Queen
The title told prospective audiences (and there were precious few of those) everything there was to know about the final entry in this decidedly dud series. Nazis spies included the inevitable Sig Rumann. Also cast: Gale Sondergaard, Gilbert Roland. (64 mins)

THE ADVENTURES OF RUSTY

A series for the moppets in which a boy (Ted Donaldson) and a dog called Rusty (played at first by Ace the Wonder Dog, and later by Flame) turn up together in a variety of adventures.

1945
The Adventures Of Rusty
Ted Donaldson has two missions here – to tame a vicious police dog as well as a new stepmother. Also cast: Conrad Nagel, Margaret Lin say. Dir: Paul Burnford. Prod: Rudolph Flothow. (69 mins)

1946

The Return Of Rusty
The adventures of a Czechoslovakian war orphan (Donaldson) who is evacuated to a small American town and is befriended by a youngster and his dog. Also cast: John Litel, Mark Dennis, Barbara Woodell. Dir: William Castle. Prod: Leonard S. Picker. (64 mins)

1947

For The Love Of Rusty
An unashamedly sentimental story about how the love of a boy (Donaldson) for his dog leads to a misunderstanding with his father (Tom Powers). A travelling vet (Aubrey Mather) helps save the day. Also cast: Ann Doran, Sid Tomack. Dir: John Sturges. Prod: John Haggott. (68 mins)

Son Of Rusty
Young Danny (Donaldson) gets involved with a bombardier (Stephen Dunne) – who is being hounded by gossip – when Danny's dog Rusty falls in love with the bombardier's dog Barb. Also cast: Tom Powers, Ann Doran. Dir: Lew Landers. Prod: Wallace MacDonald. (75 mins)

1948

Rusty Leads The Way
A tale, with its heart in the right place, of the efforts of a boy (Donaldson) to train Rusty as a seeing-eye dog for a little blind girl (Sharyn Moffett). Also cast: John Litel, Ann Doran. Dir: Lew Landers. Prod: Wallace MacDonald. (58 mins)

1949

My Dog Rusty
Only the most indulgent of family audiences could respond favourably to this yarn about a kid (Donaldson) whose lying ways result in his father (John Litel) losing a mayorial campaign. Also cast: Ann Doran, Mona Barrie. Dir: Lew Landers. Prod: Wallace MacDonald. (64 mins)

Rusty Saves A Life
A woebegone tale in which a quintet of youngsters (led by Donaldson) are supposed to inherit a property belonging to the richest man in town who dies before completing his will. However, Rusty saves the day. With Ronnie Ralph, Stephen Dunne, John Litel, Ann Doran. Dir: Seymour Friedman. Prod: Wallace MacDonald. (67 mins)

Rusty's Birthday
A final, and tearful, canine caper in which Rusty is separated from his loving owner (Donaldson) when he is inadvertently bought by some tourists – but everything came right in the end. Also cast: John Litel, Ann Doran, Ray Teal. Dir: Seymour Friedman. Prod: Wallace MacDonald. (60 mins)

Above: Rusty with Ted Donaldson

THE WHISTLER

Inspired by the CBS radio melodramas of the same name, this popular series starred Richard Dix in a set of loosely connected thrillers. The Whistler' of the title introduced each story in which Dix might play the role of either the hero or the villain.

1944

The Whistler
A diverting little thriller in which a man (Richard Dix), distraught from the death of his wife, hires a hit-man to have himself killed – only to discover that his wife is still alive. But how to stop the hit-man? Also cast: J. Carrol Naish, Alan Dinehart, Gloria Stuart, Otto Forrest. Dir: William Castle. Prod: Rudolph Flothow. (59 mins)

Mark Of The Whistler
A par-for-the-course yarn whose implausible plot concerned an itinerant bum (Richard Dix) laying claim to a dormant bank account, thereby putting his life in danger. Also cast: Janis Carter, Porter Hall, Paul Guilfoyle. Dir: William Castle. Prod: Rudolph Flothow. (60 mins)

1945

The Power Of The Whistler
Richard Dix played an amnesia sufferer-cum-homicidal maniac whose involvement with pretty Janis Carter almost leads to her death. Also cast: Jeff Donnell, Loren Tindall, Tala Birell. Dir: Lew Landers. Prod: Leonard S. Picker. (66 mins)

Voice Of The Whistler
This feeble entry in the series had Richard Dix as a wealthy man with only six months to live. Seven months later, his new wife has murder on her mind. Also cast: Lynn Merrick, James Cardwell, Rhys Williams. Dir: William Castle. Prod: Rudolph Flothow. (60 mins)

1946

Mysterious Intruder
This time Richard Dix is a private eye investigating a murder whose motive is the acquisition of a pair of recordings made by opera diva Jenny Lind. Also cast: Mike Mazurki, Barton MacLane, Nina Vale. Dir: William Castle. Prod: Rudolph Flothow. (62 mins)

Secret Of The Whistler
One of the best of the series, this entry starred Richard Dix as a mad artist who, having done away with his first wife, is preparing the same fate for spouse number two (Leslie Brooks). This one, however, is on to him. Also cast: Mary Currier, Michael Duane, Mona Barrie. Dir: George Sherman. Prod: Rudolph Flothow. (65 mins)

1947

The 13th Hour
After a grand total of 97 films, Richard Dix called it a day with this crime melodrama about the owner of a trucking company (Dix) framed for murder by a rival. Also cast: Karen Morley, Mark Dennis, John Kellogg. Dir: William Clemens. Prod: Rudolph Flothow. (65 mins)

1948

Return Of The Whistler
There was the germ of an idea, never realised, in this story about the mysterious disappearance of would-be bride (Lenore Aubert) and the attempts of her husband to be (Michael Duane) to trace her. Also cast: Richard Lane, James Cardwell, Ann Shoemaker. Dir: D. Ross Lederman. Prod: Rudolph Flothow. (63 mins)

SHORT SERIES

FIVE LITTLE PEPPERS

This series of four family-orientated programmers based on Margaret Sidney's book *Five Little Peppers And How They Grew* was directed by Charles Barton (who also produced all but the first). Edith Fellows was top-billed as Polly, the oldest, who looks after the others (Charles Peck, Tommy Bond, Jimmy Leake and scene-stealing little Dorothy Ann Seese) while their hard-working mother was played by Dorothy Peterson.

1939

Five Little Peppers
The series kicked off with a Cinderella-like plot in which the youngest Pepper comes down with measles, forcing a local rich kid (Ronald Sinclair) and his grandfather (Clarence Kolb) to remain quarantined in the Pepper home. Prod: Jack Fier. (58 mins)

1940

Five Little Peppers At Home
A sweet-as-saccharine, less-effective episode which revolved around oldtimer Clarence Kolb's financial straits and a copper-mine cave-in which traps the children. Also cast: Ronald Sinclair. (67 mins)

Out West With The Peppers
The weakest of the series found the Pepper brood in a spot of hot water at a lumber camp. Also cast: Ronald Sinclair, Pierre Warkin (in the Clarence Kolb role), Bobby Larson. (63 mins)

Five Little Peppers In Trouble
In a less than scintillating script, the Peppers find themselves in a fashionable boarding school where they became the butt of a group of snobbish rich kids. Little Dorothy Ann Seese pilfered the show with all the best lines. Also cast: Pierre Warkin, Ronald Sinclair, Bobby Larson. (63 mins)

BULLDOG DRUMMOND

The character of Hugh 'Bulldog' Drummond, a British ex-army officer yearning for his old life of adventure, was created by the novelist 'Sapper' (H. C. McNeile), and became the hero of a long series of movies – mostly made by Paramount in the Thirties. In 1947, Ron Randell starred in two Bulldog Drummond films for Columbia – but neither pleased the author's legion of devotees.

1947

Bulldog Drummond At Bay
Drummond (Randell) goes in hot pursuit of a murderer with a valuable stash of diamonds in tow. Also cast: Anita Louise, Pat O'Moore. Dir: Sidney Salkow. Prod: Louis B. Appleton Jr, Bernard Small. (70 mins)

Bulldog Drummond Strikes Back
The task for Drummond (Randell), on this uninspired occasion, was to locate a woman who, in order to appropriate a fortune, is impersonating an heiress (Gloria Henry); he soon finds himself involved in a murder. Also cast: Pat O'Moore, Anabel Shaw. Dir: Frank McDonald. Prod: Louis B. Appleton Jr, Bernard Small. (65 mins)

NERO WOLFE

Novelist Rex Stout's popular private eye reached the screen in, sadly, only two neat, low-budget thrillers – whose costs were kept to a minimum because the sybaritic, food-swilling, orchid-cultivating Wolfe did most of his sleuthing without leaving home.

1936
Meet Nero Wolfe
Wolfe (here excellently played by the rotund Edward Arnold) sets out to prove the link between the sudden death on a golf course of a college president and the slaying of a young mechanic. Also cast: Lionel Stander, Victor Jory – and Rita Cansino (later Rita Hayworth). Dir: Herbert Biberman. Prod: B. P. Schulberg. (73 mins)

1937
League Of Frightened Men
A group of Harvard graduates, three of whom have died in mysterious circumstances, hire Nero Wolfe (played by Walter Connolly) to catch the murderer before he catches any more of them. Also cast: Eduardo Ciannelli, Lionel Stander. Dir: Alfred E. Green (71 mins)

I LOVE A MYSTERY

In 1945 a series began based on a suspenseful radio show called *I Love A Mystery*, but it lapsed after only three films. Henry Levin directed and Wallace MacDonald produced them.

1945
I Love A Mystery
A preposterous, thoroughly tasteless and rather nasty little thriller, this kick-off entry involved a playboy's wife (Nina Foch) who works in league with a group of wily Orientals to provoke her husband (George Macready) into suicide. Also cast: Carole Mathews, Gregory Gaye, Lester Matthews. (68 mins)

1946
The Unknown
A familiar brew of chills and thrills, this was the tale of a contested will, set in an ancient mansion, replete with crazy inhabitants, underground passageways, mysterious shadowy figures and the obligatory stabbing or two, and featured Jim Bannon and Karen Morley. Also cast: Jeff Donnell, Robert Scott. (70 mins)

The Devil's Mask
An unassuming whodunnit that starred Jim Bannon and Barton Yarborough as a pair of detectives hired by Anita Louise to discover who murdered her father in the Amazon jungle. Also cast: Michael Duane, Mona Barrie. (66 mins)

GASOLINE ALLEY

Life in a restaurant diner was to be the background for a series centred on the Wallet family – based on Frank O. King's comic strip. It consisted of Corky Wallet (Scottie Beckett), his wife Hope (Susan Morrow), Walt Wallet (Don Beddoe), Phyllis (Madelon Mitchell), Nina (Kay Christopher) and Judy (Patti Brady), the youngest. Jimmy Lydon played Skeezix, while Dick Wessel and Gus Schilling completed the line-up as chief cook and bottle washer. However, the Wallets disappeared after just two films.

1951
Gasoline Alley
An introduction to this family involved in the catering game – with all its attendant joys and problems. Dir: Edward Bernds. Prod: Milton Feldman. (76 mins)

Corky Of Gasoline Alley
Much disruption to the Wallet family catering business is caused by the arrival of Hope's layabout cousin Elwood (Gordon Jones). Full of cliches and platitudes. Dir: Edward Bernds. Prod: Wallace MacDonald. (80 mins)

WESTERNS

Between 1930 and 1958, the studio made over 300 'B' Westerns. The majority of these ran at about an hour and were 'series' Westerns, in which an established hero returned, film after film, for new adventures. The Westerns were allotted very low budgets and, as a result, were tailored to tightly standardized production methods. An early fist-fight, an action-packed chase sequence and a villain defeated in a climactic shoot-out – plus a varying mix of Indians, Mexicans, Cavalry, stagecoaches and wagon trains – were regular ingredients. The more 'expensive' sequences, such as stampedes or Indian attacks, would be reused in other films. However, the series Westerns formed one of the studio's most reliable sources of income, for they were custom-built to fill the bottom half of the double-bill programme which Hollywood invented to coax Depression-era audiences back into cinemas.

An added attraction to the 'B' Westerns of the Thirties and Forties was the 'musical interlude', which would either be filled by a singing cowboy or by a group such as the Sons of the Pioneers or the Hoosier Hot Shots. Columbia made Western series with most of the greatest of the singing cowboys – Buck Jones, Tim McCoy, Gene Autry, Ken Maynard and Tex Ritter. Other cowboy stars included Bill Elliott, George Montgomery, Bob Allen and, most enduring and productive of them all, Charles Starrett, who made the Durango Kid one of the most popular and long-lasting of all series Western heroes.

In addition, Columbia's Western unit featured such popular 'side-kicks' as Smiley Burnett, Pat Buttram, Jock Mahoney and Jay Silverheels, and such stalwart directors as Spencer G. Bennet, Fred F. Sears, Lambert Hillyer, D. Ross Lederman, Ray Nazarro, John English, George Archinbaud and Lew Landers.

Listed below is Columbia's contribution to the Golden Age of B Westerns. Each film title is accompanied by its star, its director, its running time and a brief plot outline.

1930
Call Of The West
Matt Moore. Dir: Albert Ray. A cabaret singer falls for a rancher while in Texas and marries him. However, when he joins a posse in order to track down some rustlers, she returns to New York and a former suitor. (70 mins)

The Dawn Trail
Buck Jones. Dir: Christy Cabanne. A sheriff is holding the brother of his girlfriend for murder. (66 mins)

The Lone Rider
Buck Jones. Dir: Louis King. An outlaw turns hero as he heads the town's vigilante committee after abandoning his gang and preventing a stagecoach hold-up. (60 mins)

Men Without Law
Buck Jones. Dir: Louis King. After returning home from World War 1, a man learns that his brother has fallen in with gangsters and sets out to find him. (60 mins)

Shadow Ranch
Buck Jones. Dir: Louis King. A crooked saloon owner gains control of a valley's water supply by murdering the foreman of a ranch. Featured the song 'Ragtime Cowboy Joe'. (55 mins)

1931
The Avenger
Buck Jones. Dir: R. William Neill. A man, disguised as a Mexican bandit, sets out to track down and destroy the gang who murdered his entire family. (65 mins)

Border Law
Buck Jones. Dir: Louis King. Posing as The Pecos Kid, an ex-ranger sets out to avenge his brother's death at the hands of the notorious outlaw Shag Smith. (63 mins)

Branded
Buck Jones. Dir: D. Ross Lederman. After inheriting a ranch a man becomes involved with a pretty neighbour whose crooked foreman plans to rustle his cattle. (61 mins)

The Deadline
Buck Jones. Dir: Lambert Hillyer. A Pony Express rider, while on his last run before the introduction of the telegraph, unearths a plot by a rancher to force a company into bankruptcy and steal its land for his own personal profit. (57 mins)

Desert Vengeance
Buck Jones. Dir: Louis King. Two rival gangs of desperadoes attempt to gain supremacy in the district surrounding a small town in the Western Sierras. (55 mins)

The Fighting Marshal
Tim McCoy. Dir: D. Ross Lederman. Jailed for a crime he did not commit, a man escapes from prison, takes on the identity of a marshal and rids the town of an notorious gang of outlaws. (60 mins)

Above: Buck Jones

The Fighting Sheriff
Buck Jones. Dir: Louis King. A young girl turns against her sheriff lover when his rival tells her that he (the sheriff) was responsible for the death of her brother. (67 mins)

One Way Trail
Tim McCoy. Dir: Ray Taylor. A cowboy tries to ruin a man who murdered his brother. (60 mins)

Range Feud
Buck Jones. Dir: D. Ross Lederman. A newly appointed sheriff is forced to arrest his foster brother for murder. With John Wayne. (56 mins)

Ridin' For Justice
Buck Jones. Dir: D. Ross Lederman. A carefree, fun-loving cowboy gives the wife of a marshal a gun for protection which she uses to kill a notorious scoundrel. The cowboy is then accused of the villain's murder. (60 mins)

Shotgun Pass
Tim McCoy. Dir: Robert Quigley. A young rancher vows vengeance on his enemies for the murder of his father at the hands of the Mitchell brothers. The climax is a range war to secure a right-of-way through a pass. (60 mins)

The Texas Ranger
Buck Jones. Dir: D. Ross Lederman. A Texas Ranger takes on a gang of crooks in cattle country in order to stop a long-standing feud. (60 mins)

1932

Cornered
Tim McCoy. Dir: Reeves Eason. A sheriff and a ranch foreman both love the same girl. When the girl's father is murdered, the foreman is blamed for the crime, sent to jail, escapes, and joins an outlaw gang. (60 mins)

Daring Danger
Tim McCoy. Dir: D. Ross Lederman. A cowboy comes to the rescue of an old man and his daughter when a villain sets out to starve them off their land. (60 mins)

Fighting Fool
Tim McCoy. Dir: Lambert Hillyer. When a sheriff learns that his young brother has been killed by the 'Shadow' and his gang, he makes every effort to avenge his brother's death. (58 mins)

Fighting For Justice
Tim McCoy. Dir: Otto Brower. A man discovers that land owned by his father has been ille-

gally sold for taxes that have already been paid. The new owner, unaware of the illegality, is then murdered, and the land records destroyed. (60 mins)

Forbidden Trail
Buck Jones. Dir: Lambert Hillyer. A cowboy and a crusading girl editor join forces to oust a local land-grabber. (71 mins)

Hello Trouble
Buck Jones. Dir: Lambert Hillyer. A Texas Ranger kills one of three cattle rustlers only to discover that the dead man is a friend. (67 mins)

McKenna Of The Mounted
Buck Jones. Dir: D. Ross Lederman. A disgraced Mountie leaves the service and joins a gang of outlaws in order to bring them to justice. (66 mins)

One Man Law
Buck Jones. Dir: Lambert Hillyer. In order to protect his crooked dealings, a land speculator convinces a local cowboy to become sheriff. The new sheriff, however, soon gets wise to the speculator's activities and restores law and order. (60 mins)

Riding Tornado
Tim McCoy. Dir: D. Ross Lederman. A local boss is the brains behind a gang of rustlers. A rodeo champion brings him to justice. (59 mins)

South Of The Rio Grande
Buck Jones. Dir: Lambert Hillyer. A member of the Mexican police determines to avenge the death of his younger brother. (60 mins)

Texas Cyclone
Tim McCoy. Dir: D. Ross Lederman. In a small Arizona town, a cowboy is mistaken for another man, and almost murdered. He sets out to solve the mystery. With John Wayne. (63 mins)

Two-Fisted Law
Tim McCoy. Dir: D. Ross Lederman. After making a successful gold strike, a cowboy who was once cheated out of his ranch returns home and prevents a girl from losing her ranch to the same crook who stole his. (64 mins)

The Western Code
Tim McCoy. Dir: J. P. McCarthy. A cowboy comes to the rescue of a girl whose villainous stepfather has not only stolen her ranch, but plans to marry her then kill her brother. (60 mins)

White Eagle
Buck Jones. Dir: Lambert Hillyer. A white man masquerading as an Indian brave protects his tribe from crooks who are after their horses. (60 mins)

1933

The Whirlwind
Tim McCoy. Dir: Ross Lederman. A crooked lawman turns a father against his son. (60 mins)

California Tranil
Buck Jones. Dir: Lambert Hillyer. Two ruthless brothers who are cheating villagers out of their land in old Mexico are rounded up by an American scout. (67 mins)

The Fighting Code
Buck Jones. Dir: Lambert Hillyer. A whodunnit in which a cowboy sets out to solve the riddle of who killed his girlfriend's father. (65 mins)

Rusty Rides Alone
Tim McCoy. Dir: D. Ross Lederman. A ruthless sheepman sets out to improve his lot by driving cattle ranchers from their land. He's stopped by the cowboy hero. (58 mins)

End Of The Trail
Tim McCoy. Dir: D. Ross Lederman. After being falsely acc used of supplying guns to the Arapahoe Indians, a soldier is forced out of the army. When his adopted son is killed, he moves in with the Indians and thwarts a massacre. (60 mins)

King Of The Wild Horses
(GB: King of the Wild)
William Janney. Dir: Earl Haley. A cowboy tames a wild horse that has been cruelly treated by the bad guys.

Man Of Action
Tim McCoy. Dir: George Milford. In attempting to discover who robbed a local bank, a ranger and his buddy uncover a scheme to steal the heroine's ranch. (60 mins)

Silent Men
Tim McCoy. Dir: D. Ross Lederman. When a cattleman's special agent is suspected of being the leader of a gang of rustlers (as well as an escaped convict) he loses his job. (60 mins)

The Sundown Rider
Buck Jones. Dir: Lambert Hillyer. After being wrongly accused of rustling, a cowboy unearths a crooked plot to steal a girl's ranch because of its oil deposits. (56 mins)

The Thrill Hunter
Buck Jones. Dir: George B. Seitz. A cowboy stars in a movie and also rounds up a gang of outlaws. (58 mins)

Treason
Buck Jones. Dir: George B. Seitz. An army scout infiltrates a group of Confederate sympathizers led by a woman whose land has unjustly been taken from her in Kansas. (57 mins)

Unknown Valley
Buck Jones. Dir: Lambert Hillyer. An ex-Army scout, while searching for his father, becomes lost in the desert. He's eventually rescued by a girl belonging to a strange religious sect. (69 mins)

1934

The Fighting Ranger
Buck Jones. Dir: George B. Seitz. A ranger quits the service in order to apprehend a bunch of murderous outlaws in Mexico. A remake of Border Law (1931). (60 mins)

Law Beyond The Range
Tim McCoy. Dir: Ford Beebe. After being falsely accused of murder, a ranger is dismissed from the service. In a small town, he helps a girl newspaper editor in her crusade against the town's corrupt Mr Big. (60 mins)

The Man Trailer
Buck Jones. Dir: Lambert Hillyer. While on the run for a murder he did not commit, a cowboy prevents a stagecoach robbery and is made sheriff in return. He's then blackmailed for an incident in his past by an outlaw. (59 mins)

The Prescott Kid
Tim McCoy. Dir: David Selman. A cowboy arrives in town, is mistaken for the marshall, and corrals a bunch of crooks. (60 mins)

Square Shooter
Tim McCoy. Dir: David Selman. After spending five years in prison for a murder he did not commit, a cowboy returns home to find the real culprits of the crime. (57 mins)

The Westerner
Tim McCoy. Dir: David Selman. When a cowboy discovers that the local sheriff and his ranch foreman are operating a cattle-rustling scheme, they attempt to frame him for murder.

1935

The Gallant Defender
Charles Starrett. Dir: David Selman. When homesteaders are harassed by cattlemen a cowboy comes to their aid. Charles Starrett's first Western for the studio. (60 mins)

Justice Of The Range
Tim McCoy. Dir: Dnavid Selman. A cowboy sets out to clear his name after being accused of murdering a ranch foreman. (58 mins)

Lawless Riders
Ken Maynard. Dir: Spencer G. Bennet. A cowboy rescues a banker's daughter in a stagecoach hold-up, then sets out to apprehend an outlaw and his gang. (60 mins)

Heir To Trouble
Ken Maynard. Dir: Spencer G. Bennet. After adopting the son of his riding partner, a cowboy has to fight a rival for his girl, as well as for his mining property. (59 mins)

The Revenge Rider
Tim McCoy. Dir: David Selman. A sheriff's brother believes that the men responsible for his sibling's murder belong to the local cattlemen's association. (60 mins)

Western Courage
Ken Maynard. Dir: Spencer G. Bennet. The foreman of a dude ranch falls for a girl who is being held for ransom by outlaws. (61 mins)

Western Frontier
Ken Maynard. Dir: Albert Herman. A sheriff, posing as a medicine man, arrives in a small town in order to track down some outlaws, and discovers that his long-lost sister is the leader of the gang. Maynard's first western for the studio. (56 mins)

1936

Avenging Waters
Ken Maynard. Dir: Spencer G. Bennet. En route to selling a herd of cattle to a rancher, a cowboy becomes involved in a range feud concerning fencing rights. (56 mins)

The Cattle Thief
Ken Maynard. Dir: Spencer G. Bennet. A cattleman's agent poses as a half-wit peddler in order to infiltrate a gang of outlaws who are cheating ranchers out of their land. (57 mins)

Code Of The Range
Charles Starrett. Dir: C. C. Coleman. A cowboy helps a sheep herder to graze his flock on some cattle land – much to the chagrin of his fellow cowmen. (55 mins)

The Cowboy Star
Charles Starrett. Dir: David Selman. A celluloid cowboy, on vacation, visits a small town incognito and proves himself a real-life hero. (56 mins)

End Of The Trail (GB: Revenge)
Jack Holt. Dir: Erle C. Kenton. Two friends from childhood find themselves in love with the same girl and on different sides of the law. (70 mins)

The Fugitive Sheriff (GB: Law and Order)
Ken Maynard. Dir: Spencer G. Bennet. A cowboy is elected sheriff over the bandits' candidate, then finds himself framed for a crime he did not commit. (61 mins)

Heroes Of The Range
Ken Maynard. Dir: Spencer G. Bennet. A cowboy assists a pretty girl whose brother has been captured by outlaws. (58 mins)

The Mysterious Avenger
Charles Starrett. Dir: David Selman. A Texas ranger returns home to end a feud between his father and a rival rancher. (60 mins)

Ranger Courage
Bob Allen. Dir: Spencer G. Bennet. Outlaws dressed as Indians attack a wagon train. A ranger comes to the rescue. (58 mins)

Rio Grande Ranger
Bob Allen. Dir: Spencer G. Bennet. Two rangers clean up a border town of its outlaws. (54 mins)

Secret Patrol
Charles Starrett. Dir: David Selman. Masquerading as a woodsman, a Mountie is able to track down the killer of a collegue as well as a lumber-mill saboteur. (60 mins)

Stampede
Charles Starrett. Dir: Ford Beebe. A rancher wants a rival's land and kills to get his way. The murdered man's brother arrives on the scene and goes in search of the killer. (58 mins)

Unknown Ranger
Bob Allen. Dir: Spencer G. Bennet. A ranch ranger foils a plan concocted by rustlers to use a wild stallion in the theft of a rancher's horse. (58 mins)

1937

Dodge City Trail
Charles Starrett. Dir: C. C. Coleman. A cowboy rescues a girl from kidnappers but then he discovers she's the daughter of the gang's front man. (65 mins)

Headin' East
Buck Jones. Dir: Ewing Scott. A rancher comes to the big city to stop a group of gangsters who are making life difficult for lettuce growers. (67 inins)

Hollywood Round-Up
Buck Jones. Dir: Ewing Scott. A stunt-man is fired by a jealous leading man. He gets a job with another film company. (63 mins)

Law Of The Rangers
Bob Allen. Dir: Spencer G. Bennet. Arriving incognito in a remote settlement, two rangers come to the aid of settlers who are having a hard time at the hands of crooks. Seems the bad guys want all the water rights for themselves. (57 mins)

The Old Wyorning Trail
Charles Starrett. Dir: Folmer Blangsted. A couple of pals prevent a crook from forcing a man to sell his ranch for much less than it is worth. (56 mins)

One Man Justice
Charles Starrett. Dir: Leon Barsha. A dead ranchers look-alike agrees to impersonate the deceased man to help the local sheriff smoke out an outlaw gang currently rustling cattle belonging to the dead man's widow. (59 mins)

Outlaws Of The Prairie
Charles Starrett. Dir: Sam Nelson. A pair of Texas rangers investigate a series of stagecoach holdups. One of them is also seeking out the man who murdered his father and branded him when he was a child. (59 mins)

The Rangers Step In
Bob Allen. Dir: Spencer G. Bennet. A sheriff calls in the Texas Rangers to help stop two families feuding. (58 mins)

Reckless Ranger
Bob Allen. Dir: Spencer G. Bennet. A ranger investigates the murder of his twin brother who has been killed in cold blood by a crook intent on appropriating sheepmen's grazing rights for himself. (56 mins)

Trapped
Charles Starrett. Dir: Leon Barsha. Could a helpless cripple have murdered his rancher neighbour for his land? Starrett investigates. (55 mins)

Two Fisted sheriff
Charles Starrett. Dir: Leon Barsha. A sheriff loses his job when a pal is accused of killing his girlfriend's father. The lawman sets about apprehending the real killer. (60 mins)

Two Gun Law
Charles Starrett. Dir: Leon Barsha. An outlaw sets out to see that his adopted son follows the straight and narrow. Complications ensue. (56 mins)

Westbound Mail
Charles Starrett. Dir: Tolmar Blangsted. In order to help a young woman whose property is being sought by a miner in the belief that his gold deposit has extended into her land, an FBI agent poses as a mule-skinner. (54 mins)

1938

California Frontier
Buck Jones. Dir: Elmer Clifton. An army captain is despatched by the government to prevent Mexican ranchers in California from being forced off their land by bandits. (55 mins)

Call Of The Rockies
Charles Starrett. Dir: Allan Jones. A young woman, who is in debt to a crooked land-dealer and about to lose her ranch, is helped out by a cowboy. (54 mins)

Cattle Raiders
Charles Starrett. Dir: Sam Nelson. A cowboy is accused of murder by a pal deeply in debt to a crooked cattle dealer. (61 mins)

Colorado Trail
Charles Starrert. Dir: Sam Nelson. A father and son find themselves on opposing sides in a range war. (55 mins)

Heroes Of The Alarno
Earle Hodgins. Dir: Harry S. Fraser. Chronicling the final drive for Texas independence. (74 mins)

In Early Arizona
Bill Elliott. Dir: Joseph Levering. A quiet man becomes sheriff and cleans up a town overrun with outlaws. Bill Elliot's first western for the studio. (53 mins)

Law Of The Plains
Charles Starrett. Dir: Sam Nelson. A ranch foreman stops a gang of outlaws from threatening his boss. (56 mins)

Law Of The Texan
Buck Jones. Dir: Elmer Clifton. A mysterious figure called El Coyote is the brains behind an attempt to steal a shipment of ore. A cattle rustling attempt turns out to be a front for the operation. (54 mins)

Overland Express
Buck Jones. Dir: Drew Eberson. Renegades about to start an Indian uprising try to prevent a cowboy from launching the Pony Express at the outbreak of the Civil War. (55 mins)

Phantom Gold
Jack Luden. Dir: Joseph Levering. A cowboy, his two pals, a young boy and a dog thwart an outlaw's plan to create a gold-rush by salting an old mine. (56 mins)

Pioneer Trail
Jack Luden. Dir: Joseph Levering. A female out-law captures a ranch foreman. (55 mins)

Rio Grande
Charles Starrett. Dir: Sam Nelson . Land grabbers force a girl off her ranch. A cowboy and his pal come to her rescue. (58 mins)

Rolling Caravans
Jack Luden. Dir: Joseph Levering. A cowboy comes to the rescue of some pioneers when crooks prevent them from settling a new area. (55 mins)

South Of Arizona
Charles Starrett. Dir: Sam Nelson. In order to secure a range for themselves and rustle the rancher's cattle, a bunch of crooks murder a government ranger sent to help them. (55 mins)

Stagecoach Days
Jack Luden. Dir: Joseph Levering. A girl and her father are helped by a cowboy to secure a government mail contract for their stage line. (58 mins)

The Stranger Frorn Arizona
Buck Jones. Dir: Elmer Clifton. A railroad detective, pretending to be a cowpoke, investigates a series of robberies and murders. (60 mins)

The Thundering West
Charles Starrett. Dir: Sam Nelson. A one-time outlaw, now sheriff, is blackmailed by his former gang. Remake of The Man Trailer (1934). (58 mins)

West Of Cheyenne
Charles Starrert. Dir: Sam Nelson. A series of mysterious raids on a newly-acquired ranch results in the owner and his pals setting out to find the outlaws responsible. (53 mins)

West Of Santa Fe
Charles Starrett. Dir: Sam Nelson. A US Marshal rounds-up the murderers of a rancher. (60 mins)

Riders Of Black River
Charles Starrett. Dir: Norman Deming. A former Texas Ranger marries a girl whose brother belongs to a gang of cattle rustlers. Remake of The Revenge Rider (1935). (59 mins)

Rornance Of The Redwoods
Charles Bickford. Dir: Charles Vidor. Two loggers are in love with the samerpretty girl. When one of them is mysteriously killed, the other is blamed. (67 mins)

Spoilers Of The Range
Charles Starrett. Dir: C. C. Coleman. Outlaws try to prevent ranchers taking their stock to market in order to keep them from repaying a loan that will save their land. (58 mins)

**The Stranger Frorn Texas
(GB: The Stranger)**
Charles Starrett. Dir: Sam Nelson. A sheriff is 'disguised' as a rancher to discover who's doing the fence-cuttings and cattle rustling for which his father is being blamed. A remake of The Mysterious Avenger (1936). (54 mins)

Tarning Of The West
Bill Elliott. Dir: Norman Deming. An 'honest' businessman turns out to be the brains behind a group of outlaws who are making life difficult for a new sheriff. (55 mins)

Texas Starnpede
Charles Starrett. Dir: Sam Nelson. Cattlemen and sheepmen battle it out over the rights-of-way to water. A sheriff attempts to keep the peace. With the Sons of the Pioneers. (59 mins)

Western Caravans (GB: Silver Sands)
Charles Starrett. Dir: Sam Nelson. A local sheriff attempts to maintain the peace between ranchers and incoming settlers. (58 mins)

1939

Frontiers Of '49
Bill Elliott. Dir: Joseph Levering. In 1848 a pair of government officials go to California to curtail the activities of a bandit who forces Spanish ranchers off their property. (54 mins)

Konga, The Wild Stallion (GB: Konga)
Fred Stone. Dir: Sam Nelson. A rancher kills a man for shooting his favourite horse. He goes to jail and, years later, on release, is united with the animal who, all the while, had been cared for by his daughter. (65 mins)

The Law Comes To Texas
Bill Elliott. Dir: Joseph Levering. To restore law and order to the state of Texas, a lawyer gives up his work to form the Texas Rangers. (55 mins)

Above: Charles Starrett

**Lone Star Pioneers
(GB: Unwelcome Visitors)**
Bill Elliott. Dir: Joseph Levering. A federal marshal, diguised as an outlaw, is sent to stop bandits raiding supply wagons. The gang is holding a family hostage and using its ranch as headquarters. (56 mins)

The Man From Sundown (GB: A Woman's Vengeance)
Charles Starrett. Dir: Sam Nelson. A rancher, about to testify against an outlaw, is killed. A Texas Ranger sets out to discover who murdered him. (58 mins)

North Of The Yukon
Charles Starrett. Dir: Sam Nelson. Two Mounties, who happen to be brothers, go in search of fur thieves who murdered a trader. (59 mins)

Outpost Of The Mounties (GB: On Guard)
Charles Starrett. Dir: C.C. Coleman. A Mountie arrests his girlfriend's brother for the murder of a trading company co-owner, doubts that the man is guilty, and sets out to apprehend the real culprit. (63 mins)

1940

**Beyond The Sacramento
(GB: Power Of Justice)**
Bill Elliott. Dir: Lambert Hillyer. A cowboy single-handedly comes to the aid of Californian settlers after a spate of lawlessness. Evelyn Keyes was the heroine. (58 mins)

Blazing Six Shooters (GB: Stolen Wealth)
Charles Starrett. Dir: Joseph H. Lewis. An outlaw attempts to cheat an old man out of his land (it contains a rich silver deposit) but is prevented from doing so by a cowboy. With the Sons of the Pioneers. (61 mins)

Bullets For Rustlers (GB: On Special Duty)
Charles Starrett. Dir: Sam Nelson. A cattleman's undercover agent masquerades as a rustler in order to infiltrate a gang of outlaws. (58 mins)

**The Durango Kid
(GB: The Masked Stranger)**
Charles Starrett. Dir: Lambert Hillyer. Homesteaders clash with cattlemen-rustlers and are helped by the returning hero. (61 mins)

The Man From Tumbleweeds
Bill Elliott. Dir: Joseph H. Lewis. Wild Bill Saunders enlists paroled prisoners to help him promote law and order in a town dominated by ruthless outlaws. (59 mins)

Pioneers Of The Frontier (GB: The Anchor)
Bill Elliott. Dir: Sam Nelson. The nephew of a murdered land baron arrives to avenge his uncle's death at the hands of a lawless gunman. (58 mins)

**The Return Of Wild Bill
(GB: False Evidence)**
Bill Elliott. Dir: Joseph H. Lewis. Outlaws attempt to promote a feud between two ranchers in the hope of getting their land for themselves. One of the ranchers sends for his son, a notorious gunman. (59 mins)

Texas Stagecoach (GB: Two Roads)
Charles Starrett. Dir: Joseph H. Lewis. Hoping to monopolize two rival stagecoach lines, a crooked banker creates trouble between the owners of the respective companies. (59 mins)

Thundering Frontier
Charles Starrett. Dir: D. Ross Lederman. A cowboy comes to the assistance of the heroine whose father's business is being sabotaged. (57 mins)

Two-Fisted Rangers
Charles Starrett. Dir: Joseph H. Lewis. A cowboy brings to justice the land baron who killed his sheriff brother. (62 mins)

West Of Abilene (GB: The Showdown)
Charles Starrett. Dir: Ralph Cedar. Settlers battle it out with land-grabbers who are after their properties in the hope of re-selling the land for vast profits. (57 mins)

1941

Across The Sierras (GB: Welcome Stranger)
Bill Elliott. Dir: D. Ross Lederman. A couple of law-breakers start causing problems for Wild Bill Hickok as he is about to settle down in Oklahoma. (58 mins)

Bullets For Bandits
Bill Elliott. Dir: Wallace Fox. When a woman rancher's property is appropriated by a crook, Wild Bill Hickok arrives to save the day. With Tex Ritter. (55 mins)

Hands Across The Rockies
Bill Elliott. Dir: Lambert Hillyer. Wild Bill Hickok and his buddy Cannonball go in search of the killer of the latter's father, and, in a small town, meet a girl who not only witnessed the crime, but is being forced to marry the culprit. (55 mins)

King Of Dodge City
Bill Elliott. Dir: Lambert Hillyer. A pair of sheriffs team up to prevent an outlaw and his gang from taking over a Kansas town in 1861. With Tex Ritter. (63 mins)

Lone Star Vigilantes (GB: The Devil's Price)
Charles Starrett. Dir: Wallace Fox. At the end of the Civil War, a pair of cowboys return home to discover that the army troops in town are really bandits. With Tex Ritter. (58 mins)

**The Medico Of Painted Springs
(GB: Doctor's Alibi)**
Charles Starrett. Dir: Lambert Hillyer. While recruiting men for the Rough Riders, an army doctor becomes involved in a war between cattle raiders and sheepmen. (58 mins)

North From The Lone Star
Bill Elliot. Dir: Lambert Hillyer. Wild Bill Hickok is made marshal of the lawless town of Deadpond, then proceeds to clean up the place. (58 mins)

Outlaws Of The Panhandle (GB: Faro Jack)
Charles Starrett. Dir: Sam Nelson. A crooked

gambler who robs gold shipments opposes a cowboy and a group of cattlemen who are building a railroad. (60 mins)

The Pinto Kid (GB: All Square)
Charles Starrett. Dir: Lambert Hillyer. A cattle rustler and a bank robber attempt to lay their dirty work at the feet of honest Texans. (66 mins)

Prairie Schooners (GB: Through The Storm)
Bill Elliott. Dir: Sam Nelson. A group of settlers, led by Wild Bill Hickok, are attacked by Indians when they head west in a wagon train in search of gold. (58 mins)

The Prairie Stranger
(GB: The Marked Bullet)
Charles Starrett. Dir: Lambert Hillyer. When a doctor sets up a practice in a small Nevada town, he's accused by his already established rival of poisoning cattle. (58 mins)

Riders Of The Badlands
Charles Starrert. Dir: Howard Bretherton. A ranger and his dentist buddy go in search of an outlaw. However, the ranger is a lookalike for the bad guy and finds himself arrested. With Russell Hayden. (57 mins)

The Return Of Daniel Boone
Bill Elliott. Dir: Lambert Hillyer. A tax collector discovers his boss is cheating settlers out of their property. (56 mins)

Roaring Frontiers
Bill Elliott. Dir: Lambert Hillyer. After being sent to a small town to arrest a cowboy for murdering the local sheriff, a marshal finishes up by saving the so-called killer from a lynch mob organized by the real culprit. With Tex Ritter. (60 mins)

The Royal Mounted Patrol
(GB: Giants A'Fire)
Charles Starrett. Dir: Lambert Hillyer. The sister of a crooked lumber camp boss is the object of two Mounties' affections. With Russell Hayden, Lloyd Bridges. (59 mins)

The Son Of Davy Crockett (GB: Blue Clay)
Bill Elliott. Dir: Lambert Hillyer. Davy Crockett's son is sent by President Ulysses S. Grant to unclaimed Yucca Valley as the government's unofficial representative. His purpose: to overthrow a lawbreaker and his hired killers. (59 mins)

Thunder Over The Prairie
Charles Starrett. Dir: Lambert Hillyer. When an Indian medical student is falsely accused of murder and dynamiting a dam, a doctor comes to his aid. (60 mins)

West Of Tombstone
Charles Starrett. Dir: Howard Bretherton. When the citizens of a small town come to believe that Billy the Kid is still alive, the sheriff opens the Kid's grave – and finds it empty. With Russell Hayden. (59 mins)

The Wildcat Of Tucson
(GB: Promise Fulfilled)
Bill Elliott. Dir: Lambert Hillyer. A speculator and a bent judge attempt to cheat a group of settlers out of their land. Wild Bill Hickok and his brother put things right. (55 mins)

1942

Bad Men Of The Hills
(GB: Wrongly Accused)
Charles Starrett. Dir: Wilbam Berke. A young man investigates the murder of a marshal and is, himself, almost murdered by outlaws. With Russell Hayden. (58 mins)

The Devil's Trail (GB: Rogue's Gallery)
Bill Elliott. Dir: Lambert Hillyer. A federal marshal comes to the aid of Wild Bill Hickok after the latter is falsely accused of murder. With Tex Ritter and Noah Beery. (61 mins)

Down Rio Grande Way
(GB: The Double Punch)
Charles Starrett. Dir: William Berke. Two cowboys become involved in Texas's quest for independence. With Russell Hayden. (57 mins)

Lawless Plainsmen (GB: Roll On)
Charles Starrett. Dir: William Berke. A young woman discovers the villain behind an Indian attack during which the head of a wagon train is killed. With Russell Hayden. (59 mins)

The Lone Prairie (GB: Inside Information)
Russell Hayden. Dir: William Berke. A cattle buyer comes to the rescue of a man whose ranch is being sought after by a bunch of crooks as the property is about to have a railroad going through it. (58 mins)

North Of The Rockies (GB: False Clues)
Bill Elliott. Dir: Lambert Hillyer. A Canadian Mountie and a US marshal are at loggerheads as they set out to apprehend a bunch of fur smugglers. With Tex Ritter. (60 mins)

Overland To Deadwood (GB: Falling Stones)
Charles Starrett. Dir: William Berke. A pair of cowboys come to the aid of a young woman whose hauling operation is being sabotaged by a rival who has his sights on a lucrative railway franchise. With Russell Hayden. (59 mins)

Pardon My Gun
Charles Starrett. Dir: William Berke. A surveyor and a sheeprancher's daughter are wrongly accused of robbery and murder. (57 mins)

Prairie Gunsmoke
Bill Elliott. Dir: Lambert Hillyer. Wild Bill Hickok finds himself under suspicion and distrusted by the very ranchers he has come to protect against rustlers. With Tex Ritter. (56 mins)

Riders Of The Northland
(GB: Next In Line)
Charles Starrett. Dir: William Berke. When three Texas Rangers arrive in Alaska to investigate enemy activities, they discover that a bunch of saboteurs are constructing a runway for enemy planes. With Russell Hayden. (58 mins)

Riding Through Nevada
Charles Starrett. Dir: William Berke. A postal inspector brings to an end a series of stagecoach stick-ups by taking on the job of shotgun guard. (55 mins)

A Tornado In The Saddle (GB: Ambushed)
Russell Hayden. Dir: William Berke. A sheriff and a crooked saloon-keeper clash, with good triumphing over evil. (56 mins)

Vengeance Of The West
(GB: The Black Shadow)
Bill Elliott. Dir: Lambert Hillyer. After the murder of his family, a rancher begins to raid gold shipments. He teams with a ranger who has a warrant for his arrest and together they set out to apprehend the outlaws responsible for the slayings. With Tex Ritter. (60 mins)

1943

Cowboy In The Clouds
Charles Starrett. Dir: Benjamin Kline. By joining the Civil Air Patrol and fighting enemy agents, a cowboy does his bit for his country. (55 mins)

The Fighting Buckaroo
Charles Starrett. Dir: Willaim Berke. A cowboy arrives in town to exonerate a boyhood friend from accusations that he is in league with a group of cattle rustlers. (58 mins)

Frontier Fury
Charles Starrett. Dir: William Berke. An Indian agent attempts to find the robbers of stolen funds. (55 mins)

Hail To The Rangers (GB: Illegal Rights)
Charles Starrett. Dir: Wilham Berke. When a rancher is about to lose his range to homesteaders, an ex-ranger pal of his comes to his aid. (57 mins)

Law Of The Northwest
Charles Starrett. Dir: William Berke. Mounties are on the trail of a crooked contractor. (57 mins)

Riders Of The Northwest Mounted
Russell Hayden. Dir: William Berke. A corrupt trading post officer, leading a gang of fur thieves, is apprehended by a Mountie. (57 mins)

Robin Hood Of The Range
Charles Starrett. Dir: William Berke. The mysterious Vulcan comes to the aid of homesteaders whose properties are about to fall into the hands of the railroad. (57 mins)

Saddles And Sagebrush (GB: The Pay-Off)
Russell Hayden. Dir: William Berke. A cowboy and his pals save a rancher and his daughter from being tyrannized by outlaws. (57 mins)

Silver City Raiders (GB: Legal Larceny)
Russell Hayden. Dir: William Berke. A land-office operator claims he has a Spanish land grant which gives him possession of a property owned by a group of honest ranchers. (55 mins)

Vigilante's Ride (GB: Hunted)
Russell Hayden. Dir: William Berke. When a cowboy's younger brother is murdered by outlaws the cowboy pretends to be a bandit in order to infiltrate the gang. (55 mins)

Wyoming Hurricane (GB: Proved Guilty)
Russell Hayden. Dir: William Berke. When a crooked cafe owner murders the local sheriff, blame is placed on the boyfriend of the sheriff's daughter. (58 mins)

1944

Cowboy Canteen (GB: Close Harmony)
Charles Starrett. Dir: Lew Landers. When a ranch owner joins the army, he discovers that his newly hired hands are all female. Morale-boosting wartime fare, this was a musical-Western equivalent of Hollywood Canteen (Warner Bros., 1944), and featured musical interludes by Ray Acutt, Tex Ritter, Roy Rogers and the Mills Brothers. (72 mins)

Cowboy From Lonesome River
(GB: Signed Judgement)
Charles Starrett. Dir: Benjamin Kline. A cowboy and a group of indignant Mesa Valley ranchers break the paralysing grip a local land baron has on the community. (55 mins)

Cyclone Prairie Rangers
Charles Starrett. Dir: Benjamin Kline. Nazis in the West are prevented from sabotaging cattle, crops, and equipment by a cowboy and his pals. (55 mins)

Klondike Kate
Ann Savage. Dir: William Castle. In the late 1890's a hotel owner is nearly lynched for a murder he did not commit. With Glenda Farrell, Tom Neal. (64 mins)

The Last Horseman
Russell Hayden. Dir: William Berke. An innocent female bank-teller is recruited to aid a bunch of crooks in a bank raid, but their plans are foiled by a cowboy and his pals. (58 mins)

Riding West
Charles Starrett. Dir: William Berke. A gambler tries to prevent a man from setting up a Pony Express operation. (58 mins)

Saddle Leather Law (GB: The Poisoner)
Charles Starrett. Dir: Benjamin Kline. Two cowboys are blamed for the death of a rancher,

but the culprit is a girl who works for a crooked syndicate. (55 mins)

Sagebrush Heroes

Charles Starrett. Dir: Benjamin Kline. A radio announcer known as the Durango Kid comes to the aid of a boy who has been confined to a 'ranch of correction'. It turns out the place isn't all it should be. (55 mins)

Sundown Valley

Charles Starrett. Dir: Benjamin Kline. A war hero wants to shut down some gambling premises in a small town because the place is a magnet for men who otherwise should be working at a local gun manufacturing plant. (55 mins)

Swing In The Saddle (GB: Swing And Sway)

Jane Frazee. Dir: Lew Landers. A pretty girl arrives at a ranch by mistake, finds herself engaged to the foreman and wins a local singing contest. With Guinn Williams. Musical-Western. (68 mins)

1945

Blazing The Western Trail (GB: Who Killed Waring)

Charles Starrett. Dir: Vernon Keays. When a stagecoach operator is being forced out of business by a rival, the Durango Kid comes to his aid. With Tex Harding. (60 mins)

Both Barrels Blazing (GB: The Yellow Streak)

Charles Starrett. Dir: Derwin Abrahams. A Texas Ranger, alias the Durango Kid, is on the trail of a crook who's using an old panhandler as a front for stolen goods. With Tex Harding. (57 mins)

Lawless Empire (GB: Power of Possession)

Charles Starrett. Dir: Vernon Keays. The Durango Kid comes to the assistance of a minister and his wife who, in turn, are trying to aid settlers harassed by raiders. With Tex Harding. (58 mins)

Outlaws Of The Rockies (GB: A Roving Rogue)

Charles Starrett. Dir: Ray Nazarro. Two sheriffs, accused of aiding a gang of outlaws, are forced out of town. One of the sheriffs, however, is the Durango Kid. With Tex Harding. (55 mins)

Return Of The Durango Kid (GB: Stolen Time)

Charles Starrett. Dir: Derwin Abrahams. After being robbed by bandits on a stagecoach, a passenger takes on the guise of the masked Durango Kid and steals the money back from the gang leader. (58 mins)

Rockin' In The Rockies

The Three Stooges. Dir: Vernon Keays. A rancher, while trying to sell his land, finds himself involved with a trio of zanies. (65 mins)

Rough Ridin' Justice (GB: Decoy)

Charles Starrett. Dir: Derwin Abrahams. When ranchers find themselves opposed by a gang of outlaws, they hire the man who, hitherto, had been harassing cattlemen. (58 mins)

Rustlers Of The Badlands (GB: By Whose Hand?)

Charles Starrett. Dir: Derwin Abrahams. A trio of army scouts find themselves searching for the man who has murdered a lieutenant. With Tex Harding. (55 mins)

Sing Me A Song Of Texas (GB: Fortune Hunter)

Rosemary Lane. Dir: Vernon Keays. An old rancher cannot decide which of his two nieces should receive his wealth, so he pretends to be dead to test their reactions. With Tom Tyler. (66 mins)

Song Of The Prairie (GB: Sentiment And Song)

Hoosier Hot Shots, Ken Curtis. Dir: Ray Nazarro. The Hot Shots help a rancher-cum-bandleader open a show place called 'The Painted Post Barn Dance'. Musical. (69 mins)

Texas Panhandle

Charles Starrett. Dir: Ray Nazarro. The Durango Kid, in reality an ex-Secret Service agent, joins a wagon train and investigates a robbery. With Tex Harding. (57 mins)

1946

Cowboy Blues (GB: Beneath The Starry Skies)

Ken Curtis. Dir: Ray Nazarro. A father pretends to be a land-owner when the daughter he has not seen for years decides to pay him an unexpected visit. Musical. (66 mins)

The Desert Horseman (GB: Checkmate)

Charles Starrett. Dir: Ray Nazarro. After being wrongly accused of robbing an army payroll, a captain takes on the guise of the Durango Kid in order to track down the real culprit. With Smiley Burnette. (57 mins)

The Fighting Frontiersman (GB: Golden Lady)

Charles Starrett. Dir: Derwin Abrahams. An old who has struck gold is tortured by outlaws to make him reveal its whereabouts – until he is rescued by the Durango Kid. With Smiley Burnette. (61 mins)

Frontier Gun Law (GB: Menacing Shadows)

Charles Starrett. Dir: Derwin Abrahams. The Durango Kid goes after a group of ranch robbers known as 'The Phantoms'. With Tex Harding, Smiley Burnette. (60 mins)

Galloping Thunder (GB: On Boot Hill)

Charles Starrett. Dir: Ray Nazarro. When outlaws prevent ranchers from sending their mustang herds to the government for army use, an agent, alias The Durango Kid, is sent to investigate. With Smiley Burnette. (54 mins)

Gunning For Vengeance (GB: Jail Break)

Charles Starrett. Dir: Ray Nazarro. The Durango Kid comes to the aid of a small girl whose father is the victim of a gang of local extortionists. With Smiley Burnette. (56 mins)

Heading West (GB: The Cheat's Last Throw)

Charles Starrrett. Dir: Ray Nazarro. The Durango Kid is accused of attacking miners. The real culprit is a mine-machinery company owner. With Smiley Burnette. (54 mins)

Landrush (GB: The Claw Strikes)

Charles Starrett. Dir: Vernon Keays. The Durango Kid prevents outlaws from keeping settlers off their land. (54 mins)

Lone Star Moonlight (GB: Amongst The Thieves)

Ken Curtis. Dir: Ray Nazarro. A GI returns to the home town where he once owned a radio station to find that the station has been neglected. Not only that, but a rival station has opened as well. Musical. (69 mins)

Roaring Rangers (GB: False Hero)

Charles Starrett. Dir: Ray Nazarro. The Durango Kid discovers a sheriffs brother is behind a series of lawless acts in a small town. With Smiley Burnette. (55 mins)

Singing On The Trafl

Ken Curtis, Hoosier Hot Shots. Dir: Ray Nazarro. A sharp-shooter and a would-be radio singer come to the aid of the Hot Shots who have bought a ranch only to discover that it is not legally theirs. Musical. (69 mins)

Terror Trail (GB: Hands Of Menace)

Charles Starrett. Dir: Ray Nazarro. The Durango Kid puts an end to hostilities when a crooked rancher attempts to start a range war

by placing sheep on cattlemen's land. With Smiley Burnette. (55 mins)

That Texas Jamboree (GB: Medicine Man)

Ken Curtis. Dir: Ray Nazarro. A pretty girl runs for mayor of a western town – so does her future husband. (68 mins)

Throw A Saddle On A Star

Hoosier Hot Shots, Ken Curtis. Dir: Ray Nazarro. The Hot Shots help clinch a romance and see to it that the hero retains the rodeo championship. Musical. (67 mins)

Two-Fisted Stranger

Charles Starrett. Dir: Ray Nazarro. The Durango Kid prevents outlaws from throwing miners off their property. With Smiley Burnette. (50 mins)

1947

Buckaroo From Powder River

Charles Starrett. Dir: Ray Nazarro. When the nephew of an outlaw gang leader refuses to go along with his uncle's scheme to counterfeit government bonds, the villain plans to murder him. The Durango Kid comes to the rescue. With Smiley Burnette. (55 mins)

King Of The Wild Horses

Preston Foster. Dir: George Archainbaud. A young boy slowly befriends and finally tames a wild stallion. (79 mins)

Last Days Of Boot Hill

Charles Starrett. Dir: Ray Nazarro. The Durango Kid, supposedly dead, goes searching for gold stolen by an outlaw. Makes use of footage from Both Barrels Blazing (1945). With Smiley Burnette. (55 mins)

The Last Round-Up

Gene Autry. Dir: John English. A crooked Indian, in an attempt to prevent an aqueduct project from interfering with his takeover of range land, causes trouble with local Indians. (77 mins)

Law Of The Canyon (GB: The Price Of Crime)

Charles Starrett. Dir: Ray Nazarro. The Durango Kid puts a stop to outlaws who are forcing people to pay protection money, or have their possessions stolen. With Smiley Burnette. (55 mins)

The Lone-Hand Texan (GB: The Cheat)

Charles Starrett. Dir: Ray Nazarro. The Durango Kid prevents outlaws from sabotaging an oil driller's operation. With Smiley Burnette. (54 mins)

Over The Santa Fe Trail (GB: No Escape)

Ken Curtis. Dir: Ray Nazarro. A medicine show entertainer falls for a cowpoke. Musical-Western. (63 mins)

Prairie Raiders (GB: The Forger)

Charles Starrett. Dir: Derwin Abrahams. It's the Durango Kid to the rescue when a rancher leases land from the Department of the Interior in order to sell wild horses, and finds himself in unlawful competition with a gang of outlaws. With Smiley Burnette. (54 mins)

Riders Of The Lone Star

Charles Starrett. Dir: Derwin Abrahams. A pair of Texas Rangers seek out a notorious outlaw who hasn't reckoned with the ingenuity of the Durango Kid. With Smiley Burnette. (55 mins)

Smoky River Serenade (GB: The Threat)

Hoosier Hot Shots, Paul Campbell. Dir: Lew Landers. The Hoosier Hot Shots hold a gala concert to raise money for an elderly ranch-owner who, because of his financial situation, is being forced to sell his ranch. Musical. (67 mins)

South Of The Chisholm Trail
Charles Starrett. Dir: Derwin Abrahams. The Durango Kid rescues members of a musical troupe who are mistaken for a gang of outlaws and nearly hanged. (58 mins)

Stranger From Ponca City
Charles Starrett. Dir: Derwin Abrahams. A cowboy fetches up in a town divided by a war between the good guys and the bad. Another outing for the ubiquitous Durango Kid. With Smiley Burnette. (56 mins)

Swing The Western Way (GB: The Schemer)
Jack Leonard, Hoosier Hot Shots. Dir: Derwin Abrahams. A man pretends to own a ranch in order to impress and marry a woman he believes to be rich – and is then blackmailed by the ranch's real owner before reaching a happy musical-Western ending. (66 mins)

West of Dodge City (GB: The Sea Wall)
Charles Starrett. Dir: Ray Nazarro. The Durango Kid investigates a crime in which a crook is attempting to set up a phony power-plant after murdering a rancher for his land. With Smiley Butnette. (57 mins)

1948

Adventures In Silverado (GB: Above All Laws)
William Bishop. Dir: Phil Karlson. Author Robert Louis Stevenson, while on a stage-coach, is robbed by a masked highwayman called 'The Monk'. He then sets out to capture his attacker. Based on Stevenson's story 'Silverado Squatters'. With Smiley Burnette. (75 mins)

Arkansas Swing (GB: Wrong Number)
Hoosier Hot Shots. Dir: Ray Nazarro. The Hot Shots discover that a horse will trot like a champion only when it hears the music of a march played on a washboard. Musical. (63 mins)

Black Eagle
William Bishop. Dir: Robert Gordon. A young man becomes involved with a crooked live-stock agent. (76 mins)

Blazing Across The Pecos (GB: Under Arrest)
Charles Starrett. Dir: Ray Nazarro. The Durango Kid succeeds in preventing outlaws from starting an Indian uprising against local settlers. With Smiley Burnette. (55 mins)

Below: Gene Autry (right)

El Dorado Pass (GB: Desperate Men)
Charles Starrett. Dir: Ray Nazarro. After being sent to jail for a crime he did not commit, a cowboy escapes, and, in his guise as the Durango Kid, helps a Mexican rancher and his daughter find the man who stole their money. With Smiley Burnette. (56 mins)

Phantom Valley
Charles Starrett. Dir: Ray Nazarro. A sheriff arrives in a town where an outlaw gang has caused war between ranchers and homesteaders. More adventures for the Durango Kid. With Smiley Butnette. (53 mins)

Quick On The Trigger (GB: Condemned In Error)
Charles Starrett. Dir: Ray Nazarro. A girl's stage line is plagued by a gang, one of whose members turns out to be the girl's brother. When the brother is murdered in his cell, the local sheriff is accused of the crime. The Durango Kid comes to the rescue. With Smiley Burnette. (55 mins)

Singin' Spurs
Kirby Grant, Hoosier Hot Shots. Dir: Ray Nazarro. The Hot Shots help a neighbour to raise money in order that a tribe of Indians may obtain the means to irrigate their farms. Musical. (62 mins)

Six-Gun Law
Charles Starrett. Dir: Ray Nazarro. A rancher (the Durango Kid) is accused of murdering the local sheriff and forced to sign a confession by the gang leader, who then makes him the new sheriff in the hope of controlling him. With Smiley Burnette. (54 mins)

Smoky Mountain Melody
Ray Acuff, Guinn Williams. Dir: Ray Nazarro. Two cousins try to prevent a relative from becoming the rightful owner of Corby Ranch. Musical. (62 mins)

The Strawberry Roan (GB: Fools Awake)
Gene Autry. Dir: John English. After his son is injured by a roan, a ranch owner tries to kill the animal but is prevented from doing so by a horse-breaker. Cinecolor. (79 mins)

Trail To Laredo (GB: Sign Of The Dagger)
Charles Starrett. Dir: Ray Nazarro. A stageline operator; forced to become a fugitive by his crooked gold-smuggling partner, is helped by the Durango Kid. With Smiley Burnette. (54 mins)

The Untamed Breed
Sonny Tufts, Barbara Britton. Dir: Charles Lamont. Ranchers along the Pecos River in Texas agree to allow a man to purchase a Brahma bull in order to enhance the quality of their cattle herds. Cinecolor. (79 mins)

West Of Sonora
Charles Starrett. Dir: Ray Nazarro. After a sheriff asks his pal to become his deputy, he goes in search of a notorious outlaw and his gang. With Smiley Burnette. (52 mins)

Whirlwind Raiders (GB: State Police)
Charles Starrett. Dir: Vernon Keays. The Durango Kid on the trail of a group of crooks posing as State Police. (54 mins)

1949

Bandits Of El Dorado (GB: Tricked)
Charles Starrett. Dir: Ray Nazarro. In order to discover how criminals are escaping across the border into Mexico, a government inspector becomes a wanted man by faking the murder of a Texas Ranger. A Durango Kid adventure. With Smiley Burnette. (56 mins)

The Big Sombrero
Gene Autry. Dir: Frank McDonald. A cowboy stops a crook from marrying a girl for her property. Cinecolor. (77 mins)

The Blazing Trail (GB: The Forged Will)
Charles Starrett. Dir: Ray Nazarro. When a rancher is killed leaving a major discrepancy in his will, a sheriff and a newspaper editor expect wholesale fraud. A Durango Kid adventure. With Smiley Burnette. (56 mins)

Challenge Of The Range (GB: Moonlight Raid)
Charles Starrett. Dir: Ray Nazarro. When ranchers accuse each other of lawlessness, the Durango Kid sorts out their differences for them. With Smiley Burnette. (56 mins)

The Cowboy And The Indians
Gene Autry. Dir: John English. A rancher proves the innocence of a young Indian brave blamed for the murder of a Navajo chief. With Jay Silverheels. (68 mins)

Desert Vigilante
Charles Starrett. Dir: Fred F. Sears. While on the trail of silver smugglers along the Mexican border, a government agent meets a girl whose uncle has been murdered by the outlaws. A Durango Kid adventure. With Smiley Burnette. (56 mins)

Feudin' Rhythm (GB: Ace Lucky)
Eddy Arnold. Dir: Edward Bernds. A trouble-some social-climber who dabbles in show-business tries to get a popular hillbilly singer fired. Musical. (65 mins)

Home In San Antone (GB: Harmony Inn)
Ray Acuff. Dir Ray Nazarro. The owner of a rustic inn has problems with a kindly but klep-tomaniac uncle. (62 minis)

Horsemen Of The Sierras (GB: Remember Me)
Charles Starrett. Dir: Fred F. Sears. An under-cover agent becomes involved with two feuding families while trying to unravel the mystery of a government surveyor's murder. A Durango Kid adventure. With Smiley Burnette. (56 mins)

Laramie
Charles Starrett. Dir: Ray Nazarro. The Durango Kid prevents a full-scale war developing between the army and the Red Indians when a crooked army scout kills a chief while selling guns to the Indians. With Smiley Burnette, Jay Silverheels. (56 mins)

Law Of The Barbary Coast
Stephen Dunne. Dir: Lew Landers. A young girl takes a job in a Barbary Coast gambling house to find the man who killed her brother. (65 mins)

Loaded Pistols
Gene Autry. Dir: John English. The hero and his chums find themselves up against crooked ranchers. (70 mins)

Renegades Of The Sage (GB: The Fort)
Charles Starrett. Dir: Ray Nazarro. After the Civil War, a government agent is sent West to find out who is responsible for sab-otaging a telephone line. Suspicion falls on an ex-Confederate guerilla leader. A Durango Kid adventure. With Smiley Burnette. (56 mins)

Riders In the Sky
Gene Autry. Dir: John English. After being framed on false charges by a crooked gambler, a cowboy clears a rancher's name. (70 mins)

Riders Of Whistling Pines
Gene Autry. Dir: John English. A man believes he accidentally killed a forest ranger when, in fact, the ranger was murdered by a pair of crooked businessmen after discovering a moth infestation in the forest. (70 mins)

Rim Of The Canyon
Gene Autry. Dir: John English. Three ex-con-victs return to a town seeking revenge and find Autry and his pals instead. (70 mins)

South Of Death Valley
(GB: River Of Poison)
Charles Starrett. Dir: Ray Nazarro. While attempting to solve the riddle of the death of his gold-mining brother-in-law, a cowboy finds himself involved in a range war. A Durango Kid adventure. With Smiley Burnette. (54 mins)

1950

Across The Badlands (GB: The Challenge)
Charles Starrett. Dir: Fred F. Sears. Frequent attacks on a railway line's survey crews are investigated by the Durango Kid. With Smiley Burnette. (55 mins)

Beyond The Purple Hills
Gene Autry. Dir: John English. A sheriff arrests his buddy when the latter's father is murdered. (70 mins)

The Blazing Sun
Gene Autry. Dir: John English. A cowboy is on the lookout for a pair of bank robbers. (70 mins)

Cowtown (GB: Barbed Wire)
Gene Autry. Dir: John English. A cowboy who opposes the use of barbed wire finds himself on the outs with a pretty girl rancher, and in the middle of a range war. (70 mins)

Frontier Outpost
Charles Starrett. Dir: Ray Nazarro. The Durango Kid robs a stage carrying government gold to prevent it from being stolen by bandits. (55 mins)

Hoedown
Jock O'Mahoney, Eddy Arnold. Dir: Ray Nazarro. Musical western in which a cowboy film star arrives at a dude ranch and discovers it's a hide-out for bank-robbers. (64 mins)

Indian Territory
Gene Autry. Dir: John English. An ex-Confederate cavalryman helps expose a white man who has been stirring up Indian unrest. (70 mins)

Lightning Guns (GB: Taking Sides)
Charles Starrett. Dir: Fred F. Sears. The Durango Kid discovers the outlaws behind the sabotaging of a new dam. With Smiley Burnette. (55 mins)

Mule Train
Gene Autry. Dir: John English. A cowboy comes to the aid of two prospectors after a crooked female sheriff and a contractor steal their cement deposit. (70 mins)

Outcasts Of Black Mesa (GB: The Clue)
Charles Starrett. Dir: Ray Nazarro. The Durango Kid comes to the rescue of a young woman whose father and two partners have been killed because of their ownership of a mine. With Smiley Burnette. (54 mins)

The Palomino (GB: Hills Of The Brave)
Jerome Courtland. Dir: Ray Nazarro. When out-laws appropriate a girl's prize palomino, a cattle buyer helps her retrieve the animal. In Technicolor. (73 mins)

Raiders Of Tomahawk Creek
(GB: Circle Of Fear)
Charles Starrett. Dir: Fred F. Sears. A newly appointed Indian agent investigates the murders of several area ranchers perpetrated by his predecessor. With Smiley Burnette. (55 mins)

Sons Of New Mexico (GB: The Brat)
Gene Autry. Dir: John English. A newly-appointed executor of an estate sends the deceased man's son to a military college in order to remove him from the influence of a crooked rancher. (71 mins)

Stage To Tucson (GB: Last Stage Valley)
Rod Cameron. Dir: Ralph Murphy. Two men travel to the Southwest to investigate why numerous government stagecoaches are being hijacked and discover that secessionists are behind the incidents. (82 mins)

Streets Of Ghost Town
Charles Starrett. Dir: Ray Nazarro. Three sheriffs investigate a series of strange happenings in a ghost town caused by a blind outlaw now using his young nephew to help him find stolen booty he once hid there. A Durango Kid adventure. With Smiley Burnette. (54 mins)

Texas Dynamo (GB: Suspected)
Charles Starrett. Dir: Ray Nazarro. In order to apprehend a gang of outlaws, the Durango Kid takes on the guise of a notorious gunman known as the Texas Dynamo. With Smiley Burnette. (54 mins)

Trail Of The Rustlers (GB: Lost River)
Charles Starrett. Dir: Ray Nazarro. The Durango Kid prevents a woman and her two sons, who have discovered a water source in a valley, from running other ranchers off their land. With Smiley Burnette. (55 mins)

1951

Bonanza Town (GB: Two-Fisted Agent)
Charles Starrett. Dir: Fred F. Sears. The Durango Kid tracks down an outlaw, believed dead, but actually working in cahoots with a crooked town boss. With Smiley Burnette. (56 mins)

Cyclone Fury
Charles Starrett. Dir: Ray Nazarro. The murder of a rancher gives rise to suspicion of an agent sent to ensure the delivery of horses to the government. With Smiley Burnette. (54 mins)

Fort Savage Raiders
Charles Starrett. Dir: Ray Nazarro. A gang of army deserters, who've been raiding the countryside, are brought to justice by the Durango Kid and his pals. With Smiley Burnette. (54 mins)

Gene Autry And The Mounties
Gene Autry. Dir: John English. A couple of marshals from Montana, working together with a Mountie, apprehend a bank robber. (70 mins)

Hills of Utah
Gene Autry. Dir: John English. When a doctor arrives in a small town to investigate the murder of his father, he becomes involved in a feud between ranchers and a local mine operator. (70 mins)

Snake River Desperadoes
Charles Starrett. Dir: Fred F. Sears. White men masquerading as Indians are raiding property. The Durango Kid puts a stop to their activities. With Smiley Burnette. (55 mins)

Texans Never Cry
Gene Autry. Dir: Frank McDonald. Autry on the trail of a gang of counterfeiters. (70 mins)

The Texas Rangers
George Montgomery. Dir: Phil Karlson. Two reformed outlaws link up with the Texas Rangers in an attempt to apprehend a gang of crooks. In Technicolor. (74 mins)

Valley Of Fire
Gene Autry. Dir: John English. A crooked gambler, run out of town by a sheriff, gets his revenge by hi-jacking a wagon-load of brides. (70 mins)

When The Redskins Rode
Jon Hall. Dir: Emilio Fernandez. Pre-revolutionary melodrama, set in 1753 and in which Governor Dinwiddie and George Washington attempt to get local Indian tribes on the side of the British against the French A pretty spy tries to convince the Indian chief to do just the opposite. Technicolor. (77 mins)

Whirlwind
Gene Autry. Dir: John English. A postal inspector is seeking out a gang headed by a dishonest rancher. With Smiley Burnette. (70 mins)

The Kid From Amarilo (GB: Silver Chains)
Charles Starrett. Dir: Ray Nazarro. A gang of silver smugglers are captured along the Mexican border by a pair of US Treasury agents. With Smiley Burnette. (56 mins)

Pecos River (GB: Without Risk)
Charles Starrett. Dir: Fred F. Sears. After a series of mail holdups, a post-office investigator pretends to be a stagecoach driver in order to bring the criminals to justice. With Smiley Burnette. (55 mins)

Prairie Roundup
Charles Starrett. Dir: Fred F. Sears. After being accused of murder by a gang of outlaws, a cowboy and his pal escape jail and take on jobs on a ranch owned by a girl whose cattle the outlaws intend to steal. With Smiley Burnette. (53 mins)

Ridin' The Outlaw Trail
Charles Starrett. Dir: Fred F. Sears. The Durango Kid goes in search of a man who stole $20,000 worth of gold, discovers that the thief has been killed, and that his murderer has melted down the gold claiming it to be recently discovered. With Smiley Burnette. (54 mins)

Silver Canyon
Gene Autry. Dir: John English. An army scout is on the trail of a Union renegade leader whose activities have been denounced by the Confederacy. (70 mins)

Smoky Canyon
Charles Starrett. Dir: Fred F. Sears. In order to raise cattle prices, crooked cattlemen are depleting herds by slaughtering the animals. A government agent investigates the problem. With Smiley Burnette. (55 mins)

1952

Apache Country
Gene Autry. Dir: George Archainbaud. White conspirators supply redskins with guns and whiskey in order to keep them raiding innocent settlers as a cover-up for their bandit activities. The government sends a cowboy to round up the gang which, working undercover, he does. (62 mins)

Barbed Wire (GB: False News)
Gene Autry. Dir: George Archainbaud. A cowboy uncovers a plot in which a wealthy landowner and his men fence off large areas of land with barbed wire, thus preventing range men from driving their cattle north to the markets. (61 mins)

Blue Canadian Rockies
Gene Autry. Dir: George Archainbaud. A cowboy goes to Canada to stop his employer's daughter from marrying an outlaw and discovers that the girl has turned her home into a dude ranch and game preserve. He also learns that the place has had a series of murders. (58 mins)

Brave Warrior
Jon Hali. Dir: Spencer G. Bennet. In 1811, interference from the British threatens the peace in Indiana between settlers and Indians. Technicolor. With Jay Silverheels. (73 mins)

Cripple Creek
George Montgomery. Dir: Ray Nazarro. A pair of government agents, masquerading as bandits, infiltrate a plot by outlaws to steal shipments of gold from a mine. Technicolor. (78 mins)

The Hawk Of Wild River
Charles Starrett. Dir: Fred F. Sears. A desperado, armed with bow and arrow, and known as 'The Hawk' is responsible for a reign of lawlessness in a small town. Two government agents are sent to investigate. With Smiley Burnette. (54 mins)

Indian Uprising
George Montgomery. Dir: Ray Nazarro. While under threat of a court-martial, a cavalry captain prevents an Indian attack led by Geronimo. In SuperCinecolor. (74 mins)

Junction City
Charles Starrett. Dir: Ray Nazarro. When a stagecoach driver is accused of kidnapping his fiancée, the Durango Kid comes to his aid. Seems that he was merely hiding her from crooked guardians out to kill her for the gold mine she has inherited. With Smiley Burnette. (54 mins)

The Kid From Broken Gun
Charles Starrett. Dir: Fred F. Sears. When an exfighter is wrongly accused of murder and robbery, two of his pals ride into town to help him. (Starrett's last Western). With Smiley Burnette. (56 mins)

Laramie Mountains
(GB: Mountain Desperadoes)
Charles Starrett. Dir: Ray Nazarro. Crooked scouts attack the cavalry and are discovered by a government Indian agent. With Smiley Burnette. (53 mins)

Montana Territory
Lon McCallister. Dir: Ray Nazarro. After witnessing a murder, a young man is appointed deputy sheriff with instructions to apprehend the killers. Technicolor. (64 mins)

Night Stage To Galveston
Gene Autry. Dir: George Archainbaud. When a pair of newspapermen, once Texas Rangers, start investigating police corruption in Texas, they almost get killed trying to save the kidnapped daughter of their publisher from bent officials. (60 mins)

The Old West
Gene Autry. Dir: George Archainbaud. A horse wrangler, who is aided by a priest after being attacked, helps the minister bring religion to a small town. (61 mins)

The Rough Tough West
Charles Starrett. Dir: Ray Nazarro. When a local saloon owner makes his pal the town sheriff, he begins to believe his buddy is behind a scheme to cheat miners of their property. With Smiley Burnette. (54 mins)

Wagon Team
Gene Autry. Dir: George Archainbaud. After money is stolen in an army payroll holdup, a special investigator joins a medicine show. (61 mins)

1953

Goldtown Ghost Riders
Gene Autry. Dir: George Archainbaud. A circuit judge has to decide whether a man, who has spent ten years in jail for murder, can be tried twice for the same crime. With Smiley Burnette. (57 mins)

Jack McCall, Desperado
George Montgomery. Dir: Sidney Salkow. After being framed on a charge of supplying information to the enemy, a Southerner, who has joined the Union army, escapes, and finds the culprit. With Jay Silverheels. Technicolor. (76 mins)

Jesse James Vs. The Daltons
Brett King. Dir: William Castle. The Dalton Brothers find themselves in a shoot-out with a man claiming to be the son of Jesse James. 3-D Technicolor. (65 mins)

Massacre Canyon
Phil Carey. Dir: Fred F. Sears. A sergeant and a pair of army officers guard a shipment of rifles from marauders. (64 mins)

The Nebraskan
Phil Carey. Dir: Fred F. Sears. After being falsely accused of murder, an Indian scout almost begins a war. 3-D and Technicolor. (68 mins)

On Top Of Old Smoky
Gene Autry. Dir: George Archainbuad. A singing star, mistaken for a ranger, helps a girl whose ranch, rich in mica deposits, is being sought after by a crook. With Smiley Burnette. (59 mins)

Pack Train
Gene Autry. Dir: George Archainbaud. The bad guys are selling commodities needed by settlers to sriking miners – until a cowboy puts an end to their crooked trading. With Smiley Burnette. (57 mins)

Saginaw Trail
Gene Autry. Dir: George Archainbaud. A captain of Hamilton's Rangers, in Michigan, 1827, prevents a fur magnate from killing settlers. With Smiley Burriette. (56 mins)

Winning Of The West
Gene Autry. Dir: George Archainbaud. When a ranger refuses to shoot his outlaw brother, he loses his job. With Smiley Burnette. (57 mins)

Last Of The Pony Riders
Gene Autry. Dir: George Archainbaud. A Pony Express rider loses his job after buying a stagecoach and discovering that outlaws plan to sabotage Express operations to acquire a mail contract (Last Autry feature). With Smiley Burnette. (59 mins)

1954

Battle Of Rogue River
George Montgomery. Dir: William Castle. The signing of a peace treaty in Oregon, 1850, with local Indians, results in the formation of the State. With Jay Silverheels. Technicolor. (71 mins)

The Black Dakotas
Gary Merrill. Dir: Ray Nazarro. A rebel posing as a Yankee murders a Sioux emissary in order to start an Indian uprising. His purpose: to steal gold from the tribe. Technicolor. (68 mins)

The Law Vs Billy The Kid
Scott Brady. Dir: William Castle. On the run from the law, Billy the Kid falls in love with a rancher's daughter who is also the object of a wealthy ranch foreman's affections. Technicolor. (73 mins)

Masterson of Kansas
George Montgomery. Dir: William Castle. A trio of lawmen attempt to stop an outlaw from inciting an Indian war. With Jay Silverheels. Technicolor. (72 mins)

The Outlaw Stallion
Phil Carey. Dir: Fred F. Sears. As a ruse to steal a herd of horses from a woman and her young son, a group of thieves pose as friends. Technicolor. (64 mins)

They Rode West
Robert Francis, Phil Carey. Dir: Phil Karlson. An army camp commander and a medical officer do not see eye to eye when the latter treats a local Indian tribe during an outbreak of malaria. With Donna Reed. Technicolor. (84 mins)

1955

Apache Ambush
Bill Williams, Tex Ritter, Ray Corrigan. Dir: Fred F. Sears. After the Civil War a group of

Above: George Montgomery (left)

Union and Confederate soldiers, while on a mission to drive a herd of cattle from Texas to the northern states, find a shipment of rifles about to be sold to the Apaches and the Mexicans. A full-scale battle between Apaches and Mexicans results. (68 mins)

The Gun That Won The West
Dennis Morgan. Dir: William Castle. Two cavalry scouts are sent to make sure that the construction of a series of forts in hostile territory goes smoothly. Their chief weapon is a Springfield rifle. With Richard Denning. Technicolor. (69 mins)

Seminole Uprising
George Montgomery. Dir: Earl Bellamy. Raised by Indians, an army lieutenant is torn between the safety of his girl and orders to bring in the Seminole chief. With Karin Booth. Technicolor. (74 mins)

Wyoming Renegades
Phil Carey. Dir: Fred F. Sears. A former outlaw attempts to go straight, fails, but is finally helped by his girlfriend, who, together with a group of women in the town, ambushes the gang that is causing all the problems. With Martha Hyer. Technicolor. (73 mins)

1956

Blackjack Ketchum, Desperado
Howard Duff. Dir: Earl Bellamy. When a cattle baron attempts to take over a peaceful valley, a reformed gun-fighter jumps into acrion one more time. (76 mins)

Fury At Gunsight Pass
David Brian. Dir: Fred F. Sears. Robbers hold a town hostage, threatening to kill one citizen an hour, until money taken in a bank heist (and, in turn, stolen by the widow of the town's undertaker) is returned. (68 mins)

The Guns Of Fort Petticoat
Audie Murphy. Dir: George Marshall. A rebel, taking over an old fort, trains a group of women into a crackfire unit in order to stave off an Indian attack. At a court-marrial he's found not guilty. With Kathryn Grant. Technicolor. (81 mins)

The Phantom Stagecoach
William Bishop. Dir: Ray Nazarro. Two owners of a stagecoach line bicker over who has right-of-way. (69 mins)

Secret Of Treasure Mountain
Raymond Burr. Dir: Seymour Friedman. Two hundred years after the Apaches killed a Spaniard – who buried gold on their land, then cursed the spot – a villain and his henchmen attempt to find the gold. They fall victim to the curse and the gold remains buried. (68 mins)

The White Squaw

David Brian. Dir: Ray Nazarro. A group of Swedish immigrants attempts to drive an Indian tribe off their land by poisoning the water their cattle drink. A cattle-driving hero comes to the Indians' rescue. (75 mins)

1957

The Domino Kid

Rory Calhoun. Dir: Ray Nazarro. A man tracks down and kills five men responsible for murdering his father and stealing his cattle while he was away fighting for the Confederacy during the Civil War. (74 mins)

The Parson And The Outlaw

Anthony Dexter. Dir: Oliver Drake. While attempting to live a life of peace and quiet, Billy the Kid is forced to re-load when a local preacher friend of his is killed by outlaws. Technicolor. (71 mins)

Sierra Stranger

Howard Duff. Dir: Lee Sholem. After a prospector saves a man from lynching, the pair become good friends who find they're trouble prone. With Dick Foran. (78 mins)

Utah Blkaoin

Rory Calhoun. Dir: Fred F. Sears. After rescuing a rancher who has been hanged and left for dead, a cowboy inherits half the victim's ranch when the outlaws finally succeed in gunning-down the reprieved rancher. (75 mins)

1958

Apache Territory

Rory Calhoun. Dir: Ray Nazarro. A drifter helps an ungrateful group of settlers from being attacked by Indians. With Barbara Bates. Eastmancolor. (72 mins)

Return To Warbow

Phil Carey. Dir: Ray Nazarro. A trio of outlaws discover that the $30,000 they buried eleven years earlier has been spent by the brother of one of them. (67 mins)

1959

Gunmen From Laredo

Robert Knapp. Dir: Wallace MacDonald. With the help of an Indian girl, a rancher is sprung from jail after which he sets out to find the men who framed him and murdered his wife. Columbia Color. (67 mins)

CARTOONS

Unlike Warner Bros. or MGM, Columbia produced few cartoons of distinction. Under the supervision of Charles Mintz who, in 1930 moved his staff of animators from New York to California, the studio's first animated 'star' was Krazy Kat. Originally created by George Herriman in 1916, Krazy Kat's celluloid metamorphosis bore little relation to Herriman's cartoon-strip and was little more than a Mickey Mouse rip-off, the main difference being that Krazy Kat was bereft of a recognisable personality and had to rely for his laughs

Above: *Jack And The Beanstork*

on the sight-gags supplied by his animators. Between 1929 and 1939 Mintz churned out 98 Krazy Kat cartoons, all in black and white.

For three years, from 1929, Columbia also released Disney's output, and received an Oscar nomination for Best Cartoon (*Mickey's Orphans*) in the 1931-1932 Academy Awards. Disney, however, quit Columbia in 1932 for United Artists where he was given a more lucrative financial deal than anything Harry Cohn was prepared to consider. Cohn's refusal to renegotiate Disney's contract was, without doubt, the costliest error in Columbia's history.

After Krazy Kat, Columbia's next animated 'star' was a little boy called Scrappy who definitely suffered an attack of the cutes. There were 82 Scrappy cartoons in all, they ran from 1931 to 1940, and were made in black and white.

Though Columbia continued to produce black-and-white cartoons longer than any of the other majors – the last one being in 1947 – their 'prestige' offerings were the Color Rhapsodies (the studio's answer to Disney's profitable Silly Symphonies), and the short-lived Barney Googgle series, based on the comic strip by Billy DeBeck. Over 100

Below The Three Stooges

Rhapsodies were made between 1934 and 1949, the best being the Oscar- nominated *The Little Match Girl* (1937).

Other Screen Gems (as the cartoons were known) series included Fables, and Phantasies (both in black and white); and, in Technicolor, Fox and Crow, Li'l Abner, and Flippy.

In 1948, an independent producer called Steve Bosustow of UPA joined Columbia and, with the creation of the near-sighted Mr. Magoo, brought the kind of wealth and reputation to the studio's animation division it had heretofore never enjoyed.

With the success of the minimal-animation UPA product, Screen Gems was allowed to expire. With its demise went a tradition of animation that characterised the golden years of the short cartoon.

SHORTS

The short subject is, alas, a thing of the past today. But throughout the Thirties, Forties and Fifties, it comprised a part of every movie programme, with certain favourites generating, perhaps, more interest even than the feature itself. Every studio in Hollywood made them – none more so than Columbia, whose short-subject division, run by Jules White and Hugh McCollum, produced, quite literally, hundreds of one and two-reel shorts, (excluding those from the studio's prolific cartoon department). The most durable and popular stars of these were The Three Stooges – Moe and Curly Howard and Larry Fine. In 1946 illness forced Curly to retire from the series, his place being taken by Shemp Howard, who died in 1955. Howard was then replaced by Joe Besser. The first Stooges comedy, called *Women Haters*, appeared in May 1934; the last, *Sappy Bullfighters*, in April 1955 – making a grand total of 190 comedies in all.

Other, less durable comedy teams at Columbia included Monte Collins and Tom Kennedy, Gus Schilling and Richard Lane, Tom Kennedy and Johnny Arthur, Buster Keaton and Elsie Ames, Una Merkel and Harry Langdon, El Brendel and Shemp Howard, Wally Vernon and Eddie Quillan, and Max Baer and Maxi Rosenbloom. In addition, Columbia's short-subjects were a proving ground for such 'unknown' quantities as Lucille Ball, Walter Brennan, Bruce Bennett, Lloyd Bridges and Linda Walters (later Dorothy Comingore). Comedian Andy Clyde made 79 short comedies for the studio, and Harry Langdon – well past his prime – 20. Charley Chase also appeared in 20 comedies, and Buster Keaton in 10. Hugh Herbert did 23 and Vera Vague 17. Others appearing in Columbia two-reelers included Leon Errol (4), Polly Moran (2), Roscoe Karns (2), Billy Gilbert (3), Eddie Foy Jr (3), Joe de Rita (4), and Billie Burke (2).

DOCUMENTARIES

Feature-length documentaries have never been big box-office and, in common with all the other major Hollywood studios, Columbia released only a handful of them – a mere sixteen in all.

That said, at least half a dozen of those sixteen turned a modest profit, the best, financially as well as qualitatively, being Jacques Cousteau's *The Silent World* (1955), Peter Baylis's *The Finest Hours* (1964), Cousteau's *World Without Sun* (1964), Bruce Brown's surfing epic *The Endless Summer* (1966), and Sid Levin and Bob Abel's *hommage* to the rock 'n' roll era, *Let The Good Times Roll* (1973).

1930
Africa Speaks
Narrated by Lowell Thomas. Edited by Walter Futter. African wild-life film, featuring the widelipped Ubangi tribe. (67 mins)

1931
The Blonde Captive
Narrated by Lowell Thomas. Dir: Paul Withington, Clinton Childs. Photographic record of an expedition into the Aborigine land of North-West Australia. (75 mins)

1933
Mussolini Speaks
Narrated by Lowell Thomas. Editor/compiler: Jack Cohn. Compilation of newsreel clips celebrating the career of Il Duce. (74 mins)

1955
The Silent World (Le Mond du Silence)
Narrated by Jacques-Yves Cousteau. Dir: Cousteau and Louis Malle. Account of oceanographic exploration below the sea. (FRANCE) (82 mins)

1961
Mein Kampf (Den Blodiga Tiden)
Narrated by Leon Zitrone. Compiler Erwin Leiser. English narration: Claude Stephenson. Old newsreel footage helps illustrate Adolf Hitler's rise to power. (SWEDEN) (117 mins)

Below: *The Olympics In Mexico* (1968)

Above: *The Finest Hours* (1964)

1962
We'll Bury You
Narrated by William Woodson. Dir: Jack Leewood, Jack W. Thomas. An account of the rise of Communism. (75 mins).

1964
The Finest Hours
Narrated by Orson Welles. Dir: Peter Baylis. Tribute to Sir Winston Churchill. Technicolor. (BRITAIN) (116 mins)

World Without Sun (Le Monde Sans Soleil)
Narrated by Jacques-Yves Cousteau. Dir: Cousteau. The flora and fauna of the Red Sea's continental undersea shelf, and a descent to 1000 feet below sea level in a two-man submarine were the highlights of this underwater documentary. Technicolor. (FRANCE) (93 mins)

1966
Goal! The World Cup 1966
Narrated by Nigel Patrick. Dir: Abidine Dino, Ross Devenish. Account of the 1966 Football World Cup, hosted and won by England. Technicolor-Techniscope. (LIECHTENSTEIN/GB) (108 mins)

The Endless Summer
Narrated by Bruce Brown. Dir: Bruce Brown. Two young Californian surfers, Mike Hynson and Robert August, travel 35,000 miles in search of the perfect wave. Technicolor. (95 mins)

1967
Young Americans
Featuring The Young Americans. Dir: Alex Grass-hof. Semi-documentary about the teenage singing group The Young Americans. Technicolor. (103 mins)

1968
The Olympics In Mexico (Olimpiada en Mexico)
Narrated by Allan Jeffreys. Dir: Alberto Isaac. Official document of the 19th Olympiad in Mexico City. Technicolour, Techniscope. (MEXICO) (120 mins)

1970
Saturday Morning
Featuring Michael Solomon. Dir: Kent MacKenzie. Twenty teenagers talk about the problems of adolescence. Ektachrome. (88 mins)

1972
Wattstax
Dir: Mel Stuart. A vibrant account with music of the black experience in Los Angeles. (98 mins)

1973
Let The Good Times Roll
Featuring Chuck Berry, Little Richard, Fats Domino, Chubby Checker, Bill Haley and the Comets, Bo Diddley, The Shirelles. Dir: Sid Levin, Bob Abel. A recreation of the 1950s rock 'n' roll era. Eastmancolor. (99 mins)

1974
Birds Do It . . . Bees Do It
Narrated by Lee Bergere. Dir: Nicholas Noxon. A look at the animal kingdom's ways of lovemaking. Colour. (89 mins)

BRITISH FILMS

The first British film to be released by Columbia was *The Song You Gave Me* in August 1933. The following year saw the appearance of the studio's in-house British division, known as Columbia British. Its inaugural film was *The Lady Is Willing* which was released both in the USA and in Britain by Columbia and therefore qualifies as a main entry in the book.

For the next thirty years or so Columbia British released dozens of low-budget British films, the majority of which were made by 'local' production companies for home-grown consumption. It wasn't until 1965 that Columbia began to realize the full potential of British film production. Indeed some of the studio's biggest hits of the next decade were *A Man for All Seasons* (1966), *To Sir With Love*, *Georgy Girl* (1967) and *Oliver!* (1968). British-made successes prior to that included *The Guns Of Navarone* (1961) and *Lawrence Of Arabia* (1962). Because of Columbia's active participation in these productions (as well as in every Warwick Production) they are accorded main-entry status in this book.

The many other British films that Columbia released, but in which it had no creative or financial involvement, are outlined below – including two Eighties movies – *The Missionary* (1982) and *Educating Rita* (1983) – both of which were distributed by Columbia in the USA but not in Britain.

Films on this list have been placed under their year of production. Their release in the USA and elsewhere would usually have occurred in the following year. The British production company that originated each film is given at the end of each entry.

1933
The Song You Gave Me
Bebe Daniels, Victor Varconi. Dir: Paul Stein. Though she has three devoted beaus, a singer has eyes only for her aloof secretary. In the end she gets him. (86 mins) BIP

1934

Boomerang
Lester Matthews, Nora Swinburne. Dir: Arthur Maude. When a husband discovers that his blind wife is being blackmailed, he sets out to redeem the many wrongs he has done her in the past (82 mins) ARTHUR MAUDE

Borrowed Clothes
Anne Grey, Lester Matthews. Dir: Arthur Maude. After buying an unsuccessful dress shop, an extravagant wife is saved from bankruptcy when the original owners agree to buy the business back. (70 mins) ARTHUR MAUDE

The Feathered Serpent
Enid Stamp-Taylor, Tom Helmore. Dir: P. Maclean Rogers. Thriller in which an actress, after being accused of murder, has her innocence proven by a reporter. (72 mins) GS ENTERPRISES

Grand Prix
Milton Rosmer, Peter Hawthorne. Dir: St John L. Clowes. When a man is killed test-driving a car invented by his partner's son, the son has to prove both himself and the car's worth by winning a big race. He does, and, in so doing, also wins the love of the dead man's daughter. (71 mins) CLOWES AND STOCK

The Poisoned Diamond
Lester Matthews, Anne Grey. Dir: W. P. Kellino. After discovering a diamond mine, a man sets out to destroy a quartet of people who were once responsible for his going bankrupt. (73 mins) GRAFTON

Youthful Folly
Irene Vanbrugh, Grey Blake. Dir: Miles Mander. Romantic drama in which a working-class musician gives up his neighbourhood sweetheart for a society girl. The musician's sister implores the new girl to relinquish her brother and, in the end, the two working-class lovers are reunited. (72 mins) SOUND CITY

1935

Abdul The Damned
Nils Asther, Fritz Kortner. Dir: Karle Grüne. An account of the last years of the rule of Abdul-Hamid II, Sultan of Turkey in the early 1900s. (111 mins) BIP–CAPITOL

The Deputy Drummer
Lupino Lane, Jean Denis. Dir: Henry W. George. Musical-comedy in which a struggling composer takes a job as a drummer, is fired, then redeems himself after being re-engaged as a last-minute replacement. He also rounds up a gang of jewel thieves and gets the girl. (71 mins) ST GEORGE'S PICTURES

Opening Night
Douglas Byng, Reginald Gardiner, Doris Hare. Dir: Alex Brown. A revue centred on the opening night of a brand new cabaret nightclub. (68 mins) OLYMPIC

Trust The Navy
Lupino Lane, Wallace Lupino. Dir: Henry W. George. A pair of inept sailors aboard the HMS Improbable incur the wrath of their chief petty officer – and of a gang of smugglers. (71 mins) ST GEORGE'S PICTURES

Vanity
Jane Cain, Percy Marmont. Dir: Adrian Brunel. A self-obsessed young actress fakes her own death in order to experience the adulatory grief of her fans. However the effects of this act are soon well beyond her control. (76 mins) GS ENTERPRISES

Who's Your Father?
Lupino Lane, Peter Haddon, Joan (later Jean) Kent. Dir: Henry W. George. Comedy in which the hero finds himself dreading the arrival of his new father-in-law – for his mother has married an undertaker, and his 'dead' father suddenly reappears with the news that he is now married to a negress. (63 mins) ST GEORGE'S PICTURES

1936

The Beloved Vagabond
Margaret Lockwood, Maurice Chevalier. Dir: Kurt (later Curtis) Bernhardt. A man gives up his sweetheart so that she can save her father from ruin by marrying a count. In the meantime, he meets an orphan and takes over an orchestra founded by her grandfather. (78 mins) TOEPLITZ PRODUCTIONS

Everything In Life
Gitta Alpar, Neil Hamilton. Dir: J. Elder Wills. Musical about a temperamental diva who runs away frorn her manager and agent, falls in love with a penniless composer-pianist and, incognito, appears in a show featuring his music. (70 mins) TUDOR FILMS

Hot News
Lupino Lane, Phyllis Clare. Dir: W. P. Kellino. Comedy in which an inept English journalist is chosen to be a guest reporter on a Chicago paper. On the boat over, he confuses an heiress with a cabaret singer – and mistakes a group of ordinary travellers for smugglers. (77 mins) ST GEORGE'S PICTURES

Prison Breaker
James Mason, Andrew Engelmann. Dir: Adrian Brunel. A secret-service agent brings an international crook to justice, despite being in love with the criminal's daughter. (69 mins) GS ENTERPRISES

Royal Eagle
John Garrick, Nancy Burne. Dir: George A. Cooper. A warehouseman accused of robbery and murder proves his innocence. (69 mins) ST QUALITY FILMS

Thunder In The City
Edward G. Robinson, Luli Deste. Dir: Marion Gering. Comedy in which an American publicity agent comes to England to acquire 'dignity' and falls in love with the daughter of a nobleman. (88 mins) ATLANTIC

Toilers Of The Sea
Andrew Engelmann, Cyril McLaglen. Dir: Selwyn Jepson. A captain abandons a steamship for personal gain. The ship is eventually salvaged by an adventurer. (83 mins) LC BEAUMONT

1937

Pearls Bring Tears
Dorothy Boyd, Mark Stone. Dir: Manning Hayes. Disaster threatens when a string of pearls, on loan to a businessman as security for a deal, disappears when his wife inadvertently wears the necklace to a ball. It all comes right in the end. (63 mins) GS ENTERPRISES

The Reverse Be My Lot
Marjorie Corbett, Ian Fleming. Dir: Raymond Stross. An actress, in love with a physician's son, forces the physician to inject her with his experimental 'flu serum. The experiment is a success. (68 mins) ROCK PRODUCTIONS

21 Days (USA: 21 Days Together)
(Not released until 1940). Vivien Leigh, Laurence Olivier. Dir: Basil Dean. A man accidentally kills the husband of his girlfriend. A mentally deranged ex-clergyman is accused of the crime but dies before the case gets to court. (75 mins) LONDON FILMS-DENHAM FILMS

When The Devil Was Well
Jack Hobbs, Eve Grey. Dir: Maclean Rogers. A mother bullies her son into getting engaged to a social climber, but soon sees the error of her ways. (67 mins) GS ENTERPRISES

1938

The Awakening
Eric Elliott, Rex Walker, Eve Grey. Dir: Toni Frenguelli. In which a young woman has to decide which of the two doctors she loves will be the one she will finally marry. (64 mins) VICTORY

Chinatown Nights
H. Agar Lyons, Anne Grey. Dir: Toni Frenguelli. Dr Sin Fang, an evil Oriental, clashes with a woman whose brother has invented a powerful 'silver-ray' machine with which Fang hopes to rule 'the world. (70 mins) VICTORY

1941

Freedom Radio (USA: A Voice In The Night)
Clive Brook, Diana Wynyard, Derek Farr. Dir: Anthony Asquith. An Austrian throat specialist founds Freedom Radio to denounce the Nazis and sabotage Hitler's speeches – but his wife's fanatical brother betrays him. (95 mins) TWO CITIES

South American George
George Formby, Linden Travers. Dir: Marcel Varnel. The 'double' of a famous South American tenor agrees to change places with the tenor who would otherwise be sued for a broken contract. The lookalike, who's in love with the tenor's pretty press agent, finds himself pursued by gangsters. (92 mins) COLUMBIA BRITISH

1942

Much Too Shy
George Formby, Kathleen Harrison. Dir: Marcel Varnel. The hero, a handyman with a penchant for drawing, does head studies of three women – and finds himself in grave trouble when some pranksters add nude bodies to them. (92 mins) GAINSBOROUGH

Unpublished Story
Richard Greene, Valerie Hobson. Dir: Harold French. A war correspondent and his reporter girlfriend find themselves involved in a Nazi-backed 'peace organization'. (92 mins) TWO CITIES

We'll Meet Again
Vera Lynn, Ronald Ward. Dir: Phil Brandon. Backstage musical in which a singer, after getting herself noticed by singing in an air-raid, is signed up by BBC radio and becomes an 'airwaves sensation'. Romantic problems, however, blight her happiness. (84 mins) COLUMBIA BRITISH

1943

Bell-Bottom George
George Formby, Anne Firth. Dir: Marcel Varnel. A civilian wearing borrowed sailor's clothes is picked up by the shore patrol and has to masquerade as a sailor. He becomes a hero by exposing a nest of spies. (97 mins) COLUMBIA BRITISH

Get Cracking
George Formby, Dinah Sheridan. Dir: Marcel Varnel. Rivalry between the Major Wallop and the Minor Wallop Home Guards comes to a climax when the War Office despatches a machine gun that both sides want. (96 mins) COLUMBIA BRITISH

Rhythm Serenade
Vera Lynn, Peter Murray Hill. Dir: Gordon Wellesley. In which a teacher successfully attempts to run a nursery school for the children of munitions factory workers. (87 mins) COLUMBIA BRITISH

1944

He Stoops To Conquer
George Formby, Robertson Hare, Elizabeth Allen. Dir: Marcel Varnel. An eccentric inventor helps an odd-job man to oust dishonest local councillors. (103 mins) COLUMBIA BRITISH

One Exciting Night
(USA: You Can't Do Without Love)
Vera Lynn, Donald Stewart. Dir: Walter Forde. A woman attempts to get an impresario-cum- government-official to give her an audition – but then finds herself involved with a gang who plan to steal a valuable painting from him. (89 mins) COLUMBIA BRITISH

1945

I Didn't Do It
George Formby, Marjorie Brown. Dir: Marcel Varnel. An entertainer who is living in a theatrical boarding house becomes embroiled in the murder of an Australian acrobat. (97 mins) COLUMBIA BRITISH

29 Acacia Avenue (USA: The Facts Of Love)
Gordon Harker, Betty Balfour. Dir: Henry Cass. A crisis occurs for the Robinson family when Mr and Mrs return early from their holidays to discover that their daughter is about to embark on a trial marriage and their son is involved in his girlfriend's divorce. (83 mins) BOCA

1946

George In Civvy Street
George Formby, Ronald Shiner, Rosalyn Boulter. Dir: Marcel Varnel. A demobbed soldier faces a war with his rival in love. (The last of Formby's films.) (79 mins) COLUMBIA BRITISH

This Man Is Mine
Hugh McDermott, Glynis Johns. Dir: Marcel Varnel. When a Canadian soldier is billeted with a middle-class English family, he discovers just how eccentric an English family can be. (103 mins) COLUMBIA BRITISH

1947

The First Gentleman
(USA: Affairs Of A Rogue)
Jean-Pierre Aumont, Joan Hopkins, Cecil Parker. Dir: Alberto Cavalcanti. Costume drama that traces the reign of the Prince Regent after the Napoleonic Wars. (111 mins) TWO CITIES

1948

The Fatal Night
Leslie Armstrong, Patrick Macnee, Lester Ferguson. Dir: Mario Zampi. Spooky thriller in which a young man agrees to spend the night in a 'haunted' house as a dare – and everything goes dreadfully wrong. (50 mins) ANGLOFILM

1949

Paper Orchid
Hy Hazell, Sidney James. Dir: Roy Baker. Two newspapers compete for headlines over the sensational story of a man who is found murdered in the flat of a gossip columnist known as The Orchid. (86 mins) GANESH

1950

The Clouded Yellow
Jean Simmons, Trevor Howard. Dir: Ralph Thomas. A disgraced Secret Serviceman helps a deranged girl prove that she is innocent of the murder of a handyman. (96 mins) CARILLON

Come Dance With Me
Gordon Humphris, Yvonne Marsh, Max Wall. Dir: Mario Zampi. In order to gain entry to a swanky nightclub, a valet and a maid pose as aristocrats. (58 mins) ANGLOFILM

Midnight Episode
Stanley Holloway. Dir: Gordon Parry. Remake of the French Monsieur La Souris (1942). A busker accidentally stumbles across the body of a murdered man and finds a great deal of money in his wallet. He returns the cash to the police but keeps the wallet – much to the annoyance of the murderer . . . (78 mins) TRIANGLE

My Daughter Joy (USA: Operation X)
Edward G. Robinson, Peggy Cummins. Dir: Gregory Ratoff. A financier plans to marry off his adored daughter to an eastern potentate, despite the fact that she's in love with a newspaperman. (81 mins) BRITISH LION-LONDON FILMS

Shadow Of The Past
Terence Morgan, Joyce Howard. Dir: Mario Zampi. After seeing a mysterious woman in a house supposedly shut for two years, a man discovers that the woman is the twin sister of a murder victim. (83 mins) ANGLOFILM

State Secret (USA: The Great Manhunt)
Douglas Fairbanks Jr, Glynis Johns, Jack Hawkins. Dir: Sidney Gilliat. Chase drama in which a candidate in a forthcoming elections dies – a fact which his political supporters intend to conceal. To this end they have to track down and 'silence' the man's surgeon. (104 mins) LONDON FILMS

The Woman In Question
(USA: Five Angels On Murder)
Jean Kent, Dirk Bogarde. Dir: Anthony Asquith. Thriller in which a murdered fortune-teller is seen through the eyes of her 'help', her sister, her fiancé and a sailor. (88 mins) JAVELIN

1954

Father Brown (USA: The Detective)
Alec Guinness, Joan Greenwood, Peter Finch. Dir: Robert Hamer. Comedy in which a cross being protected by Father Brown is stolen by a master of disguise. (91 mins) FACET

1955

1984
Edmond O'Brien, Jan Sterling, Michael Redgrave. Dir: Michael Anderson. Europe, called Oceania, is ruled by Big Brother. George Orwell's prophetic novel in its first screen incarnation. (90 miles) HOLIDAY

The Prisoner
Alec Guinness, Jack Hawkins. Dir: Peter Glenville. A cardinal in an unnamed European state is interrogated, for political

Below: *Father Brown (The Detective)* (1954)

reasons, by a psychologist. He eventually 'confesses'. (94 mins) LONDON INDEPENDENT/ FACET

Storm Over The Nile
Laurence Harvey, Anthony Steel. Dir: Terence Young, Zoltan Korda. Remake of A. E. W. Nelson's celebrated novel The Four Feathers. Technicolor and CinemaScope. (107 mins) LONDON FILMS

1956

Bermuda Affair
Gary Merrill, Ron Randell. Dir: Edward Sutherland. Buddy-buddy war drama in which one of the buddies sacrifices his life for the other because he has had an affair with his best mate's wife. (77 mins) BERMUDA

Beyond Mombasa
Cornel Wilde, Donna Reed. Dir: George Marshall. Jungle adventure in which a man travels to Africa to avenge his brother's murder at the hands of an anti-white organization. He also goes in search of a uranium mine. Technicolor. (60 mins) HEMISPHERE

Fortune Is A Woman
(USA: She Played With Fire)
Arlene Dahl, Jack Hawkins, Dennis Price. Dir: Sidney Gilliat. Intrigue in which an insurance assessor discovers that a so-called valuable painting destroyed in a fire is a fake, and that the authentic one has been sold. (94 mins) JOHN HARVEL-LAUNDER-GILLIAT

The Last Man To Hang?
Tom Conway, Elizabeth Sellars. Dir: Terence Fisher. Thriller in which a man is framed by his housekeeper and accused of the murder of his neurotic wife. (75 mins) ACT FILMS

Soho Incident (USA: Spin A Dark Web)
Faith Domergue, Lee Patterson. Dir: Vernon Sewell. Thriller in which a Canadian, out for easy money, becomes embroiled in murder when he joins a crooked Soho betting gang. (77 mins) FILM LOCATIONS

Town On Trial!
John Mills, Charles Coburn, Barbara Bates. Dir: John Guillermin. Mystery involving the murder by strangulation of a good-time girl in a small country village. (96 mins) MARKSMAN

Wicked As They Come
Arlene Dahl, Herbert Marshall, Phil Carey. Dir: Ken Hughes. A gold-digger accidentally kills her wealthy husband but is saved from the gallows when the truth of her spouse's demise emerges. (94 mins) FILM LOCATIONS

1957

The Admirable Crichton
(USA: Paradise Lagoon)
Kenneth More, Cecil Parker, Sally Ann Howes. Dir: Lewis Gilbert. Second screen version (the first was in 1918) of J. M. Barrie's classic desert-island comedy. Technicolor and Vista Vision. (93 mins) MODERN SCREENPLAYS

Escapement
(USA: Zex – The Electronic Monster)
Rod Cameron, Mary Murphy. Dir: Montgomery Tully. An American investigator foils a plot in which a scientist hopes to gain control of the world by manipulating the minds of politicians and key world figures with the electronic device he has invented. (77 mins) MERTON-PARK

Kill Her Gently
Griffith Jones, Maureen Connell. Dir: Charles Saunders. An ex-mental patient, jealous of his rich wife, promises a pair of convicts money if they will murder her. But things go wrong. (75 mins) FORTRESS

The Long Haul
Victor Mature, Diana Dors. Dir: Ken Hughes. An ex-GI who stays on in England becomes a truck-driver and is seduced by the mistress of a haulage racketeer. (100 mins) MARKSMAN

Murder Reported
Paul Carpenter, Melissa Stribling. Dir: Charles Saunders. The murder of a local councillor is solved by a reporter and his boss's daughter. (58 mins) FORTRESS

Womaneater (USA: The Woman Eater)
George Coulouris, Vera Day. Dir: Charles Saunders. A mad scientist returns from the Amazon with a tree that feeds on young girls and gives out, in return, a liquid that restores life to the dead. (71 mins) FORTRESS

1958

The Camp On Blood Island
André Morell, Carl Mohner. Dir: Val Guest. Allied POWS try hard to keep the news of a Japanese surrender away from a sadistic Jap commandant. (82 mins) HAMMER

I Only Arsked!
Bernard Bresslaw, Michael Medwin. Dir: Montgomery Tully. Comedy in which soldiers and harem girls thwart a revolution and strike oil. (82 mins) HAMMER-GRANADA

Passport To Shame (USA: Room 43)
Diana Dors, Eddie Constantine. Dir: Alvin Rakoff. London cabbies rescue a young girl from a life of prostitution. (91 mins) UNITED CO-PRODUCTIONS

The Revenge Of Frankenstein
Peter Cushing, Eunice Gayson. Dir: Terence Fisher. Baron Frankenstein uses his position at a clinic to obtain limbs and a brain from the body of a dwarf. The creature that results goes on a killing rampage. Technicolor. (89 mins) HAMMER

The Snorkel
Peter Van Eyck, Betta St John, Mandy Miller. Dir: Guy Green. After drowning his wife's first husband, a man then attempts to drown her as well. His step-daughter, however, brings about his arrest. (90 mins) HAMMER

The Two-Headed Spy
Jack Hawkins, Felix Aylmer, Gia Scala. Dir: André de Toth. True story of a British spy planted into the German Officer Corps and falls in love with a female 'contact'. (93 mins) SABRE

The Whole Truth
Stewart Granger, Donna Reed, Gianna Maria Canale, George Sanders. Dir: John Guillermin. Thriller involving the murder of a film producer's mistress. (84 mins) ROMULUS-TALENT

1959

The Boy And The Bridge
Ian MacLaine, Liam Redmond. Dir: Kevin McClory. When, after a pub brawl, his dad is arrested, a youngster runs away and takes up residence with a pet seagull in a small tower in London Bridge – and then saves a woman from suicide. (90 mins) XANANDU

Don't Panic Chaps!
George Cole, Dennis Price, Nadja Regin. Dir: George Pollock. When a glamorous Italian castaway is washed ashore, British and German army units, forgotten by their respective commands and peacefully sitting out World War II on a small Atlantic island, immediately become hostile. (84 mins) ACT-HAMMER

Hell Is A City
Stanley Baker, John Crawford. Dir: Val Guest. Crime melodrama in which an escaped convict is apprehended by an inspector using marked banknotes. HammerScope. (98 mins) ASSOCIATED BRITISH-HAMMER

The Stranglers Of Bombay
Guy Rolfe, Allan Cuthbertson. Dir: Terence Fisher. In India, in 1926, a murderous cult is strangling hundreds of British East India Company passengers. (80 mins) HAMMER

The Ugly Duckling
Bernard Bresslaw, Jean Muir. Dir: Lance Comfort. Variation on the Jekyll-and-Hyde theme as a descendant of the Jekyll family discovers his sinister ancestor's transformation formula. (84 mins) HAMMER

Yesterday's Enemy
Stanley Baker, Leo McKern. Dir: Val Guest. In Burma, 1942, a British officer shoots two hostages to expose a spy. Later the situation is reversed. MegaScope. (95 mins) HAMMER

1960

The Full Treatment
(USA: Stop Me Before I Kill)
Ronald Lewis, Claude Dauphin, Diane Cilento. Dir: Val Guest. A psychiatrist leads an international racing driver to believe that he strangled his wife. Melodrama with a Riviera setting. MegaScope. (109 mins) HILARY-FALCON

Hand In Hand
Philip Needs, Loretta Parry, John Gregson, Sybil Thorndyke. Dir: Philip Leacock. Friendship between a young Jewish girl and a Roman Catholic boy. (80 mins) HELEN WINSTON

Never Take Sweets From A Stranger
(USA: Never Take Candy From A Stranger)
Gwen Watford, Patrick Allen. Dir: Cyril Frankel. A psychopathic pervert, who also happens to be the Mr Big in a small Canadian town, persuades two innocent little girls to dance naked for him in return for some sweets. He's taken to court and acquitted – but then murders a child. This time he's convicted. MegaScope. (81 mins) HAMMER

Please Turn Over
Ted Ray, Jean Kent. Dir: Gerald Thomas. All hell breaks loose when a bored teenage girl writes a lurid novel incorporating various members of her family. (87 mins) ANGLO-AMALGAMATED

Sword Of Sherwood Forest
Richard Greene, Peter Cushing. Dir: Terence Fisher. Robin Hood thwarts the Sheriff of Nottingham's plot to murder the Archbishop of Canterbury. Technicolor and MegaScope. (80 mins) HAMMER

The Terror Of The Tongs
Geoffrey Toone, Christopher Lee, Yvonne Monlaur. Dir: Anthony Bushell. In Hong Kong, 1910, a slave girl helps a seaman unmask the villain behind a gang of opium-running white slavers. Technicolor. (79 mins) HAMMER-MERLIN

The Trunk
Phil Carey, Julia Arnall. Dir: Donovan Winter. Melodrama in which a blackmailer frames a girl for the murder of her husband's ex-mistress. (72 mins) DONWIN

Visa To Canton (USA: Passport To China)
Richard Basehart, Lisa Gastoni. Dir: Michael Carreras. In China, a girl helps an American travel agent clear his half-brother who has been framed by communists. Technicolor. (75 mins) HAMMER

1961

Cash On Demand
Peter Cushing, Andre Morell. Dir: Quentin Lawrence. A bank manager is forced to help a robber in order to save his kidnapped wife and son. (66 mins) WOODPECKER-HAMMER

The Damned (USA: These Are The Damned)
Macdonald Carey, Shirley Ann Field, Viveca Lindfors. Dir: Joseph Losey. In a British seaside town an American tourist and the sister of a teenage thug set about freeing an imprisoned group of radioactive children. HammerScope. (87 mins) HAMMER-SWALLOW

The Greengage Summer
(USA: Loss Of Innocence)
Kenneth More, Danielle Darrieux, Susannah York. Dir: Lewis Gilbert. In France, a teenage girl falls in love with an English visitor and unwittingly brings about his arrest for stealing gems. From the novel by Rumer Godden. Technicolor. (99 mins) PKL

Only Two Can Play
Peter Sellers, Mai Zetterling. Dir: Sidney Gilliat. In Wales, a married librarian has an affair with the wife of a local bigwig. From Kingsley Amis's novel *That Uncertain Feeling*. (106 mins) VALE

The Pirates Of Blood River
Kerwin Matthews, Christopher Lee. Dir: John Gilling. A pirate forces a fugitive to help him raid a Huguenot settlement. Period adventure. Eastmancolor. HammerScope. (84 mins) WOODPECKER

Reach For Glory
Harry Andrews, Kay Walsh. Dir: Philip Leacock. In 1942 a soldier's evacuated son joins a group of boys in persecuting an Austrian refugee boy. (86 mins) BLAZER

Taste Of Fear (USA: Scream Of Fear)
Susan Strasberg, Ronald Lewis, Ann Todd. Dir: Seth Holt. In France a chauffeur conspires with a widow to drive a woman's crippled stepdaughter mad. (82 mins) HAMMER

Watch It Sailor!
Dennis Price, Liz Fraser, Irene Handl. Dir: Wolf Rilla. Comedy about a sailor who, on the eve of his wedding, has mother-in-law troubles as well as paternity problems. (81 mins) HAMMER

A Weekend With Lulu
Bob Monkhouse, Leslie Phillips, Alfred Marks, Shirley Eaton. Dir: John Paddy Carstairs. Comedy in which a caravan full of people is accidentally ferried to France. (89 mins) HAMMER

1962

HMS Defiant (USA: Damn The Defiant)
Alec Guinness, Dirk Bogarde, Anthony Quayle. Dir: Lewis Gilbert. In 1797 the sadistic treatment of a captain's son by a lieutenant leads to mutiny. Technicolor and CinemaScope. (101 mins) GW FILMS

The Iron Maiden
Michael Craig, Anne Helm. Dir: Gerald Thomas. An aircraft designer's vintage traction engine helps him win an American contract. Eastmancolor. (98 mins) GHW PRODUCTIONS

The L-Shaped Room
Leslie Caron, Brock Peters, Tom Bell. Dir: Bryan Forbes. A writer is in love with a French girl until he discovers she's going to have a baby. (142 mins) ROMULUS

It's Trad, Dad!
(USA: Ring-A-Ding Rhythm)
Helen Shapiro, Craig Douglas. Dir: Richard Lester. A musical in which a group of teenagers convert a pompous mayor by staging a jazz festival. (73 mins) AMICUS

Maniac
Kerwin Matthews, Nadia Gray. Dir: Michael Carreras. In France, a woman involves a tourist in the murder of her mad husband. CinemaScope. (86 mins) HAMMER

The Wrong Arm Of The Law
Peter Sellers, Lionel Jeffries. Dir: Cliff Owen. A cockney crook, posing as a French couturier, helps the police catch a gang who, in turn, are posing as the police. (94 mins) ROMULUS

1963

Siege of the Saxons
Ronald Lewis, Janette Scott, Ronald Howard. Dir: Nathan Juran. A Robin Hood-like hero prevents the dastardly Edumund of Cornwall from becoming King of England. (85 mins) AMERAN

Do You Know This Voice?
Dan Duryea, Isa Miranda, Gwen Watford. Dir: Frank Nesbitt. A man 'protecting' a witness to a child murder turns out to be the murderer. (80 mins) LIPPERT-PARROCH-MCCALLUM

The Devil-Ship Pirates
Christopher Lee, John Cairney. Dir: Don Sharp. In Cornwall, a Spanish captain captures a girl in order to force local villagers to help him repair his crippled ship. Technicolor and HammerScope. (86 mins) HAMMER

Just For Fun!
Mark Wynter, Cherry Roland. Dir: Gordon Flemyng. Musical in which a teenage group promotes a teenage party after being given the vote, and takes over the country. (85 mins) AMICUS

1964

Curse Of The Mummy's Tomb
Terence Morgan, Ronald Howard. Dir: Michael Carreras. Egypt, 1900. An Egyptian prince, cursed to eternal life, revives a 3000-year-old mummy so that it may kill the desecrators of a tomb. Technicolor and Techni-Scope. (80 mins) HAMMER-SWALLOW

The Finest Hours
Narrated by Orson Welles. Dir: Peter Baylis. Documentary tribute to Winston Churchill. (116 mins) JACK LE VIEN

The Gorgon
Peter Cushing, Richard Pasco, Barbara Shelley. Dir: Terence Fisher. Horror film set in 1910 in which a student, while investigating his father's petrification, falls in love with a nurse possessed by the spirit of Magaera, the mythical Gorgon. (83 mins) HAMMER

Nothing But The Best
Alan Bates, Millicent Martin, Denholm Elliott. Dir: Clive Donner. A real-estate agent from the wrong side of the tracks hires a degenerate to teach him how to behave in upper-crust society. He then kills his new teacher when he causes complications – and goes on to marry the boss's daughter. Eastmancolor. (99 mins) DOMINO

The Runaway
Greta Gynt, Alex Gallier. Dir: Tony Young. An MI5 agent saves a Polish chemist and a synthetic ballistic chemical from falling into the hands of Russian spies. (62 mins) LUCK-WELL

Victim Five (USA: Code Seven, Victim Five)
Lex Barker, Ronald Fraser. Dir: Robert Lynn. In Cape Town, a South African millionaire hires an American detective to solve a crime involving the murder of his valet. Technicolor and TechniScope. (88 mins) TOWERS OF LONDON FILM

1965

The Brigand Of Kandahar
Ronald Lewis, Oliver Reed. Dir: John Gilling. A half-cast lieutenant leads a band of Bengali rebels against the English. Technicolor and Cinema- Scope. (81 mins) HAMMER

Fanatic (USA: Die, Die, My Darling)
Tallulah Bankhead, Stefanie Powers. Dir: Silvio Narizzano. A religious fanatic tries to murder her dead son's American fiancée. (96 mins) HAMMER-SEVEN ARTS.

The Heroes Of Telemark
Kirk Douglas, Richard Harris. Dir: Anthony Mann. In Norway, 1942, brave Resistance workers foil a German plan to move a heavy-water plant to Berlin. Technicolor and TechniScope. (131 mins) BENTON FILMS

Life At The Top
Laurence Harvey, Jean Simmons. Dir: Ted Kotcheff. After being elected to a local council, a mill-owner's son-in-law continues an affair with a TV actress. From the novel by John Braine. (117 mins) ROMULUS

The Little Ones
Dudley Foster, Carl Gonzales, Kim Smith. Dir: Jim O'Connolly. The police pursue a youngster and his half-caste friend to Liverpool after the kids decide to run away from home. (66 mins) GOLDHAWK

Repulsion
Catherine Deneuve, Ian Hendry, John Fraser. Dir: Roman Polanski. A mentally disturbed Belgian manicurist with a sexual problem kills her boyfriend and then her landlord. (104 mins) COMPTON-TEKLI

A Study In Terror (USA: Fog)
John Neville, Donald Huston. Dir: James Hill. In the 1880s Sherlock Holmes unmasks the notorious prostitute-murderer, Jack the Ripper. Eastmancolor. (95 mins) COMPTON-TEKLI-SIR NIGEL

1966

The Wrong Box
John Mills, Ralph Richardson, Michael Caine, Peter Cook, Dudley Moore, Peter Sellers. Dir: Bryan Forbes. Two elderly Victorian brothers are trying to murder each other, for a large inheritance will fall to the survivor. From the novel by Robert Louis Stevenson. Technicolor. (110 mins) SALAMANDER

1970

Creatures The World Forgot
Julie Ege, Brian O'Shaughnessy. Dir: Michael Carreras. Stone Age horror in which all the characters communicate in grunts. Concerns the long trek of survivors of a volcanic eruption. (95 mins) HAMMER

1971

The Go-Between
Julie Christie, Alan Bates, Dominic Guard, Margaret Leighton. L. P. Hartley's story of a young lad who passes love notes between an aristocratic young woman and a farmer, with long-lasting consequences. (116 mins) MGM-EMI-WORLD FILM SERVICES

1972

The Creeping Flesh
Christopher Lee, Peter Cushing. Dir: Freddie Francis. Horror film about a Victorian scientist who has isolated 'the essence of evil' in the blood of an 'instant Monster'. (91 mins) TIGON-BRITISH WORLD FILM SERVICES

1974

Stardust
David Essex, Adam Faith. Dir: Michael Apted. The further adventures (which began in *That'll Be The Day*; 1973) of a young fairground worker and his mates who 'made it' as a successful pop group. Now our hero has 'gone solo' and is suffering the slings and arrows of fame and fortune. (113 mins) NAT COHEN-EMI-GOODTIMES ENTERPRISES

1975

Tommy
Roger Daltrey, Ann-Margret, Oliver Reed. Dir: Ken Russell. Rock opera about a deaf, dumb and blind boy who enters his own private world after witnessing the murder of his father. (108 mins) HEMDALE

1976

The Eagle Has Landed
Michael Caine, Donald Sutherland, Robert Duvall. Dir: John Sturges. World War II thriller about a Nazi plot to abduct Churchill, who is supposedly enjoying a quiet weekend on the Norfolk coast. (135 mins) ASSOCIATED GENERAL FILMS

1977

March Or Die
Gene Hackman, Terence Hill (aka Mario Giotti), Max Von Sydow, Catherine Deneuve. Dir: Richard Lester. A West Point graduate, after giving 16 years of his life to the Foreign Legion, is sent on a mission to protect a group of excavators from the Arabs. (107 mins) ENTERTAINMENT-ASSOCIATED GENERAL FILMS

1978

Warlords Of Atlantis
Peter Gilmore, Doug McClure. Dir: Kevin Connor. An undersea explorer and a naval inventor find excitement when their diving bell takes them to the sunken city of Atlantis. (96 mins) EMI

1982

The Missionary
Michael Palin, Maggie Smith, Trevor Howard. Dir: Richard Loncraine. Comedy set in Victorian times in which a missionary who has spent 10 years teaching European history to a group of African children is recalled to London where his new job is to run a slum mission for 'fallen women'. (86 mins) HAND-MADE FILMS

Monty Python Live At The Hollywood Bowl
The Monty Python Team. Dir: Terry Jones. Live coverage of the anarchic comedy team performing their bizarrely famous sketches in the USA. (80 mins) HANDMADE FILMS

1983

Educating Rita
Michael Caine, Julie Walters. Dir: Lewis Gilbert. A married hairdresser chooses an alcoholic tutor to help her acquire some education, then outgrows him. (100 mins) ACORN PICTURES

Below: *Tommy* (1975)

403

FOREIGN AND INDEPENDENT FILMS

The intention of this book is to describe and illustrate the vast body of films that were made specifically by Columbia Pictures and enlisted the particular skills of Columbia's personnel. During the golden age of the Hollywood studio system, it was not difficult to determine what was, or was not, a Columbia picture. The demarcation lines started to blur from the Sixties onwards when Columbia began to acquire and distribute movies that did not originate 'in house'. Some of these films were made in America by independent producers, but the majority were foreign-language productions which Columbia released in the USA. Many of them carry the Columbia logo and brought in revenue to the studio – and they are, of course, part of *The Columbia Story*. However, as the studio's creative involvement in these films was nil (save, perhaps, for the advertising campaign) they are of minor interest in the overall story.

Nonetheless, for the sake of completeness, these films are all listed here – by their USA title, followed by their original-language title (and their British title, if different). They have been placed under the year in which they were released in the USA, with the year of production given next to their country of origin.

As has been the case with the other studios in this on-going series, it is often difficult to establish just how independent of the studio in question the production company was, and the dividing line between the releasing studio's involvement and non-involvement is, in some cases, impossible to draw. For this reason there are films included in this appendix and others in the body of the book whose positions might well be argued either way.

1947
Pacific Adventure (AUS: Smithy)
Ron Randell, Muriel Steinbeck. Dir: Ken G. Hall. (AUSTRALIA, 1946)

1948
The Lost One
(La Signora dalle Camelie/La Traviata)
Nelly Corradi (role sung by Onelia Fineschi), Gino Mattera. Dir: Carmine Gallone. (ITALY, 1947)

1950
Faust And The Devil (La Leggenda di Faust)
Nelly Corradi (role sung by Onelia Fineschi), Italo Tajo. Dir: Carmine Gallone. (ITALY, 1948)

1954
Beat The Devil
Humphrey Bogart, Jennifer Jones, Gina Lollobrigida, Robert Morley, Peter Lorre. Dir: John Huston. (GB/ITALY, 1955)
Heidi
Elsbeth Sigmund, Heinrich Gretler. Dir: Luigi Comencini. (SWITZERLAND, 1952)

Indiscretion Of An American Wife
(Stazione Termini; GB: Indiscretion)
Jennifer Jones, Montgomery Clift. Dir: Vittorio De Sica. A De Sica Production. Filmed in Rome. English dialogue. (ITALY-USA, 1952)

1955
Special Delivery (Vom Himmel gefallen)
Joseph Cotten, Eva Bartok. Dir: John Brahm. (W. GERMANY-USA, 1955)

1957
Woman Of The River (La Donna del Fiume)
Sophia Loren, Gérard Oury. Dir: Mario Soldati. (ITALY-FRANCE, 1954)
Bitter Victory (Amère Victoire)
Richard Burton, Curt Jurgens (aka Curd Jürgens). Dir: Nicholas Ray. (FRANCE-GB, 1957)

1958
This Angry Age
(La Diga sul Pacifico; GB: The Sea Wall)
Silvana Mangano, Anthony Perkins. Dir: René Clément. Filmed in Thailand. (ITALY, 1956)

1959
Babette Goes To War
(Babette S'en Va-t-en Guerre)
Brigitte Bardot, Jacques Charrier. Dir: Christian-Jaque. (FRANCE, 1959)
The Night Heaven Fell
(Les Bijouteries du Clair de Lune)
Brigitte Bardot, Stephen Boyd. Dir: Roger Vadim. (FRANCE, 1958)
The H-Man (Bijo to Ekitai-Ningen)
Yumi Shirakawa, Kenji Sahara. Dir: Inoshiro Honda. (JAPAN, 1958)
The Warrior And The Slave Girl
(La Rivolta del Gladiatori)
Ettore Manni, Georges Marchal, Gianna Maria Canale. Dir: Vittorio Cottafavi. (ITALY-SPAIN, 1958)

1960
Battle In Outer Space (Uchu Daisensu)
Ryo Ikebe, Kyoko Anzai. Dir: Inoshiro Honda. (JAPAN, 1959)
Fast And Sexy
(Anna di Brooklyn; GB: Anna Of Brooklyn)
Gina Lollobrigida, Dale Robertson, Vittorio de Sica. Dir: Reginald Denham, Carlo Lestricati. (FRANCE-ITALY-USA, 1958)
Nights Of Lucrezia Borgia
(Le Notti di Lucrezia Borgia; GB: Nights Of Temptation)
Belinda Lee, Jacques Sernas. Dir: Sergio Grieco. (ITALY-FRANCE, 1959)

Below: *Fast And Sexy* (1960)

Above: *Fury Of The Pagans* (1962)

Swan Lake (Lebedinole Ozero)
Maya Plisetskaya, Nikolai Fadeyechev. Dir: S. Tulubyeva. (RUSSIA, 1958)
As The Sea Rages (Raubfischer in Hellas)
Maria Schell, Cliff Robertson, Cameron Mitchell. Dir: Horst Haechler. (GERMANY-YUGOSLAVIA-USA, 1959)
The Young One
(La Joven; GB: Island Of Shame)
Zachary Scott, Kay Meersman. Dir: Luis Buñuel. (MEXICO, 1960)
Queen Of The Pirates
(La Venere dei Pirati)
Gianna Maria Canale, Massimo Serrato. Dir: Mario Costa. (ITALY-W. GERMANY, 1960)

1961
The Best Of Enemies (I due Nemici)
David Niven, Alberto Sordi, Michael Wilding. Dir: Guy Hamilton. A Dino De Laurentiis production. Made in English. (ITALY, 1961)
Carthage In Flames (Cartagine in Fiamme)
José Suarez, Anne Heywood, Pierre Brasseur. Dir: Carmine Gallone. (FRANCE-ITALY, 1959)
Five Golden Hours
(Cinque Ore in Contanti)
Ernie Kovaks, Cyd Charisse, George Sanders. Dir: Mario Zampi. (GB-ITALY, 1961)
The Warrior Empress
(Saffo, Venere di Lesbo)
Tina Louise, Kerwin Matthews. Dir: Pietro Francisci (ITALY-FRANCE, 1960)

1962
Mothra (Mosura)
Franky Sakai, Emi Ito, Yumi Ito. Dir: Inoshiro Honda (plus Lee Kresel for English version). (JAPAN, 1962)
The Old Dark House
Tom Poston, Robert Morley, Janette Scott. Dir: William Castle. (USA-GB, 1962)
Fury Of The Pagans (La Furia dei Barbari)
Edmund Purdom, Rossana Podesta. Dir: Guido Malatesta. (ITALY, 1960)
The Reluctant Saint
Maximilian Schell, Ricardo Montalban. Dir: Edward Dmytryk. A Dmytryk-Weiler Independent Production. Made in Italy. (USA-ITALY, 1962)
Sundays And Cybèle
(Cybèle ou les Dimanches de Ville d'Avray)
Hardy Kruger, Patricia Gozzi. Dir: Serge Bourgignon. (FRANCE, 1962)

1963
In The French Style (A la Francaise)
Stanley Baker, Jean Seberg. Dir: Robert Parrish. (USA-FRANCE, 1963)

1964

Band Of Outsiders (Bande à Part)
Anna Karina, Sami Frey. Dir: Jean-Luc Godard. (FRANCE, 1964)

The Householder (Gharbar)
Shashi Kapoor, Leela Naidu. Dir: James Ivory. (INDIA, 1963)

The Little Prince And The Eight-Headed Dragon
Full-length animated feature. Dir: Yugo Serikawa. Animation dir: Yasuji Mori. (JAPAN, 1963)

1965

Apache Gold (Winnetou I. Teil; GB: Winnetou The Warrior)
Lex Barker, Pierre Brice, Marie Versini. Dir: Harald Reinl. (W.GERMANY-YUGOSLAVIA-FRANCE,1963)

Backfire (Echappement Libre)
Jean-Paul Belmondo, Jean Seberg, Gert Fröbe. Dir: Jean Becker. (FRANCE-ITALY-SPAIN, 1964)

The Dolls
(Le Bambole; GB: Four Kinds Of Love)
Gina Lollobrigida, Nino Manfredi, Elke Sommer. Dir: Dino Risi, Luigi Comencini, Franco Rossi, Mauro Bolognini. (ITALY-FRANCE, 1964)

Last Of The Renegades (Winnetou II. Teil)
Pierre Brice, Lex Barker, Anthony Steele. Dir: Harald Reinl. (W. GERMANY-YUGOSLAVIA-ITALY-FRANCE, 1964)

The Magic World Of Topo Gigio
Animated cartoon plus live action. Ermanno Roveri. Dir: Luca de Rico. (ITALY, 1965)

The Married Woman (Une Femme Mariée)
Macha Meril, Philippe Le Roy, Bernard Noël. Dir: Jean-Luc Godard. (FRANCE, 1964)

The Treasure Of Silver Lake
(Der Schatz im Silbersee)
Lex Barker, Pierre Brice, Herbert Lom. Dir: Harald Reinl. A Winnetou adventure. (W.GERMANY-YUGOSLAVIA, 1962)

A Virgin For The Prince aka A Maiden For The Prince (Una Vergine per il Principe/Une Vierge Pour Le Prince)
Vittoria Gassman, Virna Lisi, Philippe Le Roy. Dir: Pasquale Festa-Campanile. (ITALY-FRANCE, 1965)

1966

The Eavesdropper (El Ojo de la Cerradura)
Stathis Giallelis, Janet Margolin. Dir: Leopoldo Torre-Nilsson. (ARGENTINA-USA, 1964)

Every Day Is A Holiday (Cabriola)
Marisol, Angel Peralta. Dir: Mel Ferrer. (SPAIN, 1965)

Frontier Hellcat (Unter Geiern)
Elke Sommer, Stewart Granger, Pierre Brice. Dir: Alfred Vohrer. Another in the Winnetou series. (FRANCE-ITALY-W. GERMANY-YUGOSLAVIA, 1964)

Goal! World Cup 1966
Narrated by Nigel Patrick. Dir: Abidine Dino, Ross Devenish. (GB-LIECHTENSTEIN)

Masculin-Féminin
Jean-Pierre Léaud, Chantal Goya. Dir: Jeap-Luc Godard. (FRANCE-SWEDEN 1966)

The Mystery Of Thug Island (I Misteri della Giungla Nera)
Guy Madison, Inge Schöner, Peter Van Eyck. Dir: Luigi Capuano. (ITALY-W.GERMANY, 1964)

Rage (El Mal)
Glenn Ford, Stella Stevens, Dir: Gilberto Gazcón. (USA-MEXICO, 1966)

Rampage At Apache Wells (Der Ol Prinz)
Stewart Granger, Pierre Brice, Macha Meril. Dir: Harald Philipp. A Winnetou adventure. (W. GERMANY-YUGOSLAVIA, 1965)

Sandra (Vaghe Stelle dell'Orsa)
Claudia Cardinale, Michael Craig, Jean Sorel. Dir: Luchino Visconti. (ITALY, 1964)

Swedish Wedding Night
(Bröllopsbesvär; GB: Wedding – Swedish Style)
Jarl Kulle, Christina Schollin. Dir: Åke Falck. (SWEDEN, 1964)

The Texican
Audie Murphy, Broderick Crawford. Dir: Lesley Selander. (USA-SPAIN, 1966)

That Man In Istanbul (Estambul '65)
Horit Buchholtz, Sylva Koscina. Dir: Antonio Irasi Isasmendi. (FRANCE-ITALY-SPAIN, 1965)

Traitor's Gate
Albert Lieven, Gary Raymond. Dir: Freddie Francis. (GB-W. GERMANY, 1964)

1967

The Desperado Trail (Winnetou II. Teil)
Lex Barker, Pierre Brice. Dir: Harald Reinl. A Winnetou adventure. (W. GERMANY-YUGOSLAVIA, 1965)

The Game Is Over (La Curée)
Jane Fonda, Peter McEnery, Michel Piccoli. Dir: Roger Vadim. (FRANCE-ITALY, 1966)

Made In Italy
Anna Magnani, Walter Chiari. Dir: Nanni Loy. (ITALY-FRANCE, 1965)

A Matter Of Resistance (La Vie de Château)
Catherine Deneuve, Philippe Noiret, Pierre Brasseur. Dir: Jean-Paul Rappeneau. (FRANCE, 1965)

A Rose For Everyone (Una Rosa per Tutti)
Claudia Cardinale, Nino Manfredi. Dir: Franco Rossi. (ITALY, 1966)

1968

The Big Gundown (La Resa dei Conti)
Lee Van Cleef, Tomas Milian. Dir: Sergio Sollima. (ITALY-SPAIN, 1966)

China Is Near (La Cina è Vicina)
Glauco Mauri, Elda Tattoli. Dir: Marco Bellochio. (ITALY, 1967)

La Traviata
Anna Moffo, Franco Bonisolli, Gino Bechi. Dir: Mario Lanfranchi. (ITALY, 1966)

Payment In Blood
Guy Madison, Edd Byrnes. Dir: E.G. Rowland (aka Enzo Girolami). (ITALY, 1968)

The Queens (Le Fate: GB: Sex Quartet)
Monica Vitti, Claudia Cardinale, Raquel Welch, Capucine. Dir: Luciano Selce, Mario Monicelli, Mauro Bolognini, Antonio Petrangli. (ITALY-FRANCE, 1966)

Seven Guns For The MacGregors
(Sette Pistole per i MacGregor)
Robert Wood, Paul Carter, Manuel (Monolo) Zarzo, Agata Flory. Dir: Franco Giraldi (aka Frank Garfield). (ITALY-SPAIN, 1965)

Superargo Vs Diabolicus
(Superargo contro Diabolicus)
Ken Wood, Gérhard Tichy, Loredana Nusciak. Dir: Nick Nostro. (ITALY-SPAIN, 1966)

Up The MacGregors
(Sette Donne per i MacGregor)
David Bailey, Agata Flory. Dir: Franco Giraldi (Frank Garfield). (ITALY-SPAIN, 1966)

1969

Model Shop
Anouk Aimée, Gary Lockwood. Dir: Jacques Demy. Filmed in English. (USA-FRANCE, 1968)

Murder Czech Style (Vrazda Po Cesku)
Rudolf Hrüsinsky, Kvéta Fialová. Dir: Jírí Weiss. (CZECHOSLOVAKIA, 1966)

Serafino
Adriano Celentano, Ottavia Piccolo. Dir: Pietro Germi. (ITALY-SPAIN, 1968)

Above: *Murder Czech Style* (1969)

The Southern Star (L'Etoile du Sud)
Ursula Andress, George Segal, Orson Welles. Dir: Sidney Hayers. Made in both French and English. (FRANCE, 1968)

1970

Bed And Board (Domicile Conjugal)
Jean-Pierre Léaud, Claude Jade. Dir: François Truffaut. (FRANCE-ITALY, 1970)

Brian's Song
Billy Dee Williams, James Caan, Jack Warden. Dir: Buzz Kulik. Made for TV; subsequently released theatrically. (USA, 1970)

Claire's Knee (Le Genou de Claire)
Jean-Claude Brialy, Aurora Cornu. Dir: Eric Rohmer. (FRANCE, 1970)

Investigation Of A Citizen Above Suspicion
(Indagine Su Un Cittadino al di Sopra di Ogni Sospetto) Gian Maria Volonté, Florinda Bolkan. Dir: Elio Petri. (ITALY, 1970)

The Lady In The Car With Glasses And A Gun (La Dame dans l'Auto avec des Lunettes et un Fusil)
Samantha Eggar, Oliver Reed, Stéphane Audran. Dir: Anatole Litvak. (FRANCE, 1970)

Machine Gun McCain (Gli Intoccabili)
John Cassavetes, Peter Falk, Britt Ekland, Gena Rowlands. Dir: Giuliano Montaldo. (ITALY, 1968)

The Man With Connections (Le Pistonne)
Guy Bedos, Yves Robert. Dir: Claude Berri (FRANCE, 1969)

A Matter Of Days (A Quelques Jours près...)
Thalie Fruges, Vit Olmer. Dir: Yves Ciampi (FRANCE-CZECHOSLOVAKIA, 1969)

The Things Of Life (Les Choses de la Vie)
Romy Schneider, Michel Piccoli. Dir: Claude Sautet. (FRANCE-ITALY, 1969)

1971

Brief Season (Una Breve Stagione)
Christopher Jones, Pia Degermark. Dir: Renato Castellani. (ITALY, 1969)

The Burglars (Le Casse)
Omar Sharif, Jean-Paul Belmondo, Dyan Cannon. Dir: Henri Verneuil. (FRANCE-ITALY, 1971)

A Pocketful Of Chestnuts
(Le Castagne sono Buone)
Gianni Morandi, Stefania Casini. Dir:Pietro Germi. (ITALY, 1970)

1972

Chloë In The Afternoon (L'Après-Midi; GB: Love In The Afternoon)
Bernard Verley, Zouzou. Dir: Eric Rohmer (FRANCE, 1972)

Such A Lovely Kid Like Me (Une Belle Fille Comme Moi; GB: A Gorgeous Bird Like Me)
Bernadette Lafont, André Dusollier. Dir: Franqois Truffaut. (FRANCE, 1972)

The Valachi Papers (Joe Valachi, i Secreti di Cosa Nostra)
Charles Bronson, Lino Ventura, Walter Chiari. Dir: Terence Young. (ITALY-FRANCE, 1972)

1973

Siddhartha
Shashi Kapoor, Simi Garewal. Dir: Conrad Rooks. Filmed in India. (USA, 1972)

Traffic (Trafic)
Jacques Tati, Maria Kimberly. Dir: Jacques Tati. (FRANCE-ITALY, 1970)

White Sister (Bianco, Rosso e. . . .)
Sophia Loren, Adnano Celentano. Dir: Alberto Lattuada. (ITALY-FRANCE-SPAIN, 1972)

1974

Emmanuelle
Sylvia Kristel, Alain Cuny. Dir: Just Jaeckin. (FRANCE, 1974)

Lightening Swords Of Death (Kozure Ohkami – Ko Wo Kashi Ude Kashi Tsukamatsuru)
Tomisaburo Wakayama, Akihiro Tanikawa. Dir: Kenji Misumi. (JAPAN, 1972)

1975

Lies My Father Told Me
Yossi Yadin, Marilyn Lightstone. Dir: Jan Kadar. (CANADA, 1973)

Night Caller (Peur sur la Ville)
Jean-Paul Belmondo, Charles Denner, Lea Massari. Dir: Henri Verneuil. (FRANCE-ITALY, 1975)

1976

The Last Woman (La Dernière Femme)
Gérard Depardieu, Ornella Mun, Michel Piccoli. Dir: Marco Ferreri. (FRANCE-ITALY, 1976)

The Stranger And The Gunfighter (aka Blood Money)
Lee Van Cleef, Lo Lieh. Dir: Anthony Dawson (aka Antonio Margheriti). (HONG KONG-ITALY-SPAIN-USA, 1974)

Watch Out, We're Mad (. . .Altrimenti ci Arrabiamo)
Terence Hill, Bud Spencer, Donald Pleasence. Dir: Marcello Fondato. (ITALY-SPAIN, 1974)

1978

The Amsterdam Kill
Robert Mitchum, Richard Egan, Leslie Nielsen. Dir: Robert Clouse. (HONG KONG, 1977)

1979

Tess
Nastassia (aka Nastassja) Kinski, Peter Firth, Leigh Lawson. Dir: Roman Polanski. (FRANCE-GB, 1979)

1982

Parsifal
Armin Jordan, Michael Kutter, Edith Clever. Dir: Hans Jürgen Syberberg. (W. GERMANY-FRANCE, 1982)

Querelle
Jeanne Moreau, Brad Davis, Franco Nero. Dir: R. W. Fassbinder. (W.GERMANY-FRANCE, 1982)

Below: *Tess* (1979)

The Trout (La Truite)
Jeanne Moreau, Isabelle Huppert, Jean-Pierre Cassel. Dir: Joseph Losey. (FRANCE, 1982)

We Of The Never Never
Angela Punch McGregor, Arthur Dignam. Dir: Igor Azins. (AUSTRALIA, 1982)

Yol (The Road)
Tarik Akan, Serif Sezer. Dir: Serif Gören.(SWITZERLAND, 1982)

1983

And The Ship Sails On (E La Nave Va)
Freddie Jones, Barbara Jefford. Dir: Federico Fel- lini. (FRANCE-ITALY, 1983)

Bob Le Flambeur (Bob, The Gambler)
Roger Duchesne, Isabelle Corey, Daniel Cauchy. Dir: Jean-Pierre Melville. (FRANCE, 1955)

Danton
Gérard Depardieu, Wojciech Pszoniak. Dir: Andrzej Wajda. (FRANCE-POLAND, 1982)

Das Boot (GB: The Boat)
Jürgen Prochnow, Herbert Grönemeyer. Dir: Wolfgang Petersen. (GERMANY, 1981)

The Eyes, The Mouth (Gli Occhi, Ia Bocca)
Lou Castel, Angela Molina. Dir: Marco Bellocchio. (ITALY-FRANCE, 1982)

The Goat (La Chèvre)
Gérard Depardieu, Pierre Richard. Dir: Francis Veber. (FRANCE, 1982)

Heat Of Desire (Plein Sud)
Patrick Dewaere, Clio Goldsmith, Jeanne Moreau. Dir: Luc Béraud. (FRANCE-SPAIN, 1981)

Josepha
Miou-Miou, Claude Brasseur. Dir: Christopher Frank. (FRANCE, 1982)

La Nuit de Varennes
Jean-Louis Barrault, Marcello Mastroianni. Dir: Ettore Scola. (FRANCE-ITALY, 1982)

Le Dernier Combat (GB: The Last Combat)
Pierre Jolivet, Jean Bouise. Dir: Luc Besson. (FRANCE, 1983)

Life Goes On (La Vie Continue)
Annie Girardot, Jean-Pierre Cassel, Pierre Dux. Dir: Moshé Mizrahi. (FRANCE, 1981)

L'Invitation au Voyage
Laurent Malet, Aurore Clément, Nina Scott. Dir: Peter Del Monte. (FRANCE-ITALY 1982)

The Little Bunch (La Petite Bande)
Andrew Chandler, Hélène Dassule. Dir: Michel Deville. (FRANCE, 1983)

The Moon In The Gutter (La Lune dans le Caniveau)
Gérard Depardieu, Nastassia (aka Nastassja) Kinski. Dir: Jean-Jacques Beineix. (FRANCE-ITALY, 1983)

The Party (Le Boum)
Sophie Marceau, Brigitte Fossey, Claude Brasseur. Dir: Claude Pinoteau. (FRANCE, 1980)

Yor, The Hunter From The Future (Il Mondo di Yor)
Robert Brown, Corinne Cléry. Dir: Anthony Dawson (aka Antonio Margheriti). (TURKEY-ITALY, 1983)

1984

A Nos Amours (GB: To Our Loves)
Sandrine Bonnaire, Dominique Besnehard. Dir: Maurice Pialat

Carmen
Julia Migenes-Johnson, Placido Domingo, Ruggero Raimondo. Dir: Francesco Rosi. (FRANCE-ITALY, 1984)

Danny Boy (Angel)
Stephen Bear, Honor Heffernman. Dir: Neil Jordan (ESRE, 1982)

Dream One
Jason Connery, Mathilda Hay, Nipsey Russell. Dir: Arnaud Selignac. (FRANCE-BRITAIN, 1984)

A Love In Germany (Eine Liebe in Deütschland)
Hanna Schygulla, Marie-Christine Barrault. Dir: Andrzej Wajda. (W.GERMANY-FRANCE, 1983)

The Rehearsal (Efter Repetitionen; GB: After The Rehearsal)
Erland Josephson, Lena Ohlin, Ingrid Thulin. Dir: Ingmar Bergman (SWEDEN, 1984)

The Skin (La Pelle)
Marcello Mastroianni, Burt Lancaster, Claudia Cardinale. Dir: Liliana Cavani. (ITALY-FRANCE, 1981)

1985

Acqua e Sapone
Carlo Verdone, Natasha Hovey. Dir:Carlo Verdonedone. (ITALY, 1983)

My Other 'Husband' (Attention! Une Femme Peut en Cacher une Autre)
Miou-Miou, Roger Hanin, Eddy Mitchell. Dir: Georges Lautner. (FRANCE, 1983)

Peril (Péril en la Demeure; GB: Death In A French Garden)
Michel Piccoli, Christophe Malavoy, Nicole Garcia. Dir: Michel Deville. (FRANCE, 1985)

Sotto . . . Sotto
Enrico Montesano, Veronica Lario. Dir: Lina Wertmüller. (ITALY, 1984)

1987

The Stranger
Bonnie Bedelia, Peter Riegert. Dir: Adolfo Aristarian. (USA-ARGENTINA, 1987)

1988

The Legend Of The Holy Drinkers (La Leggendia del Santo Bevitore)
Rutger Hauer, Anthony Quayle. Dir: Ermanno Olmi. (ITALY, 1988)

1989

Hanussen
Dir: István Szabó; stars: Klaus Maria Brandauer, Erland Josephson (HUNGARY)

The Adventures of Milo and Otis
Dir: Masanori Hata; narrated by Dudley Moore (JAPAN)

1990

The Time of the Gypsies
Dir: Emir Kusturica; stars: Davor Dujmovic, Bora Todorovic (YUGOSLAVIA, 1989)

TRISTAR

TriStar, which came into being in 1984, was the brainchild of Victor Kaufman, president and CEO of CPE who, aware that all the major television networks – as well as the burgeoning cable outlets such as Showtime and Home Box Office (HBO) – were in the market for high standard new movies, came up with a competitive way of boosting their viewing figures by offering them a selection of quality productions in return for investing equity in TriStar Pictures. The deal was that this would be a three-way partnership with Columbia as the managing partner.

Because TriStar enjoyed a separate management and was creatively independent of Columbia, the ensuing ill-feeling on Columbia's part resulted in a showdown with Frank Price that ultimately cost him his job.

Nor were the TriStar personnel happy. Though management's initial brief was to make inexpensive films on tight budgets, there was no escaping the fact that in the early years of TriStar's formation, especially under the brief leadership of its first production head, the late Gary Hendler, it was considered the runt of the litter.

This situation prevailed for a couple of years, during which time the new studio's style reflected the orientation – both in the films it made and the stars it employed – of its second production head, Jeff Sagansky, who'd paid his dues in television.

It wasn't until David Matalon's stewardship in the mid-1980s, however, that TriStar became a force in its own right. It was Matalon, a hard-nosed, market-driven executive with a background more in big-screen theatrical distribution than television, who forged a profitable working relationship with Carolco, a distribution company responsible for suchTriStar successes as Total Recall (1990), Terminator 2 (1991), Universal Soldier (1992), and Cliffhanger (1993).

In 1991, a little over a year after Sony's purchase of Columbia Pictures Industries Inc. (CPII), Columbia and TriStar had merged to form Columbia-TriStar Pictures. Matalon left the company and was replaced by Mike Medavoy, who alone persuaded Sony Pictures Entertainment to green-light such hits as Sleepless In Seattle and Philadelphia, both of which had met with initial resistance, as well as Legends of the Fall. It was also Medavoy who, after the disastrous reaction to Cliffhanger's first screenings, had it recut and saw it gross over $100 million.

TriStar ceased operating at the end of 1998, ending 14 uneven, but undeniably exciting, years during which several outstanding, award-winning films were produced. At least the company closed on a high note with The Mask of Zorro as their last major release.

Above: Robert Redford and Kim Basinger in *The Natural* (1984)

Blame It On The Night
Dir: Alan Parker; stars: Byron Thames, Nick Mancuso, Leslie Ackerman

Breakin' 2: Electric Boogaloo
Dir: Sam Firstenberg; stars: Adolfo Quinones, Lucinda Dickey

The Evil That Men Do
Dir: J. Lee Thompson; stars: Charles Bronson, Theresa Saldana

Flashpoint
Dir: William Tannen; stars: Kris Kristofferson, Treat Williams, Rip Torn, Tess Harper

The Last Winter
Dir: Riki Shelach; stars: Stephen Macht, Kathleen Quinlan

Lovelines
Dir: Rod Amateau; stars: Greg Bradford, Mary Beth Evans

Meatballs Part 11
Dir: Ken Wiedehorn; stars: Richard Mulligan, John Menghatti, John Larroquette

The Muppets Take Manhattan
Dir: Frank Oz; stars: Dabney Coleman, Art Carney, Linda Lavin, Gregory Hines

The Natural
Dir: Barry Levinson; stars: Glenn Close, Robert Redford, Kim Basinger, Robert Duvall

Places In The Heart
Dir: Robert Benton; stars: Sally Field, Lindsay Crouse, Ed Harris, Amy Madigan, John Malkovich, Danny Glover

Runaway
Dir: Michael Crichton; stars: Tom Selleck, Cynthia Rhodes, Gene Simmons, Kirstie Alley

Silentnight, Deadlynight
Dir: Charles E. Sellier; stars: Lilyan Chavin, Robert Brian Wilson

Songwriter
Dir: Alan Rudolph; stars: Willie Nelson, Kris Kristofferson, Rip Torn, Melinda Dillon, Lesley Ann Warren

Supergirl
Dir: Jeannot Szwarc; stars: Faye Dunaway, Helen Slater

Where is Parsifal?
Dir: Henri Helman; stars: Tony Curtis, Orson Welles

Where The Boys Are
Dir: Hy Averback; stars: Lorna Luft, Lisa Hartman

Alamo Bay
Dir: Louis Malle; stars: Ed Harris, Amy Madigan

The Last Dragon
Dir: Michael Schultz; stars: Faith Prince

The Legend Of Billy Jean
Dir: Matthew Robbins; stars: Helen Slater, Keith Gordon, Peter Coyote, Dean Stockwell

Lifeforce
Dir: Tobe Hooper; stars: Peter Firth, Steven Railsback

Little Treasure
Dir: Alan Sharp; stars: Margot Kidder, Burt Lancaster, Ted Danson, James Hall

My Man Adam
Dir: Roger L. Simon; stars: Page Hannah, Raphael Sbarge, Austin Pendleton, Veronica Cartwright

Private Resort
Dir: George Bowers; stars: Rob Morrow, Johnny Depp

Rambo: First Blood Part II
Dir: George P. Cosmatos; stars: Sylvester Stallone, Richard Crenna, Charles Napier, Martin Cove

Real Genius
Dir: Martha Coolidge; stars: Val Kilmer, Gabe Jarrett, William Atherton, Patti D'Arbanville

Santa Claus
Dir: Jeannot Szwarc; stars: Dudley Moore, John Lithgow

Sweet Dreams
Dir: Karel Reisz; stars: Jessica Lange, Ed Harris, Ann Wedgeworth, John Goodman

Volunteers
Dir: Nicholas Meyer; stars: Tom Hanks, John Candy, Rita Wilson, George Plimpton

1986

8 Million Ways To Die
Dir: Hal Ashby; stars: Jeff Bridges, Rosanna Arquette, Andy Garcia, Alexandra Paul

About Last Night
Dir: Edward Zwick; stars: Rob Lowe, Demi Moore, Elizabeth Perkins, Jim Belushi

Band Of The Hand
Dir: Paul Michael Glaser; stars: Stephen Lang, Michael Carmine, Cameron Mitchell

The Boss Wife
Dir: Ziggy Steinberg; stars: Daniel Stern, Fisher Stevens, Christopher Plummer

Everytime We Say Good bye
Dir: Moshe Mizrahi; stars: Tom Hanks, Cristina Marsillach

Hyper Sapien: People From Another Star
Dir: Peter Hunt; stars: Sidney Penny, Ricky Paull Goldin

The Hitcher
Dir: Robert Harmon; stars: Rutger Hauer, C. Thomas Howell, Jennifer Jason Leigh

Iron Eagle
Dir: Sidney J. Furie; stars: Jason Gedrick, Louis Gossett Jr

La Cage Aux Folles 3: The Wedding
Dir: Georges Lauther; stars: Michel Serrault, Ugo Tognazzi, Michel Galabru, Stephane Audran

Labyrinth
Dir: Jim Henson; stars: David Bowie, Jennifer Connelly

Let's Get Harry
Dir: Alan Smithee; stars: Gary Busey, Robert Duvall, Matt Clark, Mark Harmon

Night Of The Creeps
Dir: Fred Dekker; stars: Jason Lively, Steve Marshall

Above: *Glory* (1989)

No Mercy
Dir: Richard Pearce; stars: Kim Basinger, Richard Gere, Jeroen Krabbe, George Dzundza

Nothing In Common
Dir: Garry Marshall; stars: Tom Hanks, Jackie Gleason, Eva-Marie Saint, Hector Elizondo, Barry Corbin, Bess Armstrong

Peggy Sue Got Married
Dir: Francis Ford Coppola; stars: Kathleen Turner, Helen Hunt, John Carradine, Maureen O'Sullivan, Nicolas Cage

RAD
Dir: Hal Needham; stars: Bart Connor, Lori Laughlan, Talia Shire, Jack Weston

Short Circuit
Dir: John Badham; stars: Ally Sheedy, Steve Guttenberg, Fisher Stevens, Austin Pendleton

Touch And Go
Dir: Robert Mandel; stars: Michael Keaton, Maria Conchita Alonso

Head Office
Dir: Ken Finkelman; stars: Judge Reinhold, Eddie Albert, Jane Seymour, Danny De Vito, Rick Moranis, Wallace Shawn

1987

Amazing Grace And Chuck
Dir: Mike Newell; stars: Jamie Lee Curtis, Gregory Peck, William L. Petersen, Dennis Lipscomb

Angel Heart
Dir: Alan Parker; stars: Mickey Rourke, Robert De Niro, Lisa Bonet, Charlotte Rampling

Blind Date
Dir: Blake Edwards; stars: Bruce Willis, Kim Basinger, John Larroquette, Joyce Van Patten

Extreme Prejudice
Dir: Walter Hill; stars: Nick Nolte, Powers Boothe, Rip Torn, Maria Conchita Alonso

Forever Lulu
Dir: Amos Kollek; stars: Alec Baldwin, Amos Kollek, Hanna Schygulla, Dr Ruth Westheimer

Gaby – A True Story
Dir: Louis Mandoki; stars: Liv Ullman, Robert Loggia, Norma Aleandro

Gardens Of Stone
Dir: Francis Ford Coppola; stars: James Caan, James Earl Jones, Dean Stockwell, Anjelica Huston, Laurence Fishburne, Sam Bottoms

High Tide
Dir: Gillian Armstrong; stars: Judy Davis, Jan Adele, Claudia Karvan

Ironweed
Dir: Hector Babenco; stars: Jack Nicholson, Meryl Streep, Carroll Baker

Light Of Day
Dir: Paul Schrader; stars: Michael J. Fox, Gena Rowlands

Like Father, Like Son
Dir: Rod Daniel; stars: Dudley Moore, Kirk Cameron, Margaret Colin

Man Of Fire
Dir: Elle Chouraqui; stars: Scott Glenn, Jade Malle, Jonathan Pryce, Danny Aiello, Joe Pesci

Monster Squad
Dir: Fred Dekker; stars: Andrew Gower, Robby Kiger

Nadine
Dir: Robert Benton; stars: Jeff Bridges, Kim Basinger, Rip Torn

The Principal
Dir: Christopher Cain; stars: James Belushi, Louis Gossett Jr, Rae Dawn Chong, Esai Morales

The Running Man
Dir: Paul Michael Glaser; stars: Arnold Schwarzenegger, Maria Conchita Alonso, Yaphet Kotto, Jim Brown

409

Above: Elijah Wood (left), Armin Mueller Stahl in *Avalon* (1990)

The Squeeze
Dir: Roger Young; stars: Michael Keaton, Rae Dawn Chong

The Suspect
Dir: Peter Yates; stars: Cher, Dennis Quaid, Liam Neeson, Joe Mantegna, Philip Bosco

1988

Bat 21
Dir: Peter Markle; stars: Danny Glover, Gene Hackman

The Blob
Dir: Chuck Russell; stars: Kevin Dillon, Shawnee Smith, Donovan Leitch, Candy Clark

Buster
Dir: David Greer; stars: Julie Walters, Phil Collins

For Keeps
Dir: John G. Avildsen; stars: Molly Ringwald, Randall Batinkoff, Kenneth Mars

High Spirits
Dir: Neil Jordan; stars: Steve Guttenberg, Peter O'Toole, Daryl Hannah, Beverly D'Angelo, Liam Neeson, Connie Booth

Iron Eagle II
Dir: Sidney J. Furie; stars: Louis Gossett Jr, Mark Humphrey, Stuart Margolin

The Kiss
Dir: Pen Densham; stars: Joanna Pakula, Meredith Salinger

Love At Stake
Dir: John Moffitt; stars: Patrick Cassidy, Kelly Preston, Bud Cort, Barbara Carrera

Made In The U.S.A.
Dir: Ken Friedman; stars: Adrian Pasdar, Christopher Penn, Lori Singer

Pound Puppies And The Legend Of Big Paw
Dir: Pierre DeCeles; stars: George Rose, B.J. Ward, Ruth Buzzi

Rambo III
Dir: Peter MacDonald; stars: Sylvester Stallone, Richard Crenna

Red Heat
Dir: Walter Hill; stars: Arnold Schwarzenegger, James Belushi, Peter Boyle, Larry Fishburne, Gina Gershon

The Seventh Sign
Dir: Carl Schultz; stars: Demi Moore, Michael Biehn, Jurgen Prochnow

Short Circuit 2
Dir: Kenneth Johnson; stars: Cynthia Gibb, Fisher Stevens, Michael McKean

Sunset
Dir: Blake Edwards; stars: Bruce Willis, James Garner, Malcolm McDowell, Mariel Hemingway, M. Emmet Walsh, Kathleen Quinlan

Sweetshearts Dance
Dir: Don Johnson, Susan Sarandon, Jeff Daniels, Elizabeth Perkins

Switching Channels
Dir: Ted Kotcheff; stars: Kathleen Turner, Christopher Reeve, Burt Reynolds, Ned Beatty

1989

The Bear
Dir: Jean-Jacques Annaud; stars: Jack Wallace, Tcheky Karyo

Chances Are
Dir: Emile Ardolino; Cybill Shepherd, Ryan O'Neal, Robert Downey Jr

Criminal Law
Dir: Martin Campbell; stars: Gary Oldman, Kevin Bacon

Deepstar Six
Dir: Sean S. Cunningham; stars: Greg Evigan, Taurean Blacque

Family Business
Dir: Sidney Lumet; stars: Sean Connery, Dustin Hoffman, Matthew Broderick

Field Of Dreams
Dir: Phil Alden Robinson; stars: Kevin Costner, James Earl Jones, Burt Lancaster, Amy Madigan

Glory
Dir: Edward Zwick; stars: Denzel Washington, Matthew Broderick, Morgan Freeman, Cliff De Young

Above: Michael Douglas and Sharon Stone in *Basic Instinct* (1992)

Johnny Handsome
Dir: Walter Hill; stars: Mickey Rourke, Ellen Barkin, Elizabeth McGovern, Morgan Freeman

Lock Up
Dir: John Flynn; stars Sylvester Stallone, Donald Sutherland

Look Who's Talking
Dir: Amy Heckerling; stars: Bruce Willis, John Travolta, Kirstie Alley, Olympia Dukakis, Abe Vigoda, George Segal

Loverboy
Dir: Joan Micklin; stars: Kate Jackson, Patrick Dempsey, Kirstie Alley, Carrie Fisher

Music Box
Dir: Constantin Costa-Gavras; stars: Jessica Lange, Frederic Forrest, Armin Mueller-Stahl, Lukas Haas, Donald Moffat

Above: *Terminator 2: Judgement Day* (1991), with Arnold Schwarzenegger, Linda Hamilton and Edward Furlong

Above: *My Best Friend's Wedding* (1997), with Julia Roberts (left) and Cameron Diaz

My First 40 Years
Dir: Carlo Vanzina; stars: Carol Alt, Elliott Gould

Russicum (a.k.a.The Third Solution)
Dir: Pasquale Squittieri; stars: Treat Williams, Danny Aiello, Rossano Brazzi, F. Murray Abraham

See No Evil, Hear No Evil
Dir: Arthur Hiller; stars: Richard Pryor, Gene Wilder, Anthony Zerbe, Joan Severance, Kevin Spacey

Sing
Dir: Richard Baskin; stars: Peter Dobson, Lorraine Bracco, Louise Lasser

Slaves Of New York
Dir: James Ivory; stars: Bernadette Peters, Adam Coleman, Mercedes Ruehl, Nick Corri

Steel Magnolias
Dir: Herbert Ross; stars: Sally Field, Dolly Parton, Shirley MacLaine, Julia Roberts, Olympia Dukakis, Daryl Hannah

Tap
Dir: Nick Castle; stars Gregory Hines, Sammy Davis Jr

Who's Harry Crumb?
Dir: Paul Flaherty; stars John Candy, Jeffrey Jones, Annie Potts, Jim Belushi

1990

Air America
Dir: Roger Spottiswoode; stars: Mel Gibson, Robert Downey Jr, Nancy Travis

Avalon
Dir: Barry Levinson; stars: Elizabeth Perkins, Aidan Quinn, Elijah Wood, Armin Mueller-Stahl

Blind Fury
Dir: Phillip Noyce; stars: Rutger Hauer, Terry O'Quinn, Lisa Blount, Meg Foster

The Freshman
Dir: Andrew Bergman; stars: Marlon Brando, Matthew Broderick, Penelope Ann Miller, Maximilian Schell

I Love You To Death
Dir: Lawrence Kasdan; stars: Kevin Kline, Tracey Ullman, River Phoenix, Joan Plowright, Keanu Reeves, William Hurt, Miriam Margolyes

Jacob's Ladder
Dir: Adrian Lyne; stars: Tim Robbins, Elizabeth Pena, Danny Aiello, Jason Alexander

Look Who's Talking Too
Dir: Amy Heckerling; stars: John Travolta, Kirstie Alley, Olympia Dukakis, Mel Brooks, Damon Wayans

Loose Cannons
Dir: Bob Clark; stars: Dan Aykroyd, Gene Hackman, Dom DeLuise, Ronny Cox

Mountains of the Moon
Dir: Bob Rafelson; stars: Patrick Bergin, Iain Glen, Fiona Shaw, Richard E. Grant

Above: Antonio Banderas (left) and Tom Hanks in *Philadelphia* (1993)

411

Above: *Jerry Maguire* (1996), with Tom Cruise and Renee Zellweger

Narrow Margin
Dir: Peter Hyams; stars: Gene Hackman, Anne Archer

Q & A
Dir: Sidney Lumet; stars Nick Nolte, Timothy Hutton

Side Out
Dir: Peter Israelson; stars: Peter Horton, C. Thomas Howell, Harley Jane Kozack

Total Recall
Dir: Paul Verhoeven; stars: Arnold Schwarzenegger, Rachel Ticotin, Sharon Stone, Ronny Cox, Michael Ironside

1991

Hook
Dir: Steven Spielberg; stars: Dustin Hoffman, Robin Williams, Julia Roberts

Another You
Dir: Maurice Phillips; stars: Gene Wilder, Richard Pryor, Mercedes Ruehl, Stephen Lang

Bingo
Dir: Matthew Robbins; stars: David Rasche, Cindy Williams, Kurt Fuller

Bugsy
Dir: Barry Levinson; stars: Warren Beatty, Annette Bening, Harvey Keitel, Ben Kingsley, Elliott Gould, Bebe Neuwirth

The Doors
Dir: Oliver Stone; stars Val Kilmer, Frank Whaley, Kevin Dillon, Meg Ryan, Kyle MacLachlan

The Fisher King
Dir: Terry Gilliam; stars: Robin Williams, Jeff Bridges, Mercedes Ruehl

Hudson Hawk
Dir: Michael Lehmann; stars: Bruce Willis, Danny Aiello, James Coburn, Sandra Bernhard, Richard E. Grant, Andie MacDowell

L.A. Story
Dir: Mick Jackson; stars: Steve Martin, Victoria Tennant, Richard E. Grant, Marilu Henner

Terminator 2: Judgment Day
Dir: James Cameron; stars Arnold Schwarzenegger, Linda Hamilton

Toy Soldiers
Dir: Daniel Petrie Jr; stars: Sean Astin, Wil Wheaton, Keith Coogan, Louis Gossett Jr

1992

Basic Instinct
Dir: Paul Verhoeven; stars: Michael Douglas, Sharon Stone, George Dzundza, Jeanne Tripplehorn

Candyman
Dir: Bernard Rose; stars: Tony Todd, Virginia Madsen, Xander Berkeley

Chaplin
Dir: Richard Attenborough; stars: Robert Downey Jr, Dan Aykroyd, Geraldine Chaplin, Anthony Hopkins, Kevin Kline

City of Joy
Dir: Roland Joffe; stars: Patrick Swayze, Pauline Collins, Om Puri, Shabana Azmi

Husbands and Wives
Dir: Woody Allen; stars Woody Allen, Juliette Lewis, Judy Davis, Mia Farrow, Sidney Pollack

Thunderheart
Dir: Michael Apted; stars: Val Kilmer, Sam Shepard

Universal Soldier
Dir: Roland Emmerich; stars: Jean-Claude Van Damme, Dolph Lundgren, Jerry Orbach

Wind
Dir: Carroll Ballard; stars: Jennifer Grey, Matthew Modine, Cliff Robertson, Jack Thompson

1993

Cliffhanger
Dir: Renny Harlin; stars: Sylvester Stallone, John Lithgow, Paul Winfield

Look Who's Talking Now
Dir: Tom Ropelewski; stars: Diane Keaton, John Travolta, Jordy Lemoine, Kirstie Alley, Danny De Vito

Manhattan Murder Mystery
Dir: Woody Allen; stars: Alan Alda, Woody Allen, Diane Keaton, Anjelica Huston

Mr. Jones
Dir: Mike Figgis; stars: Richard Gere, Lena Olin, Anne Bancroft, Tom Irwin, Bruce Altman

Philadelphia
Dir: Jonathan Demme; stars: Tom Hanks, Joanne Woodward, Denzel Washington, Jason Robards, Mary Steenburgen, Antonio Banderas, Ron Vawter

Rudy
Dir: David Anspaugh; stars: Ned Beatty, Sean Astin, Lili Taylor, Jason Miller, Robert Prosky

Sleepless In Seattle
Dir: Nora Ephron; stars: Tom Hanks, Meg Ryan, Bill Pullman, Rob Reiner, Victor Garber, Dana Ivey, Rosie O'Donnell

Below: *As Good As It Gets* (1998), with Jack Nicholson and Helen Hunt

Above: Antonio Banderas in *The Mask of Zorro* (1998)

Sniper
Dir: Luis Llosa; stars: Billy Zane, Tom Berenger, J.T. Walsh

So I Married An Axe Murderer
Dir: Thomas Schlamme; stars: Mike Myers, Nancy Travis, Brenda Fricker

Weekend at Bernie's II
Dir: Robert Klane; stars: Troy Beyer, Steve James, Terry Kiser, Barry Bostwick, Andrew McCarthy

Wilder Napalm
Dir: Glenn Gordon Caron; stars: Debra Winger, Dennis Quaid, Arliss Howard, M. Emmett Walsh

1994

Three Ninjas Kick Back
Dir: Charles Kanganis; stars: Sean Fox, Victor Wong, Dustin Nguyen

Cops and Robbers
Dir: Michael Ritchie; stars: Robert Davi, Dianne Wiest, Jack Palance

Guarding Tess
Dir: Hugh Wilson; stars: Nicolas Cage, Edward Albert, Shirley MacLaine

It Could Happen To You
Dir: Andrew Bergman; stars: Red Buttons, Isaac Hayes, Nicolas Cage, Bridget Fonda

Legends of the Fall
Dir: Edward Zwick; stars: Brad Pitt, Aidan Quinn, Anthony Hopkins, Henry Thomas

Mary Shelley's Frankenstein
Dir: Kenneth Branagh; stars Robert De Niro, Kenneth Branagh, Tom Hulce, Helena Bonham Carter, Aidan Quinn, Ian Holm

Mixed Nuts
Dir: Nora Ephron; stars: Steve Martin, Madeline Kahn, Robert Klein, Juliet Lewis

Only You
Dir: Norman Jewison; stars: Bonnie Hunt, Fisher Stevens, Marisa Tomei, Robert Downey Jr

Princess Caraboo
Dir: Michael Austin; stars: Kevin Kline, Stephen Rea, John Lithgow, Wendy Hughes, Phoebe Cates, Jim Broadbent

Threesome
Dir: Andrew Fleming; stars: Martha Gehman, Lara Flynn Boyle, Stephen Baldwin

Wagons East
Dir: Peter Markle; stars: John Candy, Richard Lewis, Robert Picardo

1995

Hideaway
Dir: Brett Leonard; stars: Jeff Goldblum, Christine Lahti, Alfred Molina

Ninjas Knuckle Up
Dir: Simon S. Sheen; stars: Chad Power, Victor Wong

Below: *Godzilla* (1998)

413

Devil In A Blue Dress
Dir: Carl Franklin; stars: Denzel Washington, Don Cheadle, Maury Chakin

Johnny Mnemonic
Dir: Robert Longo; stars: Keanu Reeves, Ice-T, Dolph Lundgren

Jumanji
Dir: Joe Johnston; stars: Robin Williams, Bonnie Hunt, Jonathan Hyde

Never Talk To Strangers
Dir: Peter Hall; stars: Rebecca De Mornay, Antonio Banderas

The Quick and the Dead
Dir: Sam Raimi; stars: Gene Hackman, Sharon Stone, Leonardo DiCaprio, Russell Crowe

Jury Duty
Dir: John Fortenburry; stars: Abe Vigoda, Shelley Winters, Pauly Shore, Tia Carrere

Magic in the Water
Dir: Rick Stevenson; stars: Mark Harmon, Sarah Wayne

1996

Mrs. Winterbourne
Dir: Richard Benjamin; stars: Shirley MacLaine, Ricki Lake, Brendan Fraser

Race the Sun
Dir: Charles Kanganis; stars: Casey Affleck, Jim Belushi, Halle Berry

Sunset Park
Dir: Steve Gomer; stars: Carol Kane, Rhea Perlman, Fredro Starr

The Fan
Dir: Tony Scott; stars: Robert De Niro, Ellen Barkin, Wesley Snipes, John Leguizamo

High School High
Dir: Hart Bochner; stars: Jon Lovitz, Tia Carrere, Louise Fletcher, John Neville

If Lucy Fell
Dir: Éric Schaeffer; stars: Ben Stiller, Elle Macpherson, Sarah Jessica Parker

Jerry Maguire
Dir: Cameron Crowe; stars: Tom Cruise, Bonnie Hunt, Renee Zellweger, Cuba Gooding Jr

Mary Reilly
Dir: Stephen Frears; stars: Julia Roberts, John Malkovich, Glenn Close

Matilda
Dir: Danny De Vito; stars: Danny De Vito, Pam Ferris, Mara Wilson

The Mirror Has Two Faces
Dir: Barbra Streisand; stars: Barbra Streisand, George Segal, Jeff Bridges, Brenda Vaccaro, Elle Macpherson, Lauren Bacall, Pierce Brosnan

1997

Beverly Hills Ninja
Dir: Dennis Dugan; stars: Chris Farley, Robin Shou, Nathaniel Parker, Billy Connolly

Donnie Brasco
Dir: Mike Newell; stars: Al Pacino, Johnny Depp, Bruno Kirby, James Russo

My Best Friend's Wedding
Dir: P.J. Hogan; stars: Julia Roberts, Cameron Diaz, Rupert Everett, Philip Bosco, Dermot Mulroney

The Pest
Dir: Paul Miller; stars: Jeffrey Jones, John Leguizamo

Rudyard Kipling's The Second Jungle Book: Mowgli and Baloo
Dir: Duncan MacLachlan; stars: Roddy McDowall, Bill Williams

Seven Years In Tibet
Dir: Jean-Jacques Annaud; stars: Brad Pitt, David Thewlis

Starship Troopers
Dir: Paul Verhoeven; stars: Clancy Brown, Michael Ironside, Dina Meyer

1998

As Good As It Gets
Dir: James L. Brooks; stars: Jack Nicholson, Helen Hunt, Greg Kinnear, Cuba Gooding Jr, Harold Ramis, Skeet Ulrich

Apt Pupil
Dir: Bryan Singer; stars: Ian McKellen, David Schwimmer, Brad Renfro, Kevin Pollack

The Big Hit
Dir: Kirk Wong; stars: Mark Wahlberg, Lou Diamond Phillips, Avery Brooks

Dancer, Texas-Pop. 81
Dir: Tim McCanlies; stars: Peter Facinelli, Ethan Embry

Godzilla
Dir: Roland Emmerich; stars: Matthew Broderick, Jean Reno, Maria Pitillo, Hank Azaria

Knock Off
Dir: Tsui Hark; stars: Jean-Claude Van Damme, Paul Sorvino, Rob Schneider

Madeline
Dir: Daisy Mayer; stars: Frances McDormand, Nigel Hawthorne

The Mask of Zorro
Dir: Martin Campbell; stars: Antonio Banderas, Anthony Hopkins, Catherine Zeta Jones, Stuart Wilson, Jose Perez, Tony Amendola

Outside Ozona
Dir: Joe C. Cardone; stars Robert Forster, Sherilyn Fenn

Slappy and the Stinkers
Dir: Barnet Kellman; stars: B.D. Wong, Bronson Pinchot

Desperate Measures
Dir: Barbet Schroeder; stars: Michael Keaton, Andy Garcia, Brian Cox, Joseph Cross, Marcia Gay Harden

Swept from the Sea
Dir: Beeban Kidron; Vincent Perez, Ian McKellen, Kathy Bates, Rachel Weisz, Joss Ackland

Urban Legend
Dir: Jamie Blanks; stars: Alicia Witt, Jared Leto, Michael Rosenbaum, Joshua Jackson, Tara Reid

Below: Tim Robbins (left) and Morgan Freeman in *The Shawshank Redemption* (Castle Rock/Columbia, 1994)

THE OSCARS®

COLUMBIA

At the beginning of the 1930s, Harry Cohn was more concerned with keeping his Gower Gulch operation above water than competing in the lofty Academy Award stakes.

It was a bonus, therefore, when the 1930-1931 Academy Award committee nominated Seton I. Miller and Fred Niblo Jr for the screenplay they wrote based on Martin Flavin's play *The Criminal Code* (1931). The boys didn't win (Howard Estabrook got it for RKO's *Cimarrron*, 1931), but at least their nomination demonstrated to the industry that Columbia was capable of making a quality movie.

Two years later Columbia's big one was Capra's *Lady for A Day* (1933) – nominated for four Oscars, including Best Picture and Best Director. Host Will Rogers, however, handed the coveted statues to *Cavalcade* (Fox) and its director Frank Lloyd.

The studio's breakthrough finally came the following year when *It Happened One Night* (1934) blitzed the award ceremony. The film took seven awards, including Best Picture and Best Director (Capra). By the end of the evening, Harry Cohn had added two more Oscars to the list: Best Sound Recording and Best Score for *One Night Of Love*.

The rest of the decade saw Oscars for *Mr Deeds Goes To Town* (1936) (Best Director – Frank Capra), *The Awful Truth* (1937) (Best Director – Leo McCarey), *Lost Horizon* (1937) (Best Art Direction/Interior Decoration; Best Editing), *You Can't Take It With You* (1938) (Best Picture, Best Director – Frank Capra), and *Mr Smith Goes To Washington* (1939) (Best Story and Screenplay).

The Forties were less auspicious. After Capra's departure in 1939, only one film, *All The King's Men* (1949) won a Best Picture Oscar, despite seven nominations, each, for *Here Comes Mr Jordan* (1941) and *The Talk Of The Town* (1942).

Throughout the Forties, though, the studio's creative and technical personnel, such as John Livadary (sound), Morris Stoloff (music), Joe Walker and Rudolph Maté

(camera), not to mention the numerous art directors, all received Oscar nominations in recognition of their outstanding contributions to films.

Things perked up in the Fifties when both *From Here To Eternity* (1953) and *On The Waterfront* (1954) won eight Oscars each, including Best Picture and Best Director (Fred Zinnemann and and Elia Kazan respectively).

In 1957 the British-made *The Bridge On The River Kwai* took seven Oscars, including Best Picture and Best Director (David Lean), thus beginning a British connection that would last throughout the Sixties. In 1962, Lean's *Lawrence Of Arabia* walked off with seven Oscars, including Best Picture; while *A Man for All Seasons* (1966) and *Oliver!* (1968) each won another six – including Best Picture and Best Director (Carol Reed and Fred Zinnemann).

Columbia's American-made movies fared less well during this period, and it wasn't until 1979 that the studio won its next Best Picture

Below: *It Happened One Night* (1934)

award – with *Kramer Vs. Kramer*. Writer-director Robert Benton's powerful domestic drama also won awards for its star Dustin Hoffman, and for Meryl Streep (Best Supporting Actress).

Only twice since 1930 have there been no nominations for Columbia: in 1974 and in 1988.

The following list tables all Columbia's Oscar nominations. The symbol • beside a name or title indicates a winner of an Academy Award.

1930-1931

WRITING
Screenplay
Seton I. Miller, Fred Niblo Jr *The Criminal Code*

1931-1932

SHORT SUBJECTS
Cartoons
Mickey's Orphans Walt Disney

1932-1933

PICTURE
Lady For A Day Frank Capra, producer

ACTRESS
May Robson *Lady For A Day*

DIRECTOR
Frank Capra *Lady For A Day*

WRITING
Adaptation
Robert Riskin *Lady for A Day*

1934

PICTURE
• *It Happened One Night* Harry Cohn, producer

WRITING
Original Story
Ernst Marischka *A Song To Remember*

CINEMATOGRAPHY
Colour
Tony Gaudio, Allen M. Harvey *A Song To Remember*

INTERIOR DECORATION
Colour
Stephen Goosson, Rudolph Sternad; Frank Tuttle (set decoration) *A Song To Remember*

SOUND RECORDING
John Livadary *A Song To Remember*

MUSIC
Song
Jule Styne (mus), Sammy Cahn (lyr) 'Anywhere' in *Tonight And Every Night*
Scoring of a Dramatic or Comedy Picture
Miklos Rozsa, Morris Stoloff *A Song To Remember*
Scoring of a Musical Picture
Marlin Skiles, Morris Stoloff *Tonight And Every Night*

FILM EDITING
Charles Nelson *A Song To Remember*

SPECIAL EFFECTS
L. W. Butler (photographic), Ray Bomba (sound) *A Thousand And One Nights*

SHORT SUBJECTS
Cartoons
Rippling Romance (Color Rhapsodies)
One-reel
Screen Snapshots 25th Anniversary Ralph Staub, producer
Two-reel
The Jury Goes Round 'n' Round (All Star Comedies) Jules White, producer

1946

ACTOR
Larry Parks *The Jolson Story*

SUPPORTING ACTOR
William Demarest *The Jolson Story*

CINEMATOGRAPHY
Colour
Joseph Walker *The Jolson Story*

SOUND RECORDING
•John Livadary *The Jolson Story*

MUSIC
Scoring of a Musical Picture
•Morris Stoloff *The Jolson Story*
FILM EDITING
William A. Lyon *The Jolson Story*

SHORT SUBJECTS
Two-reel
Hiss And Yell (All Star Comedies) Jules White, producer

1947

SHORT SUBJECTS
Two-reel
A Voice Is Born (Musical Featurette) Ben Blake, producer

1948

CINEMATOGRAPHY
Colour
William Snyder *The Loves of Carmen*

1949

PICTURE
•*All The King's Men* Robert Rossen, producer

ACTOR
•Broderick Crawford *All The King's Men*

SUPPORTING ACTOR
John Ireland *All The King's Men*

SUPPORTING ACTRESS
•Mercedes McCambridge *All The King's Men*

DIRECTOR
Robert Rossen *All The King's Men*

WRITING
Screenplay
Robert Rossen *All The King's Men*

FILM EDITING
Robert Parrish, Al Clark *All The King's Men*

WRITING
Story and Screenplay
Sidney Buchman *Jolson Sings Again*

CINEMATOGRAPHY
Colour
William Snyder *Jolson Sings Again*

MUSIC
Scoring of a Musical Picture
Morris Stoloff, George Duning *Jolson Sings Again*

SHORT SUBJECTS
Cartoons
Magic Fluke (Fox & Crow) UPA: Stephen Bosustow, producer

1950

PICTURE
Born Yesterday S. Sylvan Simon, producer

ACTRESS
•Judy Holliday *Born Yesterday*

DIRECTOR
George Cukor *Born Yesterday*

WRITING
Screenplay
Albert Mannheimer *Born Yesterday*

MUSIC
Scoring of a Dramatic or Comedy Picture
George Duning *No Sad Songs For Me*

COSTUME DESIGN
Black-and-white
Jean Louis *Born Yesterday*

SHORT SUBJECTS
Cartoons
•*Gerald McBoing Boing* (Jolly Frolics) UPA; Stephen Bosustow, executive producer *Trouble Indemnity* (Mr Magoo) UPA; Stephen Bosustow, executive producer

SCIENTIFIC OR TECHNICAL
A Class II plaque was awarded to John Livadary, Floyd Campbell, L. W. Russell and the Columbia Studio Sound Department.

1951

ACTOR
Fredric March *Death Of A Salesman*

SUPPORTING ACTOR
Kevin McCarthy *Death Of A Salesman*

SUPPORTING ACTRESS
Mildred McCarthy *Death Of A Salesman*

CINEMATOGRAPHY
Black-and-white
Frank Planer *Death Of A Salesman*

MUSIC
Scoring of a Dramatic or Comedy Picture
Alex North *Death Of A Salesman*

SHORT SUBJECTS
Cartoons
Rooty Toot Toot (Jolly Frolics) UPA; Stephen Bosustow, executive producer

1952

ACTRESS
Julie Harris *The Member Of The Wedding*

WRITING
Motion Picture Story
Edna Anhalt, Edward Anhalt *The Sniper*

COSTUME DESIGN
Black-and-white
Jean Louis *Affair In Trinidad*

SHORT SUBJECTS
Cartoons
Madeline (Jolly Frolics) UPA; Stephen Bosustow, executive producer
Pink And Blue Blues (Mister Magoo) UPA; Stephen Bosustow, executive producer

1953

PICTURE
•*From Here To Eternity* Buddy Adler, producer

ACTOR
Montgomery Clift *From Here To Eternity*
Burt Lancaster *From Here To Eternity*

ACTRESS
Deborah Kerr *From Here To Eternity*

SUPPORTING ACTOR
•Frank Sinatra *From Here To Eternity*

SUPPORTING ACTRESS
•Donna Reed *From Here To Eternity*

DIRECTOR
•Fred Zinnemann *From Here To Eternity*

WRITING
Screenplay
•Daniel Taradash *From Here To Eternity*

CINEMATOGRAPHY
Black-and-white
•Burnett Guffey *From Here To Eternity* Hal Mohr *The Four Poster*

SOUND RECORDING
•Columbia Studio Sound Dept; John Livadary, sound director *From Here To Eternity*

MUSIC
Song
Lester Lee (mus), Ned Washington (lyr) 'Blue Pacific Blues' in *Miss Sadie Thompson*
Scoring of a Dramatic or Comedy Picture
Morris Stoloff, George Duning *From Here To Eternity*
Scoring of a Musical Picture
Frederick Hollander, Morris Stoloff *The 5000 Fingers Of Dr T*

FILM EDITING
•William A. Lyon *From Here To Eternity*

COSTUME DESIGN
Black-and-white
Jean Louis *From Here To Eternity*

SHORT SUBJECTS
Cartoons
Christopher Crumpet (Jolly Frolics) UPA; Stephen Bosustow
The Tell-Tale Heart (UPA Cartoon Special) UPA; Stephen Bosustow, producer

1954

PICTURE
•*On The Waterfront* Horizon-American; Sam Spiegel, producer
The Caine Mutiny Kramer; Stanley Kramer, producer

ACTOR
•Marlon Brando *On The Waterfront*
Humphrey Bogart *The Caine Mutiny*

SUPPORTING ACTOR
Lee J. Cobb *On The Waterfront*
Karl Malden *On The Waterfront*
Rod Steiger *On The Waterfront*
Tom Tully *The Caine Mutiny*

SUPPORTING ACTRESS
•Eva Marie Saint *On The Waterfront*

DIRECTOR
•Elia Kazan *On The Waterfront*

WRITING
Screenplay
Stanley Roberts *The Caine Mutiny*
Story and Screenplay
•Budd Schulberg *On The Waterfront*

CINEMATOGRAPHY
Black-and-white
•Boris Kaufman *On The Waterfront*

ART DIRECTION/SET DECORATION
Black-and-white
•Richard Day *On The Waterfront*

SOUND RECORDING
Columbia Studio Sound Dept; John Livadary, sound director *The Caine Mutiny*

MUSIC
Scoring of a Dramatic or Comedy Picture
Max Steiner *The Caine Mutiny*
Leonard Bernstein *On The Waterfront*

FILM EDITING
•Gene Milford *On The Waterfront*
William A. Lyon, Henry Batista *The Caine Mutiny*

COSTUME DESIGN
Black-and-white
Jean Louis *It Should Happen To You*
Christian Dior *Indiscretion Of An American Wife*

SHORT SUBJECTS
Cartoons
•*When Magoo Flew* UPA; Stephen Bosustow, producer

SCIENTIFIC OR TECHNICAL
A Class III citation was awarded to John Livadary, Lloyd Russell and the Columbia Studio Sound Dept for an improved limiting amplifier as applied to sound level comparison devices

1955

PICTURE
Picnic Fred Kohlmar, producer

SUPPORTING ACTOR
Arthur O'Connell *Picnic*

DIRECTOR
Joshua Logan *Picnic*

CINEMATOGRAPHY
Black-and-white
Charles B. Lang *Queen Bee*

ART DIRECTION/SET DECORATION
Colour
•William Flannery, Jo Mielziner/Robert Priestly *Picnic*

COSTUME DESIGN
Black-and-white
Jean Louis *Queen Bee*

MUSIC
Scoring of a Dramatic or Comedy Picture
George Duning *Picnic*

FILM EDITING
•Charles Nelson, William A. Lyon *Picnic*

1956

MOTION PICTURE STORY
Leo Katcher *The Eddy Duchin Story*

CINEMATOGRAPHY
Black-and-white
Burnett Guffey *The Harder They Fall*
Colour
Harry Stradling *The Eddy Duchin Story*

ART DIRECTION/SET DECORATION
Black-and-white
Ross Bellah/William R. Kiernan, Louis Diage *The Solid Gold Cadillac*

COSTUME DESIGN
Black-and-white
•Jean Louis *The Solid Gold Cadillac*

SOUND RECORDING
Columbia Studio Sound Dept; John Livadary, sound director *The Eddy Duchin Story*

MUSIC
Scoring of a Musical Picture
Morris Stoloff, George Duning *The Eddy Duchin Story*

SHORT SUBJECTS
Cartoons
•*Mister Magoo's Puddle Jumper* UPA; Stephen Bosustow, producer
The Jaywalker UPA; Stephen Bosustow, producer
Gerald McBoing Boing On Planet Moo UPA; Stephen Bosustow, producer

DOCUMENTARY
Features
•*The Silent World* Filmad-FSJYC; Jacques-Yves Cousteau, producer

1957

PICTURE
•*The Bridge On The River Kwai* Horizon; Sam Spiegel, producer

ACTOR
•Alec Guinness *The Bridge On The River Kwai*

SUPPORTING ACTOR
Sessue Hayakawa *The Bridge On The River Kwai*

DIRECTOR
•David Lean *The Bridge On The River Kwai*

WRITING
Screenplay Based On Material From Another Medium
•Pierre Boulle *The Bridge On The River Kwai*

CINEMATOGRAPHY
•Jack Hildyard *The Bridge On The River Kwai*

ART DIRECTION/SET DECORATION
Walter Holscher/William R. Kiernan, Louis Diage *Pal Joey*

SOUND
Columbia Studio Sound Dept, John Livadary, sound director *Pal Joey*

MUSIC
Score
•Malcolm Arnold *The Bridge On The River Kwai*

FILM EDITING
•Peter Taylor *The Bridge On The River Kwai*
Viola Lawrence, Jerome Thoms *Pal Joey*

COSTUME DESIGN
Jean Louis *Pal Joey*

SHORT SUBJECTS
Trees And Jamaica Daddy UPA; Stephen Bosustow, producer

1958

WRITING
Story and Screenplay Written Directly for the Screen
Paddy Chayefsky *The Goddess*

ART DIRECTION/SET DECORATION
Cary Odell/Louis Diage *Bell, Book And Candle*

FILM EDITING
William A. Lyon, Al Clark *Cowboy*

COSTUME DESIGN
Jean Louis *Bell, Book And Candle*

1959

PICTURE
Anatomy Of A Murder Otto Preminger, producer

ACTOR
Paul Muni *The Last Angry Man*
James Stewart *Anatomy Of A Murder*

ACTRESS
Katharine Hepburn *Suddenly Last Summer*
Elizabeth Taylor *Suddenly Last Summer*

SUPPORTING ACTOR
Arthur O'Connell *Anatomy Of A Murder*
George C. Scott *Anatomy Of A Murder*

WRITING
Screenplay Based On Material From Another Medium
Wendell Mayes *Anatomy Of A Murder*

CINEMATOGRAPHY
Black-and-white
Sam Leavitt *Anatomy Of A Murder*
Colour
Leon Shamroy *Porgy And Bess*

ART DIRECTION/SET DECORATION – *Black-and-white*
Carl Anderson/William R. Kiernan *The Last Angry Man*
Oliver Messel, William Kellner/Scot Slimon *Suddenly Last Summer*

SOUND
Samuel Goldwyn Studio Sound Dept; Gordon E. Sawyer, sound director, and Todd-AO Sound Dept; Fred Hynes, sound director *Porgy And Bess*

MUSIC
Song
Dimitri Tiomkin (mus), Ned Washington (lyr) 'Strange Are The Ways Of Love' in *The Young Land*
Scoring of a Musical Picture
•André Previn, Ken Darby *Porgy And Bess*

FILM EDITING
Louis R. Loeffler *Anatomy Of A Murder*

COSTUME DESIGN
Colour
Irene Sharaff *Porgy And Bess*

1960

CINEMATOGRAPHY
Colour
Joe MacDonald *Pepe*

ART DIRECTION/SET DECORATION
Colour
Ted Haworth/William R. Kiernan *Pepe*

SOUND
Columbia Studio Sound Dept; Charles Rice, sound director *Pepe*

MUSIC
Song
André Previn (mus), Dory Langdon (lyr) 'Faraway Part Of Town' in *Pepe*
Scoring Of A Musical Picture
•Morris Stoloff, Harry Sukman *Song Without End*
Johnny Green *Pepe*

FILM EDITING
Viola Lawrence, Al Clark *Pepe*

COSTUME DESIGN
Colour
Edith Head *Pepe*

SCIENTIFIC OR TECHNICAL
A Class III citation was awarded to Arthur Holcomb, Petro Vlahos and Columbia Studio Camera Dept for a camera flicker indicating device

1961

PICTURE
The Guns Of Navarone Carl Foreman, producer

DIRECTOR
J. Lee Thompson *The Guns Of Navarone*

WRITING
Screenplay Based an Material From Another Medium
Carl Foreman *The Guns Of Navarone*

SOUND
Shepperton Studio Sound Dept; John Cox, sound director *The Guns Of Navarone*

MUSIC
Scoring of a Dramatic or Comedy Picture
Dimitri Tiomkin *The Guns Of Navarone*

FILM EDITING
Alan Osbiston *The Guns Of Navarone*

SPECIAL EFFECTS
•Bill Warrington (visual), Vivian C. Greenham (audible) *The Guns Of Navarone*

SHORT SUBJECTS
Live Action Subjects
Rooftops Of New York McCarty/Rush/Gaffrey; Robert Gaffrey, producer

1962

PICTURE
•*Lawrence Of Arabia* Horizon-Spiegel-Lean; Sam Spiegel, producer
ACTOR
Peter O'Toole *Lawrence Of Arabia*

SUPPORTING ACTOR
Omar Sharif *Lawrence Of Arabia*

DIRECTOR
•David Lean *Lawrence Of Arabia*

WRITING
Screenplay Based an Material From Another Medium
Robert Bolt *Lawrence Of Arabia*

CINEMATOGRAPHY
Colour
•Freddie Young *Lawrence Of Arabia*

ART DIRECTION/SET DECORATION
Colour
•John Box, John Stoll/Dario Simoni *Lawrence Of Arabia*

SOUND
•Shepperton Studio Sound Dept; John Cox, sound director *Lawrence Of Arabia*

MUSIC
Song
Elmer Bernstein (mus), Mack David (lyr) 'Walk On The Wild Side' in *Walk On The Wild Side*
Score
Substantially Original
•Maurice Jarre *Lawrence Of Arabia*

FILM EDITING
•Ann Coates *Lawrence Of Arabia*

1963

ACTRESS
Leslie Caron *The L-Shaped Room*

SUPPORTING ACTOR
John Huston *The Cardinal*

DIRECTOR
Otto Preminger *The Cardinal*

WRITING
Screenplay Based on Material From Another Medium
Serge Bourguignon, Antoine Tudal *Sundays And Cybele* (Which won the previous year's Academy Award for Best Foreign Language Film)

CINEMATOGRAPHY
Colour
Leon Shamroy *The Cardinal*

ART DIRECTION/SET DECORATION
Colour
Lyle Wheeler/Gene Callahan *The Cardinal*

SOUND
Columbia Studio Sound Dept; Charles Rice, sound director *Bye Bye Birdie*

MUSIC
Scoring of Music (Adaptation or Treatment)
Maurice Jarre *Sundays And Cybele*
John Green *Bye Bye Birdie*

FILM EDITING
Louis R. Loeffler *The Cardinal*

COSTUME DESIGN
Colour
Donald Brooks *The Cardinal*

SHORT SUBJECTS
Cartoons
The Critic Pintoff-Crossbow Productions;
Ernest Pintoff, producer

1964

PICTURE
Dr Strangelove Or: How I Learned To Stop Worrying And Love The Bomb Hawk Films;
Stanley Kubrick, producer

ACTOR
Peter Sellers *Dr Strangelove*

DIRECTOR
Stanley Kubrick *Dr Strangelove*

WRITING
Screenplay Based on Material From Another Medium
Stanley Kubrick, Peter George, Terry
Southern *Dr Strangelove*

DOCUMENTARY
Features
The Finest Hours Le Vien Films; Jack Le Vien,
producer

1965

PICTURE
Ship Of Fools Kramer; Stanley Kramer, producer

ACTOR
• Lee Marvin *Cat Ballou*
Oskar Werner *Ship Of Fools*

ACTRESS
Samantha Eggar *The Collector*
Simone Signoret *Ship Of Fools*

SUPPORTING ACTOR
Michael Dunne *Ship Of Fools*

DIRECTOR
William Wyler *The Collector*

WRITING
Screenplay Based on Material From Another Medium
Walter Newman, Frank R. Pierson *Cat Ballou*
Stanley Mann, John Kohn *The Collector*
Abby Mann *Ship Of Fools*

CINEMATOGRAPHY
Black-and-white
Burnett Guffey *King Rat*
• Ernest Laszlo *Ship Of Fools*

ART DIRECTION/SET DECORATION
Black-and-white
Robert Emmet Smith/Frank Tuttle *King Rat*
• Robert Clatworthy/Joseph Kish *Ship Of Fools*

MUSIC
Song
Jerry Livingston (mus), Mack David (lyr) 'The
Ballad Of Cat Ballou' in *Cat Ballou*
Scoring of Music (Adaptation or Treatment)
DeVol *Cat Ballou*

FILM EDITING
Charles Nelson *Cat Ballou*

COSTUME DESIGN
Black-and-white
Bill Thomas, Jean Louis *Ship Of Fools*

1966

PICTURE
• *A Man For All Seasons* Highland; Fred
Zinnemann, producer

ACTOR
• Paul Scofield *A Man For All Seasons*

ACTRESS
Lynn Redgrave *Georgy Girl*

SUPPORTING ACTOR
James Mason *Georgy Girl*
Robert Shaw *A Man For All Seasons*

SUPPORTING ACTRESS
Wendy Hiller *A Man For All Seasons*

DIRECTOR
• Fred Zinnemann *A Man For All Seasons*
Richard Brooks *The Professionals*

WRITING
Screenplay Based on Material From Another Medium
• Robert Bolt *A Man For All Seasons*
Richard Brooks *The Professionals*

CINEMATOGRAPHY
Black-and-white
Ken Higgins *Georgy Girl*
Colour
• Ted Moore *A Man For All Seasons*
Conrad Hall *The Professionals*

MUSIC
Song
• John Barry (mus), Don Black (lyr) 'Born
Free' in *Born Free*

Tom Springfield (mus) Jim Dale (lyr) 'Georgy
Girl' in *Georgy Girl*
Original Music Score
• John Barry *Born Free*

COSTUME DESIGN
• Elizabeth Haffenden, Joan Bridge *A Man For
All Seasons*

1967

PICTURE
Guess Who's Coming To Dinner Kramer;
Stanley Kramer, producer

ACTOR
Spencer Tracy *Guess Who's Coming To Dinner*

ACTRESS
• Katharine Hepburn *Guess Who's Coming To
Dinner*

SUPPORTING ACTOR
Cecil Kellaway *Guess Who's Coming To
Dinner*

SUPPORTING ACTRESS
Beah Richards *Guess Who's Coming To Dinner*

DIRECTOR
Stanley Kramer Guess *Guess Who's Coming
To Dinner*
Richard Brooks *In Cold Blood*

WRITING
Screenplay Based on Material From Another Medium
Richard Brooks *In Cold Blood*
Story and Screenplay Written Directly for the Screen
• William Rose *Guess Who's Coming To
Dinner*

CINEMATOGRAPHY
Conrad Hall *In Cold Blood*

MUSIC
Song
Burt Bacharach (mus), Hal David (lyr) 'The
Look Of Love' in *Casino Royale*
Original Music Score
Quincy Jones *In Cold Blood*
Scoring of Music (Adaptation or Treatment)
DeVol *Guess Who's Coming To Dinner*

FILM EDITING
Robert C. Jones *Guess Who's Coming To
Dinner*

COSTUME DESIGN
Irene Sharaff, Danilo Donati *The Taming Of
The Shrew*

SHORT SUBJECTS
Cartoons
What On Earth! National Film Board of
Canada; Robert Verrall and Wolf Koenig,
producers
Live Action Subjects
• *A Place To Stand* TDF Productions for the
Ontario Dept of Economics and
Development; Christopher Chapman,
producer

DOCUMENTARY
Short Subjects
A Place To Stand Christopher Chapman,
producer

1968

PICTURE
• *Oliver!* Romulus; John Woolf, producer
Funny Girl Rastar; Ray Stark, producer

ACTOR
Ron Moody *Oliver!*

ACTRESS
• Barbra Streisand *Funny Girl* (co-winner)

SUPPORTING ACTOR
Jack Wild *Oliver!*

SUPPORTING ACTRESS
Kay Medford *Funny Girl*

DIRECTOR
• Carol Reed *Oliver!*

WRITING
Screenplay Based an Material From Another Medium
Vernon Harris *Oliver!*

CINEMATOGRAPHY
Harry Stradling *Funny Girl*
Oswald Morris *Oliver!*

ART DIRECTION/SET DECORATION
• John Box, Terence Marsh/Vernon Dixon, Ken Muggleston *Oliver!*

SOUND
• Shepperton Studio Sound Dept *Oliver!*
Columbia Studio Sound Dept *Funny Girl*

MUSIC
Song
Jule Styne (mus), Bob Merrill (lyr) 'Funny Girl' in *Funny Girl*
Score of a Musical Picture (Original or Adaptation)
Walter Scharf *Funny Girl*
• John Green *Oliver!*

FILM EDITING
Robert Swink, Maury Winetrobe, William Sands *Funny Girl*
Ralph Kemplen *Oliver!*

COSTUME DESIGN
Phyllis Dalton *Oliver!*

SHORT SUBJECTS
Cartoons
The House That Jack Built National Film Board of Canada; Wolf Koenig and Jim MacKay, producers
Live Action Subects
Duo National Film Board of Canada

HONORARY AWARDS
Onna White for her outstanding choreography achievement for *Oliver!*

1969

SUPPORTING ACTOR
Jack Nicholson *Easy Rider*
Elliott Gould *Bob & Carol & Ted & Alice*

SUPPORTING ACTRESS
• Goldie Hawn *Cactus Flower*

Dyan Cannon *Bob & Carol & Ted & Alice*
WRITING
Story and Screenplay Based on Material not Previously Published or Produced
Paul Mazursky, Larry Tucker *Bob & Carol & Ted & Alice*
Peter Fonda, Dennis Hopper, Terry Southern *Easy Rider*

CINEMATOGRAPHY
Charles B. Lang *Bob & Carol & Ted & Alice*
Daniel Fapp *Marooned*

SOUND
Les Fresholtz, Arthur Piantadosi *Marooned*

SPECIAL VISUAL EFFECTS
• Robbie Robertson *Marooned*

SHORT SUBJECTS
Cartoons
Walking National Film Board of Canada; Ryan Larkin, producer
Live Action Subjects
People Soup Pangloss Productions: Marc Merson, producer

1970

PICTURE
Five Easy Pieces BBS Productions: Bob Rafelson and Richard Wechsler, producers

ACTOR
Jack Nicholson *Five Easy Pieces*

SUPPORTING ACTOR
Gene Hackman *I Never Sang For My Father*

SUPPORTING ACTRESS
Karen Black *Five Easy Pieces*

WRITING
Screenplay Based on Material From Another Medium
Robert Anderson *I Never Sang For My Father*
Story and Screenplay Based on Factual Material or Material not Previously Published or Produced
Bob Rafelson, Adrien Joyce *Five Easy Pieces*

MUSIC
Original Score
Frank Cordell *Cromwell*

COSTUME DESIGN
• Nino Novarese *Cromwell*

1971

PICTURE
The Last Picture Show BBS Productions; Stephen J. Friedman, producer
Nicholas And Alexandra Horizon; Sam Spiegel, producer

ACTRESS
Janet Suzman *Nicholas And Alexandra*

SUPPORTING ACTOR
Jeff Bridges *The Last Picture Show*
• Ben Johnson *The Last Picture Show*

SUPPORTING ACTRESS
• Cloris Leachman *The Last Picture Show*
Ellen Burstyn *The Last Picture Show*
Margaret Leighton *The Go-Between*

DIRECTOR
Peter Bogdanovich *The Last Picture Show*

WRITING
Screenplay Based on Material From Another Medium
Larry McMurtry, Peter Bogdanovich *The Last Picture Show*
Story and Screenplay Based on Factual Material or Material not Previously Published or Produced
Elio Petri, Ugo Pirro *Investigation Of A Citizen Above Suspicion*

CINEMATOGRAPHY
Robert Surtees *The Last Picture Show*
Freddie Young *Nicholas And Alexandra*

ART DIRECTION/SET DECORATION
• John Box, Ernest Archer, Jack Maxsted, Gil Parrondo/Vernon Dixon *Nicholas And Alexandra*

MUSIC
Song
Barry DeVorzon, Perry Botkin Jr 'Bless The Beasts And Children' in *Bless The Beasts And Children*
Original Dramatic Score
Richard Rodney Bennett *Nicholas And Alexandra*

COSTUME DESIGN
• Yvonne Blake, Antonio Castillo *Nicholas And Alexandra*

SHORT SUBJECTS
Animated Films
Evolution National Film Board of Canada; Michael Mills, producer

1972

SUPPORTING ACTRESS
• Eileen Heckart *Butterflies Are Free*
Susan Tyrrell *Fat City*

WRITING
Story and Screenplay Based on Factual Material or Material not Previously Published or Produced
Carl Foreman *Young Winston*

CINEMATOGRAPHY
Charles B. Lang *Butterflies Are Free*
Harry Stradling Jr *1776*

ART DIRECTION/SET DECORATION
Don Ashton, Geoffrey Drake, John Graysmark, William Hutchinson/Peter James *Young Winston*

SOUND
Arthur Piantadosi, Charles Knight *Butterflies Are Free*

MUSIC
Original Dramatic Score
• Charles Chaplin, Raymond Rasch, Larry Russell *Limelight* (reissue by Columbia)
John Williams *Images*

COSTUME DESIGN
Anthony Mendleson *Young Winston*

1973

ACTOR
Jack Nicholson *The Last Detail*

ACTRESS
Barbra Streisand *The Way We Were*
Joanne Woodward *Summer Wishes, Winter Dreams*

SUPPORTING ACTOR
Randy Quaid *The Last Detail*

SUPPORTING ACTRESS
Sylvia Sidney *Summer Wishes, Winter Dreams*

WRITING
Screenplay Based on Material From Another Medium
Robert Towne *The Last Detail*

CINEMATOGRAPHY
Harry Stradling Jr *The Way We Were*

ART DIRECTION/SET DECORATION
Stephen Grimes/William R. Kiernan *The Way We Were*

MUSIC
Song
• Marvin Hamlisch (mus), Alan and Marilyn Bergman (lyr) 'The Way We Were' in *The Way We Were*
Original Dramatic Score
• Marvin Hamlisch *The Way We Were*

COSTUME DESIGN
Dorothy Jeakins, Moss Mabry *The Way We Were*

1975

SUPPORTING ACTOR
Jack Warden *Shampoo*

SUPPORTING ACTRESS
• Lee Grant *Shampoo*

WRITING
Original Screenplay
Robert Towne, Warren Beatty *Shampoo*
Screenplay Based on Material From Another Medium
John Huston, Gladys Hill *The Man Who Would Be King*

CINEMATOGRAPHY
James Wong Howe *Funny Lady*

ART DIRECTION/SET DECORATION
Richard Sylbert, W. Stewart Campbell/George Gaines *Shampoo*
Alexander Trauner, Tony Inglis/Peter James *The Man Who Would Be King*

SOUND
Richard Portman, Don MacDougall, Curly Thirlwell, Jack Solomon *Funny Lady*
Arthur Piantadosi, Les Fresholtz, Richard Tyler, Al Overton Jr *Bite The Bullet*

MUSIC
Song
Fred Ebb and John Kander 'How Lucky Can You Get' in *Funny Lady*
Original Score
Gerald Fried *Birds Do It. Bees Do It*
Alex North *Bite The Bullet*
Scoring
Original Song Score and/or Adaptation
Peter Matz *Funny Lady*
Peter Townshend *Tommy*

FILM EDITING
Russell Lloyd *The Man Who Would Be King*

COSTUME DESIGN
Ray Aghayan, Bob Mackie *Funny Lady*
Edith Head *The Man Who Would Be King*

1976

PICTURE
Taxi Driver Bill/Phillips-Scorsese; Michael Phillips and Julia Phillips, producers

ACTOR
Robert De Niro *Taxi Driver*

SUPPORTING ACTRESS
Jodie Foster *Taxi Driver*

WRITING
Screenplay Written Directly for the Screen
Walter Bernstein *The Front*

MUSIC
Original Score
Bernard Herrmann *Taxi Driver*
Bernard Herrmann *Obsession*

1977

SUPPORTING ACTRESS
Melinda Dillon *Close Encounters Of The Third Kind*

DIRECTOR
Steven Spielberg *Close Encounters Of The Third Kind*

CINEMATOGRAPHY
• Vilmos Zsigmond *Close Encounters Of The Third Kind*

ART DIRECTION/SET DECORATION
Joe Alves, Dan Lomino/Phil Abramson *Close Encounters Of The Third Kind*

SOUND
Robert Knudson, Robert J. Glass, Don MacDougall, Gene S. Cantamessa *Close Encounters Of The Third Kind*
Walter Goss, Dick Alexander, Tom Beckert, Robin Gregory *The Deep*

MUSIC
Song
• Joseph Brooks (mus/lyr) 'You Light Up My Life' in *You Light Up My Life*
Original Score
John Williams *Close Encounters Of The Third Kind*

FILM EDITING
Michael Kahn *Close Encounters Of The Third Kind*

SPECIAL ACHIEVEMENT
Sound Effects Editing
Frank Warner, supervising sound-effects editor *Close Encounters Of The Third Kind*

VISUAL EFFECTS
Roy Arbogast, Douglas Trumbull, Matthew Yuricich, Gregory Jein, Richard Yuricich *Close Encounters Of The Third Kind*

1978

PICTURE
Midnight Express Casablanca-Filmworks; Alan Marshall and David Puttnam, producers

ACTOR
Gary Busey *The Buddy Holly Story*

SUPPORTING ACTOR
John Hurt *Midnight Express*

SUPPORTING ACTRESS
• Maggie Smith *California Suite*

DIRECTOR
Alan Parker *Midnight Express*

WRITING
Screenplay Based on Material From Another Medium
Neil Simon *California Suite*
• Oliver Stone *Midnight Express*

ART DIRECTION/SET DECORATION
Albert Brenner/Marvin March *California Suite*

SOUND
Tex Rudloff, Joel Fein, Curly Thirwell, Willie Burton *The Buddy Holly Story*

MUSIC
Original Song
• Paul Jabara 'Last Dance' in *Thank God It's Friday*
Original Song Score and Its Adaptation or Adaptation Score
• Joe Benzetti *The Buddy Holly Story*
Original Score
• Giorgio Moroder *Midnight Express*

FILM EDITING
Gerry Hambling *Midnight Express*

1979

PICTURE
All That Jazz co-production with 20th Century-Fox; Robert Alan Arthur, producer
• *Kramer Vs Kramer* Jaffe; Stanley R. Jaffe, producer

ACTOR
• Dustin Hoffman *Kramer Vs Kramer*
Jack Lemmon *The China Syndrome*
Al Pacino *....And Justice For All*
Roy Scheider *All That Jazz*

ACTRESS
Jane Fonda *The China Syndrome*
Marsha Mason *Chapter Two*

SUPPORTING ACTOR
Justin Henry *Kramer Vs Kramer*

SUPPORTING ACTRESS
Jane Alexander *Kramer Vs Kramer*
• Meryl Streep *Kramer Vs Kramer*

DIRECTOR
• Robert Benton *Kramer Vs Kramer*
Bob Fosse *All That Jazz*

WRITING
Screenplay Written Directly for the Screen
Robert Alan Arthur, Bob Fosse *All That Jazz*
Valerie Curtin, Barry Levinson *...And Justice For All*

Above: *Kramer Vs Kramer* (1979)

Mike Gray, T. S. Cook, James Bridges *The China Syndrome*
Screenplay Based on Material From Another Medium
•Robert Benton *Kramer Vs Kramer*

CINEMATOGRAPHY
Giuseppe Rotunno *All That Jazz*
Nestor Almendros *Kramer Vs Kramer*
William A. Fraker *1941* (co-production with Universal)

ART DIRECTION/SET DECORATION
Philip Rosenberg, Tony Walton/Edward Stewart, Gary Brink *All That Jazz*
George Jenkins/Arthur Jeph Parker *The China Syndrome*

SOUND
Arthur Piantadosi, Les Fresholtz, Michael Minkler, Al Overton *The Electric Horseman*
Robert Knudson, Robert J. Glass, Don MacDougall, Gene S. Cantamessa *1941*

MUSIC
Original Song
Marvin Hamlisch (mus), Carol Bayer Sager (lyr) 'Theme From Ice Castles (Through The Eyes Of Love)' in *Ice Castles*
Original Song Score and Its Adaptation, or Adaptation Score
•Ralph Burns *All That Jazz*

FILM EDITING
•Alan Heim *All That Jazz*
Jerry Greenberg *Kramer Vs Kramer*

COSTUME DESIGN
•Albert Wolsky *All That Jazz*

VISUAL EFFECTS
William A. Fraker, A. D. Flowers, Gregory Jein *1941*

1980

PICTURE
Tess Renn-Burrill/SFP; Claude Berri and Timothy Burrill, producers

ACTRESS
Gena Rowlands *Gloria*

DIRECTOR
Roman Polanski *Tess*

CINEMATOGRAPHY
•Geoffrey Unsworth, Ghislain Cloquet *Tess*
Nestor Almendros *The Blue Lagoon*

ART DIRECTION/SET DECORATION
•Pierre Guffroy, Jack Stevens *Tess*

MUSIC
Original Song
Lalo Schifrin (mus), Wilbur Jennings (lyr) 'People Alone' in *The Competition*
Original Score
Philippe Sarde *Tess*
FILM EDITING
David Blewitt *The Competition*

COSTUME DESIGN
•Anthony Powell *Tess*

1981

ACTOR
Paul Newman *Absence Of Malice*

ACTRESS
Marsha Mason *Only When I Laugh*

SUPPORTING ACTOR
James Coco *Only When I Laugh*

SUPPORTING ACTRESS
Melinda Dillon *Absence Of Malice*
Joan Hackett *Only When I Laugh*

WRITING
Screenplay Written Directly for the Screen
Kurt Luedtke *Absence Of Malice*

1982

PICTURE
•*Gandhi* Indo-British Films; Richard Attenborough, producer
Tootsie Mirage/Punch; Sydney Pollack and Dick Richards, producers

ACTOR
•Ben Kingsley *Gandhi*
Dustin Hoffman *Tootsie*

SUPPORTING ACTRESS
•Jessica Lange *Tootsie*
Teri Garr *Tootsie*

DIRECTOR
•Richard Attenborough *Gandhi*
Sydney Pollack *Tootsie*
Wolfgang Petersen *Das Boot*

WRITING
Screenplay Written Directly for the Screen
•John Briley *Gandhi*
Don McGuire, Larry Gelbart, Murray Schisgal *Tootsie*
Screenplay Based on Material From Another Medium
Wolfgang Petersen *Das Boot*

CINEMATOGRAPHY
•Billy Williams, Ronnie Taylor *Gandhi*
Jost Vacano *Das Boot*
Owen Roizman *Tootsie*

ART DIRECTION/SET DECORATION
•Stuart Craig, Bob Laing/Michael Seirton *Gandhi*
Dale Hennesy/Marvin March *Annie*

SOUND
•Gerry Humphreys, Robin O'Donoghue, Jonathan Bates, Simon Kaye *Gandhi*
Milan Bor, Trevor Pyke, Mike Le-Mare *Das Boot*
Les Fresholtz, Dick Alexander, Les Lazarowitz *Tootsie*

MUSIC
Song
Dave Grusin (mus), Alan and Marilyn Bergman (lyr) 'It Might Be You' in *Tootsie*
Original Score
Ravi Shankar, George Fenton *Gandhi*
Original Song Score and Its Adaptation or Adaptation Score
Ralph Burns *Annie*
Tom Waits *One From The Heart*

FILM EDITING
•John Bloom *Gandhi*
Fredric Steinkamp, William Steinkamp *Tootsie*
Hannes Nikel *Das Boot*

COSTUME DESIGN
•John Mollo, Bhanu Athaiya *Gandhi*

MAKE-UP
Tom Smith *Gandhi*

SOUND EFFECTS EDITING
Mike Le-Mare *Das Boot*

1983

PICTURE
The Big Chill Carson Productions Group; Michael Shamberg, producer
The Dresser Goldcrest/Television Ltd/World Film Services; Peter Yates, producer

ACTOR
Michael Caine *Educating Rita*
Tom Courtenay *The Dresser*
Albert Finney *The Dresser*

ACTRESS
Julie Walters *Educating Rita*

SUPPORTING ACTRESS
Glenn Close *The Big Chill*

DIRECTOR
Peter Yates *The Dresser*

WRITING
Screenplay Written Directly for the Screen
Lawrence Kasdan, Barbara Benedek *The Big Chill*
Screenplay Based on Material From Another Medium
Ronald Harwood *The Dresser*
Willy Russell *Educating Rita*

FILM EDITING
Frank Morris, Edward Abroms *Blue Thunder*

1984

PICTURE
A Passage To India G.W. Films Ltd; John Brabourne and Richard Goodwin, producers
A Soldier's Story Caldix; Norman Jewison, Ronald L. Schwary and Patrick Palmer, producers

ACTOR
Jeff Bridges *Starman*

ACTRESS
Judy Davis *A Passage To India*

SUPPORTING ACTOR
Adolph Caesar *A Soldier's Story*
Noriyuki 'Pat' Norita *The Karate Kid*

SUPPORTING ACTRESS
•Peggy Ashcroft *A Passage To India*

DIRECTOR
David Lean *A Passage To India*

WRITING
Screenplay Based on Material From Another Medium
David Lean *A Passage To India*
Charles Fuller *A Soldier's Story*

CINEMATOGRAPHY
Ernest Day *A Passage To India*

ART DIRECTION/SET DECORATION
John Box/Hugh Scaife *A Passage To India*

SOUND
Graham V. Hartstone, Nicolas Le Mesurier,
Michael A. Carter, John Mitchell *A Passage To India*

MUSIC
Song
Ray Parker Jr (mus/lyr) 'Ghostbusters' in
Ghostbusters
Phil Collins (mus/lyr) 'Against All Odds (Take
A Look At Me Now)' in *Against All Odds*
Original Score
•Maurice Jarre *A Passage To India*

FILM EDITING
David Lean *A Passage To India*

COSTUME DESIGN
Judy Moorcroft *A Passage To India*

VISUAL EFFECTS
Richard Edlund, John Bruno, Mark Vargo,
Chuck Gaspar *Ghostbusters*

1985

ACTOR
James Garner *Murphy's Romance*

ACTRESS
Ann Bancroft *Agnes Of God*

SUPPORTING ACTOR
Robert Loggia *Jagged Edge*

SUPPORTING ACTRESS
Meg Tilly *Agnes Of God*

CINEMATOGRAPHY
William A. Fraker *Murphy's Romance*

SOUND
Donald O. Mitchell, Michael Minkler, Gerry
Humphreys, Chris Newman *A Chorus Line*
Donald O. Mitchell, Rick Kline, Kevin
O'Connell, David Ronne *Silverado*

MUSIC
Original Song
•Lionel Richie (mus/lyr) 'Say You, Say Me' in
White Nights

Stephen Bishop 'Love Theme From White
Nights (Separate Lives)' in *White Nights*
Marvin Hamlisch (mus), Edward Kleban (lyr)
'Surprise, Surprise' in *A Chorus Line*
Original Score
Georges Delerue *Agnes Of God*
Bruce Broughton *Silverado*

FILM EDITING
John Bloom *A Chorus Line*

1986

MUSIC
Original Song
Peter Cetera (mus/lyr), David Foster (mus),
Diane Nini (lyr) 'Glory Of Love' in *Karate
Kid II*
Henry Mancini (mus), Leslie Bricusse (lyr)
'Life In A Looking Glass' in *That's Life*

1987

PICTURE
•*The Last Emperor* Hemdale; Jeremy Thomas,
producer
Hope And Glory Davros; John Boorman,
producer

DIRECTOR
•Bernardo Bertolucci *The Last Emperor*
John Boorman *Hope And Glory*

WRITING
Original Screenplay
John Boorman *Hope And Glory*
Screenplay Adaptation
•Mark Peploe, Bernardo Bertolucci *The Last
Emperor*

CINEMATOGRAPHY
•Vittorio Storaro *The Last Emperor*
Philippe Rousselot *Hope And Glory*

ART DIRECTION/SET DECORATION
•Ferdinando Scarfiotti/Bruno Cesari *The Last
Emperor*
Anthony Pratt/Joan Woollard *Hope And
Glory*

SOUND
•Bill Rowe, Ivan Sharrock *The Last Emperor*

MUSIC
Original Score
•Ryuichi Sakamoto, David Byrne, Cong Su
The Last Emperor

FILM EDITING
•Gabriella Cristiani *The Last Emperor*

COSTUME DESIGN
•James Acheson *The Last Emperor*

MAKE-UP
Bob Laden *Happy New Year*

1989

ART DIRECTION
Massimo Razzi, Teresa Barbasso *The
Adventures of Baron Munchausen*

COSTUME DESIGN
Gabriella Pescucci *The Adventures of Baron
Munchausen*

MAKE-UP
Maggie Weston, Fabrizio Sforza *The
Adventures of Baron Munchausen*

VISUAL EFFECTS
Richard Conway *The Adventures of Baron
Munchausen*

1990

PICTURE
Lawrence Lasker, Walter F. Parkes
Awakenings

ACTOR
Robert De Niro *Awakenings*

ACTRESS
Meryl Streep *Postcards From the Edge*

WRITING
Screenplay Based on Material From Another Medium
Steven Zaillian *Awakenings*

MUSIC
Song
Shel Silverstein (music and lyrics) 'I'm
Checkin' Out' *Postcards From the Edge*

SOUND EFFECTS EDITING
Charles L. Campbell, Richard Franklin
Flatliners

1991

PICTURE
The Prince of Tides Barbra Streisand, Andrew
Karsch

SUPPORTING ACTRESS
Kate Nelligan *The Prince of Tides*

DIRECTOR
John Singleton *Boyz 'N the Hood*

WRITING
Screenplay Written Directly for the Screen
John Singleton *Boyz 'N the Hood*

Screenplay Based on Material from Another Medium
Pat Conroy, Becky Johnston *The Prince of
Tides*

ART DIRECTION/SET DECORATION
Paul Sylbert/Caryl Heller *The Prince Of Tides*

CINEMATOGRAPHY
Stephen Goldblatt *The Prince Of Tides*

MUSIC
Original Score
James Newton Howard *The Prince Of Tides*

1992

PICTURE
A Few Good Men David Brown, Rob Reiner,
Andrew Scheinman

Above: *Bram Stoker's Dracula* (1992), with Keanu Reeves (left) and Gary Oldman

SUPPORTING ACTOR
Jack Nicholson *A Few Good Men*

ART DIRECTION/SET DECORATION
Thomas Sanders/Garrett Lewis *Bram Stoker's Dracula*

COSTUME DESIGN
• Eiko Ishioka *Bram Stoker's Dracula*

FILM EDITING
Robert Leighton *A Few Good Men*

MAKE-UP
• Greg Cannom, Michele Burke, Matthew W. Mungle *Bram Stoker's Dracula*

SOUND
Kevin O'Connell, Rick Kline, Bob Eber *A Few Good Men*

SOUND EFFECTS EDITING
• Tom C. McCarthy, David E. Stone *Bram Stoker's Dracula*

1993

PICTURE
The Remains of the Day Ismail Merchant, Mike Nichols, John Calley

ACTOR
Anthony Hopkins *The Remains of the Day*

ACTRESS
Emma Thompson *The Remains of the Day*

SUPPORTING ACTOR
John Malkovich *In the Line of Fire*

SUPPORTING ACTRESS
Winona Ryder *The Age of Innocence*

DIRECTOR
James Ivory *The Remains of the Day*

WRITING
Screenplay Written Directly for the Screen
Jeff Maguire *In the Line of Fire*

Screenplay Based on Material from Another Medium
Jay Cocks, Martin Scorsese *The Age of Innocence*
Ruth Prawer Jhabvala *The Remains of the Day*

ART DIRECTION/SET DECORATION
Dante Ferretti, Robert J. Franco *The Age of Innocence*
Luciana Arrighi, Ian Whittaker *The Remains of the Day*

COSTUME DESIGN
• Gabriella Pescucci *The Age of Innocence*
Jenny Beavan, John Bright *The Remains of the Day*

FILM EDITING
Anne V. Coates *In the Line of Fire*

MUSIC
Original Score
Elmer Bernstein *The Age of Innocence*
Richard Robbins *The Remains of the Day*

SOUND
Bill B. Benton, Chris Carpenter, D.M. Hemphill, Lee Orloff *Geronimo: An American Legend*

1994

ACTRESS
Winona Ryder *Little Women*

COSTUME DESIGN
Colleen Atwood *Little Women*

MUSIC
Original Score
Thomas Newman *Little Women*

1995

PICTURE
Sense and Sensibility Lindsay Doran

ACTRESS
Emma Thompson *Sense and Sensibility*

SUPPORTING ACTRESS
Kate Winslet *Sense and Sensibility*

WRITING
Screenplay Based on Material from Another Medium
• Emma Thompson *Sense and Sensibility*

CINEMATOGRAPHY
Michael Coulter *Sense and Sensibility*

COSTUME DESIGN
Jenny Beavan, John Bright *Sense and Sensibility*

MUSIC
Original Score
Patrick Doyle *Sense and Sensibility*

1996

ACTOR
Woody Harrelson *The People vs. Larry Flynt*

CINEMATOGRAPHY
Caleb Deschanel *I'll Fly Away Home*

1997

ART DIRECTION/SET DECORATION
Jan Roelfs/Nancy Nye *Gattaca*
Bo Welch, Cheryl Carasik *Men In Black*

MAKE-UP
• Rick Baker, David LeRoy Anderson *Men In Black*

MUSIC
Original Musical or Comedy Score
Danny Elfman *Men In Black*

Below: Emma Thompson and Hugh Grant in *Sense and Sensibility* (1994)

TRISTAR

1984

PICTURE
Places in the Heart Arlene Donovan

ACTRESS
•Sally Field *Places in the Heart*

DIRECTOR
Robert Benton *Places in the Heart*

SUPPORTING ACTOR
John Malkovich *Places in the Heart*

SUPPORTING ACTRESS
Lindsay Crouse *Places in the Heart*
Glenn Close *The Natural*

WRITING
Screenplay Written Directly for the Screen
Robert Benton *Places in the Heart*

MUSIC
Original Score
Randy Newman *The Natural*

CINEMATOGRAPHY
Caleb Deschanel *The Natural*

ART DIRECTION/SET DECORATION
Angelo Graham, Mel Bourne/Bruce
Weintraub *The Natural*

MUSIC
Original Song Score
Jeffrey Moss *The Muppets Take Manhattan*
Kris Kristofferson *Songwriter*

COSTUME DESIGN
Ann Roth *Places in the Heart*

1985

SOUND EFFECTS EDITING
Frederick J. Brown *Rambo: First Blood Part 2*

1986

ACTRESS
Kathleen Turner *Peggy Sue Got Married*
Jessica Lange *Sweet Dreams*

CINEMATOGRAPHY
Gordon Cronenweth *Peggy Sue Got Married*

COSTUME DESIGN
Theodora Van Runkle *Peggy Sue Got Married*

1987

ACTOR
Jack Nicholson *Ironweed*

ACTRESS
Meryl Streep *Ironweed*

SUPPORTING ACTRESS
Norma Aleandro *Gaby – A True Story*

1988

COSTUME DESIGN
Patricia Norris *Sunset*

1989

ART DIRECTION/SET DECORATION
Norman Garwood/Garrett Lewis *Glory*

CINEMATOGRAPHY
•Freddie Francis *Glory*

FILM EDITING
Steven Rosenblum *Glory*
Noelle Boisson *The Bear*

SOUND
•Donald O. Mitchell, Gregg C. Rudloff,
Elliot Tyson, Russell Williams II *Glory*

SUPPORTING ACTOR
•Denzel Washington *Glory*

ACTRESS
Jessica Lange *Music Box*

SUPPORTING ACTRESS
Julia Roberts *Steel Magnolias*

MUSIC
Original Score
Dean Pitchford, Tom Snow 'After All'
Chances Are

1990

WRITING
Screenplay Written Directly for the Screen
Barry Levinson *Avalon*

CINEMATOGRAPHY
Allen Daviau *Avalon*

COSTUME DESIGN
Gloria Gresham *Avalon*

MUSIC
Original Score
Randy Newman *Avalon*

SOUND
Nelson Stoll, Michael J. Kohut, Carlos
DeLarios, Aaron Rochin *Total Recall*

SOUND EFFECTS EDITING
Stephen H. Flick *Total Recall*

SPECIAL ACHIEVEMENT AWARD FOR VISUAL EFFECTS
•Eric Brevig, Rob Bottin, Tim McGovern,
Alex Funke *Total Recall*

1991

PICTURE
Bugsy Warren Beatty, Mark Johnson, Barry
Levinson

ACTOR
Warren Beatty *Bugsy*
Robin Williams *The Fisher King*

SUPPORTING ACTOR
Harvey Keitel *Bugsy*
Ben Kingsley *Bugsy*

DIRECTOR
Barry Levinson *Bugsy*

SUPPORTING ACTRESS
•Mercedes Ruehl *The Fisher King*

WRITING
Screenplay Written Directly for the Screen
James Toback *Bugsy*
Richard LaGravenese *The Fisher King*

ART DIRECTION/SET DECORATION
•Dennis Gassner/Nancy Haigh *Bugsy*
Mel Bourne/Cindy Carr *The Fisher King*

CINEMATOGRAPHY
Allen Daviau *Bugsy*
Adam Greenberg *Terminator 2: Judgment
Day*

COSTUME DESIGN
Albert Wolsky *Bugsy*
Anthony Powell *Hook*

SOUND EFFECTS EDITING
Stephen H. Flick *Total Recall*

FILM EDITING
Conrad Buff, Mark Goldblatt, Richard A.
Harris *Terminator 2: Judgment Day*

MAKE-UP
•Stan Winston, Jeff Dawn *Terminator 2:
Judgment Day*
Christina Smith, Montague Westmore, Greg
Cannom *Hook*

MUSIC
Original Score
George Fenton *The Fisher King*
Ennio Morricone *Bugsy*
Best Song
John Williams (music); Leslie Bricusse (lyrics)
Hook

SOUND
•Tom Johnson, Gary Rydstrom, Gary Summers. Lee Orloff *Terminator 2: Judgment Day*

SOUND EFFECTS EDITING
•Gary Rydstrom, Gloria S. Borders *Terminator 2: Judgment Day*

VISUAL EFFECTS
•Dennis Muren, Stan Winston, Gene Warren Jr, Robert Skotak *Terminator 2: Judgment Day*
Eric Brevig, Harley Jessup, Mark Sullivan, Michael Lantieri *Hook*

1992

ACTOR
Robert Downey Jr *Chaplin*

SUPPORTING ACTRESS
Judy Davis *Husbands and Wives*

WRITING
Screenplay Written Directly for the Screen
Woody Allen *Husbands and Wives*

ART DIRECTION/SET DECORATION
Stuart Craig/Chris A. Butler *Chaplin*

MUSIC
Original Score
John Barry *Chaplin*
Jerry Goldsmith *Basic Instinct*

FILM EDITING
Frank J. Urioste *Basic Instinct*

1993

ACTOR
•Tom Hanks *Philadelphia*

WRITING
Screenplay Written Directly for the Screen
Ron Nyswaner *Philadelphia*
Jeff Arch, Nora Ephron, David S. Ward *Sleepless In Seattle*

MAKE-UP
Christina Smith, Matthew Mungle, Judith A. Cory *Philadelphia*

MUSIC
Original Song
Bruce Springsteen 'Streets of Philadelphia' *Philadelphia*
Neil Young 'Philadelphia' *Philadelphia*
Marc Shaiman, Ramsey McLean 'A Wink and a Smile' *Sleepless in Seattle*

SOUND
Bob Breemer, Tim Cooney, Michael Minkler *Cliffhanger*

SOUND EFFECTS EDITING
Gregg Baxter, Wylie Stateman *Cliffhanger*

VISUAL EFFECTS
John Bruno, Pamela Easly, Neil Krepela, John Richardson *Cliffhanger*

Above: *Legends of the Fall* (1994), with, from left to right, Aidan Quinn, Brad Pitt, Henry Thomas and Julia Ormond

1994

ART DIRECTION
Lily Kilvert, Doree Cooper *Legends of the Fall*

CINEMATOGRAPHY
•John Toll *Legends of the Fall*

MAKE-UP
Daniel Parker, Paul Engelen, Carol Hemming *Mary Shelley's Frankenstein*

SOUND
Douglas Ganton, Paul Massey, David Campbell, Christopher David *Legends of the Fall*

1996

PICTURE
Jerry Maguire James L. Brooks, Laurence Marks, Richard Sakai, Cameron Crowe

ACTOR
Tom Cruise *Jerry Maguire*

SUPPORTING ACTOR
•Cuba Gooding Jr *Jerry Maguire*

SUPPORTING ACTRESS
Lauren Bacall *The Mirror Has Two Faces*

WRITING
Screenplay Written Directly for the Screen
Cameron Crowe *Jerry Maguire*

FILM EDITING
Joe Hutshing *Jerry Maguire*

MUSIC
Original Song
Barbra Streisand, Marvin Hamlisch, Bryan Adams, Robert 'Mutt' Lange 'I Finally Found Someone' *The Mirror Has Two Faces*

1997

PICTURE
As Good As It Gets James L. Brooks, Bridget Johnson, Kristi Zea

ACTOR
•Jack Nicholson *As Good As It Gets*

ACTRESS IN A LEADING ROLE
•Helen Hunt *As Good As It Gets*

SUPPORTING ACTOR
Greg Kinnear *As Good As It Gets*

WRITING
Screenplay Written Directly for the Screen
Mark Andrus, James L. Brooks *As Good As It Gets*

WRITING
Screenplay Based on Material From Another Medium
Paul Attanasio *Donnie Brasco*

FILM EDITING
Richard Marks *As Good As It Gets*

MUSIC
Original Musical or Comedy Score
Hans Zimmer *As Good As It Gets*
James Newton Howard *My Best Friend's Wedding*

VISUAL EFFECTS
Phil Tippett, Scott E. Anderson, Alec Gillis, John Richardson *Starship Troopers*

1998

SOUND
Kevin O'Connell, Greg P. Russell and Pud Cusack *The Mask of Zorro*

SOUND EFFECTS EDITING
David McMoyler *The Mask of Zorro*

SONY PICTURE CLASSICS

1992

ACTRESS
• Emma Thompson *Howards End*

ART DIRECTION/SET DECORATION
• Luciana Arrighi/Ian Whittaker *Howards End*

BEST PICTURE
Ismail Merchant *Howards End*

CINEMATOGRAPHY
Tony Pierce-Roberts *Howards End*

COSTUME DESIGN
Jenny Beavan, John Bright *Howards End*

DIRECTING
James Ivory *Howards End*

SCORING
Original Score Richard Robbins *Howards End*

SUPPORTING ACTRESS
Vanessa Redgrave *Howards End*

Below: Anthony Hopkins and Emma Thompson in *Howard's End* (1992)

WRITING
• Ruth Prawer Jhabvala *Howards End*

ACTRESS
Catherine Deneuve *Indochine*

BEST FOREIGN LANGUAGE FILM
• France *Indochine*

1993

ART DIRECTION
Jan Roelfs, Ben Van Os *Orlando*

COSTUME DESIGN
Sandy Powell *Orlando* 1994

BEST FOREIGN LANGUAGE FILM
• Russia *Burnt by the Sun*
Farinelli: Il Castrato

BEST FOREIGN LANGUAGE FILM
Belgium *Farinelli: Il Castrato*

1995

DOCUMENTARY
• Jon Blair *Anne Frank Remembered*
• Zhang Yimou *Shanghai Triad*

CINEMATOGRAPHY
Lu Yue *Shanghai Triad*
1996

BEST FOREIGN LANGUAGE FILM
Georgia *A Chef in Love*

WRITING
John Sayles *Lone Star*

1997

ACTRESS
Julie Christie *Afterglow*

BEST FOREIGN LANGUAGE FILM
• The Netherlands *Character*

1998

ACTRESS
Fernanda Montenegro *Central Station*

BEST FOREIGN LANGUAGE FILM
Brazil *Central Station*
Argentina *Tango*

INDEX OF PERSONNEL

Page numbers in *italic* refer to the illustrations

431

433

435

436

438

439

441

443

445

449

450

INDEX OF FILMS

453

454

455